INDIAN PHILOSOPHY

INDIAN PHILOSOPHY

JADUNATH SINHA

Volume II:

The Philosophies of the Sāṁkhya, the Yoga, Jainism, Buddhism, Advaita Vedānta and other Theistic Vedānta: Śaivism and Śāktaism

MOTILAL BANARSIDASS PUBLISHERS
PRIVATE LIMITED • DELHI

3rd Reprint: Delhi, 2017
Second Edition: Calcutta, 1978

ISBN: 978-81-208-1601-5 (Vol. II)
ISBN: 978-81-208-1603-9 (Set)

MOTILAL BANARSIDASS
41 U.A. Bungalow Road, Jawahar Nagar, Delhi 110 007
8 Mahalaxmi Chamber, 22 Bhulabhai Desai Road, Mumbai 400 026
203 Royapettah High Road, Mylapore, Chennai 600 004
236, 9th Main III Block, Jayanagar, Bengaluru 560 011
8 Camac Street, Kolkata 700 017
Ashok Rajpath, Patna 800 004
Chowk, Varanasi 221 001

MLBD Cataloging-in-Publication Data
Indian Philosophy (Vol. II)
The Philosophies of the Sāṅkhya, the Yoga, Jainism, Buddhism, Advaita Vedānta and other Theistic Vedānta: Śaivism and Śāktaism
by JADUNATH SINHA
ISBN: 978-81-208-1601-5 (Vol. II)
ISBN: 978-81-208-1603-9 (Set)
Includes, Abbreviations, Index
I. Philosophy, II. Buddhism, III. Advaita Vedanta, IV. Visistadvaita, V. Saivism & Saktaism, VI. Sinha, Jadunath.

Printed in India
by RP Jain at NAB Printing Unit,
A-44, Naraina Industrial Area, Phase I, New Delhi-110 028
and published by JP Jain for Motilal Banarsidass Publishers (P) Ltd,
41 U.A. Bungalow Road, Jawahar Nagar, Delhi-110 007

PREFACE

This volume elaborately deals with the Sāṁkhya, the Yoga, Jainism, early Buddhism, the Schools of Buddhism, the philosophies of the Ṛg-veda, the Upaniṣads, Gauḍapāda, the *Yogavāśiṣṭha*, the *Bhagavadgīta*, the *Bhāgavata*, and the *Pañcarātra*, the Vedānta systems of Śaṁkara, Bhāskara, Yadava-prakāśa, Rāmānuja, Madhva, Nimbārka, Vallabha, Caitanya, Jīva Goswāmi, and Baladeva Vidyābhūṣaṇa, Śaivism and Śāktāism. The treatment of all the systems is based upon the original Sanskrit texts. Only the Chapter on Early Buddhism is based on the authoritative English translations of the Pāli texts.

The first volume will be published shortly. It deals with the remaining systems in a comprehensive manner.

I acknowledge my indebtedness to T. W. Rhys Davids, Mrs. Rhys Davids, A. B. Keith, Anand Coomarswami, L. P. Narasu, S. N. Das Gupta, Deussen, and K. C. Bhattacharya in writing this volume. It is intended for the advanced students of the Indian and foreign Universities.

JADUNATH SINHA

39, S. R. Das Road,
Calcutta-26, India.
June 3, 1952

CONTENTS

CHAPTER I

THE SAMKHYA PHILOSOPHY

PAGE

1. Introduction. 2. Theory of Causation—Satkāryavāda—Pariṇāmavāda. 3. Prakṛti. 4. The Guṇas. 5. Evolution. 6. Unconscious Teleology. 7. Prakṛti and its Evolutes. 8. Space and Time. 9. Puruṣa. 10. Jīva. 11. Puruṣa and Buddhi. 12. Puruṣa and Prakṛti. 13. The Psychical Apparatus. 14. Factors of Knowledge. 15. The Sources of Knowledge. 16. Intrinsic Validity and Invalidity of Knowledge. 17. Theory of Error. 18. Three Kinds of Pain (Duḥkha). 19. Bondage (Bandha). 20. Liberation (Mokṣa). 21. The Means to Liberation. 22. Future Life. 23. Atheism. 24. Critical Estimate ... 1—102

CHAPTER II

THE YOGA PHILOSOPHY

1. Introduction. 2. Substance (Dharmin) and Mode (Dharma). 3. Whole (Avayavin) and Part (Avayava). 4. Different kinds of Modifications (Pariṇāma). 5. Power and Causation (Satkāryavāda). 6. Non-existence (Abhāva). 7. Particularity (Viśeṣa). 8. The Sāṁkhya and the Yoga. 9. The Place of God in the Yoga system. 10. Proofs for the existence of God. 11. The Nature of God. 12. Valid Knowledge (Pramā). 13. Three Kinds of Pramāṇa. 14. Sphoṭavāda. 15. Theory of Error. 16. The Mind (Citta) and its Modes (Vṛtti). 17. Afflictions (Kleśa). 18. The Threefold Pain (Tāpatraya). 19. Dispositions (Saṁskāra). 20. The Levels of Attention (Cittabhūmi). 21. The Path of Action (Kriyāyoga). 22. The Path of Yoga (Yogāṅga). 23. Abhyāsa and Vairāgya. 24. Kinds of Samādhi. 25. Supernormal Powers. 26. Karma and Transmigration. 27. Liberation (Kaivalya). 28. Critical Estimate 103—177

CHAPTER III

THE JAINA PHILOSOPHY

1. Introduction. 2. Relation to other Systems. 3. Valid Knowledge (Pramāṇa). 4. Perception (Pratyakṣa). 5. Mediate Knowledge (Parokṣa). 6. Anekāntavāda. 7. The Doctrine of Nayas. 8. Syādvāda : Saptabhaṅgīnyāya. 9. The Jaina refutation of one-sided (aikāntika) positions. 10. Substance, Attribute, and Modification. 11. Cause and Effect. 12. The Soul (Jīva). 13. The Theory of Karma. 14. Matter (Pudgala). 15. Dharma. 16. Adharma. 17. Space (Ākāśa). 18. Time (Kāla). 19. The Nine Categories (Padārtha). 20. The Soul and the Body. 21. Modes of Consciousness. 22. Ethical Discipline. 23. The Means to Liberation (Mokṣa). 24. The Stages in the Evolution of the Soul. 25. The Ethical Standard. 26. The Jaina refutation of Theism. 27. Critical Estimate ... 178—278

PAGE

CHAPTER IV

EARLY BUDDHISM

1. Introduction. 2. The Four Noble Truths. 3. Impermanence (Anityavāda). 4. Causality: Dependent Origination (Pratītyasamutpāda). 5. The Wheel of Existence (Bhavacakra). 6. The Doctrine of No-Self (Anātmavāda, Nairātmyavāda). 7. Karma. 8. Transmigration. 9. The Dhamma or the Norm. 10. Atheism. 11. Non-materialism. 12. Anti-metaphysical Attitude. 13. Rationalism. 14. Psychology. 15. Ethics. 16. Nirvāṇa. 17. Buddhism and the Upaniṣads. 18. Buddhism and the Sāṁkhya. 19. Buddhism and the Yoga. 20. Buddhism and Jainism. 21. Buddhism and Materialism, Fatalism and Scepticism. 22. Religion ... ... 279—348

CHAPTER V

THE SCHOOLS OF BUDDHISM

1. Introduction. 2. The Sarvāstivādin, the Vaibhāṣika and the Sautrāntika Realism. 3. The *Mahāyānaśraddhotpādaśāstra*: The Philosophy of Tathatā. 4. The Idealism of *Laṅkāvatārasūtra*. 5. The Yogācāra Vijñānavāda. 6. The Śūnyavāda of *Prajñāpāramitāsūtra*. 7. The Mādhyamika Śūnyavāda. 8. The Doctrine of Momentariness. 9. The Buddhist Epistemology and Logic ... ... 349—417

CHAPTER VI

THE BACK-GROUND OF THE VEDĀNTA

1. The Philosophy of the Ṛg-Veda: Polytheism, Henotheism, Monotheism, and Monism. 2. Religion and Ethics of the Ṛg-Veda. 3. The Spiritualistic Monism of the Upaniṣads: Brahman. 4. The Ātman and the Individual Self. 5. Intuition (Vidyā) and Intellect (Avidyā): Bondage and Liberation. 6. Cosmology. 7. Ethics. 8. Gauḍapāda's Pure Monism or Absolute Idealism. 9. The Philosophy of the *Yogavāśiṣṭha* 418—460

CHAPTER VII

THE ADVAITA VEDĀNTA OF ŚAṀKARA

1. Introduction. 2. Śaṁkara's Criticism of the Vaiśeṣika Pluralism and Atomism. 3. Śaṁkara's Criticism of the Sāṁkhya doctrine of Prakṛti as the Material Cause of the World. 4. Śaṁkara's Criticism of the doctrine of God as the Efficient Cause of the World. 5. Śaṁkara's Criticism of the Bhāgavata doctrine of God as the Efficient Cause and the Material Cause of the World. 6. Śaṁkara's Criticism of the Jaina doctrine. 7. Śaṁkara's Criticism of the Buddhist Realism. 8. Śaṁkara's Criticism of the Buddhist Subjective Idealism or Vijñānavāda. 9. The Ātman. 10. The Jīva. 11. The Sākṣin. 12. Brahman. 13. Indeterminate Brahman and Determinate Brahman. 14. Īśvara. 15. Brahman and

PAGE

Īśvara. 16. Īśvara and Jīva. 17. The Proofs for the existence of Īśvara. 18. The Material Cause and the Efficient Cause of the World. 19. Brahman and the Jīva. 20. Māyā : Avidyā. 21. The World-Appearance (Prapañca). 22. Space, Time, and Causality. 23. Creation. 24. Higher Knowledge (Parā Vidyā) and Lower Knowledge (Aparā Vidyā). 25. Scriptural Authority (Śruti), Reason (Tarka), and Intuition (Anubhava). 26. Truth. 27. The Pramāṇas. 28. Bondage. 29. Karma. 30. Future Life. 31. Mokṣa. 32. The Means to Liberation : Morality and Knowledge. 33. Ethical Thought : Dharma, Adharma, Niyoga, Springs of Action, and Freedom of the Will. 34. Religion. 35. Criticism of Śaṁkara ... ... 461—611

CHAPTER VIII

THE BACK-GROUND OF THE THEISTIC VEDĀNTA

1. The Philosophy of the *Bhagavadgītā*. 2. The Philosophy of the *Bhāgavata*. 3. The Philosophy of the *Pañcarātra* ... 612—651

CHAPTER IX

THE PHILOSOPHY OF VIŚIṢṬĀDVAITA

1. Introduction. 2. Bhāskara's Bhedābhedavada. 3. Yādavaprakāśa's Bhedābhedavāda. 4. The Sources of Knowledge. 5. Brahman : God. 6. The Jīva : Self and Consciousness. 7. Matter. 8. Causality : Satkāryavāda. 9. Creation. 10. Refutation of Śaṁkara's doctrine of Avidyā. 11. Reality of the World ... ... 652—688

CHAPTER X

THE DVAITAVĀDA OF MADHVA

1. Introduction. 2. Epistemology. 3. Viśeṣa. 4. God. 5. Prakṛti. 6. The World. 7. Reality of Difference. 8. Madhva and Rāmānuja. 9. The Jīva. 10. The Categories 689—701

CHAPTER XI

DVAITĀDVAITAVĀDA OF NIMBĀRKA

1. Introduction. 2. Brahman. 3. The Jīva. 4. Nimbārka and Bhāskara. 5. Nimbārka and Rāmānuja ... ... 702—707

CHAPTER XII

ŚUDDHĀDVAITAVĀDA OF VALLABHA

1. Introduction. 2. Epistemology. 3. Brahman. 4. Reality of the World. 5. The Jīva ... ... 708—718

PAGE

CHAPTER XIII

ACINTYABHEDĀBHEDAVĀDA OF CAITANYA

1. Caitanya's Theism. 2. Jīva Goswami's Philosophy. 3. Baladeva Vidyābhuṣaṇa's Philosophy ... ... 719—730

CHAPTER XIV

ŚAIVISM AND ŚĀKTAISM

1. The Pāśupata Philosophy. 2. The Śaiva Siddhānta. 3. The Pratyabhijñā Philosophy. 4. Śrīkāṇṭha's Śaiva Vedānta. 5. Śāktaism ... ... 731—746

INDEX 747—762

ABBREVIATIONS

ABS. = Aṇubhāṣya on Brahma Sūtra by Vallabha (BI).
ADS. = Abhidhammāttasaṁgaha.
Ait. Up. = Aitareya Upaniṣad.
AK. = Abhidharmakoṣa.
AKB. = Abhidharmakoṣabhāṣya.
AKV. = Abhidharmakoṣavyākhyā edited by Narendra Nath Law, 1949, Calcutta, C.O.S., 31.
AM. = Āptamīmāṁsā.
AMV. = Āptamimāṁsāvṛtti.
AN. = Aṅguttaranikāya.
AS. = Aṣṭasāhasrī.
BCA. = Bodhicaryāvatāra.
BCAP. = Bodhicaryāvatārapañjikā.
BG. = Bhagavadgītā.
BGB. = Buddha and the Gospel of Buddhism (Anandacoomaraswami).
BI. = Bibliotheca Indica.
BP. = Buddhist Philosophy (A. B. Keith), Oxford, 1923.
Bṛ. Up. = Bṛhadāraṇyaka Upaniṣad.
BS. = Brahma Sūtra.
CCB. = The Central Conception of Buddhism (Th. Stcherbatsky), London, 1923.
Ch.S.S. = Chaukhāmba Sanskrit Series.
Ch. Up. = Chāndogya Upaniṣad.
Ch. V. = Chāyāvyākhyā on Yoga Sūtra.
CON. = Cosmology Old and New (G. R. Jain).
C.U. = Calcutta University.
DN. = Dhīghanikāya.
DP. = Dhammapada.
DS. = Dravyasaṁgraha.
DSV. = Dravyasaṁgrahavṛtti.
EH. = Ethics of the Hindus (Sushil Kumar Maitra) C. U., Calcutta, 1925.
E.R.E. = Encyclopædia of Religion and Ethics.
GS = Gommatasāra.
HIL. = History of Indian Logic (S. C. Vidyabhushan) C. U., Calcutta, 1913.
HIP. = History of Indian Philosophy (S. N. Das Gupta) Cambridge University Press.
IIP = Introduction to Indian Philosophy (J. Sinha), Agra, 1949.
IPP. = Indian Psychology: Perception (J. Sinha), Kegan Paul, London, 1934.
JK. = Jīvakāṇḍa.
JRAS. = Journal of Royal Asiatic Society.
JTV. = Jainatarkavārtika.
KK. = Karmakāṇḍa.
Kaiṣ. Up. = Kaiṣītakī Upaniṣad.
KV. = Kathāvatthu.
L.S. = Laṅkāvatārasūtra (edited by B. Nanjio, Kyoto, 1935).
Maitr. Up = Maitrāyaṇī Upaniṣad.
MBS. = Madhvabhāṣya on Brahma Sūtra.
MK. = Mādhyamika Kārikā.
MKV. = Mādhyamikakārikāvṛtti.
MN. = Majjhimanikāya.
Māṇḍ. K. = Māṇḍukya Kārikā.
Māṇḍ. Up. = Māṇḍukya Upaniṣad.

MP. = Milindapañha.
MPS. = Mahāparinibbānasutta.
Muṇḍ. Up. = Muṇḍaka Upaniṣad.
NA. = Nyāyāvatāra.
NAV. = Nyāyāvatāravṛtti.
NV. = Nyāyavindu.
NVT. = Nyāyavinduṭīkā.
OJ. = Outlines of Jainism (J. R. Jain).
P. = Pañcāstikāyasamayasāra.
PI. = Introduction, English translation of Pañcāstikāyasamayasāra.
PKM. = Prameyakamalamārtaṇḍa.
PMS. = Parīkṣāmukhasūtra.
PNT. = Pramāṇanayatattvālokālaṁkāra.
PRK. = Prasthānaratnākara.
Pr. Up. = Praśna Upaniṣad.
PSAH.— = Positive Sciences of the Ancient Hindus (B. N. Seal) Longmans, 1912.
RBG.— = Rāmānuja Bhāṣya on Bhagavadgītā.
RBS. = Rāmānuja Bhāṣya on Brahma Sūtra.
RK. = Ratnākarāvatārikā on Pramāṇanayataṭṭvālokālaṅkara.
RM. = Rājamārtaṇḍa on Yoga Sūtra.
R.V. = Ṛg-Veda.
SAM. = Śuddhādvaitamārtaṇḍa.
SAMP.—Prakāśa on Śuddhādvaitamārtaṇḍa.
SB. = Śaṁkara Bhāṣya.
SBG. = Śaṁkara Bhāṣya on Bhagavadgītā.
SBS. = Śaṁkara Bhāṣya on Brahma Sūtra.
ŚBS. = Śrīkaṇṭha bhāṣya on Brahma Sūtra.
SBT. = Systems of Buddhist Thought (Sogen), C. U., Calcutta, 1913.
SD. = Śāstradīpikā.
SDS. = Ṣaḍdarśanasaṁgraha.
SDSM. = Ṣaḍdarśanasamuccaya.
SGB. = Gauḍapāda bhāṣya on Sāṁkhya Kārikā.
SJM. = Jayamaṅgalā on Sāṁkhya Kārikā.
SK = Sāṁkhya Kārikā.
SLS. = Studies in Laṅkāvatārasūtra (D. T. Suzuki), London, 1930.
SN. = Saṁyuttanikāya.
SPB. = Sāṁkhyapravacanabhāṣya.
SPS. = Sāṁkhyapravacanasūtra.
SS. = Sarvārthasiddhi.
SSV. = Sāṁkhyasūtravṛtti.
STK. = Sāṁkhyatattvakaumudī.
SV. = The System of the Vedānta (Deussen).
SVM. = Vedāntin Mahādeva's gloss on Sāṁkhya Sūtra.
SVM. = Syādvādamañjarī.
Śvet. Up. = Śvetāśvatara Upaniṣad.
Tait. Up. = Taittirīya Upaniṣad.
Teja Up. = Tejavindu Upaniṣad.
TDTV. = Tātparyadīpikātātparyavṛtti.
TRD. = Tarkarahasyadīpikā.
TRV. = Tattvarājavārtika.
TS = Tattvārthādhigamasūtra.
Tsāra = Tattvārthādhigamasāra.
TSV. = Tattvaślokavārtika.
TV. = Tattvavaiśāradī.
UP. = Upaniṣad.
VP. = Vardhamānapurāṇa.
VPB. = Vedāntaparibhāṣā.
VPRS. = Vedāntapārijātasaurabha.

VPS. = Vivaraṇaprameyasaṁgraha.
VRS. = Vītarāgastuti on Syādvādamañjarī.
VS. = Vedāntasāra.
VSS. = Vizianagram Sanskrit Series.
YB. = Yogabhāṣya.
YMP. = Yogamaṇiprabhā on Yoga Sūtra.
YP. = Yoga Philosophy (S. N. Das Gupta), C. U., Calcutta.
YPR. = Yoga as Philosophy and Religion (S. N. Das Gupta) Kegan Paul, London.
YS. = Yoga Sūtra
YV. = Yoga Vārtika.

CHAPTER I

THE SĀṀKHYA PHILOSOPHY

1. *Introduction*

The Sāṁkhya system advocates the ontological dualism of prakṛti and puruṣas or individual souls. It rejects the Nyāya-Vaiśeṣika categories of substance, quality, action, generality, particularity, and inherence. It rejects the Nyāya-Vaiśeṣika theism and advocates atheism. It rejects the Nyāya-Vaiśeṣika doctrine of creation of the world by God out of the pre-existing eternal atoms. It believes in the evolution of the cosmos including matter, life, and mind out of the eternal and ubiquitous prakṛti to serve the ends of an infinite number of puruṣas or individual souls. The dualism of prakṛti and puruṣas is the fundamental doctrine of the Sāṁkhya system. It is opposed to atomistic pluralism of the Vaiśeṣika, on the one hand, and uncompromising monism of the Advaita Vedānta, on the other, which regards the Brahman or the Absolute Spirit alone as the ultimate reality, and the individual souls and the world as its appearances. It agrees with the Nyāya-Vaiśeṣika and the Mīmāṁsaka in recognizing periodic creation and dissolution of the world to realize the ends of puruṣas. It recognizes unconscious finality in the evolution of prakṛti. The Sāṁkhya is an exponent of dualistic realism. It agrees with the Mīmāṁsā system in vehemently criticizing the Nyāya-Vaiśeṣika theism and strongly advocating atheism. The Sāṁkhya of the *Mahābhārata* is theistic. The classical Sāṁkhya system is atheistic. The Yoga system grafts theism on the Sāṁkhya metaphysics, and is therefore called theistic Sāṁkhya.

The Sāṁkhya system derives its name from the word *saṁkhyā*, meaning number, since it enumerates the metaphysical principles of reality. Or, the word *saṁkhyā* may mean perfect knowledge (sam khyā). The system is called Sāṁkhya, since it gives perfect knowledge of the self or puruṣas as quite distinct from prakṛti and its evolutes, body, sense-organs, mind (manas), intellect (buddhi), and egoism (ahaṁkāra), which annihilates all kinds of suffering. There is no evidence for the suggestion that the system is called Sāṁkhya because it was founded by Saṁkha.

Tradition ascribes the origin of the Sāṁkhya system to Kapila. The Sāṁkhya works, *Sāṁkhyapravacanasūtra* and *Tattvasamāsa* are ascribed to him. But there is no evidence to prove it. *Sāṁkhyakārikā* of Īśvarakṛṣṇa (200 A.D.) is the earliest available work in the Sāṁkhya system. Īśvarakṛṣṇa describes himself as a disciple of Pañcaśikha, who was a disciple of Āsuri. Āsuri was a disciple of Kapila, the founder of the Sāṁkhya system.[1] Gauḍapāda (800 A.D.) wrote a commentary on *Sāṁkhya-Kārikā*. There is no evidence to show that he was identical with the author of the commentary on the *Kārikā* on the *Māṇḍukya Upaniṣad*. Vācaspati Miśra (900 A.D.), the great scholiast, wrote a commentary on *Sāṁkhyakārikā*, known as *Sāṁkhyatattvakaumudī* which is regarded as the most authoritative work on the Sāṁkhya system. Nārāyaṇatīrtha wrote a commentary on Gauḍapāda's commentary, called *Sāṁkhya-candrikā*, which is of little value.

The *Sāṁkhyapravacanasūtra* was probably composed in the fourteenth century. Mādhava, who wrote *Sarvadarśanasaṁgraha* about 1380 A.D., does not refer to it, but based his exposition of the Sāṁkhya system on *Sāṁkhya-Kārikā*. Aniruddha (1500 A.D.) wrote a commentary on the *Sāṁkhyapravacanasūtra* known as *Sāṁkhyasūtravṛtti*. Vijñānabhikṣu (1600 A.D.) wrote a commentary on it, named *Sāṁkhyapravacana Bhāṣya* with a theistic bias. His exposition of the classical Sāṁkhya system is not so authoritative as that of Vācaspati Miśra. But Vācaspati and Vijñānabhikṣu are the two great expounders of the system. Vijñānabhikṣu wrote an independent elementary treatise called *Sāṁkhyasāra*. Vedāntin Mahādeva (1700 A.D.) wrote a commentary on the *Sāṁkhyapravacanasūtra* known as *Sāṁkhyasūtravṛttisāra*. Nāgeśa Bhaṭṭa (1700 A.D.) also wrote a commentary on it, called *Laghusāṁkhyasūtravṛtti*, which is of little value. Vedāntin Mahādeva copied Vijñānabhikṣu in the first chapter, and followed Aniruddha in his commentary on the last five chapters. Nāgeśa followed Vijñānabhikṣu faithfully in his commentary. *Tattvasamāsa* is a compendium

---

[1] SK., 70.

of the principles of reality. Mādhava (1400 A.D.) does not refer to it in his *Sarvadarśanasaṁgraha.* So it was probably of a later date. It was a table of contents of the Sāṁkhya philosophy. *Ṣaṣṭitantra* was a manual of the *Sāṁkhya-Yoga,* and not of the classical atheistic Sāṁkhya system.

1. METAPHYSICS

2. *Theory of Causation—Satkāryavāda—Pariṇāmavāda*

The Sāṁkhya theory of evolution of the cosmos out of prakṛti is based upon its theory of causation. The Sāṁkhya maintains that the effect pre-exists in the cause in a potential condition ; the effect is a modification (pariṇāma) of the cause ; it is a manifestation, development, or redistribution of the cause. The effect is not a new beginning (ārambha) as the Nyāya-Vaiśeṣika holds. It is not a new creation. It is not non-existent (asat) in the cause. It exists (sat) in the cause prior to its manifestation. So the Sāṁkhya advocates the doctrine of Satkāryavāda as distinguished from the Nyāya-Vaiśeṣika doctrine of Asatkāryavāda or Ārambhavāda. The Advaita Vedānta also holds that the effect pre-exists in the cause, and so advocates the doctrine of Satkāryavāda. But the Sāṁkhya maintains that the effect and the cause are equally real, the former being a modification (pariṇāma) of the latter, while the Advaita Vedānta maintains that the effect is an unreal appearance (vivarta) of the cause which is real. The Brahman is the ultimate reality ; it is the substratum (adhiṣṭhāna) of the world appearance. In this sense, it is the ultimate cause of all appearances (vivarta) which have only empirical reality. The Sāṁkhya, on the other hand, holds that the cause and the effect both have ontological reality,—the cause being the unmanifest condition of the effect, and the effect being the manifest condition of the cause. The Sāṁkhya advocates Pariṇāmavāda, while the Advaita Vedānta advocates Vivartavāda, both of which are different forms of Satkāryavāda.

Vācaspati mentions four views as to the relation between the cause and the effect. Some (*e.g.*, the Mādhyamika Buddhists) hold that an entity is produced by a non-entity,—an existent effect springs from non-existence or void. Some (*e.g.*, the Advaita Vedāntists) hold that a non-entity is produced by an entity. Brahman is the ultimate reality ; the world with its manifold objects is an unreal appearance of Brahman. Some (*e.g.*, the Naiyāyikas and the Vaiśeṣikas) hold that a non-entity is produced by an entity ; transient effects like dyads are produced by eternal atoms. The Sāṁkhyas hold that an entity is produced by an entity ; an existent effect is produced by an existent cause ; the effect pre-exists in the cause in a potential or unmanifested condition ; the effect is the actual or manifested condition of the cause. If the first three views are right, the existence of prakṛti cannot be inferred from its effects in the form of manifold objects of the world composed of essence (sattva), energy (rajas), and inertia (tamas). But they are not right. The cause and the effect are identical with each other ; the effect is the manifestation of the cause. This is the Sāṁkhya view. Hence the existence of prakṛti can be inferred from its multiform effects in the world.[1] The Mādhyamika view is not right. It maintains that the existent world springs from an undefinable void or non-entity (śūnya). The world cannot be identical with an undefinable void, since there can be no identity between existence and non-existence. If the Mādhyamika view is right, the existence of prakṛti cannot be inferred from the world which is its effect. The Advaita Vedāntist holds that Brahman alone is the ontological reality, and that the world is an unreal appearance (prapañca) of Brahman. There can be no identity of the undifferenced Brahman with the manifold world appearance. Further, the experience of the non-phenomenal Brahman as phenomenal appearance is illusory. But the world is real and cannot be brushed aside as an unreal appearance. So the Vedāntist view is wrong. The Nyāya-Vaiśeṣika holds that transient and unreal effects (*e.g.*, dyads) spring from eternal and real causes (*e.g.*, atoms). But there can be no identity between existence and non-existence which are contradictory to each other. Since an entity and a non-entity cannot be identical, the cause and the effect cannot be identical. If the Nyāya-Vaiśeṣika view is right, the existence of prakṛti cannot be inferred from the world, since they are not identical with each other. But this view is not right, since there can be no identity between eternal and real atoms and transient and un-

---

[1] STK., ix, pp. 141-43.

real, complex products. The Sāṁkhya holds that the cause and the effect both are real and identical with each other. Hence the existence of prakṛti can be inferred from the world, which is its effect, and identical with it.[1]

The Sāṁkhya offers the following arguments to prove the pre-existence of the effect in the cause: (1) If the effect is non-existent in the cause prior to its operation, none can bring it into existence out of the cause (asadakaraṇāt) ; blue cannot be turned into yellow even by a thousand artists. The effect is related to its cause. If it is non-existent prior to the operation of its cause, it cannot be related to it. The causal relation exists between two entities which are existent. So the effect exists both before and after the operation of the cause. Effectuation is nothing but manifestation (abhivyakti). All that is done by the cause is the manifestation of the pre-existent effect. Oil is pressed out of sesamum ; rice is threshed out of paddy ; milk is milched out of the udders of a cow. A non-entity is never found to be manifested or produced. So the effect exists prior to the operation of the cause ; it pre-exists in the cause in a latent or unmanifest condition. (2) A particular effect can be produced out of a particular material cause (upādānagrahaṇāt). A jar can be produced out of clay only ; cloth can be produced out of threads only ; curds can be produced out of milk only. There is a law that particular causes can produce particular effects (upādānaniyāmāt). This proves that the effects are pre-existent in their causes in a latent condition. If they are non-existent in their causes, the causes will be devoid of specific powers (viśeṣa) to produce non-existent specific effects. If they are admitted to have specific powers, these powers are nothing but the latent condition (anāgatāvasthā) of the specific effects. The effects are pre-existent in their causes prior to their operation, since they are related to their material causes. The cause produces the effect when it is related to it. No relation can exist between the existent cause and the non-existent effect. Hence the effect must be existent. (3) If the effect unrelated to the cause could be produced, then every effect would arise from every cause. But every effect does not arise from every cause (sarvasambhavābhāvāt). So the

[1] STK., ix, pp. 144-46.

effect is pre-existent in the cause, and the cause produces the effect when it is related to the effect ; a non-existent effect unrelated to the cause cannot be produced by the cause unrelated to the effect ; only an existent effect related to the cause can be produced by an existent cause related to the effect. (4) The effect pre-exists in the cause, since it can be produced by a potent cause only (śaktasya śakyakaraṇāt). A potent cause has causal energy to produce a particular effect. The causal energy in the cause is inferred from the perception of the effect. This accounts for regularity in the production of particular effects by particular causes. The causal energy (śakti) to produce a particular effect resides in a potent cause only. If it resides in all causes, there will be confusion, and any effect will arise from any cause. If it resides in the potent cause only, it cannot be unrelated to the effect ; the causal energy unrelated to the effect cannot produce it. So the causal energy residing in the cause must be related to the effect, and the effect must be existent in the cause. If it is non-existent, the causal energy cannot be related to it. If the causal energy is unrelated to the effect, then any effect will arise from any cause. Hence the effect must be pre-existent in its potent cause only. (5) The effect pre-exists in the cause, since it is identical in nature with its cause (kāraṇabhāvāt). The effect is not different from the cause. The cause is existent. The effect, therefore, cannot be non-existent. There can be no identity between an entity and a non-entity.

The effect is existent in the cause ; because what is non-existent can never be brought into existence ; because a determinate relation subsists between the material cause and its effect ; because all effects are not produced in all places, at all times ; because a competent cause only can produce an effect for which it is competent ; and because the effect possesses the nature of the cause.[1]

Production is manifestation (avirbhāva). Destruction is disappearance (tirobhāva). It is absorption into the cause (kāraṇalaya). It is passing into a latent condition. Production is transition from an implicit to an explicit condition. Destruction is transition from an explicit to an implicit condition. Production

[1] STK., ix; SPS., i. 114-18; SK., ix.

is unfoldment (abhivyakti). Destruction is enfoldment. Production is development. Destruction is envelopment. Production is evolution. Destruction is dissolution. Gold is transformed into ornaments. Ornaments are melted into gold. Clay is transformed into jars. Jars are powdered into clay. There is neither creation of the non-existent nor destruction of the existent.[1] This view is supported by the Gītā which says: "There is no creation of the non-existent, there is no destruction of the existent."[2] So production is not creation of a non-existent entity, but manifestation of a pre-existent latent effect.

The effect is identical with the cause in essence. The Sāṁkhya offers the following arguments to prove the identity of the cause and the effect: (1) The effect is not different from its material cause, since it is a property of the cause and inheres in it. A cloth is not different from the threads which constitute it ; it is a property of the threads and inheres in them. If an object is different from another is essence, it can never inhere in it. A cow is different from a horse. So the cow cannot inhere in the horse. But a cloth inheres in the threads ; so it is not different from them in essence. (2) There is the causal relation between the material cause and the effect constituted by it. So they are not different from each other in essence. The causal relation can never subsist between two objects which essentially differ from each other. There is no causal relation between a jar and a cloth, which are essentially different from each other. But the causal relation subsists between a cloth and the threads. So they cannot differ from each other in essence. (3) If two objects are different form each other, they can be conjoined with each other, for instance, a pool and a tree, and they can exist separately from each other, for instance, the Himalayas and the Vindhyas. But there is neither conjunction nor separate existence of a cloth and the constituent threads. So they are not different from each other in essence. The material cause and the effect cannot be brought into conjunction with each other ; nor are they capable of separate existence. Hence the material cause and the effect are not different from each other in essence. (4) The material cause and the effect are identical with each other in essence, because

[1] STK., ix. [2] BG., ii. 15.

there is quantitative equality between them. The threads and the cloth are equal to each other in weight. There is quantitative equivalence between them. The weight of the cloth does not differ from that of the constituent threads. This fact conclusively proves the essential identity between the material cause and the effect.[1]

Prakṛti is made of essence (sattva), energy (rajas), and inertia (tamas). They can neither be created nor annihilated. The cause contains these three elements. The effect also contains them. It is a mere redistribution of these three elements in another form. The Law of Causation is a form of the Law of Conservation of Energy or Persistence of Force.

The Naiyāyika criticizes the Sāṁkhya view. He offers the following arguments against it. (1) It is self-contradictory to hold that an effect is produced in the cause and the effect is destroyed in the cause ; the same cause cannot be the abode of two self-contradictory actions, *viz.*, production and destruction. (2) The cause and the effect are objects of different cognitions. We have apprehension of a cloth in the form 'This is a cloth.' But we have apprehension of the constituent threads in the form 'These are threads'. (3) The cause and the effect are objects of different words. They are spoken of by different words. We speak of a cloth in the threads. (4) The cause and the effect serve different purposes. They have different functions. Threads are woven into a cloth. They cannot cover a body. But a cloth can cover a body. Therefore the cause and the effect are different from each other.

The Sāṁkhya urges that these arguments cannot prove the essential difference between the cause and the effect. There is essential identity between them ; their difference is accidental due to manifestation and non-manifestation in one and the same thing.[2] Just as a tortoise puts out its limbs and draws them in, but does not create or destroy them, so the cause is unfolded into the effect, and the effect is dissolved into the cause. Just as the tortoise is not different from its contracting and expanding limbs, so the effects such as jars and crowns are not different from their causes such as clay and gold respectively. Just as we speak of 'trees in the forest', though they are not

[1] STK., ix.

[2] STK., ix.

essentially different from each other, so we speak of 'a cloth in the threads', though they are not essentially different from each other. The difference of functions and purposes does not prove difference in essence, since a single substance can have different functions, as the same fire can burn, cook food and give light. Nor can the uniqueness of functions prove difference among substances, since the same substance can have different functions, singly and collectively. A bearer can see the way when alone, but cannot carry a palanquin, but he can carry it in co-operation with other bearers. Similarly, the threads singly cannot cover, but can do so collectively when they develop into a cloth.[1]

Cause and effect are different states of one and the same substance. So they are distinct from each other. Their distinction is based on our practical interests. A jar can hold water, but a lump of clay cannot. They are distinct from each other because they serve different purposes. But they are not different from each other in their essential nature.[2]

The Sāṁkhya recognizes two kinds of causes, material cause (upādānakāraṇa) and efficient cause (nimittakāraṇa). The material cause enters into the constitution of the effect ; the potentiality of being reproduced in the form of the effect resides in it. The efficient cause exerts an extraneous influence on the effect ; it co-operates with the causal power inherent in the material cause and liberates it ; its causality ceases with the reproduction of the effect. Gold is the material cause of an ornament ; it enters into its constitution, and will continue to be operative as long as the ornament will last, and after its destruction it will relapse into the potential condition again. But the activity of the goldsmith is the efficient cause of the ornament ; it liberates the causal energy inherent in the material cause, and actualizes the potentiality of the effect ; its causality ceases with the production of the ornament.[3]

Patañjali urges that the efficient cause (nimittakāraṇa) in the form of liberating activity (sahakāriśakti) removes the barriers to the production of the effect (varaṇabheda).[4] It is necessary to actualize the potentiality of the effect. The effect

---

[1] STK., ix. [2] SK., xv; SGB., xv.
[3] Nanda Lal Sinha : *The Sāṁkhya Philosophy, preface,* p. ii.
[4] YS., iv. 3.

is present in a latent condition in the material cause. But it cannot pass from latency to actuality without the aid of the efficient cause. According to the Sāṁkhya, all effects are modifications of essence (sattva), energy (rajas), and inertia (tamas); any cause can produce any effect if only the obstructing barriers of a particular effect are removed. The concomitant conditions, according to Vyāsa, are place, time, form, and merit and demerit.[1] Saffron grows in Kashmir only. Paddy grows in the rainy season only. A man is born of a woman only. Pleasure and pain are felt by the soul when merit and demerit abide in it. Thus, place, time, form, and merit and demerit limit the operation of the law of causality.

The Sāṁkhya distinguishes two kinds of effects, simple manifestation and reproduction. When gold is modified into an ornament, there is causation by reproduction. When milk is transformed into cream, there is causation by simple manifestation.[2] Vyāsa distinguishes dharmapariṇāma, lakṣaṇapariṇāma and avasthāpariṇāma. When there is a change of quality or appearance, we have an instance of dharmapariṇāma, for instance, when a lump of clay is made into a jar. When there is a transition from the potential to the actual state—from the future state to the present state, or a transition from the actual to the sublatent state—from the present state to the past state, we have an instance of lakṣaṇapariṇāma. When there is a change of state due to mere lapse of time, we have an instance of avasthāpariṇāma.[3] The causal order is subordinate to the moral order. Natural causation is a means to moral causation.

3. *Prakṛti*

The Sāṁkhya infers the existence of prakṛti from the complex and manifold products in the universe. Īśvarakṛṣṇa argues for the existence of Prakṛti on the following grounds: (1) Individual things manifest to our experience are caused; they depend upon other causes which contain them in a latent condition. The cause must contain at least as much reality as

---

[1] YB., iii. 14.
[2] *The Sāṁkhya Philosophy*, Preface, p. iii.
[3] YB., iii. 15.

the effect contains. Every effect has a cause. Therefore the ultimate cause of the whole universe must be uncaused. Prakṛti is the uncaused cause of the whole world of effects which are its modifications. (2) Individual things are non-eternal or transient. They are absorbed into their causes. They are dissolved into their material causes. Therefore the ultimate material cause of the whole universe is eternal. Prakṛti is the ultimate material cause into which the whole world is dissolved. But prakṛti is never dissolved into a more primal cause. While individual things are transient, prakṛti, the ultimate cause, is eternal. (3) Individual things are limited in magnitude. They are non-pervasive or finite. An effect is pervaded by its cause. But a cause is not pervaded by its effect. The cause must contain more reality than the effect. Or, at least, it must contain as much reality as the effect does. Therefore the ultimate cause of the whole universe must be infinite and all-pervasive. The finite must ultimately depend upon the infinite. Prakṛti is the infinite and ubiquitous cause of the finite effects. (4) Individual things are active and mobile. They are subject to change and mutation. Therefore the ultimate cause of the universe is inactive and immobile. Prakṛti is subject to transformation, but devoid of motion. (5) Individual things are manifold, conditioned, determined, composed of parts, subordinate, and manifest. Therefore the ultimate cause of the universe is one, unconditioned, indeterminate, devoid of parts, independent, and unmanifest.[1]

Individual effects are manifold, while prakṛti is one. They subsist in their causes, while prakṛti does not subsist in any other cause. They are determinate, while prakṛti is indeterminate. They are composed of parts, while prakṛti is partless. They are differentiated and heterogeneous, while prakṛti is undifferentiated and homogeneous. They are subordinate to prakṛti, while prakṛti is self-subsistent and independent.[2] Prakṛti is the matrix of the whole psycho-physical universe. It is the first cause of matter, life, manas, buddhi and ahaṁkāra. The unintelligent world cannot be a transformation of an intelligent principle, since spirit cannot be transformed into matter.

---

[1] SK., x; SPS., i. 124. [2] STK., x.

Prakṛti is the state of equilibrium of sattva, rajas, and tamas.[1] Sattva, rajas, and tamas are substances. They constitute prakṛti. They are in a state of equipoise. There is neither superordination nor subordination among them. The equipoise of the guṇas is not inactivity but a kind of tension. Prakṛti is the triad of guṇas—sattva, rajas, and tamas, and not a different entity which is their substratum. They constitute prakṛti ; they are not its attributes ; they are its very form. Prakṛti is the triad of guṇas, in so far as they are not transformed into effects.[2] This is the definition of the original prakṛti (mūlā prakṛti), the root evolvent, which is not caused.[3] It is the uncaused cause or the First Cause. The definition of prakṛti as evolvent and evolved is that it is the material cause of another evolute which is its transformation. Prakṛti is imperceptible owing to its subtlety. Subtlety does not mean atomic nature, since prakṛti is all-pervasive. Subtlety means a general attribute which prevents the right cognition of it by perception.[4] Prakṛti is called pradhāna, because all effects are founded on it.[5] Prakṛti is absolutely unmanifested (avyakta), while its evolutes are manifested entities. So it is called avyakta.[6] Prakṛti cannot be called primal matter, because it is ground of all modifications, physical and psychical. It is the root cause of matter, life, and mind. All inorganic, organic, and mental products are modifications of prakṛti, which is the prius of all creation. Prakṛti is the unconscious (acetana) matrix of all modifications, physical and psychical.[7] It is the root cause of all objective existence.

The Sāṁkhya advocates dualism. It recognizes the existence of prakṛti and puruṣas. Prakṛti is unconscious. Puruṣa is conscious. Prakṛti is the object of knowledge (dṛśya). Puruṣa is the subject of knowledge or the knower (draṣṭṛ). Prakṛti cannot give rise to puruṣa. Puruṣa cannot give rise to prakṛti. So the Sāṁkhya advocates neither materialism nor spiritualism. It holds that prakṛti evolves for the sake of the puruṣas. The evolution of prakṛti is subservient to the ends of the puruṣas, experience (bhoga) and liberation[8] (mokṣa). It is not mechanical

---

[1] SPS., i. 61.
[2] SVM., i. 61.
[3] SPS., i. 67.
[4] SPB., i. 109.
[5] SPB., i. 125.
[6] SPB., i. 136.
[7] SPS., i. 126; SSV., i. 142.
[8] SK., 21; SPS., iii. 58.

but teleological. There is unconscious finality in the evolution of prakṛti.

4. *The Guṇas*

Prakṛti is constituted by sattva, rajas, and tamas. They are called the guṇas. They are not qualities but substances. They are the ultimate elements in the constitution of prakṛti. Prakṛti is the triad of the three guṇas. They are called guṇas because they are subordinate to the puruṣas, realizing their ends ; or because they are the three strands in the constitution of prakṛti even as there are three strands in a string ; or because they tie down puruṣas to empirical life. They are substances because they are capable of conjunction and disjunction, and because they are endued with qualities.[1] The guṇas are not perceived, but are inferred from their effects or modifications. They are super-sensible.[2] They are of the nature of pleasure, pain, and delusion. They are feeling substances. Sattva has the function of manifestation (prakāśa). Rajas has the function of activity (pravṛtti). Tamas has the function of restraint (niyama). Sattva manifests an object to consciousness. Rajas makes an object move and act. It is the principle of activity. Tamas is the inertia, resistance, or restraint.[3] Sattva, rajas, and tamas have the functions of manifestation, activity and restraint respectively. They produce pleasure, pain, and delusion or indifference respectively.[4] Pañcaśikha says that sattva is in the nature of pleasure in various forms such as purity or transparence, lightness, love, joy, renunciation, contentment, and the like ; rajas is in the nature of pain in various forms such as grief and the like ; tamas is in the nature of delusion in various forms such as sleep and the like.[5] Sattva is light and illumining ; it is buoyant and endued with the power of manifestation. Rajas urges sattva and tamas to act. It is incentive to action. It is the principle of motion. Tamas is heavy and obstructs activity. Sattva and tamas are inactive in themselves. They are incited to act by rajas which energizes them. Rajas is energy. It is the principle of activity. With-

---

[1] SPB., i. 61.
[2] SJM., 12.
[3] SGB., 13.
[4] SK., 12; SPS., i. 127.
[5] SPB., i. 127.

out its aid sattva and tamas cannot function.[1] Just as a lamp can burn when oil, light, and wick co-operate with one another, so the three guṇas function only in co-operation with one another. They overcome one another; they support one another; they produce their effects in co-operation with one another; they intermingle with one another. Though they are antagonistic to one another, they never exist in isolation. Sometimes sattva preponderates over rajas and tamas, overcomes them, and produces its effect, pleasure or manifestation. Sometimes rajas preponderates over sattva and tamas, overcomes them, and produces its effect, pain or action. Sometimes tamas preponderates over sattva and rajas, overcomes them and produces its effect, delusion or restraint. Sattva is the essence to be realized or manifested; tamas is the obstacle to its realization or manifestation; rajas is the energy which overcomes the obstacle and realizes the essence. They coalesce with one another, and function in co-operation with one another.[2] Rajas energizes and activates sattva and tamas which are inactive in themselves. They cannot function without its aid. It is the only principle of activity. It helps sattva to manifest itself by overcoming tamas. It helps tamas to restrain and obstruct by overcoming sattva. It urges sattva and tamas to action.[3] Just as flatulence, bile, and phlegm, though antagonistic to one another, co-operate with one another to preserve the organism, so sattva, rajas, and tamas though antagonistic to one another, co-operate with one another to produce their effects.[4]

Sattva, rajas, and tamas are infinite in number. An infinite number of individual sattva, rajas, and tamas bring about diversity of effects by conflict and co-operation, by excess and diminution. If they were single and ubiquitous, they could not bring about diversity of effects, which is due to conflict of the guṇas. If they were single individuals, they could not bring about increase and diminution.[5] They cannot be created or destroyed. They cannot change into one another. All changes are due to the combination and separation of the guṇas, which are always

---

[1] SK., 13; cp. SSV., i. 127-28.
[2] SK., 13, SGB., STK.; YB., ii. 18; SSV., i. 128.
[3] STK., 13.
[4] STK., 13; YB., ii. 18.
[5] SPB., i. 127

integrating and disintegrating. All effects are due to particular arrangements and collocations (sanniveśa) of the guṇas which are indestructible and eternal.[1] Prakṛti is eternal. It is the ultimate reality behind changing phenomena which are of the nature of manifestation (avirbhāva) and non-manifestation (tirobhāva), evolution and envelopment of the guṇas.[2] Prakṛti is eternal, but its modifications are always changing. Prakṛti is eternal, though mutable (pariṇāminitya).[3]

5. *Evolution*

Prakṛti is the substratum of the changing phenomena of the world. It is the equilibrium (sāmyāvasthā) of the guṇas, sattva, rajas, and tamas.[4] It is not a state of inactivity, but a kind of tension. The tendencies to manifestation (prakāśa) and activity (pravṛtti) are held in check by the tendency to restraint and obstruct (niyama). Infinite number of sattva, rajas, and tamas counteract their activities and bring about a state of tension. They relieve the tension and break the equilibrium under the influence of the puruṣas. The equilibrium of the guṇas is disturbed by some kind of influence of the puruṣas. Prakṛti evolves to realize their ends, experience and liberation.[5]

When the equilibrium of the guṇas is disturbed, some guṇas overpower the other guṇas, and start the process of evolution. There is neither creation nor destruction of the guṇas. The total amount of sattva, rajas, and tamas can neither be created nor destroyed, increased nor decreased. The Sāṁkhya anticipated the law of Conservation of Energy or Persistence of Force. But within the universe some guṇas can overweight the others and produce heterogeneous effects. Production is manifestation or evolution. Destruction is non-manifestation or envelopment. The Sāṁkhya clearly enunciated the doctrine of evolution. The manifold world is not created by God out of nothing. It is evolved from prakṛti, which is the First Cause. It is the matrix of the whole world of effects, physical and psychical. The world is unconscious. It cannot be transformation of a spirit which is unchangeable and immutable

[1] YB., iv. 13.
[2] TV., iv. 13.
[3] SSV., vi. 16; YB., iv. 33.
[4] SPS., i. 61.
[5] SPB., iii. 58; SK., 21.

(kūṭastha). It is the transformation of the unconscious prakṛti. All objective existence is the transformation of sattva, rajas, and tamas. Production is transformation. Prakṛti and its evolutes (vikṛti) are subject to transformation (prasavadharmin). They can never be deprived of their essential nature of modifiability, evolution and dissolution. Evolution is transformation of the homogeneous into the heterogeneous (virūpapariṇāma). Dissolution is the transformation of the heterogeneous into the homogeneous (sarūpapariṇāma).[1] The guṇas are always changing. They can never remain without modification for a moment. They are always subject to modification.[2] Evolution is due to excess of some guṇas and diminution of others. Some guṇas are increased and others are decreased. The excessive guṇas overpower the other guṇas owing to disturbance of their equilibrium, and produce heterogeneous effects. Evolution is transition from the homogeneous to the heterogeneous,—from the undifferentiated to the differentiated. It is due to the integration (samudaya) of the guṇas.[3] Dissolution is the opposite process. It is due to disintegration of the guṇas. It is counter-evolution (pratisarga). In this process heterogeneous effects are disintegrated into the homogeneous reals. Sattva, rajas, and tamas are transformed into their similar modification. Sattva is transformed into sattva. Rajas is transformed into rajas. Tamas is transformed into tamas. In dissolution the heterogeneous is transformed into the homogeneous.[4] Evolution is due to disequilibrium of sattva, rajas, and tamas, and their transformation into heterogeneous modifications. Dissolution is due to disintegration of these heterogeneous modes into the homogeneous guṇas.[5]

Evolution is transition from the potential to the actual (āvirbhāva), from the undifferentiated to the differentiated (saṁsṛṣṭaviveka), from the indeterminate or non-specific (aviśeṣa) to the determinate or specific (viśeṣa), from the unmanifest (aliṅga) to the manifest (liṅga),[6] and from the separable (yutasiddhāvayava) to the inseparable (ayutasiddhāvayava).[7] Evolution is transition from the homogeneous to the heterogene-

[1] STK., 11.
[2] STK., 15-16.
[3] STK., 15-16.
[4] STK., 15-16.
[5] SSV., vi. 42.
[6] YS., YB., ii. 19.
[7] YB., iii. 44.

ous (virūpapariṇāma). The guṇas are transformed into all the evolutes. They are neither created nor destroyed. They appear to be created and destroyed because of accretion and diminution of the individual guṇas.[1]

Prakṛti is transformed into Mahat or the cosmic intellect (buddhi). Mahat is transformed into Ahaṁkāra or the cosmic egoism. Ahaṁkāra is transformed into the eleven sense-organs, and the five tanmātras or subtle essences of sound, touch, colour, taste, and smell. The five subtle essences are transformed into the five gross elements of ether, air, fire or light, water, and earth. These are the twenty four principles.[2] In addition to these there are puruṣas. These are the twenty five principles according to the Sāṁkhya.[3]

Prakṛti evolves into Mahat or Buddhi. It is the unindividuated cosmic intellect. The cosmic Buddhi becomes individuated, and evolves into the cosmic egoism or Ahaṁkāra or Asmitā. The cosmic Ahaṁkāra is bifurcated into the subjective series and the objective series. Vācaspati holds that Ahaṁkāra in its sāttvika aspect evolves into manas, the five organs of knowledge, and the five organs of action. Ahaṁkāra in its tāmasa aspect (bhūtādi) evolves into the five subtle essences (tanmātra). Ahaṁkāra in its rājasa aspect plays its part in both. This aspect is also called the taijasa aspect. The five subtle essences evolve into the five gross elements of earth, water, light, air, and ether by a preponderance of tamas. Sattva and tamas are inactive in themselves. They are energized and moved to function by rajas which is, therefore, not ineffective.[4] In the evolution of these modifications sattva, rajas, and tamas are all present, and perform their functions, though sattva predominates in the evolution of the psychical apparatus, and tamas predominates in the evolution of the physical universe.[5]

Vijñānabhikṣu gives a slightly different account of the evolution of the cosmos. Prakṛti is modified into Mahat. Mahat is modified into Ahaṁkāra. Ahaṁkāra is modified into the eleven sense-organs, on the one hand, and the five subtle essences (tanmātra), on the other. The five subtle essences are

---

[1] YB., ii. 19.
[2] SK., 22.
[3] SPS., i. 61.
[4] STK., 25.
[5] STK., 25.

modified into the five gross elements.[1] Ahaṁkāra in its sāttvika aspect evolves into manas. Ahaṁkāra in its rājasa aspect evolves into the ten sense-organs, the five organs of knowledge and the five organs of action. Ahaṁkāra in its tāmasa aspect evolves into the five tanmātras.[2]

Patañjali says that sattva with its power of manifestation, rajas with its power of activity, and tamas with its power of restraint are modified into the known universe consisting of subtle and gross elements of matter and the psychical apparatus, the five organs of knowledge, the five organs of action, and the three internal organs, mind (manas), intellect (buddhi), and egoism (ahaṁkāra), to realize the ends of the puruṣas.[3] The modifications of the guṇas are determinate, indeterminate, manifest, and unmanifested.[4] Vyāsa says that the five tanmātras are indeterminate or non-specific (aviśeṣa) modes, and the five gross elements of matter are their determinate or specific modes (viśeṣa). Asmitā or the cosmic egoism is an indeterminate or non-specific mode, and the five organs of knowledge, the five organs of action, and the manas are its determinate or specific modes. These are the sixteen determinate or specific modes. Asmitā is an indeterminate or non-specific mode. The five subtle essences (tanmātra) of sound, touch, colour, taste and smell are indeterminate or non-specific modes. Asmitā and the five tanmātras are the indeterminate or non-specific modes of the mere being of Mahat. Prakṛti is unmanifest (avyakta) ; it is devoid of manifest signs (aliṅga). Mahat is a manifest mode (liṅga) of prakṛti ; it is a manifest sign from which prakṛti is inferred. Prakṛti is eternal. It cannot serve the ends of the puruṣas without being transformed into Mahat.[5] The guṇas in their indeterminate, determinate, and manifest conditions are non-eternal, and serve the ends of the puruṣas.[6] The purposes of the puruṣas are the efficient cause of these modifications, while the guṇas are their material cause. The manifest modes remain undifferentiated in the unmanifest prakṛti, and then they are differentiated from it. The transformations of the guṇas are subject to a causal order of succession which cannot be reversed by them (pariṇāmakramaniyama). The six in-

[1] SPB., i. 61.
[2] SPB., ii. 18.
[3] YS., ii. 18, YB.
[4] YS., ii. 19.
[5] YB., ii. 19.
[6] YB., ii. 19.

determinate modes remain undifferentiated in Mahat, and then are differentiated from it. Similarly, the five gross elements of matter and the eleven organs remain undifferentiated in the indeterminate modes, and then are differentiated from them. The determinate modes are not transformed into other modes. They are subject to change of quality (dharmapariṇāma), change of characteristic (lakṣaṇapariṇāma), and change of state (avasthāpariṇāma).[1]

Vācaspati says that the indeterminate Asmitā or egoism, with an excess of sattva, is modified into the determinate modes of the organs of knowledge. Asmitā, with an excess of rajas, is modified into the organs of action. Asmitā, with an excess of sattva and rajas both, is modified into the manas, which is both cognitive and motor organ.[2]

Vyāsa says that the subtle essence of sound has the quality of sound only. The subtle essence of touch has two qualities, sound and touch. The subtle essence of colour has three qualities, sound, touch, and colour. The subtle essence of taste has four qualities, sound, touch, colour, and taste. The subtle essence of smell has five qualities, sound, touch, colour, taste and smell. The subtle essences (tanmātra) are called the fine elements.[3] They are indeterminate or non-specific modes. The five gross elements, ether, air, light, water, and earth are the determinate or specific modes of the indeterminate or non-specific tanmātras.[4]

The atoms of the five elements are generated from the subtle essences. They are not the finest and indivisible parts of gross elements. They are evolutes of the tanmātras. The earth atom is generated from the five subtle essences of smell, taste, colour, touch and sound, of which that of smell is the chief. The water atom is generated from the four subtle essences of taste, colour, touch and sound, of which that of taste is the chief. The light atom is generated from the three subtle essences of colour, touch and sound, of which that of colour is the chief. The air atom is generated from the two subtle essences of touch and sound, of which that of touch is the chief. The ether atom is generated from the subtle essence

---

[1] YB., ii. 19.
[2] TV., ii. 19.
[3] YB., ii. 19.
[4] YB., ii. 19.

of sound.[1] The subtle essence of smell is the chief cause of the earth atom. The subtle essence of taste is the chief cause of the water atom. The subtle essence of colour is the chief cause of the light atom. The subtle essence of touch is the chief cause of the air atom. The subtle essence of sound is the cause of the ether atom.[2] Each of these subtle essences is the chief constituent of the specific kind of atom generated by it, though other subtle essence are combined with it.[3] The subtle essences are the cause of atoms. Ahaṁkāra is the cause of the subtle essences. Buddhi or Mahat is the cause of Ahaṁkāra. Prakṛti is the cause of Buddhi or Mahat. There is no cause of prakṛti. It is the First Cause. The cause is finer than its effect.[4]

The atoms are not partless and indivisible. They are effects, and so non-eternal, whereas prakṛti is the ultimate cause.[5] The Sāṁkhya analyses the atoms into the subtle essences (tanmātra), which are finer than the atoms, and traces the tanmātras finally to prakṛti.

The Sāṁkhya does not regard the atoms as the indivisible parts of the material elements as the Nyāya-Vaiśeṣika does. The atoms are the evolutes of the subtle essences which are evolved from prakṛti. The Nyāya-Vaiśeṣika regards the atoms as the material cause of the world. The Sāṁkhya, on the other hand, regards prakṛti as the material cause of the world. The Nyāya-Vaiśeṣika does not recognize the atoms of ether. It considers ether (ākāśa) to be one ubiquitous substance. The Sāṁkhya, on the other hand, recognizes the atoms of ether. Both recognize the reality of the atoms of earth, water, light, and air. The Sāṁkhya argues that just as the existence of the atoms is inferred from their qualities in their effects such as jars and the like, so the existence of prakṛti characterized by sattva, rajas, and tamas is inferred from its effect, the world composed of elements producing pleasure, pain and delusion.[6] Just as a jar made of a lump of clay is traceable to the atoms of earth through a succession of causes, so all effects including

---

[1] TV., i. 44.
[2] YB., i. 45.
[3] YV., i. 45.
[4] YB., i. 45.
[5] SSV., SVM., V. 87.
[6] SSV., i, 69, 110.

the atoms are traceable to prakṛti through a succession of causes.[1]

When the gross atoms combine with one another, their qualities are found in their products. The earth atom has solidity. The water atom has viscosity. The light atom has heat. The air atom has mobility. The ether atom has penetrability.[2] The atoms combine with one another and form aggregates (samūha). These aggregates are of two kinds, separable and inseparable. Separable aggregates are those whose parts can be separated from one another (yutasiddhāvayava), *e.g.,* a forest, a crowd, and the like. Inseparable aggregates are those whose parts cannot be separated from one another (ayutasiddhāvayava) *e.g.,* a body, a tree, an atom. An atom is an inseparable aggregate of subtle essences, one of which is the predominant element. Its parts cannot be separated from one another without breaking its integrity. A plant organism and an animal organism also are inseparable aggregates. They cannot be broken into parts without destroying their integrity.[3]

The gross atoms constitute inorganic matter, plant organisms, and animal organisms. There is continuity in the evolution of these three grades of matter. The gross atoms give rise to these modifications owing to their different arrangements (saṁsthāna).[4] The gross atoms of earth and the like are modified into jars, cows, and the like.[5] There is no difference in the constituents of inorganic things, plant organisms, and animal bodies. There are only changes in the qualities of the constituents. Changes in their qualities are due to their different arrangements.

The gross body (sthūladeha) is composed of the five elements, earth, water, light, air, and ether.[6] Some hold that it is composed of the first four elements. They do not regard ether as its constituent.[7] Others consider earth to be the only constituent of the gross body. They consider the other elements as giving an impetus to the combination of the atoms of earth. Or there are different kinds of bodies composed of either earth,

---

[1] SSV., i. 74.
[2] YB., iii. 44.
[3] YB., iii. 44.
[4] YB., iii. 13.
[5] TV., iii. 13.
[6] SPB., iii. 17.
[7] SPB., iii. 18.

water, light, air, or ether. The human body is composed of earth. The body of a spirit in the sun is composed of light.[1]

There are six kinds of bodies. Some insects are generated from moisture (uṣmaja). Birds, serpents, and the like are born of eggs (aṇḍaja). Men and others are born of wombs (jarāyuja). Plants are born of the soil (udbhijja). Some are born of the will (saṁkalpaja). Some are born of miraculous powers of penance, mantras, and the like (sāṁsiddhika)[2] Earth is the predominant element in all these kinds of bodies. The other elements are subordinate to it.[3]

Life is the common function of the three internal organs, mind (manas), intellect (buddhi), and egoism (ahaṁkāra). Some wrongly hold that the five vital forces are particular kinds of air, which perform their functions through the aid of the vital effort of the soul (jīvanayoniprayatna). They are neither different kinds of air nor their modifications. The emotions of lust and the like which are mental modes, agitate the vital powers. Hence, both emotions and vital powers must be modifications of the mind (manas.)[4]

Life is not the material cause of the body, though it is predominant in it. Life springs from a particular power of the sense-organs. In their presence life is present. In their absence life is absent. Life consists in the functioning of the sense-organs. When they cease to function, life disappears. In a dead body the sense-organs cease to function. Hence it is deprived of life. Therefore life is not the material cause of the body.[5]

The Sāṁkhya does not regard vital power as a physical (bhautika) force. Life is sustained by the powers of all the sense-organs, which are not material. It is the general function of all the sense-organs.[6] The Sāṁkhya recognizes the subtle body (sūkṣmadeha) in addition to the gross body (sthūladeha). The gross body is the vehicle of the soul's experience in its empirical life.[7] It is dissolved into its constituent elements on death. But the subtle body clings to the soul. It transmigrates into another gross body with the help of its subtle body.

[1] SPB., iii. 19.
[2] SPB., V. 111.
[3] SPB., V. 113.
[4] SPB., V. 112.
[5] SPB., ii. 31.
[6] SSV., V. 113, SVM., V. 113, SK., 29, YB., iii. 39.
[7] SPB., iii. 9.

It is called also liṅgaśarīra. It is composed of the ten sense-organs, the five subtle essences (tanmātra), mind (manas), intellect (buddhi), and egoism (ahaṁkāra). Life is the common function of the sense-organs. So the five vital forces, prāṇa, apāna, vyāna, samāna, and udāna also enter into the constitution of the subtle body.[1] These are the different forms of life. They are due to the operation of the sense-organs. The subtle body is atomic, but not devoid of parts. It is limited in magnitude. It is not absolutely atomic, since it is composed of parts.[2] Vācaspati admits the two kinds of bodies, gross and subtle.[3] But Vijñānabhikṣu recognizes another kind of body, the adhiṣṭhāna body, which supports the subtle body when the soul transmigrates to another sphere of existence. The adhiṣṭhāna body is composed of five subtle material elements. So there are three kinds of bodies.[4]

6. *Unconscious Teleology*

The Sāṁkhya does not advocate mechanical evolution of prakṛti. It believes in unconscious teleology in its evolution. Prakṛti is the matrix of all things in the world, physical and mental. The physical order is subservient to the moral order. Physical causation is governed by moral causation. Prakṛti evolves into the subtle essences, the atoms, the gross elements, and physical things, on the one hand, and into the sense-organs, mind (manas), intellect (buddhi), and egoism (ahaṁkāra), or the psychical apparatus, on the other, for the experience, enjoyment and suffering of the puruṣas in bondage.[5] The evolutes of prakṛti are adapted to their moral deserts, merits and demerits.[6] Even as unconscious trees bear fruits according to the merits and demerits of different persons, so prakṛti evolves into various modes in accordance with the merits and demerits of the bound souls owing to the beginninglessness of the empirical life.[7] Prakṛti resolves its evolutes into their constituents, and relapses into its primeval, quiescent state for the liberation of the puruṣas. Evolution is a means to the experience of the bound souls. Dissolution is a means to the liberation

[1] SPB., SSV., iii. 9.
[2] SPB., iii. 14.
[3] STK., 39-41, YB., iii. 39.
[4] SPB., iii. 11-12.
[5] SK., 21.
[6] SPS., iii. 51; ii. 46.
[7] SSV., iii. 62.

of the souls. Thus evolution and dissolution are instrumental to the experience and liberation of the souls.[1] Prakṛti unconsciously realizes the ends of the souls. Thus the Sāṁkhya believes in unconscious teleology in cosmic evolution. It believes in external teleology in the sense that prakṛti realizes the purposes of the puruṣas which are foreign to it. The Sāṁkhya advocates uncompromising dualism of puruṣas and prakṛti which are absolutely different from each other.

The Sāṁkhya advocates periodic evolution and dissolution of the world. Dissolution is relapse of prakṛti into the original quiescent state. It is the period of complete rest of the bound souls whose merits and demerits are not entirely exhausted by enjoyments and sufferings. Evolution is the transformation of prakṛti into physical things and the psychical apparatus for the experience of the bound souls. Dissolution is the complete cessation of the creative function of prakṛti owing to the puruṣa's discrimination between itself and prakṛti.[2]

7. *Prakṛti and its Evolutes*

The Sāṁkhya recognizes twenty five principles of reality. Of these puruṣa is neither a cause nor an effect. It is beyond causal change. It is an immutable spirit. It is unaffected by modal transformation. Causation is transformation of the guṇas, sattva, rajas, and tamas. The puruṣa is not composed of them, and is therefore neither a cause nor an effect.

Prakṛti is the First Cause of the aggregate of all effects in the world. It is their ultimate cause. It is not the effect of any other cause. If it had any other cause, it would lead to infinite regress. Prakṛti is a cause but not an effect. It is not a modification of any other ultimate cause.

Mahat or Buddhi, Ahaṁkāra, and the five subtle essences (tanmātra) of sound, touch, colour, taste, and smell are both causes and effects. They are effects of some causes and causes of some other effects. Buddhi is an effect of prakṛti. It is the cause of Ahaṁkāra. Ahaṁkāra is the effect of Buddhi. It is the cause of the five tanmātras or subtle essences. The subtle essences of sound, touch, colour, taste, and smell are the effects

---

[1] SK., 21; SPS., iii. 58. [2] SSV., iii. 63.

of Ahaṁkāra. They are the causes of the atoms of ether, air, light, water, and earth respectively. The essence of sound generates ether. The essence of touch generates air. The essence of colour generates light. The essence of taste generates water. The essence of smell generates earth. The essences of sound, touch, colour, taste, and smell are the chief constituents of ether, air, light, water, and earth respectively. So the seven principles of Mahat, Ahaṁkāra, and the five essences of material elements are causes (prakṛti) as well as effects (vikṛti).

The five sense-organs of knowledge, the five sense-organs of action, the internal organ of mind (manas), and the five gross elements are only effects. They are not causes of any other principles. Though the gross elements of earth, water, light, air, and ether are transformed into various inorganic things, vegetable organisms, and animal organisms, they are not to be considered as their material cause (prakṛti), since they do not give rise to other principles of reality (tattvāntara), but simply generate new qualities owing to their different collocations and arrangements (saṁsthāna).[1] The five elements and their aggregates in the form of inorganic things, plant and animal organisms are equally apprehended by the external sense-organs, and are therefore to be considered as gross matter. The inorganic things and vegetable and animal organisms are not principles of reality different from the gross elements (tattvāntara).[2] Thus, the sixteen principles of the ten external sense-organs, the internal organ of manas, and the five gross elements (mahābhūta) are only effects, and not causes.[3]

Prakṛti is unmanifest (avyakta). All its evolutes, Mahat, Ahaṁkāra, Manas, the external sense-organs, the tanmātras, and the gross elements are manifest (vyakta). The unmanifest prakṛti (avyakta) is uncaused, eternal, ubiquitous, motionless, one, self-subsistent , irresolvable, partless and independent. The manifest evolutes of prakṛti (vyakta) are caused, non-eternal, limited, mobile, manifold, subsisting in their material causes, resolvable into their elements, composed of parts, and dependent.[4] All the evolutes of prakṛti, from Mahat down to

---

[1] STK., 3.
[2] STK., 3.
[3] SGB., STK., 3.
[4] SK., 10.

the gross elements are effects produced by some causes (hetumat). They are non-eternal (anitya) because they spring from their causes. They are non-pervasive or limited (avyāpi). The effect is pervaded by its cause. The cause is not pervaded by its effect.[1] The cause is greater than its effects. The effect is less than its cause. Descartes likewise maintains that the cause contains at least as much reality as is contained in the effect. The cause contains more than the effect does. The cause can never be less than its effect. Buddhi and the other evolutes of prakṛti cannot pervade prakṛti, their material cause. So they are non-pervasive or limited. The evolutes of prakṛti are capable of motion (sakriya). The motion of the elements of earth, body, and the like is quite evident. Buddhi, ahaṁkāra, and manas, and the external senses which constitute the subtle body move from one gross body to another during transmigration. So they are capable of movement. Prakṛti is active in the sense that it is transformed into its effects. But it is devoid of physical motion (parispanda). So it is immobile (niṣkriya).[2]

The evolutes of prakṛti are manifold (aneka). Intellects, egoisms and minds are different in different individuals. The subtle essences and the gross elements also are manifold. The modifications of the gross elements also are manifold. The evolutes of prakṛti subsist in their material cause (āśrita). Though there is identity between cause and effect, there is the difference of substance and modification. The evolutes are related to their causes as modifications to their substances.[3] Buddhi subsists in its cause, prakṛti. Ahaṁkāra subsists in its cause, buddhi. The internal organ of manas, the ten external sense-organs, and the five subtle essences (tanmātra) subsist in their cause, ahaṁkāra. The five gross elements subsist in their causes, the five subtle essences of sound, touch, colour, taste, and smell. The evolutes of prakṛti are resolved into their constituent elements. The five gross elements are resolved into the five tanmātras. The five tanmātras and the eleven sense-organs are resolved into ahaṁkāra. Ahaṁkara is resolved into buddhi. Buddhi is resolved into prakṛti. The evolutes of prakṛti are endued with sound, touch, colour, taste, and smell

---

[1] STK., 10. [2] STK., 10. [3] STK., 10.

(sāvayava), while prakṛti is devoid of these qualities.[1] Or they involve inter-mingling or conjunction of constituents which can exist apart from one another. For instance, the elements of earth, water, and the like can come into conjunction with one another. The tanmātras can come into conjunction with one another. But prakṛti cannot come into conjunction with buddhi, ahaṁkāra, and the like, since they are identical with each other in their essential nature. Likewise, sattva, rajas, and tamas cannot come into conjunction with one another, since they can never exist apart from one another.[2] The evolutes of prakṛti are dependent on other principles (paratantra). Buddhi depends upon prakṛti ; ahaṁkāra depends upon buddhi ; the tanmātras and the sense-organs depend upon ahaṁkāra, and the five gross elements depend upon the tanmātras, to produce their respective effects.[3] The unmanifest prakṛti is uncaused, eternal, ubiquitous, motionless,—though not inactive,—one, self-subsistent, irresolvable, partless or devoid of conjunction or qualities, and independent. It is opposed to the manifest evolutes of prakṛti.[4] These are the dissimilarities between prakṛti and its effects (vikṛti).

The unmanifest prakṛti and its manifest effects have the following similarities. They are composed of sattva, rajas, and tamas (triguṇa), inseparable (aviveki), objects (viṣaya), common to many puruṣas (sāmānya), non-intelligent (acetana), and productive (prasavadharmin).[5] Prakṛti and its effects are composed of the three guṇas (triguṇa), sattva, rajas, and tamas. They are feeling-substances, pleasure, pain, and delusion, which are not the qualities of the puruṣa or self. Prakṛti and its effects are inseparable (aviveki). Prakṛti cannot be separated from itself. Buddhi, ahaṁkāra, and the like also cannot be separated from prakṛti owing to their identity in nature. Or, the manifest effects of prakṛti can produce their effects only in co-operation with one another. None of them can produce its effects singly, but in co-operation with others. No effect can be produced by a cause singly.[6] Prakṛti and its effects are composed of the guṇas, sattva, rajas, and tamas, which are the feeling-substances of pleasure, pain, and delusion. But they are not

---

[1] SGB., 10.
[2] STK., 10.
[3] SGB., 10.
[4] STK., 10.
[5] SK., 11.
[6] STK., 11.

cognitions or subjective modes (vijñāna). They are objective. They are objects of consciousness, external to cognitions.[1] So they are common (sāmānya) to many selves apprehending them. If they were mere cognitions, they would not be the common objects of many persons' cognitions. The cognitions of a person are peculiar to him. They are imperceptible to other persons. So they are not subjective ideas. They are external objects of knowledge. They are known objects, while the puruṣas are the knowers.[2] Prakṛti and its effects are non-intelligent or unconscious (acetana), while the puruṣas only are intelligent or conscious. Buddhi and its modes are unconscious. They appear to be conscious owing to the reflection of the puruṣas in buddhi. The mental modes are non-intelligent in themselves. But they appear to be intelligized by the puruṣas.[3] Prakṛti and its effects are always productive (prasavadharmin). They are either creative or destructive. They always undergo transformation. They either pass from the homogeneous to the heterogeneous. Or they pass from the heterogeneous to the homogeneous. They can never be deprived of similar (sadṛśapariṇāma) or dissimilar transformation (visadṛśapariṇāma).[4] They are subject to constant modification every moment.[5]

8. *Space and Time*

Space and time are not independent realities as the Nyāya-Vaiśeṣika and the Mīmāṁsaka maintain. They are generated from ether (ākāśa). They are modifications of ether.[6] Ether is modified into space and time with the help of adjuncts. So they are included in ether. They are nothing but ether modified by certain adjuncts. There is some difference between the qualified (viśeṣya) and the qualification (viśeṣaṇa). Ether is qualified by adjuncts (upādhi), and is transformed into space and time. So they are said to be generated from ether, though, in reality, they are nothing but ether.[7] Vijñānabhikṣu considers eternal space and time to be of the nature of ether. He considers them to be specific modes of prakṛti. Prakṛti is ubiquit-

---

[1] STK., 11.
[2] STK., 11.
[3] STK., 11.
[4] STK., 11.
[5] SPS., ii. 10.
[6] STK., 5.
[7] SSV., SVM., ii. 12.

ous. So time and space also are ubiquitous. But limited times and spaces are generated from ether in conjunction with their limiting adjuncts. Infinite space and time are in the nature of ether. But finite space and time are products of ether.[1]

Vijñānabhikṣu says in *Yogavārtika* that the one eternal space is not a metaphysical reality. There is no proof for its existence. The limited spaces, east, west, north, south, and the like are conceivable in relation to one another. They are conceived as parts of ether. They are products of ether. They cannot exist apart from ether. They are not independent entities. We understand by space ether limited by such adjuncts as determine east, west, and the like. Ether is the permanent substratum of limited spaces. There is no one eternal space, in reality, apart from limited spaces which are products of ether co-existing with one another. The difference between space and time lies in that time consists of moments which are not co-existent, while space is an order of co-existent points.[2]

Vācaspati says that the Sāṁkhya does not recognize time as an independent reality. The Vaiśeṣika considers time to be one eternal, ubiquitous substance which appears to be many on account of its limiting adjuncts. The Sāṁkhya maintains that the past, the present, and the future are determined by specific modes or adjuncts (upādhi) which alone are real, and that one real time is useless. One eternal time cannot be divided into past, present, and future.[3]

Vyāsa gives a clear account of the nature of time. A moment is the indivisible unit of time even as an atom is the indivisible unit of a material substance. A moment is the duration of time which an atom in motion requires to leave one point in space and reach the next point. Sequence is the continuous flow of moments. Moments alone are real. Sequence is conceived by the intellect. Two moments cannot co-exist simultaneously. There can be no sequence between two simultaneous moments. Sequence is the posteriority of a subsequent moment to an antecedent moment. So the present moment alone is real and existent ; the past and future moments are unreal and non-existent. Therefore their aggregates are non-existent.

---

[1] SPB., ii. 12. [2] YV., iii. 52. [3] STK., 33.

The past is past. The future is not yet come. They are non-existent at the present moment. So the past, the present, and the future moments cannot form aggregates. Sequence is the continuity in the flow of moments. There are no aggregates of moments or sequences in reality. They are made into aggregates by the intellect. Hours, days, months, and the like are merely intellectual aggregates (buddhisamāhāra). They are not real aggregates of moments (vastusamāhāra). One, infinite, eternal time is an intellectual construction (buddhinirmāṇa). It appears to be a reality to empirical consciousness. The intellect constructs aggregates of moments and conceives hours, days, months, years, and ultimately one infinite time. These are mental constructs. Moments alone are real. They follow a definite order or sequence. Sequence is succession of events occurring in moments. This sequence of momentary events is known as time.[1]

In reality, the present moment alone is real. The past moments and the future moments are unreal. They exist in a subtle condition at the present moment in the form of modifications. They are past and future in relation to the present moment. The entire universe undergoes modifications at the present moment. All its modifications occur at the present moment. They do not occur at the past and future moments since they are non-existent.[2] The intellect constructs the idea of sequence out of the present moments occurring one after another in a definite order. Vācaspati says that sequence is not real, but mental. It is subjective (kālpanika). It is not objective (vāstava).[3] Vijñānabhikṣu says that there is no time apart from moments. The aggregates of moments are imaginary aggregates made by the intellect (buddhikalpitasamāhāra). There is no proof for the existence of one eternal time. All causes and effects occur in moments. All uses and actions refer to limited times.[4] Our empirical life does not presuppose one eternal time. So the Sāṁkhya considers the moment alone to be real time. The moment apart from an event is an abstraction. It is a particular modification of sattva, rajas, and tamas. All events are transformations of the guṇas. The moment is a real mode of the guṇas.[5]

---

[1] YB., iii. 52.
[2] YB., iii. 52.
[3] TV., iii. 52
[4] YV., iii. 52.
[5] YV., iii. 52.

Vyāsa points out that the past and the future are not altogether non-existent. They exist in subtle forms in the present condition. The future is what will be manifested. The past is what has been manifested. The present is what is engaged in its activity. The future, the past, and the present are objects of knowledge. If they were non-existent, they would not be apprehended. So the past and the future exist in reality.[1] The past and the future do not exist in an object in the same form as the present exists in it. The present exists in a substance in the form of a particular manifest modification of sattva, rajas, and tamas. The past and the future do not exist in such a manifest condition in a substance. The future exists in it in its potential condition which will be manifested. The past exists in it in its sub-latent condition which was manifested. The past and the future exist in a substance in a subtle (sūkṣma) unmanifest condition. The present only exists in it in a manifest, actual (vyakta) condition.[2]

9. *Puruṣa*

The Sāṁkhya advocates dualism of prakṛti and puruṣa. They are entirely different from each other. They have opposite characteristics. Prakṛti is composed of the three guṇas, sattva, rajas, and tamas. Puruṣa is not composed of the guṇas. Prakṛti is non-discriminating. Puruṣa is discriminating. Or prakṛti is an aggregate. Puruṣa is simple. Prakṛti is the object of knowledge. Puruṣa is the subject of knowledge. Prakṛti is common to many persons. Puruṣa is different in different bodies. Prakṛti is non-intelligent or unconscious. Puruṣa is intelligent or conscious. Prakṛti is productive. It is transformed into modifications. Puruṣa is non-productive. It is not subject to modification.[3] Puruṣa is neither a cause nor an effect.[4] It is unchangeable and immutable. All things change every moment except the conscious self or puruṣa.[5] Prakṛti is active. Puruṣa is inactive. Prakṛti is constant in the midst of mutations (pariṇāminitya). Puruṣa is constant beyond all mutations (kūṭasthanitya).[6] The essential difference between prakṛti and

---

1 YB., iv. 12.
2 YB., iv. 12; iv. 13.
3 SK., 11.
4 SK., 3.
5 STK., 6.
6 YB., iv. 33, SSV., vi. 13.

puruṣa lies in that the former is the unconscious and known object, while the latter is the conscious knower or subject. Prakṛti with all its modifications, manas, buddhi, and ahaṁkāra are unconscious. Only puruṣa is conscious.

The Sāṁkhya puts forward the following arguments to establish the existence of the puruṣa. (1) Prakṛti, Mahat, Ahaṁkāra and the like are aggregates of sattva, rajas, and tamas, and therefore means to the ends of other beings, like beds, chairs, and the like. They are unconscious (acetana). They serve the ends of conscious spirits or puruṣas. The body is an aggregate of the five gross elements. It is enjoyed by the puruṣa, even as a bed is enjoyed by it.[1] The puruṣa is not an aggregate. It is different from the body, manas, buddhi, and ahaṁkāra, which are aggregates of sattva, rajas, and tamas.[2] (2) All knowable objects are non-intelligent (acetana), non-discriminating (aviveki), objects (viṣaya) of knowledge. They are composed of the three guṇas, sattva, rajas, and tamas (triguṇa). Therefore, they presuppose the intelligent (sacetana), discriminating (viveki), subject of knowledge (jñātṛ), devoid of the three guṇas (atriguṇa). All knowable objects presuppose the knowing subject or self.[3] (3) All non-intelligent products of prakṛti, inorganic things, plant organisms, and animal organisms, must be controlled and directed by the intelligent spirits or puruṣas even as non-intelligent chariots move when they are controlled and guided by charioteers. Matter is inert. It cannot act by itself. It can act only when it is controlled by a spirit. So all material objects of the world require guidance by intelligent puruṣas. Prakṛti and its activities are guided by the selves which supervise them.[4] (4) Prakṛti is composed of sattva, rajas, and tamas. They are held by some Sāṁkhyas to be feeling-substances, pleasure, pain, and delusion. They are objects of experience (bhogya). They presuppose the subjects of experience or experiencers (bhoktṛ). Or, pleasure and pain are objects of experience. They are modes of the intellect (buddhi) or mental modes. Pleasure is an agreeable feeling. Pain is a disagreeable feeling. Pleasure affects the self agreeably. Pain affects it disagreeably. Therefore, pleasure and pain, which are mental modes, presuppose the self or puruṣa

[1] SK., 17; SGB., 17; STK., 17.
[2] SPB., i. 140.
[3] SGB., STK., 17.
[4] SGB., STK., 17; SPB., i. 142.

which experiences them. The intellect (buddhi) cannot be the experiencer (bhoktṛ). It is non-intelligent and unconscious. Pleasure and pain are mere modes of buddhi. Therefore, buddhi cannot be the experiencer. It cannot be self and not-self, subject and object at the same time, since it is self-contradictory. The self, which is different from buddhi, is the experiencer of pleasure and pain, which are its modes. Each self feels its own pleasure and pain, which are modes of its buddhi. Pleasure and pain are experienced by the self which is different form them.[1] Others put the argument thus: All knowable objects (bhogya, dṛśya) presuppose the existence of the knower (bhoktṛ, draṣṭṛ). There can be no known or knowable objects without the knowing subjects. There can be no not-self without self.[2] Experience belongs to the immutable self. It cannot belong to the body, or the intellect, which is not-self or object, and cannot, therefore, become self or subject.[3] (5) Some spiritual aspirants strive and struggle to achieve liberation. Liberation consists in absolute cessation of three kinds of suffering. It is complete negation of pain. Buddhi and the like are themselves in the nature of sufferings. They are modes of buddhi. So buddhi can never be relieved from sufferings. It is only the self, which is distinct from buddhi and the like, which can be relieved from sufferings and achieve liberation.[4]

The Sāṁkhya recognizes the existence of many selves or puruṣas and puts forward arguments for their existence. (1) Birth, death, and the sense-organs are different in different persons. If there were one self (puruṣa) only, the birth of one person would lead to the birth of all, the death of one would lead to the death of all, and the defects in the sense-organs in one would lead to the same defects in the sense-organs in all. Deafness, dumbness, and lameness of one would make all others deaf, blind, dumb, and lame.[5] Madness of one would make all others mad. So there are many puruṣas; there are different selves in different bodies.[6] The puruṣa is immutable. It is incapable of birth and death. Birth consists in the connection of a self with a unique aggregate of body, sense-organs, buddhi, and

---

[1] STK., 17.
[2] STK., 17.
[3] SPB., i. 143.
[4] STK., 17; SPB., 1. 144.; SK., 17.
[5] SGB., 18.
[6] STK., 18; SPS., vi. 45.

mental modes. Death consists in the self's severance of connection with the unique aggregate or mind-body-complex. The self, which is unchangeable, is neither born nor dies. Different souls are connected or disconnected with different mind-body-complexes.[1] (2) If there were one self in different bodies, the activity of one person would lead to the activity of all. But, in fact, different persons are engaged in different kinds of activity. Some are engaged in the pursuit of virtue. Some are engaged in the pursuit of vice. Some are engaged in cultivating detachment. Others are engaged in acquiring knowledge. Hence, there are different selves engaged in different kinds of activity.[2] Activity is the expression of a volition, which is a mode of the internal organ (buddhi). The self is inactive. Activity is attributed to it owing to its connection with the buddhi, which is active. If there were one self in all bodies, it would move them all at the same time. But, in fact, different bodies move at different times. So there are different souls in different bodies.[3] (3) Different selves are equipped with different moral endowments. Gods are endowed with buddhi in which sattva predominates. Men are endowed with buddhi in which rajas predominates. Beasts are endowed with buddhi in which tamas predominates.[4] Again, among men some are happy owing to the excess of sattva; some are unhappy owing to the excess of rajas; others are under delusion owing to the excess of tamas.[5] So there are many selves, which are devoid of the guṇas, but are endowed with different mind-body-complexes with an excess of either sattva, rajas, or tamas. The Sāṁkhya rejects the Advaita Vedānta doctrine of one self.[6]

The Sāṁkhya recognizes the plurality of souls and the spiritual unity of each soul. Puruṣa is distinct from its material vestment, the body, manas, buddhi, and ahaṁkāra.[7] It is distinct from prakṛti and its effects. It is devoid of sattva, rajas, and tamas. It is discriminating. It is simple. It is the knower. It is not common to many persons. It is intelligent or conscious. It is non-productive.[8] It is beyond causality. It is neither cause nor effect.[9] It is eternal and immutable (apari-

[1] STK., 18; SPB., i. 149.
[2] SGB., 18.
[3] STK., 18.
[4] STK., 18.
[5] SGB., 18.
[6] SK., 18.
[7] SPS., i. 139.
[8] SK., 11.
[9] SPB., i. 61; SK., 3.

ṇāminitya), while prakṛti is eternal and mutable (pariṇāminitya).[1] It is beyond time and space. Eternal time and space are nothing but ether. Limited space and time are modes of ether. Ether is a mode of prakṛti.[2] Puruṣa is conscious (cetana). It is not an object (aviṣaya). So it is the witness (sākṣin), the seer (draṣṭṛ). The conscious self only is the seer. An unconscious object cannot be the seer. A witness is one to whom objects are shown. Prakṛti shows its effects and modifications to the self which is their witness, even as a plaintiff and a defendant show their object of dispute to a witness. The self is the witness to which buddhi shows its mental modes.[3] It is inactive (akartṛ). The guṇas are active. Buddhi is active, since it is composed of the guṇas. Puruṣa appears to be active owing to its connection with buddhi. But it is not really active.[4] Buddhi is unconscious. But it appears to be conscious owing to its connection with puruṣa.[5] Thus, puruṣa is conscious but inactive. It is ubiquitous (vyāpin).[6] It is devoid of movement (niṣkriya).[7] It is said to have movement owing to its limiting adjunct, the body, which is capable of movement even as all-pervading ether is said to have movement owing to its limiting adjuncts, jars and the like.[8] It is indifferent (madhyastha, udāsīna). It is free from pleasure, plain, and delusion, since it is devoid of the guṇas. It is free from attachment and aversion. It is free (kevala). It is distinct from the guṇas. It is entirely free from entanglements in the meshes of prakṛti. It is, in its intrinsic nature, free from all kinds of pain.[9]

Puruṣa is eternal (nitya), pure (śuddha), conscious (buddha), and liberated (mukta). It is eternal in the sense that it is beyond the temporal order. It is not determined by time. It is non-temporal. It is free from virtue and vice. It is devoid of merit and demerit which are the modes of buddhi. It is eternally conscious. Its essential nature of consciousness never ceases. It is eternally free. Pain is a mode of buddhi. It is wrongly appropriated by the puruṣa owing to non-discrimination. Puruṣa wrongly ascribes pain to itself from which it is absolutely free. Bondage is phenomenal. It is due to confusion of

---

[1] YB., iv. 33.
[2] SPB., ii. 12.
[3] STK., 19.
[4] STK., 19.
[5] SK., 20.
[6] SPS., 1. 12-13.
[7] SPS., 1. 49.
[8] SPS., 1. 51.
[9] STK., 19.

the puruṣa with buddhi. When the confusion is dispelled by discrimination, puruṣa realizes its intrinsic freedom.[1]

Puruṣa is the seer (draṣṭṛ). It is the knower. But it is not an inert (jaḍa) substance, which acquires the attribute of consciousness in conjunction with the manas, as the Nyāya-Vaiśeṣika holds. Matter does not manifest itse'f. If the self were an inert, material substance, it would require another conscious substance to manifest it. The parsimony of hypotheses demands that the self itself be of the essence of consciousness (prakāśarūpa), which manifests all things in the world.[2] Consciousness is not a mode (dharma) of the self, since it is devoid of the guṇas, and therefore unmodifiable. The self is immutable and not liable to modification. So consciousness cannot be a mode of the self.[3] The self cannot be known, when cognition which is of the nature of manifestation is not known. There is no relation of substance and quality or mode between the self and cognition. Cognition is not its quality, since it is capable of conjunction with objects, and does not depend upon a substratum to support it. Cognition is, therefore, neither a mode (dharma), nor a quality (guṇa) of the self. It constitutes its essence (svarūpa). The self is essentially conscious.[4]

The self is distinct from matter (jaḍa). It is the knower, the seer (draṣṭṛ). Matter is an object of knowledge (dṛśya). The self is of the essence of consciousness (dṛśimātra)[5] It manifests or apprehends matter. Manifestation (prakāśa) is not its mode. But it constitutes its essence.[6] Matter is unconscious. It does not manifest itself. It is manifested by the self. If the self also were a material substance, it would be manifested by some other entity. So the self should be considered to be of the nature of manifestation (prakāśarūpa).[7] If the self were material (jaḍa), it would not be the witness (sākṣin) or known in dreamless sleep. But we have an experience, 'I slept soundly.'[8] The self is the witness in three grades of empirical life, waking,

[1] SPB., i. 19.
[2] SPS., SSV., i. 145.
[3] SSV., i. 146; SPS., i. 146; YV., ii. 20; SPB., i. 146.
[4] SPB., i. 146.
[5] YS., ii. 20.
[6] SSV., vi. 50.
[7] SSV., 1. 145.
[8] SSV., i. 148, 160, 161.

dream, and dreamless sleep.[1] The self is a witness in the sense that it is of the essence of cognition only.[2]

Śaṁkara, the Vedāntist, holds that the self is of the essence of consciousness and bliss (cidānandarūpa). But the Sāṁkhya considers pleasure and pain to be unconscious modes of buddhi which do not affect the conscious self. It is devoid of pleasure and pain.[3] The self is devoid of the guṇas and therefore unchangeable. So bliss cannot be a mode (dharma) of the self. If bliss were the essence (svarūpa) of the self, it would be experienced in empirical life which is full of suffering. Consciousness is cognition. Bliss is pleasure. If the self were of the nature of consciousness and bliss, it would be affected by duality.[4] Pleasure is not a particular kind of cognition. The self is of the nature of immutable cognition.[5] So it is of the essence of cognition. Empirical cognition is a mental mode. But transcendental cognition is the essence of the self.

The self is free from attachment and aversion. Attachment is craving for pleasureable objects. Aversion is antipathy towards painful objects.[6] They are modes of buddhi. The self is free from desire (icchā) and aversion (dveṣa).

The self is inactive (akartṛ). The guṇas are active. The self appears to be active in connection with them.[7] Volition (prayatna), which is expressed in action (pravṛtti), is a mode of the internal organ or buddhi. It is attributed to the self owing to its connection with buddhi.[8] Sometimes egoism (ahaṁkāra) is said to be active. Volition (kṛti) is a mode of egoism. The self, which is immutable, cannot have volition.[9] Ahaṁkāra is a mode of buddhi. Buddhi is a mode of the guṇas, sattva, rajas, and tamas. So volition is said to be a mode of the guṇas, buddhi, or ahaṁkāra.[10] The self is inactive in the sense that it is devoid of desire, aversion and volition.[11]

---

1 SPS., iii. 26.
2 Candrikā on SK., 19.
3 STK., 17.
4 SSV., v. 66.
5 SPB., V. 66.
6 YS., ii. 7-8.
7 SK., SGB. 20.
8 STK., 18; SSV., i. 106; i. 52; i. 153.
9 SPS., SPB., SSV., vi. 54.
10 Candrikā on SK., 19; Sk., 20; STK., 18.
11 SPS., vi. 54.

The self is free from merit (dharma) and demerit (adharma). It is devoid of moral deserts (adṛṣṭa). It is eternally pure. It has neither virtue nor vice.[1] It does not acquire moral qualities. Purity constitutes its essence. The self is devoid of the guṇas. So merit and demerit are not its modes.[2] They are the modes of egoism or buddhi.[3]

The self is free from disposition (saṁskāra). It is the impression left by a past cognition. It is revived by certain conditions and gives rise to recollection.[4] It is a modification of buddhi. The self is devoid of the guṇas. It is immutable ; so it cannot be the substratum of disposition. Buddhi is the substratum of all dispositions.[5] They do not subsist in the external senses, manas, and ahaṁkāra. Even blind and deaf persons can remember things seen and heard in the past. Even when manas and ahaṁkāra are destroyed by right knowledge of reality, there is recollection. So dispositions are modes of buddhi, and subsist in it.

Thus, the Sāṁkhya differs from the Nyāya-Vaiśeṣika and the Mīmāṁsaka in holding that the self is devoid of pleasure, pain, desire, aversion, volition, merit, demerit, and disposition. The Sāṁkhya considers them to be modes of buddhi (buddhipariṇāma).

The Sāṁkhya differs from the Nyāya-Vaiśeṣika in considering cognition to be the essence (svarūpa) of the self and not to be its accidental quality (dharma) acquired in conjunction with the manas and the body as the latter holds. The Sāṁkhya differs from the Advaita Vedānta in considering bliss or pleasure to be a mode of buddhi, whereas the latter regards the self as of the essence of bliss. The Sāṁkhya differs from the Buddhist in regarding the self as an eternal (nitya) immutable (kuṭastha) spirit distinct from the stream of consciousness or mental modes. The Buddhist regards the self as an aggregate of mind-body-complex (saṁghāta) or a stream of cognitions, feelings, and volitions (vijñānasantāna). The Sāṁkhya conceives the self as the transcendental self (sākṣin, draṣṭṛ) beyond the temporal series of changing empirical modes. It is beyond time, space,

---

[1] SPB., i. 19.
[2] SSV., i. 52; SSV., vi. 62; SPS., V. 25.
[3] SSV., vi. 62.
[4] SSV., ii. 43, 44.
[5] SPB., ii. 42.

and causality. The Sāṁkhya differs from the Cārvāka in regarding the self as an immaterial, incorporeal, conscious principle distinct from the body, the sense-organs, manas, buddhi, and ahaṁkāra. The Cārvāka identifies the self with the body.

The Sāṁkhya criticizes the Cārvāka doctrine that consciousness is a product of the material elements of the body. Consciousness is not found in the different parts of the body. So it is not its natural property. Nor can it be a property of the aggregate of the elements, since it is not a property of the constituent elements.[1] So consciousness is not a natural property of the body. In dreamless sleep and death the body becomes unconscious. If consciousness were its natural property, it would exist in the dead body and during dreamless sleep.[2] The Cārvāka argues that consciousness is produced by the aggregation of the elements of the body, though they are devoid of it, even as intoxicating power (mādakaśakti) is produced by the aggregation of molasses and other ingredients, though they are devoid of it. This is wrong. No quality can exist in a product, which does not exist in its cause. If consciousness exists, in a subtle form, in each element of the body, then only it can appear in the joint product of all the elements. Intoxicating power exists in a subtle form in each ingredient of liquor. So it appears in a manifest condition, when all the ingredients are mixed up together. But consciousness is not experienced in each element of the body. If it is said to be inferred from the manifestation of consciousness in the whole body, it is a gratuitous hypotheseis. It is better to assume the existence of one, eternal self, which is of the nature of consciousness, than to assume many consciousnesses in the constituent elements of the body. The parsimony of hypotheses demands the existence of one eternal self which is of the nature of consciousness. Consciousness cannot be a property of a corporeal body. It is the essential nature of an incorporeal, immaterial spirit or self.[3] If the self were identical with the body, then there would be different souls in childhood, boyhood, youth, and old age, and the soul would perish along with death of the body.[4] Further, we never experience our bodies to be ourselves, but instruments of our experience. We

---

[1] SSV., iii. 20.
[2] SPB., iii. 21.
[3] SPS., iii. 22; SPB., iii. 22.
[4] SSV., vi. 2.

speak of our bodies. We never speak of ourselves as bodies.[1] Therefore the self is not identical with the body.

10. *Jīva*

The Sāṁkhya draws a distinction between the transcendental self and the empirical self, and calls the former puruṣa and the latter jīva. The puruṣa is an eternal, ubiquitous, immaterial, inactive, immobile, eternally pure, conscious, and free spirit. It is non-temporal, non-spatial, and non-causal. It is devoid of the guṇas. It is the noumenal self. It is unchangeable and immutable. It has no empirical modes. It has no empirical cognitions, feelings, and volitions. It is devoid of pleasure, pain, desire, aversion, volition, merit, demerit, and disposition, which are unconscious mental modes. It is of the nature of consciousness (citsvarūpa). It is a conscious (cetana) subject (aviṣaya), seer (draṣṭṛ), or witness (sākṣin). It is not active. It appears to be active in conjunction with buddhi.

The puruṣa, in itself, is not an agent, or enjoyer, since it is immutable. The jīva is an agent, and enjoyer. The self (puruṣa) as determined by the body and the sense-organs is the jīva. It can act and enjoy in their presence. It cannot act and enjoy in their absence.[2] The self, in its intrinsic nature, is not a jīva. If it were an active jīva, it would cease to be immutable.[3] The jīva is the self determined by the body and the sense-organs, endowed with the powers of enjoying and acting.[4] The self (ātman) appears to be active on account of its proximity to buddhi in which it is reflected. The acts of doing, enjoying, and guiding are attributed to it which is really inactive. Activity of the self is illusory.[5] The bodily acts of eating and the like also belong to the jīva, and not to the self which is immutable. Aniruddha defines the jīva as the self determined by the body, the external sense-organs, manas, ahaṁkāra, and buddhi.[6] The self (ātman) which is devoid of empirical cognition (vṛttijñāna), merit, demerit, and other mental modes is the ātman. But it becomes the jīva, when it is determined by the body and connected with manas through

[1] SSV., vi. 3.
[2] SPS., vi. 63.
[3] SSV., vi. 63.
[4] SVM., vi. 63; SSV., i. 106.
[5] SSV., i. 96.
[6] SSV., i. 97; vi. 63.

its relation to life which contains an aggregate of air, light, and the like. Merit, demerit, knowledge, ignorance, pleasure, pain, and the like are modes of buddhi or ahaṁkāra in conjunction with the external senses, which are in communion with their objects. Buddhi is transparent owing to the excess of sattva in it. The self is reflected in it. So it wrongly thinks itself to be active. This false appropriation of activity belongs to the jīvātman, or the self reflected in buddhi, not to the self (ātman). The self reflected in buddhi appears to be active, though buddhi alone, the reflecting medium, is active, even as the moon reflected in water appears to tremble, though, in reality, water trembles. The self (ātman) is immutable, and free from attachment to the guṇas. So its activity is false. Activity implies change or modification. Attachment is the spring of action. So the self cannot be active. The jīvātman becomes identical with the ātman when its material vestment is destroyed by intense meditation. When meditation matures, dispositions gradually diminish and manas is destroyed. When the manas is destroyed, dispositions are destroyed. When dispositions are destroyed, the body is annihilated, and no other body can be produced. Then the jīvātman is deprived of its limiting adjuncts, the body, and the manas, and becomes identical with the ubiquitous ātman, and free from merit, demerit, and activity.[1]

Vijñānabhikṣu defines the jīva as the self limited by egoism (ahaṁkāra). Vital acts belong to the jīva or the empirical self. They do not belong to the puruṣa or the transcendental self. The jīva differs from the puruṣa or the paramātman in that the former is limited by the adjuncts of the internal organ, while the latter is the pure self free from all determinations.[2] Vijñānabhikṣu defines the jīva also as the self reflected in the internal organ or buddhi, which is active, as distinguished from the puruṣa or the pure self which is immutable and of the nature of transcendental consciousness, and therefore inactive.[3]

The pure or transcendental self is the puruṣa, the ātman, or the paramātman. It is not identical with Brahman of the Advaita Vedāntist, which is one, non-dual. The Sāṁkhya recognizes many pure selves, which are irreducible to one self. The empirical self, or the self as limited and determined by

---

[1] SSV., vi. 59; SSV., i. 97; SSV vi. 63; SSV., vi. 59.
[2] SPB., vi. 63. [3] SPB., i. 97.

its psycho-physical organism, the body, the senses, the manas, buddhi, and ahaṁkāra is the jīva or the jīvātman. All empirical cognitions (vṛttijñāna), feelings, emotions, volitions, actions, merit and demerit belong to the empirical self. The transcendental self is free from all these mental modes. The empirical self is limited in time and space in its experience. The transcendental self is eternal and ubiquitous. It is beyond time and space. When the limiting adjunct (upādhi) of the psycho-physical organism is completely destroyed, the jīva becomes identical with the puruṣa, and realizes its intrinsic freedom. It is divested of all empirical modes including merit, demerit, disposition, and activity. It is manifested as pure, transcendental consciousness entirely free from all entanglements in prakṛti.[1] So the jīva is a mixture of matter and spirit, prakṛti and puruṣa. When it completely breaks the shackles of prakṛti it becomes the puruṣa.

The Sāṁkhya is uncompromising in its dualism of puruṣa and prakṛti. Puruṣa is the seer (draṣṭṛ) or witness (sākṣin). It is of the nature of transcendental consciousness (dṛśimātrā), as distinguished from empirical cognitions (vṛttijñāna). The body, manas, buddhi, ahaṁkāra, and all their modes are the modes of prakṛti. They are unconscious objects. They constitute the material vestment of the puruṣa. They constitute the empirical self. Puruṣa is the subject self. Jīva is the object self. Puruṣa is the seer (draṣṭṛ). Jīva is the seen (dṛśya). The Nyāya-Vaiśeṣika self (ātman) is the empirical self or jīva of the Sāṁkhya. It is an object (viṣaya) of internal perception or intuition. It is endued with cognition, pleasure, pain, desire, aversion, volition, merit, demerit, and disposition. The Sāṁkhya regards all these as modes of buddhi, which cannot belong to the immutable self.

The Sāṁkhya distinction between the pusuṣa and the jīva resembles the Advaita Vedānta distinction between the Ātman and the jīva. According to the Advaita Vedānta, the Ātman is pure, eternal, undifferenced consciousness, while the jīva is the pure consciousness limited or determined by the internal organ (antaḥkaraṇa). The jīva is the Ātman limited by the adjunct (upādhi) of the psychical apparatus, which is a mode

---

[1] SSV., vi., 59.

of its avidyā. Avidyā is a fragment of māyā or cosmic nescience which is peculiar to an individual jīva. But the Sāṁkhya recognizes the reality of many puruṣas or pure selves, while the Advaita Vedānta believes in one Ātman only. Some Sāṁkhyas hold that the puruṣa is reflected in buddhi. Some Advaita Vedāntists hold that the Ātman is reflected in the internal organ (antaḥkaraṇa).

Every jīva has a subtle body (liṅgaśarīra) formed of the ten sense-organs, manas, buddhi, and ahaṁkāra, and the five subtle essences.[1] It is the basis of rebirth.[2] The gross body is born of the parents. But the subtle body is not so born.[3] The gross body is the effect of the subtle body. The enjoyment (bhoga) of the subtle body is real, while that of the gross body is apparent, which has no enjoyment in death.[4] The subtle body is the medium of enjoyment. The jīva enjoys its empirical life through it. Merit and demerit (karma) are the individuating principles. The jīvas differ from one another on account of their different moral deserts. They are distinguished from one another by their distinct moral equipments.[5] Merit (dharma) and demerit (adharma) are modes of ahaṁkāra. Ahaṁkāra is an evolute of buddhi. So they are also modes of buddhi.[6] The bondage of the jīva is due to the subtle body through which merit and demerit, which are modes of buddhi or ahaṁkāra, are wrongly appropriated by the self or puruṣa. The bondage of the puruṣa is only phenomenal. So long as the subtle body continues, merit and demerit are wrongly owned by the puruṣa. When it achieves discrimination (viveka), merit and demerit are destroyed, and therefore no longer appropriated by it, and it attains liberation. Discrimination is the knowledge of distinction between puruṣa and prakṛti, the transcendental self and the not-self including the empirical self or jīva. Discrimination leads to the destruction of merit and demerit, which dissolves the subtle body, annihilates empirical life, and leads to liberation.[7] The transcendental self (puruṣa) should not be identified with the subtle body, since it is an aggregate (saṁghāta) of manas, buddhi, ahaṁkāra, the

---

[1] SSV., iii. 9.
[2] SPS., iii. 16.
[3] SPS., iii. 7.
[4] SPS., SSV., SVM., iii. 8.
[5] SPS., iii. 10.
[6] SPS., SSV., vi. 62.
[7] SPS., SSV., vi. 67-70.

external senses, and the five subtle essences of material elements, and therefore a means to the realization of the purposes of the puruṣa.[1]

11. *Puruṣa and Buddhi*

The jīva, the empirical self, has empirical cognition (vṛttijñāna), pleasure, pain, desire, aversion, volition, merit, demerit, and disposition. The puruṣa, the pure self, is devoid of these mental modes. But it is reflected in buddhi, wrongly identifies itself with its reflection in buddhi, and thinks all its modes to be its own, though, in reality, it is immutable and devoid of modes. Aniruddha says that the jīva, the empirical self, or the self limited by its psychical apparatus, is the actor (kartṛ), enjoyer (bhoktṛ), and guide (adhiṣṭhātṛ), since the self (puruṣa) is reflected in buddhi owing to its proximity.[2] The luminous self (puruṣa) is reflected in the internal organ of buddhi which is intelligized by it, since it appears to be conscious owing to the reflection. The unconscious buddhi intelligized by the reflection of the self in it is the guide owing to the proximity of the self.[3] The puruṣa itself is neither an actor nor an enjoyer. But it appears to be active owing to its reflection in buddhi. It wrongly thinks itself to be an active agent owing to the reflection.[4] Its false sense of activity is due to its reflection in buddhi owing to its proximity to buddhi.[5] Prakṛti is an object of enjoyment (bhogya). Puruṣa is the enjoyer (bhoktṛ). The pure self (puruṣa) is immutable (kūṭastha) and cannot, therefore, be an enjoyer. But it appears to be an enjoyer owing to its reflection in buddhi. Buddhi and the other sense-organs act for the realization of the purposes of the puruṣa which is reflected in buddhi and appropriates the merits and demerits subsisting in it.[6] Aniruddha holds that the self only is reflected in buddhi, but buddhi is not reflected in the self. He follows Vācaspati's view.

Patañjali says that the seer which is of the nature of consciousness and devoid of modes appears to have mental modes.[7] Vyāsa clearly distinguishes between puruṣa and buddhi. The

---

[1] SPS., SSV., iii. 13.
[2] SPS., SSV., i. 96.
[3] SPS., SSV., i. 99.
[4] SPS., SSV., i. 106.
[5] SPS., SSV., i. 164.
[6] SSV., i. 143.
[7] YS., ii. 20.

puruṣa is of the nature of consciousness. It is the seer of buddhi and its modes. It is reflected in buddhi. So the modes of buddhi appear to be its own modes.[1] The puruṣa is different from buddhi in nature. First, buddhi is mutable. Its objects are sometimes known and sometimes unknown. It knows the objects into which it is modified. It does not know the objects into which it is not modified. The mental modes conform to their objects. This shows the mutability of buddhi. But the puruṣa always knows the modes of buddhi without being modified into them. This shows that it is immutable. Thus, buddhi is mutable(pariṇāmin), while Purusa is immutable (apariṇāmin). Secondly, buddhi serves the purposes of a puruṣa (parārtha) since it is an aggregate of sattva, rajas, and tamas, while the puruṣa realizes its own purposes (svārtha). Buddhi is an instrument of the self. It is its psychical organ which realizes its ends. Buddhi is subordinate to the self which is independent. Thirdly, buddhi is modified into all objects and yields determinate knowledge of them. So it is formed of sattva, rajas, and tamas. It is unconscious (acetana). The puruṣa is conscious (cetana). It is the seer of buddhi and its modes. It is the knower. Buddhi is the known. Though the puruṣa is different from buddhi, yet it is not absolutely different from it. Though the puruṣa is pure or devoid of the guṇas, it thinks the modes of buddhi to be its own modes. The self is reflected in buddhi, knows its modes and appears to be identical with it, though it is never, in reality, identical with it.[2] Thus the puruṣa appears to be endued with the mental modes of pleasure, pain and the like, which are unconscious. Pañcaśikha says, "the immutable conscious self, devoid of movement and transference, is reflected in the mode of buddhi, modified into the form of an object, and wrongly appropriates the mental mode as its own, and manifests it. The mental mode (buddhivṛtti) receives the reflection of the self ; the cognition (jñānavṛtti) of the self, imitating as it does the mental mode, appears to be non-different form it."[3]

Vācaspati holds that the conscious puruṣa, devoid of mental modes, is reflected in the unconscious buddhi modified into cognition, pleasure, and other modes, wrongly identifies itself

---

[1] YB., ii. 20. [2] YB., ii. 20. [3] YB., ii. 20, iv. 22.

with buddhi, and thinks the mental modes to be its own, though, in reality, it is immutable.[1] The puruṣa knows buddhi when it is reflected in it. External objects are known, when they come into contact with buddhi which receives the reflection of the self. Buddhi is modified into the forms of its objects. The self is reflected in the mirror of buddhi which is modified into these forms. Then only the self knows them. The self is immutable. It can never be modified into buddhi which is formed of sattva, rajas, and tamas. It is devoid of the guṇas. So it can know objects by being reflected in buddhi, not by being modified into it.[2] Vācaspati holds that the self is reflected in buddhi, but buddhi is not reflected in the self. Vijñānabhikṣu states Vācaspati's view thus: The self manifests a function or mode of buddhi only when it is reflected in the mode. The mental mode is known by the self only when it receives its reflection. There is no reflection of the mental mode in the self.[3]

But Vijñānabhikṣu holds that the pure self is the knower (pramātṛ), the mode of buddhi (buddhivṛtti) modified into the form of its object is the means of knowledge (pramāṇa), the reflection of the mode of buddhi with the form of its object in the self is valid knowledge (pramā), and the object of the mode of buddhi in which the self is reflected is the object of knowledge (prameya). The self is the witness (sākṣin) of the mode of buddhi, since it directly knows it. It is the knower (draṣṭṛ) of external objects through the modes of buddhi. It has direct knowledge of mental modes but indirect knowledge of external objects.[4] The self cannot be modified into the form of an object, since it is immutable. But an object can be known by the self only when it acts upon the self and modifies it. To obviate this difficulty, Vijñānabhikṣu assumes that the mode of buddhi being modified into the form of its object does not modify the self, but is reflected in the self. This reflection of the mode of buddhi in the self constitutes the knowledge of the self. Here there is no transference (uparāga) of the mode of buddhi to the self, but there is reflection of it in the self leading to a false sense of identity (abhimāna) between puruṣa and buddhi. The modes of buddhi cast their reflections in the self, without

[1] STK., 4.
[2] TV., ii, 20.
[3] SPB., i. 87.
[4] SPB., i. 87.

which it can never have knowledge of objects. So the self is reflected in the transparent buddhi, and buddhi is reflected back in the self. The self cannot have knowledge of objects without this double reflection.[1] There is a peculiar relation between puruṣa and buddhi. It is neither contact nor causation. But it is double reflection between them. There is mutual reflection of the self in buddhi as well as of buddhi in the self. The reflection of the self in buddhi is assumed to account for the knowledge of the self by itself. The self can know itself only through the aid of its reflection in buddhi. It cannot know itself directly, since it cannot be the knower and the known at the same time. This reflection of the self in buddhi is called the appearance of the self (cidāveśa). It leads to a false sense of identity between them. The reflection of buddhi in the self is assumed to account for the knowledge of buddhi modified into the forms of objects by the self. The self cannot know objects by being modified into them, since it is immutable. But it can know them when buddhi modified into their forms is reflected in it. The reflection of buddhi in the self is the cause of its knowledge of all objects.[2] Vijñānabhikṣu explains his view more explicitly in the *Yogavārtika*. How can the immutable self, which cannot be modified into objects, know them? The objects are shown to it by budhi. The modes of buddhi with the forms of objects are reflected in the self, and thus known by it.[3] Though the self is of the essence of consciousness and immutable, the reflections of the modes of buddhi with the forms of objects appear to be the modes of the self. The modes of buddhi appear to be the modes of the self on account of mutual reflection of the self in buddhi and of buddhi in the self. So the reflection of buddhi in the self must be admitted. Otherwise, all objects would be always known by the self, since it is immutable, eternal, and ubiquitous, and consequently, related to them all. Like the reflection of buddhi in the self, that of the self in buddhi also must be admitted. Otherwise, the self would not be known. If it were known by itself directly, it would be subject and object of knowledge at the same time, which is self-contradictory. The self does not know itself directly. It can know itself only through the

[1] SPB., i. 87.
[2] SPB., i. 99; YV., i. 2, 4.
[3] YV., i. 2, 4.

aid of its reflection in buddhi, even as we cannot see our face directly, but only its image in a mirror. So the self can know itself through its reflection in buddhi .The false sense of identity is due to the mutual reflection of the self in buddhi, and of buddhi in the self. 'I am an actor'. 'I am happy'. 'I know'. These experiences are due to the double reflection of the self and buddhi in each other.[1] Thus Vijñānabhikṣu's view differs from that of Vācaspati. The former assumes double reflection of the self in buddhi and of buddhi in the self, while the latter assumes single reflection of the self in buddhi. These theories are assumed to account for the relation of the self to buddhi and external objects. The Sāṁkhya-Yoga posits buddhi as the intermediary between the self and external objects. Buddhi is modified into the forms of the objects. It also receives the reflection of the self. It is the meeting point between the self and objects. Buddhi appears to be an intelligent knower on account of the reflection, though it is, in reality, an unintelligent object . It is coloured by 'the self and the objects.[2] Vācaspati holds to the reflection of the self in buddhi, while Vijñānabhikṣu holds to the reflection of buddhi in the self in addition to it.

Vyāsa says that the self can have an intuition (prajñā) of itself by concentrating attention on its reflection in buddhi. It is the pure self that knows its reflection in buddhi. The pure self is the knower. Its reflection in buddhi is known. The sattva of buddhi intelligized by the reflection of the self in it does not intuit the pure self.[3] Vācaspati makes it more clear. Unconscious matter is manifested by the conscious self. The self cannot be manifested by matter. The mode of buddhi is unconscious, and cannot, therefore, manifest the self. The conscious self, which is self-luminous, manifests unconscious matter. It manifests the unconscious mode of buddhi in which it is reflected. The pure self is the knowing subject, and the buddhisattva which takes in the reflection of the self and is modified into its form is the object of self-apprehension. The pure self is the knower, while the empirical self is the known.[4] The pure self can intuit itself when it concentrates its attention on its reflection in a mode of buddhi, and withdraws it from

---

[1] YV., i. 4; IPP., pp. 232-36.
[2] YS., iv. 23, YB., iv. 23.
[3] YB., iii. 35.
[4] TV., iii, 35

the mental mode.[1] But Vijñānabhikṣu holds that the self knows itself through the reflection, in itself, of the mode of buddhi, which takes in the reflection of the self and is modified into its form, just as it knows an external object through the reflection, in itself, of the mode of buddhi which assumes the form of the object.[2] There is double reflection of the self in buddhi and of buddhi in the self in the supernormal intuition of the self also. But Vijñānabhikṣu holds that the same self cannot be subject and object of knowledge at the same time. The self as determined by the mode of buddhi modified into its form is the subject of self-apprehension, while the pure self undetermined by the mental mode is the object of self-apprehension.[3]

This interpretation appears to be wrong. The pure self is the knower. The self as reflected in buddhi is known. The pure self can intuit itself only through the empirical self determined by the mode of buddhi in which it is reflected by concentrating its attention on its own reflection apart from the mode in which it is reflected. The pure self cannot intuit itself directly.

Vyāsa holds that the mind (citta, buddhi) becomes the object of knowledge of the self by mere proximity (sannidhi), like a magnet. Buddhi does not come into contact with the self in order to be known by it. It attracts the self by mere proximity and is known by it. So there is a beginningless relation (anādisambandha) between puruṣa and buddhi, which is the cause of its experience of mental modes (cittavṛtti-bodha).[4]

Vācaspati urges that there can be no contact between the incorporeal puruṣa and the corporeal buddhi in time or space, but that there is a proximity (sannidhi) in the form of a special fitness (yogyatā). There is special fitness between puruṣa and buddhi, so that the former is the experiencer (bhoktṛ) and the latter is the experienced (bhogya) without coming into contact with each other in time or space. Though experience (bhoga) is a modification of buddhi into external objects, it appears to be the puruṣa's experience owing to the false sense of identity with buddhi (abhimāna). Hence, though the puruṣa does not come into contact with buddhi, it seems to have the experience

---

[1] IPP, p. 235.
[2] YV., iii. 34.
[3] YV., iii. 34.
[4] YB., 1. 4.

of the modes of buddhi, though it is not modified by them. The beginningless relation of the immutable self with the mutable buddhi, in the form of the owner (svāmin) and the owned (sva) is due to beginningless ignorance (avidyā) or false identification of the self with buddhi (abhedasamāropa).[1]

Vijñānabhikṣu contends that there is no special kind of fitness (yogyatā) between puruṣa and buddhi, which makes the former the experiencer (bhoktṛ) and the latter the experienced (bhogya). If there were such fitness, it would be eternal, and could not be terminated by discriminative knowledge (vivekajñāna), and the puruṣa would never be released. If the fitness be supposed to be non-eternal, conjunction (saṁyoga) between puruṣa and buddhi would serve the purpose, because it is non-eternal. Both fitness and conjunction, which are non-eternal, would make the puruṣa mutable and non-eternal. Fitness has not been mentioned in the *Sāṁkhyapravacanasūtra* and the *Sāṁkhya Kārikā.* So it is not authoritative. It is an unwarranted innovation on the part of Vacaspati. A special kind of conjunction (saṁyogaviśeṣa) between puruṣa and buddhi is the cause of bondage.[2] There is a real conjunction between puruṣa and prakṛti. But conjunction is not modification (pariṇāma). Modification of a thing implies production of some particular property in it in addition to the general attributes of the class. If it were not so, ubiquitousness of the immutable self could not be proved. Nor is mere conjunction attachment (saṅga). It is conjunction that is the cause of modification which is denoted by attachment. So Vijñānabhikṣu concludes that there is a special conjunction between puruṣa and prakṛti, that is the cause of bondage.[3]

12. *Puruṣa and Prakṛti*

The distinction between puruṣa and prakṛti has been discussed. The relation between them is a crux of the Sāṁkhya philosophy. Prakṛti is active but unconscious. Puruṣa is inactive but conscious[4]. Prakṛti acts to realize the ends of puruṣas. It evolves the world for their experience (bhoga). It

---

[1] TV., 1. 4.
[2] SPB., 1. 19.
[3] SPB., 1. 19.
[4] SK., 20.

dissolves the world for their liberation (apavarga)[1]. Prakṛti is the state of equilibrium of sattva, rajas, and tamas[2]. It is the material cause (upādānakāraṇa) of the world. The equilibrium of the guṇas is disturbed by the proximity (sānnidhya) of the puruṣas. Just as a magnet attracts iron by its mere proximity, so the puruṣas move prakṛti by their mere proximity. Just as the magnet is the unmoved mover of iron, so the puruṣas are the unmoved movers of prakṛti[3]. The union (saṁyoga) of puruṣa and prakṛti is the cause of evolution of the latter, even as the union of a lame man and a blind man is the cause of the movement of the latter[4]. A lame man of good vision mounting on the shoulders of a blind man of sure foot guides the latter in his movements. Likewise, the inactive, conscious puruṣa guides the evolution and dissolution of the unconscious active prakṛti. The puruṣa is compared to a lame man. Prakṛti is compared to a blind man. Just as a lame man guides a blind man, so puruṣas guide prakṛti. Prakṛti is blind and unconscious. It evolves the manifold world under the guidance of puruṣas to realize their ends.[5]. The evolution of prakṛti is not mechanical. It is teleological. It serves the ends of puruṣas. But its teleology is unconscious. Prakṛti is unconscious. It unconsciously realizes the ends of puruṣas. There is unconscious teleology in the evolution of prakṛti. It is suggested by other analogies. The non-intelligent prakṛti acts to realize the ends of puruṣas, even as non-intelligent milk flows for the nourishment of the calf[6], or even as non-intelligent trees bear fruits under the influence of merits and demerits for the enjoyment of puruṣas. The diversity of effects is due to the variety of merits and demerits of the jīvas.[7] (Dharmabhedena kāryavaicitryam.) Prakṛti is the material cause (upādānakāraṇa) of the world. It can be transformed into a variety of effects owing to the variety of merits and demerits which are their efficient cause (nimitakāraṇa).[8] (Karmavaicitryāt sṛṣṭivaicitryam.) The activities of prakṛti are adapted to the moral deserts of jīvas. Natural causation of prakṛti is subordinate to moral causation. The evolution

---

[1] SK., 21; SPS., i. 144; ii. 1; iii. 58.
[2] SPS., i. 61.
[3] SPS., i. 96; SPB., i,. 96.
[4] SK., 21.
[5] SK., 57, SPS., iii. 59.
[6] SSV., ii. 1; iii. 62.
[7] SPS., SSV., V. 20.
[8] SPS , SSV., SPB., vi. 41; iii. 51.

(sarga) of prakṛti is subservient to the experience of the empirical individuals. Its dissolution (pralaya) is subservient to their liberation.[1] Prakṛti is one. But puruṣas are many. Some wrongly identify themselves with prakṛti and its evolutes; manas, buddhi, and ahaṁkāra, and enjoy the manifold objects of the world. Prakṛti evolves the manifold world for them. They are in bondage due to non-discrimination (aviveka). Others attain discrimination (vivekajñāna) between themselves and prakṛti and its evolutes, and realize their intrinsic freedom. They achieve liberation. Prakṛti ceases to evolve the world for them. It dissolves the world for the liberation of puruṣas. The evolution of prakṛti continues even after the liberation of some puruṣas for the enjoyment of others, since there are innumerable puruṣas[2]. The evolution of the manifold universe continues till the puruṣas attain discrimination (vivekajñāna) between themselves and prakṛti. Prakṛti never loses its innate nature to evolve[3]. Non-discrimination (aviveka) is the cause of evolution. Discrimination (vivekajñāna) is the cause of dissolution[4]. Bondage is due to non-discrimination between puruṣa and prakṛti. Liberation is due to discrimination between them. Puruṣas are eternally liberated. Their bondage and liberation are only phenomenal (ābhimānika)[5]. In reality, prakṛti has bondage and liberation. Bondage is activity of prakṛti for the puruṣas devoid of discrimination. Liberation is the cessation of its activity for the puruṣas which have attained discrimination. Prakṛti is never divested of its active nature[6]. It retires from its creative activity after accomplishing discrimination of the puruṣas, even as a dancing girl retires from dance after entertaining the spectators[7]. It acts for the liberation of the puruṣas, and ceases to act after achieving their liberation, even as a person in bondage strives for freedom from bondage, and becomes inactive after achieving freedom, since his desire has been fulfilled[8].

The puruṣa is the pure self. It is eternally pure, transparent, conscious, and free. Its bondage and liberation are

---

[1] SK., 21, 56-59; SPS., i. 144; ii. 1.
[2] SPS., SSV., SPB., ii. 4-5; SPB, ii. 4; YS., iii. 22.
[3] SPS., SSV., iii. 47.
[4] SPS., SSV., iii., 47; iii. 63.
[5] SPS., SSV., iii. 71.
[6] SPS., SSV., iii. 72.
[7] SK., 59; SPS., SSV., iii. 69.
[8] SPS., SSV., vi. 43.

merely phenomenal. It wrongly identifies itself with prakṛti and its evolutes, manas, buddhi, and ahaṁkāra owing to non-discrimination. It does not actually transfer itself to buddhi, but wrongly identifies itself with it owing to non-discrimination. There is no actual transference (uparäga) of the self to buddhi. But there is the reflection of the self in buddhi or ahaṁkāra, which leads to a false sense of identiy (abhimāna) between them. There can be no transeunt causation between them, since there can be no conjunction (saṁyoga) between them. The puruṣa seems to be identical with buddhi, even as a white crystal seems to be tinged with red colour in proximity to a red flower. The false sense of identity between puruṣa and prakṛti is due to non-discrimination.[1] Puruṣa is is absolutely heterogeneous in nature to prakṛti. It comes to be indirectly related to prakṛti through its evolute, buddhi, which is transparent owing to the excess of sattva, and catches its reflection. Puruṣa is related to buddhi through its reflection (pratibimba) in it, as Vācaspati holds. Or it is related to buddhi through its reflection in buddhi, which is reflected back in itself, as Vijñānabhikṣu holds. The Sāṁkhya finds it extremely difficult to account for the relation between puruṣa and prakṛti, since it starts with uncompromising dualism. The theory of reflection is a poor intellectual device to relate the two heterogeneous realities to each other.

13. *The Psychical Apparatus*

Buddhi, ahaṁkāra, manas, and the external senses constitute the psychical apparatus. It is the instrument of knowledge and action. The empirical self (jīva) acquires knowledge of the world through it. It acts upon the world through it. The jīva or empirical individual acts upon the world through it.

Mahat or Buddhi evolves from Prakṛti. In its cosmic aspect, it is the cause of the manifold world. It is called Mahat. In its psychical aspect, it is the highest sense-organ in an individual. It is called Buddhi. Buddhi evolves from Prakṛti owing to the preponderance of the element of sattva. It is transparent. The conscious self is reflected in it. Buddhi is

---

[1] SPS., SSV., vi. 27-28.

active but unconscious. But it appears to be conscious owing to the reflection of the self in it. The self is conscious but inactive. It appears to be active owing to its reflection in buddhi. Owing to the preponderance of sattva, buddhi can manifest itself and other things when the self is reflected in it. The specific function of buddhi is determination (adhyavasāya). It is either theoretical or practical. It is definite knowledge of objects[1]. Or it is resolution to perform an action[2]. When it has excess of sattva, it has such modes as virtue (dharma), knowledge (jñāna), detachment (vairāgya), and supernormal powers (aiśvarya). Virtue leads to happiness (abhyudaya) and liberation (niḥśreyasa). Knowledge is discrimination between puruṣa and prakṛti. Detachment is absence of attachment. Supernormal powers are minuteness, lightness, greatness, attainment of remote objects, non-obstruction to the will, control over physical things and forces, lordliness or creation and destruction of things, and fulfilment of resolution. When buddhi is vitiated by tamas, it has contrary modes, vice (adharma), ignorance (ajñāna), attachment (avairāgya), and powerlessness (anaiśvarya).[3] Empirical cognition (vṛttijñāna),[4] pleasure, pain,[5] desire, aversion,[6] volition or action,[7] disposition (saṁskāra),[8] merit (dharma) and demerit (adharma)[9] are modes of buddhi. They are unconscious mental modes. They are not qualities of the self (puruṣa) as the Nyāya-Vaiśeṣika holds. The self thinks these modes of buddhi to be its own owing to its false sense of identity with buddhi in which it is reflected.[10] Buddhi is the highest sense-organ. The external sense-organs, manas, and ahaṁkāra function for buddhi, while buddhi functions for the self. Buddhi is the immediate instrument through which the self knows external objects definitely. The external sense-organs give indeterminate perception of objects. Manas turns it into determinate perception. Ahaṁkara leads to appropriation of determinate perception by the empirical self. Buddhi turns it into definite knowledge, and determines its conative attitude towards its object. Ascertainment (niścaya) and resolution (adhyavasāya) are the

---

[1] SGB., 23.
[2] STK., 23.
[3] STK., 23; SPS., SSV., SPB., ii. 13-15.
[4] STK., 23.
[5] STK., 5.
[6] Candrikā on SK., 19.
[7] Ibid, 19; STK., 18.
[8] SPB., ii. 42.
[9] SPS., SSV., ii. 46; vi. 62.
[10] STK., 5.

functions of buddhi. It directly shows objects of knowledge to the self[1]. When manas and ahaṁkāra are destroyed by discriminative knowledge, recollection persists, which is due to revival of dispositions. They subsist in buddhi which is the receptacle of all dispositions. Recollection (smṛti), thinking (cintā) and meditation (dhyāna) also are the functions of buddhi. Reflection (manana) is a function of buddhi. Meditation is its highest function. It is a kind of thinking. Manas supervises the function of the external senses. Ahaṁkāra supervises the function of manas. Buddhi supervises the function of ahaṁkāra. So buddhi is the supreme sense-organ.[2]

Ahaṁkāra is an evolute of Mahat or Buddhi.[3] It is self-sense or egoism (abhimāna).[4] Every person has, at first, knowledge of an object, and then appropriates it to himself. This sense of 'I' and 'mine' is the function of ahaṁkāra. 'This is I.' 'I know this.' 'I do this.' 'This is my good'. 'I know sound, colour, taste, touch, or smell'. 'These objects are mine'. The self-sense is the specific function of ahaṁkāra. It is apperception or self-appropriation. Buddhi performs its function through its aid. It determines its practical reaction to an object definitely known and apperceived with the help of ahaṁkāra thus: 'This is to be done by me'. Ahaṁkāra is the effect of buddhi. Its material cause is buddhi which has the specific function of determination (niścayavṛtti). So buddhi is inferred from ahaṁkāra as its cause.[5] Ahaṁkāra is not mere self-sense or egoism (abhimāna). It is a substance, an internal organ, which has the function of self-sense. It is inferred as the cause from its effects, the subtle essences (tanmātra) and the sense-organs. Ahaṁkāra, which has the function of self-sense, is their material cause.[6] In dreamless sleep the self-sense of ahaṁkāra is destroyed but it persists as the substratum of dispositions (vāsanā).[7] Merit (dharma) and demerit (adharma) are the modes of ahaṁkāra. It is the effect of buddhi. So they are modes of buddhi also.[8] The self is not an agent (kartṛ),

[1] SPB., ii. 40.
[2] SPS., SPB., ii. 40-47; SPS., SSV., i. 71.
[3] SK., 22; SPS., i. 62, 72.
[4] SK., 24; SPS., ii. 16.
[5] STK., 24; SPB., i. 64, 72; ii. 16; Candrikā on SK., 24; Laghuvṛtti on SDSM., 37.
[6] SPB., i. 63.
[7] SPB., i. 63.
[8] SPS., SSV., vi. 62.

since it is immutable (apariṇāmin). Ahaṁkāra is the agent. Activity follows the self-sense, which is the function of ahaṁkāra.[1]

Manas evolves from ahaṁkāra in its sāttvika aspect.[2] It is the central organ partaking of the nature or organs of knowledge and action both. It supervises the functions of both kinds of sense-organs. They cannot exercise their functions without the guidance of manas. Without the supervision of manas there can be no sense-perception or action.[3] The ten sense-organs are different modifications of the central organ, manas, owing to the different modifications of the constituent guṇas, sattva, rajas, and tamas aided by merit and demerit.[4] The manas becomes identical with the visual organ and the like, in connection with them, and exercises the diverse functions of vision, and the like.[5]

Manas is not atomic. If it were atomic, it would be eternal. But it is not eternal. It is an evolute of ahaṁkāra. So it is evolved and dissolved. It is not devoid of parts, since it can be connected with many sense-organs at the same time.[6] It is not without a cause. Ahaṁkāra is its cause.[7] Manas is not all-pervading (vibhu), since it is an instrument (karaṇa), a sense-organ, like an axe, which is of limited dimension. It is the instrument of experiences connected with the whole body. This shows that manas is of intermediate magnitude. Further, it is capable of movement. The self goes to another sphere of existence after death with the aid of its adjunct (upādhi), manas. The self, which is all-pervading, is incapable of movement. Only its adjunct, manas, is capable of movement. So it is not all-pervading.[8] Thus manas is neither atomic nor all-pervading, but of intermediate magnitude, and possessed of parts.[9] Manas has the function of assimilation and discrimination (saṁkalpa). It reflects upon an object intuitively apprehended by an external organ, and determines it as like this and unlike this, and thus yields determinate perception of it. It knows the object in a subject-predicate-relation (viśeṣaṇaviśeṣyabhāva).

---

[1] SPS., vi. 54; SPB., vi. 54.
[2] SK., 25; SPS., ii. 18.
[3] SK., 27; SPS., SSV., SVM., ii. 26.
[4] SPS., SSV., ii. 27.
[5] SPB., ii. 27.
[6] SPS., SPB., v. 71.
[7] SSV., v. 71.
[8] SPB., v. 70.
[9] SPB., v. 69, 71.

The external sense-organs yield indeterminate perception. Manas yields determinate perception. This is the view of Vācaspati.[1] But Vijñānabhikṣu holds that the external sense-organs yield determinate perception. According to him, indecision and decision are the functions of manas. Decision (saṁkalpa) is the desire to do (cikīrṣā).[2]

Buddhi, ahaṁkāra, and manas are the three internal organs. They are the door-keepers, while the external sense-organs are the doors. The former are the organs of elaboration of the sense-material given by the latter. The former apprehend the past, present, and future objects, while the latter apprehend only present objects.[3] Buddhi, ahaṁkāra, and manas are the forms of the internal organ.[4] Their specific functions are determination, self-sense, and assimilation and discrimination respectively.[5] Vital acts are the general functions of all the sense-organs.[6] Vijñānanbhikṣu describes them as the general functions of the three internal organs only.[7] There are ten external sense-organs, five organs of knowledge (buddhīndriya) and five organs of action (karmendriya). The former are cognitive organs. The latter are motor organs. The former are eyes, ears, nose, tongue, and skin. The latter are the vocal organ, hands, legs, the organ of evacuation, and the organ of reproduction.[8] The visual organ apprehends colour ; the gustatory organ apprehends taste ; the olfactory organ apprehends smell ; the auditory organ apprehends sound ; the tactual organ apprehends touch. Speaking is the function of the vocal organ ; grasping, that of the hands ; walking, that of the legs ; evacuation, that of the evacuative organ ; reproduction, that of the generative organ.[9]

The sense-organs are the instruments of the self. They are the effects of ahaṁkāra, and organs of knowledge and action.[10] The self is the knower (draṣṭṛ) ; the cognitive sense-organs are the instruments of knowledge.[11] Though the self is immutable and therefore inactive, it moves the motor sense-organs to act, even as a magnet moves a piece of iron without itself moving, or a king makes his soldiers fight without himself fighting. The

---

[1] SK., STK., 27.
[2] SPB., ii. 30.
[3] SK., 33, 35.
[4] SPS., SSV., ii. 19; SPB., ii. 16.
[5] SK., 29; SPS., SSV., ii. 30.
[6] SK., 29; SPS., SSV., ii. 31.
[7] SPB., ii. 31.
[8] SK., 26.
[9] SK., 28; STK., 26; SPS., SPB., ii. 19, 28.
[10] SPB., ii, 19.
[11] SPS., ii. 29.

activity of the self consists in moving the aggregate of causes or sense-organs to act. The sense-organs are the instruments of the self, which are engaged in activity.[1] The sense-organs are evolved to realize the ends of the self. They act also to fulfil the merits and demerits of the empirical self.[2] The volition or activity of the self is not responsible for the evolution of the sense-organs, since it is immutable and inactive.[3] The sense-organs act by themselves for the sake of the self, even as milk flows of itself from the udder of the cow for nourishment of the calf.[4]

All sense-organs are supersensible. They cannot be perceived. They are wrongly identified with eyes, ears, tongue, nose, and skin which are their physiological seats (adhiṣṭhāna). They are powers (śakti) behind the seats.[5] The ten external sense-organs are the different powers of the one chief sense-organ, manas, which is both cognitive and motor organ.[6] The sense-organs are not material (bhautika) but products of ahaṁkāra. Their material cause is ahaṁkāra, the internal organ. They are endued with the power of manifestation.[7] They are psychical powers. Manas, in conjunction with the eyes, ears, and the like, becomes identical with them, and has the functions of vision, hearing, and the like. Thus, it assumes the different forms of the sense-organs.[8] All sense-organs evolve and dissolve. They have origin and end. They are not eternal. Manas is not eternal as the Nyāya-Vaiśeṣika holds.[9]

II. Epistemology

14. *Factors of Knowledge*

Knowledge involves four factors: (1) the knower (pramātṛ); (2) the known (prameya); (3) the means of knowledge (pramāṇa); (4) the result of knowing or valid knowledge (pramā). Kapila defines valid knowledge as determinate knowledge of an object not known before.[10] According to Vijñānabhikṣu the pure self is

[1] SPB., ii. 29.
[2] SPS., SPB., ii. 36.
[3] SPB., ii. 35.
[4] SPS., SPB., ii. 37.
[5] SPS., SPB., ii. 23.
[6] SPB., ii. 26.
[7] SPB., ii. 20.
[8] SPB., ii. 27.
[9] SPB., ii., 32.
[10] SPS., SSV., i. 87.

the knower (pramātṛ) ; the mode of buddhi modified into the form of the object is the means of knowledge (pramāṇa) ; reflection of the mode of buddhi with the form of the object in the self is valid knowledge (pramā) ; the object apprehended by the mode of buddhi reflected in the self is the known (prameya). The self is the witness (sākṣin) of the mode of buddhi. It knows the mental mode directly. It knows external objects indirectly through the medium of the mental mode. It is their knower or seer (draṣṭṛ). The mode of buddhi is the means of knowledge. The knowledge of the self, which is the result of the mode of buddhi, is valid knowledge.[1] Vyāsa also holds the same view.[2] But the self is of the nature of consciousness. It is eternal and unchangeable. It cannot suffer any change as a result of the mode of buddhi. Vijñānabhikṣu urges that the self, though eternal and immutable, as coloured by the object of knowledge is the result of the mode of buddhi. Or, its consciousness coloured by the object of knowledge is the result of the cognitive act of buddhi.[3] Vijñānabhikṣu holds that the mode of buddhi modified into the form of an object is reflected in the self, which knows the object, though, being immutable, it cannot be modified into the object. If the mode of buddhi be not reflected in the self, it can never know the object. The self directly knows the mode of buddhi. It knows an external object indirectly through the mode of buddhi which is reflected in it. Vijñānabhikṣu holds that the mode of buddhi is reflected in the self and that the self also is reflected in the mode of buddhi. But Vācaspati holds that the self only is reflected in the mode of buddhi and manifests it, but that there is no reflection of the mode of buddhi in the self.[4] Vācaspati defines valid knowledge (pramā) as the mode of buddhi which apprehends an object, undoubted, real, and not known before, or the knowledge of the self, which is the result of it.[5] He regards the mental mode and the knowledge of the self both as valid knowledge. This definition excludes doubt, illusion, and recollection. Valid knowledge is definite and determinate knowledge (avadhāraṇa). Doubt is indefinite knowledge. Valid knowledge apprehends an object as it really is. Illusion is

---

[1] SPB., i. 87; YV., i. 7.
[2] YB., i. 7.
[3] SPB., i. 87.
[4] SPB., i. 87.
[5] STK., 4.

wrong knowledge. It mistakes one object for another. It does not apprehend an object as it really is. Valid knowledge is novel knowledge. Recollection is the knowledge of an object which is already known.[1] Vācaspati defines valid knowledge also as the knowledge due to the self's identification with its reflection in the mode of buddhi modified into the form of an object.[2] Vijñānabhikṣu says that if the knowledge of the self be regarded as valid knowledge, then the mode of buddhi should be regarded as the means of valid knowledge. If the mode of buddhi be regarded as valid knowledge, the intercourse of a sense-organ with an object should be regarded as the means of valid knowledge.[3]

15. *Sources of Knowledge*

The Sāṁkhya recognizes three means of valid knowledge (pramāṇa), perception, inference, and scriptural testimony. Iśvarakṛṣṇa defines perception as determinate knowledge of an object due to its intercourse with a sense-organ.[4] Vācaspati explains the characteristics of perception. First, it must have a real object, either external or internal. This characteristic distinguishes perception from illusion. Earth, water, and the like are the external objects. Pleasure, pain and the like are the internal objects. Gross objects are perceived by us. Subtle essences (tanmātra) are perceived by the yogins. Secondly, a particular kind of perception is brought about by the intercourse of a particular sense-organ with a particular kind of object. Visual perception is brought about by the intercourse of the visual organ with colour. This characteristic distinguishes perception form inference, memory, and the like. Thirdly, perception involves the operation of buddhi. When the sense-organs are stimulated by their objects, tamas of buddhi is overcome and its sattva becomes manifest and brings about determinate knowledge (adhyavasāya). Determinate knowledge consists in the reflection of the self in buddhi modified into an object.[5] This characteristic distinguishes perception from doubt or indefinite knowledge.[6] Kapila defines perception as the

---

[1] STK., 4; SPB., i. 87.
[2] STK., 4.
[3] SPB., i. 87.
[4] SK., 5.
[5] STK., 6.
[6] STK., 5.

cognition or the mode of buddhi which assumes the form of an object.[1] Buddhi goes out through a sense-organ to an object after the intercourse of the sense-organ with the object, and is modified into its form. The mode of buddhi assuming the form of the object produces its knowledge in the self. This is perception.[2] Perception brought about by the sense-object-intercourse is normal (laukika). The intuition of the yogin is supernormal (alaukika). It is not external perception brought about by the sense-object-intercourse. It apprehends past, future, remote, and subtle objects through buddhi aided by merit produced by intense meditation. It is brought about by the intercourse of buddhi with past, future, remote, and subtle objects. The future is present in a latent state. The past also is present in a certain condition. Tamas of buddhi is removed by the sense-object-intercourse in normal perception. It is removed by merit brought about by intense meditation in supernormal perception. When tamas is removed from buddhi and its sattva comes out, it goes out to an object and manifests it. Thus, the Sāṁkhya recognizes perception of the yogin.[3]

It distinguishes two stages of perception, indeterminate (nirvikalpa) and determinate (savikalpa), and regards them as valid. Vācaspati defines indeterminate perception as immediate apprehension of an object, pure and simple, devoid of the relation between the qualified object and its qualifications, like the apprehension of a baby and a dumb person. He quotes Kumārila's definition of indeterminate perception. He defines determinate perception as definite cognition of an object as qualified by its generic and specific characters and other properties. It is perceptual judgment which distinguishes between the qualified object and its qualifications and relates them to each other. It involves analysis and synthesis, assimilation and discrimination. Indeterminate perception is the function of the external sense-organs of knowledge. Determinate perception is the function of the internal organ, manas. The external senses apprehend an object as merely 'this' or 'unlike this.' It assimilates the object to like objects, and discriminates it from unlike objects. Assimilation and discrimination involved in determinate perception are the functions of manas. The external senses

---

[1] SPB., i. 89. [2] SPB., i. 89. [3] SPS., SPB., i. 90-91.

yield indeterminate perception or non-relational apprehension of an object. Manas yields determinate perception involving analysis and synthesis, assimilation and discrimination, subject-predicate relation. It is relational apprehension of an object.'[1]

But Vijñānabhikṣu holds that both indeterminate and determinate perception are given by the external sense-organs. Vācaspati wrongly holds that the external senses give indeterminate perception, while manas turns it into determinate perception. Vijñānabhikṣu cites the authority of Vyāsa who holds that the external senses perceive an object as endued with generic and specific characters.[2] But Vācaspati seems to be right. Assimilation and discrimination are the functions of manas. They cannot be ascribed to the external senses.

Aniruddha defines perception as direct and immediate apprehension of an object, untainted by any defect. It is indeterminate and determinate. Indeterminate perception is simple apprehension of an object free from all association of name, class, and the like. It is a presentative process. Determinate perception is relational apprehension of an object qualified by its name, class, and the like which are remembered owing to revival of dispositions by similarity, and other conditions. It is a presentative-representative process. It involves perception and recollection. Both indeterminate and determinate perception are valid, since they apprehend objects as they really are, which were not known before. Determinate perception involves recollection of name, class, and the like. But the recollection does not affect the perceptual character of the knowledge. It is an auxiliary condition which helps the main cause of determinate perception, *viz.*, the intercourse of a sense-organ with an object. So determinate perception is valid.[3]

Vācaspati describes the functions of the external and internal sense-organs in the process of perception. An external sense-organ stimulated by an external object gives indeterminate perception of it. Then manas turns it into determinate perception by analysis and synthesis, assimilation and discrimination. Then ahaṁkāra appropriates and apperceives it, and turns the

---

[1] STK., 27, IPP., pp. 38-39.
[2] SPB., ii. 32; YB., i. 7; IPP., p. 39.
[3] SSV., i. 89; IPP., pp. 37-39.

impersonal apprehension of the object into a personal experience. Then buddhi turns it into definite knowledge and assumes a practical attitude to react to it. Then the self is reflected in the mode of buddhi modified into the form of its object. The self wrongly identifies itself with its reflection in buddhi assuming the form of the object, and has knowledge of the object. In dim light a person at first apprehends an object as something undiscriminated, then attentively reflects upon it and knows it to be a terrible thief by his bow and arrow, then thinks him in reference to himself (*e.g.*, 'he is running towards me'), and then resolves 'I must fly from this place'. This example illustrates the successive functions of an external sense-organ, manas, ahaṁkāra, and buddhi.[1] Sometimes the succession of the functions of the external and internal organs is so rapid, that they seem to occur simultaneously. When a person perceives a tiger in utter darkness illumined by a sudden flash of lightning, and runs away from it at once, the functions of the visual organ, manas, ahaṁkāra, and buddhi seem to occur at the same moment, though really they are successive.[2] The external sense-organs can apprehend external objects, while the internal organs can apprehend internal objects, pleasure, pain, and the like. The former can apprehend only present objects, while the latter can apprehend past and future objects as well.[3]

Īśvarakṛṣṇa defines inference as the knowledge which is preceded by the knowledge of the sign (liṅga) and the signate (liṅgin), or the middle term (vyāpya) and the major term (vyāpaka). Vācaspati explains it as the knowledge which is preceded by, or based on, the knowledge of the relations of the middle, the major, and the minor terms to one another. Inference is the knowledge derived from the major and minor premises.[4] Kapila defines inference as the knowledge of the major term derived from the knowledge of invariable concomitance between it and the middle term. Invariable concomitance (pratibandha) is the uniform accompaniment of the middle term and the major term. It is pervasion (vyāpti). The middle term (*e.g.*, smoke) is pervaded by the major term (*e.g.*, fire). Inference is the knowledge of the major term (*e.g.*, fire)

[1] STK., 30.
[2] STK., 30; SPS., ii. 32.
[3] SK., 33.
[4] SK., 5; STK., 5.

derived from the knowledge of invariable concomitance between the middle term (*e.g.*, smoke) and the major term (*e.g.*, fire).[1] On perception of smoke, the middle term, the existence of fire, the major term, is inferred on the ground of the knowledge of invariable concomitance between smoke and fire. What is unperceived is inferred from what is perceived through the knowledge of a universal relation between them. The Sāṁkhya recognizes five members of a syllogism : (1) statement (pratijñā) ; (2) reason (hetu) ; (3) example (dṛṣṭānta) ; (4) application (upanaya) ; (5) conclusion (nigamana), like the Nyāya.[2]

Vyāpti is the invariable concomitance of both the major term and the middle term, or of one.[3] Causedness and non-eternality are coextensive ; they always coexist with each other. Non-eternality (sādhya) is inferred from causedness (sādhana). Smokiness and fieriness are not coextensive with each other. The former is pervaded by the latter, but the latter is not pervaded by the former. Smokiness is invariably accompanied by fieriness. Vyāpti is the relation of constant co-existence between the attributes of the objects denoted by the middle term and the major term.[4] It is a relation between things, but not a separate principle (tattvāntara). It is nothing but constant concomitance of attributes. If it were a separate principle, it would involve the assumption of an entity in which the quality of vyāpti would subsist.[5]

What is the ground of vyāpti ? How do we know it ? We know it by the observation of concomitance attended with the non-observation of non-concomitance of the middle term and the major term. We cannot know it by the observation of a single instance of concomitance, since it is liable to be contradicted by a contrary instance. We perceive the co-existence of an ass and a fire in a washerman's house. But we cannot infer the existence of fire from that of an ass. We observe many instances of fire not accompanied by asses. So generalisation is the result of frequent observation of agreement in presence and agreement in absence of the middle term and the major term. One single

---

[1] SPS., i. 100; SPB., i. 100.
[2] SPS., SSV., SPB., v. 27.
[3] SPS., v. 29.
[4] SVM., v. 29.
[5] SPS., SPB., v. 30.

instance of their co-existence is not sufficient to prove their constant co-existence.[1]

The middle term has five characteristics. First, it (*e.g.*, smoke) must be present in the minor term (*e.g.*, the hill). Secondly, it must be present in all positive instances (*e.g.*, kitchen). Thirdly, it must be absent from all negative instances (*e.g.*, a lake) in which the major term does not exist. Fourthly, it must be characterized by the absence of a contradictory reason leading to an opposite conclusion. Fifthly, it must be non-incompatible with the minor term.[2] The middle term is well known ; it is connected with the major term ; it is present where the major term is present ; it is absent where the major term is absent.[3]

Aniruddha mentions six kinds of inference : (1) Anvayin, or by agreement ; (2) Vyatirekin, or by difference ; (3) Anvaya-vyatirekin, or by agreement and difference ; (4) Pūrvavat, or from cause to effect ; (5) Śeṣavat, or form effect to cause ; (6) Sāmānyatodṛṣṭa, or based on non-causal concomitance.[4] Vācaspati divides inference into two kinds, *viz.*, Vīta and Avīta. The Vīta is based upon affirmative concomitance or universal agreement in presence. For instance, whatever is smoky is fiery, the hill is smoky, therefore the hill is fiery. The Avīta is based upon negative concomitance or universal agreement in absence. For instance, what is non-different from other elements has no smell ; the earth has smell ; therefore the earth is different from other elements. Vācaspati sub-divides the Vīta into two kinds, *viz.*, Pūrvavat and Sāmānya-todṛṣṭa. Pūrvavat inference is based on observed uniformity of concomitance of the middle term and the major term. For instance, fieriness of the hill is inferred from its smokiness on the ground of the observed uniformity of concomitance of smokiness and fieriness in the kitchen and other places. Sāmānyatodṛṣṭa inference is not based on observed uniformity of concomitance between the middle term and the major term, but on the similarity of the middle term with what is invariably concomitant with the major term. For instance, the existence of the sense-organs, which are imperceptible, is inferred from the perceptions of colour, sound, and the like,

[1] SPS., SSV., v. 28.
[2] SSV., v. 27.
[3] SSV., i. 100.
[4] SSV., i. 100.

because they are of the nature of actions, like the act of cutting. The existence of an axe, an instrument, which is required for the act of cutting, has been observed. But the sense-organs, which are supersensible, are inferred as organs or instruments of perceptions because perceptions are actions like the act of cutting. Here, the sense-organs are not inferred from the observed uniformity of concomitance between perceptions and the sense-organs. They are inferred from the fact that perceptions are actions, like the act of cutting, and require instruments in the shape of the sense-organs, like it. The Avīta is Śeṣavat or Pariśeṣa inference. It is inference by exclusion of all other alternatives to it. It is inference by elimination. For instance, sound is a specific quality of ether, because it is not a specific quality of earth, water, fire, air, space, time, manas, and the self. So by elimination of the other alternatives we infer that sound is the specific quality of ether, the remaining substance.[1] Gauḍapāda gives the following examples of Pūrvavat, Śeṣavat, and Sāmānyatodṛṣṭa. Rainfall is inferred from the rising of clouds. This is Pūrvavat inference. We taste a drop of water of the sea and perceive it to be saline. From this we infer that the remaining water of the sea also is saline. This is Śeṣavat inference. We perceive the successive positions of the moon. From this we infer its movement. Or, we perceive mango trees blossoming in a place. From this we infer that mango trees have blossomed in other places also. These are Sāmānyatodṛṣṭa inferences.[2] Vijñānabhikṣu mentions three kinds of inference, *viz.,* Pūrvavat, Śeṣavat, and Sāmānyatodṛṣṭa. Pūrvavat is an inference of an object (*e.g.,* fire) which belongs to a class of objects perceived, since fire has been perceived along with smoke in the kitchen and other places. Śeṣavat is inference by difference. It literally means that which has an object not known before as its subject-matter. In it the object to be inferred is not already known. For example, the difference of earth from all other substances is inferred form the generic character of earth or earthness, since it was not established before. Sāmānyatodṛṣṭa is an inference which is different from Pūrvavat and Śeṣavat. In this kind of inference, an imperceptible object is inferred from a mark of inference, which is a

[1] STK., 5. [2] SGB., 5.

property of the subject of inference, on the ground of the knowledge of uniform concomitance between a similar mark of inference and a perceived object. For instance, the imperceptible sense-organs are inferred from perceptions of colour and the like, which are so many acts, on the ground of the observed uniform concomitance between the act of cutting and an axe, the instrument of cutting. The existence of puruṣa and prakṛti is inferred by Sāmānyatodṛṣṭa inference.[1]

Vedic testimony is authoritative statement. It is another source of valid knowledge. The Sāṁkhya does not recognize secular testimony as an independent source of valid knowledge, since it depends on perception and inference. Valid testimony is true revelation.[2] The Vedas are relevations of supersensible realities, which are beyond the range of perception and inference, to inspired seers.[3] They are not composed by any person. They are impersonal.[4] They are not composed by God, since there is no proof for His existence. God is non-existent. So the Vedas are not of divine origin.[5] They are not composed by the liberated souls, since they are devoid of attachment and therefore inactive. Though they are omniscient, they are inactive, since they are free from attachment which is a spring of action. The bound souls are not omniscient, and therefore not competent to compose the Vedas dealing with supersensible realities.[6] The Vedas are not of personal origin (apauruṣeya), but not eternal. They are non-eternal. To be not of personal origin and to be eternal are not invariably accompanied by each other. In sprouts there is no concomitance between them. They are evidently not produced by any person, but yet they are not eternal.[7] Likewise, the Vedas are not of personal origin, and yet non-eternal. They are revelations of eternal truths to the enlightened seers. The statements regarding their eternality refer to the continuity of revelation of similar truths to the seers in different cycles.[8] The Vedas of the previous cycle were remembered by Kapila at the beginning of the next.[9] Vedic testimony is self-evident (svataḥpramāṇa). It is free from doubt and discrepancy, since it is not of personal origin.[10] Its authority

[1] SPB., i. 103.
[2] SPS., SSV., i. 101.
[3] SPS., v. 41.
[4] SPS., v. 46.
[5] SSV., SPB., v. 46.
[6] SPS., SSV., SPB., v. 47.
[7] SPS., SSV., v. 48.
[8] SPB., v. 45.
[9] STK., 5.
[10] STK., 5.

does not depend upon the true knowledge of the person who makes the statement. The Vedas have an intrinsic power of revealing truths.[1] They are the embodiments of the intuitions of enlightened seers. Vedic testimony is self-evident. It is not irrational. The assertions of the Buddha are irrational and antagonistic to the Vedas. So they are not trustworthy.[2]

Testimony is an authoritative statement. It takes the form of a sentence. The meaning of a sentence is the object to be proved by it. The sentence is not its property which may serve as the mark of inference. Nor does a sentence, expressing a meaning, depend upon the knowledge of the relation between a mark of inference and the object inferred. A sentence composed anew by a new poet can express its meaning and denote an unknown object. So testimony is not inference.[3] It is a distinct source of knowledge.

Comparison (upamāna) is not a distinct source of knowledge. The knowledge derived from the authoritative statement 'the wild cow (gavaya) is like a cow', is nothing but testimony. The knowledge that the word 'gavaya' (wild cow) denotes some object resembling the cow is nothing but inference. The object which is designated by a particular word by experienced persons, comes to be denoted by the word, in the absence of any other object which could be so denoted. For instance, the class 'cow' (gotva) is denoted by the word 'cow'. Likewise, the knowledge that 'the word *gavaya* denotes an object resembling a cow' is an inference, since it has been asserted by experienced people. The knowledge of similarity of the wild cow present to the visual organ with the cow is nothing but perception. The knowledge of the perceived wild cow's similarity with a remembered cow also is mere perception. The wild cow's similarity with the cow is the same as the cow's similarity with the wild cow. There is not one similarity in the cow, and another similarity in the wild cow. Similarity of one species with another consists in both having a common collocation of their various parts, which is one and the same. If the common collocation of parts is perceived in the wild cow, it is perceived in the cow also, which is remembered. There is

---

[1] SPB., v. 51.
[2] STK., 5.
[3] STK., 5.

no distinct object of comparison so that it may be regarded as a distinct source of knowledge.[1]

Presumption (arthāpatti) is included in inference. It is said to consist in the assumption of an unperceived object to reconcile two inconsistent facts. We perceive the non-existence of Chaitra, who is living, in his house. So we assume that he is outside his house. This assumption reconciles his living with his non-existence in his house. The Sāṁkhya holds that the so-called presumption is nothing but inference. Whatever finite thing exists, must exist elsewhere, if it does not exist in one place. Chaitra, who exists, does not exist in his house. So he must exist somewhere outside his house. Chaitra's existence outside his house is inferred from his non-existence in the house, which is perceived, and serves as the mark of inference. Chaitra's existence somewhere else does not set aside the fact of his non-existence in the house, therefore, his non-existence in the house can serve as a reason (hetu) from which his existence elsewhere can be inferred. Nor does his non-existence in the house set aside his existence altogether ; so he may exist outside the house, though he does not exist in the house. There is no inconsistency between Chaitra's non-existence in the house and his mere existence. So presumption, as a distinct source of knowledge, is not required to remove inconsistency between two facts. It is nothing but inference.[2]

Inclusion (sambhava) also is included in inference. Lesser weights are included in greater ones. This is known by the so-called inclusion. But it is merely inference. There is uniformity of concomitance between a lesser weight and a greater weight. The latter cannot exist without the former. Therefore we infer the existence of a lesser weight in a greater weight. This is inference.[3]

Tradition (aitihya) is not valid knowledge. It is mere succession of rumour, whose first speaker is unknown. For instance, 'a demon lives in this tree'. This statement, handed down by tradition, is doubtful, since its first speaker is not known. Valid testimony is an authoritative statement of a person who is trustworthy. Tradition is not valid testimony.[4]

---

[1] STK., 5.
[2] STK., 5.
[3] STK., 5.
[4] STK., 5.

Negation (abhāva) is nothing but perception. The non-existence of a jar on the ground is nothing but a particular modification of the ground characterized by its absence. All things are subject to modification every moment, except the self which is immutable. Such modifications are perceptible. The particular modification of the ground characterized by the absence of the jar is perceived. So the so-called negation is nothing but perception. There is no distinct object of negation or non-apprehension. So negation is not a distinct source of knowledge. Non-apprehension may be due to long distance, close proximity, abnormality of the sense-organs, inattention, extreme subtlety, a barrier, obscuration, and mixture with other similar things. So non-apprehension (anupalabdhi) does not prove non-existence.[2]

16. *Intrinsic Validity and Invalidity of Knowledge*

The Sāṁkhya holds that validity and invalidity belong to knowledge itself.[3] Valid knowledge is definite knowledge of a real object which was not known previously.[4] Novelty, reality of the object, and definiteness are the characteristics of valid knowledge. Perception, inference, and Vedic testimony are three kinds of valid knowledge.[5] The Vedas are self-evident. Their validity is inherent in them. They have an inherent power of manifesting their objects. They have intrinsic validity.[6] Validity of knowledge is generated by the complement of causes which produce the knowledge of the power inherent in it. It is not produced by an additional quality, or excellence (guṇa) as the Nyāya holds. Validity of knowledge is ascertained by the natural power of the truth to apprehend its validity. Valid knowledge reveals its own validity. Its intrinsic validity is known from the manifestation of its own inherent power, and also from its leading to action immediately[7]. Validity of knowledge is inherent in it. It does not depend on any excellence in its causes. The validity of the Vedas is self-evident. It does not depend on their being composed by a trust-

[1] STK., 5.
[2] SK., 7-8.
[3] SDS., p. 232.
[4] SPS., SSV., i. 87.
[5] SPS., i. 88.
[6] SPS., v. 51.
[7] ṢSV., v. 51.

worthy person. The Vedas reveal truths by their own inherent power. If their validity depends on other conditions than themselves, their invalidity will depend on the defects in their causes. In fact, validity and invalidity are intrinsic characters of knowledge itself. Some knowledge is intrinsically valid. Other knowledge is intrinsically invalid.[1] Workability (arthakriyākāritva) is the test of reality (sattā). An unreal thing (*e.g.*, the horn of a hare) is not capable of effective action. So it cannot produce valid knowledge. Pleasure is real, since it is capable of fruitful action, and whatever is capable of fruitful action is real.[2] Workability is the mark of reality. Unworkability is the mark of unreality. In the state of dissolution all things except the puruṣas are unreal, since they cannot lead to effective action.[3] Valid knowledge prompts fruitful action. Invalid knowledge fails to prompt fruitful action. But validity of knowledge does not depend on fruitful action, and invalidity of knowledge, on unfruitful action. They are inherent in knowledge itself.[4]

17. Theory of Error

The Sāṁkhya advocates the theory of Sadasatkhyāti. In the illusory perception 'this is silver', when a nacre is mistaken for silver, the cognition of 'this' is real (sat), and the cognition of 'silver' is unreal (asat). The cognition of 'this' apprehends an object present to the visual organ, and it is not contradicted; so it is real. The cognition of 'silver' apprehends silver which is not present to the visual organ, and it is contradicted by a sublating cognition 'this is not silver'; so it is not real. Thus an illusion apprehends both a real object and an unreal object.[5]

The Mādhyamika holds that an illusion apprehends a non-existent (asat) object. This theory is called Asatkhyāti. The illusory perception 'this is silver' apprehends non-existent silver as identical with nacre. This is wrong. A non-existent object (*e.g.*, the horn of a man) is not capable of prompting fruitful action. Nor can it produce knowledge.[6]

---

[1] SVM., v. 51.
[2] Yad yad arthakriyākāri tat tat sat. SPB., v. 27.
[3] SPB., i. 154.
[4] SSV., SVM., v. 51.
[5] SPS., SSV., v. 56; IPP., P. 297.
[6] SPS., SSV., v. 52.

Prabhākara holds that an illusion consists of two cognitions, perception and recollection. The illusory perception 'this is silver' consists of the perception of 'this' which is real and the recollection of 'silver'. Non-discrimination of these two elements from each other (bhedāgraha) leads to action. This theory is called Akhyāti or Vivekākhyati. This is wrong. Apprehension of non-difference or identity (abhedagraha) is found to lead to action. The illusory perception 'this is silver' is contradicted by the sublating cognition 'this is not silver'. Valid knowledge cannot be contradicted.[1]

The Advaita Vedāntist holds that an illusion apprehends an undefinable (anirvacanīya) object which is neither real nor unreal nor both. If it were unreal, it could not produce immediate knowledge or perception. If it were real, it could not be contradicted by a sublating cognition. It cannot be both real and unreal, since it is self-contradictory. So it is undefinable. This theory is called Anirvacanīyakhyāti. This is wrong. The object of the illusion is defined as 'this is silver'. So it cannot be undefinable.[2]

The Naiyāyika holds that an illusion apprehends an object as another. It is wrong perception. It mistakes one object for another. This theory is called Anyathākhyāti. For instance, in the illusion 'this is silver' a nacre is perceived as silver. This is wrong. One object is never manifested to consciousness as another object.[3]

The Sāṁkhya holds the doctrine of Sadasatkhyāti. In the illusion 'this is silver' the cognition of 'this' is real, and the cognition of 'silver' is unreal.[4]

18. *Three kinds of pain (Duḥkha).*

As the science of medicine has four divisions, disease, removal of disease or health, the cause of disease, and cure, so metaphysical ethics has four divisions, pain, absolute destruction of pain, the cause of pain, and the means to the removal of pain. Three kinds of pain are to be avoided (heya). Total destruction of three-fold pain is avoidance (hāna). The cause of the avoidable (heyahetu) is non-discrimination (aviveka) due

[1] SPS., SSV., v. 53.
[2] SPS., SSV., v. 54.
[3] SPS., SSV., v. 55.
[4] IPP., PP., 296-97.

to conjunction of puruṣa with prakṛti. The direct and immediate knowledge of the distinction between puruṣa and prakṛti (vivekakhyāti) is the means to the total destruction of three-fold pain (hānopāya).[1]

There are three kinds of suffering or pain, ādhyātmika, ādhibhautika and ādhidaivika. The pains due to bodily disorders and mental agitation caused by emotions and passions are of the first kind. The pains caused by men, beasts, birds, reptiles, and the like are of the second kind.[1] The pains caused by supernatural agencies, planets, ghosts, demons, and the elements, *e.g.*, heat and cold, are of the third kind.[2] The past pain is past and does not need destruction. The present pain will be destroyed after the second moment. The future pain should be destroyed.[3]

Every person strives to get rid of pain. It is the main spring of action. When we are hungry, we strive to satisfy our hunger. So satisfaction of hunger is a good (puruṣārtha) to us.[4] Medicines are good, since they remove physical pain. Company of a beautiful wife, enjoyment of sweets, and the like are good, since they remove mental pain. Certain methods prescribed by the moral science are good, since they remove the pain caused by men and beasts. Incantations, prayers, and the like are good, since they remove the pain caused by supernatural agencies. Virtue (dharma), wealth (artha), happiness (kāma), and liberation (mokṣa) are good (puruṣārtha). But the first three are not the supreme good, since they are exhaustible, and yield physical pleasure brought about by external objects. Liberation is the supreme good (atyantapuruṣārtha), since it is eternal and of the nature of manifestation.[5] It consists in absolute cessation of threefold pain.[6] It consists in non-production of pain in future due to total destruction of its cause.[7] Liberation is the highest good, since it is one, eternal, and complete negation of all kinds of suffering.[8]

19. *Bondage* (*Bandha*)

The self or puruṣa is eternally liberated, enlightened, and pure. It is devoid of association with the guṇas. But it has

---

[1] SPB., i. 1.
[2] STK., 1; SPS., SSV., SPB., i. 1.
[3] SPB., i. 1; YS., ii. 16.
[4] SPS., i. 3.
[5] SPS., i. 1.
[6] SPS., i. 1.
[7] SPS., SSV., i. 2.
[8] SPS., SSV., i. 5.

a false sense of bondage owing to non-discrimination between itself and prakṛti, or its product, the mind-body-complex.[1] Is the self bound or liberated? If it is bound by nature, it can never be divested of it, and achieve liberation. If it is liberated by nature, it need not strive for liberation, and be engaged in meditation and the like.[2] It is not really bound ; nor is it liberated from bondage. But it is eternally liberated. It is liberated by nature.[3] Bondage and liberation of the self are only phenomenal, and not real. They do not really belong to the self. Its apparent bondage is due to non-discrimination. Its apparent liberation is due to discrimination.[4] Bondage and liberation really belong to prakṛti. The activity of prakṛti for the undiscriminating self is bondage. Its inactivity for the discriminating self is liberation.[5] The self has a mere sense or feeling (abhimānamātra) of bondage and liberation though it is not really bound or liberated.[6] The self is free from association with the guṇas. It can have no real connection with pain. So it cannot strive to get rid of it. Pain is a modification of buddhi. The self is reflected in the mental mode and erroneously identifies itself with it. This false sense of identity of the self with the mental mode of pain is bondage. The self is not really tinged with pain.[7] This is the view of Aniruddha and Vācaspati. Vijñānabhikṣu holds that the mental mode of pain in which the self is reflected and is intelligized by it, is reflected back in the self, so that it can have experience of pain.[8] Buddhi is really tinged with pain. The self appears to be tinged with it. When a crystal is placed near a red flower, it is not really tinged with red colour, but appears to be so tinged owing to its proximity to a red flower. Likewise, the self, which is free from association with the guṇas, is not really tinged with the mental mode of pain, but it appears to be tinged with it and feels it to be its own experience owing to the superimposition of egoism on it.[9] Vijñānabhikṣu considers bondage to be a mere feeling (abhimāna) of the self's being coloured by mental modes reflected in it owing to non-discrimination, even as there is the appearance of a red crystal owing to the reflection of a red flower in the

---

[1] SPS., SSV., i. 19.
[2] SSV., i. 159.
[3] SSV., i. 160; SSV., ii. 1.
[4] SPS., SSV., iii. 71.
[5] SPS., SSV., iii. 72.
[6] SSV., ii. 8.
[7] SPS., SSV., VI. 27.
[8] SPB., i. 1.
[9] SPS., SSV., Vi. 28.

crystal, which is not discriminated from the reflection, though the crystal is not really tinged with red colour.[1] Thus bondage of the self is not real, but phenomenal.

Bondage is not natural (svābhāvika) to the self. Heat is natural to fire. It can never be divested of it. Similarly, if bondage be natural to the self, it can never be liberated from bondage. If the self is bound by nature, it can never be released even in a hundred births. There is no bondage due to the nature of the self ; nor is there release from its non-existence. Bondage and release are due to error (vikalpa) ; they are not real. If bondage were natural, destruction of nature would bring about destruction of the self itself.[2] Its nature is permanent. So its bondage also is permanent. Therefore the instructions laid down by the scriptures are irrelevant.[3] But it may be argued that bondage is the natural condition of the self, which can be destroyed by appropriate means, even as a piece of white cloth is coloured by a dye, or the natural power of germination in a seed is destroyed by fire.[4] This is wrong. An effect pre-exists in the cause in a latent state. The whiteness of the cloth is not destroyed, but is enveloped by the dye, and is developed or manifested again after washing. Likewise, when the seed sprouts, it is not destroyed, but is enveloped or overpowered. Its non-reappearance is due to the diversity of nature.[5] All production is development or manifestation (āvirbhāva). All destruction is envelopment or involution (tirobhāva). The natural whiteness of a cloth is not destroyed by a dye, but is enveloped by it. The natural power of germination is not destroyed by fire, but overpowered by it. So the natural condition of bondage cannot be said to be destroyed by meditation and the like. The disappearance of the power of pain cannot be said to be release, since the absolute cessation of pain is felt to be the *summum bonum* by persons.[6]

The bondage of the self is not due to relation to time. Time is eternal and all-pervading. So it is related to all souls, bound as well as released. So released souls also would be bound by being related to time.[7]

---

[1] SPB., Vi. 28.
[2] SPS., SSV., SPB., i. 7.
[3] SPS., i. 8.
[4] SPS., SSV., SPB., i. 10.
[5] SPS., SSV., i. 11.
[6] SPB., i. 11.
[7] SPS., SPB., i. 12.

The bondage of the self is not due to relation to space. Space is eternal and all-pervading. So it is related to all souls, bound as well as released. So released souls also would be bound by being related to space.[1]

The bondage of the self is not due to organic condition, since it is a property of the body, which is subject to change, while the self is unchangeable. The property of the unconscious body cannot entangle the conscious self, which is a different entity, in bondage. If the condition of the body can bring about the bondage of the soul, it can bring about the bondage of the released soul also.[2] Organization cannot be a property of the self, since it is devoid of the guṇas, while organization is a condition of the organism, which is an aggregate of the guṇas.[3]

The bondage of the self is not due to actions, since they are not property of the self.[4] Prescribed or prohibited actions cannot bring about the bondage of the self, since they are property of the body, which is different from the self. If the property of the body can bring about the bondage of the soul, which is quite different from it, it can cause the bondage of the released soul as well. So the bondage of the self cannot be caused by actions.[5]

The bondage of the self is not due to prakṛti. Prakṛti cannot entangle the self in bondage without depending on a particular conjunction of the self with buddhi. If it can cause its bondage without a particular conjunction, the self would experience pain and be in bondage during the state of dissolution.[6] But the Sāṁkhya holds that the self does not feel pain during dissolution. So bondage is accidental (aupādhika) and due to the accident of a particular conjunction of the self with prakṛti.[7] It is phenomenal. It is not noumenal. Just as a white crystal appears to be red owing to its proximity to a red flower, so the eternally pure and liberated self appears to be in bondage owing to the reflection of pain, a mode of buddhi, in the self. The self itself is eternally free from pain. It appears to experience pain and be in bondage owing to its

[1] SPS., SSV., SPB., i. 13.
[2] SPS., SPB., SSV., i. 14.
[3] SPS., SPB., i. 15.
[4] SPS., i. 16.
[5] SPB., i. 16.
[6] SPS., SPB., i. 18.
[7] SPB., i. 19.

reflection in it and its non-discrimination of itself from the reflection.[1] The self can never be bound without non-discrimination. But its bondage due to non-discrimination is a mere appearance.[2]

Bondage is not due to avidyā or nescience. Avidyā is unreal and therefore cannot bring about bondage. It is either prior non-existence of knowledge or its posterior non-existence. In either case, it is unreal, and cannot cause bondage of the real self. An unreal thing is not capable of producing an effect (arthakriyā). So bondage cannot be caused by nescience,[3] as the Advaita Vedāntists hold. If avidyā is held to be real, it undermines their monism. They hold Brahman alone to be real. If they admit the reality of avidyā also, they would uphold dualism. The dualists hold that avidyā is real and beginningless. Therefore it cannot be destroyed, and the instruction as to the destruction of bondage is useless.[4] Avidyā cannot be said to be both real and unreal, since such a thing has never been observed.[5]

Bondage is not due to vāsanā as the Buddhists hold. Vāsanā consists in the soul's being coloured by external objects. The soul is an impermanent stream of ideas. It is coloured by the desire for external objects. This view is wrong. Buddhi is the seat of desires which are its modes. The self is free from desires. So it cannot be bound by desires. Further, the self, according to the Buddhists, is not permanent. Desires also are not permanent. Therefore they cannot cause its bondage.[6] The stream of ideas or the self cannot be said to be bound by the stream of desires owing to their being coloured by external objects, since internal psychoses cannot be coloured by external objects owing to the difference of space. Two objects in different points of space cannot colour each other.[7] So the Sāṁkhya concludes that bondage is due to non-discrimination (aviveka) between puruṣa and prakṛti, and liberation is due to discrimination (viveka). Bondage and liberation are not real, but apparent.[8]

[1] SPB., i. 19.
[2] SSV., i. 19.
[3] SPS., SSV., i. 20.
[4] SPS., SSV., SPB., i. 21-22.
[5] SPS., i. 23-24.
[6] SPS., SSV., i. 27.
[7] SPS., SSV., i. 28.
[8] SPS., SSV., i. 57-58; i. 155.

20. *Liberation (Mokṣa)*

The self is liberated by nature. It is eternally pure, enlightened, and liberated.[1] It appears to be in bondage. It appears to be liberated from bondage. Its apparent bondage is due to its non-discrimination between itself and prakṛti. Its apparent liberation is due to discrimination between them.[2] Liberation consists in absolute cessation of pain, which is the highest good. Supreme happiness is not the highest good, since it is exhausted.[3] Happiness is always mixed with pain. There is no unalloyed happiness in our empirical life. So, though pain gives rise to suffering, happiness does not necessarily give rise to desire for it. Every body seeks to get rid of pain. But every body does not seek pleasure.[4] Pleasure is always attended with pain. So it is regarded by the wise as pain.[5] Liberation does not consist in happiness, but in total negation and non-production of pain.[6] Virtue, wealth and happiness are good to the self. But they are not the highest good, since they are exhausted and yield sensuous pleasure due to external objects. Liberation is the highest good (atyanta-puruṣārtha), since it is eternal manifestation.[7] Supreme happiness unmingled with pain, not eclipsed afterwards by pain, attained as soon as it is desired, may be called heaven. But it is exhausted and followed by pain. So it is not the highest good. Pleasure and pain are modes of buddhi. They are not attributes of the self. Disembodied isolation (videhakaivalya) of the self is the highest good.[8] The disembodied self which has realized its distinction from prakṛti and its evolutes is beyond pleasure and pain.[9]

Liberation does not consist in the manifestation of bliss (ānandābhivyakti) as some Vedāntists hold. In the state of release there is no relation of an attribute and the possessor of an attribute. If the manifestation of bliss exists at all times, it exists even in the state of bondage and empirical existence. If it is brought about by appropriate means, it must necessarily perish, and there will be no permanent release.[10] If it is the

---

[1] SPS., i. 19.
[2] SPS., SSV., iii. 71.
[3] SPS., SSV., Vi. 5.
[4] SPS., SSV., Vi. 6.
[5] SPS., SSV., Vi. 8.
[6] SPS., i. 1-2.
[7] SSV., i. 1.
[8] SPB., i. 5.
[9] SPB., i. 19.
[10] SPS., SSV., V. 74.

essential nature of the self, it is eternal, and cannot be effected by any means.[1]

Liberation does not consist in the annihilation of specific attributes of the self (viśeṣaguṇocchitti). If its specific attributes only are annihilated, its generic attributes will persist, in connection with which it cannot have release.[2] In fact, the self is devoid of attributes. Cognition, pleasure, pain, desire, aversion, volition, merit, demerit, and disposition are modes of buddhi. They are not attributes of the self. So the annihilation of them does not constitute release.[3]

Liberation does not consist in the soul's upward movement to supra-mundane space (viśeṣagati). The Jaina holds that the soul is co-extensive with the body, and it moves upward to supra-mundane space in the state of release. This is wrong. The soul is inactive and devoid of motion. It cannot move upward. Further, it is not co-extensive with the body. If it were so, it would be capable of contraction and expansion in order to transmigrate into smaller or larger bodies, and it would be non-eternal, being possessed of parts.[4] If it is said to move with the help of its subtle body, its transport to heaven or supra-mundane space is not liberation, since subtle body is the cause of empirical existence (saṁsāra).[5]

Liberation does not consist in the destruction of the dispositions of the forms of cognitions imprinted on them by external objects (ākāroparāgocchitti) as some Buddhists hold. The self is the stream of momentary cognitions. Their modifications into the forms of objects constitute bondage. The annihilation of the dispositions (vāsanā) of these forms constitutes release. This view is wrong. Release, on this view, is momentary, and cannot be an object of desire.[6] The self is momentary. The stream of transparent cognitions is momentary. Their modifications into the forms of objects are momentary. Their destructions also are momentary, which are found even in empirical life. So they cannot constitute release.[7]

Liberation does not consist in total annihilation of the self which consists of cognitions (sarvocchitti). The extinction of

---

[1] SPB., V. 74.
[2] SPS., SSV., V. 75.
[3] SPB., V. 75.
[4] SPS., SSV., V. 76.
[5] SPB., V. 76.
[6] SPS., SPB., V. 77.
[7] SVM., V. 77.

the self can never be an object of desire.[1] The extinction of all objects cannot be brought about. Nor it is desirable.[2]

Liberation is not void (śūnya) as the Mādhyamika Buddhists hold. It is not an object of desire. No practical means can be applied to bring about void.[3] The annihilation of all cognitions and their objects amounts to extinction of the self. It can never be the object of human endeavour.[4] The Buddhists contend that if the self persists in the state of release, it has aversion to what is antagonistic to it, and attachment for what is favourable to it, which being the cause of bondage, cannot lead to release. The Sāṁkhya replies that attachment and aversion, in themselves, do not cause bondage, but particular forms of attachment and aversion entangle the soul in bondage. Just as the Buddhists admit that the stream of cognitions, in itself, does not cause bondage, since the stream of transparent cognitions, free from impressions of objects, is a means to release, so the Sāṁkhya admits that aversion to what is antagonistic to the isolation of the self from prakṛti, and attachment for the existence of the self divested of all its adjuncts (upādhi) do not cause bondage, but, on the contrary, cause release.[5]

Liberation does not consist in the attainment of the objects of enjoyment in heaven or supra-mundane space. Conjunction with a space ends in disjunction from it. Conjunction with a time also ends in disjunction from it. Conjunction with a particular act also ends in disjunction from it. An act is exhausted and leads to empirical existence (saṁsāra).[6] Ownership is not release on account of its perishableness.[7] The Cārvāka wrongly holds that independence (svātantrya) or ownership (svāmya) is release, since it is perishable.

Liberation does not consist in conjunction of the soul with Brahman, as some Vedāntists hold. The individual soul is not a part of Brahman, since it is devoid of parts. Conjunction ends in disjunction. So the soul which is conjoined with Brahman in the state of release, will be disjoined from it and will cause bondage again. It may be argued that there is no more disjunction of the soul from Brahman after release owing to the

[1] SPB., V. 78.
[2] SSV., V 78.
[3] SSV., V. 79.
[4] SPB., V. 79.
[5] SSV., v. 79.
[6] SPS., SSV., V. 80.
[7] SPB., V. 80.

absence of the cause of transmigration. But, then, there is no use of assuming the conjunction of the soul with Brahman. The absence of the cause of transmigration itself will lead to release.[1] The Sāṁkhya does not recognize the existence of Brahman or the Lord. So it does not regard absorption (laya) of the soul in Brahman as release. Absorption or destruction of one's self (svalaya) is not an object of desire.[2]

Liberation does not consist in the acquisition of supernatural powers, *e.g.,* attenuation, levitation, heaviness, reaching remote places, unrestricted fulfilment of desire, lordliness, control, and free movement. They are effects, and therefore perishable. So they cannot constitute release.[3] The soul's connection with these supernatural powers must end in its disjunction from them. Thus release will be followed by bondage. So acquisition of supernatural powers is not release.[4]

Liberation is not the attainment of supreme power like that of Indra, the king of heaven, since it is not eternal.[5] Even this supreme power is perishable like supernatural powers.[6] So it is not release.

The Sāṁkhya holds that liberation is the absolute negation of three-fold suffering or pain.[7] The supreme release (paramukti) is total annihilation of three-fold pain without leaving any trace of it. It is brought about by discrimination (viveka) only, and not by any other means.[8] Release partly resembles deep sleep and ecstasy (samādhi) which are lacking in consciousness of external objects and feeling of pain.[9] But it differs from them because they contain dispositions, while there is complete destruction of them in release. In deep sleep and ecstasy there is temporary arrest of mental functions, while in release there is complete destruction of mental functions or their complete reabsorption in prakṛti.[10] In the state of release there is complete isolation (kaivalya) of the self from prakṛti and its evolutes, the mind-body-complex. There is destruction of mental functions, and not mere arrest of them. There is destruction of all dispositions. Release is either embodied (jīvanmukti) or disembodied isolation (videhamukti) of the self. In the former

[1] SPS., SSV., V. 81.
[2] SPB., V. 81.
[3] SPS., SSV., V., 82.
[4] SFB., V., 82.
[5] SSV., V. 83.
[6] SPB., V. 83.
[7] SPS., i. 1.
[8] SPS., SSV., iii. 84.
[9] SPS., SSV., V. 116.
[10] SPS., SSV., V. 117, 118.

traces of dispositions persist, which preserve bodily life. In the latter even these traces are completely destroyed and the body is dissolved.[1] Discrimination leads to release. But it is of different degrees. Persons of intense discrimination have no experience. Persons of moderate discrimination have experience in the form of continuance of dispositions. They are the fruitions of their previous actions. They wear them away by their experience. They are devoid of attachment and aversion, which have been destroyed by knowledge.[2] They achieve embodied release. Their bodily existence is not an obstacle to their release. Traces of dispositions of previous births continue their bodily existence. But it no longer hinders their experience of isolation. Their attachment and aversion are destroyed. Merits and demerits cease to accrue to them. Still traces of potencies of previous births compel them to continue in their embodied existence. This is the state of embodied isolation (jīvanmukti).[3] The dispositions of merit and demerit which are the fruitions of the actions in previous births, preserve bodily existence, and are worn out by experience.[4] Just as a wheel continues to revolve for some time even when the staff is withdrawn, owing to its momentum, so persons of moderate discrimination continue to live an embodied life on account of the persistence of traces of dispositions, not completely worn out, which can preserve their bodies. They do not achieve disembodied isolation at once. When they wear out all traces of dispositions by experience, they are disjoined from their bodies and achieve disembodied isolation.[5] There are traces of dispositions (saṁskāra-leśa) in embodied release. There is total annihilation of even these traces in disembodied release.[6] There is annihilation of buddhi also, in which they subsist, and of which they are modes.[7] During dissolution merits and demerits persist in the subtle body in a dormant state. At the time of creation they are activated and create a body, which is a fit medium for the enjoyment of their fruits.[8] The souls transmigrate to different

[1] SPB., V. 119.
[2] SPS., SSV., iii. 77.
[3] SSV., SVM., V. 77, 78.
[4] STK., 67.
[5] SK., STK., SGB., 67; SPS., SSV., iii. 82.
[6] SK., STK., SGB., 68; SPS., SVM., iii. 83, 84.
[7] SPB., i. 1.
[8] SSV., iii. 6.

forms of embodied life in accordance with the merits and demerits subsisting in their subtle bodies. When they are almost worn out by appropriate means, they achieve embodied release. When they are completely destroyed along with the subtle body without leaving any trace behind, the gross body is dissolved, and the souls achieve disembodied isolation (videha-kaivalya). This is the real kind of liberation.[1] In disembodied release there are no empirical cognitions of external objects,[2] which are known through the medium of buddhi which is destroyed. There is no experience of pain.[3] There is no possibility of reappearance of pain. There are no germs of pain in the forms of merits, demerits, and dispositions.[4] The self remains in its pristine purity, transparence, and freedom. It remains in its essential nature of transcendental consciousness, free from empirical cognitions, devoid of association with buddhi and its modes, attachment and aversion, pleasure and pain, merit and demerit, virtue and vice.[5]

The self is neither bound, nor released, nor transmigrates from one body to another. Prakṛti, in the form of buddhi, ahaṁkāra, tanmātras, and the sense-organs, is bound, released, and transmigrates. The self has neither bondage nor release. Prakṛti binds and liberates itself. The subtle body with merit and demerit is entangled in bondage.[6] Prakṛti binds itself with its seven-fold forms, virtue, dispassion, lordliness, vice, ignorance, attachment, and powerlessness. It liberates itself by knowledge.[7] Prakṛti acts for the release of the self.[8] It shows its activities to the self and then desists from them. When the self apprehends the distinction of the self from prakṛti, it becomes completely fulfilled. So prakṛti withdraws its creative acts from it.[9] When it withdraws its acts, the self remains in its intrinsic nature (svastha) as its spectator (prekṣaka).[10] It realizes its innate purity, and remains as its indifferent seer (upekṣaka).[11] Liberation is the indifference of prakṛti and puruṣa to each other. The indifference of prakṛti consists in its in-

---

[1] SPB., V. 116.
[2] SSV., iii. 79; V. 116.
[3] SVM., V. 116.
[4] SVM., iii. 83, 84.
[5] SPS., i. 19; SPB., V. 116.
[6] SK., SGB., 62.
[7] SK., SGB., 63; SPS., SSV., iii. 73.
[8] SK., 58.
[9] SK., 59; STK., 44.
[10] SK., 65.
[11] SK., 66.

activity towards the discriminating puruṣa. The indifference of puruṣa consists in its lack of attachment for prakṛti.[1]

21. *The Means to Liberation*

Virtue (dharma) leads to transmigration to higher spheres of empirical life. Vice (adharma) leads to transmigration to lower spheres of empirical life. They are the causes of future life. Error leads to bondage. Knowledge leads to release. Excess of energy (rajas) is the cause of attachment. Attachment is the cause of bondage. Excess of purity or essence (sattva) is the cause of dispassion. It is the cause of absorption in prakṛti (prakṛtilaya). It is absorption of puruṣa in prakṛti, buddhi, ahaṁkāra, and the tanmātras. Ignorance persists in this condition. True knowledge is the cause of release.[2] It is discrimination (vivekakhyāti) or apprehension of distinction between puruṣa and prakṛti.[3] It is not theoretical knowledge, but direct and immediate knowledge of the self, as distinct from buddhi, ahaṁkara, and the like.[4]

Discrimination is release.[5] Non-discrimination is bondage.[6] Non-discrimination, bondage, and transmigration are identical with one another, since they are related to one another as cause and effect. Non-discrimination is the cause of bondage. Bondage is the cause of transmigration.[7] Non-discrimination is non-eternal. It is destroyed by discrimination even as darkness is destroyed by light.[8] Discrimination leads to liberation. Is it related to the self or not? If it is related to it, it affects its immutability. If it is not related to it, it cannot liberate it. Its relation to the self is not real, but phenomenal. The self appears to have discrimination owing to its proximity to buddhi in which it is reflected.[9] Discrimination arises from listening to the instruction of an adept (śravaṇa), reflection (manana) on it, and intellectual conviction (nididhyāsana). It is direct and immediate knowledge of the self as distinct from prakṛti and its evolutes.[10] Suffering is due to ignorance, desire, merit, and demerit. Ignorance is error. Its disposition is the cause of

---

1 SPS., SSV., iii. 65.
2 SK., SGB., STK., 44, 45.
3 STK., 44.
4 SSV., V. 85; SPB., Vi. 43.
5 SPS., SSV., Vi. 18.
6 SPS., Vi. 16.
7 SSV., Vi. 16.
8 SPS., SSV., Vi. 13, 14.
9 SSV., i. 57, 58.
10 SSV., i. 59.

desire. Destruction of suffering is total extinction of its cause, and non-production of suffering in future. It can be accomplished by the true knowledge of the self, which is its means. The knowledge of the self destroys ignorance.[1] Liberation can be achieved by knowledge. It is the knowledge of distinction between the self and the not-self or the guṇas.[2]

Action cannot bring about release. Performance of empirical duties (kāmyakarma) for the fulfilment of desires leads to enjoyment. Performance of non-empirical duties (akāmakarma)[3] leads to knowledge. Performance of obligatory duties (nityakarma) purifies the mind.[4] Action is empirical or phenomenal (māyika) like a dream. Knowledge is real or noumenal like waking experience.[5] Combination of knowledge and action (jñānakarmasamuccaya) cannot bring about release, since action is not ultimately real, in the sense that it cannot produce an absolute result.[6] Action is full of pain. So, if liberation were effected by action, it would be full of pain. Action is transitory. So its result, liberation, would be transitory.[7] Vedic rites involve violence or killing animals, and consequently entail suffering. Suffering produces suffering. It cannot destroy ignorance or non-discrimination.[8] Vedic rites involve impurity and sin of killing. So their effects are transitory and relative.[9] The Sāṁkhya condemns animal sacrifice like Buddhism and Jainism. Performance of duties without any desire (niṣkāma karma) brings about knowledge. Knowledge brings on release. In this sense, duties for the sake of duties free from empirical motives indirectly lead to release.[10]

Knowledge is the direct means to release. It is discrimination of the self from prakṛti and its evolutes. It is direct knowledge of the self. It annihilates suffering.[11] It is aided by subsidiary means, *viz.*, sense-control, purity of mind, posture, breath control, withdrawal of mind from external objects, concentration of mind on different parts of the body, meditation, and complete arrest of mental functions.[12] Desire for objects is

---

[1] SSV., ii. 1.
[2] SK., 44; STK., 23.
[3] SSV., iii. 25.
[4] SVM., iii. 26.
[5] SSV., SVM., iii. 26.
[6] SSV., SVM., iii. 27.
[7] SPS., SSV., i. 84.
[8] SPB., i. 84; SK., 2.
[9] SPB., i. 6.
[10] SSV., i. 85; iii. 73.
[11] STK., 2.
[12] SSV., Vi. 57; iii. 32.

arrested in samādhi.[1] The sense of identity of the self with ahaṁkāra due to non-discrimination is arrested by meditation, fixation of mind on different parts of the body, constant practice, dispassion, and total suspension of mental functions.[2] Meditation is the destruction of attachment which is due to the excess of rajas.[3] Its perfection can be achieved by the arrest of mental functions, which can be perfected by sense-control, purity of mind, breath control, withdrawal of mind from external objects, concentration of mind on the navel and the like, posture of the body, and performance of specific duties relating to one's caste and station in life.[4] Mental functions can be arrested by dispassion and constant practice of meditation also. Discrimination gives rise to higher dispassion which arrests all mental functions and brings about release.[5] Then prakṛti withdraws its activities and stops creation.[6] All sufferings are completely annihilated. The self becomes completely fulfilled.[7] The yoga practices are recognized by the Sāṁkhya as subsidiary means to liberation.

22. *Future Life*

Non-discrimination is the cause of bondage. Bondage is the cause of transmigration.[8] The self is eternally pure and free. It is neither bound nor released. It does not transmigrate. The self reflected in buddhi, or the empirical individual (jīva), transmigrates. It transmigrates with the help of the subtle body (liṅgadeha) which is composed of buddhi, ahaṁkāra, manas, five subtle essences, and ten sense-organs.[9] Virtue leads to heaven. Vice leads to hell.[10] Virtue is the cause of exaltation (abhyudaya) and the highest good (niḥśreyasa). Virtue arising from Vedic rites leads to happiness on earth and in heaven. Virtue arising from the practice of the eight-fold yoga leads to embodied release.[11] Virtue and vice are modes of buddhi or ahaṁkāra. The self determined by ahaṁkāra, or the jīva, has

[1] SSV., Vi. 26.
[2] SSV., Vi. 27-29.
[3] SPS., SSV., iii. 30.
[4] STK., 23; SPS., SSV., iii. 31, 32.
[5] SPB., ii. 3.
[6] SPB., iii. 63.
[7] SPB., iii. 84.
[8] SVM., Vi., 16.
[9] SPS., SSV., iii. 9.
[10] SK., STK., 44.
[11] STK., 23.

virtue and vice. But they cannot touch the self which is eternally pure, and devoid of them.[1] Virtue and vice are the causes of the relationship of the owner and the owned (svasvāmi-sambandha) between puruṣa and prakṛti. Puruṣa is the owner. Prakṛti is owned. This relationship causes bondage. It is destroyed by discrimination which dawns when the unseen agencies of virtue and vice are destroyed, and the relationship of the owner and the owned between puruṣa and prakṛti is destroyed.[2] This relationship continues so long as the subtle body transmigrates to a gross body.[3] Liberation arises from the complete extinction of transmigration. Transmigration is destroyed by the destruction of the relationship of the owner and the owned between puruṣa and prakṛti. This relationship is destroyed by knowledge or discrimination. Knowledge arises from the extinction of the unseen agencies of virtue and vice.[4]

Virtue and vice are the causes of empirical life. Virtue is the cause of transmigration to a higher sphere. Vice is the cause of transmigration to a lower sphere. Greater and greater moral excellences lead to births in higher and higher spheres of empirical existence. But transmigration or cycle of births and deaths ought to be avoided.[5] It is full of suffering. There is no unalloyed happiness in empirical life. Happiness is always mixed with pain. Even happiness in heaven is perishable. When virtue is worn out, the jīva is again born in a lower sphere. So even birth in the highest sphere of empirical life is not release. Total extinction of empirical life or transmigration is release.

The jīva is born as a god in the upper region or heaven owing to predominance of sattva. It is born in the nether region of hell owing to predominance of tamas. It is born in the middle region owing to predominance of rajas. In men rajas predominates over sattva and tamas. So their lives are full of suffering.[6] Pain is a specific mode of rajas. Persons acquire virtue and vice by actions. Virtue brings them happiness. Vice brings them misery.[7]

---

[1] SPS., SSV., SVM., V. 25; Vi. 62; SPB., i. 19.
[2] SPS., SSV., Vi. 67.
[3] SSV., Vi. 69.
[4] SPS., SSV., Vi. 70.
[5] SPS., SSV., iii. 52.
[6] SK., SGB., STK., 54; SPS., iii. 48-50.
[7] STK., 54.

The self is superimposed on the subtle body and appears to suffer owing to non-apprehension of distinction between them.[1] The self is devoid of movement. It does not transmigrate from one body to another. The self as determined by the subtle body undergoes transmigration.[2] The subtle body is the seat of dispositions (saṁskāra) of actions performed in previous births. It is the seat of virtue and vice. It is the real seat of pleasure and pain. The gross body enjoys and suffers through it.[3] Conjunction of the subtle body with a gross body is birth. Its disjunction from the gross body is death.

Birth in a particular kind of gross body is determined by the dispositions (bhāva) which are the results of acts.[4] Suffering continues till the subtle body persists, which is the seat of dispositions.[5] Enjoyment and suffering are not possible without a subtle body and a gross body. Their instruments, the external senses and the internal organs, are not possible without dispositions, virtue, and vice.[6] The subtle body endowed with dispositions transmigrates.[7] Dispositions, virtue, and vice determine the different kinds of gross bodies with which the subtle bodies are invested. The germ-plasm (kalala) generated by the parents is the physiological cause of the gross body. But psychical tendencies brought about by acts done in the previous birth, and moral deserts of the empirical individual are its predisposing causes.[8] The empirical individual passes through different grades of embodied existence from the lowest to the highest, according to its moral deserts.[9] The law of karma operates through dispositions.[10] Liberation is the total extinction of transmigration (saṁsārocchitti) which abounds in suffering. It is the absolute extinction of suffering.

IV. THEOLOGY

23. *Atheism*

The Sāṁkhya believes in future life. But it does not recognize the existence of God. God is not the creator of the

[1] STK., 55.
[2] STK., 62.
[3] SSV., iii. 8.
[4] SK., 40, 52.
[5] SK., 55.
[6] STK., 52.
[7] SGB., 43.
[8] SK., STK., 43; SPS., iii. 10, 46.
[9] SPS., iii. 52.
[10] SK., 40.

world. Prakṛti is its material cause. Virtue and vice of the souls are its efficient cause. Prakṛti evolves into the manifold world in accordance with their moral deserts. Transcendental influence of the souls disturbs the equilibrium of prakṛti and starts its evolution. Prakṛti evolves for their experience. It dissolves for their release. God is not the creator, preserver, or destroyer of the world.

Vācaspati interprets the Sāṁkhya doctrine as atheism. From Mahat down to gross elements, earth, water, light, air and ether, all things are produced by prakṛti. They are not created by God. Brahman is not their material cause. Intelligent spirit cannot be the material cause of the unintelligent world. Spirit is immutable. It cannot be modified into the world. Nor is it produced by prakṛti supervised by God. God is an inactive spirit. Therefore He cannot supervise prakṛti, and help it produce the world. A carpenter is active, and therefore can manipulate his tools. But God, being inactive, cannot supervise prakṛti.

It may be argued that prakṛti is unconscious and therefore cannot act by itself without the supervision of an intelligent spirit. Individual souls, though intelligent, cannot supervise prakṛti, because they are ignorant of its nature. Hence, there must be an omniscient supervisor of prakṛti. He is God. The Sāṁkhya replies that prakṛti, though unintelligent, acts to realize the ends of individual souls, even as milk flows from the udder of a cow for the nourishment of the calf. Prakṛti is not conscious of the ends, even as milk is not conscious of nourishment. Even if God be supposed to be the supervisor of prakṛti, what is His motive of creation? A wise person's action is actuated by self-interest (svārtha) or benevolence (kāruṇya). But God can be moved by neither of them. God is said to be an eternally fulfilled Being. All His desires are fulfilled. He cannot be moved by unfulfilled desires. Nor can He be moved by compassion for others' suffering. There is no suffering before creation, since the bodies, the senses, and the objects necessary for creatures' suffering are not yet existent. God cannot be said to be moved by compassion for suffering subsequent to creation. This would involve mutual dependence. Creation would depend upon compassion. Compassion would depend upon creation. Further, if God created the world out of compassion, He would create only happy creatures. If the manifoldness of the world be said to be due to variety of merits and demerits (karmavaicitrya) of the souls, there is no need of postulating God as their supervisor. Prakṛti is unintelligent. It can be moved neither by self-interest nor by benevolence. It acts unconsciously to realize the ends of puruṣas. It evolves the world for their experience. It dissolves it for their liberation. The existence of God is a gratuitous hypothesis.[1]

Aniruddha refutes the Nyāya argument for the existence of God. The Nyāya argues that the earth and the like are produced by an intelligent agent, God, out of the pre-existing atoms, even as a jar is produced by a potter out of pre-existing clay. God is the efficient cause of the world. Aniruddha contends that God, with or without body, cannot be an active agent. So he cannot be the efficient cause of the world.[2] Further, is He bound or liberated? If He is bound, He has conjunction with merits and demerits, and therefore He cannot be the Lord. If He is free, He cannot be an active agent, since He is devoid of cognition, desire to act, and volition. He cannot be the Lord, if he is bound or free. Nor can He be like an individual soul which has attained embodied release (jīvanmukti), since such a soul is not found to be possessed of lordship.[3] Again, if God were the independent creator (svatantra kartā) of the world, He could create it without the aid of past deeds or merits and demerits of the individual souls. But the Nyāya holds that He creates the manifold world in accordance with their merits and demerits acquired by past deeds. Then merits and demerits may be regarded as the cause of the world. There is no necessity for God to supervise them. If God depends on merits and demerits of souls, He loses His independence. Again, God has no motive for creation. He is moved by neither self-interest nor benevolence. He has no unfulfilled desires. So He is devoid of self-interest. If He were moved by benevolence, He would create a happy world only. But it abounds in misery. So it cannot be the creation of a benevolent creator. Further, even benevolent acts are done for some selfish ends. No acts are absolutely selfless. There is no need of God for the creation of the world. The

---

[1] STK., 57. [2] SSV., i. 92. [3] SSV., i. 93.

merits and demerits of individual souls are enough to serve as the efficient cause of the world, while prakṛti is its material cause.[1]

The Nyāya argues that God is the author of the Vedas. But the Sāṁkhya contends that they are impersonal, since their personal author does not exist. The existence of God has been disproved.[2] The Vedas are impersonal. They are embodiments of eternal truths. They are revealed to seers. God is neither perceived,[3] nor inferred,[4] nor proved by Vedic testimony.[5] The Vedic texts 'He is the knower of all and the creator of all' and the like are really eulogies of the released souls, or the souls endowed with supernatural yogic powers. They do not refer to the Lord.[6] There is no proof for the existence of God, as conceived by the Nyāya. Aniruddha gives an atheistic interpretation of the Sāṁkhya system.[7] The Sāṁkhya criticism of the proofs for the existence of God closely resembles Kumārila's criticism. Vācaspati and Aniruddha think that the Sāṁkhya denies the existence of God.

But Vijñānabhikṣu thinks that the Sāṁkhya is not avowedly atheistic. It holds that the existence of God cannot be proved. It does not deny the existence of God. The *Sāṁkhya Sūtra* says 'because there is no proof for the existence of God (īśvarāsiddheḥ).[8] It does not say 'because God does not exist' (īśvarābhāvāt). This negation of God is a bold assertion (prauḍhivāda) of some thinkers who do not find any necessity for God in the Sāṁkhya system. The main objects of the system are the supreme good of the self and discrimination between the self and prakṛti, the means to its realization. The main object of the Vedānta, on the other hand, is the Lord. Theism lays stress on His lordliness. It enjoins the aspirants' vision of His perfect, eternal, and pure lordliness. But the Sāṁkhya exclusion of God is intended to enjoin dispassion for His lordliness which is an obstacle to the practice of discrimination (vivekābhyāsapratibandha). The Sāṁkhya does not condemn the theistic theory. The *Mahābhārata* describes the Sāṁkhya as the highest knowledge. Its superiority to all other systems is only in respect

---

[1] SSV., V. 2; i. 82.
[2] SPS., V. 46; SSV., V. 46; V. 41, 128.
[3] SVM., Vi. 65.
[4] SSV., i. 82; V. 2; i. 92-94.
[5] SSV., V. 46.
[6] SPS., SSV., i. 95.
[7] SSV., iii. 57.
[8] SPS., i. 92.

of discrimination between the self and the not-self, but not in respect of the exclusion of God. The Sāṁkhya exclusion of God is a concession to current views (abhyupagamavāda) or a dogmatic assertion (prauḍhivāda). Its atheism may be deliberately intended to hinder the knowledge of sinners. Thus there is no contradiction between the Vedānta and the Yoga, on the one hand, and the Sāṁkhya, on the other. The Sāṁkhya atheism is only for practical purposes.[1]

Vijñānabhikṣu admits the reality of a supreme puruṣa. The original puruṣa (ādipuruṣa) turns prakṛti into Mahat by mere conjunction, even as a magnet attracts a piece of iron by mere proximity. Though the supreme puruṣa is devoid of desire or volition, He is an agent (kartṛ) by mere conjunction. He moves prakṛti to evolve into Mahat by mere conjunction or proximity.[2] The puruṣas are absorbed in prakṛti by dispassion for Mahat and the like. They are not released. They again appear as Lords. They are emergent Lords.[3] The puruṣa absorbed in prakṛti in the previous creation becomes in the next creation the original Puruṣa (ādipuruṣa) or the Lord (Īśvara) who is the knower of all and the doer of all.[4] He is the created Lord. The existence of the eternal Lord is an object of controversy. The original puruṣa is supreme, universal, and endowed with the power of knowing all and doing all. He gives an impetus to prakṛti by His mere proximity like a magnet.[5] Viṣṇu with the adjunct of Mahat is the preserver. He is said to be the supreme Lord, Brahmā. In the Sāṁkhya system the causal Brahman is intended to be the genus of Puruṣa, free from the guṇas, since God is not admitted.[6] Vijñānabhikṣu tries to reconcile the Sāṁkhya dualism with the Vedānta monism.

V. CRITICAL ESTIMATE

The Sāṁkhya advocates dualism of puruṣa and prakṛti. Puruṣa is spirit. Prakṛti is primal matter. Both are independent realities. Puruṣa cannot be reduced to prakṛti. Prakṛti cannot be reduced to puruṣa. This is ontological dualism. The Sāṁkhya advocates neither materialism nor spiritualism, but dualism of

[1] SPB., Introduction.
[2] SPB., i. 96.
[3] SPB., iii. 54.
[4] SPB., iii. 56.
[5] SPB., iii. 57.
[6] SPB., Vi. 66.

puruṣa and prakṛti. It advocates uncompromising dualism, and vehemently attacks the monism of the Vedānta which recognizes Brahman or Absolute Spirit as the ultimate reality, and the materialism of the Cārvāka.

The Sāṁkhya regards puruṣa as the seer (draṣṭṛ), the knower, or the self, and prakṛti as the seen (dṛśya), the known, or the not-self. But if puruṣa and prakṛti are the self and the not-self, they are correlative to each other, and cannot exist apart from each other. If there is no not-self to be known, there can be no knowing self. If there is no knowing self, the not-self cannot be known. The self implies the not-self, and the not-self implies the self. Therefore they presuppose the existence of a higher reality of which they are expressions. They are moments in the life of the Absolute, which are organically related to each other. The Sāṁkhya dualism logically leads to Absolute Idealism. But it does not bring out the logical implications of its dualism, and rejects the concept of God as an unwarranted hypothesis.

The Sāṁkhya dualism is mitigated by the assumption that prakṛti acts to realize the ends of puruṣas. It evolves the manifold world for their experience (bhoga). It dissolves the world for their liberation (mokṣa). Prakṛti is the means. Puruṣas are the ends. Therefore prakṛti is subordinate to puruṣas. Prakṛti and puruṣas are not independent and co-ordinate realities. Though prakṛti does not owe its existence to puruṣas, its activity and inactivity serve their ends. If puruṣas were non-existent, prakṛti would lose all its functions. So prakṛti is not co-ordinate with puruṣas, but subordinate to them. The Sāṁkhya implicitly gives primacy to puruṣas over prakṛti and paves the way for idealism. If prakṛti is subordinate to puruṣas and realizes their purposes, who subordinates it to them? Who adapts the activities of prakṛti to the purposes of puruṣas? Brahman, the Absolute, or God can adapt them to each other, of which prakṛti and puruṣas are different expressions. But the Sāṁkhya is avowedly atheistic, and rejects the notion of God as a dogmatic assumption. Rāmānuja regards prakṛti and individual souls as dependent modes of God,—the three realities being inseparably related to one another. Absolutism, like that of Rāmānuja, is the logical consequence of the Sāṁkhya dualism.

The Sāṁkhya starts with uncompromising dualism of prakṛti and puruṣa, and therefore finds it extremely difficult to relate them to each other. It makes use of analogies to explain their relation. The puruṣa is intelligent but inactive. Prakṛti is non-intelligent but active. The intelligent puruṣa acts upon prakṛti and guides its evolution and dissolution, even as a lame man with good vision mounted on the shoulders of a blind man of sure foot guides his movements to come out of a forest. This argument is a false analogy. The lame man is not inactive. He communicates his ideas through words to the blind man, and thus acts upon him and guides his movements. The blind man is not non-intelligent. He is intelligent and understands the meanings of the words uttered by the lame man. He understands his orders and carries them out. This analogy would make the puruṣa active and prakṛti intelligent. The Sāṁkhya argues that the intelligent and inactive puruṣa moves non-intelligent but active prakṛti to action, even as a magnet attracts iron without itself moving. This argument also is a false analogy. Wherever there is action of one thing upon another, some influence must pass out of the former to the latter. Action is transeunt causation. The puruṣa must be active in order to move prakṛti to action. Action of the inactive puruṣa on the active prakṛti is inconceivable. The Sāṁkhya argues that the unconscious but active prakṛti acts to realize the purposes of puruṣas, even as unconscious milk flows out of the udders of a cow for the nourishment of her calf. This argument also is a false analogy. Both the cow and the calf are intelligent animals. The cow's instinctive love for her calf helps the flow of milk out of her udders. The calf consciously draws milk from its mother's udders to satisfy its hunger. This argument would make puruṣa active and prakṛti intelligent. The Sāṁkhya further argues that unconscious prakṛti acts to realize the ends of puruṣas, even as unconscious water flows downward by its very nature. This argument also is a false analogy. All causality is will-causality. Physical causation is divine causation. Water flows downward at the will of God. The action of water is the volition of God.

There is no mere mechanical or natural causation. All causation is spiritual and teleological. All teleology is conscious and intelligent. There is no unconscious teleology, which is a contradiction in terms. Teleology or purpose implies foresight. Purposive action is the execution of a preconceived purpose. If prakṛti acts to realize the purposes of puruṣas, it must be intelligent and conscious of their purposes. Or, it must be an instrument of the Absolute Spirit or God, who is conscious of the purposes of puruṣas, and guides its activities to realize them, so that the intelligent and purposive acts of God moves the seemingly unconscious purposive action of prakṛti. Unconscious finality of prakṛti is as unintelligible as unconscious teleology of the Implicit Will of Schopenhauer, or of the Unconscious Idea of Hartmann. Mechanical causation in the world is subservient to spiritual causation of God. Natural causation is the vehicle of moral causation. The seemingly mechanical causation of prakṛti is adapted to the moral deserts of the individual souls by God who is the inner controller of the realm of nature and the realm of spirits. The Sāṁkhya dualism of prakṛti and puruṣas cannot account for the adaptation of the activities of prakṛti to the ends of puruṣas. Its logical consequence is theism.

Buddhi is the finest evolute of prakṛti. Sattva predominates in it and makes it transparent. The puruṣa knows external objects through buddhi which is modified into their forms. How is it related to buddhi? Vyāsa holds that buddhi does not come into contact with the self in order to be known. It attracts the self by mere proximity (sannidhi) and is known by it. There is a beginningless relation between puruṣa and buddhi, which makes the former an experiencer (bhoktṛ) and the latter experienced (bhogya). Experience is knowledge. Knowledge implies conation or activity. It is not mere sentience. The self knows an object in order to fulfil a purpose. Mere proximity cannot account for the self's act of knowledge. The self must act upon buddhi in order to know it. But the Sāṁkhya conceives the self to be inactive. Vācaspati holds that there can be no contact between the incorporeal puruṣa and the corporeal buddhi in time and space. But there is a proximity (sannidhi) in the form of a special kind of fitness (yogyatā) between puruṣa and buddhi which makes the former an experiencer and the latter experienced without coming into contact with each other in time or space. If there is a special kind of fitness between puruṣa and buddhi, which makes the former a knower and the latter known, the relation can never be dissolved. The puruṣa will ever continue to be the knower of buddhi, and buddhi will ever be known. The special kind of fitness between them, being eternal, can never be terminated. The self's false sense of identity (abhimāna) with the modes of buddhi due to ignorance (avidyā) or non-discrimination (aviveka) will never be resolved. Therefore the self will never realize its intrinsic freedom. The assumption of special fitness between puruṣa and buddhi amounts to the assumption that they are intimately related to each other as the knowing self and the known object, and are inseparable from each other. They exist as correlative to each other, and can never exist apart from each other. They are correlated moments of a higher unity or Absolute Spirit.

Vijñānabhikṣu holds that there is a particular conjunction (saṁyogaviśeṣa) between puruṣa and prakṛti or buddhi, which is the cause of bondage. But there can be conjunction between two corporeal entities of intermediate magnitude. The puruṣa is incorporeal and ubiquitous. Prakṛti also is ubiquitous. There can be no conjunction between two ubiquitous entities. Buddhi of an individual person is of intermediate magnitude. The puruṣa is ubiquitous. So there can be no particular conjunction between them. Even if there is any, it is eternal and cannot be dissolved. Hence there can be no liberation.

The Sāṁkhya holds that the conscious puruṣa wrongly identifies itself with an unconscious mode of buddhi and thinks it to be its own mode. This wrong identification (abhimāna) of the self with buddhi is due to the reflection (pratibimba) of the self on the transparent buddhi, according to Vācaspati. It is due to mutual reflection of the self on buddhi and of buddhi on the self, according to Vijñānabhikṣu. This theory of reflection, single or double, is a mechanical device to relate the two absolutely heterogeneous entities, the conscious puruṣa and the unconscious buddhi, to each other. The real remedy lies in rejecting uncompromising dualism of puruṣa and prakṛti. The Sāṁkhya regards buddhi as an instrument (karaṇa) of the self. Therefore the self should be regarded as an agent (kartṛ). The self acts upon its instrument or organ in order to know an object. But the Sāṁkhya does not recognize the self as an active agent. It recognizes buddhi as an instrument (karaṇa), but does not recognize the self as an active agent (kartṛ). Buddhi is an instrument of knowledge. The self is the knower (draṣṭṛ) but not an actor (kartṛ). The Sāṁkhya starts with the assumption that puruṣa and prakṛti or buddhi are entirely disparate in character, and therefore cannot bring them into relation to each other.

The puruṣa is essentially conscious. Transcendental cognition (cit) constitutes its essence. Empirical cognition (vṛttijñāna) does not characterize it. Pleasure and pain are modes of buddhi. Desire, aversion, and volition are modes of buddhi. Merit, demerit and disposition also are modes of buddhi. So the Sāṁkhya puruṣa is the transcendental self, characterized by non-empirical cognition, devoid of feeling and conation, moral deserts, and dispositions. The self is mere sentience. It differs from the Nyāya-Vaiśeṣika self which is a substance endued with the qualities of cognition, pleasure, pain, desire, aversion, volition, merit, demerit, and disposition. The Sāṁkhya self is essentially knower (citsvarūpa), while the Nyāya-Vaiśeṣika self is an inert substance which acquires knowledge in conjunction with body and manas. The former regards knowledge as the essence of the self, while the latter regards it as an accident of the self. The former regards the self as the knower (draṣṭṛ) only, while the latter regards it as the knower (jñātṛ), enjoyer (bhoktṛ), and doer (kartṛ). The Advaita Vedānta regards the self as a transcendental reality (sat) characterized by non-empirical knowledge (cit) and bliss (ānanda). The Sāṁkhya, on the other hand, regards it as divested of pleasure which is a mode of buddhi. Both regard it as of the essence of non-empirical knowledge (citsvarūpa). Both regard it as inactive (akartṛ). The inactive self seems to be active owing to its reflection in buddhi which is active. This is the Sāṁkhya view. The inactive self seems to be active owing to its reflection in egoism (ahaṁkāra) which is active. This is the Advaita Vedānta view. Both recognize the existence of the jīva or empirical self. It is the transcendental self (puruṣa or ātman) limited by the adjunct (upādhi) of the subtle body. So there is great resemblance between the Sāṁkhya view and the Advaita Vedānta view as to the nature of the self. But there is a fundamental difference between them. The Sāṁkhya recognizes the plurality of puruṣas, while the Advaita Vedānta recognizes the existence of one Ātman. The former advocates spiritualistic pluralism, while the latter advocates spiritualistic monism.

The Sāṁkhya conception of the self is abstract. The puruṣa is the noumenal self. It is immutable. It is devoid of the guṇas and their mutation. It is beyond empirical modes of cognition, feeling, and conation. It is beyond time, space, and causality. There is no modal change in it. All changes and modes of consciousness pertain to buddhi which is an unconscious mode of prakṛti. Such a transcendental, non-temporal self cannot be related to changing mental modes which are modifications of buddhi. The self cannot be related to buddhi and its changing modes. The Sāṁkhya cannot relate the self to the modes of buddhi, as Kant cannot relate the noumenal self to the empirical self. The Nyāya conception of the self is concrete, while the Sāṁkhya conception of the self is abstract.

The Sāṁkhya does not recognize the social character of the puruṣas. They are spiritual beings owing to their social intercourse with one another. They are interdependent members of the society. But the Sāṁkhya does not explain the relation of puruṣas to one another. The question does not occur to the Sāṁkhya thinkers. This is a serious defect of the Sāṁkhya system. It invents many hypotheses to explain the relation of puruṣa to prakṛti and buddhi. But it does not think it proper to explain the relation of puruṣas to one another.

The Nyāya-Vaiśeṣika and the Mīmāṁsaka reduce the world to atoms, which are the indivisible units of matter. The Sāṁkhya reduces the atoms to tanmātras. It reduces the atoms of earth, water, light, and air to the subtle essences (tanmātra) of touch, colour, taste, and smell. It reduces the indivisible material substances into their constituent subtle qualities. It reduces the tanmātras to sattva, rajas, and tamas which constitute prakṛti, primal matter. Thus the Sāṁkhya is more thorough-going in its analysis of the world. It regards sattva, rajas, and tamas as feeling substances. Sattva is pleasure substance. Rajas is pain substance. Tamas is delusion substance. They are subjective-objective. They are the ultimate reals constituting the psycho-physical universe. They are the constituents of matter, life, and mind. Tamas or inertia predominates in the inorganic world. Rajas or energy predominates in the organic world. Sattva or essence predominates in the psychical world. They are inseparable from one another. They are always in conflict with one another and enter into the relation of superordination and subordination to one another. Sattva overcomes rajas and tamas and predominates over them in mind (citta, buddhi). Tamas overcomes rajas and tamas and predominates over them in matter. Sattva is the principle of manifestation. Rajas is the principle of activity. Tamas is the principle of obstruction. They are the unanalysable elements of the whole world of matter, life, and mind. They are the inseparable and indivisible units of the mutable world. All changes and mutations in the material, organic, and psychical world are the different collocations of sattva, rajas, and tamas. But what is their relation to one another? The Sāṁkhya does not explain it. Why should it regard them as the ultimate reals? If atoms can be reduced to tanmātras, and tanmātras to sattva, rajas, and tamas, the guṇas also may be reduced to one ultimate matter-stuff. The Sāṁkhya conception of guṇas is a bold hypothesis which plays an important part in the Bhagavat Gitā and the Vedānta.

Prakṛti is the state of equilibrium of sattva, rajas and tamas. The Sāṁkhya cannot satisfactorily explain how their equilibrium is disturbed and evolution of prakṛti begins. The Yoga holds that God disturbs the equilibrium of prakṛti and starts its evolution. He directs the evolution of prakṛti and dissolves the world into prakṛti. The Sāṁkhya does not believe in God. Some transcendental influence of puruṣas disturbs the equilibrium of prakṛti and starts its evolution, though they are inactive. They move prakṛti to action without moving themselves. They are unmoved movers of prakṛti, even as Aristotle's God is the unmoved mover of matter, and the efficient cause of its evolution. But how can the multiplicity of puruṣas move prakṛti to action and make it evolve into the universe, and ultimately dissolve it into itself? Is evolution or dissolution of the world subjective or objective? Is it ideal or real? The Sāṁkhya maintains that non-discrimination (aviveka) of puruṣas is the cause of evolution of prakṛti, and their discrimination (viveka) is the cause of its dissolution. Vyāsa says that when some puruṣas achieve discrimination, the evolution of prakṛti does not stop, but continues for the experience of the other puruṣas which are innumerable.[1] This

---

[1] YB., iv. 33.

shows that evolution is real and objective and is not affected by the discrimination of some puruṣas. It does not affect the liberated puruṣas which are divested of all experience, enjoyment and suffering. It affects only the bound puruṣas which have not achieved discrimination. Thus the Sāṁkhya contention that non-discrimination is the cause of evolution and discrimination is the cause of dissolution is meaningless. If prakṛti evolves for the non-discriminating puruṣas and dissolves for the discriminating puruṣas simultaneously, its evolution and dissolution are not real, since they counteract each other. In fact, if they depend upon ignorance and real knowledge, which are subjective, they themselves become subjective. If they are subjective, prakṛti becomes a useless fiction. But the Sāṁkhya is realistic and insists on the ontological reality and objectivity of prakṛti and its evolution and dissolution. But all puruṣas cannot be bound simultaneously and cause evolution of prakṛti, and all cannot be liberated simultaneously and cause its total dissolution. If evolution and dissolution are real and objective, they cannot depend upon subjective factors. The Sāṁkhya explanation of them is entirely unsatisfactory.

If prakṛti is essentially active, its activity and mutation will ever continue, and there can be no liberation of puruṣas. If it is essentially inactive, it will never act and evolve the world, and there can be no bondage of puruṣas. Prakṛti, indeterminate, non-specific, and devoid of qualities, is an abstraction. It is difficult to derive the richness and variety of the empirical world from such an abstract qualityless entity.

The Sāṁkhya conceptions of bondage and liberation are not satisfactory. The puruṣa is eternally free and liberated (nityamukta). It is neither bound nor liberated. Its bondage and liberation are apparent (māyika). They are not real (tāttvika). They are accidental (aupādhika). They are due to its association with the not-self, or the body, the external sense-organs, manas, ahaṁkāra, and buddhi, and its false identification with them. Bondage is due to these adjuncts (upādhi) which limit the self. It is due to non-discrimination (aviveka) between the self and its adjuncts, the mind-body-complex. Liberation is due to discrimination (viveka) between them. Bondage is due to ignorance (avidyā). Liberation is due to knowledge (jñāna). But if bondage and liberation are apparent or phenomenal, the empirical life of the self in bondage struggling to achieve liberation is only a magic show empty of meaning and value. The puruṣa, the transcendental self, is eternally pure, enlightened, and free. It is neither bound, nor liberated, nor transmigrates from one body to another. The jīva, empirical self, or the pure self limited by the subtle body, is entangled in bondage, transmigrates from one body to another, and is liberated from bondage. The pure self is not affected by these empirical modes. The distinction between the pure self (ātman) and the empirical self (jīva) is a subterfuge to evade the difficulty. If the empirical life of the self is real, its bondage, moral struggle, and achievement of liberation must be real. To speak of bondage, transmigration, and liberation as apparent and unreal is to play fast and loose with the moral life of the self. The Sāṁkhya holds that prakṛti is in bondage and achieves liberation. Its activity and evolution constitute bondage. Its inactivity and dissolution constitute liberation. The indifference of prakṛti to its activity, or the absence of attachment of puruṣa for its activity, is liberation. But bondage and liberation can belong to a conscious spirit only. They cannot belong to an unconscious entity. Stocks and stones can neither be bound nor liberated. Bondage and liberation of prakṛti are meaningless.

The Sāṁkhya ethics is intellectualistic. Moral life is essentially intellectual. It consists in dispelling non-discrimination or ignorance and achieving discrimination or knowledge. Liberation can be achieved by direct and immediate knowledge of the self (ātmajñāna) as distinct from buddhi, ahaṁkāra and the like. Action is empirical or phenomenal (māyika) like a dream. Knowledge is real or noumenal like a waking experience. Performance of empirical duties motivated by desires leads to enjoyment (bhukti). Performance of non-empirical duties unmotived by desires leads to knowledge. Performance of obligatory duties purifies the mind. Thus niṣkāma karma only yields saving knowledge which leads to liberation. Discriminative knowledge only brings on liberation. The yoga discipline is subsidiary to the attainment of discrimination. Thus the Sāṁkhya ethics is predominantly intellectualistic.

The Sāṁkhya is pessimistic in its outlook on life. Life is full of pain. The total destruction of three-fold suffering is liberation. It is not a state of transcendental bliss. Bliss is pleasure. Pleasure is always mixed with pain. In the liberated state the self realizes its pristine purity and transcendental consciousness. It becomes free from empirical cognition, pleasure, pain, desire, aversion, virtue, vice, and disposition. It is divested of all empirical mental modes. Love is a mode of buddhi. So the liberated self is devoid of love. The Sāṁkhya conceives the self as essentially non-moral, beyond virtue and vice. Such a destiny hardly satisfies the aspirations of man. Infinite knowledge, infinite love, infinite good will, infinite righteousness, and infinite bliss should characterize the liberated self.

The Sāṁkhya atheism cuts the ground from under the feet of the dogmatic theist. It will appeal to the modern realist, naturalist, positivist, humanist, and agnostic. It shows the weak links in the chain of arguments for the existence of God. But without the hypothesis of a cosmic spirit it is impossible to explain the cosmic order, and the relation of prakṛti to puruṣas, and of puruṣas to one another. The Sāṁkhya dualism of prakṛti and puruṣas is entirely unsatisfactory as a metaphysical doctrine.

CHAPTER II

THE YOGA PHILOSOPHY

1. *Introduction*

The Yoga adopts the Sāṁkhya metaphysics and grafts the concept of God on it. It is called the theistic Sāṁkhya, while the Sāṁkhya system is called the atheistic Sāṁkhya.[1] The Yoga recognizes the reality of prakṛti and its evolutes, countless puruṣas, and God. Prakṛti is the material cause of the world. God is its efficient cause. He is not the creator of prakṛti. Nor is He the creator of puruṣas. Prakṛti and puruṣas are co-eternal with God. He disturbs the equilibruim of sattva, rajas, and tamas, and starts the evolution of prakṛti. He is the creator of the Vedas. He reveals them for enlightenment of puruṣas at the end of each cyle. He associates and dissociates puruṣas and prakṛti in accordance with their merits and demerits (adṛṣṭa), and brings about evolution and dissolution of the world. He removes obstacles to the evolution of prakṛti. He removes obstacles to the achievement of liberation by puruṣas.

The Sāṁkhya believes in the reality of twenty-five principles, prakṛti, mahat, ahaṁkāra, manas, ten external sense-organs, five tanmātras, five gross elements, and puruṣas. The Yoga assumes the reality of these twenty five principles and adds the principle of God to them.

It recognizes the reality of twenty six principles. The Yoga adopts the Sāṁkhya ontology with slight variations. It agrees with the Sāṁkhya in holding that bondage is due to nondiscrimination (aviveka) between puruṣa and prakṛti, and liberation is due to discrimination (viveka) between them. But it lays stress on the practice of yoga as an indispensable means to discriminative knowledge (vivekakhyāti). This is the special feature of the Yoga system.

Patañjali was the author of the *Yoga Sūtra*. He systematized the Yoga conceptions in it. It is the first work in the

[1] SDS., p. 266.

system. It is doubtful whether Patañjali, the author of the *Yoga Sūtra,* was the famous grammarian, the author of the *Mahābhāṣya,* who flourished in the second century B. C. Vyāsa's commentary on the *Yoga Sūtra,* called *Yoga-Bhāṣya* or *Vyāsa-Bhāṣya* (400 A.D.) is the most important and authoritative work in the system. Vācaspati (900 A.D.), the great scholiast, wrote a glossary on it called *Tattvavaiśāradī.* Vijñānabhikṣu (1600 A.D.) also wrote a glossary on it called *Yoga Vārtika.* These three works are the standard expositions of the Yoga principles. Bhojadeva (1000 A.D.) wrote a commentary on the *Yoga Sūtra* called *Rājamārtaṇḍa.* It is known as *Bhojavṛtti.* It is a popular manual, and hardly discusses deep metaphysical problems. Nāgeśa (1700 A.D.) wrote a commentary on the *Yoga Sūtra* called *Chāyāvyākhyā.* He faithfully followed Vijñānbhikṣu in his interpretation of it. Nārāyaṇatīrtha wrote two commentaries on it called *Yogasiddhāntacandrikā* and *Sūtrārthabodhinī.* Rāmānanda Sarasvatī wrote a commentary on it called *Yogamaṇiprabhā.* Our exposition of the Yoga principles is mainly based on *Vyāsa-Bhāṣya, Tattvavaiśāradī,* and *Yogavārtika,* though the other works also have been consulted.

1. Metaphysics

The Yoga views of the nature of prakṛti, puruṣa, their relation to each other, time, space, causality, and atoms, have been discussed in the last chapter. Here some special metaphysical problems of the Yoga philosophy will be discussed.

2. *Substance (dharmin) and Mode (dharma)*

The Yoga holds that modes (dharma) are modifications (pariṇāma) of a substance (dharmin), which persists in them. Vyāsa defines a substance (dravya) as an aggregate of generic and specific qualities (sāmānyaviśeṣasamudāya).[1] An earthy substance has the generic quality of earthness (pṛthivītva) and the specific qualities of smell, taste, colour, touch, and sound. These qualities are its modes. They subsist in it. It persists in them. Though the modes change, the substance abides. A substance (dharmin) is characterized by generic and specific

[1] YB., iii. 44.

qualities (sāmānyaviśeṣātmā), and it persists in its manifest and unmanifest modes (dharma).[1] There are no qualities apart from a substance. There are no self-subsistent modes. They subsist in a permanent substance.

The Buddhists hold that there are only impermanent modes without any permanent substance.[2] They come into being and pass away. A substance is a mere aggregate of passing modes. It is identical with them. There is no permanent substance apart from the modes. Being is change. Change is momentary. Nothing is permanent. There is no permanent substance which persists in the midst of the changing modes. There is no permanent self apart from a stream of momentary cognitions. There is no permanent thing apart from an aggregate of changing qualities or modes.

Vyāsa urges that if there were no permanent self, there would be no reaping of fruits of one's actions and there would be no recollection. If the self were a stream of cognitions, one cognition would perform an action and another would reap its fruit, and one cognition would perceive an object and another would remember it. Reaping the fruits of one's actions and recollection presuppose a permanent self. If there were no permanent thing, there would be no recognition of it (*e.g.*, 'this is that jar'). But there is a distinct recognition of it as perceived in the past in spite of the change of its qualities or modes. This clearly proves that there is a permanent substance behind the changing modes. A substance is not identical with modes. It is not a mere aggregate of modes. The Buddhist view is wrong.[3]

The Vaiśeṣika holds that substance is a substratum in which its qualities abide. At the first moment of its production it is devoid of qualities. It is endued with qualities at the second moment. Its qualities are destroyed when it is destroyed. So it is a permanent entity in which qualities subsist. It is different from its qualities. Substance and quality are independent categories (padārtha). Generic and specific qualities inhere in a substance.

But the Yoga urges that though there is a permanent substance apart from its qualities or modes, it is not entirely

[1] YB., iii. 14.
[2] YB., iii. 14; ChV., iii. 13, p. 151.
[3] ChV., iii. 13.

different from them. A substance is partly different from, and partly identical with, its qualities.[1] There is not only difference, but also indentity between them. We distinctly perceive a cloth as white. The cloth is different from its white colour, but it is also identical with it.[2] A substance is identical with its generic and specific qualities (sāmānyaviśeṣātmā). It does not possess them. They do not inhere in it. There is identity (tādātmya) between a substance and its qualities.[3] The substance (dharmin) is sometimes spoken of as the generic character (sāmānya), since it is common to its qualities or modes (dharma). The qualities or modes are sometimes spoken of as the specific character (viśeṣa), since they are its particular modifications.[4]

The Yoga holds that there is identity in difference (bhedābheda) between a substance and its qualities or modes. If there were absolute difference between them, they would not be related as substance and mode. If there were absolute identity between them, a substance could not be its own mode. A cow and a horse are different from each other. So they are not related to each other as substance and mode. A horse is identical with itself. So it cannot be its own mode.[5] But a cloth is partly different from its white colour, and partly identical with it. So a substance is partly different from, and partly identical with, its modes. Vyāsa says: "A quality is merely the nature of the substance; it is the changes in the substance that are manifested by the qualities."[6]

Dharmin and dharma are relative terms. What is a dharma in relation to a dharmin, is a dharmin in relation to another dharma. The five tanmātras of sound, touch, colour, taste, and smell produce the atom of earth. So they are a dharmin in relation to earth, which is a dharma. Earth produces a jar. So earth is a dharmin in relation to a jar, which is a dharma.[7]

---

[1] Dharmiṇaśca bhinnābhinnarūpatayā sarvatrānugamaḥ. RM., iii. 15, p. 48.

[2] YV., iii. 43, p. 241.

[3] TV., i. 7, p. 23.

[4] RM., iii. 14, p. 47. Sāmānyaṁ dharmirūpaṁ, viśeṣaḥ dharmaḥ. TV., iii. 14, p. 214.

[5] TV., iii. 13, p. 208.

[6] Dharmisvarūpamātro hi dharmo dharmivikriyaiveṣā dharmadvārā prapañcyate. YB., iii. 13.

[7] YB., iii. 15.

3. *Whole (Avayavin) and Part (Avayava)*

An object of perception is a complex product of atoms. It is a whole composed of parts. The Yoga regards the whole (avayavin) as partly different from, and partly identical with, its parts (avayava). If the whole were different from its parts or atoms, it could not subsist in them, and share in their nature. If it were identical with them, it would be subtle and manifold like its constituent atoms. So it is neither entirely different from, nor entirely identical with, its constituent parts or atoms. If the whole were different from its parts, it could not be their product. If it were identical with them, they could not produce it. So the whole is partly different from, and partly identical with, its parts. There is identity in difference between them.[1]

Vyāsa says, "The whole produces a single cognition ; it is an object ; it is a particular aggregate of atoms ; it exists in each part in its entirety ; it is partly identical with its parts ; it emerges with the qualities of its causes and disappears when some other effect arises ; it is one, great or small, tangible, active , and non-eternal ; it is an object of action."[2] The whole produces a single cognition (*e.g.,* a jar.) So it is a single entity. Many atoms cannot produce a single cognition. Therefore the whole is not a mere aggregate of parts as the Buddhist realists hold. It is not a mere cognition (vijñāna) as the Buddhist idealists hold. It is of the nature of an object (arthātmā). It is an object of knowledge. A mere cognition cannot be its own object. It cannot act upon itself and know it. It is real. It is a particular modification of atoms in the shape of an extended thing (aṇupracayaviśeṣātmā). It is a product of atoms. It is not a product of dyads and triads as the Vaiśeṣika holds. A gross object is directly produced by atoms. Dyads and triads are non-existent. The whole is partly identical with, and partly different from, its constituent atoms. There is no contradiction in it. Difference is mutual exclusion. Identity is inseparability. The whole is inseparable from its parts, and yet it is different from them. A single whole is the product of manifold parts. There is a peculiar relation of identity of nature (svarūpasambandhaviśeṣa) between them.

---

[1] TV., i. 43, pp. 90-91.

[2] YB., i. 43.

The whole exists in each part in its entirety ; it is the common quality (sādhāraṇadharma) of its constituent subtle parts. It can be perceived, even when all its parts are not perceived. A jar is a particular aggregate of earth atoms. It appears when some other product appears. It disappears when it is broken into fragments. The whole acquires certain new qualities which are not possessed by its parts. For instance, it has a large dimension, while its constituent atoms are atomic. The whole is an object of perception, while its constituent atoms are imperceptible. The whole is an object of action, while its subtle parts cannot be used. Thus the whole is partly different from, and partly identical with, its parts. It is a particular arrangement (saṁsthānaviśeṣa) of atoms, which is identical with them.[1] The Buddhist realists hold that the whole is a mere aggregate of atoms. It is not a real entity (avastuka). It is not an entity apart from a collection of atoms. The Yoga urges that atoms are not perceived, but a whole complex thing is perceived. So it is an illusion or false knowledge. There is no right knowledge, since it apprehends complex things.[2] If the whole be a mere aggregate of atoms, there cannot be a cognition of a single extended object, since atoms are many and non-extended. If the aggregate be said to be different from the component atoms, it is another name for the whole. The functions of the whole cannot be done by the component parts. A jar can contain water, but its component atoms cannot do so. Hence the existence of the whole must be admitted.[3]

Atoms also are not simple and indivisible. They are wholes composed of tanmātras. The Yoga does not regard them as devoid of parts like the Vaiśeṣika. An atom is a complex whole composed of tanmātras. For instance, an earth atom is a complex whole composed of five tanmātras of smell, taste, colour, touch, and sound. It is an object of single cognition. So it is a single whole made of parts.[4] An atom is composed of parts. It is non-eternal. But the Vaiśeṣika holds that an atom is partless and eternal. He believes in dyads and triads. The Yoga denies their existence.

---

[1] YB., TV., YV., i. 43.
[2] YV., i. 43, p. 75.
[3] YB. i. 43.
[4] TV., i. 44, p. 94.

4. *Different Kinds of Modifications (pariṇāma)*

Sattva, rajas, and tamas are the constituents of all phenomena in the world. They are the constituents of all physical and mental phenomena. All effects are particular arrangements (sanniveśaviśeṣamātra) of the guṇas. They undergo modifications and produce various effects.[1]

Modification (pariṇāma) is the production or appearance of one quality in a stable substance on the destruction or disappearance of another quality in it.[2] Substance persists in the midst of its changing qualities. They constitute its nature whose change is manifested by them.

The modification of the non-specific modes (aviśeṣa) into the specific modes (viśeṣa) is called tattvāntarapariṇāma. When egoism (ahaṁkāra) is evolved from mahat or buddhi, or when the tanmātras or the sense-organs are evolved from egoism, or when the five gross elements are evolved from the five tanmātras, the modification is called tattvāntarapariṇāma. It is the evolution of an entirely new category of existence (tattvāntara). When the tanmātras are evolved from ahaṁkāra, there is not merely a change of quality, but a change of existence. Though the tanmātras are evolved from ahaṁkāra, the traces of ahaṁkāra are not easily traceable in them. They acquire properties which differ widely from those of ahaṁkāra. They are wholly different from ahaṁkāra from which they are evolved. So when the atoms are evolved from the tanmātras, they are wholly different from the latter, since they acquire sensible properties which are absent from them.[3] Thus the evolution of the specific modes (viśeṣa) from the non-specific modes (aviśeṣa) is called tattvāntarapariṇāma.[4] No independent categories of existence are evolved from the specific modes. They undergo modifications by change of quality (dharmapariṇāma), change of mark (lakṣaṇapariṇāma), and change of state (avasthāpariṇāma).[5]

The five tanmātras of sound, touch, colour, taste, and smell, and egoism (asmitā) are the non-specific modes of the guṇas. The five atoms of ether, air, light, water, and earth

---

[1] YB., iv. 13.
[2] YB., iii. 13.
[3] YPR., pp. 40-41.
[4] YB., ii. 19.
[5] YB., ii. 19.

are the specific modes of the five tanmātras of sound, touch, colour, taste, and smell, which are non-specific modes. The eleven sense-organs are the specific modes of egoism (asmitā), which is a non-specific mode. The five cognitive organs, auditory, tactual, visual, gustatory, and olfactory, are the specific modes of egoism with sattva as the predominant element. The five motor organs,—vocal, prehensive, locomotive, excretory, and generative,—are the specific modes of egoism with rajas as the predominant element. The manas is the specific mode of egoism with sattva and rajas as present in equal proportion. The eleven sense-organs and the five kinds of atoms are the specific modes. The evolution of the specific modes from non-specific modes is called tattvāntarapariṇāma.[1] But the specific modes, the eleven sense-organs and the five kinds of atoms, undergo modifications by change of quality (dharmapariṇāma), change of mark (lakṣaṇapariṇāma), and change of state (avasthāpariṇāma).[2] These substances are modified by change of qualities (dharmapariṇāma) ; qualities modified by change of marks (lakṣaṇapariṇāma) ; and marks are modified by change of state (avasthāpariṇāma).[3] For instance, a lump of clay is modified into a jar. The substance of earth leaves the quality of a lump and acquires the quality of a jar. This is change of quality (dharmapariṇāma). The quality of a jar passes from the latent condition to the actual condition, from the unmanifest condition to the manifest condition. This is change of mark (lakṣaṇapariṇāma). The new jar becomes old in course of time. It undergoes change every moment, which is imperceptible. The accumulation of these momentary changes due to lapse of time is perceived as change of state (avasthāpariṇāma).[4]. A man passes through childhood, adolescence, youth, and old age. This is change of state.[5] These three kinds of modifications are modifications of a substance. It is permanent. But its qualities, marks, and states change. It is the persisting factor among its changing modifications. Qualities appear and disappear. But the substance does not change. It is not turned into another substance. Gold is turned into a necklace. The

---

[1] YB., ii. 19.
[2] YB., ii. 19.
[3] YB., iii. 13.
[4] YB., iii. 13.
[5] TV., iii. 13.

necklace is turned into an ear-ring. The ear-ring is turned into a bangle. Here gold is the permanent substance which does not change. But only its qualities (dharma) change. Similarly, marks and states also undergo modification. For instance, the substance of earth does not pass from the latent or future condition to the actual or present condition. Nor does it pass from the actual condition to the sublatent or past condition. It does not pass from the future to the present, and from the present to the past condition. It does not undergo modification by change of marks (lakṣaṇapariṇāma). It is only a quality or mode of earth (*e.g.*, a jar) which undergoes modification by change of quality, change of mark, and change of state. For instance, the jar (dharma) is turned into powder of earth. This is change of quality (dharmapariṇāma). The jar passes from the latent or future condition to the actual or present condition, and from the actual condition to the sublatent or past condition. Thus a quality or mode (dharma) only undergoes modification by change of mark (lakṣaṇapariṇāma). Again, the jar (dharma) passes from a new condition to an old condition due to accumulation of its momentary changes in course of a long period. Thus a quality or mode (dharma) only undergoes modification by change of state (avasthāpariṇāma). A substance is not turned into another substance among the specific modes of the guṇas. The modifications of the earth substance by change of quality, mark, and state can never leave their earthy nature. They cannot modify the earth into any other kind of substance. Thus all kinds of modifications of a specific mode are modifications of its qualities (dharma). One substance cannot be modified into another. Earth cannot be changed into water. The modification of one quality of a substance into another (dharmapariṇāma) may be said to be a change of state (avasthāpariṇāma). Similarly, the modification of one mark of a quality into another (lakṣaṇapariṇāma) also may be said to be a change of state (avasthāpariṇāma). Quality (dharma), mark (lakṣaṇa), and state (avasthā) may be called dharma.[1] So the modifications of the same substance may be said to be dharmapariṇāma, lakṣaṇapariṇāma, and avasthāpariṇāma from different points of view.[2] None of these three kinds

[1] TV., iii. 13, p. 204.

[2] TV., iii. 13, p. 204.

of modifications transcends the nature of the substance ; they all subsist in it ; they all share in its nature. So the modification of the same substance is common to the three kinds of modifications. Thus, in reality, there is only one modification of a substance, since the substance and its qualities are partly identical with each other. This one modification is spoken of as three-fold, since the substance is partly different from its qualities or modes. Thus the three kinds of modifications are one from the point of view of identity of a substance with its modes, and the one modification appears to be three-fold from the point of view of the difference of a substance from its modes. Modes constitute the mere essence of a substance (dharmisvarūpamātra). The change of its nature is manifested by its qualities. The guṇas are always active and restless. They cannot remain inactive and devoid of modifications by change of qualities, marks, and states for a single moment.[1]

There is a definite temporal order among the modifications of a substance by change of qualities, marks, and states. The powder of earth is changed into a lump of earth. The lump of earth is changed into a jar. The jar is changed into broken pieces. The fragments are changed into particles of earth. This is the temporal order among the qualities (dharma) of earth. The lump of earth disappears, and the jar appears This is the temporal order of modifications of qualities (dharmapariṇāmakrama) in the production and destruction of a jar. It is irreversible. The jar passes from the latent, unmanifest, or future condition to the actual, manifest, or present condition. Then it passes from the actual condition to the sublatent or past condition. The future is modified into the present, and the present is modified into the past. The past is not modified into any other modification by change of mark. The future, the present, and the past: this is the temporal order of the modifications by change of mark (lakṣaṇapariṇāmakrama). It is irreversible. The jar passes from the new state to the old state after the lapse of a long period. It undergoes change of state (avasthāpariṇāma) every moment. But it is not perceptible. It can be perceived only after a long time. The old state can be perceived when it becomes

[1] YB., iii. 13.

prominent after a long period. For instance, new rice becomes brittle after two or three years and is perceived as old. This is the temporal order of the modifications by change of state (avasthāpariṇāma). It is irreversible. Change of qualities (dharmapariṇāma) or change of marks (avasthāpariṇāma) does not occur every moment. But change of state (avasthāpariṇāma) occurs every moment, though it is not perceived. So it is different from change of quality and change of mark.[1] The Yoga gives a dynamic view of the world.

5. *Power and Causation—Satkāryavāda*

The Yoga advocates the theory of Satkāryavāda or Pariṇāmavāda. There is no production of a non-existent thing. There is no destruction of an existent thing.[2] A non-existent thing cannot be produced. What was existent in an unmanifest condition appears in a manifest condition. Production is manifestation (avirbhāva). Destruction is envelopment (tirobhāva).[3] A present cause contains its effect in a latent condition.[4] It is turned into what is already contained in its nature.[5] Milk is turned into curd which it contained in a potential condition. All effects are particular collocations of the guṇas (guṇasanniveśaviśeṣa). Sattva, rajas, and tamas are the ultimate constituents of all phenomena.[6] They are the material cause (upādānakāraṇa) of all effects. They undergo various modifications, but are neither generated nor destroyed. They appear to be generated and destroyed on account of their modes passing from the latent to the actual condition, and from the actual to the sublatent condition.[7] The Vaiśeṣika holds that the effect is a new beginning (ārambha) ; it had prior non-existence (prāgabhāva) before its production ; it has posterior non-existence (dhvaṁsābhāva) after its destruction. What is called prior non-existence by the Vaiśeṣika is called the latent, unmanifest, or future condition (anāgatāvasthā) of the effect by the Yoga. It does not believe in non-existence (abhāva). It is identical with the locus (adhikaraṇa). The Yoga holds that what is non-existent in the cause cannot be produced by it.

[1] YB., iii. 15; YPR., pp. 70-75.
[2] YB., iv. 12; TV., ii. 19, p. 149.
[3] YB., iii. 11.
[4] YV., iv. 11, p. 270.
[5] TV., ii. 18.
[6] YB., iv. 13.
[7] YB., ii. 19.

What exists in a subtle condition in it can be produced by it. The causal power in the form of an unmanifest condition is turned into an effect.[1] What is called posterior non-existence by the Vaiśeṣika is called the sublatent condition by the Yoga. The effect passes from the present or actual to the past or sublatent condition. It is not completely destroyed. It is destroyed as a mode (dharma) but continues to exist in a subtle condition in its material cause (dharmin). It is not perceived owing to its subtlety.[2]

The material cause (upādānakāraṇa) possesses the power (śakti) to produce a particular effect. Power exists in the causal substance (dharmin) to produce a specific effect.[3] It is a quality that is inferred from the production of a particular effect. Earth can produce a jar. Threads can produce a cloth. These causal powers are not perceived. They are inferred from the production of different effects. They are of the nature of dharma. So they are not different from the causal substances (dharmin) in which they reside. They are latent conditions (anāgatāvasthā) of their effects prior to their production.[4] The potent cause cannot be deprived of its causal power, since they are identical with each other.[5]

The causal energy (kāryakāriśakti) or the latent condition of an effect is liberated by an efficient cause (nimittakāraṇa) or concomitant condition (sahakāriśakti). It cannot generate a non-existent effect. It can only manifest a pre-existent latent effect in the material cause. A slab of marble is the material cause of a statue which exists in a potential condition in it. It is liberated by chiselling which is its efficient cause. Mustard is the material cause of oil which exists in a latent condition in it. It is liberated by pressing which is its efficient cause. Paddy is the material cause of rice which exists in an unmanifest condition in it. It is liberated by husking which is its efficient cause.[6] Potential energy (śakti) is stored up in a collocation of the guṇas, the sum of material causes, which is liberated by the action of the efficient cause, which removes the barriers,

[1] YB., YV., ii. 19.
[2] YB., iii. 13.
[3] Yogyatāvacchinnā dharmiṇaḥ śaktireva dharmaḥ. YB., iii. 14, SPB., i. 117.
[4] SPB., i. 115; YB., iii. 14; TV., iii. 15.
[5] ChV., iii. 14, p. 148.
[6] SPB., i. 129.

liberates the causal energy, and produces the effect which is a fresh collocation of the guṅas.[1] The efficient cause can only make the latent effect actual. It cannot produce a non-existent effect.[2] Its function consists in the removal of the barriers which prevent the potential causal energy from being actualized. It removes the counteracting forces (āvaraṇaśakti) and liberates the causal energy (kāryakāriśakti) in the material cause.[3]

Prakṛti evolves manifold things for the enjoyment and suffering of the jīvas or empirical individuals according to their merits and demerits. Sattva, rajas, and tamas are the ultimate material causes of all effects. Merit (dharma) and demerit (adharma) are their effects. They are modifications of the mind (citta) which is an evolute of the guṇas. Effects cannot move their causes to action. So merit and demerit cannot move the guṇas to action, and make them produce manifold effects. They can only break the barrier (varaṇabheda, āvaraṇabhaṅga), remove the counteracting forces, and liberate the causal energy (kāryakāriśakti). When the counteracting forces are removed by merit and demerit (pratibandhāpanayana), which are the efficient causes, the material causes themselves are modified into particular effects. Merit and demerit do not interfere with the material causes, but only liberate the potential causal energy in them, and manifest particular effects. Merit only overpowers demerit. Demerit only overpowers merit. They do not move the material causes to act. Thus merits and demerits of the jīvas are the efficient causes of the production of various effects out of their material causes. God is the efficient cause of the world because He disturbs the equilibrium of sattva, rajas, and tamas, and removes the necessary barriers (akhilāvaraṇabhaṅga) to the production of particular effects out of them. He also has a negative function. He removes obstacles (pratibandhāpanaya) to the evolution of prakṛti to adjust it to the merits and demerits of the empirical individuals. God and merits and demerits liberate the causal powers in the material causes. Physical agents, which are efficient causes, counteract the manifestation of other effects (kāryāntarābhivyaktipratibandhaka).

---

[1] PSAH., pp. 14-15.

[2] Sataśca phalasya vartamānīkaraṇe sāmarthyaṁ nāpūrvajanane. YB., iv. 12.

[3] YPR., p. 84.

Thus the efficient causes have a negative function of counteracting the opposing forces (āvaraṇaśakti)[1]

The Yoga holds that all effects exist potentially in all causes.[2] Sattva, rajas, and tamas are the material causes of all effects, which are their particular arrangements. But they do not produce all effects simultaneously. Their causal efficiency is regulated by the law of place, time, form, and merit and demerit (deśakālākāranimittāpabandha).[3] Saffron grows in Kashmir, but not in Panchal. Its seeds germniate in a particular environment. This is the limitation of place. Clouds are not produced in summer. Different crops grow in different seasons. This is the limitation of time. A female deer cannot give birth to a human being. This is the limitation of form. A person endowed with demerit does not enjoy happiness. A person endowed with merit does not feel unhappiness. This is the limitation of merit and demerit.[4] A sprout is not produced from a piece of stone. A particular arrangement of parts prevents the production of it from the stone. But the will of God can remove all barriers and turn even a stone into a sprout, even poison into nectar.[5] In fact, concomitant conditions only remove the counteracting forces which prevent the production of particular effects.[6]

6. *Non-existance* (*Abhāva*)

The Vaiśeṣika regards non-existence (abhāva) as an independent category. He recognizes four kinds of non-existence : (1) prior non-existence ; (2) posterior non-existence ; (3) mutual non-existence ; (4) absolute non-existence. The Yoga does not recognize non-existence as a separate category. It identifies non-existence with a particular state (avasthāviśeṣa) of its locus (adhikaraṇa).[7] It agrees with Prabhākara who denies non-existence and identifies it with its locus. There is non-existence of a jar on the ground. The Yoga identifies it with a particular state of the ground. There is no additional entity called non-

---

[1] YB., ix. 3; YV., ChV., iv. 3.
[2] Sarvaṁ sarvātmakam. YB., iii. 14.
[3] YB., iii. 14.
[4] YB., TV., Ch.V., iii. 14.
[5] YV., iii. 14, p. 205.
[6] Vastutaḥ sahakārikāraṇāṁ pratibandhanivartakataiva. ChV., .iii. 14, p. 150.
[7] YV., i. 16, p. 31.

existence.[1] The Vaiśeṣika holds that an effect had prior non-existence (prāgabhāva) before its production ; it has posterior non-existence (dhvaṁsābhāva) after its destruction. The effect is non-existent in the cause. The Vaiśeṣika upholds the theory of Asatkāryavāda. The Yoga advocates the theory of Satkāryavāda. It identifies the so-called prior non-existence of the effect with its latent condition (anāgatāvasthā) in its material cause.[2] The effect pre-exists in its cause in a latent condition. The Yoga identifies the so-called posterior non-existence of the effect with its sublatent condition in its material cause.[3] Mutual non-existence (anyonyābhāva) is difference. The non-existence of a jar in a cloth and the non-existence of a cloth in a jar are nothing but difference between them.[4] Absolute non-existence (atyantābhāva) is unreal. It is subjective imagination (kalpanā).[5] Thus the Yoga rejects non-existence as an ontological category.

The Sāṁkhya also identifies it with its locus.[6] It regards prior non-existence as the latent condition of an effect,[7] and posterior non-existence as its sublatent condition. It regards them both as positive entities (bhāvarūpa). The present condition of the effect is its manifestation (abhivyakti).[8]

7. *Particularity* (*Viśeṣa*)

The Vaiśeṣika recognizes particularity (viśeṣa) as an independent category. It is the distinguishing mark of an eternal substance. Time, space, self, manas, ether, and atoms have particularity. Complex substances like a jar and a cloth can be distinguished from each other by their parts. But one atom of earth can be distinguished from another atom of earth by its particularity (viśeṣa). All eternal substances have particularities which distinguish them from one another. But particularities distinguish themselves from one another (svato vyāvartaka). They do not require other particularities to distinguish

---

[1] Na hyabāvo'smanmate atirikto'sti, adhikaraṇasyāvasthāviśeṣasyaivābhāvatvāt. YV., i. 16, p. 31.
[2] YV., ii. 19, p. 137; iv. 11, p. 270; i. 43, p. 75.
[3] YB., iii. 13; YV., iii. 14, p. 202.
[4] YV., i. 43, p. 73.
[5] YS., i. 9.
[6] SPB., v. 56.
[7] SPB., i. 115.
[8] SPB., i. 122.

them from one another. Particularities (viśeṣa) inhere in the eternal substance. They also are eternal.

But the Yoga rejects the category of particularity (viśeṣa). Atoms are not partless. They are composed of parts. Different kinds of atoms are composed of different tanmātras. They also can be distinguished from one another by their arrangements of parts (saṁsthāna). Genus, space, time, mark, and distance also can distinguish two atoms of the same kind from each other. So particularity (viśeṣa) as an independent category is unnecessary.[1]

8. *The Sāṁkhya and the Yoga*

The Sāṁkhya recognizes the existence of twenty five principles, while the Yoga recognizes the existence of God in addition to them. The Sāṁkhya believes in prakṛti and puruṣas. The Yoga believes in prakṛti, puruṣas, and God. The Sāṁkhya is atheistic (nirīśvara), while the Yoga is theistic (seśvara). It is called theistic Sāṁkhya. Vyāsa calls the Yoga *Sāṁkhya-pravacana* in the *Yoga Bhāsya*. Madhavācārya also calls it *Sāṁkhyapravacana*.[2] The Sāṁkhya regards non-discrimination (aviveka) as the cause of bondage, and discrimination (viveka) as the cause of liberation. The Yoga accepts the Sāṁkhya view. But it lays stress on the practice of yoga which is an indispensable means to the realization of absolute freedom. This is the main contribution of the Yoga philosophy. The Sāṁkhya regards knowledge as the means of liberation. The Yoga regards knowledge, concentration, and action as the means of liberation.

Both the Sāṁkhya and the Yoga trace bondage to illusion (avidyā). But the Sāṁkhya regards it as negative knowledge or, non-apprehension of the difference between puruṣa and prakṛti (vivekākhyāti),[3] while the Yoga regards it as positive false knowledge.[4] Avidyā consists in thinking the impure, non-eternal, pain, and not-self to be the pure, eternal, pleasure, and the self respectively.[5] The Sāṁkhya holds the Akhyāti theory

[1] YB., iii. 53.
[2] SDS., p. 266.
[3] RM., iv. 33.
[4] YS., i. 8.
[5] YS., ii. 5.

of illusion, while the Yoga holds the Anyathākhyāti theory of illusion. The former regards it as non-discrimination (avivekakhyāti) or lack of complete knowledge. The latter regards it as false knowledge (mithyājñāna) or knowing one object for another. It is a positive mistake. The former regards it as non-apprehension of distinction. The latter regards it as misapprehension.[1] Kapila describes the Sāṁkhya view as Sadasatkhyāti. Illusion consists in perception of a real object and recollection of an unreal object.[2] These two elements are not distinguished from each other. This view is similar to the view of Prabhākara.

The Sāṁkhya holds that the future purposes (anāgata puruṣārtha) of the puruṣas move prakṛti to action. There is unconscious teleology in the activities of prakṛti. But the Yoga holds that God makes the future purposes of the puruṣas His own purpose in directing the activities of prakṛti. He consciously realizes their purposes in the evolution of prakṛti. There is conscious teleology in cosmic evolution.[3] Puruṣas are not the movers of prakṛti. God is its prime mover. He makes the fulfilment of their purposes His own purpose in starting and directing the course of evolution. He consciously adapts its evolution to the purposes of the puruṣas' experience and liberation.[4]

The Sāṁkhya and the Yoga give slightly different accounts of the evolution of prakṛti. The Sāṁkhya holds that prakṛti develops into mahat ; mahat develops into ahaṁkāra ; ahaṁkāra develops into the five tanmātras, the five sensory organs, the five motor organs, and manas or the central sensory-motor organ ; the five tanmātras develop into the five gross elements.[5] But the Yoga holds that prakṛti develops into mahat ; mahat (asmitāmātra) develops, on the one side, into ahaṁkāra or asmitā, manas, the five sensory organs, and the five motor organs, and, on the other, develops into the five tanmātras, which develop into the five gross elements. There are two parallel lines of evolution of mahat into the subjective series

[1] Vidyāviparītaṁ jñānāntaram avidyā. YB., ii. 5; YV., i. 8, p. 21; HIP., 1, pp. 260-61 n.; YPR., p. 164.
[2] SPS., v. 56.
[3] TV., iv. 3; YSB., iv. 3.
[4] YPR., pp. 89-90.
[5] SK., 22, SGB. STK.

and the objective series. The subjective series consists of ahaṁkāra, manas, and the ten external sense-organs. The objective series consists of the five tanmātras. The five tanmātras develop into the five kinds of atoms of ether, air, light, water, and earth. The five kinds of atoms develop into the five gross elements.[1]

The *Sāṁkhyakārikā* does not mention atoms. The *Sāṁkhya-pravacanasūtra* distinctly mentions atoms (aṇu) and regards them as composed of parts. Vijñānabhikṣu says that aṇus mean atoms (paramāṇus) of the elements. They are not dyads or triads. They are non-eternal. They are composed of the tanmātras.[2] Vyāsa traces the evolution of atoms from the tanmātras.[3] It is erroneous to say that the Sāṁkhya did not believe in atoms, while the Yoga believed in them.

The Yoga develops the doctrine of modification (pariṇāma) and considers its three forms, dharmapariṇāma, lakṣaṇapariṇāma, and avasthāpariṇāma. The Sāṁkhya does not discuss them. Vijñānabhikṣu describes the action of the cause as producing the vartamānalakṣaṇapariṇāma of its effect.[4]

The Sāṁkhya conceives liberation to be absolute extinction of the three kinds of pain. The Yoga conceives it to be complete isolation of the self (kaivalya) or its realization of its intrinsic essence of transcendental consciousness. The Sāṁkhya invents the hypothesis of reflection to relate the puruṣa to buddhi. The Yoga posits conjunction between puruṣa and prakṛti due to beginningless nescience (avidyā). Bondage is due to their conjunction. Liberation is due to their disjunction. The disjunction can be effected by complete annihilation of mental functions and subconscious dispositions (vāsanā) by a severe discipline of body and mind. Disembodied isolation can be accomplished by the annihilation of the mind (citta) itself. Perfect insight or discriminative knowledge (vivekakhyāti) is not enough to accomplish liberation. The Yoga lays greater stress on the freedom of the self which can break off shackles by its own unceasing efforts with the aid of God.

---

[1] YB., ii. 19; PSAH., pp. 10-11; YPR., pp. 59-60.
[2] SPB., v. 87-88.
[3] YB., i. 45.
[4] SPB., i. 120.

II. THEOLOGY

God

9. *The Place of God in the Yoga system*

Patañjali grafts the concept of God on the Sāṁkhya metaphysics and makes it theistic. The Yoga system is theistic (seśvara) while the Sāṁkhya system is atheistic (nirīśvara). Mādhavācārya describes Patañjali as the founder of the theistic Sāṁkhya (seśvarasāṁkhya-pravartaka).[1] He recognizes three realities, prakṛti, puruṣas, and God. But he does not regard God as an integral part of his system. Īśvarapraṇidhāna is one of the means to yoga or complete arrest of mental activities, which is the chief subject of his discussion. It means either devotion to God,[2] or resignation of all actions or renunciation of their fruits to Him.[3] God helps the aspirants achieve yoga. He removes their obstacles to the attainment of yoga. He removes the barriers (varaṇabheda) to the transformation of prakṛti into various effects. But he does not move it to action (aprayojaka). Even as a peasant floods lower fields by removing the barriers from higher fields full of water, so God removes obstacles to the transformation of prakṛti into various modes without energizing it into activity. God is the inactive efficient cause of the evolution of prakṛti.[4] Patañjali does not distinctly mention God as its efficient cause.[5] Vyāsa regards merits and demerits of puruṣas as its efficient cause, since they overcome demerits and merits which obstruct prakṛti, and help it transform itself into various effects. But they do not move it to action.[6] Vyāsa does not regard God as the efficient cause of the evolution of prakṛti. Bhojadeva faithfully follows Vyāsa.[7] But Vācaspati clearly states that God is the efficient cause of the evolution of prakṛti into various effects, whose function consists in the removal of barriers (pratibandhāpanayana) for the fruition of merits and demerits.[8] They are the effects of

---

[1] SDS., p. 266.
[2] YS., i. 23.
[3] YS., YB, ii. 1.
[4] TV., YV., iv. 3.
[5] YS., iv. 3.
[6] YB., iv. 3.
[7] RM., iv. 3.
[8] TV., iv. 3.

prakṛti. Effects cannot move their cause to action. Therefore merits cannot move prakṛti to transform itself into various effects. They cannot be the efficient cause of its evolution. They can merely remove obstacles in the shape of opposite demerits. Demerits also can merely remove obstacles in the shape of opposite merits. Nor can the ends of puruṣas (puruṣārtha) move prakṛti to action. But God moves it to action for the realization of their ends by mere presence.[1] Vijñānabhikṣu also agrees with Vācaspati. They hold that prakṛti is the material cause of the world, while God is its efficient cause in the sense that He disturbs the equilibrium of sattva, rajas, and tamas, removes all barriers to their redistribution into various modes, and guides their evolution for the enjoyment and liberation of puruṣas.[2] Prakṛti is the potential cause of all effects which are mere redistribution of its constituents, sattva, rajas, and tamas. They can be transformed into all kinds of effects. But, in fact, they are transformed into particular effects owing to certain concomitant causes. Time, merits and demerits, and God liberate the causal powers of prakṛti to transform itself into particular modes.[3] Merits and demerits remove barriers in the shape of opposite demerits and merits. Time awakens merits and demerits and ripens them for fruition. Other accessory causes remove other barriers to the modification of prakṛti into particular effects. God removes all barriers (akhilāvaraṇabhaṅga) to the transformation of prakṛti into particular effects.[4] He starts the evolution of prakṛti and guides it for the realization of the ends of puruṣas' enjoyment and liberation. The Yoga does not believe in the unconscious teleology of prakṛti. But it believes in external teleology. God consciously realizes the ends of puruṣas through the evolution of prakṛti which He guides from without. God is the *Deus ex machina*. He somehow relates prakṛti to puruṣas. He somehow adapts the heterogeneous and homogeneous transformation of prakṛti to the moral deserts of the empirical individuals for their enjoyment and liberation. But He is not organically related to prakṛti and puruṣas. He is not their immanent-spirit.

---

[1] TV., iv. 3.
[2] YV., iv. 3.
[3] YV., iv. 3.
[4] YV., ChV., iv. 3.

10. *Proofs for the Existence of God*

Patañjali gives an ontological argument,[1] for the existence of God. The law of continuity points to His existence. God is the supreme Being who is the emobodiment of the highest degree of omniscience. Magnitude admits of degrees, higher and lower. Ether (ākāśa). has the largest magnitude. Atoms have the smallest magnitude. So knowledge admits of degrees. God is the highest limit of knowledge.[2] Knowledge of the past, present, future, remote, and supersensible objects, individual and collective, is found in different degrees, small and great ; it increases more and more, and reaches its culmination in God who is omniscient. He is the highest limit of omniscience.[3] Vyāsa applies the law of continuity to power and lordship (aiśvarya). There are different degrees of lordship. They point to the existence of the highest Lord. God is the repository of the greatest power, unequalled and unsurpassed (sāmyātiśayavinirmukta). He is the highest embodiment of power. Power increases more and more and culminates in God. He is the supreme Lord. He is omnipotent. If there were a more powerful Lord than God, He would be the highest Lord. If there were another equally powerful Lord, their wills would be thwarted by each other. So God is the Supreme Person whose lordship is unrivalled and unexcelled.

The Vedas refer to God. Therefore He must exist. The scriptures are authoritative. They cannot deceive us. They are the creations of God. But is it not an argument in a circle? The Vedas are authoritative because they are the creations of God, the perfect person. God exists because the Vedas bear testimony to His existence. The existence of the Vedas depends upon God. The existence of God depends upon the Vedas. But Vyāsa urges that there is a beginningless relation (anādi sambandha) between the Vedas and the pre-eminence of God.[4] The Vedas may be said to be the *ratio cognoscendi* of the existence of God. God may be said to be the *ratio essendi* of the Vedas. We may know the existence of God through the Vedas, though God creates them and is prior to them in existence.

---

[1] Cp., Anselm.
[2] YS., RM., i. 25.
[3] Niratiśayaṁ sarvajñabījam. YS., i. 25.
[4] YB., i. 24.

God is the Prime Mover of prakṛti. He upsets the equilibrium of prakṛti and starts the evolution of the world. He cannot create, preserve or destroy prakṛti which is the material cause of the world. He is the inactive efficient cause of the world. He removes all barriers to the transformation of prakṛti into various effects. He guides the evolution of the world for the enjoyment of some puruṣas and liberation of others.[1] He adapts the modifications of prakṛti to the moral deserts of the puruṣas. God mechanically relates prakṛti to puruṣas from without. He is not immanent in them. He does not control them from within. The individual souls are unconscious of their merits and demerits. They cannot bring about their fruition in the shape of enjoyment and suffering due to experience of the evolutes of prakṛti. Prakṛti is unconscious. It cannot act and unfold its evolutes to individual selves for their enjoyment and suffering in accordance with their merits and demerits. God is omniscient and omnipotent. He knows the merits and demerits of individual selves. He knows prakṛti and its infinite potentialities. He removes all barriers and starts and directs the evolution of prakṛti for the enjoyment and suffering of some individual selves, and brings it to an end for the liberation of others.[2] God is the unmoved Mover of prakṛti and the efficient cause of the world. He is the Moral Governor (adhiṣṭhātṛ) of the individual selves.[3]

Prakṛti and puruṣas are independent realities. They cannot associate themselves with each other. They cannot dissociate themselves from each other. But their association (saṁyoga) is the cause of the evolution of prakṛti and the empirical life of the puruṣas, and their dissociation (viyoga) is the cause of the dissolution of the world and the liberation of the puruṣas. Their association and dissociation cannot be accounted for without the will of God.[4] He has no end of His own (svaprayojana). He is eternally fulfilled. But compassion for creatures (bhūtānugraha) is the end which moves Him to effect conjunction and disjunction between puruṣas and prakṛti. His merciful resolution to liberate all empirical individuals through their moral education is the end of creation and dissolution which depend upon conjunction and disjunction of prakṛti

[1] YB., iv. 33.
[2] TV., YV., iv. 3; ii. 22.
[3] YV., i. 26.
[4] RM., i. 25.

and puruṣas. God brings about their conjunction and disjunction.[1]

11. *The Nature of God*

Patañjali describes God as a particular self (puruṣaviśeṣa) untouched by afflictions, actions, fruits, and dispositions.[2] He is the perfect self free from all taint of imperfections. He is eternally free from afflictions (kleśa), ignorance, egoism, attachment, aversion, and fear of death. He is eternally fulfilled. He does not perform actions (karma), good, bad, and indifferent. He does not experience fruits of actions (vipāka), enjoyment and suffering. He has no dispositions (āśaya) of past experiences. Empirical individuals are subject to all these afflictions, actions, fruits, and dispositions. But God is eternally free from them. He is not a liberated (mukta) self which was subject to afflictions in the past. He is not a self absorbed in prakṛti (prakṛtilīna) during dissolution, which will be subject to afflictions and consequent empirical life in the future after creation. He had no relation to afflictions in the past ; He has none at present ; He will have none in future. He is eternally liberated. He is the eternal Lord.[3] God is omniscient. His knowledge is infinite. He knows the past, present, future, and supersensible objects individually and collectively. He has intuitive knowledge of the whole universe. His knowledge is supreme and perfect.[4] God is the supreme Lord. He is omnipotent. His power is infinite. His lordship is unequalled and unexcelled.[5] There is no other Lord equal to him, or superior to Him. The Yoga system believes in monotheism. God is one. If there were two rival Lords, they would be of equal or unequal powers. If they had equal powers, they would thwart each other's will, and fail to realize their ends. If they had unequal powers, the superior Lord would be the true Lord, and the other would be inferior to Him.[6] Though the Yoga system believes in one supreme God, it recognizes the existence of many gods who are entangled in empirical life owing to ignorance (avidyā).[7] God

[1] RM., i. 26.
[2] YS., i. 24.
[3] YB., i. 24.
[4] YB., i. 25.
[5] YB., i. 24.
[6] YB., i. 24.
[7] YS., YB., i. 19.

has eternal knowledge (jñāna), desire (icchā), and will (kṛti), which do not lapse even during dissolution.[1] He is immutable (kūṭasthanitya). He is free from the mutations of sattva, rajas, and tamas.[2] But He assumes pure sattva (prakṛṣṭasattva) untainted by rajas and tamas to create the scriptures. His excellence of sattva is expressed in them. They bear testimony to the pre-eminence of His sattva. God teaches true wisdom (jñāna) and morality (dharma) to the individual selves through the scriptures. He cannot create them without supreme knowledge and capacity for action, which depend upon pre-eminence of sattva. So He assumes pre-eminent sattva (prakṛṣṭasattva) to create the scriptures and enlighten mankind. He has supreme knowledge (jñāna), perfect righteousness (dharma), complete detachment (vairāgya), and infinite power (aiśvarya) owing to His pre-eminent sattva.[3] There is an eternal relation between words (vācaka) and their objects (vācya). God's convention (saṅketa) merely manifests the relation. He does not create it.[4] So God manifests the eternal relation between the scriptures and His pre-eminence of sattva.[5] God is the pure (śuddha), blissful (prasanna), free (kevala), and transcendental (anupasarga) self. He is immutable and eternal (kūṭasthanitya). He is uncaused and indestructible. He is free from afflictions. He is devoid of merits and demerits. He is not subject to birth. He is not entangled in empirical life, enjoyment and suffering. He is non-empirical or noumenal self.[6] He is beyond time[7] and space. He is eternal and all-pervading.

God is omniscient, omnipotent, contented, independent, and ubiquitous. He has eternal knowledge and eternally manifested powers. He has ten eternal qualities—knowledge, detachment, lordship, austerity, veracity, forgiveness, patience, creative power, self-knowledge, and superintendence. God is eternally fulfilled. He has perfect detachment. He has no selfish end. But His creative act is moved by compassion for empirical individuals (bhutānugraha). Their liberation is the motive of His creation. He is supremely merciful to the

[1] YV., i. 24.
[2] YB., TV., i. 29.
[3] YB., TV., RM., i. 24.
[4] YB., i. 27.
[5] TV., i. 24.
[6] YB., TV., i. 29.
[7] YS., i. 26

creatures.[1] God creates or reveals the Vedas in the beginning of each world-epoch for the enlightenment and liberation of the individual selves. He is the promulgator of moral codes. The Vedas prescribe right and wrong actions. God is the Supreme Teacher (paramaguru).[2] He was the teacher of the ancient sages. They were limited by time. God, unlimited by time, was their teacher.[3]

God favours the aspirants who are devoted to Him, and fulfils their desires.[4] Repeated practice of devotion to Him removes all obstacles to yoga.[5] They are disease, inactivity of mind, doubt, inadvertence, laziness of body and mind, thirst for enjoyment, illusion, non-attainment of the condition of ecstasy, and instability of mind even in ecstasy.[6] Pain, mental excitement, bodily restlessness, and irregularity of breathing accompany the distractions.[7] All these are removed by repeated practice of concentration on one principle.[8] Repeated concentration on God also removes all these mental and bodily distractions, and enables the mind to attain ecstasy (samādhi) and liberation (mokṣa).[9] Devotion to God[10] and dedication of all actions and resignation of their fruits to Him[11] facilitate the attainment of yoga. The grace of God is recognized.[12] He is expressed by the mystic syllable *Om*.[13] He is revealed to a person who constantly recites it and meditates on Him.[14]

The relation of God to prakṛti and puruṣas is not inseparable and organic. He is not the creator, preserver, or destroyer of prakṛti which is eternal, though mutable. He does not energize it to activity. He merely upsets the equilibrium of prakṛti and removes all obstacles to the effectuation of material causes, sattva, rajas, and tamas. He indirectly helps evolution and dissolution of the world. He is not the immanent spirit in it realizing His purpose in it. He is loosely connected with the world. He is not the creator or destroyer of the puruṣas. They are eternal and all-pervading. They

---

[1] YB., TV., i. 25.
[2] YB., ii. 1.
[3] YS., YB., i. 26.
[4] YS., YB., i. 23.
[5] YS., TV., i. 32.
[6] YS., TV., i. 30.
[7] YS., i. 31.
[8] YS., i. 32.
[9] YB., TV., YV., i. 23; ii. 1.
[10] YS., YB., i. 23.
[11] YS., YB., ii. 1.
[12] YB., i. 23; i. 25; iii. 6.
[13] YS., i. 27.
[14] YS., YB., i. 28.

are uncaused and indestructible. They are entangled in empirical life owing to ignorance (avidyā). They can work out their own salvation unaided by God. He is not their indwelling spirit. God is not organically related to them. But if they are devoted to Him or dedicate all their actions and their consequences to Him, He removes all their distractions and helps them to attain liberation. He is loosely connected with the puruṣas. This is an unsatisfactory concept of God.

III. Epistemology

12. *Valid knowledge* (*Pramā*)

The nature of valid knowledge has been discussed in the last chapter. Vijñānabhikṣu holds that the pure self is the knower (pramātṛ), that the mental mode (buddhivṛtti) apprehending an object is the means of valid knowledge (pramāṇa), that the reflection of the mental mode assuming the form of the object in the self is valid knowledge (pramā), and that the object apprehended by the reflected mental mode is the object of valid knowledge (prameya)[1] But Vācaspati differs from Vijñānabhikṣu in holding that the self is reflected in the mental mode and identifies itself with it which is modified into the form of an object. The reflection of the self in the apprehending mental mode is valid knowledge (pramā). The mental mode is not reflected in the self. The knowledge is not generated in the self.[2] They both agree in holding that the self is the knower, that the mental mode is the means of valid knowledge, and that the object apprehended by the mental mode is the object of valid knowledge.

The Yoga advocates realism.[3] It holds that external objects are real, and are apprehended as they are in themselves by mental modes. There is correspondence between the mental modes and their objects. The modes of buddhi are modified into their forms. The forms of cognitions correspond to the forms of their objects. Vyāsa says that valid knowledge apprehends a real object (bhūtārthaviṣaya).[4] Vācaspati defines it as

[1] YV., i. 7, p. 19.
[2] TV., i. 7, p. 23.
[3] J. Sinha: *Indian Realism,* Ch. V.
[4] YB., i. 8.

knowledge of an object which was not known previously (anadhigata), leading to fruitful action (vyavahārahetu).[1] Novelty excludes recollection from valid knowledge. Workability is the pragmatic test of truth. It consists in attainment of good (hitaprāpti) and avoidance of evil (ahitaparihāra).[2] Nāgeśa defines valid knowledge as novel knowledge agreeing with its object (avisaṁvādijñāna). Novelty and correspondence are the marks of truth.[3] Vyāsa points out that error is contradicted by valid knowledge.[4] This implies that valid knowledge is not contradicted. Thus novelty, correspondence, noncontradiction, and serviceability are the marks of truth. The pramāṇas are the means of valid knowledge.

13. *Three kinds of Pramāṇa*

Patañjali, like the Sāṁkhya, recognizes three pramāṇas, perception, inference, and testimony.[5] Vyāsa defines perception as the mental mode which apprehends a real object possessing generic and specific characters, which particularly apprehends its specific properties, when buddhi goes out to an external object through the channel of the external sense-organs and is modified into its form.[6] Vācaspati brings out the implications of the definition. First, perception as valid knowledge apprehends a real object. It does not mistake one object for another. It apprehends an object as it really is. Secondly, perception apprehends an external object directly. It does not apprehend the form of a cognition (jñānākāra). It does not indirectly apprehend an external object through the medium of a cognition. Perception is direct or presentative. It is not indirect or representative. Thirdly, the form of cognition corresponds to the external object because buddhi goes out to it and is modified into its form. Fourthly, perception apprehends neither generality (sāmānya) only, nor particularity (viśeṣa) only, nor a substance in which they inhere, but both generality and particularity characterizing an object (sāmānyaviśeṣātmā), in which apprehension of particularity is the predominant factor (viśeṣā-

[1] TV., i. 7, p. 21.
[2] TV., i. 7, p. 27.
[3] ChV., i. 7, p. 11.
[4] YB., i. 8.
[5] YS., i. 7.
[6] YB., i. 7.

vadhāraṇapradhāna). The Advaita Vedāntist holds that indeterminate perception apprehends generality or Being only. The Buddhist holds that it apprehends specific individuals (svalakṣaṇa) only. The Nyāya-Vaiśeṣika holds that it apprehends a substance in which both generality and particularity inhere. But the Yoga holds that perception apprehends an object identical with its generic and specific qualities. There is no relation of inherence between the qualities and the substance. There is identity (tādātmya) between them. Perception apprehends both generality and particularity characterizing an object, but the apprehension of generality is subordinated to that of particularity in it. This characteristic distinguishes perception from inference in which the apprehension of generality is the predominant factor. Perception is immediate apprehension (sākṣātkāra).[1]

Vyāsa defines inference as definite knowledge in which apprehension of generality is the predominant factor (sāmānyāvadhāraṇapradhāna) and which depends upon the knowledge of invariable concomitance between the mark of inference and the inferred property, the latter pervading the former and being present in all homogeneous instances and being absent from all heterogeneous instances.[2] The distinctive feature of inference lies in that it apprehends generality (sāmānya), since it depends upon the knowledge of invariable concomitance between generalities of the mark of inference (*e.g.*, smoke) and the inferred property (*e.g.*, fire). All their particular instances cannot be known. So the relation of invariable concomitance between all particular instances of smoke and all particular instances of fire cannot be known. The object of inference, according to Vācaspati, is the substance endued with the inferable property.[3] When the existence of fire is inferred from the existence of smoke perceived in a hill, the generality of fire is already known, the hill is perceived, but the hill possessing fire is inferred.[4] This is the view of Pārthasārathi Miśra also.

A trustworthy person, who has perceived or inferred an object, instructs another person by words to communicate his knowledge of it to him. The hearer's knowledge of the object derived from the words of the instructor is called testimony

[1] TV., i. 7.
[2] YB., i. 7.
[3] TV., i. 7.
[4] Cp. SD., pp. 177-78; IIP., p. 210.

(āgama). The instructor must be free from error, inadvertence, fraudulence, inefficiency of the sense-organs, and the like defects. He must have knowledge of the reality and compassion for the hearer. He must have perceived or inferred the object himself. And he must be trustworthy in character. If he can produce similar knowledge of the object perceived or inferred in another person by his words, the latter's knowledge is called testimony. If the instructor has not perceived or inferred the object himself, and if his character is not trustworthy, testimony is not valid. A trustworthy instructor communicates his valid knowledge to another person for the latter's attainment of good and avoidance of evil. God is the original instructor. He is omniscient. So the Vedas revealed by Him are valid.[1] Perception is stronger than inference and testimony, as a means of valid knowledge.[2]

Inference and testimony both apprehend generality. Testimony is verbal knowledge. It is derived from words. Words denote classes, and not individuals. So all subtle, hidden, and remote objects cannot be apprehended by inference or testimony. Nor can they be apprehended by normal perception. They cannot be said to be non-existent because they are not objects of ordinary perception. They are apprehended by the highest yogic intuition which apprehends all truths (ṛtambharā prajñā). It is different from testimony and inference since it apprehends all supersensible individuals. It is absolutely valid. It is free from all taint of falsehood.[3] The Yoga believes in yogic intuition which is the highest wisdom. It is the perfect vision of the reality.

14. *Sphoṭavāda*

How does a word manifest an object? The Yoga holds that neither uttered letters nor heard sounds can manifest it. They produce cognitions which leave their subconscious impressions (saṁskāra) in the mind. They appear and disappear in quick succession. They cannot produce a word-image because they do not co-exist with one another. The last vocal letter or audible sound produces a perception which, with the

---

[1] TV., YV., i. 7. [2] YB., i. 35. [3] YS., YB., i. 48, 49.

help of the subconscious impressions of the previous letters or sounds, produces a word-image or padasphoṭa which comprehends all the constituent letters in one thought and signifies an object.

The vocal organ of the speaker produces letters (varṇa). It generates a vocal sound which moves in air waves and reaches the ear-drum of the hearer. When it comes into contact with the auditory organ, it produces an audible sound (dhvani). The auditory organ of the hearer apprehends only a modification of the audible sound. Neither vocal sounds (varṇa) nor audible sounds (dhvani) signify objects. But a succession of letters and audible sounds appearing and disppearing in a definite temporal order produce one thought-form (padasphoṭa) which signifies an object. All letters have the power of manifesting endless meanings. But they cannot do so singly. When they combine with other letters in a definite order of sequence, they produce one word-image and manifest one object determined by convention. They appear and disappear in rapid succession. They are not produced simultaneously. But they are brought together and comprehended by one thought-form or word-image (padasphoṭa) which manifests an object. One word is the object of one thought (ekabuddhiviṣaya). It is produced by one effort of the speaker (ekaprayatna). It is devoid of parts (abhāga). It is not composed of letters (avarṇa) appearing in succession (akrama). It is not an objective whole composed of parts. Letters composing an audible word are successive. They are not co-existent and synchronous. So they cannot be parts of an audible word, which is devoid of letters and their succession. A word is a thought-form (bauddha) produced by the perception of the last letter aided by the subconscious impressions of the cognitions of the previous letters. This word-image in thought is called padasphoṭa, without which mere letters cannot signify an object.[1] Uttered letters or vocal sounds are produced by the vocal organ. Heard letters or audible sounds are produced by the auditory organ. But the word-image (padasphoṭa) is a particular modification of buddhi. It is a mental mode. It is a thought-form. It is called a sphoṭa because it manifests or illumines an object.[2]

---

[1] YB., iii. 17.

[2] YB., TV., YV., ChV., iii. 17.

Words are combined together into a sentence. They do not convey its meaning singly or together. They are uttered in rapid succession. They are not synchronous. So they cannot form one objective whole. They appear in succession and produce one thought-form, through their subconscious impressions, which conveys a meaning. This thought-form of a sentence is called vākyasphoṭa. It is a particular mode of buddhi. It is a mental mode. It is not an objective whole. It is an ideational structure without which a sentence cannot convey any judgmental meaning. The same words in various combinations produce different thought-forms which convey different meanings. Mere expectancy (ākāṁkṣā), fitness (yogyatā), proximity (sannidhi) and knowledge of intention (tātparyajñāna) urged by the Nyāya are not sufficient to make a sentence intelligible. The words must produce a judgment-form (vākyasphoṭa) in the mind, with the help of these accessory conditions, which conveys a judgmental meaning. The word *vākyasphoṭa* does not occur in the Yoga literature. But the theory propounded by Vyāsa, Vācaspati, Vijñānabhikṣu, and Nāgeśa implies the notional existence of vākyasphoṭa admitted by the Grammarians. The Yoga view approaches the Anvitābhidhāna view which holds that words express a meaning only when they are combined with one another as parts of a sentence. It is different from the Abhihitānvayavāda which holds that words themselves can express meanings by the power of denotation (abhidhā), and are subsequently connected into a sentence.[1]

Verbal cognition is due to confusion of words (śabda), objects (artha), and cognitions (jñāna) with one another. They are distinct from one another. But we erroneously identify them with one another and comprehend them in one act of thought by illusion (adhyāsa). Convention is memory consisting in confusion of words with their meanings or objects, so that a word appears to be an object, and an object appears to be a word. The word 'cow' and the object 'cow' are confused with each other. They are also confused with the cognition 'cow'. There is no real identity of words and objects. But they appear to be identical with each other owing to confusion

---

[1] YPR., pp. 185-86; IIP., p. 224.

(adhyāsa) which makes for convention (saṅketa). The convention is due to the confusion of words and word-images with their objects according to the Yoga, while it is due to the will of God according to the Nyāya.[1]

15. *Theory of Error*

The nature and kinds of valid knowledge have been discussed. Valid knowledge agrees with its object (avisaṁvādi jñāna). There is correspondence between them. Error or illusion, according to the Yoga, is false knowledge (mithyā-jñāna) which apprehends one object as another (atadrūpa-pratiṣṭha).[2] It is opposed to valid knowledge. It is positive misapprehension.[3] A shell is mistaken for silver.[4] The Yoga advocates the doctrine of Anyathākhyāti. It is clearly stated by the aphorism which describes ignorance (avidyā) as positive misapprehension of the non-eternal, the impure, the painful, and the not-self as the eternal, the pure, the pleasant, and the self respectively. Avidyā is false knowledge. It apprehends one thing as a different thing.[5] The Yoga differs from the Sāṁkhya which regards avidyā as mere non-discrimination (avivekamātra). The metaphysical error (avidyā) consists in non-discrimination between the self (puruṣa) and the not-self (prakṛti).[6] The illusion (bhrama) consists in non-discrimination between the given element (*e.g.*, 'this') and the ideal element (*e.g.*, 'silver'). The Sāṁkhya advocates the doctrine of Akhyāti (non-apprehension) or Vivekākhyāti (non-apprehension of distinction) or Sadasatkhyāti (apprehension of a real object and an unreal object).[7] But the Yoga advocates the doctrine of Anyathākhyāti like the Nyāya-Vaiśeṣika. But there is a slight difference between the Yoga view and the Nyāya-Vaiśeṣika view. The Yoga holds that in the illusion 'this is silver' the internal cognition of silver is attributed to the perceived object or shell.[8] The idea of silver, which is an internal form of cognition (jñānākara), is attributed to the external object or shell perceived. The shell is present here and now. It is mis-

---

1 YB., YV., iii. 17; YPR., pp. 178-80, 184-87.
2 YS., i. 8.
3 YB., ii. 5.
4 RM., i. 7, 8.
5 YS.., ii. 5.
6 RM., iv. 33.
7 SPS., v. 56.
8 YV., i. 8, p. 21.

taken for silver because the idea of silver is attributed to it. But the Nyāya-Vaiśeṣika holds that an external remote object (*e.g.*, silver) is attributed to a present object (*e.g.*, shell), so that one object is perceived as another. An internal cognition (jñānākāra) is attributed to a perceived external object according to the Yoga, while an unperceived external object is attributed to a perceived external object according to the Nyāya-Vaiśeṣika. The subtle distinction between the Nyāya-Vaiśeṣika doctrine of Anyathākhyāti and the Yoga doctrine of Anyathākhyāti has been drawn by Vijñānabhikṣu.[1] Doubt is included in illusion. It is a judgment in the form 'Is it this or not this?' It is indefinite knowledge.[2] Illusion is invalid knowledge. It is contradicted by valid knowledge. The illusion of silver is contradicted by the perception of shell. The illusion of double moon is contradicted by the perception of one moon.[3]

IV. Psychology

16. *The Mind (Citta) and its Modes (Vṛtti)*

The Sāṁkhya treats manas, buddhi, and ahaṁkāra as the three internal organs with different functions though they are inter-related to one another, and constitute the psychical apparatus. The Yoga treats them as one and speaks of the citta and its modes. Patañjali generally speaks of the citta.[4] Sometimes he refers to buddhi as its equivalent.[5] Vyāsa also generally speaks of the citta, but sometimes mentions buddhi and manas as its equivalents.[6] Vācaspati distinctly says that the word *citta* means the internal organ (antaḥkaraṇa) of buddhi.[7] We shall treat them as equivalents of mind. The mind is an evolute of prakṛti. It is composed of the triad of sattva, rajas, and tamas. Sattva is the principle of illumination (prakhyā) and pleasure (sukha). Rajas is the principle of activity (pravṛtti) and pain (duḥkha). Tamas is the principle of inertia

[1] YV., i. 8, p. 21.
[2] YB., i. 30.
[3] YB., YV., RM., i. 8.
[4] YS., i. 2, 30, 33, 37; ii. 54; iii. 2, 11, 12, 19, 34, 38; iv. 16, 18, 21, 23, 26.
[5] YS., iv. 21, 22.
[6] YB., i. 2; iv. 21, 23.
[7] TV., i. 1, p. 6.

(sthiti) and delusion (moha).[1] Sattva preponderates over rajas and tamas in the mind and makes it transparent and manifest objects.[2] The mind with an excess of satvva can manifest all objects. But it cannot do so because it is covered by tamas. When the tamas is removed by the activity of rajas with regard to an object, the mind can manifest it. When it is purged of all impurities, it can manifest all objects.[3] The mind is unconscious (acetana). The self or pure conciousness is reflected in it and intelligizes it. The unconscious mind appears to be conscious owing to the reflection of the self in it.[4] The transparent mind is coloured by the knowing self and the known objects. It is coloured by the pure self and appears to be the knower (grahītṛ). It goes out to an external object through a sense-organ, is coloured by it, and modified into its form (grāhya). It is modified into an apprehending mode (grahaṇa). It appears to be the knower, the knowledge, and the known, though, in reality, the pure self is the knower, a mental mode is the knowledge, and an external object is known. A discriminating person can clearly distinguish these three factors of knowledge from one another.[5]

The mind is a known object (dṛśya). It cannot manifest itself. It is manifested or known by the self which is self-luminous.[6] The self is immutable. The mind is modifiable. The modes of mind are not sometimes known and sometimes unknown by the self. They are always known by it. So the mind is mutable, but the self is immutable.[7]

The Sāṁkhya holds that the mind is neither atomic nor all-pervading but of intermediate magnitude, co-extensive with the body it occupies. The mind is small in a small body. It is large in a large body.[8] But the Yoga distinguishes between the kāraṇacitta and the kāryacitta. The former is the causal mind. The latter is the effect-mind. The former is all pervading (vibhu). The latter is limited and capable of expansion and contraction. The mind in itself is all-pervading, but its modes expand and contract.[9] Each individual self has a ubiquitous mind. There are countless selves with countless minds which

---

[1] YB., i. 2., ii. 18.
[2] TV., i. 1, p. 11.
[3] YB., iv. 31.
[4] YB., ii. 20.
[5] YS., YB., iv. 23.
[6] YS., iv. 19.
[7] YS., iv. 18.
[8] ChV., iv. 10, p. 197.
[9] YB., iv. 10.

are all-pervading and eternal like ether, which are the instruments of their enjoyments and sufferings. But they are limited by the mass of dispositions of desires due to false knowledge (avidyā) which obstruct their powers of manifesting objects, even as the all-pervading ether is limited by finite adjuncts, a jar, a palace, and the like.[1]

The mental modes expand and contract owing to merit and demerit and some internal and external efficient causes. Merit is the cause of expansion. Demerit is the cause of contraction. External actions, prayer, charity, salutation and the like, are the causes of expansion Mental acts, faith, striving, recollection, concentration, and intuition also are the causes of expansion. Mental acts, being of the nature of wisdom and detachment, transcend all powers. The super-normal power born of yoga is the cause of expansion. It can make the mind all-pervading and manifest all objects. A yogin can know all objects simultaneously. So his mind must be all-pervading. Its super-normal power born of yoga can completely remove the crust of tamas which covers knowledge, and manifest all objects. The impurities of the normal mind contract its modes and make its knowledge limited. It can be related to external objects only through the sense-object-intercourse. But the mind of a yogin can dispense with the sense-object-intercourse and be related to all objects and manifest them through a supernormal power born of yoga, which makes it all-pervading.[2] The yogin can restore his mind to its original ubiquity by the practice of yoga. The supernormal mind is not limited by space and time, which are but mental constructs (buddhinirmāṇa). The normal empirical mind only is limited by them. A yogin can attain omniscience. Our knowledge is fragmentary.

There are three levels of empirical consciousness, the subconscious, the conscious, and the superconscious. Perception, inference, testimony, illusion, memory, imagination, feeling, emotion, and volition are conscious mental modes. Cognitive, affective, conative dispositions, and pre-dispositions of past lives are subconscious mental modes. The complete arrest of mental modes and eradication of all mental impurities lead to the emergence of the superconscious intuition (prajñā) which

---

[1] YV., iv. 10, pp. 297-98. [2] YB., YV., ChV., iv. 10.

comprehends all present, past, future, remote, and subtle objects.[1] These are the three levels of mental or empirical consciousness. Besides these, the self has transcendental consciousness which is objectless and eternal, and constitutes its essence. This is supramental non-empirical consciousness. The self has consciousness of objects, through the mind (citta). When the mind is destroyed or merged in prakṛti, the liberated self has transcendental objectless consciousness.

The mind is the substance (dharmin) which abides in its states. It persists in its changing modes (dharma). The mental modes or processes (vṛtti) are always changing, since sattva, rajas, and tamas which constitute the mind are restless and active.[2] The mind is modified by change of quality (dharmapariṇāma), change of mark (lakṣaṇapariṇāma), and change of state (avasthāpariṇāma).

Patañjali speaks of the mind as a stream (cittanadī) of mental modes. But it is not a mere flux of mental states with no substance persisting in it as the Buddhists hold. They regard the mind as a mere psychic continuum of cognitions, feelings, volitions, and dispositions (vijñānasantāna).

There are five kinds of mental modes, valid knowledge (pramāṇa), illusion (viparyaya), imagination (vikalpa), sleep (nidrā) and recollection (smṛti). The first two have been discussed under epistemology.

Imagination (vikalpa) is a mental mode which is objectless and depends upon the mere cognition of a word. For instance, the idea of the horn of a hair or the idea of a sky-flower is imagination. These ideas are objectless. They have no real objects corresponding to them. They are excited in the mind by the corresponding words. In valid knowledge there are three elements, a word, an object, and a cognition. But in imagination the object is absent. There is an idea corresponding to a mere word. Imagination attributes difference to non-different things. We speak of 'consciousness of the self'. Here we treat consciousness as an attribute of the self which is a substance. But, in reality, consciousness *is* the self ; it is its essence. Imagination attributes also non-difference to different things. We speak of 'the distracted mind'. Distraction

---

[1] YB., i. 47-49.

[2] TV., i. 1, p. 11; YB., ii. 15.

is a state of the mind which is a substance. There is a difference between a substance and its state. But here we treat the mind and its distracted state as identical. Imagination is not valid knowledge, since it is objectless. It is not illusion, since, though it attributes difference to identity and identity to difference like an illusion, it continues to be a cause of action even when it is contradicted by valid knowledge, while an illusion cannot induce action when it is contradicted. We continue to speak of 'consciousness of the self,' 'distracted mind', 'horn of a hair', 'sky-flower', and the like, though we know that there are no objects corresponding to them.[1]

Sleep (nidrā) is a mental mode which apprehends the absence of all waking and dream states. It is a particular kind of apprehension (pratyayaviśeṣa), since it is remembered on waking from sleep. Recollection presupposes previous apprehension. I remember: I slept happily; my mind is transparent; it produces clear knowledge. This is recollection of sleep under the influence of sattva. Or I remember: 'I slept unhappily; my mind is restless and wandering'. This is recollection of sleep under the influence of rajas. Or I remember: 'I slept heavily; my body is heavy; my mind is fatigued and lazy'. This is recollection of sleep under the influence of tamas. So the Yoga regards sleep as a distinct mental mode apprehending absence of waking and dream cognitions. The Nyāya holds that sleep is mere absence of all cognitions, since the external sense-organs and the mind are inoperative. But the Yoga holds that it is a distinct apprehension. It is a mental mode (vṛtti) as distinguished from the mere absence of all determinate cognitions. It is an indefinite and indeterminate mode of consciousness. The Advaita Vedānta regards sleep as a mental mode which apprehends nescience (ajñāna). The Yoga regards it as a mental mode which apprehends tamas which conceals the buddhisattva. Tamas overpowers sattva and rajas of the mind in sleep. When sattva influences tamas in sleep, we have sāttvika sleep. When rajas influences tamas in sleep, we have rājasa sleep. When tamas completely overpowers sattva and rajas in sleep, we have tāmasa sleep.[2] Recollection (smṛti) is a mental mode which reproduces a past apprehension

---

[1] YS., YB., TV., YV., i. 9.

[2] YS., YB., TV., YV., i. 10.

of an object. Apprehension (anubhava) manifests an object and its cognition. It leaves a subconscious impression or disposition (saṁskāra) in the mind. It produces recollection (smṛti) which reproduces both the object and the apprehension. But in apprehension the cognition is prominent, while the object is prominent in recollection.[1] Recollection cannot apprehend more than the object perceived in the past. It may apprehend less than the perceived object. There can be recollection of valid knowledge, illusion, imagination, sleep, and memory, which are perceptions as experiences. All cognitions as cognitions are perceived by the self. They leave behind mental dispositions which produce recollections.[2] Dispositions and recollections due to their revival are of the same kind. Dispositions and perceptions which produce them are of the same kind. Dispositions produce recollections. Recollections again produce dispositions. Their causal relation and temporal sequence cannot be broken even by the barrier of time and space.[3] Dispositions are the causes of recollections. Perception of similar objects, merit and demerit, thinking, and the like are only excitants of dispositions. Revival of dispositions depends upon the removal of obstructions like sleep and other defects.[4] There are two kinds of recollection. The object of one kind is imaginary (bhāvitasmartavya). Dream is this kind of recollection. Its objects are imaginary. The object of another kind is not imaginary (abhāvitasmartavya). Waking recollection is of this kind.[5] The five kinds of mental modes are either afflicted (kliṣṭa) or unafflicted (akliṣṭa). The former are the causes of afflictions and bring about merit and demerit. The latter bring about discrimination between self and not-self and counteract the causal activity of sattva, rajas, and tamas. Afflictions are false knowledge, egoism, attachment, aversion, and instinctive fear of death.[6]

False knowledge (avidyā) is the cause of all other kinds of afflictions.[7] So afflicted mental modes are due to avidyā and lead to bondage. Unafflicted mental modes are due to discriminative knowledge, and loosen bondage. They are opposed

---

[1] YB., i. 11.
[2] YB., TV., YV., i. 11.
[3] YB., iv. 9.
[4] YV., iv. 3.
[5] YB., i. 11.
[6] YS., ii. 3.
[7] YS., ii. 4.

to each other. Still they are interspersed with each other. Unafflicted mental modes occasionally intervene in the stream of afflicted mental modes. Afflicted mental modes occasionally intervene in the stream of unafflicted mental modes. There are momentary flashes of discriminative knowledge and detachment in persons entangled in empirical life. There are occasional lapses into ignorance and passions in persons who are habitually enlightened and detached. Afflicted states produce afflicted dispositions. Unafflicted states produce unafflicted dispositions. The wheel of empirical life is a perpetual cycle of afflicted and unafflicted mental modes and dispositions. When they are completely destroyed by discriminative knowledge, the mind attains the translucent nature of the self or is merged in prakṛti.[1] The Yoga enjoins complete arrest of all mental modes.

17. *Afflictions* (*Kleśa*)

Patañjali mentions five kinds of afflictions (kleśa), false knowledge (avidyā), egoism (asmitā), attachment (rāga) aversion (dveṣa), and instinctive fear of death (abhiniveśa).[2] False knowledge (avidyā) consists in knowing the non-eternal as eternal, the impure as pure, the painful as pleasant, and the not-self as the self.[3] The impermanent earth is known as permanent. The impure and ugly body composed of blood, flesh, and bone is known as pure and beautiful. Thus vice is known as virtue ; evil is known as good. Worldly enjoyments, which are really full of pain, are known as pleasure. The not-self is known as the self. The external objects, conscious or unconscious, which are means of enjoyment, the body, which is the vehicle of enjoyment, and the mind, the internal organ of enjoyment, are known as the self. Vyāsa clearly states that avidyā is positive false knowledge. It is neither valid knowledge nor absence of valid knowledge. But it is opposed to right knowledge.[4] Vijñānabhikṣu distinguishes between the Sāṁkhya view and the Yoga view. The Sāṁkhya regards avidyā as non-discrimination (aviveka) or lack of adequate knowledge, while the Yoga regards it as a determinate knowledge (viśiṣṭa-jñāna)

---

[1] YB., i. 5.
[2] YS., ii. 3.
[3] YS., ii. 5.
[4] YB., ii. 5.

which apprehends one object as another as the Vaiśeṣika holds.[1] Egoism (asmitā) consists in false identification of the conscious self and the unconscious buddhi with each other. Experience (bhoga) is due to this false sense of identity or egoism. When the discriminative knowledge of the self as distinct from the mind emerges, experience ceases, and the self realizes its intrinsic freedom or isolation (kaivalya). The self is eternally pure, indifferent, and conscious. But buddhi is impure, full of attachment and aversion, and unconscious. The self is immutable. But buddhi is mutable. Confusion of them with each other leads to bondage. Discrimination of them from each other leads to liberation.[2] Vijñānabhikṣu distinguishes between avidyā and asmitā. Avidyā consists in the self-sense which apprehends the difference and identity between the self and buddhi in a general way. It does not apprehend the absolute identity between them. But asmitā succeeds avidyā and is produced by it. It consists in attributing the qualities of buddhi to the self in such forms as 'I am the ruler', 'I am happy', and the like. It apprehends the absolute identity between the self and buddhi. Avidyā is the cause of asmitā.[3]

Attachment (rāga) is the desire for an object which yielded pleasure in the past and is remembered now. It springs from the recollection of pleasure. It also arises from the apprehension of pleasure. Attachment is yearning for an object perceived or remembered, which is the means of pleasure. It is due to avidyā. Pleasant objects are really painful. Painful objects are wrongly known as pleasant. A liberated person is free from attachment.[4]

Aversion (dveṣa) is anger towards an object which yielded pain in the past and is remembered now. It springs from the recollection of pain. It springs also from the apprehension of pain. It is produced by an object perceived or remembered, which is the means of pain. Aversion is a kind of desire. It arises from the thwarting of attachment. It is due to avidyā. Pain is not an attribute of the self which is indifferent. A liberated person is free from aversion.[5]

Fear of death (abhiniveśa) is instinctive. It is not due to perception, inference, or testimony in this birth. It is due to

---

[1] YV., ii. 5, p. 97.
[2] YS., YB., TV., ii. 6.
[3] YV., ChV., ii. 6.
[4] YS., YB., YV., ChV., ii. 7.
[5] YS., YB., ii. 8; YV., ChV., ii. 8.

the predispositions of the apprehension of pain of death in many past births. It is common to the wise and the ignorant. It is the expression of the instinctive urge to cling to life. It is the manifestation of the primitive will to live. It is a kind of desire. It is the strongest desire. It is due to avidyā. It springs from misapprehension of the body as the self.[1]

The afflictions are so called because they afflict the empirical self and bind it to empirical life of birth and death. They are caused by false knowledge (avidyā). So they are regarded as its different kinds. Egoism (asmitā) consists in mistaking the not-self for the self. Attachment (rāga) consists in mistaking the impure for the pure. Aversion consists in mistaking the really painful for the pleasant. Fear of death consists in mistaking the transient for the eternal[2] Afflictions strengthen the causal efficiency of sattva, rajas, and tamas, with the aid of seen and unseen agencies, and bring about the causal series, buddhi, ahaṁkāra, sense-organs, and the body. They are the springs of actions. Actions generate merit (dharma) and demerit (adharma). They generate birth (jāti), length of life (āyuḥ) and enjoyment and suffering (bhoga). All afflictions are due to false knowledge (avidyā) which can be destroyed by right knowledge.[3] The Yoga, like Spinoza, regards emotions and passions as intellectual disorders which can be cured by true knowledge.

Egoism, attachment, aversion, and fear of death are either dormant (prasupta), or attenuated (tanu), or intercepted (vicchinna), or manifest (udāra) or functioning on particular objects. They are dormant when they exist in the mind as subconscious potencies (śakti) or seeds (bīja) which are manifested by their proper objects. The minds which are merged in prakṛti (prakṛtilīna) have dormant afflictions. They are awakened and generate birth and death. But the subconscious potencies of afflictions are completely burnt up by perfect discriminative knowledge (prasaṁkhyāna) in persons who have achieved embodied release (jīvanmukti). The burnt seeds of afflictions can no more germinate and bring on birth and death.

---

[1] YS., YB., YV., ChV., ii. 9.

[2] YS., ii. 5-9; H. D. Bhattacharya : *Yoga Psychology, The cultural Heritage of India,* Vol. 1, p. 339.

YB., ChV., ii. 3.

The afflictions are attenuated, when they are overpowered by the thought of opposite excellences. The yogins have attenuated afflictions which become fit for being exterminated. The afflictions are intercepted, when others come into the focus of consciousness. When attachment comes to the focus, anger is intercepted and sinks into the subconscious. When attachment for one woman comes to the focus, attachment for some other woman sinks into the subconscious and will come to the focus in future. The latter attachment is in an intercepted condition. The afflictions are manifested when they function on particular objects. Attachment felt for a woman is in a manifest condition. The persons attached to worldly enjoyments have intercepted and manifest afflictions. False knowledge (avidyā) is the cause of all other kinds of afflictions in their dormant, attenuated, intercepted, and manifest conditions.[1] Egoism can be overcome by discrimination between the self and the not-self. Attachment and aversion can be overcome by indifference. Instinctive fear of death can be overcome by fearlessness due to extirpation of the will to live. False knowledge can be overcome by right knowledge. The will to live is the strongest desire. It can be destroyed only when the mind is destroyed. It cannot be destroyed by mere knowledge.[2] Afflictions are subtle (sūkṣma) in the form of potencies (saṁskāra). They can be destroyed with the mind, when it is merged in Prakṛti.[3] The Yoga enjoins complete arrest of afflictions and their dispositions.

18. *The Threefold Pain* (*Tāpatraya*)

Patañjali mentions three kinds of pain, pariṇāmaduḥkha, tāpaduḥkha, and saṁskāraduḥkha. Worldly pleasures are ultimately painful. Thirst for sensual pleasures is never completely quenched by enjoyment. It is aggravated by enjoyment. So sensual pleasures are painful because their consequences are painful. The consequential pain involved in sensual pleasures is pariṇāmaduḥkha. Attachment to sensual pleasures involves aversion to those who thwart the desire for their attainment. Aversion or anger is painful. This kind of

[1] YS., YB., TV., ii. 4.
[2] YV., ii. 9, p. 100.
[3] YS., YB., ii. 10.

pain is tāpaduḥkha. Apprehension of pleasure generates a disposition (saṁskāra) of pleasure. Apprehension of pain generates a disposition of pain. These dispositions generate recollections of pleasure and pain. The recollections of pleasure and pain produce attachment and aversion. These produce mental, verbal, or bodily actions. Actions benefit or injure others, and so produce merit (dharma) and demerit (adharma). Merit produces pleasure. Demerit produces pain. Thus the cycle of pain due to dispositions goes on. This is saṁskāraduḥkha.

The mind by its very nature suffers from pain. It is composed of sattva, rajas, and tamas, which are contrary in their nature and always active. They are in constant conflict with one another. So the mind always undergoes modifications which are attended with pain. There is a conflict among pleasure, pain, and delusion. There is a conflict between knowledge and ignorance, virtue and vice, detachment and passion, powerfulness and powerlessness. So pain is inherent in the nature of mind and mental modes. All is painful to a discriminating person.[1] Avidyā is the cause of all these kinds of pain. Right knowledge (samyagdarśana) is the cause of its destruction. So a yogin takes refuge in it.[2] The three kinds of pain described by the Yoga are subtler than the three kinds of pain described by the Sāṁkhya, *viz.*, pain caused by physical objects (ādhibhautika), pain caused by bodily and mental disorders (ādhyātmika), and pain caused by supernatural agencies (ādhidaivika). The Yoga, like the Sāṁkhya, was profoundly influenced by the pessimism of Buddhism. It enjoins complete extirpation of all kinds of pain which also are recognized by the Yoga.[3]

19. *Dispositions* (*Saṁskāra*)

The Yoga speaks of the cognitive, affective, and conative dispositions.[4] It speaks of the prenatal dispositions of past births. They may be called predispositions. Valid knowledge,

---

[1] Duḥkhameva sarvaṁ vivekinaḥ. YB., ii. 15.
[2] YB., YV., R.M., ii. 15.
[3] YB., i. 31.
[4] P. V. Pathak : *The Heyapakṣa of Yoga*, pp. 120-29.

perception, inference, and testimony, illusion, imagination, sleep, and recollection leave subconscious impressions in the mind, which generate their recollections.[1] These subconscious impressions are cognitive dispositions (jñānaja saṁskāra). They are the causes of recollections. Afflictions are feelings and emotions. They are the springs of action. False knowledge, egoism, attachment, aversion, and fear of death leave behind subconscious impressions in the mind. They are affective dispositions (kleśasaṁskāra).[2] They do not produce recollections. They produce afflictions. Emotional dispositions produce emotions. Good actions produce merit (dharma). Bad actions produce demerit (adharma).[3] Merit and demerit are conative dispositions (karmāśaya). They produce fruits (vipāka) in the forms of birth (jāti), duration of life (āyuṣ) and experience (bhoga).[4] The same mind clings to the empirical self which transmigrates from one body to another modified by the predispositions (vāsanā) of the good and bad actions performed in all the previous births. These predispositions constitute the racial unconscious transmitted from the individual's own past lives to the present life.[5] Thus cognitive dispositions produce recollections. Affective dispositions produce afflictions or emotions. Conative or volitional dispositions, virtue and vice, produce birth, duration of life, and experience.[6] Mental modes, afflicted and unafflicted, and their dispositions perpetually go round and round in the wheel of life.[7] All dispositions are attributes of the mind (cittadharma).[8] The Yoga enjoins extirpation of all psychic dispositions.[9] The subconscious can be controlled by the conscious. The subconscious dispositions can be extirpated by mental discipline.[10]

20. *The Levels of Attention* (*cittabhūmi*)

Vyāsa mentions five levels of attention or stages of the mind: (1) distracted (kṣipta), (2) infatuated (mūḍha), (3) occasionally steady (vikṣipta), (4) one-pointed (ekāgra), and

---

[1] YB., i. 11.
[2] YB., i. 5; ii. 4, 10.
[3] YS., ii. 12.
[4] YS., ii. 13.
[5] YS., iii. 18; iv. 8, 9.
[6] TV., iii. 18, p. 230.
[7] Vṛttisaṁskāracakramaniśam āvartate. YB., i. 5.
[8] YB., iii. 9.
[9] YB., i. 18.
[10] N. K. Brahma: *Philosophy of Hindu Sādhanā*, p. 130.

(5) restrained (nirūddha.[1] (1) The distracted (kṣipta) mind, being overpowered by rajas, becomes extremely unsteady and extroverted (bahirmukha) and flits constantly from one object to another, which is the source of pleasure or pain. (2) The infatuated mind (mūḍha) being overpowered by tamas, is fixed on unrighteous actions under the influence of anger and other violent emotions. It loses the power of distinguishing between right and wrong. It also sinks into listlessness, drowsiness and sleep under the influence of tamas, and has dispersed attention or absolute inattention. (3) The occasionally unsteady (vikṣipta) mind being influenced by sattva, though unsteady for the most part, becomes occasionally steady, withdraws itself from painful objects, and fixes itself on pleasurable objects.[2] Its persistent unsteadiness is either natural or due to physical or mental distractions.[3] These three stages of mind are unfit for concentration (samādhi). (4) The one-pointed (ekāgra) mind, under the influence of pure sattva, is withdrawn from all other objects and focussed on one object, either physical or mental, and has an unflickering cognition of it. There is complete introversion in this mono-eidic stage.[4] The restrained (niruddha) mind, under the influence of pure sattva, arrests all mental functions, and retains only subconscious dispositions according to Vācaspati.[5] Vijñānabhikṣu also holds the same view.[6] But Bhojadeva opines that there is complete suspension of all mental modes and subconscious dispositions in the restrained (niruddha) stage of mind. Yoga or complete arrest of mental functions is possible in the last two stages.[7] All mental modes are attended with pleasure, pain, and delusion, and should be suppressed.[8] The Yoga enjoins the complete suppression of all mental modes and eradication of all mental dispositions by rigid discipline of the body, the vital forces, and the mind, and moral practices.

V. *Ethics*

The Yoga enjoins the path of action (kriyāyoga) and the path of knowledge (jñānayoga) for the attainment of complete freedom or isolation (kaivalya) of the self. The path of know-

---

1 YB., i. 1.
2 RM., i. 1.
3 TV., i. 1.
4 Ekāgre bahirvṛttinirodhaḥ. RM., i. 1.
5 TV., i. 1, p. 7.
6 YV., i. 1, p. 4.
7 RM., i. 1.
8 YV., i. 1, p. 6.

ledge includes the yogic practices (yogāṅga). This is superior to the path of action which is intended for persons of inferior intellectual and moral equipment. The path of severe mental discipline and cultivation of right knowledge is suitable for introverts. The path of action is suitable for extroverts. Both the paths may be followed by a person. Performance of righteous actions and dedication of them and their fruits to God will purify the mind and make it fit for concentration. Then the body, the vital forces, the sense-organs, and the mind can be controlled and disciplined till all mental modes and their dispositions are completely eradicated and the self shines in its eternal glory and effulgence.

21. (I) *The Path of Action* (*kriyāyoga*)

The Yoga gives a psychological analysis of voluntary action. Feelings and emotions (kleśa) are the springs of action. Pleasure generates attachment. Pain generates aversion. Attachment or aversion generates volition (prayatna). Volition generates mental, verbal, or bodily action (ceṣṭā). Voluntary action either benefits others or injures others. Socially useful action produces virtue or merit (dharma) in the self. Socially injurious action produces vice or demerit (adharma) in it. Merit is the predisposing cause of pleasure. Demerit is the predisposing cause of pain. Thus the cycle of afflictions (kleśa), actions (karma), merit and demerit or potencies of actions (karmāśaya), and their fruitions in the form of birth (jāti), duration of life (āyuṣ), and experience (bhoga) goes on. False knowledge (avidyā) is the root cause of this cycle of afflictions and actions.[1]

The Yoga gives an ethical division of voluntary actions. It recognizes four kinds of actions, black, white and black, white, and neither white nor black. Actions of vicious persons such as killing and the like are black or unrighteous. They produce vice or demerit (adharma). Actions which are done through the aid of external agents either benefit others or injure others. If they are benificial to others, they produce virtue or merit. If they are injurious to others, they produce vice or demerit. Animal sacrifice with the help of a priest is white-black. It

[1] YB., iv. 11.

gives pain to the animal, and is therefore black or unrighteous. It involves payment of fees to the priest, and is therefore white or righteous. It is partly righteous and partly unrighteous. Austerities, recitation of the mystic syllable *Om*, the study of the scriptures, and meditation are independent of external agents. They are not injurious to others. They produce only virtue or merit. They are white or righteous actions. Yogins who have overcome their afflictions never commit sins and give pain to others. So they do not produce vice or demerit. They completely surrender their actions and their fruits to God. They perform their duties without any attachment. So their actions do not produce virtue or merit. They are neither white nor black. They are beyond good and evil. Such yogins are liberated in an embodied state. They will attain disembodied release after the death of their bodies.[1] White, black, and white-black actions produce merit and demerit. They revive dispositions of similar actions favourable to their fruitions in the forms of birth, duration of life, and experience. But non-white-non-black actions do not produce merit and demerit. They do not give rise to embodied existence.[2]

Introverts are fit for the yoga. But extroverts (vyutthitacitta) are unfit for it. They should adopt the path of action (kriyāyoga). They can purge their minds of merit, demerit, and dispositions of avidyā and other afflictions accumulated in innumerable births by continuous performance of enjoined duties without disturbing the harmony of the bodily humours. Extroverts should undergo penances, recite the mystic syllable *Om*, study the scriptures, and surrender all their actions and their fruits to God.[3] If all actions and their fruits are resigned to God, they lead to absorptive concentration (samādhi) which gives rise to intuition (prajñā) which can know all things in remote time and space.[4] Kriyāyoga can attenuate afflictions and generate samādhi. It makes afflictions unfit for actuating actions and producing merit and demerit. It has the same action on afflictions as discriminative knowledge has on them. Just as the fire of discriminative knowledge (prasaṁkhyānāgni) almost burns up their seeds or dispositions, so actions free from attachment and dedicated to God make them unfit for producing effects.

---

[1] YS., YB., iv. 7.
[2] YS., YB., iv. 8.
[3] YS., YB., ii. 1.
[4] YS., YB., ii. 45.

When afflictions are attenuated and become unproductive, discriminative intuition of the self (prajñā) free from all taint of afflictions emerges and can destroy the productivity of the guṇas, sattva, rajas, and tamas, and bring on release. Thus the path of action (kriyāyoga) also leads to absorptive concentration (samādhi), discriminative knowledge (sattvapuruṣānyatākhyāti), intuition (prajñā), and liberation.[1]

22. (II) *The Path of Yoga: Yogāṅga*

Patañjali defines yoga as complete suppression of all mental modes or processes (cittavṛttinirodha).[2] Vyāsa defines it as absorptive concentration (samādhi). It is a universal attribute of the mind.[3] All persons can attain yoga by repeated practice (abhyāsa) and detachment (vairāgya).[4] The distracted (kṣipta), infatuated (mūḍha) and occasionally steady (vikṣipta) minds are not fit for yoga. The one-pointed (ekāgra) and restrained (niruddha) minds are fit for it.[5] "Yoga can be known by yoga; yoga can be accomplished by yoga; he who is not deluded by occult powers (siddhi) delights in yoga for ever".[6] The yogin only knows the nature of yoga. He only can attain yoga by severe mental discipline or yogic practices. Yoga generates occult powers, clairvoyance, clairaudience, thought-reading, thought-transference, and the like. If the yogin is infatuated with them, he falls from yoga. If he is indifferent to them, he will delight in yoga for ever. The yogic practices only can lead the yogin from a lower stage to a higher stage. Yoga is not theoretical or speculative. It is practical. The art of yoga is a matter of constant practice and severe discipline of the body, the vital forces, and the mind. It is pre-eminently an art of mental discipline.

The Yoga enjoins the practice of restraints (yama), observances (niyama), bodily posture (āsana), breath control (prāṇāyāma), withdrawal of the sense-organs (pratyāhāra), fixation of attention (dhāraṇā), meditation (dhyāna), and absorptive concentration (samādhi) as aids to yoga (yogāṅga).[7]

---

[1] YB., ii. 2.
[2] YS., i. 2.
[3] YB., i. 1.
[4] YS., i. 12.
[5] RM., i. 2.
[6] YB., iii. 6.
[7] YS., ii. 29.

(i) The first discipline of restraint (yama) consists in non-injury (ahiṁsā), truthfulness in thought and speech (satya), non-stealing (asteya), sexual restraint (brahmacarya), and non-acceptance of unnecessry gifts.[1] These are negative virtues. Non-injury (ahimsā) consists in the absence of cruelty to all creatures in all possible ways and at all times. It is tenderness, good will, and kindness for all living beings.[2] Ahiṁsā is non-killing. Killing (hiṁsā) is the root of all evils. So it must be shunned by all means. Non-injury is the root of all other negative (yama) and positive virtues (niyama). So absolute non-injury is prescribed by the Yoga system.[3] 'Thou shalt not kill.' Animal sacrifice for a religious purpose is forbidden. The Sāṁkhya, the Yoga, Buddhism, and Jainism agree on this point. Truthfulness consists in the harmony between true thoughts and words in conformity with the good of all creatures. The words must be spoken for the good of all creatures. They must not be spoken for doing harm to others. If they are spoken for the purpose of doing harm to others, they cannot be regarded as true and righteous. Truthfulness in violation of the good of others amounts to falsehood. It must be in harmony with the welfare of the sentient creation. Absolute truthfulness regardless of its social consequences or welfare of humanity and animal kingdom is forbidden. The Yoga is not egoistic and ascetic in its ethical attitude. It is altruistic and has a ring of Ideal Utilitarianism in it. Truthfulness involves harmony of thoughts with facts which must be guaranteed by the speaker. A truthful person must vouch for the truth of his words. He ought to state what he has perceived, or inferred, or derived from a reliable authority. If his words deceive the hearer, or produce error in him, or are unintelligible to him, they are not true. A truthful person must have valid thoughts in his mind, speak them out correctly, excite similar thoughts in the hearer's mind, and his words must be conducive to the welfare of all creatures.[4] Truthfulness involves harmony of the speaker's thoughts with facts, harmony of his thoughts with his words, harmony of his words with the hearer's thoughts, and harmony of his words with the welfare of the sentient creation. Veracity

[1] YS., ii. 30.
[2] YB., ii. 30.
[3] YB., RM., ii. 30.
[4] Sarvabhūtahitaṁ satyaṁ brūyāt, YB., ii. 30.

must be consistent with the welbeing of humanity (lokahita). If its consequence is injurious to others, it is not real veracity, but a semblance of it (satyābhāsa). The Yoga gives a strict but humanitarian conception of truthfulness. Hypocrisy, flattery, deceit, and truthful words injurious to society are falsehood.[1] 'Thou shalt not lie in thought, word, and deed'. Theft is immoral misappropriation of others' possessions. Non-stealing (asteya) consists in not merely misappropriating the property of others. It is not merely non-thieving as an overt act. It is lack of greed (aspṛhā). It is an ast of mind (mānasa vyāpāra). 'Thou shalt not steal'. 'Thou shalt not covet others' wealth'. Sexual purity (brahmacarya) consists in restraint of the sexual organ and all other sense-organs with regard to the object of sex-gratification. Recollection of the sexual act, talk about it, sport and secret conversation with a woman, watching her limbs, sexual desire, and resolution to indulge in sexual pleasure, and overt sexual act are the eight kinds of sex-gratification. Sex-restraint consists in restraining the sex-organ and all other sense-organs with regard to its object.[2] 'Thou shalt not commit adultery.' 'Thou shalt not lust after a woman'. The Yoga enjoins absolute sexual continence. Non-acceptance of gifts (aparigraha) consists in abstaining from acquiring objects of enjoyment. It consists in non-acquisition and non-possession. A person devoid of greed realizes that acquisition, preservation and expenditure of wealth are tainted with the faults of attachment and violence or exploitation. Hence he eschews wealth and other objects of enjoyment. Non-acceptance of gifts consists in accepting nothing but what is absolutely necessary for one's bare subsistence.[3] 'Thou shalt not own and possess any property'. These are the yamas or negative virtues. They are universal categorical imperatives. They are the great vows which must be observed by all. They are unconditionally obligatory. They are not limited by time, place, caste, or purpose.[4] The fishermen earn their livelihood by killing and selling fish. A person may resolve that he will not kill a living creature in a place of pilgrimage. Or he may resolve that he

[1] YB., TV., YV., ii. 30.
[2] YB.; YV., ii. 30.
[3] YB., RM., TV., ii. 30.
[4] Jātideśakālasamayānavacchinnāḥ sārbhaumā mahāvratam. YS., ii. 31.

will not kill life on an auspicious day. Or he may resolve that he will not kill life except for gods and Brahmins. Kṣatriyas kill only in the battle field. All these acts of killing (hiṁsā) are absolutely forbidden. Non-killing, truthfulness, non-stealing, sexual restraint, and non-acceptance of anything but what is absolutely necessary for bare subsistence ought to be observed unconditionally and universally, unlimited by caste or profession, place, time, and purpose without any exceptions. They are the great vows which are universally obligatory. They ought to be observed in all spheres, in all possible ways, with regard to all objects. They are unexceptionable.[1] These correspond to the great vows (mahāvrata) of the Jainas.

(2) The second discipline of observance (niyama) consists in cleanliness (śauca), contentment (santoṣa), austerities (tapas), study of the scriptures (svādhyāya), and resignation of all actions to God (īśvarapraṇidhāna). Cleanliness is of two kinds, external (bāhya) and internal (ābhyantara). The former is cleanliness of the body by means of water and other purifying articles. The latter is cleanliness of the mind by purging it of all impurities, attachment, aversion, pride, conceit, envy, and the like by cultivating good will, compassion, and cheerfulness. Contentment consists in lack of desire to acquire anything but what comes of itself without exertion and what is absolutely necessary for bare livelihood. Austerities consist in the habit of enduring hunger and thirst, heat and cold, sitting and standing, non-speaking, non-communication of desires even through gestures, and observance of vows involving physical hardships. Svādhyāya consists in studying the scriptures, or reciting the mystic syllable *Om*, and meditating on God. Īśvarapraṇidhāna consists in surrendering all actions to God, the supreme teacher.[2] It does not mean meditation on, or devotion to God, which is included in samādhi or absorptive concentration. The restraints (yama) are negative virtues unlimited by time, place, and other circumstances. The observances (niyama) are positive virtues limited by time, place, and other circumstances. They are not universal great vows.[3]

Sins are counteracted by thoughts and habits of opposite virtues.[4] Vicious habits are broken by cultivating opposite

---

[1] YB., ii. 31. [2] YB., ii. 32. [3] YV., ii. 32.
[4] Vitarkabādhane pratipakṣabhāvanam. YS., ii. 33.

virtuous habits. Sins are of three kinds. They are either done (kṛta), or caused to be done (kārita), or approved (anumodita). They are actuated by greed, anger, and delusion. They are extremely violent, or mild, or the least intense. They are counteracted by the constant thought that they produce infinite pain and false knowledge. They cannot be overcome by fixing our thoughts on them but on the opposite virtues.[1] The mind is purged of its impurities by cultivating good will (maitrī) for all happy beings, compassion (karuṇā) for all distressed creatures, cheerfulness (muditā) towards all virtuous persons, and indifference (upekṣā) to all vicious persons.[2] Attachment (rāga) and aversion (dveṣa) also are overcome by good will or friendliness (maitrī).[3] Good will, compassion, and cheerfulness are the three thoughts (bhāvanā). By focussing the mind on them powers of good will (maitrībala), kindness (karuṇābala), and cheerfulness (muditābala) are acquired. Focussing the mind on these three thoughts brings about absorptive concentration (samādhi). Concentration generates these powers unfailingly. Indifference (upekṣā) to vicious persons is not a thought (bhāvanā). The mind cannot be focussed on it. So it cannot bring on absorptive concentration. So it cannot produce power of indifference.[4] We have already discussed that afflictions (kleśa) are overcome by the thought of opposite excellences (pratipakṣabhāvanā). False knowledge (avidyā) is overcome by right knowledge. Egoism (asmitā) is overcome by discrimination of the self from the not-self. Attachment (rāga) and aversion (dveṣa) are overcome by indifference. Fear of death (abhiniveśa) is overcome by fearlessness.[5] Bad emotions and passions are overcome by good emotions and passions. This is a great psychological truth discovered by the Yoga system long ago. It is a commonplace of modern Ethics. Mackenzie says, "It is generally better to escape from our defects, not by thinking about them and trying to elude them, but by fixing our attention on the opposite excellences. It certainly seems a more effectual method as a rule to expel our evil propensities by developing good ones rather than by seeking directly to crush the evil ones."[6]

---

[1] Pratipakṣabhāvanāhetorheyā vitarkāḥ. YB., ii. 34.
[2] YS., i. 33.
[3] RM., i. 33.
[4] YB., iii. 25.
[5] TV., ii. 4, p. 110.
[6] *Manual of Ethics*, 1935, p. 341.

(3) The third discipline is bodily posture (āsana). It is a steady and pleasant posture of the body. It should not move. It should not be painful. It should not distract the mind. There are many kinds of postures, padmāsana, vīrāsana, bhadrāsana, svastika, and the like. The various postures of the body are the means of controlling it and keeping it healthy and fit. They tone up the nervous system. They can be learnt from experts. The control of the body is the basis of the yoga disclipline.[1]

(4) The fourth discipline is breath control (prāṅāyāma). It consists in controlling natural breathing and subjecting it to a definite law. It consists in slow and deep inspiration (pūraka), retention of breath (kumbhaka), and slow expiration (recaka).[2] These three functions should be performed for definite periods. The time of inspiration, the time of retention of breath, and the time of expiration should be in the proportion : 1, 4 and 2. The vital forces move the body. The mind has desire and will which are expressed in bodily actions. So regulation of the vital forces leads to control of the mind. Breath control is conducive to concentration of mind. It removes the crust of affliction from illumination of the sattva of the mind. It removes the demerit which obscures discriminative knowledge. Breath control is the supreme austerity. It purges the mind of impurities and generates illumination of knowledge.[3] It can be learnt only under the guidance of experts.

(5) The fifth discipline is withdrawal of the external sense-organs from their objects (pratyāhāra) due to withdrawal of mind from them. If the mind is withdrawn from external sensible objects, the external senses are automatically withdrawn from them. They do not follow their objects, but they follow the mind. They are fixed on those objects only on which the mind is fixed. The restraint of the external senses depends upon the restraint of the mind. It can be acquired by repeated practice, resolute will, and sense control.[4]

The five disciplines of restraint (yama), observance (niyama), bodily posture (āsana), breath-control (prāṅāyāma), and sense-control (pratyāhāra) are the external aids to yoga

---

[1] YS., RM., YB., ii. 46.
[2] YS., ii. 49, 50.
[3] YS., ii. 53; YB., RM., ii. 52.
[4] YS., YB., YMP., ii. 54.

(bahiraṅgasādhana). The last three disciplines, fixation of mind (dhāraṇā), meditation (dhyāna), and absorptive concentration or ecstasy (samādhi) are the internal aids of yoga (antaraṅgasādhana). They directly lead to conscious ecstasy (samprajñātasamādhi).[1]

(6) The sixth discipline is fixing the mind on a particular object (dhāraṇā). The object is either intra-organic or extra-organic. The mind is fixed on the navel, the heart, the tip of the nose, the tip of the tongue, the middle of the eye-brows, the throat, and the like. Or it is fixed on an external object, the idol or image of a deity. Bodily posture controls the body. Breath control regulates the vital forces. Withdrawal of the senses from their objects controls the senses. Fixation of attention controls the mind. It requires withdrawal of the mind from other objects. It prepares the mind for meditation.[2]

(7) The seventh discipline is meditation (dhyāna). It consists in the continuous flow of the same cognition of the object of attention undisturbed by any other cognition.[3] Fixation of attention on an object to the exclusion of other objects leads to meditation, if the cognition produced by it continues unbroken for a long time. There is a continuous stream of similar cognitions of the contemplated object undisturbed by dissimilar cognitions.[4]

(8) The eighth discipline is absorptive concentration or ecstasy (samādhi). It is the manifestation of the object of meditation only devoid of the cognition of meditation.[5] Dhāraṇā is fixation of attention on an object undisturbed by the cognition of any other object. Dhyāna is unbroken flow of the same cognition for a long time. There is manifestation of the object, meditation, and the self in it. Samādhi is manifested in it (arthamātranirbhāsa). The self and the act of meditation are not manifested (svarūpaśūnyamiva). Only the object of meditation is manifested. If such samādhi continues for a long time, it is called conscious ecstasy (samprajñāta samādhi). When there is no manifestation of the object also,

---

[1] YB., iii. 1; YS., YB., iii. 7.
[2] YS., YB., YMP., iii. 1.
[3] Paratyayaikatānatā dhyānam. YS., iii. 2.
[4] RM., iii. 2.
[5] YS., iii. 3.

it is called superconscious ecstasy (asamprajñāta samādhi).[1] Fixation (dhāraṇā), meditation (dhyāna), and absorptive concentration (samādhi) on the same object together are called saṁyama. They are the internal aids (antaraṅgasādhana) to conscious ecstasy, while restraint, observance, bodily posture, breath control, and withdrawal of the senses from their objects are the external aids (bahiraṅgasādhana) to it. But they are the external aids to superconscious ecstasy.[2]

The performance of the eightfold aids to yoga (yogāṅga), external and internal, purges the mind of its afflictions, manifests right knowledge, which goes on increasing with the gradual removal of impurities, and culminates in discriminative knowledge of the true nature of the pure self as distinct from prakṛti and its evolutes, body, sense-organs, and mind (citta). When the impurities of afflictions, false knowledge, egoism, attachment, aversion, and the will to live are completely destroyed, the pure sattva of the mind attains perfection, and is modified into discriminative knowledge (vivekakhyāti). The performance of the aids to yoga is the cause of dissociation of afflictions from the mind (viyogakāraṇa). It is the cause of attainment of discriminative knowledge (prāptikāraṇā). Vyāsa mentions nine kinds of causes: (1) cause of production (utpattikāraṇa); (2) cause of existence (sthitikāraṇa); (3) cause of manifestation (abhivyaktikāraṇa); (4) cause of modification (vikārakāraṇa); (5) cause of knowledge (pratyayakāraṇa); (6) cause of attainment (prāptikāraṇa); (7) cause of dissociation (viyogakāraṇa); (8) cause of changing one thing into another (anyatvakāraṇa); (9) cause of preservation (dhṛtikāraṇa). The mind is the cause of production of a cognition. Experience and liberation are the cause of the existence and continuance of the mind. Light is the cause of manifestation of colour. Fire is the cause of modification of rice into cooked rice. Another object modifies the mind into a different mode or cognition. The knowledge of smoke is the cause of the knowledge of fire. The performance of the aids to yoga (yogāṅga) is the cause of attainment of discriminative knowledge. It is the cause of dissociation of impurities from the mind. The goldsmith is the cause of turning gold into an ornament. The body is the cause

---

[1] YMP., iii. 3.

[2] YS., YB., iii. 4, 7, 8.

of preservation of the sense-organs. The gross elements are the cause of preservation of the body and other physical objects. These are the nine kinds of causes.[1] The buddhisattva is in the nature of pleasure and manifestation. When it attains supreme perfection (prakarṣātiśaya), it naturally attains pleasure and discriminative knowledge. But they are not manifested because they are obscured by demerit (adharma) and tamas. When they are removed by merit (dharma) or performance of the yogāṅgas, the light of discriminative knowledge shines forth.[2] Vijñānabhikṣu states that the yogāṅgas are prescribed for inferior aspirants (mandādhikārin) ; the path of action (kriyāyoga), penances, study of the scriptures, and resignation of all actions and their fruits to God, is intended for the mediocre aspirants (madhyamādhikārin) or extroverts (vyutthitacitta). Repeated practice (abhyāsa) and detachment (vairāgya) are intended for the superior aspirants (uttamādhikārin) or introverts.[3]

Patañjali says that penance, regular study of the scriptures, or dedication of all actions to God, repeatedly practised for a long period, exhausts the afflictions gradually and generates concentration.[4] When the afflictions are attenuated by the performance of actions (kriyāyoga), the mental modes afflicted by pleasure, pain, and delusion, which are their manifest functions, should be arrested by meditation (dhyāna) on discriminative knowledge (prasaṁkhyāna) till they become incapable of producing effects almost like burnt seeds (dagdhabījakalpa). The manifest modes of afflictions can be arrested by continuous human effort of meditation. But their subtle dispositions (saṁskāra) are destroyed only when the mind in which they subsist is destroyed or merged in cosmic egoism (asmitā). Dispositions are modes of the mind. When the substance is destroyed, its modes are bound to be destroyed. When the mind attains liberation, it is merged in its cause. When the mind is merged in cosmic egoism (asmitā), all subtle dispositions of afflictions, feelings, emotions, and passions are destroyed.[5]

---

[1] YB., ii. 28.
[2] TV., ii. 28, pp. 169-70; YMP., ii. 28.
[3] YV., ii. 28.
[4] YS., ii. 2.
[5] YS., YB., TV., YV., RM., ii. 10, 11.

23. *Abhyāsa and Vairāgya*

The superior aspirants or introverts can attain absorptive concentration or trance (samādhi) by continuous and steadfast practice (abhyāsa) and detachment (vairāgya). The stream of mind flows in two directions. It flows through the downward channel of discriminative knowledge towards isolation (kaivalya) or complete independence of the self. It flows through the downward channel of non-discrimination towards empirical life (saṁsāra). It flows for good. It flows for evil. Empirical cognitions of objects are obstructed by detachment. Discriminative knowledge is manifested by steadfast practice of discrimination between the self and the not-self. The complete suspension of all mental functions depends on these two conditions, steadfast habit of discrimination (abhyāsa) and detachment (vairāgya). The path of enjoyment is obstructed by dispassion for worldly objects. The path of liberation is opened by steadfast habit of discrimination.

Steadfastness (abhyāsa) consists in continuous efforts in performing the eightfold yoga practices which are the external and internal aids to yoga. It leads to the blissful unruffled state of mind (sthiti) due to the continued flow of mental modes dominated by sattva which completely overpowers rajas and tamas. The mind is not ruffled by joys and sorrows in this state. Sounds, tastes, smells, colours, good and evil things of the world cannot excite pleasure or pain in it. The mind attains the state of one-pointedness (ekāgratā). Steadfastness becomes firmly rooted (dṛḍhabhūmi), when it is continued uninterruptedly for a long period. When the aspirant continues the habit of performing the yogāṅgas with austerity, absolute sex-restraint, meditation, and devotion, he acquires firm steadfastness, and is not soon overpowered by dispositions of empirical cognitions (vyutthānasaṁskāra), and entrapped by worldly enjoyments. Extroversion is remedied by introversion. Restlessness of mind can be completely overcome by steadfast habit of concentration. Firm steadfastness can bring about the restrained condition (nirodha) of the mind.[1]

Detachment (vairāgya) is of two kinds, inferior (apara) and superior (para). Inferior detachment (apara vairāgya) consists

[1] YS., RM., YB., TV., YV., i. 12-14.

in aversion to the objects of worldly and heavenly enjoyments.[1] The aversion is due to extirpation of desire for them. It is due to the understanding of their painful consequences. Women, food and drink, lordliness, and the like are the objects of worldly enjoyment. Disembodied condition of merging in the sense-organs (vaidehya), merging in prakṛti (prakṛtilayatva), and unalloyed heavenly bliss are the objects of other-worldly enjoyments. Inferior detachment consists in complete indifference to sensible and supersensible objects of enjoyment even when the mind comes into contact with them owing to the realization of their painful consequences and discrimination of the self from the not-self. Inferior detachment is of four kinds: (1) yatamānasaṁjñā; (2) vyatirekasaṁjñā; (3) ekendriyasaṁjñā; (4) vaśikārasaṁjñā. The yatamānasaṁjña consists in the endeavour to destroy the afflictions of attachment, aversion, and other emotions and passions which direct the sense-organs to their objects. Interest is the subjective condition of attention. If it is destroyed, attention to objects ceases. They fail to evoke interest and therefore cannot attract attention. The sense-organs are directed to their objects by the mind. If it is purged of attachment and aversion, it acquires complete indifference to the objects of enjoyment.[2] The endeavour to destroy the impurities of mind is yatamānavairāgya. Vyatirekasaṁjñā consists in determining attachments to what objects have not been destroyed, and in endeavouring to destroy them. It is the effort to destroy the attachments that still persist in the mind and direct the sense-organs to certain objects. This is vyatirekavairāgya. Ekendriyasāṁjñā consists in the continuance of eagerness (autsukya) for enjoyment in the mind even after the sense-organs are withdrawn from their objects. The subtle subconscious impressions of enjoyments persist in the mind in this condition. This is ekendriyavairāgya. Vaśikārasaṁjñā consists in destroying even the eagerness of the mind for enjoyment by extirpating the subconscious impressions of enjoyments.[3] It is absolute indifference to all temporal and non-temporal objects of enjoyment[4]. The mind shakes off thraldom to them completely. They become its slaves.

---

[1] Cp. DP., 120, xiv. 9, xxvi. 35, xxvi. 28.
[2] CP., DP., xxv. 18, 19; xxv. 10.
[3] Cp. DP., xxvi. 1.
[4] Cp., DP., xxvi. 28.

Vaiśikāravairāgya is the complete conquest of the sensible and supersensible objects of enjoyment. It is due to the knowledge of their consequential painfulness.

Superior detachment (para vairāgya) consists in complete indifference to the guṇas with their manifest and unmanifest modifications due to steadfast practice of discriminative knowledge of the self. The mind is purged of rajas and tamas and dominated by sattva which makes it pure and transparent.

Supreme detachment is the culmination of transparence of mind. It is mere clarity of discriminative insight (jñānaprasādamātra). The aspirant who has acquired supreme detachment knows that he has attained complete freedom or isolation, that his afflictions have been uprooted, and that his cycle of birth and death has been broken. Supreme detachment is the culmination of knowledge which includes isolation in an embodied state.[1] It is embodied release (jīvanmukti). In inferior detachment there are traces of rajas left in the mind. But in superior detachment even these traces are destroyed and the pure sattva of mind shines forth. Tamas is completely removed by the pre-eminence of sattva in both the conditions. In supreme detachment there is absolute clarity of discriminative knowledge of the self. It is another name for embodied liberation (jīvanmukti). It is dharmameghasamādhi which consists in indifference to the discriminative knowledge of the self untainted by any desire for fruits.[2]

24. *Kinds of Samādhi*

We have seen that Vyāsa defines yoga as concentration (samādhi), which is a universal property of mind, and can be acquired by all. The distracted (kṣipta), torpid (mūḍha), occasionally steady (vikṣipta) states of the mind are unfavourable to concentration. The one-pointed (ekāgra) and restrained (niruddha) states are favourable to it. Samādhi is either conscious (samprajñāta) or superconscious (asamprajñāta). The former manifests the real nature of an object, wears off afflictions, loosens the ties of bondage in the shape of merit and demerit and inclines the mind to the restrained state. The

[1] Jñānasyaiva parākāṣṭhā vairāgyam. YB., i. 16.
[2] YS., YB., TV., YV., YMP., i. 15, 16; YS., iv. 29.

latter consists in the suppression of all mental functions.[1] The former is concentration on an object (sabīja). The mind is concentrated on an object and identifies itself with it. The latter is objectless concentration. The mind is not concentrated on an object. It is devoid of all mental modes and dispositions.[2]

Conscious trance (samprajñāta samādhi) is of six kinds. (1) Savitarka samādhi is the concentration in which the mind identifies itself with a gross object (sthūla artha) together with its name (śabda) and cognition (jñāna). In it the object is not manifested to consciousness in its pure form but associated and identified with its name and cognition, though the object, the name, and the cognition are quite distinct from one another. It is called savitarka, since its object appears in trance-consciousness (samādhiprajñā) as associated with the determinations of its name and cognition (śabdārthajñānavikalpānuviddha). (2) Nirvitarka samādhi is the concentration in which the mind identifies itself with a gross object devoid of association with its name and cognition. In it the object is manifested to trance-consciousness in its pure form (arthamātranirbhāsa) free from the recollection of its name. Even the cognition of the object is not manifested to trance-consciousness (svarūpaśūnyeva). This kind of conscious trance is free from all determinations (vikalpaśūnya).[3] (3) Savicāra samādhi is the concentration in which the mind identifies itself with subtle tanmātras associated with the notions of time, space, and causality, and endued with manifest qualities, which are apprehended by one cognition.[4] (4) Nirvicāra samādhi is the concentration in which the mind identifies itself with subtle tanmātras devoid of sublatent, actual, and latent qualities, and yet capable of being endued with these qualities, and free from associations with time, space, and causality. Subtle tanmātras are manifested to trance-consciousness in their true nature devoid of all determinations which are attributed to them. Even cognitions of the tanmātras are not manifested to trance-consciousness (svarūpaśūnyevārthamātrā prajñā) in this kind of samādhi.[5] The subtle objects of concentration are not only

---

[1] YB., i. 1.
[2] YS., i. 46, 51.
[3] YB., i. 42; YS., YB., i. 43.
[4] YB., TV., i. 44.
[5] YB., TV., iv. 44.

the tanmātras, but also egoism (ahaṁkāra), buddhi, and prakṛti.[1] (5) Ānandānugata samādhi is the concentration in which the mind identifies itself with the gross sense-organs, the products of egoism (ahaṁkāra) in which sattva with its bliss predominates. The mental mode "I am happy" is manifested to trance-consciousness as a direct and immediate apprehension (sākṣātkāra).[2] It does not admit of two kinds, sānanda and nirānanda.[3] (6) Asmitānugata samādhi is the concentration in which the mind identifies itself with egoism (asmitā) identified with the self. There is a direct and immediate apprehension of the mental mode 'I am' identified with the pure self. It does not admit of two kinds, sāsmita and nirasmita.[4]

Vyāsa comprehends all kinds of conscious trance (samprajñāta samādhi) under three classes: (1) grāhya samādhi or concentration on external objects, gross and subtle; (2) grahaṇasamādhi or concentration on the sense-organs; (3) grahītṛ-samādhi or concentration on the self. In these trance-cognitions the mind is coloured by, and completely identified with, the objects, the sense-organs, and the self. This identification is called samāpatti.[5] Vācaspati includes vitarkānugata and vicārānugata samādhis apprehending gross objects and tanmātras in grāhyasamādhi, ānandānugata samādhi apprehending the sense-organs in grahaṇasamādhi, and asmitānugata samādhi apprehending egoism in grahītṛsamādhi.[6]

Vijñānabhikṣu holds a different view. Vitarkānugata samādhi is concentration on gross objects and sense-organs, in which there is immediate apprehension of their infinite peculiarities unknown before. It is either savitarka or nirvitarka. Vicārānugata samādhi is concentration on tanmātras, ahaṁkāra, mahat and prakṛti, in which there is immediate apprehension of their infinite peculiarities (aśeṣaviśeṣasāksātkāra). It is either savicāra or nirvicāra. Ānandānugata samādhi is concentration on extreme bliss owing to the predominance of sattva. There is immediate apprehension of the bliss in the form 'I am happy'. It does not admit of two kinds, sānanda and nirānanda. Asmitānugata samadhi is concentration on the pure self, in which there is direct apprehension of it in the form 'I am'.

---

[1] YS., YB., i. 45.
[2] TV., YV., i. 17.
[3] YV., i. 17.
[4] YV., i. 17.
[5] YS., YB., i. 41.
[6] YV., i. 41.

It has either the finite self (jīvātman) or the supreme self (paramātman) for its object. It does not admit of two kinds, sāsmita and nirasmita. Direct apprehension of the pure self (kevalapuruṣajñāna) is indeterminate (nirvikalpa) only. It cannot be determinate.[1]

Savitarka, nirvitarka, savicāra, and nirvicāra samādhis are called sabīja samādhi. They are concentration on objects which are their basis (ālambana). The first two are concentration on gross objects. The last two are concentration on subtle objects.[2] They are kinds of samprajñāta samādhi or conscious trance. They are called sabīja also because they contain seeds (bīja) of bondage. They are devoid of discriminative knowledge which dispels false knowledge (avidyā).

Nirvicāra samādhi or concentration on subtle objects free from all determinations of time, space, and causality, purges the mind of the impurities of rajas and tamas and makes it translucent owing to the predominance of sattva. It generates the purity of mind (adhyātmaprasāda). It acquires clarity or intuition which clearly apprehends objects in their real nature without temporal order. It is like the vision of one who sees all objects from the top of a mountain.[3] The intuition (prajñā) of the yogin whose mind is pure and translucent and purged of all afflictions and impurities apprehends only truth (ṛta). So it is called ṛtambharā prajñā. It is free from all taint of falsehood. It directly apprehends all particular qualities of subtle, hidden, and remote objects, and souls. It is different from the knowledge derived from inference and testimony which apprehend generalities (sāmānya) only. Ṛtambharā prajñā apprehends particular qualities of supersensible objects directly.[4]

The dispositions (saṁskāra) of the intuition of nirvicāra samādhi overpower and counteract the dispositions of empirical cognitions (vyutthānasaṁskāra). When they are overpowered, they cannot generate empirical cognitions in the form of recollections. When empirical cognitions are arrested, concentration is generated. Concentration gives rise to intuition (prajñā). Intuitions produce dispositions. Dispositions of intuitions destroy afflictions, false knowledge, egoism, attach-

[1] YV., i. 17.
[2] YS., YB., i. 46.
[3] YS., YB., i. 47.
[4] YS., YB., i. 48, 49.

ment, aversion, and will-to-live. So they prevent the mind from generating experience or enjoyment and suffering. The mind functions till discriminative knowledge dawns upon it.[1]

Superconscious trance (asamprajñāta samādhi) is called nirbīja because it is objectless and devoid of avidyā which is the seed of bondage. It arises from the complete suppression or destruction of conscious trance (samprajñāta samādhi) and its dispositions. The dispositions of superconscious trances overpower and counteract the dispositions of conscious trances. The dispositions of superconscious trances are destroyed along with the mind which is merged in prakṛti. When the mind is destroyed, the pure self remains in its essential nature (svarūpapratiṣṭha). It is said to be then liberated (mukta).[2]

Superconscious trance is objectless (nirālambana). There is complete suppression of all mental modes. But their dispositions are left in the mind (saṁskāraśeṣa). This kind of trance can be brought about by supreme detachment (para vairāgya) which is its means. Steadfast practice of supreme detachment makes the mind objectless, since all desires for objects are extirpated. When the mind is no longer modified into objects, it ceases to have modes. When its modes are destroyed, it seems to be destroyed. This is superconscious trance which is objectless and free from cognitions, feelings, and conations, but not free from dispositions. It cannot be brought about by inferior detachment which is not absolutely free from all attachment for objects. Inferior detachment can generate conscious trance. Superior detachment can generate superconscious trance.[3]

The superconscious trance of disembodied souls (videha) and persons whose minds are merged in prakṛti (prakṛtilaya) is due to avidyā or false knowledge. Their minds are not destroyed. They persist with their dispositions and cling to the souls. There is a semblance of apprehension of complete freedom or isolation (kaivalya). There is no extirpation of avidyā in them. They attain these supernatural conditions by concentrating their minds on prakṛti and its evolutes. They attain inferior release resembling heavenly bliss. They may fall from this condition and be born again.[4]

---

[1] YS., YB., i. 50; iii. 9, 10.
[2] YS., YB., i. 51.
[3] YS., YB., i. 18.
[4] YS., YB., i. 19.

The superconscious trance of the yogins is due to faith (śraddhā), power (vīrya), recollection of truth or meditation (smṛti), concentration (samādhi), and intuition (prajñā). Faith is purity or clarity of mind. It protects the aspirant like mother. It does him great good. Desirous of discriminative knowledge he makes efforts. These generate meditation on truth. Meditation gives rise to concentration or conscious trance. The trance generates discriminative intuition (prajñā-viveka). Steadfast practice of this intuition and dispassion for its objects generates superconscious trance. Thus conscious trance is an aid to superconscious trance.[1]

Samādhi can be attained by single-minded devotion to God (īśvarapraṇidhāna) also. The grace of God falls on His devotee who meditates on Him with extreme devotion. God grants him samādhi by His grace. So His devotee attains it without his own efforts.[2] All distractions of attention are completely overcome by devotion to God.[3] The Yoga recognizes the path of devotion to God (bhaktiyoga).

The stability of mind can be attained by concentration on the mind of a person who has attained embodied release and shaken off all attachments. It can be attained by concentration on dream-cognitions or sleep-cognitions, or by meditation on attractive objects. It can be attained by concentration on subtle objects as we have already seen.[4]

25. *Supernormal Powers*

The third book, Vibhūtipāda of the *Yoga Sūtra,* is devoted to the description of supernatural powers that arise from steadfast practice of yogāṅgas and concentration on different objects. But these occult powers are obstacles to the aspirant. The steadfast habit of performing the yogāṅgas generates supernormal powers which are devoid of philosophical significance. Each yogāṅga brings its own reward. Non-injury destroys enmity of all other animals. Even ferocious wild animals do no harm to the person who is a votary of ahiṁsā. Truthfulness makes a person's words infallible. He can make others virtuous and capable of attaining heaven by benedictory words which are

---

[1] YS., YB., i. 20.
[2] YS., YB., i. 23.
[3] YB., i. 29.
[4] YS., i. 37-40.

fraught with potent suggestive forces. Non-stealing or non-covetousness brings untold wealth from all directions. Absolute sex-restraint generates unfailing powers to impart knowledge to disciples. Non-acceptance of unnecessary gifts generates the power of knowing the past, present, and future births. These supernormal powers arise from steadfast habit of performing restraints.[1] Bodily cleanliness generates hatred for one's own body and aversion to contact with other's bodies. Mental cleanliness generates purity of mind, complacence, one-pointedness, conquest of the senses, and capacity for intuition of the self. Contentment generates supreme bliss. It is due to the extinction of desires. Sensual pleasure is not even a fraction of this bliss. Austerities destroy all impurities of mind, and generate supernormal powers of the body and the sense-organs. They produce minuteness (aṇimā), lightness (laghimā), largeness (mahimā), reaching remote objects (prāpti), unobstructed fulfilment of desires (prākāmya), absolute control over physical objects (vaśitva), fulfilment of resolutions (yatrakāmāvasāyitva), and hyperæsthesia of the sense-organs, clairvoyance, clairaudience, and the like. Recitation of a mantra generates vision of the desired deity. Resignation of all actions to God generates conscious ecstasy which produces intuition of desired objects in other times, places, and births. These supernormal powers arise from the steadfast habit of performing observances (niyama).[2] Bodily posture generates endurance of heat and cold, and the like. It facilitates breath control. Complete mastery over breath control destroys demerits and afflictions which obscure discriminative knowledge, and produces capacity for fixation of attention. Withdrawal of the senses from their objects generates absolute control over them. Sense-conquest is either extinction of attachment for sensible objects. Or it is perception of them without pleasure or pain due to extinction of attachment and aversion. Fixation of attention, meditation, and concentration, called saṁyama, generate the light of intuition (prajñāloka).[3]

Saṁyama on three kinds of modifications by change of quality, change of mark, and change of state (dharmalakṣaṇāvasthāpariṇāma) generates intuition of the past and the future.[4]

---

[1] YS., YB., ii. 35-39.
[2] YS., YB., ii. 40-45.
[3] YS., YB., ii. 48, 49, 52, 53, 55; iii. 5.
[4] YS., iii. 16.

Saṁyama on ones's own predispositions generates intuition of the past births. Concentration on others' predispositions generates intuition of their past births. Direct apprehension of the predispositions arises from concentration on them. This apprehension generates intuition of the past births.[1] Concentration on the mental modes of another person through their bodily expressions generates intuition of his mind with its modes. But it does not produce intuition of their objects. Thus concentration brings about thought-reading and insight into another's mind.[2] Concentration of the light of intuition on subtle, hidden, and remote objects generates knowledge of them.[3] Concentration on the light of the brain generates vision of the siddhas living in the region between the earth and heaven.[4] Saṁyama on the heart, which is the seat of the mind, generates knowledge of the mind.[5] Concentration on the pure self through its reflection in the mental mode generates knowledge of the self.[6] Intuitive knowledge (prātibhajñāna) arises spontaneously without instruction. It is the precursor of discriminative knowledge. It can apprehend all objects.[7] Concentration on moments and their temporal order generates discriminative intuition (vivekajajñāna) of all objects with their modifications. This intuition can distinguish those objects from one another, which cannot be distinguished from one another by their universals (jāti), peculiar marks (lakṣaṇa), and positions in space (deśa). It directly apprehends all objects with their modes without temporal sequence (akrama) in the present moment (ekakṣaṇopārūḍha). It is complete knowledge (paripūrṇa jñāna). It is the saving knowledge (tārakajñāna).[8]

Concentration on the sun generates knowledge of the cosmos. Concentration on the moon produces knowledge of the arrangement of the stars. Concentration on the pole star generates knowledge of their movements. Concentration on the navel produces knowledge of the structure of the body. Concentration on the cavity in the throat destroys hunger and thirst.[9] Concentration on the pure self produces knowledge of subtle, hidden, remote, past, and future objects, and hyperæsthesia of

---

[1] YS., YB., iii. 18.
[2] YS., iii. 19, 20.
[3] YS., iii. 25.
[4] YS., iii. 32.
[5] YS., iii. 34.
[6] YS., iii. 35.
[7] YS., YB., iii. 33.
[8] YS., YB., iii. 52-54.
[9] YS., iii. 26-30.

the sense-organs, perception of supersensible sound, touch, sight, taste, and smell.[1]

When merit and demerit are attenuated by mental discipline, the mind of the yogin can enter into another body with his sense-organs.[2] The yogin can assume many bodies by power of yoga. He produces many minds (nirmāṇacitta) out of asmitā (egoism) by mere resolution. He produces one mind which can regulate all these created minds and control their resolutions and actions.[3] Concentration on omens of death or one's own merits and demerits produces knowledge of the time and place of one's death.[4] Mastery over udāna vital force by concentration on it generates the power of voluntary death.[5] Concentration on samāna vital force generates effulgence of the body.[6] Saṁyama on gross elements generates minuteness (aṇimā), lightness (laghimā), largeness (mahimā), and power of reaching remote objects (prāpti). Saṁyama on their nature produces non-obstruction to desires (prākāmya). Saṁyama on the tanmātras generates the power of controlling animate and inanimate physical objects (vaśitva). Saṁyama on sattva, rajas, and tamas generates the power of creating and destroying physical objects (īśitva). Saṁyama on their power of generating experience and liberation produces the power of fulfilling the desires with regard to physical objects (yatrakāmavasāyitva). The yogin can overcome the qualities of physical objects by acquiring mastery over them through concentration (bhūtajaya). He can enter into a rock. Water cannot drench him. Fire cannot burn him. The strong wind cannot remove him from one place to another. He can become invisible to all. But these miracles are not due to the suspension of the laws of nature. A powerful yogin cannot turn one thing into another, but can change the powers of things.[7] Saṁyama on the nature of physical elements generates supernatural powers of the body, beauty, charm, strength, and hardness of a thunder.[8] Conquest of the senses (indriyajaya) arises from concentration on the sense-organs, their causes, egoism, sattva, rajas, and tamas, their apprehension of objects, and conduciveness to experience and liberation. It gives rise

[1] YS., YB., iii. 36.
[2] YS., YB., iii. 38.
[3] YS., YB., iv. 4, 5.
[4] YS., iii. 22.
[5] YS., iii. 39.
[6] YS., iii. 40.
[7] Na ca śakto'pi padārthaviparyāsaṁ karoti. YB., iii. 45.
[8] YS., iii. 46.

to quick movement of mind, movement of the senses to their objects without any aid of the body, and control over prakṛti and its evolutes.[1] Concentration on the discriminative knowledge of the self and buddhi generates the power of controlling all unconscious objects (sarvabhāvādhiṣṭhātṛtva), and omniscience (sarvajñātṛtva) or knowledge of all objects with their arrangements of sattva, rajas, and tamas, endued with manifested, actual, and unmanifest qualities without their sequence. It generates omniscience and omnipotence. Omniscience destroys all afflictions and merits and demerits. This is the siddhi called viśokā. The yogin becomes the master (vaśin).[2]

The supernormal powers are achievements to the extroverts (vyutthitacitta) who are devoid of concentration. But they appear to be harmful to the introverts absorbed in concentration (samāhitacitta) because they are hindrances to the knowledge of the self.[3] They are either congenital or due to drugs, mantras, austerities, and concentration.[4] The Yoga system does not mention miracles due to black magic. It describes the miraculous powers born of concentration by the way. They do not form its vital part. But an account of the system will be incomplete without any mention of them. The Yoga is preeminently a science of mental discipline.

26. *Karma and Transmigration*

The different kinds of actions, black, white-black, white, and non-white-non-black, have already been described. Black actions produce vice or demerit (adharma, pāpa). White-black actions produce both virtue (dharma, puṇya) and vice. White actions produce virtue or merit only. Non-white-non-black actions of yogins produce neither virtue nor vice.[5] Virtue and vice are called karmāśayas or potencies of actions. They are subconscious dispositions of actions. They are ultimately due to afflictions, false knowledge, egoism, attachment, aversion, and will-to-live (kleśamūla). The afflictions are manifested as different emotions and passions. So merit and demerit arise from desire, greed, delusion, and anger.

---

[1] YS., YB., iii. 48.
[2] YS., YB., iii. 49.
[3] YS., YB., iii. 37.
[4] YS., iv. 1.
[5] YB., iv. 7.

The karmāśayas bear fruits either in the present life (dṛṣṭajanmavedanīya) or in another unknown life (adṛṣṭajanmavedanīya). Merits (puṇyakarmāśaya) arising from steadfast recitation of mantras, austerities, and concentration, or devotion to great saints, noble souls, deities, or God bear fruit in this life. Demerits (papakarmāśayas) due to repeated harm done to frightened, sick, and poor persons, confident protegés, noble souls or hermits doing penances bear fruits in the present life. They are dṛṣṭajanmavedanīya. Other kinds of karmāśayas ripen and fructify in other future lives. They are adṛṣṭajanmavedanīya. The merits and demerits of the yogins who have burnt up their afflictions by severe mental discipline ripen and bear fruits in the present life.[1]

The karmāśayas bear fruits in the forms of birth (jāti), duration of life (āyuṣ), and experience (bhoga) with the aid of afflictions which are the concomitant conditions of their fruitions. They cannot bear fruits if afflictions are destroyed by discriminative knowledge.[2] Merits (puṇykarmāśaya) produce pleasure, and demerits (pāpakarmāśaya) produce pain.[3] One karmāśaya does not produce one birth, since many karmāśayas of this life and previous lives would require infinite number of births for their fruition. One karmāśaya does not produce many births for the same reason. Many karmāśayas combine with one another, with some as principal and others as subordinate, and produce one birth. Principal karmāśayas are ready to bear fruits. They fructify earlier than subordinate ones. Subordinate karmāśayas produce their effects after some delay. Accumulated virtuous and sinful karmāśayas (sañcitakarma) of this life, being overpowered by those of the previous births (prārabdha karma), combine with similar karmāśayas, cause the death of the person, and produce one birth in order to produce their fruits. They determine not only birth, but also length of life and experience or enjoyment and suffering. They are the causes of three fruitions (trivipāka). Some produce experience and length of life. They are the causes of two fruitions (dvivipāka.) Others produce only experience. They are the causes of one fruition only (ekavipāka).

---

[1] YS., YB., ii. 12.
[2] YS., YB., ii. 13.
[3] YS., ii. 14.

The same mind (citta) clings to the soul through many births. It is variegated with predispositions (vāsanā) of afflictions (kleśa), merits and demerits (karma), and fruitions (vipāka) of many births. They are anekabhavika or generated by many births. They are the latent deposits of actions of many lives. They are different from the potencies of actions that accumulate in one life. The former are prārabdha karma. The latter are sañcita karma. The predispositions of past lives are the cause of the instinctive tendencies peculiar to the species in the present life.

The karmāśayas accumulating in one life (ekabhavika) are either of appointed fruition (niyatavipāka) or of unappointed fruition (aniyatavipāka). The former bear fruits in this life. The latter will become fruitful in other lives. This rule applies to dṛṣṭajanmavedanīyakarmas of appointed fruition. It does not apply to adṛṣṭajanmavedanīya-karmāśayas of unappointed fruition (aniyatavipāka). They may have three different courses: (1) They may be destroyed without fruition. (2) They may be merged in the principal action. (3) They may remain for a long time, being overpowered by the principal action of appointed fruition, since adṛṣṭajanmavedanīyakarmāśayas of unappointed fruition are not manifested at the time of death. They may be destroyed. They may be merged in the principal karmāśayas as subordinate to it. They may remain for a long time, being overpowered by principal karmāśayas, till they are awakened by similar karmāśayas and enabled to bear fruits. There is no certainty about the time, place, and occasion of the ripening and fruition of the adṛṣṭajanmavedanīyakarmāśayas of unappointed fruition. Hence the course of karmāśayas is said to be varied and inscrutable.[1]

The Yoga doctrine of Karma and transmigration has great similarity with the Jaina doctrine. It believes in transmigration of the human soul into an animal body and a divine body. It believes in the continuity of the same mind through innumerable lives, in which predispositions (vāsanā) of many births are imbedded. They can be destroyed by destroying avidyā and other afflictions which are their causes, merits and demerits, birth, length of life, and experience which are their effects,

---

[1] YB., ii. 13; YPR., pp. 103-12; YP., pp. 322-26.

the mind which is their substrate, and objects of experience. These can be destroyed by discriminative knowledge of the self.[1]

27. *Liberation* (*Kaivalya*)

In empirical consciousness (vyutthāna) the self wrongly identifies itself with mental modes which assume the forms of objects, and in which it is reflected. But in liberation the self remains in its essential condition (svarūpe avasthāna). There is a beginningless relation (anādisambandha) between the self and the buddhi due to avidyā on account of which the self erroneously identifies itself with buddhi, and is entangled in bondage.[2] Life is full of pain. All is pain to the discriminating person.[3] The threefold pain (tāpatraya) discussed already is due to avidya.[4] It can be destroyed by right knowledge (samyagdarśana). Just as medical science treats of diseases, the cause of diseases, the cure of diseases, and the medicines for diseases, so the science of liberation treats of saṁsāra or empirical life of bondage, the cause of saṁsāra, liberation, and the means of liberation. Saṁsāra abounding in misery is to be avoided (heya) ; the conjunction (saṁyoga) of puruṣa with prakṛti is the cause of the avoidable saṁsāra (heyahetu) ; the absolute extinction of their conjunction is avoidance (hāna) ; right knowledge is the means of avoidance (hānopāya).[5] Future pain is to be avoided. The conjunction of the self with the buddhi is its cause.[6] Avidyā is the cause of the conjunction. When it is destroyed, the conjunction is destroyed, and the self is liberated, and remains in its essential condition.[7] When the self realizes its intrinsic nature, it is liberated.[8]

Discriminative knowledge untainted by avidyā is the means of liberation. When afflictions and their seeds or dispositions are burnt by discriminative knowledge, and are made incapable of producing their effects, the sattva of the mind becomes predominant and translucent, and the stream of discriminative knowledge (vivekapratyayapravāha) becomes pure and un-

[1] YS., YB., iv. 11.
[2] YB., i. 3, 4.
[3] Sarvaṁ duḥkhaṁ vivekinaḥ. YB., ii. 15; Cp. DP., xx. 6.
[4] Cp. DP., xviii. 9.
[5] YB., ii. 15.
[6] YS., ii. 16, 17, 23.
[7] YS., YB., ii. 24, 25.
[8] Draṣṭuḥ svarūpopalabdhiḥ apavargaḥ. YB., ii. 23

tainted (aviplavā vivekakhyāti). This is the means of achievement of liberation.[1] When the potencies of afflictions (kleśabīja) are burnt up, they cannot produce their effects. When they are destroyed along with the mind, the pure self does not suffer threefold pain (tāpatraya). When the manas is merged in prakṛti with its sattva, rajas, and tamas, the self is completely dissociated from the guṇas (ātyantikaguṇaviyoga), and realizes its essential nature (svarūpapratiṣṭhā) as transcendental consciousness (citiśakti). When the self shakes off attachment even to the discriminative knowledge of itself, it attains absolute freedom or isolation (kaivalya). This is the culmination of supreme detachment (para vairagya)[2] When the self acquires supreme detachment for even discriminative knowledge of itself, it acquires dharmameghasamādhi, which is the highest stage of conscious ecstasy (samprajñātasamādhi). It is a continuous flow of discriminative knowledge.[3] It destroys all afflictions (kleśa), actions (karma), and merits and demerits (karmāśaya) with their roots or dispositions. When they are destroyed, the discriminating (vidvān) self becomes liberated, even while living an embodied life. This is called embodied release (jīvanmukti).[4] When the dispositions of all mental modes, afflicted and unafflicted, are destroyed, the self acquires superconscious ecstasy (asamprajñāta samādhi). When all mental modes and their dispositions are completely arrested, the self is disentangled from the meshes of prakṛti, becomes pure (amala) and isolated (kevala), shines forth with its light of intrinsic transcendental consciousness (svarūpamātrajyoti),[5] and becomes omniscient.[6] When the guṇas are merged in prakṛti after accomplishing the purposes of the self, experience and liberation, the self attains disembodied release (videhakaivalya). It consists in remaining in its essential nature (svarūpapratiṣṭhā) or transcendental consciousness (citiśakti) free from empirical consciousness due to mental modes.[7]

The self is eternally pure and liberated. It is said to be entangled in bondage and liberated from bondage in relation to prakṛti or buddhi. When the modes of buddhi are attributed

[1] YS., YB., ii. 16.
[2] YB., ii. 50.
[3] YS., YB., iv. 29.
[4] YB., iv. 30.
[5] YB., ii. 27; iv. 55.
[6] YS., iv. 31.
[7] YS., YB., iv. 34.

to the self, it is said to be bound. When they are completely destroyed or merged in their cause, prakṛti, they are no longer attributed to the self, and it is said to be liberated. Bondage and liberation of the self are not real.

28. *Critical Estimate*

The Yoga metaphysics is the Sāṁkhya dualism of prakṛti and puruṣas with God added to it. The conception of God does not mitigate the dualism. God is not the creator of prakṛti and puruṣas. He is not the material cause of the world. He is its efficient cause only in the sense that He disturbs the equilibrium of prakṛti and starts its evolution and guides it and adapted it to the merits and demerits (adṛṣṭa) of the puruṣas. He removes the barriers to the production of effects by the material causes. The relation of God to prakṛti is external. He is not its immanent spirit. The relation of God to the puruṣas also is external. He is not their immanent spirit. God removes obstacles of the moral aspirants to their achievement of liberation. But God's aid is not necessary for liberation. Devotion to God or resignation of all actions to God is one of the means of liberation. God can be dispensed with for attaining freedom from bondage. The yoga is a method of self-help and severe mental discipline. God is loosely connected with prakṛti and puruṣas.

The relation of prakṛti to puruṣas is said to be conjunction. But how there can be conjunction between an incorporeal ubiquitous spirit (puruṣa) and a corporeal ubiquitous prakṛti passes comprehension. Avidyā of the puruṣa has been credited with miraculous powers. It brings about conjunction between puruṣa and prakṛti. But what is the cause of avidyā? The Yoga does not answer the question. Its psychology and ethics are based on the conception of avidyā. The Yoga ontology is open to many of the objections which have been urged against the Sāṁkhya ontology. Its conceptions of time, space, and different kinds of modifications are of great philosophical significance.

The Yoga psychology is intellectualistic. It regards emotions as intellectual disorders. Emotions are called afflictions. They are due to false knowledge (avidyā). They can be destroyed by right knowledge. The Yoga had a clear conception of the subconscious impressions or dispositions (saṁskāra). It refers to emotional dispositions (kleśasaṁskāra), cognitive dispositions (jñānajasaṁskāra), conative dispositions (karmāśayas), and predispositions of past lives (vāsanā). They can be known directly by concentration (samādhi). They can be destroyed by discriminative knowledge.

The Yoga system anticipated the doctrine of Psycho-analysis which prescribes methods of unearthing the repressed unconscious complexes and tackling them rationally. But they differ from each other in fundamental respects. The Yoga advocates rationalism. Psycho-analysis advocates irrationalism. The former adopts asceticism. The latter adopts hedonism or self-expression. The former is intellectualistic, while the latter is voluntaristic. The former regards all emotions as intellectual disorders or effects of false knowledge. The latter regards all judgments as coloured by unconscious whishes.

The Yoga ethics is intellectual eudaemonism. Perfect knowledge of the self as transcendental consciousness (citiśakti) is the *summum bonum* of human life. It is free from bliss. It is devoid of will. The buddhi is will. It is endued with bliss. The puruṣa is pure non-empirical consciousness. Freedom (kaivalya) is self-realization. It is the existence of the pure self in its essential condition (svarūpapratiṣṭhā).

The Yoga ethics is asceticism inasmuch as it inculcates extirpation of love, hatred, and all other emotions and desires including the will-to-live. It enjoins strict observance of non-injury, in body, mind, and speech, truthfulness consistent with the welfare of all creatures, non-stealing and greedlessness, absolute sex-restraint, and non-acceptance of unnecessary gifts, purity of body and mind, contentment, penances, recitation of mantras, dedication of all actions to God, habits of pure thoughts and virtuous actions, control of body, sense-organs, and mind. It is the art of discipline of body, life, and mind. It aims at liberation of the self.

The Yoga ethics is not egoistic inasmuch as it is not indifferent to the welfare of mankind (lokahita) and the sentient creation (sarvabhūtahita). Good will or friendship (maitrī) for all happy creatures, compassion (karuṇā) for all miserable creatures, cheerfulness or joy (muditā) for all virtuous persons, and indifference (upekṣā) to all vicious persons are described as the means of stability and complacence of the mind. They are stressed by Jainism and Buddhism also. Thus the Yoga is altruistic in outlook. It defines virtue as benevolence, and vice as malevolence. Hence the Yoga is not egoistic, though it is predominantly ascetic and concerned with achievement of the transcendental condition of the self. The Yoga method of self-realization is a bold achievement of the Hindu mind. Its ethics seems to be profoundly influenced by the Jaina and Buddhist ethics. Its doctrine of karma and transmigration bears the stamp of the Jaina doctrine.

CHAPTER III

THE JAINA PHILOSOPHY

1. *Introduction*

According to the Jaina tradition Ṛṣabha was the founder of Jainism. It was taught by twenty four Tīrthaṅkaras who attained liberation. Ṛṣabha was the first, and Vardhamāna was the last Tīrthaṅkara. Vardhamāna, the last prophet, was a contemporary of Buddha. He was born in 599 B.C. and died in 527 B.C.[1] The Jaina scriptures are founded on his teachings. He was called the Jina, spiritual conqueror, Mahāvira, great hero. He was not the founder of Jainism. He reformed the creed of Pārśvanātha, the twenty third Tīrthaṅkara, who is said to have died 250 years before Vardhamāna. Parśvanātha was probably a historical person. The other Tīrthaṅkaras are legendary. The orthodox Jainas believe that the Jaina religion is eternal, and that it has been revealed by Tīrthaṅkaras in every one of the endless epochs of the world. Vardhamāna organized his disciples into a regular order with lay and monastic members of both sexes.

There are two main sects of Jainism, Śvetāmbaras and Digambaras. They agree in believing in all the fundamental tenets of Jainism. They differ in inessential tenets. The Digambaras hold that the Tīrthaṅkaras live without food, that a monk who owns any property and wears clothes cannot attain liberation, and that no woman can attain liberation. They disown the canonical works of the Śvetāmbaras. They themselves have none. The Digambaras are sky-clad or nude. The Śvetāmbaras are clothed in white. The schism took place in 82 A.D.[2]

The Jaina philosophy was developed out of the canonical works of the Jainas. Many glosses and commentaries were written on the sacred texts. Philosophical literature was first written in Prakrit, and then in Sanskrit. Umāsvāmi or

---

[1] HIL., p. 159.

[2] HIL., p. 159.

Umāsvāti (135—219 A.D.) wrote *Tattvārthādhigamasūtra*.[1] It is a sacred epitome of Jainism. It is a Śvetāmbara extra-canonical work. But it is revered by the Svetāmbara and the Digambara sects both. It contains all the fundamental principles of Jainism. It has many commentaries. *Sarvārthasiddhi* of Pūjyapāda, *Tattvārthaślokovārtika* of Vidyānandisvāmi, and *Rājavārtika* of Akalaṅkadeva (750 A.D.) are important among them. Amṛta Candra Sūri's (905 A.D.) *Tattvārthasāra* is an important work. Kundakundācārya was the author of *Pañcāstikāyasamayasāra* which deals with five astikāyas or extended beings, jīva, pudgala, dharma, adharma, and ākāśa. He was greatly revered by the Digambara sect. He was probably born in 52 B.C.[2] Nemicandra (tenth century A.D.) wrote (1) *Dravyasaṁgraha*, compendium of the substances ; (2) *Gommatasāra*, dealing with the jīva, bondage, the cause of bondage, and the ways of breaking bondage ; (3) *Labdhisāra*, a treatise on attainment (labdhi) of those things which lead to perfect conduct, (4) *Kṣapaṇasāra*, dealing with bondage, passions (kaṣāya), soul-tints (leśyā), and the means of removing passions ; (5) *Trilokasāra*, dealing with the three regions of the universe. *Dravyasaṁgraha* is an important Jaina work. It deals with the six substances, jīva, pudgala, dharma, adharma, ākāśa, and time, the seven tattvas, the nine padārthas, and the means of liberation. Brahmadeva wrote a commentary on it several centuries later.[3] *Nyāyāvatāra* of Siddhasena Divākara (480—550 A.D.), *Jaina Tarkavārtika* with Śāntyācārya's commentary, *Syādvādamañjarī* of Malliṣena (1292 A.D.), *Āptamīmāṃsā* of Samantabhadra (600 A.D.), *Parīkṣāmukhasūtra* of Māṇikyanandi (800 A.D.) with its commentary, *Parīkṣāmukhasūtralaghuvṛtti* of Anantavīrya (1039 A.D.), *Prameyakamalamārtaṇḍa* of Prabhācandra (825 A.D.), *Pramāṇatattvālokālaṅkāra* of Vādi Deva Sūri (1086—1169 A.D.) are important works on the Jaina theory of knowledge and Logic. Hemacandra Sūri's (1088—1172 A.D.) *Yogaśāstra* is an important work on the Jaina ethics. Haribhadra Sūri (1129 A.D.) wrote *Ṣaḍdarśanasamuccaya* dealing with the different

[1] J. L. Jaina : English Translation of *Tattvārthādhigamasūtra*, p. vii.
[2] A. Chakravartinayanar : English Translation of *Pañcāstikāyasamayasāra*, Introduction, p. vii.
[3] S. C. Ghoshal : English Translation of *Dravyasaṁgraha*, Introduction.

systems of Hindu philosophy, Buddhism and Jainism. Guṇaratna (1409 A.D.) wrote a commentary on it called *Tarkarahasyadīpikā.* It contains a short and excellent account of Jainism. Mādhavācārya's *Ṣaḍdarśanasaṁgraha* contains a succint account of the Jaina metaphysics.

The Jaina philosophy is dualism of the soul (jīva) and the non-soul (ajīva). There are innumerable souls, earth-souls, water-souls, fire-souls, air-souls, plant-souls, animal-souls, human-souls, and god-souls. The soul is an eternal spiritual substance. It cannot be derived from matter. It is an immaterial principle. It transmigrates from one body to another. The ajīva is matter (pudgala), the principle of motion (dharma), the principle of rest (adharma), space (ākāśa), and time (kāla). Matter is either an atom (aṇu) or an aggregate (skandha) of atoms. All atoms are homogeneous. Karma is a kind of subtle matter which enters into the soul, and causes its bondage. Matter cannot be derived from the soul. The soul and matter are entirely heterogeneous. This is dualism. There is no God. The Jaina advocates atheism. The world is self-existent and eternal. All objects of the world are multiform (anekānta) and endued with infinite qualities and relations (anantadharmaka). This is relative pluralism. The reality can be considered from different points of view or nayas. The nayas are the standpoints. The different systems of philosophy are only partial views of the reality. Jainism is the complete view of the reality. It embodies the absolute truth. All judgments are relative and probable. No judgments are absolute. This is syādvāda. There are seven ways of predication. This is called saptabhaṅgīnyāya. The Jaina ethics is ethics of ahiṃsā and asceticism. The Jaina religion is the worship of the Tīrthaṅkaras and the attainment of liberation by sheer self-exertion. It is the religion of self-help. Divinity is innate in the human soul. It shines forth in its innate glory when it completely extirpates the veil of karma-matter that covers the soul and obscures its infinite knowledge, infinite perception, infinite bliss, and infinite power.

2. *Relation to other Systems*

The Upaniṣads recognize the reality of the Brahman and consider changes to be appearances. They consider the permanent substance (*e.g.*, clay) to be real, and its changes of form to be names and forms (nāmarūpa) or unreal appearances.[1] The Advaita Vedānta develops the monism of the Upaniṣads into Absolutism. It regards the Brahman as pure identity of consciousness devoid of all changing qualities and states which are branded as appearances. The Buddhists, on the other hand, recognize the reality of changing qualities, and deny the reality of the substance underlying them. They consider the substance to be a figment of imagination. The so-called substance is a mere conglomeration of changing qualities. There is no permanent substance behind them. The Upaniṣads affirm the reality of substance, and deny the reality of changing qualities. The Buddhists affirm the reality of changing qualities, and deny the reality of substance. The Upaniṣads provide the thesis. The Buddhists provide the antithesis. The Jainas reconcile the thesis and the antithesis in a synthesis. They affirm the reality of both substance and qualities related to each other in an organic unity. Substance is not bare identity as the Upaniṣads hold. It is not mere plurality as the Buddhists hold. It is identity-in-difference. The Jainas consider a real entity to be a permanent substance in which some new qualities are generated, some old qualities are destroyed, and some qualities persist. By virtue of the persisting qualities a substance is said to be permanent. Thus Jainism is a reconciliation of Upaniṣadic monism and Buddhist pluralism.

Jainism agrees with the Sāṁkhya in denying the existence of God, and advocating dualism of matter and spirit. The Jaina dualism of jīva and ajīva corresponds to the Sāṁkhya dualism of puruṣa and prakṛti. Both are atheistic. Both recognize the reality of infinite eternal souls. Both emphasize the ethics of ahimsā. Both are pessimistic in outlook. The Sāṁkhya dualism is more radical than the Jaina dualism. The puruṣa, according to the Sāṁkhya, can never be united with prakṛti, since they are heterogeneous in their nature. But the jīva, according to the Jaina, is united with the particles of karma-matter, and entangled in bondage. The Sāṁkhya does not advocate panpsychism. But the Jaina advocates panpsychism, and believes in earth-souls, water-souls, fire-souls, air-souls,

---

[1] Ch. Up., vi. 1.

plant-souls, animal-souls, and human souls. The puruṣa is regarded by the Sāṁkhya as the knower (jñātṛ) only, devoid of feeling and activity. but the jīva is regarded by the Jaina as the knower (jñātṛ), enjoyer (bhoktṛ), and active agent (kartṛ). It has cognition, feeling, and activity. The Sāṁkhya traces the world to eternal prakṛti from which atoms are evolved. Jainism traces the world to eternal homogeneous atoms.

Jainism agrees with the Yoga in considering a substance (dharmin) to be partly identical with, and partly different from, its changing qualities and modes (dharma), and permanent in the midst of its changing modes. It agrees with it in recognizing the reality of modifications of a substance by change of quality (dharmapariṇāma), change of mark (lakṣaṇapariṇāma), and change of state (avasthāpariṇāma).[1] It agrees with it in emphasizing the ethics of ahiṁsā and ascetic morality. But it differs from the Yoga in denying the existence of God. Jainism is atheistic, while the Yoga is theistic. The Sāṁkhya, the Yoga, Jainism, and Buddhism advocate pessimism, and hold that liberation can be attained by right knowledge. Jainism stresses the importance of right faith and right conduct also.

Jainism agrees with Buddhism in not believing in the existence of God, in rejecting the authority of the Vedas, and in emphasizing the ethics of ahimsā. But it differs from Buddhism in recognizing the eternity of the souls and the reality of permanent material substances endued with changing qualities. Buddhism regards the soul as a stream of cognitions (vijñānasantāna), and a material substance as a conglomeration of changing qualities.

Jainism agrees with the Mīmāṁsā in recognizing the reality of atoms, self-existence and eternity of the world, the reality of infinite eternal souls, and in denying the existence of God. It differs from the Mīmāṁsā in rejecting the authority of the Vedas, eternal relation between words and their meanings, the ethics of ritualism, and in advocating the ethics of ahiṁsā and rigoristic morality.

Jainism agrees with the Nyāya-Vaiśeṣika in recognizing the reality of eternal atoms, space, time, infinite eternal souls which are knowers, enjoyers, and active agents. But it differs

[1] SVM., pp. 17-18.

from it in rejecting the existence of God, and the authority of the Vedas.

The Jaina contributions to Logic are unique. Relative pluralism (anekāntavāda), the doctrine of standpoints (nayavāda), relativity of judgments (syādvāda), and sevenfold predication (saptabhaṅgīnyāya), are special contributions of the Jainas to Logic. The Jaina attitude to the world is scientific and positivistic. Jainism steers a middle course between Absolutism and radical pluralism.

The Jaina philosophy will be considered under five heads: (1) Epistemology and Logic, (2) Metaphysics, (3) Psychology, (4) Ethics, and (5) Atheism.

I. EPISTEMOLOGY AND LOGIC

3. *Valid knowledge* (*Pramāṇa*)

Māṇikya Nandi defines valid knowledge as the determinate cognition of itself and an object, which has not been known before. It has practical efficiency. It leads to the selection of good and the avoidance of evil.[1] It is a determinate cognition. It apprehends itself and an object as it really is. Its object must be novel and not known before. Valid knowledge has pragmatic utility. It is capable of prompting action which selects a good or rejects an evil. The Jaina regards valid knowledge as pramāṇa.

The Jaina definition sets aside the Buddhist idealist view that valid knowledge apprehends itself only, since there is no external object. But the Jaina contends that if the external object is non-existent, there can be no cognition. The definition sets aside the views of the Naiyāyikas, the Mīmāṁsakas, and others who hold that valid knowledge apprehends an external object only, since it cannot apprehend itself. The Jaina contends that a cognition can apprehend an object, only when it apprehends itself. Knowledge, like a lamp, illumines itself as well as an external object. The definition sets aside the Naiyāyika, the Sāṁkhya, and the Mīmāṁsaka view that indeterminate perception is valid. The Jaina does not admit

[1] PMS., i. 1, 2.

the existence and validity of indeterminate perception (nirvikalpa pratyakṣa) because it does not apprehend specific qualities (viśeṣa), and prompt successful action. The definition excludes recollection from valid knowledge, since it apprehends an object which was known before. The definition excludes illusion, doubt, and indefinite cognition from valid knowledge.[1]

Vādi Deva Sūri defines valid knowledge as determinate cognition which apprehends itself and an object, and which is capable of prompting activity which attains a desirable object or rejects an undesirable object.[2] This definition does not exclude recollection and recognition from valid knowledge. Siddhasena defines valid knowledge as cognition, which apprehends itself and an object, and which is not contradicted.[3] *Jainatarkavārtika* also defines valid knowledge as cognition, which apprehends itself and an object, which is free from contradiction, and which is the cause of attainment of good and avoidance of evil.[4] These definitions do not exclude recollection from valid knowledge. Harmony of knowledge with its object, practical efficiency, and non-contradiction are the marks of truth. Correspondence (avisaṃvādakatva), pragmatic utility (pravartakatva) or capability of leading to the attainment of the intended object (arthaprāpakatva), and uncontradictedness (abādhitatva) characterize truth.[5] Māṇikya Nandi regards novelty (anadhigatatva) also as a mark of truth.

The result of valid knowledge is cessation of ignorance, avoidance of evil, selection of good, and indifference. It is partly distinct and partly non-distinct from valid knowledge. The person who has valid knowledge removes his ignorance, avoids evil, selects good, and becomes indifferent on account of knowledge of truth.[6]

A cognition in itself is valid, since it cannot contradict itself. It is valid or invalid in relation to its object. If it is in harmony with its object, it is valid. If it is not in harmony with its object, it is invalid.[7] The validity (prāmāṇya) of knowledge consists in its agreement with its object, and the invalidity (aprāmāṇya) of knowledge consists in its disagree-

---

[1] PNT., i. 6.
[2] PNT., i. 2, 3.
[3] NA., i. 1.
[4] JTV., i. 1, 2.
[5] *Pramāṇaparīkṣā*, p. 52.
[6] PMS., v. 1-3.
[7] RK., i. 19, p. 41.

ment with its object. Both validity and invalidity of knowledge arise from extraneous circumstances, *viz.*, the proficiency (guṇa) or the deficiency (doṣa) respectively in their originating causes. But they are known by themselves in habitual cognitions, and they are known from extraneous circumstances, *viz.*, the knowledge of harmony or disharmony, and the presence or absence of contradicting experience in unhabitual cognitions.[1]

Invalid knowledge is the determinate knowledge of an object in what it does not exist.[2] Its invalidity consists in its disharmony with the real nature of its object. It is of three kinds, illusion (viparyaya), doubt (saṁśaya), and indefinite cognition (anadhyavasāya).[3] Illusion is determinate knowledge of one object as a different object. The perception 'this is silver' in a shell is an illusion.[4] The Jaina, like the Nyāya-Vaiśeṣika and the Yoga, advocates the doctrine of Anyathā-khyāti. Doubt is the knowledge of an object as either this or that in the absence of validating knowledge or contradicting knowledge, *e.g.*, 'Is this a post or a man?'[5] Indefinite knowledge (anadhyavasāya) is bare knowledge of 'something' devoid of specific qualities. It is indistinct knowledge such as tactual apprehension of something by a person walking on grass.[6] Invalidity of knowledge consists in its disagreement with the real nature of its object. Knowledge is invalid with regard to its object. It is not invalid in itself. It does not disagree with itself. Invalidity of knowledge arises from defects in the causes of knowledge. It is due to extraneous circumstances. It is known by contradicting knowledge (bādhakajñāna), if it is not habitual. But if it is habitual, its invalidity can be known by itself.[7]

Valid knowledge is of two kinds, immediate knowledge or perception (pratyakṣa) and mediate or indirect knowledge (parokṣa).[8]

4. *Perception* (*Pratyakṣa*)

Perception is distinct (spaṣṭa) knowledge.[9] Distinctness (vaiśadya) consists in the apprehension of an object with its

[1] PNT., RK., i. 20, p. 41.
[2] PNT., i. 7.
[3] PNT., i. 8.
[4] PNT., i. 9, 10.
[5] PNT., i. 11, 12.
[6] PNT., RK., i. 13, 14.
[7] RK., i. 20.
[8] PNT., ii. 1.
[9] PNT., ii. 2.

specific qualities (viśeṣa) without the mediation of any other knowledge.[1] It is independent of other pramāṇas. It apprehends an object as 'this'. It apprehends its specific qualities distinctly. Knowledge of 'thisness' and particular qualities (viśeṣaprakāśana) constitute distinctness (spaṣṭatva) of perception. It apprehends more than what is apprehended by inference and testimony. It is stronger than indirect knowledge as a kind of valid knowledge.[2]

There are two kinds of perception, empirical (sāṁvyavahārika) and transcendental (pāramārthika). Empirical perception is practical. It is uncontradicted perception which promps successful action in the form of attainment of a desired object or rejection of an undesired object. It depends on the sense-organs and other conditions. Our ordinary perception is empirical. Transcendental perception depends upon mere proximity to the self. It does not depend upon the sense-organs and other conditions. It is revelation of knowledge of all objects due to the extirpation of the karma-matter that enters into the soul. It is non-sensuous. It is independent of the sense-organs.[3] Empirical perception is either sensuous (indriyanibandhana) or non-sensuous (anindriyanibandhana).[4] Sensuous perception is due to the external sense-organs stimulated by external objects. It apprehends external objects with sensible qualities. Non-sensuous perception is mental perception. It apprehends pleasure, pain, cognition, and volition through the manas which is not a sense-organ.[5] Both sensuous perception and mental perception apprehend a part of an object distinctly.[6] They cannot apprehend an object with all its infinite qualities and relations. They distinctly apprehend an aspect of an object. Knowledge is a revelation from within the self due to the removal of the crust of karma-matter covering it. An object and light are not the cause of knowledge. A cognition reveals an object without being produced by it, even as a lamp illumines an object without being produced by it. Causal theory of knowledge is rejected. Theory of knowledge as manifestation is accepted. If the cause of knowledge were its object, then the sense-organs, which are said to be the

---

[1] PMS., ii. 4.
[2] PNT., ii. 3.
[3] PNT., RK., ii. 4; PMS., ii. 11.
[4] PNT., ii. 5.
[5] PNT., RK., ii. 5; TRD., p. 208.
[6] PMS., ii. 5.

cause of knowledge, would be objects of knowledge. But they are imperceptible. They are not known by the cognition generated by them.[1] A particular perception has a special fitness (yogyatā) to apprehend or manifest a particular object, when the crust of karma-matter covering the soul and obscuring the knowledge is attenuated or destroyed.[2] Umāsvāmi speaks of five sense-organs, organ of touch, organ of taste, organ of smell, organ of vision, and organ of hearing.[3] He divides the sense-organs into two kinds, physical sense-organs (dravyendriya) and the psychical senses (bhāvendriya).[4] The five kinds of sense-organs are the physical sense-organs. The psychical senses are the sense-faculties of the soul. They are the attainment (labdhi) of manifestation of the soul's sensibilities due to the subsidence or destruction of the karma-matter, and the attention (upayoga) of the soul to the sense-faculties.[5] Siddhasena speaks of a part of the self itself from which karma-matter subsides or is destroyed as the sense-organ. It is not anything other than the self. He does not recognize physical sense-organs. The so-called physical organs are the windows of the soul through which it perceives external objects on account of the subsidence or destruction of karma-matter covering the soul in those parts. The soul pervades the whole body even as light illumines the room which it occupies. So the soul is the proper sense-organ.[6] The presence of an external object, light, the capacity of the physical sense-organs, and the like are the external conditions of perception. But the real cause of perception is the removal of the crust of karma-matter which obscures the knowledge of the object. Knowledge is a revelation from within the self. The Jaina does not recognize the existence and validity of indeterminate perception (nirvikalpa pratyakṣa) as prior to determinate perception, since it cannot determine the nature of its object with its specific qualities, and it cannot lead to attainment of good and avoidance of evil.[7] Valid knowledge is determinate cognition (vyavasāyātmaka-jñāna) which apprehends itself and an object. Indeterminate

---

[1] PMS., ii. 6, 8, 10.

[2] PMS., ii. 9.

[3] TS., ii. 15, 19.

[4] TS., ii. 16.

[5] TS., ii. 18.

[6] Jīvapradeśa eva karmakṣayopaśamatvād indriyaṁ nānyat. . . Ātmā ca indriyam. JTV., p. 98.

[7] RK., i. 2.

perception is not determinate cognition. It neither apprehends itself nor apprehends an object definitely. So it is not valid. It is not vivid or distinct (spaşṭa) cognition. So it is not perception. The Jaina denies the existence and validity of indeterminate perception, while the Buddhist denies the validity and perceptual character of the so-called determinate perception. Determinate perception is indeterminate perception of individual things-in-themselves (svalakşaṇa) and imagination of categories (kalpanā). Imagination deprives it of its perceptual character and makes it invalid.

Sense-perception has four stages, avagraha, īhā, avāya, and dhāraṇā, (1) Avagraha is the first impression of an object endued with inferior generic characters arising from the formless cognition of mere beinghood just after the intercourse of a sense-organ with an object. The object is a substance endued with qualities and modes. The eyes, the ears, and the like are the physical sense-organs. They are rightly stimulated by the objects which exist in a proper place. The stimulation of the peripheral organs by the objects generates a formless cognition which apprehends mere beinghood. It gives rise to the first impression of the object endued with the generic characters inferior to mere beinghood, *e.g.*, the generic character of man, and the like. For example, an object is perceived as a man, and not as mere being. All perception is determinate. There is no indeterminate perception.[1] Avagraha is of two kinds, vyañjanāvagraha and arthāvagraha. Vyañjanāvagraha is the implicit (avyakta) apprehension of an object with its sensory qualities. There can be no apprehension of mere sensory qualities, since the incorporeal (amūrta) sensory qualities, colour, smell, taste, and the like, cannot have intercourse (sannikarşa) with the sense-organs. Arthāvagraha is the explicit (vyakta) apprehension of an object with its sensory qualities. Implicit apprehension is prior to explicit apprehension which gives rise to īhā.[2] (2) Īhā is the enquiry to know the particular features (viśeṣa) of the object apprehended by the first impression (avagraha). For example, is the man perceived as an inhabitant of Karnāṭa, Lāṭa, or any other region? (3) Avāya is the right determination of the particular features (viśeṣa nirṇaya) of the

[1] PNT., ii. 8; TRD., p. 208. [2] SS., i. 17, 18.

object, which the self desires to know. For example, the man perceived is definitely known to be an inhabitant of Karṇāṭa. (4) Dhāraṇā is the firm retention of the perception of the object, which is the cause of its recollection in future. Retention (dhāraṇā) is the cause of recollection (smṛti). Perception produces a disposition (saṃskāra), a particular power of the self (ātmaśaktiviśeṣa), which generates its recollection in future.[1] An object perceived in the sky as white is avagraha. Is the white object a row of herons or a flag? The desire to know it is īhā. The white object is definitely known to be a row of herons through its particular features such as flying upward and downward and movements of the wings. This is avāya. The firm retention of the perception is dhāraṇā. It is the cause of the recollection: 'This is that row of herons which I perceived in the morning'. This is the order of the different stages of perception.[2]

Transcendental (mukhya, pāramārthika) perception depends upon the self alone. It is independent of the sense-organs and the manas. The self directly perceives objects on account of the subsidence or destruction of the karma-matter covering it and obscuring knowledge, independently of the sense-organs and other conditions. It is either incomplete (vikala) or complete (sakala). Incomplete transcendental perception is of two kinds, avadhi and manaḥparyāya. (1) Avadhi is the perception of sensible objects independent of the sense-organs and the manas due to the subsidence or destruction of the crust of karma-matter obscuring avadhijñāna. It is caused by right intuition, right faith, and right conduct. It is clairvoyance, clairaudience, and the like. It is intuitive perception of remote sensible objects. (2) Manaḥparyāyajñāna is telepathic knowledge of the processes of other minds. It is direct or immediate knowledge (sākṣātkārijñāna). It is caused by the destruction of a particular kind of karma-matter obscuring the knowledge, which is due to the purity of restraint or right conduct. It is thought-reading. (3) Complete (sakala) transcendental perception is the omniscient's immediate knowledge (kevalajnāna) of all substances and their modes in their infinite aspects. It arises from the annihilation of the entire crust of karma-matter due

---

[1] PNT., RK., ii. 8-10; TRD., p. 208; *Pramāṇaparīkṣā*, p. 68.
[2] SS., i. 15.

to right intuition, right faith, and right conduct reaching the acme of perfection.[1]

5. *Mediate knowledge* (*Parokṣa*)

Mediate knowledge is indistinct (aspaṣṭa). It is devoid of perceptual vividness. It is of five kinds, recollection (smṛti), recognition (pratyabhijñāna), induction (tarka), deduction (anumāna), and testimony (āgama).[2]

(1) Recollection (smaraṇa) is the knowledge of an object perceived in the past as 'that' due to revival of its disposition (saṃskāra), which is a particular power of the self. It is revived and produces its effect in the form of recollection. Recollection is the effect of the revival of the disposition of the previous perception of an object. It remembers either conscious beings or unconscious things. Not only previous perception produces recollection. But even previous recollection, recognition, induction, deduction, and testimony may leave behind dispositions in the soul, which produce recollections. Some hold that recollection is not valid knowledge (pramāṇa), since it depends upon previous perception, and knows an object known already by it. Inference depends upon induction for its production. But it does not depend upon any other kind of knowledge in knowing its object. But recollection knows its object with the help of the past knowledge revived. So it is not valid knowledge. But the Jaina urges that recollection depends upon previous perception for its production. It arises from its disposition in the self. But it does not depend upon previous perception in knowing its object. Valid knowledge determines the nature of an object as it really is. Recollection, like serial perception (dhārāvāhikapratyakṣa), determines the real nature of an object perceived in the past. So it is valid knowledge (pramāṇa).[3]

(2) Recognition (pratyabhijñāna) is the composite cognition (saṁkalanātmakajñāna) produced by perception and recollection. It apprehends an object in the forms: 'this is that', 'this is like that', 'this is different from that', 'this is correlated

---

[1] PNT., RK., ii. 18-23; PMS., ii. 12
[2] PNT., iii. 1, 2.
[3] PNT., RK., iii. 3, 4; PMS., iii. 3, 4.

to that', and the like. 'This is that Devadatta'. 'A wild cow is like a cow'. 'A buffalo is different from a cow'. 'This is remote from that'. 'This is called a tree'. 'This individual is a cow'. These are recognition. Recognition apprehends identity, similarity, difference, correlation, relation of sign and signate, and the like. It apprehends the generic property (sāmānya) in the form of similar collocation of parts (sadṛśa-pariṇama) in different animate individuals, or a common substance in inanimate things.[1]

Recognition is a distinct kind of valid knowledge. It knows a present perceived object as known in the past, *e.g.*, 'this is that Devadatta'. Perception knows 'this'. Recollection knows 'that'. But recognition knows 'this is that'. It knows an object as it really is. It is in harmony with its real nature. It knows an object which is not known by any other kind of valid knowledge. It knows relations, identity, similarity, dissimilarity, relation of sign and signate, correlation, and the like, between a present perceived object and an object perceived in the past and remembered now. 'Thisness' cannot be known by recollection. 'Thatness' cannot be known by perception. The objects such as 'this is that', 'this is similar to that', 'this is dissimilar to that', and the like are known by recognition which is a distinct kind of valid knowledge. It is in harmony with its object. It is not contradicted by any other kind of valid knowledge. It is not perception, since it is not direct and immediate knowledge, and it is devoid of perceptual vividness. It is a distinct kind of valid knowledge.[2] Comparison (upamāna) is included in recognition. It is not treated as a distinct kind of valid knowledge.

(3) Induction (tarka) is a knowledge of the invariable concomitance (vyāpti) of the middle term with the major term in the past, the present, and the future, arising from the observation of their co-presence and co-absence in the form 'If this is present, that is present, and if this is absent, that is absent'. It is also called ūha. Vyāpti is of two kinds, anvayavyāpti and vyatirekavyāpti. Smoke arises only if there is fire. Wherever there is smoke, there is fire. This is anvaya-vyāpti. Smoke does not arise, if there is no fire. Wherever

---

[1] PMS., iii. 5, 6, PNT., iii. 5, 6. [2] PKM., pp. 97-98.

there is no fire, there is no smoke. This is vyatirekavyāpti.[1] Vyāpti is universal accompaniment (avinābhāva) of the middle term by the major term in simultaneity or succession. Simultaneity is the relation between the middle term and the major term which co-exist with each other. Succession is the relation between the cause and the effect. The genus of a Śiṃśapā tree and the genus of a tree co-exist with each other. The former is pervaded by the latter. The former is the middle term. The latter is the major term. Fire is the cause of smoke. Smoke is the middle term. Fire is the major term. The universal attendance of the middle term by the major term is determined by induction (tarka).[2]

(4) Deduction or inference (anumāna) is the knowledge of the major term derived from the knowledge of the middle term. Fire is inferred from smoke.[3] 'Smoke' is the middle term. 'Fire' is the major term. Inference is based on universal accompaniment of the middle term by the major term in simultaneity or succession. It is based on vyāpti derived from induction (tarka). There are three terms in an inference, the middle term (sādhana, hetu), the major term (sādhya) and the minor term (pakṣa). The middle term is that which is definitely known to be inseparably connected with the major term.[4] If the major term (*e.g.*, fire) does not exist, the middle term (*e.g.*, smoke) cannot exist. If the former exists, the latter exists. This is the only mark of the middle term. The Jainas do not recognize the five marks of the middle term recognized by the Naiyāyika, *viz.*, presence in the minor term (pakṣadharmatva), presence in all positive instances (sapakṣasattva) in which the major term exists, absence in all negative instances (vipakṣāsattva) in which the major term does not exist, non-incompatibility with the minor term (abādhitaviṣayatva), and absence of counteracting reasons leading to a contradictory conclusion (asatpratipakṣatva), since they may lead to fallacies (hetvābhāsa).[5] The major term (sādhya) is the inferable object not contradicted, and not certainly known.[6] It is the object of inference. It is not contradicted by any other kind of valid

[1] PNT., RK., iii. 7, 8; PMS., ii. 7-8; TRD., pp. 209-10.
[2] PMS., iii. 12-14.
[3] PMS., iii. 9.
[4] PMS., iii. 10.
[5] PNT., RK., iii. 11-13.
[6] PMS., iii. 15; PNT., iiii. 14.

knowledge. Nor is it definitely known. The minor term is that in which the middle term exists, and whose connection with the major term is to be proved. It is not excluded from perception. It is absolutely necessary to state the minor term in an inference.[1] In the inference 'the hill is smoky, therefore, the hill is fiery' 'the hill' is the minor term. The middle term 'smoke' exists in it, and the existence of the major term 'fire' in it is to be proved.

There are two kinds of inference, inference for oneself (svārtha) and inference for others (parārtha).[2] In inference for oneself a person perceives the reason (hetu) or middle term (sādhana), remembers the inseparable connection between the reason (hetu) and the inferable object or the major term (sādhya) determined by induction (tarka), and at once knows the major term.[3] Inference for others consists in the statement of the middle term, the major term, and the minor term. It consists of two propositions. (1) 'The hill is fiery ; (2) because it is smoky'. The example (dṛṣṭānta) is not present here.[4] This is intended for intelligent persons. For less intelligent persons the inference includes the example (dṛṣṭānta) and consists of three propositions: (1) 'The hill is *fiery* (major term) ; (2) because it is *smoky* (middle term) ; (3) whatever is smoky is fiery, as the *kitchen* (example)'.[5] The example is the object in which the middle term is perceived to be accompanied by the major term. There are two kinds of examples, affirmative and negative. The affirmative example (anvaya dṛṣṭānta) shows that the middle term is pervaded by the major term, *e.g.*, 'wherever there is smoke, there is fire, as in the kitchen'. The negative example (vyatirekadṛṣṭānta) shows that the absence of the major term is followed by the absence of the middle term, *e.g.*, 'wherever there is no fire, there is no smoke, as in a lake.[6] The affirmative example shows the inseparable connection between the middle term and the major term by homogeneousness (sādharmya) : (1) 'The hill is fiery ; (2) because it is smoky ; (3) whatever is smoky is fiery, as the kitchen'. Here 'smoke' and 'fire' abide homogeneously in the kitchen. The negative example shows the inseparable connec-

---

[1] NA., i. 13, 14.
[2] PMS., iii. 47, 48; PNT., iii. 9.
[3] PNT., RK., iii. 10.
[4] PNT., iii. 23, 28.
[5] PNT., iii. 42.
[6] PNT., iii. 43-47.

tion between the middle term and the major term by contrariety (vaidharmya): (1) 'The hill is not smoky; (2) because it is not fiery; (3) whatever is not fiery is not smoky, as a lake'.[1] Here the absence of 'fire' and the absence of 'smoke' abide in the lake. The example (dṛṣṭānta), the application (upanaya), and the conclusion (nigamana) are necessary to convince persons of dull intellect of the truth of an inference. The application is reassertion of the presence of the middle term in the minor term in which the presence of the major term is to be proved. The conclusion is reassertion of the presence of the major term in the minor term.[2] Inference for dull persons consists of five propositions: (1) 'The hill is fiery (pakṣavacana); (2) because the hill is smoky (hetuvacana); (3) whatever is smoky is fiery, as the kitchen (dṛṣṭānta); (4) the hill is smoky (upanaya); (5) therefore, the hill is fiery (nigamana)'.[3] The Naiyāyika holds that these five members are indispensably necessary for a demonstrative syllogism to convince others. The Sāṁkhya and the Mīmāṁsā hold that the conclusion, the reason (hetu), and the example (dṛṣṭānta) are the three members of a syllogism.[4]

Some Jaina logicians, like the Buddhists, prefer internal universal concomitance (antarvyāpti) to external universal concomitance (bahirvyāpti). Internal universal concomitance (antarvyāpti) occurs when the minor term (pakṣa) itself as the common abode of the middle term (hetu) and the major term (sādhya) reassures the inseparable connection between them, thus: (1) 'The hill (minor term) is fiery (major term); (2) because the hill is smoky (middle term).' Here the minor term (*e.g.*, the hill) shows the inseparable connection between the middle term (*e.g.*, smoke) and the major term (*e.g.*, fire), which is their common abode. External universal concomitance (bahirvyāpti) occurs when an example (dṛṣṭānta), which is not an essential part of the inference, is introduced from outside as the common abode of the middle term and the major term to reassure the inseparable connection between them, thus: (1) 'The hill is fiery (major term); (2) because it is smoky (middle term); (3) just as a kitchen (example)'.

---

[1] PNT., iii. 45-48; NA., 18, 19.
[2] PNT., iii. 49, 51.
[3] PNT., iii. 53.
[4] RK., iii. 28.

Here the example (*e.g.*, the kitchen) is introduced from outside as the common abode of the middle term (*e.g.*, smoke) and the major term (*e.g.*, fire) to reassure the inseparable connection between them. Some Jaina logicians hold that the internal universal concomitance (antarvyāpti) alone is sufficient to establish the major term, so that the external universal concomitance (bahirvyāpti) is superfluous. When the internal universal concomitance exists, the external universal concomitance is superfluous. When the former does not exist, the latter is useless.[1]

The best form of an inference for the dullest persons consists of ten members (daśāvayava) : (1) proposition (pratijñā), *e.g.*, 'non-injury to life is the greatest virtue' ; (2) the limitation of the proposition (pratijñāvibhakti), *e.g.*, 'non-injury to life is the greatest virtue, according to the Jaina Tīrthaṅkaras'; (3) the reason (hetu), *e.g.*, 'non-injury to life is the greatest virtue, because those who observe the vow of non-injury to life are loved by the gods, and it is an act of merit to honour them' ; (4) the limitation of reason (hetuvibhakti), *e.g.*, 'only those who observe the vow of non-injury to life reside in the highest place of virtue' ; (5) the counter-proposition (vipakṣa), *e.g.*, 'but those (Brahmins) who kill animals in sacrifices are loved by the gods and reside in heaven' ; (6) the opposition to the counter-proposition (vipakṣapratiṣedha), *e.g.*, 'those who kill animals in sacrifices are not loved by the gods and do not reside in heaven because they violate the instructions of the Tīrthaṅkaras who speak absolute truth' ; (7) the example (dṛṣṭānta), *e.g.*, 'the Arhats do not cook food to avoid killing insects, but beg food of the householders' ; (8) doubting the validity of the example (āśaṅkā), *e.g.*, 'but the Arhats share the householders' sins for killing insects in cooking food for them' ; (9) removing the doubt (āśaṅkāpratiṣedha), *e.g.*, 'the Arhats do not share the householders' sins because they go to their houses unexpectedly, and beg food of them, which was not intentionally cooked for them' ; (10) the conclusion (nigamana), *e.g.*, 'non-injury to life is the greatest virtue'. Bhadrabāhu was an exponent of the ten-membered syllogism.[2] Vātsyāyana criticized the ten-membered syllogism in his com-

[1] NA., E.T., 20, pp. 18-19. [2] HIL., pp 165-67; RK., iii. 42.

mentary on the *Nyāyaśūtra*[1] and established the five-membered syllogism.

(5) Testimony (āgama) is the knowledge of objects derived from the words of reliable persons. Words manifest their objects by their natural denotative power and convention. For example, the north pole exists.[2] A reliable person (āpta) is one who knows objects as they really are, and expresses his ideas correctly. He is free from attachment and aversion. His words are in harmony with their objects. They do not contradict the nature of their objects.[3] Testimony is of two kinds, secular (laukika) and non-secular (lokottara). Testimony of Janaka and others is secular. Testimony of Tīrthaṅkaras is non-secular. The Jainas do not believe in the authority of the Vedas. They recognize the authority of the Tīrthaṅkaras only who attained perfection and became omniscient. Testimony is a proposition (vacana) composed of a sentence, words and letters. Audible letters are made of atoms of sounds. A word is a collection of interdependent letters. It is independent of letters in other words. A sentence is a collection of interdependent words. A word denotes an object by virtue of its natural denotative power and convention. Just as a lamp illumines an object, so a word manifests an object by its natural power. But it differs from a lamp in that it depends upon convention to produce knowledge of an object. But its truth or falsehood depends upon excellence (guṇa) or imperfection (doṣa) of the speaker.[4]

Umāsvāmi divides knowledge into five kinds: (1) sense-knowledge (mati), (2) testimony (śrūti), (3) clairvoyance (avadhi), (4) thought-reading (manaḥparyaya), and (5) omniscience (kevalajñāna).[5] Sense-knowledge (mati) and testimony (śrūti) are mediate knowledge (parokṣa). Sensitive knowledge is acquired through the medium of external sense-organs. Testimony is acquired through the medium of the scriptures. So both are indirect or mediate knowledge, since they depend upon external conditions. Clairvoyance (avadhi), thought-reading (manaḥparyaya), and omniscience (kevalajñāna) are immediate knowledge or perception (pratyakṣa).[6] They are

[1] NS., i. 32.
[2] PMS., iii. 94-96; PNT., iv. 1.
[3] PNT., iv. 4, 5.
[4] PNT., RK., iv. 6-12.
[5] TS., i. 9.
[6] TS., i. 11, 12.

direct knowledge of the soul without any external help. Of these the first two are incomplete direct knowledge due to subsidence and partial destruction of knowledge-obscuring karmas, and the last one is complete direct knowledge due to total destruction of the knowledge-obscuring karmas.

6. *Anekāntavāda*

The Jainas hold that a real thing is endued with an infinite number of qualities and modes (anantadharmaka). It is comprehended by valid knowledge.[1] It has infinite modes in the past, the present, and the future. They are co-existent or successive. The co-existent modes are qualities. The successive modes are modifications. All objects of knowledge are manifold or multiform (anekānta). They have infinite qualities and relations which distinguish them from the other objects. For example, a gold jar exists as a specific substance with its specific qualities in a particular place at a particular time. It does not exist as other substances in other places at other times. When its generic qualities such as beinghood, knowability, comprehensibility, and the like are considered, it is not distinguished from the other homogeneous and heterogeneous subtances. When it is considered as a substance (dravya), it exists as an aggregate of atoms ; it does not exist as a substance in the sense of space (ākāśa), the principle of motion (dharma), the principle of rest (adharma), and the other substances. Thus, it exists as a substance in one sense only, and it does not exist as a substance in the other senses. It exists as a substance in the sense that it is an aggregate of atoms, not in the sense that it is a soul, dharma, adharma, space and time. There are infinite souls (jīva). There are infinite non-souls (ajīva). So the qualities of the other substances are infinite. They do not exist in the gold jar. It exists as a collection of earth atoms. It does not exist as a collection of water atoms, fire atoms, and air atoms. It exists as a collection of earth atoms in the sense that it is made of a metal which is a modification of earth ; it does not exist as a lump of clay, and the like. It exists as a collection of gold atoms, and not of silver

---

[1] *Saḍdarśanasamuccaya,* 55.

atoms or atoms of other kinds of metal. It exists as a collection of gold atoms in the sense that it is made of melted and pure gold, and not impure gold. It exists as made of melted and pure gold moulded by Devadatta, and not by Yajñadatta. It exists as made of melted and pure gold moulded by Devadatta into the shape of a jar, and not of a jug, a pitcher, and the like. It exists as moulded into the shape of this jar, and not any other jar. As a substance its own qualities are not many. But the qualities of the other substances are infinite. It is distinguished from them by their infinite qualities. It exists in its own place. It exists in the middle part of the world. It exists neither in the upper world nor in the lower world. In the middle world it exists in India, and not in other countries. It exists at Pataliputra, and not in other towns. It exists in the house of Devadatta, and not in others' houses. It exists in one part of his house, and not in its other parts. Its own qualities in its own place are not many. But the qualities of the things in other places are infinite. It is distinguished from them by their infinite qualities. It exists in its own time. It exists in the present cycle, and not in the past and future cycles. In the present cycle it exists in the present year, and not in the past years. It exists in the spring season, and not in the other seasons. In the present spring season it exists to-day, and not in the other days. To-day it exists in the present moment, and not in other moments. One thing has infinite qualities in time, since it exists in innumerable moments. The qualities of the other things in time are infinite. The gold jar is distinguished from them by infinite qualities. In its essential qualities it exists as endued with yellow colour, and not as blue colour. It exists as endued with a particular degree of yellow colour. It exists as endued with a particular taste in a particular degree. It exists as endued with a particular smell in a particular degree. It exists as endued with roughness or smoothness, heat or cold, lightness or heaviness, in particular degrees. In number it exists as the first, the second, the third, and the like from near and remote substances. In magnitude it exists either as minute or large, short or long, and the like in relation to the other substances. It can be distinguished from other substances by infinite magnitudes. In spatial position it exists as near, nearer, nearest, remote, remoter, remotest, and the like in relation to other substances. In temporal order it exists as prior or posterior, near or remote by moments, hours, and the like in relation to other substances. It exists as comprehended by perception or inference by an infinite number of souls. The comprehended object must differ according as its comprehending modes of knowledge differ. So the gold jar must be endued with infinite natures according as it is comprehended by infinite cognitions of infinite souls. It produces pleasure, pain, acceptance, avoidance, indifference, desire, merit, demerit, bondage of karma, disposition, anger, pride, delusion, greed, attachment, aversion, and the like in countless souls. It exists as endued with upward movement, downward movement, contraction, expansion, locomotion, flow, evacuation, filling, holding water, and the like at different times in different degrees. It exists as endued with innumerable qualities which differentiate it from the other similar substances. It exists as endued with innumerable qualities which differentiate it from the other dissimilar substances. It exists in infinite relations to the other substances in infinite time. Thus all things possess infinite qualities and infinite relations.[1] Hence one who comprehends one thing completely comprehends all things completely, and one who comprehends all things completely comprehends one thing completely.[2] The world is a system of inter-related objects possessing infinite qualities and infinite relations. This is the Jaina doctrine of relative pluralism (anekāntavāda). It naturally leads to the doctrine of nayas which are the different standpoints from which things are considered as possessing particular qualities and relations.

7. *The Doctrine of Nayas*

This doctrine is a peculiar feature of the Jaina epistemology. Pramāṇa and naya are the different ways of knowing the reality. They enrich our knowledge of real things. Pramāṇa is the valid knowledge of the multiform (anekānta) object. It is comprehension of an object endued with many qualities (anekāntapratipatti). Naya is the valid know-

---

[1] TRD., pp. 212-18.
[2] *Ibid.*, pp. 222-23.

ledge of one part, aspect, quality, or mode of a multiform object (ekadharmapratipatti).[1] Naya is a part of pramāṇa. It is partial valid knowledge. It is not complete valid knowledge.[2] A naya apprehends a part or aspect of a real thing comprehended by valid knowledge. It ignores the other parts or aspects of the thing. It is the standpoint of the knowing person embodying a particular purpose (saṁkalpa) to understand a particular aspect of a thing to the exclusion of other aspects.[3] He becomes indifferent to the other aspects of the thing for the time being. Nayas are the points of view from which things are considered. They are partial views of reality. They are inadequate to the whole reality. They do not consider things as they are in themselves. They consider them in their relations. They give relative truths. They do not give absolute truth. When the partial views (ekāntapratipatti) are taken as the complete view (anekāntapratipatti), they become invalid. When nayas or relative truths are mistaken for absolute truths, they become nayābhāsas. They are invalid because they deny the truth of the other aspects of things not relevant to the knower's purpose. They are false standpoints.[4]

Nayas are mainly of two kinds, dravyanaya and paryāyanaya. Dravyanaya considers a thing as a substance (dravya) in which qualities and modes are unified. It emphasizes the substantial aspect of a thing, and ignores its qualitative and modal-aspects. Paryāyanaya considers a thing as a conglomeration of qualities and modes, and ignores its substantial aspect.[5] Dravyanayas are of three kinds, naigamanaya, saṁgrahanaya, and vyavahāranaya.[6] They are also called arthanayas. They refer to objects or meanings (artha). Paryāyanayas are of four kinds, ṛjusūtra. śabda, samabhirūḍha, and evambhūta.[7] They are also called śabdanayas. They refer to words (śabda).

(1) Naigamanaya is interpreted in two ways. First, Pūjyapāda takes it as the standpoint which emphasizes the purpose (saṁkalpa) of a series of actions, which is not yet completely accomplished. A person going with an axe, being asked for what purpose he is going, answers, "I am going to bring a prastha,

---

[1] AMV., 106.
[2] SS., i. 33.
[3] PNT., vii. 1.
[4] PNT., vii. 2.
[5] PNT., vii. 5; SVM., p. 203; SS., TSV., i. 33.
[6] PNT., vii. 6.
[7] PNT., vii. 27.

a wooden measure'. He is going to cut a bamboo and make a prastha out of it. The measure is the purpose to be realized in the action. A person collecting fuel and water, being asked what he is doing, answers, 'I am cooking rice'. It refers to the purpose of a series of actions not yet completely accomplished.[1] Secondly, Candraprabha Sūri interprets naigamanaya in another manner. It is the common-sense point of view which considers things as possessing both generic (sāmānya) and specific qualities (viśeṣa) which are not distinguished from each other.[2] Hemacandra Sūri also is of the same view.[3] The Advaita Vedānta denies the specific qualities (viśeṣa). Buddhism denies the generic qualities (sāmānya). The Jaina holds that a thing is an organic unity of both generic and specific qualities, which are equally real. The universal (sāmānya) is not real apart from the particular (viśeṣa). The particular is not real apart from the universal. They are abstractions apart from each other. A real thing cannot exist apart from either. This is the concrete view of the Jaina. The naigamanaya is the standpoint of the Nyāya and the Vaiśeṣika systems according to the Jaina. They hold that a thing is the complex of the universal and the particular, which are equally real and primary and different from each other. So far they agree with the Jaina. But they consider the distinction between the universal and the particular to be absolute, while the Jaina considers it to be relative. They consider them to be absolutely different from each other, while the Jaina considers them to be partially different (kathañcidbhinna) from each other. The naigamanaya becomes naigamābhāsa at the hands of the Naiyāyikas and the Vaiśeṣikas.[4]

(2) Saṁgrahanaya is the class point of view. It refers to mere generality (sāmānyamātra) devoid of all specific qualities (viśeṣa). It considers things from the general point of view, ignores the special features, and treats them as mere 'being'. The saṁgrahanaya is of two kinds, parasaṁgraha and aparasaṁgraha. Parasaṁgraha is the highest class view. All individual things in the world may be considered from the most general point of view as mere 'being' irrespective of their parti-

---

[1] SS., i. 33; TRV., i. 5, 33; PKM., p. 204.
[2] NAV., 29, p. 47.
[3] SVM., VRS., p. 202.
[4] PI., pp. liv-lv.

cular features.[1] The Advaita Vedānta considers the world as mere one 'being', and denies the plurality of things. Its standpoint, according to the Jaina, is parasaṁgrahanayābhāsa.[2] Aparasaṁgrahanaya is the inferior class view. It refers to the inferior classes as distinct from the highest class 'Being'. This standpoint considers dharma, adharma, space, time, soul, and non-soul as identical with one another, since they have substantiality.[3] It considers all earth vessels as earth irrespective of their particular features. This is the inferior class view.[4] When the intermediate generalities alone are regarded as real, and the individuals are regarded as unreal, the standpoint becomes aparasaṁgrahanayābhāsa.[5] The Saṁkhya commits this error, since it considers all material things, the living bodies, the sense-organs, manas, buddhi, and ahaṁkāra as modes of prakṛti irrespective of their essential differences.

(3) Vyavahāranaya is the practical point of view based on sense-perception. We generally perceive particular things, and react upon them. We do not react upon classes, but upon individuals. When things are considered as individuals, they become practically useful. Individual things are objects of practical use. Vyavahāranaya is the practical standpoint which considers the particular individuals alone, without taking cognizance of their generic qualities (sāmānya) and specific qualities (viśeṣa).[6] When distinctions of real things are denied, and those of imaginary things are recognized, the standpoint is called vyavahāranayābhāsa. The Cārvākas recognize the reality of the elements of earth, water, fire, and air which are objects of practical use, and reject the reality of the soul. Materialism is vyavahāranayābhāsa.[7]

(4) Ṛjusūtranaya is the standpoint which considers only the present momentary modes of a thing apart from the permanent substance. It does not consider the past modes which have vanished, and the future modes which have not yet come into existence. For example, 'pleasure exists at the present moment.' The transient mode of pleasure at the present

---

[1] PNT., vii. 15, 16; SVM., VRS., p. 202.
[2] PNT., vii. 17, 18.
[3] PNT., vii. 19, 20.
[4] SS., i. 33.
[5] PNT., vii. 21.
[6] SVM., VRS., p. 202.
[7] PNT., vii. 25, 26.

moment is considered, and its substrate, the soul, is ignored. Ṛjusūtranaya is literally the straight standpoint which considers a thing at the present moment without any reference to the past and the future. It is the extreme opposite of saṃgrahanaya. The former denies all continuity and identity. The latter denies all changes and differences. Ṛjusūtra considers the modes of a thing at the present moment only. It is narrower than vyavahāranaya which considers individual things with a certain duration.[1] When only the transitory modes of the present mode are considered to be real, and the substance in which they abide is denied, the standpoint becomes ṛjusūtranayābhāsa. The Buddhist standpoint, according to the Jaina, is ṛjusūtranayābhāsa, since it considers the transitory modes of the present moment to be real, and denies the reality of the substance, which is their abode, which exists in the past, present, and future, and which is apprehended by recognition.[2] The remaining three are śabdanayas.

(5) Śabdanaya is the standpoint which refers to words and their meanings. A word implies a particular object, an attribute, a relation, or an action. Each word has its own meaning. Different words also may refer to the same object. The relation between words and their meanings is relative. It is not absolute. Words differing in gender, number, person, case, and the like may refer to the same object. *Puṣya* (masculine), *Tārā* (feminine), and *Nakṣatra* (neuter) mean the same object,—star.[3] *Dārāḥ* (plural) and *Kalatra* (singular) mean the same object,—wife. 'The potter makes a pot? 'A pot is made by the potter'. The word 'pot' is used in the objective case in the first sentence, and in the nominative case in the second sentence. But they refer to the same object. 'The north pole was (babhūva), is (bhavati), and will be (bhaviṣyati)'. Here śabdanaya considers the differences in the north pole corresponding to the verbs in the past, the present, and the future tenses, and ignores its identity in the past, the present, and the future.[4] When we consider the relation of words to their meanings to be absolute, we commit an error. The Gramma-

[1] PI., p. lviii.
[2] PNT., vii. 28-31; SS., i. 33; SVM., VRS., p. 202; PKM., p. 205.
[3] SS., i. 33.
[4] PNT., vii. 33.

rians commit śabdanayābhāsa, since they consider the relation of words to their meanings to be absolute.[1]

(6) Samabhirūḍhanaya refers to the different meanings of words according to their roots. *Indra* literally means 'all prosperous'. *Śakra* literally means 'all powerful'. *Purandara* literally means 'destroyer of the enemies.' Samabhirūḍhanaya emphasizes the literal meanings of the words, and ignores their identical derivative meaning. The three words have the same derivative or conventional meaning. They refer to the king of gods in heaven.[2] Samabhirūḍhanaya is a special application of śabdanaya. It distinguishes the synonyms from one another, and applies each word appropriately to a specific object according to its etymological meaning. If it ignores the identity of the derivative meaning of the synonyms, it becomes samabhirūḍhanayābhāsa. The Grammarians commit this error.[3]

(7) Evambhūtanaya is a special application of samabhirūḍhanaya. It restricts a word to one particular meaning which emphasizes one particular aspect of an object suggested by its root. The word *'gau'* literally means a moving animal. A moving cow is a *gau*. When it is at rest, it should not be called a *'gau'*. It should be designated by a different word. This is the standpoint of evambhūtanaya. It uses a word in its strict etymological sense, and applies it to an object possessing practical efficiency at the present moment. It applies the word *Śakra* to a man who is actually strong, implied by the word.[4] If we ignore the nature of the object which is not strictly implied by the etymological meaning of the word, we commit an error. The Grammarians, according to the Jaina, commit evambhūtanayābhāsa.[5]

According to the Jainas, the Nyāya and the Vaiśeṣika adopt naigamanaya ; the Advaita Vedānta and the Sāṁkhya adopt saṁgrahanaya ; the Cārvākas adopt vyavahāranaya ; the Buddhists adopt ṛjusūtranaya ; the Grammarians adopt śabdanaya, samabhirūḍhanaya, and evambhūtanaya.[6]

---

[1] NAV., 29, p. 47; PNT., vii. 34.
[2] PNT., vii. 36, 37; PKM., p. 205; SVM., VRS., p. 202; SS., i. 33.
[3] PNT., vii. 38.
[4] SS., i. 33; SVM., VRS., p. 202; PNT., vii. 40, 41; PKM., p. 206.
[5] PNT., vii. 42, 43.
[6] SVM., VRS., p. 203; NAV., 29, p. 47.

Each preceding naya has a greater extent than the succeeding one. Naigamanaya has the greatest extent. Evambhūtanaya has the least extent.[1] Naigamanaya deals with real (bhāva) and unreal things (abhāva). So it is of greater extent than saṁgrahanaya which deals with real things only. It deals with the 'being' of all real things. So it is of greater extent than vyavahāranaya which deals with a part of the real, *e.g.*, individual things. It deals with individual things existing in the past, the present, and the future. So it is of greater extent than ṛjusūtranaya which deals with the present modes only of individual things. It deals with their present modes. So it is of greater extent than śabdanaya which deals with words conveying different meanings in different tenses. Śabdanaya dealing with the expression of the real is of greater extent than samabhirūḍhanaya which deals with only one particular expression. It is of greater extent than evambhūtanaya which deals with that particular expression which applies to the thing in its present activity.[2]

A substance has infinite powers. It can be known from various points of view.[3] The nayas are partial views. They are not adequate to the complete reality. They give relative truths. They do not give absolute truths. All predications are relative. All affirmations and negations are relative to time, place, and circumstances. They are not unconditional and absolute. So the doctrine of nayas is related to Anekāntavāda and Syādvāda.

8. *Syādvāda: Saptabhaṅgīnyāya*

Absolute judgments are possible in Ekānta or one-sided systems. But they are not possible in the Anekānta philosophy of the Jaina. All objects are multiform (anekānta) according to him. From their many-sided nature it follows that all judgments are relative. They are true under certain conditions. They are conditional or hypothetical. No judgments are absolutely true. The word 'perhaps' should be added to all judgments to indicate their

---

[1] SS., i. 33.
[2] SVM., VRS., p. 205; TS., E.T., p. 47.
[3] SS., i. 33.

conditional character. This is Syādvāda or the doctrine of relativity of judgments. There are seven different ways of making judgments about a substance or an attribute as follows: (1) 'Perhaps S is (syāt asti)'; (2) 'Perhaps S is not (syāt nāsti)'; (3) 'Perhaps S is, is not (syāt asti nāsti)'; (4) 'Perhaps S is indescribable (syāt avaktavyam)'; (5) 'Perhaps S is and indescribable (syāt asti avaktavyam)'; (6) 'Perhaps S is not and indescribable (syāt nāsti avaktavyam)'; (7) 'Perhaps S is, is not, and indescribable (syāt asti nāsti avaktavyam)'. The first is an affirmative judgment (vidhi). The second is a negative judgment (niṣedha). The third is an affirmative judgment and a negative judgment in succession. The fourth is simultaneous affirmative judgment and negative judgment. The fifth is an affirmative judgment combined with simultaneous affirmative judgment and negative judgment. The sixth is a negative judgment combined with simultaneous affirmative judgment and negative judgment. The seventh is successive affirmative judgment and negative judgment combined with simultaneous affirmative and negative judgment.[1]

1. 'Perhaps S is'. From the point of view of its own substance, place, time, and nature, a thing exists. The jar exists as an earthen substance possessing dark colour in winter at Pataliputra.

2. 'Perhaps S is not'. From the point of view of substance, place, time, and nature, a thing does not exist as other things. The jar does not exist as a watery substance possessing red colour in spring at Kanyakubja.

3. 'Perhaps S is and is not.' The jar exists as its own substance in its own place at a particular time with its own nature. It does not exist as another substance in another place at another time with another quality.

4. 'Perhaps S is indescribable' The presence of its own nature and the absence of its contradictory nature both are in a thing together. But it cannot be expressed. But it cannot be absolutely indescribable. What is absolutely indescribable like Māyā of the Advaita Vedānta is unintelligle and meaningless. It means that we cannot find an idea which includes both the thesis and the antithesis at the same time.

---

[1] SVM.; VRS., pp. 276-77.

5. 'Perhaps S is and indescribable'. When a predicate is affirmed of a thing with reference to its own substance, place, time, and nature, and a predicate is affirmed of it as described above and denied of other things as different substances in other places and times and with different natures simultaneously, we have affirmation and indescribability.

6. 'Perhaps S is not and indescribable'. When a predicate is denied of other substances in other places at other times and with different natures, and a predicate is simultaneously affirmed of the thing and denied of other things, we have negation and indescribability.

7. 'Perhaps S is, is not, and indescribable'. When a predicate is affirmed of a thing as its own substance in its own place at its own time and with its own nature, and it is denied of other substances in other places at other times and with other natures, and affirmation and denial are made simultaneously, we have affirmation, negation, and indescribability. The Jainas admit only the sevenfold judgments (saptabhaṅgīnyāya).[1] Of these the affirmative judgment that a thing is in its own substance, its own place, its own time, and with its own nature, and the negative judgment that a thing is not in other substances, other places, other times, and with other natures are the main. The five other judgments are combinations of them. Affirmation implies negation. Negation implies affirmation. A thing is existent with its own nature, and non-existent with other natures. A positive thing is distinguished from other things. A thing devoid of all distinctions is inconceivable. The Jainas advocate relative pluralism (anekāntavāda). Syādvāda or relativity of judgments and Saptabhaṅgīnyāya or sevenfold judgments are logical corrollaries of it.

Śaṁkara and Rāmānuja criticize Saptabhaṅgīnyāya on the ground that contradictory attributes such as existence and non-existence cannot at the same time belong to one and the same thing. A thing cannot be hot and cold at the same moment. Light and darkness cannot co-exist in the same place. Śaṁkara and Rāmānuja misunderstand the Jaina doctrine. The Jainas hold that a real thing is not a pure identity devoid of all differences. It is complex in nature. It is a permanent sub-

---

[1] TDTV., 14.

stance endued with different qualities and modes. It is real because it is a unity-in-difference. It comprehends and reconciles differences in itself. Two contradictory attributes cannot exist in one and the same thing in the same part at the same moment. The Jainas admit it. But they can co-exist in the same thing in different parts. A tree as a whole is unmoving while its branches are moving. In a sense, a tree is both moving and unmoving. Contradictory attributes may co-exist in the same thing in different relations. The same person may be father in relation to A and son in relation to B. The Jainas emphasize manifold nature of real things which are endued with infinite qualities, modes, and relations to the other things. They have identity-in-difference. The Vedāntists emphasize pure identity and deny plurality. The Jainas emphasize manifoldness of inter-related reals and deny pure identity. They are anti-Absolutists. They are advocates of relative pluralism.[1]

II. Ontology

9. *The Jaina refutation of one-sided (aikāntika) positions*

Is existence (bhāva) unreal? If existence is unreal, and only non-existence (abhāva) is real, then perception, inference, and testimony are non-existent and unreal, and can neither establish the thesis that non-existence is real, nor refute the antithesis that existence is real.[2] So existence is real.

Is non-existence (abhāva) unreal? The Jaina admits, like the Vaiśeṣika, four kinds of non-existence, prior non-existence (prāgabhāva), posterior non-existence (pradhvaṁsābhāva), mutual non-existence (anyonyābhāva), and absolute non-existence (atyantābhāva). If there were no prior non-existence, a produced substance would be beginningless. If there were no posterior non-existence, it would be endless. If there were no mutual non-existence, all things would be identical in nature. If there were no absolute non-existence, a sky-flower, a hare's horn, etc., could be spoken of together. There is a difference between mutual non-existence and absolute non-existence. There is mutual non-existence of a cloth and a jar in each

[1] PI., pp. lxxvi-lxxx.
[2] AMV., 12.

other. There is absolute non-existence of matter in the soul.[1] So non-existence is real and fourfold.

The Jaina holds that a thing is both existent (sat) and non-existent (asat) in different relations. It is existent in its own substance in its own place at its own time and with its own nature. It is non-existent as other substances in other places at other times and with other natures. This is the doctrine of Syādvāda.[2] Thus affirmation (vidhi) and negation (niṣedha) both are real in different relations, and they are not self-contradictory.[3]

Is the substance (dravya, dharmin) real apart its attributes? Or are attributes (dharma) real apart from the substance? The Jaina holds that the substance is neither devoid of attributes nor a conglomeration of attributes. The substance is the abode of attributes. It is the permanent substratum of changing attributes. It is one, but its attributes are many. It is partly different from, and partly identical with, its attributes. Both substance (dharmin) and attributes (dharma) are real in relation to each other. Attributes depend upon substance.[4]

Is a real thing one or many? It is one as a substance. But it is endued with many attributes which change in time. Thus it is both one and many in different senses.[5]

Is the non-dual alone real? If the reality is non-dual (advaita), the differences that are perceived are unreal. There can be no difference between agents and actions, and between one action and another. One cannot be produced out of one. If non-duality is real, there can be no duality (dvaita) of good actions and bad actions, merit and demerit, this world and the next world, knowledge and ignorance, bondage and liberation. If non-duality is established by a reason, then there is a duality of the reason (hetu) and the inferred object (sādhya). If non-duality is established by mere verbal statement, duality as well may be established by it. Non-duality (advaita) is unmeaning without duality (dvaita). So the reality cannot be regarded as non-dual or one devoid of differences as the Advaita Vedānta holds.[6] What contradicts our experience is

---

[1] AMV., 10, 11.
[2] AMV., 15.
[3] AMV., 47.
[4] AMV., 22.
[5] AMV., 23; SVM., VRS., p. 111.
[6] AM., 24-27; SVM., VRS., p. 101.

not true. Differences are actually perceived. So they cannot be regarded as unreal.[1]

Is distinctness alone real? If distinctness (pṛthaktva) or difference (bheda) alone is real, it is either distinct or non-distinct from the different objects. If it is distinct from them, they are non-distinct from one another, which contradicts our experience, and is therefore false. Further, distinctness cannot be related to the objects in which it is supposed to inhere. If distinctness is not distinct from the different objects, then one distinctness exists in many different objects without any modification. But this is inconceivable. So both the alternatives are untenable. If partial identity is denied, there can be no aggregate (samudāya) of co-existent qualities or succesive modes, nor psychic continuum (santāna) to which discrete psychoses belong, nor its continuance after death (pretyabhāva) and transmigration. If all objects are distinct from one another, there can be no similarity among them.[2] So distinctness alone cannot be real.

Is the reality eternal? If the reality is eternal, there can be no modification. There can be no cause or effect. There can be no valid knowledge (pramāṇa) and its result (phala) in the shape of acceptance, rejection, or indifference. Valid knowledge manifests the reality. And the reality is manifested by valid knowledge. If both valid knowledge and the reality are eternal, they cannot be related to each other as the manifester (vyañjaka) and the manifested (vyaṅgya). Manifestation implies change. The eternal is unchanging. If the reality is eternal, it can never be produced, like the self (puruṣa) of the Sāṁkhya. If modification (pariṇāma) is real, the reality cannot be eternal. Modification consists in the destruction of some quality and production of some other quality. But there is neither production nor destruction in the eternal. But modification is known by valid knowledge. So it is real. Therefore the reality cannot be eternal. If there is no modification, there can be no right actions or wrong actions, merit or demerit, bondage, transmigration, or liberation, or their agent, the self. Thus eternalism leads to negation of the self (nairātmyavāda).[3] The reality cannot be eternal as the Advaita Vedāta holds.

---

[1] AS., 24.
[2] AMV., AS., 28, 29.
[3] AMV., AS., 37-40.

Is the reality momentary? If the reality is momentary (kṣaṇika), there can be no recognition of permanent objects. In the absence of recognition, there can be no actions to produce different things. Further, if the reality is momentary, the self is a series of momentary psychoses, which is incapable of continuation after death and transmigration.[1] If the self were a series of momentary mental processes, one member of the series would do an action, and another would reap its fruit, one would be in bondage, and another would be liberated.[2] The momentary psychoses would not be members of the same series, and their origin, existence, and destruction would be unreal.[3] But the reality is partially permanent because it is recognized as such. Recognition apprehends the identity of an object in the past and the present time (*e.g.*, 'this is that Devadatta'). Therefore a real object is not an aggregate of momentary states. It is neither eternal nor momentary. It is partially permanent in the midst of changing qualities and modes.[4] Hence the reality is not momentary as the Buddhists hold.

Is generality (sāmānya) entirely different from particularity (viśeṣa)? If it were so, the same object would not be apprehended by an assimilative cognition (anuvṛtti) and a discriminative cognition (vyāvṛtti). But, in fact, a man is apprehended as similar to other persons and different from other persons. He is known as possessed of generic as well as specific qualities.

Is generality entirely identical with particularity? If it is so, then either of them is non-existent, and the two words 'generality' and 'particularity' cannot be used. An object possesses both generality and particularity because it is known as such. Generality is known by an inclusive cognition (anuvṛttipratyaya). Particularity is known by a discriminative cognition (vyāvṛttipratyaya).[5] There is no generality apart from particularity. There is no particularity apart from generality. Both are unreal apart from each other. The same object possesses generality as well as particularity. It possesses identity (aikya) as well as distinctness (pṛthaktva).[6]

---

[1] AMV., 41.
[2] AM., 51.
[3] AM., 54.
[4] AMV., 56; SVM., VRS., p. 16.
[5] SVM., VRS., pp. 13, 100.
[6] AMV., 33.

How are attributes (dharma) related to a substance (dharmin)? The Vaiśeṣikas hold that attributes are different from a substance, and that there is a relation of inherence (samavāya) between them. If they are absolutely different from each other, attributes cannot be said to be the attributes of a substance, and a substance cannot be said to be the abode of attributes. Inherence (samavāya) is said to be an independent category (padārtha). It is a relation between a substance and its attributes or actions ; it is a relation of abode (ādhāra) and what abides (ādheya) ; it is a relation between two inseparable entities (ayutasiddha), which are the container and the contained ; it generates the cognition 'this is contained in this abode' (ihapratyayahetu). The Jaina urges that we have not three distinct cognitions of a substance, an attribute, and inherence (samavāya) between them. A substance is perceived through its attributes. Attributes also are perceived along with a substance. They constitute its nature. They are partly different from, and partly identical with it. No separate relation between them is perceived. So there is no independent relation called inherence (samavāya) between a substance and its attributes. The genus of earth (pṛthivītva) is said to inhere in earth (pṛthivī). But the Jaina urges that the so-called genus of earth is nothing but the existence of earth. It is the very nature (svarūpa) of earth. It is not a different entity (vastvantaram). If inherence is an independent relation between a substance and its attributes, how can inherence be related to a substance and attributes? If substance were related to attributes by inherence, then inherence also would require another inherence to be related to a substance, and it also would require another inherence to be related to attributes. And these two inherences would require other inherences, and so on *ad infinitum*. Further, if the genus of earth required inherence to be related to earth, then inherence also would require the genus of inherence (samavāyatva) to subsist in it in the relation of inherence, and so on *ad infinitum*. The Vaiśeṣikas hold that inherence is one, eternal, ubiquitous, and incorporeal. The Jaina contends that if inherence is of such a nature, then the colours of a jar should inhere in a cloth, because inherence is one, eternal, and ubiquitous, just as one, eternal, ubiquitous space (ākaśa) is related simultaneously to all material things without any distinction. Further, if inherence is one, then when one substance in which attributes inhere is destroyed, inherence in all other substances will be destroyed. But if inherence in that one substance only is supposed to be destroyed, then it becomes non-eternal. Hence inherence is nothing but inseparability of existence.[1]

Is the reality subjective or objective? Are cognitions alone real? Or are external objects alone real? The Jaina is a realist. He holds that external objects are real, and are apprehended by cognitions. Cognitions exist in the self. External objects exist in the world. Cognitions are of the nature of manifestation (prakāśa). Objects are inert (jaḍa) Cognitions manifest external objects. So both are real. Both subjective idealism and materialism are invalid.[2] There is partial identity as well as partial difference between apprehending cognitions and apprehended objects. Their partial difference has been indicated above. Their partial identity (tādātmya) is shown by similarity between the forms of cognitions and the forms of objects.[3] The Jaina realism has been discussed elaborately in *Indian Realism* (Ch. IV).

10. *Substance, Attribute, and Modification*

A substance (dravya) has the characteristic of existence (sat). It is a real entity.[4] It possesses generation (utpāda), destruction (vyaya), and permanence (dhrauvya). Some new qualities are generated in it. Some old qualities are destroyed in it. Some qualities remain permanent in it.[5] Permanence means indestructibility and continuity of the essence of the substance. Recognition apprehends permanence of a substance in the form 'this is that'.[6] When prominence is given to the indestructible essence of a thing, and its changing qualities are subordinated to its essence, it is called a substance. It is permanent (nitya) in regard to its essential qualities (sāmānya), and impermanent (anitya) in regard to its changing qualities (viśeṣa).[7] A substance is possessed of attributes (guṇa) and

---

[1] SVM., VRS., pp. 36-39.
[2] SVM., VRS., p. 140.
[3] AMV., AS., 30.
[4] TS., v. 29.
[5] TS., v. 30.
[6] TS., SS., v. 31.
[7] TS., SS., v. 32.

modifications or modes (paryāya). Attributes coexist with one another in the substance (anvayin). Modes succeed one another in it (vyatirekin).[1] Modes are changes in the attributes of a substance.[2] They are partly different from their substance, since even when they are destroyed their substance persists. They are partly identical with their substance, since they cannot exist apart from their substance, and they are nothing but its modifications.[3] Sometimes attributes are said to be co-existent modes. Successive modes are said to be modes proper.

Like the Vaiśeṣikas the Jainas hold that attributes (guṇa) abide in substances, but that they are devoid of attributes. Attributes cannot exist without a substance. But there can be no attribute of an attribute. But many attributes can coexist in the same substance at the same time in the same point of space. They subsist in a permanent substance. But modes are accidental modifications of a substance. Attributes are synchronous, while modes are successive. So they are different from each other, though they subsist in a substance.[4]

A substance is partly different from, and partly identical with, generation (utpāda), destruction (vyaya), and permanence (dhrauvya). So it is said to be united with them.[5] The Jaina agrees with the Yoga in considering a substance to be partly different from, and partly identical with, its generated, destroyed, and permanent qualities. A substance is characterized by creation, destruction, and permanence.[6] What maintains its identity through its many attributes and modes, and what is not different from beinghood (sattā) is called a substance.[7] First, it has existence (sattā). Secondly, it has permanence through generation and destruction. Generation is appearance of a new form. It is not creation out of nothing. Destruction is disappearance of the old form. It is not absolute annihilation. Creation and destruction are phases in the development of a substance. Permanence is persistence of the essential nature. Thirdly, a substance is the substratum of attributes and modes. It is dynamic and concrete. These three characteristics are inseparable from one another.[8]

---

[1] TS., v. 38.
[2] TS., v. 42.
[3] SS., v. 42.
[4] TS., SS., v. 41.
[5] SS., v. 30.
[6] P., 8.
[7] P., 9.
[8] TDTV., 10.

From the standpoint of substance, a substance is neither created nor destroyed ; it has only existence. But from the standpoint of modes, a substance has creation, destruction, and permanence.[1] A substance is both permanent and changing. It is permanent as a substance. It is changing as modes. A substance is permanent through its changing modes.[2]

A substance cannot exist without modes. Modes cannot exist without a substance. They cannot exist apart from each other.[3] They are partially different from, and partially identical with, each other.[4] The relation of a substance to its mode is that of matter to its form. There can be no matter without form. There can be no form without matter.

A substance cannot exist without attributes. Attributes cannot exist without a substance. They cannot exist apart from each other. They are non-different (avyatirikta) from each other in their nature.[5] They are partly different from and partly identical with each other.[6]

If a substance is entirely distinct from its attributes, then it may be transformed into infinite other substances. If the attributes are entirely distinct from a substance and can exist apart from it, there is no necessity for a substance. Both the alternatives are untenable. Hence a substance and its attributes are not entirely distinct from each other.[7]

According to the Advaita Vedānta a substance alone is real, and its qualities are unreal appearances. According to the Buddhist the so-called substance is unreal, and it is a mere aggregate of qualities. According to the Jaina a substance and its qualities both are real. Qualities depend on a substance which is their substratum. The substance is manifested through its qualities. It exists (sat) ; it is a real entity. It is permanent (dhruva) through the appearance (utpāda) and disappearance (vyaya) of its qualities. Both substance and qualities are real. They are partly distinct and partly non-distinct from each other. The Jaina view resembles the Yoga view.

The Jaina philosophy rejects the Buddhist view that a substance and its qualities are absolutely non-distinct from each

[1] P., 11.
[2] TDTV., 11.
[3] P., 12.
[4] TDTV., 12.
[5] P., 13.
[6] TDTV., 13.
[7] P., 50.

other. It rejects the Nyāya-Vaiśeṣika view that they are absolutely different from each other, and related to each other by inherence (samavāya). It rejects the view that they are absolutely different and absolutely non-different from each other at the same time, since it is self-contradictory.[1] It holds that they are distinguishable from each other in thought only. They are not distinct and separable in real nature. They are partially different and partially non-different from each other. There is distinctness (pṛthaktva) as well as identity (ekatva) between substance and qualities.[2] They are co-existent (samavartin) with each other, non-distinct (apṛthagbhūta), and inseparable (ayutasiddha) from each other. The relation between substance and qualities is not one of combination. There is unity between them.[3]

11. *Cause and Effect*

The Jaina agrees with the Sāṁkhya in holding that there can be neither destruction of existing substances nor creation of non-existent ones. But there can be creation and destruction of its qualities and modes. The substance is permanent though its qualities and modes are created and destroyed. It persists through its changing qualities which appear and disappear. A substance is said to be created and destroyed because of its qualities and modes.[4] It is permanent, though its qualities and modes are constantly changing.

If the effect is pre-existent (sat) in the cause, it cannot be produced again. An unproduced effect can neither exist, nor can it be destroyed like a sky-flower. So the Sāṁkhya theory of Satkāryavāda is wrong: If the effect is non-existent (asat) in the cause, it cannot be produced anew. There can be no creation out of nothing. So the Nyāya theory of Asatkāryavāda also is wrong. If the cause is absolutely destroyed the effect cannot be produced out of nothing. Prdouction and destruction are in the nature of actions or modifications. They are not possible without a substance in which they subsist (nirādhāra). The effect partly pre-exists in the cause and is partly non-existent in it. The cause continues in the effect. It cannot be momentary as the Buddhists hold. A momentary

---

[1] P., 51.
[2] P., 53.
[3] P., 56.
[4] P., 15.

cause cannot produce an effect. It is destroyed in a moment. So it cannot produce an effect. An absolutely existent or absolutely non-existent thing cannot be produced. The Jaina holds that the effect is partly existent in the cause, and partly non-existent in it. So he reconciles the truths of Satkāryavāda and Asatkāryavāda. The effect is a modification of the causal substance, and yet it is a new emergence.[1] The cause and the effect are partly distinct (pṛthak) and partly non-distinct (eka) from each other.[2]

The Nyāya-Vaiśeṣika holds that an effect (*e.g.*, a jar) is different from its material cause (*e.g.*, earth atoms), and inheres in it. The effect is a whole (avayavin) which inheres in its material cause or parts (avayava). But the Jaina contends that the whole is one and partless, and so it cannot exist in many parts. If it is supposed to have parts, it loses its unity. Further, if the whole is different from the parts in space or time then they are not inseparable from each other like a jar and a cloth, and they cannot coexist in the same space because both are corporeal, and being different from each other must exist in different portions of space. There is no relation of inherence (samavāya). Thus the Jaina rejects the Nyāya-Vaiśeṣika theory of causation.

The Jaina recognizes six substances (1) soul (jīva) ; (2) the principle of motion (dharma) ; (3) the principle of rest (adharma) ; (4) space (ākāśa) ; (5) matter (pudgala) ; and (6) time (kāla). The last five substances are called non-soul (ajīva). The first five substances are extensive like body (kāya), and occupy more than one unit of space. So they are called astikāyas. Soul, matter, dharma, adharma, and space are extensive substances. Time is unextended ; it has no extent in space. It is composed of innumerable moments which are not coextensive with one another. So time is a substance. But it is not extensive (astikāya). The nature of the substances will be discussed one after another.

12. *The Soul (Jīva)*

The soul (jīva) is an eternal spiritual substance. It is incorporeal or formless (amūrta). It is immaterial. It is different

[1] AM., 42; AS., 21, 42. [2] AS., 29.

from the body or the sense-organs. But it is coextensive with the body it occupies (svadehaparimāṇa), even as the light of a lamp is coextensive with the room in which it exists.[1] Cognition, feeling, and conation are its qualities. It is the knower (upayogamaya), the enjoyer (bhoktṛ), and the active agent (kartṛ). It possesses knowledge (jñāna) and perception (darśana). Consciousness is not its accidental quality as the Nyāya-Vaiśeṣika holds, but it constitutes its essence. The soul is not different (udāsīna) or inactive (akartṛ) as the Sāṁkhya holds. It is the enjoyer of the fruits of its actions. It feels pleasure and pain. It is active. It has freedom of the will. It can freely do right actions or wrong actions, and acquire merit (puṇya) or demerit (pāpa). It is the master (prabhu) of its own destiny. It freely enters into bondage. It freely liberates itself from bondage. It is united with particles of karma-matter in the state of bondage. It is separated from karmic matter in the state of liberation. The liberated soul moves upward to the summit of mundane space (lokākāśa).[2]

From the practical standpoint (vyavahāranaya), that is called the soul which is possessed of the five sense-organs, and four vital forces (prāṇa), strength (bala), duration of life (āyuṣ), inspiration and expiration (āṇa-prāṇa) in the past, the present, and the future. But from the ontological standpoint (niścayanaya), that is called the soul which has consciousness (cetanā).[3] The soul (jīva) is absolutely different from the non-soul (ajīva). What is devoid of pleasure and pain and desire of doing good and avoiding evil is non-soul (ajīva).[4] The soul is conscious. It has knowledge, feels pleasure and pain, desires good and avoids evil. It has cognition, affection, and conation. It knows and perceives objects, desires pleasure, fears pain, does good and evil, and enjoys the fruits of its actions.[5] The five sense-organs and the body are its accidental adjuncts (upādhi). They are not conscious. But the soul is the principle of consciousness which manifests itself and other objects.[6]

The soul is a spiritual substance. As a spiritual entity, it has neither beginning nor end—it is eternal. It has both beginning and end, as endued with the psychical qualities in

---

[1] TS., v. 16.
[2] DS., 2; P., 27, 132.
[3] DS., 3.
[4] P., 132.
[5] P., 129.
[6] P., 128.

the states of emergence (audayika), subsidence (aupaśamika), and destruction and subsidence (kṣayopaśamika) of karmic matter. But as endued with the psychical qualities in the state of annihilation (kṣāyika) of karmic matter, it has beginning, but no end. When it is disentangled from karma-matter, it realizes its true nature and becomes immortal. Though the soul is really eternal, it undergoes birth and death because of its accidental association with karma-matter.[1] The disembodied bound soul has a subtle body composed of karma-matter through which it transmigrates to other bodies. The liberated soul shakes off the karmic body and moves upward to the summit of mundane space and abides there for ever. It cannot step beyond because there is no principle of motion (dharma) in supramundane space.[2]

The jīva is active because of its association with karmic matter. In the perfect state it is absolutely free from karmas. It is practically inactive in this state. It transcends the causal series in the state of liberation.[3] The soul is the lord of its own destiny. It is the agent of its own actions, and the enjoyer of their fruits. It is blinded by ignorance (moha) on account of its bondage to karma-matter created by itself, and roams about in the world of birth and death (saṃsāra). The faithful (bhavya) soul liberates itself from bondage by adopting the path of right faith, right knowledge, and right conduct. But the unfaithful (abhavya) soul roams about in the world of saṃsāra for ever. But both kinds of souls are the lords of their own career. The destiny of each jīva is entirely self-determined.[4]

Knowledge (jñāna) constitutes the essence of the self. If the self is entirely distinct from knowledge, then both are unconscious (acetana). If they are separable (yutasiddha), the self cannot become conscious by conjunction with knowledge, since the self is devoid of consciousness in its essential nature and knowledge as a quality does not subsist in a substance. If the self is entirely distinct from knowledge, it cannot be the knower by union with knowledge because both are unconscious. Consciousness cannot be generated by non-conscious elements individually or collectively. If consciousness is an adventitious quality of the self, then before acquiring conscious-

[1] P., 59, 60.
[2] P., 79.
[3] P., 105.
[4] P., 75.

ness it must be either thinking or unthinking. If it is thinking, acquisition of knowledge is useless. If it is unthinking, then its unthinking nature is either adventitious or innate. If it is adventitious, it cannot acquire knowledge because it is incompatible with its former acquisition. If it is innate, then its thinking nature also may be innate. Thought or knowledge (jñāna) is not an adventitious quality of the self as the Nyāya-Vaiśeṣika and Prabhākara hold. It is its intrinsic essence. The self is the knower (jñānin) by its very nature. It does not become the knower by union with the adventitious quality of knowledge.[1] Infinite knowledge, infinite perception, infinite bliss, and infinite power for right action are innate in the soul. But they are obscured by karma-matter in the state of bondage. When the shackle of karma-matter is completely broken, the soul realizes omniscience, eternal bliss, and infinite power.

The soul is a spiritual substance. So it is non-spatial or unextended. But it is considered to be an extensive substance (astikāya) because it illumines the whole body with its consciousness like the light of a lamp which illumes the whole room which it occupies.[2] The soul has no physical expansion. It has spiritual manifestation. It pervades the whole body by spiritual illumination. Just as a piece of red ruby placed in a cup of milk imparts its lustre to the milk, so the soul residing in a body imparts its consciousness to the whole body.[3] It is distinct from the body, though it appears to be identical with it when it functions in it. It assumes different bodies because of different karmas in the cycle of saṁsāra. The same soul exists in different bodies in different births. In its spiritual nature it is quite different from its bodies. It is incorporeal while its bodies are corporeal.[4]

The souls are of the essence of consciousness (cetanātmaka). Perception and knowledge are their essential characteristics. The souls are of two kinds, bound (saṁsārin) and liberated (mukta). The former are limited by adjuncts (sopādhi). They have either gross body or subtle body. The latter are free from bodily adjuncts (nirupādhi). They have neither gross

---

[1] P., TDTV., 54, 55.
[2] TS., v. 16.
[3] P., 33.
[4] P., TDTV., 34.

body nor subtle body. The former are impure. The latter are pure. The former have finite knowledge and finite perception owing to karmic matter which limits them. The latter have infinite knowledge and infinite perception owing to annihilation of karmic matter.[1] The former have false knowledge and perception, emotions and passions. The latter have omniscience, infinite bliss, and infinite power. Each class of jīvas contains infinite number of individuals. The perfect souls retain their identity and individuality. They conserve the moral values achieved by them. Jainism, like the Sāṁkhya, advocates uncompromising pluralism of souls.[2]

The omniscient soul pervades the whole universe by its consciousness.[3] Even the bound soul occupies innumerable space-points.[4] Though it occupies innumerable space-points, it can occupy the space of a small body or a large body by the contraction (saṃhāra) and expansion (visarpa) of the space-points, like a lamp. It is like a lamp which illumines a small room or a large room.[5] Jainism is undecided as to spatiality or non-spatiality of the soul. Mundane souls support one another. We are members of one another. We cannot live apart from one another.[6] The perfect souls are absolutely unconditioned. They are neither causes nor effects. They have no causal relation to the cycle of saṃsāra. They are absolutely incorporeal and perfectly spiritual. They are entirely free from karma-matter. They are transcendental souls. But the imperfect souls are united with karma-matter. Though in themselves incorporeal, they are embodied and associated with particles of karma. The perfect souls are devoid of life-principles (dravyaprāṇa), but they have their psychical counterparts (bhāvaprāṇa). They are free from the limitation of the body. They are approximately of the dimension of the last body.[7]

The jīvas are either embodied or disembodied. The former are bound (saṁsārin). The latter are perfect (siddha). The bound souls are either faithful (bhavya) or unfaithful (abhavya).[8] The faithful souls attain liberation. The unfaithful souls never attain liberation. They roam in the world for ever. The

---

[1] P., TDTV., 117.
[2] P., TDTV., 31, 32.
[3] TS., v. 8.
[4] TS., v. 15.
[5] TS., v. 16.
[6] TS., v. 21.
[7] P., 35.
[8] P., 127.

embodied souls are either non-moving (sthāvara) or moving (trasa).[1] Earth, water, fire, and air are endowed with souls. Earth-souls, water-souls, fire-souls, and air-souls have one sense-organ, *viz.*, touch associated with intense stupor (moha). These are elemental souls. They live in elementary bodies. They live and die, and are reborn in the same or another elementary body. They are either gross or subtle. The subtle elementary lives are invisible. Plants also are endowed with souls. They have the sense of touch only. All the five kinds of non-moving souls have four kinds of life-principles, strength of body, respiration, duration of life, and the sense of touch. They are microscopic organisms endowed with souls. How souls can exist in fire is unintelligible. The non-moving souls have no mental modes. But they are not unconscious. They are subconscious like a fœtus in an egg, or an embryo in a womb, or a man in a swoon. They have dormant consciousness. They have life and potency of consciousness.[2] Plants are jīvas with the sense of touch. "Of some plants each is the body of one soul only, but of other plants each is an aggregation of embodied souls which have all functions of life, as respiration and nutrition, in common. That plants possess souls is an opinion shared by other Indian philosophers. But the Jainas have developed this theory in a remarkable way. Plants in which only one soul is embodied are always gross ; they exist in the habitable part of the world only. But those plants of which each is a colony of plant-lives may also be subtle, *i.e.*, invisible, and in that case they are invisible all over the world. These subtle plants are called nigoda ; they are composed of an infinite number of souls forming a very small cluster, have respiration and nutrition in common, and experience the most exquisite pains. Innumerable nigodas form a globule, and with them the whole space of the world is closely packed. The nigodas furnish the supply of souls in place of those who have attained nirvāṇa. But an infinitesimally small fraction of one single nigoda has sufficed to replace the vacancy caused in the world by the nirvāṇa of all the souls that have been liberated from the beginningless past down to the present. Thus it is evident that the saṃsāra will never be empty of living

[1] TS., ii. 12.

[2] P., 118-120; TS., ii. 13.

beings."[1] Some ensouled organisms have two sense-organs. Sea snail, cowrie shell, conch shell, mother o' pearl, and earthworm have the senses, touch and taste. They are moving souls (trasa).[2] The louse, the bug, the ant, the scorpion, and other insects have three senses, touch, taste, and smell. The gad-fly, the mosquito, the fly, the bee, the black bee, the moth, and the like have four senses, touch, taste, smell, and sight. Higher animals living on land and in water, and birds have five senses, touch, taste, smell, sight, and hearing.[3] Some souls have a mind or reason (saṁjñin, samanaska). They can distinguish between right and wrong. Others have no mind or reason (asaṁjñin, amanaska). They cannot distinguish between right and wrong. Human souls are rational. Animal souls, plant-souls, and elemental souls are irrational.[4] The embodied souls are of these five kinds. The Jainas believe in panpsychism.

There are five kinds of bodies. In addition to the gross body there are four subtle bodies. The karmic body (kārmaṇa śarīra) is composed of infra-atomic karma-particles. This is the innermost body. It has no bodily functions. The soul transmigrates with the help of this karmic body. All embodied souls have the igneous body (taijasa śarīra) which in common persons causes assimilation of food, and in meritorious persons gives effect to their benedictions and curses. Then some saints have the translocation body (āhāraka śarīra) which causes their transportation to a Tīrthaṅkara at a distance to consult him and remove their doubts. Gods and denizens of hell have the transmutation body (vaikriyika śarīra) which they can change at will. All men and animals have the gross physical body (audārīka śarīra).[5] Of the physical body, the transmutation body, the translocation body, the igneous body, and the karmic body, each succeeding one is subtler than the preceding one.[6] All mundane souls have the igneous body and the karmic body ; their connection with them is without beginning.[7] The souls have four gatis, celestial (deva), hellish (nāraka), human (mānuṣya), and subhuman (tiryak).[8] Gatis are conditions of the soul's existence.

---

[1] *Lokaprakāśa*, vi. 31ff, E.R.E., vol. vii, p. 469; cp. IP., vol. I, p. 332.

[2] TS., ii. 14.

[3] P., 121-24; TS., ii. 15.

[4] TS., ii. 11, 24; GTS., JK., 660-61.

[5] TS., ii. 36; E.R.E., p. 469n.

[6] TS., ii. 37.

[7] TS., ii. 41, 42.

[8] P., 61.

That by which the soul is tinged with its merit (puṇya) and demerit (pāpa) is called the leśyā. The thought-paints generated by the accumulation of karma-matter are called bhāva-leśyā. The actual tinging of the soul by karma-matter is called dravya-leśyā. Black, indigo, grey, fiery, lotus, and white are the different kinds of the soul-paints. Thought-paints are due to the actions of the body and the mind (yoga) and passions (kaṣāya).[1]

13. *The Theory of Karma*

Karmas are infra-atomic particles of matter (karmabargaṇā). They are produced by passions and actions of mind, body, and speech moved by desire, aversion, and delusion. There are four destructive (ghātīya) karmas and four non-destructive (aghātīya) karmas. The former are (1) knowledge-obscuring (jñānāvaraṇīya), (2) perception-obscuring (darśanāvaraṇīya), (3) obstructive (antarāya), (4) deluding (mohanīya). The latter are (5) age-determining (āyuṣ), (6) character-determining (nāma), (7) family-determining (gotra), and (8) feeling-determining (vedanīya).[2] (1) The knowledge-obscuring (jñānāvaraṇīya) karmas obscure five-fold right knowledge, sense-knowledge (mati), testimony (śruti), clairvoyance (avadhi), telepathic knowledge of other minds (manaḥparyāya), and omniscience (kevala.)[3] (2) The perception-obscuring (darśanāvaraṇīya) karmas obscure right visual perception (cakṣuṣ), non-visual perception (acakṣuṣ), perception of distant objects (avadhi), perfect perception (kevala), sleep (nidrā), deep sleep (nidrānidrā), restless sleep (pracalā), very restless sleep (pracalāpracalā), and somnumbulism (styānagṛddhi).[4] (3) The obstructive (antarāya) karmas obstruct the inborn energy of the soul and prevent it from doing good actions in spite of the desire to do them. They obstruct charity (dāna), gain (lābha), enjoyment (bhoga), the means to enjoyment (upabhoga), and power (vīrya).[5] (4) The deluding (mohanīya) karmas are mainly of two kinds, according as they delude right belief (darśanamohanīya), and right conduct (cāritramohanīya). The former obscure right belief,

---

[1] GS., JK., 489, 490, 494.
[2] TS., viii. 4.
[3] TS., viii. 6.
[4] TS., viii. 7.
[5] TS., viii. 13.

wrong belief, and right belief mixed with wrong belief. The latter affect passions (kaṣāyavedanīya), *viz.*, anger, pride, deceit and greed, and slight passions (akaṣāyavedanīya), *viz.*, laughter, attachment, aversion, sorrow, fear, disgust, female sex-feeling, male sex-feeling, and an eunuch's sex-feeling.[1] (5) The age-determining (āyuṣ) karmas determine the duration of hellish life, animal life, human life, and celestial life.[2] (6) The namakarmas determine the transmigration of the soul to hellish, animal, human, and celestial life, the genus, the number of sense-organs, the different kinds of bodies, the skeleton, the nervous system, the build of the body, the limbs, and the like. They determine the peculiarities of the body, the special qualities and faculties, character and personality of an individual. They determine the birth in a high family or a low family.[3] (8) The feeling-obscuring (vedanīya) karmas are of two kinds according as they produce pleasure and pain. They obscure the innate blissful nature of the soul.[4]

Actions of mind, body, and speech produce subtle modifications of the soul called bhāvakarmas. These produce infra-atomic particles of matter called dravyakarmas, which flow into the soul and stick to it. Passions (kaṣāya) make the karma-particles stick to the soul.[5] The soul is actually united with karma-matter and entangled in bondage. All knowledge, feeling, and volition are produced from within by removing the veil of karma-matter. External objects are only concomitant conditions of the removal of the veil of karma-matter. The soul is the material cause (upādāna kāraṇa) of its thoughts. The karma-matter is their efficient cause (nimitta kāraṇa).[6] Emotions (bhāva) are conditioned by karma-matter (dravyakarma). Karma-matter, in its turn, is conditioned by emotional states of the soul (bhāvakarma).[7] Karma is a kind of subtle matter. It is the subtle medium through which it is connected with the gross body composed of matter.

The soul is in its natural (pāriṇāmika) state, when its pure thought-activities are independent of karmas. It is in its opera-

---

[1] TS., viii. 9.
[2] TS., viii. 10.
[3] TS., viii. 11, 12.
[4] TS., viii. 8; E.R.E., vol. 7, p. 469.
[5] GS., JK., 492; P. TDTV., 65.
[6] P., 65, 67.
[7] P., 66.

tive (audayika) state, when karmas operate and bear their fruits. It is in its subsiding (aupaśamic) state, when the destructive karmas are prevented from producing their fruits. It is in its purified (kṣāyika) state, when the destructive karmas are annihilated. It is in its mixed (miśra) or purified-subsiding (kṣāyopaśamika) state, when some karmas are destroyed, some subside or are prevented from bearing fruits, and some are operative. The souls of good men are in this state.[1]

14. *Matter (Pudgala)*

The non-soul extensive substances (ajīvāstikāya) are: (1) dharma or the principle of motion; (2) adharma or the principle of rest; (3) ākaśa or space; (4) pudgala or matter.[2] They are extensive and occupy more than one space-unit (pradeśa). Time (kāla) is not an extensive substance because indivisible particles of time (kālāṇu) exist in space-points without mixing with one another. There are five kinds of ajīva, *viz.*, matter (pudgala), dharma, adharma, space (ākaśa), and time (kāla).[3] They constitute the world.

Matter is a non-soul (ajīva) substance which has touch, taste, smell, and colour.[4] Material substances have form or shape (rūpa).[5] Matter exists in the form of an atom (aṇu) or an aggregate (skandha).[6] Atoms are indivisible units of matter. Aggregates are composed of atoms. Atoms arise from the division (bheda) of aggregates. They are the furthest limit of division (antya).[7] They cannot arise from combination (saṃghāta) or from combination with division (saṃghātabheda).[8] An atom is one (eka), indivisible (avibhāgin), indestructible (śāśvata), and corporeal or formed (mūrta) unit of matter.[9] It is eternal (nitya). It is the marker (kartṛ) of aggregates. It is the breaker (bhettṛ) of aggregates. It is a constituent unit of an aggregate. An aggregate (skandha) is broken into atoms. It is spatial, yet non-spatial. It occupies only one unit of space (pradeśa). It is the determinant of time and number.[10]

---

[1] TS., SS., ii. 1; GS., JK., 8.
[2] TS., v. 1.
[3] VP., xvi. 15.
[4] TS., v. 23.
[5] TS., v. 5.
[6] TS., v. 25.
[7] P., 84.
[8] TS., SS., v. 27.
[9] P., 84, 85.
[10] P., 87; TS., v. 11.

It is without beginning, middle, and end.[1] It is capable of modifications (pariṇāmaguṇa).[2] Atoms are combined into aggregates. The aggregates are minute or large. They can grow or decay. They can increase or decrease. They have the qualities of touch, taste, smell, colour, and sound. But atoms each have one taste, one smell, one colour, and two tactile qualities. They are the causes of sounds. But they are devoid of sounds.[3] There are five kinds of taste, bitter, pungent, sour, sweet, and astringent. There are two kinds of smell, agreeable and disagreeable. There are five kinds of colour, blue, yellow, white, black, and red. There are eight kinds of touch, softness, hardness, heaviness, lightness, cold, heat, smoothness, and roughness.[4] Atoms have non-manifest (avyakta) or imperceptible qualities. They become manifest (vyakta) in their aggregates (skandha).[5] Of the eight kinds of tactile qualities an atom has temperature, *i.e.*, heat or cold and degrees of roughness or smoothness. It has neither heaviness nor lightness. It is devoid of sound (aśabda). But it is the cause of sound (śabdakāraṇa). Sound is generated by aggregates. An aggregate is composed of molecules or compounds of atoms. Sound is generated by striking of aggregates against one another (skandhaprabhava). Sound is the quality of an aggregate which occupies many space-points. An atom occupies only one space-point. So it cannot have sound.[6] Sound is not the quality of ether (ākāśa) as the Vaiśeṣika holds. If it were the quality of ether, it would be heard in a vacuum in which ether is present.[7] Atoms are homogeneous. They have no qualitative differences.[8] They are subtle (sūkṣma). They are imperceptible to us. But they can be perceived by the omniscient only. An atom occupies one space-point (pradeśa). The same space-point is occupied by its qualities, touch, taste, smell, and colour. If the atom were divested of its qualities, it would be annihilated.[9] The homogeneous atoms produce the four elements of earth, water, fire and air.[10]

The Jaina agrees with the Yoga in holding that one moment (kālāṇu) is the time taken by one atom to move from one space-

---

[1] P., TDTV., 85.
[2] P., 85.
[3] P., 88.
[4] SS., v. 23.
[5] TDTV., 85.
[6] TDTV., 85; TS., v .
[7] P., 85, 86; CON., p. 90.
[8] P., TDTV., 88.
[9] TDTV., 85.
[10] P., 85

point to the next space-point.[1] The change of position of an atom is the measure of time. An atom is also the measure of number (saṃkhyā) or quantity. It is a unit of an aggregate. So the number of atoms determine the quantity of the aggregate (dravyasaṃkhyā). One atom occupies one space-time. Many atoms occupy many space-points. So they also indirectly cause quantitative differences of space (kṣetrasaṃkhyā). They indirectly determine also quantitative differences of their aggregates. Modifications of matter are due to integration (saṃghāta) or disintegration (bheda) of their constituent atoms. So atoms cause quantitative differences of their modes (bhāvasaṃkhyā). The motion of an atom from one space-point to the next space-point is the measure of an instant of time. So its motion through many space-points determines the quantitative differences in time (kālasaṃkhyā). Thus an atom is the direct unit of material things. It is the indirect unit of space, time and change. Atoms are the cause of quantitative difference and qualitative difference of physical objects.[2]

The Jaina holds that one atom of matter (aṇu) and one particle of time (kālāṇu) exist in one unit of space (pradeśa). Matter, time, and space are three inseparable units of the physical world. They cannot be separated from one another, though they are different in their nature. Matter-space-time-units are the elementary substances of the dynamic world. Karma-particles are infra-atomic matter. They are finer than atoms.

Atoms are combined into aggregates (skandha). Aggregates are formed by integration (saṁghāta). Large aggregates are divided into small aggregates. So aggregates are formed by disintegration (bheda). Some aggregates are formed by integration and disintegration (saṁghātabheda).[3] When two primary atoms are combined, a binary aggregate occupying two space-points is formed. When a binary aggregate is combined with a primary atom, a tertiary aggregate occupying three space-points is formed. In this way aggregates of varying quantities numerable (saṃkhyeya), innumerable (asaṃkhyeya), infinite (ananta), infinitely infinite (anantānanta) are formed.[4]

Atoms are linked (bandha) with one another in virtue of their smoothness and roughness. A binary aggregate is due

---

[1] Vyāsa, YB., iii. 52.
[2] P., TDTV., 87; E.T., p. 85-86.
[3] TS., v. 26.
[4] TS., v. 10.

to the union (śleṣa) of a smooth atom with a rough atom.[1] An atom cannot unite with another atom with the minimum degree of smoothness or roughness (jaghanyaguṇa).[2] Atoms with equal degrees of smoothness or roughness cannot unite with one another.[3] An atom with two degrees of smoothness or roughness can unite with an atom of four degrees of smoothness or roughness, but neither less nor more.[4] In such a union the atom with a higher degree of smoothness or roughness absorbs the atom with a lower degree of smoothness or roughness into itself.[5] Atomic linking is due to mere juxtaposition (saṃyoga).

Aggregates (skandha) have manifest qualities of touch, taste, smell, colour, and sound. They possess sound, while atoms are devoid of sound. They have hardness, softness, heaviness, lightness, heat, cold, roughness and smoothness. They have atomic linking, dimension, small or great, figure, divisibility, opacity, and radiant heat-light.[6]

Matter is the basis of body, speech, respiration, and manas. It makes possible pleasure, pain, life, and death.[7] Whatever is perceived by the senses, the sense-organs, body, the physical manas (dravyamanas) or the brain, and karma particles are corporeal (mūrta). All these are matter (pudgala).[8] Matter is knowable, enjoyable, and corporeal.

15. *Dharma*

The Jainas do not use the word *dharma* in the sense of virtue or merit (puṇya), which is a subjective quality of the self, as the Nyāya-Vaiśeṣika does. Nor do they use it in the sense of Moral Law or Ought, which is a transcendental and objective category, as Prabhākara does. They use it in the peculiar sense of the imperceptible medium of motion of matter and souls. Dharma is an ontological reality. It is a part of the physical universe. It is the principle of motion.

Dharma is supersensible. It is devoid of sensible qualities, taste, colour, smell, sound, touch, lightness, and heaviness.

---

[1] TS., SS., v 33.
[2] TS., v. 34.
[3] TS., v. 35.
[4] TS., v. 36.
[5] TS., v. 37.
[6] PSAH., p. 95.
[7] TS., v. 19, 20.
[8] P. 89.

It is perceptible to the omniscient soul (kevalin) only. It is formless or incorporeal (amūrta), inactive (niṣkriya), and eternal (nitya). It is co-extensive with mundane space (lokākāśa). It is not discrete. It is continuous (spṛṣṭa) because its units of space are inseparable (ayutasiddhapradeśa). Though it is co-extensive with mundane space, it is regarded as occupying innumerable units of space (asaṃkhyātapradeśa) from the practical point of view. It is without any gaps. It is motionless. It is incapable of being moved. It cannot impel matter and souls to move (niṣpreraka). It cannot impart motion to them. They move by their very intrinsic nature. When they begin to move, it assists their movement, even as water without moving itself assists the movement of fish which move about in it. Dharma is the neutral (udāsīna), external (bahiraṅga), auxiliary cause (sahakārikāraṇa) of motion of matter and living beings which move on account of their own material causes. It pervades mundane space. So it is called dharmāstikāya. It is a real substance. It persists in the midsts of appearance and disappearance of its modes.

Water neither moves with the moving fish nor does it impel them to move. The fish move owing to their own spontaneous activity. They are not moved by water. It simply assists their movements by its mere existence. It is the helping medium of their motion. So dharma merely assists the motion of matter and living beings (gamanānugrahakara). It neither moves by itself nor generates motion in other things. It gives scope (prasara) to motion (gati) of living beings (jīva) and non-living bodies (pudgala). Dharma by its mere existence conditions motion without being its efficient cause, since it is devoid of movement. It is the fulcrum of motion without which it would not be possible. It is the neutral cause (udāsīnahetu), not the principal or efficient cause (mukhyahetu) of motion. If it were its efficient cause, motion of matter and living beings would never cease, since dharma continues to exist for ever. Their motion is due to their spontaneous activity. Dharma is only an external (bahiraṅga), neutral (udāsīna) or non-efficient, auxiliary cause (sahakārikāraṇa) of motion. It is the support (āśraya) of motion. It is one, incorporeal, imperceptible, inactive, all-pervading, continuous medium of motion. It is akin to ether in modern physics.[1]

16. *Adharma*

The Jainas do not use the term *adharma* in the sense of vice or demerit as the Nyāya-Vaiśeṣika does. It is not a subjective quality of the self. It is an objective category. It is a constitutive principle of the universe. Adharma, like dharma, is one, eternal (nitya), formless (amūrta), inactive (kriyāhīna) substance which is co-extensive with mundane space (lokākāśa). It pervades the world. So it is called adharmāstikāya. It is an extensive substance. It is non-atomic and non-discrete in structure. It is simple. It is not composite. It is incorporeal (amūrta) and formless (arūpa). Its structure is not constituted by space-points (pradeśa). It is devoid of sensible qualities of material things (pudgala). It is supersensible. It is perceptible to the omniscient soul (sarvajña) only. It is an external (bahiraṅga), neutral (udāsīna) or non-efficient, auxiliary cause (sahakārikāraṇa) of rest (sthiti) of moving and stationary living beings (jīva) and material things (pudgala), even as the shade of a tree is the auxiliary cause of rest of the travellers, or even as the earth is the auxiliary cause of the rest of creatures. Adharma is not the principal or efficient cause (mukhyahetu) of rest of living beings and non-living things. It does not generate their rest. Nor does it impel them to rest. But it merely assists the rest of stationary things or things in motion, living or non-living like the earth. Moving things, animate or inanimate, are not brought to rest by the earth. It simply supports the rest of stationary and moving things. If there is no earth to support, stationary and moving things will have no power to rest. Likewise adharma merely helps or supports the rest of stationary and moving things, without which they would not be able to rest.[2] It is the support of rest. It is akin to gravitation in modern physics.[3]

---

[1] DSV., 17; VP., xvi. 29; TS., iii. 33, 34; *Candraprabhacaritam*, xviii. 69, 70; P., TDTV., 90, 91, 92, 95, 96, SS.; TSV., 8, 17; CON., pp. 18-22; DS., 17, pp. 52-54.

[2] P. 93.

[3] DS., 18, pp. 54-56; VP., xvi. 30; TS., 36; *Candraprabhacaritam*, xviii. 71; DSV., 18; P., 93; SS., v. 8, 17.

Adharma assists the rest of matter and living beings which are stationary. It is the auxiliary cause of their rest. It is the principle of rest. Its nature is similar to that of dharma. It differs from dharma in being the principle of rest. It is the continuous medium of rest. But for its existence, flying atoms would have been scattered in infinite space and produced a chaos. It binds them to the centre of the world. It guarantees the stability of the structure of the world.[1]

Dharma and adharma are co-extensive with mundane space. They do not exist in space-points. They are non-atomic and non-discrete. They do not exist in supramundane space (alokākāśa). They are the non-efficient, neutral, auxiliary causes of motion and rest. Dharma is the principle of motion. Adharma is the principle of rest. They do not generate motion and rest. They are not their efficient causes (mukhyahetu). They are their external (bahiraṅga) and neutral (udāsīna) causes. But for the presence of dharma, there would have been no motion of matter, and the world would have been static and immobile. But for the presence of adharma, the atoms would have been scattered to infinite space, and the world would have been reduced to a chaos. Adharma binds them to the centre of the world, and helps the production of a cosmos. It is the medium of rest and equilibrium which is a modification (pariṇāma) of matter and soul. Motion and rest are due to the instrinsic nature of things themselves. They are not caused by dharma and adharma. They are not the efficient causes of motion and rest. If they were so, then the things that are in motion would continue to be so for ever, and the things that are at rest would continue to be so for ever. But the moving things come to rest, and the stationary things begin to move. Therefore dharma and adharma are neutral, auxiliary causes of motion and rest respectively. They are their common supports (sādhāraṇāśraya). They guarantee the dynamic nature and the cosmic structure and stability of the world. They do not function beyond the world in supramundane space which is devoid of motion and rest, matter and soul.[2]

---

[1] SS., v. 17.
[2] P., TDTV., 94, 96; SS., v. 17.

Dharma and adharma are non-living (ajīva) or not-self. They are entities in the physical universe. They are devoid of sensible qualities. They are incorporeal or formless (amūrta), inactive (niṣkriya), co-extensive with mundane space (lokākāśavyāpin), continuous, and inseparable (ayutasiddha-pradeśa) principles. They are not efficient causes. They are external, neutral, auxiliary causes of motion and rest respectively.[1] Dharma is the indispensable condition of motion. Adharma is the indispensable condition of rest. Dharma is akin to ether. Adharma is aking to gravitation.[2]

17. *Space (Ākāśa)*

The Nyāya-Vaiśeṣika, the Sāṁkhya, the Vedānta, and the Mīmāṁsā use the word *ākāśa* in the sense of ether which is one of the five elements. But the Jainas use it in the sense of space. Ākāśa or space is one, eternal (nitya), pervasive (vyāpaka), incorporeal or formless (amūrta), giving accommodation (avakāśa-prada) to living beings, matter, dharma, adharma, and time. It contains infinite space-points (pradeśa)[3]. Interpenetrability (avakāśadāna) is the function of space.[4] Space is of two kinds, mundane space (lokākāśa) and supramundane space (alokākāśa). Mundane space accommodates all jīvas, material things (pudgala), dharma, adharma, and time.[5] They are not distinct from the world. They together constitute it. But space is both identical with and distinct from the world. It is infinite, and contains the world. So mundane space is distinct from the world, and yet identical with it because it is conterminous with it.[6] Beyond the world there is supramundane space (alokākāśa). It is pure (śuddha) space. It is infinite (ananta), eternal (nitya), formless (amūrta), inactive (kriyāhīna), devoid of substances (dravyavarjita), and perceived by the omniscient souls only (sarvajñadṛṣṭigocara).[7] In supramundane space there is only pure space (ākāśa). There is no dharma, adharma, matter, soul, or time in it. Souls and material things are confined to mundane space. They are held together by dharma and adharma which are confined to mundane space. Dharma,

[1] TS., v. 17.
[2] P., p. 96; CON., p. 44.
[3] P., 97, 98; DS., 19; *Tsāra*, iii. 38; VP., xvi. 31; TS., v. 9.
[4] TS., v. 18.
[5] DS., 19, 20.
[6] P., 98; CON., pp. 45-48.
[7] VP., xvi. 33.

adharma, and mundane space are inseparable (apṛthagbhūta) and co-extensive (samānaparimāṇa). They constitute one inseparable unity. They interpenetrate one another. Hence they are one in locality. But they are different in their functions. Motion (gati) is the function of dharma. Rest (sthiti) is the function of adharma. Accommodation or inter-penetration (avakāśa) is the function of space (ākāśa). Dharma and adharma are confined to the world (loka). They are incorporeal and devoid of sensible qualities. They are the constituent elements of the world. They can be distinguished from one another by their functions only. Jīvas can be distinguished from one another by their conscious qualities. Material things can be distinguished from one another by their sensible qualities. But akāśa, dharma, and adharma can be distinguished from one another by their functions only, because they are incorporeal and devoid of sensible qualities. They are three distinct incorporeal principles in the world.[1] They are eternal, uncreated, and of immense magnitudes. Atoms and souls also are eternal and uncreated. Space contains souls, matter, dharma, adharma, and time.

Dharma, adharma, and mundane space are confined to the world. They are co-extensive, incorporeal, and devoid of sensible qualities. What is the use of postulating the existence of dharma and adharma? Ākāśa may be credited with the functions of assisting motion and rest in addition to accommodation or interpenetration. This hypothesis is illegitimate. There is ākāśa beyond the world (alokākāśa). There is no motion or rest in it. No atoms or jīvas can step beyond mundane space into supramundane pure space. Therefore space (ākāśa) is not the cause of motion and rest. If space were the condition of motion and rest of souls and material things, there would be the disappearance of supramundane space devoid of motion and rest and destruction of the world (loka). Therefore dharma and adharma are the conditions of motion and rest respectively. Space is not their cause. They depend upon independent principles.[2]

Space is imperceptible. It is inferred from the fact that extended substances can exist in some place only. Space is

[1] P., TDTV., 103.
[2] P., TDTV., 99-102.

what accommodates them. It is the necessary condition of their existence. Space does not make things extended. They are extended by their very nature. But they require a locus in which they can exist. Space is the locus of extension. It is not the same as extension. Space is occupied by substances; substances occupy space.

18. *Time* (*Kāla*)

Time is a real substance.[1] It is not a subjective category of the mind. The Jainas distinguish between absolute or real time (pāramārthika kāla) and relative or empirical time (vyāvahārika kāla). Absolute time is the auxiliary cause of continuance (vartanā) of substances. Relative time is the auxiliary cause of changes (parivartana) or modifications (pariṇāma) of substances.[2] Continuance (vartanā), modification (pariṇāma), motions or activities (kriyā), temporal remoteness (paratva), and temporal proximity (aparatva), or oldness (jīrṇatva) and newness (navatva) of substances are the functions of time. Continuance is the function of real time. Modifications, activities, oldness, and newness are the functions of empirical time.[3] Substances continue in time. Their modifications are changes in time. Their movements or successive positions occur in time. Their oldness and newness depend upon the passage of time.

Time has no extension. So it is not an extended substance (astikāya).[4] Extension is of two kinds, monodimensional, or longitudinal extension (ūrdhvapracaya) and multi-dimensional extension (tiryakpracaya). The moments of time exist in a monodimensional series, and have only linear extension. The other substances, living beings, matter, space, dharma, and adharma exist in a two-dimensional series, and have surface extension (tiryakpracaya). Time has one dimension. It is a lineal order. The moments of time do not coexist with one another. Though time is not an extensive substance (astikāya), it is a real substance because it indirectly helps endurance and modifications of other substances.[5]

[1] TS., v. 39. [2] DS., 21.
[3] Ts., SS., v. 22; VP., xvi. 34; *Tsāra.*, iii. 45-48.
[4] P., 109.
[5] P., 109; E.T., p. 110; PI., pp. xxviii-xxix; CON. p. 227.

Real time (kāla) is one, eternal, formless, without beginning or end, and devoid of varieties. Empirical time (samaya) has a beginning and an end, and consists of varieties, seconds, minutes, hours, and the like. Moments are momentary, but hours, days, weeks, and the like have long duration. Real time (niscayakāla) is an eternal substance. Empirical time (vyavahārakāla) is momentary or temporary because it is a modification (paryāya) of real time.[1] Real time, when limited, produces empirical time. It is the material cause (upādānakārana) of empirical time. One time (kāla) is modified into infinite moments (samaya).[2]

Empirical time (samaya) is the auxiliary cause of changes (parivartana), modifications (pariṅāma), movements (kriyā), and temporal priority (paratva), and posteriority (aparatva) of substances. It is apparent time. It consists in motion of the sun in rising and setting. It is the auxiliary cause of the modifications of substances in the form of oldness and newness. Empirical time is the indicator of real time. Some deny real time behind empirical time which consists in acts (kriyā) or motions of the sun in rising and setting. But this view is wrong. There must be real time which assists the production of these acts or movements. There must be real time behind apparent time. Real time is limited by acts or movements of substances and becomes apparent time. Real time is inferred from the modifications of substances brought about by apparent time. Rice is put into water and heated and turned into cooked rice during a period of time. The existence of real time is inferred from the continuity (vartanā) of rice in the midst of its slow changes brought about by empirical time. Real time does not produce its continuity, but indirectly assists its continuity, just as empirical time does not produce its modifications, but indirectly assists production of its modifications. Some Jaina writers do not regard time as a separate substance, but regard it as a mode (paryāya) of other substances. But this is wrong. Modifications of substances presuppose the existence of empirical time. If there is no empirical time, there can be no modifications of substances. Substances themselves are the material cause (upādānakāraṇa) of their modi-

[1] P., TDTV., 108.
[2] DSV., 21; TS., v. 39, 40.

fications. But empirical time is their auxiliary cause (sahakāri kāraṇa).

A substance (dravya) has permanence (dhrauvya), origin (utpāda), and destruction (vyaya). It is endued with qualities (guṇas) and modes (paryāya). Time is a permanent substance through origin and destruction of its modifications, moments, minutes, and the like which constitute empirical time. Their origin and decay depend upon other causes. The qualities of real time are either generic or specific. Its generic qualities are unconsciousness, incorporeality, subtlety or imperceptibility, absence of sensible qualities, such as lightness, heaviness, and the like. Its specific qualities are aiding continuity of other substances. Origin and destruction of empirical time are its modifications. The particles of time (kālāṇu) are infinite (ananta) in number. There are as many particles of time (kālāṇu) as there are space-units (pradeśa) of mundane space (pratilokākāśapradeśabhinna). Each time-particle exists in each space-unit. It is inactive. It functions in itself. Continuity is aided by real time. Modifications are aided by empirical time.[1] Real time is one. But it is composed of innumerable moments, past, present, and future, which are its modifications or limitations.[2] Time is the real substance that assists the continuity of substances through their successive modifications and ensures orderliness of evolution. Time guarantees orderly evolution of the world.[3] Time causes evolution and dissolution. Creative evolution of the world is aided by utsarpiṇī kāla. Dissolution of it is aided by avasarpiṇī kāla.[4]

Time is confined to the mundane space (lokākāśa). It does not exist in supramundane space. It exists in mundane space in all its space-points. Innumerable particles of time existing in innumerable space-points are confined to mundane space. They do not step beyond it to pure supramundane space.[5] Each particle of time (kālāṇu) exists in its own capacity in each space-point of mundane space, and is devoid of activity.[6] Different particles of time exist in different space-points.[7]

---

[1] SS., v. 39. [2] TS., SS., v. 40.
[3] C. R. Jain : *Key of Knowledge*, p. 758.
[4] CON., p. 230.
[5] TSV., v. 40, p. 440; DS., 22.
[6] Tsāra., iii. 40. [7] VP., xvi. 35.

They never mix with one another. This characteristic distinguishes time from all other substances. Time consists of separate successive particles, while the other substances are collections of indivisible parts which are inseparable from one another.[1] Just as space is the receptacle (ādhāra) of innumerable substances, and its own receptacle, so time is the auxiliary cause of its own modifications and those of the other substances.[2] Infinite particles of time (samaya) are the modifications of one real time.[3] A particle of time (samaya) or moment (kālāṇu) is the time taken by an atom of matter to move from one space-point to the next space-point. The atoms of matter can combine with one another and form aggregates (skandha), but particles of time cannot combine with one another. Each particle of time exists separately. Though an atom of matter may be said to occupy many space-points with reference to its existence in an aggregate, a particle of time cannot be said to occupy many space-points, because it cannot combine with other particles of time. Time is not a subjective cognition (vijñāna). It is a real substance. It has qualities and modifications. It is the substratum of conjunction and disjunction of substances.[4] The Jaina conception of time is realistic. Matter, space, and time are inseparable from one another. M-S-T may be said to be the unit of the dynamic world. Atoms of matter, space-points, time-points, motion (gati) and rest (sthiti) as assisted by dharma and adharma constitute the world.

19. *The Nine Categories* (*Padārtha*)

The Jainas recognize the reality of nine verities, *viz.*, (1) soul (jīva), (2) non-soul (ajīva), (3) merit (puṇya), (4) demerit (pāpa), (5) inflow (āsrava), (6) bondage (bandha), (7) stoppage (samvara), (8) shedding of karma (nirjarā), (9) liberation (mokṣa). Jīva is living being or soul. Ajīva is a non-living being or non-soul. Matter (pudgala), dharma, adharma, space (ākāśa), and time (kāla) constitute ajīva. Puṇya is virtue or merit. Pāpa is vice or demerit. Āsrava is the inflow of karma-matter into the soul. Bandha is bondage, or invest-

---

[1] DS., E.T., p. 63.
[2] DSV., 22, p. 27.
[4] TSV., v. 39, 1, p. 439.
[3] TS., v. 40.

ment of the soul by karma-matter. Samvara is the stoppage or arrest of the inflow of karma-matter into the soul. Nirjarā is partial destruction of the accumulated karma-matter. Mokṣa is liberation of the soul from bondage. It is complete destruction of the accumulated karma-matter. It is complete separation of the soul from the karma-matter. Of these nine categories jīva and ajīva are the primary existences (bhāva). Merit, demerit, āsrava, bandha, samvara, nirjarā, and mokṣa are the conditions of the soul (jīva), which arise from its different relations to karma-matter (pudgala).[1]

Pure thought or good will is an auspicious modification (śubhapariṇāma) of the soul. It is subjective righteousness, virtue or merit (bhāvapuṇya). It produces an auspicious modification of karma-matter. It is called objective virtue (dravya puṇya). Subjective virtue produces objective virtue. Objective virtue facilitates subjective virtue. Auspicious modification of karma-matter facilitates purity of thought. Impure thought or bad will is an inauspicious modification (aśubhapariṇāma) of the soul. It is subjective unrighteousness, vice, or demerit (bhāvapāpa). It produces an inauspicious modification of karma-matter. It is called objective vice (dravyapāpa). Subjective vice produces objective vice. Objective vice facilitates subjective vice. Inauspicious modification of karma-matter aggravates evil disposition. Thus bhāvakarmas and dravya karmas interact upon each other.[2] Auspicious thought activities (bhāva) produce virtue (puṇya). Inauspicious thought-activities (bhāva) produce vice (pāpa). Auspicious bhāvas consist of freedom from delusion, acquisition of right faith and knowledge, practice of reverence, observance of the five vows, *viz.*, truthfulness, non-injury, chastity, non-acceptance of unnecessary gifts, and non-stealing, subduing of the four passions, anger, pride, deceit, and greed, control of the senses, and practice of penances. They produce virtue or merit (puṇya). Virtue produces pleasure. Inauspicious bhāvas are the opposites of auspicious bhāvas. They produce vice or demerit (pāpa).[3] Vice produces pain. Subjective virtue (bhāvapuṇya) produces auspicious karmas (dravyapuṇya) such as pleasure-bearing (sadvedya), good-life-determining (śubhāyuṣ),

[1] P., TDTV., 116.
[2] TDTV., 139.
[3] DSV., 38.

good-character-determining (śubhanāma), and good-family-determining (śubhagotra) karmas. Subjective vice (bhāvapāpa) produces inauspicious karmas (dravyapāpa) such as pain-bearing (asadvedya), bad-life-determining (aśubhāyuṣ), bad-character-determining (aśubhanāma), bad-family—determining (aśubhagotra) karmas.[1] Consciousness, bliss, and innate purity constitute the essential nature of the soul. So it cannot be said to have virtue, vice, bondage, and liberation. But it acquires virtue and vice according as it has auspicious and inauspicious thought-activities (bhāva) which produce auspicious and inauspicious karma-particles.[2] The Jaina recognizes the reality of subjective virtue and objective virtue, and subjective vice and objective vice. Objective virtue (dravyapuṇya) is auspicious karma-matter (satkarmapudgala). Objective vice (dravyapāpa) is inauspicious karma-matter (asatkarmapudgala). This is the distinctive feature of the Jaina doctrine of virtue and vice.

Āsrava is the influx of karma-matter. There are two kinds of Āsrava: (1) Bhāvāśrava, (2) Dravyāsrava. The modification of the soul which generates the influx of karma-matter into the soul is subjective influx (bhāvāsrava). The physical influx of karma-matter into the soul is objective influx (dravyāsrava).[3] Bhāvāsrava is the modification of the soul through the five senses. It consists in thought-activities. It causes the physical influx of karma-matter into the soul, which is called dravyāsrava. Bhāvāsrava is related to thought-activities (jīvapariṇāma). Dravyāsrava is related to karma-matter (karmapariṇāma). Āsrava is the effect of bodily, verbal, and mental actions.[4] Āsrava is the cause of bondage of the soul. It is said to be the channel through which karma-matter enters into the soul.[5] Āsrava is the spring of virtue or vice. Bhāvāsravas are of two kinds, bhāvapuṇyāsrava and bhāvapāpāsrava. Purity of mind, attachment to excellences of saints, and activities of body, speech, and mind prompted by compassion are called bhāvapuṇyāsrava. They generate the influx of pure karma-matter into the soul. They are the springs of virtue. They produce pure karma-matter (puṇyadravyakarma).[6] Reverence for saints, following preceptors, and active pursuit of virtue consti-

---

[1] TS., viii. 25, 26.
[2] DSV., 38.
[3] DS., 29.
[4] TS., vi. 1, 2.
[5] Tsāra, iv. 3.
[6] P., TDTV., 142.

tute praiseworthy attachment. Compassion consists in feeling sympathy for the thirsty, the hungry, and the distressed, and efforts to alleviate their misery. These are bhāvapuṇyāsravas.[1] Anger, pride, deceit, and greed agitate the mind. They produce impurity of the mind. Inordinate attachment to worldly things, impure emotions, insatiable hankering for and indulgence in sensual pleasures, causing anguish to others, slandering others are the springs of vice. Animal instincts, food-seeking instinct, fear-instinct, sex-instinct, and acquisitive instinct,—the soul-defiling emotions, indulgence in sensual pleasures, misery, wrath, impure thoughts, and infatuation also are the springs of vice. They are called bhāvapāpāsrava. They produce impure karma-matter called dravyapāpakarma.[2]

Bhāvāsravas are of five kinds: (1) false belief (mithyātva), (2) want of control (avirati), (3) inadvertence (pramāda), (4) bodily, verbal, and mental activities (yoga), and (5) passions (kaṣāya)[3] (1) False belief (mithyātva) is of five kinds, a false belief taken to be true (ekānta), a right belief and a false belief both taken to be true (viparīta), a false belief known to be false, but retained owing to old habit (vinaya), doubt as to truth or falsity of a belief (saṃśaya), and lack of any belief due to want of exercise of reason (ajñāna). (2) Lack of control (avirati) is of five kinds, injury (hiṃsā), falsehood (anṛta), stealing (caurya), incontinence (abrahma), and desire to possess things (parigrahākāṅkṣā). (3) Inadvertence (pramāda) is of five kinds, contemptible talk (vikathā), passions (kaṣāya), *e.g.*, anger, pride, deceit, and greed, abuse of the five senses (indriya), sleep (nidrā), and attachment to worldly objects (rāga). Each passion is of four degrees of intensity, excessive, intense, moderate, and mild. Thus there are sixteen passions. The other passions (no-kaṣāya) are laughter (hāsya), sense-indulgence (rati), languor (arati), sorrow (śoka), fear (bhaya), hatred (jugupsā), male sex-feeling (puruṣa veda), female sex-feeling (strīveda), and eunuch's sex-feeling (napuṃsakaveda).[4] Bhāvāsravas produce dravyāsravas or actual influx of eight kinds of karma-matter into the soul,—jñānāvaraṇīya, darśanāvaraṇīya, vedanīya, mohanīya, āyuṣ, nāma, gotra, and antarāya. The karma-matter which flows into the soul is very subtle (sūkṣma-

[1] P., 143, 144.
[2] P., 146, 147.
[3] DS., 30.
[4] DSV., 30, E.T.,pp. 74-77.

sūkṣma) and therefore imperceptible.[1] The Jainas use the Prakrit word *āsava.* The Buddhists also use the Pali word āsava corresponding to the Sanskrit word āsrava, and take it in the sense of defilements or depravities. They describe various kinds of āsravas. Some scholars think that the Buddhists borrowed the concept of āsava from the Jainas.[2]

The conscious state which causes the investment of the soul by karma-matter is called subjective bondage (bhāvabandha). The actual investment of the soul by karma-matter is objective bondage (dravyabandha). It is actual interpenetration of karma-particles with the soul.[3] Bhāvabandha is the alliance of the soul with conscious states generated by attachment and aversion.[4] Dravyabandha is the actual union of the soul with karmic matter. The soul, being defiled with passions, assimilates matter fit to form karma-particles. Bondage is this assimilation of karmic matter into the soul.[5] Bhāvabandha is the auspicious or inauspicious modifications of the soul tinged with attachment, aversion, and delusion. Dravyabandha is the actual interpenetration of the soul with auspicious or inauspicious modifications of karma-particles.[6] The union of karma-matter with the soul is due to the actions of mind, body, and speech (yoga). They directly bring about the interpenetration of karma-particles into the soul. Bondage is a particular modification of karma-particles by which they interpenerate the soul. It is due to emotions (bhāva) of soul tinged with desire, attachment, aversion, and delusion. These states are brought about by deluding (mohanīya) karma which causes spiritual delusion. Yoga is the external condition (bahiraṅgakāraṇa) of bondage, since it directly brings about the union of karma-matter into the soul. The emotions of the soul are the internal cause (antaraṅgakāraṇa) of bondage.[7] Umāsvāmi mentions wrong belief (mithyādarśana), vowlessness (avirati), carelessness (pramāda), passions (kaṣāya), and modifications of the soul due to actions of mind, body, and speech (yoga) as the conditions of bondage.[8] But Kundakundācārya shows that these psychical conditions themselves are the effects of desire,

---

[1] DS., 31.
[2] S. C. Ghoshal., DS., E.T., p. 72.
[3] DS., 32.
[4] VP., xvi. 43.
[5] TS., viii. 2.
[6] P., TDTV., 154.
[7] P., TDTV., 155.
[8] TS., viii. 1.

attachment, aversion, and delusion. They cannot bring about bondage in the absence of desire, attachment, and the like. Hence they are merely the subsidiary conditions of bondage. The psychical dispositions (jīvabhāva) brought about by desire, attachment, aversion, and delusion are the internal cause of bondage.[1]

Objective bondage (dravyabandha) is of two kinds, bondage of the soul to good (puṅya) karmas, and its bondage to bad (pāpa) karmas. It is of four kinds according to the nature (prakṛti) of karma, duration (sthiti) of bondage, intensity (anubhāga), and number of (pradeśa) of karma-particles interpenerating the soul.[2] Different kinds of karmas, knowledge-obscuring (jñānāvaraṇīya), perception-obscuring (darśanāvaraṇīya), feeling-obscuring (vedanīya), deluding (mohanīya), age-determining (āyuṣ), character-determining (nāma), family-determining (gotra), and obstructive (antarāya),—determine the nature of bondage. The karma-matter is combined with the soul for a longer or shorter duration. It may be mild or strong so that its fruition is mild or strong, immediate or delayed. The particles of karma-matter may be few or many, and interpenetrate the soul to a small or great extent. These are the four kinds of actual bondage.[3] The nature and extent of bondage are due to the activities of mind, speech, and body. The duration and intensity of bondage are due to emotions and passions (kaṣāya), attachment, aversion, and the like. Passions are the internal cause of bondage. Activities of mind, speech, and body are the external cause of bondage.[4]

First, there is a psychical disposition which generates the influx of karmic matter into the soul. This is bhāvāsrava or subjective influx. Second, the subjective influx generates the physical influx of karma-matter into the soul. This is dravyāsrava. Third, there are emotional states due to desire, attachment, aversion and delusion. They produce subjective bondage or bhāvabandha. Fourth, the subjective bondage produces physical bondage (dravyabandha) or union of the soul with karma-particles. It is interpenetration (saṃśleṣa) of the soul with karma-matter.[5]

[1] P., TDTV., 156.
[2] TS., viii. 3.
[3] TS., viii. 3; DS., 33.
[4] DSV., 33; P., 155; SS., viii. 3.
[5] VP., xvi. 43, 44.

Samvara is the opposite (pratipakṣa) of āsrava.[1] Āsrava is the influx of karma-matter into the soul. Samvara is the arrest or stoppage of the influx of karma-matter into the soul.[2] As there are two kinds of āsravas, bhāvāsrava and dravyāsrava, so there are two kinds of samvaras, bhāvasamvara and dravyasamvara. The modification of consciousness (cetanāpariṇāma) which is the cause of stopping the influx of karma-matter into the soul is called bhāvasamvara. This is subjective inhibition. The actual stoppage of the influx of karma-matter into the soul is called dravyasamvara. This is objective inhibition. The bhāvasamvaras are the five vows (vrata), the five careful attitudes (samiti), the three kinds of restraints (gupti), the ten kinds of observances (dharma), the twelve kinds of meditations (anuprekṣā), the twenty kinds of victory over trouble (parīṣahajaya), and the five kinds of right conduct (cāritra).[3] These will be discussed under the heading of Ethics. Kundakundācārya regards the voluntary suppression of enjoyment of sensuous pleasures, the taints of emotions and passions (kaṣāya), and the animal instincts (saṃjñā) as the subjective inhibition (bhāvasamvara), since it is the cause of arrest of the influx of karma-matter into the soul.[4] The voluntary suppression of attachment, aversion, and delusion is the subjective inhibition. The arrest of beneficial (śubha) and harmful (aśubha) modifications of karmas caused by the suppression of the emotions is the objective inhibition.[5] All actions of mind, body, and speech, yielding pleasure and pain should be avoided, because they attract beneficial and harmful karma-particles to the soul. Virtue and vice both should be avoided, since both produce karma-matter. Virtue produces pleasure. Vice produces pain. The moral aspirant should be indifferent to pleasure and pain. The states of consciousness are pleasant (śubha), unpleasant (aśubha), and pure (śuddha). Only pure states of consciousness should be cultivated.[6] The actual stoppage of all karma-matter through the great vows and meditation is the objective inhibition (dravyasamvara).[7]

---

[1] Commentary on Sthānāṅga, I.
[2] TS., ix. 1.
[3] TS., ix. 2; DS., 34, 35.
[4] P., 148.
[5] P., TDTV., 149.
[6] P., 149, 150.
[7] VP., xvi. 67, 68.

Destruction of karmas is called nirjarā. It is of two kinds, bhāvanirjarā and dravyanirjarā. The pure thought activities which cause the destruction of karmas through penances after their fruits are enjoyed constitute bhāvanirjarā. It is the subjective shedding. The destruction of karmas is dravyanirjarā. It is the objective shedding.[1] Bhāvanirjarā is the pure modification of the soul which facilitates the separation of karmas from the soul. Dravyanirjarā is their actual separation from the soul. Bhāvanirjarā is of two kinds, savipāka or akāma and avipāka or sakāma. When karmas are separated from the soul of themselves after their fruits are enjoyed, this is called savipāka nirjarā. It is non-voluntary (akāma). When karmas are separated from the soul by penances before their fruits are enjoyed, this is called avipāka nirjarā. It is voluntary (sakāma). All beings have savipākanirjarā for their karmas disappear after their fruits are enjoyed on earth, or in hell or heaven. Avipākanirjarā is generated voluntarily by penances which destroy karmas before their fruits are enjoyed. The mirror of the soul is soiled by the dust of karmas. When they are destroyed or removed from the soul, it becomes transparent.[2]

A person should practise inhibition (samvara) to stop all further influx of karmas, and destroy the karmas, which have interpenetrated the soul, by means of penances. The dust of karmas is completely washed off by the practice of penances (tapas) and meditation (dhyāna) upon the self with its pure thought with the controlled senses. The fire of meditation is born of freedom from attachment, aversion, delusion, and actions of mind, body, and speech. It burns up all beneficial and harmful karmas. Meditation completely determined by right faith, right knowledge, and right conduct, on the pure self unrelated to objects is the cause of annihilation of karmas (nirjarā).[3] The nature and kinds of meditation and penances will be discussed in connection with the Jaina Ethics.

Nirjarā leads to mokṣa. The modification of the soul, which is the cause of destruction of all karmas, is called bhāvamokṣa. It is subjective liberation. The actual separa-

---

[1] DS., 36.
[2] Tsāra, vii. 2-4; VP., xvi. 90; DS., E.T., pp. 93-96.
[3] P., 151-153, 159.

tion of all karmas from the soul is called dravyamokṣa. It is objective liberation.[1] Nemicandra distinguishes bhāvamokṣa from dravyamokṣa in this manner. Kundakundācārya considers the destruction of the four destructive (ghātīya) karmas,—knowledge-obscuring (jñānāvaraṇīya), perception-obscuring (darśanāvaraṇīya), deluding (mohanīya), and obstructive (antarāya) karmas,—to be bhāvamokṣa, and the destruction of the four non-destructive (aghātīya) karmas,—bliss-obscuring (vedanīya), age-determining (āyuṣ), character-determining (nāma), and family-determining (gotra) karmas,—to be dravyamokṣa.[2] According to Umāsvāmi the destruction of the four destructive karmas leads to perfect knowledge or omniscience (kevalajñāna), and the destruction of all kinds of karmas and the soul's complete separation from them lead to liberation (mokṣa).[3] Hence bhāvamokṣa is freedom from the four destructive karmas, and dravyamokṣa is freedom from the four non-destructive karmas. In the state of liberation the soul realizes infinite knowledge (anantajñāna), infinite perception (anantadarśana), infinite bliss (anantasukha), and infinite power (anantavīrya). These four infinite qualities are called ananta-catuṣṭaya. The liberated soul becomes God.[4] Thus the Jainas believe in the innate divinity of each soul. But they do not recognize the reality of God as the creator of the world. Infinite knowledge and infinite perception are innate in the soul. Spotless conduct leads to the realization of these infinite qualities.[5] The liberated soul is absolutely self-determined, since it is firmly established in its intrinsic nature, and free from relations to other souls and objects.[6] It intuits itself as constituted by infinite knowledge and infinite perception which constitute its essential nature, and is therefore absolutely self-determined.[7] But the conduct of a bound soul is self-determined as well as other-determined. It is self-determined when it is determined by its essential qualities. It is other-determined when it is determined by its accidental qualities. When the soul is moved by attachment and aversion to other things, and experiences pleasure and pain, it is other-determined (parasa-

---

[1] DS., 37.
[2] P., TDTV., 160
[3] TS., x. 1, 2.
[4] P., TDTV., 158.
[5] P., 161.
[6] P., 166.
[7] P., 165.

maya). When it is self-determined (svasamaya), or determined by its essential nature, it is liberated from the bondage of karma-matter.[1] The self determined by pleasant mental states yielding virtue (puṇya), and painful mental states yielding vice (pāpa), which produce good karmas and bad karmas, is other-determined.[2] The liberated soul transcends virtue and vice and attains absolute purity. It shines forth in its innate glory. Right belief (samyagdarśana), right knowledge (samyagjñāna), and right conduct (samyak cāritra) are three jewels (triratna) which are the means of liberation. They exist in the soul. So the soul itself is the cause of its liberation.[3] Right faith, right knowledge, and right conduct will be discussed under the heading of Ethics.

III. Psychology

20. *The Soul and the Body*

Jainism adopts a dualism of soul (jīva) and body. The soul is the knower, the enjoyer, and the active agent. Knowledge constitutes its essence. The self and knowledge cannot be separated from each other.[4] The self has three fundamental modes of consciousness—cognition, feeling and conation. Feeling is experience of the fruits of karma. In the order of psychic evolution feeling appears first, then conation, and at last knowledge. Plant-souls have feeling ; animal souls have feeling and conation ; human souls have feeling, conation, and knowledge. The perfect souls have pure knowledge.[5] Body is corporeal. It is matter (pudgala). It is knowable. It is enjoyable.[6] The relation of the self to the body is that of the knower to the known. Jainism advocates dualism of soul and body, and avoids mentalism and materialism. It does not reduce body to ideas of the soul. Nor does it reduce the soul to an epiphenomenon of the body. The soul is a spiritual substance. The body is a material substance. The mundane soul is embodied. The liberated soul is disembodied. The former is of the same dimension as the body in the sense that it

[1] P., 162; 163.
[2] P., 164.
[3] DS., 39, 40.
[4] P., 40, 49, 55.
[5] P., 38, 39.
[6] P., 89.

illumines the whole body like the light of a lamp. It is associated with karmic matter (karmasaṃyukta). The latter is disembodied and absolutely free from karmic matter.[1] Jainism seems to advocate the theory of parallelism between soul and body. "Karmic matter itself through its own essential nature brings about its own changes. Jīva, too, in the same manner, through its own impure states of thought that are conditioned by karma, brings about its own thought changes."[2] "The mental states and the states of karma (matter) form two independent series. A change in karmic matter is determined by the antecedent physical change. Similarly the mental change in the jīva is entirely determined by the antecedent mental change. In short, the jīva is the primary condition of mental changes, and karmic matter, of its own changes. The physical changes of karmic matter cannot be attributed to jīva nor the mental changes of jīva to matter."[3] The soul which brings about changes in itself is the cause of its own modifications of consciousness. It is not the cause of changes in karmic matter, which are distinctly physical in nature.[4] Jainism admits that modifications of karmas are the concomitant causes of the emotional states (bhāva) of the soul, but that they are not their material cause. It also admits that beneficial and harmful states of consciousness are the concomitant causes of good karmas and bad karmas, but that they are not their material cause. It seems to hold a kind of psycho-physical parallelism. Mental states may be the efficient cause (nimitta kartṛ) of karmic states, but not their material cause (upādāna kartṛ). Similarly, karmic states may be the efficient cause (nimitta kartṛ) of mental states, but not their material cause (upādāna kartṛ).[5] The soul is the direct material cause of its own emotions, though they are conditioned by changes in karmic matter. The soul is their material cause. Karmic matter is their efficient cause. The soul is their immediate cause, while karmic matter is their indirect cause. Emotions cannot occur apart from the corresponding changes in karmic matter. But they cannot be said to be really caused by karmic matter, since they are states of the soul and can be directly

[1] P., 27., E.T., pp. 24-26.
[2] P., 68.
[3] P., 68, E.T., p. 69.
[4] P., 67.
[5] P., 66, E.T., pp. 67-68.

caused by it, though they are indirectly conditioned by karmic matter. Emotional states are indirectly conditioned by karmic matter. Karmic changes are indirectly conditioned by changes in the soul. They are indirectly conditioned by each other. They are not directly caused by each other. They are parallel to each other.[1] Jainism thus seems to uphold psycho-physical parallelism. It does not seem to uphold interactionism. It seeks to explain psycho-physical parallelism by contiguous co-existence of soul and body. "The jivas and karma-vargaṇas co-exist and by the mere fact of contiguity jiva and karmic matter are brought together."[2] But Jainism regards objective bondage (dravya-bandha) as interpenetration (anyonyapraveśa) or union (saṃśleṣa) of the soul and karmic matter. This union can hardly be explained by psycho-physical parallelism. The commentator on *Pañcāstikāyasamayasāra* explains the union of karmic matter with the soul by contiguous co-existence. The soul is united with karmic matter even as a casket filled with collyrium powder becomes black by mere contact (añjanacūrṇapūrṇasamudgakanyāyena).[3] The jīva creates its own impure states tinged with attachment, aversion, and delusion owing to its beginningless bondage. But there karmic matter exists in the same place. The impure mental states are the concomitant condition (nimitta kāraṇa) of changes in karmic matter. Particles of karma interpenetrate the space-points of the soul, and are united with it by their own nature.[4]

21. *Modes of Consciousness*

Jainism recognizes three modes of consciousness, cognition, feeling, and conation. Feeling is the experience of pleasure and pain, which are the fruits of karmas (karmaphalacetanā). Knowledge (jñāna) and perception (darśana) are the cognitions. They constitute the essence of the self. Conation and activity are found in a mundane soul. They are actuated by attachment, aversion, and delusion which are the main springs of

---

[1] P., 63-66.
[2] P., 70, E.T., pp. 70-71.
[3] P., 70.
[4] Tadā ātmabhāvameva nimittīkṛtya jivapradeśeṣu parasparāvagāhenānupraviṣṭāḥ svabhāvaireva pudgalāḥ karmabhāvamāpadyante. P, TDTV., 71.

action. The actions of a mundane soul are self-determined, when they are determined by pure thoughts, and other-determined when they are determined by emotions and passions. The actions of a perfect (siddha) soul are absolutely self-determined, since they are determined by the intrinsic purity of the soul. A liberated soul has infinite power, but no activity. It has infinite knowledge, infinite perception, infinite bliss, and infinite power. Life and consciousness are co-extensive. Life is always attended with consciousness. Life is an attribute of the soul.

There are five kinds of knowledge: (1) sensitive knowledge (mati), (2) testimony (śruta), (3) knowledge of remote objects (avadhi), (4) telepathic knowledge of other minds (manaḥparyāya), and (5) omniscience (kevalajñāna). Knowledge is either immediate (pratyakṣa) or mediate (parokṣa). Perception is direct or immediate knowledge. It is of two kinds, empirical and transcendental. Empirical perception is either sensuous or non-sensuous or mental. Sense-perception has four stages, avagraha, īhā, avāya, and dhāraṇā. Transcendental perception is incomplete or complete. Avadhi and manaḥparyāya are incomplete transcendental perception. Kevalajñāna is complete transcendental perception. Perception is always determinate (savikalpa). There is no indeterminate (nirvikalpa) perception. Perception involves sensations. Sensations are of five kinds, tactual, gustatory, olfactory, visual, and auditory. Tactual sensations are lightness and heaviness, softness and hardness, roughness and smoothness, cold and heat. These include sensations of temperature, pressure, and kinæsthetic or motor sensations. Olfactory sensations are agreeable smell and disagreeable smell. Gustatory sensations are pungent, bitter, sweet, sour, and astringent tastes. Visual sensations are black, blue, yellow, white, and pink colours. Auditory sensations are sounds caused by men, and those caused by nature (*e.g.*, thunder, roar of ocean, etc.). The sounds caused by men are uttered or unuttered. Unuttered artificial sounds are musical sounds of drums (tata), musical sounds of stringed instruments as vīṇā (vitata), musical sounds of bells (ghana), sounds produced from conches and the like (suṣira).[1] Sounds are produced by the striking of molecules

[1] SS., v. 24.

of matter against one another. The sense-organs are of two kinds, the physical sense-organs (dravyendriya) and their psychical counterparts (bhāvendriya). The physical senses (dravyendriya) are the sense-organs and the protective coverings. The pupil is the internal visual organ. The eye-lid is its protective cover. There are five physical sense-organs, tactual, gustatory, olfactory, visual, and auditory. The so-called five organs of action (karmendriya) are not sense-organs proper. The psychical senses (bhāvendriya) consist of partial destruction and subsidence of knowledge-obscuring karma (labdhi) and conscious attention of the soul (upayoga).[1] Manas is of two kinds, dravyamanas and bhāvamanas. The former is made of karmic matter. The latter is the purity of the soul caused by the subsidence and partial destruction of knowledge-obscuring karma. Manas is not regarded as a sense-organ.[2] Sometimes the soul itself is regarded as a sense-organ, since even sense-knowledge is revealed from within the soul owing to the partial destruction of karma-matter covering the soul.[3] Retention (dhāraṇā) is the last state of perception. Perception is retained in the self. Impression (saṃskāra) is a particular power of the self (ātmaśaktiviśeṣa). Mediate (parokṣa) knowledge is indistinct, while immediate knowledge or perception is distinct. It is of five kinds, recollection, recognition, induction, deduction, and testimony which have already been discussed. Feelings are of three kinds, pleasure, pain and indifference. Attachment, aversion, and delusion are affective-conative states. They are springs of action. Passions (kaṣāya) are anger, pride, deceit, and greed in different degrees of intensity. Emotions (nokaṣāya) are mirth or laughter (hāsya), indulgence (rati) languor (arati), sorrow (śoka), fear (bhaya), disgust (jugupsā), sex-feeling of a woman (strīveda), sex-feeling of a man (puṃveda), and an eunuch's sex-feeling (napuṃsakaveda).[4] Instincts (saṃjñā) are of four kinds, food-seeking instincts (āhārasaṃjñā), instinct of fear (bhayasaṃjñā), sex-instinct (maithunasaṃjñā), and acquisitive instinct (parigrahasaṃjñā).[5] When karmas are annihilated, infinite transcendental knowledge, infinite transcendental bliss, and infinite power

[1] TS., SS., ii. 15-19.
[2] SS., ii. 11.
[3] JTV., p. 98.
[4] TS., viii. 9.
[5] P., TDTV., 147.

surge up in the perfect soul. It fills the whole universe with its omniscience.

IV. Ethics

22. *Ethical discipline*

The subjective inhibition (bhāvasamvara) is brought about by (1) vows (vrata), (2) careful attitudes (samiti), (3) restraints (gupti), (4) observances (dharma), (5) meditations (anuprekṣā), (6) victory over troubles (pariṣahajaya), and (7) right conduct (cāritra).[1]

(1) The vows (vrata) are of five kinds, *viz.*, non-injury (ahiṃsā), truthfulness (satya), non-stealing (asteya), sex-restraint (brahmacarya), and non-acceptance of unnecessary gifts (aparigraha). The five vows of the Jainas correspond to the five restraints (yama) of the Yoga system.[2] They are negative duties. They consist in abstention from injury, falsehood, stealing, sex-indulgence, and acceptance of unnecessary gifts. They are called small vows (aṇuvrata), when there is limited abstention from them. They are called great vows (mahāvrata), when there is total abstention from them. The Jaina vows are included in the duties of householders and monks according to Buddhism.[3] The sins corresponding to the duties of ahiṃsā, truthfulness, non-stealing, sex-restraint, and non-acceptance of unnecessary gifts are injury (hiṃsā), falsehood (anṛta), stealing (steya), sex-gratification (abrahma), and worldly attachment (mūrcchā). Injury consists in hurting the life of a creature by actions of mind, body, and speech moved by passions (pramattayoga). Falsehood consists in speaking untruth which gives pain to living beings through bodily and mental actions due to passions. Theft is misappropriation of others' property not given by them through vibrations of passions. Even covetousness is stealing. Incontinence consists in all acts of sex-indulgence due to attachment of man and woman for each other. It is sex-gratification through vibrations of passions. It nourishes injury, falsehood, and theft. Covetousness consists in attachment to the living and non-living objects

---

[1] TS., SS., ix. 2.
[2] YS., ii. 30.
[3] Rhys Davids: *Buddhism*, pp. 138-40.

of enjoyment, and in acquisition, preservation, and improvement of them. It is due to egoism or the sense that the external objects of enjoyment are mine. It is due to vibrations of passions. Covetousness nourishes injury, falsehood, theft, and incontinence.[1]

Vowers should be free from deceit (māyā), wrong belief (mithyā), and desire for enjoyment of wordly objects (nidāna). They are of two classes, householders and monks. Householders should observe small vows (aṇuvrata). Monks should observe great vows (mahāvrata). Small vows are partial abstention from sins. Great vows are total abstention from sins.[2] Householders should not kill animals. They should not tell agreeable lies under the influence of affection, infatuation, and other emotions even in times of danger. They should not make use of others' property without permission, even when it is deserted by the owner owing to hurtful fear. They should not commit adultery. They should be chaste in their married life. They should put a voluntary limit upon their possessions in life. These are the five small vows.[3] Monks should not kill or injure any kind of life. They should not indulge in falsehood in thought, word, and deed. They should not covet others' possessions under any circumstances. They should completely extirpate their attachment to objects of enjoyment. They should totally abstain from indulgence in sex-thoughts, sex-words, and sex-acts. They should not possess any property, and accept any gifts except what is absolutely necessary for bare subsistence. They should observe the vows with the utmost rigour and vigilance.[4] They should not commit sins, cause sins to be committed, and approve of sins.

For the achievement of steadfastness in the performance of the five vows five kinds of meditations (bhāvanā) are enjoined. The meditations for the vow of non-injury are restraint of speech (vāggupti), restraint of mind (manogupti), careful walking (īryā), care in lifting and laying down things (ādānanikṣepaṇasamiti), and thorough examination of food and water before eating and drinking them (ālokitapānabhojana). The meditations for the vow of truthfulness are suppression of anger (krodha), greed (lobha), cowardice (bhīrutva), mirth

[1] TS., SS., vii. 13-17.
[2] TS., SS., vii. 18, 19, 20, 2.
[3] SS., vii. 20.
[4] *Ibid*, vii. 2.

or laughter (hāsya), and truthful words in accord with the reality (anuvīcivaṣaṇa). The meditations for the vow of stealing are residence in a solitary place (śunyāgāravāsa); residence in a deserted house (vimocitāvāsa), residence in a place where one may not prohibit others (paroparodhākaraṇa), purity in receiving alms (bhaikṣaśuddhi), and abstention from wrangling with co-religionists (saddharmāvisaṃvāda). The meditations for the vow of chastity are giving up hearing stories exciting attachment for women, giving up seeing their beautiful bodies, giving up recollection of past enjoyment of women, giving up exciting and sweet drinks, and giving up adornment of the body. The meditations for the vow of non-covetousness are giving up attachment to pleasant sensible objects, and aversion to unpleasant sensible objects. These are evidently intended for the monks.[1]

The moral aspirants should meditate upon the fact that sins are destructive of welfare (abhyudaya) and liberation (niḥśreyasa) and are therefore censurable, and are themselves pain, since they are the causes of pain. They should meditate on good-will or friendship (maitrī) for all living beings, delight (pramoda) at the sight of virtuous persons, compassion (kāruṇya) for distressed creatures, and indifference (mādhyasthya) to vicious persons. Buddhism and the Yoga system also enjoin cultivation of love for all creatures, compassion for the distressed men and animals, joy for the virtuous, and indifference to the vicious persons.[2] The aspirants should meditate on the transitoriness of the world and life and impurity, unsubstantiality, transitoriness, and painfulness of the body.[3] Buddhism also enjoins meditations on them.[4]

The householders should observe seven supplementary vows. They should set a limit to the distance in all directions beyond which they should not travel in their lives (digvirati). They should further restrict their movements for a specific period within the limited area to suit their requirements (deśavirati). They should abstain from purposeless sins (anarthadaṇḍavirati). They are of five kinds, thinking ill of others

---

[1] *Ibid*, vii. 3-8.
[2] *Sutta-Nipāta*, 149, 150; YS., i. 33.
[3] TS., SS., vii. 9-12.
[4] Rhys Davids: *Buddhism*, pp. 170-71.

(apadhyāna), preaching of sin (pāpopadeśa), thoughtless actions (*e.g.*, breaking the branches of a tree, etc.) (pramādācarita), giving the means of injury to others (hiṃsādāna), and hearing of bad talks (aśubhaśruti). These are the three subsidiary vows (guṇavrata). The householders should daily meditate on the self, the cycle of existence full of pain, and the way to liberation in a quiet place once, twice, or thrice a day (sāmāyika). They should fast once a week, and spend the day in reading scriptures and meditating on the self (proṣadhopavāsa). They should limit the quantity of their food and drink, perfumery, dress, ornaments, beds, houses, and conveyances. They should for ever give up honey, liquor, and meat. They should abstain from killing animals (upabhogaparibhogaparimāṇa). They should feed holy persons every day out of their own food, who may turn up at their houses at the proper time (atithisaṃvibhāga). These are the four disciplinary vows (śikṣāvrata). They prepare the householders for the discipline of ascetic's life. Thus laymen ought to observe five aṇuvratas, three guṇavratas, and four śikṣāvratas. They ought to observe twelve vows. They should also prepare themselves for peaceful death by detachment and suppression of passions (sallekhanā).[1]

The partial transgressions (aticāra) of the vows are described by Umāsvāmi. Those of the small vow of non-injury (ahiṃsāṇuvrata) are tying up an animal or detaining a human being (bandha), beating (badha), mutilating (cheda), overloading (atibhārāropaṇa) an animal or a human being, and with-holding food or drink from an animal or a human being due to anger or carelessness.[2] Those of the small vow of truthfulness (satyāṇuvrata) are preaching false doctrines (mithyopadeśa), divulging the secret actions of man and woman (rohobhyākhyāna), deceptive falsehood such as perjury, diplomacy, and the like (kūṭalekhakriyā), misappropriation of a part of entrusted money (nyāsāpahāra), and divulging the secrets of others indicated by their gestures owing to jealousy (sākāramantrabheda).[3] Those of the small vow of stealing (asteyāṇuvrata) are abetment of theft (stenaprayoga), receiving stolen property (tadāhṛtādāna), illegal trade with alien enemies

---

[1] *Ibid*, vii. 21, 22.
[2] TS., SS., vii. 25.
[3] TS., SS., vii. 26.

(viruddharājyātikrama), buying articles of merchandise with higher weights and measures and selling them with lower weights and measures (hīnādhikamānonmāna), adulteration of food and other articles with artificial substitutes (pratirūpaka-vyavahāra). Hoarding, blackmarketing, profiteering, bribery, smuggling, adulteration, and any kind of dishonesty in trade are partial transgressions of the duty of non-stealing. Those of the small vow of chastity (brahmacaryāṇuvrata) are match-making for persons of other families (paravivāhakaraṇa), adultery with an immoral married woman (itvarikāparigṛhītā-gamana), adultery with an immoral unmarried woman (itvarikā-aparigṛhitāgamana), unnatural sexual intercourse (anaṅga-krīḍā), and intense sexual craving (kāmatīvrābhiniveśa). These are the partial transgressions of the householder's duty of being content with sexual intercourse with his own wife (svadāra-santoṣavrata).[1] The partial transgressions of the small vow of limitation of property (parigrahaparimāṇavrata) are to exceed the limit of fields (kṣetra), houses (vāstu), gold and silver (hiraṇya, suvarṇa) cattle (dhana), corn (dhānya), maid-servants (dāsī), male servants (dāsa), clothes and articles of toilet (kupya) owing to excessive greed.[2] The partial transgressions of the subsidiary vows (guṇavrata) and the instructive vows (śikṣā-vrata) also are mentioned.[3] Those of peaceful death (salle-khaṇāvrata) are desire for longer life (jīvitāśaṃsā), desire for quick death (maraṇāśaṃsā), attachment for friends (mitrānu-rāga), repeated recollection of past enjoyments (sukhānu-bandha), and desire for happiness in the next world (nidāna).[4]

(2) Careful attitudes (samiti) are of five kinds, *viz.*, the use of the trodden path to avoid injury to insects (īryā), gentle and good talk (bhāṣā), receiving alms properly (eṣaṇā), care in lifting and laying down things (ādānanikṣepa), excreting in solitary places (utsarga). These are the means to avoid injury to life.[5] They stop the inflow of karma-matter due to carelessness.

(3) Restraints (gupti) are of three kinds, *viz.*, restraint of body (kāyagupti), restraint of speech (vāggupti), and restraint of mind (manogupti). Restraint means control of the natural

[1] *Ibid*, vii. 28.
[2] *Ibid*, vii. 29.
[3] *Ibid*, vii. 30-36.
[4] *Ibid*, vii. 37.
[5] *Ibid*. ix. 5.

functions. Restraints are conducive to purification of the self. They are not conducive to worldly enjoyments.[1]

(4) Observances (dharma) are of ten kinds, *viz.*, cultivating habits of excellent forgiveness (uttama kṣamā), excellent humility (uttama mārdava), excellent straightforwardness (uttama ārjava), excellent cleanliness (uttama śauca), excellent truthfulness (uttama satya), excellent restraint (uttama saṁyama), excellent austerities (uttama tyāga), excellent indifference (uttama ākiñcanya), and excellent celibacy (uttama brahmacarya).[2] They stop the influx of karma-matter due to transgression of the observances.

(5) Meditations (anuprekṣā) are of twelve kinds, *viz.*, meditation on the transitoriness of the world (anitya), meditation on our having no other refuge than truth (aśaraṇa), meditation on the cycles of empirical life (saṃsāra), meditation on one's sole responsibility for his own good and bad actions (ekatva), meditation on the distinctness of the soul from the non-soul, mind, body, friends, and relatives (anyatva), meditation on the uncleanness of the body (aśuci), meditation on the influx of karma-matter into the soul (āsrava) due to sense-pleasures and passions, meditation on the inhibition of the influx of karma-matter into the soul (saṁvara), meditation on the destruction of karma-matter which has entered into the soul (nirjarā), meditation on the nature of the world (loka), meditation on the difficulty of acquiring right faith, right knowledge, and right conduct (bodhidurlabha), and meditation on the right path (dharma) to liberation.[3] They remove negligence in the performance of duties and produce intense efforts in their performance.

(6) Conquest of troubles (pariṣahajaya) is of various kinds, *viz.*, hunger, thirst, cold, heat, bite of gnats and mosquitoes, nakedness, languor, mental agitation due to the sight of women, fatigue of walking, continuous sitting, sleeping on hard ground, anger due to insult, ill-feeling against the enemy who comes to kill, desire to beg in times of urgent need, failure to get alms, pains of disease, contact with thorny shrubs, disgust at dirt, desire for respect or reward, pride of wisdom, despair arising from failure to attain knowledge, and despair

---

[1] TS., SS., ix. 4. [2] *Ibid*, ix. 6. [3] *Ibid*, ix. 7.

arising from failure to attain the desired fruits even after penances. These are the twenty-two kinds of victory over troubles.[1]

(7) Right conduct (cāritra) is of five kinds, equanimity due to non-injury, sex-restraint, non-stealing, non-acceptance of gifts for a certain period (sāmāyika), paying penalties for faults due to inadvertence and recovering equanimity (chedopasthāpanā), purity due to absolute non-injury to living beings (parihāraviśuddhi), conduct in which only subtle greed is present (sūkṣmasāmparāya), and perfect conduct purged of all passions (yathākhyāta).[2] These kinds of right conduct completely stop the influx of karma-matter into the soul.

The subjective disposition of the soul, which causes destruction of karma-matter which has entered into the soul (bhāvanirjarā) is brought about by penances (tapas).[3] Penances are of two kinds, external (bāhya) and internal (āntara). The external penances are of six kinds, fasting (anaśana), eating less than one's fill (avamodarya), taking a vow to accept food from a householder, only if a certain kind of food is given without letting him know the vow (vṛttiparisaṃkhyāna), giving up delicacies such as ghee, milk, curd, sugar, salt, and oil (rasaparityāga), sleeping in a solitary place devoid of animate beings (viviktaśayyāsana), and mortification of the body (kāyakleśa).[4] The internal penances are of six kinds, *viz.*, atonement for sins (prāyaścitta), reverence (vinaya) for respectable persons, service of the saints (vaiyāvṛtya), study of the scriptures (svādhyāya), giving up attachment to the body (vyutsarga), and concentration (dhyāna).[5] There are nine kinds of atonements, *viz.*, confession of sins to the preceptor (ālocana), repentance for sins (pratikramaṇa), confession and repentance (tadubhaya), giving up a particular food or drink for which there is great attachment (viveka), giving up attachment to the body (vyutsarga), austerities of a particular kind (tapas), cutting short the period of performance of an austerity by a fortnight or a month (cheda), expulsion from the order for some time (parihāra), and re-admission into the order (upasthāpanā).[6] There are four kinds of reverence, *viz.*, reverence for

[1] TS., SS., ix. 9.
[2] *Ibid*, ix. 18.
[3] *Ibid*, ix. 3.
[4] *Ibid*, ix. 19.
[5] *Ibid*, ix. 20.
[6] *Ibid*, ix. 22.

right knowledge (jñāna), reverence for right belief (darśana), reverence for right conduct (cāritra), proper forms of respect, bowing, folding the hands, and the like (upacāra) before respectable persons, and remembering their virtues in their absence.[1] Service is of ten kinds, *viz.*, service of the head (ācārya) of an order of saints, a preceptor (upādhyāya) in the order, a saint undergoing penances (tapasvin), a student saint (śaikṣa), an invalid saint (glāna), brothers of the same order (gaṇa), fellow-disciples (kula), the whole order (saṅgha), a saint (sādhu), and a popular saint (manojña).[2] Study is of five kinds, *viz.*, reading (vācanā), questioning (pṛcchanā), reflection (anuprekṣā), proper recitation (āmnāya), and delivering sermons (dharmopadeśa).[3] Renunciation (vyutsarga) is of two kinds, *viz.*, renunciation of external objects such as houses, cattle, corns and the like, and renunciation of internal objects such as passions, and suppression of the will-to-live.[4] Concentration (dhyāna) is fixation of thought on one particular object for a long time. It is uninterrupted like the unflickering flame of fire. It is steady thought of a particular object uninterrupted by any other thought. It continues up to forty-eight minutes in a person of strong nervous system.[5] Concentration is of four kinds, *viz.*, painful (ārta) concentration, unrighteous (rudra) concentration, righteous (dharmya) concentration, pure (śukla) concentration.[6] Painful concentration is due to loss of a cherished object, attainment of an undesirable object, desire for the attainment of an object, and sorrow. Unrighteous concentration is due to injury, falsehood, theft, and preservation of wealth.[7] Righteous concentration is on the principles of the right faith (ājñāvicaya), removal of wrong belief (apāyavicaya), fruition of the eight kinds of karmas (vipākavicaya), and constitution of the universe (saṃsthānavicaya).[8] Pure concentration is of four kinds, *viz.*, concentration on the self with its different attributes (pṛthaktvavitarka), concentration on one aspect of self (ekatvavitarka), concentration on the pure self with fine vibrations (sūkṣmakriyāpratipātin), and complete concentration on the pure self without any vibrations (vyupara-

---

[1] TS., SS., ix. 23.
[2] *Ibid*, ix. 24.
[3] *Ibid*, ix. 25.
[4] *Ibid*, ix. 26.
[5] *Ibid*, ix. 27.
[6] *Ibid*, ix. 28.
[7] TSāra, vii. 36.
[8] TS., ix. 36.

takriyānivartin).[1] Painful concentration and unrighteous concentration are the causes of bondage. Righteous concentration and pure concentration are the causes of liberation.[2] Penances destroy the karma-matter that has entered into the soul. They are the causes of shedding of karmas (nirjarā).

23. *The Means to Liberation* (*Mokṣa*)

Right faith (samyak darśana), right knowledge (samyak jñāna), and right conduct (samyak cāritra) constitute the path to liberation. They must be determined by the pure nature of the self. If faith, knowledge, and conduct are determined by external things, and moved by attachment and aversion, they cannot lead to liberation. Devotion to an Arhat, Siddha, or Saṅgha produces beneficial karma which yields celestial happiness. But it does not liberate the soul from karmic matter. Absolute freedom from attachment is necessary for liberation. Devotion is an affection which disturbs the tranquillity of mind. Nirvāṇa is attained through devotion to one's self, absolutely free from attachment to any other thing or person. Extirpation of emotions and passions is necessary for liberation. Knowledge of the reality, devotion to the Tīrthaṅkaras and the scriptures, self-control and penance lead to the happiness of heaven, but not to liberation. Nirvāṇa is attained by realization of the true nature of the self. Right conduct is the main constituent element of the path. Only faithful souls (bhavya jīva) are eligible for it. They have faith in it and aspire to it. They are of good dispositions. Faithless souls (abhavya jīva) are not eligible for it. They are of intrinsic evil dispositions. They roam in the world of birth and death for ever.[3]

The self is the abode of the three jewels of right faith, right knowledge, and right conduct. They exist in the self only. So they, being centred in the self, are the cause of liberation. Or the self itself, possessing the three jewels, is the cause of liberation.[4] Right faith is sincere belief in the essential principles of Jainism, jīva, ajīva, āsrava, bandha, saṃvara, nirjarā, and mokṣa. Right knowledge is the knowledge of the self and the not-self, free from doubt, illusion, and

[1] TS., ix. 39.
[2] *Ibid*, ix. 29.
[3] P., TDTV., 171-79; 113.
[4] DS., 39-40.

uncertainty.[1] In mundane souls knowledge (jñāna) is preceded by perception (darśana). But in the perfect soul (kevalin) knowledge and perception arise simultaneously.[2] From the ordinary point of view, vows (vrata), careful attitudes (samiti), and restraints (gupti) constitute right conduct. Doing beneficial actions and abstaining from harmful actions constitute right conduct.[3] But, from the realistic point of view, the arrest of all actions, external and internal, constitutes right conduct. The external acts of body and speech and the internal acts of the mind moved by attachment and aversion produce beneficial karmas and harmful karmas which are attached to the soul and cause saṃsāra. So right conduct consists in checking all kinds of acts which cause saṃsāra. By this means a person becomes free from all influx of beneficial and harmful karmas, realizes the real nature of his self, and attains liberation.[4] From the ordinary and realistic points of view, liberation can be attained by meditation. Freedom from attachment, aversion, and delusion is favourable to meditation. They disturb the calm of the mind. Indifference to beneficial and harmful things is the necessary pre-requisite of meditation.[5] Repetition of mantras and meditation on them are enjoined.[6] All acts of body, speech, and mind should be restrained, and all faculties should be turned inward, and thought should be concentrated on the pure self. This is excellent concentration.[7] Penances, vows, and knowledge of the scriptures are indispensable aids to meditation.[8]

Liberation is the absolute separation of the soul from all karmic matter in the absence of the causes of bondage and destruction of all karmas which have entered into the soul. The destruction of all accumulated karmic matter leads to the self's realization of its intrinsic purity (svātmasaṃprāpti).[9] When karmas are burnt by right faith, right knowledge, and right conduct, they do not cause birth and death, even as scorched seeds do not germinate.[10] First, deluding (mohanīya) karmas, which are the causes of saṃsāra, are entirely destroyed by right faith, right knowledge, and right conduct, when the

[1] DS., 42.
[2] DS., 44.
[3] DS., 45.
[4] DSV., 46.
[5] DSV., 47-48.
[6] DS., 49.
[7] DSV., 56.
[8] DS., 57.
[9] Tsāra., viii. 2, 4.
[10] *Ibid*, viii. 7.

influx of a new karma-matter is stopped, and the accumulated karma-matter is worn out. Then obstructive (antarāya), knowledge-obscuring (jñānāvaraṇīya), and faith-obscuring (darśanāvaraṇīya) karmas are simultaneously destroyed. Lordship appears in the soul separated from the four kinds of karma-matter. The person is called the supreme Lord (parameśvara). He becomes pure, enlightened (buddha), free from bodily and mental diseases, omniscient or all-knowing (sarvajña), and all-perceiving (sarvadarśin). He is called the Victor (jina) or the Kevalin. He attains nirvāṇa when the other four kinds of karmas, feeling-obscuring (vedanīya), age-determining (āyuṣ), character-determining (nāma), and family-determining (gotra), are completely destroyed. The liberated soul moves upward to the summit of mundane space.[1] It realizes infinite knowledge, infinite perception, infinite bliss, and infinite power (anantacatuṣṭaya). The Jaina ethics stresses complete moral discipline of the soul.

24. *The Stages in the Evolution of the Soul*

There are fourteen stages in the evolution of the soul. They are called guṇasthānas. They are (1) false belief (mithyātva), (2) downfall (sāsādana), (3) mixed belief (miśra), (4) vowless right belief (aviratasamyaktva), (5) partial vow (deśavirata), (6) imperfect vow (pramattavirata), (7) perfect vow (apramattavirata), (8) initiation to pure concentration (apūrvakaraṇa), (9) incessant pursuit of higher thought-activity (anivṛttakaraṇa), (10) desireless condition clouded by subtle greed (sūkṣmasamparāya), (11) desireless condition (upaśantamoha), (12) freedom from delusion (kṣīṇamohạ), (13) omniscience in an embodied condition (sayogakevalin), and (13) omniscience devoid of vibrations (ayogakevalin). After the last stage the soul becomes liberated (siddha).[2]

In the first stage a person has a false belief. He has no faith in Jainism. In the second stage he has a fall from the stage of right belief to a false belief. In the third stage he has a mixture of right belief and false belief. In the fourth stage he has a right belief, but does not observe vows. He can

---

[1] Tsāra., viii. 20, 21, 22, 24. 25, 27.
[2] GS., JK., 9, 10.

control intense passions, but cannot control mild passions. In the fifth stage he observes the vows of non-injury, truthfulness, non-stealing, continence, and non-covetousness with partial success. In the seventh stage he succeeds in practising the vows without any transgression. In the eighth stage he checks the expressions of mild passions and feels an ineffable joy. He is initiated into a higher life which is the beginning of pure meditation (śukladhyāna). In the ninth stage he incessantly pursues pure meditation on the self and acquires purer states. In the tenth stage he subdues subtle forms of greed. In the eleventh stage he subdues all desires and acquires control over deluding karmas. In the twelfth stage he destroys all deluding karmas. In the thirteenth stage he destroys all faith-obscuring, knowledge-obscuring, bliss-obscuring, and obstructive karmas, and attains omniscience with soul-vibrations. He becomes sayogakevalin. In the fourteenth stage he attains omniscience without soul-vibrations. He becomes ayogakevalin. He attains perfect liberation.

The soul suffers from five kinds of evils, wrong belief, vowlessness, carelessness, passions, and vibratory activity of body, speech, and mind. It gets rid of wrong belief at the end of the first stage, vowlessness at the end of the fourth, carelessness at the end of the sixth, passions at the end of the tenth, and vibratory activity at the end of the thirteenth stage. It gradually advances from wrong belief to right belief, then to vows, then to careful vows, then to passionlessness, and, at last, to arrest of all its vibrations due to the activities of body, speech, and mind. Thus the stage of perfection is attained by right belief, right knowledge, and right conduct, passionlessness, and perfect tranquillity of the soul.[1]

25. *The Ethical Standard*

According to the Jainas, perfection or self-realization is the highest good. The self has the innate qualities of infinite knowledge, infinite perception, infinite bliss, and infinite power. These qualities are obscured by karma-matter which flows into and interpenetrates the self. When karma-matter is completely

[1] OJ., pp. 105-07; DSV., 13, E.T., pp. 37-39; GS., JK., E.T., pp. 56-57; GS., KK., E.T., pp. 41-43.

destroyed and the self is absolutely dissociated from it, it realizes its innate perfection. The Jainas are exponents of perfectionism or eudæmonism. But the self does not acquire perfection as an adventitious quality. It is innate in itself. It is obscured by the veil of karma-matter due to wrong belief, attachment, aversion, delusion, and passions. When the veil is removed by right belief, right knowledge, vows, penances, meditation, passionlessness, and perfect tranquillity, the self-realizes its innate perfection. Virtue (puṇya) produces beneficial (śubha) karmas. Vice (pāpa) produces harmful (aśubha) karmas. So the self must transcend virtue and vice both. Perfection is transcendental purity. It is super-moral. Purity (viśuddhi) consists in the existence of the self in its innate nature (svatmani avasthānam).[1] Asceticism is the means to the realization of perfection. It consists in extirpation of passions. Though friendship or good-will (maitrī) for all, delight (pramoda) at the sight of the virtuous, compassion (kāruṇya) for the distressed, and indifference (upekṣā) to the vicious are emphasized, they are treated as subsidiary aids to self-culture. Even ahiṃsā in thought, word, and deed is an aid to self-realization. Perfection is attained by complete cessation of activities of body, speech, and mind because they disturb the tranquillity of the soul. Thus perfection or self-realization is the highest good. But asceticism or passionlessness is the means to its attainment. Ahiṃsā is the fundamental and basic virtue. Truthfulness, non-stealing, sex-restraint, and non-covetousness are based upon ahiṃsā. The Jaina ethics is pre-eminently ethics of ahiṃsā.

The Jaina ethics emphasizes purity of motives as distinguished from consequences of actions. It considers an action to be right if it is actuated by a good intention (abhisandhi), though it leads to unhappiness of others. It considers an action to be wrong if it is actuated by a bad intention, though it leads to happiness of others. An intention is pure when it is devoid of attachment, aversion, delusion, and passions. It is impure when it is distressing and aggressive. A distressing or afflicting (ārta) intention is manifested in an effort to avoid the unpleasant or to attain the pleasant, or in absorption

[1] AS., 95.

in the experience of pain, or desire for the attainment of power not yet acquired. An aggressive (raudra) intention is manifested in injury to life, untruth, theft, and preservation of property. An intention is pure when it is of the nature of meditation on Duty (dharma) or of the nature of meditation on the pure self. Righteousness depends on purity of motive or intention. Unrighteousness depends on impurity of motive or intention. They do not depend on external consequences of happiness of others. Thus the Jaina ethics stresses subjective morality, though it gives due consideration to the consequences of actions.[1]

The Moral Law (niyoga) is a command of a perfect omniscient person. It is not a command of God because there is no God. The omniscient person (arhat) has realized his innate perfection. So he can prescribe the means for its realization. Every person can realize his innate perfection by obeying the Moral Law. He can attain super-moral purity (viśuddhi) by right belief, right knowledge, and right conduct. The Moral Law is ultimately the self. It is essentially self-imposed. Though it appears to be imposed from without by an omniscient person (arhat) who has realized his innate perfection, it is really imposed by the self upon itself. It is imposed by the ideal self upon the actual self. The intrinsic perfection of the self demands its realization. This demand of the perfect self is moral obligation. But in the moral consciousness it takes the form of a personal prescription of a superior person (āptapuruṣa) to an inferior person.[2]

According to some, the Moral Law (niyoga) is pure objective duty (śuddha kārya) as distinguished from subjective prompting (preraṇā). According to others, niyoga is pure subjective prompting or moral impulsion (śuddhapreraṇā) as distinguished from objective duty (kārya). According to others, niyoga is objective duty supported by subjective moral impulsion (preraṇāsahitakārya). According to others, niyoga is subjective prompting expressed in objective duty (kāryasahitapreraṇā). Moral impulsion is primary. Objective duty gives form to moral impulsion. According to others, the niyoga is authoritative. It derives its authority from the self which is

[1] AMV., AS., 95; TSV., ix. 30-37; EH., pp. 227-29, 323-24.
[2] EH., pp. 159-61.

the light of consciousness. The authority of the self is transferred by projection (upacāra) to objective duty (kāryasyaiva upacaritapravartakatvam). According to others, niyoga is the relation between objective duty and subjective impulsion (kāryapreraṇāyoḥ sambandhaḥ). It is the relation between a person and his present duty. According to others, niyoga is the aggregate of subjective prompting, objective duty, and the relation between them (tatsamudāya). It is the concrete experience consisting of subjective and objective factors. According to others, niyoga is free from subjective impulsion and objective duty. It is absolute, categorical imperative. It is the transcendental reality or Brahman (tadubhayavinirmukta) which appears to be subjective prompting and objective duty which are its phenomenal forms. According to others, niyoga is the agent as working out his end (yantrārūḍha atma). It is the agent realizing his moral end through a particular action. According to others, niyoga is an object which is conducive to fulfilment of the self (bhogarūpa). But an object of fruition (bhogya) necessarily implies an experiencing subject (bhoktṛ). Self-fulfilment implies self-appropriation. But an object of fruition is to be accomplished (sādhya). It is not yet accomplished (siddha). Hence niyoga is neither subjective moral impulsion nor pure objective duty, but an object of fruition (bhogya) of the self. According to others, niyoga is the agent himself (puruṣa eva). It is the agent qualified by duty (kāryaviśiṣṭapuruṣa). The agent is both the accomplisher (sādhaka) and the accomplished (sādhya). Vidyānanda refutes all these theories of moral obligation.[1]

V. Atheism

26. *The Jaina refutation of Theism*

The Naiyāyika argues that the world, which is of the nature of an effect, must have an efficient cause, just as a pot is made by a potter. God is the efficient cause (nimittakāraṇa) of the world. He has created the world out of preexisting eternal atoms which are its material cause (upādānakāraṇa). "The world is not infinite, it is of intermediate magni-

---

[1] EH., pp. 151-58; *Aṣṭasāhasrī*.

tude. It consists of parts. So it is of the nature of an effect. It is produced by an intelligent agent, *viz.,* God who has direct knowledge of the material cause or atoms, desire to create the world, and the volition to do so."[1]

The Jaina disputes the nature of the world as an effect. He asks what the Naiyāyika means by the assertion that the world is of the nature of an effect. Does he mean by effect that which consists of parts (sāvayavatva)? What does he mean by that which consists of parts? Does he mean by it (1) having conjunction with parts (avayavasaṃyogitva), or (2) having inherence in parts (avayavasamavāyitva), or (3) being produced by parts (avayavajanyatva), or (4) a substance inhering in parts (samavetadravyatva)? What does he mean by a substance inhering in parts? It means either a substance which possesses the mere relation of inherence (samavāyasambandhamātravaddravyatva), or (5) a substance inhering in other parts (anyatra samavetadravyatva). (6) Or a substance consisting of parts means that which is apprehended as consisting of parts (sāvayavabuddhiviṣayatva). The Jaina refutes all these alternatives. (1) If a substance made up of parts means that which has conjunction with parts, then ether (ākāśa) consists of parts, and is an effect, since it has conjunction with parts. But the Naiyāyika holds that ether is one, partless, and eternal. So the first alternative is wrong. (2) If a substance made up of parts means that which inheres in parts, then generality (sāmānya) consists of parts, and is an effect, since the genus of jar (ghaṭatva) inheres in an individual jar, and in all its parts. But the Naiyāyika holds that a generality is one, partless, and eternal. So the second alternative is wrong. (3) If a substance consisting of parts means that which is produced by parts, then there is no difference between the middle term (sādhana) *viz.,* 'consisting of parts' and the major term (sādhya) *viz.,* 'effect'. A substance produced by parts (sādhana) is identical with an effect (sādhya). Therefore 'being produced by parts' cannot prove an 'effect'. They are identical with each other. So the third alternative is wrong. (4) If a substance consisting of parts means a substance which possesses the mere relation of inherence, then ether (ākāśa) consists of

[1] J. N. Sinha : *Introduction to Indian Philosophy,* pp. 99-100.

parts, and is an effect, since its qualities and the genus of substance inhere in it. But the Naiyāyika holds that ether is eternal. So the fourth alternative is wrong. (5) If a substance consisting of parts means a substance inhering in other parts, then there is no difference between the middle term (sādhana) and the major term (sādhya). Inherence of a composite substance in its parts which are its material cause has to be proved. The Jainas reject inherence as a relation. So the fifth alternative is wrong. (6) If a substance consisting of parts means that which is apprehended as consisting of parts, then the self consists of parts, and is an effect, since it is apprehended as consisting of parts and pervading the body. But the self is eternal. It is not an effect. If the self is said to be partless (niravayava) and yet extensive (vyāpaka), then a partless atom also will be extensive. But an indivisible atom has no extensive magnitude. So the sixth alternative is wrong. Therefore a substance consisting of parts cannot be an effect, and the world is not an effect because it consists of parts.[1]

If God is the creator of the world, he creates it with a body or without a body. He cannot create it without a body, just as a jar is not created by a potter without a body. Creation involves movement which is not possible without a body. If God creates the world with a body, it is either perceptible or imperceptible. It is not perceptible, since grass, plants, rainbow, clouds, and the like are found to be spontaneously generated without its aid. If God's body is imperceptible, what is its cause? If a special greatness (māhātmyaviśeṣa) is its cause, there is no reason to prove it, and it involves mutual dependence. God's imperceptible body depends upon his special greatness, and His special greatness depends upon His imperceptible body. Our body is caused by our merits and demerits. But God's body cannot be caused by His merit and demerit because He is devoid of merit and demerit. Our merits and demerits also cannot be the cause of His imperceptible body. Therefore God cannot have a perceptible or imperceptible body. He cannot create the world without a body also.[2]

Even if we grant that the world is an effect, it does not follow that it is produced by one independent creator without

[1] SDS., iii. 17.
[2] SVM., pp. 26-27.

accessories. If it is produced by one God, all effects in the world such as human productions may be produced by Him, and particular causes of particular effects are not necessary. Further, the world may be produced by the co-operation of many gods, even as a palace is made by the co-operation of many masons or as a bee-hive is made by the co-operation of many bees. The Naiyāyika argument that many gods will conflict with one another, frustrate one another, and produce a chaos is invalid. If a society of bees can construct a bee-hive, a society of gods can create the world.[1]

Does God create variety in the world with the aid of the merits and demerits of the creatures or without their aid? If He depends on them, He ceases to be the independent Lord. If He does not depend upon them, why does He make some creatures happy and others unhappy? Then He is kind to some, and unkind to others, and thus guilty of partiality. If merits and demerits of creatures make them happy and unhappy, they become the Lord (īśvara), and God ceases to be the Lord (aniśvara).[2] The Law of Karma can account for variety in the world. The variety of the moving animals is due to fruition of the beneficial and harmful karmas produced by them. The variety of conscious plants also is due to fruition of their good and bad karmas. The variety of inanimate things is eternally existing in order to be objects of enjoyment of the conscious, moving, and non-moving souls. The Jainas explain variety in the world by the Law of Karma, and dispense with God as the Lord of Karma (karmādhyakṣa).[3]

Even if God exists, He canot be eternal, ubiquitous, and omniscient. If God is eternal, is He of the nature of creative act or not of the nature of creative act? If He is of the nature of creative act which is eternal, He can never desist from creating the world. If He desists from the creative act, He cannot be of the nature of creative act. Until the creative act is completed, not a single effect can be produced. If He is not of the nature of creative act, He can never create the world, since He cannot acquire creativity. Moreover, if He is absolutely eternal, He can neither create the world nor destroy it, since creation and destruction imply change, and God is admitted

---

[1] SVM., pp. 27-28.
[2] *Ibid*, pp. 24-25, 33.
[3] *Ibid*, p. 31.

to be unchangeable and immutable. Creation and destruction are two distinct acts. They cannot be made by an eternal God who is not liable to change. Does God destroy the world by the same nature by which He creates the world? Or does He do so by a different nature? If He does so by the same nature, then creation and destruction of the world will be simultaneous owing to His identity of nature. If He does so by a different nature, then He is liable to change, and is not eternal. Diversity of nature is the characteristic of a non-eternal thing. The theist admits that God creates the world with the aid of rajas or energy, preserves it with the aid of purity or sattva, and destroys it with the aid of tamas or delusion. His different functions depend upon His different natures which are inconsistent with His eternal nature. Even if God is eternal, why does He not always create? If He does not always create owing to His volitions, then His volitions which depend upon His mere existence should impel Him to create always. If His different volitions are the causes of His different creations, then He ceases to be eternal. Eternal God cannot create the world.[1]

If God is the creator of the world, what is the motive of His creation? An intelligent being exerts himself owing to self-interest or compassion for others. So God being intelligent must create the world to serve His self-interest or out of compassion for His creatures. But He is an eternally fulfilled being. He has no unfulfilled desires. He has no self-interest. So He cannot create the world to fulfil His selfish end. Nor can He be moved by compassion for creatures. Compassion is desire to remove the sufferings of others. But before creation there is no suffering which is felt by the self through the mind, body, and sense-organs in intercourse with objects, which are not yet created. If God feels compassion for sufferings of creatures before their creation, then creation will depend upon compassion, and compassion will depend upon creation and sufferings consequent on it. Hence God has no motive for creation.[2] If God creates the world in sport (krīḍā), then His creative act is purposeless like the play of a child. If creation follows from His nature (svabhāva), then all effects may spring

[1] SVM., pp. 33-34.
[2] *Ibid*, pp. 34-35.

from the nature of their causes, and the hypothesis of God is unwarranted.

God cannot be ubiquitous. Is He ubiquitous through His body or through His knowledge? If He pervades the universe through His body, there is no scope for the production of effects by human agents. All human productions must be ascribed to God. But this is contradicted by perception. If God pervades the universe through His knowledge, the Jainas also admit that an omniscient person (sarvajña) pervades the universe with an overflow of his omniscience. But they do not believe in God. But the Upaniṣads speak of Brahman as pervading different parts of the universe through different parts of its body. Does God create the whole universe directly through His bodily activity or by mere will (saṁkalpamātra)? If He creates it through His bodily activity like a carpenter, He will take infinite time to create mountains and other effects. If He creates it by mere will, then other gods also may create them by mere will. Further, if God is all-pervading, He creates impure creatures in hell also. The Naiyāyika may urge that the omniscient person fills the whole universe with omniscience, and is therefore tainted with pains and imperfections known by Him according to the Jainas. But this argument is invalid. Knowledge does not get at its object (aprāpyakārin). It knows its object, while it remains in the self. Mere knowledge of pain and imperfection does not taint its purity. It cannot be said that knowledge gets at its object (prāpyakārin), since it is a quality of the self, and therefore it cannot go out to its object. If it goes out to its object, then the self will become non-intelligent. A quality cannot be detached from its substance. It may be argued that knowledge can leave its substrate, the self, and go out to its object, even as the rays of light leave the sun and go out to an object. But this argument is wrong. The rays of the sun are of the nature of substances. They are molecules of light. They are not qualities of the sun. But knowledge is a quality of the self. So it cannot leave the self and go out to an object. Hence God is not ubiquitous.[1]

God cannot be omniscient. His omniscience cannot be proved by perception, inference, and testimony. Perception is

---

[1] SVM., pp. 28-30.

produced by the intercourse of the sense-organs with sensible objects. So it cannot apprehend the omniscience of God, which is supersensible. Divine omniscience cannot be proved by inference which depends upon the recollection of invariable concomitance (vyāpti) between the mark of inference (liṅga) and the inferred property (liṅgin) after perception of the mark of inference. But there is no mark of inference (hetu) which is invariably accompanied by omniscience of God, which is the object of inference. Divine omniscience is supersensible and far remote from us. Its invariable accompaniment with any mark of inference is not apprehended. The variety of the world cannot be said to be the mark of inference. It cannot prove divine omniscience, since it has already been said to be due to the Law of Karma. Testimony also cannot prove omniscience of God. Does testimony depend upon God or some other reliable authority? If it depends upon God, He loses His greatness because great souls do not boast of their own glories. Further, scriptures consist of letters and sounds produced by different parts of the body. God has no body. So He cannot be the creator of the scriptures. If the scriptures depend upon some other agent, he is either omniscient or not omniscient. If he is omniscient, then there are two omniscient beings. But the theist does not admit two omniscient beings. He believes in one God only who is omniscient. If the agent is not omniscient, he is not trustworthy. Further, the scriptures prove a non-omniscient agent. They cannot prove omniscience of their agent, since they are full of conflicting statements. They sometimes enjoin non-killing of all creatures. Sometimes they enjoin killing of animals in sacrifices. In fact, the Jainas reject the authority of the Vedas.[1] They do not recognize the existence of God. They do not believe in His eternity, ubiquity, independence, mercifulness, and omniscience. The Jainas are avowed atheists. The world is eternal and self-existent. Particular things in the world are created out of their material causes and destroyed into them. There is no creation out of nothing. There is no destruction of something into nothing. The phenomena in the world are governed by the law of causality subservient to the moral Law of Karma.

---

[1] SVM., pp. 30-32.

But though the Jainas do not believe in God, they believe in the innate divinity of each soul. Every soul can realize its intrinsic divinity by self-effort. It can realize its infinite knowledge, infinite perception, infinite bliss, and infinite power. In this sense, Jainism is not atheism. The Jainas worship the Tīrthaṅkaras or Arhats with devotion. They worship also the Siddhas, Ācāryas, Upādhyāyas, and Sādhus. They are called five Parameṣṭhins. The Jainas are full of religious fervour in their worship of the great souls.[1] They worship their idols. They believe in worship, prayer, faith, and devotion. They recite mantras. They lay stress on meditation, penances, and right conduct for the realization of innate divinity. But their practical religion consists in tenderness for animal life. They have developed an instinctive horror of killing animals and insects. They are scrupulous vegetarians. Jainism forbids killing life, causing life to be killed, and approving of killing life. It is a religion without God. It is a religion of self-help. It does not believe in grace. It believes in the inexorable Law of Karma.

VI. CRITICAL ESTIMATE

The Jaina doctrine of relativity of judgments (syādvāda) implies an absolute standpoint. Relativity implies the absolute. Knowledge of the relative as relative implies transcendence of the relative and knowledge of the absolute. Absolute relativism is suicidal. Radical probabilism does not satisfy the human intellect, and cannot guide us in our practical life. The Jainas advocate realistic pragmatism. Knowledge has practical utility. Valid knowledge leads to selection of good (hitaprāpti) and rejection of evil (ahitaparihāra). But merely relative and probable knowledge cannot lead to fruition of our desires. Valid knowledge accords with the reality. If it is merely probable, it cannot accord with the reality. The Jainas admit that the omniscience of the Kevalin is perfectly valid. It is not infected with relativity. It may be regarded as absolute knowledge. The judgments of the omniscient soul are absolutely valid. So the Jaina relativism is not applicable to the knowledge of the perfect person.

---

[1] DS., 50- 54.

The Jaina doctrine of standpoints (nayavāda) shows catholicity of outlook and a comprehensive grasp of the nature of the reality. All the different systems of Hindu philosophy and Buddhism emphasize particular aspects of the reality, and regard them as the whole truth. Jainism regards them as partial aspects of the reality. But it cannot reconcile them with one another adequately. It betrays a spirit of ecclecticism in its doctrine of standpoints.

The Jaina doctrine of relative pluralism (anekāntavāda) is an empirical survey of the world. Everything in the world has an infinite number of qualities and relations (anantadharmaka). It is related to all other things in the world in time and space. The world is a plurality of inter-related things so that one who knows any one of them completely knows the whole universe completely, and one who knows the whole universe completely, knows each thing in it completely.[1] The Jaina emphasizes plurality of things, though he regards them as inter-related to one another. But if they are inter-related to one another, they form a system of inter-related parts. They are members of one whole. The relations among them are not external. But they are internal. They enter into the being of the reals. The inter-related reals are not real apart from their relations. They are, therefore, expressions of one reality which is unity-in-difference. Such a reality can only be a spirit. One infinite spirit is expressed in the inter-related reals. The reality is an expression of the Absolute. Jainism is a halfway house between radical pluralism and spiritual monism or Absolutism. It is relative pluralism. But it logically leads to Absolutism. Complete inter-relatedness is an expression of a teleological spiritual principle which inter-relates the parts to one another to realize its purpose. The world is a purposive whole. But Jainism fights shy of this conclusion and halts at relative pluralism. It is avowedly anti-absolutistic.

The Jaina dualism of jīva and ajīva, soul and matter is unsatisfactory. The jīva is the knower, enjoyer and active agent. Matter is the object of knowledge, enjoyment, and activity. The self and the not-self are related to each other as subject and object. The self cannot have consciousness

[1] SVM., p. 4.

without the not-self or object. But the Jaina believes in the independent existence of the object apart from consciousness. He advocates realism. But if the self cannot have consciousness apart from the object, it also cannot exist apart from consciousness. The self and the not-self, subject and object, are correlative to each other. If they are correlative to each other, they imply the existence of a universal spirit or the Absolute which is expressed in both and relates them to each other. Absolute dualism of soul and matter is metaphysically unsound. The Jaina admits that knowledge (jñāna) and its object (jñeya) are partly different from and partly identical with each other.[1] If so, the object is akin to the subject and cannot be brute matter. It must be at least partly spiritual in nature. Dualism cannot account for knowledge.

The Jaina doctrine of knowledge as revelation from within the self is hardly tenable. The self is omniscient. But its omniscience is veiled by the crust of karma-matter. The sense-object-intercourse does not produce knowledge, but simply removes the veil of karma-matter and reveals knowledge of the self. This doctrine minimizes the function of object in producing knowledge. Knowledge is due to the interaction of subject and object. It is rather due to the communion of the self with an object. Both are indispensable to knowledge. Cut out the object, and knowledge becomes impossible. Knowledge is revelation of an object by the self. It is not mere revelation from within. The self is not the only contributory factor in knowledge.

The Jaina doctrine of knowledge as subservient to practical life has a ring of modernism. But knowledge exists in its own right apart from its practical efficiency. Knowledge is valid apart from its pragmatic utility. It is invalid apart from its practical inutility. Knowledge as subservient to pragmatic utility becomes subjective, relative, and humanistic. But the Jaina combines pragmatism with realism like the Naiyāyika, and saves his doctrine of knowledge from the charge of subjectivism.

The Jaina has not a clear conception of the self, spirit, or soul. He cannot distinguish between life and soul. He

---

[1] AMV., 30.

ascribes soul to a plant. Jīva means a living being. The mundane jīva is a soul with a body. The soul is co-extensive with the body. It is an extensive substance (astikāya). It assimilates karma-matter into it. There is inter-penetration (saṃśleṣa) of karma-matter into the soul. It is associated with karma-matter (karmasaṃyukta). Yet the soul and the body cannot interact upon each other. The activities of soul and body are parallel to each other. The Jaina is undecided as to the nature of the soul and its relation to the body. The soul is a spirit. So it cannot be extended. Matter cannot attach to it. The soul cannot be associated with matter. The mundane soul is spirit associated with matter. But the perfect soul is pure spirit free from matter. It has upward movement (ūrdhvagati). It rises up to the summit of mundane space when it is dissociated from matter. The Jaina conception of the jīva is a primitive animistic conception of the soul embodied in matter. It is not so refined as the Vedānta conception of the Ātman as pure spirit.

The Jaina doctrine of panpsychism resembles monadism of Leibnitz. The whole world is full of souls. There are earth-souls, water-souls, fire-souls, and air-souls. There are plant-souls. There are animal-souls. There are human souls. There are celestial souls. According to Leibnitz the world is full of monads or spiritual atoms. The Jaina does not believe in God. But Leibnitz believes in God whose pre-established harmony accounts for the relation of monads to one another. The Jaina advocates dualism of matter and soul. But Leibnitz reduces matter to souls or monads. The Jaina recognizes atoms. But Leibnitz denies their reality, and recognizes only monads or spiritual atoms. So there is superficial similarity between them. Panpsychism betrays ignorance of the distinction among the different degrees of reality, matter, life, and soul. It is due to primitive tendency to animism.

The Jaina conception of a dynamic reality in which atoms, space-points, and time-points are inseparable from one another is a bold adventure of thought which anticipates modern discoveries of physics. Matter, space, and time are inseparable aspects of the real world. The principle of motion (dharma) and the principle of rest (adharma) are posited to account for the dynamism, stability, and coherence of the world. The Jaina does not inter-relate matter, space, time, dharma, and adharma systematically with one another. He does not relate matter and soul to each other. He does not inter-relate the souls to one another. Inter-relation of atoms, souls, time, space, dharma, and adharma to one another inevitably points to the existence of the Absolute which is expressed in them and inter-lates them to one another. But Jainism does not bring out the implications of its doctrine, stops short of Absolutism, and halts at relative pluralism which is not logically tenable.

The Jaina criticism of theistic arguments resembles the Sāṁkhya and the Mīmāṃsaka criticisms. They are all atheistic. But these anti-theistic arguments have been refuted by the later Naiyāyikas. The Jainas reject the notion of God as the creator of the world or the Lord of Karma. But they deify the Tīrthaṅkaras and worship them. Their religion of self-help without God or His grace is unique in the history of the world.

The Jaina ethics of ahiṃsā has great importance in the modern age of mass slaughter of men. Ahiṃsā is non-injury to life in thought, word, and deed. Noble attachment (praśasta rāga), compassion (anukampā), and freedom from impurity of the heart (citta-akāluṣya) constitute the spring of righteousness (puṇyāsrava).[1] Compassion consists in the feeling of sympathy for the distressed and actively relieving their sufferings. Mere feeling of sympathy is not adequate. It must be expressed in active relief of the distress of others. Charity is sympathy and active relief. Common persons cultivate this kind of charity. But wise persons cultivate a higher kind of compassion. They cultivate compassion for the bound souls and help them achieve their liberation from bondage. Thus compassion is lower and higher.[2] The Jaina ethics stresses meditation on love (maitrī) for all creatures, compassion for the distressed (kāruṇya), delight (pramoda) at the virtuous, and indifference (upekṣā) to the vicious. These are social virtues. They make for social harmony. But they are regarded as the means of self-culture. Their social significance is not emphasized. Social welfare is not the goal of morality. Self-perfection or self-realization is the highest good. Complete

[1] P., TDTV., 145.

[2] P., TVTV., 144.

eradication of emotions and passions is indispensable for self-realization for they disturb the tranquillity of the soul. Even devotion to the Arhat, which is a kind of noble attachment, should be eradicated. Complete passionlessness and inactivity of the mind, body, and speech are necessary for perfection. Thus the Jaina ethics is rigoristic and ascetic, though it recognizes the social virtues of benevolence, charity, and love. But it cannot be said to be egoistic. It upholds eudæmonism as to the *summum bonum* and rationalism and asceticism as to the means of its attainment. It regards transcendental purity (viśuddhi) of the soul as the highest good, beyond virtue and vice which generate beneficial and harmful karma-particles or impurities. This is purism or rationalism. The Jaina ethics of ahiṃsā and universal love and good-will is a grand contribution to ethical thought. These should be the foundation of the new order.

CHAPTER IV

EARLY BUDDHISM

1. *Introduction*

We shall discuss Buddhism in two chapters under the heads: Early Buddhism and the Schools of Buddhism. In this chapter we shall discuss the main teachings of Buddha and the relation of Buddhism to the other systems of thought, and indicate the main differences between the Hīnayāna and the Mahāyāna Buddhism. In the next chapter we shall deal with the four main philosophical schools of the Vaibhāṣika, the Sautrāntika, the Yogācāra, and the Mādhyamika.

The teachings of Buddha are to be found in the three *Piṭakas* or Baskets of the Law which constitute the Pāli canonical literature. They are (1) *Sutta* or tales, (2) *Vinaya* or discipline, and (3) *Abhidhamma* or doctrine. The *Sutta piṭaka* has five divisions, called *Nikāyas.* They are *Dīghanikāya,* or collection of long suttas, *Majjhimanikāya,* or collection of middle suttas, *Saṁyuttanikāya* or collection of joined suttas, *Aṅguttaranikāya,* or collection of miscellaneous suttas, and *Khuddakanikāya,* or collection of short suttas. The last has fifteen divisions: (1) *Khuddakapāṭha,* or collection of small texts, (2) *Dhammapada,* four hundred and twenty-three verses epitomizing the teachings of Buddha, (3) *Udāna,* eight-two suttas embodying praise, (4) *Itivuttaka,* stories regarding sayings of Buddha, (5) *Suttanipāta,* seventy suttas, (6) *Vimānavatthu,* stories of celestial palaces, (7) *Petavatthu,* stories of departed spirits, (8) *Theragāthā,* stanzas of monks, (9) *Therīgāthā,* stanzas of nuns, (10) *Jātaka,* former births, (11) *Niddesa,* explanations of some suttas of Sāriputta, (12) *Patisambhidāmagga,* road of discrimination and intuitive insight, (13) *Apadāna,* legends, (14) *Buddhavaṁsa,* stories of twenty-four preceding Buddhas and Gotama, and (15) *Cariyāpiṭaka,* basket of conduct, Buddha's meritorious actions. The *Vinaya piṭaka* dealing with the discipline of the monks has three divisions: (1) *Vibhaṅga,* (2) *Khandaka* divided into *Mahāvagga,* large section, and *Cullavagga,* small section, and (3) *Parivārapāṭha.*

The *Abhidhammapiṭaka,* dealing with psychological ethics and metaphysics, has seven divisions: (1) *Dhammasaṅgaṇi,* enumeration of conditions of life, (2) *Vibhaṅga,* disquisitions, (3) *Kathāvatthupakaraṇa,* book of subjects of discussion, (4) *Puggalapaññati* or *Paññati,* declaration of personality, (5) *Dhātukathā,* account of elements (dhātu), (6) *Yamaka,* pairs, (7) *Paṭṭhānapakaraṇa,* book of causes.[1] This Pāli Canon embodies the doctrine known as the Theravāda, or the doctrine of the Theras or the Elders. It is also known as the Sthaviravāda. All canonical works were completed before 241 B.C. when the third council was held. *Milinda Pañha* (Questions of King Milinda), the dialogue between the Greek King, Menander (100 B.C.), and the Buddhist teacher, Nāgasena, is of great philosophical importance. Buddhghosa's (500 A.D.) *Visuddhimagga* is a compendium of Theravāda doctrines. His *Atthasālinī* is a commentary on *Dhammasaṅgaṇi.*

The Upaniṣads teach that the eternal (nitya) Ātman alone is real. It is identical with Braman. It is the transcendental reality (sat), consciousness (cit) and bliss (ānanda). Buddha teaches the opposite truth. Everything is impermanent (anitya). There is no permanent self (anātman). All is suffering (duḥkha). The self is an impermanent mind-body-complex (samudāya). There is no Brahman, God, or the Absolute as Creator of the world. It is self-existent. It is without beginning or end. It is unsubstantial (nissatta) and soulless (nijjīva). There are no permanent substances. There are only impermanent qualities (dhamma) or phenomena. They are subject to the inexorable law of becoming or dependent origination (pratītyasamutpāda). They are produced by their causes and conditions. The law of causation is subservient to the Moral Law. It is the Law of Karma. It is the Law of Righteousness (Dhamma). All is impermanent Becoming, flow and flux. Change is the stuff of reality. The world is dynamic. The soul is fluid. It grows and develops. It is an impermanent series with no personal identity. It is a psychical continuum of transitory psychoses, which transmigrates from one body to another. Life is full of suffering. Suffering is due to craving or will-to-live (tṛṣṇā). Will-to-live is due to ignorance (avidyā).

---

[1] Childer's *Pali Dictionary.*

Ignorance is false knowledge of the impermanent as the permanent. It is delusion of individuality. It is the root of the cycle of birth and death. It cannot be killed by philosophical knowledge. Buddha adopts anti-metaphysical attitude. There are ten indeterminable questions which are insoluble. Philosophical wrangling is unavailing. It generates self-conceit and scepticism. Buddha adopts moral pragmatism. His teachings aim at the total extinction of suffering and attainment of nirvāṇa here on earth. Nirvāṇa is the cooling of passions. It is perfect peace and equanimity. It is perfect enlightenment (bodhi). The way to nirvāṇa is the eightfold path (aṣṭāṅgamārga) of right conduct (śīla), concentration (samādhi) and insight (prajñā). The delusion of individuality or egoism must be extirpated. When egoism is eradicated, will-to-live (tṛṣṇā) or craving is destroyed. The round of birth and death is ended, and nirvāṇa is attained. Ahiṃsā, non-injury in thought, word, and deed, is the corner-stone of moral life. Universal goodwill and friendship (maitrī), compassion (karuṇā) for the distressed, joy (muditā) for the virtuous, and indifference (upekṣā) to the vicious are inculcated. Purity of inner life is emphasized. Purity of overt actions is not enough. Religion of animal sacrifice, ritualism, ceremonialism, and legalism is condemned. Hereditary caste distinctions are condemned. Buddha teaches neither Being nor Non-Being, but Becoming. He teaches neither self-indulgence nor self-mortification, but the middle path of right view, right speech, and right conduct. He teaches the religion of ahiṃsā. It is the religion of self-help. Everyone has to work out his own salvation which does not depend on the grace of God. Buddha asks his disciples not to depend upon authority but on reason. He asks them to be a light unto themselves (ātmadīpa), a refuge to themselves. He turns the wheel of the Law (dharmacakra) which is irresistible. He lays the foundation of the kingdom of righteousness.

2. *The Four Noble Truths*

The whole of the teachings of Buddha is summed in the four noble truths (ārya satya) : (1) There is suffering (duḥkha). (2) It has a cause (samudāya). (3) It can be stopped (nirodha). (4) There is a way to stop suffering (mārga).

Siddhārtha or Gautama (567 B.C.—487 B.C.) was overwhelmed with grief at the sight of disease, old age, and death. He was overpowered by abundant misery in the world. He renounced the world to find out the remedy for suffering. He discovered its cause and the way to stop it. He found the way to peace on earth, and preached it to the world. He became enlightened or Buddha.

The first noble truth is suffering. "Birth is attended with pain ; decay is painful ; disease is painful ; death is painful. Union with the unpleasant is painful, painful is separation from the pleasant ; any craving that is unsatisfied, that too is painful. In brief, the five aggregates which spring from attachment are painful."[1] The cause and conditions of individuality are painful. "The whole world is on fire ; where is the scope for merry-making."[2] Sensual pleasure is transitory. It endures for one moment. It is a prelude to pain. Pleasure is pain itself. "Sorrow comes from merriment. Fear comes from merriment."[3] All physical and mental loss is sorrow. The loss of objects of sensual pleasure leads to sorrow.[4] More tears have been shed by men than all the water which is in the great oceans.[5] Nowhere can man find a place on earth where he will not be overpowered by death.[6] The world is completely unsubstantial. It is void of Being It is perpetual Becoming. It is like an arrow stuck in the heart. He who has been pierced by this arrow runs here and there, restless with agony. When he draws out the arrow, he sits quietly.[7] The world is afflicted with death and decay. Therefore the wise do not grieve, knowing the nature of the world. Mere weeping or grieving is unavailing. When a house is on fire, it must be extinguished by water. A man, who is pierced by the arrow of grief, must draw it out.[8] Life is full of suffering. All created things are grief and pain.[9] The world is the vale of suffering.

The second noble truth is concerning the origin of suffering. Thirst (tṛṣṇā) or craving which generates the cycle of birth and death is the cause of suffering. It is threefold : (1) thirst

[1] *Foundation of the Kingdom of Righteousness*, 5.
[2] DP., 146.
[3] DP., 213.
[4] *Visuddhimagga*, xvii.
[5] SN.
[6] DP., 128.
[7] *Attadaṇḍasutta*, 936-39.
[8] *Sallasutta*, 581, 584, 591, 592.
[9] DP., 278.

for sensual pleasures (kāma tṛṣṇā), (2) thirst for being (bhavatṛṣṇā), and (3) thirst for wealth and power (vibhavatṛṣṇā).[1] "Verily, it is thirst or craving, causing the renewal of existence, accompanied by sensual delight, seeking satisfaction now here, now there—that is to say, the craving for the gratification of passions, or the craving for a future life, or the craving for success in this present life. This is the noble truth concerning the origin of suffering."[2] Thirst, craving, or will-to-live is the cause of suffering. All pain arises from individuality (upādhi) which is due to avidyā. Avidyā is due to will-to-live which is the root cause of suffering.

The third noble truth is the extinction of suffering. It is complete destruction of thirst, craving, or will-to-live. It is renunciation of thirst, separation from it, freedom from it, giving no room to it.[3] "Verily, it is the destruction in which no passion remains, of this very thirst ; the laying aside of it, the getting rid of it, the being free from it, the harbouring no longer of this thirst. This is the noble truth concerning destruction of suffering."[4] Delusion of individuality, desire for mind-body-complex (nāma-rūpa), and egotism are the causes of suffering. Destruction of egoism and will-to-live leads to extinction of attachment, aversion, delusion, and suffering.[5] Nibbāna is the extinction of desire, doubt, and sensual pleasures based on the reflection of nothingness.[6] It is total extinction of suffering, decay, and death. It is grasping at nothing, and possessing nothing.[7] It is perfect calm and tranquillity undisturbed by desires and passions like the depth of the ocean.[8] It is complete desirelessness. All desires for this life and the next life are extinguished in it. Non-grasping is attained by the knowledge of impermanence and voidness.[9] "He who overcomes this fierce thirst (tṛṣṇā), sufferings fall off from him, like water-drops from a lotus leaf. Dig up the root of thirst,

---

[1] MN., i. 5. 4. Jung also holds that the will-to-live, the sex-instinct, and the will-to-power are the primal urges of human nature.
[2] *Foundation of the Kingdom of Righteousness*, 6.
[3] MN., i. 140.
[4] *Foundation of the Kingdom of Righteousness*, 7.
[5] *Attadaṇḍasutta*, 944-54.
[6] *Upasīvamāṇavapucchā*, 1069.
[7] *Kappamāṇavapucchā*, 1093.
[8] *Tuvaṭakasutta*, 920.
[9] *Vāseṭṭhasutta*, 634, 643.

that the tempter may not crush you again and again."[1] The nibbāna is insuperable, unchangeable, matchless.[2]

The fourth noble truth is the way to the extinction of suffering. It is the eightfold path: (1) Right Belief (samyak dṛṣṭi); (2) Right Resolve (samyak saṁkalpa); (3) Right Speech (samyak vāk); (4) Right Conduct (samyak karma); (5) Right Livelihood (samyak ājīvikā); (6) Right Effort (samyak vyāyāma); (7) Right Mindfulness (samyak smṛti); (8) Right Concentration (samyak samādhi).[3] When the four noble truths are grasped, craving or will-to-live (tṛṣṇā) is extirpated, that which leads to birth is destroyed, and there is no more birth.[4] The four noble truths are suffering, the origin of suffering, the destruction of suffering, and the eightfold way of destruction of suffering.[5] The eightfold path consists of moral conduct (śīla), concentration (samādhi), and insight (prajñā). Insight includes right belief and right resolve. Moral conduct comprises right speech, right conduct, and right livelihood. Concentration comprehends right effort, right mindfulness, and right concentration. The eightfold path is the best way to freedom from suffering. It leads every aspirant to the complete extinction of suffering.[6] Buddhism is pessimism in so far as it looks upon life as suffering. But it is optimism in so far as it aims at extinction of suffering in this life.

3. *Impermanence* (*Anityavāda*)

Existence is impermanent. All is flux. Nothing is permanent. All things, mental and physical, are transitory. They do not endure for long. They are transient and fleeting. Impermanence is the inexorable law of all existence. There are five things which are inevitable. What is subject to old age must grow old. What is subject to sickness must be sick. What is subject to death must die. What is subject to decay must decay. What is liable to pass away must pass away.[7] These cannot be over-ruled by supra-mundane God or by any

---

[1] DP., 336-37.
[2] *Pārāyanasutta,* 1148.
[3] MN., i. 140.
[4] MPS., ii. 2.
[5] DP., 191; DN., ii. 9, 5; MN., iii. 4, 11.
[6] DP., 273, BGB., pp. 90-93. [7] AN., ii.

mundane agency. Brāhmanism accepts the perpetual cycle of birth and death. Buddhism stresses the perpetual succession of Becoming. There is no Being. There is only Becoming.[1] Some believe in Being. Some believe in Non-Being. Both are extreme views. Buddhism believes in Becoming. "Everything *is*: this is one extreme view. Everything *is not*: this is the second extreme view. Avoiding both these extremes, Buddha teaches the Norm by the Mean. And the gist of the doctrine of the Mean is that life is a becoming, or coming to be."[2]

Everything is becoming, change, flux. It is a phenomenon enduring for a moment and then passing away. It is produced by preceding phenomena. It produces succeeding phenomena. The world is a succession of transient phenomena. There is no permanent being. All things are transient phenomena. All substances are mere aggregates of impermanent qualities (dhamma). They are void of permanence and substantiality. The world is unsubstantial and impermanent.

All individuals are series of momentary states of consciousness. There is no permanent soul behind the series of momentary psychoses. There is only a succession of momentary mental processes. A past mental process has lived. But it neither lives, nor will it live. A future mental process will live. But it neither lives nor has it lived. A present mental process does live. But it has neither lived, nor will it live.[3] The life of an individual lasts only while a mental process lasts. An individual is a child, a boy, a youth, a man, an old man. He is a succession of changes. There is no identity in his body and mind. His body continually changes from one state to another. His mind also continually changes from one mental process to another. There is continuity but no identity. There is only a continuous succession of bodily and mental changes. We attribute identity to them for our practical convenience owing to their continuity. The changes are causally connected with one another. Each component state is absolutely determined by its antecedent conditions. It is not a causeless event. The world of Becoming is governed by the Law of Causality (pratītyasamutpāda). It is without beginning or end.[4]

---

[1] BGB., pp. 93-94.
[2] SN., ii. 17; iii. 135; Mrs. Rhys Davids, *Buddhism*, p. 83.
[3] *Visuddhimagga,* Ch. viii. [4] BGB., pp. 95-96.

Every individual is an aggregate of component elements. It comes into being and passes away. Its elements come together and produce it. Individuality is the effect of aggregation. Aggregation is becoming. Becoming is becoming different. Becoming different is not possible without disintegration. Disintegration is dissolution. Thus individuality is becoming. It is unstable and impermanent.[1]

All existences are essenceless and impermanent.[2] This is the universal law. The physical world and the psychical world are devoid of self. They are unsubstantial. They are transient. They are void. The empirical individual is an aggregate of the body, perceptions, feelings, dispositions, and self-consciousness, which are impermanent. Impermanence is misery. Whatever is impermanent is full of misery.[3] Heraclitus said, "All things are in a state of flux." Bergson holds that all is flow and flux. The Upaniṣads stress eternal Being or Brahman. Buddhism stresses impermanent Becoming. It is the antithesis of Upaniṣadic Absolutism. It gives a dynamic view of Reality. Change is the stuff of reality. Buddha reconciles Being and Non-Being in Becoming. He says, " 'Every thing is'—this is one extreme. 'Everything is not' is another extreme. The truth is the middle."[4] It is perpetual Becoming. Becoming is subject to universal causation. "Whatever exists arises from causes and conditions, and is in every respect impermanent."[5] All composite things undergo origination (utpāda), maintenance (sthiti), decay (jarā), and destruction (nirodha). All undergo modification. All are impermanent.[6] All component things are impermanent, unstable, and disintegrating. They are without substance and temporary. Form (rūpa) is impermanent. The eye is impermanent. Cognition is impermanent. Qualities are impermanent. All conscious and unconscious components are impermanent. They come together, take individual forms, and break up. All components and composite things are impermanent. Animals, gods, men, plants, and inorganic things are all impermamaent.[7]

---

[1] Rhys Davids: *Early Buddhism*, p. 57.
[2] *Uragasutta*, 5.
[3] BP., pp. 56-60.
[4] SN.
[5] MPS.
[6] SBT., pp. 12-13.
[7] MPS., ii. 10.

4. *Causality: Dependent Origination* (*Pratītyasamutpāda* or *Paṭiccasamuppāda*)

All existence is impermanent. It is becoming. All becoming is subject to the Law of Causation. Causation is dependent origination. "I will teach you the Dhamma", says Buddha, "that being present, this becomes; from the arising of that, this arises. That being absent, this does not become; from the cessation of that, this ceases."[1] Pratītyasamutpāda means arising (samutpāda) after getting (pratītya). It means the production of an effect out of a complement of cause and conditions. When the cause and conditions disappear, the effect appears. Buddhism believes in Asatkāryavāda. The effect emerges from the destruction of its cause and conditions. It follows necessarily from the doctrine of impermanence. The cause and the effect both are impermanent. The cause vanishes; then the effect emerges. The cause cannot continue in the effect. They cannot be synchronous. The cause must be prior to the effect. The effect arises from an aggregate of cause (hetu) and conditions (pratyaya). A seed is the cause of a plant. But soil, water, light, and manure are its conditions. A distinction is made between a hetu and a pratyaya. A hetu is the principal cause, and a pratyaya is a concomitant condition in Sarvāstivāda. Sometimes they are used synonymously. When they are distinguished, various kinds of conditions are described. One cause cannot produce an effect. It must be aided by other concomitant conditions to produce it. An effect arises from a cause and a complement of co-operating conditions.

The Law of causality or dependent origination applies to the past, the present, and the future. It is without beginning or end. It is applicable to all composite entities (saṁskṛta dharma), mental and physical. It is not applicable to non-composite entities (asaṁskṛta dharma) like space, since they are eternal. Buddhism believes in transient causation. The cause transmits its causal energy to its effect. Causation is development or transformation. Buddhism does not believe in immanent causality, in which a substance appears to be manifested as its qualities. Causation is dynamic, not static. Static view of causation is erroneous. The world-process is an active self-

[1] MN., ii. 32; i. 1, 9; i. 1, 2; i. 3, 8.

development. According to the Sarvāstivādin, "the cause never perishes but only changes its name, when it becomes an effect, having changed its state. For example, clay becomes a jar having changed its state ; and in this case the name clay is lost and the name jar arises."[1]

The Piṭakas imply that the Moral Law (Dharma) of right and wrong actions and their consequences, happiness and unhappiness, is a part of the cosmic order. They substitute a natural moral order for the moral design of a creative Deity. Niyama means process. Buddhaghoṣa (500 A.D.), a great scholiast, speaks of five kinds of niyama : (1) "Kammaniyama, order of act and result ; (2) utu-niyama, physical inorganic order, (3) bīja-niyama, order of germs, physical-organic order ; (4) citta-niyama, order of mind ; (5) dhamma-niyama, order of the norm, or the effort of nature to produce a perfect type."[2] The kamma-niyama expresses the universal fact that certain kinds of bodily, verbal, and mental actions bring pleasure to the agent and his fellows, while certain other actions bring pain to both. The utu-niyama is inorganic order. The bīja-niyama is organic order. The citta-niyama is mental order. The dhamma-niyama is the universal cosmic moral order. It expresses the fact that the effort of nature is to produce a perfect type.[3] The Piṭakas do not mention the fivefold order. In later realistic Buddhism there is a distinct recognition of inorganic order, organic order, and moral order. "The Buddhists distinguish between (1) causation among elements of dead matter, where the law of homogeneity (sabhāga hetu) between cause and result reigns, (2) causation in the organic world, where we have the phenomenon of growth (upacaya), and (3) causation in the animate world, where the operation of moral causation (vipāka hetu) is superimposed upon the natural."[4] Thus Buddhism regards the cosmic order as self-developing according to causal law without any creator, and without beginning or end. It has a scientific conception of the world.

---

[1] Āryadeva's commentary on MS, xx. 9; SBT., pp. 139-40.
[2] Mrs. Rhys Davids : *Buddhism,* p. 119.
[3] *Ibid,* pp. 119-20.
[4] Stcherbatsky : *The Central Conception of Buddhism,* 1923, p. 31.

The doctrine of dependent origination is opposed to accidentalism (yadṛcchāvāda) which denies the law of causality, and regards an event as an accidental happening. It is opposed to naturalism (svabhāvavāda) which ascribes an effect to its own inherent nature, for example, heat is inherent in the nature of fire. It is opposed to fatalism (niyativāda), which regards all things, good and bad, as unalterably fixed and pre-determined by fate. It is opposed to supernaturalism. An event is not generated by the supernatural intervention of God. It is produced by an antecedent natural event. Accidentalism and naturalism were advocated by materialists. Supernaturalism was advocated by Brāhminism. The Buddhist doctrine of causation was a great contribution to philosophical thought. All existences, physical and psychical, are subject to the law of universal causation. All that exist, are produced. Existence is becoming or production. Nothing is uncaused. Nothing is eternal. All are in the grip of causality. There is no transcendental cause of the world. There is no first cause.

5. *The Wheel of Existence* (*Bhavacakra*)

Buddha says, "He who knows dependent origination, knows dharma. He who knows dharma, knows dependent origination. The five aggregates of material form or body (rūpa), feeling (vedanā), perception (saṁjñā), disposition (saṁskāra), and self-consciousness (vijñāna) originate from their causes and conditions (pratītyasamutpanna)."[1] An empirical individual is an aggregate of five groups (skandha) of body, feeling, perception, disposition, and self-consciousness. The mind-body-complex (nāmarūpa) is produced by ailments. "Ailment (āhāra) is caused by thirst or craving (tṛṣṇā). Craving is caused by feeling (vedanā). Feeling is caused by contact (sparśa). Contact is caused by five sense-organs and mind (ṣaḍāyatana). They are caused by mind (nāma) and body (rūpa). They are caused by consciousness (vijñāna). Consciousness is caused by dispositions (saṁskāra). Dispositions are caused by ignorance (avidyā)."[2] The twelve members in the chain of causation are stated thus: "By reason of ignorance dispositions; by reason

[1] MN., i. 3, 8.

[2] MN., i. 4. 8.

of dispositions consciousness ; by reason of consciousness name and form (or mind-body-complex) ; by reason of name and form contact ; by reason of contact feeling ; by reason of feeling thirst ; by reason of thirst grasping ; by reason of grasping becoming ; by reason of becoming birth ; by reason of birth old age and death and grief."[1] By the destruction of ignorance, the dispositions are destroyed ; by the destruction of the dispositions, consciousness is destroyed ; by the destruction of consciousness, mind-body-complex is destroyed ; by the destruction of mind-body-complex, the six sense-organs are destroyed ; by the destruction of the six sense-organs, contact is destroyed ; by the destruction of contact, feeling is destroyed ; by the destruction of feeling, thirst is destroyed ; by the destruction of thirst, grasping is destroyed ; by the destruction of grasping, becoming or will-to-be-born is destroyed ; by the destruction of becoming, birth is destroyed ; by the destruction of birth, old age and death and grief are destroyed. Thus (1) ignorance (avidyā), (2) dispositions (saṁskāra), (3) consciousness (vijñāna), (4) name and from (nāmarūpa) or mind-body-complex, (5) six sense-organs (ṣaḍāyatana), (6) contact (sparśa), (7) feeling (vedanā), (8) thirst or craving (tṛṣṇā), (9) grasping (upādāna), (10) becoming (bhava), (11) birth (jāti), and (12) old age and death (jarāmaraṇa) are the twelve links in the chain of causation.

Ignorance (avidyā) is the root cause of suffering. It gives rise to birth and death. It is the false sense of individuality. It is knowledge of the impermanent series of mental and bodily processes as the permanent self. It is misconception of a series of transient phenomena as a permanent entity. It generates dispositions (saṁskāra). The dispositions of ignorance in the past life produce an initial consciousness (vijñāna) in the embryo. This consciousness generates the new mind-body-complex (nāmarūpa). If consciousness did not enter into the womb, name and form or mind-body-complex would not arise in the womb.[2] The mind-body-complex produces the five external sense-organs and the internal sense-organ or mind (ṣaḍāyatana). They produce sense-contact (sparśa) with sensible objects or qualities. The sense-contact produces feeling

[1] DN., ii. 55ff.; MN., i. 4, 8; AN., i. 177.
[2] *Mahānidānasutta,* ii. 2; MPS., ii. 6.

(vedanā) due to sense-experience. The feeling produces thirst (tṛṣṇā). Thirst produces grasping or clinging to objects (upādāna). Grasping produces becoming or will-to-be-born (bhava). The will-to-be-born in the present life produces rebirth (jāti) in the future life. Rebirth produces old age and death (jarāmaraṇa). The cycle of birth and death moves in this manner. The twelve links in the chain of causation are: (1) ignorance (avidyā), (2) dispositions (saṁskāra) belonging to the past life; (3) initial consciousness (vijñāna), (4) mind-body-complex (nāmarūpa), (5) six sense-organs (ṣaḍāyatana), (6) contact (sparśa), (7) feeling (vedanā), (8) thirst (tṛṣnā), grasping (upādāna), (9) will-to-be-born (bhava) belonging to the present life; (11) rebirth (jāti), (12) old age and death (jarāmaraṇa) belonging to the future life. Thus the twelve links extend to three lives, the past, the present, and the future. This is the view of the Hīnayānists. The Sthaviravādin and the Sarvāstivādin hold this view.[1] The Mādhyamikas regard dependent origination with the twelvefold chain of causation as relative truth (saṁvṛtisatya). The Yogācāras regard the first ten links as belonging to the present life, and the last two as belonging to the future life. Further, they group the twelve links under four heads. They consider ignorance and dispositions to be seed-producing potencies, consciousness and feeling to be seeds, thirst, grasping, and becoming to be conditions of producing seeds, and rebirth, old age and death to be manifested effects.

Ignorance is the cause of egoism or individuality. The false knowledge of individuality generates thirst, craving, or will-to-live (tṛṣnā). It is the cause of rebirth which is suffering. Thus craving due to ignorance is the cause of suffering. It is the original sin. It is the cause of bondage. Deliverance is the extinction of craving or the will-to-live. It is the extirpation of egoism. It is the eradication of root ignorance. The disposition of ignorance produces the initial consciousness which generates the mind-body-complex. The cycle of birth and death does not presuppose the existence of a permanent self. It does not depend upon the intervention of a transcendental Deity.[2]

---

[1] AK., iii. 20; ADS., viii. 3.

[2] BP., p. 110.

6. *The Doctrine of No-Self (Anātmavāda, Nairatmyavāda)*

"Look upon the world," says Buddha, "as void, having destroyed the view of oneself as really existing, so one may overcome death ; the king of death will not see him who thus regards the world".[1] The doctrine of No-Self means two things: (1) The self is an aggregate of impermanent mental and bodily processes. (2) The world is devoid of substances ; it is unsubstantial and void ; it is an aggregate of impermanent qualities.

The self is impermanent. It is an aggregate. It is the mind-body-complex. It is a series of successive mental and bodily processes which are impermanent. There is no permanent self. The self is a stream of cognitions (vijñānasantāna), "Conscious existence is like the current of a river which still maintains one constant form, one seeming identity, though not a single drop remains to-day of all the volume that composed the river yesterday."[2] In the river the drops of water change constantly. But still there is continuity.[3] Similarly, in the self there is a continuity of constantly changing mental processes. Sometimes they are intermittent. So the self is sometimes compared to sleep and dream. The course of organic life (bhavaṅgagati) is compared to dreamless sleep, in which consciousness is evoked by external stimuli, which is compared to dream. Conscious processes break in upon the stream of the subconscious processes. "The Pāli word *bhavaṅga* expresses both the objective aspect of vital functioning and the subjective aspect of our subconsciousness, or mental state, when we are not attending."[4] The self is an aggregate of body (rūpa) and four kinds of mental processes, feeling (vedanā), perception (saṁjñā), disposition (saṁskāra) including will (cetanā), and self-consciousness (vijñāna). It is called pudgala, jīva, ātmā, sattā. The body is not permanent. It is an aggregate of vital organs and their functions. It is an aggregate of changing qualities.

Buddha is emphatic on the denial of the permanent self in the following texts. "The world is empty of a self, or of

---

[1] *Mogharājamāṇavapucchā,* 1118.
[2] *Compendium of Philosophy,* pp. 8-9.
[3] Haraclitus said, "you cannot step twice into the same river, for fresh waters are ever flowing in upon you."
[4] Mrs. Rhys Davids : *Buddhism,* p. 76.

anything of the nature of a self. The five seats of the five senses, and the mind, and the feeling that is related to mind: all these are void of a self or of anything that is self-like".[1] "When one says 'I', he refers either to all the skandhas combined or any one of them and deludes himself that that was 'I'. One could not say that the rūpa was 'I' or that the vedanā was 'I' or any other skandha was 'I'. There is nowhere to be found in the skandhas 'I am'."[2] "Since neither self nor ought belonging to self can really and truly exist, the view that holds that this I who am world, who am self, shall hereafter live permanent, persisting, eternal, unchanging, abide eternally; is not this utterly and entirely a foolish doctrine?"[3] "This self of mine is the knower, the enjoyer of the fruits of my good and bad actions; it is eternal and immutable, it will continue for infinite time: this thought is very childish."[4] "The material form or body (rūpa) is not-self; feeling (vedanā) is not-self; perception (saṁjñā) is not-self; disposition (saṁskāra) is not-self; self-consciousness (vijñāna) is not-self. All dharmas are not-self."[5] The five aggregates are impermanent. They are not the so-called permanent self. Belief in permanent self is called Satkāyadṛṣṭi. It is a wrong view of the self.[6] The last text does not mean that the self is eternal and transcendental, behind and beyond the impermanent empirical self as Dr. Keith, Dr. Radhakrishnan, and Edmond Holmes wrongly interpret it.[7] It clearly means that the five aggregates constitute the not-self. There is no permanent or eternal self. The self is an empirical aggregate. There is no self beyond them. This is the unique and original teaching of Buddha. It is not an echo of the teaching of the Upaniṣads as some scholars think. The Upaniṣads teach the reality of the permanent Self or Ātman. Buddha teaches the reality of the impermanent not-self or anātman. The former recognize the reality of the transcendental or noumenal self, while the latter recognizes the reality of the empirical self.

---

[1] SN., iv. 54.
[2] SN., iii. 130.
[3] MN., Sutta Piṭaka, i. 138.
[4] *Ibid*, i. 1, 2.
[5] *Ibid*, i. 4, 5; i. 1. 2; i. 3. 2; iii. 1. 9; iii. 5. 2; iii. 5. 4; iii. 5. 5.
[6] MN., iii. 1, 9.
[7] BP., pp. 64-65; *Indian Philosophy*, Vol. I, pp. 386-88; *The Creed of Buddha*, pp. 165ff.

Once Buddha kept silent on the existence or non-existence of the self. The wandering monk Vacchagotta said, "Is there the ego?" Buddha was silent. Again he said, "Is there not the ego?" Still Buddha kept silent. When the monk departed, Buddha said to Ānanda that the affirmative answer would lead to eternalism (śāśvatavāda), and that the negative answer would lead to annihilationism (ucchedavāda). But both are wrong views. The ego or self is not eternal as some hold. Nor is the self non-existent as others hold. If the self is non-existent, there can be no transmigration and reaping of the fruits of actions. The truth lies in the middle of the two extreme views. The phenomenal or empirical self exists.

Nāgārjuna says in his commentary on the *Prajñāpāramitā-sūtra*: "The Tathāgata sometimes taught that the ātman exists and at other times he taught that the ātman does not exist. When he preached that the ātman exists and is to be receiver of misery and happiness in the successive life as the reward of his own Karma, his object was to save men from falling into the heresy of Nihilism (Ucchedavāda). When he taught that there is no ātman in the sense of a creator or perceiver or an absolutely free agent, apart from the conventional name given to the aggregate of the five skandhas, his object was to save men from falling into the opposite heresy of Eternalism (Śaśvatavāda). Now which of these two views represents the truth? It is doubtless the doctrine of the denial of ātman. . . . The two doctrines were preached by Buddha for two different purposes. He taught the existence of the ātman when he wanted to impart to his hearers the conventional doctrine; he taught the doctrine of anātman (no-self) when he wanted to impart to them the transcendental doctrine."[1] Similarly, Dharmapāla says in his commentary on *Vijñānamātraśāstra*, "The existence of the ātman is affirmed in the Canon only provisionally and hypothetically and never in the sense of its possessing a real and permanent nature."[2] Vasubandhu says in his commentary on *Abhidharmakośa*, "Whoever believes in the existence of ātman in its transcendental sense, exposes himself to the heresy of Eternalism, and whoever does not believe in the existence of ātman in its conventional sense, runs the risk

---

[1] SBT., pp. 18-19. [2] *Ibid*, p. 19.

of destroying the seeds of his own good Karma."[1] Thus he exposes himself to the heresy of Nihilism. Therefore the eternal, transcendental, noumenal self is unreal while the impermanent, empirical, phenomenal self is real.

There is a sermon of Buddha which is made out to indicate the existence of the self as distinct from the five aggregates. "O Brethren, I will explain to you the burden, the taking up of the burden, the laying aside of the burden, and the carrier of the burden. Of these, the burden is the five aggregates, which are the substrates of personal life ; the taking up of the burden is the craving for a continuation of life, accompanied by a sense of satisfaction ; the laying aside of the burden is emancipation ; the carrying out of the burden is the individual."[2] The individual, therefore, is distinct from the five aggregates. Otherwise the burden-bearer and the burden would be the same. Dr. Keith and Dr. Radhakrishnan interpret the text in this sense.[3] But this is a wrong interpretation. It is in flat contradiction to the main trend of Buddha's teaching on anātmavāda. Dr. S. K. Mukherjee rightly observes, "the individual spoken of as the carrier of the burden is nothing distinct from the aggregates: the preceding aggregates which culminate in the succeeding aggregates, are called the burden, and the latter are the burden carrier, being the inheritor of all that has gone before."[4] The bearer of the burden is not the permanent self.

In *Milindapañha* the Buddhist teacher Nāgasena instructs the king Milinda on the nature of the self by means of the parallel of the chariot. Just as a chariot is nothing but an aggregate of the wheels, the axle, and the body, so the self is nothing but a name of the five aggregates of body, feelings, perceptions, dispositions, and self-consciousness. The five aggregates constitute the empirical individual.[5] There is no eternal self behind the collection of the five aggregates. The mind is a collection of mental processes. The body is a collection of bodily processes. The empirical individual is a mind-body-complex. There is no permanent noumenal self. Personal identity is an illusion. It is ignorance (avidyā). The imperma-

[1] AK., p. 19.
[2] SN., iii. 25.
[3] BP., p. 82; *Indian Philosophy*, Vol. I, p. 387.
[4] *The Buddhist Philosophy of Universal Flux*, C.U., 1935, p. 190.
[5] *Milindapañha*, pp. 25ff.

nent series of mental and bodily processes is mistaken for the permanent self. Continuity produces an illusion of identity. It accounts for moral responsibility, reward and retribution, and transmigration.[1]

Buddhaghoṣa emphatically denies the existence of the permanent self. "Of ought within called self which looks forward or looks around, there is none!" "There is no permanent entity or self which acquires these states. These are to be understood phenomenally. There is no other essence or existence or personality or individuality whatever."[2] Buddhaghoṣa regards the self as a complex of mental and bodily constituents, even as a chariot is a complex of the wheels, the axle, and the body.[3] The empirical individual is the totality of the five skandhas, both mind and body. It must be kept free from metaphysical conception of the permanent soul. Mrs. Rhys Davids opines that Buddhism is emphatically a system of philosophy which extrudes the Ego.

The Buddhist theory of impermanent empirical self anticipated Hume's theory of the self. "For my part," says Hume, "when I enter most intimately into what I call *myself,* I always stumble on some particular perception or other, of heat or cold, light or shade, love or hatred, pain or pleasure. I never can catch myself at any time without a perception and never can observe anything but the perception. . . . What we call mind is nothing but a heap or bundle of different perceptions united together by certain relations, and supposed, though falsely, to be endowed with a certain simplicity and identity." Personal identity is an illusion engendered by rapid succession of impressions and ideas. Nāgasena and Buddhaghoṣa, like Hume, deny the permanent soul-substance. They regard it as a mere collection of the five aggregates. Unlike Hume, they include the bodily constituents also in the empirical self or individual.

The later Buddhist philosophers, Nāgārjuna, Vasubandhu, Diṅnāga, Dharmakīrti, Dharmottara, Śāntarakṣita and others deny the reality of the permanent self. The great Hindu philosophers, Vyāsa, Vācaspati, Jayanta Bhaṭṭa, Śrīdhara, Udayana, Kumārila, Prabhākara, Vijñānabhikṣu,

---

[1] *Ibid,* pp. 40ff.
[2] *Dhammasaṅgaṇi,* E.T., preface, pp. xxxvi—xxxvii.
[3] *Visuddhimagga; Atthasālinī,* 308.

Saṁkara, Rāmānuja, and others criticize the Buddhist doctrine of the impermanent empirical self severely. The Jaina philosophers also criticize the Buddhist doctrine of the impermanent empirical self. Hence it is quite clear that Buddhism believed in the impermanent self.

But some scholars opine that Buddha believed in the eternal noumenal self. Dr. Radhakrishnan says, "Buddha clearly tells us what the self is not, though he does not give any clear account of what it is. It is, however, wrong to think that there is no self at all according to Buddha. . . . The discussion of the burden and its bearer makes out that the skandhas which are the burden and the pudgala which is the bearer are distinct entities. . . . What we know is the phenomenal self. Buddha knows that there is something else. He is never willing to admit that the soul is only a combination of elements, but he refuses to speculate on what else it may be. The Upaniṣads arrive at the ground of all things by stripping the self of veil after veil of contingency. At the end of the process they find the universal self which is none of these finite entities, though the ground of them all. Buddha holds the same view, though he does not state it definitely."[1] Dr. Keith quotes certain texts in favour of the view that Buddha believed in the eternal noumenal self. He writes, "In the Alagaddūpamā Sutta of the *Majjhima*[2] there is a striking denial by the Buddha following on an exposition of the doctrine of the not-self. The accusation is made that the Buddha holds the destruction of a real entity. This he denies absolutely; what he bids men throw off is the non-ego consisting of the five constituents, bodily form, perception, feeling, the dispositions, and intellect; . . . the real entity is not destroyed by the laying aside of the constituents. This view may be strengthened by the observation that the Buddhist formula applied to everything in nature is applied by the Sāṁkhya school to the whole of material and spiritual nature, but with the single aim of expressing the absolute otherness of the self from nature. . . . The person is neither identical with the aggregates, nor yet is he distinct from them; the relationship is properly described as ineffable. . . . It accords with the position asserted by Sāriputta in his discussions with Sāti, for there we find that the Tathāgata is declared neither to be five aggregates nor to be different from them."[3] Dr. Radhakrishnan expresses the same view in the same language. He writes, "In the *Alagūddūpamā Sutta*[4] the accusation is made that the Buddha teaches the doctrine of the destruction of a real entity, but he denies it absolutely. He argues that he bids men throw off only the non-ego consisting of the five constituents, bodily form, perception, feeling, the dispositions and intellect. . . . . This view is corroborated by the Buddhist formula: This is not mine: I am

[1] *Indian Philosophy*, Vol. I, 1922, pp. 386-88.
[2] i. 140 ff.
[3] BP., 1933, pp. 64, 65, 67, 82, 84. [4] *Majjhima*, i. 140.

not this: this is not myself'. These negations aim at expressing the absolute difference of self from not-self or object. . . . . . Is the person identical with the five aggregates? To this question, the usual answer is given that the relationship is ineffable (avācya). . . . . Sāriputta, in his discussions with Sāti, observes that the Tathāgata is declared neither to be the five aggregates nor to be different from them."[1] The Buddha "implies the reality of a universal spirit which is not to be confused with the changing empirical aggregate."[2] This interpretation involves the heresy of eternalism (śāśvatavāda). It is against the bulk of the Pāli texts and the predominant note of phenomenalism in the teachings of Buddha. The texts cited above can be interpreted in an empirical way. Edmond Holmes also opines that Buddha believed in the eternal universal self.[3]

The doctrine of No-self (anātmavāda) means also that the world is unsubstantial and soulless. All external things are aggregates of changing qualities. There is no permanent substance apart from impermanent qualities. The permanent identical substance is a fiction of imagination. Buddhism denies the reality of substances apart from qualities. It recognizes the reality of phenomena only, physical and mental. It advocates phenomenalism. Early Buddhism believes in the phenomenal self and the phenomenal world. All forms of existence, material and psychical, are impermanent, soulless, and full of misery. They are subject to the inexorable law of becoming.[4]

7. *Karma*

Brahmanism makes too much of the self. Buddhism puts Dharma (Dhamma) in its place. It stresses energy, effort, endeavour. Will is the man alive. Will is the man in action. Knowledge is will.[5] Buddha says, "Very pure will we become in deed, word, thought. We will neither exalt the self nor despise the other man."[6] "Rouse thyself by thyself, examine thyself by thyself; thus self-protected and attentive wilt thou live happily, O Bhikṣu!"[7] "For self is the lord of self, self is the refuge of self; therefore curb thyself as the merchant curbs a good horse."[8] "Self is the lord of self, who else could be the lord? With self well subdued, a man finds a lord such

[1] *Gautama the Buddha*, 1945, pp. 52-55.
[2] *Ibid*, p. 55.
[3] *The Creed of Buddha*, Ch. iv.
[4] AN., i. 286; SN., ii. 25; DN., ii. 198; BP., p. 60.
[5] Mrs. Rhys Davids, *Buddhism*, p. 21.
[6] *Mahā-assapura-sutta, Ibid*, p. 23.
[7] DP., xxv. 379.
[8] DP., xxv. 380.

as few can find."[1] Thus Buddhism emphasizes freedom of the will. Is it consistent with the empirical conception of the self as the collection of the five aggregates (skandha)? In the empirical self some part may be regarded as dominant and others as dominated by it. The will is the dominant element in the individual. Sometimes the intellect (vijñāna) is compared to the guardian of a city, who, standing at the cross roads, controls the traffic.[2] Intellect is will. Intellect is the theoretical aspect of will. Will is the practical aspect of intellect. Vasubandhu says, "Karma is will (cetanā) and voluntary action."[3]

Buddhism regards the self as a collection of empirical aggregates or congeries of mental phenomena. In and through them it seeks to trace the working of moral causation. To look beneath or behind them for a 'thing in itself' or noumenal self it holds to be a dangerous superstition.[4] "On the ruins of the animistic view, Buddhism had to reconstruct a new personality, wholly phenomenal, impermanent, law-determined, yet none the less able, and alone able, by indomitable faith and will, to work out a personal salvation, a personal perfection."[5]

Buddhism lays great stress on freedom of the will, moral effort, energy, and activity. We are the masters of our own destiny. We make ourselves pure by our own free good volitions and actions. We make ourselves impure by our own free bad volitions and actions. "By onself the evil is done, by oneself one suffers; by oneself evil is left undone, by oneself one is purified. Purity and impurity belong to oneself, no one can purify another."[6] Man is the architect of his own destiny. He can work out his own salvation by free moral actions. "Work out your own salvation with diligence."[7] Buddhism, like Jainism, is a religion of self-help. Salvation does not depend upon the grace of extra-mundane God. It has to be wrought by a man himself by earnest moral efforts. Moral autonomy is the foundation of Buddhist ethics. "Beings are owners of their actions (karma), heirs of their actions; their actions are their matrix; their actions are their lineage, and by their actions

---

[1] DP., xii. 160.
[2] MP., p. 62.
[3] AK., iv. i; cp. AN., Vol. iv, 415.
[4] *Rhys Davids, Dhammasaṅgaṇi,* E.T., preface, pp. xxxiv-xxxv.
[5] *Ibid,* p. xciv.
[6] DP., xii. 165.
[7] MPS., vi. 10.

are they established."[1] Nāgasena says, "It is through a difference in their karma that men are not all alike, but some long-lived, some short-lived, some healthy and some sickly, some handsome and some ugly, some powerful and some weak, some rich and some poor, some of high degree and some of low degree, some wise and some foolish."[2] Man is what he has made himself. His past actions are the determinant of what he is, as his present actions of what he will be. Man is the builder of his own character and destiny. The past self is wrought up into the present self. The future self is a projection of the present self. The self never is, but is always becoming, evolving, to experience the fruits of its free actions in future lives. The self is not static, but fluid.

Our happiness is the result of our past good deeds. Our misery is the result of our past evil deeds. Our past good and evil actions in this life or the past life have brought about our present weal or woe. They are not caused by capricious Deity, the decree of an inexorable Fate, or blind chance. They are the inevitable results of our past free actions.[3] "Whatever a man does through his body, speech, or thought, are to be called his own for they follow him when he departs from his life like a shadow that leaves him not."[4] Karma is the connecting link between one life of an individual and another. Though Buddhism denies the existence of imperishable individual soul, it recognizes the unbroken continuity of karma or action. Though it rejects the immortality of the soul, it does not deny the continuity of personality.[5] The Buddhist conception of karma is moral, while the Jaina conception of it is physical. The Buddhist holds that karma, though mental, can interfere with the disposition of atoms and determine their growth.[6]

8. *Transmigration*

Karma leads to rebirth. There is no transmigration of an eternal soul from one body to another. There is mere continuity of the same series of mental processes. The last mental

---

[1] MN., iii. 203.
[2] MP., Warren: *Buddhism in Translations*, p. 215.
[3] AN. [4] SN. [5] SBT., pp. 50 ff.
[6] Stcherbatsky: *The Central Conception of Buddhism*, p. 34.

act ceases, and transmits its causal energy to the first mental act in a new embryonic germ-cell. The last conscious act dies away, another conscious act arises in a new organism. This is called rebirth. There is neither absolute identity nor absolute difference. The fruit arises in the same psychical series in which the act was done. The child is trained ; the youth reaps its fruits. The child and the youth are neither absolutely identical with each other, nor absolutely different from each other. In rebirth there is transmigration of character from the last conscious act in one life to the first conscious act in the next life. Moral responsibility attaches to the same series.[1] Buddha says, "To say 'one acts, another reaps the fruits of those acts', is not true. And to say 'one and the same both acts and is affected by the result' is not true. I teach a Midway between both extremes, to wit, the doctrine of Becoming by way of Cause."[2]

Buddha explains transmigration by the example of the flame of a lamp. A lamp burns throughout the night. But the flame of light does not remain the same throughout. There is a continuous change in the flame ; there is no identity in the flame but continuity in the different flames of light of the lamp. Similarly, the last flash of consciousness of a person in one life goes out, and it kindles the first flash of consciousness in the embryo in the next life. The psychical series continues uninterrupted, but its members continually change, appearing for a moment and then disappearing.

Buddha explains transmigration by the example of the different modifications of milk. Milk is modified into curds ; curds are transformed into butter ; butter is converted into melted butter. The same series continues, but its members continue changing. There is unbroken continuity in the series, but no permanent identity. Similarly, the psychic series continues in transmigration, but there is no identity of the permanent soul. The first conscious act in the new birth is produced by the last conscious act in the preceding birth, which is modified by the accumulated dispositions (saṁskāra) of all the psychoses of this birth. Thus there is transmigration of the impermanent psychical series, though there is no identity of the permanent and eternal soul.[3]

---

[1] *Visuddhimagga.*

[2] SN., ii. 20; Mrs. Rhys Davids, *Buddhism,* p. 134. [3] MP.

"When an individual dies, a new individual is born and inherits his karma ; what transmigrates is not a person, but his karma".[1] Dr. Rhys Davids opines that Buddha did not teach the transmigration of souls. "What he did teach would be better summarized as the transmigration of character. After death of any being, there survived nothing at all but the being's 'karma', the result of its mental and bodily actions."[2] Professor Poussin writes, "The series passes into another existence, and lives a new section of life, under new conditions. It cannot be said that acts are the sole material cause of re-incarnation. It is the 'series' as a whole, with all its moral and material elements, that is incarnated. The new being is what its acts have made it."[3]

The Upaniṣads taught the Law of Karma. The Jaina stressed it and taught that a person could modify his future becoming by cancelling his past acts through his free actions. He had a materialistic conception of karma. Good actions produce auspicious karma-matter. Bad actions produce inauspicious karma-matter. Both kinds of karma-matter invest the soul. But Buddha has a moral conception of the Law of Karma. He teaches that man's actions are an index of his becoming or character, and that his becoming is modified by his acts. Free actions determine character. Character partly determines actions.

9. *The Dhamma or the Norm*

The word *Dhamma* is used generally in five senses: (1) scriptural texts, (2) quality (guṇa), (3) cause (hetu), (4) unsubstantiality (nissatta) and soullessness (nijjīva), and (5) the Law or Norm. There are no substances but only unsubstantial phenomena or attributes. There are mental and physical phenomena. They are devoid of soul or core of reality. They are unsubstantial. They are subject to the law of dependent origination (pratītyasamutpāda). They are subject to the inexorable law of Becoming, appearance and disappearance. The law of dependent origination is subject to the Law of Karma.

---

[1] AKV., iii. 24.
[2] *The Hibbert Lectures,* 1881, pp. 91-92.
[3] E.R.E., vii, *Karma,* p. 674.

Buddha says, "By Karma the world exists, by Karma mankind exists, beings are bound by karma as the linch-pin of a chariot keeps the wheel on."[1] The variety in the world is due to karma. (Karmajaṁ lokavaicitryam.) The Law of Karma governs all physical and mental phenomena. It is the supreme law. It is the law of moral causation to which physical causation is subservient. M. Poussin writes, "The whole universe with all its variety is the result of acts. It is the effect of the combined mass of the acts of all beings."[2]

In the Ṛgveda Ṛta represents the physical order and the moral order. It is independent of gods. It is an impersonal law. Buddhism regards Dhamma as an impersonal Law. It is the supreme all-embracing Law. "It denotes the laws of nature. It applies to the law of impermanence. It applies to the chain of causation. The various members of the chain stand in a relation of accordance with law (dhamma-ṭhiti). The progress to enlightenment on the part of the individual is regulated by law. Dhamma applies equally to law in the sphere presided over by the king and his judges. It denotes whatever is righteous or good. It expresses the characteristic of any person or thing. It comes to be used as a synonym of cause or ground. (hetu)."[3]

Dhamma is sometimes used in the sense of truth or reality. Such phrases as 'insight into Dhamma' (dhammavipassanā) and 'the eye of Dhamma' (dhamma-cakkhu) are used. Dhamma sometimes denotes more than mere truth ; it signifies the essence of things or the reality. The way of Dhamma takes the place of the way of the Brahman.[4] The eightfold path is called the Brahmayāna or the Dhammayāna. The Tathāgata is said to be the Dhammakāya, Brahmakāya, one with the Dhamma, one with the Brahman.[5] The Dhamma is used as a synonym of the Ātman, Brahman, or the Absolute.[6] It is equivalent to the highest reality. It is immanent in the reality. The Tathāgata is an embodiment of it. It is the Good immanent in the universe. Sometimes it is the semi-personification of the Good.[7]

---

[1] *Vāselṭhasutta*, 654; *Kathāvatthu*, E.T., p. 315.
[2] E.R.E., vii, p. 674.
[3] BP., pp. 69-70.
[4] SN., i. 141.
[5] DN., iii. 81, 84.
[6] SN., v. 6; DN., ii. 100.
[7] MP., p. 207; BP., pp. 71-74; cp. *Gautama the Buddha*, pp. 48-52.

Thus Dhamma is sometimes taken in the sense of the Moral Law immanent in the universe.

10. *Atheism*

The whole universe of phenomena is subject to the law of dependent origination (pratītyasamutpāda). There is no scope for God, an extra-mundane Creator. The law of dependent origination is not supervised by a person. Material and mental phenomena, plants, animals, men, and gods are subject to origin and destruction. They are determined by their causes and conditions. Buddha ridicules the conception of God, who is the eternal and immutable creator of the universe which is temporary, perishing and mutable. Brahmā, the first created being, may think owing to delusion that he is the omniscient and omnipotent Creator of the universe, past, present, and future. But, in fact, he is as subject to origin and destruction as any other effect.[1] Buddha says, "Brahmā is subject to delusion (avidyā). He thinks the non-eternal and impermanent Brahmaloka as eternal and permanent. But it also is subject to birth and death."[2] None among the Brāhmaṇas versed in the three Vedas has actually seen Brahmā, the Creator, but everybody has heard it from others, who, in their turn, have heard it from others, and so on. Tradition is no argument for the existence of God. The blind are misled by the blind.[3] Buddha, as a rationalist, cannot rely on tradition.[4] Brahmā himself confesses that he does not know where the elements of earth, water, light, and air are completely destroyed, that he is not omniscient. Buddha says that the four elements are completely destroyed in Nirvāṇa which is devoid of origin, continuance, and destruction, and which is ever shining.[5]

The variety in the world is due to karma. (Karmajaṁ lokavaicitryam). All things are transformations. There is neither creation nor destruction. The world has neither beginning nor end. All phenomena in the world are caused by other phenomena, which, in their turn, are caused by other

[1] DN., *Pāthikasutta*, iii. 1.
[2] MN., *Brahmanimantikasutta*, i. 5, 9.
[3] *Tevijja-sutta*, DN., i. 12-15.
[4] Rahul Sāṁkṛtyāyan : *Darśana-digdarśana* (Hindi), pp. 520-26.
[5] *Kevaṭṭa-sutta*, 11.

phenomena. Nothing is self-caused (svatantra). Nothing is uncaused. Every phenomenon in the universe, physical, organic, or mental, is determined by a number of conditions. The whole universe is a chain of causally connected phenomena, which is not determined by anything beyond the series of phenomena. The contingent world is not determined by a necessary Being which transcends the phenomena. There is no intervention of a supernatural Being, God, or the Absolute, in the phenomenal series of causes and effects. There are no uncaused phenomena. They are not self-caused or self-existent. They are not spontaneous emergences. They are not produced by their nature (svabhāvavāda). They do not come into existence by chance. They are not accidental occurrences. They are not pre-determined by Fate. They are determined by the totality of antecedent conditions on which they are dependent. The antecedent causal conditions vanish, and immediately after their disappearance their effects appear. This is the doctrine of dependent origination (pratītyasamutpāda). It emphasizes the conditional and dependent nature of all existence. There is no First Cause or Creator of the world. It is without beginning or end. Buddhism agrees with Jainism on this point. Both adopt a scientific attitude towards the world. Physical causation, organic causation, mental causation, and moral causation are parts of the Dhamma or the Law. There is no room for God. Buddha says, "Without beginning and end is this world-process (saṁsāra)." "A fruit does not originate of itself, nor is it made by another ; it originates in virtue of its cause ; it ceases on the cessation of its cause".[1] There can be no First Cause. We experience no absolute beginning. We experience no absolute end. Dependent origination is without beginning or end. It has no Lord presiding over it (asvāmika). It has no soul (anātmaka) to inspire it. The causal or cosmological argument is invalid.

It may be urged that every law has a law-giver. The law of dependent origination must be supervised by God. But this is wrong. The causal order is there. It is not intended or designed by God. It is the observed causal sequence of phenomena in the world. It is not caused or designed by God. There

---

[1] SN.

is no purpose in nature. There is no conscious agent who adapts the phenomena of the world with a purpose. Teleological argument is argument by analogy which is very weak.

In a conversation with Anāthapiṇḍika Buddha argues as follows: "If the world had been made by Īśvara, there should be no change nor destruction, there should be no such thing as sorrow or calamity, as right or wrong, as all things, pure and impure, must come from him. If sorrow and joy, love and hate, which spring up in all conscious beings, be the work of Īśvara, he himself must be capable of sorrow and joy, love and hatred, and if he has these, how can he be said to be perfect? If Iśvara be the maker, and if all beings have to submit silently to their maker's power, what would be the use of practising virtue? The doing of right or wrong would be the same, as all deeds are his making and must be the same with their maker. But if sorrow and suffering are attributed to another cause, then there would be something of which Īśvara is not the cause. Why, then, should not all that exists be uncaused too? Again, if Īśvara be the maker, he acts either with or without a purpose. If he acts with a purpose, he cannot be said to be all-perfect, for a purpose necessarily implies satisfaction of a want. If he acts without a purpose, he must be like a lunatic or suckling babe. Besides, if Īśvara be the maker, why should not people reverently submit to him, why should they offer supplications to him when sorely pressed by necessity? And why should people adore more gods than one? Thus the idea of Īśvara is proved false by rational argument, and all such contradictory assertions should be exposed. (Aśvaghoṣa's *Buddhacarita*). If the theists say, God is too great for man to be able to comprehend Him, then it follows that His qualities also surpass our range of thought, and that we can neither know Him nor attribute to Him the quality of creator. (*Bodhicāryāvatāra*)[1]". "If the world has not been created by Īśvara, may not all existence be a manifestation of the Absolute, the Unconditioned, the Unknowable behind all appearances? Said the Blessed One to Anāthapiṇḍika: 'If by the Absolute is meant something out of relation to all known things, its existence cannot be established by any reasoning (hetuvidyāśāstra). How can we know

[1] P. Laksmi Narasu: *The Essence of Buddhism,* 1908, pp. 188-89; cp. *Indian Philosophy,* Vol. I, pp. 456-57 n.

that any thing unrelated to other things exists at all? The whole universe, as we know it, is a system of relations; we know nothing that is, or can be, unrelated: How can that which depends on nothing and is related to nothing produce things which are related to one another and depend for their existence upon one another? Again, the Absolute is one or many. If it be only one, how can it be the cause of the different things which originate, as we know, from different causes? If there be as many different Absolutes as there are things, how can the latter be related to one another? If the Absolute pervades all things and fills all space, then it cannot also make them, for there is nothing to make. Further, if the absolute is devoid of all qualities (nirguṇa), all things arising from it ought likewise to be devoid of all qualities (nirguṇa). But in reality all things in the world are circumscribed throughout by qualities. Hence the Absolute cannot be their cause. If the Absolute be considered to be different from the qualities, how does it continually create the things possessing such qualities and manifest itself in them? Again, if the Absolute be unchangeable, all things should be unchangeable too, for the effect cannot differ in nature from the cause. But all things in the world undergo change and decay. How then can the Absolute be unchangeable? Moreover, if the Absolute which pervades all is the cause of everything, why should we seek liberation? For we ourselves possess this Absolute and must patiently endure every suffering and sorrow incessantly created by the Absolute. (*Aśvaghoṣa's Buddhacarita*)."[1]

Yasomitra argues that God cannot be the cause of the world, since if He were the cause, all things in it would be produced simultaneously. But they are produced in succession. The cause being present, the effect must be produced. God is always present. Therefore the entire world must be produced all at once. But, in fact, effects are produced in a serial order (kramasambhava). The germ-cell (kalala), the sprout, and the like gradually undergo mutation and development, and grow into a full-grown person, a tree, and the like. They are produced by the totality of their own causes and conditions. If they had been produced by God, they would have been produced

---

[1] *The Essence of Buddhism*, 1908, pp. 198-99; cp. *Indian Philosophy*, Vol I, pp. 457-58 n.

simultaneously. The serial order of effects may be said to be due to the will (chanda) of God. God wills that the effects be produced in a definite temporal sequence. Let A be produced first. Let B be produced after A, and so on. Then God has a variety of wills (chandabheda), which is the cause of a variety of effects. Then there is no one cause of multiplicity of effects. This hypothesis does not fare better than the hypothesis of a multiplicity of causes for a multiplicity of effects. If the variety of God's wills be said to be simultaneous because of His oneness, then all effects in the world should be produced simultaneously. If their non-simultaneous production depends on other concomitant conditions besides God's volitions, then they would depend upon other conditions, and so on to infinity. Thus there would be infinite regress (anavasthā). Buddhism also believes in beginningless world-process (anādi saṁsāra). Then the hypothesis of God becomes useless. It may be argued that even if God's volitions be simultaneous, their effects may be successive because the volitions would determine the definite serial order of their effects. This argument is wrong. After the volitions, there are no specific causes of specific effects (viśeṣābhāva). In the absence of specific causes there can be no specific effects. Hence, if the volitions of God be simultaneous, the effects in the world must be simultaneous. If the latter depend on other concomitant conditions, there will be infinite regress, and God will not be the sole cause of the world. Even if God is its sole cause, it is no credit to Him, since the world abounds in evils and miseries. Further, if God is the cause of the world, human efforts (puruṣakāra) will be useless. A gardener makes efforts to sow seeds in the cultivated field, makes it fertile by manure, weeds out weeds, and irrigates the field in order to grow plants. His efforts are unavailing, if God is the sole cause of plants. In the presence of the cause, the effect is present. In the absence of the cause, the effect is absent. If we apply this rule, seeds, manure, water, soil and the like are the causal conditions of plants. The causal activity of God is not perceived in the production of them. If God together with the causal conditions be said to be their cause, it amounts to irrational devotion to God (bhaktivāda). The causal conditions are adequate to produce their effects. They do not require the aid of God. On the other hand, if God requires their aid, He is not true Lord (īśvara). But God may be said to be the First Cause (ādisarga īśvarahetukaḥ[1]), and causal conditions may be called the second causes. In that case human efforts will not be useless. If effects are produced by their causes, which, in their turn, are produced by their causes, until we reach God, the First Cause, then God also should have a cause. The so-called First Cause is not uncaused. Hence God is not the cause of the world.[2]

Dr. Radhakrishnan criticizes the arguments against God as the creator of the world and reproduces long passages from *"The Essence of Buddhism"* in his *Indian Philosophy* (Vol. I). But in his *Gautama the Buddha* he opines that Buddha believed in the super-personal Absolute. He writes, "The Buddha set himself against all personal conceptions of God. . . . The nature of absolute reality is supra-logical. . . . . The Buddha pointed out the reality of nirvāṇa, of an absolute self and of an absolute reality which he chose to call dharma."[3] "If the Buddha declined to define the nature of this Absolute or if he contented himself with negative definitions, it is only to indicate that absolute being is above all determinations."[4] Dr. Radhakrishnan thinks that Buddha believed in the eternal self, the Absolute, or the eternal justice (dharma), and that he looked upon nirvāṇa as timeless or eternal existence of the self. He interprets Buddha's silence on ultimate ontological questions as implying the existence of the Absolute. But reading Absolutism into Buddha's teachings is extremely hazardous and unwarranted by the bulk of the texts in the Pāli canon. Poussin opines that Buddhism does not believe in the Absolute.[5] Dr. Das Gupta opines that "there is no Brahman or supreme permanent reality" in Buddhism.[6]

11. *Non-Materialism*

Though Buddha denies the existence of the permanent self (ātman) and the Creator of the world or God (īśvara), he is not a materialist. He does not reduce the mind or mental processes to the material elements. He does not identify the soul with the body. Nor does he regard it as quite distinct from the body. Is the soul identical with the body? Or is it distinct from the body? It is an indeterminable (avyākṛta) question. If it is quite distinct from the body and eternal and immutable, it cannot be purified by moral conduct,

---

[1] AKV., p. 174.
[2] AKV., pp. 171-74.
[3] P., 66.
[4] P. 62.
[5] E.R.E., ix. p. 377.
[6] HIP., Vol. I, p. 111.

concentration, and insight. This conception is subversive of morality. If, on the other hand, it is identical with the body, it is dissolved with the body, and cannot reap the fruits of its actions.[1] Buddha believes in the Law of Karma, future life, and transmigration. He believes in the complete extinction of suffering and achievement of perfect peace or nirvāṇa here on earth. He believes in the attainment of holiness or sanctification of life. Thus he rejects materialism and accepts spiritualistic outlook on life. He refutes the materialism of Pāyāsi who holds that there is neither future life, nor reaping of fruits of good and bad actions, nor rebirth of souls. Pāyāsi argues that none have returned after death from the next world and vouched for its existence, that even the virtuous, who are sure of heaven, are reluctant to die, that the dead body does not become lighter after death, and that none has seen the soul depart from the body.[2] Buddha refutes these arguments.

Early Buddhism admits the reality of four permanent elements, earth, water, fire, and air which undergo changes. It sometimes includes ether in the elements, and sometimes treats it as a derivative. The external stimuli interact upon the sense-organs and produce consciousness. Early Buddhism believes in naive realism and causal theory of knowledge.

12. *Anti-metaphysical Attitude*

Buddha solves only one practical problem. How to exterminate suffering? Philosophical wrangling does not solve this problem. Idle theoretical speculation does not soothe the agony of suffering. It generates self-conceit, arrogance, and scepticism. It does not draw out the arrow of agony. So Buddha discourages philosophizing and emphasizes self-control, thoughtfulness, energy, activity, moral conduct, purity of mind, goodwill, love, compassion, and peace. He says, "The Tathāgata is free from all theories." He rules out ten questions relating to the world, the relation of the soul and the body, and the condition after the attainment of nirvāṇa. These are indeterminable. They are as follows: (1) Is the world eternal? (2) Is it non-eternal? (3) Is it finite? (4) Is it infinite? (5) Is the

[1] AN., iii.

[2] DN., ii. 10.

soul identical with the body? (6) Is it distinct from the body? (7) Does the Tathāgata exist after death? (8) Does he not exist after death? (9) Does he both exist and not exist after death? (10) Does he neither exist nor not-exist after death?[1] These questions are fruitless for moral life. They are not conducive to detachment, peace, enlightenment, and nirvāṇa. So these metaphysical puzzles are ruled out. Wrangling over philosophical views is useless. Self-command is the way to perfection.[2] The whole world is on fire. Extinguish the fire. Do not waste a moment in useless disputes. Overcome the torrent of passions and attain perfect peace and calm (nirvāṇa)[3] Philosophical views lead to disputes; they do not lead to purity, but in the realization of nirvāṇa there is no dispute.[4]

13. *Rationalism*

Buddha teaches rationalism to his disciples and condemns faith in tradition and authority. He advises them to trust in their own reason and believe in what commends itself to their reason. He says to the Kālāma princes, "It is natural that doubt should arise. Do not believe in traditions merely because they have been handed down for many generations; do not believe in a written statement of an old sage. After observation and analysis, when it agrees with reason and is conducive to the good of all, accept it and act upon it."[5] Authority is no source of truth. Its validity must be tested by reason and personal experience. Tradition is like a number of blind men leading one another. The first man does not see; neither does the middle one see; nor does the last one see. Tradition is an exceedingly weak argument. Buddha makes a distinction between the mere reception of truth and the knowledge of truth which involves rational conviction. He says, "One must not accept my Dharma from reverence, but first test it as gold is tested by fire." "You must trust to yourselves. You can take nothing from me. You must be righteous through your own efforts. You must depend on yourselves for the extinction of all suffering."[6] "Three things shine before the world and

---

[1] DN., i. 187; MN., ii. 2, 3. p. 431-485.
[2] *Khaggavisāṇasutta*, 21.
[3] *Dhaniyasutta*, 4.
[4] *Mahāviyūhasutta*, 895, 910.
[5] AN., *Kālāmasutta*.
[6] MN., i. 265.

cannot be hidden. They are the moon, the sun, and the truth proclaimed by the Tathāgata. There is no secrecy about them." Buddhism has no esoteric or occult doctrines. "He who questions the validity of reason by arguments contradicts himself."[1] "One must not rely upon another's opinion. Obedience to an authority can have no value by itself. To attain knowledge, instruction is necessary, but it should be confirmed and assimilated by personal experience."[2] Thus Buddha teaches rationalism.[3]

But Buddha himself attained nirvāṇa by intuition (prajñā) and enlightenment (bodhi). So every one must attain intuition by his own free efforts. He must work out his own salvation by intuition. This intuition is supra-rational. It is not achieved by discursive intellect. It is the crown of the eightfold path. Boundless is the enlightenment of Buddha. He alone knows where the elements of earth, water, fire, and air are completely destroyed. He is omniscient. So faith in Buddha is necessary. The intelligible parts of his doctrine should be understood by reason. But its unintelligible depths which are understood by Buddha only should be accepted on faith. The nature of the action of Karma is not comprehensible. It has to be accepted on faith. There is no discredit in it.[4] The word of Buddha must refer to truth, it must refer to the law ; it must decrease sin ; it must lead to nirvāṇa.[5] This is the pragmatic test of the truth of his word accepted on faith. Hence anything that is well said is said to be a word of Buddha.

Faith is an indispensable preliminary to entrance upon the path. It is a prelude to right knowledge. Faith in the complete enlightenment of Buddha and his word leads to correct knowledge and conviction. Faith is sometimes said to be the means of attaining nirvāṇa. The teaching of Buddha saves the faithful, but destroys the faithless.[6] Thus faith in the authority of Buddha, independent reflection or individual reason, and individual insight and intuition have their place in the life of an aspirant. Intuition is the consummation of

---

[1] *Jātakamāla*, the story of Mahābodhi.
[2] *Bodhisattvabhūmi*.
[3] *The Essence of Buddhism*, ch. ii.
[4] AN., iv. 82; ii. 80; DN., iii. 138.
[5] BCAP., ix. 43.
[6] AN., iii. 21; *Sumaṅgalavilāsinī*, p. 31.

moral discipline. It is based upon faith in, and rational comprehension of the Law. Faith, reason, and intuition are harmoniously blended in Buddhism as a religion.[1]

14. *Psychology*

The Buddhist psychology is empirical. It is psychology without the self. The mind is the stream of transient psychoses, each of which has origin, existence, and termination. It is not a substance persisting in the midst of changes. It is a series of phenomena combined into a unity. Consciousness is the relation between subject and object. Each psychosis is awakened by an external stimulus. Visual consciousness is produced by the contact of the eye with a visible object. Auditory consciousness is produced by the contact of the ear with a sound. Thought is excited by the contact of the mind with a mental object. If the stimulus ceases, consciousness ceases.[2] Sometimes consciousness (citta), mind (manas), and intelligence (vijñāna) are identified.[3] Sometimes consciousness is included in the elements (vijñānadhātu). It is an irreducible element. Manas is the intellectual function of consciousness. Vijñāna is the sense-response. Citta is the subjective aspect of consciousness.[4] The individual is mind-body (nāmarūpa). Personality (attabhāva) is an aggregate of transient mental processes. The mind is ever changing as it arises and disappears.[5] It is like an ape clutching a bough, giving it up, and clutching another. It moves from one object to another. It becomes conscious of one object ; the consciousness of it sinks into the subconscious ; then it becomes conscious of another object. It is a manifold of psychic factors. Body and mind are impermanent without a soul.[6]

Bhavaṅga is the subconscious continuity of organic life. Consciousness springs out of the subconscious and lapses into the subconscious. Bhavaṅga is the potential state of consciousness. It is subliminal consciousness. In deep sleep the consciousness (citta) becomes one with the subconscious (bhavaṅga)

[1] BP., pp. 33-39.
[2] MN., iii. 2. 2.
[3] DN., i. 213; AN., 170.
[4] Rhys Davids : *Buddhist Psychology*, p. 19.
[5] SN., ii. 95.
[6] SN., iii. 57.

or flow of organic life, and does not discern what is pleasant and what is unpleasant.[1]

Three degrees of consciousness are recognized: the subconscious, the conscious, and the superconscious. Subconsciousness is concerned with desire (kāma), the material (rūpa), or the immaterial (arūpa). Normal consciousness (kāmacitta) is concerned with objects of desire. Supernormal consciousness is sublime. It is concerned with the material (rūpaloka), the immaterial (arūpaloka), or the supra-mundane (lokuttara).[2]

The individual consists of five aggregates: (1) a corporeal aggregate or body (rūpa); (2) feeling (vedanā); (3) perception (saṁjñā); (4) disposition (saṁskāra); (5) intellect or self-consciousness (vijñāna). The rūpaskandha includes the body, the sense-organs, the sensible objects, and sensations.[3] The vedanā-skandha comprises feelings. There are three kinds of feeling, pleasure, pain, and neutral feeling. Pleasure arises from the experience of a desired object. Pain arises from the experience of an undesired object. Neutral feeling arises from the experience of an object which is neither desired nor undesired. Sense-contact is the cause of feelings.[4] Pleasure has stationariness as pleasant, change as unpleasant; pain has stationariness as painful, change as pleasant. Neutral feeling has knowledge as pleasant, not-knowing as painful.[5] Pleasure and pain are opposed to each other. Neutral feeling is the absence of pleasure and pain. It is comparable with ignorance which is the absence of knowledge. Pleasure is produced by an agreeable object. It does not want to change it. Pain is produced by a disagreeable object. It wants to get rid of it. Vedanā is not sensation. "Because of the sixfold field of sense, contact; because of contact, vedanā; because of vedanā, craving". Sensation generates feeling; feeling generates craving or desire. Cognition is prior to feeling. Feeling is prior to conation. Buddhaghoṣa points out: "There is no subject who feels; it is only feeling that feels because of some object which is in causal relation to it." Neutral feeling or indifference is distinct from equanimity (tatramajjhatthatā), which is an

[1] *Buddhist Psychology*, pp. 171-72.
[2] *Compendium of Philosophy*, p. 12.
[3] SN., ii. 86.
[4] SN., iii. 101.
[5] MN., i. 303: *Buddhist Psychology*, p. 47.

emotion. Joy is an emotion akin to pleasure. Grief is an emotion akin to pain. Feeling is either bodily or mental. Joy is pleasure mingled with excitement. Grief is pain mingled with excitement.

The saṁjñāskandha includes determinate perceptions of objects to which names are attached involving recognition. It does not include nameless indeterminate perceptions or sensations which are included in the rūpaskandhā.[1] Saṁjñā includes cognitive assimilation of sense-impressions and cognitive assimilation of ideas by naming. The former is perception of resistance (paṭigha-saññā), while the latter is perception of the name (adhivacana-saññā) by the central sense (mano). Thus there are two stages of saṁjñā-consciousness: (1) contemplating sense-impressions; (2) recognizing them by naming.[2] They are resistance-perception and designative perception.

The saṁskāraskandha includes composite mental states and synthetic mental activity. All mental dispositions or conformations, intellectual, emotional, and volitional are saṁskāras.[3] They are compound psychoses. Elementary psychoses are combined into dispositions which imply synthetic activity. They bear fruit in actions. Fifty mental properties are included in them in the *Abhidhamma*. They are mental aggregates. They include will, attention, concentration, zest, faith, energy, mindfulness, insight, righteousness, modesty, discretion, disinterestedness, non-covetousness, non-hatred, equanimity and various other groups. Volition (cetanā) is the active side operating in them.

The vijñānaskandha includes the intellectual process or self-consciousness. It includes object-cognitions and self-cognitions. Feeling, perception, and self-consciousness are inseperable from one another. Vijñāna is awareness of mind. What one feels, one perceives; what one perceives, one is conscious of. Sense-cognitions are visual, auditory, olfactory, gustatory, and tactual. The senses of smell, taste, and touch are subordinated to that of sight. Touch is accorded its due importance. The mental cognition is recognized. The sense-impressions are co-ordinated by the mind, the central sense. The five external senses are the doors. The mind is the inward door

[1] AKB., pp. 50 ff.
[2] *Buddhist Psychology*, pp. 49-50. [3] SN., iii. 87.

of sense. The sense-cognition is a process of natural causation. The visual consciousness is the product of the contact of the eye with a visible object. Feeling arises from the sense-experience. Contact gives rise to the series: feeling, perception, thought, will (cetanā), concentration (ekāggatā), sense of vitality (jivitendriya), and attention (manasikāra).[1] Peripheral contact gives rise to feeling. It is the response to the consciousness of the new stimulus. Where there is no peripheral contact, there is no feeling.[2]

The Nikāyas mention attending, perceiving remembering, comparing, discerning, and thinking as cognitive processes. They speak of thinking, volition, desire, and endeavour.[3] Thinking gives rise to desire. Through desire we divide objects into what we like and what we dislike.[4] From contact feeling arises; from feeling, perception; from perception, thinking; from thinking, mental clinging.[5] Thus perception arouses thinking. What we perceive, we think about.[6] Vitakka is thinking. Takka is argument. Vitakka is discursive intellection. It is not intuition. Vicāra is persistence in discursive thinking. It is the continuation of vitakka. Cintā also is intellection.[7] Manasikāra is attention. Sāti is mindfulness. It is the opposite of mental distractedness. It is thoughtful awareness. It is the essential condition of concentration of mind and ethical training. Mindfulness (sāti) and self-awareness (sampaññā) are coincident with each other. They involve intense attention.[8] Self-awareness is deliberate intellection. Vicaya and vimaṅsā are equivalent to self-awareness. But they emphasize the volitional aspect of discursive thinking. Cintā is speculation. Lokacintā is speculation about the world. Diṭṭhi is belief. It is allied to speculation. Knowledge or gnosis is nāna. Insight is paññā. It is illumination or intuition. It is not ratiocination. Jhāna is meditation. Samādhi is rapt concentration. Sublime meditations (brahmavihāra) are the higher intellectual functions suffused with the emotions of love, pity, sympathetic joy, and equanimity. Jhāna leads to intuition (paññā) of the four Truths. It is

---

[1] MP., p. 56.
[2] SN., iv. 171.
[3] SN., ii. 153; MN., i. 480; ii. 173.
[4] DN., ii. 178.
[5] MN., i. iii.
[6] MN., i. iii.
[7] SN., v. 447.
[8] DN., i. 70; AN., v. 115.

higher knowledge (abhiññā). It is complete knowledge (pariññā). These are the processes of ideation.

Cetanā, sañcetanā, and saṅkappa mean volition. Cetanā is will. Thinking generates volition. Volition produces action.[1] Cetanā is effort of volition. Saṅkappa is purpose or design of the mind with regard to an object. Volition is transformed into action, mental, verbal, or bodily. Its function is twofold. In its psychological aspect it determines the activities of its concomitant mental constituents. In its ethical aspect it determines its own consequences.[2]

The three primary emotions, attachment (lobha) with its forms, greed, lust, and passion, aversion (dosa) with its forms, anger, hate, and malevolence, and delusion (moha) or ignorance are mentioned. The opposite emotions are disinterestedness (alobha), amity (adosa), and true knowledge (amoha).[3] Amoha is intuition (paññā). Friendship (mettā), pity, or sympathy with suffering (karuṇā), joy, or sympathy with happiness (muditā) are altrustic emotions.[4] They are different forms of amity (adosa).

Manasikāra is attention. Yonisomanasikāra is intensive attention. It is essential to suppression of sensuality, malevolence, laziness, distraction, and doubt, and to the production of the spiritual qualities.[5] It leads to liberation. It gives rise to joy, zest, calm, happiness, and concentration. Intensive attention leads to true knowledge of things as they are in their causal relation. True knowledge generates dispassion. Dispassion generates freedom.[6] Early Buddhism contains germs of analytical psychology. It is empirical psychology without the Ego. The identity of personality is due to continuity of the psychical series. There is no identity, but there is continuity.[7]

15. *Ethics*

An act is will or volition (cetanā). It is expressed in vocal or bodily act. It has a mental side and a bodily side.

---

[1] AN., iii. 415.
[2] *Compendium of Philosophy,* p. 16.
[3] AN., i. 134.
[4] AN., i. 183.
[5] SN., v. 85, i. 14.
[6] DN., iii. 288.
[7] *Buddhist Psychology;* BP., pp. 84-91; *Campendium of Philosophy*, pp. 1-16.

Mental acts are acts *par excellence*. There are no vocal or bodily acts without mental acts.. "We are what we think; we are what we will." (*Poussin*) There are two kinds of acts, pure acts and impure acts. The former are free from depravities (āsava) involving ignorance and desire. Pure acts are free from passions (kleśa).. They are free from ignorance and desire. They have no retribution. They destroy becoming. They prepare the way to nirvāṇa. Meditation on the four noble truths is a pure act. Acts which lead to nirvāṇa are pure. All other acts are impure. They are either good or bad, meritorious or demeritorious. Acts which lead to pleasant retribution are good. Acts which lead to unpleasant retribution are bad. Acts which are done with the intention of attaining happiness in this world are bad. Acts which are done with the intention of attaining happiness in the world beyond are good. Sometimes acts done with the intention for the good of others are said to be good, and acts done with the intention for the harm of others are said to be bad. Utilitarian morality is hinted at here. Sometimes three kinds of acts are distinguished: good (kuśala), bad (akuśala), and indifferent (avyākṛta). Good acts are beneficial. Bad acts are pernicious. Indifferent acts are neither beneficial nor pernicious. The good acts are free from greed, hatred, and delusion. The bad acts are tainted with them. Acts are also classified as meritorious (puṇya), demeritorious (apuṇya), and fixed (āniñjya). A meritorious act leads to happiness in the sphere of desire. A demeritorious act leads to unhappiness in the sphere of desire. A fixed act leads to fruits in a higher sphere. An act leading to nirvāṇa is good (kuśala), since it is pure, but not meritorious (puṇya). Acts are also divided into four kinds. "Every bad act is black; the act that is good in relation to the higher spheres is white; the act that is good in relation to the sphere of desire is white-black, because, being always weak, it is always mixed with evil. It is good in itself, but co-exists in the 'series' along with bad acts."[1] Bad or black acts produce impurity. Good or white acts produce purity. Good-bad or white-black acts produce both purity and impurity. Non-white-non-black acts or acts which are neither good nor

---

[1] E.R.E., vii, p. 675.

bad produce neither purity nor impurity, but contribute to the destruction of karmas.[1] This fourfold classification of acts is found in the Jaina and the Yoga systems also.

We must distinguish in an act the volitional preparation, the act proper, and the consequence. Moral responsibility attaches to all these stages of an act. A voluntary act is done with full knowledge of what a person is doing. We must take into account the subjective and objective elements of an act in order to pass moral judgment upon it.[2] Motive and intention, the act, and the consequence are the objects of moral judgment. For moral evaluation of an act of charity, we must take into account the qualities of the donor and his attitude, the qualities of the object given, the qualities of the receiver, and the consequences of the act.[3]

Buddha rejects both Being and Non-Being and believes in Becoming. He adopts the metaphysical mean. He rejects both self-indulgence and self-mortification, and enjoins the ethics of moderation. He preaches the doctrine of the ethical mean. "There are two extremes which he who has gone forth ought not to follow—habitual devotion, on the one hand, to the passions, to the pleasures of the sensual things, a low and pagan way of seeking satisfaction, ignoble, unprofitable, fit only for the worldly-minded ; and habitual devotion, on the other hand, to self-mortification, which is painful, ignoble, unprofitable. There is a Middle Path discovered by the Tathāgata—a path which opens the eyes, and bestows understanding, which leads to peace, to insight, to the higher wisdom, to nirvāṇa. Verily ! it is this Aryan Eightfold Path ; that is to say, Right Views, Right Aspiration, Right Speech, Right Conduct, Right mode of livelihood, Right Effort, Right Mindfulness, and Right Rapture."[4]

(1) Right view or belief (samyak dṛṣṭi) consists in right knowledge of the four noble truths, which leads to nirvāṇa. It is not theoretical speculation which does not lead to dispassion, self-control, and peace.

(2) Right resolve (samyak saṁkalpa) consists in the determination to uproot attachment to sensual pleasure, ill-will towards others, and desire to do harm to them. Mere right

[1] *Atthasālinī*, 89.
[2] *Abhidhammabhāṣya*, Ch. iv.
[3] E.R.E., vii, p. 676.
[4] *Early Buddhism*, p. 51.

knowledge of right and wrong does not help the aspirant reach his goal. It must be expressed in right resolve to do what is right and desist from doing what is wrong. Right resolve is aspiration towards renunciation, benevolence, and compassion.

(3) Right speech (samyak vāk) is an outwar1 expression of right resolve. It is an outward expression of right resolve. It consists in abstention from lying, slander, abuse, harsh words, and frivolous talk. One should speak what is right (dhamma), not what is unrighteous (adhamma). One should speak what is pleasing, not what is unpleasing. One should speak what is true, not what is false. One should speak well. One should speak what does not pain oneself nor hurt others. Truth should be in harmony with right and good. The just stand firm in what is true, in what is good, and in what is right.[1] Enmity cannot be pacified by harsh words, but by good-will.[2] One useful word which pacifies the mind, is far better than a thousand useless words.[3]

(4) Right conduct consists in abstention from the destruction of life, theft, sex-indulgence, lying, the use of intoxicating liquors, eating between meals, attending social entertainments, the use of unguents and ornaments, the use of luxurious beds, and the handling of gold and silver which are binding upon the monks.[4] The first five duties are binding on lay men. They should observe chastity in their married life. These sins should neither be committed, nor caused to be committed, nor approved. Lay men have specific duties. Parents should train their children in virtue and restrain them from vice, give them education, get them married decently, and give them their property. Children should support their old parents, perform family duties, protect their patrimony and matrimony, make themselves their worthy heirs, and honour their memory after their death. Pupils should honour their teachers by rising in their presence, by ministering to them, by obeying them, by supplying their wants, and by attending to their instructions. Teachers should show affection to their pupils, train them in virtue, instruct them in arts and science, speak well of them, and protect them from danger. The husband should respect his wife, treat her kindly, be faithful to her, make others respect her, and

---

[1] *Subhāsitasutta.*
[2] DP., i. 5.
[3] DP., viii. 1.
[4] *Dhammikasutta.*

give her suitable clothes and ornaments. The wife should show affection to her husband, manage her household rightly and frugally, be faithful to her husband, be hospitable to kinsmen and relatives, and show skill and diligence in all matters. An honourable man should treat his friends as equals, speak politely to them, offer them presents, promote their interests, and share with them his prosperity. They should guard him from danger, protect his property when he is careless, offer him shelter in danger, adhere to him in misfortune, and show kindness to his family. The master should take care of his servants, give them work according to their strength, give them suitable wages and food, tend them in sickness, share with them unusual delicacies, and give them occasional holidays. They should revere him, stand up before him, retire later to rest, be content with what is given them, work cheerfully and well, and speak well of him. A lay man should minister to monks, show them affection in thoughts, words, and acts, welcome them readily, and supply their wants. They should dissuade him from vice, exhort him to virtue, show kindness to him, instruct him in religion, remove his doubts, and point the way to nirvāṇa. Liberality, courtesy, kindness, and unselfishness should be cultivated by all.[1]

(5) Right livelihood (samyak ājīvikā) consists in earning living by honest means. Trades in arms, animals, flesh, liquor, and poison are forbidden.[2] Earning livelihood by under-weights, fraudulence, bribery, ingratitude, crookedness, mutilation, persecution, confinement, robbery, and plunder is forbidden.[3]

(6) Right effort (samyak vyāyāma) consists in constant vigilance, effort, and activity which are necessary for self-control, sense-restraint, arrest of evil thoughts, stimulation of good thoughts, and concentration of the mind on universal goodwill. Restless mind is not conducive to good thoughts, good emotions, and good conduct. Right effort consists in suppressing evil states and stimulating good states. The following five methods are recommended to expel an evil thought: "(1) Attend to some good idea ; (2) face the danger of the consequences of letting the bad idea develop into action ;

[1] *Sigālovāda Sutta; Tevijja Sutta,* ii; Rhys Davids: *Buddhism,* pp. 144-47.

[2] AN., 5.

[3] DN., p. 269.

(3) become inattentive to the bad idea ; (4) analyse its antecedents, and so paralyse the sequent impulse ; (5) coerce the mind with the aid of bodily tension."[1] This method is similar to the Yoga method of meditation on opposite thoughts (pratipakṣabhāvanā). The will is controlled by right effort. "On the mind depends the practice of dharma, and on the practice of dharma depends the attainment of bodhi."[2]

(7) Right mindfulness (samyak smṛti) consists in recollection of the impurity of the body, the nature of feeling, pleasure, pain, and neutral feeling, the nature of mind endowed with greed, hatred, and delusion, the nature of dharmas, five aggregates, sense-organs, sensible objects, means to enlightenment, and four noble truths. Right mindfulness is an indispensable pre-requisite of right concentration.[3]

(8) Right concentration (samyak samādhi) consists of four meditations. It is the crown of the eightfold path. The first Jhāna is a state of joy born of seclusion, accompanied by reflection and investigation, in which sensuality is destroyed. The second Jhāna is a state of joy born of deep tranquillity, without reflection or investigation, which are suppressed ; in it thought is tranquilized, and intuition predominates. The third Jhāna is a state of neutral consciousness in which all passions are destroyed. The fourth Jhāna is a state of complete tranquillity and self-possession in which joy and sorrow are destroyed.[4] Buddhism stresses right conduct (śīla), right concentration (samādhi) and right insight (prajñā). Śīla and samādhi lead to insight. Right insight purges the mind of lust (kāmāsava), becoming (bhavāsava), and ignorance (avidyāsava).[5] All should meditate on love and friendship (maitrī) for all creatures, compassion (karuṇā) for distressed creatures, joy (muditā) for virtuous persons, and indifference to all vicious persons. These are called the four sublime meditations (brahmabihāra). The four meditations are associated with the meditation on the impurity of the body (aśubha-

[1] *The Essence of Buddhism*, p. 170; cp. *Indian Philosophy*, Vol. I, p. 422.
[2] Cittādhīno dharmo dharmādhīno bodhiḥ. *The Essence of Buddhism*, p. 175; cp. *Indian Philosophy*, Vol. I, p. 423.
[3] *Mahasatipittana Sutta*, ii. 9.
[4] *Mahāsudassana Sutta*, ii; Rhys Davids : *Buddhism*, pp. 175-76.
[5] *Dhammacakkapavattana Sutta*, 4.

bhāvanā). It impresses on the mind the impermanence of the body and creates dispassion for it. These meditations are enjoined by Jainism and the Yoga also.

The four paths are sometimes spoken of. The first path is conversion (srotāpanna). It consists in taking refuge in Buddha, the Law (Dhamma), and the Order, and practising the Law. It destroys egoism, doubt, and belief in the efficacy of rites and ceremonies. The second path is that of those who have conquered sensuality, malevolence, and delusion to a great extent. They will be born once more and attain liberation in the next birth (sakṛdāgāmin). The third path is that of those who will completely destroy their lust, hatred, and delusion and attain nirvāṇa in their present life (anāgāmin). The fourth is that of the Arhats, who are freed from the will-to-be-born, pride, self-righteousness, and ignorance. They are full of infinite love and good-will for all in the whole world.[1]

There are ten fetters or evil states of mind: (1) delusion of self (sakkāya-diṭṭhi); (2) doubt (vicikicchā); (3) belief in rites (sīlabbata parāmāsā); (4) lust (kāma); (5) hatred (patigha); (6) desire for rebirth on earth (rūparāga); (7) desire for rebirth in heaven (arūparāga); (8) pride (māna); (9) self-righteousness (uddhacca); and (10) ignorance (avijjā). Freedom from the first five fetters makes the aspirant an Arhat. Freedom from the last five leads to nirvāṇa. It is the fruit of the fourth path.[2]

There are four intoxicants or taints (āsava): (1) sensuality (kāmāsava), (2) desire for rebirth (bhavāsava), (3) ignorance of the four noble truths (avijjāsava), and (4) the holding of heretical views (diṭṭhāsava). Āsavas are depravities of the mind. The Jainas take āsava in the sense of influx of karma-matter into the soul. But the Buddhists take it in the sense of taints or impurities of the mind.

There are ten afflictions (kilesa). They are specific passions such as greed (lobha), hatred (dosa), delusion (moha), pride (māna), heresy (diṭṭhi), doubt (vicikicchā), idleness (thīna), boastfulness (udhacca), shamelessness (ahirika), and hardness of heart (anottāpa). They are effects of āsavas. Greed (lobha), hatred (dosa), and delusion (moha) are said to be the root

[1] *Mettasutta;* BGB., pp. 101-02; *The Essence of Buddhism,* pp. 181-82.

[2] *Ratana Sutta; Cetokhilasutta.*

afflictions. They are the springs of actions, verbal, bodily, and mental. This view of afflictions partly resembles the Yoga view of five afflictions, ignorance (avidyā), egoism (asmitā), attachment (rāga), aversion (dveṣa), and delusion (moha).

There are ten sins: three sins of the body, four sins of speech, and three sins of the mind. The three sins of the body are killing, stealing, and adultery. The four sins of speech are lying, slander, abuse, and frivolous talk. The three sins of the mind are greed, hatred, and delusion. Intention determines whether an act is a sin or not.

Buddhism emphasizes purity of the inner life. Mere pure external conduct does not suffice. The heart must be purified. The mind must be purged of all impurities. Greed, hatred, and delusion must be destroyed. Anger, envy, jealousy, must be rooted out. All passions that ruffle the calm of the mind must be extirpated. The mind must be sanctified. "A bad mind and wicked deeds defile a man. Killing, cutting, binding, stealing, speaking falsehood, fraud, deception, adultery: this is what defiles one (āmagandha),—but not the eating of flesh. Neither penances, nor hymns, nor oblations, nor sacrifices, nor observances purify a mortal who has not conquered his doubt."[1] "The man who has the strength of understanding, is endowed with virtue and pure actions, is composed, delights in meditation, is thoughtful, free from ties, free from harshness, and free from passion, him the wise call a Muni."[2] Buddha stresses an internal view of morality, and severely condemns ritualism and ceremonialism.

The Buddhist morality is altruistic. Though nirvāṇa is the highest good, it is realized through universal good-will and love (maitrī). Buddha says, "May all beings be happy and secure. Let no one deceive another, let him not despise another in any place, let him not out of anger or resentment wish harm to another. As a mother at the risk of her own life, protects her son, her only son, so let him cultivate boundless love towards all beings. Let him cultivate towards the whole world—above, below, around—a heart of love unstinted, unmixed with different or opposing interests. Let a man maintain this mindfulness all the while he is awake, whether he

[1] *Āmagandha Sutta*, 241, 248.
[2] *Munisutta*, 211; *Hemavatasutta*, 173.

is standing, walking, sitting, or lying down. This state of heart (cetovimukti) is best in the world."[1] "Let his mind pervade one quarter of the world with thoughts of love, and so the second, and so the third, and so the fourth."[2] We should pervade the whole world with love, pity, sympathy, and equanimity.[3] Universal love (maitrī), compassion (karuṇā) for the distressed, joy (muditā) for the virtuous, and indifference (upekṣā) to the vicious are enjoined. Love generates compassion, joy, and indifference. So love is higher than these. So the Buddhist ethics is altruistic.

The ethics of ahiṁsā is the keynote of Buddhism. "Let one refrain even from hurting any creature, both those that are strong, and those that tremble in the world."[4] "Let a man overcome anger by love ; let him overcome evil by good ; let him overcome the greedy by liberality, and the liar by truth. For hatred does not cease by hatred at any time ; hatred ceases by love, this is its true nature."[5] "Let us live happily, not hating those who hate us ! Among men who hate us let us dwell free from hatred."[6] "Good men melt with compassion even for one who has wrought them harm."[7] "Returning good for good is noble, but returning good for evil is nobler still."[8] "To the man who foolishly does me wrong I shall return the protection of my ungrudging love ; the more the evil that comes from him, the more the good that shall go from me."[9] "The virtuous, when injured, grieve not so much for their own pain as for the loss of happiness incurred by their injuries".[10] Hatred should be conquered by love ; harm should be conquered by good. Evil recoils upon one who offends a harmless, pure, and innocent person. Hatred generates hatred. A harsh word excites a harsh word. A blow incites a blow. Patience is the highest virtue. "Victory breeds hatred, for the conquered is unhappy. He who has given up both victory and defeat, he, the contented, is happy."[11] We should be

---

[1] *Metta Sutta*, 146-50; *The Essence of Buddhism*, p. 74; *Early Buddhism*, p. 61.

[2] *Tevijja Sutta*, iii. 1.

[3] *Mahāsudassana Sutta*, ii 8-11.

[4] *Dhammika Sutta*, 393.

[5] DP., 223, 5.

[6] DP., 197.

[7] *Avadānakalpalatā*.

[8] *Bodhicaryāvatāra*.

[9] *Sūtra of forty-two sections*.

[10] *Jātakamālā; The Essence of Buddhism*, p. 72.

[11] DP., 125, 133, 184, 201.

tolerant with the intolerant, mild with fault-finders, free from passion among the passionate. We should not offend any one by body, word, or thought.[1] A man is not just, if he carries a matter by violence ; he is just, if he leads others, not by violence, but by law and equity.[2] Poison does not affect one who has no wound ; evil does not affect one who does not commit evil.[3] Non-injury, in thought, word, and deed, love, good-will, patience, endurance, and self-purification constitute the Buddhist morality.

Buddhist morality is the mean between self-indulgence and self-mortification. Gautama underwent severe penances and self-torture which proved fruitless. They could not lead to nirvāṇa. Self-torture emaciates the body and fills the mind with evil thoughts. It is painful and unprofitable. If the fires of lust, hatred, and delusion are not quenched, self-mortification can lead us nowhere. Craving for pleasure springs from egoism. When egoism is rooted out, lust is extinguished, craving for worldly and heavenly pleasures is quenched. One free from egoism and passions may satisfy his natural appetites, but their satisfaction does not defile him. On the other hand, self-indulgence is enervating and degrading. It disturbs the calm and purity of the mind. But to satisfy hunger and thirst, to keep the body in good health, to protect it from heat and cold, to save it from fatigue, to cover it comfortably and decently are necessary to keep the mind strong and pure. This is the Middle Path that avoids both extremes. The Dharma spurns both pursuit of pleasures and self-mortification. It aims at purity of heart and purity of conduct. It aims at equanimity, peace, and enlightenment. Buddha condemns the austerities of the Jainas.

Thirst (tṛṣṇā) is the root of all desires. It is the will-to-live. It is the root of all suffering. So it must be rooted out by the conquest of conscious desires. Desires can be conquered by strong will (chanda), strenuous endeavour, and active discipline. Moral life is not quietism and inactivism. Indolence is the root of all moral diseases. Earnestness, diligence, and watchfulness are indispensable for morality. Lust, anger, malice, pride, and ignorance can be conquered by universal love and bene-

---

[1] DP., 405, 406, 391. [2] DP., 256-57. [3] DP., 124.

volence, compassion, and cheerfulness. Self-perfection can be attained by self-abnegation.[1]

But Buddha prefers a monk's life to a householder's life. "Full of hindrances is household life, a path defiled by passion: free as the air is the life of him who has renounced all worldly things. How difficult is it for the man who dwells at home to live the high life in all its fulness, in all its purity, in all its bright perfection!"[2] So Buddha goes forth from a household life into the homeless state. Social intercourse interferes with one's freedom. It gives rise to affections. Pain arises from affections. Compassion for friends and companions fetters the mind. Affections for children give rise to pain. Separation from them is painful. Their death is heart-rending. Love yields sorrow and suffering. So social intercourse should be cut off, and friendship with individual persons should not be cultivated. Love of the Law (Dharma) is supreme. Narrow selfish love should be consumed by universal selfless love. One who is at home in the whole world, not hostile to any body, is contented.[3] "From love comes grief, from love comes fear; he who is free from love knows neither grief nor fear." "Let no man love anything; loss of the beloved is evil; those who love nothing and hate nothing, have no fetters."[4] A monk should be as calm as the depth of the ocean unruffled by the wind of desires. He should not desire anything in the world.[5] This is the note of asceticism in Buddhism. But a householder also can attain nirvāṇa by strenuously cultivating truth, justice, firmness, and liberality. His life should be disciplined by the Law (Dhamma).[6]

The Buddhist ethics is charged with intellectualism. Passions are intellectual disorders. They spring from egoism or the false sense of individuality which generates thirst (tṛṣṇā) or will-to-live. Egoism is due to ignorance. Ignorance can be destroyed by the knowledge of the noble truths. Intuition (prajñā) and enlightenment (bodhi) lead to nirvāṇa. Virtue is knowledge. So the Buddhist ethics is intellectualistic. But this charge is wrong. Right conduct (śīla), concentration

---

[1] *The Essence of Buddhism*, Ch. vii.
[2] *Tevijja Sutta*, i. 47.
[3] *Khaggavisāna Sutta.*
[4] DP., 215, 211.
[5] *Tuvaṭakasutta*, 6, 8.
[6] *Ālavakasutta*, 2, 8.

(samādhi), and intuition (prajñā) are the prerequisites of enlightenment. Purity of heart and purity of conduct are the first step to enlightenment. Discipline of the intellect, emotion, and will is necessary for it. Sanctification of the whole personality is a prelude to enlightenment. Universal love and benevolence, compassion, and cheerfulness are stressed for moral culture. So Buddhism is not intellectualistic.

Buddha does not recognize hereditary caste distinctions. "Not by birth does one become an outcaste, not by birth does one become a Brāhmaṇa ; by deeds one becomes an outcaste, by deeds one becomes a Brāhmaṇa."[1] "By actions one is a husbandman, by actions one is a merchant, by actions one is an artisan, by actions one is a servant."[2] All castes are equal. He is a Brāhmaṇa, who is free from anger, hatred, arrogance, hyprocrisy, cruelty, hostility, greed, passions, and all taints of mind. He is self-controlled, subdued, desireless, virtuous, temperate, mild, wise, and tranquil in thoughts, words, and deeds.[3] He has laid aside the burden and attained nirvāṇa. He is an outcaste who cherishes hatred, who steals, commits adultery, speaks falsehood, practises fraud, deception, violence, and returns evil for good. The *Therigātha* mentions Angulimala, the robber, Sunita, the scavenger, Svapāka, the dog-eater, Svāti, the fisherman, Nanda, the cowherd, and Upāli, the barber among the elders. Ambapāli, the courtesan, Vimalā born of a prostitute, Pūrna, a slave woman's daughter, and Chāpā, a hunter's daughter are mentioned. This clearly shows that Buddhism was catholic and humanitarian in outlook. It was a reform movement. It was a social and religious reform.[4]

16. *Nirvāṇa*

The third noble truth is the extinction of suffering. It is nirvāṇa (nibbāna). It is the ideal, the highest good, the *summum bonum*. It is the *raison d'être* of the Buddhist discipline. "The law and discipline is impregnated with but one flavour, with the taste of nirvāṇa."[5] De la Vallée Poussin considers four conceptions of nirvāṇa as pure annihilation, as a

---

[1] *Vasalasutta*, 21.
[2] *Vaseṭṭhasutta*, 57, 58.
[3] *Vaseṭṭhasutta*, 31-38, 62.
[4] *The Essence of Buddhism*, p. 97.
[5] *Cullavagga*, ix. 1. 4.

state of happiness, as an inconceivable state, or as a changeless state in the Pāli Canon.[1]

(1) Nirvāṇa literally means 'cooled' or 'extinguished'. "As a flame blown about by the violence of the wind goes out, cannot be reckoned as existing, even so a Muni delivered from mind and body, disappears, and cannot be reckoned as existing. For him who has disappeared there is no form ; that by which he is, exists for him no longer."[2] Passions are compared to 'fires'. Passionlessness is the 'cooling' of the fires. Nirvāṇa is the extinction of greed, hate, anger, and delusion which are called 'fires', and of the impurities (āsava), sensuality, will-to-be-born, and ignorance.[3] It is the extinction of becoming or rebirth (bhavanirodha).[4] The Piṭakas frequently make use of 'kindling' and 'putting out' fires. The individual is said to be on fire with passions. The four paths are described as the process of extinguishing the fires. Nirvāṇa is described as the state of coolness (sitibhāvā).[5] It is the complete extinction of passions and consequent suffering. It is not extinction of existence. It is not annihilation.[6] It can be attained in this life. Suffering can be completely extinguished in this life.[7] It is not heaven to be realized after death. It is to be realized in this life by one who is grounded in virtue and disciplined according to the Moral Law. It is deliverance from the sense of individuality.[8] It is to be realized here and now as Buddha realized it at the beginning of his ministry.[9] It is not inaction. It is compatible with active intellectual and social life. Buddha lived an active life after attaining nirvāṇa. It is not renunciation of actions, but the purging of all actions of attachment, aversion, and delusion. It is renunciation of all the bases of rebirth, destruction of craving, will-to-live, and becoming.[10] In it the physical form remains, but the will-to-live (tṛṣṇā) is completely destroyed. It is similar to jīvanmukti conceived by the Upaniṣads. Only the Buddhist self is

---

[1] E.R.E., Vol. IX, pp. 376-79.

[2] *Upasīvamāṇavapucchā*, 1073-75.

[3] SN., iv. 251, 261, 371; V. 8.

[4] Mrs. Rhys Davids : *Buddhism*, pp. 180-81.

[5] SN., i; Vinaya Texts, i. 134.

[6] MN., i. 304.

[7] MN., ix.

[8] AN., iii. 359.

[9] BGB., p. 116.

[10] AN., ii. 118; DN., iii. 130; Mrs. Rhys Davids : *Buddhism*, pp. 178-

not permanent. The chain of causation is broken for ever. The last act of cognition (vijñāna) transmigrates no longer. There is now no continuity of the empirical consciousness beyond this life.[1] The liberated person's old karma is exhausted ; no new karma is produced ; longing after future life is destroyed ; the will-to-live being destroyed, and no new craving for becoming springing up within him, he is extinguished like a lamp.[2] Nirvāṇa is not annihilation. It is consistent with embodied life in which there is complete extinction of craving or will-to-live (tṛṣṇā) with impurities of mind (āsava).

Rhys Davids says, "It is the extinction of that sinful, grasping condition of mind, which would otherwise, according to the great mystery of Karma, be the cause of renewed individual existence. Nirvāṇa is the same thing as a sinless, calm state of mind, and may best be rendered 'holiness', perfect peace, goodness, and wisdom."[3] Mrs. Rhys Davids says, "More positively expressed, this riddance is pictured, intellectually, as light, insight, truth, higher 'saving' knowledge ; emotionally, as happiness, calm, coolness, content, good, peace, safety ; volitionally, as freedom, self-mastery, supreme opportunity, saintly companionship."[4] It is perfect insight, perfect calm, and perfect freedom. It is completely disciplined intellect, emotion, and will.

It is a state of enlightenment (bodhi) which removes all ignorance. It is a state of perfect equanimity which removes attachment, aversion, and delusion. It is a state of stainless purity and good-will. It is a state of perfect self-possession and unconditioned freedom. It is a state of perfect peace.[5] The liberated person has complete insight, complete passionlessness, unruffled calm, perfect self-control, tranquil mind, tranquil words, and tranquil deeds.[6] But he is devoid of egoism or the sense of individuality, since his mental grasping (upādāna), ignorance (kleśa), and craving (tṛṣṇā), which produce a new individual of five aggregates, are completely destroyed. There is extinction of individual existence.[7] Schrader wrongly

---

[1] BP., p. 128.
[2] *Ratana-sutta*, 7, 14; T. W. Rhys Davids : *Buddhism*, 1912, p. 111.
[3] *Buddhism*, pp. 111-12.
[4] *Buddhism*, p. 184.
[5] *Sāmaññaphala-sutta*, *Dialogues*, 1, p. 84.
[6] DP., 90, 94-96.
[7] *Parinibbānasutta*, J.R.A.S., vol. viii, p. 238.

holds that there is a feeling of infiniteness in nirvāṇa with no loss of individuality.[1] This interpretation is against the spirit of the Buddhist texts.[2] Buddha's silence on the condition of Tathāgata after death is due to the fact that it is not conducive to dispassion, calm, insight, enlightenment, nirvāṇa.[3] It is an indeterminable question.

(2) In the Pāli texts nirvāṇa has sometimes been described as a state of bliss. The liberated person is free from evil desire ; he has a steadfast mind ; he has perfect knowledge of the noble truths ; he has obtained the fruit of the fourth path, and is immersed in ambrosia, and enjoys nirvāṇa.[4] The Piṭaka synonyms for nirvāṇa are "the ambrosial or the immortal (amātā), the non-deceasing (acchūta), the beyond-end (acchanta), the no-whence-fear (akutobhaya), the beyondless security (anuttara yogakkhema)".[5] "Nirvāṇa is the farther shore (para), the island (dvīpa), the endless (atyanta), the immortal (amṛta), the immortal state (amṛta pada), the *summum bonum* (niḥśreyasa)."[6] *Dhammapada* describes nirvāṇa as a state of bliss, crown of happiness, perfect peace, free from greed, hate, and delusion.[7] The Arhants, meditative, persevering, ever energetic, attain to nirvāṇa, the highest bliss.[8] Nirvāṇa is happiness or holiness which is distinct from pleasure. Pleasure is an empirical feeling. It is transitory and therefore painful. Nirvāṇa is the highest good. It is the blissful end.[9]

(3) Nirvāṇa is deep, immeasurable, unfathomable as the ocean.[10] It is inconceivable.[11] It is an existence that is beyond reason and conception.[12] Dr. Keith says, "All emperical qualifications are unfitted to describe the ineffable."[13] Dr. Das Gupta also opines that nirvāṇa is indescribable in terms of worldly experience. It cannot be described as positive or negative.[14] It is a non-empirical, ineffable state.

---

[1] *Pali Text Society Journal,* 1905.
[2] HIP., i, p. 109.
[3] SN., ii. 223.
[4] *Ratanasutta,* vii. 14.
[5] Mrs. Rhys Davids : *Buddhism,* pp. 181-82.
[6] Poussin : E.R.E., vol. ix, article on Nirvāṇa.
[7] DP., 202-03
[8] DP., 23.
[9] AN., v. 414.
[10] SN., iv. 374.
[11] *Alaguddūpamāsutta.*
[12] SN., iii. 109.
[13] BP., p. 129.
[14] HIP., Vol. I, p. 109.

(4) Buddha says, "There is something that is not born (ajāta), not produced (abhūta), not created (akṛta), not compounded (asaṁskṛta). Were there not something not born, there would be no possible exit for what is born."[1] Rāhul Saṁkṛtyāyan opines that these negative epithets should not be interpreted in the positive sense of eternal existence.[2] But Dr. Radhakrishnan interprets nirvāṇa as "becoming one with the eternal reality, which Buddha does not explicitly admit."[3] "Nirvāṇa is timeless existence, and so Buddha must admit the reality of a timeless self."[4] It is "peace and rest in the bosom of the eternal."[5] Radhakrishnan interprets nirvāṇa in the Mahāyāna sense of eternal existence. But this interpretation of nirvāṇa in early Buddhism involves the heresy of eternalism. Oldenberg rightly remarks, "For the Buddhists, the words 'there is something uncreated' merely signify that the created can free himself from the curse of being created." Nirvāṇa is neither annihilation (ucchedavāda) nor eternal existence (śāśvatavāda). It is an ineffable state of perfect wisdom, perfect peace, and perfect self-command. The sisters describe nirvāṇa as sorrowlessness, purity, fulfilment of moral efforts, liberty, true happiness, freedom from longing, perfect serenity and calmness, complete self-mastery, extinction of rebirth and all suffering.[6]

Two kinds of nirvāṇa are described: (1) Sa-upādi-śeṣa-nirvāṇa; (2) Anupādi-śeṣa-nirvāṇa. The former means nirvāṇa with residual vital conditions or with the remainder of mental grasping (upādāna), the cause of rebirth. The latter means nirvāṇa without residual vital conditions or without remainder of mental grasping (upādāna). Parinirvāṇa literally means 'completely gone out'. One who is perfectly disciplined and calmed is said to be parinibbuta or perfected.[7] The early Pāli texts regard nirvāṇa as a moral condition to be attained in this life. The later Sanskrit texts regard Parinirvāṇa and

---

[1] *Udāna*, viii. 3; *Itivuttaka*, 43.
[2] *Darśanadigdarśana*, p. 533.
[3] *Indian Philosophy*, Vol. I, p. 450.
[4] *Ibid*, p. 451.
[5] *Gautama the Buddha*, p. 60.
[6] *Psalms of the Sisters*, xxxi; Mrs. Rhys Davids: ***Buddhism***, pp. 185-86.
[7] *Ibid*. pp. 191-92.

Anupādiśeṣanirvāṇadhātu as death with no life to follow.[1] The conception of nirvāṇa was modified by the later Buddhist schools, the Hīnayāna and the Mahāyāna.

17. *Buddhism and the Upaniṣads*

The Upaniṣads regard the phenomena of the world as names and forms (nāmarūpa) or appearances of Brahman which is the transcendental reality. Early Buddhism regards them as impermanent qualities (dhamma) of the permanent elements behind them. The Upaniṣads regard the eternal Brahman as real and phenomena as unreal appearances, while later Buddhism regards the impermanent qualities as real and permanent substances as unreal appearances and rejects the conception of the transcendental Absolute. The Upaniṣads recognize the eternal as the reality, while Buddhism recognizes the non-eternal or impermanent as the reality. The former recognize the reality of Being or Brahman, while the latter recognizes the reality of Becoming. Thus Buddhism is the antithesis of the philosophy of the Upaniṣads. The phenomena are real and produced by their antecedent causes and conditions according to Buddhism which advocates the doctrine of Pratītyasamutpāda or dependent origination which is a form of Asatkāryavāda. The phenomena are unreal appearances (vivarta) of Brahman according to the Upaniṣads which advocate the doctrine of Vivartavāda or Satkāraṇavāda. The cause is real, but the effect is its unreal appearance. But according to Buddhism both cause and effect are real. The earlier Upaniṣads reject the conception of transcendent personal God as the creator of the universe. Buddhism also rejects the conception of God. The Upaniṣads teach the futility of rituals and sacrifices and substitute for them a religion of ethical purity and intuition. They stress the knowledge of the Brahman or the Ātman. 'That thou art'. The individual soul is identical with the universal soul. The intuition of their identity is the means of release. Buddhism is a revolt against ritualism and ceremonialism. It preaches the religion of ahiṁsā and universal love and good-will. It inculcates the purity of the heart, ethical

[1] Rhys Davids: *Buddhism*, p. 117.

purity, and intuition. The Upaniṣads teach that ignorance (avidyā) is the cause of bondage, because it is the spring of desire, and that knowledge of the identity of the individual soul with Brahman removes ignorance. Buddhism also holds that ignorance is the cause of bondage, because it is the cause of craving, thirst, or will-to-live (tṛṣṇā) which is the root of all desires. The knowledge of the noble truths, right conduct, right concentration, and insight eradicate ignorance and craving. The Upaniṣads regard individuality (upādhi) due to ignorance as the cause of bondage. Individuality is due to manas, buddhi, ahaṁkāra, the sense-organs, and the vital forces. Buddhism also regards individuality (upādhi) or the five aggregates (skandha) or the mind-body-complex (nāma-rūpa) due to ignorance and craving as the cause of bondage. Both regard ignorance (avidyā) as false knowledge. But while the Upaniṣads regard avidyā as knowledge of the permanent as the impermanent, Buddhism regards it as knowledge of the impermanent as the permanent. Both believe in the Law of Karma and transmigration. The Upaniṣads believe in the transmigration of the individual soul (jīvātman) from one body to another. Buddhism believes in the continuity of the individual stream of consciousness and transmigration of the last cognition (vijñāna) to another body appropriate to its moral equipment. Though there are superficial points of resemblance between the Upaniṣads and Buddhism, they are radically opposed to each other in their fundamental outlooks. The Upaniṣads stress the reality of Brahman, the eternal Absolute, while Buddhism stresses the reality of impermanent phenomena and rejects the reality of the permanent self and the eternal Brahman. The former advocate eternalism and absolutism, while the latter advocates phenomenalism and philosophy of change and flux. Buddhism is the antithesis of Upaniṣadic absolutism.[1]

18. *Buddhism and the Sāṁkhya*

The Sāṁkhya and Buddhism both are pessimistic in their outlook. Both hold that life is full of suffering, that ignorance is the cause of suffering, that the saving knowledge which

[1] Cp. BGB., pp. 187-94.

destroys egoism or individuality is the cause of liberation. Both regard pleasure and pain alike as suffering because pleasure is always mixed with pain or a prelude to pain. Both regard liberation as total extinction of suffering. Secondly, both recognize the constant changes in the world process and look upon the world as dynamic. But the Sāṁkhya regards the impermanent phenomena as changes of the guṇas, sattva, rajas, and tamas which are the eternal substances constituting Prakṛti, while early Buddhism regards them as impermanent changes with permanent elements of earth, water, fire, and air underlying them. Both regard the phenomena as governed by the law of causation. The Sāṁkhya believes in Satkāryavāda, while Buddhism believes in Pratītyasamutpāda which is a form of Asatkāryavāda. Thirdly, the Sāṁkhya regards ignorance as non-discrimination between the eternal self (puruṣa) and prakṛti and its evolute, buddhi in which it is reflected, while Buddhism regards ignorance as the false knowledge of the impermanent stream of consciousness and bodily processes as the permanent self, or as the delusion of individuality. Fourthly, Buddhism regards the group of the five aggregates (skandha) as the self and rejects the eternal self, while the Sāṁkhya recognizes the reality of the eternal spirits (puruṣa). Fifthly, both reject the reality of God as the creator of the world. Both are atheistic. Sixthly, both believe in transmigration. The Sāṁkhya believes in the transmigration of the empirical self (jīva), or the self limited by the adjuncts of the sense-organs, manas, ahaṁkāra, and buddhi bearing the impressions of the previous deeds, from one body to another, while the transcendental self (puruṣa) is not affected by birth and death. Buddhism denies the eternal self and believes in the transmigration of the last vijñāna of the stream of cognitions, modified by the impressions of the previous deeds from one body to another. Seventhly, the Sāṁkhya regards bondage and liberation as apparent only, the eternal self (puruṣa) being ever free and liberated because it is transcendental. Egoism (ahaṁkāra) binds it to prakṛti and entangles it in apparent bondage. The saving knowledge or discrimination between the eternal self (puruṣa) and egoism, an evolute of prakṛti, cuts the bond, and makes the self realize its intrinsic freedom. Buddhism regards bondage and liberation as real. Egoism, the delusion of individuality, the sense of 'I' and 'mine' due to ignorance, is the cause of suffering and bondage. Ignorance can be destroyed by knowledge of the truth. But Buddhism emphasizes good conduct and moral purity (śīla) along with concentration (samādhi) and intuition (prajñā).[1] But, though there are important similarities between the Sāṁkhya and Buddhism, there are important dissimilarities between them. The Sāṁkhya believes in the eternal mutable Prakṛti and the eternal immutable puruṣas. But Buddhism rejects them both and recognizes the reality of the impermanent series of psychical and bodily processes and the impermanent world process.

19. *Buddhism and the Yoga*

The Yoga argees with Buddhism in pessimistic outlook. It holds that all is suffering to the discriminating,[2] that there is suffering, that there is a cause of suffering, that there is extinction of suffering, and that there is a way to stop suffering.[3] This closely resembles the four noble truths of Buddhism. The Yoga holds that empirical life (saṁsāra) is suffering, that the conjunction of the eternal self (puruṣa) and prakṛti in the form of buddhi due to ignorance (avidyā) is the cause of suffering, that complete dissociation of the eternal self from buddhi is the extinction of suffering, and that discriminative knowledge of the eternal self is the means of release. Buddhism also holds that ignorance (avidyā) which generates egoism and thirst (tṛṣṇā) for the continuance of individuality is the cause of bondage, and that it is destroyed by right knowledge. Secondly, the Yoga concentration (samādhi) in its different stages closely resembles the Buddhist Jhāna of four kinds. The terms 'savicāra' 'nirvicāra', 'savitarka', and 'nirvitarka', and samāpatti' occur in both. Thirdly, the Yoga ethics of non-killing (ahiṁsā), truthfulness, non-stealing, sex-restraint, and noncovetousness (yama) which are universal and unconditional duties (sārvabhauma mahāvrata) obligatory at all times, in all places, under all circumstances corresponds closely to the Buddhist ethics.[4] Fourthly, the Yoga ethics of friendship

---

[1] Cp. BGB., pp. 194-96; BP., pp. 140-43.
[2] Duḥkhameva sarvaṁ vivekinaḥ. YS., ii. 15.
[3] YB., ii. 15.
[4] YS., YB., ii. 31, 32.

(maitrī) for all creatures, joy (muditā) for the virtuous, compassion (karuṇā) for the distressed, and indifference (upekṣā) to the vicious exactly corresponds to the Buddhist ethics of sublime meditations (brahmavihāra).[1] This is the common feature of Jainism, Buddhism, and the Yoga. But the Yoga ethics is ascetic, while the Buddhist ethics advocates the morality of the middle path between asceticism and hedonism, self-denial and self-indulgence. Fifthly, the Yoga afflctions (kleśa) correspond to the Buddhist defilements (kleśa). The terms 'Citta' and 'Nirodha', 'impermanence', 'impure', 'misery', and 'not-self' occur in both systems. Both recognize the necessity of the five qualities of faith (śraddhā), energy (vīrya), recollection (smṛti), concentration (samādhi), and intuition (prajñā) for trance.[2]

But there are fundamental dissimilarities between the Yoga and Buddhism. First, the Yoga believes in God, the eternal souls (puruṣa), and the eternal prakṛti underlying the phenomena of nature. But Buddhism rejects all these eternal realities. It recognizes the reality of impermanent qualities (dhamma) or phenomena, mental and physical. Secondly, the Yoga advocates Satkāryavāda which regards effects as modifications (pariṇāma) of the permanent substances, satta, rajas, and tamas, while Buddhism advocates Pratītyasamutpāda or Asatkāryavāda which regards effects as non-extent in their causes and conditions by which they are produced. Both give a dynamic view of the world.[3]

20. *Buddhism and Jainism*

There are great similarities between the Buddhist ethics and the Jaina ethics. First, both inculcate the universal and unconditional duty of ahiṁsā or non-killing and non-injury in thought, word and deed. Both enjoin truthfulness, non-stealing, sex-restraint, and non-covetousness. Both lay down rules of morality for lay disciples and monks and nuns. Both enjoin universal good-will and friendship for all creatures, compassion for the distressed, joy for saints, and indifference to vicious persons. Both enjoin meditation on the impurity of the body and the impermanence of the world. Both enjoin meditation and concentration. But Jainism is ascetic and enjoins severe

[1] YS., i. 33. [2] YS., i. 20. [3] BP., pp. 143-45.

penances and austerities, while Buddhism preaches the morality of the mean between self-indulgence and self-mortification, though Buddha preferred the life of a monk to that of a householder. He ridiculed the Jainas who practised severe austerities. Both Buddhist and Jaina ethics speak of 'āsrava and 'samvara', and emphasize the need of unruffled calm and passionlessness for liberation. Secondly, both repudiate the authority of the Vedas, deny the existence of God, and recognize the self-existence of the world which is without beginning or end. Thirdly, both emphasize the Law of Karma and transmigration. But Jainism has a materialistic conception of Karma, while Buddhism has a psychical and moral conception of Karma. Jainism believes that bodily, verbal, and mental acts produce subtle karma-matter which envelopes the soul and produces retribution. Buddhism believes that they produce impressions in the stream of consciousness and bear fruits. Fourthly, both give a dynamic view of the world. Fifthly, both are religions without God. Both are religions of self-help.

But there are fundamental differences between the ontology of Jainism and that of Buddhism. Jainism believes in the eternal souls (jīva), while Buddhism rejects them. Buddhism believes in Asatkāryavāda, while Jainism believes in Satkāryavāda or Pariṇāmavāda. Buddhism believes in impermanent qualities (dhamma) only, while Jainism believes in permanent substances which are partly different from, and partly identical with, their qualities and modes. The Buddhist nirvāṇa is indescribable and ineffable, while the Jaina mokṣa is the omniscience of the eternal soul attended with infinite bliss and infinite power. Thus early Buddhism is more radically opposed to Brāhmanism than Jainism, though both reject the authority of the Vedas, the supremacy of the Brahmans, hereditary caste distinctions, Vedic rites and animal sacrifices, and deny the existence of God. Jainism believes in eternal souls, while Buddhism rejects them and believes in impermanent streams of consciousness.

21. *Buddhism and Materialism, Fatalism, and Scepticism*

In the Pāli canon, the materialist, Ajita Keśa Kambala, the fatalist, Makkhaḷi Gośāla, the inactivist, Purṇa Kāśyapa, the eternalist, Prakruddha Kātyāyana, the sceptic, Sañjaya

Velaṭṭhiputta and the relativist, Nigaṇṭha Nātaputta or Jaina[1] are mentioned. Buddha criticizes their doctrines. Ajita is a materialist. He holds that a living body is composed of the four elements, earth, water, fire, and air. When a person dies, earth returns to earth, water to water, fire to fire, and air to air, and the sense-organs pass into space. There is no future life. There is no survival of individuality after death. Good and bad actions bear no fruits. Gifts and sacrifices are fruitless. There is annihilation on death. Wisdom avails not to prevent it. There is no true birth, from father, or mother, or super-natural. There is no heaven or hell.[2] Ajita is a materialist and annihilationist. His doctrine resembles that of the Lokāyatas, who held that the soul was identical with the body.[3] The view of Ajita is made more clear by Pāyāsi who holds that the soul is not an entity distinct from the body. The sword is distinct from the sheath, and they are perceived as distinct from each other. But the soul is never perceived as distinct from the body. There is no future life or rebirth. Actions have no results. There is annihilation on death.[4] Buddha's attitude towards materialism has been discussed. Buddha believes in the soul as the mind-body-complex, good and bad actions and their fruits, future life and rebirth. He is not a materialist. But he regards the question whether the soul is identical with or distinct from the body as indeterminable (avyākṛta).

Makkhali Gośāla of the Ājīvika or Ājīvaka school is a fatalist or determinist.[5] He holds that the world is governed by necessity. Fate determines everything. There is no power, force, or energy in living beings. They are rigidly governed by fate. That which is to happen, must happen ; that which is not to happen, cannot happen. All things are unalterably fixed and determined by fate. Every living being lives, acts, enjoys, suffers, and dies in the manner in which it is destined to do so.[6] The purity and impurity of mind are uncaused.

---

[1] SN., iii. 1. 3; DN., i. 2.

[2] DN., i. 2; MN., ii. 1. 10; ii. 6. 6; SN., iii.

[3] Barua : *Pre-Buddhistic Indian Philosophy*, 1921, pp. 290-96; BP., pp. 97, 135.

[4] DN., ii. 10. [5] MN., ii. 3. 6.

[6] *Dialogues of Buddha*, ii, 72-73; *Pre-Buddhistic Indian Philosophy*, p. 310.

They are not determined by causes. Men become pure or impure without any cause. There is neither increase nor decrease, neither progress nor decline.[1] Buddhaghoṣa explains Gośāla's view as naturalism (svabhāvavāda). Nature means the inherent nature of each thing. Every thing is determined by its own inherent nature.[2] No act of penance or righteousness can counteract the force of destiny or nature.[3] Buddha is a staunch advocate of freedom of the will ; he holds that man can make or mar his fortune by free moral efforts ; he believes in future life, transmigration, and nirvāṇa which entirely depend upon our free volitions and actions. He advocates causalism (hetuvāda) and holds that all phenomena are produced by their causes and conditions. He rejects non-causalism (ahetuvāda) or naturalism (svabhāvavāda).

Purṇa Kāśyapa is an advocate of inactivism (akriyāvāda) or non-action. The soul is passive (niṣkriya). It neither acts nor causes others to act. Good and bad actions do not affect the soul. Good actions such as acts of charity, sacrifices, and the like bring no merits. Bad actions such as killing all creatures, oppression, and the like bring no demerits.[4] Buddha charges Purṇa Kāśyapa with the doctrine of fortuitous origin (adhicca-samuppāda) or accidentalism as contrasted with his doctrine of dependent origination (paṭiccasamuppāda).[5] He describes him also as a non-causalist (ahetu-apaccaya-vādin).[6] According to accidentalism, something comes out of nothing, whereas according to the doctrine of dependent origination, nothing comes out of nothing.[7] Dr. Keith opines that Purṇa Kāśyapa's doctrine is clearly fatalistic.[8] Fatalism is implied in the passive nature of the soul. Buddha is emphatic on the free volitions and actions of the self by which it can reap good or bad fruits. Purṇa Kāśyapa is an inactivist (akriyāvādin) and non-causalist (ahetuvādin), whereas Buddha is an activist (kriyāvādin) and causalist (hetuvādin). Inactivism is subversive of morality.

---

[1] DN., ii. 1.

[2] *Sumaṅgala Vilāsinī*, i. 161; *Pre-Buddhistic Indian Philosophy*, p. 311.

[3] BP., p. 136.

[4] DN., i. 53; SN., iii. 69.

[5] *Dialogues of Buddha*, II, pp. 41-42.

[6] SN., iii. 169.

[7] DN., i. pp. 28-29; *Pre-Buddhistic Indian Philosophy*, pp. 279-80.

[8] BP., p. 136.

Prakruddha Kātyāyana holds that there are seven permanent elements, earth, water, fire, air, pleasure, pain, and soul. Pleasure and pain are the principles of change. He also believes in subtle elements or atoms and pores in organic bodies. He denies the void. Actions bear no fruits. There is no slayer or cause of slaying.[1] Buddha interprets Kātyāyana's doctrine as eternalism, since the elements are eternal and imperishable. They are neither created nor caused to be created. He considers Kātyayāna's doctrine to be a doctrine of non-action (akriyāvāda), since the elements are combined and separated by pleasure and pain, and there is no freedom of the will or voluntary action. There is no act of killing or hearing or instructing. Inactivism (akriyāvāda) cuts at the root of morality.[2] Dr. Keith thinks that Kātyāyana's doctrine is, in effect, complete fatalism.[3]

Sañjaya Velaṭṭhiputta is a sceptic. He refuses to assert or deny any form of the four possible propositions: A is B; A is not B; A is both B and not B; A is neither B nor not B.[4] Buddha calls him an eel-wriggler given to equivocation and wriggling. "We neither know the good nor the evil as it really is."[5] The future life, fruits of actions, the liberated person, and gods are unknown and unknowable. Whether they are, or whether they are not, or whether they are and are not, or whether they are neither is unknowable.[6] But Buddha urges that right view is necessary for the extinction of suffering.

The Jaina leader, Nigaṇṭha Nātaputta, forbids drinking of unstrained water because it is full of minute living beings, forbids the commission of all sins, claims to be sinless by forbidding the commission of sins, and is constantly engaged in prohibiting the commission of sins. He stresses penances and self-mortification. He claims to be omniscient.[7] Buddha condemns self-tortures and asceticism. He stresses purity of the mind and conquest of greed, hatred, and delusion. He prescribes the middle path between self-mortification and self-indulgence.

---

[1] DN., i. 2.
[2] *Pre-Buddhistic Indian Philosophy*, pp. 282-86.
[3] BP., p. 136.
[4] DN., i. 58; BP., p. 137.
[5] *Pre-Buddhistic Indian Philosophy*, pp. 328-29.
[6] DN., i. 2.
[7] DN., i. 2; MN., ii. 2. 6; i. 2. 4.

The Jaina accuses Buddha of hedonism, while Buddha accuses the Jaina of rigorism and asceticism.[1] Thus Buddha refutes all the contemporary thinkers of the opposite schools.[2] But he is not a philosopher. He does not give a system of philosophy. He is a founder of a new religion based on sublime morality.

22. *Religion*

Buddhism is a religion without God like Jainism. It believes in transmigration and future life, though it does not believe in the permanent self. It emphasizes the Law of Karma or moral causation. It aims at the extinction of suffering by extinguishing craving or desire. It aims at inner and outer purity of life, the purity of the heart, and the purity of external conduct. It rejects rites, ceremonies, sacrifices, and penances. It stresses, like Jainism, the ethics of ahiṁsā, non-injury in thought, word, and deed. It enjoins extinction of egoism and ignorance. It aims at enlightenment and nirvāṇa on earth. Nirvāṇa is insight, peace, and selfless will. Buddhism is a religion of self-help. Liberation does not depend on the grace of God. It has to be wrought by one's own moral efforts.

Buddhism admits the reality of Brahmā, Indra, and other gods. But it makes them subject to birth and death. They are subject to ignorance and passions. Buddha is greater than gods. Buddhism believes in heaven and hell. Righteous actions lead to heaven. Vicious actions lead to hell. But nirvāṇa can be attained by complete extinction of desires for earthly or heavenly happiness. It is above heaven. Buddha emphasizes the Law (Dhamma). He turns the wheel of the Law (Dhammacakka) which is irresistible. He lays the foundation of the kingdom of righteousness.[3]

Buddhism is catholic. It is open to all nations, races, castes, and creeds. Buddha says, "Know, Vasettha, that (from time to time) a Tathāgata is born in the world, a fully Enlightened One, blessed and worthy, abounding in wisdom and goodness, happy, with knowledge of the world, unsur-

---

[1] BP., pp. 137-38.
[2] *Darśanadigdarśana* (Hindi), pp. 485-95; *Bauddha Darśana* (Hindi), pp. 30-42.
[3] *Selasutta*, 554; *Dhammacakkapavattanasutta*.

passed as a guide to erring mortals, a teacher of gods and men, a Blessed Buddha. He, by himself, thoroughly understands, and sees, as it were, face to face this universe—the world below with all its spirits, and the worlds above, of Māra and of Brahmā —and all creatures, gods and men, he then makes his knowledge known to others. The truth does he proclaim both in its letter and spirit, lovely in its origin, lovely in its progress, lovely in its consummation: the higher life doth he make known, in all its purity and in all its perfectness."[1] "Subdue thy doubt about me, have faith in me, O Brahmana, difficult to obtain is the sight of Buddhas repeatedly."[2] Faith and reason both lead to salvation. Rational conviction, self-control, and moral purity are essential to it. Buddha does not grant liberation to men, but he teaches them the way to achieve liberation.

Buddhism is a rational religion. There is no secret in it. Buddha does not make any distinction between esoteric and exoteric doctrines. He denounces all secret doctrines. Secrecy belongs to false doctrines and occult priestcraft. The religion of Buddha shines by its light.[3] It is the negation of mysticism. Buddhism is a religion of individual freedom and endeavour. Buddha says, "O Ānanda, be ye lamps unto yourselves. Be ye refuges to yourselves. Hold fast to the Dhamma as a lamp. Hold fast as a refuge to the Dhamma. Look not for refuge to any one beside yourselves."

Buddhism is a missionary religion. The gift of the Dhamma is the greatest of all gifts. "Go ye, O Bhikṣus, for the benefit of the many, for the welfare of mankind, out of compassion for the world. Preach the doctrine which is glorious in the beginning, glorious in the middle, and glorious in the end, in the spirit as well as in the letter. Proclaim to them a life of holiness. They will understand the doctrine and accept it." These words of the Master inspired his followers to spread the religion far and wide.[4]

In course of time a schism took place between the Hīnayāna and the Mahāyāna which differ in many respects. First, the Hīnayāna is conservative, whereas the Mahāyāna is catholic

---

[1] *Tevijja Sutta; Buddhist Suttas*, SBE., xi. pp. 186-87.
[2] *Selasutta*, 559. [3] AN.; MPS.
[4] *The Essence of Buddhism*, Ch. II.

and progressive. Secondly, the former regards the Buddha as a historical person, while the latter regards the Buddha as the transcendental, eternal, and absolute, who saves all beings through his triple body (trikāya), Dharmakāya, Sambhogakāya, and Nirmāṇakāya. Thirdly, the former believes in one Buddha, the historical Gautama, while the latter believes in an infinite number of Boddhisattvas who take a vow to attain perfection and liberate all sentient creatures. Fourthly, the former aims at the attainment of Arhathood or individual liberation, while the latter aims at the attainment of Bodhisattvahood to liberate all. The former aims at individual liberation, while the latter aims at universal liberation. Fifthly, the former believes that one person attained Buddhahood, while the latter believes that all may attain it because they have the Buddha-nature and desire for enlightenment (Bodhi). Sixthly, the former opposes nirvāṇa to saṁsāra, while the latter believes that saṁsāra is not the negation of nirvāṇa which has to be achieved in and through saṁsāra. The former emphasizes the monk's life of renunciation, while the latter emphasizes the life of a householder. Seventhly, the former looks upon suffering as something to be escaped from, while the latter regards it as a means to liberation. In the Mahāyāna, the Bodhisattva voluntarily and joyfully undergoes suffering for the liberation of all beings. Eighthly, the former regards nirvāṇa as cessation of transmigration, while the latter regards it as transcendental experience of Śūnyatā. The former considers it to be a negative state, while the latter considers it to be a positive state. Ninthly, the former stresses abstention from evil, while the latter stresses cultivation of perfections (pāramitās) and doing positive good to others. The former is negative and self-centred in outlook, while the latter is positive and altruistic in outlook. Tenthly, the former is realistic, whereas the latter is idealistic. The former believes in the reality of the external world and individual minds or streams of consciousness, while the latter believes in One Mind, Ālayavijñāna, which constructs the imaginary world. Lastly, the former believes in the impermanence of all phenomena, physical and mental, while the latter believes in the Śūnyatā or Emptiness, which is the noumenon behind the impermanent phenomena. Phenomena are manifestations of the noumenon, Śūnyatā. The law of change is supreme in the world of phenomena or relativity, but Śūnyatā is supreme in the world of Nirvāna, which is above all relativity.[1] The Hīnayāna religion is based on the Pāli canon, the original teaching of Buddha, and preserves its monastic and rationalistic elements. The Mahāyāna religion possesses no canon, and develops a mystical and devotional religion. Hīnayāna Buddhism is called Southern Buddhism, since it flourished in Ceylon and Burma. Mahāyāna Buddhism is called Northern Buddhism, since it prevailed in Tibet, China, and Japan.

The Hīnayāna and the Mahāyāna resemble each other in the following respects. First, enlightenment is the goal of Buddhism. It aims at removal of ignorance and achievement of enlightenment. Secondly, the world is without beginning or end. All phenomena are subject to the law of causation. There is no first cause. Thirdly, all is transitory, impermanent flow and flux. There is no Being. There is only Becoming. Fourthly, there is no permanent Ego or Self. There is only an impermanent stream of consciousness. Fifthly, the Law of Karma governs moral phenomena. Sixthly, transmigration is due to karma. Actions in empirical life produce karma. Transmigration leads to suffering. Seventhly, ignorance is the cause of suffering. Lastly, the Eightfold Noble Path and the perfections (pāramitās) destroy ignorance.[2]

The Hīnayāna is called Theravāda or Sthaviravāda, or the doctrine of the Elders. It is the small vehicle. It can carry a few to salvation. The Mahāyāna is the great vehicle. It is large enough to carry all to salvation. It was developed out of the doctrine of the Mahāsaṅgikas. They coined the word Bodhisattvayāna which soon became Mahāyāna. They hinted at the idea of the Buddha-nature in all and its flowering in Enlightenment. The Mahāsaṅgika Buddhology was developed into the Mahāyāna idea of Triple Body (trikāya). Universal salvation is the kernel of the Mahāyāna religion. Idealistic monism is its philosophical foundation. All are governed by causation. Mind is the origin of all causation. "Mind, Buddha, and Beings are one."[3]

The Hīnayānists believed in the historical Buddha who attained liberation in this life. The Mahāsaṅgikas conceived

---

[1] B. L. Suzuki : *Mahāyāna Buddhism,* 1948, pp. 14-15.
[2] *Ibid,* pp. 17-18. [3] *Ibid,* Ch. I.

of the Buddha as supramundane and transcendental. The Mahāyānists believed in the Triple Body (trikāya) of Buddha: Dharmakāya, Law-body, or the Absolute, immanent in all beings; Sambhogakāya, Bliss-body, or God; and Nirmāṇakāya, Transformation-body, Divine Incarnation, Avatāra, the historical Buddha. The Dharmakāya is the transcendent Absolute. It is the permanent, undifferentiated, all-comprehending Truth. It is the Norm of all existence. In the *Awakening of Faith* it is the Absolute Truth, the eternal, the blissful, the pure, the immutable Truth. It is Suchness (Tathatā). It is the Tathāgata's womb (Tathāgatagarbha), the source of all individuals endowed with love, compassion, and selfless will. In the *Laṅkāvatāra* it is the transcendent reality from which all beings derive their existence. It is the Absolute Truth, the transcendent Dharma, which constitutes the essence of Buddha. The Dharmakāya is also called Svabhāvakāya, since it abides in itself with its intrinsic nature. The Mādhyamika regards the Dharmakāya as the Śūnya, the transcendent reality. The Yogācāra regards it as the Absolute. In later Mahāyāna the Dharmakāya is personified as Ādi-Buddha, the Supreme Being, whose power (śakti) is Prajñāpāramitā, the highest wisdom. The Sambhogakāya is the Bliss-body in heaven. It is personal God who teaches the Bodhisattvas. It becomes Nirmāṇakāya, Transformation-body, for the benefit of common people. Human incarnations or historical Buddhas are the Nirmāṇakāya.[1] The Dharmakāya is the Absolute Truth (paramārtha). It is manifested as Sambhogakāya, Bliss-body, in heaven to celestial beings. It is manifested on earth as Nirmāṇakāya, Transformation-body, to human beings. The Dharmakāya is the Absolute. The Sambhogakāya is God. The Nirmāṇakāya is Avatāra. Every individual can attain Buddhahood. Amitābha Buddha rules over the heaven Sukhavatī. The historical Gautama and the Bodhisattva Avalokiteśvara are associated with him. The Tathāgata reveals himself as an earthly Buddha out of love for men to lead them to salvation.[2]

The Mahāyāna lays the greatest stress on the conception of Bodhisattva. A Bodhisattva is a future Buddha. All human beings are future Bodhisattvas. The Hīnayānists taught their

---

[1] *Mahāyāna Buddhism*, pp. 46-47; BGB., pp. 238-39.
[2] BGB., pp. 250-51.

followers to become Arhats through enlightenment. The Mahāyānists taught their followers to become Bodhisattvas and lead humanity to liberation through enlightenment. A Bodhisattva takes four vows to liberate all beings, to destroy evil passions, to learn the Truth and teach it to others, and to lead all beings to Buddhahood. He must be full of love and compassion (mahākaruṇācitta) for all creatures. He must practise the perfections (pāramitās). Six perfections were recognized: generosity (dāna), good conduct (śīla), patience (kṣānti), energy (vīrya), meditation (dhyāna), and wisdom (prajñā). Four perfections were added later: device (upāya), resolution (praṇidhāna), strength (bala), and knowledge (jñāna).

A Bodhisattva passes through ten stages (bhūmi) in his career. The first is the stage of joy (pramuditā); in it he feels joy because he devotes himself to the work of a saviour; he realizes the selflessness (nairatmya) of the self, and of other things; he realizes the Norm (dharmatā) as the common nature of them all. The second is the stage of purity (vimalā) free from egoism and sin; in it he practises moral precepts, meditation (dhyāna) and trance (samādhi). The third is the stage of illumination (prabhākarī); in it he practises bhāvanās or sublim meditations and patience and forbearance; he shines wi... tolerance with people; he sheds anger, hatred, and delusion. The fourth is the radiant (arciṣmatī) stage; in it he practises the greatest energy in good actions and meditation. The fifth is the invincible (sudurjayā) stage; in it he practises meditation on the four noble truths, which leads to transcendental knowledge (prajñā). The sixth stage is called turned towards (abhimukhī); in it he turns to the chain of causation (pratītya-samutpāda) and unsubstantiality; he is right in face of Nirvāṇa; he transcends good and evil, and achieves transcendent purity; he is now Arhat or Bodhisattva. The seventh stage is called far going (dūraṅgamā); he becomes an adept in all means of leading others to salvation; he feels great compassion for them, and helps them in their troubles; he seeks enlightenment which will enable him to effect universal salvation. The eighth stage is called immovable (acalā); in it he attains supreme knowledge, transcends duality of selfishness, knows all things as rooted in Suchness (Tathatā), and teaches the Dharma to others. The ninth stage is called the good (sādhumatī) ; endowed with the highest knowledge, he becomes a preacher of the Law, and prepares the creatures for Nirvāṇa. The tenth stage is called cloud of the Law (dharmamegha) ; in it he is enshrined in the heart of the Dharmakāya, acquires the powers of a Buddha, and reaches the end of his career.[1] The Hīnayāna and the Mahāyāna conceptions of liberation will be considered in the next chapter under metaphysics.

The main Mahāyāna religious works are the following :— (1) *Aṣṭasāhasrikāprajñāpāramitā* (200 A.D.) ; (2) *Samādhirāja ;* (3) *Suvarṇaprabhāsa* (rendered into Chinese in 420 A.D.) ; (4) *Bajracchedikā* (rendered into Chinese in 401 A.D.) ; (5) *Daśabhūmīśvara* (rendered into Chinese in 300 A.D.) ; (6) *Saddharmapuṇḍarīka* (250 A.D.) ; (7) *Gaṇḍavyuha* (rendered into Chinese in 400 A.D.) ; (8) *Kāraṇḍavyūha* (rendered into Chinese in 270 A.D.) ; (9) *Sukhāvatīvyūha* (100 A.D.) ; (10) *Buddhacarita* (100 A.D.) ; (11) *Bodhicaryāvatāra ;* and (12) *Sikṣāmuccaya* (700 A.D.).

[1] *Mahāyāna Buddhism,* pp. 54-57 ; BP., pp. 291-92.

CHAPTER V

The Schools of Buddhism

1. *Introduction*

The Hīnayāna Buddhism gave rise to two main schools, the Vaibhāṣikas and the Sautrāntikas. The Mahāyāna Buddhism gave rise to two main schools, the Yogācāras and the Mādhyamikas. The Vaibhāṣikas and the Sautrāntikas sprang out of the Sarvāstivādins. The Sarvāstivādins hold that everything exists. The elements (dharmas), mental and physical, are real. The Vaibhāṣikas hold that external objects are real and perceptible. The Sautrāntikas hold that external objects are real and inferable. The Yogācāras hold that external objects are nonexistent, and are mere cognitions (vijñāna). The Mādhyamikas deny the absolute reality of external objects and subjective cognitions, and regard them as essenceless, but they affirm the reality of the Śūnya. The Śūnya is not void or nothing, but predicateless Absolute. The Vaibhāṣikas and the Sautrāntikas are realists. The Yogācāras are idealists (vijñānavādins). The Mādhyamikas are Śūnyavādins. They are not Nihilists but phenomenalists and Absolutists. There were many other minor schools among the Hīnayānists and the Mahāyānists. Treatment of them is beyond the scope of this work. An account of the four main schools, the Vaibhāṣika, the Sautrāntika, the Yogācāra, and the Mādhyamika will be given here.

The Theravāda or Sthaviravāda gave rise to a number of schools during the second and first century B.C. Its main branch was known as the Hetuvādins or Sarvāstivādins in the second century. The Sarvāstivādins include the Vaibhāṣikas and the Sautrāntikas. Vasubandhu (450 A.D.) wrote *Abhidharmakośa,* which is a compendium of the Vaibhāṣika philosophy. He wrote also a commentary on it named *Abhidharmakośabhāṣya* in which he criticized some views of the Vaibhāṣikas. He had strong sympathies for the Sautrāntika philosophy, and later adopted the Yogācāra Vijñānavāda. The Vaibhāṣika school probably derived the name from *Vibhāṣā,* a commentary on the *Abhidharma.* Kumāralāta was the founder of the Sautrāntika school. The name was derived from the *Sūtras* which were regarded as the authority. They adhered to the *Sūtras* alone, though they accepted some Sarvāstivādin and Vaibhāṣika views. Yaśomitra, a Sautrāntika, wrote a commentary on *Abhidharmakośa* named *Abhidharmakośavyākhyā.*

2. *The Sarvāstivādin, the Vaibhāṣika, and the Sautrāntika Realism*

The conception of dharma is the foundation of Buddhist metaphysics. Dharmas are irreducible elements. All things, mental and physical, are produced by the elements. All compound things are produced by the co-operation of a plurality of subtle, ultimate, indivisible, and unanalysable elements of matter, mind, and forces. These elements are technically called dharmas. Buddhism uses the term in this unique sense. Hence it is characterized by Stcherbatsky as Radical Pluralism (saṁghā tavāda). The elements are realities ; all compound things are mere names denoting groups of separate elements. Every element is a separate (pṛthak) entity. There is no inherence of one element in another. Hence there is no substance apart from its qualities, no matter beyond the separate sensible qualities, and no soul beyond the separate mental qualities. Elements are momentary (kṣaṇika) ; they have no duration ; they exist in the present moment. The elements co-operate with one another (saṁskṛta). Their co-operative activity is controlled by the law of causation (pratītyasamutpāda). The world-process is a process of combination of seventy two kinds of subtle momentary elements. Dharmas proceed from their causes (hetuprabhava) and advance towards extinction (nirodha). They produce the phenomenal world under the influence of ignorance (avidyā). They are appeased and destroyed under the influence of enlightenment (prajñā). There is complete stoppage of the process of phenomenal life in the case of a Buddha. Hence the elements are broadly divided into suffering (duḥkha), cause of suffering (duḥkhasamudāya, avidyā) extinction (nirodha), and cause of extinction (mārga, prajñā). The world-process tends towards the final goal of total suppression,

Absolute Calm : all co-operation of the elements becomes extinct, and is replaced by immutability (asaṁskṛta, nirvāṇa).[1]

The Sarvāstivādins hold that every thing exists. Matter and mind exist. Matter consists of elements. Mind also consists of elements. Elements are dharmas. There are seventy five kinds of dharmas which constitute the whole of reality. There are eleven material compounds. Mind is one compound. There are forty six mental compounds. There are fourteen non-mental compounds. There are three uncompounded dharmas. They are ether (ākāśa), unplanned destruction (apratisaṁkhyānirodha), and deliberate destruction (pratisaṁkhyānirodha). Ether (ākāśa) is an eternal, ubiquitous, material substance. Freedom from obstruction constitutes its essence. It may be regarded as absolutely real space. Apratisaṁkhyānirodha is the essential nature of things as ever perishing without cause or non-perception of things due to the absence of the necessary conditions. Pratisaṁkhyānirodha is complete liberation from bondage which endures for ever, and which is attained by enlightenment.

Matter obstructs the sense-organs. The atom is the unit of matter. It is invisible, inaudible, intangible, and untastable. It is indivisible. It is not permanent. Activity is its essential nature. It is a centre of energy. There are four kinds of atoms of general matter. They are earth atoms, water atoms, fire atoms, and air atoms. Earth atoms have hardness. Water atoms have cohesion (saṁgraha). Fire atoms have heat. Air atoms have motion (īraṇā). There are special atoms of colour, sound, touch, and taste. The sense-organs are made of very subtle translucent matter (rūpaprasāda). It is shining. It has no weight. It disappears at death. Still it is atomic. There are five kinds of special atoms which constitute the five sense-organs. The atoms are imperceptible. Only the combined atoms appear in phenomenal reality. The simple atoms are regarded as transcendental reality.[2]

The Vaibhāṣikas recognize the reality of mind and matter. Mind is composed of elements. Matter is composed of elements. There is no permanent soul. Existence is either transient or eternal. Space and Nirvāṇa are

[1] CCB., pp. 73-74.
[2] BP., pp. 160-61; CCB., pp. 12-15; AK., AKV., i. 12-13.

eternal. The elements of matter, mind, and forces are transient or phenomenal. The elements of phenomenal reality are past, present, and future. The past and the future elements are as real as the present ones. There are only four elements, earth, water, fire, and air. Earth is hard. Water is cool. Fire is warm. Air is mobile. Ether (ākāśa) is not recognized as an element. External objects are real. They are aggregates of atoms. The atom has six sides. It is invisible, inaudible, intangible, and untastable. It is indivisible. Atoms cannot penetrate one another. The perceptible atom (aṇu) is an aggregate of imperceptible atoms (paramāṇu). A distinction is made between a saṁghātaparamaṇu and a dravyaparamāṇu. Saṁghātaparamāṇu is the subtlest state of visible matter (rūpaskandha). Dravyaparamāṇu has nothing of matter (rūpāpacitaṁ dravyam); it is devoid of parts. There are eight dravyaparamāṇus, *viz.*, earth, water, fire, and air, and smell, taste, colour, and touch in the kāmadhātu.[1]

The Vaibhāṣikas criticize the Sautrāntaka doctrine of inferability of external objects from their cognitions as contradictory language (viruddha bhāṣā). If all external objects are inferred from their cognitions, then there are no objects of perception. There is therefore no observation of invariable concomitance (vyāpti) of the middle term with the major term, which is the ground of inference. Hence inference is not possible. This contradicts all actual experience. The Sautrāntika position is not tenable. There are two kinds of objects. Some are apprehended by indeterminate perception (grāhya), and others are apprehended by determinate perception (adhyavaseya). Indeterminate perception is free from conceptual construction (kalpanā). Determinate perception is perception wrought up by conceptual construction, which is therefore not valid. The validity of inference can be tested by fruitful action. The Vaibhāṣikas recognize the reality of external objects, and regard them as objects of perception.[2] They advocate direct realism.

The Sautrāntikas are representationists. They advocate indirect realism. They recognize the reality of external objects. But they regard them as objects of inference on the following

---

[1] AKV., ii. 22; Introduction, p. xx.
[2] SDS., ii. 55-56.

grounds: (1) External objects produce their cognitions, and imprint their forms on them. The forms of cognitions are similar to those of external objects. When cognitions come into being, their objects have ceased to be. Present cognitions cannot perceive past objects. Therefore external objects are inferred from their cognitions. The forms of objects are inferred from those of their cognitions. Cognitions are copies or representations of their objects, which are their archetypes. This doctrine is similar to representationism of Descartes and Locke. Just as we infer nourishment from a thriving look, nationality from language, and affection from flurried movements, so knowable objects are inferred from forms of cognitions. The objects mould the cognitions without losing their nature. (2) Cognitions are formless and homogeneous. They are diversified by their objects. Different external objects produce different cognitions, and impress their forms on them. The internal forms of cognitions are representations of the external forms of objects. We directly perceive cognitions. We infer external objects from their cognitions. If there were no objects, there would be no diversity of cognitions. (3) The object-cognitions appear at certain times only, while the subject cognitions are uniformly present. The Ālayavijñāna is of the nature of subject-cognitions (ahamāspada). But the object-cognitions (pravṛttivijñāna) are of the nature of 'this' (idamāspada). The stream of subject-cognitions is uniformly present. But the object-cognitions appear and disappear at certain times. Therefore they must be produced by external objects. (4) External objects exist and produce perceptions of colours, sounds, tastes, odours, temperatures, pressures, pleasure and pain. Perceptions are produced by external objects, which are the basic condition (ālambana pratyaya), the immediately preceding cognitions, which are the antecedent condition (samanantara pratyaya), the concomitant condition (sahakāri pratyaya), for instance, light in visual perception, and the sense-organs, which are the dominant condition (adhipati pratyaya).[1]

The Sautrāntika criticizes the Yogācāra Vijñānavāda in the following manner. The Yogācāra denies the reality of external

---

[1] SDS., ii. 45-47.

objects, and reduces them to cognitions (vijñāna). This position is not tenable. (1) The Yogācāra argues that an external object (*e.g.*, blue) and its cognition (*e.g.*, cognition of blue) are invariably perceived at the same time. The external object can never be perceived apart from its cognition. So the object is identical with its cognition. But this argument is wrong. "A sensation and its content are necessarily experienced together. The sensation is the experience of its content. But this does not prove that sensation is identical with its content."[1] (2) The object is different from its cognition. The cognition is internal (antarmukha) or subjective, while the object is external (bahirmukha) or objective. The object is independent of its cognition. They cannot always be referred to the same time and the same space. Therefore they are different from each other. (3) If the object were a mere cognition, it would be apprehended as 'I' (aham), and not as 'this' (idam). But a blue object is never perceived as '*I* am blue', but as '*this* is blue'. It is 'given'. It is not-self. It is not a mode of the self. (4) The Yogācāra argues that an internal cognition appears to be an external object owing to illusion, though it does not exist. The distinction of cognition and object is illusory. Cognition alone is real. It is, in reality, distinctionless. The Sautrāntika urges that if external objects are absolutely non-existent, an internal cognition cannot appear to be an external object. It would be as absurd as to say 'Vasubandhu looks like the son of a barren mother.' The illusion of externality presupposes valid knowledge of externality somewhere. The sense of externality can never be derived from mere subjective cognitions. (5) The Yogācāra argument involves mutual dependence (anyonyāśraya). The Yogācāra argues: The object is identical with its cognition because the appearance of distinction between them is illusory. Again, the distinction between cognition and its object is illusory because they are, in reality, identical with each other. The argument involves vicious circle. (6) External objects are actually perceived by us. We undoubtedly perceive them, and react to them. We pass over the cognitions of external objects. So it is wrong to argue that internal cognitions appear to be external

[1] *Indian Realism*, p. 36.

objects. (7) The Yogācāra argues that a variety of object-cognitions is due to the variety of impressions (vāsanā) within the stream of cognitions. The instinctive roots or seed-potentialities of ignorance imbedded in the Ālayavijñāna from beginningless time generate a variety of perceptions of sense-data. The beginningless uninterrupted stream of impressions of difference is the cause of the variety of perceptions of difference.[1] But impressions (vāsanā) can produce recollections only. They cannot produce perceptions of external objects. The series of the Ālayavijñāna in an individual is always present. The impressions are deposited in it. The Ālayavijñāna or the receptacle consciousness with the impressions being always present, the perceptions of objects would be always present. But, in fact, object-cognitions appear at certain times and disappear at other times. Therefore they cannot be generated by impressions.[2]

The Sautrāntikas affirm the reality of external objects composed of atoms. But they do not admit contact of atoms with one another. Atoms are partless, and cannot therefore come into contact with one another. If atoms touch one another, they would interpenetrate one another, and would not be able to increase the dimension of their aggregate. Vasumitra says, "If the atoms of which the objects are composed could really come into contact, they would be existing during the next moment." Every atom being momentary, its contact with another atom is impossible because it would take place in another moment. Bhadanta says, "There is no such thing as contact. Contact is only a name for the close vicinity of two apparitions."[3]

Nāgasena argues that time is due to ignorance. For the enlightened there is no time. For the unenlightened, whose dispositions (saṁskāra) have not borne fruit and been dissolved, there is time. There is continuity between the present, the past, and the future. The Sarvāstivādins maintain the existence of the past, the present, and the future. The Vibhajyavādins maintain the existence of the present elements and those past elements which have not yet produced their results, and the non-existence of the future elements and those past elements which have produced their results. The Vaibhāṣikas maintain

---

[1] Anādiravicchinnapravāhabhedavāsanaiva nimittam, SDS., ii. 39.
[2] SDS., ii. 48. [3] CCB., p. 60.

the existence of the past, the present, and the future. The elements which have produced their effects are past. The elements which are producing their effects are present. The elements which have not yet produced their effects are future. The past, the present, and the future are real. If the past were not real, actions done in the past could not produce their fruits in the present. The canon recognizes merely origin and destruction, or origin, decay, and destruction. The Vaibhāṣikas recognize origin, existence, decay, and destruction. These four moments of existence, which are considered as four kinds of forces, combine with the essence of an entity, and produce their impermanent manifestations. The Sautrāntikas contend that the Vaibhāṣika doctrine involves the heresy of eternalism. They deny the reality of the past and the future, and affirm the reality of the present alone. They maintain that there is no distinction between an entity, its efficiency or productivity, and its appearance. Entities emerge from non-existence ; they exist for a moment ; then they disappear. They are momentary. Only momentary entities are capable of causal efficiency. The present alone is real. The past and the future are unreal. "The future was not real before becoming present, and the past was not real after having been present."[1] Hence the present moment alone is real.[2] The Sautrāntikas developed the doctrine of impermanence (anityatva) into that of momentariness (kṣaṇikatva). Every thing is by its very nature perishing. There is no cause of its destruction. It exists for one moment only, and then vanishes.

The Sthaviravādins considered ākāśa to be a material derivative. Nāgasena describes it as uncaused and unproduced, out of time, imperceptible by the sense-organs, but perceptible by the mind. Ākāśa is described in another passage as infinite, boundless, immeasurable, incomprehensible, resting upon nothing, and unobstructed by anything. The Vaibhāṣikas consider ākāṣa to be uncompounded (asaṁskṛta). It does not obstruct anything. Nor is it obstructed by anything. It is not mere absence of obstruction. It is a positive entity. It is not perceptible. It is inferred from non-obstruction (anāvaraṇa) of

---

[1] CCB., p. 42.

[2] MP., pp. 50 ff.; AK., V. 24 ff.; AKV., i. 20; TRD., p. 46; KV., ii. 7; xxii. 8; BP., pp. 163-68.

other elements. It is eternal, immutable, and underivative. The Sautrāntikas also consider ether or space to be unconditioned and eternal.[1]

The Vaibhāṣikas consider Nirvāṇa to be a positive state of existence in which all passions have been completely extinguished, and the chances of the re-appearance of miseries have been eliminated. They regard ether or space (ākāśa), pratisaṁkhyānirodha, and apratisaṁkhyānirodha as uncompounded (asaṁskṛta) and eternal elements. Pratisaṁkhyānirodha is the dissociation of the elements from the impurities caused by enlightenment (pratisaṁkhyā) and the consequent non-production of their effects. It is also the dissociation of the mind from the impurities of affections and passions caused by enlightenment. It is a positive state of Nirvāṇa which is eternal and manifested by pure enlightenment. Apratisaṁkhyānirodha is complete non-emergence of impurities and miseries by the complete removal of their causes and conditions, especially of ignorance (avidyā). It is the complete extinction of the causal efficiency of the elements, and non-production of their effects. It is non-perception of dharmas caused by the absence of conditions, and not produced by enlightenment.[2] The Vaibhāṣikas maintain the existence of two kinds of elements, the one representing their eternal nature (dharmasvabhāva), and the other representing their momentary manifestations in actual life (dharmalakṣaṇa). "When all manifestations are stopped, all forces extinct, remains the lifeless residue. It is impersonal, eternal death, and it is a separate element, a reality, the reality of the elements in their lifeless condition. This reality is very similar to the reality of the Sāṁkhya's undifferentiated matter (prakṛti) ; it is eternal, absolute death."[3] Both kinds of nirodha are uncompounded (asaṃskṛta), unconditional, and eternal. They are not products of other dharmas. They are not causes of other dharmas. They are neither causes nor effects. Nirvāṇa is absolute annihilation of all the compounded dharmas (saṁskṛtadharma). It is complete dissociation of the elements from one another without any

---

[1] MP., pp. 271, 388; AK., i. 5; AKV., i. 5, pp. 16-17; BP., pp. 168-69; SBT., p. 161.

[2] AK., AKV., i. 6; SBT., p. 164; *Buddhist Philosophy of Flux*, Ch. XXVI.

[3] Stcherbatsky : *The Conception of Buddhist Nirvāṇa*, pp. 27-28.

chance of their combining with one another in future and producing individuality and phenomenal life. The Sautrāntikas, unlike the Vaibhāṣikas, reject the reality of the eternal elements, and admit the reality of the momentary manifestations only. They consider Nirvāṇa to be "the absolute end of the manifestations, the end of passion and life, without any positive counterpart. Nirvāṇa means only the end of the process of life, without any lifeless substance (dharma) as the residue or the substratum *in which* life has been extinguished."[1] Guṇaratna describes the Nirvāna of the Sautrāntikas as the absolute cessation of the stream of consciousness induced by constant meditation on the soullessness of all phenomena.[2] The Sautrāntikas consider asaṁskṛta dharmas as negative.

The Vaibhāṣikas enumerate six kinds of causes: (1) the efficient cause (kāraṇahetu); (2) co-operative causes (sahabhūhetu); (3) allied cause (sabhāgahetu); (4) united causes (saṁprayuktahetu); (5) omnipresent causes (sarvatragahetu); (6) and causes of fruition (vipākahetu). When visual consciousness arises on account of contact of the eyes with an object, the eyes are the efficient cause of the consciousness. When right knowledge is attained by the three paths, with which arise feeling, determinate perception, and volition, these are the co-operative causes of the right knowledge. When a person is endowed with faith, watchfulness, non-covetousness, and other virtues and attains purity through them, they are the allied causes of purity. When a person knows that his faith is based on knowledge, his knowledge is the united cause of his faith. When a person's false views affect all his bodily, verbal, and mental actions, which lead to evil states, his false views are the omnipresent cause of his evil states. When an effect is due to one's past karma, it is called the cause of its fruition.[3]

The Sautrāntikas hold that all things are momentary and perishing by their very nature, which depend on their causes, and exist by virtue of their dependence. "Causation is necessary succession of determined effects; its dependence constitutes the whole nature (dharmatā), suchness (tathatā), of things; they have no other reality. Their production is in the nature

[1] *The Conception of Buddhist Nirvāṇa*, p. 29.
[2] TRD., p. 47; *The Buddhist Philosophy of Flux*, p. 256.
[3] A.K., ii. 49; Introduction, p. xxviii; BP., pp. 177-78.

of magic (māyā) ; no real causality can be attributed to the impermanent ; their action and causality are merely their becoming. Hence we cannot talk rationally of the destruction of things by a cause."[1]

3. *Mahāyānaśraddhotpādaśāstra*: *The Philosophy of Tathatā*

Mahāyānaśraddhotpādaśāstra is ascribed by tradition to Aśvaghoṣa, the famous author of *Buddhacarita,* who flourished in the reign of King Kaniṣka (100 A.D.). But there is no reliable evidence for it. Aśvaghoṣa was a Brahmin converted into Buddhism. The doctrine of Tathatā or Suchness elaborated in this book resembles the Absolutistic Monism of the Upaniṣads and the Advaita Vedānta. It is believed that Aśvaghoṣa smuggled Upaniṣadic Absolutism into the Mahāyāna Buddhism. The book was composed in Sanskrit. The Sanskrit original is lost. It was rendered into Chinese by Paramārtha in 554 A.D., and by Śikṣānanda in 700 A.D. D. T. Suzuki rendered the Chinese version into English under the title *The Awakening of Faith.* Rev. Timothy Richard also rendered it into English under the same title. It is not authentic. Our account of the philosophy of Tathatā is based upon Suzuki's version.

The ultimate reality is called Suchness (Tathatā). It is the supreme, transcendental reality. It is the Absolute. It is the unconditioned noumenon. It is trans-empirical and non-phenomenal. It is one. It is non-dualistic and undifferenced. It is beyond the dualism of subjects and objects. It is beyond the distinction between what discriminates and what is discriminated. It is the fundamental essence of the whole universe. It is the essence of all beings. It is immanent in them. It is eternal. It remains in the past, the present, and the future. It is the essence of the Tathāgatas. Without it they cannot become Tathāgatas. Suchness is the immanent essence of the universe.

Tathatā is Śūnyatā. Śūnyatā is Tathatā. Suchness is Void. Void is Suchness. Suchness has two aspects, immutable Suchness, or Void-in-itself, and conditioned Suchness, or no-Void. The immutable Suchness is the Transcendental Mind or the Absolute Soul. The conditioned Suchness is the empirical mind

[1] BP., p. 178.

subject to birth and death. The immutable Suchness is the one all-inclusive Mind. It is not subject to birth and death. It is not liable to increase or decrease. It does not increase in the Buddha and Bodhisattvas. It does not decrease in other beings. It is the eternal, pure, blissful light of wisdom (prajñā) which illumines the entire universe. "Suchness has two aspects, transcendental and phenomenal, absolute and relative.[1] The conditioned Suchness is manifested in the empirical world. The Absolute Suchness and the conditioned Suchness are one and the same. The world is merely a fragment of the Absolute Bhūtatathatā. The finite mind's Bodhi only can grasp the Absolute Suchness. Why it becomes conditioned is inexplicable."[2]

Suchness has two aspects, Bhūtatathatā and saṁsāra. As Bhūtatathatā it is one reality. As saṁsāra it appears as many phenomena. Suchness as Bhūtatathatā is the supreme reality. It harmonizes all contradictions. It directs the course of events in the world. It is Nirvāṇa, and brings absolute peace. It is Bodhi, perfect wisdom, the source of intelligence. It is Dharmakāya, and the main spring of love and wisdom. It is the Highest Good (kuśalamūla). It is the heart of enlightenment (bodhicitta). It is the Highest Truth (paramārthasatya). It is Bhūtakoṭi, the essence of Being. It is the Tathāgatagarbha, the womb of the Tathāgatas.[3]

Bhūtatathatā is the Absolute and Infinite ground of the universe. It has neither existence nor non-existence, nor both, nor neither. It is neither unity nor plurality, nor both, nor neither.[4] It is transcendent ; it transcends the conditional and relative world. It is immanent in the phenomenal world as its permanent ground and essence. It is absolute, infinite, immutable, and imperishable. It is Dharmadhātu, the great all-comprehending whole. Absolute Suchness is One Soul. It is absolute sameness (samatā) in all phenomena. It is uncreated and eternal.[5] It is distinctionless. It is unnameable and inexpressible. It is beyond subject and object. It is incomprehensible. It is beyond the range of perception and intellectual knowledge. It can be grasped by supra-intellectual intuition

---

[1] Cp. Nirguṇa Brahma and Saguṇa Brahma of the Advaita Vedānta.
[2] D. T. Suzuki : *Outline of Mahāyāna Buddhism.*
[3] SBT., pp. 253-54.
[4] *The Awakening of Faith,* p. 59.
[5] *Ibid,* pp. 55-56.

(prajñā). The relative, conditional, phenomenal, and dualistic world of subjects and objects is comprehended by discriminative intellect. But the Absolute Suchness is grasped by non-discriminative intuition. It is beyond all intellectual categories. It may be called negation (śūnyatā) in this sense. But negation (sūnyatā) also is void (śūnya) in its nature. Neither that which is negated nor that which negates is real in itself. Only the one, eternal, immutable Soul, which is the immanent essence of the whole universe, is real. It may be called affirmation in this sense. But there is no affirmation in it by the intellect, since it is beyond all intellectual categories. No conceptual constructions can be predicated of it. It is one, non-empirical, non-phenomenal, unconditioned, pure, Absolute Soul, which can be grasped only by intuition which transcends intellectual comprehension.[1]

Absolute Suchness is beyond relativity. Saṁsāra is the empirical world of relativity. It is devoid of ontological reality. When it is viewed apart from its relativity and particularity, it is found to be the same as Bhūtatathatā, the ultimate ground of the universe. Bhūtatathatā is One Soul. But it appears to be many empirical minds and manifold world owing to ignorance (avidyā). When ignorance is dispelled by intuition (prajñā), manifoldness of empirical minds and empirical objects vanishes, and One Soul shines forth. Multiplicity is subjective and unreal ; oneness is real : it is the ontological reality.[2]

Aśvaghoṣa attempts to account for the relation between Absolute Suchness and conditioned Suchness by the principle of avidyā. It is nescience or ignorance. It is the principle of individuation. "Nescience is a spark of consciousness that spontaneously flashes from the unfathomable depths of Suchness. Awakening of consciousness marks the first step towards the rising of the universe from the abyss of self-identity of Suchness. For the unfolding of consciousness implies the separation of the perceiving and the perceived, the subject and the object."[3] Ignorance (avidyā) is as inexplicable as Suchness. It is analogous to Māyā in the Advaita Vedānta. Avidyā is a spontaneous expression of Suchness. It is the principle of

---

[1] SBT., pp. 257-58; HIP., I, pp. 130-31.
[2] Mrs. B. L. Suzuki : *Mahāyāna Buddhism*, 1948, p. 108.
[3] D. T. Suzuki : *Outline of Mahāyāna Buddhism.*

relativity. It awakens subjectivity, and creates egoism. Egoism is avidyā in the sense of confused subjectivity. It is setting up self-will over against the absolute will. "On account of the human mind not being able to comprehend the oneness of the totality of things (dharmadhātu), the mind is not in accord with the Truth or Reality ; and then delusion or subjectivity ensues ; this is called ignorance or avidyā."[1]

The universe as a whole is the Infinite Mind. The finite mind is a microcosm. It can realize in its inmost depths of consciousness what the cosmic mind feels. When it transcends subjectivity and objectivity created by avidyā, it is in communion with the Infinite Mind. Tathāgatagarbha is the transcendental soul of man. It is pure and free as the expression of Suchness in man. But when it comes under the Law of Karma, it undergoes birth and death. The human soul is an individuation of Tathāgatagarbha, and it is called Ālayavijñāna. Ālayavijñāna is an individual expression of the cosmic Tathāgatagarbha in the human mind. When Ālayavijñāna comes under the influence of birth and death, it is polarized into an empirical subject and an empirical world. Citta is a state of Suchness, in which there is no awakening of mental modes. When manas is evolved, mental modes appear in it.[2]

Absolute Suchness is related to the phenomenal world through the Ālayavijñāna which has two aspects, enlightenment and non-enlightenment or ignorance. The Ālayavijñāna binds us to saṁsāra, and leads us to enlightenment. As enlightenment it is pure, bright, and true ; as non-enlightenment it is impure, dark, and false. The Ālayavijñāna of Aśvaghoṣa includes relative (paratantra) and absolute (pariniṣpanna) knowledge, while the Ālayavijñāna of the Yogācāra Vijñānavādin includes relative knowledge only. It binds us to the empirical world of saṁsāra. It leads us to enlightenment or Nirvāṇa.[3]

Enlightenment and non-enlightenment are relative to each other. Non-enlightenment is a non-entity. So enlightenment also is meaningless. They have significance only in relation to each other. Enlightenment is the intrinsic purity of the mind free from the hindrances of intellectual (jñeyāvaraṇa) and emotional depravities (kleśāvaraṇa), and the impurities of the

[1] SBT., p. 265.
[2] *Outline of Mahāyāna Buddhism,* Ch. V-VI. [3] SBT., pp. 258-59.

creative instinctive memory (smṛti). It is the universal Dharmakāya of all Tathāgatas. It is the unity of all (dharmadhātu). It is the foundation of all existence. It is the essence of the universe. It is Absolute Suchness. It is the pure, eternal light of consciousness. When the oneness of the universe is not recognized, non-enlightenment or ignorance appears with particularities. Non-enlightenment has two aspects, root and branch. The former is ignorance itself. The latter is determination to persist in ignorance. The former is the ignorance of the true nature of Suchness. The latter is the ignorance which makes us cling to empirical objects which are mere subjective creations of the mind. Ignorance and enlightenment are one in their essence. Ignorance is illusory and relative knowledge. Enlightenment is absolute knowledge. When one attains Nirvāṇa, ignorance becomes enlightenment. Ignorance is empirical knowledge of apparent multiplicity and individuality. Enlightenment is absolute knowledge of real unity and universality. Enlightenment is the truth of non-enlightenment or ignorance. Ignorance is, in its ultimate nature, identical with enlightenment. It is, in its apparent nature, different from enlightenment. Ignorance in one sense is destructible, and in another sense it is indestructible. In its ultimate nature as enlightenment it is indestructible. In its apparent nature as non-enlightenment it is destructible. Non-enlightenment has no existence of its own apart from its relation to enlightenment *a priori*.[1] The relation of enlightenment to non-enlightenment may be illustrated by the simile of the water of the ocean and its waves. The waves arise in the ocean, when its water is stirred up by the wind. When the wind ceases, the waves subside, but the water of the ocean remains the same. "Likewise when the mind of all creatures, which in its own nature is pure and clean, is stirred up by the wind of ignorance (avidyā), the waves of mentality (vijñāna) make their appearance. These three, the mind, ignorance, and mentality, have no existence, and they are neither unity nor plurality. When the ignorance is annihilated, the awakened mentality is tranquillized, whilst the essence of wisdom remains unmolested."[2] The Ālayavijñāna is in its true nature pure, eternal, and im-

---

[1] *The Awakening of Faith;* SBT., pp. 260-61.
[2] *The Awakening of Faith.*

mutable. But it is stirred up by the wind of avidyā into mental modes. When the wind of avidyā is calmed, it is restored to its original purity and enlightenment, and mental modes disappear. Non-enlightenment is manifested in three ways: (1) as the Ālayavijñāna through the activity of ignorance (avidyā-karma) producing suffering; (2) as an ego or perceiver; and (3) as an external world which is not self-existent but dependent on the perceiving ego.

The unreal external world acts upon the mind, and generates six phenomena. First, it produces in the mind the feelings of the agreeable and the disagreeable. Secondly, it produces in it the retention of agreeable and disagreeable feelings in succession. Thirdly, it produces in it a desire to cling to agreeable and disagreeable things, which arises from the memory of such feelings. Fourthly, it produces in it attachment to names (saṁjñā) by which it defines all real things. Fifthly, it excites actions in it on account of attachment to names attributed to unreal external objects, which indivilualizes them. Sixthly, it generates misery in the mind due to its actions. Misery entangles it in bondage and deprives it of its intrinsic freedom. All these phenomena are creations of avidyā.

The Ālayavijñāna becomes an ego (manas), when avidyā manifests itself in it. The ego is called activity-consciousness (karmavijñāna), since the unenlightened mind is disturbed by the activity of ignorance. It is called evolving consciousness (pravṛttivijñāna), since it evolves an unreal external world when it is disturbed by ignorance. It is called representation-consciousness, since it represents an external world as presented by the five senses. It is called particularization-consciousness, since it discriminates between particular things, pure and defiled. It is called succession-consciousness, since it retains the impressions of all experiences with the help of attention, and provides for retribution of actions, memory of the past, and anticipation of the future. All objects, corporeal (rūpaloka), incorporeal (arūpaloka), and desired (kāmaloka) are the subjective creations of the Ālayavijñāna owing to the influence of avidyā and instinctive memory (smṛti). When it is disturbed by avidyā, multiplicity appears. When it is stilled by the removal of avidyā, multiplicity vanishes. Ālayavijñāna is practically identical with Suchness. Absolute Suchness is related to conditioned Suchness or empirical world through Ālayavijñāna. All things are primarily the Absolute Soul, which is the pure light of wisdom (prajñā). Empirical minds, mental modes, and empirical objects are awakened in it owing to ignorance. They are mere subjective constructions of the unenlightened mind. Aśvaghoṣa does not deny the empirical reality of the perceiving egos and the perceived objects. But he denies their ontological reality. When ignorance is destroyed by enlightenment, the mind realizes its identity with the Absolute Suchness or Infinite Mind, and apparent multiplicity of subjects and objects vanishes. Avidyā projects the plurality of minds and objects in the unity of the Absolute Suchness. There is a great resemblance between Aśvaghoṣa's Tathatā and the Brahman of the Advaita Vedānta, and between Aśvaghoṣa's avidyā and the Māyā of the Advaita Vedānta. Avidyā is as mysterious and inexplicable as Māyā or cosmic nescience which veils the Brahman and projects the world of plurality.

There is interperfuming of Suchness and ignorance by each other. Suchness is pure, undefiled, and free from all taint of ignorance. On the other hand, ignorance has no purity. Suchness is defiled by the perfuming power of ignorance. Ignorance leads us to purity by the perfuming power of Suchness.[1] It perfumes Suchness and produces confused subjectivity, which, in its turn, perfumes ignorance, and produces an external world of subjectivity. The external world created by subjectivity acts upon the mind, and generates attachment in it. Attachment individualizes objects, and gives rise to clinging to them. Thus avidyā is the spring of individuation and particularization.

Again, Suchness perfumes ignorance, pours the love (maitrī) and compassion (karuṇā) of all Buddhas and Bodhisattvas on the individual, and induces in his mind aversion to birth and death and longing for Nirvāṇa. This aversion and longing perfume Suchness. Owing to this perfuming influence, the individual realizes that he is in possession of Suchness in himself, which is pure and undefiled, and that all external objects are mere subjective creations of the Ālayavijñāna. He no more particularizes and clings to particular objects. He practises the

[1] *The Awakening of Faith*, pp. 84-85.

means of liberation, and performs actions in accordance with the dharma. He destroys ignorance, and attains enlightenment or Nirvāṇa. The Ālayavijñāna is no longer disturbed by ignorance, and ceases to have individuating mental modes. Ignorance vanishes, and Nirvāṇa is attained. Nirvāṇa is Suchness (Tathatā) free from all taint of ignorance.

Suchness is "the effulgence of great wisdom ; the universal illumination of the dharmadhātu (universe), the true and adequate knowledge, the mind pure and clean in its nature ; the eternal, the blessed, the self-regulating and the pure, the immutable and the free."[1] It is universal illumination ; but it has no objects to illumine. It is the pure eternal light of consciousness. It is non-dualistic and distinctionless. But avidyā infects it with duality, and generates the Ālayavijñāna and the external world which is its subjective creation. When avidyā is destroyed, the universal illumination manifests itself.[2]

4. *The Idealism of Laṅkāvatārasūtra*

Laṅkāvatārasūtra is a very important work on the Mahāyāna metaphysics. The date of its composition is not definitely known. It was translated into Chinese by Guṇabhadra in 443 A.D., by Bodhiruci in 513 A.D., and by Śikṣānanda in 700—704 A.D. Winternitz opines that it was not written earlier than 400 A.D. He holds that it teaches a modification of Śūnyavāda and Vijñānavāda. D. T. Suzuki opines that it was composed at a time when the two schools of the Yogācāra and the Mādhyamika were not differentiated from each other.[3] It is not a book on systematic philosophy. It is a sketch-book containing important notes on the Mahāyāna religion. The different strands of thought contained in it are sketched below.

The predominant note in the book is that the "Mind only" (cittamātra) is real, and that the external world is not real. The external objects are unreal like dreams (māyāsvapna), mirage (mṛgatṛṣṇā), sky-flower (khapuṣpa), reflections of trees

---

[1] *The Awakening of Faith*, p. 96.

[2] *The Awakening of Faith; Outline of Mahāyāna Buddhism*, Ch. V-VI; HIP., I, pp. 129-38; BP., pp. 252-56; SBT., Ch. VII; *Mahāyāna Buddhism*.

[3] Winternitz : *A History of Indian Literature*, Vol. II, pp. 332-33; SLS., p. 170.

in water, the circle of a revolving fire-brand (alātacakra), an imaginary city in the clouds (grandharvanagara), and the like. They are unreal like illusions, hallucinations, dreams, and day-dreams. They do not exist ; they are mere imaginary constructions (vikalpamātra) of the mind. All phenomena (dharma), apart from the cognitions of the mind, are unreal like illusions.[1] The self (pudgala), the stream of cognitions (santati), the aggregates (skandha), the causes (pratyaya), the atoms (aṇu), prakṛti, and God, the so-called creator of the world, are all imaginary constructions of the mind only.[2] Causation is either external or internal. The five aggregates (skandha), the five elements (dhātu), the five sense-organs and the mind, and the five sensible objects, and the intelligible objects are said to be produced. But they are nothing but imaginary constructions of the mind. Action is said to be produced by craving. Craving is said to be produced by ignorance. But these links in the chain of internal causation are nothing but imaginary constructions of the mind.[3] The meditator, meditation, and the object of meditation are its mere imaginary constructions (kalpanāmātra). The four stages of one who has entered into the stream (srotāpanna), one who will be born once (sakṛdāgāmin), one who will not be born (anāgāmin), and an Arhat are delusions of mind (cittavibhrama).[4] Saṁsāra and nirvāṇa are mental creations. Even the Dharmakāya is unreal like an unreal dream (māyāsvapnasvabhāva).[5] So every object of knowledge is an idea of the mind (citta) only.

Citta, Manas, and Vijñāna are spoken of as different because of appearances. In fact, the eight kinds of vijñānas have no specific qualifying marks ; there is nothing to be qualified (lakṣya) ; there is no qualifying mark (lakṣaṇa). As there is no differentiation in the waves of the ocean, so there is no modification of the citta in the form of vijñānas or cognitions. Citta accumulates karma or potencies of actions ; Manas investigates ; the Vijñāna distinguishes, and the five sense-cognitions discriminate the perceptible world. Blue, red, and other sensible objects are not the waves or modifications of the citta ; they are said to be the modes of mind for the sake

[1] LS., ii. 149-60, 1-2.
[2] LS., ii. 139.
[3] LS., ii. pp. 82-83.
[4] LS., ii. 177-78.
[5] LS., ii. 4, 7, 8.

of the ignorant. The body (deha), enjoyment (bhoga), and the objects of enjoyment (pratiṣṭhāna) are the cognitions of men.[1]

This doctrine of the reality of the mind only (cittamātra) appears to be subjective idealism. External objects are mere imaginary creations of the mind. They are mere subjective ideas. Sometimes they are spoken of as ideas of one's own mind (svacitta). It is devoid of known objects (grāhyavarjita).[2] They are imaginary constructions of one's own mind (svacittadṛśyavikalpa).[3] This lends colour to subjectivism. But this is a wrong interpretation of the idealism of *Laṅkāvatarasūtra*.

The Citta is identical with the Ālayavijñāna. It is the All-conserving Mind. The ocean of the Ālayavijñāna is stirred up by the wind of objects, and rolls on dancing with the waves of the various cognitions (vijñāna). The seven vijñānas which are the waves of the ocean are produced in conjunction with the mind (manas). Just as the ocean is stirred up into manifold waves, so the Ālayavijñāna is stirred up into a variety of cognitions.[4] Ālayavijñāna is pure citta or mind, devoid of mental cognitions (manovijñāna) and impurities.[5] Citta is known in two ways,—as the knower (grāhaka) and the known (grāhya), and is neither eternal nor subject to destruction.[6] The pure citta or mind is identical with the Ālayavijñāna. Object-cognitions (pravṛttivijñāna) arise from the Ālayavijñāna.[7] The mind-only (cittamātra) or the Ālayavijñāna only is real.

The Ālayavijñāna is the repository of the potencies of all past actions. The dispositions (vāsanā) of actions accumulated in it from beginningless time produce a variety of object-cognitions. They are not produced by external objects. But they are produced by the Ālayavijñāna from within itself owing to the maturation of dispositions (vāsanā) accumulated in it from beginningless time.[8] They are imaginary constructions of the all-conserving Mind or Ālayavijñāna. It is the womb of the Tathāgatas (Tathāgatagarbha).

The Ālayavijñāna does not appear to be the individual mind. It is the all-conserving Universal Mind. T. D. Suzuki

---

[1] LS., ii. 104-10.
[2] LS., ii. 109.
[3] LS., p. 44.
[4] LS., ii. 99-103.
[5] LS., Sagāthaka, 238-39.
[6] LS., iii. 65.
[7] LS., p. 44.
[8] LS., pp. 44-45.

observes. "The Ālaya being super-individual holds in it not only individual memory but all that has been experienced by sentient beings. When the sūtra says that in the Ālaya is found all that has been going on since beginningless time systematically stored up as a kind of seed, this does not refer to individual experiences, but to something general, beyond the individual, making up in a way the background on which all individual psychic activities are reflected. Therefore the Ālaya is originally pure ; it is the abode of the Tathāgatahood, where no defilements of the particularizing intellect and affection can reach. In short, the world starts from memory ; memory in itself as retained in the universal Ālaya is no evil, and when we are removed from the influence of false discrimination the whole vijñāna system woven around the Ālaya as centre experiences a revulsion toward true perception (parāvṛtti). This is the gist of the *Laṅkāvatāra*."[1] Suzuki says, "According to my way of interpreting the *Laṅkāvatāra,* which may not be correct, the Ālaya is a sort of universal consciousness, and Manas individual empirical consciousness. At the back of the six vijñānas there must be Manas, the principle of individuation, and also the Ālaya, which goes even beyond the foundation of consciousness".[2] There is no discrimination in the Ālayavijñāna. It is the store-house of the dispositions of all past experiences and actions of sentient creatures. The Manas is the active source of all the mental activities which apprehend particular objects. Sogen interprets the Ālayavijñāna as the subconscious mind. It must, then, be the individual subconscious mind.[3] The universal Ālayavijñāna may be expressed in the individual as the subconscious mind.

Suzuki's interpretation of the Ālayavijñāna as the super-individual all-conserving Mind appears to be valid, though the *Laṅkāvatārasūtra* does not mention it distinctly anywhere. Thus it teaches a kind of absolute idealism like the Yogācāra. It teaches the ultimate reality of pure consciousness, 'Vijñapti-Mātra', Prajñaptimātrā.[4] Winternitz holds that the Vijñānavāda of *Laṅkāvatārasūtra* is similar to the doctrine of Maitreya-

---

[1] SLS., p. 184.
[2] SLS., pp. 195-96.
[3] SBT., p. 214.
[4] LS., pp. 26, 33, 96, 168, 169, 267, 270.

nātha, Asaṅga and other Vijñānavādins. Its idealism cannot be branded as pure subjectivism or solipsism. It is a kind of absolute idealism. So far its doctrine is identical with that of the Yogācāra.

The *Laṅkāvatārasūtra* teaches the selflessness (nairātmya) or unsubstantiality of all phenomena (dharma). Unsubstantiality of the soul (pudgala) and all phenomena is said to be its main teaching. It is difficult to understand it.[1] The world is like a sky-flower. It is devoid of origin and destruction. It is neither existent nor non-existent. It is neither eternal nor transient. All objects (bhāva) are essenceless (niḥsvabhāva). They are devoid of origin and destruction. The self-natures (svabhāva) of all objects known by the mind cannot be ascertained. So they are undefinable (anabhilāpya) and essenceless (niḥsvabhāva). All objects are unproduced and essenceless in the state of concentration (samādhi). They are not produced; nothing is produced by them. All dharmas are non-dual (advaya); they are not affected by duality. They are, in their ultimate nature, distinctionless and non-dual like the complete extinction of empirical life (saṁsāraparinirvāṇa). They are Śūnyatā. It is non-dual, irrelative, unconditioned, absolute. It is neither eternal nor ephemeral. It is the absolute essence of all phenomena. It is their ultimate ground. Hence the mind should be concentrated on the unborn (anutpāda), non-dual (advaya), essenceless (niḥsvabhāva) Śūnyatā.[2]

There are seven kinds of Śūnyatā: (1) Lakṣaṇaśūnyatā; (2) Bhāvasvabhāvaśūnyatā; (3) Apracaritaśūnyatā; (4) Pracaritaśūnyatā; (5) Sarvadharmanirabhilāpyaśūnyatā; (6) Paramārthāryajñānamahāśūnyatā; (7) Itaretaraśūnyatā. (1) All objects are interdependent on one another; they have no special characteristics in themselves; they are indeterminate in their nature; they cannot be determined by reference to other objects; hence they are undefinable by specific characteristics (lakṣaṇaśūnyatā). (2) All objects are devoid of positive essences, since they arise from non-existence of their essences or self-natures; this characteristic constitutes their essencelessness (bhāvasvabhāvaśūnyatā). Individualization is the imaginary construction of the mind. (3) All aggregates (skandha) are devoid of activities

[1] LS., p. 1; ii. 6.
[2] LS., ii. 1-4, 175, p. 76.

which appear to be real, since Nirvāṇa, free from activity, is already embedded in them. The non-acting of the skandhas is characterized as emptiness (apracaritaśūnyatā). (4) The skandhas are devoid of selfhood and all that belongs to selfhood. Their activities are due to the combination of causes and conditions, and therefore phenomenal appearances. They are characterized by emptiness (pracaritaśūnyatā). (5) All dharmas are devoid of self-natures which can be defined ; they depend for their existence upon our imagination (parikalpita) ; hence they are undefinable or unnameable. This unnameability is a form of emptiness (nirabhilāpyaśūnyatā). (6) When the ultimate reality (paramārtha) is realized in our inner consciousness, all theories, all wrong ideas, and all the traces of beginningless memory (vāsanā) are completely wiped out, and the ultimate reality becomes perfectly empty. This constitutes Great Emptiness of Ultimate Reality (mahāśūnyatā). (7) We distinguish objects from one another by some specific qualities which are not possessed by other objects. The absence of the distinguishing qualities of things in one another is emptiness of reciprocity (itaretaraśūnyatā).[1] The doctrine of Śūnyatā was emphasized by the Mādhyamika. The Śūnyatā is not Void or non-entity. It is the absolute ground of all phenomena.

The positive side of the doctrine of emptiness (śūnyatā) is known as the doctrine of Suchness (Tathatā). The *Laṅkāvatāra-sūtra* insists that when the world is viewed as empty (śūnya), it is grasped in its Suchness (Tathatā). Suchness can be grasped by absolute knowledge (pariniṣpannajñāna) which is the highest degree of knowledge.[2] Tathatā, Śūnyatā, Nirvāṇa, and Dharma-dhātu are synonymous. It is the ontological reality. It is neither positive nor negative ; it is beyond being (bhāva) and non-being (abhāva). It is devoid of positive and negative characters of our empirical consciousness.[3] Tathatā is realized in our inner consciousness (pratyātmatathatājñeya).[4] The conception of Suchness (Tathatā) makes the idealism of *Laṅkāvatārasūtrā* undoubtedly absolutistic. Thus it teaches a kind of Absolute Idealism.

It recognizes three degrees of knowledge: (1) imaginary (parikalpita), (2) relative (paratantra) ; and (3) absolute (pari-

---

[1] LS., pp. 74-75; SLS., pp. 288-89.
[2] LS., ii. 134; vi. 6.
[3] LS., iii. 30-31.
[4] LS., 57, 61, 68, 75, 242.

niṣpanna), like the Yogācāra. The first is the common-sense knowledge of multiplicity unconnected with one another. It includes illusory knowledge also. The second is intellectual knowledge of objects as causally connected with, and dependent upon, other objects. It is relative knowledge. It serves our practical purposes. It is conventional, empirical, or practical knowledge. The highest knowledge of Suchness (Tathatā), the absolute ground of all phenomena, is absolute knowledge. When a rope is mistaken for a snake, we have imaginary (parikalpita), or illusory knowledge. When it is known as a rope depending upon its cause and conditions, we have relative or dependent (paratantra) knowledge. When it is known as Suchness (Tathatā), we have absolute (pariniṣpanna) knowledge. It is right knowledge (samyagjñāna). It is the highest intuition. It is supra-intellectual knowledge. It is the highest wisdom (prajñā).

The imaginary (parikalpita) knowledge apprehends multiplicity, though there is none. It is an imaginary construction of the mind in a state of confusion. The relative (paratantra) knowledge is free from illusions or imaginary creations of the confused mind. It apprehends objects as dependent upon other objects. It is the empirical knowledge of appearances. It is not yet the highest knowledge. The mind tainted by intellectual disorders (jñeyāvaraṇa) and passions (kleśāvaraṇa) has relative knowledge of appearances, affected by duality and relativity.[1] The pure mind purged of intellectual and affective taints has absolute knowledge of Suchness (Tathatā) which is unconditioned and unaffected by all dualism and relativity. This is absolute knowledge.[2] These three degrees of knowledge are recognized by the Yogācāra.

Laṅkāvatārasūtra, like the Mādhyamika, recognizes two kinds of knowledge : Saṁvṛti, apparent or empirical knowledge, and Paramārtha, absolute or transcendental knowledge. The Parikalpita and the Paratantra knowledge both are empirical knowledge ; they are concerned with illusions and appearances. The Paratantra knowledge of empirical appearances serves our practical purposes (vyavahāra). It is intellectual knowledge.

---

[1] LS., pp. 97, 134-35.
[2] LS., ii. 183, 185, 186, 193, 194, 199, 202, 134, pp. 56-57; SLS. 67-68, pp. 157-63.

But it cannot grasp the ontological reality. Apparent truth (saṁvṛtisatya) prevails in the world of illusory (parikalpita) and relative (paratantra) knowledge. Absolute truth (paramārthasatya) prevails in the realm of absolute (pariniṣpanna) knowledge. The distinction between truth or reality (bhūtakoṭi) and its reflected image or semblance (pratibimba) corresponds to that between Saṁvṛti and Paramārtha.[1]

Our intelligence has two kinds of knowledge: pravicayabuddhi and pratiṣṭhāpikābuddhi. The former knows a thing as either this or the other, either both or not-both, either existent or non-existent, either eternal or non-eternal. But all these cannot be the predicates of all phenomena. The latter creates imaginary constructions such as hot, liquid, moving, solid, and the like, and arranges them in a logical order of cause and effect, subject and predicate, and the like. It is logical knowledge. It establishes propositions. It is intellectual knowledge. Pravicayabuddhi also is intellectual knowledge. It is not the highest knowledge (pariniṣpannajñāna).[2]

Three stages of knowledge are recognized: (1) mundane knowledge (laukikajñāna) of common people who comprehend things as either existent or non-existent; (2) supra-mundane knowledge (lokottarajñāna) of the Śrāvakas and Pratyekabuddhas who comprehend things by their individualities and generalities; (3) the highest supra-mundane knowledge (lokottaratamajñāna) of Buddhas and Bodhisattvas who comprehend the unsubstantiality (nairātmya) of all phenomena, beyond being and non-being, origin and destruction. It is the highest knowledge. It is the supreme wisdom (āryajñāna) of the Bodhisattva, which enables him to enter into the inmost nature (svapratyātma) of all the Buddhas.[3] It is the inner realization of the absolute truth (paramārthagocara), the eternal unthinkable (nityam acintyam) Suchness (Tathatā).[4]

There are four stages of meditation: (1) Bālopacārika; (2) Arthapravicaya; (3) Tathatālambana; and (4) Tāthāgata. (1) The Bālopacārika meditation consists in concentration on the doctrine of soullessness and impermanence, misery, and

[1] LS., ii. 187; Sagāthakam, 299, 54-55, pp. 163-64.
[2] LS., pp. 122-23.
[3] LS., p. 157; SLS., pp. 139-40.
[4] LS., pp. 59-60.

impurity. It is practised by the Śrāvakas and Pratyekabuddhas. (2) The Arthapravicaya meditation consists in concentration on the soullessness and unsubstantiality of all dharmas which cannot be distinguished from one another by their individualities and generalities. (3) The Tathatālambana meditation consists in concentration on Suchness (Tathatā) behind soullessness of all dharmas or phenomena which are imaginary constructions of the mind, and are mere appearances of Suchness. (4) The Tāthāgata meditation consists in concentration on the inner realization (pratyātmāryajñāna) of Suchness, which is the inconceivable reality.[1]

Nirvāṇa is the revulsion (parāvṛtti) of the mind into its pure state of emptiness of the self-nature of all its activities on the cessation of the dispositions (vāsanā) of all cognitions, and of the dispositions of mental cognitions, manas, and the Ālaya-vijñāna. It is the inner realization of Suchness which is free from the imaginary constructions of being and non-being, the eternal and the transient, and individualities and generalities. It differs from the Nirvāṇa of the Śrāvakas and the Pratyekabuddhas, which is a state of desirelessness arising from the knowledge of the generalities and individualities of things, untainted by errors and illusions due to absence of attachments. It is not death, since it is not followed by rebirth. It is not destruction, since compound things only are liable to destruction. Thus it is different from death or destruction. It is the inner realization of the eternal, unthinkable Suchness which is the essence of the mind. It is the intuition of the Absolute. Nirvāṇa is realized when one sees into the abode of Suchness which is formless and beyond origin and destruction.[2] It is Tathatā (Suchness), Tattva (Thatness) realized in the inmost consciousness of the Tathāgata. It is a state of pure intuition. It is the supreme wisdom, which is eternal, and arises from its intrinsic nature.[3]

Aṣṭasāhasrikā Prajñāpāramitāsūtra emphasizes the idea of Emptiness (śūnyatā), while *Laṅkāvatārasūtra* emphasizes the self-realization of the transcendental truth of no-birth, though it discusses the various kinds of Śūnyatā. When there is no actual perception of the truth, no actual seeing of the origin

[1] LS., pp. 97-98.
[2] LS., pp. 98-99, 200.
[3] SLS., p. 147.

of things, all these philosophical views end in nihilism.[1] *Prajñāpāramitāsūtra* teaches that what is known as mind in discursive reasoning is no-mind (acitta), though Mind cannot be reached without it. There is Mind that is no-mind, that is neither being nor non-being, neither to be perceived nor grasped. This view of no-mind-ness (acittatā) corresponds to the *Laṅkāvatāra* view of Cittamātra or mind only. "Both start from the untenability or unknowability of ultimate reality which is beyond the dualism of being and non-being, of birth and death ; and while the one ends in a form of negativism, the other comes to the affirmation that there is nothing but Mind. At the bottom of these two propositions, however, there is but one experience, for both aim at the realization of one and the same fundamental truth."[2]

The Yogācāra Vijñānavāda emphasizes the subjectivity of external objects of perception, which are mere names and our own subjective creations without any foundation in realities. The mind particularizes and discriminates individual objects, and is deluded into believing that they are real, and becomes attached to them. "When the vijñāna takes no hold on an objective world, it abides in the Vijñaptimātratva, for when there is nothing to be grasped, there is no grasping."[3] This is the gist of the Vijñānavāda as presented by Asaṅga and Vasubandhu. *Laṅkāvatāra* agrees with the Yogācāra Vijñānavāda that the world is a subjective creation of the mind, but it emphasizes the reality of Mind-only (cittamātra). The 'Citta-Mātra' is not the individual empirical mind which functions as Manas and Vijñāna. It is the principle of mentality. It is prior to all discrimination. It is prior to the duality of subject and object. It is the Ālayavijñāna, the universal Mind. It is beyond particularization. It is grasped by non-discriminating wisdom (avikalpa jñāna), supreme wisdom (āryajñāna), enlightenment (prajñā). It is realized in the inmost recess of consciousness. It is called the Mind (citta).[4] "The transcendent mind, or Mind itself, or 'Mind-only' is the chief subject of the text[5]." *Laṅkāvatāra* is metaphysical in its outlook, while the Yogācāra Vijñānavāda is epistemological in its standpoint.

---

[1] LS., pp. 40-41.
[2] SLS., p. 286.
[3] *Triṁśikāvijñaptikārikā*, 28.
[4] SLS., pp. 279-81.
[5] SLS., p. 281.

The doctrine of subjectivity of the external world is emphasized by the Yogācāra Vijñānavāda. The doctrine of negativism or emptiness of all phenomena is emphasized by *Prajñāpāramitāsūtra* and the Mādhyamika. The doctrine of Tathatā is emphasized by the *Mahāyānaśraddhotpādaśāstra.* It is adopted by the Yogācāra Vijñānavāda also. All these doctrines are found in *Laṅkāvatārasūtra* with an emphasis on the reality of the Transcendental Mind (cittamātra). It does not teach subjectivism or solipsism. We have adopted Suzuki's interpretation of the idealism taught by it.

5. *The Yogācāra Vijñānavāda.*

The Vaibhāṣika advocates direct realism. He recognizes the reality of external objects which are directly perceived. The Sautrāntika advocates indirect realism. He recognizes the reality of external objects, which are inferred from their cognitions produced by them. External objects produce their cognitions and imprint their forms on their cognitions. There is likeness (sārūpya) between the forms of cognitions (jñānākāra) and the forms of objects (viṣayākāra). The cognitions are directly perceived. The external objects are inferred from them as their causes. This doctrine is representationism. It paves the way for subjective idealism which reduces external objects to ideas (vijñāna). The Yogācāra denies the reality of external objects and reduces them to subjective cognitions. He advocates Vijñānavāda. Asaṅga (450 A.D.) wrote *Yogācārabhūmiśāstra,* an important work on it. The name *Yogācāra* may be derived from it. The Vijñānavādins used to practice yoga, and hence might be called Yogācāras. Maitreyanātha (400 A.D.) was the founder of the school. Asaṅga and his brother Vasubandhu (500 A.D.), Diṅnāga (600 A.D.), Dharmakīrti (700 A.D.), Śāntarakṣita (800 A.D.), and Kamalaśīla (800 A.D.) were important writers of the school.

The Yogācāras do not recognize the reality of external objects. They reduce them to cognitions (vijñāna). Therefore they are called Vijñānavādins. Their main arguments are summarized here. *Laṅkāvatārasūtra* regards external objects as unreal and false like dreams, day-dreams, illusions, and hallucinations. It regards them as transformations of the Ālayavijñāna, the cosmic mind, which is stirred up into the waves of mental modes. Object-cognitions are the modes of the cosmic mind. There are no objects apart from cognitions. When they are examined by the intellect, they are found to be indefinable (anabhilāpya) and essenceless (niḥsvabhāva). Object-cognitions (pravṛttivijñāna) arise from the Ālayavijñāna or receptacle consciousness.[1]

Vasubandhu recognizes the reality of consciousness (vijñapti) only, which manifests non-existent objects like the illusory hair and double moon. Citta, manas, vijñāna, and vijñapti are synonyms. Objects are self-creations of thought. The self-evolving thought, or cosmic mind (Ālayavijñāna) transforms itself, on the one hand, into different subjects, and into different objects, on the other. All dharmas, subjective and objective, are fruitions (vipāka) of the seeds or dispositions (vāsanā) conserved in the Ālayavijñāna. One pure consciousness (vijñaptimātra) is the ground of the all-conserving mind. There are no external objects. They are transformations of the Ālayavijñāna into the form of knowable objects.[2]

Dharmakīrti reduces the so-called external material objects to sense-data which are nothing but sensations or cognitions (vijñāna). When we perceive an object, we perceive only its colour, length, breadth, thickness, weight, smoothness and the like sensible qualities. We can never perceive or infer the material object apart from the sense-data. We never perceive it as an external object. We perceive only colours, sounds, tastes, smells, temperatures and pressures through the sense-organs. These sense-cognitions are elaborated by the mind (manas) which reflects upon them. Neither the mind nor the sense-organs perceive the external material objects. They are nothing but cognitions (vijñāna). When we examine them thoroughly, they disappear into nothingness; only their cognitions are left behind. Feelings of pleasure and pain are felt by the mind as subjective mental modes. It is quite evident. Even the so-called external objects are forms of cognitions. The apprehending cognition (grāhaka) and the apprehended object (grāhya), subject and object, are the forms of cognition which is one and self-identical. The distinction of subject and

[1] LS., pp. 22, 44, 46-47, 95-96, 116.
[2] *Viṁśikā, Triṁśikā; Sthiramati's Bhāṣya.*

object falls within cognition (vijñāna). The object is not outside cognition. Subject does not exist without object. Object does not exist without subject. They are inseparable from each other. They are forms or aspects of the same cognition. Cognition (vijñāna) is the only reality. It is in its essential nature formless. But it assumes the forms of subject (grāhaka) and object (grāhya), cognitional forms and object forms. Object-cognitions are due to the revival of the impressions (vāsanā) deposited in the mind. They are not excited by external objects. Vijñāna is the only reality. The inner and the outer are its forms. The distinction of subject and object is illusory. We stick to it for the practical purposes of our life. The distinction is not real. Dharmakīrti's arguments remind us of Berkeley's arguments.[1]

Śāntarakṣita and Kamalaśīla give the following arguments for the non-existence of external objects. (1) A cognition is self-aware (svasaṁvedana). Its essential nature consists in self-awareness. It reveals itself. It is self-revealing consciousness. It does not apprehend an external object. It is not apprehended by the permanent self, since it is non-existent. There is neither a permanent self nor an external object. There is only a series of self-aware cognitions (vijñāna). Cognitions manifest themselves as cognitions of blue, yellow, and the like, though there are no external objects. Vijñāna alone is the reality. (2) An object is said to be unconscious and material. A cognition is conscious and mental. There is no relation of identity or causation between them. A cognition is not identical with an object. It cannot generate an object. Nor can an object generate a cognition. Hence a cognition can never apprehend an external object. (3) "A formless (nirākāra) cognition cannot come into connection with an external object. So it cannot apprehend it. The cognition is devoid of the form of the object. Therefore it cannot apprehend its real nature, since it has no mode (prakāra) to represent it."[2] Illusory cognitions arise owing to avidyā, which reveal unreal forms, though there are no external objects corresponding to them. (4) The Sautrāntika holds that an external object imprints its form on the cognition

[1] *Pramāṇavārtika,* iii. 202, 209, 212, 213, 215, 217, 219, 253-55; *Darśanadigdarśana,* pp. 755-57.
[2] *Indian Realism,* pp. 17-18.

produced by it so that there is similarity between the form of the cognition and the form of the object. If there is complete similarity between them, the cognition is unconscious like its object. If there is partial similarity between them, the part of the cognition which is not similar to its object apprehends it. Therefore every cognition can apprehend every object. Further, a uniform cognition apprehends a multiform object. An unextended cognition apprehends an extended object. Therefore there is no correspondence between a cognition and its object. Even a cognition with a form cannot apprehend an external object. (5) A cognition with a different form (anyākāra) cannot apprehend an external object. If a cognition with one form apprehends an object with another form, then every cognition would apprehend every object, and a particular cognition would not be necessary to apprehend a particular object. Therefore a cognition can never apprehend an external object either with or without its form or with another form. So the cognition alone is the only reality. (6) The cognized object and the cognition are invariably apprehended together (sahopalambha). Therefore they are identical with each other. Śāntarakṣita says, "The cognition of blue is non-distinct from the cognition of the cognition of blue". Kamalaśīla says, "There is one and the same cognition of the cognized object (jñeya) and of the apprehending cognition (jñāna)." (7) There is no evidence for the existence of an external object. It cannot be preceived by a formless cognition or by a cognition with a form. A formless cognition cannot come into relation with an object. A cognition invested with the form of an object perceives its own form. It does not perceive the form of its object. So an external object cannot be perceived. Nor can it be inferred from the harmony between it and the cognition. Harmony means either the capacity for leading to the attainment of the object or the capacity for fruitful actions. The external object can never be attained because it is non-existent. Cognitions can lead to fruitful actions. Therefore an external object cannot be inferred. (8) Even if an external object exists, it must be perceived either as an aggregate of atoms or as a complex whole made of atoms or as a gross object not composed of atoms. The first alternative is not tenable. Atoms are imperceptible. Only gross objects are perceived. Atoms cannot produce the cognition of a gross object. The second alternative cannot be maintained. The external object cannot be a complex whole made of atoms. The relation between the whole and the parts cannot be explained. The third alternative also is untenable. The external object cannot be a gross object not composed of atoms. Its nature cannot be defined. So it does not exist. It is an unreal appearance. Cognition is the only reality.[1]

Mādhavācārya (1400 A.D.) gives the following arguments of the Yogācāras against the existence of external objects. Dharmakīrti says, "One who does not perceive cognitions cannot perceive their objects." But cognitions are aware of themselves (svasaṁvedana). They do not perceive external objects. (1) An external object does not exist. If it exists, it is either produced by an entity or not. If it is produced by an entity, it cannot have permanent existence. If it is not produced by an entity, it can have no existence, for to exist is to come into being. (2) An external object cannot produce a cognition by which it is apprehended. When the cogntion is produced, the object has ceased to be. Therefore it apprehends a past object. But we perceive a present object. Therefore a cognition cannot apprehend an external object; it apprehends itself. If a past object can be apprehended by a cognition produced by it, then the sense-organs also would be apprehended by a cognition which is produced by them. But the sense-organs are imperceptible. (3) If an external object exists, it is either an atom or a whole (avayavin) composed of parts or atoms. It cannot be an atom, since it is imperceptible. Nor can it be an aggregate of atoms. If it is an aggregate of atoms, it is either different or non-different from the atoms. If it is different from the atoms, it cannot be said to be composed of atoms. If it is non-different from the atoms, they cannot produce the cognition of a gross body. Further, an atom cannot combine with other atoms either partially or entirely. It cannot combine partially because it is partless. It cannot combine entirely because total interpenetration of atoms cannot produce grossness in the aggregate of atoms. Therefore the external object does not exist. (4) An external

[1] *Ibid*, pp. 12-34; *Tattvasaṁgraha* and *Tattvasaṁgrahapañjikā*, Vol. I, pp. 559-75, 552-53.

object independent of a cognition does not exist ; so a cognition manifests itself. A cognition is self-aware. There is no cognized object apart from the cognition. There is no other cognition to apprehend it. There is no subject (grāhaka) or object (grāhya). A cognition apprehends itself. It is self-subsistent. (5) If an external object exists, a cognition can never enter into relationship with it, and therefore can never perceive it. Uniform relation between a cognition and its object can be explained by identity only. Causality cannot account for it. Therefore the cognized object is identical with the apprehending cognition. (6) The identity of the object with its cognition is inferred from the simultaneous perception of them. Whenever we perceive an object (*e.g.*, blue), we perceive also the cognition of the object (*e.g.*, the cognition of blue) at the same time. Therefore the object is identical with the cognition. The apparent difference between them is an illusion like the appearance of the double moon. A cognition, which is devoid of parts, appears to be divided into subject (grāhaka) and object (grāhya), though the apprehending cognition is identical with the apprehended object. The cognition reveals or apprehends itself. That which is apprehended by a cognition is not different from it. (7) Though the cognition is devoid of the distinction of subject and object, it appears to be polarized into the duality of the apprehending cognition (grāhaka) and the apprehended object (grāhya) owing to the dispositions of beginningless avidyā or ignorance (anādyupaplavavāsanā). The instinctive roots or impressions of the uninterrupted stream of beginningless illusion of difference are the cause of the illusory appearance of the distinction between a cognition and its object. (8) The distinction between real things and imaginary things falls within consciousness. Some cognitions which are capable of fruitful actions are treated as real things. Others which are not capable of fruitful actions are treated as unreal things. The difference between a real sweetmeat and an imaginary sweetmeat is a difference between an effctive cognition and an ineffective cognition. Pragmatic utility and inutility are the tests of reality and unreality. Therefore external objects are unreal. They are nothing but their cognitions.[1] All these

---

[1] SDS., ii. 34-41.

arguments tend to show that the Yogācāra Vijñānavāda was subjective idealism. Kumārila calls it nirālambanavāda because it recognizes the reality of self-subsistent cognitions without any basis (ālambana) in external objects. The Nyāya-Vaiśeṣika, the Mīmāṁsaka, the Sāṁkhya, the Yoga, the Vedāntists, and the Jaina criticize the Vijñānavāda as subjective idealism. Their criticisms have been elaborately discussed in *Indian Realism*. But the Vijñānavādins believed in Tathatā, Śūnyatā, or the Absolute, and the Ālayavijñāna. Belief in Tathatā or Suchness makes the doctrine absolutism. The Ālayavijñāna is not the individual mind. It is the cosmic mind, which is expressed in the individual mind also. Cognitions and objects are transformations of the cosmic Ālayavijñāna. Therefore Vijñānavāda is objective idealism. Vasuvandhu recognizes the reality of one eternal pure consciousness (vijñaptimātratā). The Ālayavijñāna is superimposed on it. Subjective cognitions and objective phenomena are its transformations. Vasubandhu's Vijñānavāda is absolute idealism. The nature of the Ālayavijñāna is indefinite. Various accounts of it are given. There were various phases of Vijñānavāda.

Maitreyanātha, the founder of Vijñānavāda, describes three degrees of knowledge: (1) illusory (parikalpita) knowledge; (2) dependent or empirical (paratantra) knowledge; and (3) absolute (pariniṣpanna) knowledge. Illusory (parikalpita) knowledge consists in false ascription of an idea of imagination to an object produced by its cause and conditions. For instance, a rope is mistaken for a snake; the imaginary idea of snake is wrongly attributed to a rope which is produced by its cause and conditions, though it is ultimately an idea. An illusion is the apprehension of a subjective idea (ātmakhyāti). Empirical (paratantra) knowledge is knowledge of objects produced by their causes and conditions. Empirical objects, which are not self-existent, but dependent on other objects, are apprehended by empirical or relative knowledge. The knowledge of a rope as a rope is relative. It serves the practical purposes of our life. It is ordinary (laukika) and pragmatic knowledge. Absolute (pariniṣpanna) knowledge is knowledge of one, nondual, ontological reality. Suchness (Tathatā) is the absolute reality. It is grasped by non-discriminative knowledge. When the rope is known in its ultimate nature as Suchness, its knowledge is absolute. Absolute knowledge is supra-intellectual intuition. It is non-discriminative (avikalpa). There is no distinction of subject and object in it. It is non-dual and distinctionless. Empirical knowledge is relative, conventional, practical, intellectual and discriminative. It apprehends empirical objects or phenomena produced by other phenomena. There is distinction of the cognizer (grāhaka) and the cognized (grāhya) in paratantra knowledge, though the distinction is unreal and imaginary. Illusory (parikalpita) knowledge is imaginary and useless. It apprehends illusory objects. Empirical (paratantra) knowledge apprehends phenomena. Absolute (parinişpanna) knowledge apprehends Tathatā.[1] The relative truth (saṁvṛti-satya) of the Mādhyamika comprises the parikalpita knowledge and the paratantra knowledge of the Yogācāra. The absolute truth (paramārtha-satya) of the Mādhyamika corresponds to the parinişpanna knowledge of the Yogācāra. It is enlightenment (prajñā).

Asaṅga, a disciple of Maitreyanātha, distinguishes three grades of reality. (1) There is the parikalpitasattā, imaginary reality in which a name or an idea of an object caused by an illusion is attributed by imagination. (2) There is the paratantrasattā, relative, contingent, or dependent reality, in which the three characteristics of the cognizer (grāhaka) and the cognized (grāhya) are based on the law of relativity. The cognized objects are of three kinds, an apparent word, an apparent object, and an apparent body. The cognizers are of three kinds, mind, sense-cognitions, and conceptual constructions (vikalpa). The relative reality is characterized by a distinction between the cognizer and the cognized in their various forms. (3) There is the parinişpannasattā, absolute reality, which is beyond empirical existence, non-existence, and both, which is the same in all positive and negative beings, and which is beyond saṁsāra and nirvāṇa. It is entirely free from empirical categories. It is the ontological reality. It is Tathatā. It is neither existent nor non-existent, neither such (tathā) nor non-such (atathā), neither generated nor destroyed, neither liable to increase nor liable to decrease, neither purified nor defiled. It is the absolute reality (paramārtha).[2]

---

[1] *Madhyāntavibhāga*, p. 19.
[2] *Mahāyānasutrālaṅkāra*, xi. 39-41; vi. i; SBT., p. 230.

Tathatā is the eternal reality. It exists in the past, the present, and the future. It is not born. It is not subject to modification. It is unchangeable, immutable, and eternal. It is the supreme reality (bhūtakoṭi), the essence of all beings. It is uncaused, unconditioned, necessary, and absolute. It is the essence of the whole universe (dharmadhātu). It is the noumenon. It is inseparable from the empirical world of phenomena which are its manifestations. Phenomena cannot exist apart from their noumenon or Suchness. It is grasped by absolute knowledge which is supernormal (lokottara)[1] The Vijñānavādin believes in the existence of the absolute reality, Tathatā, like the author of *Laṅkāvatārasūtra*. He advocates absolutistic monism.

Tathatā is the eternal noumenon. "It is the transcendental essence of all things in the universe. It is termed 'Suchness' because its essential nature is real and eternal. But its real nature is indefinable." Vasubandhu describes the nature of Tathatā in this manner. Dharmapāla says that Suchness is a provisional name, that it is said to have a positive nature (bhāva) because it may be mistaken for nothingness, and that it may be called Śūnyatā or emptiness. But it is called 'reality', since it is neither illusory nor subjective.[2] It is non-dual, one. It is beyond existence and non-existence, suchness and non-suchness, birth and death, decrease and increase, purity and impurity. The Bodhisattva knows the emptiness of the illusory reality (abhāvaśūnyatā), the emptiness of the empirical reality of phenomena (tathābhāvaśūnyatā), and the emptiness of the absolute reality (prakṛtiśūnyatā). He knows the nature of emptiness.[3] Thus Tathatā is absolutely essenceless and indefinable. The Yogācāra believes in the doctrines of Tathatā and Śūnyatā. *Laṅkāvatārasūtra* also believes in both. Śūnyatā is not nothingness but essencelessness.

Asaṅga and Vasubandhu (500 A.D.) regard the absolute reality as one pure consciousness (vijñaptimātratā), which is pure and eternal. Nirvāṇa consists in entering into this eternal, blissful consciousness. Thus the ultimate reality, which is one, self-identical, eternal, pure consciousness, and pure bliss, is

---

[1] *Madhyāntavibhāga*, p. 41; SBT., p. 246.
[2] SBT., pp. 229-30.
[3] *Mahāyānasūtrālaṅkāra*, xiv. 34.

different from the Tathatā of Aśvaghoṣa, and very similar to the Brahman of the Upaniṣads.[1] It is foundational consciousness. It is the ground of the Ālayavijñāna which evolves the individual subjects and the objective universe. It is the foundation of the cosmic consciousness and the individual consciousness.

According to Vasubandhu all appearances, subjective and objective, are transformations of the eternal principle of pure consciousness (vijñaptimātratā). The external objects are self-creations or transformations of the pure consciousness in its manifestation as the Ālayavijñāna under the influence of the dispositions (vāsanā) of past experiences. They are false imaginative constructions like dreams. Perceptions are like dream-cognitions. Both are generated by dispositions (vāsanā) of past experiences. Perception and memory are equally self-creations of knowledge. Perceptual cognition is one form of self-creation of knowledge in which objects are experienced as presented to us. Memory is another form of self-creation of knowledge, which depends on perceptual cognition. Both are evolved from within the mind ; both are mental creations ; both are self-evolutions of thought. Perceptual cognitions are not produced in the mind by external objects. The external world is self-creation of thought. The individual centres of consciousness can communicate with one another through their own specific experiences without any common medium of the objective world. There is a real transformation of the self-evolving thought into the individual subjects, on the one hand, and the objective world of perceived objects, on the other. The individual subjects seem to perceive an objective world external to them, though there is no distinction between the subjective and the objective, both being equally self-evolutions of thought. Vasubandhu regards subjects and objects as real transformations of the self-evolving thought, while Aśvaghoṣa regards them as illusory transformations of Tathatā through ignorance. The knowable objects, according to Vasubandhu, are not material, but real transformations of knowledge. The ground of transformation, the vijñāna or consciousness, exists. There are no external objects, but there are only the transformations of consciousness in the form of knowable objects.[2]

[1] Das Gupta : *Indian Idealism,* pp. 120, 123.
[2] *Triṁśikā, Indian Idealism,* pp. 110-12.

The eternal and unchangeable, pure consciousness, the vijñaptimātra, is beyond all experiences. It is transcendent and non-empirical. It is the ground of the Ālayavijñāna, the evolving cosmic consciousness, which is transformed into the individual subjective centres and the external objective world. The nature of the pure transcendent consciousness is indeterminable and unthinkable. Even the Ālayavijñāna with its transformations is an imposition on it. The subjective centres and the objective appearances are merged in this pure consciousness in the state of nirvāṇa. The subjective and objective appearances have their foundation in the pure consciousness. It is their ground and essence. They are unreal apart from it.[1]

The pure consciousness (vijñaptimātra) is one, homogeneous, and undifferenced. It cannot account for the variety of subjective centres and external world. So the Vijñānavādin makes the hypothesis of the Ālayavijñāna. Sthiramati says that it is called Ālaya because it contains the seeds or potentialities of all dharmas which produce defilements, or because all dharmas of the world are the effects of the seed-potentialities preserved in it, or because it exists in all dharmas in the form of a cause. All dharmas or subjective and objective phenomena exist in a potential state in the Ālayavijñāna ; it exists in them as their cause. It is the cause of the world which is its effect. The Ālayavijñāna and the world are intimately related to each other as cause and effect.[2] Vasubandhu compares the modes of the Ālayavijñāna to the tide of the ocean which creates the mental properties of contact, feeling, and the like under the influence of the dispositions (vāsanā) of good and bad karmas. It is the repository of the dispositions (vāsanā) or seeds (bīja) of the past experiences of all individuals. It is the constantly changing stream of consciousness. All individual subjects and all objective phenomena spring out of it and merge into it. It is the universal cosmic consciousness. It exists in each individual stream of consciousness as the subconscious mind. The world is the expression of the Ālayavijñāna or cosmic consciousness.[3]

According to Vasubandhu the present experiences create

[1] *Indian Idealism*, pp. 119-20.
[2] *Triṁśikābhāṣya*, p. 18; *Abhidharmasūtra, Madhyāntavibhāga*, p. 28.
[3] *Triṁśikā Kārikā*, 4, pp. 21-22; *Vijñaptimātratāsiddhi*, pp. 19-21.

impressions or seed-potentialities (bīja) in the Ālayavijñāna, and the impressions already deposited in it manifest themselves as present experiences of the seven kinds of cognitions (vijñāna). The present experiences again deposit their impressions in the Ālayavijñāna. It is the repository of the innate and acquired impressions. The objective world is its creation. The Ālaya-vijñāna is called the first transformation of consciousness. The Manovijñāna is called the second transformation of consciousness. The six vijñānas are called the third transformation of consciousness.[1]

Citta, according to Asaṅga, is the ultimate source of all things. It has two aspects, phenomenal (lakṣaṇa) and noumenal (bhāva). The former is changeable, whereas the latter is unchangeable. Again, citta has twofold reflection. It is endued with attachment and the like which are the one set of reflections. It is endued with faith and the like which are the other set of reflections. The moral and immoral dharmas do not exist apart from it. Their impressions are preserved in the Ālayavijñāna. They are the fruitions (vipāka) of the impressions deposited in it. They are its manifestations. The Ālayavijñāna is the repository of the seeds full of defilement (sāsravabīja) and of the seeds free from defilement (anāsravabīja). The former comprise the seeds of suffering and the cause of suffering. The latter comprise the seeds of the path to the extinction of suffering and the extinction of suffering. The Ālayavijñāna contains the seeds of defilement and enlightenment. Saṁsāra and nirvāṇa are due to the defiled and undefiled seeds deposited in the Ālayavijñāna. All pravṛttidharmas which move the individuals in the world of saṁsāra spring from it. All nivṛttidharmas which lead them to enlightenment spring from it. The former spring from the seeds full of defilement. The latter spring from the seeds free from defilement. The Ālayavijñāna is the active principle which makes the six kinds of cognitions (vijñāna) move according to the law of karma.[2]

The Ālayavijñāna is the constantly changing stream of consciousness. It is the cosmic consciousness which is transformed into the visual cognitions, the auditory cognitions, the gustatory

[1] *Vijñānamātraśāstra;* SBT., pp. 215, 219.

[2] *Mahāyānasūtrālaṅkāraśāstra,* xi, 34; *Vijñānamātraśāstra;* SBT., pp. 211-13.

cognitions, the olfactory cognitions, the tactual cognitions, and the mental cognitions, on the one hand, and the sense-data of colours, sounds, tastes, smells, and temperatures, and thoughts, on the other. Attention, sense-contact, feeling, determinate perception, and volition are its mental properties.[1] All phenomena, subjective and objective, mental and physical, are transformations of vijñāna. They spring from the cosmic consciousness (Ālayavijñāna) like its waves. The individual cognitions (pravṛttivijñāna) and the world of sense-data are its transformations.[2]

The pure consciousness (vijñaptimātra) is eternal and unmodifiable. "It is from the interfunctioning of avidyā or ignorance that there arises the cosmic consciousness of Ālayavijñāna, which contains within it the seed-potentialities of all notions representing subjective centres, objects and their cognitions. On the ground of the Ālayavijñāna cognitional forms are synthesized with particular subjective centres and their works in a spatio-temporal order, and in this sense the Ālayavijñāna may be regarded as the universal repository of all subjects and their experiences. The Ālayavijñāna is only a hypothetical state which may be regarded as much an imposition on the pure consciousness and as false as are the ordinary experiences."[3] Dr. Das Gupta opines that the Ālayavijñāna is the cosmic consciousness which is transformed into the individual subjects and their experiences, on the one hand, and into the spatio-temporal order, on the other. But he thinks it to be a false imposition on the pure consciousness. It is a hypothetical state. The Ālayavijñāna is the cosmic collective consciousness which contains the seed-potentialities of all subjective and objective phenomena or dharmas. Its relation to the pure consciousness (vijñaptimātra) is unintelligible. The pure consciousness is eternal and unchangeable. How it can be transformed into the active cosmic consciousness or Ālayavijñāna is inexplicable. It may be a false superimposition on the pure consciousness due to ignorance (avidyā). But if it is a mere superimposition, the individual subjects and their experiences and the spatio-temporal world cannot be regarded as its real trans-

[1] *Vijñaptimātratāsiddhi*, pp. 19-21.
[2] *Yogācārabhūmi; Darśanadigdarśana*, p. 718.
[3] *Indian Idealism*, pp. 120-21.

formations. The Ālayavijñāna is not the Ātman of the Upaniṣads. The Ātman is unchangeable and immutable. But the Ālayavijñāna is the growing, developing, and mutable cosmic, consciousness. The pure consciousness (vijñaptimātra) corresponds to the Ātman. It is one, eternal, and immutable. It does not contain the seed-potentialities of the past experiences. But the Ālayavijñāna is their receptacle. It is the intermediate principle which relates Tathatā with the empirical world in *Mahāyānaśraddhotpādaśāstra* and *Laṅkāvatārasūtra*. It is the intermediate principle that relates the pure consciousness (vijñaptimātra) with the empirical egos and the empirical world according to Asaṅga and Vasubandhu. There are slight variations in the different works as to its nature. Suzuki regards the Ālayavijñāna of *Laṅkāvatārasūtra* as the super-individual mind. Das Gupta regards the Ālayavijñāna of Asaṅga and Vasubandhu as the cosmic consciousness. Keith also regards it as the cosmic consciousness. Ananda Coomarswami also regards it as the cosmic mind. "There does exist", he writes, "a cosmic, not impersonal, Mind, called Ālayavijñāna, the All-containing, or ever-enduring, Mind. All things in the universe rest in, or rather consist of this substrate. It is sometimes confused with Suchness, but actually it corresponds rather to the saguṇa (qualified) than the nirguṇa (unqualified) Brahman of the Brāhmans. According to the Yogācāras, it is in this Cosmic Mind that the germs of all things exist in their ideality. In other words, the objective world consists entirely of mind-stuff, and it is the illusion born of ignorance that projects the real ideas into an external and phenomenal universe."[1] Thus the Yogācāra Vijñānavāda appears to be objective idealism.

The Ālayavijñāna, the receptacle consciousness, is the foundation both of the external and the internal world ; it is the essence of the inanimate world ; it is the life that grows in the organic world. It attains sensation and perception in animals. It attains retention, association, discrimination, and thought in the higher animals and men. It is the energy that produces matter, life, and mind. This is the cosmic evolution of the Ālayavijñāna.

"The receptacle consciousness gives rise to the corres-

---

[1] BGB., p. 252.

ponding receptacle consciousness of the individual, as well as to the sense-organs and sense-objects. Then develops—from the influence of past impressions—the defiled mind (kliṣṭa-manas) which distinguishes subject and object; fecundated by the receptacle consciousness, it becomes aware of a world as external, and confers on it mental determinations of form and shape. Then develops mind or normal consciousness (manovijñāna), which discriminates the various phenomena, and it, fecundated by the receptacle consciousness, develops the conception of like and dislike. Then come the five forms of consciousness corresponding to the sense-organs, visual, aural, nasal, taste, and touch consciousness, which fecundated by the receptacle consciousness, give the presentation of the world of experience. The interaction of the whole body of these factors is necessary for the knowledge of the world; without, for instance, sight consciousness there could be no vision of colour; without the infected mind one could not discriminate form or size, and without the receptacle consciousness neither the individual nor the world would exist. Mind is the cause proper (hetu), infected mind and the receptacle consciousness the conditions (pratyaya), and the experienced world the fruit. The ordinary mind sees in the infected mind the final reality; Bodhisattvas recognize beneath it the receptacle consciousness as its prius."[1]

Four kinds of nirvāṇa are distinguished. (1) Nirvāṇa is equivalent to the Dharmakāya, the body of the Law, the pure essence of the universe. Every individual, in his inner essence, is one with the Dharmakāya. He possesses nirvāṇa in his essential nature. (2) Upādhiśeṣanirvāṇa, or nirvāṇa with residue of vital basis is enlightenment achieved by an individual, who still continues to work out his accumulated karmas. (3) Anupādhiśeṣanirvāṇa, or nirvāṇa without residue of vital basis is complete liberation of death. (4) Nirvāṇa without basis (apratiṣṭhita) is absolute enlightenment which generates determination to bring enlightenment and supreme bliss to all creatures. It is superior to the enlightenment of the Śrāvakas and the solitary Buddhas.[2]

---

[1] BP., pp. 256-57.
[2] *Vijñānamātraśāstra;* BP., pp. 257-58.

6. *The Śūnyavāda of Prajñāpāramitāsūtra*

Pañcaviṁśatisāhasrikā Prajñāpāramitā emphasizes the essencelessness and emptiness (sūnyatā) of all phenomena and ends in negativism. It mentions twenty kinds of Śūnyatā. (1) Adhyātmaśūnyatā : The visual, auditory, olfactory, gustatory, tactual, and mental cognitions are devoid of an eternal soul ; they are soulless phenomena without any noumenal substrate. (2) Bahirdhāśūnyatā : The sensible qualities of colour, sound, odour, taste, and touch are phenomena devoid of noumenal essences ; they are devoid of permanent entities. (3) Adhyātma-bahirdhāśūnyatā : The eyes, the ears, the nose, the tongue, the skin, and the manas are devoid of colour, sound, odour, taste, and touch. The sensible qualities of colour, sound, odour, taste, and touch are devoid of eyes, ears, nose, tongue, body, and manas. They are devoid of permanent noumenal substrates. They are essenceless. (4) Śūnyatāśūnyatā : All dharmas are essenceless ; even essencelessness is essenceless. Śūnya is not an ontological reality which can be achieved. It also is essenceless. (5) Mahāśūnyatā : Directions are relative to one another ; the eastern direction is relative to the western direction ; the northern direction is relative to the southern direction ; the upward direction is relative to the downward direction. They are not really eastern, western, northern, southern, upward, and downward. They are essenceless and imaginary. This is called Mahāśūnyatā. (6) Paramārthaśūnyatā : Paramārtha is nirvāṇa which is the negation of phenomena. Nirvāṇa is essenceless. It has no noumenon. (7) Saṁskṛta-śūnyatā : Compound things generated by desires (kāmadhātu), material elements (rūpadhātu), and immaterial formless elements (arūpadhātu) are essenceless phenomena devoid of noumena. (8) Asaṁskṛtaśūnyatā : Non-composite things are devoid of origin, continuance, and destruction. But non-production, non-continuance, and non-destruction are mere conceptual constructions. They are relative to each other. Composite and non-composite beings are relative to each other. Both are essenceless, unsubstantial phenomena devoid of noumena. (9) Atyanta-śūnyatā : That whose end is not perceived is atyanta ; it is essenceless. Eternal is one end. Destruction is the other end. There is nothing between them which can distinguish the eternal from the transitory, which are essenceless. (10) Anavarāgraśūnyatā: The beginning, the middle, and the end are relative to one another and therefore essenceless. They are mere phenomena devoid of intrinsic essences: The beginning is devoid of beginning. The middle is without the middle. The end is endless. (11) Anavakāraśūnyatā: Anavakāra is anupādhiśeṣa nirvāṇa which can never be removed. Removal is an act which is relative to the act of non-removal. Non-removal is relative to removal. It is essenceless. It is a mere phenomenon without a noumenal essence. (12) Prakṛtiśūnyatā: The natures of all produced or unproduced things can neither be produced nor destroyed by Śrāvakas, Pratyekabuddhas and Tathāgatas. They can neither be changed nor kept unchanged. They are essenceless phenomena. (13) Sarvadharmaśūnyatā: All dharmas, produced and non-produced, are relative to one another, and therefore essenceless. All the five skandhas, the sense-organs, the āyatanas, the vijñānas, the contacts, and the feelings are produced (saṁskṛta-dharma). They are mere phenomena devoid of noumenal essences. (14) Svalakṣaṇaśūnyatā: All composite and non-composite things have their specific characters (svalakṣaṇa) or individualities by which they are recognized by us. Visibility is the specific character of colour. Apprehensibility is the specific character of feeling. Denotation is the specific character of a name. Impressibility is the specific character of a disposition. Manifestation is the specific character of a vijñāna. These specific characters are devoid of essences, since they are produced by their causes and conditions. They are mere phenomena without noumenal essences. (15) Anupalambhaśūnyatā: The past, the present, and the future are relative to one another; they cannot be conceived apart from one another. The future cannot be perceived in the past. The past cannot be perceived in the future. The past and the future cannot be perceived in the present. The present cannot be perceived in the past and the future. So the past, the present, and the future are mere essenceless phenomena. Time is a mere conceptual construction. (16) Abhāvasvabhāvaśūnyatā: Composite things are produced by the conjunction of certain other things. They have no intrinsic nature (svabhāva), since they are produced by the conjunction of their causes and conditions. Their natures depend upon their causes and conditions. Even conjunction is essenceless. So composite things are devoid of their intrinsic natures which are essenceless phenomena. (17) Bhāvaśūnyatā: The fivefold aggregate (pañcaskandha), which is said to be the soul, is essenceless. An aggregate is a collection of its constituents. It is not self-existent. It depends upon its constituents. So it is an essenceless phenomenon. (18) Abhāvaśūnyatā: Non-composite (asaṁskṛta) things, ākāśa (space), pratisaṁkhyā-nirodha, and apratisaṁkhyānirodha are mere negations of empirical objects. They are mere phenomena devoid of noumenal essences. (19) Svabhāvaśūnyatā: All objects are supposed to have their intrinsic natures (svabhāva) which are not produced but manifested by the supernormal insight of the enlightened persons. But they are mere essenceless phenomena, and cannot therefore be manifested. (20) Parabhāvaśūnyatā: Things have an ontological reality which is self-existent. It is called dharmatā. It is not affected by the birth and death of Tathāgatas. It is eternal. It cannot be produced by other things.[1] *Prajñāpāramitā* emphasizes the relativity and emptiness, essencelessness, or phenomenality of all objects of empirical knowledge, though it recognizes the ontological reality of the eternal Dharmatā behind all phenomena. *Laṅkāvatāra* emphasizes the transcendental reality, Dharmatā, Tathatā, or Tattva which can be realized in the inmost recess of consciousness by supra-intellectual intuition. *Prajñāpāramitā* gives a philosophy of relativism, negativism, and phenomenalism.

7. *The Mādhyamika Sūnyavāda*

The *Prajñāpāramitāsūtras* dogmatically asserted the emptiness (śūnyatā) of all phenomena without giving any reasons. the Mādhyamikas, Nāgārjuna (200 A.D.) and his followers, established the doctrine of Śūnya by employing dialectics. Nāgārjuna wrote *Mūlamādhyamikakārikā,* his own commentary on it named *Akutobhayā* preserved in Tivetan rendered into Chinese by Kumārajīva (405 A.D.), *Vigrahavyāvartanī, Suhṛllekha,* and some other works. Āryadeva (200 A.D.) wrote *Catuḥśataka, Cittaviśuddhiprakaraṇa,* and *Hastabālaprakaraṇa.* Buddhapālita (600 A.D.) wrote a commentary on

[1] *Pañcaviṁśatisāhasrikā Prajñāpāramitā,* edited by N. Dutt, C.O.S., 28, 1934, pp. 195-98.

Mādhyamikakārikā. Bhāvaviveka (600 A.D.) wrote *Mādhyamikakārikāvyākhyā, Madhyamahṛdayakārikā, Madhyamārthasaṁgraha,* and *Hastaratna.* Candrakīrti (700 A.D.) wrote *Prasannapadā,* a famous commentary on *Mādhyamikakārikā, Mādhyamikāvatāra,* and *Catuḥśatakaṭīkā.* Śāntideva (700 A.D.) wrote *Śikṣāsamuccaya* and *Bodhicaryāvatāra.* Nāgārjuna was not the originator of Śūnyavāda. The relation of *Mādhyamikakārikā* to *Prajñāpāramitā* cannot be determined.

All Buddhists, Hīnayāna and Mahāyāna, believe that the empirical world consists of impermanent phenomena governed by the law of cause and effect. The Vaibhāṣikas maintain the existence of eternal atoms which are manifested as impermanent phenomena. The Sautrāntikas maintain the existence of momentary atoms and elements and their aggregates. Both believe in the real existence of the world, and dispense with a personal Creator or God. But the Mahāyānists believe in the Absolute Reality or Śūnya which is eternal. The Yogācāras regard it as the basis of the Ālayavijñāna which creates all empirical minds and phenomenal objects. They regard the world as the self-creation of the cosmic mind, and consider external objects to be subjective ideas of the mind. The Mādhyamikas regard external objects and subjective cognitions to be equally essenceless (niḥsvabhāva) with the Śūnya as their eternal basis. The Yogācāras recognize the existence of Tathatā, and identify it with Śūnyatā. They stress the subjectivity of the external world. Therefore they are called Vijñānavādins. The Mādhyamikas regard subject and object, and all objects of thought as relative and conditional, and therefore essenceless. They posit the reality of the Śūnya which is the eternal and absolute reality. It is predicateless. It is not void or nothingness. The Mādhyamikas are relativists, phenomenalists, and absolutists. But sometimes they tend towards scepticism, and sometimes towards mysticism. Aśvaghoṣa's philosophy of Tathatā is, in all essential points, the same as the Mādhyamika Śūnyavāda, except its belief in the existence of the All-conserving Mind (Ālayavijñāna), as a stage in the evolution of Suchness (Tathatā) in which consciousness is awakened.[1]

---

[1] Stcherbatsky: *The Conception of Buddhist Nirvāṇa,* p. 32.

Nāgārjuna believes in three degrees of truth or knowledge. The Śūnya is the absolute truth (paramārtha satya). It corresponds to parinişpanna knowledge of the Vijñānavādin. It is beyond the phenomena. The relative world of phenomena is conventional or relative truth (saṃvṛti satya). Saṃvṛti is the veil of ignorance (avidyā). It veils the nature of the reality. It is that nature of a thing which is determined by its cause and conditions. It is the relative, contingent, and dependent nature of phenomena. Saṃvṛti satya corresponds to dependent knowledge (paratantrajñāna) of the Vijñānavādin. Saṃvrti is of two kinds, lokasaṃvṛti and alokasaṃvṛti. Lokasaṃvṛti is the relative truth of the external objects which are recognized by common people as empirical realities. Alokasaṃvṛti is the illusory truth of illusions of a yellow conch-shell, double moon, and the like, which are not shared by common people, but which are perceived by the perverted sense-organs of certain individuals. Lokasaṃvṛti is also called tathyasaṃvṛti. Alokasaṃvṛti is also called mithyāsaṁvṛti. The former is relative, conventional, or pragmatic truth. The latter is illusory truth. It corresponds to parikalpita knowledge of the Vijñānavādin. Absolute truth cannot be attained without relative truth, which is the indispensable step to it. Those who do not understand the distinction between the two kinds of truth cannot know the real depth of Buddha's teaching. The transcendental truth (paramārtha satya) cannot be taught without the aid of the conventional or relative truth (lokasaṃvṛti), and Nirvāṇa cannot be attained without attaining the transcendental truth. The Mādhyamika does not deny the relative truth of the empirical world of phenomena, which is admitted to be real by common people, but he denies its absolute truth. He affirms the absolute truth of the Śūnya or the Absolute which explains the world of phenomena. The Absolute is the truth of the phenomenal world.[1] The Mādhyamika philosophy is so called because it adopts the mean between extreme affirmation and extreme negation.[2] It adopts absolutism on the basis of relativism. The Śūnya is the Absolute. It is the essence of the relative world.

---

[1] MK., xxiv. 8-10; MKV., p. 492; BCAP., p. 352; BCA., p. 353.
[2] MK., xxii, p. 445.

Nāgārjuna was one of the greatest philosophers in ancient India. He was a great dialectician, like Bradley, and showed by his dialectics that all categories of thought were self-discrepant and therefore relative, essenceless or ultimately unreal. Subject and object, substance and quality, whole and part, cause and effect, time, space, relation, compounded and uncompounded dharmas, change, motion, rest, self-nature (svabhāva), other-nature (parabhāva), knowledge, self, God, saṁsāra, and Nirvāṇa are self-discrepant and therefore relative or ultimately unreal. Some of the important categories are discussed here.

Substance does not exist apart from qualities. Qualities do not exist apart from substance. Substance is a mere aggregate of qualities. Substance and qualities are correlative to each other. Colour, sound, taste, smell, heat and cold are mere sensations which depend upon the eyes, the ears, the tongue, the nose, and the skin. They are meaningless apart from the sense-organs. They are mere sense experiences. We do not know the real nature of a substance. Substance is a mere relation that harmonizes its qualities with one another. All relations are transient and unreal. Substance and quality are relative to each other, and therefore unreal. Substance is regarded as a mere collection of qualities from the conventional point of view. It is not an ontological reality.

Nothing has its own independent nature (svabhāva). Heat is not the essential nature of fire, for its heat is generated by its cause and conditions, and therefore produced and transient. The essential nature of a thing must be independent of other things. If a thing has no essential nature (svabhāva), it cannot have other-nature (parabhāva). In the absence of self-nature and other-nature, it is not a positive entity (bhāva). Nor is it a negative entity or non-entity (abhāva). Self-nature, other-nature, being, and non-being cannot be predicated of any thing.[1] The characteristics (lakṣaṇa) cannot exist apart from the characterized thing (lakṣya). The characterized thing cannot exist apart from the characteristics. They are relative to each other. Therefore they are not real.[2]

---

[1] MK., xv. 3-6; MKV., p. 265.
[2] MK., v. 4-5.

Causality is unintelligible. A thing cannot be produced by itself, by another, by both, or by neither. If a thing exists in itself, it cannot be produced by itself. If it is produced by another, then light would be produced by darkness. If it is neither produced by itself nor by another, it cannot be produced by both. If it is not produced by itself or by another, then any thing would come into being at any time. An effect is said to be produced by its causes, basic cause or support (ālambana-pratyaya), immediately preceding cause (samanantara-pratyaya), concomitant cause (sahakāri-pratyaya), and dominant cause (adhipati-pratyaya). But its essential nature (svabhāva) cannot exist in its causes. The cause and the effect can neither be like each other nor unlike each other. Neither the existent (sat) nor the non-existent (asat) can be produced. Neither of them can have a cause. The dharma that comes into being is neither existent nor non-existent, nor both. Neither the present, nor the past, nor the future can be produced. Sometimes the effect is said to be produced by a collocation of conditions (sāmagrī). If the effect exists in the totality of conditions, it should be perceived in it. But it is not perceived in it. If it does not exist in the totality of its cause and conditions, then it cannot be produced by it. It may be produced by other causes and conditions. If the cause (hetu) is destroyed without giving rise to the effect, then the effect produced after the destruction of its cause would be causeless. The effect cannot come into being along with the totality of its cause and conditions at the same time. Cause and effect cannot be simultaneous. The two horns of a cow springing together cannot be the cause of each other. If the effect comes into being before the totality of its cause and conditions, then it would be uncaused, and would not require any cause and conditions. If the effect comes into being after its cause is destroyed and transfers its influence to it, then the destroyed cause would again be born. The present effect cannot be related to the past cause. There can be no relation between the present and the past, the known and the unknown. The identity between the cause and the effect cannot be established; nor can difference between them be established. If the cause is identical with the effect, we cannot speak of them as cause and effect. If they are different from each other, then the cause would be the same as the non-cause. Again, if the cause produces the effect, does it produce it with its essential nature or without its essential nature? It cannot produce the effect with or without its essential nature. Therefore causality is inconceivable and self-contradictory. The relation of cause to effect is incomprehensible. Causality is relative and empirical. It is not an ontological reality. In the absence of production there are neither compounded (saṁskṛta) nor uncompounded (asaṁskṛta) dharmas.[1]

If there is no production, there can be no destruction. There is no death without birth. There is no destruction without production. Production and destruction cannot exist together because they are self-contradictory. There can be no change or modification. One thing cannot change into another. A young man cannot become old. Youth and old age, which are contradictory qualities, cannot co-exist in the same person at the same time. An old man is already old. He cannot be united with old age. If milk becomes modified into curd, then one thing leaves its nature and becomes another. But if one thing changes into aother, then any other thing may change into curd. When milk exists, there is no curd. No object has its essential nature (svabhāva). Everything is essenseless (niḥsvabhāva). Hence it is irrational to speak of change of the nature of one thing into another. Causality itself is unintelligible. It cannot account for change.[2]

There is neither destruction nor production, neither transitoriness nor eternality, neither unity nor plurality, neither coming nor going. Dependent origination is not real. The highest good is the cessation of all phenomena (prapañcopaśama). The whole world is devoid of origin and destruction. Production, existence, and destruction are only apparent or phenomenal.[3]

Pratītyasamutpāda means either production of the non-existent depending on causes (hetu) and conditions (pratyaya) or production of each and every destructible individual. Candrakīrti rejects both the meanings. The canon speaks of

---

[1] MK., i. 1, 3; iv. 6; vii. 20, 21; xx. 3, 4, 6, 8, 9, 12, 13, 19, 21; vii. 34; vii; *Ratnāvalī*, 46, 47, 50.

[2] MK., xxi. 1, 2, 3; xiii. 3, 4, 5, 6.

[3] MKV., pp. 3, 11; MK., vii. 34; xviii. 11.

the production of particular phenomena arising from other phenomena on which they depend. Visual cognition is produced by the contact of the eyes with a visible object. But there can be no contact between the eyes and the object. Visual cognition cannot be related to the eye and the object. Momentary dharmas cannot come together and produce other dharmas either before or after they come into existence or at the same time. Every individual person is a collection of mental and material dharmas. Every physical object is a collection of material dharmas. There is no existence apart from dharmas. There is no substratum (dharmin) in which dharmas subsist. Momentary dharmas alone are real. But they are not self-existent. They depend upon other dharmas. But dependent origination is merely phenomenal. It is a mere appearance due to ignorance. It is not a real law. There is, in reality, neither origination nor destruction. There can be no production of a thing by itself, by another, by both, or by neither. It is an unintelligible appearance. 'This happening, that happens'. This doctrine of pratītyasamutpāda really means that dharmas or phenomena come one after another, for they are essenceless. As they are essenceless (niḥsvabhāva), they are neither produced nor destroyed. They are void (śūnya) in the sense that they are devoid of independent reality (svabhāvaśūnya). Dependent origination is relativity of existence. Relativity is an appearance or phenomenon. Dependent origination is Śūnyatā or a designation (prajñapti). It is the middle path.[1]

The world is said to be a net-work of relations. But relations (saṁsarga) are unintelligible. Relation can exist between two distinct things. But they are not distinct from each other. A thing which is produced by another thing, cannot exist apart from it. A sprout cannot exist apart from a seed. The sprout is not therefore distinct from the seed. They are not distinct from each other. So they cannot be related to each other. No two things are ultimately distinct from each other. Therefore they cannot be related to each other. If, again, two things are distinct from each other, they cannot be related to each other. Two self-existent and unrelated things cannot

[1] MKV., xxvi, p. 542; *The Conception of Buddhist Nirvāṇa,* p. 43.

be related to each other. If the distinctness of A is independent of B, then the distinctness of B also is independent of A. A and B are independent of each other. If two things are identical with each other, they cannot be related to each other. Identity and relation cannot exist together. Therefore there are no relations and relata. Relations are unintelligible and phenomenal. They are not ultimately real.[1]

The whole and its parts are relative to each other. The whole cannot exist apart from the parts. The parts cannot exist apart from the whole. Neither is self-existent. They are dependent on each other. They exist in relation to each other. Their relatedness makes them mere appearances. They are not ontological realities. They are conditional and phenomenal.[2]

The genus (jāti) and the individual (vyakti) are relative to each other. The genus or generality cannot exist apart from the individuals. In fact, there is no generality at all. The so-called genus of cow (gotva) is nothing but mere negation of non-cow. The existence of a cow means its non-existence as a horse, a buffalo, and the like. Generality (sāmānya) is mere apoha or distinction of an individual from other things. Knowledge involves distinction. Distinction is a relation. There is no absolute knowledge. All knowledge is relational. Neither generic properties (sāmānya) nor specific properties (viśeṣa) of individuals can be known. They are mere phenomena. They are not ultimately real.

Motion (gati) is unintelligible. A moves from B to C. But A cannot exist in B and C at the same time. Motion means co-existence of the same thing in two positions. A is not passing the path which has already been passed. A is not passing the path which has yet to be passed. The path which has neither been passed nor is yet to be passed is incomprehensible. There is no third path except the path which has already been passed and the path which is yet to be passed. The path which has already been passed is over. The path which is yet to be passed is not yet. There is no present path which is being passed at present. Therefore motion is impossible. This reminds us of Zenos' argument against the

---

[1] MK., xvi. 3, 5-8.
[2] MKV., pp. 190, 213, 225.

existence of motion. If there is no motion, there can be no moving agent (gantṛ). If there is no act, there can be no agent of the act. If the moving thing is different from motion, then the moving thing can exist without motion, and motion can exist without a moving thing. The moving thing cannot be identical with motion, since there cannot be a moving thing without motion. They can neither be identical with, nor different from each other. In fact, motion, the moving thing, and the path traversed are unreal appearances. They are not ultimate realities.[1]

Rest (sthiti) is inconceivable. Does a moving thing (gantṛ) rest? Or does a non-moving thing (agantṛ) rest? A moving thing cannot rest, since motion and rest are contradictory to each other. The same thing cannot have motion and rest at the same time. A non-moving thing also cannot rest, since it is already at rest. There is no third thing which is neither moving nor non-moving, which may rest. Motion and rest are relative to each other, and therefore are not ultimate realities. They are mere appearances or phenomena.[2]

Time is unintelligible. The past, the present, and the future are relative to each other. They are not self-existent. They exist in relation to each other. The past is that nature of an object which was produced, and has been destroyed. The present is that nature of an object which has been produced but not destroyed. The future is that nature of an object which has not yet come into being. If the present and the future exist depending upon the past, then they would exist in the past, since a thing which depends upon another thing must exist at the time when it exists. If they do not exist in the past, they cannot depend upon the past. If they do not depend upon the past, they are non-existent like the horns of an ass. Just as the present and the future are non-existent apart from the past, so the past and the future are non-existent apart from the present, and the present and the past are non-existent apart from the future. The present, the past, and the future are unreal without relation to one another. They are relative and conditioned existence. Therefore they are mere appearances or phenomena. Time exists only in

[1] MK., ii. 1, 6, 7, 8, 14, 18-21, 25.
[2] MK., ii. 15.

relation to things (bhāva). It cannot exist apart from them. Things are unreal. Therefore time is unreal. It may be argued that time exists because quantities of time, *e.g.*, moments, hours, days and the like exist. If time had been non-existent, these durations would have been non-existent. This argument is wrong. There is no unchanging (kūṭastha) time distinct from moments, hours, and the like, which may be known through them. Time does not exist as a compounded element (saṃskṛtasvabhāva) or as an uncompounded element (asaṁskṛtasvabhāva). Therefore time is a mere name (saṁjñāmātra), a mere convention (vyavahāramātra), a mere phenomenal appearance (saṃvṛtimātra).[1]

Space (ākāśa) is said to be characterized by non-obstruction. It does not exist before its characteristic comes into existence. If it exists before its characteristic comes into existence, then it would be devoid of its characteristic. But space which is unobstructed cannot exist. There is no being devoid of its characteristic. If unobstructed space exists, it cannot take on its characteristic of non-obstruction. If space devoid of non-obstruction exists, then also it cannot be characterized by non-obstruction. Then unobstructedness of space cannot be established. Nor can its obstructedness be established. Space is devoid of colour, form, or visible matter. It is a mere negation (abhāvamātra). It is a mere name (nāmamātra). There can be no form (rūpa) without material elements. Nothing exists, which is not produced. Nothing is eternal (śāśvata). Eternal space is a mere imagination of unthinking people. It is a mere name (saṁjñāmātra), a mere convention (vyavahāramātra), a mere phenomenal appearance (saṁvṛtimātra). Spatial relations are relative and therefore phenomenal. They are not absolutely real.[2]

The Vātsiputrīyas and Sāṁmitīyas believe in the existence of the soul (pudgala) which is neither identical with, nor different from, the mental aggregates (skandha). It is not different from the aggregates, since it will then be the Ātman of the heretical schools. It is not identical with them, since it will then be split up into a multiplicity. It is an indefinable and inexpressible principle of individuality. The personalists

[1] MK., MKV., xix. 1-6, pp. 382-89.
[2] MKV., pp. 24, 129, 271, 389, 413, 505, 528.

(pudgalvādin) argue that if the self does not exist prior to the acts of seeing, hearing, and the like, who will see or hear? So the self exists prior to the acts of knowing as the agent.[1]

Nāgārjuna contends that if the self exists without the acts of seeing, hearing, and the like, then these acts of knowing also can exist without the self. The personalists may argue that the self does not exist prior to all the acts of seeing and the like, but it exists prior to each act. Nāgārjuna urges that if the self does not exist prior to all the acts of seeing, it cannot exist prior to each act of seeing. If it is the same self that sees, that hears, and that feels, then the self must exist prior to each act. If one self sees, another self hears, and another feels, then there are many selves in a person. The self does not exist in the elements by which the acts of seeing, hearing, and feeling are generated. The self does not exist prior to the acts of seeing, or together with them, or posterior to them. If the acts of seeing can take place before the self comes into being, there is no use of it at all. But there can be no acts without an agent.[2]

If the self is identical with the five aggregates (skandha), then it is subject to origin and destruction. If it is different from them, then it cannot be characterized by the five aggregates. The self and the aggregates are related to each other as subject (upādātṛ) and object (upādāna), and therefore cannot be identical with each other. Subject and object must be distinct from each other. If the self does not exist, the mental aggregates cannot be said to belong to it. The aggregates are due to egoism which is not absolutely real. Egoism is destroyed when the aggregates are known to be unreal. When egoism is destroyed, the aggregates are no longer generated. The consciousness (vijñāna) is not the self; the self is not endued with consciousness; there is no self in consciousness; there is no consciousness in the self. Body, perception, feeling, disposition, and consciousness cannot exist in the self; nor can the self exist in them. The aggregates are soulless. The self is soulless. They have no core of reality in them. Buddha has taught neither the existence nor the non-existence of the self or ego.[3]

---

[1] MK., ix. 2.
[2] MK., MKV., ix. 2, 4, 7-12.
[3] MK., MKV., xviii. 1-6.

The self is said to be actor (kartṛ). But the actor and the act (kriyā) are both unreal. The actor is one who acts. If the actor exists, it cannot act. The actor itself is the agent of activity. It cannot exist as devoid of activity. Then there is no need of its acting again. Therefore the act would be without an actor. The actor, the act, and the object of activity (karma) are relative to one another. Therefore they are not absolutely real. If acts do not exist, their results, merit and demerit, do not exist. If merit and demerit do not exist, their fruitions in heaven and liberation and the path to them do not exist. Thus the actor, the act, the object of action, merit, demerit, bondage and liberation, and the way to liberation are unreal.[1]

Karma is said to mature after some time and bear fruit (karmaphala). If karma persists till its fruition, it becomes permanent. If it is transient, it cannot produce its fruit after an interval of time. If karma produces its fruits by its inherent nature (svabhāva), it must then be permanent, since nature cannot be altered. If karma is permanent, it cannot be the result of activity. If it is not the result of activity, then there will be attainment of unacquired merit and demerit (akṛtābhyāgama), and there will be no distinction between the virtuous and the vicious. If karma, either produced or unproduced by its causes and conditions, does not exist, then the actor does not exist. If karma and the actor do not exist, then the fruit of action also does not exist. If the fruit of action does not exist, the enjoyer of the fruit (bhoktṛ) does not exist. Therefore karma and fruit of karma are as unreal as dream, mirage, and day-dream. They are not absolutely real.[2]

Knowledge is inexplicable. The eyes, the ears, the nose, the tongue, the skin, and the manas are the sense-organs. Colour, sound, smell, taste, touch, and thought are the objects of these sense-organs. They exist in relation to each other. Colour cannot exist apart from the eye ; the eye cannot exist apart from colour. Sound, smell, taste, touch, and thought cannot exist apart from the ears, the nose, the tongue, the skin, and the mind ; they also cannot exist apart from sound, smell, taste, touch, and thought. The sense-organs cannot

---

[1] MK., viii. 1-6.
[2] MK., xvii. 6, 22-24, 30, 33.

apprehend their objects. The eye cannot see itself, and therefore cannot see another object. It may be argued that the eye can see another object, though it cannot see itself, even as fire can burn another object, though it does not burn itself. This is a false analogy. The act of seeing is unreal like the act of burning. That which has already been seen (dṛṣṭa) is not being seen. That which has not yet been seen (adṛṣṭa) is not being seen. The object of seeing must be either what has already been seen or what has yet to be seen. The object already seen is non-existent now. The object not yet seen also is non-existent at present. Therefore the object of seeing is non-existent. In the absence of the object the act of seeing is non-existent. Knowledge is impossible. The knower and the known are non-existent. Knowledge depends upon the knower and the known. If the knower and the known are non-existent, knowledge also is non-existent. Knowledge is relative and phenomenal. It is not absolutely real.[1]

The Vaibhāṣikas regard nirvāṇa as an ultimate, unconditioned, uncompounded (asaṁskṛta dharma) reality because it possesses a character (dharma), a reality (vastu), an individuality (svalakṣaṇa), an existence of its own (svabhāva). It fits in with the definition of reality. The Sautrāntikas regard nirvāṇa as a negative reality. The Mādhyamikas define reality as not relative or dependent (anapekṣasvabhāva). Their conception of relativity (śūnyatā) covers all conditional and eternal elements. The absolute becomes meaningless and devoid of individual reality without the relative. The relative becomes meaningless without the absolute. The phenomenal is meaningless without the non-phenomenal. According to the principle of relativity the Hīnayāna nirvāṇa or absolute becomes just as relative as the other ultimates of this system. The Mādhyamika abandons the Hīnayāna conceptions of reality and causation, together with the ultimate reality of the senses and the sense-data, of the mind and mental properties, and of all the elements of matter, mind, and forces. The Vaibhāṣikas regard nirvāṇa as something real (dharma) in which consciousness and life are extinct for ever. The Sautrāntikas regard it as the cessation of the world-process including the cessation of consciousness.

---

[1] MK., MKV., iii. 1-7.

In both cases something real is assumed to exist before nirvāṇa and to disappear afterwards. This makes nirvāṇa not only relative, but a product of causes (saṁskṛta). According to the Mādhyamika there is no difference between nirvāṇa and saṁsāra. "The universe viewed as a whole is the Absolute, viewed as a process it is the Phenomenal."[1] Nāgārjuna says, "Having regard to causes and conditions constituting all phenomena, we call this world a phenomenal world. This same world, when causes and conditions are disregarded, *i.e.*, the world as a whole, *sub specie æternitatis*, is called the Absolute.[2]

Nirvāṇa is the realization of unreality and essencelessness of the whole world of becoming. Nāgārjuna says, "There is no production (utpāda), no destruction (uccheda), no annihilation (nirodha), no eternality (śāśvata), no unity (ekārtha), no plurality (nānārtha), no coming in (āgamana), no going out (nirgama). The highest good is the cessation of all phenomena." Nirvāṇa is neither lost nor acquired ; it is neither destroyed nor does it persist ; it is neither produced nor annihilated. It is neither positive nor negative. It is total extinction of all relation to positive and negative beings. If it is positive, it is a product subject to decay and death. If it is absolute negation of suffering and birth, then it is non-eternal. The negation of suffering and birth is impermanent. So nirvāṇa is impermanent. Birth and death both should be avoided. So nirvāṇa is neither positive nor negative. There is no difference between saṁsāra and nirvāṇa. All dharmas are essenceless. None of them is finite or infinite. None of them is eternal or non-eternal. All essenceless things are indefinable and pure in their nature. The highest good is the cessation of all phenomena and the extinction of all afflictions and knowledge. The impermanent aggregates are neither bound nor liberated.[3]

The Mādhyamika rejects plurality of external objects and internal cognitions because of their relativity, and posits the existence of the unique, indefinable (anirvacanīya) Essence of Being, the One-without-a-second. All the elements have relative and contingent reality. The Śūnya only has absolute reality. "The unique reality, although declared to be un-

---

[1] *The Conception of Buddhist Nirvāṇa*, p. 48.
[2] *Ibid*, pp. 45-48; MK., xxv. 9.
[3] MK., MKV., xxv. 3, 4, 5, 6, 10, 19, 22, 23, 24; xvi. 5, 8.

characterizable (anirvacanīya), has been variously described as the element of the elements (dharmadhātu), as their relativity (śūnyatā), as thisness (idaṃtā), as their relation to thisness (idaṃpratyayatā), as suchness (tathatā), as the suchness of existence (bhūtatathatā), as the matrix of the Lord (tathāgatagarbha), and lastly as the cosmic body of the Lord, as Buddha's Dharmakāya."[1] Buddha and nirvāṇa are identical with each other. Buddha is neither relational nor non-relational, nor both, nor neither. Such characteristics are conventional (prajñapti). They are imputed characters. The real eternal Buddha is cognized by mystic intuition.[2] Sometimes śūnya and aśūnya both are said to be unreal because they are relative to each other.[3]

Nāgārjuna's doctrine is the middle path (madhyamā pratipat) between existence and non-existence, between essencelessness (śūnya) and essence of being (aśūnya).[4] Śūnyatā is not produced by other causes (aparapratyaya) ; it is absolute calm (śānta) ; it is not expressed by empirical definitions and characteristics (prapañca) ; it is one (anānārtha) ; it is apprehended by supra-intellectual intuition (nirvikalpa).[5] All dharmas are essenceless. They are relative and contingent. They are in their essence inexpressible (anakṣara). They are manifested as calm and pure in the state of enlightenment.[6] The reality has been called Śūnya in order to refute all other views. But those who cling to the view of śūnyatā are incurable.[7] Nāgārjuna uses the word *Śūnyatā* in two senses, the relative and the Absolute. All dharmas are relative (śūnya). But they are grounded in the Absolute (śūnya). Relativism is not the absolute truth. The relative is the way to the Absolute, which cannot be attained without the help of the relative. Nirvāña cannot be attained without knowing the Absolute.[8] Though the relative has been branded as unreal like an illusion, a reverie, a dream, a magic show and the like, yet it has some reality. It has contingent reality which can serve the practical purposes of our life. It has empirical reality. It is unreal in

---

[1] *The Conception of Buddhist Nirvāṇa*, p. 47.
[2] *Ibid*, p. 44; MKV., xxii. 11, pp. 443-44.
[3] MK., xiii. 7.
[4] MKV., p. 445.
[5] MKV., p. 491.
[6] MKV., pp. 500, 539.
[7] MK., xiii. 8.
[8] MK., xxiv. 10.

relation to the Absolute (śūnya).[1] The Absolute is inexpressible (anakṣara). It can be described by imputed characters (samāropa) only.[2] All relative and contingent phenomena become extinct in the Absolute (śūnyatā).[3] It cannot be called śūnya or aśūnya, or both, or neither, but it is called sūnya in order to indicate its nature (prajñaptyartham). Śūnya is nirvāṇa. Nirvāṇa is the state of Dharma (dharmatā). It is devoid of birth and death. It is beyond the reach of thought and language. It is incomprehensible by the intellect. It is indefinable and inexpressible by words. All phenomena completely cease in it. All knowledge of phenomena ceases in it.[4] All phenomena are essenceless (ādiśānta). They have no independent reality. They depend upon other phenomena. They become extinct in the Absolute.[5] The Absolute is neither existent, nor non-existent, nor both, nor neither. It is beyond these four empirical categories.[6] It is transcendent and unconditioned. It is the absolute ground of the empirical world of phenomena. Nāgārjuna is not a mere relativist, a phenomenalist, or a sceptic. He is an Absolutist. He is a monist. He is a mystic and intuitionist. Intellect gives an empirical world of relativity and plurality. Intuition gives the noumenon or the Absolute One which is the ultimate truth of all phenomena which are lost in it (prapañcopaśama). Nāgārjuna is not a negativist or a nihilist. His position is similar to that of Bradley. Only he does not in any way characterize the Absolute. His Śūnya is similar to the nirguṇa Brahman of the Upaniṣads, which is beyond thought and language. Nāgārjuna influenced Gauḍapāda, Śaṁkara, and Śaṁkarite dialecticians.

The Vaibhāṣika advocates radical pluralism of the eternal atoms and their momentary manifestations governed by the law of dependent origination. The Sautrāntika advocates radical pluralism of momentary atoms and phenomena determined by dependent origination. The Yogācāra reduces them to subjective ideas of the Ālayavijñāna. The cosmic all-conserving

---

[1] MKV., pp. 41, 173, 177, 334, 347, 457, 528.
[2] MKV., p. 264.
[3] MK., xviii. 5.
[4] MK., xxii. 11; MKV., pp. 350, 351, 364.
[5] MK., vii. 16; xviii. 5.
[6] MK., i. 7; SDS., ii. 31.

Mind creates empirical minds and empirical objects under the influence of instinctive dispositions (vāsanā). The world is an ideal construction of the Ālayavijñāna which is grounded in Tathatā. The Yogācāra is not a subjective idealist. He is an objective idealist. The Mādhyamika denies the ontological reality of external objects and subjective cognitions because they are relative and contingent, and affirms the ontological reality of the Śūnya or Absolute. Nāgārjuna is an Absolutist. He is not a nihilist. But his Absolute is transcendent, and cannot be related to the relative and phenomenal. The One is the ground of the many which are not its expressions.

8. *The Doctrine of Momentariness*

The Sautrāntika developed the doctrine of impermanence into the ontological doctrine of momentariness. All schools of later Buddhism believed in the doctrine of momentariness. The Vaibhāṣikas believed in the reality of the eternal elements and their momentary manifestations. The Sautrāntikas rejected the eternal elements. The following arguments are advanced to prove the momentariness of all existence. Whatever is existent is momentary like a mass of clouds. Existence (sattva) consists in causal efficiency or production of effects (arthakriyākāritva). The cause produces its effect either simultaneously or successively. Only momentary causes can produce their effects either simultaneously or successively. Permanent entities are not capable of simultaneous or successive production of effects, since the alternatives cannot be proved. When a permanent entity produces its effect at the present time, has it capacity of producing its effect in the past and the future? If it has the capacity, it must produce past and future effects in the present moment, since what is capable of producing an effect at a particular time must produce it at that time. If it has not the capacity, it can never produce past and future effects, since what does not produce an effect at a particular time is not capable of producing it at that time. A piece of stone can never produce a sprout. A permanent entity does not produce past and future effects at the present moment. So it is not capable of producing them at present. Capacity of production and production of effects must go together. Causal efficiency cannot exist without production.

If a permanent entity is said to produce its effects in succession with the help of concomitant conditions (sahakāri kāraṇa), do the concomitant conditions render any aid to the permanent entity or not? If they do not, they are unnecessary, and can be dispensed with. If they do, is the aid (upakāra) different or non-different from the permanent entity? If the aid is different from it, then the adventitious aid should be regarded as the cause, and not the permanent entity, since wherever the adventitious aid is present the effect is present and wherever it is absent the effect is absent. If it is urged that a permanent entity by its very nature produces its effect only when the concomitant conditions co-operate with it, then it can never be separated from the concomitant conditions in order to produce its effect because it can never be divested of its nature. Further, does the supplementation (atiśaya) produced by the concomitant conditions produce another supplementation or not? If it produces another supplementation, it will require other concomitant conditions, and so on to infinity. It will lead to infinite regress. If the supplementation does not produce another supplementation, then the permanent entity in co-operation with the concomitant conditions acquires a supplementation (atiśaya) and produces an effect. If the permanent entity does not require the help of concomitant conditions, then the aid or supplementation will always be present, and will always produce the effect. But it is contradicted by experience. Then does the supplementation, though it depends on the permanent entity for the production of the effect, produce the effect independently of the permanent cause (*e.g.*, a seed) or as dependent on it? On the first alternative, the seed would not be the cause of a sprout. On the second alternative, there will be infinite regress. The supplementation will produce another supplementation in the permanent cause, and so on to infinity. If the aid or supplementation is non-different from the permanent cause, then the so-called permanent cause ceases to be permanent, since it was devoid of supplementation before and it now acquires supplementation. A permanent cause is incapable of causal efficiency.

A permanent entity cannot produce its effect simultaneously. If it produces its effect simultaneously or all at once, does it persist after production of its effect or not? If it persists in future, then it will continue to produce the effect which it has already produced. But the effect which has already been produced need not be produced again. If the permanent cause does not persist after production of its effect, then it cannot be said to be permanent. Those entities are different from each other, which are endued with contradictory attributes like heat and cold. The cloud perpetually changes its colour; so it is a series of momentary entities.

It cannot be argued that a permanent entity has capacity to produce its effect at one time, and has no capacity to produce it at another time, since what produces an effect at a particular time possesses the capacity to produce it at that time, and what is incapable of producing an effect at a particular time does not produce it at that time. A stone can never produce a sprout at any time. Thus a permanent entity cannot produce its effect simultaneously or in succession. Only momentary entities are capable of causal efficiency. All existence is momentary. Existence (sattva) consists in causal efficiency (arthakriyā). Causal efficiency exists in momentary entities only. Permanent entities are incapable of causal efficiency.[1]

We attribute identity to a continuous series of similar momentary things. Identity is an illusion produced by similarity and continuity of a series of momentary entities. There is no identity or permanence of an external thing. The flame of a lamp appears to be the same, though it changes from moment to moment. The stream of water appears to be the same, though it changes every moment. All objects of the world are undergoing destruction every moment. But they appear to persist owing to illusion.

The Sautrāntikas laid stress on the conception of the self as a series of momentary cognitions (vijñānasantāna). There is no permanent self behind the continuous series of mementary cognitions. The preceding cognition leaves an impression (vāsanā) which modifies the succeeding cognition. There is

[1] SDS., ii. 12-23.

transference of impression (vāsanāsaṁkrama) from one cognition to another, which accounts for memory. Memory does not require a permanent self which is the substratum of impressions, and which recollects an object perceived in the past. A future member of the same series of cognitions remembers a past momentary object perceived by a past member of the same series. Recognition is a collection of perception and recollection. It does not presuppose a permanent self; nor does it apprehend a permanent object such as '*this* is *that* Devadatta'. The stream of momentary cognitions can account for memory and recognition both. Thus neither the self nor an external object is permanent and identical. Both are series of momentary entities.

The Buddhist doctrine of momentariness is severely criticized by the Jaina, the Nyāya-Vaiśeṣika, the Mīmāṁsaka, and the Vedāntist. The Jaina criticism of momentariness is given here. First, if the self is not permanent, there can be no reaping of fruits, since one member of the series of momentary cognitions exerts, and another member of the series enjoys its fruit. But it is absurd that one acts and another reaps its fruit. We have a distinct recognition of personal identity in the form 'I acted in the past, and the same I enjoy the fruit of my action at present'. There is persistence of the permanent self in the past, the present, and the future. Recognition proves the permanence of the self. Secondly, the argument that whatever is existent is momentary like a cloud is invalid. Is the momentariness of the cloud proved by the same inference or by another inference? It cannot be proved by the same inference, since the momentariness of the cloud is not admitted by the Jaina, whereas the example must be admitted to be real by both disputants. It cannot be proved by another inference, since that inference will prove momentariness of all existence, and the first inference that seeks to prove momentariness of existence becomes fruitless. Thirdly, causal efficiency (arthakriyākāritva) cannot constitute existence (sattva), since an illusory object also can produce an effect, and would therefore be real. There is snake-bite of an illusory snake, which frightens and depresses a person. But the snake is not real. The Jaina holds that a substance is identical in the midst of originating, perishing, and persisting qualities.

Fourthly, it may be contended that the permanent substance possesses the contrary attributes of possessing causal efficiency and not possessing causal efficiency at the same time, and therefore consists of many momentary entities. The Jaina replies that an existent entity is multiform (anekānta), and may possess contrary attributes. Fifthly, in a series of momentary entities there can be no causal relation. When one member of the series is destroyed, it cannot transfer its causal energy to the succeeding member of the series. The succeeding cognition cannot be modified by the preceding cognition in the same series, since it is completely destroyed and cannot leave any impression behind to modify the succeeding cognition. If the self is nothing but a series of momentary cognitions (vijñānasantāna), then there would be loss of acquired merit (kṛtapraṇāśa) and acquisition of unearned merit or demerit (akṛtakarmabhoga), and there would be no transmigration and liberation, and there would be no recollection. Therefore the self is a permanent spiritual substance. Sixthly, the doctrine of momentariness cannot account for knowledge. The object (jñeya) does not exist at the time when cognition (jñāna) comes into existence. The cognition does not exist when the object comes into existence. If they do not exist at the same time, the cognition cannot apprehend an object. If there is no knowledge, all practical life will collapse. If the momentary object and the momentary cognition are simultaneous, they cannot be related to each other as cause and effect, like the two horns of a cow springing up simultaneously. The momentary object cannot produce the momentary cognition, and be apprehended by it. An unapprehended object cannot be the basic condition (ālambanapratyaya) of the cognition. It cannot be argued that a momentary object imprints its form on a succeeding momentary cognition, since a momentary cognition cannot assume the form of the preceding momentary object. Further, it is useless to hold that cognitions assume the forms of their objects. Formless cognitions can apprehend different objects by virtue of their fitness (yogyatā). This is the Jaina view. Perceptual cognition, devoid of the form of the object, apprehends the object. It does not reflect the form of the object like a mirror. If it reflects its form, then it would reflect its remoteness and nearness. But, in fact, it is in the self, and is not apprehended as remote and near. Further, if it reflects the form of its object, then it would be inert like its object. If it does not reflect the inertness of the object, it should not reflect also blueness and the like. Hence the Sautrāntika doctrine of momentariness is not valid.[1]

9. *The Buddhist Epistemology and Logic*

Dharmottara (900 A.D.) defines valid knowledge as the knowledge that is in harmony with its object.[2] A knowledge can be known to be in harmony with its object, if it leads the knower to the actual attainment of the object. The knowledge does not produce its object, and induces the knower to attain it. But it induces the knower to attain its object. It cannot make the person attain its object at once. It is not the immediate cause of the attainment of the object. Ṛight knowledge leads to recollection of an object perceived in the past. The recollection gives rise to desire. Desire gives rise to action. Action leads to attainment of the object (arthaprāpti). Attainment of the object apprehended by right knowledge is its result (pramāṇaphala). Does right knowledge of an object lead to the attainment of the same object? It leads to the attainment of an object-moment in the same series. Right knowledge also leads to the avoidance of an undesired object. Dharmottara gives pragmatic test of the truth, like the Naiyāyika. He advocates realistic pragmatism.[3]

There are two kinds of valid knowledge, perception and inference. Dharmakīrti (700 A.D.) defines perception as a non-erroneous presentation devoid of all determinations or conceptual constructions.[4] It is the immediate apprehension of an object in its uniqueness (svalakṣaṇa), unassociated with names and other determinations (kalpanā). Indeterminate perception alone is perception. It is valid, since it apprehends the uniqueness or individuality of an object devoid of all qualifications. But the so-called determinate perception is not perceptual in character, since it is a presentative-representative

---

[1] SDS., iii. 1-9.
[2] NVT., p. 5. [3] NVT., pp. 5-8.
[4] Kalpanāpoḍham abhrāntaṁ pratyakṣam. NV., p. 11.

process involving determinations. It is invalid because determinations (vikalpa) are not real forms of objects but ideal constructions of the mind superimposed upon indeterminate and unqualified objects. It is invalid because it apprehends an object associated with its name which does not enter into its constitution. Indeterminate perception is valid, but determinate perception is not valid. The former apprehends an object in its uniqueness, while the latter apprehends an object associated with conceptual constructions, such as genus, substance, quality, action, and name. These conceptual constructions invalidate determinate perception. In indeterminate perception there is similarity (sārūpya) between the form of the cognition and the form of its object. Perception is of four kinds, sense-perception (indriyajñāna), mental perception (monovijñāna), self-awareness (svasaṁvedana), and yogic intuition (yogipratyakṣa). Sense-perception is the immediate apprehension of an object through a sense-organ. Visual perception of a colour belongs to this kind. Mental perception is produced by sense-perception, which is its immediately preceding cause (samanantarapratyaya), and the objective datum, which comes into being in the second moment, and which is similar to the object of sense-perception. When the visual organ continues to function, there is sense-perception of colour. When it ceases to function, there is mental perception of colour. Manovijñāna is not mental perception (mānasapratyakṣa) of the Nyāya-Vaiśeṣika and the Mīmāṁsaka. All cognitions (citta) and feelings (caitta) are aware of themselves (svasaṁvidita). They are self-luminous. They apprehend themselves. They are not apprehended by the self which is nonexistent. Each cognition immediately apprehends itself rightly without any determinations. So this self-aware cognition is perception. Yogic intuition is direct and distinct perception of the real nature of objects brought about by the most intense meditation. It is not brought about by the sense-organs. It is indeterminate and in harmony with its object. These are the four kinds of perception. Sense-perception is brought about by the object, which is the basic condition (ālambanapratyaya), the immediately preceding cognition, which is the immediate antecedent (samanantarapratyaya), the auxiliary condition (*e.g.*, light in the case of visual perception), and the sense-organ, which is the dominant condition (adhipatipratyaya). This is the Sautrāntika theory of perception.[1]

Perception apprehends the unique individuality (svalakṣaṇa) of an object, which is the ontological reality. A real object is characterized by the capacity to produce fruitful activity (arthakriyāsāmarthya). That which is different from it is the generic character of an object (sāmānyalakṣaṇa). It is its common character. It is apprehended by inference. Inference is of two kinds, inference for one's own sake (svārtha) and inference for the sake of others (parārtha). The former is the knowledge of an inferable property (sādhya) from the knowledge of a mark of inference (liṅga) which abides in the minor term or the subject of inference (pakṣa), or in cases which are homologous (sapakṣa), or which does not abide in cases which are heterologous (vipakṣa). The middle term (liṅga) must have three characteristics. It must abide in the minor term. It must abide in homologous instances. It must not abide in heterologous instances. The homologous instance is one in which both the probans (hetu) and the probandum (sādhya) abide. The heterologous instance is one in which the probans and the probandum never reside. If the reason or probans possesses these three characteristics, it will invariably lead to the inference of the probandum. Only the following reasons (hetu) possess the three characteristics: (1) a reason which is identical in essence with the probandum (svabhāva); (2) a reason which is an effect (kārya) of the probandum; and (3) a reason which is not perceived (anupalabdhi) in negative instances. 'This is a tree because it is a Śiṁśapā tree'. This inference is based on uniformity of identity in essence (tādātmya), which is a uniformity of co-existence. 'There is fire here because there is smoke here.' This inference is based on uniformity of causation (tadutpatti), which is a uniformity of succession. Smoke is the effect of fire. The cause is inferred from its effect. The non-existence of fire here is inferred from the non-existence of smoke here. Non-perception of smoke proves its non-existence. The non-existence of a Śiṁśapa tree here is inferred from the non-perception of a tree here. The non-existence of smoke is inferred from the non-perception of fire here.[2] The probandum

[1] NV., NVT., pp. 17-21.
[2] NV., pp. 35, 38-41, 48-49.

is directly inferred from the probans which has inseparable connection with it (avinābhāva). Inference for the sake of others (parārthānumāna) resembles inference for one's own sake (svārthanumāna) in all essential characteristics, but it differs from it in the fact that it is formally stated in the form of a syllogism. "Inference for the sake of others is of two kinds: (1) positive or homogeneous (sādharmyavat); and negative or heterogeneous (vaidharmyavat) as follows: (1) Sound is non-eternal, because it is a product, all products are non-eternal as a pot (positive). (2) Sound is non-eternal, because it is a product, no non-eternal *i.e.,* eternal thing is a product as ether (negative)."[1] There are three members of a syllogism. The Buddhist rejects the five-membered syllogism of the Naiyāyika. The three members are the conclusion, the minor premise, and the universal major premise with an example. Inference is based on vyāpti or inseparable connection (avinābhāva) between the probans and the probandum. Inseparable connection between them is based upon causality or identity in essence. Dharmakīrti recognizes three fallacies of the middle term (hetvābhāsa): (1) unproved (asiddha); (2) uncertain (anaikāntika); and (3) contradictory (viruddha). (1) 'Sound is eternal, because it is visible'. This inference involves the fallacy of unproved middle, because visibility of sound is not admitted by either party. (2) 'Sound is non-eternal, because it is knowable'. This inference involves the fallacy of uncertain middle, because the knowable include the eternal as well as the non-eternal (3) 'Sound is eternal, because it is a product'. This inference involves the fallacy of contradictory middle, because 'product' is opposed to 'eternal'.[2]

[1] HIL., p. 312.
[2] HIL., pp. 310-13; *The Buddhist Doctrine of Flux,* ch. xvii, xix, xx-xxiv.

CHAPTER VI

THE BACK-GROUND OF THE VEDĀNTA

1. *The Philosophy of the Ṛg Veda: Polytheism, Henotheism, Monotheism, and Monism.*

The Vedas and the Upaniṣads form the back-ground of the Vedānta. They are called the Śruti. The Hindus implicitly believe in their authority. The orthodox systems of philosophy, the Nyāya, the Vaiśeṣika, the Mīmāṃsā, the Sāṁkhya, the Yoga, and the Vedānta employ reason in subordination to the authority of the Vedas. But the heterodox systems, the Cārvāka, the Buddhist, and the Jaina repudiate their authority. They are believed to be revelations of truths to the seers (ṛṣi). They embody their intuitions.

There are four Vedas, Ṛg Veda, Sāma Veda, Yajur Veda, and Atharva Veda. Each of them has three divisions, *viz.*, the Saṁhitās, the Brāhmaṇas, and the Āraṇyakas. The Saṁhitās are collections of sacred texts mostly in verse. The Brāhmaṇas are commentaries in prose. The Āraṇyakas are forest treatises. The Upaniṣads are mostly parts of the Āraṇyakas. The Saṁhitās and the Brāhmaṇas are called Karmakāṇḍa, the portion pertaining to rituals. The Āraṇyakas are called Upāsanākāṇḍa, the portion relating to meditation. The Upaniṣads are called Jñānakāṇḍa, the portion dealing with supreme knowledge. The Ṛg Veda, Sāma Veda, and Yajur Veda are said to be the triad (trayī), and considered to be the original Vedas. The Atharva Veda is a later addition. The Ṛg Veda is the most ancient record of the Indo-Aryan religious thought. The Sāma Veda contains the hymns of the Ṛg Veda to be chanted in sacrifices. The Yajur Veda contains large portions of the Ṛg Veda with slight variations. The Atharva Veda also contains many mantras of the Ṛg Veda. Tilak assigns the Vedic hymns to 4500 B.C., the Brāhmaṇas to 2500 B.C., and the early Upaniṣads to 1600 B.C. Maxmüller dates the Vedas 1200 B.C.; Haug puts them at 2400 B.C., and Jacobi assigns them to 4500 B.C. They may be assigned to about 1500 B.C.

The Vedic religion traverses the whole gamut of polytheism, organized polytheism, henotheism, monotheism, and monism. The Vedic poets were simple children of nature. They wondered at the grand and sublime, beautiful and useful aspects of nature, and were thrilled into ecstasy. They clothed the powers of nature with the glory of supernatural and superhuman spirits akin to mankind. They broke forth into songs in honour of the gods of fire (Agni), the sun (Sūrya), the dawn (Uṣas), the earth (Pṛthivī), the rain-cloud (Parjanya), the storms (Maruts), the winds (Vāyu, Vāta), the sky (Dyaus), the bright sky and day (Mitra), the dark sky and evening (Varuṇa), the morning sun (Savitṛ), and the like. The Vedic gods are the spirits presiding over diverse powers of nature. They are not distinct personalities like the gods of the Purāṇas. They are hypostatized or personified natural forces. They are endowed with great physical power, beauty, fierceness, intelligence, wisdom, omniscience, mercifulness, benevolence, justice, and righteousness. They are not confined to a particular place. They are pervasive entities. They are not natural objects or phenomena. They are supernatural and superhuman spirits governing the phenomena of nature, friendly and benevolent to the worshippers, and terrific and deadly to their haters. They are mighty, fierce, invincible, wise, merciful, omniscient, pervasive, righteous, truthful, and benevolent. They are easily propitiated by hymns, adoration, prayer, oblations, offerings, and sacrifices. They are givers of wealth, strength, happiness, sons and grandsons, victory in battles, and a life of a hundred years. They are also givers of wisdom and moral qualities. They are born of father and mother, and yet immortal. Mortals are elevated to the rank of immortals. There is kinship between mortals and immortals. The nature of gods will be clear from the description of a few gods.

The fire-god, Agni, is the domestic god. He is the Lord of the house. He is the youngest, resplendent, and beautiful god. He is mighty, great, invincible, and destructive. He is wise, righteous, omniscient, and benevolent. He is the mediator between men and gods. He is the messenger of gods. He carries the oblations to the gods. He brings them to the sacrifices. He is the steward of both worlds. He shines on heaven and earth. He has a twofold birth, celestial and terrestrial. He pervades all spaces of the atmosphere. "Thou, O Agni, the flaming one, art born from the Heavens, thou art born from the Waters and the flint ; thou art born from the forests and the herbs ; thou art born bright, O Lord of men, to men."[1] Agni is the divine leader of the divine tribes, the guardian of the seasons. He is infallible. His blessings are flawless. He is intent upon right (ṛta) and true. In him all commands, all wishes dwell. He adheres to his own power of mind. He knows all rules. He has proclaimed his rules to the mortals. He knows everything that leads us astray. He protects us from sin that defiles us. He is the friend and protector of his worshippers. They live in his companionship, protected by him. He is the self-dependent god. He promotes the worshipper's prayer. He releases men from all sins committed in thoughtlessness. He reigns over immortality.[2]

The Maruts are the storm-gods. They are endowed with terrible vigour and strength. They cause men and mountains to tremble. They drench the earth with rain. They wash away all sins of men. They are brisk, active, indefatigable, powerful, and impetuous. They throw down what is firm. They are all-knowing, true, flawless searchers and purgers of sins. Their bounties are never-ceasing. They raise the rain from the sea, and rain it down on earth. They are of great bounty, immortal, righteous, and merciful to the worshippers. Their greatness is infinite.[3]

Indra holds the earth, the sky, and the heaven. He unites the immeasurable earth and the sky. He is the father of the Maruts, the sun, the dawn, and the fire-god. He is the terrific destroyer of enemies in the battle-field. He is the killer of the demon Vṛtra. He is the Lord of the world. He is resplendent, ever-young, and infinitely great. He is a voracious drinker of soma juice. He is the possessor of infinite wealth. He is the giver of food, wealth, prosperity, victory, and long life. He entered into the earth and the sky, and created the world. He is the creator of the waters. He is bountiful, generous,

---

[1] R.V., ii. 1. 1.

[2] R.V., i. 59. 2; i. 141. 10; i. 188. 3; 1. 145. 1-5; i. 149, 4; i. 189. 1, 6; iii. 20. 4; iii. 25. 3; iv. 4. 10, 12, 14; iv. 6. 1; iv. 12. 3-4; v. 1. 7, 11; v. 4. 3; v. 8. 6-7; v. 21. 3; v. 28. 2, 5, 6.

[3] R.V., i. 37. 4, 12; i. 38. 6, 9; i. 64. 8, 10-12; i. 87. 4; i. 166. 7; v. 55. 5; v. 58. 8; v. 87. 5-6.

self-controlled, and immortal. He is great, grave, and fierce. He pervades the world. He is the protector of the worshippers.[1]

The different gods are the personifications of the different powers of nature. They are sometimes worshipped individually. This is not naturalism, but anthropomorphic polytheism. The Vedic poets were not worshippers of nature. They worshipped supernatural and superhuman deities pervading the whole or considerable part of nature and beyond and endowed with some qualities of the supreme god-head.

Sometimes the gods were invoked in groups. A number of dual gods such as Mitra and Varuṇa, Indra and Agni, Agni and Soma were invoked. Sometimes three gods working together such as Aryaman, Mitra and Varuṇa, or Agni, Soma and Gandharva were praised. Sometimes four deities such as Bhāratī, Ilā, Sarasvatī and Māhī were worshipped.[2] Sometimes many gods together were praised. 'May Mītra and Varuṇa, Aditi, the Sindhu, the Earth, and the Sky grant us happiness and long life.'[3] Sometimes all the gods together, Viśve Devās, were praised and invoked. 'Sit down on the sacrificial altar, O Vasus, O Viśve Devās, O Ādityas, worthy of worship.' 'May all gods protect us for our welfare.'[4] Thus gods were inter-related to one another. When all gods were worshipped together, they were implicitly conceived as partial aspects of one supreme God. A collection of gods working in harmony paved the way for one God. This stage may be called organized polytheism.

The gods were gradually related to one another as the major and the minor (aṅgapratyaṅgabhāva), as dependent on one another (anyonyāśraya), and as generating one another (anyonyotpatti). Heaven and Earth are the mothers of Agni. Rudra is the father of the Maruts. Aditi is the mother of the Ādityas. The Aśvis are brothers. This relationship organizes the plurality of nature-gods. Indra maintains the Earth and the Sky in their places. He is the major god. The Earth and the Sky are the minor deities. The Maruts maintain the Sun, the Wind, and the Fire gods in the sky. They are superior

[1] R.V., iii. 30. 5, 18, 22; iii. 31. 3, 9, 15, 18, 22; iii. 32. 7, 8, 10, 17; iii. 34. 11; iii. 36. 10, 11; iii. 37. 1; iii. 46. 1, 4.

[2] R.V., i. 36. 4; i. 75. 5; i. 79. 3; i. 141. 9; i. 142. 4, 9.

[3] R.V., i. 94. 16; i. 95. 11.

[4] R.V., ii. 3. 4; iv. 46. 3; v. 51. 13.

to the three gods. Varuṇa, Mitra and Aryaman kindle Agni. They are glorious through Agni. They are inter-dependent on one another.[1] This religion is organized polytheism.

Among the multitude of nature-gods any one is treated as the supreme god for the time being when he is worshipped. Maxmüller calls this religion henotheism.[2] 'O Agni, thou art mighty Indra, the wide-ruling Viṣṇu, the king Varuṇa whose laws are firm, the wondrous Mitra, Aryaman, the lord of beings. Thou art Rudra, the Maruts, the Winds, and Pūṣan. Thou art Savitṛ, a bestower of treasures, Bhaga, the lord of wealth, Ṛbhu, Aditi, Bhāratī, Iḍā, and Sarasvatī. Thou art united with all the gods and equal to them in strength, nay, thou surpassest them, when thy power has expanded over Heaven and Earth.'[3] Agni is identified here with many gods and treated as superior to them. This is Henotheism. It is a step from polytheism to monotheism.

All gods are inspired by the same divine power. Their great divinity is one. There is unity and order in the phenomena of nature. Agni is kindled on the altar of sacrifice, it is kindled in the forest ; it is kindled in the sky. The sun rises in the east and sets in the west every day. Day succeeds night. Night succeeds day. The sky rains water on earth ; the earth sends moisture to the sky. The same creator creates beasts, birds, and men. He gives rain, produces crops, and sustains men with food. All the diverse phenomena of nature are the works of gods who are endowed with the same divine power. The order in nature paves the way for monotheism.[4]

The conception of Ṛta further harmonizes the gods with one another, and makes for monotheism. Ṛta is the physical order. Everything in the world has its own sphere. The sun moves in the sky. The priest offers oblations at the altar. But Ṛta reigns everywhere, in the sky, in the sun, in the sacrifice, in the mountain, and in truth.[5] The gods follow the laws of Ṛta. They acquired divinity and immortality by serving Ṛta rightly. Varuṇa walks round the earth on the straight path of Ṛta. Agni lay in the womb of Ṛta. Ṛta is the course

[1] R.V., i. 141. 4, 9; i. 143. 1; ii. 33. 1; iii. 30, 4, 9; iv. 29. 1; i. 36, 4.
[2] *The Six Systems of Indian Philosophy*, 1903, p. 40.
[3] R.V., ii. 1. 3-5. [4] R.V., iii. 55. 1-22.
[5] R.V., iv. 40. 5.

of nature. It is the natural order. Sacrifices should conform to Ṛta. It is the law of rites. It is the customary law or social law. It is the law of truth, right and justice. It is the moral law. Agni has proclaimed his rules to mortals, for he is intent on Ṛta or Right, and is true. Varuṇa is the custodian of the moral law. He adheres to the right, and punishes sins.[1] The physical order and the moral order point to the existence of one supreme God whose law is unalterable and inviolable. But Ṛta is an impersonal order which upholds the gods and the world. The conception of Ṛta paves the way for monotheism.

Hiraṇyagarbha arose in the beginning. He alone was the lord of all that is. He established the earth and the heaven. He gives breath and strength ; his commands are followed by other gods ; his shadow is death and immortality. He is the sole king of the whole universe. He rules the mountains, the sea, and the rivers. He governs men and beasts. He alone is God above all gods. He began the earth, the heaven, and the mighty waters. He is no other than Prajāpati, the Lord of all creatures.[2] Hiraṇyagarbha or Prajāpati may claim the rank of Supreme God.

Viśvakarmā is the creator of the entire universe. He is the Seer of all. His eyes are everywhere, his face is everywhere, and he is of all hands and all feet. He, that one God, creates the sky and the earth. He is the world-architect.[3]

There is a Cosmic Person (parama puruṣa) whose body is the whole universe. He has a thousand heads, a thousand eyes, a thousand feet. He pervades the whole terrestrial space and transcends it. Whatever was or whatever will be—all that is Puruṣa. He is the lord of immortality. He is untouched by the fruits of actions (karma). All creation is his grandeur, but he is ever superior to the entire creation. The whole of the universe is only one-fourth of his being, the remaining three-fourths remain in celestial immortality.[4] The inner nature of the Parama Puruṣa is transcendental, though he is immanent in the whole universe. He is both immanent and

---

[1] R.V., i. 65. 3; i. 68. 4; i. 79. 3; iii. 1. 11; iii. 2. 1, 8; iii. 7. 2; iii. 10. 2; iv. 7. 7; i. 75. 5; i. 145. 5; i. 2. 8; iv. 85. 7-8.
[2] R.V., x. 121. 1-10.
[3] R.V., x. 81. 2-4.
[4] R.V., x. 90. 1-3.

transcendent. The Puruṣa Sūkta teaches panentheism. These are the monotheistic tendencies in the Ṛg Veda.

Monotheism leads to monism. The Vedic poets conceived One Reality which is manifested in diverse ways. 'There is One Reality; sages call it by various names; they call it Agni, Yama, Mātariśvan'.[1] 'That One' (tad ekam) is not personal; it is neither male nor female; it is neuter. It is an impersonal principle which breathed by itself without breath. There was nothing other than it.[2] The Nāsadīya Sūkta clearly brings out the pure monism of the Ṛg Veda:

'Then there was neither existence nor non-existence; there was no sky, nor heaven beyond. Then there was neither death nor immortality. There was neither day nor night nor distinction between them. There was the sole One (tad ekam) that breathed by itself without breath; there was nothing other than the One. Then there was darkness without light. All was engulfed in the primal cause. That One was born by the power of austerity (tapas). There first arose desire or will in the Cosmic Mind and from the first one sprang the seed of creation. The wise sages realized in their heart the bond of what is in what is not. He from whom this creation arose, the Highest Seer in the highest heaven knows.'[3] This is pure spiritualistic monism. That One (Tad Ekam) was later identified with Brahman or Ātman.[4]

2. *Religion and Ethics of the Ṛg Veda*

The Vedic religion was simple chanting of hymns, adoration, and prayer. Sacrifices were made, in which milk, butter, honey, the soma juice, and food were offered to the gods. There was animal sacrifice.[5] Prayers and sacrifices were intended for obtaining cattle, wealth, sons and grandsons, a life of hundred years, victory in battles, and happiness and bliss. Health, wealth, and happiness were the goal of prayer

---

[1] Ekaṁ sat viprā vahudhā vadanti agniṁ yamaṁ mātariśvānam āhuḥ. i. 164. 46.

[2] R.V., x. 129. 1, 2.

[3] R.V., x. 129. 1-4, 7.

[4] *The Six Systems of Indian Philosophy*, Ch. II; S. K. Das: *A Study of the Vedānta*, Ch. II; B. N. Seal: *A Syllabus of Indian Philosophy*, p. 2; *The Cultural Heritage of India*, Vol. I, pp. 14-19; *Vedic Hymns*, S.B.E., Vol. XXXII, XLVI.

[5] R.V., ii. 7. 5; i. 43. 4.

and sacrifices. There was an optimistic outlook on life. The gods were considered to be friendly to the worshippers. They were regarded as father, brother, friend, companion, protector, and forgiver of sins. They were regarded as deadly and destructive to the enemies. They crushed haters of gods, sorcerors, and cheats. They were the custodians of the moral laws. They promoted the welfare of the virtuous and punished the vicious. They maintained the physical order and the moral order. Ṛta was the germ of the Law of Karma. The virtuous were transported to heaven, and the vicious were condemned to hell, the nether region of darkness. Transmigration was yet to come. Mokṣa was not conceived. Virtue was truth. Sin was untruth (anṛta). The gods purged the worshippers of their sins.[1] Virtue was rewarded ; vice was punished.[2] The path of the fathers (pitṛyāna) and the path of the gods (devayāna) were mentioned.[3] To be united with the gods and to attain immortality were also regarded as the goal of religion.[4] Religion aimed at earthly happiness and heavenly bliss.

Ṛta is the moral law. It is truth and righteousness. The gods are the custodians and followers of the moral laws.[5] Varuṇa is of fixed, unswerving right conduct (ḍrḍhavrata). Sin is untruth and unrighteousness. It is falsehood (anṛta) and delinquency. Virtue is rewarded. Vice is punished. Virtue is not only external conduct in conformity with the moral law. It is also the purity of the inner life. The gods descry the impure motives and intentions, and punish them.[6] They know the pure thoughts of the worshippers, and promote their prayer.[7] Duties to men and duties to gods were recognized. Charity and hospitality to men and kindness to animals were enjoined. Falsehood, treachery and fraudulence were condemned. Witchcraft, spells, sorcery, and black magic were despised. Gambling was denounced, though it was prevalent. War was not condemned. Ethics of non-violence (ahiṁsā) was absent. Violence is to be met by violence. Strength bends before strength.[8] 'Let us stand straight that we may walk and

[1] R.V., iii. 7. 10; iv. 12. 4.
[2] R.V., iv. 5. 4.
[3] R.V., x. 88. 15.
[4] R.V., v. 4. 11.
[5] R.V., i. 65. 3; i. 68. 4.
[6] R.V., i. 189. 6; iv. 5.4.
[7] R.V., iv. 6. 1.
[8] R.V., vi. 66. 9; v. 87. 5; vii. 56. 19.

live."[1] The Buddhist ethics of ahiṁsā was unknown to the Vedic age. Asceticism was foreign to the spirit of the Vedic people, though it might be practised by a few people. The world is said to have been created by the austerity (tapas) and self-abnegation of the Cosmic Spirit. There was no caste system, though the Puruṣa Sūkta refers to the four classes. There was no child marriage. Women enjoyed a high position in society. They did not observe 'purdah'. Some women were composers of mantras. "One in the many, unity in variety, is the perennial message of the Vedic India. The last Sūkta of the Ṛg Veda breathes this out unequivocally thus: Assemble, speak together, let your minds be of one accord. . . Let all priests utter the mantras in a common way. Common be their assembly, common be their mind, so be their thoughts united. . . United be the thoughts of all, that all may live happily, that ye may all happily reside."[2] This is the ethics of the Ṛg Veda.

3. *The Spiritualistic Monism of the Upaniṣads : Brahman*

Śaṁkara commented upon Īśa, Kena, Kaṭha, Praśna, Muṇḍaka, Māṇḍukya, Aitareya, Taittirīya, Śvetāśvatara, Chāndógya, and Bṛhadāraṇyaka Upaniṣads. These are generally regarded as authoritative. There are numerous other Upaniṣads. The early Upaniṣads were composed between 1000 B.C. and 500 B.C. The Ṛg Veda spoke of One Reality (ekam sat) which is spoken of in various ways by the sages.[3] It spoke of That One (tad ekam) which created the world.[4] The Upaniṣads call it Brahman. Brahman is Ātman. It is the Reality of the reality. It is the transcendental reality behind the empirical reality.[5] 'All this is nothing but Brahman'. 'All this is certainly Brahman'. 'All this is certainly Ātman'. 'There was one, non-dual reality before creation of the world'. There was one Ātman in the beginning.'[6] It is the cause of all created things. 'It is their substratum in which they subsist'. It is their ultimate ground and essence. It is one devoid of plurality. It is one beyond many. 'There is

[1] R.V., i. 36. 14.
[2] R.V., x. 191. 2-4; *The Cultural Heritage of India,* Vol. I, p. 19.
[3] R.V., i. 164. 46.
[4] R.V., x. 129. 1, 2.
[5] Satyasya satyam. Bṛ. Up. ii. 1. 20.
[6] Ch. Up., iii. 4. 1; vii. 25. 2; vi. 2. 1; Ait. Up., i. 1; Nṛ. Up., 7.

nothing other than it.' 'There is nothing higher than it.' 'It is one without any second'. It is pure identity without difference.[1] The supreme principle is called Brahman because it is the ubiquitous cosmic principle. It is called Ātman because it is one eternal homogeneous consciousness (ekātma-pratyayasāra).[2]

All gods spoken of by the Vedas subsist in Brahman. None can excel it. None can transcend it. They cannot exist without it. Brahman is their essence. It is the ground of the order of nature. Ṛta is grounded in Brahman. 'Fire burns, the sun rises, the wind blows, and death overtakes creatures at its command'. The uniformities of nature are sustained by Brahman.[3] The Vedic poets conceived the super-natural deities presiding over the forces of nature and the physical and moral order (ṛta) sustained by them. They had a glimpse of the One Reality. The Upaniṣadic seers conceived it as one Brahman or Ātman. They unambiguously advocate spiritualistic monism or Absolute Idealism. This is the bed-rock of the Hindu religion and philosophy.

The Upaniṣads speak of higher (para) Brahman and lower (apara) Brahman. The former is formless (amūrta), unmanifest (aśabda), immortal (amṛta), abiding (sthita), and transcendental (tyat). The latter is formed (mūrta), manifest (śabda), mortal (martya), fleeting (yat), and empirical (sat). The former is imperishable and immutable (akṣara). The latter is perishable and mutable. The former is transcendental (śānta) or non-phenomenal (niṣprapañca), undecaying (ajara), immortal (amṛta), redeeming (abhaya), and unexcelled (para). There is no reality beyond it. It is devoid of all attributes and determinations. It is unqualified, indeterminate, and unconditioned.[4] It is the Absolute. Apara Brahman is qualified (saguṇa), determinate (saviśeṣa), conditioned (sopādhi), formed (mūrta), and manifest (śabda). It is personal God. They are not two Brahmans. But one Brahman viewed from the transcendental standpoint is indeterminate, and viewed from the empirical standpoint is determinate. The indeterminate

---

[1] Ch. Up., vi. 8. 4; Bṛ. Up., iv. 4. 19; iv. 3. 23; Śvet. Up., iii. 9.
[2] Maṇḍakya Up. i. 7. [3] Kaṭh. Up., ii. i. 3; ii. 33.
[4] Bṛ. Up., ii. 3. 1; Pr. Up., v. 2; Kaṭha Up., i. 2. 16; Pr. Up., v. 2; v. 7; vi. 7; Maitrī Up., vi. 3.

Brahman is sometimes conceived to be real, and the determinate Brahman is conceived to be unreal.[1]

Higher Brahman is unqualified (nirguṇa). It is atributeless. It is indeterminate. 'This Ātman is not this, not this.'[2] It is devoid of determinations. It is the supreme reality. There is nothing beyond it. It is imperishable (akṣara), immortal (amṛta), transparent (śubhra), immaculate (nirañjana), pure (śuddha), characterless (alakṣaṇa), non-phenomenal (prapañcopaśama), non-dual (advaita), calm (śānta), partless (niṣkala), inactive (niṣkriya), *summum bonum* (śiva). It is neither small nor great. It is neither short nor long. It is devoid of sensible qualities such as colour, sound, taste, smell, and touch. It is not any of the elements. It is neither ether, nor air, nor fire, nor water, nor earth. It is neither eye nor ear, nor life, nor manas. It is without beginning or end. It is without any prior and without any posterior. It is without inside and without outside. It is not a part. It is partless. It is neither existent (sat) nor non-existent (asat). It is one. It is non-empirical (kevala). It is the highest Good (śiva). It is imperceptible (adṛśya), unknowable (agrāhya), inconceivable (acintya), inexpressible (avyapadeśya), and unusable (avyavahārya). It transcends the known and the unknown.[3]

Nirguṇa Brahman is unconditioned (nirupādhi). It is beyond space, time, and causality. It is non-spatial, non-temporal, and non-causal. "Brahman, in contrast with the empirical system of the universe, is not like it in space but is spaceless, not in time but timeless, not subject to but independent of the law of causality."[4]

Brahman is spaceless. It is devoid of spatial characters. The Upaniṣads express it in the following manner. Brahman is the subtlest of the subtle and the greatest of the great. It is neither short nor long. It has neither inside nor outside. It is near. It is remote. It is immanent in the whole universe. It transcends the whole universe. Brahman is below and above, behind and before, in the north and the south, in the east and the west; it is the entire universe. It is limitless in the east,

---

[1] Maitrī Up., vi. 3. [2] Bṛ. Up. iv. 4. 22.

[3] Kaṭha Up., iii. 15; Muṇḍaka Up., i. 6; Ch. Up., iv. 15. 1; Īśa Up., 8; Kena Up., 3, 4; Śvet. Up. iv. 18; Māṇḍukya Up., i. 7, 12; Māṇḍukya Kārikā, i. 26; Bṛ. Up. ii. 3. 1; iii. 8. 8.

[4] Deussen: *The Philosophy of the Upaniṣads*, p. 150.

limitless in the west, limitless in the north, limitless in the south, limitless above, limitless below, limitless in all directions. For it there exist neither east and other directions nor across nor below. It is indivisible (aṇu) like the point of a needle. It is partless. It resides in the heart, smaller than a grain of barley or mustard. It is greater than the earth, greater than the sky, greater than heaven, greater than all these worlds. The whole of space is interwoven with Brahman. It is omnipresent and ubiquitous. Thus Brahman is spaceless, and yet it is the ground of space.[1]

Brahman is timeless. It is eternal (nitya), abiding (śāśvata), and ancient (purāṇa). It is without beginning and end. It is independent of the past and future. It is Lord of the past and future. It transcends all three times (kālātīta). It is untouched by time which changes into days and years in the empirical world. Brahman is not in time. Birth, growth, and death of created things happen in time. Time is formless and formed. That which is prior to the sun is the timeless (akāla), without parts (akala). But that which begins with the sun is formed time, which has parts. Brahman is timeless, and yet it is the ground of time.[2]

Brahman is non-causal. It is independent of causality; changes are governed by causality. Brahman is unchanging, and therefore not subject to causality. It is imperishable (akṣara). It is unborn (aja) and undying (amṛta). It is immutable. It is independent of cause and effect. It is independent of becoming (sambhūti) and unbecoming (asambhūti). It is unageing, undying, eternal, immutable, and imperishable. Change is a mere name, an appearance. The unchangeable and imperishable (akṣara) Brahman alone is real. It transcends the category of causality, and yet it is the ground of the empirical world subject to causality.[3]

Brahman is immobile, and yet it moves to a remote place. It is fixed, and yet it goes everywhere. It is unmoved, and

---

[1] Śvet. Up., iii. 20; v. 8; vi. 5, 17, 19; Bṛ. Up., iii. 8. 7, 8; ii. 5, 19; Iśa, iv. 5; Ch. Up., vii. 25; iii. 14. 3; Maitrāyaṇī Up., vi. 17; Praśna Up., vi. 5; Kaṭha Up., ii. 20; Muṇḍaka Up., ii. 2. 9; Maitrī, vi. 15.

[2] Kaṭha Up., i. 2. 14, 18; i. 3. 15; ii. 1. 5, 12, 13; Bṛ. Up., iv. 4. 15, 16; iii. 8. 7; Śvet. Up. v. 13; vi. 5; Maitrī Up., vi. 14, 15.

[3] Kaṭha Up., i. 2. 14, 16, 18; i. 3. 2, 15; ii. 2. 1; Muṇḍaka Up., i. 2. 13; Bṛ. Up., iv. 4. 20; iii. 8. 9, 11; Ch. Up., vi. 1. 3; Iśa Up., 12-14; Praśna Up., v. 7; Śvet. Up., vi. 6-8.

yet it moves faster than the mind. It is the unmoved mover. Motion is change. Brahman is changeless. It is static in its transcendental nature, and dynamic in its empirical manifestations.[1] It is beyond virtue and vice. It is supermoral.[2]

Nirguṇa Brahman is one, non-dual, undifferenced (nirviśeṣa). It is indeterminate. There is no other than it. It is devoid of duality and distinction. There is no distinction of subject and object in it. There is neither knower nor known in it. It is distinctionless. It is infinite (bhūmā), all-comprehending, one. There is no plurality in it. Plurality is an appearance (nānā iva).[3] This position is pure monism. Śaṁkara recognized the ontological reality of Nirguṇa Brahman only.

Nirguṇa Brahman is acosmic (niṣprapañca). It is unknowable by the sense-organs, mind, and intellect. It is imperceptible by the sense-organs. It is incomprehensible by the mind. It is unknowable by the intellect. It can be realized by subtle concentrated intellect. It is grasped by the introverted mind. It is known by intuition (prajñāna). It is realized by spiritual illumination (adhyātmayoga). It is inexpressible in words.[4]

Though acosmic Brahman is devoid of attributes (guṇa), yet it has three essential characters (svarūpalakṣaṇa). The essential Brahman is pure being, pure consciousness, and pure bliss. It is not empirical being. It is transcendental being. It is not empirical consciousness. It is transcendental consciousness beyond subject and object. It is transcendental bliss. It is beyond empirical pleasure and pain, joy and sorrow. It is, in its essential nature, infinite (ananta) being (sat), consciousness (cit), and bliss (ānanda).[5] Brahman is described as being, consciousness, and bliss in *Sarvopaniṣatsāra.*[6]

Brahman is the Reality of the reality. It is the infinite reality. It is existent (sat), non-existent (asat), and immortal (amṛta). The immortal is veiled by the reality. The transcend-

---

[1] Kaṭha Up., i. 2. 21; Iśa Up., 4, 5.
[2] Kaṭha Up., i. 2. 14.
[3] Kaṭha Up., ii. 1. 10, 11; Bṛ. Up., ii. 4. 14; ii. 1. 19; iv. 3, 31; Ch. Up., vi. 2. 1.
[4] Kaṭha Up., i. 2. 24; i. iii. 12; ii. 1. 2; ii. 3. 12; Muṇḍaka Up. iii. 1. 18; Kena Up., i. 3, 5; Tait. Up. ii. 4. 1; Bṛ. Up., iii. 9. 28.
[5] Tait. Up. ii. 1; iii. 5. 1; iii. 6. 1; Bṛ. Up., iii. 9. 28.
[6] 21.

ental reality is the ground of the empirical reality. Brahman is neither existent nor non-existent. It is higher than the existent and the non-existent. These texts indicate that Brahman is the supreme transcendental reality beyond empirical being and non-being.[1]

Brahman is self-luminous consciousness. It is the light of lights. It is the supreme light. All things are illumined by it. They are revealed by its light. It is of the essence of consciousness. It is one, infinite, absolute, undifferenced consciousness (ekātmapratyayasāra). It does not know anything inside it. Nor does it know anything outside it. Nor does it know anything inside and outside both. It is one universal consciousness (prajñānaghana). It is subject-objectless consciousness.[2] Sometimes Brahman is described as the eternal knower (vijñātṛ). It is the unborn and immortal seer. It is the witness (sākṣin), the pure consciousness (kevala cetas). It is the seer (draṣṭṛ). It is the subject. It is not an object (idam).[3]

Brahman is bliss (ānanda). It is the quintessence of bliss (rasa). The individual soul partakes of this bliss, and becomes joyful. Who would live and breathe, if the whole space were not pervaded by infinite bliss? The finite creatures partake of a particle of the infinite bliss of Brahman, and are sustained by it. Brahman is dearer than wealth, dearer than sons, dearer than all other things. It is the dearest of all. Husband, wife, wealth, and sons are not dear in themselves, but for the Ātman that is their immanent spirit. Anything other than Brahman is full of pain and sorrow. But there is absolute negation of pain in Brahman. It is beyond hunger and thirst, grief and delusion, decay and death. It is sinless. Brahman is beyond subject and object, beyond duality and distinction. So it is bliss. Brahman is infinite (bhūmā). The infinite is bliss. There is no bliss in the finite and little. Brahman is the infinite and absolute. So bliss constitutes its essence.[4]

---

[1] Bṛ. Up., i. 6. 3; ii. 1. 10; ii. 3. 6; Kaṭha Up., ii. 2. 2; Praśna Up., ii. 5; Muṇḍaka Up., ii. 2. 1; Śvet. Up., iv. 18.

[2] Bṛ. Up., iv. 3. 6; iv. 4. 16, 22; iv. 5. 13; iv. 3. 21; iv. 5. 13; Māṇḍukya Up., i. 7; Kaṭha Up., ii. 1. 13; ii. 2. 15.

[3] Br. Up., ii. 4. 14; iii. 4. 2; iii. 7. 23; iii. 8. 11; vii. 24. 1; Kena Up., i. 4-8; Praśna Up. vi. 5; Śvet. Up., vi. 14.

[4] Bṛ. Up., iii. 9. 28; iv. 3. 19, 20, 21, 32; i. 4. 8; ii. 4. 5; iii. 4, 2; iii. 5. 1; iii. 7. 23; Ch. Up., vii. 23. 1; vii. 24. 1; i. 6. 7; viii. 1. 5;

Brahman conceived as qualified (saguṇa) is God (īśvara). The Absolute in relation to the empirical world is God (īśvara). The cosmic (saprapañca) Brahman is the creator, preserver, and destroyer of the world (tajjalān). All creatures spring out of Brahman (tajja). They live in Brahman (tadan). They are re-absorbed in Brahman (talla).[1] Brahman is the Lord (īś, īśa, īśāna, īśvara) of all. He is the Lord of Lords. He is the Lord of deities. He is the supreme Lord (parameśvara). He is the Infinite Person (mahān puruṣa). He is the origin and end of all creatures. He is their inner guide (antaryāmin). He is the inner guide of the entire universe. He is the Moral Governor (vidhātṛ). He awards fruits (vasuda) to individual souls in accordance with their merits and demerits.[2] He is omniscient and perfect. He is not enhanced by their good actions. He is not decreased by their bad actions. He is all-perfect and full. He is unequalled and unexcelled. He supports and furthers virtue, and avoids and punishes vice. He is the Lord of the wealth of greatness. He is possessed of infinite excellences. He is worthy of adoration. He is the support of all. He is the refuge of all. He can be realized by His grace. He cannot be realized by knowledge or austerities.[3] This is theism.

God is immanent in the world. He transcends the world. He is both transcendent and immanent. The world is in God. It is not God. God is not the world.[4] This is panentheism.

God is immanent in the whole world. He is immanent in the individual souls. He inspires good persons to do right actions and elevates them. He inspires bad persons to do wrong actions and degrades them. Individual souls have no freedom of the will.[5] God is all-acting (sarvakarmā), all-wishing (sarvakāma), all-smelling, all-tasting.[6] This is pantheism. Rāmānuja recognized the ontological reality of saguṇa Brahman.

---

viii. 7. 1; Kaiṣ. Up. iii. 8; Maitr. Up., vi. 23; iii. 8; Teja Up., 8; Maitrī Up., vi. 21; vii. 7; Tait. Up., ii. 4, 7, 9.

[1] Ch. Up., iii. 15. 1; Tait. Up., iii. 1.

[2] Īśa Up., 1; Bṛ. Up., iv. 4. 22, 24; Śvet. Up., iii. 19; vi. 6-8; iii. 12; Māṇḍukya Up., 6; Ch. Up., iv. 15. 2-4.

[3] Śvet. Up., iii. 16-17, 1-2; iv. 11; vi. 7, 17; Bṛ. Up., v. 6. 1; iv. 4. 22; iii. 7. 23; Kaiṣ. Up., iii. 8; Īśa, Up., 8; Kaṭha Up., i. 2. 23.

[4] Īśa, 5; Tait. Up., ii. 6; Ch. Up., iii. 12. 6; Maitrī Up., vii. 11.

[5] Kaiṣ. Up., iii. 8; iv. 18.

[6] Ch. Up., iii. 14. 4.

4. *The Ātman and the Individual Self*

Brahman is the cosmic principle. Ātman is the psychic principle. It is the inner self in man. Brahman is Ātman. The cosmic principle is the psychic principle. The universal spirit is the self in man. It is the immanent spirit in him. It is his inner guide (antaryāmin). Brahman is the soul (ātman) of all. 'The eternal knower is thy soul, the inner guide, the immortal'. It is the knower, but is not known. It is the foundational consciousness which is the ground of the universe. It is the ground of our empirical consciousness. The eternal, universal light of consciousness resides in our heart and illumines all objects of our knowledge. 'It is thy soul that is within all.'[1] 'That of which the whole universe is composed, that is, the real, that is the soul, that art thou, O Śvetaketu.' 'Tat tvam asi'. 'I am Brahman.' 'Ahaṁ brahmāsmi.' 'This soul is Brahman.' 'Ayam ātmā brahma.'[2] The identity of the individual soul with the universal soul was emphasized by Śaṁkara. Rāmānuja recognized the individual soul to be a real mode (prakāra) of the universal soul.

Māṇḍukya Upaniṣad speaks of the four stages of the individual soul and the universal soul. The individual soul in the waking condition is called the Viśva which knows and enjoys gross external objects. The individual soul in the condition of dream is called the Taijasa which knows and enjoys subtle internal objects or cognitions. The individual soul in the condition of dreamless sleep is called the Prājña which is one homogeneous mass of consciousness and bliss (prajñānaghana). It does not apprehend external objects or internal cognitions. The individual soul in the fourth ecstatic (turīya) condition is called the Ātman which is one universal consciousness (ekātmapratyayasāra) which knows neither external objects nor internal cognitions, which is not a mass of consciousness, which is neither consciousness (prajña) nor non-consciousness (aprajña). It is one, non-dual, non-empirical or transcendental consciousness. The Ātman is universal superconsciousness.[3] It can be realized by supra-intellectual intuition. There are

[1] Bṛ. Up., iii. 4. 5; iii. 7. 3; Ch. Up., viii. 1. 3; iii. 13. 17; Kaiṣ. Up., iii. 8.
[2] Ch. Up., vi. 11. 3; Bṛ. Up., i. 4. 10; ii. 5. 1.
[3] *Ibid*, i. 2-4.

four stages of Brahman corresponding to the four stages of the individual soul. The entire universe of gross objects constitutes the body of Virāṭ or Vaiśvānara. The totality of subtle bodies constitutes the body of Hiraṇyagarbha. The cosmic nescience (māyā) constitutes the body of Sūtrātmā or Īśvara. He is self-conscious with Māyā as the non-ego or object of consciousness. The cosmic consciousness beyond cause and effect, ego and non-ego, is called Brahman. It is pure transcendental consciousness which is subject-objectless. It is transcendental bliss and perfect freedom (ānanda). Thus the Ātman is Brahman. The turīya or intuitive self is Brahman.[1]

Taittirīya Upaniṣad describes five sheaths of the individual self. (1) The bodily self is called the bodily sheath (annamaya koṣa). It is dependent on food. The self is identified with the body and its organs. (2) Penetrating the bodily sheath we find within it the vital sheath (prāṇamaya koṣa). The vital forces, which animate the body, constitute its parts. The vital self is dependent on vital breath. (3) Within the vital sheath there is the mental sheath (monomaya koṣa). The mental self is dependent on manas. Volitions directed to selfish ends constitute the mental sheath. (4) Within the mental sheath there is the intellectual sheath (vijñānamaya koṣa). Intellectual knowledge which is discriminative and involves the distinction of subject and object constitutes the intellectual sheath. The intellectual self is dependent on the intellect. (5) Deeper still within the intellectual sheath there is the blissful sheath (ānandamaya koṣa). Subject-objectless transcendental consciousness and bliss constitute the blissful self. It is non-empirical. It is ānanda or absolute freedom. In fact, ānanda does not constitute a sheath of the self. But it constitutes the very essence of the self.[2] Ranade opines that the problem of sheaths is the problem of substance. Matter, life, mind, and intellect cannot be regarded as the ultimate principle of things. Intuitive bliss is the source of reality.[3]

Kaṭha Upaniṣad describes the Ātmān as the disembodied spirit that is not born, that does not die, though the body dies, that is unborn (aja), eternal (nitya), immutable (śāśvata),

[1] *Ibid*, i. 9-12; *Vedāntasāra* (Jacobi's edition), pp. 7-25.
[2] Tait. Up., iii. 1. 2-6.
[3] *A Constructive Survey of Upaniṣadic Philosophy*, 1926, p. 144.

and ancient (purāṇa). The cosmic spirit, Brahman, is immanent in the individual self. The great all-pervading self, which is formless and disembodied, exists in all individual embodied souls. The universal soul is immanent in the individual soul.[1] Kaṭha Upaniṣad draws a distinction between the individual soul and the universal soul. They are opposed to each other like light and darkness. The individual soul is bound to empirical life. The universal soul is free from empirical life. The individual soul earns merits and demerits by its actions, and enjoys them. But the universal soul is super-moral and free from merits and demerits. It does not enjoy the fruits of an individual's actions, though it is immanent in his soul. It is the indifferent spectator of the individual soul's enjoyment of fruits of its actions. The individual soul associated with the sense-organs, manas, buddhi, and ahaṁkāra, which are its adjuncts, is the enjoyer (bhoktṛ). The universal soul is beginningless, endless, and eternal. It is the witness of all. Eternal consciousness is its essence. The universal timeless soul is the master and sustainer of the individual temporal soul that enjoys the fruits of its actions (madhvada). The one universal self, the self of all creatures, which is the indwelling spirit in the individual soul, is not touched by its sorrows and imperfections.[2]

Kaṭha Upaniṣad distinguishes the individual self from the body, the sense-organs, manas, and buddhi. Body is the chariot or material vehicle. Ātman is the charioteer. Intellect or buddhi is the driver. Manas is the bridle. The sense-organs are the horses. Objects are the field. The sense-organs are directed by manas. Manas is directed by buddhi. The individual soul associated with the sense-organs, manas, and buddhi is the empirical soul. Manas is superior to the sense-organs. Buddhi is superior to manas. Ātman is superior to buddhi.[3] Avyakta or unmanifest Prakṛti is superior to Mahat or cosmic intellect. The supreme puruṣa, the universal soul, is superior to Avyakta. It is the highest reality. There is nothing higher than it.[4]

---

[1] Kaṭha Up., i. 2. 12, 18, 19, 20, 22.
[2] *Ibid,* SB., i. 3. 1, 4, 15; ii. 1. 5; ii. 2. 11; Śvet. Up., iv. 6-7; Muṇḍaka Up., iii. 1. 1-2.
[3] *Ibid,* i. 3. 3, 4, 5, 6, 10.
[4] *Ibid,* i. 3. 11.

The individual soul has no freedom of the will. The universal soul causes those individual souls to do right actions, which it desires to raise higher. It causes those individual souls to do wrong actions, which it desires to degrade lower. It is the immortal, eternal soul, which is perfect, and which is not increased by their good actions or decreased by their bad actions. Omnipotent God is the agent (kartṛ) of actions of all individual persons. He does all their actions.[1] Individual souls have no freedom of the will. The eternal universal self that is the inner guide of the whole universe is also the inner guide (antaryāmin) of the vital forces, the sense-organs, manas, and intellect of the individual persons. All finite souls are grounded in the universal soul. The eternal, universal self immanent in them is the unknown knower, the unseen seer, the unheard hearer, the unreflected reflector, the uncomprehended comprehender. How can the knower (vijñātṛ) be known? It can be known by intuition (prajñāna). It can be realized by spiritual illumination (adhyātmayoga).[2] The Upaniṣads do not attach adequate importance to the individual souls. They do not recognize their freedom of the will. They make too much of the all-immanence of the universal spirit in them.

Śvetāśvatara Upaniṣad distinguishes between the universal soul and the individual soul. Both are unborn (aja). The former is omniscient (jña), while the latter is ignorant (ajña). The former is omnipotent (īśa), while the latter is impotent (anīśa). Muṇḍaka Upaniṣad describes the individual soul as sorrowful on account of its ignorance and impotence, which shakes off all sorrow when it has an intuition of the universal soul dwelling within it.[3]

5. *Intuition* (*Vidyā*) *and Intellect* (*Avidyā*) : *Bondage and Liberation*

Higher knowledge of Brahman as pure identity devoid of difference is intuition (vidyā). Lower intellectual knowledge of the empirical world of plurality of individual objects and selves is ignorance (avidyā). Intuition brings about release.

[1] Kaiṣ. Up., iii. 8; iv. 18.
[2] Bṛ. Up., iii. 7. 3-23; ii. 5. 15; iii. 4. 2; iii. 8. 11; Kena Up., 1-8; Kaṭha Up., i. 2. 12, 24.
[3] Śvet. Up., i. 9; Muṇḍaka Up., iii. 1. 2.

Intellect ties the individual self to the empirical life of birth and death. Vidyā is mokṣa. Avidyā is saṁsāra. Vidyā and avidyā are opposed to each other. Vidyā leads to self-realization which is the highest good (śreyas). Avidyā leads to the fulfilment of desires or happiness (preyas). Avidyā is non-discrimination of the eternal and the non-eternal. Vidyā is discrimination between them. Avidyā leads to transmigration, heaven and hell. Vidyā leads to mokṣa or extinction of transmigration. It leads to complete destruction of suffering. It leads to realization of Brahman (brahmaprāpti). Avidyā is the sphere of actions (karma). Actions unenlightened by knowledge lead to darkness. One cannot cross death by actions springing from avidyā or illusion of difference. One can attain immortality (amṛta) by vidyā or knowledge.[1]

Vidyā is knowledge of pure identity. Duality of subject and object is apparent. Ātman is the ontological reality. It is one transcendental consciousness which is beyond the distinction of subject and object. It can be known by intuition (prajñāna). Plurality is a mere name, an appearance, a matter of words. It is not an ontological reality. Knowledge of plurality of empirical objects in time and space, and subject to causality is avidyā. Intellectual knowledge of phenomena through the categories of time, space, and causality is avidyā. It is not real knowledge. It cannot grasp the pure identity of Ātman or Brahman. It is one, eternal, undifferenced consciousness. Avidyā ties us to the world of appearance. Vidyā leads us to realization of our Brahmanhood. Avidyā is intellectual or discriminative knowledge. Vidyā is intuitive or non-discriminative knowledge.

The individual soul's individuality is due to avidyā. Avidyā is the cause of individuality. It produces the body, the sense-organs, manas, buddhi and ahaṁkāra which constitute its individuality. The jīva sleeps under the influence of beginningless nescience (māyā) and is entangled in the bondage of empirical life. When it awakes to the sense of its intrinsic identity with Ātman, it realizes that it is the one eternal Brahman which is ever-awake, which never sleeps or dreams.[2] The self is never covered by nescience ; it is pure

[1] Kaṭha Up., S.B., i. 2. 4, 5; Īśa Up., 9, 10, 11; Bṛ. Up., iv. 4. 10.
[2] Māṇḍukya Kārikā, 1. 16.

and transparent by nature ; it is for ever enlightened and liberated. Only knowledge of its intrinsic purity and freedom constitutes its liberation.[1] When an individual completely shakes off his individuality due to avidyā, he can realize his essential Brahmanhood. Knowledge of pure identity is not the cause of liberation. It is itself liberation. One who knows Brahman becomes Brahman.[2] The individual soul is always Brahman. It never becomes Brahman. Only it knows its Brahmanhood. This knowledge is direct intuitive realization. It is not indirect, mediate knowledge. Lack of this knowledge is bondage. So long as the individual soul erroneously identifies itself with the body, the sense-organs, and the like, it is haunted by desires of wealth and happiness. So long as it is haunted by desires, it undergoes birth and death. Like corns it dies and is born again in accordance with its merits and demerits.[3] But when it is free from desire of objects, and desires the self only, it becomes immortal. It abandons name and form, shakes off individuality, and enters into the supreme spirit, even as a stream disappears in the ocean. What can it desire, which has all? It has realized the bliss of Brahman, and is free from fear. Where there is the consciousness of duality or plurality, there is fear. Where there is the consciousness of pure identity, all fear vanishes. One who transcends individuality, overcomes sorrow. Brahman or Ātman is pure bliss. When it is realized, all sorrow vanishes. One who has realized Ātman, becomes free from doubt. In the pure light of intuition (vidyā) all doubts relating to intellectual knowledge (avidyā) vanish. The knowledge of Ātman is intutitive. It is not discursive. Immediate intuition is not shaken by doubt. One who has realized Ātman transcends good and evil deeds. He is free from desires. So he is incapable of evil deeds. Knowledge makes all actions ineffective. Actions depend upon individuality. Individuality depends upon avidyā. When avidyā is dispelled by true knowledge (vidyā), the sense of individuality is destroyed. Actions cannot lead to liberation. Knowledge of Ātman is liberation.[4] Liberation can be realized

[1] *Ibid*, iv. 98.

[2] Brahmavid brahmaiva bhavati.

[3] Kaṭha Up., i. 1. 6.

[4] Bṛ. Up., iii. 5; iv. 4. 23; i. 4. 2; Ch. Up., iii. 14. 4; iv. 14. 3; vii. 1. 3; viii. 4. 2; viii. 12. 1; Tait Up., ii. 4; Muṇḍ. Up., iii. 2. 2, 8; ii. 2. 6; Īśa, 2; *The Philosophy of the Upaniṣads*, pp. 344-55.

here on earth. Embodied life is no bar to its realization. When the unconditioned universal self reveals itself to the individual self, all desires in its heart are extirpated, and the mortal self becomes immortal. It realizes its Brahmanhood even in its embodied life. When all knots of the heart are broken, the mortal embodied self becomes immortal. It does not transmigrate to any other sphere of life.[1]

6. *Cosmology*

The Upaniṣads suggest some theories of creation of the world. Bṛhadāraṇyaka Upaniṣad says, "As a spider ejects its thread from its body, and as fire emits sparks, so all lives, all beings, all gods, all creatures spring from this Ātman."[2] Muṇḍaka Upaniṣad likewise says, "As a spider ejects and retracts threads, as the plants shoot forth on the earth, as the hairs spring from a living body, as sparks come out from a red-hot fire, so various kinds of living beings spring forth from the imperishable Brahman, again return to it."[3] This is the doctrine of emanation. The world emanates from the fulness of Brahman and returns to it. Chāndogya Upaniṣad says, "There was one only without a second in the beginning. It created heat or fire. From heat water was created. From water food (earth) was created."[4] Ātman created fire, water, and earth. Muṇḍaka Upaniṣad says, "The imperishable Brahman created qualified Brahman ; qualified Brahman created life, manas, sense-organs, ether, air, fire, water, and earth."[5] Qualified Brahman or God created ether, air, fire, water and earth. He created plants and animals born of wombs and eggs. This is the doctrine of creation. Taittirīya Upaniṣad says, "The Ātman desire to become many and propagated itself. It practised self-mortification and created the entire universe and entered into it."[6] Creation is an act of self-abnegation. The world and beyond are created by Ātman by self-renunciation. Creation is self-sacrifice. It implies that creation is self-expression and self-communication of God to the creatures. Creation is a moral act of willing self-sacrifice. Bṛhadāraṇyaka

---

[1] Kaṭha Up., ii. 3. 13-16.
[2] Bṛ. Up., ii. 1. 20.
[3] Muṇḍ. Up., i. 1. 7; ii. 1. 1.
[4] Ch. Up., vi. 2. 1-3.
[5] Muṇḍ. Up., ii. 1. 2-3; Tait. Up., i. 2. 4.
[6] Tait Up., ii. 6.

Upaniṣad says, "The universe was not unfolded in the beginning; it was unfolded in name and form (nāmarūpa). Ātman entered into it up to the finger-tips, as a knife is hidden in a sheath."[1] This text suggests that creation is a passage from an undifferentiated condition to a differentiated condition. If differentiation is real, the process is evolution. If it is not real, creation is a mere appearance. Creation is unfoldment. Dissolution is enfoldment. It is either evolution (pariṇāma) or appearance (vivarta).

Svetāśvatara Upaniṣad says, "God is the magician (māyin), and māyā is prakṛti." "He created the world out of prakṛti and covered Himself in it." "The power of God was hidden in His own qualities." "God is the Lord of prakṛti and individual souls (kṣetrajña)."[2] Here though God is described as a magician, His māyā is prakṛti which is subordinate to Him. Prakṛti is the power of God. Creation is manifestation of the power of God. But there are many texts which convey the idea that creation is an appearance. "Brahman is the transcendental reality, which is concealed by the empirical reality, which is a universe of names and forms". "Brahman is the reality of reality". "It moves and plans, as it were". "There is duality, as it were". "There is plurality, as it were". "Change is a mere name, a matter of words"[3] Chāndogya Upaniṣad suggests the doctrine of Vivartavāda or Satkāraṇavāda. The effect is a mere appearance of the cause. Earth is real. All its modifications are its unreal appearances. Iron is real. All its modifications are its unreal appearances. The cause is real. But its effects are its unreal appearances.[4]

The Upaniṣads suggest the doctrines of triplication (trivṛtkaraṇa) and quintuplication (pañcīkaraṇa) of the elements. Fire, water, and earth are combined in such a manner that one of them becomes the principal element while the other two become subordinate elements. In fire the element of fire is the principal constituent, while the elements of water and earth are subordinate. In water the element of water is the principal constituent, while fire and earth are subordinate. In

[1] Bṛ. Up., i. 4. 7.

[2] Śvet. Up., iv. 10; vi. 10; i. 3; vi. 16.

[3] Bṛ. Up., i. 6. 3; ii. 1. 20; iv. 3. 7; ii. 4. 14; iv. 4. 19; Maitrī Up., vi. 24; Ch. Up., vi. 1. 4-6.

[4] Ch. Up., vi. 1. 4-6.

earth the element of earth is the principal constituent, while fire and water are subordinate. This is the doctrine of the triplication of the elements.[1] Praśna Upaniṣad speaks of earth (pṛthivī) and earth-essence (pṛthivīmātra), water (ap) and water-essence (ap-mātra), fire (tejas) and fire-essence (tejas-mātra), air (vāyu) and air-essence (vāyumātra), ether (ākāśa) and ether-essence (ākāśamātra).[2] The five essences of the elements are combined in such a manner that one of them becomes the principal constituent, while the other four elemental essences become subordinate. The earth-essence, the water-essence, the fire-essence, the air-essence, and the ether-essence are the principal constituents of the elements of earth, water, fire, air, and ether respectively. The doctrine of the essences of elements was developed by the Sāṁkhya into the doctrine of tanmātras or subtle essences of elements.

7. *Ethics*

Kaṭhopaniṣad draws a distinction between happiness (preyas) and the highest Good (śreyas). He who seeks happiness is deprived of the highest Good. He who seeks the highest Good attains his real well-being. The discriminating person rejects happiness and selects the highest Good. The non-discriminating person rejects the highest Good and selects happiness. Fulfilment of desires yields pleasure or happiness. It is temporary and unsubstantial. The highest good is realization of the eternal universal self in man. Vidyā or supra-intellectual intuition leads to self-realization. Avidyā or intellect is directed to objects of desire in the empirical world.[3] The universal self can be realized by the purity of the manas, intellect, egoism, and the sense-organs (dhātuprasāda) and extirpation of all desires (akratu).[4] Intuition of the self depends on moral purity and self-renunciation. Ātman can not be realized by one who does not desist from forbidden conduct, who is not self-controlled, whose mind is not concentrated on the self, and whose mind is not free from desires for earthly pleasures. It can be realized by intuition (prajñāna) which depends upon complete self-control, desirelessness, and

[1] Ch. Up., vi. 3. 3.
[2] Pr. Up., iv. 8.
[3] Kaṭha Up., i. 2. 1-4.
[4] *Ibid*, i. 2. 20.

concentration of mind.[1] Moral purity is the indispensable prerequisite of knowledge of Ātman. Direct knowledge of Ātman or one universal self in multiplicity of individual persons leads to eternal peace and indefinable transcendental bliss.[2] Thus Kaṭhopaniṣad ethics is anti-hedonistic and eudaemonistic. The highest good is self-knowledge or self-realization. It depends on complete desirelessness and perfect self-control and moral purity. The method of attaining self-knowledge is asceticism and purism.

Karma is not excluded from moral life. Prescribed actions should be performed without any desire or motive. Niṣkāma karma purifies the mind.[3] It is only a preliminary step to self-knowledge. Direct and immedite knowledge of the universal self in all creatures and above them is the highest good (niśreyasa). It is mokṣa.[4] Penance or self-mortification (tapas), sense-control (dama), unmotived and selfless duties (karma), and study of the Vedas are the means of liberation. Truthfulness (satya) is its foundation. It should be observed rigidly in mind, body, and action. It includes non-deceit and non-crookedness. Truthfulness is the foundation of all virtues. Falsehood leads to utter ruin. Those who are crooked, mendacious and fraudulent can never attain purity.[5] Asceticism (tapas), liberality (dāna), uprightness (ārjava), non-injury to life or harmlessness (ahiṁsā), and truthfulness (satyavacana) are one's gifts for the priests.[6] A student should observe celibacy (brahmacarya), practise austerities (tapas), cultivate faith (śraddhā), study the scriptures, and earnestly seek the knowledge of the self.[7] Right living (ṛta), truthfulness (satya), austerities (tapas), self-restraint (dama), tranquillity (śama), maintenance of sacrificial fires (agni), Agnihotra sacrifice, hospitality, humanity, duties to wives, children and grandchildren, learning and teaching the Vedas are the duties of a householder.[8] Theft, drinking liquor, adultery, and murder are forbidden. Sacrifice and good actions are the main duties of a householder.[9] He should later retire from the world, and adopt the life of Vānaprastha. He should give up desire for worldly

[1] *Ibid,* i. 2. 24.
[2] *Ibid,* ii. 2. 13-14.
[3] Īśa Up., 2.
[4] ***Ibid,*** 6.
[5] Kena Up., iv. 8; Pr. Up., i. 16; vi. 1.
[6] Ch. Up., iii. 17.
[7] Kena Up., i. 10; v. 3.
[8] Tait. Up., i. 9.
[9] Ch. Up., v. 10. 9, 10.

possessions and enjoyments (vittaiṣaṇā), desire for children (putraiṣaṇā), and desire for the world (lokaiṣanā), and retire to a forest.[1] Ascetic practices with meditation may not lead to the knowledge of the Ātman. Asceticism and fasting are only the means by which one seeks to know the Ātman. They are not indispensable to the knowledge of the Ātman according to some ; they are the indispensable means to it according to others.[2] The Sannyāsin renounces the world and wanders about homeless. He should abandon all desire, cultivate knowledge, and practise truthfulness, non-covetousness, non-injury, and chastity. He should live at peace with all creatures. He should completely overcome lust, anger, desire, infatuation, deceit, pride, envy, self-will, presumption, and falsehood. He is not elated by praise and angered by censure. His impulses are perfectly stilled ; he abides only in knowledge of the self ; he is firmly established in the Ātman. Self-restraint (yama), observances (niyama), posture (āsana), breath-control (prāṇā-yāmā), withdrawal of the sense-organs from their objects (pratyāhāra), fixation of mind (dhāraṇā), meditation (dhyāna), and concentration or trance (samādhi) also are enjoined. The self can be known by spiritual illumination (adhyātmayoga). Self-restraint (dama), tranquillity (śama), suppression of the sense-organs (uparati), endurance (titikṣā), and concentration (samādhi) are necessary for the knowledge of the self. Evil does not overcome one who has known the Self ; he overcomes all evil. Evil does not burn him ; he burns all evil. Free from evil, free from sin, free from doubt, he becomes a Brāhmaṇā.[3] The ethics of the Upaniṣads is eudæmonism with a blend of asceticism or moral purism. It does not aim at intellectual perfection devoid of moral purity. It aims at direct realization of the Self by means of selfless and unmotived performance of duties, cultivation of virtues and suppression of vices, rigid self-control and extinction of desires. The ethics of the Upaniṣads is not intellectualistic. It aims at super-moral purity, perfect equality with Brahman, which is beyond good and evil prevalent in the empirical world. This is the highest

---

[1] Bṛ. Up., iii. 5. 1.

[2] Maitr. Up., i. 2; iv. 3; Ch. Up., ii. 23, 1; Bṛ. Up., iv. 4. 22; Jāvāla Up., 4.

[3] Bṛ. Up., iv. 4. 23; *The Philosophy of the Upaniṣads*, pp. 364-95.

stage of moral life. It is the beatific vision of the super-moral Ātman. It is a state of mystic experience of the supreme reality.[1]

8. *Gauḍapāda's Pure Monism or Absolute Idealism*

Gauḍapāda (600 A.D.), the teacher of Govinda, the teacher of the great Advaita Vedāntist, Śaṁkara, developed his philosophy of Pure Monism or Absolute Idealism in his Māṇḍukya Kārikā. He wrote a commentary on Māṇḍukya Upaniṣad in verses. He was profoundly influenced by the great Mādhyamika dialectician, Nāgārjuna (200 A.D.). His doctrine is Absolutism (bramavāda) blended with Nāgarjuna's relativism, phenomenalism, and subjcetivism.

There are four stages of the Ātman. It is Viśva in the waking condition ; it knows external objects. It is Taijasa in the dream state ; it knows dream-cognitions. It is Prājña in dreamless sleep ; it is a mass of consciousness (ghanaprajña). The Viśva enjoys gross objects. The Taijasa enjoys subtle objects or cognitions. The Prājña enjoys bliss (ānanda). The Ātman in these three states is the knowing subject (bhoktṛ) of certain objects (bhogya). But the Ātman is beyond them all. It is subject-objectless transcendental consciousness. The non-dual intuitive self (turīya) is the master of them. It is neither cause nor effect. The Prājña is the cause which contains the potentialities of ignorance. The Taijasa and the Viśva are both cause and effect. The Prājña knows neither itself nor an object other than itself. But the intuitive self is always all-knowing ; its consciousness is never extinct.[2] Ātman is Brahman.

The jīva is not an ontological reality. It has empirical reality. It sleeps under the influence of beginningless Māyā or cosmic nescience and believes itself to be real. But when it awakes from the sleep induced by Māyā, it realizes its eternal, non-dual (advaita) nature. When it destroys its false sense of individuality, it realizes its identity with Ātman or Brahman.[3] The jīva is an unreal appearance. The world (prapañca) also is a false appearance. The world-appearance is infected with duality. All duality (dvaita) is a mere

---

[1] Kaṭha Up., ii. 2. 14; Bṛ. Up., iv. 4. 20; Muṇḍ. Up., iii. 1. 3, 8.
[2] Māṇḍ. K., i. 1-15. [3] Māṇḍ. K., i. 16.

appearance (māyāmātra). Non-duality (advaita) is the ontological reality (paramārtha satya). If the world-appearance were existent, it would be destroyed. But it is an unreal appearance.[1] Brahman or Ātman is the ontological reality. Neither the jīva nor the world is real.

Gauḍapāda lays the foundation of Advaita Vedānta which was elaborated by Śaṁkara and his followers later. Nāgārjuna called the ontological reality Śūnya which is the predicateless absolute. Gauḍapāda calls it Brahman or Ātman which is one, eternal, non-dual, pure consciousness. It is non-dual (advaita), non-phenomenal (prapañcopaśama), good (śiva), and calm (śānta) like the Śūnya of Nāgārjuna.[2] Gauḍapāda, like Nāgārjuna, distinguishes between two degrees of truth, *viz.*, ontological truth (paramārtha satya) and empirical truth (saṃvṛti satya). Brahman has ontological truth; the world-appearance has empirical truth.[3] The empirical truth is saṃvṛti or veil of appearance. It is also called conventional truth (prajñapti).[4] Gauḍapāda does not regard the Śūnya as the ontological reality. Like Asaṅga, the Vijñānavādin, Gauḍapāda also mentions three degrees of knowledge, *viz.*, absolute knowledge (paramārtha), empirical knowledge (paratantra saṃvṛti), and illusory knowledge (kalpitasaṃvṛti)[5] Gauḍapāda uses the word 'niṣpanna' to indicate the highest state of realization of Brahman.[6] Thus he was acquainted with the Vijñānavādin's three degrees of knowledge, *viz.*, absolute knowledge (pariniṣpanna jñāna), empirical knowledge (paratantra jñāna), and illusory knowledge (parikalpita jñāna). The Vijñānavādin calls the ontological reality Tathatā. But Gaudapāda calls it Brahman. It is one, eternal (aja), distinctionless (akalpaka) consciousness. It reveals itself to itself. There is no distinction between the supra-intellectual, non-discriminative intuition which apprehends Brahman and its object, Brahman.[7] It cannot be grasped by intellectual, discriminative knowledge. It can be realized by superconscious trance (nīrvikalpa samādhi), when the manas is not merged

---

[1] Māṇḍ. K., i. 17, 18.
[2] Māṇḍ. Up., i. 12; Māṇḍ. K., i. 29.
[3] Māṇḍ. K., i. 17; ii. 1, 4, 32.
[4] *Ibid*, iv. 24, 25, 73.
[5] *Ibid*, iv. 73. 24.
[6] *Ibid*, iii. 46.
[7] *Ibid*, ii. 33, 34.

in nescience as in sleep, but becomes identical with Brahman.[1] Gauḍapāda, like *Laṅkāvatārasūtra,* distinguishes between mundane knowledge (laukika jñāna) and supra-mundane knowledge (lokottara jñāna). Mundane knowledge is empirical knowledge of objects and cognitions. The knowledge of cognitions without their objects is called pure mundane knowledge (suddha laukika jñāna). Supra-mundane knowledge is pure intuition of subject-objectless pure consciousness. It is neither knowledge of objects nor knowledge of cognitions. It is trans-empirical knowledge.[2]

Gauḍapāda, like the Vijñanavādin, argues that empirical objects are the subjective creations of the mind (citta). The mind does not apprehend an external object. Nor does it apprehend an illusory object (arthābhāsa). External objects are not real. Illusory objects have no existence apart from the mind. It cannot apprehend an object either in the past, or the present, or the future. So its cognitions are objectless, uncaused, and illusory. Neither cognitions are produced, nor are objects produced.[3] All objects of consciousness (cittadṛśya) are creations of the mind ; all cognitions are objectless (avastuka) like dreams. Waking perceptions are as false as dream-cognitions. Dream-objects (*e.g.,* elephants, mountains, etc.) are unreal because they cannot exist in a small body. All empirical objects are unreal like them because they are due to avidyā (saṁvṛti). There is no difference between the objects of waking perceptions and those of dream-cognitions. They are equally unreal. Just as dream-objects are non-existent in the beginning and at the end and therefore unreal, so objects of waking perceptions are non-existent in the beginning and at the end and therefore non-existent. They are transient. They are caused and destroyed. Therefore they are unreal. In dream we make a distinction between the real and the unreal. The objects apprehended in the external world in dream are real. But the objects imagined by the mind and apprehended as within it are unreal. In the waking condition also the objects imagined by the mind are unreal, while those apprehended by it in the external world are real. Hence both dream-objects and objects of waking perceptions are equally

[1] *Ibid,* iii. 35, 37.
[2] *Ibid,* iv. 87-88.
[3] *Ibid,* iv. 26-28.

unreal.[1] The world is unreal like dream, magic show (māyā), day-dream (gandharvanagara). All phenomena (dharma) are false (mṛṣā) like dreams ; they are appearances of Brahman owing to saṃvṛti or veil of nescience.[2] Just as in dreams the mind overpowered by avidyā or Māyā appears to be subject and object (dvayābhāsa), so in the waking condition it appears to be subject and object under the influence of avidyā. The one (advaya) mind is real ; duality is an appearance in waking cognitions and dreams both. Just as objects of dream-cognitions do not exist apart from the mind, so objects of waking cognitions do not exist apart from the mind. Both are equally mind-dependent and subjective creations.[3] The mind and the objects of cognition are dependent on each other ; the mind cannot be conscious without objects ; objects cannot be known without the mind. Their mutual dependence shows their essencelessness (lakṣaṇāśūnyam ubhayam). Objects of cognitions are not real ; they have no existence apart from the mind.[4] The mind is objectless (nīrviṣaya) ; it is always unattached (asaṅga). The empirical mind (grāhaka) and empirical objects (grāhya) are due to agitation of the mind (cittaspandita).[5]

All are appearances of one, eternal, pure consciousness, Brahman or Ātman.[6] Just as a moving fire-brand appears to be straight or crooked, so one eternal cognition (vijñāna) appears to be subject (grāhaka) and object (grāhya).[7] This is the argument of the Vijñānavādin like Vasubandhu. Just as the fire-brand does not appear to be straight or crooked when its movement is stopped, so one eternal cognition (vijñāna) does not appear to be subject and object when avidyā is destroyed. It appears to be empirical minds and empirical objects when it is agitated by avidyā.[8] They are mere appearances (ābhāsa) like the straight or crooked movement of a moving fire-brand.[9] They cannot arise from anything distinct from the one eternal cognition (vijñāna), since they arise only when it becomes active ; they do not abide in anything distinct from it when it becomes inactive (nispanda), nor are they re-

[1] *Ibid*, iv. 36, 37; ii. 1, 4, 5-7, 9, 10.
[2] *Ibid*, ii. 31; iv. 33.
[3] *Ibid*, iv. 61-66.
[4] *Ibid*, iv. 67.
[5] *Ibid*, iv. 72.
[6] *Ibid*, iv. 46.
[7] *Ibid*, iv. 47.
[8] *Ibid*, iv. 49.
[9] *Ibid*, iv. 50.

absorbed in it, since they are unreal.[1] They are mere unreal appearances (ābhāsa) ; they are not real. So they cannot be produced by the eternal cognition, since they cannot be related to it as effect and cause. They are always inconceivable (acintya). They are indefinable and inexplicable.[2] One substance can be the cause of another substance, and a non-substance can be the cause of a non-substance. But the Ātman is neither a substance nor a non-substance ; so it can be neither a cause nor an effect. It is neither a substance, nor a cause, nor any other empirical category.[3] Empirical objects (dharma) are not produced by the mind (citta). The mind is not produced by empirical objects. They are all appearances of the one eternal cognition (vijñānasvarūpābhāsamātra) or Ātman which transcends the category of causality.[4] All dharmas mysteriously appear in the Ātman, though they are neither eternal nor perishable. A seed is an appearance (māyāmaya). A sprout that springs from it is an appearance. It is neither eternal nor perishing. It is an inexplicable appearance. So all dharmas are mere appearances.[5] Causality is an appearance. So long as the intellect views the empirical world through the category of causality, empirical life (saṁsāra) persists. When we transcend the empirical category of causality and view the world *sub specie æternitatis,* empirical objects vanish and empirical life (saṁsāra) ceases.[6] All empirical objects are due to nescience (saṃvṛti) ; they are not eternal ; considered as existent (sat) Brahman they are eternal (aja), and can never be absolutely annihilated.[7] Nāgārjuna also holds the same view. Only he substitutes the Śūnya for Brahman. Empirical objects (dharma) are not really produced ; their production is illusory like magic or māyā (māyopama), and Māyā is not real.[8] All dharmas are uncaused (aja) and inexpressible ; so they can be said to be neither eternal nor non-eternal.[9]

There is neither production nor destruction ; neither bondage nor liberation; neither a seeker of liberation nor a liberated person. Duality is an unreal appearance. One non-dual Brahman alone is real.[10] It appears as manifold empirical

---

[1] *Ibid,* iv. 51.
[2] *Ibid,* iv. 52.
[3] *Ibid,* iv. 53.
[4] *Ibid,* iv., 54.
[5] *Ibid,* iv. 59.
[6] *Ibid,* iv. 56.
[7] *Ibid,* iv. 57.
[8] *Ibid,* iv. 58.
[9] *Ibid,* iv. 60.
[10] *Ibid,* ii. 32.

objects. Duality and multiplicity are its appearances. One non-dual (advaya) Brahman or Ātman alone is good.[1] The multiple world-appearance is neither real in itself nor as Brahman ; no object is different from Brahman ; nor is it non-different from Brahman. The non-phenomenal (prapañco-paśama), non-dual (advaya) Brahman is absolutely devoid of distinction (nirvikalpa).[2] This is the reality within and without. One who knows it becomes identical with it (tattvībhūta).[3] One eternal pure consciousness is devoid of origin, activity, and objects. But it appears to be generated and active, and apprehend objects.[4] Neither the mind (citta) is generated, nor are the empirical objects (dharma) generated.[5] All dharmas are, in reality, beginningless and like the sky. They are one eternal Brahman. There is no plurality anywhere. All dharmas are, in reality, eternally in the nature of eternal consciousness (ādibuddha). He who realizes this becomes immortal. The eternal consciousness is self-revealing. All dharmas are by nature eternally calm (ādiśānta), uncaused, eternally pure and liberated, homogeneous (sama) and non-different (abhinna). Their eternality and homogeneity are beyond doubt.[6] The intuition of the one, eternal, homogeneous consciousness is mokṣa. The knowledge of difference in it is saṁsāra. All selves are naturally pure and transparent and unveiled by nescience ; they are eternally enlightened and eternally liberated.[7] Gauḍapāda converts the Śūnya of Nāgārjuna into Brahman, though he uses the same language and the same arguments. Gauḍapāda, like Nāgārjuna, argues that Ātman, which is by nature self-revealing, is misunderstood by common people, since they know it as neither existent nor non-existent, nor both existent and non-existent, nor neither existent nor non-existent, as neither stable nor unstable, nor both, nor neither. But the enlightened (buddha, sambuddha) person transcends the relativity of intellectual knowledge and intuits the one, homogeneous, eternal Ātman.[8]

Gauḍapāda, like Nāgārjuna, denies causation for similar reasons. Nothing can be produced by itself or by any other

[1] *Ibid*, ii. 33.
[2] *Ibid*, ii. 34, 35.
[3] *Ibid*, ii. 38.
[4] *Ibid*, iv. 45.
[5] *Ibid*, iv. 46.
[6] *Ibid*, iv. 1, 10, 11, 91-93.
[7] *Ibid*, iv. 92.
[8] *Ibid*, iv. 83, 85, 93, 95-100.

thing, since an existent (sat), or non-existent (asat), or both existent and non-existent (sadasat) thing cannot be produced. An existent thing need not be produced. A non-existent thing cannot be produced like a hair's horn. If a thing is both existent and non-existent at the same time, it is self-contradictory and therefore impossible. A thing cannot be produced by itself, or by another, or by both, or by neither.[1] A cause cannot be produced by its beginningless effect. An effect also cannot be produced by a beginningless cause. An uncaused effect cannot produce a cause. An uncaused cause cannot produce an effect. This is the nature of things. That which has no cause cannot be produced. Therefore both cause and effect are uncaused.[2] If cognitions are said to be produced by objects in order to account for their variety, one eternal Brahman can adequately account for variety of empirical objects and empirical cognitions. Cognitions and objects are its mere appearances. Objects have no existence apart from the mind which apprehends them. Extra-mental objects, past, present, or future, cannot produce cognitions, and cannot therefore be apprehended by them. Therefore neither cognitions nor objects are produced. Their production is an appearance. Cognitions spring from that whose nature is uncaused (aja) or eternal, and can never be altered. They are mere appearances of one eternal Brahman. If there is production, beginningless saṁsāra cannot have an end, and mokṣa produced by discriminative knowledge cannot be endless. But, in fact, saṁsāra is ended, and mokṣa is endless. So there is no causation.[3] Because there is no production, all are uncaused (aja) and eternal. In fact, unreal appearances can never spring from the real Brahman. A non-existent thing cannot be produced by a non-existent cause ; nor can an existent thing be produced by a non-existent cause. An existent thing cannot be produced by an existent cause. So a non-existent cause can never produce an existent thing. Cause and effect are supposed to be distinct from each other. If duality is real, then cause and effect are supposed to be distinct from each other. If duality is real, then cause and effect are real. But duality is an appearance. So cause and effect are mere

[1] *Ibid*, SB., iv. 22.
[2] *Ibid*, iv. 23.
[3] *Ibid*, iv. 23-30.

appearances. If one eternal (aja) Brahman is real, cause and effect cannot be real. Hence non-production (ajāti) is real. One eternal (aja) Brahman appears to be many caused effects which are unreal appearances. All dharmas are uncaused and eternal (aja) in their essential nature. They appear to spring into existence owing to nescience (saṁvṛti). Their production is apparent, and not real. It is māyā which does not exist.[1] Thus there is no real causation.

The Sāṁkhya holds that eternal (aja) prakṛti is modified into mahat, ahaṁkāra and the like, which are its effects. The effects are non-different from the cause. But how can prakṛti which produces effects be uncaused, and how can it remain eternal when it is modified into effects? If an effect is not different from its cause, it is eternal and uncaused (aja) like prakṛti which is its cause. If the effect is non-eternal, then its cause, prakṛti, is non-eternal, since the effect is non-different from the cause. There is no example to show that an uncaused cause produces an effect. If the effect is produced by a cause which is produced by another cause, then there will be infinite regress.[2] Therefore prakṛti cannot be the cause of all effects in the world.

Some hold that merits and demerits are the cause of birth, and that birth is the cause of merits and demerits. They cannot account for the beginningless relation of mutual dependence or reciprocal causation between birth and merits and demerits. If a cause produces an effect, and the effect produces the cause, then a father can produce a son, and the son also can produce his father, which is absurd. We must admit priority and posteriority in the production of cause and effect. If they are produced simultaneously, they cannot be related to each other as cause and effect like the two horns of cow springing into existence together. Causation must be sequence. The cause must be an antecedent of its effect. The effect must be its consequent. Simultaneity cannot account for causation. If the cause be produced by its effect, it cannot be established as its cause. If it cannot be established as its cause, how can it produce its effect? If the cause is produced by its effect and the effect is produced by the cause, which of them is produced

[1] *Ibid*, iv. 38, 40, 43, 45, 46, 57, 58.
[2] *Ibid*, iv. 11-13.

first so that it may produce the other? If they are produced simultaneously they cannot be related to each other as cause and effect. Simultaneity cannot explain the order of production. Causal order is intelligible only if causation is successive. If seed and sprout are said to be produced by each other, the beginninglessness of their mutual causation cannot be established. If priority and posteriority of cause and effect cannot be determined, it proves the unreality of production (ajāti). If an effect were really produced, its prior cause would certainly be known. Therefore there is no real production.[1] These arguments of Gauḍapāda are similar to those of Nāgārjuna.

Gauḍapāda mentions different theories of creation. Some regard it as manifestation of the glory of God (vibhūti). Others regard it as unreal like dream and magic show (svapnamāyāsarūpa). Others maintain that God created the world by mere fiat of will (icchāmātra). Others hold that time created the world. Some maintain that God created the world for enjoyment (bhoga), while others hold that He created it for His sport (krīḍā). Gauḍapāda rejects all these views and maintains that it is the inherent nature (svabhāva) of God that He should create the world. He is eternally fulfilled (āptakāma) and so cannot have any desire.[2] Brahman associated with Māyā (prāṇa) produces all inanimate objects. The cosmic consciousness (cetas) produces all jīvas or individual souls.[3] The world-appearance is mere māyā; one eternal Brahman is the only reality.[4] Brahman is unconditioned (para) and conditioned (apara). Unconditioned Brahman is one eternal consciousness beyond space, time, and causality. Conditioned Brahman is God who is transcendent to and immanent in all creatures.[5] God is Brahman associated with Māyā. He imagines the multiple world and souls by His own power of Māyā (svamāyayā).[6] God imagines the variety of cognitions and the variety of objects.[7] He creates objects through His power of Māyā and is deluded, as it were, by His creation.[8] The world is neither different nor non-different from Brahman.[9] One Brahman is equally present every-

---

[1] *Ibid*, iv. 14-20.
[2] Māṇḍ. K., i. 7-9.
[3] *Ibid*, i. 6.
[4] *Ibid*, i. 17.
[5] *Ibid*, i. 25-28.
[6] *Ibid*, ii. 12.
[7] *Ibid*, ii. 13.
[8] *Ibid*, ii. 17.
[9] *Ibid*, ii. 34.

where. All things are uncaused (ajāti), eternal Brahman.[1] Creation is not real.

The jīva or individual soul is said to be born, as it were, from the universal soul or Brahman in conjunction with body (saṁghāta) which is its adjunct (upādhi), even as the ether limited in a jar (ghaṭākāśa) is said to be born from the ubiquitous ether (mahākāśa) though, in reality, they are identical with each other. When the jar is destroyed, the ether in it is merged in the ubiquitous ether. So when the body is destroyed, the individual soul becomes the universal soul. The adjunct of body individualizes the jīva. When the limiting adjunct is destroyed, it realizes its identity with Brahman. Though the universal soul is one, the individual souls are many owing to their limiting adjuncts. When one individual soul feels pleasure or pain, other jīvas do not feel pleasure or pain, even as the ether limited by one jar soiled by dust, smoke and the like does not soil the ether limited by any other jar with these impurities. The ether is ubiquitous, but the ether limited in a jar is small. Its small extent and different function such as containing water are due to the adjunct, *viz.*, the jar, though, in reality, it is identical with the ubiquitous ether. Ether is one ; its differences are due to its limiting adjuncts. Likewise Brahman is one ; its empirical plurality as jīvas is due to its limiting adjuncts. Just as the ether limited in a jar is neither a part nor a modification of the ubiquitous ether, so the jīva is neither a part nor a modification of Brahman. Just as the ubiquitous ether appears to be soiled with smoke to ignorant persons, so the universal soul appears to be subject to birth and death to ignorant persons. Just as the ether is incapable of birth, death, and movement, so the universal soul, which is the reality in the jīva, is incapable of birth, death, and transmigration. All adjuncts of body and the like are the products of avidyā of the individual soul (ātmamāyā). They are not ontological realities. They are imaginary creations of the jīva deluded by avidyā. The universal soul (paro jīvaḥ) is the self of the five sheaths, the bodily sheath, the vital sheath, the mental sheath, the intellectual sheath, and the blissful sheath. Identity of the individual soul with the universal soul is real. Difference between them is

[1] *Ibid*, iii. 2.

accidental. Their difference is due to the limiting adjuncts of the bodies and the like. When jīvas are said to spring out of Brahman like the sparks of a fire, their non-difference from it is emphasized. There is absolutely no difference between them.[1] When the jīva breaks the delusion of avidyā, it realizes its identity with Brahman.[2] The jīva is never born.[3]

A person can achieve self-knowledge, eternal peace, sorrowlessness, and fearlessness by rigid control of mind, which is extremely difficult. He should meditate on painfulness of all things, withdraw his mind from all objects of desire and enjoyment, and all empirical objects subject to origin and destruction, and concentrate it on the eternal Brahman. He should transquillize the distracted mind, fix it on the discrimination of one Brahman, and not allow it to be distracted again by empirical objects of enjoyment. Supreme happiness springs from concentration of the mind on Brahman. But the aspirant should not enjoy the happiness ; he should remain absolutely indifferent to it by means of discriminative knowledge of Brahman, and identify his concentrated mind with it with great effort. In such a superconscious trance the mind is identified with Brahman, and does not apprehend empirical objects. Such self-knowledge or self-realization is realization of one's intrinsic nature ; it is calm and attended with supreme indescribable bliss ; it is nirvāṇa ; it is knowledge of the eternal self by itself ; it is above distinction of subject and object. This is called *asparśayoga* in which there is intuitive experience of Brahman devoid of experience of all empirical objects. This is the highest good. It is extremely difficult of realization.[4]

Gauḍapāda assimilated the teachings of Nāgārjuna and the Vijñānavādins and grafted on them the Absolutism (brahmavāda) of the Upaniṣads. His Absolutism is blended with the relativism and phenomenalism of Nāgārjuna, and subjectivism of the Vijñānavādins. His Brahman is non-dual (advaya), non-phenomenal (prapañcopaśama), distinctionless (nirvikalpa), and beyond time, space, and causality like the Sūnya of Nāgārjuna. It appears to be manifold owing to saṁvṛti or avidyā. Causality is unreal. There is neither production nor destruction, neither bondage nor liberation. The reality is non-dual. There

---

[1] *Ibid,* iii. 3-14.
[2] *Ibid,* i. 16.
[3] *Ibid,* iii. 48.
[4] *Ibid,* iii. 40-47, 39.

are neither empirical subjects nor empirical objects. There is only one eternal Brahman; it is devoid of empirical characters; it is incomprehensible and indefinable. It can be realized by supra-intellectual intuition. It can be characterized as neither existence nor non-existence, nor both, nor neither. What is non-eternal from the empirical standpoint, is eternal from the ontological standpoint. All dharmas are false appearances due to saṁvṛti or nescience. There are two degrees of truth, ontological and empirical. These teachings of Gauḍapāda bear the stamp of Nāgārjuna's teachings.[1]

The unconditioned Brahman of Gauḍapāda corresponds to the pure eternal consciousness (vijñaptimātratā) of Vasubandhu. God (īśvara) or conditioned Brahman corresponds to the Ālaya-vijñāna of the Vijñānavādins, which creates the empirical minds and the empirical objects. The world-appearance is the subjective creation of the mind agitated by avidyā (cittaspandita). It is unreal like dream, mirage, and reverie. Dreams and waking perceptions are equally unreal. One eternal cognition (vijñāna) alone is real. It is devoid of distinction of subject and object, which is imaginary. All objects of cognitions are unreal.[2] These teachings of Gauḍapāda are influenced by the Vijñānavāda of Asaṅga, Vasubandhu and others. But his doctrines of Brahman and Māyā and the identity of the world-appearance and the jīvas with Brahman are derived from the Upaniṣads. Gauḍapāda says, "This was not spoken by Buddha."[3] Śaṁkara in commenting on it says, "The non-dual ontological reality devoid of cognition, cognized object, and cognizer was not taught by Buddha. It is the teaching of the Vedānta."

8. *The Philosophy of the Yogavāśiṣṭha*

The *Yogavāśiṣṭha* was composed in the seventh or eighth century. It contains the teachings of Vaśiṣṭha to Rāmacandra. Its philosophy resembles the Absolute Idealism of Gauḍapāda and Śaṁkara, relativism of Nāgārjuna, and the Vijñānavāda of *Laṅkāvatārasūtra,* Asaṅga and Vasubandhu. So its philosophy is summarized here.

---

[1] *Ibid,* ii. 32, 33, 35; iii. 26, 37, 47; iv. 29, 33.
[2] *Ibid,* iv. 36, 45, 47-52, 61, 62, 72.
[3] Naitad buddhena bhāṣitam. *Ibid,* iv. 99.

Vaśiṣṭa affirms the reality of the unconditioned Brahman (para brahma). It is the supreme reality. It is indefinable and inexpressible. It is absolutely indeterminate and characterless. "It is neither spirit nor matter, neither being nor non-being, neither ego nor non-ego, neither one nor many."[1] It is neither part nor whole, neither substance nor non-substance, neither existent nor non-existent, neither self nor not-self. Matter and spirit are differentiations within it. Being and non-being are neutralized by each other in it. Self and not-self are relative to each other. The unconditioned Brahman cannot be affected by relativity. It is beyond time, space, causality, change, and other empirical categories. It is neither static or dynamic. Its inherent nature (svabhāva) cannot be defined. It is indeterminate. It is one, eternal, homogeneous, pure consciousness (cinmātra). It is subject-objectless. It is śūnya because it transcends all forms of individuation ; it is aśūnya because all individual things emanate from it. It is like the essenceless Śūnya of the Śūnyavādins, the Brahman of the Vedāntins, and the Vijñānamātra or pure consciousness of the Vijñānavādins. It is like the Tathatā of Aśvaghoṣa, which is neither existent nor non-existent nor both nor neither, neither one nor many, nor both one and many at once.[2] It is the ultimate Reality. It is the reality of the whole world. It is immanent in the entire universe. Whatever exists is Brahman.[3]

The unconditioned Brahman or Absolute consciousness (cinmātra) creates Brahmā, the Cosmic Mind, by intensifying its consciousness partly. Brahmā is personal God. He emerges from Absolute Consciousness (Brahman) like a dream personality (svapnapuruṣa) owing to its stress (spanda) or vibration. Brahmā is the Cosmic Mind. Imagination (saṁkalpana) is the essential characteristic of mind. The world is the creation or imagination of Brahmā. Brahmā, the Cosmic Mind, originates from the Absolute Brahman, as a wave originates from an undisturbed ocean. The emergence of Brahmā is due to a vibratory movement (spanda) in the Absolute Consciousness. Just as Tathatā of Aśvaghoṣa, which is unconditioned, becomes relative

---

[1] *Yogavāśiṣṭha*, v. 72. 41.

[2] *The Awakening of Faith*, p. 59.

[3] *Yogavāśiṣṭha*, v. 72. 42-43; iii. 5. 5-7; iii. 9. 49; iii. 91. 36; vi. 47. 2; B. L. Ātreya : *The Philosophy of the Yogavāśiṣṭha*, ii. ch. xi.

and conditioned in Ālayavijñāna, so the Absolute Brahman of Vaśiṣṭha becomes Brahmā by its spiritual outflow. Absolute Brahman is beyond time, space, and causality. But Brahmā is its individualized form limited in time and space by its own power out of sport. Just as Ālayavijñāna is the intermediate principle between Tathatā and the empirical world, so Brahmā connects the Absolute Brahman with the empirical world. Just as Ālayavijñāna is the self-affirmation of Tathatā, so Brahmā is the self-affirmation of the Absolute Brahman.[1] Brahmā is the creator of the world. He is the dreamer of the world-dream. It is His imagination or thought-construction (manorājya).[2]

The unconditioned Brahman of Vaśiṣṭha is not a pure unity without difference like that of Gauḍapāda and Śaṁkara. It is full of infinite powers and potentialities. Creative power is one of them. Multiplicity of empirical objects exist in a potential form in the Absolute Consciousness. They are aspects of the creative or imaginative activity of the Cosmic Mind. Creative activity is the vibratory movement (spəndaśakti) of the Absolute Consciousness. It is imaginative power (saṁkalpaśakti). This creative power is called Prakṛti, the will of God (śivecchā), the Māyā of the world (jaganmāyā). Prakṛti is the creative power of the Absolute Consciousness. The multiplicity of the world is the manifestation of the creative power of the Absolute Conciousness. Prakṛti originates from Brahman, which is the eternal illuminating consciousness, called Puruṣa. The creative power (spandaśakti) and the Pure Consciousness (cinmātra) are always identical in essence (ekātmā). Pure consciousness (śiva) cannot exist without its vibratory movement (spandaśakti), of Prakṛti, which is identical in essence with Pure Consciousness (saṁvinmātra).[3] This doctrine resembles Śaivism.

The world is expansion (bṛṁhana) of Brahman ; the expansion of Brahman is the world. The world is the flashing of the Absolute Consciousness which is pure and transparent. All that exists, is Brahman. All that is produced, exists, and is destroyed is Brahman. The world is the vibration of the Self

[1] *Yogavāśiṣṭha,* iii. 55. 47; vi. 186. 65; iii. 3. 34; iii. 1. 15; iii. 100. 25; iv. 42. 4, 5, 6; iv. 44. 14, 15; iii. 2. 54, 55; *The Philosophy of the Yogavāśiṣṭha,* ii. ch. ix.

[2] *Yogavāśiṣṭha,* iii. 3. 15, 33.

[3] *Yogavāśiṣṭha,* iii. 67. 2; vi. 85. 14; iii. 96. 70; iii. 96. 71; vi. 84. 3; vi 83. 14; vi. 85. 18, 19; *The Philosophy of the Yogavāśiṣṭha,* ii. ch. x.

(Ātmā) or Pure Consciousness. It exists in a potential form in Brahman even as a tree exists in a potential condition in a seed. Empirical plurality are differentiations of the one homogeneous pure consciousness. They are harmonized with one another in the concrete unity of the Absolute Consciousness, which is a unified whole. The manifold world is the manifestation or differentiation of the Absolute Consciousness, apart from which it has no existence. The being of the world is the being of Absolute Consciousness (citsattā). The being of Absolute Consciousness is the being of the world. It is the inherent nature of the Absolute Consciousness to manifest itself as the manifold world. Its power of manifestation is imaginative construction. Brahmā emerges as a dream personality within the Absolute Consciousness. This is the first creative act. Then the world is the imaginative construction of Brahmā or Cosmic Mind. The multiplicity of the world do not impair the unity of the Absolute. Just as the unity of consciousness is preserved in the plurality of dream-objects, so the plurality of empirical objects do not impair the unity of the Absolute Consciousness (cidākāśa). Multiplicity of empirical objects are vibrations of the one Absolute Consciousness even as waves are the vibrations of one ocean. In reality, the Absolute and the world are the same, though the world appears to be different from Brahman.[1]

The relation of the world with the Absolute is identity (tādātmya), non-difference (abhinnatā), or non-otherness (ananyatva). As gold ornaments are not different from gold, and as waves are not different from water, so the world is not different from Brahman. Origination, existence, destruction, agent, instrument, and action, time, space, causation, change, substance—all are Brahman. The being of the world is the being of the Absolute Consciousness. The world is the embodiment of Pure Consciousness (cidavapuṣ).[2]

Vaśiṣṭha, like Nāgārjuna and Gauḍapāda, argued that the Absolute is the eternal reality. It has no beginning, middle, or end. It persists for ever.[3] The world is an appearance. It

[1] *Yogavāśiṣṭha,* vi. 2. 27; vi. 99. 18; iii. 100. 11, 28; iii. 11. 20; vi. 35. 6; vi. 191. 10, 11; iii. 14. 75; vi. 47. 29; vi. 144. 23; iv. 36. 16; *The Philosophy of the Yogavāśiṣṭha,* ii. ch. xii.

[2] *Yogavāśiṣṭha,* iii. 1. 17; iii. 61. 4; iii. 100. 30; vi. 60. 28; iii. 14. 74; *The Philsophy of the Yogavāśiṣṭha,* ii. ch. xiii.

[3] *Yogavāśiṣṭha,* v. 5. 9; iv. 45, 46; v. 5, 9; MK. xi. 2; Māṇḍ. K., iv. 31.

is false (mithyā). It is unreal like a dream or an illusion (bhrāntimātra). It is a mixture of reality and unreality (sadasanmaya). It is neither real nor unreal like a dream or an illusion. So long as dream continues, it is real to the dreamer. So long as illusion lasts, it is real to the experiencer. So long as the identity of the world-appearance with Brahman is not realized by intuition, it is real to the individual mind. Thus the world partakes of both reality and unreality. It is an appearance (pratibhāna).[1] It is unreal (asatya). But it appears to be real (satyābha). It is a mere subjective creation, an imaginary construction (kalpanāmātra). There is no difference between dream and waking perception. They are equally subjective creations of mind. Vaśiṣṭha, like Gauḍapāda, does not distinguish between dreams and waking perceptions.

The individual mind (jīva) is an atom of consciousness (cidaṇu), or a monad. It is the Absolute Consciousness manifesting itself as a creative agent. It is an individualized form of the Absolute Consciousness through its own will-power. It is an embodiment of the self-affirmed will of the Absolute, which becomes consciousness of an objective world. It imagines its own world of objects and clings to them owing to ignorance. It forgets its identity with the Absolute. It forgets the identity of the world with the Absolute. Individuality is self-alienation of the Absolute from itself. Brahman is pure subject-objectless consciousness. But the individual mind (jīva) is the subject conscious of empirical objects. It is empirical consciousness with objectivity. It is a pulsation of the Absolute Conciousness, which partakes of subjectivity and objectivity both. It is called the jīva because it is the living principle in the body. It binds itself to its body like a silk-worm. It binds itself to a net-work of objects created by its own imagination.[2]

Bondage is due to ignorance or the sense of individuality. When individuality is annihilated and the knowledge of one's identity with the Absolute dawns, liberation is achieved. Ignorance is bondage. True knowledge is liberation. Intense desire for objects is bondage. Attachment is bondage. It is

[1] *Ibid*, iii. 44. 27; vi. 114. 20; iii. 65. 5; iii. 54. 21.

[2] *Yogavāśiṣṭha*, iii. 96. 3; iii. 4. 43; iii. 96. 40; iii. 91. 37; iii. 91. 40; v. 13. 53; vi. 188. 4; iv. 42. 31; iv. 42. 34; *The Philosophy of the Yogavāśiṣṭha*, ii. ch. iv.

due to ignorance. It is destroyed by the knowledge of identity with Brahman. Liberation can be achieved by destruction of mind or individuality through detachment from all desires. Meditation on the self beyond the body, the senses, the mind, the intellect and the individual ego (jīva), and realization of identity of the Self with Brahman lead to liberation. From the Absolute point of view there is neither bondage nor liberation.[1]

[1] *Yogavāśiṣṭha*, ii. 2. 5; iii. 1. 22; iii. 114. 23; v. 73. 36; vi. 128. 46-47; *The Philosophy of the Yogavāśiṣṭha*, iii. ch. ii.

CHAPTER VII

THE ADVAITA VEDĀNTA OF ŚAṀKARA

1. *Introduction*

Śaṁkara (788—820 A.D.) was the greatest philosopher among the Indian thinkers in intellectual eminence. He was relentless in his criticism of the other systems. He was zealous and untiring in the exposition of his own system of Absolute Idealism (advaitavāda). He defeated many eminent contemporary philosophers in philosophical discussions. The intellectual atmosphere was surcharged with his Absolute Idealism in his times. He wrote commentaries on the principal Upaniṣads, the *Brahmasūtra,* and the *Bhagavad Gītā.* He wrote commentaries on Kena, Kaṭha, Īśa, Praśna, Muṇḍaka, Māṇḍukya, Chāndogya, Bṛhadāraṇyaka, Śvetāśvatara, Aitareya, and Taittirīya Upaniṣads. Our exposition of his Absolute Idealism (Advaita Vedānta) is based on the commentaries on the *Brahmasūtra* and the Upaniṣads. He worte many other minor works which are not of philosophical importance. His commentary on the *Brahmasūtra* is called the *Śārīraka Bhāṣya.* Vācaspatimiśra (900 A.D.) wrote a commentary on it called *Bhāmatī.* Amalānanda (1300 A.D.) wrote a commentary on *Bhāmatī* called *Kalpataru.* Appayadīkṣita (1600 A.D.) wrote a commentary on *Kalpataru* called *Kalpataruparimala.* Govindānanda wrote a commentary on Śaṁkara's *Śārīraka Bhāṣya* called *Ratnaprabhā.* Padmapāda wrote an elaborate gloss on the first four sūtras of the *Brahmasūtra* called *Pañcapādikā.* Prakāśātman (1200 A.D.) wrote a commentary on it called *Pañcapādikāvivaraṇa.* Vidyāraṇya (1400 A.D.) wrote a gloss on it called *Vivaraṇaprameyasaṁgraha.* Śrī Harṣa's *Khaṇḍanakhaṇḍakhādya* (1200 A.D.) is the greatest work on Advaita Vedānta dialectics. Dharmarāja's *Vedāntaparibhāṣā* is an important work on Advaita Vedānta Logic.

Śaṁkara emphasizes the monistic tendency in the Upaniṣads and develops it into a systematic Advaitavāda. He emphasizes the reality of the unconditioned and unqualified (nirguṇa)

Brahman, and regards God (īsvara), the individual souls (jīva) and the world (jagat) as appearances due to an indefinable principle called Māyā (cosmic nescience) which is neither real, nor unreal, nor both, nor neither. God is Brahman associated with Māyā in its excellent aspect. The jīva is Brahman associted with Māyā (avidyā) in its inferior aspect. The jīva is, in essence, identical with Brahman or Ātman. Brahman is one, eternal, pure, transcendental consciousness. It transcends the duality of subject and object. It transcends the empirical categories of space, time, substance, causality, change, and the like. It is transempirical and non-phenomenal. It is pure identity. It is one homogeneous consciousness. It is not the subject or knower. It is devoid of distinction, external and internal. The world is an appearance (prapañca) of Brahman. It is nondifferent from Brahman. Ignorance is bondage. True knowledge is liberation. Bondage is due to avidyā which generates a false sense of individuality. It is due to knowledge of difference and multiplicity. Liberation is pure intuition of Brahman,—knowledge of identity. Jñāna leads to liberation. Karma does not lead to liberation. It belongs to a lower order. Śaṁkara is untiring in re-iterating the importance of renunciation (sannyāsa) of worldly life and dedication of life to the pursuit of knowledge of Ātman or Brahman. But he does not discard ethics and religion. Śaṁkara recognizes the empirical reality (vyāvahārikasattā) of the individual souls (jīva) and the world-appearance (jagatprapañca) for practical purposes. But he maintains the ontological reality (pāramārthikasattā) of the unconditioned and unqualified Brahman only. He advocates unqualified monism (advaita) or non-dualism. He advocates Absolutism like Nāgārjuna. But he converts the Śūnya of Nāgārjuna into Brahman, which is one eternal transcendental being (sat), consciousness (cit) and bliss (ānanda). His Brahman is like the one, eternal, pure consciousness (vijñānamātra) of the Yogācāra Vijñānavādins. He himself calls it Vijñaptimātra and Vijñānamātra.[1] But his idealism cannot be branded as subjecticism. He severely criticizes the subjective idealism of some Buddhist idealists. He advocates Vivartavāda in his theory of causation. The effect is an appearance (vivarta) of the cause. It pre-exists

[1] SB., Māṇḍ. K., iv. 60, 62.

in the cause. Śaṁkara advocates Satkāryavāda in the form of Vivartavāda. Dr. Das Gupta calls it Satkāraṇavāda. Brahman, the cause, is real. The world, its effect, is its appearance (vivarta). Śaṁkara discredits intellect, which gives false knowledge (avidyā), and stresses the importance of intuition (anubhava), which is right knowledge (samyagdarśana). But he does not discredit reason (tarka), which he subordinates to Śruti or intuition of the seers. Śaṁkara severely criticizes the other schools of philosophy, both orthodox and heterodox. His criticism of the other systems will be given first. Then an exposition of his system will be given.

I. CRITIQUE

2. *Śaṁkara's Criticism of the Vaiśeṣika Pluralism and Atomism*

Śaṁkara criticizes the early Vaiśeṣika doctrine of six categories, *viz.*, substance (dravya), quality (guṇa), activity (karma), generality (sāmānya), particularity (viśeṣa), and inherence (samavāya). The Vaiśeṣika regards them as independent categories or existences possessed of different characteristics. Still it regards quality, action, generality, particularity, and inherence as dependent on substance. Quality cannot exist apart from a substance. Activity cannot exist apart from a substance. Generality cannot exist apart from individual substances. Particularity cannot exist apart from eternal individual substances. Inherence is a relation between a substance and a quality or an action, a whole and a part, a generality and an individual, and particularity and an eternal substance. But a substance can exist apart from a quality or an activity. Therefore quality, activity, generality, particularity, and inherence should be regarded as identical with substance (dravyātmaka). If they are all independent categories (padārtha), quality, action, generality, particularity, and inherence should exist independently of substance. Therefore the Vaiśeṣika pluralism is not logically tenable.

Inherence (samavāya) cannot be regarded as an independent category. It is said to be an inseparable relation (ayutasiddhi) between substance and quality, substance and action, whole and part, generality and individuals, and particularity and eternal substances. But a substance in the first moment of its production can exist apart from its qualities ; it is endued with its qualities in the second moment of its existence. Thus, though qualities cannot exist apart from a substance, a substance can exist apart from them. The effect, the whole prior to its production, cannot be inseparably related to its cause, the parts. Generality can exist apart from individuals. But individuals cannot exist apart from generality. Therefore inherence cannot be said to be inseparable relation (ayutasiddhi). Inherence is a relation. A relation cannot exist apart from the relata. The being of the relation depends on the being of the relata.

Inherence is said to be inseparability of existence (ayutasiddhatva). Is it inseparability in space (apṛthagdeśatva), or inseparability in time (apṛthakkālatva), or inseparability in nature (apṛthaksvabhāvatva)? If it is inseparability in space, it contradicts the Vaiśeṣika doctrine that whiteness of a cloth, which inheres in it, occupies the space of the cloth, while the cloth occupies the space of its constituent threads. So inherence is not inseparability in space. If it is inseparability in time, then the two horns of a cow growing together would inhere in each other, which is not admitted. If it is inseparability in nature, it is nothing but identity (tādātmya). Śaṁkara does not recognize inherence as an independent category or relation. He reduces it to identity.[1]

If the relation of inherence is required to relate a substance to its quality, then it being an independent category would require another inherence to relate itself to the substance, and the second inherence would require a third, and so on to infinity. Thus it would involve infinite regress (anavasthā).[2] Therefore inherence is not an independent category. It is mere identity (tādātmya).

The Vaiśeṣika advocates atomism. There are four kinds of atoms, earth atoms, water atoms, fire atoms, and air atoms. Atoms are indivisible units of matter. Two atoms are conjoined into a dyad. Two dyads are conjoined into a quartrad. Atoms are globular and minute. Dyads also are minute. But quartrads are large. Conjunction of atoms is creation of the world.

[1] SBS., ii. 2. 17. [2] SBS., ii. 2. 13.

Disjunction of atoms is its dissolution. Prior to creation conjunction of atoms is due to activity brought about by the unseen agency (adṛṣṭa). Śaṁkara considers the earlier Vaiśeṣika doctrine which does not believe in God as the creator of the world.

Śaṁkara criticizes the earlier Vaiśeṣika atomism. Conjunction of atoms must be due to an activity (karma). When atoms are in motion they come into conjunction with one another. Activity is an effect. So it must have a cause. If it has no cause, it cannot come into existence. If it has a cause, it must be volition (prayatna) or impact (abhighāta). The individual souls are unconscious and devoid of volition prior to creation. They acquire volition in conjunction with body after creation. There is no body before creation. Therefore the souls have no volition at the time. Hence the original activity before creation cannot be due to volition. It cannot be due to impact which is due to gravity and viscidity. They are always present in atoms. So activity due to them would be always present. Activity posterior to creation cannot be the cause of the original act prior to creation.

If the original act (karma) be said to be due to the unseen agencies (adṛṣṭa) or merits and demerits of souls, they inhere in the souls or atoms. In either case they are non-intelligent (acetana), and cannot act independently or move atoms to act without being supervised by an intelligent (cetana) principle. The souls are non-intelligent prior to creation. If the unseen agencies inhere in the souls, they cannot produce activity (karma) in the atoms because there is no relation between them. If there is a relation between the unseen agencies (adṛṣṭa) and the atoms, the relation being always present, activity in the atoms would always be present and lead to unceasing creation. There being no particular cause of the original creative act, there would be no conjunction of the atoms leading to creation.

Supposing the atoms come into conjunction with one another, they are conjoined either wholly or partly. If they are wholly conjoined, they would interpenetrate one another, and never lose their atomic dimension, and produce large dimensions in their aggregates. If they are partly conjoined, they would cease to be partless and indivisible. If the atoms have imaginary parts, their conjunction also would become imaginary. There being no conjunction, which is the non-inherent cause of dyads, quartrads, and the like, these aggregates would not be produced.

Just as there can be no creation in the absence of the cause of the creative act, so there can be no dissolution in the absence of the destructive act. Just as an activity is necessary to bring about conjunction of the atoms, so an activity is necessary to bring about disjunction of the atoms. The unseen agencies (adṛṣṭa), merits and demerits of the souls, can bring about their enjoyments and sufferings. They can never cause dissolution. Therefore the Vaiśeṣika cannot account for creation and dissolution.[1]

Further, atoms are naturally active, or inactive, or both, or neither. If they are naturally active, their activity would never cease, and there would be no dissolution. If they are naturally inactive, their inactivity would never cease, and there would be no creation. They cannot be both active and inactive because it is self-contradictory. If they are naturally neither active nor inactive, then their activity and inactivity would be due to an extraneous cause such as the unseen agencies (adṛṣṭa) and the like. And these being always present, there would be perpetual activity or perpetual inactivity of the atoms, or perpetual creation or perpetual dissolution. If the unseen agencies are supposed to be dependent and non-eternal, then there would be perpetual inactivity of the atoms, and there would be no creation.[2]

Earth has smell, taste, colour, and touch. Water has taste, colour, and touch. Fire has colour and touch. Air has touch. Their atoms also must have the corresponding qualities, since the qualities of the material cause produce qualities in the effect. A larger number of qualities would require a larger dimension. A smaller number of qualities would require a smaller dimension. Therefore the earth atoms would be larger than the water atoms, which would be larger than the fire atoms, which would be larger than the air atoms. Therefore the atoms cannot be said to be indivisible and of the minutest magnitude. If the four kinds of atoms are supposed to be homogeneous, then smell would be perceived in water, smell and taste, in

---

[1] SBS., ii. 2. 12.

[2] SBS., ii. 2. 14.

fire, smell, colour, and taste, in air. But they are not perceived in these substances. Hence atoms cannot be the material cause of the world.[1]

3. *Śaṁkara's Criticism of the Sāṁkhya doctrine of Prakṛti as the Material Cause of the World*

The Sāṁkhya maintains that prakṛti, the triad of sattva, rajas, and tamas, is stimulated to activity by the transcendental influence of the puruṣas or individual souls and evolves into the world to effect their experience (bhoga) and liberation (apavarga). Śaṁkara urges that non-intelligent (acetana) prakṛti can never act and evolve the world without being supervised by an intelligent (cetana) principle. Clay is made into a pot when it is supervised and moulded by a potter. A pot has a particular arrangement (viśiṣṭākārā racanā) which can be made only by an intelligent potter. Unconscious prakṛti cannot produce the world with a particular arrangement (racanā), order, and harmony, and adapted to the merits and demerits of the individual souls, without being supervised by an intelligent principle. Sattva, rajas, and tamas are said to be in the nature of pleasure, pain, and delusion (sukhaduḥkhamohātmaka). They are feeling substances. They produce all external objects, internal organs, and mental modes. This is wrong. Pleasure, pain, and delusion are subjective (āntara). They cannot produce external objects. The same external object can produce pleasure, pain, or delusion according to the difference of mental dispositions (bhāvanāviśeṣa). So it cannot be made of pleasure, pain, and delusion. The Sāṁkhya argues that sattva, rajas, and tamas which are of limited magnitude, come into relation (saṁsarga) with one another, and produce external and internal objects, just as seeds of limited magnitude produce limited sprouts, when they come into relation with one another. This argument is wrong. A chair, a bed and the like are made out of their stuff only when it is supervised by an intelligent principle. The cause-effect relation is always found to be supervised by an intelligent agent.[2]

Prakṛti is in a state of equilibrium prior to creation. How is the equipoise (sāmyāvasthā) of sattva, rajas, and tamas dis-

---

[1] SBS., ii. 2. 16. [2] SBS., ii. 2. 1.

turbed? How do they come to be related to one another as principal (aṅgin) and subordinate (aṅga), and assume a tendency to act in order to produce specific effects? They are non-intelligent (acetana) and independent (svatantra). Therefore they cannot act by themselves and produce specific effects. Non-intelligent clay cannot turn into a specific pot without being supervised by an intelligent potter. A non-intelligent chariot cannot move without being supervised by intelligent horses. Therefore non-intelligent prakṛti cannot produce the world since it cannot act. The original creative act (pravṛtti) of prakṛti and its disequilibrium prior to creation are inexplicable.

It may be urged that an intelligent principle cannot act without the aid of a non-intelligent thing. An intelligent horse can act and move a non-intelligent chariot. What is the cause of activity? Is it the intelligent horse or the non-intelligent chariot? Activity is perceived in the latter. Therefore it may be said to be due to the non-intelligent thing in which activity is perceived. This is wrong. When an intelligent principle is present, activity in the non-intelligent thing is present. When an intelligent principle is absent, activity in the non-intelligent thing is absent. Therefore the cause of activity of a non-intelligent thing must be the intelligent principle. Prakṛti is non-intelligent. It cannot be the cause of its own activity.

The Śāṁkhya may argue that the Ātman, the one, eternal, pure consciousness (vijñānasvarūpamātra), cannot be the cause of activity. Śaṁkara argues that the inactive Lord (īśvara), who is ubiquitous, immanent in the entire universe, omniscient, and omnipotent, can act and create the world, even as an inactive magnet can move a piece of iron, or as inactive objects can move the sense-organs. But how can there be activity of the Lord in the absence of any thing to be acted on? Śaṁkara argues that the diverse names and forms (nāmarūpa) presented by Māyā, Avidyā, or cosmic nescience are acted upon (pravartya) by the Lord who is the active agent (pravartaka). God is the efficient cause of the world. Māyā, the power of God, is its material cause. Thus God is both the efficient cause and the material cause of the world. Unconscious prakṛti cannot be the cause of the world.[1]

---

[1] SBS., ii. 2. 2.

The Sāṁkhya argues that non-intelligent prakṛti acts by its very nature in order to realize the ends of puruṣas, even as unconscious milk flows out of the udders of a cow by its very nature for the nourishment of the calf, or as unconscious water flows by its very nature for the good of the people. This argument is wrong. Milk and water act because they are supervised by an intelligent principle (cetanādhiṣṭhita). The cow consciously and willingly emits milk out of her udders out of affection for her calf. The calf also voluntarily draws milk from her udders. Water flows at the will of the Lord. It also depends on the low ground in order to flow. All unconscious objects must be guided by a conscious spirit in order to act. Therefore unconscious prakṛti cannot act by its own nature without the guidance of a conscious spirit.[1]

Prakṛti consists of sattva, rajas, and tamas. They exist in a state of equilibrium before creation. Prakṛti cannot act or cease to act without them. It does not depend on an extraneous condition in order to be active or inactive. Puruṣas are indifferent (udāsīna) and inactive. So they cannot move prakṛti to activity or inactivity. Prakṛti is independent. Why it acts sometimes and is modified into mahat and the like, and why it ceases to act sometimes and dissolves the world cannot be explained by the Sāṁkhya. But God is omniscient, omnipotent, and endowed with the power of Māyā. Therefore He can create and destroy the world at His will, or in sport, or by His diverse nature, or in accordance with the merits and demerits of the individual souls.[2]

The Sāṁkhya may argue that a conscious, inactive puruṣa moves unconscious prakṛti to activity, even as a lame man of good vision mounted on the shoulders of a blind man of sure foot guides him in his movements, or as an unmoved magnet moves a piece of iron. This argument is wrong. The lame man guides the blind man by his words. But the puruṣa is devoid of the guṇas and activity, and it cannot therefore move prakṛti to activity. How can the inactive puruṣa move prakṛti to activity? It cannot move prakṛti to activity by mere proximity (sannidhi) as a magnet attracts a piece of iron by mere

---

[1] SBS., ii. 2. 3.

[2] SBS., *Bhāmati,* ii. 2. 4.

proximity, since proximity of the puruṣa to prakṛti is eternal, and therefore the activity of prakṛti would be eternal. Prakṛti is unconscious, and the puruṣa is inactive, and there is no *tertium quid* to relate them to each other. Therefore the puruṣa cannot move prakṛti to activity. If fitness (yogyatā) between them be said to relate them to each other, then fitness being eternal, they would be eternally related to each other, and there would be no liberation of the puruṣa. But Śaṁkara holds that the supreme Ātman is inactive in itself, but it becomes active in association with Māyā.[1] Therefore prakṛti cannot be active under the influence of a puruṣa.

Further, prakṛti is a state of equilibrium of the constituent guṇas, sattva, rajas, and tamas, when they are not related to one another as principal and subordinate. They do not depend on any external condition of that time. Therefore they can never acquire quantitative inequalities and start evolution of the world. They cannot pass from the homogeneous to the heterogeneous condition. There is no external moving power to upset the equipoise of the guṇas. Therefore they cannot evolve into mahat, ahaṁkāra, and the like which are composed of the guṇas in unequal quantities (guṇavaiṣamyanimitta).[2]

The Sāṁkhya may urge that sattva, rajas, and tamas are restless (cala), which have capacity for acquiring quantitative inequalities even in a state of equipoise. But Śaṁkara contends that even then the unconscious guṇas cannot produce the world with a particular arrangement. If they are supposed to be conscious, then the Sāṁkhya position that unconscious prakṛti is the material cause of the world is undermined. Even if the guṇas have the capacity for acquiring quantitative inequalities and heterogeneity (vaiṣamaya) in the state of equipoise, they cannot become heterogeneous in the absence of an efficient cause. If they are thrown into a state of disequilibrium and become heterogeneous in the absence of an efficient cause, then they would always be heterogeneous, and cannot acquire the homogeneous state of equilibrium.[3] Therefore prakṛti cannot be the cause of the world.

---

[1] SBS., ii. 2. 7.
[2] SBS., ii. 2. 8.
[3] SBS., ii. 2. 9.

4. *Śaṁkara's Criticism of the doctrine of God as the Efficient Cause of the World.*

Some philosophers hold that God is only the efficient cause of the world. The Yoga holds that God, the supervisor (adhiṣṭhātṛ) of prakṛti and puruṣas, is the efficient cause of the world. Prakṛti is its material cause. Prakṛti, puruṣas, and God are different from one another. The Śaivas also hold that God is the efficient cause of the world, while prakṛti is its material cause. The later Naiyāyikas and the Vaiśeṣikas also maintain that God is the efficient cause of the world, while the atoms are its material cause.

Śaṁkara argues that first, if God is the efficient cause of the world, He is partial and subject to attachment and aversion, and cannot therefore be the Lord, since He creates good, mediocre, and bad creatures. Secondly, if the different lots of creatures be said to be due to their own merits and demerits (prāṇikarma) in accordance with which God creates them, then God's creative activity would depend on the creatures' merits and demerits, and their moral deserts would depend on the will of God, and thus there would be mutual dependence (anyonyāśraya). The creatures' merits and demerits (karma) are unconscious, and so they cannot move God to action. If the reciprocal activity of Gods' creative will and the creatures' merits and demerits be said to be beginningless (anādi), it would not solve the difficulty. Each creative will of God would depend on prior merits and demerits of creatures, and their merits and demerits would depend on prior creative will of God. The supposition that unconscious merits and demerits of creatures move God to action is as irrational as the supposition that a series of blind men lead one another. Thirdly, a defect (doṣa), attachment, aversion, or any other emotion or passion, is the spring of action. None is engaged in action without being actuated by an emotion or passion for his own good or for the good of others. Persons are engaged in actions even for others' good with a selfish motive. Self-interest is the primary motive of their actions. Therefore God's creative act must be actuated by a selfish motive, and thus He would lose His divinity and Lordship. Fourthly, the Yoga holds that God is a particular self (puruṣaviśeṣa) free from all taint of afflictions (kleṣa), actions (karma), fruitions (vipāka), and merits and demerits (āśaya). But if God is a particular puruṣa, He is indifferent (udāsīna), and cannot therefore become active. Indifference or inactivity and activity contradict each other.[1] Fifthly, God is said to be the ruler (īśitṛ) of prakṛti and puruṣas, though He is distinct from them. If He is distinct from them, He cannot rule over them without some relation with them. There can be no conjunction (saṁyoga) between them, since they are all ubiquitous and partless. There can be no inherence (samavāya), since there is no relation of the container (āśraya) and the contained (āśrayin) between them. There can be no other relation between them, which may be inferred from the cause-effect relation between them, since God's causality of the world has not yet been established.[2] Sixthly, God cannot act on prakṛti since it is imperceptible and devoid of colour and other sensible qualities. A potter can act on clay which is perceptible and possessed of sensible qualities.[3] The Yoga may argue that just as the self (puruṣa) acts on the sense-organs, which are imperceptible and colourless, so God acts on prakṛti which is imperceptible and colourless. This argument is wrong. The self acts on the sense-organs for its enjoyment and suffering (bhoga). But God is incapable of enjoyment and suffering. He is not subject to empirical life like the empirical self (jīva). Seventhly, an earthly king can rule over his subjects only with the help of a body, but God cannot have a body and sense-organs, and therefore cannot rule over prakṛti. Body comes into existence after creation. It cannot exist before creation. If God is disembodied, He cannot act on prakṛti and create the world out of it. Only an embodied intelligent being can act upon some unconscious material and produce an effect out of it. If God is supposed to have a body, He becomes subject to empirical life and ceases to be God.[4] Lastly, God is said to be omniscient and unlimited. Prakṛti and souls (puruṣa) also are unlimited. They are yet different from one another. Does omniscient God know the unlimited magnitude of Himself, prakṛti and the souls? Or does He not know it? If He knows it, the magnitude of

---

[1] SBS., ii. 2. 37.
[2] SBS., ii. 2. 38.
[3] SBS., ii. 2. 39.
[4] SBS., ii. 2. 40.

Himself, prakṛti and each soul must be limited, since every object whose magnitude is known is found to be limited. If God, prakṛti, and souls are of limited magnitude, they must be non-eternal, since all limited things are non-eternal. The souls are said to be infinite in number. But God, being omniscient, must know their number. But the souls will gradually attain liberation. When all souls will attain liberation, prakṛti will have no purpose to realize, and therefore be devoid of evolution and dissolution, and cease to exist. If prakṛti ceases to exist, God will have nothing to know and act upon, and therefore cease to be omniscient and the efficient cause of the world. God is different from prakṛti and souls. So they must be limited by one another. Being limited, they must have origin and end. If God does not know the magnitude of prakṛti and souls, He ceases to be the omniscient Lord. Therefore God cannot be the efficient cause of the world, prakṛti being its material cause.[1] Thus Śaṁkara refutes the doctrine of the Yoga and the Śaivas. These arguments invalidate the later Nyāya-Vaiśeṣika doctrine also which regards God as the efficient cause of the world and the eternal atoms as its material cause.

5. *Śaṁkara's Criticism of the Bhāgavata doctrine of God as the Efficient Cause and the Material Cause of the World*

The Bhāgavatas maintain that God is the efficient cause and the material cause of the world. Śaṁkara also holds that God is the efficient cause and the material cause of the world. This doctrine is taught by the Upaniṣads. So Śaṁkara criticizes the Bhāgavata doctrine of fourfold manifestations (caturvyūha) of God, which revolts against their monism. The Bhāgavatas maintain that Vāsudeva is one supreme God, who is pure consciousness and the ontological reality. He manifests Himself as Vāsudeva, Śaṁkarṣaṇa, Pradyumna, and Aniruddha. These are the four manifestations of one God. Vāsudeva is the supreme soul (paramātman). Saṁkarṣaṇa is the individual soul (jīva). Pradyumna is the manas or mind. Aniruddha is the ahaṁkāra or egoism. Vāsudeva is the root cause (parā prakṛti) of

[1] SBS., ii. 2. 41.

Saṁkarṣaṇa, Pradyumna, and Aniruddha. They are the effects of parā prakṛti. The individual soul can attain God by recitation of mantras, worship, devotion, and meditation. Śaṁkara does not object to the manifestation of God in diverse ways or the attainment of God by the individual soul by devotion and meditation. But he firstly contends that Saṁkarṣaṇa, the individual soul, cannot be born of Vāsudeva or the supreme soul. If it is born, it must be non-eternal. If it is non-eternal, it cannot attain God. If it is born, its liberation becomes impossible.[1] Secondly, manas, which is the internal organ, cannot be generated by the individual soul. An agent, Devadatta, cannot produce an instrument, an axe. Therefore Saṁkarṣaṇa cannot produce Pradyumna. One instrument cannot produce another instrument. Egoism (ahaṁkāra) cannot be produced by mind (manas). Aniruddha cannot be produced by Pradyumna.[2] Thirdly, if Vāsudeva, Saṁkarṣaṇa, Pradyumna, and Aniruddha be regarded as Lords (īśvara) possessed of supreme knowledge, rulership, power, strength, heroism, and effulgence, equally faultless, immaterial, and eternal, then it leads to polytheism. If one God can explain the entire universe, the hypothesis of many Gods is unwarranted and unjustified. Parsimony of hypothesis demands one God. In fact, the Bhāgavatas themselves look upon Vāsudeva as one supreme God, and the four embodiments (caturvyūha) as possessed of equal powers of Lordship. Therefore Saṁkarṣaṇa cannot be born of Vāsudeva, Pradyumna of Saṁkarṣaṇa, and Aniruddha of Pradyumna, since the cause is not greater than its effect. All the four embodiments of God are possessed of equal powers of Lordship. Therefore they cannot be related to each other as cause and effect.[3] Fourthly, if there is only one God, there cannot be the relation of substance and attributes in Him. The Bhāgavatas maintain that knowledge, rulership, power, strength, heroism, and effulgence are qualities of these four Lords, though they are one God or supreme soul. The attributes are different from the substance. They do not constitute its essence. Śaṁkara does not admit any difference between a substance and its attributes. Therefore the Bhāgavata doctrine is not tenable.[4]

---

[1] SBS., ii. 2. 42.
[2] SBS., ii. 2. 43.
[3] SBS., ii. 2. 44.
[4] SBS., ii. 2. 45.

6. *Śaṁkara's Criticism of the Jaina doctrine*

The Jainas maintain the existence of the soul (jīva), non-soul (ajīva), influx (āsrava), stoppage (samvara), shedding (nirjarā), bondage (bandha), and liberation (mokṣa). In brief, there are two realities, jiva and ajīva. There are five extensive substances (astikāya): soul, matter (pudgala), dharma or principle of motion, adharma or principle of rest, and space. The Jainas uphold relativity of judgments (syādvāda) which admit of sevenfold predication (saptabhaṅgīnyāya): (1) Perhaps S is (syādasti) ; (2) Perhaps S is not (syad nāsti) ; (3) Perhaps S is indescribable (syād avaktavya) ; (4) Perhaps S is and is not (syād asti nāsti) ; (5) Perhaps S is and indescribable (syād asti avaktavyaḥ) ; (6) Perhaps S is not, and indescribable (syād nāsti avaktavyaḥ) ; (7) Perhaps S is, is not, and indescribable (syād asti nāsti avaktavyaḥ). These seven kinds of judgments are applicable to oneness, eternity, and all other predicates.

Śaṁkara contends that this doctrine is irrational. The same thing cannot be hot and cold at the same time in the same portion. Nothing can be existent and non-existent at the same time. The same thing cannot possess contradictory qualities at the same time. We have already pointed out that this criticism of Śaṁkara is unjust. Again, Śaṁkara urges that the Jainas maintain the existence of seven categories or entities of distinct characteristics. But according to the doctrine of Syādvāda their number is seven, not seven, indescribable and the like. Their characters cannot be definite ; they are such, not such, indescribable, and the like. The natures of entities are indefinite. The natures of cognitions also are indefinite. The views of the Jainas also must be indefinite and therefore doubtful and invalid. The knower (pramātṛ), knowledge (pramāṇa), the known object (prameya), and the result of knowledge (phala) are indefinite and uncertain. Therefore none can have faith in the Jaina views and adopt them to attain liberation. This criticism of Śaṁkara is cheap. He does not criticize the Jaina doctrine of Syādvāda itself, but he shows the absurdity of its application to the Jaina views. Similarly, Śaṁkara urges that extensive substances (astikāya) are either five, or more, or less, or indescribable. They cannot again be said to be indescribable, for they cannot be described if they are indescribable. It is self-contradictory that they are indescribable and can yet be described. Right knowledge, which is the result of ascertaining their true nature, either is, or is not, and indescribable. Wrong knowledge also opposed to right knowledge either is, or is not, or indescribable. Heaven and liberation also either are, are not, or indescribable. They are either eternal, non-eternal, and the like. The nature of the liberated souls also, who are worshipped by the Jainas, is uncertain and indefinite. The nature of soul, matter, dharma, adharma, time, and space is uncertain and indefinite, since it is one and many, eternal and non-eternal, distinct and non-distinct, and the like, which is self-contradictory. Therefore the Jaina views are not tenable.[1]

Śaṁkara refutes the Jaina doctrine of the soul as co-extensive with the body. The Jainas maintain that the dimension of the soul is co-extensive with that of the body ensouled by it. Things of limited dimension are non-eternal. If the soul possess the dimension of the body, it must be non-eternal. The same person has a small body in childhood, a bigger body in boyhood, and a still bigger body in youth. Therefore the dimension of his soul undergoes change. It is smaller in childhood, bigger in boyhood, and still bigger in youth. Again, the human soul transmigrates into an elephant body or an ant body. How does it occupy a larger body or a smaller body than a human body? If the soul be said to have an infinite number of parts which expand in a large body, and contract in a small body, are some of them destroyed in a small body? If they are not destroyed, an infinite number of parts cannot exist in a small body. If they are destroyed, then the soul exists in one part only and is therefore minute (aṇu), and cannot be co-extensive with the body. Further, that the parts of the soul are limited to the body and yet unlimited cannot be inferred.[2] The Jainas may argue that the parts of the soul are increased in a large body, and decreased in a small body. Śaṁkara contends that the soul then undergoes modification, and is therefore non-eternal. If it is non-eternal, it cannot attain liberation. If there is no liberation, there is no bondage. If the soul consists of unlimited parts which increase or decrease, it is non-

[1] SBS., ii. 2. 33. [2] SBS., ii. 2. 34.

eternal and incapable of bondage and liberation. If some of its parts be said to be produced, what is their cause? They cannot be produced by material elements. Consciousness cannot be produced by unconscious matter. If some parts of the soul are said to be destroyed, into what are they absorbed? They cannot be absorbed in matter for the same reason. Consciousness cannot merge into unconscious matter. If some parts are added to the soul and some are taken away from it, it has no definite and permanent dimension. The soul cannot for the same reason be said to be increased and decreased in succession. The soul undergoing modification is non-eternal. If it be said to be a stream of consciousness (santāna) and yet eternal, the stream is either a real substance (vastu) or an unreal substance (avastu). If it is a real substance, it undergoes modification and is therefore non-eternal. If it is not a real substance, the Jaina advocates the Buddhist doctrine of soullessness (nairātmya-vāda) or non-existence of the permanent soul.[1]

The Jainas maintain that the dimension of the liberated soul is fixed and unchangeable. Śaṁkara contends that if the dimension of the liberated soul is fixed, then those of the soul in the beginning and in the middle also must be fixed. The three dimensions of the soul are the same. They do not differ from one another. Therefore the dimension of the soul is either minute or large, and not co-extensive with the body. The Jaina doctrine of the soul as co-extensive with the body is not tenable.[2]

7. *Śaṁkara's Criticism of the Buddhist Realism*

The Sarvāstivādins maintain the existence of all external objects and internal things or minds. There are the elements (bhūta) and the aggregates composed of them (bhautika). There are minds (citta) and mental properties (caitta). Earth, water, fire, and air are the elements. Colour and the other sensible qualities and the sense-organs are composed of the material elements. The earth atoms are hard; the water atoms are viscid; the fire atoms are hot; the air atoms are mobile. They are combined into aggregates, and constitute gross earth, water, fire, and air. The minds are composed of the five groups

---

[1] SBS., ii. 2. 35.

[2] SBS., ii. 2. 36.

(pañcaskandha) of sensation, perception, feeling, disposition, and self-consciousness.

First, Śaṁkara contends that the formation of these two kinds of aggregates (saṁghāta) cannot be accounted for by the Sarvāstivādins. The material elements and the mental elements are unconscious (acetana), and cannot combine themselves with one another. The emergence of consciousness of the mind (cittābhijvalana) depends upon the aggregation of the elements. There is no other permanent conscious (cetana) agent which can experience, control, and combine the unconscious elements into aggregates. Unconscious elements cannot combine themselves with one another without being guided by a permanent conscious agent. But the Sarvāstivādins do not recognize the existence of permanent souls and God. If unconscious elements act by themselves without the aid of an external agent, their activity would never cease, and there would be perpetual creation, and no dissolution or liberation. The Ālayavijñāna cannot be said to combine the unconscious elements into aggregates, because its relation to each constituent mental element cannot be established. It is either different or non-different from the constituent cognitions. If it is different from them, it is nothing but the permanent self of the Vedāntins. If it is non-different from them, it is momentary. But momentary entities cannot act ; they come into being and perish. Therefore the momentary Ālayavijñāna cannot combine the unconscious elements into aggregates. If the aggregates are not produced, there would be collapse of mundane life.[1]

Secondly, the Sarvāstivādins may urge that though there is no permanent intelligent agent who may experience, control, and combine the unconscious elements into aggregates, yet the mutual causality of avidyā and the other members of the twelve-fold chain of causation (bhavacakra) can account for mundane life. Avidyā, disposition, initial consciousness, mind-body, the six sense-organs, contact, feeling, desire, clinging, will-to-be-born, rebirth, old age and death are the links in the wheel of existence. The mutual causation of these members of the causal series can account for the formation of aggregates. This argument is wrong. Even if the preceding member can pro-

[1] SBS., ii. 2. 18.

duce the succeeding member of the causal series, there is no cause of the formation of aggregates. If avidyā and the like be said to presuppose the formation of aggregates, which therefore must exist, it must be assigned to a cause, which is not forthcoming. If the Vaiśeṣikas, who admit the existence of eternal atoms and eternal enjoying souls, cannot account for the formation of aggregates, far less can the Buddhist realists, who admit the existence of momentary atoms and momentary cognitions, can account for it.

Avidyā and the like cannot be said to be the cause of the formation of aggregates, because they themselves come into existence subsisting in the aggregates. They depend upon aggregates or mind-body-complexes for their existence. Therefore they cannot be their efficient cause. The Sarvāstivādins may urge that in the beginningless cycle of birth and death aggregates succeed one another in an unbroken chain, and that avidyā and the like, subsisting in them, succeed one another in an uninterrupted series. In that case, the aggregates produce either similar aggregates or both similar and dissimilar aggregates. In the first case, a human body cannot be transformed into a celestial body, or a hellish body, or an animal body. In the second case, a human body can turn, in a moment, into an elephant body, then into a celestial body, and again into a human body. Both these views are contrary to Buddhism. Further, an aggregate (saṁghāta) is for the enjoyment of a soul. But the Buddhists deny the existence of a permanent enjoying soul. Therefore enjoyment is for itself, and liberation is for itself. If a bound soul exerts itself for the attainment of liberation, it must persist in bondage, endeavour, and liberation. If it persists for a duration of time, it contradicts the doctrine of momentariness. Therefore the formation of aggregates cannot be established in the absence of an enjoyer, even if avidyā and the like be supposed to cause each other.[1]

Thirdly, even in the twelvefold chain of causation the preceding member cannot produce the succeeding member, because they are momentary. When the succeeding member is produced, the preceding member is destroyed. There cannot be any

---

[1] SBS., ii. 2. 19.

relation of cause and effect between the preceding moment and the succeeding moment. The preceding moment, which is already destroyed, or which is being destroyed, entering upon the state of non-existence cannot be the cause of the succeeding moment. If the preceding moment in a state of existence and in the stage of completion be said to be the cause of the succeeding moment, then the preceding moment in a state of existence exercises causal efficiency, and therefore must persist for more than one moment. If the existence of the preceding moment itself be said to be its causal efficiency, then it cannot produce the succeeding moment, since the effect cannot be produced by its cause unless it is related to it, and there can be no relation between cause and effect, which are momentary. If the cause be supposed to exist till the effect has been produced, it ceases to be momentary. If the cause be said to produce its effect without being related to it, then any cause can produce any effect. But a specific cause only can produce a specific effect. Therefore a cause must be related to its effect in order to produce it. Cause and effect can never be related to each other, if they are momentary. Further, do production and destruction constitute the nature (svarūpa) of the thing, or its different state, or another thing? In the first case, the thing, its production and destruction would be synonymous. In the second case, the thing would cease to be momentary, since its production would be its first state, its existence its second state, and its destruction its third state. In the third case, production and destruction would be quite different from the thing, which would therefore become permanent and unaffected by origin and destruction. If production and destruction be said to depend upon perception and non-perception respectively, then they are attributes of the percipient, and not of an external thing, which is therefore permanent. Hence there is no mutual causality of avidyā and the other members of the twelvefold chain of causation. If the effect be said to be produced without a cause, then everything would be produced everywhere, and there would be no restriction in the production of effects. But the Sarvāstivādins maintain that minds and mental properties are produced by the fourfold cause, the basic cause (ālambana pratyaya), the immediately preceding cause (samanantara pratyaya), the auxiliary cause (sahakāri pratyaya), and the dominant cause (adhipatipratyaya). So effects cannot be produced without causes. If the preceding moment be said to exist till the succeeding moment is produced, then the cause and the effect would be simultaneous, and it would contradict the doctrine of momentariness.[1]

Fourthly, the Buddhist doctrine of momentariness is irrational. If all entities are momentary, the knowing soul also is momentary. But it cannot be momentary, since it perceives a thing and remembers it later. The soul that remembers it is the same as that which perceived it before. There is identity of the soul in perception and recollection of the same object. We never find that one person perceives an object and another remembers it. We experience personal identity from birth to death. This flatly contradicts the doctrine of momentariness. But the Buddhists may urge, like Hume, that the sense of personal identity is an illusion generated by the rapid succession of many different momentary cognitions which are similar to one another. Continuity of different similar cognitions produces the illusion of personal identity. But Śaṁkara contends that the knowledge of 'this is like that' presupposes the existence of a permanent self which apprehends the two cognitions, compares them with one another, and comprehends similarity between them. The Buddhists may argue that one of the two cognitions apprehends similarity between them. Then that cognition would exist for two moments, and thus contradict the doctrine of momentariness. If the cognition 'this is like that' be different from the cognitions of 'this' and 'that,' and do not depend upon them, then it contradicts our experience. The use of the two words 'this' and 'that' points to the existence of different things which are comprehended by the self in a judgment of similarity. If there be one cognition which comprehends similarity, then the expression 'this is similar to that' would be meaningless. The identity of an object cannot be said to be due to similarity, since it is not apprehended as similar to some other object, but as the same object. The same object that was perceived by me in the past is remembered by me now. Identity cannot be due to similarity.[2] Śaṁkara's criticism of the Buddhist doctrine of Asatkāryavāda will be discussed under causality.

[1] SBS., ii. 2. 21.

[2] SBS., ii. 2. 25.

Fifthly, the Sautrāntikas consider pratisaṁkhyānirodha, apratisaṁkhyānirodha, and ākāśa to be negative in character. Do deliberate destruction and unplanned destruction belong to the series or the momentary elements of the series? The series cannot be destroyed, since the elements are related to one another as cause and effect in an unbroken chain in it. The elements also cannot be completely destroyed without any relation to the other elements. Recognition testifies to the uninterrupted identity of an object in its different states, which persists through them. It does not testify to the complete extinction of an object unrelated to other objects. Hence both kinds of extinction are not possible.[1] The Buddhist realists maintain that extinction of avidyā is included in deliberate destruction (pratisaṁkhyānirodha) and unplanned destruction (apratisaṁkhyānirodha). Śaṁkara asks whether extinction of avidyā is generated by right knowledge or by itself. If it is generated by right knowledge, then it contradicts the Buddhist doctrine that all things are by nature transient and momentary. If it is generated by itself, then the instructions about the eightfold path are useless.[2] Ākāśa cannot be said to be negative in character because it is described by the Upaniṣads as a positive element produced by Brahman or Ātman. It is also inferred from sound as the substance which possesses this quality. The Buddhists maintain that air subsists in ākāśa, which is not therefore negative in nature. Then, again, pratisaṁkhyānirodha, apratisaṁkhyānirodha, and ākāśa are said to be negative and yet eternal. If they are eternal, they must be positive entities. Negative entities can be neither eternal nor non-eternal.[3] Hence the Sarvāstivāda is not tenable.

8. *Śaṁkara's Criticism of the Buddhist Subjective Idealism or Vijñānavāda*

Śaṁkara gives the following arguments of the Yogācāras to prove the non-existence of external objects. (1) If external objects exist, they are either atoms or aggregates of atoms. But they can be neither, and are therefore non-existent. (2) Even those, who admit the existence of external objects,

---

[1] SBS., ii. 2. 22.
[2] SBS., ii. 2. 24.
[3] SBS., ii. 2. 24.

admit different forms of their cognitions. But if forms of cognitions are admitted, they suffice for the practical purposes of our life, and the existence of external objects becomes unnecessary. (3) Objects and their cognitions are invariably perceived together (sahopalambhaniyama). Therefore they are identical with each other. Objects *are* ideas. (4) Waking cognitions apprehend themselves like dream-cognitions. Both are similar to each other. Both are not produced by external objects. (5) The variety of waking cognitions (pratyayavaicitrya) is due to the variety of dispositions (vāsanāvaicitrya). Śaṁkara refutes these arguments. (1) External objects are actually perceived, and therefore their existence cannot be denied. We do not perceive cognitions, but external objects. The Yogācāras argue that internal cognitions appear like external objects. Śaṁkara urges that if external objects are non-existent and never perceived, internal cognitions cannot appear like external objects. Viṣṇumitra cannot appear like the son of a barren mother. External objects are actually perceived as external. They are not perceived as if they were external. (2) It cannot be argued that their existence is not possible. Actuality determines possibility. Possibility cannot determine actuality. Actuality is determined by valid knowledge. The existence of external objects is ascertained by all kinds of valid knowledge. Therefore it must be real. (3) Invairiably simultaneous perception of an object and its cognition does not prove their identity. It proves their difference. They are always perceived together because they are related to each other as the manifested and the manifester. The object is manifested by its cognition. The cognition manifests the object. If there is no object, the cognition cannot be produced. If there is no cognition, the object cannot be apprehended. Consciousness is common to all cognitions. But it is diversified by different objects such as a jar and a cloth. The variety of cognitions is due to the variety of objects. So there is a difference between objects and cognitions. The Yogācāras look upon the distinction of subject (grāhaka) and object (grāhya) as falling within the stream of momentary cognitions. But the preceding momentary cognition cannot apprehend the succeeding momentary cognition, since the former vanishes when the latter comes into existence. The Yogācāras admit the existence of cognitions because they are perceived. Śaṁkara argues that we must admit the existence of external objects also because they are actually perceived. If the Yogācāras argue that cognitions apprehend themselves because they are self-luminous like a lamp, whereas external objects are not self-luminous, Śaṁkara contends that cognitions can never act upon themselves and apprehend themselves even as fire cannot burn itself. It is the common experience of all that a cognition apprehends an external object distinct from itself. The apprehending cognition is different from the cognized object. Momentary cognitions cannot apprehend their production and destruction. They can be apprehended by the permanent witness self (sākṣin). The sākṣin is eternal, self-existent and self-manifest. But cognitions are non-eternal, dependent, and known by the sākṣin. Cognitions are not self-luminous, while the self is self-luminous. The Yogācāras may argue that the self of the Vedāntist is in the nature of immediate experience (anubhavarūpa) or cognition (vijñāna) which apprehends itself, and that momentary cognitions also can likewise apprehend themselves. Śaṁkara contends that the self is different from cognitions. The self is permanent while cognitions are momentary. The self is the knower or manifester while cognitions are known or manifested by it. The self is one and eternal while cognitions are many and non-eternal. The self knows the plurality, origin, and destruction of empirical cognitions, which are not self-existent and self-manifest or self-aware. So the Vedantist doctrine is quite different from the Yogācāra subjective idealism. Evidently Śaṁkara was not acquainted with the Vijñānavāda of Vasubandhu and others who maintained the existence of one, eternal, pure cognition (vijñaptimātratā).[1] (4) Waking perceptions are not similar to dream-cognitions. The former are not contradicted while the latter are contradicted by waking perceptions. The former are perceptions apprehending present objects while the latter are recollections apprehending absent objects perceived in the past. The former apprehend external objects while the latter apprehend themselves. So waking perceptions are not objectless (nirālambana) like dream-cognitions.[2] (5) The variety of perceptions is not due to the variety of dispositions. Dispositions are the impressions of perceptions. Perceptions apprehend

[1] SBS., ii. 28.
[2] SBS., ii. 2. 29.

external objects. The Yogācāras deny the existence of external objects. So there are no perceptions. In the absence of a variety of perceptions there can be no variety of dispositions. The hypothesis of a beginningless series of dispositions (vāsanā) and perceptions involves infinite regress (anavasthā). It is as absurd as a chain of blind persons leading one another. Perceptions account for dispositions. Dispositions cannot account for perceptions. Further, dispositions (vāsanā) are impressions (saṁskāra). Impressions cannot exist without a substratum. But the Yogācāras cannot offer any substratum for them. The Ālayavijñāna cannot be their substratum, since it is as impermanent as object-cognitions (pravṛttivijñāna). If it is permanent, eternal, immutable (kūṭastha), and all-knowing, it cannot be the substratum of dispositions. It contradicts the Buddhist doctrine of momentariness. The eternal self is the witness self (sākṣin) of the Vedantist.[1] The Nihilist doctrine (śūnyavāda) is summarily dismissed by Śaṁkara. It is disproved by all kinds of valid knowledge.[2]

II. ONTOLOGY

9. *The Ātman*

The Ātman, according to Śaṁkara, is the universal self. It is Brahman, the Absolute, the supreme reality. The jīva is the individual self. It is the Ātman limited by the body, the sense-organs, manas, buddhi, and the like, which are its limiting adjuncts (upādhi). The Ātman is the transcendental, non-empirical, metaphysical self. The jīva is the empirical, phenomenal, psychological self.

The Ātman is the reality in the jīva. It is the foundational consciousness which sustains the jīva. Its existence cannot be denied. One who denies its existence is the Ātman.[3] Every person knows the existence of his self. He never knows its non-existence.[4] Whoever denies it affirms its existence. The

[1] SBS., ii. 2. 30, 31; *Indian Realism*, pp. 227-41.

[2] SBS., ii. 2. 31, 32.

[3] Ātmanaḥ pratyākhyātum aśakyatvāt. Ya eva nirākartā tasyaiva ātmatvāt. SBS., i. 1, 4.

[4] Sarvo hi ātmāstitvaṁ pratyeti, na nāhamasmīti. SBS., i. 1. 4.

self is always present. It is present even in the act of denial of its existence.[1] The Ātman is self-proved (svayaṁsiddha). It cannot be proved by the means of valid knowledge (pramāṇa) which cannot function without it. The Ātman is the foundation of all pramāṇas. It is their presupposition. They prove the existence of those things which are not self-proved. The Ātman exists prior to all pramāṇas.[2] Śaṁkara starts with the existence of the Ātman which is self-proved. His argument reminds us of that of Descartes. : *Cogito ergo sum* : 'I think, therefore I exist.' But Śaṁkara starts with the existence of the Ātman, the universal self, which is the ontological reality of the individual self, whereas Descartes starts with the existence of the individual self.

The Ātman is of the nature of undifferenced consciousness (nirviśeṣacaitanya) which reveals the empirical self (jīva). It is subject-objectless universal consciousness. It is trans-empirical or non-phenomenal (niṣprapañca). It is of the essence of consciousness and bliss (caitanyānandaghana). It is devoid of enjoying nature (bhoktṛtva) and activity (kartṛtva). But it appears to be an enjoying and active agent owing to its limiting adjuncts.[3]

The Ātman is one, eternal, homogeneous consciousness in its essential nature (nityaikarasavijñaptimātrasattāka). It is of the nature of eternal consciousness (nityabodhasvarūpa). It is the witness of all cognitions (sarvapratyayasākṣin).[4] It is their knower (sarvapratyadarśin). Its essence consists in the mere power of consciousness (cicchaktisvarūpamātra). It is pure (śuddha) or transcendental, undifferentiated, eternal consciousness devoid of origin and destruction.[5] Presentations appear and disappear. But the Ātman is the eternal principle of consciousness which reveals and apprehends them.[6] It is the eternal, universal consciousness, which is self-luminous. It

[1] Ya eva nirākartā, tadeva tasya svarūpam, sarvadā vartamānasvabhāvatvāt. SBS., ii. 3, 7.

[2] Ātmā tu pramāṇādivyavahārāśrayatvāt prāgeva pramāṇādivyavahārāt sidhyati. SBS., ii. 3, 7; A. C. Mukherjee : *The Nature of Self*, p. 128.

[3] SBS., *Bhāmatī*, i. 1, 1.

[4] SB., Māṇḍ. K., iv. 60, 92; SB., Īśa Up., 6.

[5] Sarvapratyayadarśitve copajananāpāyavarjitadṛksvarūpatānityatvaṁ viśuddhasvarūpatvam ātmatvaṁ nirviśeṣataikatvaṁ ca sarvabhūteṣu siddhaṁ bhavet. SB., Kena Up., ii. 4.

[6] Cp. Green. *The Nature of Self*, pp. 175-76.

shines by its own light. It is not revealed by any other consciousness. It reveals all cognitions. It reveals all objects which cannot reveal themselves.[1] It is neither subject (grāhaka) nor object (grāhya). It is the eternal consciousness which is present in the adjunct of the internal organ (buddhi), and reveals all its modes (buddhipratyayasākṣin).[2] The distinction of subject and object is due to avidyā. When avidyā is destroyed, the distinction vanishes.[3] The manas apprehended as the self appears to be subject and object. The Ātman is non-dual and beyond subject and object.[4] It is the eternal light of consciousness, which is of the nature of self-luminosity, and does not depend on any other cognition to manifest it. It is the eternal cognition which apprehends itself.[5]

The Ātman is of the nature of pure consciousness (caitanyamātrasvarūpa). It is of the nature of eternal consciousness (nityadṛksvarūpa). It is eternally pure, conscious, and liberated. It is the eternal, unchangeable, irrelative, formless, one, supreme reality. It is different from the jīva. But the jīva is not different from it. The Ātman is its reality.[6]

The Ātman is not an enjoying (bhoktṛ) and active agent (kartṛ). It is devoid of merit and demerit. It does not experience the fruits of actions. It does not enjoy and suffer. It is inactive since it is immutable. It is not subject to birth and death. Transmigration is due to avidyā. It is empirical existence. Ātman has non-empirical, transcendental existence due to right knowledge.[7] Ātman in itself unconditioned by an adjunct is not an enjoyer. When it is limited by the adjuncts of buddhi and the like, it becomes an enjoyer.[8] Ātman is devoid of activity. If it were active, it would be changed by its acts, and be non-eternal. It is unchangeable and eternal. So it cannot be the abode of its own activity or activity of any other thing. It cannot act in itself ; nor can it be acted on

[1] SB., Pr. Up., vi. 2.
[2] SB., Muṇḍ. Up., i. 6; ii. 6.
[3] SB., Māṇḍ. K., iii. 35.
[4] SB., Māṇḍ. K., iii. 30.
[5] Tena ātmasvarūpeṇa ajena jñānena ajaṁ jñeyam ātmatattvaṁ svayameva avagacchati. SB., Māṇḍ. K., iii. 33.
[6] Paramātmano jīvād anyatvaṁ draḍhayati, jīvaṣya tu na parasmād anyatvaṁ pratipipādayiṣati. SBS., i. 3, 19.
[7] SBS., i. 1. 4; i. 2. 11, 12; ii. 3. 19; SB., Kaṭha Up., i. 13; ii. 5.
[8] Na hi kevalasyātmano bhoktṛtvam asti, buddhyādyupādhikṛtameva tasya bhoktṛtvam. SB., Kaṭha Up., i. 3, 4.

by any other thing. It is devoid of all activity.[1] Activity is due to egoism (ahaṁkāra) which is the adjunct of the jīva. Egoism is not knowledge which constitutes the essence of the Ātman, since it is an object of knowledge.[2] The jīva is a doer. It is an active agent ; it performs duties and bears responsibility.[3] The Ātman is not naturally active. If it were so, it would not be liberated. The jīva is active. Its activity is due to the adjunct of buddhi or ahaṁkāra. Activity is of the nature of pain.[4] The Ātman is of the nature of bliss which is always revealed in it. So it cannot be active. The jīva is not of the nature of bliss.[5] Activity is a quality of buddhi, which is superimposed on the Ātman, and attributed to it. Activity and power of feeling pleasure and pain are due to avidyā.[6]

The Ātman is not an agent (kartṛ). It is not an object of activity (karma). It is beyond space, time, and causality. It is non-dual. It is one. It appears to be many jīvas owing to avidyā. It is not subject to empirical life of birth and death. It is not active. It does not experience pleasure and pain.[7] It is eternally pure, conscious, liberated, eternal, unageing, immortal, fearless, and non-dual.[8] It is undifferenced (nirviśeṣa). It is distinctionless. There are no distinctions of subject and object, agent (kāraka), activity (kriyā), and fruit (phala) in it. These distinctions are due to avidyā.[9] The same Ātman cannot be the knower (jñātṛ) and the known (jñeya) at the same time, since it is devoid of parts. It is not an agent of the act of knowing (jñānakartṛ).[10] It is of the nature of the light of consciousness (caitanyajyotiḥsvabhāva). It reveals all objects by its light of consciousness.[11] It is the witness of all cognitions or mental modes (sarvabuddhipratyayasākṣin).[12] It is of the nature of knowledge (upalabdhisvarūpa). It is of the nature of

[1] SBS., i. 1. 4.

[2] Ahaṁkārapūrvakaṁ api kartṛtvaṁ nopalabdhur bhavitum arhati, ahaṁkārasyāpy upalabhyamānatvāt. SBS., ii. 3. 40.

[3] SBS., ii. 3. 33.

[4] Na svābhāvikaṁ kartṛtvam ātmanaḥ sambhavati, anirmokṣaprasaṅgāt, . . . kartṛtvasya duḥkharūpatvāt. SBS., ii. 3. 40.

[5] SBS., i. 1. 16, 19; SB., Muṇḍ. Up., ii. 7, 8.

[6] Avidyāpratyupasthāpitatvāt kartṛtvabhoktṛtvayoḥ. SBS., ii. 3. 40.

[7] SB., Pr. Up., vi. 3.

[8] SB., Ait. Up., i. 1.

[9] SB., Ch. Up., vii. 24. 1.

[10] SB., Tait. Up., ii. 1.

[11] SB., Bṛ. Up., iv. 3. 21.

[12] SB., Kaṭha Up., i. 13.

undifferenced consciousness (nirviśeṣacinmātra). Pleasure, pain, desire, aversion, volition and activity appear and disappear. They belong to the empirical self (jīva). They do not belong to the Ātman. If they belonged to it, it would be non-eternal like them. It would be made of parts and modifiable like the body. These are due to the adjunct of buddhi which is attributed by avidyā.[1]

The Nyāya-Vaiśeṣika holds that knowledge (jñāna) is a quality of the Ātman. It is its accidental quality due to its conjunction with manas. It inheres in the Ātman which is in itself an unconscious substance (acetana dravyamātra). But Śaṁkara urges that the Ātman, according to the Nyāya-Vaiśeṣika, is partless, omnipresent, and always conjoined with manas, and that it would therefore always have recollections and the like, which is not a fact of experience. The Ātman is unqualified (nirguṇa), undifferenced (nirviśeṣa), and different from all other things (sarvavilakṣaṇa). It is irrelative (asaṅga). Its relationship to other things is irrational, and contradicts Śruti and Smṛti. It cannot be related to manas, which is dissimilar to it. So knowledge cannot be its accidental quality. It constitutes its essence. The Ātman is of the nature of the eternal light of knowledge which never lapses. It is the knower of all cognitions. It is not the individual self. It is the universal self. It is Brahman.[2]

Kumārila holds that the Ātman is the agent of the act of knowledge. But Śaṁkara urges that it is not the agent endowed with the potency of knowing activity (bodhakriyāśaktimān). It is of the nature of knowledge (bodhasvarūpa). Knowledge is produced and destroyed. When it is produced, the Ātman is modified by the act of knowledge, and becomes determinate and qualified (saviśeṣa). When knowledge is destroyed, it is divested of knowledge, and becomes a mere indeterminate and unqualified substance. Thus it becomes composed of parts, modifiable, non-eternal, and impure or empirical. The Ātman is the eternal consciousness devoid of origin and destruction. It is pure and undifferenced consciousness. It is devoid of the distinction of

---

[1] Avidyādhyāropitabuddhyupādhikṛta. SB., Māṇḍ. K., iii. 5.

[2] Tasmāt nityāluptavijñānasvarūpajyotirātmā brahma. SB., Kena Up., ii. 4.

knowledge, known, and knower (jñānajñeyajñātṛbhedarahita).[1] It is eternal (aja). It is neither cause nor effect.[2] It is one, eternal, homogeneous, undifferenced consciousness in its essential nature.[3] It is of the nature of eternal consciousness. Conciousness constitutes its essence. It is not its adventitious quality due to its conjunction with body and manas.[4]

The Buddhists hold that the Ātman is a stream of momentary cognitions, which apprehend themselves. But Śaṁkara urges that if momentary cognitions apprehend themselves, then memory, recognition, and personal identity cannot be explained.[5] The Śruti has it, "The knowledge of the Ātman or knower is never destroyed." Śaṁkara holds that the Ātman is unconditioned (nirupādhi), eternal, and one, which is of the nature of self-luminous knowledge. It is not apprehended by any other knowledge. It does not depend upon any other knowledge to apprehend it, even as light manifests itself, and does not depend upon any other light to manifest it.[6] Its knowledge never lapses, even as the sun is never divested of its power of illumination.[7]

The Ātman is Brahman. The transcendental Self is the Reality. The psychic principle is the cosmic principle. The Ātman is the eternal consciousness, which is the foundation of the empirical universe. It is the Absolute. It is one, nondual, undifferenced, unconditioned, and indeterminate consciousness. 'Know the Ātman itself to be the indeterminate Brahman'.[8] 'The supreme, infinite Brahman is the essence of the Ātman.[9]

10. *The Jīva*

The Ātman is the supreme, universal Self. It is non-dual or one. It is partless (niravayava) and omnipresent (vibhu) like

---

[1] SB., Māṇḍ. K., iv. 1, 99.
[2] SB., Māṇḍ. K., iv. 53.
[3] SB., Māṇḍ. K., iv. 60.
[4] SBS., ii. 3. 18.
[5] SBS., ii. 2. 25.
[6] Saṁvedanasvarūpatvāt saṁvedanāntarāpekṣā na sambhavati, yathā prakāśasya prakāśāntarāpekṣāyā na sambhavaḥ, tadvat. SB., Kena Up., ii. 4.
[7] SB., Māṇḍ. K., i. 12.
[8] Ātmānameva nirviśeṣaṁ brahma viddhi. SB., Kena Up. i. 5.
[9] Tadveda ātmasvarūpaṁ brahma niratiśayaṁ bhūmākhyaṁ brahmeti viddhi. *Ibid*, i. 5.

space. The jīva is the Ātman limited or individuated by the adjuncts of the body, the sense-organs, manas, buddhi, and ahaṁkara. It is the psychophysical organism. It is the empirical self or ego. The Ātman is one. But it appears to be many individual selves (jīva) owing to its limiting adjuncts (upādhi).[1] The internal organ (antaḥkaraṇa) is the adjunct of the Ātman. It takes the forms of manas, buddhi, vijñāna, and citta. Vijñāna means ahaṁkāra.[2] Thus the internal organ in its fourfold form is the individuating principle of the jīva. The Ātman is the universal self. The jīva is the individual self. The Ātman is the transcendental self. The jīva is the empirical self. It is neither a part nor a modification of the Ātman.[3] It is its appearance. The adjuncts of the body, the sense-organs, manas, buddhi, and the like are creations of avidyā (ātmamāyāvisarjita).[4] They are not real. The jīva is a construction of māyā or avidyā. When avidyā is destroyed, the jīva remains in its essential nature as the Ātman, which is its reality. The jīva is the Ātman limited by avidyā. When avidyā is destroyed, the underlying reality or the Ātman persists.[5] The jīva is reality and appearance. When appearance vanishes, reality remains.

The jīva is the knower (pramātṛ), enjoyer (bhoktṛ), and active agent (kartṛ). It acquires merit and demerit ; and experiences their fruits. It is subject to transmigration. It lives an embodied life in the spatio-temporal world subject to causality. It is capable of bondage and liberation. Though it is non-different from the Ātman, the supreme Self, and immortal in its essential nature, mortality is attributed to it owing to its actions motived by desires due to avidyā.[6] The difference between the jīva and the Ātman is not real (pāramārthika), but

---

[1] Para evātmā dehendriyamanobuddhyupādhibhiḥ paricchidyamāno bālaiḥ śārīra ityupacaryate. SBS., i. 2. 6. Ekasyaiva tu bhedavyavahāra upādhikṛtaḥ, yathā ghaṭākāśo mahākāśa iti. SBS., i. 2, 20; SB., Māṇḍ. K., iii. 3.

[2] SBS., ii. 3. 32; SB., Māṇḍ. Up., i. 3.

[3] SB., Māṇḍ. K., iii. 7.

[4] SB., Māṇḍ. K., iii. 15.

[5] Māyānirmitasya jīvasya avidyayā pratyupasthāpitasya avidyānāśe svabhāvarūpatvāt paramārthataḥ ko nu enaṁ janayet. SB., Māṇḍ. K., iii. 25.

[6] Avidyākṛtatvāt saṁsāritvasya pāramārthikatvācca asaṁsāritvasya. SBS., i. 2. 11. Yadyapi vijñānātmā paramātmano'nanya eva tathāpi avidyākāmakarmakṛtaṁ tasmin martyatvaṁ adhyāropitam. SBS., i. 2. 17.

phenomenal due to the limiting adjuncts caused by avidyā.[1] The origin of the jīva from the Ātman is not real. It is a limitation of the Ātman. The origin of the limiting adjunct of the mind-body aggregate is said to be the origin of the jīva. On the destruction of the psychophysical organism the jīva merges in the Ātman, the supreme Self.[2]

The relation of the Ātman to the adjunct of buddhi is due to false knowledge which is dispelled by right knowledge. It does not cease until the knowledge of identity of the jīva with Brahman dawns upon it. The empirical life of the jīva is annulled by right intuition (samyagdarśana). The jīva is not an ontological reality. It is an imaginary construction of the adjunct of buddhi. It has no existence apart from buddhi which is the individuating principle.[3] There is no ontological difference among the jīvas, which owe their empirical difference to the adjuncts of the mind-body aggregates, even as there is no real difference among the limiting spaces, there being only one all-pervading space.[4]

The jīva is the embodied self. It has a gross body (sthūla śarīra), a subtle body (liṅga śarīra), and a causal body (kāraṇa śarīra). The gross body is composed of the five gross elements, the sense organs, and the vital forces. The subtle body is made of the seventeen elements, *viz.*, the five organs of perception, the five organs of action, the five vital forces, manas, and buddhi. The jīva transmigrates with its subtle body which is the basis of its moral equipment. The causal body is made of avidyā or false knowledge of the not-self as the self.[5] The jīva is the conscious ruler of the body, and the sustainer of its vital forces.[6]

The waking self knows external objects through the sense-organs. The dreaming self knows dream-cognitions through the manas with the aid of subconscious impressions, when the external organs cease to function. The sleeping self is one homogeneous mass of consciousness and bliss. The intuitive (turīya) self is the Ātman, which is unconditioned (nirupādhi), non-

---

[1] Avidyāpratyupasthāpita-kāryakaraṇopādhinimitto'yaṁ śārīrāntaryāmiṇorbhedavyapadeśo na pāramārthikaḥ. SBS., i. 2. 20.

[2] SB., Māṇḍ. K., iii. 3, 4.

[3] Paramārthatastu na jīvo nāma buddhyupādhiparikalpitasvarūpavyatirekeṇāsti. SBS., ii. 3. 30.

[4] SB., Māṇḍ. K., iii. 6.

[5] SB., Īśa Up., 8.

[6] SBS., i. 1, 6.

dual, homogeneous, distinctionless, devoid of genus and species, quality and activity, non-objective, non-empirical, unchangeable, unprovable, and indefinable. It is present in the waking, dreaming, and sleeping self. It is the ultimate reality. It is the universal self. It is the eternal consciousness which apprehends all.[1]

The jīva is an object of self-consciousness (ahaṁpratyayaviśaya). The Ātman is the witness (sākṣin) which reveals the jīva. It is the pure Self. It is self-luminous. It is apprehended by intuition (aparokṣa). The jīva is its limited form (upahita rūpa), though there is ontological identity between them. The Ātman reveals self-consciousness (ahaṁpratyaya) which cannot reveal it. It is a mental mode which is unconscious. It is illumined by the Ātman. Mental modes have origin and destruction. But the Ātman is eternal, immutable, and indestructible.[2] The empirical self (jīva) is an object of self-consciousness (asmatpratyayaviṣaya). The transcendental self is apprehended by supra-intellectual intuition (aparokṣa).[3]

11. *The Sākṣin*

Saṁkara does not make any distinction between the Ātman and the Sākṣin. He regards the Ātman, the eternal, universal self in the jīva, as the witness (sākṣin) of all cognitions (sarvapratyayasākṣin) or mental modes (buddhipratyayasākṣin).[4] Cognitions are produced and destroyed. But their witness is eternal. Cognitions are mental modes. They are objects (viṣaya) of consciousness. They are not self-luminous. They do not apprehend or manifest themselves. They are apprehended by the witness self (sākṣin) which is self-luminous.[5] Ātman is not an object of self-consciousness (ahaṁpratyayaviṣaya). Self-consciousness is a mental mode which is unconscious. It cannot reveal the Ātman. It is the Ātman that is the witness (sākṣin) of self-consciousness.[6] Vācaspati also regards the Ātman

---

[1] SB., Māṇḍ. Up., i. 3-7.

[2] SBS., *Bhāmatī*, i. 1, 4.

[3] Na tāvad ekāntenāviṣayaḥ, asmatpratyayaviṣayatvāt, aparokṣatvācca pratyagātmaprasiddheḥ. SBS., i. 1. 1.

[4] SB., Māṇḍ. K., iv. 60, 92; SB., Īśa Up., 6; SB., Muṇḍ. Up., i. 6; ii. 6.

[5] SBS., ii. 2, 28, 31.

[6] **Nanvātmā ahaṁpratyayaviṣayatvāt upaniṣatsveva vijñāta ityanupapannam, na, tatsākṣitvena pratyuktatvāt. SBS., i. 1, 4.**

conditioned by the mind-body-aggregate as the jīva, and the pure Ātman as its witness.[1] Therefore the pure, transcendental, unconditioned Ātman is the witness self, which is the ontological reality in the empirical self (jīva). There is no difference between the Ātman and the Sākṣin. But a distinction is made in the later Advaita Vedānta.

Dharmarājādhvarindra distinguishes between the jīva and the Sākṣin. The Sākṣin, the witness self, is the eternal consciousness conditioned by the internal organ, which does not enter into its being and qualify it. The jīva is the eternal consciousness determined by the internal organ, which enters into its being and qualifies it.[2] The Ātman is the pure, eternal consciousness. When it is conditioned (upahita) by the internal organ, it becomes the witness self (sākṣin). When it is determined (avacchinna) or qualified by the internal organ, it becomes the jīva. The internal organ is a qualification (viśeṣaṇa) of the eternal consciousness in the jīva. But it is a condition (upādhi) of the eternal consciousness in the Sākṣin. "Antaḥkaraṇa is not separable from the individual self (jīva) because it enters as a constituent element into the individual self; but it is separable from the Witness Self (Jīva-Sākṣin), because it limits it merely as an adventitions condition. The antaḥkaraṇa is a constituent factor of the individual self (Jīva), but it is merely an adventitious condition of the Witness Self (Jīva-Sākṣin)."[3] A qualification or attribute (viśeṣaṇa) qualifies a being. But a condition or limitation (upādhi) does not qualify it.[4] Both particularize the universal consciousness. The Sākṣins differ in the different jīvas. They are different from the Ātman, which is the eternal, universal, unconditioned, and unqualified consciousness.[5]

The author of *Kaumudī* holds that the Sākṣin is a special form of the Lord, which permits the jīva to act or refrain from action, but which is itself an indifferent spectator. The Lord is the witness (sākṣin), knower, pure, and attributeless.[6] The Witness Self immediately apprehends the avidyā pertaining to the jīva in deep sleep.

The author of *Tattvaśuddhi* holds that the Witness Self is the Brahman, but that it appears to belong to the jīva, even as this—element in the illusion 'that is silver' really belongs to nacre, but appears to belong to silver.

Some maintain that the jīva conditioned by the avidyā is the Witness Self (sākṣin), since it is possessed of immediate intuition, and devoid of activity. It is a spectator, but not a doer. The jīva is devoid of

---

[1] Tasyopahitaṁ rūpaṁ jīvah, śuddhaṁ tu rūpaṁ tasya sākṣī. *Bhāmati*, SBS., i. 1, 4.

[2] Tatra jīvo nāmāntaḥkaraṇāvacchinnacaitanyaṁ, tatsākṣī tu antaḥkaraṇopahitacaitanyam. VPB., p. 103.

[3] IPP., p. 374.

[4] VPB., p. 103.

[5] *Siddhantaleśasaṁgraha* (Calcutta, 1897), pp. 153-55.

[6] Svet. Up.

attachment, indifferent and self-luminous, and can therefore be the Witness Self. It is in itself inactive, but it appears to be active owing to its false identity with the internal organ.[1]

Vidyāraṇya defines the Witness Self (sākṣin) as the unchanging, immutable consciousness, which is the substratum of the subtle body and the gross body. It directly knows and controls the two bodies, without being modified by them. The Witness Self is conscious but inactive. It illumines the body, manas, buddhi, egoism, and the like, and their functions. When they cease to function, it shines by itself. Its presence in the empirical self accounts for the sense of personal identity, memory, recognition, and unity of apperception. It is the inactive spectator in the jīva. This definition of the Witness Self is given in *Kūṭasthadīpa* of *Pañcadaśī*. Vidyāraṇya compares the Witness Self to a lamp on the stage, which illumines the manager, the actress, and the audience, and shines by itself in their absence in the *Nāṭakadīpa* of *Pañcadaśī*. The Witness Self illumines the empirical self, the internal organ, and the objects, and shines by itself in their absence in deep sleep. It is the immutable consciousness, which is the substratum of the illusion of the jīva in its false identification with egoism on which the eternal consciousness is reflected.[2] Thus the sākṣin is different from the jīva. But it does not belong to the constitution of Brahman or Ātman.[3]

The author of *Tattvapradīpikā* defines the Witness Self as the pure, unqualified Brahman, which is the substratum of all jīvas, and which wrongly identifies itself with them.[4]

12. *Brahman*

Brahman is the only ontological reality.[5] It is the supreme, perfect, absolute reality. This is the etymological meaning of the word. The existence of Brahman is proved as the self of all beings. Every one knows the existence of his own self. No one knows that he does not exist. The existence of the Self (Ātman), which is self-existent and self-proved (syayaṁsiddha), proves the existence of Brahman.[6] The Ātman is the ontological reality in the empirical self (jīva). It is the foundational consciousness, which is the transcendental ground of the

[1] *Siddhāntaleśasaṁgraha*, pp. 244-50.

[2] Cidābhāsaviśiṣṭāhaṅkārarūpajīvabhramādhiṣṭhāna - kūṭastha - caitanyātmā sākṣī. *Ibid*, p. 242.

[3] *Ibid*, pp. 234-42.

[4] Sarvapratyagbhūtaṁ viśuddhaṁ brahma jīvābhedena sākṣī. *Ibid*, p. 243. See also T. M. P. Mahādevan : *The Philosophy of Advaita*, pp. 173-78; M. N. Sircar : *The System of Vedantic Thought and Culture*, pp. 155-58.

[5] Ekameva hi paramārthasatyaṁ brahma. SB., Tait. Up., ii. 6.

[6] Sarvasyātmatvāt brahmāstitvaprasiddhiḥ. SBS., i. 1. 1.

empirical self. It is the foundational consciousness, which is the transcendental ground of the empirical universe. The Ātman is Brahman.[1] There is one, eternal, universal consciousness. This is the only ontological reality. Śaṁkara gives this ontological proof for the existence of Brahman.

'Brahman is Truth or Existence, Knowledge, and Infinite.' 'Brahman is Knowledge and Bliss'.[2] Brahman is existence or being, knowledge, and bliss. It is the only ontological being or reality. It is infinite, eternal, supreme knowledge or conciousness. It is infinite, eternal, supreme bliss. Existence is knowledge. Knowledge is existence. They cannot be sundered from each other. The Absolute is existence or being and knowledge or consciousness. Being *is* consciousness. Consciousness *is* Being. Brahman is infinite (*bhūmā*). It is limitless. It is immortal (amṛta) and imperishable (akṣara). It is not limited by time, space, and objects. It is eternally fulfilled (nityatṛpta). So it is of the nature of bliss. It is full of bliss. Existence, knowledge, and bliss constitute its essence. They are its essential characters (svarūpalakṣaṇa). They are neither its parts nor its properties. They constitute its nature. They distinguish Brahman from the world-appearance which is unreal (anṛta), non-intelligent (jaḍa), and of the nature of pain (duḥkha).[3]

Truth is freedom from contradiction.[4] It is never sublated. Absolute truth can never be contradicted. Truth is existence. Existence is constant and unalterable. Brahman is absolute existence. Appearance (prapañca) is relative existence. The world-appearance is not constant and invariable.[5] It is sublated by the knowledge of Brahman. It has contingent existence. It can be thought away. But we can never think away existence itself. Existence is Truth. Existence is the ontological reality. Brahman is Existence. 'Brahman is the being of all beings.'[6] Brahman is absolute existence. It is not relative, dependent, contingent existence. It is irrelative, independent, absolute

---

[1] Ātmā ca brahma. SBS., i. 1. 1.

[2] Satyaṁ jñānam anantaṁ brahma. Tait. Up., ii. 1. 1. Vijñānam ānandaṁ brahma. Bṛ. Up., iii. 9. 28.

[3] SBS., i. 3. 9, 10.

[4] Satyatvaṁ bādharāhityam. *Pañcadaśī*, iii. 29.

[5] SB., Tait. Up.

[6] Satyasya satyam. Bṛ. Up., ii. 1. 20; ii. 3. 6.

existence. Therefore it is one, non-dual, without the second. Brahman is pure, transcendental, trans-empirical being. It is absolutely affirmative or positive, absolutely simple, absolutely indeterminate.[1] It is free from negation and limitation. It is not changeable and mutable. It is immutable and eternal. It is free from all determinations (nirviśeṣa). It is not limited by any conditions (nirupādhi).

Brahman is non-spatial, non-temporal, non-causal, and trans-empirical existence. It transcends the past, the present, and the future. It transcends causes and effects, which are empirical phenomena. It transcends all empirical existence (sarvavyavahāragocarātīta).[2] It is free from all differences of space, time (digdeśakālādibhedaśūnya), attributes, motion, fruits, and the like. It is one attributeless (nirguṇa) and indeterminate (nirviśeṣa) real being (sat). But it appears to be non-being (asat) to persons of dull intellect.[3] Though it is devoid of attributes or phenomenal qualities, it appears to them to be possessed of attributes.[4] Brahman is attributeless (nirguṇa). But it appears to be qualified by attributes (saguṇa) to the intellect perverted by avidyā. Indeterminate Brahman is apprehended by right intuition.[5] Brahman is devoid of all adjuncts and determinations. It is devoid of genus, quality, activity, and other determinations.[6] The higher Brahman (para brahma) is devoid of phenomenal attributes and determinations (sarvadharmaviśeṣavarjita).[7] It is the supreme (niratiśaya) reality. There is nothing higher than this. It is the highest reality.[8] It transcends all phenomena (sarvaprapañcavivarjita). It is noumenal and immutable.[9]

Brahman only is the reality. All else are a mere false appearance. Brahman, expanded in the form of effects, appears as mere names and forms. It is the ground of the entire

---

[1] *The System of Vedantic Thought and Culture,* p. 5.

[2] SB., Kaṭha Up., i. 2. 14.

[3] Digdeśaguṇagatiphalabhedaśūnyaṁ hi paramārthasad advayaṁ brahma mandabuddhīnām asad iva pratibhāti. SB., Ch. Up., viii. 1. 1.

[4] Yadyapi sat nirguṇaṁ, tathāpi mandabuddhīnāṁ guṇavattvasya iṣṭatvāt satyakāmādiguṇavattvaṁ ca vaktavyam. SB., Ch. Up., viii. 1. 1.

[5] Samyakpratyayaikaviṣayaṁ nirguṇam ātmatattvam. SB., Ch. Up., viii. 1. 1.

[6] Na tajjātyādiviśeṣaṇavad brahma. SB., Kena Up., i. 3; ii. 1.

[7] SB., Pr. Up., v. 2.

[8] SB., Pr. Up., v. 7.

[9] SB., Pr. Up., v. 7.

universe of phenomenal appearances. This entire universe is Brahman itself.[1] Brahman is one. It has no genus (sāmānya) and species (viśeṣa). It has no activity. It has no quality. It is indefinable.[2] One eternal Brahman appears to be manifold appearances owing to avidyā. It is partless. It cannot split itself into many appearances. One partless Brahman cannot be differentiated into the manifold world and a plurality of empirical selves. If it does, it ceases to be partless and imperishable. So duality or plurality is not metaphysically real.[3] Brahman is immortal (amṛta) by nature. It can never be divested of its nature, even as fire can never lose its heat.[4] Brahman is the ontological ground of the manifold, empirical world. There are many universals (sāmānya) and particulars (viśeṣa), genera and species, conscious and unconscious, in this world. They are arranged in a hierarchy of higher and lower genera and species, and comprehended in the highest genus, Brahman, which is pure consciousness.[5] When the universal is known, all the particulars included in it are known.[6] When Brahman, the highest universal, is known, all the particular empirical appearances are known, since it is their ultimate ground. They are non-different from Brahman. They have no reality apart from it. Brahman is said to be the highest universal (mahāsāmānya) to indicate its all-comprehensiveness.[7]

Brahman is devoid of all difference, homogeneous, heterogeneous, and internal. There is no other reality similar to it, from which it may differ. There is no other reality dissimilar to it, from which it may differ. There are no other realities within it, which differ from one another, as branches, leaves, flowers, and fruits differ from one another in a tree. Brahman is pure identity. It is absolutely undifferenced. It is devoid

---

[1] Brahma eva satyaṁ, sarvaṁ tadvikāraṁ nāmadheyamātram anṛtam itarat. Brahmaivedaṁ viśvaṁ samastam idaṁ jagat. SB., Muṇḍ. Up., ii. 2, 12.

[2] SB., Māṇḍ. Up., i. 7.

[3] SB., Māṇḍ. Up., i. 19.

[4] SB., Māṇḍ. Up., i. 21.

[5] Aneke hi vilakṣaṇāś cetanācetanarūpāḥ sāmānyaviśeṣāḥ. Teṣāṁ pāraṁparyagatyā ekasmin mahāsāmānye antarbhāvaḥ prajñānaghane. SB., Bṛ. Up., ii. 4. 9.

[6] Sāmānyasya grahaṇena tadgatā viśeṣā gṛhītā bhavanti. SB., Bṛ. Up., ii. 4. 7.

[7] Cf. Plato : The Idea of the Good is the highest of all Ideas.

of homogeneous (sajātīyabheda), heterogeneous (vijātīyabheda), and internal difference (svagatabheda).

Brahman is limitless and infinite (ananta). It is limitless in space. It is omnipresent. It is limitless in time, since it is not an effect which is limited in time. It it limitless in relation to objects. One object is limited by another different from it. But there is no difference in Brahman. So it is limitless. It is infinite. It is the cause of all phenomena in the sense that it is their substratum. All phenomena are non-different from it. They are effects. All effects are unreal. They do not really exist apart from their cause.[1] There are no other realities except Brahman. It is infinite in space, time, and reality. Hence it is the infinite, non-spatial, non-temporal, non-causal, trans-empirical reality.[2]

Brahman is of the nature of existence (sat) and consciousness (cit). Existence itself is consciousness. Consciousness itself is existence. There is no difference between them. Existence and consciousness constitute their essence. Hence the questions whether Brahman is characterized by existence, consciousness, or both are meaningless. Brahman is devoid of all difference. There is no existence which is not consciousness. There is no consciousness which is not existence. Existence *is* consciousness. Consciousness *is* existence.[3] Brahman is of the nature of eternal knowledge or consciousness. It is not different from its knowledge. Knowledge of Brahman is non-different from its essence. It is its essence, as illumination is the essence of the sun, or as heat is the essence of fire. Brahman is eternal knowledge devoid of subject and object.[4] It is the eternal, transcendental consciousness devoid of the distinction of knowledge, known, and knower.[5] It is subject-objectless consciousness (sarvaviṣayavarjita).[6] It is free from all

---

[1] Sarvānanyatvaṁ brahmaṇaḥ sarvavastukāraṇatvāt. Anṛtatvāt kāryavastunaḥ. Na hi kāraṇavyatirekeṇa kāryaṁ nāma vastuto'sti. SB., Tait. Up. ii. 1.

[2] Ata eva niratiśayasatyatvam. SB., Tait. Up., ii. 1.

[3] Sattaiva bodhaḥ, bodha eva ca sattā, nānayaḥ parasparavyāvṛttir asti. SBS., iii. 2. 21.

[4] Yattu brahmaṇo vijñānaṁ tat savitṛprakāśavad agnyuṣṇatvavacca brahmasvarūpāvyatiriktaṁ svarūpam eva tat. SB., Tait. Up., ii. 1.

[5] Jñāna-jñeya-jñātṛbhedarahitaṁ paramārthatattvadarśanam. SB., Māṇḍ. Up., iv. 1.

[6] *Ibid*, i. 37.

relation to empirical objects.[1] It is eternal consciousness. It never lapses. It is always awake. It is devoid of dream or sleep.[2] It is not subconsciousness or unconsciousness. It transcends phenomena, or names and forms. It is indefinable by any name. It is indescribable by any form. It is trans-empirical. It is eternally self-luminous. It is devoid of self-expression (āvirbhāva) and self-concealment (tirobhāva).[3] It is devoid of non-apprehension and misapprehension. It is the eternal, transcendental consciousness.[4] It is the light of lights.[5] It is the eternal light of consciousness (cinmātrajyotiḥ).[6] It is the witness of all (sarvekṣitṛ).[7] It is the Inner Self (pratyagātman) of all creatures. The Ātman of all knowers is Brahman. Therefore it cannot be known by knowers or empirical selves.[8] It can be known by superconscious intuition.[9]

Brahman is the foundational, eternal knowledge which is self-luminous. It does not depend upon any means of knowledge. It manifests itself like the sun.[10] It is distinctionless. It transcends the distinction of subject and object. Subject-object-distinction is due to avidya.[11] Brahman is the Ātman in the jīva. When the jīva transcends its empirical vestments, and realizes its essential nature of selfhood, it knows Brahman as non-different from itself, even as heat is non-different from fire. Eternal, indeterminate knowledge is non-different from Brahman, the ontological reality.[12] Brahman is of the nature of one, undifferenced consciousness, which manifests itself, and does not depend upon any other knowledge to manifest it. It is eternally self-luminous like the sun.[13] It is the eternal light of consciousness which manifests the entire universe.[14]

---

[1] *Ibid,* i. 39.
[2] SB., Māṇḍ. K., i. 16; iii. 36.
[3] Contrast Vallabha.
[4] SB., Māṇḍ. K., iii. 37.
[5] Jyotiṣām jyotiḥ. Muṇḍ. Up., ii. 2, 10.
[6] Kena Up., i. 4.
[7] SB., Kena Up., iii. 2.
[8] Sarvasya hi vedituḥ svātmā brahma. SB., Kena Up., ii. 1.
[9] Samādhinimittaprajñāvagamya. SB., Māṇḍ. K., iii. 37.
[10] SBS., i. 1. 5.
[11] SB., Māṇḍ. Up., iii. 35.
[12] Akalpakaṁ ajaṁ jñānaṁ jñaptimātraṁ jñeyena paramārthasatā brahmaṇā abhinnam. Tena ātmasvarūpeṇa ajena jñānena ajaṁ jñeyam ātmatattvaṁ svayameva avagacchati. SB., Māṇḍ. K., iii. 33.
[13] Nityaprakāśasvarūpa iva savitā nityavijñānaikarasaghanatvāt na jñānāntaram apekṣate. *Ibid,* iii. 33.
[14] SBS., i. 1. 24.

Brahman is impersonal or supra-personal, since personality implies distinction between self and not-self. Brahman is distinctionless. It is not the knower. It is not the will, since the will implies becoming, change, mutation. It is not an active agent, since activity would make it mutable and non-eternal. It is not an enjoyer of joy and sorrow, since it is devoid of merits and demerits. It is supermoral.[1]

Brahman is eternally fulfilled (nityatṛpta). It is the accomplished (niṣpanna) reality. It is the full or perfect (purṇa) reality. It cannot be divested of its fullness or perfection. It is the infinite reality. Hence bliss (ānanda) constitutes its essence. Infinitude (bhūmā) is bliss. Finitude is limitation and misery.[2] Brahman is transcendental bliss. It is freedom or liberation. It is supreme, unexcelled, and indescribable. It is without origin. It is eternal. Eternal bliss is non-different from Brahman. Omniscient Brahman itself is bliss.[3] It is supreme, infinite bliss.[4] It is full of infinite bliss (ānandamaya).[5] Finite creatures feel the bliss of Brahman tainted by avidyā. They feel empirical joy, which springs from the relation of subject and object. But the subject-object-distinction is due to avidyā. When avidyā is destroyed, the distinction of subject and object vanishes, and the Ātman or Brahman shines forth in its essential nature of infinite bliss.[6] Undifferenced, intrinsic bliss is nothing but Brahman or the supreme Self ; it is not due to the relation between subject and object.[7] It is non-empirical, transcendental, immortal bliss, which is devoid of all evil, misery, and effort. It shines in the Ātman or Brahman.[8] It is apprehended by superconscious intuition.

Brahman is the eternally accomplished being. It is not becoming. It is not subject to increase and decrease. It does not grow and develop. It is perfect and full. It does not acquire perfection. It does not move from imperfection to

---

[1] SB., Kaṭha Up., i. 2. 14.
[2] Na hi alpe sukham asti. Bhumaiva sukham. Ch. Up., vii. 23. 1.
[3] Sarvajñaṁ brahmaiva sukham. SB., Māṇḍ. K., iii. 47.
[4] Brahmānandasya niratiśayatvāvadhāraṇāt. SBS., i. 1. 13.
[5] SBS., i. 1. 16.
[6] SB., Tait. Up., ii. 7, 8.
[7] Abhinnaḥ svābhāvika ānandaḥ paramātmaiva, na viṣayaviṣayisaṁbandhajanitaḥ. SB., Tait. Up., ii. 8.
[8] SB., Muṇḍ. Up., ii. 8.

perfection. It is not a tendency to perfection. It is immutable and unchangeable. It is static. It is not dynamic. It is inactive and immobile. It is non-teleological. It does not realize an end or purpose, external or immanent.

The existent Brahman is an object of enquiry. It does not depend upon the activity of a person.[1] The knowledge of Brahman is the supreme end of life, since it exterminates avidyā completely, which is the cause of empirical life of birth and death.[2] Brahman can be known from the Śruti. The knowledge of Brahman is derived from reflection on the meaning of the scriptural texts. It cannot be derived from inference and the other pramāṇas. Inference cannot prove the existence of Brahman independently of the Śruti, which is an embodiment of intuition (anubhava). It contains authoritative statements of those who had intuitions of truths. Reason is subordinate to intuition. It can strengthen our belief in the existence of Brahman known from the Śruti. The knowledge of Brahman derived from it culminates in intuition, which immediately apprehends the eternally existent reality.[3] The Vedas are breathed by God who is omniscient and omnipotent. They are the means of knowing Brahman indirectly.[4] Intuition is the means of knowing it directly. Valid knowledge depends on a real object. The knowledge of Brahman also depends on the existence of Brahman which is eternally existent.[5] The scriptures do not prove Brahman to be of the nature of an object (idam). They only remove the knowledge of plurality due to avidyā. They prove that Brahman is identical with the inner self, which is not an object of knowledge or not-self. They remove the knowledge of difference of knowledge, knower, and known.[6] They prove the identity of Brahman with the Ātman.

---

[1] Bhūtaṁ brahma jijñāsyaṁ, nityanirvṛttatvāt na puruṣavyāpāratantram. SBS., i. 1. 1.

[2] Brahmāvagatirhi puruṣārthaḥ niḥśeṣasaṁsārabījāvidyādyanarthanirvahaṇāt. SBS., i. 1. 1.

[3] Śrutyādayaḥ anubhavādayaśca yathāsambhavam iha paramāṇam, anubhavāvasānatvāt bhūtavastuviṣayatvācca brahmavijñānasya. SBS., i. 1. 2.

[4] SBS., i. 1. 3.

[5] Bhūtavastuviṣayāṇāṁ prāmāṇyaṁ vastutantram. Tatraivaṁ sati brahmavijñānamapi vastutantrameva, bhūtavastuviṣayatvāt. SBS., i. 1. 2.

[6] SBS., i. 1. 4.

13. *Indeterminate Brahman and Determinate Brahman*

The Upaniṣads speak of the higher Brahman (parabrahma) and the lower Brahman (aparabrahma). The former is unconditioned (nirupādhi), indeterminate (nirviśeṣa), and attributeless (nirguṇa). The latter is conditioned (sopādhi), determinate (saviśeṣa), and qualified by attributes (saguṇa). The former is trans-empirical and non-phenomenal (niṣprapañca). The latter is empirical and phenomenal (saprapañca). The former is transcendent. The latter is transcendent and immanent. Existence, consciousness, and bliss constitute the essence of the indeterminate Brahman. They are its essential characters (svarūpalakṣaṇa). Brahman conditioned by māyā or avidyā is the Lord (īśvara), who is the creator, preserver, and destroyer of the empirical world, and moral governor. Īśvara is the determinate Brahman. He is a phenomenal appearance of the indeterminate Brahman, which is free from all conditions and determinations (vigatasarvopādhiviśeṣa). Indeterminate Brahman is indefinable and inexpressible. It is the Witness of all known phenomena, and therefore itself unknown. It is imperceptible by the sense-organs. It is incomprehensible by the manas. It is inexpressible by speech. It is known by right intuition (samyagdarśanaviṣaya).[1] Brahman, in its essential nature, transcends all empirical life. But it appears to be the Lord of the empirical selves (jīva) and the empirical world of phenomena, when it is conditioned by avidyā, which is neither real nor unreal but indefinable, through its undifferentiated and differentiated empirical names and forms.[2] Indeterminate Brahman transcends the duality of the worshipper and the worshipped. It is the transcendent essence of God, devoid of all determinations and attributes. It is the substratum of all. It is manifested as empirical phenomena of names and forms. It is the universal life principle of all.[3] Creation is an unreal appearance due to avidyā. It does not affect the non-dual, identical nature of Brahman.[4]

Īśvara is the determinate Brahman. He is omniscient and omnipotent creator, preserver, destroyer, and moral governor of the world.[5] Omniscience and omnipotence are the characteristics

---

[1] SB., Bṛ. Up., ii. 2. 1; SBS., iii. 2. 23.
[2] SBS., ii. 1. 27.
[3] SBS., i. 1. 20, 22, 23.
[4] SBS., ii. 1. 28.
[5] SBS., i. 1. 4.

of the determinate Brahman conditioned by avidyā or māyā.[1]

Brahman is not both indeterminate and determinate. It is indeterminate in itself. It appears to be determinate owing to the limiting adjunct of avidyā and its products. Brahman is indeterminate and undifferenced. It cannot assume different forms. It is in itself non-different. But it appears to be different, God and the individual self, the worshipped and the worshipper, for the sake of prayer. The difference is due to adjuncts of avidyā.[2] The empirical reality of the worshipper and the worshipped depends upon difference which is apparent due to avidya.[3] Their duality is an empirical appearance due to ignorance. It is destroyed, when avidyā is dispelled by right knowledge.[4] One Brahman free from limiting adjuncts is the object of intuition, and it is the object of worship when it is conditioned by the limiting adjuncts.[5] Phenomenal Īśvara is the object of worship, but the indeterminate Brahman is not the object of worship, since it is beyond actor and activity, acceptance and rejection. When the knowledge of the identity of Brahman dawns, all knowledge of duality vanishes. Indeterminate Brahman is realized by supra-intellectual intuition.[6] In this sense, twofold Brahman is known, Brahman free from all adjuncts and Brahman qualified by the adjuncts of empirical names and forms.[7]

14. *Īśvara*

Īśvara is the determinate Brahman. He is not the unconditioned, indeterminate, attributeless Brahman. He is personal God. He is Brahman conditioned by māyā or cosmic nescience. Though Brahman is attributeless (nirguṇa), it is said to be endowed with empirical attributes (saguṇa) for the sake of prayer.[8] Brahman is one. There is no duality of the

---

[1] *Bhāmatī*, SBS., i. 1. 2.

[2] Samastaviśeṣarahitaṁ nirvikalpam eva brahmopadiśyate. SBS., iii. 2. 11. Upādhikṛtatvāt akārabhedasya. Bhedasyopāsanārthatvād abhede tātparyāt. SBS., iii. 2. 12.

[3] Upāsyopāsakabhāvo'pi bhedādiṣṭhāna eva. SBS., i. 2. 4.

[4] SBS., i. 1. 11.

[5] Ekamapi brahma apekṣitopādhisambandhaṁ nirastopādhisambandhañca upāsyatvena jñeyatvena ca vedānteṣu upadiśyate. SBS., i. 1. 11.

[6] SBS., i. 1. 4.

[7] Dvirūpaṁ hi brahmāvagamyate nāmarūpavikārabhedopādhiviśiṣṭaṁ, tadviparītañca sarvopādhivivarjitam. SBS., i. 1. 11.

[8] Nirguṇamapi sat brahma nāmarūpagatair guṇaiḥ saguṇam upāsanārtham upadiśyate. SBS., i. 2. 14.

ruler and the ruled in it. It appears to be the omniscient and omnipotent creator, preserver, and destroyer of the world owing to the differentiation of the seeds of empirical names and forms due to avidyā.[1] The empirical names and forms projected by avidyā are the seeds of the entire world of phenomena (prapañca). They are neither real nor unreal, but indefinable. They are the magic power (māyāśakti) of God, who is different from them. But they are non-different from him. Īśvara is Brahman conditioned by the adjuncts of empirical names and forms due to avidyā. Without them Brahman cannot appear to be Īśvara.[2] He is one, immutable, eternal, pure consciousness (Brahman). But he appears to be manifold owing to māyā or avidyā. But he is not, in reality, different from Brahman or pure consciousness.[3] Omniscience, omnipotence, and Lordship depend upon the limiting adjuncts of avidyā. They are not ultimately real. When they are destroyed by right knowledge, the distinction of the ruler and the ruled vanishes, and one Brahman shines forth. Īśvara is a phenomenal appearance.[4] He is eternal, pure, conscious, free, and omniscient. But he is conditioned by the adjunct of pure sattva of māyā. He is not an enjoyer. He is a looker on. He is the eternal Witness of the individual souls and their objects of enjoyment and suffering, and their guide. He guides them by merely witnessing them. His mere knowledge is enough for their guidance.[5]

God is omnipresent, independent, and one. There is none equal to him. There is none superior to him. He is the inner self of all. He is the controller of the entire world. He is of the nature of pure consciousness. But he produces multiform objects with the aid of the different impure adjuncts, of names and forms[6] by dint of his inconceivable power. He is self-subsistent, subsisting in his own greatness, and omnipresent.

---

[1] Avidyātmakanāmarūpabījavyākaraṇāpekṣatvāt sarvajñatvasya. SBS., ii. 1. 14.

[2] SBS., ii. 1. 14.

[3] Eka eva parameśvaraḥ kūṭasthanityo vijñānadhātur avidyayā māyayā māyāvivad anekadhā vibhāvyate, nānyo vijñānadhāturasti. SBS., i. 3. 19.

[4] SBS., ii. 1. 14.

[5] Īśvaro nityaśuddhabuddhamuktasvabhāvaḥ sarvajñaḥ sattvopādhir īśvaro naśnāti. Preraryitā hyasāvubhayor bhojyabhoktror nityasākṣitvasattāmātreṇa. SB., Muṇḍ. Up., iii. 1.

[6] Nāmarūpādyaśuddhopādhibhedavaśena. SB., Kaṭha Up., ii. 2. 12.

He does not subsist in any other substratum.[1] He is non-different from Brahman, though it is different from him. God is Brahman conditioned by māyā. Brahman is the pure eternal consciousness. God is the witness or knower of the empirical world. God is the knower ; the world is his object. Brahman is unconditioned. God is conditioned by the pure sattva of māyā, and creates the world of phenomena. He is the material cause and the efficient cause of the world.[2] He is inactive in his essential nature, but active in association with māyā.[3] He is omniscient. His knowledge is unobstructed by nescience (avidyā). It is non-sensuous and intuitive. It is independent of the body and the sense-organs.[4] He is the Witness of the world. He illumines the universe (bhāmani).[5]

God is the creator, preserver, and destroyer of the world (tajjalān). The world is born out of him, sustained by him, and absorbed in him. He is immanent in the world. He is the inner Self of all.[6] He is the immortal, inner ruler (antaryāmin) of all.[7] He is the Moral Governor. He controls and awards fruits to the individual souls in accordance with their actions (vāmani).[8] He is the Lord of the Law of Karma (karmādhyakṣa). He creates empirical objects for the enjoyment and suffering of the individual souls according to their merits and demerits. He creates various creatures according to the variety of their actions in the previous births.[9] He is not subject to empirical life. He does not enjoy and suffer. He is devoid of merits and demerits. So he does not feel joys and sorrows which are due to false knowledge (avidyā). God is not subject to avidyā. He is omniscient. He has no false knowledge. So he has no trace of enjoyment and suffering.[10] The jīvas enjoy and suffer under the influence of avidyā. God is a mere spectator. He makes them enjoy and suffer.[11] He is

[1] Na hi anādhārasya svamahimapratiṣṭhasya sarvavyāpinaḥ parameśvarasyādhāra upadiśyate. SBS., i. 1. 20.
[2] Cetanaṁ brahma jagataḥ kāraṇaṁ prakṛtiśca. SBS., ii. 1. 11.
[3] SBS., ii. 2. 7.
[4] SBS., i. 1. 5.
[5] SB., Ch. Up., iv. 14. 4; SBS., i. 2. 13.
[6] SBS., i. 2. 1.
[7] SBS., i. 1. 21.
[8] SB., Ch. Up., iv. 14. 2, 3.
[9] SB., Ait. Up., 1. 3.
[10] SBS., iv. 1. 3; i. 2. 8; i. 1. 20.
[11] SBS., i. 2. 9, 11.

free from all taint of sins and imperfections. He controls and distributes the fruits of actions (vāmanī).[1] He is the founder of the moral order. He is the harmonizer of the conflicting members of the society. He holds them together, and sustains the moral organism. He is the protector of all creature.[2]

God is omnipresent and immanent in all. He is their inner guide. He subsists in his greatness and infinitude. But he is said to exist in some particular substratum for the sake of prayer.[3] Though he is omnipresent, he becomes gracious to the devotee who worships him as residing in his heart.[4] Though he is formless, he assumes various forms of his own accord to favour his worshippers.[5] Śaṁkara sometimes uses the word 'Brahman' to indicate Īśvara. But they must not be confused with each other.

.15. *Brahman and Īśvara*

Brahman is the pure, trans-empirical, unconditioned, indeterminate, eternal, subject-objectless consciousness. Īśvara is Brahman conditioned by māyā. He is reality and appearance. Brahman is the reality in him. He is non-different from it. Brahman is the impersonal or supra-personal foundational knowledge or consciousness. Īśvara is the supreme person. He is the empirical Lord of the world of phenomena. He is the intermediate principle between Brahman and the empirical world. He is the knower or subject of the world, which is the object of his knowledge. Even before creation of the world, the undeveloped seeds of names and forms (avyākṛtanāmarūpabīja) are the objects of his knowledge. His creation of the world depends on the differentiation of the seeds of empirical names and forms, which are of the nature of avidyā.[6] They are neither real nor unreal, but indefinable. They are, as it were, the inner nature of Īśvara. They are the seeds of the phenomena of the empirical world. They are the power of Īśvara, which is called māyā or prakṛti. So Īśvara depends upon the adjuncts

[1] SBS., i. 2. 13; SB., Ch. Up., iv. 14, 2. 3.
[2] SB., Bṛ. Up., iv. 4. 22; SBS., i. 1. 20.
[3] SBS., i. 1. 20.
[4] SBS., i. 2. 7.
[5] SBS., i. 1. 20.
[6] Avidyātmakanāmarūpabījavyākaraṇāpekṣatvāt sarvajñātvasya. SBS., ii. i. 14.

of names and forms caused by avidyā, and is different from them.[1] He controls and guides the empirical selves which depend on the adjuncts of the body, the sense-organs, manas, buddhi and the like in their empirical life, which are the products of avidyā. His Lordship, omniscience and omnipotence depend on the limitation of the empirical names and forms which are of the nature of avidyā. All these adjuncts are destroyed by the right knowledge of Brahman. There is no ontological reality of the difference between the Lord and creatures.[2] Īśvara is real in empirical life only. He is a phenomenal appearance. He has empirical reality. He has no ontological reality. In trans-empirical life there is neither creator nor creation.[3] One Brahman, free from adjuncts, is realized by intuition. Limited by adjuncts, it is worshipped as the Lord. So Īśvara has no reality apart from Brahman. Intuition of Brahman leads to embodied release (jīvanmukti) at once. But worship of Īśvara leads to gradual liberation. (kramamukti).[4] Brahman is pure Being. Īśvara is Becoming. Brahman is the causal Brahman (kāraṇabrahman). Īśvara is the effect Brahman (kārybrahman).[5] Brahman is inactive. Īśvara is active. He wills, creates, preserves, and destroys the world. He maintains the moral order. He creates the Vedas, and promulgates the moral laws. His oneness is not affected by creation of the many appearances.[6]

16. *Īśvara and Jīva*

Both Īśvara and jīvas are empirical realities. But Īśvara is the ruler whereas jīvas are the ruled. Īśvara is limited by the excellent adjunct of the pure sattva of māyā. But jīvas are limited by the impure adjuncts of avidyā, the mind-body-aggregate. So Īśvara rules the jīvas.[7] They are related to each

---

[1] Īśvarasyātmabhūte ivāvidyākalpite nāmarūpe tattvānyatvābhyām anirvacanīye saṁsāraprapañcabījabhūte īśvarasya māyā śaktiḥ prakṛtiḥ, tābhyām anyaḥ īśvaraḥ. Evam avidyākṛtanāmarūpopādhyanurodhīśvaro bhavati. SBS., ii. 1. 14.

[2] Avidyātmakopādhiparicchedāpekṣameveśvarasyeśvaratvaṁ sarvajñatvaṁ sarvaśaktitvañca, na paramārthato vidyayāpāstasarvopādhisvarūpe ātmanīśitrīśitavyasarvajñatvādivyavahāra upapadyate. SBS., ii. 1. 14.

[3] Paramārthāvasthāyām īśitrīśitavyādivyavahārābhāvaḥ pradarśyate. Vyavahārāvasthāyāṁ tu īśvarādivyavahāraḥ. SBS., ii. 1. 14.

[4] SBS., i. 1. 11.

[5] SB., Bṛ. Up., v. 1. 1.

[6] SB., Ch. Up., vii. 14. 1.

[7] Niratiśayopādhisampannaśca īśvaro nihīnopādhisampannān jīvān praśāsti. SBS., ii. 3. 45.

other as master and servant. Jīvas are favoured (upakārya) by God. He favours them. He is their benefactor (upakāraka). They are parts of God, as it were. God is devoid of parts. Jīvas cannot be his real parts. Pure consciousness is the common element in both, as heat is common to fire and its sparks.[1] Brahman is the reality in both. God and the individual souls are phenomenal appearances. Brahman is limited by the pure sattva of māyā, and appears to be Īśvara. It is limited by the impure adjuncts of avidyā, the psychophysical organisms, and appears to be jīvas. Īśvara is non-different from Brahman. Jīvas also are Brahman in their essential nature.[2] But Īśvara is not deluded by the influence of māyā, and therefore not subject to empirical life, and consequent misery.[3] Jīvas, on the other hand, feel misery of empirical life owing to non-discrimination between the Self and the not-self or its adjuncts. Īśvara is not affected by the miseries of the jīvas.[4] Jīvas are neither the supreme Self, nor different entities, but its reflections (ābhāsa).[5] Though Īśvara and jīvas are appearances of Brahman, they are not identical with each other. Īśvara is the Lord. He is the creator of the empirical world of names and forms. Jīvas are devoid of Lordship. They cannot create the world of phenomena.[6] Īśvara is omniscient, omnipotent, and perfect. Jīvas have finite knowledge, limited powers, and imperfections. Īśvara is eternally enlightened and liberated. Jīvas are bound, and liberated by right knowledge. Though Īśvara is the inner ruler of all beings, his powers are manifested in different degrees in the jīvas according to the different degrees of purity of their minds (cittopādhiviśeṣatāratamya) which are their limited adjuncts.[7] Īśvara is perfect. He is not increased by their good actions. He is not decreased by their bad actions. He is not improved or degraded by their right or wrong actions. He causes those jīvas to do right actions whom he intends to liberate from bondage. He causes those to do wrong actions whom he intends to degrade.[8] Īśvara is the

---

[1] Caitanyañcāviśiṣṭaṁ jīveśvarayoḥ, yathā agnivisphuliṅgayor auṣṇyam. SBS., ii. 3. 43.

[2] Sarveṣāmeva nāmarūpakṛta-kāryakāraṇasaṁghātapraviṣṭānāṁ jīvānāṁ brahmatvam āhuḥ. SBS., ii. 3. 43.

[3] SBS., ii. 1. 9.

[4] SBS., ii. 3. 46.

[5] SBS., ii. 3. 50.

[6] SBS., ii. 4. 20.

[7] SBS., i. 1. 22.

[8] SBS., i. 1. 28.

directive cause (kārayitṛ) of human actions and enjoyments and sufferings. Jīvas are active agents and enjoyers.[1] They do right and wrong actions, acquire merits and demerits, and feel joys and sorrows. But Īśvara is free from merits and demerits, sinless and perfect. So he does not feel joys and sorrows.[2] Īśvara is not affected by the enjoyments of the jīvas, since he has right knowledge. Enjoyments are due to false knowledge.[3] Empirical life (saṁsāritva) and non-empirical life (asaṁsāritva) are opposed to each other like light and darkness. The former is due to avidyā. The latter is due to right knowledge. Īśvara is omniscient, and devoid of false knowledge. So he is not subject to empirical life (asaṁsārin). But the jīvas have false knowledge, and so undergo miseries of empirical life (saṁsārin).[4] Sinlessness and transcendental purity constitute their essential nature. They are Brahman in their metaphysical nature. Their imperfection is due to their limiting adjuncts.[5] The divine nature of the jīvas is manifested, when the right knowledge of their identity with Brahman dawns upon them. It is not manifested so long as the right knowledge of their identity with Brahman does not dawn upon them. Manifestation of their divinity is due to right knowledge. Non-manifestation of it is due to false knowledge. So the difference between Īśvara and jīvas is not real, but apparent due to false knowledge.[6]

The author of *Prakaṭārthavivaraṇa* defines Īśvara as the reflection of Brahman in cosmic nesience (māyā), which is beginningless and indefinable, which is the source of the elements, and which is connected with the eternal consciousness only. He defines the jīvas as the reflections of Brahman in numberless limited portions of māyā called avidyā, which is possessed of the powers of veiling (āvaraṇa) the nature of Brahman and projecting (vikṣepa) a plurality of appearances. Māyā is cosmic nescience. Avidyā is the jīva's share of it. It is a part of māyā. Māyā is the adjunct (upādhi) of Īśvara. Avidyā is the adjunct of the jīva. The distinction between māyā and avidyā is drawn by the

[1] SBS., i. 2. 11.

[2] Viśeṣo hi bhavati śārīraparameśvarayoḥ, ekaḥ kartā bhoktā dharmādharmasādhanaḥ sukhaduḥkhādimāṁśca, ekastadviparīto'pahatapāpmatvādiguṇaḥ. Ekesya bhogaḥ, netarasya. SBS., i. 2. 8.

[3] SBS., i. 2. 8.

[4] SBS., i. 2. 11.

[5] SBS., i. 3. 19.

[6] Vivekavijñānābhāvād anāvirbhūtasvarūpaḥ san vivekajñānād āvirbhūtasvarūpa ityucyate. Evaṁ mithyājñānakṛta eva jīvaparameśvarayor bhedo na vastukṛtaḥ. SBS., i. 3. 19.

Advaita Vedāntists after Śaṁkara.[1] The author of *Tattvaviveka* also regards Īśvara as the reflection of Brahman in māyā, in which pure sattva is predominant and not overcome by rajas and tamas. He regards the jīvas as the reflections in fragments of māyā called avidyā, in which impure sattva is overcome by rajas and tamas. Māyā, in which the power of projecting a plurality of appearances (vikṣepa) is predominant, is the adjuct of Īśvara. Avidyā, in which the power of veiling the nature of Brahman (āvaraṇa) is predominant, is the adjunct of the jīva. Avidyā is called ignorance (ajñāna). The relation to Brahman is common to both māyā and avidyā. The jīva is ignorant owing to relation to ajñāna. But Īśvara is not ignorant owing to the absence of relation to ajñāna. He is omniscient.[2] The author of *Saṁkṣepaśārīraka* defines Īśvara as the reflection of Brahman in avidyā. He defines the jīva as the reflection of Brahman in the internal organ (antaḥkaraṇa). Avidyā is the cause of the antaḥkaraṇa. Avidyā is the causal adjunct (kāraṇopādhi). The antaḥkaraṇa is the effected adjunct (kāryopādhi). Here avidyā is identified with cosmic nescience (māyā), and the antaḥkaraṇa is identified with avidyā. The theory of reflection is advocated.[3] The author of *Pañcapādikāvivaraṇa* regards the jīva as the reflection of Īśvara in ajñāna. Both Īśvara and the jīva are not reflections. Īśvara is independent. The jīva is dependent. When ajñāna is completely destroyed, the Ātman becomes identical with Brahman.[4] The author of *Pañcadaśī* in *Citradīpa* defines Brahman as the unconditioned, pure consciousness, Īśvara as Brahman conditioned by māyā, Hiraṇyagarbha or Sūtrātmā as Brahman conditioned by the subtle essences of the elements taken together, and Virāt as Brahman conditioned by the gross elements taken together.[5] Again he divides consciousness (caitanya) into four kinds : (1) Brahman, (2) Īśvara, (3) Kūṭastha, and (4) Jīva. Brahman is the unconditioned consciousness. Īśvara is the reflection of Brahman in the impressions (vāsanā) in the minds of all creatures, which subsist in the tamas of māyā hanging in Brahman. The Kūṭasṭha is the immutable consciousness, which is the substrate (adhiṣṭhāna) of the gross and subtle bodies, and which is limited by them. The jīva is the reflection of Brahman in the internal organ (antaḥkaraṇa) superimposed on the immutable consciousness (kūṭastha). Thus Īśvara is the reflection of Brahman in māyā tinged with the impressions of all creatures, while the jīva is the reflection of Brahman in the antaḥkaraṇa.[6] In *Brahmānanda* Brahman is defined as pure consciousness. Īśvara is Brahman conditioned by māyā, pure, devoid of adjuncts which are products of avidyā. Hiraṇyagarbha is Brahman conditioned by the aggrgeate of all subtle bodies, which are the products of unquintupled subtle essences of the elements. Virāt is Brahman condi-

[1] *Siddhāntaleśasaṁgraha*, p. 99.
[2] *Ibid*, pp. 101-02.
[3] *Ibid*, p. 103.
[4] *Ibid*, pp. 130-32.
[5] Ch. vi. 2.
[6] Ch. vi. 13, 15, 16; *Siddhāntaleśasaṁgraha*, pp. 105-07.

tioned by the aggregate of all gross bodies, which are the products of quintupled subtle essences of the elements. Gross elements are the products of their subtle essence. The subtle essences are the products of māyā composed of sattva, rajas and tamas. Viśva is an individual self limited by an individual gross body with which it wrongly identifies itself in the waking condition. Taijasa is an individual self limited by an individual subtle body with which it wrongly identifies itself in dream. Prājña is an individual self limited by an individual gross body with which it wrongly identifies itself in deep sleep. It is the witness of mere nescience when the antaḥkaraṇa is dissolved (ajñānamātrasākṣin). Turīya is the universal Self or Brahman devoid of phenomenal appearances (niṣprapañca).[1] Sadānanda also defines Īśvara as pure consciousness conditioned by māyā or cosmic nescience in which pure sattva predominates. The jīva is pure consciousness conditioned by avidyā, individual nescience in which sattva is overcome by rajas and tamas. So Īśvara is omniscient and omnipotent, while the jīva has finite knowledge and limited power.[2] Dharmarājādvarīndra defines Īśvara as pure consciousness qualified (viśiṣṭa) by māyā or cosmic nescience, Īśvarasākṣin as pure consciousness conditioned (upahita) by māyā, jīva as pure consciousness as qualified (viśiṣṭa) by the antaḥkaraṇa, and jīvaśākṣin as pure consciousness conditioned (upahita) by the antaḥkaraṇa. The difference between qualification (viśeṣaṇa) and an adjunct (upādhi) has been explained already. A qualification enters into the being of the qualified entity. But an adjunct does not enter into the being of the conditioned entity. It simply limits it from outside. There are many jīvas and jīvasākṣins. There is one Īśvara. There is one Īśvarasākṣin.[3] So many subtle distinctions were drawn in later Advaita Vedānta among the variants of pure consciousness according to different adjuncts.

17. *The Proofs for the existence of Īśvara*

Saṁkara gives the cosmological, teleological, and moral arguments for the existence of God. Determinate Brahman or Īśvara is the cause from which proceed the origin, subsistence, and dissolution of this world of appearances which are differentiations of names and forms, which includes many agents and enjoyers, which is the abode of fruits of their actions determined according to space, time, and causality, the arrangement of which is inconceivable even by the mind. Omniscient and omnipotent God is the cause of the world.[4] He is the cause

[1] *Siddhāntaleśasaṁgraha*, pp. 118-22.
[2] *Vedāntasāra*, 13, 15.
[3] VPB., pp. 102-05.
[4] Asya jagato nāmarūpābhyām vyākṛtasyānekakartṛbhoktṛsaṁyuktasya pratiniyatadeśakālanimittakriyāphalāśrayasya manasāpyacintyaracanārūpasya janmasthitibhangaṁ yataḥ sarvajñāt sarvaśakteḥ kāraṇād bhavati, tad brahma. SBS., i. 1. 2.

of the creation, subsistence, and dissolution of the world.[1] He is the material cause (upādānakāraṇa) and the efficient cause (nimittakāraṇa) of the world.[2] Atoms are not its material cause as the Vaiśeṣika maintains. Prakṛti is not its material cause as the Sāṁkhya maintains. Īśvara is its material cause. The undifferentiated names and forms, which are the seeds of phenomena of the empirical world, which are of the nature of nescience (avidyā) constitute the nature, as it were, of Īśvara.[3] They are the cause of the subtle essences of the elements. So Īśvara is the material cause of the world. He is also its efficient cause. He differentiates the undifferentiated seeds of names and forms, creates the subtle essences of the elements out of them (sūkṣmabhūta), combines them with one another in definite proportions, and produces the gross elements.[4] So Īśvara is the material cause and the efficient cause of the world.[5] He is omniscient. He is the Witness (sākṣin) of the world. He wills the world into existence. His immediate knowledge (īkṣitṛtva) is the cause of creation. Non-intelligent prakṛti cannot create the world.[6] Īśvara creates, preserves, and dissolves the world.[7] He supports the sky, the sun, and the moon.[8] He maintains the world. He dissolves the world into himself, even as a magician withdraws his magic power into himself by his mere will without an effort.[9] Īśvara is the uncaused cause of the world. He cannot spring from any other cause. He is pure being (sanmātra). He cannot spring from another pure being, since the cause must be superior to the effect. Nor can he spring from a differentiated being (viśeṣa), since heterogeneity can spring from homogeneity (sāmānya), but homogeneity cannot spring from heterogeneity (viśeṣa). Jars and the like can spring from clay, but clay cannot spring from them. Īśvara is homogeneous, and cannot therefore spring from a differentiated being. Nor can he spring from non-being, since non-being is a non-entity, and an entity cannot spring from a non-entity. Being cannot spring from non-being. Īśvara is not a modification

[1] SBS., i. 1. 4, 5.
[2] SBS., i. 1. 5, 11, 22; i. 2. 1, 10, 21, 22; ii. 1. 1, 22.
[3] SBS., ii. 1. 14.
[4] Akṣaram avyākṛtaṁ nāmarūpabījaśaktirūpaṁ bhūtasūkṣmam īśvarāśrayaṁ tasyaivopādhibhūtam. SBS., i. 2. 22; Cp. ii. 1. 14.
[5] SBS., i. 2. 23.
[6] SBS., i. 1. 5; ii. 2. 1-10.
[7] SBS., i. 2. 1.
[8] SBS., i. 3. 10, 11, 16.
[9] SBS., ii. 1. 21.

(vikāra) or effect. If he were an effect, his cause would be produced by another, and so on to infinity. It would lead to infinite regress (anavasthā). He is the cause. But he is uncaused.[1] He is the First Cause (mūlaprakṛti). This is the cosmological argument for the existence of God.[2] The hypothesis of many Lords is useless. One Īśvara is enough to create the world.[3]

It is objected that Īśvara is different (vilakṣaṇa) from the world in nature, and so cannot be its cause. Īśvara is conscious and pure. The world is unconscious and impure. So they cannot be related to each other as cause and effect. Gold cannot be the cause of pots of clay. Clay cannot be the cause of gold ornaments. The cause and its effect are homogeneous in nature. Clay is the cause of pots of clay. Gold is the cause of gold ornaments.[4] Śaṁkara replies that unconscious hairs, nails, and the like are found to spring from conscious persons. Conscious scorpions are found to spring from unconscious cow-dung. So the cause and its effect may be heterogeneous. If it be urged that earth is the common element in persons and hairs and nails, and cow-dung and scorpions, then Śaṁkara replies that the characteristic of being (sattā) is common to Īśvara and the world. Is Īśvara different from the world, because the world is devoid of all the characteristics of Īśvara, or of some one or other characteristic, or of consciousness? First, if Īśvara and the world were absolutely identical, they would not be related to each other as casue and effect. The cause must be superior to the effect, and Īśvara is superior to the world. Secondly, existence (sattā) is common to Īśvara and the world. Thirdly, the Vedāntist admits that the unconscious world is the effect of conscious Īśvara. So Īśvara is the material cause of the world.[5]

It is further objected that if the world springs from, and is dissolved in Īśvara, then its grossness or materiality (sthaulya), compositeness (sāvayavatva), non-intelligence (acetanatva), limitedness (paricchinnatva), impurity (aśuddhi) and the like must defile him. Therefore Īśvara cannot be the cause of the world.[6] Śaṁkara replies that the effect loses its specific qualities when it is absorbed in its cause, and does not qualify it with them. Pots lose their specific qualities, when they are dissolved into clay. Ornaments lose their specific qualities, when they are melted into gold. They do not corrupt their material causes with their specific qualities. So the world loses its specific qualities when it is reabsorbed into Īśvara, and does not defile him with them.[7] Cause and effect are non-different (ananya) from each other. It means that an effect is identical with its cause, but it does not mean that a cause is identical

---

[1] Sa kāraṇaṁ, na cāsya kaścij janitā. Śvet. Up., vi. 9.
[2] SBS., ii. 3. 9.
[3] SBS., ii. 2. 44.
[4] SBS., ii. 1. 4.
[5] SBS., ii. 1. 6.
[6] SBS., ii. 1. 8.
[7] SBS., ii. 1. 9.

with its effect.[1] The world is of the nature of Īśvara, but he is not of the nature of the world. The cause is real. The effect and its qualities are unreal. They are superimposed by avidyā on the cause. So they cannot defile their cause. Just as a magician is not affected by his magic illusion at any time, so Īśvara also is not affected by his māyā of world-appearance.[2]

It may be urged that if the world loses its specific qualities, and enters into a state of non-distinction from Īśvara in dissolution, then many enjoyers and objects of enjoyment cannot emerge from him again at the next creation, since there is no cause of his differentiation.[3] Śaṁkara replies that just as the soul enters into a state of non-distinction or unity in deep sleep and trance, and returns to a state of distinction on waking from them owing to the non-destruction of false knowledge, so the individual souls not yet liberated emerge from Īśvara again because the seeds of their karmas are not yet completely destroyed. They are reborn to wear off their store of merits and demerits due to false knowledge.[4]

It is further objected that if the bound souls, who enter into a state of non-distinction from Īśvara in dissolution, emerge from him again at the next creation even after the annihilation of all their karmas, then the liberated souls also may spring from him, and be reborn in the world.[5] Śaṁkara replies that the liberated souls are not reborn because their false knowledge has been annihilated. Their seeds of karmas have been completely destroyed[6]

It is further objected that Īśvara cannot be the cause of the world, since he is then accused of partiality and cruelty. He creates some creatures as extremely happy, some creatures as extremely unhappy, and others as partly happy and partly unhappy. He must then have attachment and aversion like ordinary mortals. He must be partial to those creatures who are happy, and cruel to those who are miserable. But Īśvara is described by the scriptures to be of pure and transparent nature. To this Śaṁkara replies that inequalities in the fortunes of the creatures are due to the merits and demerits acquired by them in their previous births. God creates creatures of varying fortunes in accordance with their merits and demerits. He is not to blame for inequalities in their fortunes. As rain is the common cause (sādhāraṇa kāraṇa) of plants whereas the various kinds of seeds are the specific causes (asādhāraṇa kāraṇa) of their various kinds such as rice, barley, and the like, so God is the common cause of various kinds of creatures whereas their various karmas or merits and demerits are their specific causes. God's favour and disfavour depend upon specific karmas of creatures.[7] But it may

---

[1] Ananyatve'pi kāryakāraṇayoḥ, kāryasya kāraṇātmakatvam, na tu kāraṇasya kāryātmakatvam. SBS., ii. 1. 9.

[2] Paramātmāpi saṁsāramāyayā na saṁspṛśyate. SBS., ii. 1. 9.

[3] SBS., ii. 1. 8.

[4] SBS., ii. 1. 9.

[5] SBS., ii. 1. 8.

[6] SBS., ii. 1. 9.

[7] SBS., ii. 1. 34; ii. 3. 42.

be urged that karmas depend upon bodies which are non-existent before creation. There being no karmas before creation, there can be no creation of creatures of varying fortunes. To this Śaṁkara replies that saṁsāra is beginningless (anādi) so that karmas of the individual souls in a previous cycle determine their varying fortunes in a subsequent cycle, just as seeds are the cause of sprouts and sprouts are the cause of seeds in a beginningless series.[1] If the world had a beginning, then inequalities of happiness and misery would be uncaused. Īśvara cannot be their cause. Avidyā alone, which is uniform, cannot produce them. Avidyā may be their cause with the aid of karmas produced by the impressions of afflictions. The souls cannot assume embodied life without karmas, and karmas cannot exist without bodies. So on the doctrine of the world having a beginning we are led to a logical see-saw. The world must, therefore, be beginningless.[2] The empirical selves are active agents in the state of avidyā owing to their adjuncts, bodies, sense-organs, and the like. But their activity depends upon God's permission. In all their activities God is the directive cause. But though their activities depend upon God, they themselves do their actions, and God only directs them to do their actions in accordance with their merits and demerits acquired by their previous actions. God himself does not perform the actions of empirical selves. If he performs them, the free efforts of the jīvas would be useless. Śaṁkara seems to recognize the empirical freedom (puruṣakāra) of the jīvas conceded by God, and exercised by them under his direction to pursue good or evil in their empirical life. But they have no ontological reality, and therefore cannot have real freedom.[3]

God creates without implements. But a potter makes pots out of clay with the aid of a wheel, thread, a staff, and the like. But Īśvara is the sole material cause and efficient cause of the world. This is inconceivable. To this Śaṁkara replies that Īśvara is transformed into the world as milk is transformed into curd by its very nature.[4] If the material cause requires the aid of concomitant conditions, they merely aid its causal power to issue into effect. But Īśvara is perfect (paripurṇaśaktika). He does not require concomitant conditions to achieve perfection. He is transformed into the manifold world with his various powers.[5] Just as gods and ṛṣis create material things by sheer meditations, so Īśvara, though intelligent, creates the world out of himself without the aid of external conditions.[6] He creates it through sheer force of meditation. But if Īśvara transforms himself unaided into the

---

[1] SBS., ii. 1. 35. [2] SBS., ii. 1. 36.

[3] Avidyāvasthāyāṁ jīvasya īśvarāt tadanujñayā kartṛtvabhoktṛtvalakṣaṇasya saṁsārasya siddhiḥ. Sarvāsveva pravṛttiṣvīśvaro hetukartā. Parāyatte'pi hi kartṛtve karotyeva jīvaḥ, kurvantaṁ hi tam īśvaraḥ kārayati, pūrvatarañca prayatnam apekṣya. Īśvarasya cātyantānapekṣatve laukikasyāpi puruṣakārasya vaiyarthyam. SBS., ii. 3. 41, 42.

[4] Kṣīravat dravyasvabhāvaviśeṣāt. SBS., ii. 1. 24.

[5] SBS., ii. 1. 24.

[6] Cetanam api brahma anapekṣya bāhyaṁ sādhanaṁ svata eva jagat srakṣyati. SBS., ii. 1. 25.

world, he is wholly transformed into it, and ceases to exist after creation. If he is partly transformed into the world, he ceases to be partless. If he has parts, he is not eternal.[1] Īśvara is described by the Upaniṣads to be the cause of the world, and yet to exist as distinct from his modifications. So he is transcendent and immanent. He is immanent in the world, and yet transcends it. He remains immutable, though he is modified into the world.[2] Īśvara is Brahman conditioned by māyā, which is the matrix of empirical names and forms. He creates the world with their aid. The muitiplicity of names and forms projected by avidyā do not affect the integrity and partlessness of Īśvara, because they are unreal.[3] Just as one and the same self creates many dream-objects during sleep, which do not affect its identity, so one and the same Īśvara creates manifold objects which do not affect his unity.[4] In fact, creation is not real. The appearance of names and forms in space and time and subject to causality, which are mere projections of avidyā, is called creation. They are not realy. The texts about creation prove the non-difference of the world from Īśvara.[5]

It is objected that Īśvara cannot create the world because he has no motive for creation. All voluntary actions are guided by the idea of ends. But Īśvara has no ends. He has no unfulfilled desires. He is eternally fulfilled (paritṛpta). But there can be no actions without ends.[6] Śaṁkara replies that God's creation is an act of sport. Creation springs from his very nature. It is not determined by any external ends. The nature of a being cannot be challenged. God's sportive act of creation springs from his infinite powers.[7] Creation is empirically real. It is not ontologically real. It proves the identity of the world with Brahman.[8] Īśvara is the cause. The world is the effect. The effect is non-different from its cause. So the entire world is non-different from Īśvara.[9]

It is further objected that the empirical self is identical with Brahman. The Śruti says, 'Thou art that', 'Brahman created an empirical self and entered into it', 'Brahman entered into the empirical self and created the world of names and forms'. Thus creation of the world by God

---

[1] SBS., ii. 1. 26.

[2] Yathā hi brahmaṇo jagadutpattiḥ śrūyate, evaṁ vikāravyatirekeṇāpi brahmaṇo'vasthānaṁ śrūyate. Tasmād asti avikṛtiṁ brahma. SBS., ii. 1. 27.

[3] Vācārambhaṇamātratvāt avidyākalpitasya nāmarūpabhedasya na niravayavatvaṁ brahmaṇaḥ kupyati. SBS., ii. 1. 27.

[4] SBS., ii. 1. 28.

[5] Na ceyaṁ paramārthaviṣayā sṛṣṭiśrutiḥ, avidyākalpitanāmarūpavyavahāragocaratvāt brahmātmabhāvapratipādanaparatvācca. SBS., ii. 1. 33.

[6] SBS., ii. 1. 32.

[7] Īśvarasya anapekṣya kiñcit prayojanāntaraṁ svabhāvādeva kevalaṁ līlārūpā pravṛttir bhaviṣyati .. Parameśvarasya līlaiva kevaleyaṁ aparimitaśaktitvāt. SBS., ii. 1. 33.

[8] SBS., ii. 1. 33.

[9] Kāryasya kāraṇād ananyatvam. Ataśca kṛtsnasya jagato brahmakāryatvāt tadananyatvācca. SBS., ii. 1. 20.

is its creation by an empirical self (jīva). Śaṁkara answers that if the independent jīva were the creator of the world, he would create only what is beneficial to him, and he would not create the complex tissue of evils, birth, death, old age, disease, and the like. No independent person creates a prison for himself and enters into it.[1] So individual selves cannot create the world. They have no power of Lordship over the world. Even liberated selves cannot create, maintain and dissolve the world. Only God can do so.[2]

The word is full of unity, order, and harmony. Its arrangement is inconceivable even by the mind (manasāpi acintya-racanārūpa).[3] There are adjustments and adaptations in the world which can be adequately explained by Īśvara only. Non-intelligent things without being guided by an intelligent being cannot serve the purposes of human beings. Houses, palaces, beds, seats, pleasure-gardens and the like, which are adapted to the attainment of pleasure and avoidance of pain, are contrived by intelligent artists. So the entire world adapted to the enjoyment of fruits of various actions of individual souls, including the elements and the bodies of the different species with a definite arrangement of organs capable of being the vehicles of enjoyment and suffering, is contrived by omniscient and omnipotent Īśvara. The arrangement of the world including adjustments of the organs in various kinds of organisms cannot be even conceived by the most intelligent artists. So it must be contrived by Īśvara who is the intelligent designer of the world. Non-intelligent prakṛti cannot account for it. Just as clay is made into a pot by a potter, so prakṛti also must be shaped into the world by an intelligent being. God is the designer of the world. He acts upon the undifferentiated seeds of empirical names and forms, which constitute māyā, and fashions them into a definite arrangement.[4] This is the teleological argument for the existence of God.

God is the omnipresent, omniscient, and omnipotent self of all beings. Though he is devoid of activity, he can incite all to activity through the influence of avidyā. Avidyā projects the names and forms or empirical objects to be acted on. God acts on them, and creates a particular arrangement in the empirical world. Non-intelligent prakṛti cannot create it. It cannot

[1] Na hi kaścid aparatantro bandhanāgāram ātmanaḥ kṛtvānupraviśati. SBS., ii. 1. 21.

[2] SBS., iv. 4. 17.

[3] SBS., i. 1. 2.

[4] SBS., ii. 2. 1, 2; SB., Ait. Up., i. 3.

be transformed into the world. It cannot dissolve it into itself. But God can create and destroy the world, since he is omniscient, omnipotent, and endowed with the power of cosmic nescience (māyā).[1] God is inactive in his essential nature, but active in association with māyā.[2] Therefore omniscient and omnipotent God possessed of the power of māyā is the cause of the world.[3]

God is the Lord of the Law of Karma (karmādhyakṣa).[4] He awards fruits to the individual selves in accordance with their karmas or merits and demerits. He is the giver of the fruits of actions. He creates various objects for the enjoyments and sufferings of the individual selves according to their karmas, since he knows them and the place and the time of their fruition.[5] God is the directive cause of the jīvas' actions and their merits and demerits produced by them. He is the giver of fruits (vāmanī).[6] Human efforts are various ; so their fruits also are various. God gives various fruits to jīvas according to their karmas.[7] Actions are destroyed in a moment. They cannot produce their fruits in future. Non-entities cannot produce entities. Actions cannot be said to produce their fruits before they are destroyed, which are enjoyed by the jīvas in future. This is not tenable. Fruits are fruits when they are enjoyed by the jīvas. Joys and sorrows related to them and felt by them are the fruits of their actions. The Mīmāṁsaka holds that actions produce an unseen power (apūrva) which produces the fruits in proper time. This view also is wrong. Apūrva is non-intelligent. It cannot act and produce any effects without the guidance of an intelligent agent. So God produces the fruits of actions.[8] This is the moral argument for the existence of God.

God is the source of the scriptures which reveal injunctions and prohibitions constituting the moral laws. He is the promulgator of them. The will of God is the moral standard. Whatever is enjoined by him is right. Whatever is forbidden by him is wrong. These prescriptions of God are embodied in the Vedas which are breathed out by him.[9] This

[1] SBS., ii. 2. 2, 4.
[2] SBS., ii. 2. 7.
[3] SBS., ii. 1. 37.
[4] SBS., i. 1. 4; ii. 3. 41.
[5] SBS., iii. 2. 38.
[6] SBS., i. 2. 13.
[7] Dharmādharmayorapi hi kārayitṛtveneśvaro hetur vyapadiśyate phalasya ca dātṛtvena. SBS., iii. 2. 41.
[8] SBS., iii. 2. 38.
[9] SBS., i. 1. 3.

also may be regarded as the moral argument for God's existence.

The proofs are inadequate to prove the existence of Īśvara. Inference and other means of valid knowledge cannot prove his existence. The Śruti is the only means of knowing his existence.[1] Reason strengthens its verdict. It is subordinate to the Śruti.[2]

18. *The Material Cause and the Efficient Cause of the World*

Śaṁkara regards Īśvara as the material cause (upādāna kāraṇa) and the efficient cause (nimitta kāraṇa) of the world. Īśvara is Brahman conditioned by māyā with its pure sattva as its limiting adjunct. Māyā is the power of Īśvara. It is his nature, as it were (ātmabhūta iva). Māyā is the matrix of undeveloped seeds of names and forms. Īśvara differentiates them into subtle elements, and quintuples them into the gross elements. He transforms them into the world. It is the appearance (vivarta) of Brahman. But it is the transformation (pariṇāma) of Īśvara, though he is immutable in his essential nature. He is immanent in the world-appearance (prapañca). He transcends it, and persists in his immutable nature. Brahman is transcendental. It transcends all empirical phenomena. It is trans-empirical (niṣprapañca). This is the view of Śaṁkara.

But widely divergent views were held by Śaṁkara's followers. Sarvajñātmamuni, the author of *Saṁkṣepaśārīraka*, regards the pure Brahman as the material cause of the world. The Śruti says, "Ākāśa was generated from the Ātman." The Ātman is the absolute Brahman. A material cause is that which produces an effect non-different from itself.[3] Prakāśānandayati, the author of *Pañcapādikāvivaraṇa*, regards Īśvara or Brahman as conditioned by māyā as the material cause of the world. Pure Brahman is trans-empirical. It cannot be the material cause of the empirical world of phenomena.[4] Prakāśānanda, the author of *Vedāntasiddhāntamuktāvalī*, regards māyā as the material cause of the world. Brahman is transcendental and non-causal. It is above cause and effect. But it is figuratively called the material cause of the world, since it is the substratum of māyā, which is the material cause of the world.[5] The author of *Padārthatattvanirṇaya* regards Brahman and māyā both as the material cause of the world. Brahman is the cause of its being

---

[1] SBS., i. 1. 3. [2] SBS., i. 1. 2.

[3] Svābhinnakāryajanakatvam upādānatvam. *Siddhāntaleśasaṁgraha*, (Jīvānanda edition), 1897, p. 91.

[4] *Ibid*, pp. 71-73. [5] *Ibid*, pp. 98-99.

(sattā), while māyā is the cause of its materiality (jāḍya). Brahman is its material cause, since it is an appearance (vivarta) of Brahman. Māyā is its material cause, since it is a modification (pariṇāma) of māyā.[1] Vācaspati Miśra regards Brahman, the object of nescience subsisting in the jīva, as the material cause of the world, and māyā as an auxiliary condition. Brahman itself appears as the empirical world of phenomena with the aid of materiality of māyā which subsists in the jīva.[2] Pure Brahman cannot be the cause of the materiality of the world, which must be traced to māyā which is said to subsist in the jīva. Māyā subsists in the jīva, and has Brahman for its object.[3] Brahmānanda Sarasvatī and Madhusūdana regard the jīva, which is the substratum of avidyā, as the material cause of the world, and avidyā as its instrumental cause. Amalānanda, the author of *Kalpataru*, regards Brahman as the material cause, and avidyā as subsisting in the jīva as the instrumental cause of the empirical world. Brahman appears as the manifold world. It is its material cause. Avidyā subsisting in the jīva is its instrumental cause. Vidyāraṇya regards Īśvara as the material cause of the objective world, and the jīva, of the subjective world.[4] Some maintain that the empirical world is a modification of māyā subsisting in Īśvara, who is therefore its material cause, while the internal organ and the like are the effects of avidyā subsisting in the jīva, which is the product of the gross elements evolved by māyā subsisting in Īśvara. Thus Īśvara supporting māyā is the material cause of the external world, while the jīva supporting avidyā is the material cause of the internal world.[5] Dharmarājādhvarīndra regards māyā as the material cause of the world. Partless Brahman cannot be transformed into the world. It cannot be the material of the empirical world. But it is the substratum (adhiṣṭhāna) of the world-appearance, even as a rope is the substratum of the illusion of a snake.[6] Brahman is the support of māyā which is transformed into the world. So māyā is its material cause. Trans-empirical Brahman cannot be modified into the world. Some regard the jīva as the material cause of the subjective order and the objective order. It projects the external world of appearances and the internal world of dreams.[7] Mahādevānanda Sarasvatī regards Īśvara or pure consciousness conditioned by māyā as the cause of the world. As conditioned by the power of knowledge (jñānaśakti) Īśvara is the efficient cause,[8] and as conditioned by the power of nescience (ajñāna) which has

---

[1] Tatra brahma vivartamānatayā upādānam avidyā pariṇamamānatayā. *Ibid*, p. 90.

[2] Jīvāśritamāyāviṣayīkṛtaṁ brahma svata eva jāḍyāśrayaprapañcākāreṇa vivartamānatayā upādānam iti māyā sahakārimātram. *Ibid*, pp. 96-97.

[3] Māyā jīvapadā brahmaviṣayā. [4] *Pañcadaśī*, ch. iv. 1-14.

[5] *Siddhānталeśasaṁgraha*, pp. 81-82.

[6] VPB., p. 325.

[7] Jīva eva svapnadṛṣṭavat svasmin īśvarādisarvakalpakatvena sarvakāraṇam ityapi kecit. *Siddhāntaleśasaṁgraha*, p. 88. *System of Vedāntic Thought and Culture*, pp. 97-99; *A study of the Vedānta*, pp. 251-54.

[8] *Advaitacintāmaṇi*, p. 41.

the power of projection (vikṣepaśakti) he is the material cause.[1] Thus different views were held by Śaṁkara's followers as to the material cause and the efficient cause of the world.

19. *Brahman and the Jīva*

Āśmarathya regards the jīva as partly different and partly non-different from Brahman, even as the sparks are partly different and partly non-different from the fire. As the sparks issuing from a fire are not absolutely different from the fire, because they both are of the nature of fire ; and, on the other hand, are not absolutely non-different from the fire, because in that case they could be distinguished neither from the fire nor from one another ; so the jīvas also are neither absolutely different from Brahman, because they both are of the nature of consciousness ; nor absolutely non-different from Brahman, because in that case they could be distinguished neither from Brahman nor from one another, and if they were identical with Brahman and omniscient, instruction to them would be useless. Hence the jīvas are different and non-different from Brahman.[2]

Auḍulomi regards the jīva as different from Brahman, when it becomes impure in contact with the adjuncts of body, sense-organs, manas, and buddhi. But he regards it as non-different from Brahman, when it is divested of the limiting adjuncts by right knowledge and meditation. The bound jīva is different from Brahman. The liberated jīva is non-different from Brahman. The jīva loses its individuality, and realizes its identity with Brahman in the state of liberation.[3]

Kāśakṛtsna regards the jīva as identical with Brahman. The jīva is not different from the immutable Īśvara or Brahman.[4] Though Āśmarathya regards the jīva as different from Brahman, he seems to hold that they are related to each other as effect and cause, since the jīva depends upon Brahman. Auḍulomi looks upon difference and non-difference of the jīva from Brahman as due to different conditions. It is different from Brahman in the state of bondage. It is non-different from

---

[1] *Advaitacintākaustubha*, pp. 34, 51.

[2] *Bhāmatī*, SBS., i. 4. 20. Thibaut : E.T. SBS., Vol. I, p. 227. Cp. *Indian Philosophy*, Vol. II, p. 605.

[3] SBS., i. 4. 21.

[4] Kāśakṛtsnasya avikṛtaḥ para eva īśvaro jīvo nānya iti matam. SBS., i. 4. 22.

Brahman in the state of liberation. Kāśakṛtsna's view accords with the Śruti which says: 'That thout art'. The jīva is identical with Brahman. It is not a modification, since if it were so, it would be merged in prakṛti or māyā in dissolution, and would not be immortal (amṛta). So the names and forms, which subsist in the adjuncts, are attributed to the jīva. Its origin from Brahman like that of the sparks issuing from fire is really the origin of its limiting adjuncts. The jīva is identical with Brahman. This is the view of Kāśakṛtsna.

Śaṁkara adopts this view. There is no ontological difference between the individual self and Brahman. Their difference is empirical due to the limiting adjuncts of body, senses, manas, and buddhi composed of empirical names and forms imagined or constructed by avidyā.[1] The text 'Tat tvam asi' clearly shows it. The purity of indeterminate Brahman is the real nature of the jīva. Its enjoyments, sufferings, and the like are its accidental nature due to its limiting adjuncts.[2]

The jīva is not a part of Brahman, since Brahman is devoid of parts. It is not a modification of Brahman, since Brahman is unchangeable.[3] Brahman, the eternal, transcendental consciousness, is the substratum of the empirical selves and the entire empirical universe, which cannot exist apart from it.[4] The jīva limited by the adjuncts of body, vital forces, senses, and the like subsists in Brahman.[5] It is the reality of the jīva. It cannot exist without Brahman. One, eternal, self-luminious consciousness exists in the heart of the jīva. On meditating on it the jīva is liberated.[6] The Śruti praises non-difference (ananyatva) of the jīva from Brahman, and condemns their difference. The difference between them is not real. It is empirical or phenomenal. It is due to the limiting adjuncts which account for bondage and suffering. Just as the space limited by a jar (ghaṭākāśa) is non-different from the infinite

---

[1] Vijñānātmaparamātmanoravidyāpratyupasthāpita — nāmarūparacita-dehādyupādhinimitto bhedo na pāramārthikaḥ. SBS., i. 4. 22.

[2] Tat paraṁ brahma. Tacca apahatapāpmatvādidharmakaṁ, tadeva jīvasya pāramārthikaṁ svarūpam, netarat, upādhikalpitam. SBS., i. 3, 19.

[3] SBS., iv. 3. 14; SB., Maṇḍ. K., iii. 7.

[4] Etad yadāspadaṁ sarvaṁ, tad ātmabhūtaṁ bhavatām, mūrtāmūrtayoḥ tadvyatirekeṇābhāvāt. SB., Muṇḍ. Up., ii. 2. 1.

[5] Caitanyāśrayo hi prāṇendriyādisarvasaṁghātaḥ. SB., Muṇḍ. Up., ii. 2. 2.

[6] SB., Kaṭha Up., ii. 2. 1.

space (mahākāśa), so the empirical self is non-different from Brahman. The difference is due to the limiting adjuncts. Non-difference of the jīva from Brahman is primary, while their difference is secondary.[1]

Śaṁkara seems to hold both the theory of limitation (avaccheda) and the theory of reflection (pratibimba). The jīva is Brahman limited by the adjuncts (upādhi) of the body, the senses, manas, buddhi, and the like, even as space within a jar is the ubiquitous space limited by the jar.[2] This analogy suggests the theory of limitation. Again, the jīva is a reflection of Brahman in avidyā, even as the image of the sun in the water in a jar is the reflection of the sun in the water.[3] This analogy suggests the theory of reflection.

"The individual soul, as identified with the material body is the jīva or dehin; the unity of all these jīvas, the collective or cosmic self in the walking state is Virāj in Vaiśvānara. As identified with the subtle body, the individual is the liṅgin or taijasa, and the unity of all taijasas is Hiraṇyagarbha or Sūtrātman. Lastly, as identified with the kāraṇa-śarīra, the individual is prājña, and the unity of all prājñas is Īśvara. From Īśvara to Virāj, from prājña to dehin, is the order of sṛṣṭi or progressive materialization, the reverse being that of pralaya or progressive idealization of de-individualization."[4]

20. *Māya: Avidyā*

Śaṁkara uses the two words synonymously. Brahman conditioned by māyā is Īśvara. Māyā is his power or energy (śakti). It is the source of the names and forms which are modified into the phenomena of the world. The names and forms are neither real nor unreal, but indefinable. They cannot be defined as being (sat) or non-being (asat). They are indefinite. They are the seeds of phenomena of the empirical world. They constitute the nature of Īśvara, as it were.[5] Īśvara depends upon the limiting adjuncts of these names and forms which spring from

[1] SB., Māṇḍ. K., iii. 13. 14.

[2] SBS., i. 2. 6; i. 3. 7; i. 2. 21; ii. 1. 14; ii. 3. 17; SB., Māṇḍ. K., iii. 4-7, 9; SB., Muṇḍ. Up., iii. 2. 5, 7; ii. 1. 1.

[3] SBS., ii. 3. 50; iii. 2. 18; SB., Muṇḍ. Up. iii. 2. 7; ii. 2. 4; iii. 2. 7; Praśna Up., vi. 2.

[4] K. C. Bhattacharya: *Studies in Vedantism,* C. U., 1909, p. 45. Cp. *Indian Philosophy,* Vol. II, p. 552.

[5] Īśvarasyātmabhūte iva avidyākalpite nāmarūpe tattvānyatvābhyām anirvacanīye saṁsāraprapañcabījabhūte īśvarasya māyā śaktiḥ prakṛtir iti. SBS., ii. 1. 14.

avidyā or māyā.[1] Omniscience and creatorship of Īśvara depend on the manifestation of the seeds of the world in the form of names and forms which are of the nature of avidyā.[2] Īśvara is the omniscient knower. He knows the entire universe, which is the object of his knowledge. Even before creation, the unmanifest seeds of names and forms, which are developed by Īśvara into the world, are the objects of his knowledge.[3] His omniscience, omnipotence, and Lordship depend on the limiting adjuncts produced by avidyā. He knows, creates, and rules over the empirical world of names and forms, which are of the nature of avidyā.[4] Īśvara himself imagines different forms in himself through his own māyā.[5] He himself creates subtle essences and gross elements[6] out of the seeds of names and forms. They are of the nature of Īśvara, but he is different from them. He is eternal, pure, conscious, and free in his nature. Names and forms are like the foam of transparent water.[7] He manifested the unmanifest names and forms, which are his own self, and created the entire world.[8] So names and forms do not exist apart from Īśvara ; they constitute his nature. They are his energy (śakti). Brahman is the only reality. So names and forms, in all conditions, are of the nature of Brahman. But Brahman is not of the nature of names and forms.[9] Names and forms are germs of the empirical world. They are not real in themselves. Their reality is Brahman. But Brahman is not empirical. It is absolutely trans-empirical. One, uncaused Brahman is real. The world appears to be born owing to māyā. It is an imaginary construction of māyā[10]

---

[1] Avidyākṛtanāmarūpopādhyanurodhīśvaro bhavati. SBS., ii. 1. 14.

[2] Avidyātmakanāmarūpabījavyākaraṇāpekṣatvāt sarvajñatvasya. SBS., ii. 1. 14.

[3] Tattvānyatvābhyām anirvacanīye nāmarūpe avyākṛte vyācikīrṣite. SBS., i. 1. 5.

[4] Avidyātmakopādhiparicchedāpekṣam īśvarasya īśvaratvaṁ sarvajñatvaṁ sarvaśaktitvañca. SBS., ii. 1. 14.

[5] SB., Māṇḍ. K., ii. 12; iii. 24; SB., Ait. Up., i. 1. 2.

[6] SB., Māṇḍ. K., ii. 13.

[7] Yaḥ kāraṇaṁ sarvasya jagato, yadātmake nāmarūpe, yaśca tābhyāṁ nāmarūpābhyāṁ vilakṣaṇaḥ svato nityaśuddhabuddhamuktasvabhāvaḥ. SB., Bṛ. Up., i. 4. 7.

[8] Sa eṣo avyākṛte ātmabhūte nāmarūpe vyākurvam brahmādistambaparyanteṣu. SB., Bṛ. Up., i. 4. 7.

[9] Ato nāmarūpe sarvāvasthe brahmaṇaivātmavatī. Na brahma tadātmakam. SB., Tait. Up., ii. 6.

[10] SB., Māṇḍ. K., iii. 27.

Brahman cannot be defined by a name. It cannot be known by any form. It is devoid of names and forms.[1] Creation is not real. It is a creation of avidyā.[2] One eternal, immutable Brahman appears to be the manifold world owing to māyā. Duality of empirical selves (jīva) and empirical objects (prapañca) is not ontologically real.[3] Brahman, the ontological reality, is not touched by names and forms. Pure consciousness is common to them. They are of the nature of pure consciousness. They are, in reality, Brahman.[4] Brahman is neither a substance, nor a non-substance. So it cannot be a cause or an effect of any thing. All empirical objects are generated by avidyā (saṁvṛti). They are created and destroyed from the empirical standpoint. But they are eternal Brahman from the ontological standpoint.[5] Gauḍapāda borrowed the concept of saṁvṛti from Nāgārjuna. Śaṁkara borrowed it from Gauḍapāda, and converted it to avidyā. Production of empirical objects is due to avidyā. Māyā is avidyā.[6] Avidyā is mentioned in the Upaniṣads. Production is due to māyā. It is unreal like māyā. Is māyā, then, not real? No. Māyā does not exist.[7] Māyā is neither being (sat), nor non-being (asat), but indefinable (anirvacanīya). Brahman is the ontological reality. It is formless. But it assumes diverse forms owing to its limiting adjuncts. It is one in itself. But it appears to be manifold owing to adjuncts (upādhi).[8] Brahman is real (sat). Māyā is unreal (asat). There is no relation between them.[9] How is brahman related to māyā is an illegitimate question. The differences of empirical objects are mere appearances. They do not affect the immutability and transcendental identity of Brahman. They are not metaphysically real. Brahman is, in itself, changeless and non-empirical. But it

[1] *Ibid.*, iii. 36.

[2] SB., Māṇḍ. K., iii. 19.

[3] SB., Ait. Up., iii. 23.

[4] Te nāmarūpe yasya brahmaṇo antarā vartete nāmarūpābhyām aspṛṣṭaṁ tad brahma nāmarūpavilakṣaṇam. Cinmātrānugamāt citsvarūpataiva gamyate. SB., Ch. Up., viii. 14. 1.

[5] Saṁvṛtiḥ avidyāviṣayo laukikavyavahāraḥ, tayā saṁvṛtyā jāyate sarvam. Paramārthaśadbhāvena tu ajaṁ sarvam ātmaiva. SB., Māṇḍ. K., iv. 57.

[6] Avidyālakṣanā anādimāyā. *Ibid,* iii. 36.

[7] Māyayā janma tat māyopamam. Māyā nāma vastu tarhi? Naivaṁ, sā ca māyā na vidyate. *Ibid,* iv. 58.

[8] Anekāni hi nāmarupopādhikṛtāni brahmaṇo rūpāṇi, na svataḥ. SB., Kena Up., ii. 1.

[9] Na hi sadasatoḥ sambandhaḥ. SB., Māṇḍ. K., i. 7.

appears to be modified into the empirical world through indefinable names and forms.[1] Brahman is not modified into the world. The Śruti regarding modification of Brahman into the world really conveys the identity of the world-appearance with trans-empirical Brahman.[2] The world is not a modification (pariṇāma) of Brahman. It is its mere appearance (vivarta). A modification is transformation of a cause into an effect of the same order of reality. But an appearance is perversion of a cause into an effect of a different order of reality.[3] The world is a perversion of Brahman. It is its mere appearance. Its reality is Brahman. Brahman is devoid of all determinations. It cannot have infinite powers. The multiplicity of appearances is a construction of avidyā.[4]

Only Īśvara, who is omniscient and omnipotent, can create the world through his infinite powers out of the unmanifest seeds of names and forms, which constitute his nature, as it were, and which are his magic power (māyāśakti). He can create the world out of his māyāśakti which is the matrix of names and forms.[5] Creation is beginningless (anādi) from the empirical standpoint. It is an eternal, sportive act of Īśvara, undetermined by an external end, issuing from his nature. But creation is unreal from the ontological standpoint.[6] Īśvara, endowed with māyā, is active or inactive.[7] He is, in his essential nature, inactive. But he becomes active in relation to his māyā.[8] Īśvara is the creator of the world, in relation to māyā, which is the object of his activity.[9] Out of relation to it, he is Brahman. He is not a separate reality apart from Brahman. The same Brahman is indeterminate and attributeless, unrelated

---

[1] Avidyākalpitena nāmarūpalakṣanena rūpabhedena vyākṛtāvyākṛtātmakena tattvānyatvābhyām anirvacanīyena brahma pariṇāmādisarvavyavahāraspadatvaṁ pratipadyate, pāramārthikena ca rūpeṇa sarvavyavahārātitaṁ apariṇatam avatiṣṭhate. SBS., ii. 1. 27.

[2] SBS., ii. 1. 7.

[3] Pariṇāmo nāma upādānasamasattākakāryāpattiḥ, vivarto nāma upādānaviṣamasattākakāryāpattiḥ. VPB., p. 141. *Siddhāntaleśasaṁgraha*, pp. 67-68.

[4] Na pratiṣiddhasarvaviśeṣasyāpi brahmaṇaḥ sarvaśaktiyogaḥ sambhavati ityetadapi avidyākalpitarūpabhedopanyāsenoktameva. SBS., ii. 1. 31.

[5] SB., Kaṭha Up., ii. 2. 12. [6] SBS., ii. 1. 31.

[7] Īśvarasya mahāmāyatvāt pravṛttyapravṛttī. SBS., ii. 2. 4.

[8] Paramātmanaḥ (īśvarasya) svarūpavyapāśrayam audāsīnyam, māyāvyapāśrayañca pravartakatvam. SBS., ii. 2 7.

[9] SBS., ii. 2. 1.

to the limiting adjunct of māyā, and it is determinate and qualified in relation to this adjunct.[1] Īśvara may be said to be an intermediate principle between indeterminate Brahman and the empirical world from the empirical standpoint. Indeterminate Brahman cannot be related to the world-appearance. It is immutable and inactive.[2] It cannot create the world. Only Īśvara, determinate Brahman, can be related to it. He can create it out of his māyā. Māyā is cosmic nescience. It is called mahāmāyā. Īśvara is called mahāmāyin.[3] Māya is an indefinable principle. It is ontologically unreal, since Brahman is the only ontological reality. But it is not absolutely unreal like a hare's horn. It is real enough to project the multiple world of appearances. They are modifications (pariṇāma) of names and forms, which are creations or constructions of avidyā or māyā.[4] They are modifications (parināma) of māyā. But they are appearances (vivarta) of Brahman.

Māyā is not an independent principle like prakṛti of the Sāṁkhya. It is dependent on Īśvara. It is his energy (śakti). It contains the unmanifest seeds of names and forms, which are transformed into the subtle essences and the gross elements. Īśvara is immanent in them as their inner self and guide. He transcends them all in his essential nature.[5] One Īśvara, who is, in reality, the eternal and immutable consciousness, appears to be many owing to māyā or avidyā. But there is no other conscious principle than the eternal and immutable consciousness or Brahman, either Īśvara or the jīva.[6]

Māyā is called *avyakta,* since it cannot be defined as real or unreal.[7] It is called *avyakta* also because it consists of subtle essences of the elements. They exist in an unmanifest condition in it. They exist in the condition of seed-potentialities of appearances. They exist as unmanifest names and forms.

---

[1] SBS., i. 1. 11. [2] SBS., ii. 1. 14.

[3] Sarvajñaṁ sarvaśakti mahāmāyañca tad brahma. SBS., ii. 1. 37.

[4] Avidyākṛta, avidyākalpita, avidyāpratyupasthāpita. SBS., i. 1. 4, 17; i. 2. 22; i. 3. 19; ii. 1. 22, 27, 31, 33; ii. 2. 2.

[5] Akṣaram avyākṛtaṁ nāmarūpabījaśaktirūpaṁ bhūtasūkṣmaṁ īśvarāśrayaṁ tasyaiva upādhibhūtam. SBS., i. 2. 22.

[6] SBS., i. 3. 9.

[7] Avyaktā hi sā māyā tattvānyatvanirūpaṇasya aśakyatvāt. SBS., i. 4. 3; SB., Kaṭha Up., i. 3. 11; SB., Īśa Up., 12; SB., Muṇḍ. Up., ii. 1. 2.

The empirical world consists of manifest names and forms.[1] Māyā is the subtle condition of the world prior to creation. It is dependent on Īśvara. He creates the world with māyā, his creative energy. He is inactive without māyā.[2] Māyā is sometimes called *ākāśa*. It is sometimes called *akṣara,* or the indestructible. It is of the nature of avidyā.[3] Avidyā is false knowledge. It is absence of true knowledge. It is non-apprehension of the reality. It is misapprehension of it as manifold appearances. It is beginningless. It is the cause of saṁsāra. It exists in the form of seeds or karmas in the jīvas.[4] Avidyā veils the nature of the Ātman or Brahman.[5] The jīva subject to avidyā cannot know its inner Self, Brahman, within it.[6] Māyā consists of sattva, rajas, and tamas. Pure sattva not overcome by rajas and tamas is the adjunct of Īśvara.[7] Māyā is the sumtotal of causal powers of all effects. It subsists in Īśvara, being permeated by him.[8] Māyā is deep sleep, as it were, or cosmic nescience subsisting in, and dependent on, Īśvara, in which bound empirical selves, ignorant of their essential nature, sleep.[9] This is the state of dissolution prior to creation. Īśvara creates the world out of this state of cosmic nescience (māyā). The bound jīvas also are reborn at the time of creation to exhaust the store of karmas.

The later Advaita Vedāntists distinguished between māyā and avidyā. Mahādevānanda Sarasvatī defines ajñāna as positive nescience, composed of sattva, rajas, and tamas, neither real nor unreal, but indefinable, and capable of being annulled by right knowledge. Ajñāna is twofold, māyā and avidyā. Māyā is made of pure sattva. Avidyā is made of impure sattva. Māyā is the adjunct of Īśvara. Avidyā is the adjunct of the jīva. Ajñāna has power of knowledge (jñānaśakti) and power of activity (kriyāśakti). Sattva not overcome by rajas and tamas

---

[1] Idam eva vyākṛtaṁ nāmarūpavibhinnaṁ jagat prāgavasthāvāṁ parityaktavyākṛtanāmarūpaṁ bījaśaktyavastham avyaktaśabdayogyaṁ darśayati. SBS., i. 4. 2.

[2] SBS., i. 4. 3.

[3] Avidyātmikā hi sā bījaśaktiḥ. SBS., i. 4. 3.

[4] Jīvaḥ tattvāpratibodharūpeṇa bījātmanā anyathāgrahaṇalakṣaṇena cānādikālapravṛttena māyālakṣanena svapnena svapnān paśyan suptaḥ. SB., Māṇḍ. K., i. 16.

[5] Avidyādoṣeṇa vidyamānasya ātmanas tiraskaraṇāt. SB., Īśa Up., 3.

[6] Avidyayā saṁvṛtaṁ sat (brahma) na lakṣyate. SB., Muṇḍ. Up., iii. 1. 7.

[7] Sattvopādhir Īśvaraḥ. SB., Muṇḍ. Up., iii. 1. 1.

[8] Avyaktaṁ sarvakāryakāraṇaśaktisamāhārarūpaṁ paramātmani otaprotabhāvena samāśritam. SB., Kaṭha Up., i. 3. 11.

[9] Parameśvarāśrayā māyāmayī mahāsuṣuptiḥ, yasyāṁ svarūpapratibodharahitāḥ śerate saṁsāriṇo jīvāḥ. SBS., i. 4. 3.

is the power of knowledge. Rajas and tamas not overcome by sattva are the power of activity. The power of activity is twofold, power of veiling (āvaraṇśakti) and power of projecting (vikṣepaśakti). Tamas not overcome by rajas and tamas is āvaraṇaśakti. Rajas not overcome by sattva and tamas is the vikṣepaśakti. Māyā has predominance of the power of projecting plurality of appearances. Avidyā has predominance of the power of veiling the nature of Brahman.[1] One ajñāna is called māyā and avidyā according to the predominance of the power of projection (vikṣepaśakti) and that of the power of veiling (āvaraṇaśakti).[2] Sadānanda also defines ajñāna in the same manner. He divides nescience (ajñāna) into collective (samaṣṭi) and individual (vyaṣṭi). The collective nescience with pure sattva predominant in it is the adjunct of Īśvara. It is māyā. The individual nescience with impure sattva predominant in it is the adjunct of the jīva. It is avidyā. Ajñāna has vikṣepaśakti by which it produces the multiple world-appearance. It has āvaraṇaśakti by which it obscures the nature of Brahman in the jīva and the world, and binds it to saṁsāra.[3] Māyā is cosmic nescience. Avidyā is individual nescience. Prakāśātman agrees with Śaṁkara that māyā and avidyā are identical in nature. But he holds that vikṣepaśakti is predominant in māyā which projects the world-appearance, while āvaraṇaśakti is predominant in avidyā which veils the nature of Brahman.[4] Vācaspati recognizes original nescience (mūlā avidyā) and fragmentary nescience (tūlā avidyā).[5] Beginningless positive root nescience is the cause of the world. It is the adjunct of Īśvara. Individual nescience is the adjunct of the jīva. The locus of avidyā is the jīva. The object of avidyā is Brahman.[6] Brahman, the object of nescience subsisting in the jīva, is perverted into the world with the aid of materiality of māyā subsisting in Brahman.[7] The avidyā in the jīva is turned into the subjective order and the objective order. Vidyāraṇya regards māyā as made of pure sattva, and avidyā as made of impure sattva. Īśvara is the reflection of Brahman in māyā. The jīva is the reflection of Brahman in avidyā.[8] Māyā and avidyā are one. Māyā produces effects, depending on the will of Īśvara. Its effects are perversions or appearances of Brahman. It has excessive power of projecting appearances. Avidyā is independent of the jīva. It veils the nature of Brahman. It has excessive power of veiling the real nature of the jīva and the world.[9] Māyā is the adjunct of Īśvara. Avidyā is the adjunct of the jīva. Nescience (ajñāna) is positive (bhāvarūpa). It is perceived in the forms 'I am ignorant', 'I do not know myself nor anybody else'. Thus nescience is perceived. Here negation of knowledge is not perceived, since negation implies the object negatived. 'I do not know'. This perception

---

[1] *Advaitacintākaustubha,* pp. 27-34.
[2] *Ibid,* p. 38.
[3] VS., pp. 8-14.
[4] Ekasminnapi vastuni vikṣepaprādhānyena māyā ācchādanaprādhānyena avidyā iti vyavahārabhedaḥ. *Pañcapādikāvivaraṇa,* p. 32.
[5] *Bhāmatī,* Śloka 1.
[6] Jīvapadā brahmaviṣayā.
[7] *Siddhāntaleśasaṁgraha,* pp. 96-97.
[8] *Pañcadaśī,* i. 14-15.
[9] VPS., p. 38.

apprehends general nescience. It does not apprehend negation of a particular object. Perception of nescience is different from perception of negation of a particular object. It can be known by non-apprehension (anupalabdhi). In dreamless sleep general nescience is perceived. It leaves an impression behind. On waking from sleep it is revived, and brings about the recollection 'I did not know anything during deep sleep'. Thus nescience is perceived.[1] Nescience is known by inference also. 'I did not know it before; I know it now'. The knowledge of the object removes the veil of nescience obscuring it, even as a streak of light removes the veil of darkness covering an object. Nescience is the material cause of illusions.[2]

Pārthasārathi Miśra, a follower of Kumārila, criticizes the Advaita Vedānta concept of avidyā. Is avidyā false knowledge? Or is its cause different from it? If it is false knowledge, it either belongs to Brahman or jīvas. Brahman is of the nature of eternal right knowledge. It cannot have false knowledge. Jīvas also are non-different from Brahman in their real nature. So they cannot have false knowledge. Thus false knowledge does not exist. Therefore, its cause, which is different from it, cannot exist. If false knowledge or its cause be said to exist separate from Brahman, then monism is undermined. If avidyā exists in Brahman, what is its cause? It cannot be anything different from Brahman. Nor can it be Brahman, since it is of the nature of right knowledge. It cannot contradict its nature. Therefore the concept of avidyā is irrational.[3]

24. *The World-Appearance (Prapañca)*

The empirical world (saṁsāra) is the unfoldment of undifferentiated names and forms, which are the objects of avidyā or false knowledge. It is the abode of empirical agents, acts, and their fruits. It consists of formed and formless objects imagined by avidyā. It is superimposed on the Ātman or Brahman. Brahman is different from empirical names and forms. Though it is one, eternal, pure or trans-empirical, conscious, and free, it appears to be the manifold world of appearance variegated by differences of agents, acts, and fruits. Knowledge of Brahman dispels avidyā, which is the seed-potentiality of attachment, aversion, and actions.[4] The world is the scene of retribution. Here the jīvas experience the fruits

---

[1] VPS., pp. 16-17; *Pañcapādikāvivaraṇa*, pp. 12-13.

[2] *Pañcapādikāvivaraṇa*, p. 12. VPS., pp. 17-18.

[3] SD., pp. 313-14.

[4] SB., Bṛ. Up., i. 1. 1; SB., Ait. Up., i. 1. 1; SB., Ch. Up., iii. 16. 1; vi. 1. 1; vi. 3. 3.

of their actions done in the past. The empirical objects are the material of their enjoyments and sufferings.[1]

Empirical objects are constructions of avidyā. Avidyā is imaginary. Its constructions are empirically real. They are not ontologically real. But the knowledge of the empirical objects is a means to the knowledge of Brahman.[2] Avidyā is the means of acquiring vidyā.[3] Brahman is free from imaginary constructions of avidyā (sarvakalpanāvarjita).[4] Avidyā produces difference. Difference infects saṁsāra. It is infected with duality of subjects and objects. Duality is a creation of avidyā. Subjects and objects are not ontologically real. They have only empirical reality.[5]

Duality which infects the world-appearance is mere māyā. Non-duality or Brahman is ontologically real.[6] Duality is the object of avidyā. Non-duality is the object of vidyā. When avidyā is destroyed by vidyā, duality vanishes, and non-dual Brahman shines forth.[7] When Brahman is known, duality does not exist.[8] Empirical selves and empirical objects are not metaphysically real.[9] Sometimes the duality of subjects and objects is said to be mental construction.[10] The mind is, in reality, the Ātman. It has no objects.[11] When it is purged of the taint of avidyā in trance, it becomes non-dual Brahman. It no longer perceives subjects and objects.[12] It becomes one, pure, undifferenced consciousness.[13]

---

[1] Sarvaprāṇikarmaphalopādānādhiṣṭhānabhūta. SB., Ait. Up., i. 1. 3.

[2] Yaḥ padārthaḥ vidyate, sa kalpitasaṁvṛtyā; kalpitā ca sā, paramārthapratipattyupāyatvena saṁvṛtiśca sā, tayā yaḥ asti, paramārthena nāsti asau na vidyate. SB., Māṇḍ. K., iv. 73.

[3] Cp. Nāgārjuna.

[4] *Ibid*, iv. 76.

[5] *Ibid*, iv. 94, 88; i. 12; ii. 1.

[6] Prapañcākhyaṁ māyāmātraṁ dvaitaṁ, advaitaṁ paramārthataḥ. *Ibid*, i. 17.

[7] Māṇḍ. Up., Introduction; i. 3.

[8] Jñāte paramārthatattve, dvaitaṁ na vidyate. SB., Māṇḍ. K., i. 18. *Ibid*, i. 29; iii. 18, 19.

[9] *Ibid*, ii. 1.

[10] Sarvaṁ grāhyagrāhakavat cittaspanditam eva dvayam. *Ibid*, iv. 72. Cp. LS., Yogācāra.

[11] *Ibid*, iv. 72.

[12] Yadā grāhyagrāhakāvidyākṛtamaladvayavarjitaṁ, tadā param advayaṁ brahmaiva tat saṁvṛttam. *Ibid*, iii. 35.

[13] Nivṛttasya dvaitaviṣayāt, cittasya brahmasvarūpā sthitiḥ advayavijñānaikaghanarasalakṣaṇā. *Ibid*, iv. 80.

The world-appearance is false. It is mere Māyā.[1] It is unreal like the illusory snake in a rope.[2] It is as unreal as magic elephants, rope-snakes, mirage, dreams, and the like.[3] It is unreal (asat), even as dream and magic are unreal.[4] Both external objects and mental modes are unreal (asat), like the illusory snake in a rope, and the like.[5] But though the world-appearance is unreal, it is not absolutely unreal (alīka) like a hare's horn,[6] or a barren woman's son. They do not come into being in reality or through māyā.[7] The world has not illusory reality. Even illusions are not objectless (nirāspada). They have foundation in empirical objects. The illusory snake is existent (sat) in the rope, which appears to be a snake owing to avidyā. The illusory water in a mirage is existent (sat) in the sandy desert, which appears as water in the sun owing to avidyā. The rope and the desert are empirical objects.[8] Illusions are not without basis in objects. They are wrong perceptions of empirical objects. A rope is mistaken for a snake. A nacre is mistaken for silver. A post is mistaken for a person. A desert is mistaken for a mirage. The illusions cannot exist separated from the empirical objects, which are their substrates. They are unreal (anṛta) in comparison with their substrates.[9] Śaṁkara says, "The water in a mirage is unreal (asat). The water we use is real (sat)."[10] By this he means that the former is unreal, while the latter has empirical reality, but not ontological reality. The empirical objects in the world are unreal (asat) in comparison with Brahman, which is the only ontological reality. They have relative or pragmatic reality (āpekṣika satya). They

---

[1] *Ibid*, i. 17.

[2] Ayaṁ prapañco māyā rajjusarpavat. *Ibid*, i. 18.

[3] *Ibid*, i. 27.

[4] Yathā svapnamāye dṛṣṭe asadrūpe, tatha viśvam idaṁ asad dṛṣṭam. *Ibid*, ii. 31.

[5] *Ibid*, ii. 38.

[6] *Ibid*, iv. 17.

[7] Bandhyāputro na tattvena māyayā vāpi jāyate. SB., Māṇḍ. K., i. 6.

[8] Dṛṣṭaṁ ca rajjusarpādīnām avidyākṛtamāyābījotpannānāṁ rajjvātmanā sattvaṁ, na hi nirāspadā rajjusarpamṛgatṛṣṇikādayaḥ kvacit upalabhyante. SB., Māṇḍ. K., i. 6. Rajjur api sarpavikalpasya āspadībhūtā. *Ibid*, ii. 32; iii. 29.

[9] Na hi sarpa-rajata-puruṣa-mṛgatṛṣṇikādivikalpāḥ, rajju-śukti-sthāṇūṣarādi-vyatirekeṇa avastvāspadāḥ śakyāḥ kalpayitum. SB., Māṇḍ. Up., i. 7.

[10] Sacca paramārthodakādi. Asacca marīcyudakādi. SB., Pr. Up., iv.

are objects of empirical knowledge and practical use.[1] They are real in comparison with illusory objects. Śaṁkara does not deny the empirical reality of the world. Illusory objects are unreal (anṛta). They do not serve practical needs. Empirical objects have pragmatic reality. They serve the practical purposes of life. They have fixed laws.[2] They have relative reality. They are real until mokṣa is realized. When the jīva realizes its identity with Brahman, it is no longer deluded by the apparent plurality of the world.[3] But until the intuition of Brahman is attained, the objects of practical use, secular and religious activities, have empirical reality.[4]

It is entirely erroneous to suppose that Śaṁkara treats the world as illusory, or as absolutely real.[5] He recognizes the relative (āpekṣika), empirical, or pragmatic (vyāvahārika) reality of the world. He accords more reality to it than to illusions which are false (anṛta). He accords less reality to it than to Brahman, which is the only ontological reality. Illusions are more real than ideas of absolutely unreal things like hare's horns, since they subsist in empirical objects. They are not without foundation in reality (nirāspada). The world-appearance is false (mithyā) in comparison with Brahman. Just as illusions subsist in empirical objects, which are their reality, so the world-appearance subsists in Brahman, which is its reality. Brahman is the substratum (adhiṣṭhāna) of the world-appearance (sarvakalpanāspada).[6]

Dharmarājādhvarīndra recognizes three grades of reality : (1) ontological reality (pāramārthika sattā); (2) empirical reality (vyāvahārika sattā); and (3) illusory reality (prātibhāsika sattā). Brahman is the ontological reality. The world in space and time, and subject to causality is the empirical reality. The jīvas and Īśvara also are empirical realities. Illusions, dreams, and the like are illusory existences. The spatio-temporal world subject to causality is not an ontological reality like Brahman. It is not an illusion of the empirical self. It is real and independent of the jīvas. It is a creation of Īśvara out of his māyā.[7]

---

[1] Satyaṁ ca vyavahāraviṣayaṁ na paramārthasatyam. Ekam eva hi paramārthasatyaṁ brahma. Iha punar vyavahāraviṣayam āpekṣikaṁ satyaṁ, mṛgatṛṣṇikādyanṛtāpekṣayodakādi satyam ucyate. Anṛtam ca tadviparītam. SB., Tait. Up., ii. 6.

[2] SB., Kaṭha Up., ii. 3. 2. [3] SB., Māṇḍ. K., ii. 18.

[4] Sarvo'yaṁ laukiko vaidikaśca vyavahāro'vidyāviṣayaḥ. SB., Māṇḍ. K., ii. 32.

[5] Kokileswar Sastri : *An Introduction to Advaita Philosophy*, Ch. III.

[6] *Ibid.*, ii. 33. [7] VPB., ch. i.

Śaṁkara elaborates Gauḍapāda's arguments for the falsity of the empirical objects from the ontological standpoint: (1) All objects of waking perceptions and dream-cognitions are known (dṛśya). Whatever are known, are unreal, like objects of dream-cognitions.[1] Cognizability (dṛśyatva) and falsity (asatyatva) are common to objects of waking perceptions and dream-cognitions. What are known, are products of avidyā.[2] Śaṁkara agrees with Gauḍapāda that the objects of knowledge (dṛśya) have no ontological reality. Only Brahman, the eternal subject-objectless consciousness is the ontological reality. But he differs from Gauḍapāda in holding that waking perceptions are dissimilar to dream-cognitions, since the latter are contradicted by waking perceptions while the former are not contradicted.[3] Gauḍapāda tends towards subjectivism, though he is an absolutist, but Śaṁkara is uncompromising in his anti-subjectivism. He refutes Vijñānavāda, and establishes the empirical reality of external objects of waking perceptions. (2) The objects of waking perceptions are unreal, since they do not exist in the beginning and at the end, like the illusory objects.[4] All things with origin and destruction are false appearances. They are unreal, but appear to be real.[5] The real is eternal. Plato also is of the same view. Objects of waking perceptions are unreal like objects of dream-cognitions, since both have origin and end, and both serve practical ends. Even in dreams persons feel the satisfaction of eating and drinking.[6] The non-eternal are unreal. (3) Just as the objects of dreams, illusions, and reveries appear to be real, though they are unreal, so the world infected with duality and plurality appears to be real, though it is metaphysically unreal.[7] This argument is common to the Yogācāras, Nāgārjuna, Gauḍapāda, and Śaṁkara. But Śaṁkara recognizes different degrees of reality. Brahman is the ontological reality. The world, jīvas, and Īśvara have empirical reality. Dreams, illusions, and reveries have illusory reality. They are unreal (anṛta) from the empirical standpoint. Hare's horns, barren woman's sons, and the like are absolutely unreal (alīka).

---

[1] SB., Māṇḍ. K., ii. 4.
[2] Avidyābījaprasūtaṁ vedyam. *Ibid*, i. 12.
[3] SBS., ii. 2. 29.
[4] *Ibid*, ii. 6.
[5] *Ibid*, iv. 31-32.
[6] *Ibid*, ii. 7.
[7] Yathā ca svapnamāye dṛṣṭe asadrūpe, tathā viśvam idam dvaitaṁ samastam asad dṛṣṭam. *Ibid*, ii. 31.

They have not even illusory reality. Śaṃkara never denies the pragmatic or relative reality of the empirical objects of the world. Nāgārjuna also recognizes three degrees of reality; (1) Ontological reality (paramārtha satya); (2) empirical reality (lokasaṁvṛti); and (3) illusory reality (alokasaṁvṛti). (4) What is always present, is real. Brahman, the eternal consciousness, is never absent. It is eternally present everywhere.[1] But the world is created and dissolved. So it is unreal. The eternal being is real. The non-eternal world is unreal. (5) Brahman is real, since it never loses its essential nature. It is unchanging and immutable.[2] The world is unreal, since it is changeable and mutable. (6) Brahman is non-spatial, non-temporal, and non-causal. It is not limited in space. It is not limited in time. It is not subject to causality. Therefore it has ontological reality. The world, on the other hand, is spatio-temporal and determined by causality. It is limited in time and space. It is the reign of the law of causality. Time, space, and causality are empirical categories. They are not metaphysically real. So the world is unreal. Brahman is the whole reality. It is not limited in space. If it were so limited, it would be corporeal, with origin and end, subsisting in another entity, composed of parts, non-eternal, and produced.[3] But Brahman is incorporeal, unborn, imperishable, self-subsistent, partless, eternal, and uncaused. The world, on the other hand, is corporeal, born, perishable, dependent on Brahman, composed of parts, non-eternal, and caused. So it has no ontological reality. Brahman transcends the past, the present, and the future. It is not limited by time.[4] So it is metaphysically real. But the world is limited by time. So it has no ontological reality. Brahman transcends cause and effect. So it is real. But empirical objects are causes and effects. So they have no ontological reality.[5] Brahman is uncaused (ajāti, aja). Empirical objects are caused; their causation is due to avidyā.[6] (7) Imperishable Brahman known by higher knowledge (parā vidyā) is real. The perish-

---

[1] Sarvatra avyabhicārāt jñasvarūpasya satyatvam. SB., Māṇḍ. Up., i. 7.

[2] Ātmā na vyeti svarūpāt na vyabhicarati na cyavate. SB., Māṇḍ. K., i. 10; SB., Bṛ. Up., ii. 4. 12.

[3] SB., Muṇḍ. Up., iii. 2. 6.

[4] SB., Kaṭha Up., i. 2. 14.

[5] *Ibid*, i. 2. 4

[6] SB., Māṇḍ. K., ii. 2, 19, 20, 21, 24, 27, 38; iv. 14, 22, 38, 40.

able world, the object of lower or empirical knowledge (aparā vidyā), and the abode of fruits of actions, is unreal (anṛta). It has relative or empirical reality (āpekṣika satya). Akṣara Brahman, the source of the world, is real, while the world is unreal.[1] Modifications (vikāra) are objects of empirical knowledge. So they are unreal (anṛta).[2]

The whole world subsists in Brahman. It is the substratum (āspada) of the world-appearance, even as a rope is the substratum of the illusion of a snake.[3] It is the Self of all jīvas. It is the reality of formed and formless things. They cannot exist apart from it.[4] All beings subsist in the eternal consciousness, which is real, while the beings subsisting in Brahman are unreal.[5] Brahman alone is true. All its apparent modifications are false.[6] That is the essence of a thing which does not depend upon any other thing. It is its reality (tattva). That is not the essence of a thing which depends upon some other thing, since it does not exist in its absence. The essence of a thing consists in its immutability (avikriyā), since it does not depend upon another thing.[7] So the essence (tattva) of empirical things is Brahman. Their mutations are unreal appearances. The world of mutations is unreal (anṛta). It is nothing but Brahman. There is no reality called the world other than Brahman.[8]

There is causation in the world of empirical objects. But there is no causation in Brahman, the ontological reality. There is ontological non-difference of the empirical world from indeterminate Brahman. There is causation in the world of empirical objects. Empirical causation is mutation, modification, or transformation (pariṇāma). The world is the modification or evolute of māyā, power of Īśvara. Īśvara, determinate Brahman, is the material cause and the efficient cause of the world, because he is an appearance of Brahman. But there is non-difference (abheda) between indeterminate Brahman and the empirical world. Ontological non-difference is the truth of empirical

---

[1] SB., Muṇḍ. Up., ii. 1. 1.
[2] *Ibid*, ii. 1. 2.
[3] *Ibid*, ii. 2. 12.
[4] *Ibid*, ii. 2. 1.
[5] Caitanyāśrayā hi sarve prasiddhāḥ. Tad etat sarvāśrayam akṣaraṁ brahma. Tad etat satyam. *Ibid*, ii. 2. 2.
[6] Brahma eva satyaṁ, sarvaṁ tadvikāram anṛtam. *Ibid*, ii. 2. 12.
[7] Dravyasya hi tattvam avikriyā, parānapekṣatvāt. Vikriyā na tattvaṁ, parāpekṣatvāt. SB., Tait. Up. ii. 8.
[8] Puruṣa (brahma) eva idaṁ viśvaṁ sarvam. Na viśaṁ nāma puruṣād anyāt kiñcid asti. SB., Muṇḍ Up., ii. 1. 10.

causation. The world is the appearance (vivarta) of indeterminate Brahman. It is not its modification. It is the ground (adhiṣṭhāna) of the world-appearance. Śaṁkara advocates Vivartavāda from the ontological standpoint, and Pariṇāmavāda from the empirical standpoint.

An effect does not exist apart from its cause. It is unreal.[1] Gold ornaments are non-different from gold. But gold is not of the nature of gold ornaments. Earthen vessels are non-different from earth. But earth is not of the nature of earthen vessels. Though effect and cause are non-different from each other, the effect partakes of the nature of the cause, but the cause does not partake of the nature of the effect.[2] The effect is non-different from the cause. The entire world is an effect or appearance of Brahman. So it is non-different from Brahman.[3] The world is the effect or appearance. Indeterminate Brahman is its cause or ground. So the world-appearance is ontologically non-different from indeterminate Brahman. The aggregate of empirical objects, which are appearances of indeterminate Brahman, cannot exist apart from Brahman. The world-appearance cannot exist apart from Brahman, its ground and reality. It has only empirical reality. Its ontological reality is Brahman.[4]

Creation is real from the empirical standpoint. It is unreal from the ontological standpoint. Texts relating to creation of the world by Brahman aim at proving its non-difference (abheda) from, or identity (ekatva) with, Brahman.[5] The differences in the world are not due to creation. They are products of avidyā. They are names and forms. They are empirical appearances. Creation is not ontologically real.[6] A thing composed of parts is modified into a different thing owing

---

[1] Anṛtatvāt kāryavastunaḥ. Na hi kāraṇavyatirekeṇa kāryaṁ nāma vastuto' asti. SB., Tait. Up., ii. 1.

[2] Ananyatve'pi kāryakāraṇayoh, kāryasya kāraṇātmakatvaṁ, na tu kāraṇasya kāryātmakatvam. SBS., ii. 1. 9.

[3] Kāryasya kāraṇād ananyatvam. Ataśca kṛtsnasya jagato brahmakāryatvāt tadananyatvācca. SBS., ii. 1. 20.

[4] Kāryaṁ bahuprapañcaṁ jagat, kāraṇaṁ paraṁ brahma. Tasmāt kāraṇāt paramārthato' ananyatvam vyatirekeṇa abhāvaḥ kāryasya avagamyate. Brahmavyatirekeṇa kāryajātasya abhāvaḥ. SBS., ii. 1. 14.

[5] Tasmād utpattyādiśrutayaḥ ātmaikatvabuddhyavatārāyaiva, na anyārthāḥ kalpayituṁ yuktāḥ. SB., Māṇḍ. K., iii. 15.

[6] Na ceyaṁ paramārthaviṣayā sṛṣṭiśrutiḥ, avidyākalpitanāmarūpavyavahāragocaratvāt, brahmātmabhāvapratipādanaparatvācca. SBS., ii. 1. 33.

to mutation of its parts. Earth is modified into vessels. But one, uncaused, partless Brahman cannot be modified into the manifold objects of the world. One immutable Brahman appears to be the multiform world owing to māyā. It does not really become the manifold world.[1] Brahman is eternal and immutable. It has neither cause nor effect.[2] There is no causal relation from the ontological standpoint.[3]

External objects are subjective ideas according to the Yogācāras. They are objective entities, which are empirically real, but ontologically unreal according to Śaṁkara. He is not a subjective idealist.[4] Saṁkara agrees with Vasubandhu that Brahman or pure, eternal consciousness is the ontological reality, and that subjects and objects are creations of avidyā. But Śaṁkara differs from Vasubandhu in holding that one Brahman appears to be manifold subjects and objects owing to avidyā, while Vasubandhu holds that subject-cognitions and object-cognitions are transformations of one, pure, eternal consciousness (vijñaptimātratā).

Gauḍapāda says, "The multiple objects of the world are not real as Brahman ; they are not real in themselves. They are neither different nor non-different from Brahman".[5] Śaṁkara says, "The empirical world does not appear to be different from Brahman, when it is known in its real nature to be one Brahman, even as the illusory snake does not appear to be different from a rope, when it is known to be a rope. The empirical objects are not non-different from one another, and from Brahman, since they are unreal".[6] They are constructions of māyā or avidyā. It is the absence of the knowledge of Brahman. It is destroyed by the intuition of Brahman.[7] Liberated persons do not perceive external objects

[1] SBS., Māṇḍ. K., ii. 19. SBS., ii. 1. 14.

[2] Na hi nityasya kūṭasthasya ātmano hetuphalātmakatā sambhavati. SB., Māṇḍ. K., iv. 14.

[3] Paramārthatastu na kasyacit kenacid api prakāreṇa kāryakāraṇabhāva upapadyate. SB., Māṇḍ. K., iv. 40.

[4] Asatyeva ghaṭādau ghaṭādyābhāsatā vijñānavādinā abhupagatā, tad anumoditam asmābhir api bhūtadarśanāt. SB., Māṇḍ. K., iv. 28.

[5] Nātmabhāvena nānedaṁ na svenāpi kathañcana. Na pṛthaṅ nāpṛthak kiñcit. Māṇḍ. K., ii. 34.

[6] SB., Māṇḍ. K. ii. 34.

[7] Avidyālakṣaṇā anādimāyā. Sā ca avidyā ātmasatyānubodhena niruddhā. *Ibid,* iii. 36.

as different from Brahman because they are not deluded by false knowledge.[1] Those, who have realized their identity with Brahman, do not apprehend the distinction of agents, actions, and fruits. They know the identity of the ontological reality. They apprehend plurality as a mere construction of false knowledge. Right knowledge of identity dispels false knowledge of plurality.[2] But until the right knowledge of identity of Brahman dawns, knowledge of falsity of the world-appearance with the distinction of knowers, knowledge, and known objects, does not arise. So the empirical objects of the world are known to be real in our secular and religious life until their identity with Brahman is known. Therefore the world-appearance has empirical reality.[3] The difference between empirical truth and falsehood remains intact until the identity of Brahman is realized. The moral and religious life also remains unaffected. Morality and religion have empirical truth. They are not annulled.[4]

Pārthasārathi Miśra criticizes the Advaita Vedāntist doctrine of falsity of the world-appearance. The world is said to be the appearance of Brahman. The world-appearance is not non-existent (asat), since it is actually perceived. Perception cannot be sublated by scriptural testimony. Perception is stronger than inference, testimony, and the other pramāṇas. It may be argued that the world-appearance is not non-existent (asat), since it is perceived, nor that it is ontologically existent (sat), since it is sublated by the knowledge of Brahman, but that it is indefinable (anirvacanīya). This argument is wrong. What is other than the existent is non-existent. If the world-appearance is not existent, it must be non-existent. If it is not non-existent, it must be existent. The existent and the non-existent are contradictory terms. There is no intermediate possibility between them. It may be argued that what is never known, for example, hare's horns, is non-existent, that what is known, but not sublated is existent, for example, Brahman, but that what is known, but sublated, for example, the world-appearance, cannot

---

[1] Na hi muktānāṁ bhrāntidarśanābhāve ātmavyatirikto bāhyo'rtha upalabhyate. *Ibid,* iv. 25.

[2] Darśayati brahmātmatvadarśinaṁ prati samastasya kriyākārakaphalalakṣaṇasya vyavahārasya abhāvam. Ekatvam evaikaṁ pāramārthikaṁ darśayati, mithyājñānavijṛmbhitañca nānātvam. Ekatvajñānena nānātvajñānam apanudyate. SBS., ii. 1. 14.

[3] Yāvaddhi na satyātmaikatvapratipattiḥ, tāvat pramāna-prameyaphala-lakṣaṇeṣu vyavahāreṣu anṛtabudddhir na kasyacid utpadyate. Tasmāt prāg brahmātmatāprabodhād upapannaḥ sarvo laukiko vaidikśca vyavahāraḥ. SBS., ii. 1. 14.

[4] Prāk cātmaikatvāgater avyāhataḥ sarvaḥ satyānṛtavyavahāro laukiko vaidikaśca. SBS., ii. 1. 14. See R. P. Singh : *The Vedānta of Śaṅkara,* 1949, pp. 267-71.

be defined as existent or non-existent. This argument is wrong. What is known, but sublated, for example, illusions, is non-existent. There is no difference between hare's horns and a mirage. If the world-appearance is sublated, it is non-existent, but not indefinable. But it is not sublated by the knowledge of Brahman during empirical life. The liberated person also cannot have sublating knowledge, since his organs of knowledge have been destroyed, and no knowledge can arise without the senses. He cannot have recollection, since all his impressions have been destroyed. So perception of the world cannot be sublated. So the world-appearance is not false.[1]

22. *Space, Time, and Causality*

Brahman is non-spatial, non-temporal, and non-causal. The empirical world is spatial, temporal, and determined by causality. Space, time, and causality are categories of empirical knowledge. They imply plurality which is a construction of avidyā. Avidyā is empirical knowledge.[2] Space implies co-existence of a plurality of objects.[3] Time implies succession of a plurality of events. Causation implies sequence of causes and effects. The space-time-cause world is an object of empirical knowledge (aparā vidyā). It is not an object of higher knowledge (parā vidyā). Only Brahman is known by right intuition (samyak darśana). Space, time, and causality have empirical reality. They have no ontological reality. They apply to empirical objects. They do not apply to Brahman, which transcends them.[4]

Brahman is one, uncaused, indivisible, partless, and devoid of inside and outside. It is therefore non-spatial.[5] Empirical objects are many, caused, divisible, composed of parts, and have inside and outside. They are therefore spatial. Brahman has nothing prior or posterior to it.[6] It is eternal. It is always present. It transcends the past, the present, and the future. It is above temporal sequence. It is non-temporal or timeless.[7] But empirical objects are limited in time. Brahman is uncaused (aja). It transcends cause and effect.[8] But empirical

[1] SD., pp. 311-13.
[2] SB., Māṇḍ. K., ii. 32.
[3] Bāhyānām anyonyaparicchedyatvām. *Ibid,* ii. 14.
[4] SB., Māṇḍ. K., iii. 2, 19, 20, 24, 27, 38; iv. 14, 22, 38, 40; Muṇḍ. Up., ii. 2. 6; Kaṭha Up., i. 2. 4. 14.
[5] SBS., ii. 3. 7; SB., Māṇḍ. K., ii. 38.
[6] SB., Māṇḍ. K., i. 26.
[7] SB., Māṇḍ. Up., i. 1; SB., Kaṭha Up., ii. 1. 5, 13.
[8] SB., Māṇḍ. K., i. 26; iv. 14, 40, 54, 57; SB., Kaṭha Up., i. 3. 15.

objects are produced by their causes, and produce effects. Whatever is limited in space, is limited in time, and produced by a cause. Therefore empirical objects are spatial, temporal, and caused.[1]

There is no causality from the ontological standpoint. Brahman is the ontological reality. It is not subject to causality. It is neither a cause nor an effect. Brahman is the cause (kāraṇa) of the world-appearance in the sense that it is its ground (adhiṣṭhāna) or substrate (āśraya). Causation implies distinction of cause and effect, their temporal sequence, and modification of cause into effect. But Brahman is distinctionless, non-temporal, and immutable. So Brahman is not a cause in the empirical sense. Brahman is the substratum (āspada) of the world-appearance, even as a rope is the substratum of an illusory snake. Brahman is not transformed into the world. It is unchangeable and unmodifiable. The world is an appearance (vivarta) of indeterminate Brahman. It is non-different (ananya) from it. It is identical with it in reality. Identity is the truth of causality, which has only empirical reality.

Though Śaṁkara denies causality from the ontological standpoint, he does not deny it from the empirical standpoint. He advocates Satkāryavāda or pre-existence of the effect in its cause. He criticizes the Nyāya-Vaiśeṣika doctrine of Asatkāryavāda or Ārambhavāda, which maintains that an effect is a new beginning (ārambha), and that it does not pre-exist in its cause. It springs from its material cause, and subsists in it in the relation of inherence (samavāya). The effect (*e.g.*, curds) is different from its cause (*e.g.*, milk). It inheres in the cause. Śaṁkara argues that an effect must pre-exist in its cause, and that if it does not pre-exist in it, it can never arise from it. Oil cannot be pressed out of sand. It can be pressed out of oil-seeds only, because it pre-exists in them. So the effect pre-exists in its cause as non-different from it prior to its production, and it is non-different from its cause after its production.[2] The effect is said to be non-existent in its cause, because it exists in an unmanifest (avyākṛta) or undeveloped condition in its cause, and becomes manifest (vyākṛta) or developed in the state of the effect.[3] The effect pre-exists in its cause as non-different from it, since particular effects spring from particular causes. Curds spring from milk. Jars spring from earth. Golden ornaments spring from gold. Curds do not spring from earth. Jars do not spring from milk. If the effect did not pre-exist in its cause, then any effect would spring from any cause, and there would be no restriction of

[1] Yaddhi loke iyattāparicchinnaṁ vastu ghaṭādi, tadantavad dṛṣṭam. SBS., ii. 2. 41.

[2] SBS., ii. 1. 16.

[3] SBS., ii. 1. 17.

specific effects to specific causes. If a cause had no distinctiveness (viśeṣa), then any cause would produce any effect. If the effect were non-existent in its cause prior to its production, then its non-existence being common to all causes, any effect would spring from any cause. If it is urged by the Nyāya-Vaiśeṣika that though non-existence of an effect prior to production is common to all causes, a specific cause has a specific power (ātiśaya) to produce a specific effect, then Śaṁkara argues that it undermines the doctrine of Asatkāryavāda, and establishes the doctrine of Satkāryavāda. The effect pre-exists in its cause in the form of a specific power (atiśaya, śakti). Power is not different from the cause. Nor is it non-existent. It is the essence of the cause. The effect is the essence of the causal power. Causal power is identical with the cause. The effect is identical with the causal power.[1] Further, the effect does not inhere in its material cause, since inherence (samavāya) between cause and effect, distinct from each other, would require another inherence to relate itself to the cause, and so on to infinity. The Nyāya-Vaiśeṣika treats cause, effect, and inherence as independent entities; therefore it must posit an infinite series of inherences to relate cause and effect to each other. This infinite regress (anavasthā) can be avoided, if essential identity (tādātmya) of the effect with its cause is admitted. If it were not admitted, cause and effect would be isolated from each other, and could not be related to each other. Further, whether the effect, which is a whole, exists in each part of its material cause entirely or partially is unintelligible. If inherence itself be said to relate the effect to its cause, then conjunction also would relate the two things conjoined without the aid of inherence. But the Vaiśeṣika maintains that conjunction is a quality (guṇa) of the conjoined things, which is related to them through inherence. But Śaṁkara denies the relation of inherence between a substance (dravya) and its quality (guṇa), and admits essential identity (tādātmya) between them. If the effect does not pre-exist in its cause before its production, its production by an agent would be meaningless. Production is an act, and its presupposes an active agent. An act without an agent is inconceivable. If production is said to be the relation of the effect to its cause, how can the non-existent effect be related to the existent cause? Two existent things only can be related to each other. An existent thing and a non-existent thing cannot be related to each other, since the latter is a non-entity. The effect must be existent to be related to its cause.[2] It may be objected that if the effect pre-exists in its cause, the activity of the agent would be unnecessary. Śaṁkara replies that the activity of the agent arranges the material cause into the form of effect. Oil pre-exists in oil-seeds, but not in the form of oil. A person presses oil out of them. The effect pre-exists in its cause in a potential condition. It is made actual by the activity of an agent. An unrolled cloth pre-exists in a rolled cloth. An agent's activity merely unfolds the rolled cloth, and

---

[1] Kāraṇasya ātmabhūtā śaktih, śakteśca ātmabhūtaṁ kāryam. SBS., ii. 1. 18.

[2] Cp. The Sāṁkhya.

spreads it out.[1] An effect is, therefore, a manifestation of its potential form pre-existing in its cause. It is an unfoldment of the causal power, in which it is dormant. A cause is the unmanifest condition of its effect. The effect is the manifest condition of its cause.[2] Therefore the effect is non-different from, or identical in essence with, its cause.[3] Further, if the effect were non-existent in its cause, the activity of the agent would be objectless, since a non-entity cannot be its object. Even hundred strokes of a sword cannot cut the ether. The agent's activity cannot be said to act on the material cause, since action on one thing cannot produce another thing. A potter cannot make a gold pot out of clay with a staff and a wheel. If the effect be said to be a specific power (atiśaya) of the material cause itself, then it pre-exists in the cause before its production in this form. Curds pre-exist in milk in a potential condition; when it takes the form of curds, it is called an effect. The effect is never non-different from its cause. A root cause gradually unfolds itself successively as a series of effects. The cause continues in the effect. Thus the pre-existence and non-difference of the effect from its cause are known from the cause.[4] Īśvara, the cause of the world, exists in all times. The world also, the effect or creation of Īśvara, exists in all times. Being is one. So the effect, the world, is non-different from the cause, Īśvara. Its being is the being of Īśvara.[5] Śaṁkara advocates Satkāryavāda in the form of Vivartavāda. The effect is the appearance (vivarta) of the cause. The cause is real; the effect is unreal. Das Gupta call the doctrine Satkāraṇavāda.[6]

Śaṁkara elaborates Gauḍapāda's arguments to prove that causality is an empirical category applicable to finite objects, and that it is inapplicable to Brahman, which is beyond causal relation. Causation implies change. Change is mutation. Mutation is becoming different or alteration. Alteration is possible in the empirical world of finite things.[7] But one, non-dual Brahman cannot be different from itself. It is changeless and immutable. It can only appear to be different from itself. One appears to be many. It never becomes many. But how it appears to be many is inexplicable māyā. Brahman is the reality of the world-appearance. It is the ground of the spatio-temporal, causality-bound world of names and forms.

---

[1] SBS., ii. 1. 19. [2] Cp. The Sāṁkhya.

[3] Kāryasya kāraṇād ananyatvam. SBS., ii. 1. 21.

[4] Kāryasya prāgutpatteḥ sattvam ananyatvañca kāraṇād avagamyate. SBS., ii. 1. 18.

[5] Yathā ca kāraṇaṁ brahma triṣu kāleṣu sattvaṁ na vyabhicarati, evaṁ kāryam api jagat triṣu kāleṣu sattvaṁ na vyabhicarati. Ekaṁ ca punaḥ sattvam, ato'pyananyatvaṁ kāraṇāt kāryasya. SBS., ii. 1. 16.

[6] HIP., i. p. 468. See Deussen: *The System of the Vedānta*, pp. 256-60. Cp. *Indian Philosophy*, Vol. II, pp. 528-30.

[7] SB., Tait. Up., ii. 8.

All mutations are differentiations of names and forms. Brahman is different from them. Even names and forms cannot exist apart from it. Thus the world-appearance subsists in Brahman.[1] Space, time, and causality cannot be applied to Brahman.[2]

Citsukha criticizes the Nyāya definition of cause as the unconditional, invariable, and immediate antecedent of an event, or as an aggregate of conditions. An antecedent cannot be a cause. If it were so, an ass would be the cause of smoke in a washerman's house. Time is one. It does not exist in time. Time being one, there can be no antecedence and sequence. But it may be argued that though time is one, it is manifold through its adjuncts (upādhi) in the form of changes or phenomena, and therefore there can be antecedence and sequence. But this argument involves vicious circle. Antecedence and sequence of real time depends upon antecedence and sequence of phenomena; antecedence and sequence of phenomena depends upon the antecedence and sequence of real time. Then a cause is said to be an invariable antecedent. What is an invariable antecedent? If it means that it being always present, the effect is present, then an ass being always present in a washerman's house, it would be the cause of smoke. If it means that it is an antecedent which does not depend upon other conditions (ananyathāsiddha), then the space occupied by an ass being an antecedent, it would be the cause of smoke. If it means an antecedent that contributes to the production of the effect, the nature of its contribution to the effect except its mere antecedence is unintelligible. Antecedence is known. But production is never known.[3] If the invariable antedecent means an antecedent in the presence of which the effect must come into being, then the seed is not the cause of a sprout, because though the seed is present, the sprout may not spring up. If it is said that a cause can produce an effect only when it is aided by its accessory conditions (sahakāri kāraṇa), then the nature of the cause and its relation to the auxiliary conditions is not intelligible. Again, the same effect is produced by different causes at different times. There is plurality of causes. Then the cause cannot be an invariable antecedent; it does not invariably precede the effect. If a specific cause (kāraṇaviśeṣa) be said to be the cause of a specific effect (kāryaviśeṣa), then it may be urged that the same kind of clay can produce different vessels. Therefore the invariable antecedent cannot be the cause. The Nyāya defines a cause of collocation of conditions (sāmagrī). What is a collocation? It is either a collocation of conditions or something in addition to them.

[1] Na ca brahmaṇo'nyannāmarūpābhyām arthāntaraṁ sambhavati, sarvasya vikārajātasya nāmarūpābhyām eva vyākṛtatvāt. Nāmarūpayorapi nirvahaṇaṁ niraṅkuśaṁ na brahmaṇo'anyatra sambhavati. SBS., i. 3. 41.

[2] Na deśakālādiviśeṣasaṁyogaḥ paramātmanaḥ kalpayituṁ śakyate. SBS., iv. 3. 14. Digdeśakālādibhedaśunyaṁ brahma. SB., Ch. Up., viii. 1. 1. SB., Tait. Up., ii. 1; Bṛ. Up., ii. 4. 12.

[3] Cp. Hume.

On the first view, the effect would be produced by the individual conditions being scattered in the world. On the second view, something in addition to the conditions is either eternal or non-eternal. If it is eternal, the effect would always be produced. If it is non-eternal, the individual conditions being its cause, and being always present, the effect would always be produced. The collocation (sāmagrī) cannot be said to be the last activity (vyāpāra) of the conditions immediately preceding the production of the effect, because whether all the conditions individually or collectively cause the activity is not intelligible. Further, if the conditions are active before activity comes into being, then an infinite series of activities would be required to relate them to the activity which produces the effect. If the conditions are inactive before activity comes into being, they may produce the effect directly without first producing the activity. If the causal activity itself has activity (vyāpāra) before it produces the effect, then there will be infinite regress. If it has no inactivity before it produces the effect, the inactive conditions themselves may produce the effect without the intervening activity. The conception of causal activity (vyāpāra) is useless.[1] The idea of unconditional antecedence or necessity also is incomprehensible. Thus the Nyāya definition of cause is invalid. Causality is indefinable, incomprehensible, and inexplicable.[2] Prakāśānanda asks : Is the effect existent (sat) or non-existent (asat) in the cause before its production ? If it is existent, the activity of the cause is useless, and production of it becomes meaningless. If it is non-existent, hare's horns also would be produced because they are non-existent in a cause. If production is said to be mere manifestation (abhivyaktimātra) brought about by the activity of a cause, then the manifestation also is either existent or non-existent in the cause, and the same difficulties would arise. The effect is, therefore, neither existent nor non-existent, but indefinable (anirvacanīya). All effects are produced by beginningless, indefinable nescience (ajñāna). Nescience has various powers, and can produce infinite variety of effects through them.[3]

23. *Creation*

There is an order in cosmic evolution and dissolution. Dissolution is the reverse order of creation.[4] There are cycles of creation and dissolution. The world is evolved out of māyā, and dissolved into it. Māyā is the energy of Īśvara. So the world is born out of Īśvara, and re-absorbed in him. Īśvara is the creator, preserver, and destroyer of the world. Māyā is the matrix of the seeds of names and forms. It is dependent on Īśvara. When the world is created, it remains non-different

[1] Cp. Hume. [2] *Tattvapradīpikā*, pp. 313-16.
[3] *Vedāntasiddhāntamuktāvalī* (Jīvānanda edition), pp. 78-81.
[4] SBS., ii. 3. 15.

from Īśvara. When it is destroyed, it remains in the form of seed-potentialities of names and forms, non-distinct from māyā, the power of Īśvara.[1] The world is non-different from Īśvara. It exists in an effect state (kāryāvasthā) after creation. It exists in a causal state (kāraṇāvasthā) after dissolution. It is the sphere of moral and religious life. Īśvara creates empirical objects for the enjoyments and sufferings of the individual selves. He adapts the world (kṣetra) to the moral deserts of the empirical selves (kṣetrajña). It is the abode of the fruits of actions of creatures.[2] The world is a moral order. Īśvara is the Moral Governor.

Īśvara created ether (ākāśa), air, fire, water, and earth in due succession.[3] Ākāśa is one, infinite, imponderable, inert, and all-pervasive.[4] Śaṁkara rejects the view that ākāśa is a negative entity, the mere absence of obstruction. It is a positive entity, which is inferred from the quality of sound.[5] It is not eternal as the Nyāya-Vaiśeṣika maintains. It is an effect of māyā. Air is generated from ether ; fire, from air ; water, from fire ; and earth, from water.[6] Śaṁkara recognizes the distinction between the subtle elements (sūkṣmabhūta) and the gross elements (mahābhūta) like the Sāṁkhya. The Upaniṣads mention the five subtle elements (tanmātra).[7] Sureśvara explains the order of creation thus. From māyā of Īśvara, the matrix of unmanifest (avyākṛta) names and forms, is generated the subtle essence of sound (śabdatanmātra). It is the subtle element of ether. It has the quality of sound only. The subtle element of air is generated from it. Its essence is touch. The subtle element of fire is generated from them. Its essence is colour. The subtle element of water is generated from them. Its essence is taste. The subtle element of earth is generatd from them. Its essence is smell. Ether has sound. Air has sound and touch. Fire has sound, touch, and colour. Water has taste in addition to these. Earth has smell in addition to these qualities. Gross elements are generated from the subtle elements by quintuplication (pañcikaraṇa). Each subtle

[1] SB., Ait. Up., i. 2.
[2] SB., Ait. Up., i. 3; SB., Muṇḍ. Up., iii. 1. 1.
[3] SBS., ii. 3. 7.
[4] PSAH., pp. 85-86. Cp. *Indian Philosophy,* Vol. II, p. 591.
[5] SBS., ii. 2. 22, 24.
[6] SBS., ii. 3. 8-13.
[7] Pr. Up., iv. 8, SB.

element is divided into half. Each half is divided into four equal parts. Each half of a subtle element is combined with $\frac{1}{8}$ of each of the other elements, and thus a gross element is produced.

Gross ether $= \frac{1}{2}$ ether essence (tanmātra) $+ \frac{1}{8}$ air essence $+ \frac{1}{8}$ fire essence $+ \frac{1}{8}$ water essence $+ \frac{1}{8}$ earth essence.

Gross air $= \frac{1}{2}$ air essence $+ \frac{1}{8}$ ether essence $+ \frac{1}{8}$ fire essence $+ \frac{1}{8}$ water essence $+ \frac{1}{8}$ earth essence.

Gross fire $= \frac{1}{2}$ fire essence $+ \frac{1}{8}$ ether essence $+ \frac{1}{8}$ air essence $+ \frac{1}{8}$ water essence $+ \frac{1}{8}$ earth essence.

Gross water $= \frac{1}{2}$ water essence $+ \frac{1}{8}$ ether essence $+ \frac{1}{8}$ air essence $+ \frac{1}{8}$ fire essence $+ \frac{1}{8}$ earth essence.

Gross earth $= \frac{1}{2}$ earth essence $+ \frac{1}{8}$ ether essence $+ \frac{1}{8}$ air essence $+ \frac{1}{8}$ fire essence $+ \frac{1}{8}$ water essence.[1]

Saṁkara recognizes triplication (trivṛtkaraṇa) mentioned in the Upaniṣads. Triplication is the combination of the three subtle essences of earth, water, and fire. Ether and air cannot combine with the other elements.[2] Gross fire $= \frac{1}{2}$ fire essence $+ \frac{1}{4}$ water essence $+ \frac{1}{4}$ earth essence. Gross water $= \frac{1}{2}$ water essence $+ \frac{1}{4}$ fire essence $+ \frac{1}{4}$ earth essence. Gross earth $= \frac{1}{2}$ earth essence $+ \frac{1}{4}$ fire essence $+ \frac{1}{4}$ water essence. Thus the gross elements (mahābhūta) are compounds of the subtle elements (sūkṣmabhūta). "The Sūkṣma Bhūtas are forms of homogeneous and continuous matter, without any atomicity of structure ; the Mahābhūtas are composite ; but even these are regarded as continuous, and without any atomic structure. The Vedānta speaks of Aṇu not as an ultimate indivisible discrete constituent of matter, but as the smallest conceivable quantum of matter."[3] Gross ether has manifest sound ; gross air, sound and touch ; gross fire, sound, touch, and heat and light ; gross water, taste in addition to these qualities ; and gross earth, smell in addition to these.[4] Sureśvara ascribes these qualities to the subtle elements. Sadānanda ascribes them to the gross elements. The subtle elements possess them in an unmanifest condition. The gross elements possess them in a manifest condition. The gross elements produce the different kinds of substances by transformation (pari-

[1] *Pañcīkaraṇavārtika*, 2-10. VPB., pp. 356, 362.
[2] SBS., ii. 4. 20; SB., Ch. Up., vi. 3. 3.
[3] B. N. Seal : PSAH., p. 88. Cp. *Indian Philosophy*, Vol. II, p. 592, n.
[4] VS., p. 41; SB., Pr. Up., vi. 4; SB., Muṇḍ. Up., ii. 1 3.

ṇāma). "Matter is constantly undergoing change of state."[1] The gross elements produce compounds, which possess like qualities with the constituents ; or they produce compounds, which possess unlike qualities.[2] The cosmic system consisting of the fourteen worlds is composed of the gross elements with the excess of tamas in various forms of integration and disintegration.[3] Īśvara himself creates the subtle and gross elements out of his māyā by volition.[4] In dissolution earth becomes water ; water, fire ; fire, air ; air, ākāśa ; and ākāśa is reabsorbed in Īśvara's māyā.[5]

The physical organism is made of all the five gross elements. It is the gross body (sthūla śarīra). Its different constituents form different parts of the body. The chief prāna, the cosmic life, which is the energy inherent in all natural forces, is a creation of Īśvara. The prāṇa is the energy inherent in the physical organism. It is neither air nor activity of the sense-organs. The organs of knowledge and the organs of action cannot produce the vital force of the organism as the Sāṁkhya holds. Life is a subtle physical force (adhyātmavāyu) pervading the organism. It is prior to the senses, and regulates the development of the organism.[6] It is subtle (aṇu) and pervades the body.[7] There are five vital forces, prāṇa, apāna, vyāna, udana, and samāna. Prāṇa resides at the nasal cavity ; it regulates inspiration and expiration. Apāna resides at the anus ; it helps evacuation. Vyāna pervades the body ; it sustains the whole organism. Udāna resides at the throat ; it has upward movement. Samāna resides at the navel ; it digests and assimilates food and drink. The five vital forces arise from the five subtle elements collectively with the excess of rajas.[8] The five organs of knowledge (jñānendriya), ears, skin, eyes, tongue, and nose arise from the five subtle elements individually with the excess of sattva, which manifests objects. The five organs of action (karmendriya), vocal organ, hands, feet, excretive organ, and generative organ arise from the subtle elements individually with the excess of rajas, whose function

---

[1] PSAH., p. 89. Cp. *Indian Philosophy*, Vol. II, p. 593.
[2] PSAH., p. 90.
[3] VS., 42; VPB., pp. 364-65.
[4] SBS., ii. 3. 13.
[5] SBS., ii. 3. 14.
[6] SBS., ii. 4. 9. PSAH., pp. 242-43.
[7] SBS., ii. 4 13.
[8] SBS., ii. 4. 12; VS., p. 18; VPB., pp. 359-61.

is activity.[1] The external sense-organs are physical (bhautika). There are four kinds of gross bodies, uterine (jarāyuja), *e.g.*, human and animal bodies ; born of eggs (aṇḍaja), *e.g.*, bodies of birds and reptiles ; born of moisture (svedaja), *e.g.*, bodies of bugs and mosquitoes, and plant bodies (udbhijja). Plants have souls (kṣetrajña). They are capable of suffering. They suffer the fruits of their demerits with their bodies.[2] Animals have no intelligence ; they are miserable. Men have intelligence and will ; they are partly happy and partly miserable. Gods are happy ; they have greater knowledge and power.[3]

Manas, buddhi, ahaṁkāra, and citta are the internal organs. Assimilation (saṁkalpa) and discrimination (vikalpa) are the functions of manas. Determination (niścaya) is the function of buddhi. Self-sense (abhimāna) is the function of ahaṁkara. Recollection (anusandhāna) is the function of citta.[4] The internal organs also are physical ; they arise from the five subtle elements collectively with the excess of sattva.[5] The subtle body (sūkṣma śarīra) is composed of the five organs of knowledge, the five organs of action, the five vital forces, and manas and buddhi. Citta and ahaṁkāra are included in manas and buddhi. The subtle body is made of the five subtle elements. It clings to the jīva till it attains liberation. It helps it transmigrate from one body to another.[6] The causal body (kāraṇa śarīra) is the cause of the subtle body and the gross body. It is the individual nescience (ajñāna), which is an appearance of the eternal consciousness (caitanyābhāsa). It is not ontologically existent, since it is destroyed by the knowledge of the Ātman. It is not absolutely non-existent, since it is known by perception, and capable of fulfilling our practical purposes. It is not both existent and non-existent, since it is self-contradictory. It is not different from the Ātman, which is the only reality. It is not non-different from it, since it deludes the jīva, and veils its real nature. It is not both different and non-different from the Ātman, since it is self-contradictory. It is not divisible into parts, since it is not an effect. Nor is it indivisible and partless, since it is modified into the body, the senses,

[1] VS., pp. 17-18; VPB., pp. 357-58; SB., Kaṭha Up., ii. 3. 6.
[2] VS., pp. 21-22; VPB., pp. 365-66; SBS., iii. 1. 20, 24.
[3] SBS., ii. 1. 25, 34.
[4] *Pañcīkaraṇavārtika*, 33, 34.
[5] VS., p. 17; VPB., p. 357.
[6] VS., p. 17; VPB., p. 363.

manas and buddhi. Nor is it both divisible and indivisible, since it is self-contradictory. It is indefinable (anirvacanīya). It is destroyed by the knowledge of the identity of the Ātman with Brahman.[1] The entire aggregate of effects and organs is of the nature of names and forms. They are assembled to serve the ends of individual selves.[2] Śaṁkara resolves all activity—physical, vital, and psychical—into modes of motion, subtle cosmic motion (sarvalokaparispanda).[3]

Śaṁkara recognizes the empirical reality of the world. He recognizes different degrees of reality in it. Though eternal and immutable Īśvara is one, who is modified into the empirical world, there are degrees of reality which manifest his powers in different degrees. He is immanent in all living creatures. But they can comprehend his powers in different degrees owing to different degrees of avidyā perverting their minds (cittopādhiviśeṣatāratamya).[4] The inorganic, organic, and psychic worlds are higher and higher stages through which Īśvara reveals his nature.[5] There is a gradual diminution of knowledge, power, and the like in the series of beings from men down to blades of grass. There is a gradually increasing manifestation of knowledge, power, and the like in the series of beings from men up to Hiraṇyagarbha.[6] There are different degrees of manifestation of bliss in men, gandharvas, and gods.[7] Though Śaṁkara recognizes different degrees of reality in the empirical world, he does not treat them as ontologically real. They have only relative or empirical reality. This important point must not be lost sight of.

III. Theory of Knowledge

24. *Higher Knowledge (Parā Vidyā) and Lower Knowledge (Aparā Vidyā)*

Śaṁkara distinguishes between the ontological reality and the empirical reality. The former is known by true knowledge (vidyā) or higher knowledge (parā vidyā). The latter is known

---

[1] *Pañcīkaraṇa*, 39-41; *Pañcīkaraṇavivaraṇa*, Ch. S.S., 1923, pp. 56-61; SB., Īśa Up., 8.
[2] SB., Pr. Up., iv. 8; SB., Kaṭha Up. ii. 2. 5.
[3] PSAH., pp. 90-91.
[4] SBS., i. 1. 12.
[5] SB., Ait. Up.
[6] SBS., i. 3. 30.
[7] SB., Tait. Up., ii. 4. *An Introduction to Advaita Philosophy*, p. 113.

by false knowledge (avidyā) or lower knowledge (aparā vidyā). Brahman is known by higher knowledge. It is trans-empirical subject-objectless consciousness. There is no distinction of the knower, the knowledge, and the known in it. It is not conditioned by space, time, and causality, which are empirical categories. The spatio-temporal world bound by causality is known by lower knowledge. It is known through the categories of space, time, and causality by empirical knowledge. It involves the distinction of the knower and the known.[1] True knowledge (vidyā) is intuition (anubhava), which is supra-intellectual integral experience (samyag darśana). It is higher immediacy. False knowledge (avidyā) is discursive, intellectual knowledge. It is categorized, empirical, fragmentary knowledge. Higher knowledge is absolute knowledge of identity. Lower knowledge is relative and pragmatic knowledge of difference.[2] Though they are opposed to each other, relative knowledge is a step to absolute knowledge. Intellect is a means to intuition.[3]

Brahman is the Ātman. It is the eternal, universal, foundational knowledge. It is the reality underlying the empirical world and the empirical selves. It cannot be known by sense-perception and intellectual knowledge. It can be known by higher knowledge or intuition. Lower knowledge is inadequate to grasp it.

The Ātman is the reality (satya). The empirical world including the body, the senses, and the internal organs, which is not-self (anātman), is ontologically unreal (anṛta). But avidyā impels the empirical self (jīva) to identify the Ātman with the psychophysical organism. It leads to confusion (adhyāsa) of the Ātman with the not-self, the witness (viṣayin) with the known object (viṣaya). Confusion consists in superimposition of the not-self (anātman) on the transcendental Self or Ātman[4] and superimposition of the Ātman on the not-self.[5] Avidyā is the false knowledge of the self (Ātman) in the mind-body aggre-

[1] Jñāna-jñeya-jñātṛbhedarahitaṁ paramārthatattvadarśanam. S.B., Māṇḍ. K., iv. 1. Sarvaṁ dvaitam *avidyā-vijṛmbhitam*. Ibid, iii. 43; i. 12.

[2] Sarvo'yaṁ laukiko vaidikaśca vyavahāro' vidyāviṣya eva. *ibid*, ii. 32. Aparavidyāviṣayaṁ karmaphalalakṣaṇaṁ satyam āpekṣikam. SB., Muṇḍ. Up. ii. 1. 1.

[3] 3 SB., Iśa Up., 11; S.B., Māṇḍ. K., iii. 25.

[4] Pratyagātmanyapyanātmādhyāsaḥ. SBS., i. 1. 1.

[5] Ātmānātmanor itaretarādhyāsaḥ. SBS., i. 1. 1.

gate, which is not-self.[1] Vidyā is the true knowledge of the Ātman as distinct from the mind-body aggregate. The Ātman is the witness of all. It illumines the internal organ, which is the object of self-consciousness (ahaṁpratyaya). It is a known object or not-self (anātman). It is superimposed on the Ātman. This confusion (adhyāsa) is false knowledge. It is the cause of agency and enjoyment. It is evident to all. It is beginningless, endless, and natural.[2] It is endless in the sense, that it continues till true knowledge of the Ātman is attained. False knowledge is destroyed by true knowledge of identity of the Ātman with Brahman.[3] The Ātman or Brahman is apprehended by integral experience.[4] It cannot be known by empirical knowledge.

"It is not possible for us to discover any true relation between the consciousness (dṛk) and the objects of consciousness (dṛśya). Consciousness must be admitted to have some kind of connection with the objects which it illumines, for had it not been so, there could be any knowledge at any time irrespective of its connections with the objects. But it is not possible to imagine any kind of connection between consciousness and its objects, for it can neither be contact (saṁyoga) nor inherence."[5]

25. *Scriptural Authority* (*Śruti*), *Reason* (*Tarka*), *and Intuition* (*Anubhava*)

The knowledge of Brahman is first acquired from the scripture (śruti), which is confirmed by reasoning (tarka), which culminates in intuition (anubhava) or integral experience (samyagdarśana). The scriptural authority is self-certifying. It bears testimony to the existence of Brahman. Hearing (śravaṇa), reflection (manana), and meditation (nididhyāsana) lead to intuitive apprehension of Brahman.[6] The scripture must be admitted to be the means of knowing Brahman.[7] Scripture reveals the nature of all objects like a lamp. It is like the

---

[1] Dehādiṣu anātmasu ātmabuddhir avidyā. SBS., i. 3, 2.
[2] Ayam anādir ananto naisargiko' dhyāso mithyāpratyayarūpaḥ kartṛtvabhoktṛtvapravartakaḥ sarvalokapratyakṣaḥ. SBS., i. 1. 1.
[3] Mithyājñānāpāyaśca brahmātmaikyavijñānād bhavati. SBS., i. 1. 4.
[4] Paramātmaivāyaṁ samyagdarśanaviṣayabhūtaḥ. SBS., i. 3. 13.
[5] HIP., Vol. I, 1922, pp. 447-48. Cp. *Indian Philosophy,* Vol. II, 1927, pp. 504-05.
[6] SBS., i. 1. 2, 4; ii. 1. 4.
[7] Śāstrapramāṇakaṁ brahma abhyupagantavyam. SBS., i. 1. 4.

omniscient Being. Brahman or Īśvara is the cause of Śruti.[1] The identity of the Ātman with Brahman cannot be known by any other means than the scripture.[2] The knowledge of Brahman is the result of reflection on the meaning of the scriptural texts regarding it. It cannot be derived from inference and the other means of knowledge.[3] The scripture is authoritative because it embodies intuition. Its authoritativeness is independent of other conditions.[4] The identity of the Ātman with Brahman can be known by intuition due to meditation (ārṣajñana).[5] It is apprehended by yogic intuition.[6] Thus an individual passes from implicit faith in authority to personal freedom of reason and intuition. The Śruti is authoritative because it embodies intuition of the absolute reality.[7]

But Śaṁkara does not abjure reason. He subordinates reason to the scripture. Hearing (śravaṇa) must be followed by reflection (manana). Reflection includes reason (tarka). But mere reasoning ungrounded in faith in the scripture cannot lead to realization of the Ātman. Reasoning in conformity with the scripture is conducive to the intuition of Brahman, and therefore should be employed.[8] Reason unaided by the scripture never leads to absolute truth ; it deludes us.[9] Inference in harmony with the scripture is a valid means of knowledge of the ontological reality. Reason must be admitted to be auxiliary to the scripture.[10] In matters which can be known from the scripture mere reasoning cannot be relied on. Reasonings independent of the scripture depend upon theoretical speculations of individuals, since speculations are unrestricted and devoid of proper foundation.[11] Speculations of a feeble intellect are disproved by those of a strong intellect, and these, in their turn, are disproved by speculations of a stronger intellect. They never come to rest. The profound absolute truth, which leads to liberation, cannot be inferred without the authority of the

---

[1] SBS., i. 1. 3.
[2] SBS., i. 1. 4.
[3] SBS., i. 1. 2.
[4] Vedasya hi nirapekṣaṁ svārthe prāmāṇyam. SBS., ii. 1. 1.
[5] SBS., i. 1. 30.
[6] SBS., iii. 2. 24.
[7] S. K. Das : *The System of the Vedanta,* Ch. I.
[8] Śrutyanugṛhīta eva hy atra tarko' anubhavāṅgatvena āśrīyate. SBS., ii. 1. 6.
[9] Kevalasya tarkasya vipralambhakatvaṁ darśayiṣyati. SBS., ii. 1. 6.
[10] Śrutyaiva ca sahāyatvena tarkasya abhyupetatvāt. SBS., i. 1. 2.
[11] Nirāgamāḥ tarkā apratiṣṭhitāḥ, utprekṣāyā niraṅkuśatvāt. SBS., ii. 1. 11.

scripture.[1] Scriptural knowledge leads to perfect knowledge. It is of one kind, since it is determined by its object. Brahman is self-existent and eternal. So the perfect knowledge of it is identical.[2] But discursive knowledge is never uniform. Rational speculations come into conflict with one another. Divergent intellectual knowledge cannot yield perfect knowledge (samyag jñāna). But the Vedas are eternal. The knowledge produced by them is the same in all times and places. Its validity cannot be disproved by speculators at any time. So the knowledge derived from the Upaniṣads is perfect knowledge (samyag jñāna).[3] Perfect knowledge culminates in perfect intuition (samyag darśana) of Brahman.[4] Reasoning which follows the scripture can prove the existence of conscious Brahman or Īśvara as the material cause and the efficient cause of the world.[5] But reasoning cannot prove the existence of indeterminate Brahman, which is inscrutable. It can be known from the scripture only.[6]

The perfect intuition of Brahman is integral experience (anubhava). It is the immediate intuition of Brahman (brahmasākṣātkāra).[7] It annuls avidyā, and reveals the nature of Brahman. It does not depend upon the act of a person. It depends upon the existence of Brahman, which is apprehended by it. Brahman reveals itself to intuitional consciousness.[8] Śaṁkara cannot be branded as a subjectivist. He makes knowledge depend upon its object, which exists in itself. Brahman is not an object of activity. The scripture does not prove it to be an object. Scriptural knowledge annuls the difference imagined by avidyā. It removes the distinction of the knower, the known, and knowledge. Brahman is not an object, but it is the inner self.[9] Knowledge of duality depends upon intellect.

---

[1] Na hīdam atigambhīraṁ bhāvayāthātmyaṁ muktinibandhanam āgamam antareṇa utprekṣitum api śakyam. SBS., ii. 1. 11.
[2] Tat samyag jñānam ekarūpam, vastutantratvāt. SBS., ii. 1. 11.
[3] SBS., ii. 1. 11.
[4] Anubhavāvasānaṁ brahmavijñānam. SBS., ii. 1. 4.
[5] Āgamānusāritarkavaśena cetanaṁ brahma jagataḥ kāraṇam prokṛtiś ca. SBS., ii. 1. 11.
[6] Śrutyavagāhyam eva idam atigambhīraṁ paraṁ brahma, na tarkāvagāhyam. SBS., ii. 1. 31.
[7] *Bhāmatī*, SBS., i. 1. 2.
[8] Na puruṣavyāpāratantrā brahmavidyā, vastutantraiva. SBS., i. 1. 4.
[9] Pratyagātmatvena aviṣayatayā pratipādayad avidyākalpitaṁ vedyaveditṛvedanābhedam apanayati. SBS., i. 1. 4.

Intellectual knowledge involves the distinction of subject and object. Brahman is one and non-dual. It is known by perfect intuition. Intuition is the knowledge of identity or unity. It annuls the intellectual knowledge of duality. Īśvara can be known by meditation. It involves the duality of the deity and the devotee. But Brahman is non-dual. It can be realized by intuition.[1] Intellect doubts, reflects, and investigates. It cannot yield absolutely certain knowledge. Valid knowledge is determined by its object. Perfect knowledge of Brahman is determined by its real object.[2] Intellect gives knowledge of plurality. Intuition gives knowledge of unity. Intellect gives false knowledge. Intuition gives right knowledge. False knowledge destroys right knowledge.[3] Vidyā results in integral experience.[4] Integral experience is intuitional consciousness of the identity of the Ātman.[5] The perfect knowledge of Brahman is non-different from its object, the ontological reality. The Ātman or Brahman reveals itself to intuitional consciousness, which is immediate and indeterminate.[6] The intuition is eternal (aja). Brahman is eternal (aja). When avidyā is annulled, intuition of Brahman shines forth. The Ātman reveals itself to itself. Intellectual knowledge is determinate (savikalpa). Intuition is indeterminate (avikalpa). Intellect knows the real through the empirical categories. Intuition knows it without categories and determinations. (vikalpa). When the mind transcends its limits and becomes supramental, it apprehends the non-dual reality.[7] The reality is revealed to the perfectly restrained (niruddha) mind. When the seeds of avidyā, the potencies of attachment and aversion are exterminated, the mind is perfectly restrained. The completely restrained mind purged of all taint of avidyā itself becomes non-dual Brahman.[8] In intuitional consciousness the mind is identified with Brahman.

---

[1] SBS., i. 1. 4; SB., Māṇḍ. K., iii. 1.

[2] Vikalpanās tu puruṣabuddhyapekṣāḥ; na vastuyāthātmyajñānaṁ puruṣabuddhyapekṣam, vastutantram eva tat. Brahmavijñānam api vastutantram eva, bhūtavastuviṣayatvāt. SBS., i. 1. 2.

[3] SBS., ii. 1. 14; iv. 1. 19; SB., Māṇḍ. K., iii. 17.

[4] Anubhavārūḍham eva vidyāphalam. SBS., iii. 4. 15.

[5] Ātmaikatvabuddhir eva samyag darśanam. SB., Māṇḍ. K., iii. 17.

[6] Akalpakaṁ jñānaṁ paramārthasatā brahmaṇā abhinnam. SB., Māṇḍ. K., iii. 33.

[7] Manaso hi amanībhāve dvaitaṁ nopalabhyate. SB., Māṇḍ K., iii. 31 · iii. 34. Cp. Yogācāra and Nāgārjuna.

[8] *Ibid*, iii. 34, 35.

Integral experience (samyag darśana) is the immediate intuition of the identity of the Ātman in all beings. It is the vision of God in the entire universe and the self. It is the intuition of indeterminate Brahman in the empirical world. It is the experience of many as rooted in one Brahman.[1] It is the realization of the non-dual Ātman.[2]

26. *Truth.*

Śaṁkara regards the distinction of the knower (pramātṛ), the known (prameya), and the means of knowledge (pramāṇa) as empirical. All empirical life depends upon this distinction. The Ātman, which is irrelative, cannot be the knower. The knower being non-existent, there can be no means of knowledge.[3] All pramāṇas result in the knowledge of the identity of the Ātman with Brahman. When the non-dual Ātman is known, the distinction of the knower and the means of knowledge vanishes.[4] Śaṁkara recognizes non-contradiction (abādhitatva) as the test of truth. The knowledge of the non-dual Ātman is valid, since it is not contradicted.[5] Vācaspati defines truth as uncontradicted, novel, and undoubted knowledge.[6] Dharmarajādhvarīndra defines truth as novel, uncontradicted knowledge of an object.[7] Novelty is the given element in knowledge. It was not acquired already. Harmony or coherence is the test of truth. Śaṁkara emphasizes this idealistic test of truth. But he recognizes correspondence and practical efficiency also as tests of truth. Correspondence is the realistic test. Practical efficiency is the pragmatic test. The truth of the knowledge of objects depends upon them. Perception, inference, and the other pramāṇas depend upon their objects for their validity. Correspondence is the test of empirical truth.[8] Valid

---

[1] SBG., v. 7; x. 10; xiii. 26, 30.

[2] Advaitātmadarśanaṁ samyagdarśanam. *Ibid*, xviii. 20; iv. 24, 26, 33, 34, 37, 41, 42; v. 7, 9, 25-27; vi. 1, 32; viii. 11; x. 10; xii. 2, 12; xiii. 2, 18, 26, 28, 30; xiv. 18; xviii. 20, 50, 66. *The Nature of Self*, pp. 341-52.

[3] SBS., i. 1. 1.

[4] SBS., i. 1. 4.

[5] Na ceyam avagatir bhrāntiḥ bādhakāntarābhāvāt. SBS., ii. 1. 14.

[6] Abādhitānadhigatāsandigdhabodhajanakatvaṁ hi pramāṇatvaṁ pramāṇānām. *Bhāmatī*, SBS., i. 1. 4.

[7] Anadhigatābādhitārthaviṣayajñānatvam. VPB., p. 20.

[8] SBS., i. 1. 4.

knowledge is produced by the means of knowledge, which has for its object the real nature of an existent object. It cannot be made or unmade by the empirical self. It is determined by the object. It does not depend upon the command of the self. The knowledge which corresponds with the real nature of its object is valid.[1] Correspondence is the test of absolute truth also. Brahman ought to be known by valid knowledge because it is the highest Good.[2] The knowledge of Brahman is valid, because it corresponds with its real nature. Integral experience is determined by the real nature of Brahman.[3] The scripture gives the knowledge of Brahman. It dispels avidyā. Though the validity of the scripture is self-certifying, it can be known by the pragmatic test of its fruitful consequence.[4] Dharmarājādhvarīndra defines valid knowledge as uncontradicted knowledge of an object or as the knowledge of an object as it really is, which is conducive to fruitful activity.[5] This definition applies to apprehension and recollection alike. It recognizes correspondence, practical efficiency, and coherence as tests of truth. Error or illusion will be discussed in the next section.

Dharmarājādhvarīndra recognizes intrinsic validity (svataḥ prāmāṇya) of knowledge as to its origin and knowledge. Validity of knowledge arises from the general conditions of knowledge untainted by deficiencies. It is not due to special proficiencies (guṇa) as the Naiyāyika maintains. It is directly known by the Winess Self (sākṣin), which apprehends the knowledge. It is not known from adventitious conditions. Invalid knowledge arises from the general conditions of knowledge vitiated by deficiencies. It is due to extraneous conditions (parataḥ aprāmāṇya). It is known from fruitless activity prompted by it.[6]

---

[1] Bhūtavastuviṣayānāṁ prāmāṇyaṁ vastutantram. SBS., i. 1. 2. Jñānaṁ tu pramāṇajanyaṁ, yathāvastuviṣayaṁ ca, na hi tat puruṣatantraṁ, vastutantram eva hi tat. SBS., iii. 2. 21.

[2] SBS., i. 1. 2.

[3] Brahmavijñānam api vastutantram eva bhūtavastuviṣayatvāt. SBS., i. 1. 2. Samyagdarśane vastutantratvāt jñānasya. SBS., iv. 1. 7.

[4] Ātmavijñānasya phalaparyantatvāt na tadviṣayasya śāstrasya prāmāṇyaṁ śakyaṁ pratyākhyātum. SBS., i. 1. 4.

[5] Pramātvam abādhitārthaviṣayakajñānatvam. VPB., pp. 19-20. Saṁvādipravṛttyanukūlaṁ tadvati tatprakārakajñānatvaṁ prāmāṇyam. VPB., p. 333.

[6] VPB., pp. 332-38.

27. *The Pramāṇas*

Śaṁkara recognizes perception, inference, scriptural testimony,[1] comparison,[2] presumption, and non-apprehension as the sources of valid knowledge.[3] Dharmarājādhvarīndra also enumerates six kinds of pramāṇas, which yield empirical truth.[4]

(1) *Perception.*—There is one eternal consciousness. It is Brahman. When it is determined by the internal organ (antaḥkaraṇa), it is called the subject-consciousness (pramātṛcaitanya). The empirical self (jīva) is the subject-consciousness. When the eternal consciousness is determined by mental modes, it is called the knowledge-consciousness (pramāṇa-caitanya). When it is determined by an empirical object, it is called the object-consciousness (viṣayacaitanya). In external perception the mind goes out to an empirical object through a sense-organ, and is modified into its form. This mental mode assuming the form of the object is called vṛtti. So the knowledge-consciousness (pramāṇa-caitanya) or consciousness determined by the mental mode coincides with the object-consciousness (viṣayacaitanya). There is identification of the apprehending mental mode with the object. The mental mode conforms to the empirical object. The mental order conforms to the given order. In external perception the mental mode and the object occupy the same position in space. This mark distinguishes perception from inference. "In inference, the mind only *thinks* of the inferred object but does not go out to meet it. In perception the given element and its interpretation are welded together in a unity, while in inference they are kept distinct."[5] The perceptive process and the object occupy the same point of time. They occupy the present time. The memory of pleasure is not perception. Memory is a present mental mode. But pleasure remembered is past. The apprehending mental mode and the apprehended object occupy different time-positions. The object should be capable of being perceived. Fitness (yogyatva) for being perceived is a mark that distinguishes perception from scriptural testimony, which apprehends supersensible objects like merit (dharma) and demerit (adharma). In the bare perception

---

[1] SBS., iii. 1. 11.
[2] SB., Muṇḍ. Up., i. 2. 12.
[3] SB., Bṛ. Up., iii. 3. 1.
[4] VPB., p. 38.
[5] K. C. Bhattacharya: *Studies in Vedantism,* C. U., 1909, p. 54. Cp. *Indian Philosophy,* Vol. II, 1927, p. 489.

of an object there is only identification of the knowledge-consciousness (pramāṇa-caitanya) with the object-consciousness (viṣaya-caitanya). But in the perception of the object *as object* there is not only identification of the knowledge-consciousness (pramāṇa-caitanya) with the object-consciousness (viṣaya-caitanya) but also identification of the knowledge-consciousness (pramāṇa-caitanya) with the subject-consciousness (pramātṛ-caitanya). The apprehending mental mode is referred to the empirical self and identified with it.[1] In internal perception of pleasure the apprehending mental mode is identified with the mental mode of pleasure, or the knowledge-consciousness (pramāṇa-caitanya) coincides with the object-consciousness (viṣaya-caitanya).

Perception is indeterminable (nirvikalpa) or determinate (savikalpa). Indeterminate perception is non-relational apprehension. 'That thou art'. This verbal knowledge is indeterminate perception. There is no subject-predicate relation in it. Determinate perception is relational apprehension. 'I know the jar'. This is determinate perception. There is subject-predicate relation in it. Perception is either sensuous or non-sensuous. Perception through the sense-organs is sensuous. Mental perception is non-sensuous, since the manas is not a sense-organ. In sensuous perception the mind goes out to an external object through a sense-organ, and is modified into its form. In mental perception the mind does not go out to an object. Mental modes of pleasure, pain, and the like are perceived in it. Perception, again, refers to an object (jñeya) or a cognition (jñapti). An object is perceived through the medium of a mental mode (vṛtti). A cognition is directly perceived by the self without an intervening mental mode. Perception is, again, divided into perception of the Witness Self (jīvasākṣin) and perception of the Divine Witness (īśvarasākṣin). The eternal consciousness (Brahman) limited by the internal organ is the jīva. When it is conditioned by the internal organ, it is the jīvasākṣin. The eternal conciousness limited by māyā is Īśvara. When it is conditioned by māyā, it is Īśvarasākṣin.[2]

Error or Illusion.—In the illusory perception 'this is silver' the visual organ perverted by a defect comes into contact with a nacre, and generates a mental mode in the form of 'this-

[1] IPP., p. 129. [2] VPB., pp. 39-20; IPP., pp. 47-49, 128-39; 373-76.

consciousness'. The consciousness of 'this' is perception. There is identification of 'this-consciousness' with the knowledge-consciousness and the subject-consciousness. The mental mode goes out through the visual organ to the bright object ('this'), and is modified into its form. This is perceptive process. Then avidyā in the form of nacre in the object-consciousness which is identified with the subject-consciousness, is transformed into the objective illusory silver and the subjective illusion of silver with the aid of the impression of silver revived by the perception of brightness, which is common to the nacre and the silver, and a defect in the visual organ. The illusory silver, which is a modification of avidyā, exists in 'this-consciousness' subsisting in avidyā. All effects are modifications of avidyā, and subsist in it. The consciousness of 'this' is valid perception. The consciousness of 'silver' is a memory image. But illusion fuses them into a unitary psychosis, which is perceptual. Illusory silver has illusory reality (prātibhāsika sattā), while real silver has empirical reality (vyāvahārika sattā). Illusion is contradicted by right perception.[1] Illusory silver is neither existent nor non-existent, but indefinable (anirvacanīya). The Advaita Vedānta advocates the theory of Anirvacanīyakhyāti.

The Mādhyamika maintains that in an illusion a non-existent thing (*e.g.*, silver) is apprehended as existent. This doctrine is called Asatkhyāti. An illusion without foundation in an object is not possible. The illusion of an imaginary city has its foundation in the sky. An illusion without any substrate is inconceivable. An absolutely non-existent thing cannot be apprehended as existent. The Śūnya cannot be the substrate of the illusion of silver. If it were so, the illusion would be apprehended as 'the Śūnya is silver', and not as 'this is silver'. Further, when the illusion is sublated, the Śūnya would be apprehended. But it is not apprehended. So the doctrine of Asatkhyāti is not tenable.[2]

The Yogācāra maintains that in an illusion a subjective idea is apprehended as an external object. There are no external objects. There are only ideas (vijñāna). The internal idea of silver appears to be a real external object. This doctrine is called Ātmakhyāti. The Sautrāntika ascribes perception to four

[1] VPB., pp. 121-37; IPP., pp. 282-83.
[2] VPS., pp. 41-42.

causes. The auxiliary cause (sahakāri pratyaya), *e.g.*, light, is the cause of distinctness of perception. It is not the cause of the perception of silver. The dominant cause (adhipati pratyaya), *e.g.*, the eye, is the cause of visual perception. It is not the cause of the perception of silver. The immediately preceding cause (samanantara pratyaya), *e.g.*, the immediately antecedent cognition, is not the cause of an illusion. The antecedent cognition of a jar cannot produce the cognition of silver. An external object (ālambana pratyaya) is not the cause of the illusion of silver, since the Vijñānavādin denies the existence of external objects. If the cognition of silver be said to be due to the impression (saṁskāra) of it, the impression is either permanent or momentary. If it is permanent, the Buddhist doctrine of momentariness is undermined. If it is momentary, the momentary impression being known, it contradicts the doctrine of the existence of mere cognitions (vijñānamātravāda). If the illusion of silver be said to be a cognition of silver in the series of beginningless cognitions, appearing to be an external object, is the silver unproduced or produced? If it were unproduced, the illusory cognition of silver would not be apprehended as an emergent cognition. If it is produced, it is produced by an external object or a cognition. It cannot be produced by an external object, since it does not exist. It cannot be produced by a pure cognition, since it is of the nature of liberation. If it is said to be produced by an impure cognition due to a vitiated cause, either the cognition of the cause itself apprehends illusory silver or some other cognition apprehends it. The cause and the effect are momentary, and exist at different times, so the antecedent cognition of the cause cannot perceive the succeeding illusory silver. Some other pure cognition cannot apprehend illusory silver. If it could, any cognition would apprehend any object. If some other impure cognition apprehends it, it is either produced by silver or not produced by it. If it is produced by silver, silver must exist as an external object, since it prompts activity. If it is not produced by silver, it cannot apprehend silver, since that is the object of a cognition, which imparts its form to it. So silver cannot be apprehended in the illusion of silver. The doctrine of Ātmakhyāti is not tenable.[1]

---

[1] VPS., pp. 34-35.

Prabhākara advocates the doctrine of Akhyāti or Vivekākhyāti. He maintains that in the illusion 'this is silver' there are two cognitions, the perception of 'this' and the recollection of 'silver', that there is non-apprehension (akhyāti) of the distinction (viveka) between them, and that non-discrimination between the given element and the ideal element due to obscuration of memory (smṛtipramoṣa) constitutes the illusion. Prabhākara maintains that all apprehension is valid, and that there is no logical error. Truth depends on practical efficiency. Error depends on practical inefficiency. A cognition in itself is valid. But if it prompts fruitless activity, it is invalid. In cognitions as such there is no error.[1] Vidyāraṇya criticizes the Prābhākara doctrine of Akhyāti. What is non-apprehension (akhyāti)? It is either mere absence of apprehension, or cognition of a person seeking one object prompting activity in respect of another object, or cognition of many objects as undistinguished from one another. On the first view, there would be illusion in deep sleep only, and there would be no illusion in waking and dream. On the second view, there would be no illusion where there is no activity owing to quick sublation or laziness. On the third view, distinction, the counter-entity of non-distinction, is either apprehension of difference (bhedagraha) or non-apprehension of non-difference (abhedāgraha). It is not apprehension of difference, since in the illusion 'this is silver' there is apprehension of difference between the general (sāmānya) and the particular (viśeṣa), and therefore there cannot be non-distinction between them. It is not non-apprehension of non-difference, since there is apprehension of difference, and consequently, there is no non-apprehension of non-difference, and therefore there can be no non-distinction. The Prābhākara urges that non-discrimination (aviveka) is non-apprehension of non-relation (asaṁsargāgraha), and that illusion consists in not cognizing the presentation of 'this' and the memory image of 'silver' to be non-related. Non-apprehension of non-relation cannot be as between apprehension and memory, since in that case 'I am a man' would not be an illusion. But, in fact, it is an illusion, in which there is non-apprehension of non-relation between two apprehensions. Non-apprehension of non-relation cannot be as between any two

---

[1] VPS., pp. 26-28.

things, since in that case 'the cloth is white' would be an illusion as there is non-apprehension of non-relation in it, while it is a valid cognition. Non-apprehension of non-relation cannot be as between two things devoid of knowledge of relation, since it involves the same defect. Therefore the doctrine of Akhyāti is not tenable.[1]

The Naiyāyika and the Bhāṭṭa Mīmāṁsaka maintain that in the illusion 'this is silver' there is misapprehension of nacre as silver. They advocate the doctrine of Anyathākhyāti. One object, *e.g.*, 'nacre' is apprehended as otherwise (anyathā) *i.e.*, as 'silver' which exists in some other place. Vidyāraṇya asks whether otherwiseness belongs to the cognition, or to the result, or to the object. If it belongs to the cognition, the cognition of silver has for its basis or object nacre. Then, is the nacre the object of the cognition of silver, because it imparts its form to the cognition, or because it is the object of activity prompted by the cognition? The first alternative is untenable. Nacre cannot impart its form to the cognition of silver. The second alternative also cannot be maintained. The perception of a tiger prompts the use of a sword. But the sword is not the object of the cognition of a tiger. Otherwiseness cannot belong to the result or manifestation, which is common to valid knowledge and illusion. There is no difference in the manifestation brought about by valid knowledge and illusion. Otherwiseness cannot belong to the object. Is otherwiseness in the object identity of nacre with silver? Or is it transformation of nacre into silver? If it is identity of nacre with silver, is there absolute difference between them, or difference and non-difference? They cannot be absolutely different, since absolutely different things cannot be identical. They cannot be different and non-different, since in that case 'this is silver' would not be an illusion like the cognition 'the cow is short-horned'. If nacre is modified into silver, there can be no sublation. Therefore the doctrine of Anyathākhyāti is untenable.[2]

---

[1] VPS., pp. 28-29.

[2] VPS., pp. 33-34. *The Philosophy of Advaita*, pp. 78-79. IPP., pp. 283-305. The Naiyāyika criticizes the Advaita Vedānta doctrine of Anirvacanīyakhyāti thus: "If the illusory object, silver, is created in the absence of silver, we could see anything of which we have an idea, *i.e.*, there could be no difference between image and percept." (*Studies in Vedantism*, 1909, p. 56. Cp. *Indian Philosophy*, Vol. II, 1927, p. 132).

(2) *Inference.*—Inference is produced by the knowledge of invariable concomitance (vyāpti) of the middle term with the major term as such. The knowledge of vyāpti is its instrumental cause (karaṇa). The residual impression of it is the intermediate function (vyāpāra) which generates inference. The Nyāya regards the knowledge of the existence of the probans, pervaded by the probandum, in the subject of inference (tritīyaliṅgaparāmarśa) as the instrumental cause (karaṇa) of inference. But the Advaita Vedānta does not regard it as a cause of inference, far less an instrumental cause. Vyāpti is the co-existence of the middle term and the major term in all the substrata of the middle term. It is known by observation of concomitance of the middle term with the major term, and non-observation of their non-concomitance. The number of instances is not material to inference. Concomitance may be observed once or many times. Observation of concomitance only is the ground of inference. Vyāpti does not depend upon the agreement in absence between the middle term and the major term. Inference is of one kind. It is Anvayi. It depends upon the agreement in presence between the middle term and the major term. It is founded on their positive concomitance. It is not Kevalānvayi like the inference 'this pot is knowable, because it is nameable'. The Navya Nyāya calls it a Kevalānvayi inference, because there is no agreement in absence (vyatirekavyāpti) between the middle term (*e.g.*, 'nameable') and the major term (*e.g.*, 'knowable'). Concomitance between 'not-nameable' and 'not-knowable' cannot be ascertained, because the terms do not stand for existents. "According to Vedānta, there is no Kevalānvayi inference ; as Brahman is the constant ground of all differenced reality, the negation of all things is existent."[1] All attributes abide in Brahman, since every attribute is the counter-entity (pratiyogi) of its absolute negation (atyantābhāva), though Brahman is devoid of attributes. There is absolute negation of all attributes in Brahman. There is no Anvaya-vyatireki inference, which is said to be based on agreement in presence and agreement in absence between the middle term and the major term, since knowledge of vyatirekavyāpti, agreement in absence, is not a cause of inference. There is no Kevalavyatireki inference, since

[1] *Studies in Vedantism*, p. 60.

knowledge of negative concomitance of the absence of the major term and the absence of the middle term cannot generate inference. 'Where there is no fire, there is no smoke.' This is vyatirekavyāpti. Concomitance of the absence of fire and the absence of smoke cannot produce the inference of the existence of fire from the existence of smoke. What is called Kevalavyatireki inference is presumption (arthāpatti). Thus the Advaita Vedānta rejects the three kinds of inference, Kevalānvayi, Kevalavyatireki, and Anvaya-vyatireki, recognized by the Navya Nyāya. There are two kinds of inference, inference for oneself (svārtha) and inference for others (parārtha). The former is generated by the impression of vyāpti. The latter consists of three members only, proposition (pratijñā), reason (hetu), and example (udāharaṇa), or example, application (upanaya), and conclusion (nigamana). Three members can show vyāpti and existence of the middle term in the subject of inference. The two other members of the Nyāya syllogism are redundant.[1] The Nyāya states a demonstrative syllogism thus: (1) 'The mountain is fiery (pratijñā). (2) Because it is smoky (hetu). (3) Whatever is smoky, is fiery, as the kitchen (udāharaṇa). (4) The mountain is smoky (upanaya). (5) Therefore, it is fiery (nigamana).' The Advaita Vedānta agrees with the Mīmāṁsā in advocating the three-membered syllogism.[2]

(3) *Comparison* (*upamāna*).—Comparison is the means of the knowledge of similarity. A person, who has perceived a cow in a town, goes to a forest, and perceives a wild cow. He has an apprehension 'this animal is similar to a cow' owing to the intercourse of his eyes with the animal. Then he has an apprehension 'my cow is similar to this animal'. This knowledge of similarity of a cow with a wild cow is acquired by comparison. The knowledge of similarity existing in a wild cow with a cow (gavayaniṣṭhagosādṛśyajñāna) is the instrumental cause (karaṇa). The knowledge of similarity existing in a cow with a wild cow (goniṣṭhagavayasādṛśyajñāna) is the result. This knowledge of similarity cannot be acquired from perception, since the cow is not present to the eyes. Nor can it be acquired from inference, since similarity existing in a wild cow with a cow cannot serve as a mark of inference (liṅga) as follows: 'My cow is similar to

---

[1] VPB., ch. ii.
[2] IIP., pp. 209, 213.

this wild cow ; because she is the correlate of similarity existing in this wild cow ; whatever is the correlate of similarity with another thing is similar to it, as Caitra, the correlate of similarity existing in Maitra, is similar to Maitra.' The Advaita Vedānta contends that the reason or mark (liṅga) must exist in the minor term (pakṣa), but that the reason 'similarity existing in a wild cow with a cow' does not exist in the minor term 'my cow'. Therefore, it cannot prove the existence of the major term 'similarity existing in my cow with a wild cow'. Therefore the knowledge of similarity existing in my cow with a wild cow cannot be acquired from inference. It is acquired from comparison, which is neither perception nor inference, but a distinct means of valid knowledge.[1] *A* presented suggests its similar *B*. Then we have the knowledge that *A* is similar to *B*. The similarity of *B* with *A* is apprehended (anubhavasiddha). It is not inferred through the function of vyāpti. It is not perceived, since *A* alone is perceived.[2]

The Advaita Vedānta view of comparison is similar to the Mīmāṁsā view. Kumārila and Prabhākara regard comparison as the knowledge of similarity of a perceived object (*e.g.*, a wild cow) *in* a remembered object (*e.g.*, a cow). Comparison is the knowledge of similarity of the remembered cow with a perceived wild cow. It depends upon the knowledge of similarity of the wild cow with the cow.[3] The Nyāya, on the other hand, holds that comparison is the knowledge of similarity of an unfamiliar object (*e.g.*, a wild cow) with a familiar object (*e.g.*, a cow).[4]

(4) *Presumption* (*arthāpatti*).—"Arthāpatti is the supposition of the premises, reason, or cause from the conclusion, consequence, or effect. It is like the framing of a hypothesis from given facts."[5] It is the assumption (āpatti) of a fact (artha) to account for another inexplicable fact. The postulation of a hypothesis to explain the inexplicable fact is called arthāpatti. It is presumption, postulation, or implication. The knowledge of the fact to be explained (upapādyajñāna) is the instrumental cause (karaṇa). The knowledge of the fact that explains (upa-

[1] VPB., ch. iii.
[2] *Studies in Vedantism*, pp. 62-63. *The System of Vedantic Thought and Culture*, p. 203.
[3] SD., p. 208, PP., p. 71; IIP., p. 214-16.
[4] NS., i. 1. 6; IIP., p. 215.
[5] *Studies in Vedantism*, p. 67.

pādakajñāna) is the result (phala). A person is known not to eat in the day time, and yet gets stout. His stoutness is to be explained (upapādya). It cannot be explained without postulating his eating at night. In the absence of his eating at night his stoutness cannot be explained. Eating at night explains the unintelligible fact (upapādaka). This assumption (kalpanā) of a hypothesis is called (arthāpatti). It is the supposition of a cause. The effect is given. The cause is assumed.[1]

The Advaita Vedānta agrees with Kumārila's view that arthāpatti is assumption of some unperceived fact to account for some inconsistency in perceived facts.[2] Prabhākara maintains that there must be an element of doubt as to the truth of the two inconsistent facts perceived. Presumption removes the element of doubt. We know that a person is alive, and perceive his absence from his house. This perception generates a doubt whether he is alive or dead. The doubt is removed by the presumption of his living somewhere else.[3] This view is wrong. If the person's living be doubtful, his going out of his house cannot be assumed. If his living is certain, then only the presumption is made.

Presumption cannot be regarded as an inference, since the universal major premise cannot be based on positive concomitance (anvayavyāpti). Negative concomitance (vyatirekavyāpti) is not admitted by the Advaita Vedānta. The Kevalavyatireki inference based on negative concomittance is nothing but presumption.[4]

(5) *Non-apprehension* (*a n u p a l a b d h i*).—Non-existence (abhāva) is known by non-apprehension or non-cognition. It cannot be known by the other pramāṇas. Non-apprehension is the unique pramāṇa which cognizes negation or non-existence.[5] The non-existence of a jar on the ground is known by non-apprehension. When the jar is removed from the ground, we perceive the ground, the locus (adhikaraṇa) of the non-existence of the jar, but we do not perceive the non-existence itself. We know the non-existence by non-apprehension. Though the locus of non-existence is perceived, the non-existence itself is not perceived. "The percept of the locus, *minus* that thing, is there-

---

[1] VPB., ch v.
[2] SD., p. 214; IIP., p. 225.
[3] PP., pp. 113-15; IIP., p. 226.
[4] VPB., ch. v.
[5] VPB., ch. vi.

fore the percept of the minusness or abhāva."[1] Non-existence is known by non-apprehension. It can never be known by perception. The perceptive process is directed only to the locus of the non-existence, but not to the non-existence itself. The non-existence is known by appropriate non-apprehension (yogyānupaladbhi). The object of abhāva must be capable of being perceived. The object, which is absent, must be fit for being perceived. If it is not capable of being perceived, its non-existence cannot be known by non-apprehension. A jar is capable of being perceived. If the jar had been present, it would have been perceived. Merit (dharma) and demerit (adharma) are supersensible. They cannot be perceived. So their non-existence cannot be known by non-apprehension. The thing that is absent, must be of the same order of reality as its locus which is perceived. The negation must not be absolute negation, but it must be the negation of something perceptible.[2]

Prabhākara maintains that the non-existence of a thing is non-different from its bare locus (adhikaraṇa). The non-existence of a jar on the ground is nothing but the bare ground. When we perceive a jar on the ground, we perceive the ground as related to the existence of the jar. But when the jar is absent, we perceive the bare ground only.[3] The Sāṁkhya also holds that non-existence of a thing is identical with its bare locus.[4] Perception of the mere locus is erroneously called non-apprehension. Perception of the bare ground is a positive cognition. It is not non-cognition. The Advaita Vedānta, like Kumārila, contends that if the non-existence of a jar on the ground were identical with the bare ground, it would be perceived even when the jar is present on the ground.[5] The Advaita Vedānta regards non-existence as non-different from its locus. It considers the world-appearance to be non-different from Brahman, its locus. But it maintains that non-existence is known by non-apprehension, and that it is not known by the perception of its locus. But the author of *Vedāntaparibhāṣā* admits the four kinds of non-existence, prior non-existence, posterior non-existence, mutual non-existence, and absolute non-existence recognized by the Nyāya-Vaiśeṣika. The Naiyāyika

[1] *Studies in Vedantism*, p. 68.
[2] *Studies in Vedantism*, p. 69.
[3] PP., p. 123; IIP., p. 232.
[4] STK., 5.
[5] SD., pp. 235-36; IIP., pp. 233-34.

advocates the adjectival theory of non-existence. He considers non-existence to be an attribute of the locus. The ground is qualified by the non-existence of a jar. The non-existence of the jar on the ground is perceived through the visual organ which is in conjunction with the ground qualified by the non-existence of the jar. Non-existence is perceived through the sense-object-intercourse called viśeṣaṇatā.[1] The Advaita Vedānta rejects this view, since viśeṣaṇatā cannot be a mode of sense-object-intercourse. If it were so, there would be the cognition of the non-existence of a jar on the ground which is hidden by a wall, since it is qualified by the non-existence of the jar.[2]

(6) *Testimony* (*āgama*).—A sentence refers to an objective relation. That sentence is a valid source of knowledge, which refers to an objective relation, which is not contradicted by any other means of valid knowledge.[3] A sentence must fulfil four conditions in order to convey a meaning. It must have syntactical connection (ākāṅkṣā) among its essential parts. The verb must demand a subject, a transitive verb an object, and the like. A sentence must have fitness (yogyatā) or compatibility of meaning among its parts. The objective relation conveyed by a sentence must be free from contradiction. It must be harmonious. 'He wets the ground with fire'. This sentence is meaningless. The objective relation conveyed by it is self-contradictory. A sentence must have proximity of its parts (āsatti). If the words 'bring', 'a', and 'cow' are uttered at the interval of one hour each, they do not form a sentence, and convey any meaning. They must be uttered in close succession to form a sentence. A sentence must have an objective intention (tātparya). *'Saindhavam ānaya'*. It means either 'bring a horse' or 'bring salt'. If a person utters the sentence while taking his meal, it obviously means 'bring salt'. Fitness (yogyatā) is the formal compatibility of meaning. Intention (tātparya) is compatibility in a material reference. It is correspondence of the subjective

[1] SM., p. 263; IIP., p. 77.

[2] *The Six Ways of Knowing*, BK., iii. *The Philosophy of Advaita*, pp. 39-44. *The System of Vedantic Thought and Culture*, pp. 214-17. *Thought and Reality*, Part II, ch. iv. *Studies in Vedantism*, pp. 68-70.

[3] VPB., p. 239.

intention of the speaker with the objective relation conveyed by the sentence.[1]

A sentence is composed of words. The Nyāya maintains that words denote individuals (vyakti), connote the genus (jāti), and suggest configuration (ākṛti), or that words denote individuals endued with the genus and configuration. But the Advaita Vedānta maintains that a word denotes a genus (jāti), and not individuals, since individuals are infinite in number. How, then, can it denote an individual? The genus and the individual are apprehended by the same cognition produced by a word at the same time.[2] Śaṁkara admits the existence of universals which are not born, while individuals are born and die. Words are related to universals, not to individuals, since individuals are infinite in number. There is an eternal relation between words and their meanings.[3]

Words are composed of sounds. Sounds are not created, but only manifested. When a letter (varṇa) is uttered, it is not created anew but only manifested in an audible form (dhvani). The sound-form is eternal, but its manifestation alone is in time. The word is eternal. It existed in all previous cycles. It is remembered by Īśvara, and manifested to us. The Veda is eternal. It embodies eternal truths. It is revealed by Īśvara in the beginning of each cycle. "To Īśvara, who is eternally free in intelligence and volition, all these remembrances before each creation are one, and all these creations are but timeless actualization of the same Vedas or objective reason. To the individual, however, the manifestation in a particular cycle is new."[4] The Vedas are self-evident. Their authoritativeness is independent of other conditions.[5] They are eternal. They embody eternal truths.[6] The Advaita Vedānta theory of knowledge is elaborately treated in other books.[7]

---

[1] *Studies in Vedantism*, pp. 66-67. VPB., pp. 241-60.
[2] VPB., p. 369.
[3] SBS., i. 3. 28.
[4] *Studies in Vedantism*, 1909, p. 65. Cp. *Indian Philosophy*, Vol. II, p. 496.
[5] SBS., ii. 1. 1.
[6] SBS., i. 3. 29.
[7] D. M. Datta: *The Six Ways of Knowing*. *Studies in Vedantism*, pp. 51-70. *The System of Vedantic Thought and Culture*, pp. 175-217. *The Philosophy of Advaita*, pp. 9-60.

IV. EHICS

28. *Bondage*

The Ātman is the reality of the empirical self (jīva). It is Brahman. It is one, eternal, universal consciousness. It is eternally liberated (nityamukta). Its bondage is due to ignorance (avidyā). Avidyā generates the psychophysical organism, which limits the universal consciousness, and makes it appear as the individual self. Thus avidyā is the cause of bondage. It is intellectual knowledge infected with the duality of subject and object. Avidyā is removed by intuition (vidyā) of the identity of the Ātman with Brahman. Vidyā, true insight, integral experience, leads to liberation. It is liberation. Bondage is ignorance. Liberation is higher knowledge.

False knowledge is the knowledge of difference between the individual self and Īśvara due to non-discernment of the accidental nature of the jīva owing to its limiting adjunct of the psychophysical organism.[1] It is the cause of bondage and suffering.[2] It is destroyed by the knowledge of the Ātman or Brahman.[3] The mind-body-complex, attachment, aversion, delusion, enjoyment, and activity constitute the empirical nature of the individual self. It is due to avidyā. When avidyā is destroyed, its intrinsic pure divine nature is known, even as the real nature of a rope is known when the illusion of a snake is destroyed.[4] Integral experience uproots avidyā, which is the root cause of saṁsāra. It destroys rebirth due to conjunction of the Ātman with the mind-body-complex, which is caused by avidyā.[5] The Ātman is eternally liberated, but its intrinsic freedom is not known because it is covered by avidyā. Liberation is not an achievement, but a discovery. It is like the discovery by a prince brought up by a shepherd, of his sovereignty when his identity is disclosed to him.[6]

Śaṁkara repeatedly speaks of avidyākāmakarma. Āvidyā is the cause of desire (kāma). Desire takes the forms of attachment and aversion. These are called faults (doṣa) or afflictions

---

[1] Dehādisaṁghātopādhisambandhāvivekakṛteśvarasaṁsāribhedamithyābuddhiḥ. SBS., i. 1. 5.

[2] SBS., ii. 3. 46.

[3] Tadavagatyā mithyājñānasya saṁsārahetor nivṛttiḥ. SBS., i. 1. 4.

[4] SBS., i. 3. 19.

[5] SBG., xiii. 26.

[6] SB., Bṛ. Up., ii. 1. 20.

(kleśa). They are due to intellectual disorders (avidyā). They are the springs of action. They produce actions (karma). Actions are either righteous or unrighteous. Righteous actions produce merits (dharma). Unrighteous actions produce demerits (adharma). Merits and demerits are residual impressions (vāsanā), potencies (saṁskāra), or dispositions (karmāśaya) of righteous and unrighteous actions. They are also called karmas. They produce their fruits (phala) in the shape of joys and sorrows in the present life or in a future life. They are the cause of rebirth or transmigration. Until the merits and demerits, which are the seeds of actions (karmabīja) are completely burnt up by the fire of integral experience of the Ātman or Brahman, the wheel of birth and death continues to revolve. When they are exterminated by true insight, transmigration ceases, and mokṣa is realized.[1]

29. *Karma*

Śaṁkara assumes the Law of Karma. As you sow, so you reap. None can escape the consequences of his actions. "Man is entirely formed of desire (kāma) ; according as his desire is, so is his volition (kratu) ; according as his volition is, so he does the works (karma) ; according as he does the works, so does he become. One, who performs good works, becomes righteous. One, who commits bad works, becomes unrighteous."[2] Merits and demerits are the causes of rebirth. Righteous and unrighteous actions actuated by emotions and passions due to desire produce rebirth. So desire is the root cause of transmigration. If desire is extirpated, actions cannot produce merits and demerits. So actions motived by desire bring about rebirth.[3]

The kind of body to be assumed by a transmigrating soul depends upon its moral equipment.[4] The empirical world is the moral sphere of retribution of the works done in previous births. The mind-body-complex is the instrument forged by avidyā intended to produce the retribution in the form of happiness and misery. The works of a single birth have to be atoned for in

---

[1] SB., Tait. Up., Introduction; SB., Ch. Up., vi. 15. 2; SB., Ait. Up., ii. 1; iv. 1; SB., Māṇḍ. Up., i. 4; Pr. Up., iv. 5; SB., Muṇḍ. Up., i. 1. 8; i. 2. 7; i. 2. 12; iii. 3. 1, 2.

[2] Bṛ. Up., iv. 4. 5.

[3] SB., Bṛ. Up., iv. 4. 5.

[4] SBS., iv. 1. 12.

several succeeding births. Perfect knowledge consumes the ungerminating accumulated merits and demerits, and stops transmigration. But it cannot at once put an end to the present bodily existence because it is determined by the works of a previous birth, whose seed has already germinated, and cannot therefore be consumed. The present life will continue till full retribution of these works is achieved.[1]

God is the dispenser of the Law of Karma. He awards the fruits of actions to the creatures. He makes them happy and unhappy in accordance with their merits and demerits. The individual souls are responsible for their actions. They can make or mar their fortunes by their own deeds or misdeeds. If they act up to the Vedic injunctions (vidhi), and refrain from prohibited acts (niṣedha), they acquire merits. If they commit forbidden acts, they acquire demerits. Merits produce happiness. Demerits produce unhappiness. God distributes happiness and misery among creatures in accordance with their merits and demerits with strict impartiality. He is the Lord of Karma (karmādhyakṣsa).[2] Karmas are unintelligent. They cannot produce their fruits in particular times and places without the guidance of God.[3] There are different grades of persons, who experience different degrees of happiness and misery in accordance with their different degrees of merits and demerits due to avidyā through different kinds of organisms.[4]

The Law of Karma does not undermine human freedom. The individual is responsible for his acts. He acquires merits and demerits by his free actions. He is actuated by his impulses (prakṛti) and inborn predispositions (saṁskāra). But he can counteract and conquer them because of his infinitude. He can control his impulses, extirpate his desires, and realize his intrinsic freedom. He can transcend his psychophysical individuality, and realize his transempirical noumenal freedom. When he acquires intuition of the Ātman, he destroys avidyā, the cause of individuality, and frees himself from subjection to the Law of Karma. The Moral Law operates in the empirical

---

[1] SBS., iv. 1. 15; SV., pp. 353-54.
[2] SB., ii. 3. 41, 42; iii. 2. 38, 41.
[3] SBS., iii. 2. 38.
[4] Avidyādoṣavatāṁ dharmādharmatāratamyanimittaṃ śarīropādānapūrvakaṁ sukhaduḥkhatāratamyam. SBS., i. 1. 4.

world of phenomena. It does not bind the transcendental Ātman. It is eternally free.[1]

30. *Future Life*

Śaṁkara believes in the transmigration of the empirical self (jīva). The self is distinct from the body. It does not perish with the death of the body. Birth is union of the soul with a body. Death is separation of it from the body.[2]

The Cārvākas maintain that consciousness is an epiphenomenon of the body, and that the self is the conscious body. When the material elements are combined into an organism, they produce consciousness, even as unintoxicating ingredients undergo fermentation and produce intoxicating liquor.[3] Consciousness exists so long as the body exists. It does not exist when the body is destroyed. So it is a quality of the body. Hence the self is not distinct from the body.[4]

Śaṁkara refutes the materialistic doctrine of the Cārvākas. Consciousness is the essence of the self. It exists so long as the self exists in the body. It disappears when the self departs from the body. After death the body persists, but consciousness disappears. So it is not a property of the body. Colour is a property of the body, since it persists in it even after death, and is perceived by others. But consciousness does not persist in the body after death, and is not perceived by others. Further, consciousness may not disappear after death, but continue without any organism. Again, if consciousness were a property of the body, it could not perceive the body. Consciousness cannot act upon itself. It can apprehend other objects, but cannot apprehend itself. Therefore consciousness is distinct from the body. It is found to be accompanied by the body, because it is its organ. But it does not always depend upon the body. When the body is inactive in sleep, consciousness appears in diverse forms in dreams. Further, recognition and recollection presuppose the identity of the self. It is identical, permanent, incorporeal spirit, the essence of which is consciousness.[5]

Śaṁkara maintains that the empirical self transmigrates with a subtle body.[6] It is subtle in its essence and dimension, and capable of movement. It is transparent, irresistible, and invisible. It has infra-sensible touch and colour.[7] It contains

---

[1] SBG., ii. 33, 34, 37; xviii. 20, 22, 41; vii. 27; viii. 3; SB., Kena Up. i. 1; SBS., i. 1. 4. Kokileshwar Shastri: *An Introduction to Advaita Philosophy*, ch. iv.

[2] SBS., ii. 3. 16.

[3] Caitanyaṁ madaśaktivad vijñānaṁ caitanyaviśiṣṭaḥ kāyaḥ puruṣaḥ. SBS., iii. 3. 53.

[4] IIP., pp. 20-22.

[5] SBS., iii. 3. 54; IIP., pp. 26-27.

[6] SBS., iv. 2. 21.

[7] SBS., iv. 2 9.

the seed of a future body in the shape of merits and demerits (karma). The kind of body to be assumed on rebirth is determined by the karmas acquired in the previous births. Knowledge (vidyā), character (karma), and impression of past experience (pūrvaprajñā) pursue the empirical self during transmigration.[1]

The Ṛg-Veda believes in future life, but does not speak of transmigration of the soul. "The souls of the good pass after death into Yama's heaven of light where they lead a blissful life in the company of the Fathers (pitaraḥ)[2]; the wicked are shut out from it and pass into the nether darkness".[3] The Upaniṣads speak of three paths. "The Wise after death, will be carried over higher and higher upon the Devayāna that is the Path of the Gods, onwards into Brahman, whence there is no return. The doers of works go upwards by the Pitṛyāna, the Path of the Fathers into the luminous realm on the moon, enjoy there the fruit of their works and then descend once more into a new incarnation, differing according to the moral character of the previous life. Finally, those who possess neither knowledge nor works come to the third place, that is, they are reborn as lower animals[4] or plants, without having tasted bliss on the moon".[5] Thus the Upaniṣads believe in transmigration. But the knower of Brahman becomes Brahman here and now; he neither migrates nor enters into Brahman.[6]

Śaṁkara combines all the three views. He believes in double retribution for the good and the evil in the Beyond and in a new rebirth. He combines the Vedic view with the Upaniṣadic view. Those who follow customary morality go through the path of the fathers. Those who acquire knowledge (vidyā) go through the path of the gods. Those who commit sins do not go to the moon. They go downward to hell, exhaust their sins by suffering, and again rise to the earth. There are seven kinds of hell. Those souls which are unfit for departing through the path of the gods and the path of the fathers are born again and again as small short-lived insects.[7] Those who desire to know Brahman, practise celibacy, faith, truthfulness, and other virtues or worship personal God, go through the path of the gods to Brahmaloka or heaven, and attain gradual liberation

---

[1] SBS., iii. 4. 11; ii. 1. 5-8.
[2] Rig Veda, x. 14. 10.
[3] Rig Veda, xi. 152. 4; SV., p. 357. Cp. *Indian Philosopy,* Vol. II, p. 647.
[4] Kaṭha Up., v. 7.
[5] SV., pp. 357-58. Cp. *Indian Philosophy,* Vol. II, p. 647.
[6] Bṛ. Up., iv. 4. 6.
[7] SBS., iii. i. 13, 15, 17.

(kramamukti). They gradually acquire knowledge of their identity with Brahman, and attain absolute liberation. They do not return to the world.[1] Those, who have exterminated avidyā by perfect knowledge or integral experience, realize absolute freedom. They never return to embodied existence.[2] The knower of indeterminate Brahman destroys avidyā and other afflictions, and attains absolute eternal life.[3] His desires and karmas are extirpated. He becomes entirely desireless and blessed. He neither moves nor departs. He identifies himself with omnipresent Brahman, and attains Brahmanhood. His life, senses and subtle elements constituting his subtle body are dissolved into indeterminate Brahman.[4] This is the highest state of impersonal, absolute immortality. Bondage and transmigration are due to false knowledge. They cannot be ended without perfect knowledge. Transmigration continues till the saving knowledge is attained.[5]

31. *Mokṣa*

The experience of Brahman is the supreme end, because it completely destroys avidyā, which is the root cause of saṁsāra, the round of birth and death.[6] The Ātman is the reality of the individual self. It is Brahman. It is the eternal existence, consciousness, and bliss. The experience of the identity of the Ātman with Brahman is the highest good, because it destroys all afflictions. Brahman is an eternally accomplished fact. It is neither acceptable nor avoidable. It is not an object of activity.[7] It cannot be acquired by actions. It can be experienced by intuition only.

The Ātman is disembodied, transempirical, and eternal. It is eternally liberated. Liberation is its ontological nature. It is unchangeable, eternal, omnipresent, unmodifiable, eternally fulfilled, undivided, self-luminous, supermoral, non-temporal, and disembodied. It transcends virtue and vice. It transcends the

---

[1] SBS., iv. 3. 5, 7, 9, 10.

[2] SBS., iv. 4. 22; iv. 2. 7.

[3] Ātyantikam amṛtatvam. SBS., iv. 2. 12.

[4] SBS., iv. 2. 13, 15.

[5] SBS., iv. 2. 8.

[6] Brahmāvagatir hi puruṣārthaḥ. Niḥśeṣasaṁsārabījāvidyādyanarthanivarhaṇāt. SBS., i. 1. 1.

[7] Heyopādeyaśūnyabrahmātmāvagamādeva sarvakleśaprahāṇāt puruṣārthasiddheḥ. SBS., i. 1. 4.

past, the present, and the future.[1] Mokṣa is the intrinsic nature of the Ātman. It is eternal. It is hidden by avidyā. When avidyā is removed by vidyā, mokṣa is realized.[2] It is life eternal and absolute. It consists in existence in the essential condition of the Ātman.[3] It is existence in the essential state of Brahman.[4] It is absolute existence (brāhmī sthiti).[5] The individual self (jīva), which knows Brahman, attains eternal peace and rest.[6] It becomes Brahman.[7] Mokṣa is extinction of the individual self in the Absolute (brahmanirvāṇa).[8] Individuality is due to avidyā. When it is destroyed by vidyā, the individual self is merged in the Absolute. It realizes its intrinsic transcendental and absolute nature. The transcendental Ātman is the highest Good (śiva). It is Good because it transcends duality. Non-duality is good ; it is free from fear.[9] Saṁsāra is empirical life. It is infected with duality of subject and object. Mokṣa is the highest Good (niḥśreyasa). It consists in the complete cessation of empirical life, with its cause, avidyā. It is nirvāṇa, total extinction of all misery involved in empirical life.[10] Bondage is due to avidyā. Mokṣa is due to vidyā.[11] It is realization of Brahmanhood.[12] The knower of Brahman becomes Brahman. His karmas are worn off. He enjoys eternal bliss. He becomes free from fear, delusion, doubt, and sorrow.[13]

Mokṣa is not produced (utpādya). It is eternal. So it does not depend upon bodily, verbal, and mental actions. It is independent of actions. It is not a modification of the Ātman. It is not modifiable (vikārya). If it were so, it would be non-eternal. It is not attainable (āpya). It is the essential nature of the Ātman. So it cannot be attained.[14] Even if it were

---

[1] Idaṁ tu pāramārthikaṁ kūṭasthaṁ nityaṁ sarvavyāpi sarvavikriyārahitaṁ nityatṛptaṁ niravayavaṁ svyaṁjyotiḥsvabhāvaṁ yatra dharmādharmau saha kāryeṇa kālatrayaṁ ca na upāvartate, tat aśarīraṁ mokṣākhyam. SBS., i. 1. 4.

[2] Avidyāpratibandhamātro hi mokṣo na anyapratibandhaḥ, nityatvāt ātmabhūtaṭvāt ca. SB., Muṇḍ., iii. 2. 9.

[3] Ātmanaḥ svarūpeṇa avasthānam. SB., Māṇḍ. K., ii. 32.

[4] Brahmarūpeṇaiva avasthānam. SBG., ii. 72.

[5] BG., ii. 72. [6] SB., Māṇḍ. K., iii. 40.

[7] Brahmabhūto bhavati. SBG., ii. 71.

[8] SBG., ii. 72. SB., Muṇḍ. Up., iii. 2. 6.

[9] SB., Māṇḍ K., i. 12; ii. 33. [10] SBG., Introduction ; ii. 71.

[11] Māṇḍ. K., iii. 5.

[12] Brahmabhāvaśca mokṣaḥ. SBS., i. 1. 4.

[13] SBS., i. 1. 4; SB., Muṇḍ. Up., iii. 2. 9; ii. 2. 9.

[14] Svātmasvarūpatve sati anāpyatvāt. SBS., i. 1. 4.

different from the essential nature of the Ātman, it would not be attainable. The Ātman is omnipresent, and so its mokṣa is eternally present in it (nityāpta-svarūpa). Mokṣa does not admit of refinement (saṁskārya). Refinement consists in producing excellence in the object refined, or in removing its defects. Mokṣa is the essential nature of Brahman. It does not admit of production of any excellence in it. It is of the nature of supreme perfection.[1] It is the essential nature of Brahman, which is eternally pure, and does not require any purging of imperfections.[2] It cannot be said to be hidden in the Ātman, which is manifested by an activity, since the Self cannot be an object of activity. If it were modified by activity, it would be non-eternal. It is neither an object of its own activity nor activity of any other agent. So it cannot be refined by activity. Mokṣa is the intrinsic nature of the Ātman, which is identical with Brahman. It is eternal and unchangeable. It consists in the intuition of the Ātman or Brahman. Bondage is the ignorance of its essential nature. Mokṣa is the knowledge of it. There is no trace of activity in it.[3] Activity can lead to production, attainment, modification, and refinement.[4] Mokṣa is not in the nature of any of these, and cannot therefore be brought about by activity.

The jīva is identical with Īśvara. Divinity is its essential nature. Its bondage is due to its ignorance of its divine nature. Its liberation is due to its knowledge of its divine nature.[5] The divinity of the individual self is hidden by the veil of avidyā, which is destroyed by the grace of God, when it meditates on him, and makes strenuous efforts to know its essential divinity. Divine knowledge and sovereignty are hidden by avidyā in the jīva, and it appears to be different from Īśvara owing to its connection with the mind-body-complex.[6] When avidyā is completely destroyed, there is no more rebirth. Bondage is due to the adjuncts (upādhi) which are generated by avidyā.[7] When they are destroyed, the jīva realizes its intrinsic liberation.[8]

---

[1] Anādheyātiśayabrahmasvarūpatvāt mokṣasya. SBS., i. 1. 4.
[2] Nityaśuddhabrahmasvarūpatvāt mokṣasya. SBS., i. 1. 4.
[3] SBS., i. 1. 4.
[4] SB., Tait. Up., i. 11; Bṛ. Up., iii. 3. 1; Muṇḍ. Up. i. 2. 12.
[5] Īśvarasya svarūpāparijñānāt bandhaḥ, tatsvarūpaparijñānāt tu mokṣaḥ. SBS., iii. 2. 6.
[6] SBS., iii. 2. 6.
[7] SBS., iii. 2. 11.
[8] SBS., iii. 2 9.

The jīva is identical with Brahman. It is, in its essence, one eternal and immutable consciousness, which is obscured by avidyā. When it is destroyed, its absolute nature shines forth.[1] The jīva is, in its real nature, Brahman, which is self-luminous.[2] Brahman manifests other objects. But it is not manifested by any other entity.[3]

Perfect knowledge is of one kind, since it depends upon its object, Brahman, which is identical with its nature.[4] Identity of the Ātman with Brahman is natural.[5] The identity consciousness is the consciousness of all as identical with the Ātman (sarvātmaikatva). When the intuitional consciousness of the identity of the whole universe with the Ātman or Brahman is attained, the jīva is purged of all desires for any other objects, since they are non-existent. The intuitional consciousness of identity is not illusory, since it results in the cessation of avidyā, and is not contradicted.[6] Mokṣa is a state of desirelessness. When Brahman is known, there remains no duty to be performed. The sense of duty is transcended. Mokṣa is the supreme state of beatitude or blessedness.[7] It is not a lapse into immorality. But it is a supermoral state of fulfilment. The sense of duty is not the chief element in the highest state of beautitude. There is nothing to be desired or rejected in it.[8] The person who has realized beatitude transcends moral obligation. Injunctions and prohibitions are useless to him, who has acquired integral experience, since he has no sense of command imposed upon him by Īśvara. He has transcended the sense of duality.[9] Virtue and vice both are causes of bondage. Virtue leads to heaven. Vice leads to hell. Virtue generates supramundane happiness, which is empirical and transient. Vice generates intense suffering in hell. Vidyā destroys both, and puts an end to transmigrations. It destroys all karmas. Virtue

---

[1] SBS., i. 3. 19. [2] SBS., i. 3. 22.

[3] Brahma hi anyad vyanakti, na tu brahma anyena vyajyate. SBS., i. 3. 22.

[4] Samyakjñānam ekarūpaṁ vastutantratvāt. SBS., ii. 1. 11.

[5] Svābhāvikī brahmātmatā. SBS., ii. 1. 14.

[6] SBS., ii. 1. 14.

[7] Brahmāvagatau satyāṁ sarvakartavyatāhāniḥ kṛtakṛtyatā ceti. SBS., i. 1. 4.

[8] Akartavyapradhānam ātmajñānaṁ hānāya upādānāya vā na bhavati. SBS., i. 1. 4.

[9] SBS., ii. 3. 48.

also obstructs liberation. Knowledge is superior to virtue. Vidyā is the higher saving knowledge. It destroys all merits and demerits, and leads to liberation after death.[1]

Mokṣa is an accomplished fact. It is discovered by intuition. It cannot be produced by activity. Actions are useless in achieving liberation.[2] Mokṣa is a state of actionlessness (naiṣkarmya). It is existence in the essential state of the Ātman, which is a state of inactivity.[3] Activity belongs to the empirical self (jīva). It does not pertain to the transcendental Self (ātman). It is the effect of lower knowledge (aparā vidyā) or avidyā. It is possible in the empirical world of duality and plurality, where there is a distinction of the agent, action, object, and fruit, means and ends.[4] It is not possible in the realm of the eternal, absolute, transcendental, non-dual reality or Ātman. Mokṣa is not a state of activity, which is painful.[5] It is eternal bliss, which always shines in the Self.[6] It is the highest state of ecstasy (yoga). It leads to liberation, which never ceases.[7]

The person, who has intuition of the Ātman, takes delight in it (ātmarati). He is contented with it (ātmatṛpta). He sports with it (ātmakrīḍa). He does not take delight in external objects. He shakes off all attachment to them. He withdraws his mind completely from them, fixes it on the Ātman, and realizes the eternal bliss inherent in it.[8] He, who has realized the Ātman as the reality of the universe, is delighted in it, sports with it, is united with it, and filled with supreme bliss, and becomes autonomous.[9] Eternal bliss is the essence of the Ātman. It never ceases. But it is hidden by the limiting adjuncts of the psychophysical organism.[10] The adjuncts are due to avidyā. When avidyā is destroyed by integral experience, the transcen-

---

[1] SBS., iv. 1. 4.

[2] Mokṣasya akāryatvāt mumukṣoḥ karmānarthakyam. SBG., iii. 1.

[3] Niṣkriyātmasvarūpeṇaiva avasthānam. SBG., iii. 4.

[4] Samastam aparavidyākāryaṁ sādhyasādhanalakṣaṇaṁ kriyākārakaphalabhedabhinnaṁ dvaitam. SB., Muṇḍ. Up., i. 2. 11.

[5] SBS., ii. 3. 40.

[6] SB., Muṇḍ. Up., ii. 2. 8.

[7] SBG., iv. 1.

[8] SB., Muṇḍ. Up., iii. 1. 4; SBS., iv. 1. 2.

[9] Ch. Up., vii. 25. 2.

[10] Svarūpasya anapāyitvāt upādhikṛtasvarūpatirobhāvāt. SBS., iii. 2. 35.

dental bliss of the Ātman manifests itself.[1] The bliss arising from the intuition of the Ātman is indescribable. It is supreme and transempirical. It is self-luminous. It cannot be enjoyed by non-discriminating persons through their sense-organs. It can be enjoyed by discriminating persons only, who have extirpated their primal desires (eṣaṇā) for enjoyment, and realized their essential nature.[2] The Ātman is Brahman, which is infinite (bhūmā). It is in the nature of supreme bliss, which is infinite, eternal, and transcendental. It springs from the realization of the Ātman as the essence of the whole universe (sarvātmabhāva). It transcends all relation to empirical objects, avidyā, desires, and actions. The self-luminous Ātman is supreme bliss. It is the highest consummation of happiness.[3] It is an object of intuition. It is different from empirical pleasure, which is due to sense-object-contact. It is non-sensuous. It is hidden by avidyā, and split up into fragments.[4] Empirical pleasure is an imperfect reflection of it.

What, being known by the Self, is sought to be achieved by it, is the end. There are two kinds of ends, the supreme end and the subordinate ends. Happiness and extinction of misery are the supreme ends. The means to their attainment are the subordinate ends. Happiness is either infinite (niratiśaya) or finite (sātiśaya). Finite happiness is empirical and sensuous. It imperfectly reflects the infinite bliss of the Ātman. Infinite happiness or bliss is Brahman itself.[5] Mokṣa is attainment of Brahman, which is infinite bliss.[6] It is not transportation to heaven or enjoyment of celestial happiness, since it is produced by virtue and non-eternal, and liable to lapse into earthly life.[7]

Mokṣa is existence of the Ātman in its essential condition of infinite bliss. When it realizes its identity with Brahman, desires due to avidyā are extirpated. Desires are the cause of pain. Finite objects produce desires. They cannot yield permanent satisfaction. But Brahman is free from desires. It is eternal bliss.[8] Sensuous pleasure is due to the sense of duality. It arises from contact of a sense-organ with an object. But supreme bliss does not arise from contact of the senses with

---

[1] SB., Kaṭha Up., ii. 2. 12; iii. 1. 4.
[2] *Ibid*, ii. 2. 14.
[3] Sarvātmabhāvaḥ svabhāvaḥ asya. Evam avidyākāmakarmādisarvasaṁsāradharmasambandhātītaṁ rūpam asya. Svayaṁjyotir ātmaiṣa parama ānandaḥ. Sa eṣa sukhasya parā kāṣṭhā. SB., Bṛ. Up., iv. 3. 34.
[4] SB., Bṛ. Up., iv. 3. 32.
[5] VPB., pp. 406-07.
[6] Ānandātmakabrahmāvāptiśca mokṣaḥ śokanivṛttiśca. *Ibid*, p. 407.
[7] *Ibid*, p. 408.
[8] SB., Ch. Up., vii. 24. 1.

external finite objects. It is independent of the body, life, and the senses.[1] It is supreme, infinite, and eternal. It can never be derived from the senses.[2] It is the acme of happiness. It springs from realization of identity of the Ātman with Brahman.[3] It exists in the inner Self, which is divine in nature. It is the Self of all.[4] The bliss arising from all-self-hood (sarvātmabhāva) is unique and indescribable. It is known by yogic intuition. It is known by eternal knowledge, which is mokṣa. It is supreme isolation (kaivalya).[5]

The knower of the Ātman (ātmavit) is the knower of the whole universe (kṛtsnavit).[6] He has integral experience. He does not cease to have cognitions of external objects. But his cognitions of them are not tainted by attachment, aversion, delusion, and other imperfections. He is neither attracted nor repelled by them. He knows them as non-different from Brahman. His knowledge of Brahman runs through cognitions of them. It is not obstructed, hidden, or destroyed by them.[7] His desires are withdrawn from external objects, and turned inward to the Ātman. His desires for untruth are sublimated into desires for Truth.[8] He does not dissolve the empirical world of plurality, but he destroys the sense of plurality. His knowledge of plurality is transmuted by the intuition of Identity. He throws off the sway of empirical objects. If he dissolved the world of plurality, his liberation would liberate all.[9] Saṁkara believes in embodied release. This clearly shows that integral experience does not dissolve the empirical world.

The knower of Brahman exists in Brahman.[10] He lives, moves, and has his being in Brahman. He realizes eternal bliss, which is the essence of the Ātman. He eschews empirical pleasure completely.[11] It arises from false knowledge (avidyā). But transcendental bliss arises from true insight.[12]

Mokṣa is realization of Brahmanhood (brahmabhāva). It is realization of the self in the entire universe.[13] It is the highest Good (niḥśreyasa). It is the supreme end.[14] Knowledge of the

[1] SB., Ch. Up., vii. 25. 2.
[2] SBG., vi. 21.
[3] SBG., vi. 27, 28.
[4] SB., Kaṭha Up., ii. 1. 6.
[5] SB., Māṇḍ. K., iii. 47.
[6] SBG., iii. 29.
[7] SB., Ch. Up., vii. 26. 2.
[8] SB., Ch. Up., viii. 1. 5.
[9] SBS., iii. 2. 21.
[10] BG., vi. 20.
[11] SB., v. 20, 21.
[12] SB., Kaṭha Up., ii. 1. 1-4.
[13] Sarvātmabhāvo mokṣaḥ. SB., Bṛ. Up. iv. 4. 6.
[14] SB., Bṛ. Up., iv. 4. 23.

Ātman is independent of space, time, and causality. But knowledge of objects depends on these empirical categories. The Ātman can be known by transempirical knowledge. It can be known by supra-intellectual intuition. But the empirical world can be known by intellectual knowledge. Knowledge depends upon its object (vastutantra). But activity (kriyā) depends upon an agent (puruṣatantra). So the Ātman of Brahman cannot be realized by activity. But it can be known by intuition.[1]

The essential nature of the Ātman is beyond pleasure and pain, good and evil, virtue and vice. They are connected with the body, which is a product of avidyā. The Ātman is disembodied and incorporeal. It is not touched by these empirical qualities. Avidyā is the cause of pain. When it is annulled by the intuition of the essential identity of the Ātman (ātmaikatvasvarūpadarśana), there is no possibility of connection with pain.[2] Mokṣa is the transempirical and noumenal state of the Ātman.

Śaṁkara recognizes gradual liberation (kramamukti) and liberation on earth (jīvanmukti). The person who meditates on the mystic syllable *Om,* the symbol of Brahman, goes to Brahmaloka or heaven after death. He retains his personality there, and gradually acquires integral experience of Brahman. This is gradual release (kramamukti).[3] Worship of determinate Brahman or personal God leads to destruction of sins, attainment of sovereignty, and gradual release.[4] Indeterminate Brahman cannot be comprehended by persons of dull intellect.[5] But the person, who acquires intuition of indeterminate Brahman, becomes Brahman here and now. He realizes his infinitude and absoluteness in the embodied state. He becomes immortal in his mortal coil. He enters into life eternal. He is purged of avidyā, desires, and actions, virtue and vice, and becomes infinite and eternal spirit (brahmaprāpta).[6] Perfect knowledge of Brahman leads to embodied release. But imperfect knowledge of it leads to gradual release.[7] Worship of personal God leads to attainment of Brahmaloka. It brings about residence with God (sālokya) and affinity in nature with him (sārūpya).[8] But perfect knowledge of Brahman leads to

[1] SB., Bṛ. Up., iv. 5. 15.
[2] SB., Ch. Up., viii. 12. 1.
[3] SBS., i. 3. 13.
[4] SBS., iii. 2. 21.
[5] SB., Kena Up., iv. 5.
[6] SB., Kaṭha Up., ii. 2. 1; ii. 3. 14-18; SB., Muṇḍ. Up. iii. 2. 9.
[7] SB., Kaṭha Up., ii. 3. 4.
[8] SBS., iv. 4. 21.

embodied release.[1] It does not destroy the body at once. It burns up only those unseen potencies (karma) which have not yet begun to bear fruit, whether they are acquired in the present life or in a previous birth. But it does not destroy those potencies which have fashioned the present life. When they are exhausted by enjoyment and suffering through continuance of life, complete liberation is attained. This is disembodied release. "As a potter's wheel continues for a time to revolve, even after the vessel has been completed so also life continues after liberation, since it contains no cause to check the impetus already gained."[2] As a man suffering from eye disease, continues to see two moons owing to the force of the impression (saṁskārā), even when he is convinced of the existence of one moon only, so too the knowledge of the empirical world persists for some time owing to the force of its impression, even after a man has attained knowledge of its unreality. The knowledge of Brahman attained by a person in his embodied condition cannot be refuted by another. It is a fact of experience.[3] The knower of Brahman becomes omnipresent spirit, and realizes absoluteness here and now.[4] Mokṣa is not production of anything new, but mere cessation of bondage owing to annulment of avidyā.[5] It is the complete cessation of saṁsāra ; it is beginningless, endless, unageing, undying, immortal, fearless, pure, and faultless ; it is existence in the essence of the Ātman ; it is non-dual supreme bliss ; it is the object of integral experience.[6]

32. *The Means to Liberation : Morality and Knowledge*

Saṁkara is the staunchest advocate of knowledge as the only means of liberation. Bondage is ignorance. Liberation is true knowledge. It is attained by integral experience. It is the experience of all beings in the Ātman and the experience of the Ātman in all beings. It is the experience of the identity of the Ātman with Brahman without any distinction.[7] The

---

[1] SBS., iii. 2. 21.
[2] SV., p. 425. Cp. *Indian Philosophy,* Vol. II, p. 645.
[3] SBS., iv. 1. 15. SV., pp. 424-26.
[4] SBS., iv. 2. 14.
[5] Phalatvasiddhir api mokṣasya bandhananivṛttimātrāpekṣā na apūrvopajananāpekṣā. SBS., iv. 4. 2.
[6] SB., Muṇḍ. Up., i. 11. 1. [7] SBG., vi. 29.

person, who has acquired integral experience, remains in the highest condition of Brahmanhood.[1] Knowledge of the Ātman (ātmavidyā) is the highest good.[2] Mystic experience of Identity of the Ātman is the highest consummation of knowledge.[3] Integral experience consumes all merits and demerits, which cause rebirth.[4] It destroys grief, delusion, and other afflictions, which obscure the knowledge of the Ātman.[5] It quickly leads to realization of mokṣa.[6] The yoga is the stability of integral experience.[7] It can be attained by total extinction of all desires for external objects of enjoyment.[8] It can be acquired by meditation on Brahman by the concentrated mind free from all taint of attachment, aversion, and the other afflictions, and withdrawn from external objects of enjoyment.[9] Those, who have extirpated all desires for enjoyment here and hereafter, acquire integral experience.[10] They shake off false egoism, and do not identify the Ātman with the mind-body-complex.[11] They are suffused with universal good will, amity, and compassion. They are freed from enmity to all. They are full of forgiveness. They uproot their self-love. They become indifferent to their own joys and sorrows.[12] They experience Brahman in all, and treat all as equal.[13] They renounce all desires and actions, acquire integral experience, and enter into life eternal.[14] They enjoy eternal bliss inherent in their inner Self, merge in Brahman, and become Brahman even while alive.[15] They realize their identity with Brahman or eternal Being, Consciousness, and Bliss. They exist in Brahman. They realize their intrinsic freedom. They are not born again.[16] Integral experience is not discursive knowledge. It is direct experience of Brahman. It is accompanied by supreme eternal bliss.[17]

Saṁkara's ethics is branded as intellectualistic, since he regards higher knowledge as the only means of liberation, and

---

[1] SBG., vi 31.
[2] SB., Kaṭha Up., i. 2. 7.
[3] Jñānasya hi parā niṣṭhā yad ātmaikatvavijñānam. *Ibid,* i. 2. 8.
[4] Samyag darśanaṁ sarvakarmaṇāṁ nirbījatve kāraṇāṁ. SBG., iv 37.
[5] SBG., iv. 42.
[6] SBG., iv. 39.
[7] SBG., x. 7.
[8] Nivṛttasarvabāhyaiṣaṇā. SBG., x. 10.
[9] SBG., xi. ii; SB., Māṇḍ. K., iv. 2.
[10] SBG., x. 2.
[11] SBG., xii. 5.
[12] SBG., xii. 20.
[13] SBG., v. 18.
[14] SBG., xii. 13.
[15] SBG., v. 24.
[16] SBG., v. 17, 18.
[17] SBG., xiii 27.

knowledge of the self as the highest good.[1] But this is a misconception. Though the Truth (Ātman) is the Good (niḥśreyasa), the saving knowledge is the result of rigid self-control and virtuous life. Morality precedes spiritual realization. The indispensable propædeutic to the knowledge of Brahman is discrimination of the eternal and the non-eternal (nityānityaviveka), detachment from enjoyments on earth and heaven (ihāmutraphalabhogavairāgya), restraint of the internal organs or tranquillity (śama), control of the external senses (dama), withdrawal of the mind from external objects of enjoyment (uparati), endurance of heat and cold (titikṣā), concentration of the mind on Brahman (samādhi), faith in the instructions of preceptors and the Vedānta (śraddhā), and desire for liberation (mumukṣutva).[2] These moral qualifications make a person fit for the study of the Vedānta and enquiry into the nature of Brahman (brahmajijñāsā). Non-killing or non-injury (ahiṁsā), truthfulness (satya), celibacy (brahmacarya), non-acceptance of gifts except for bare subsistence or non-covetousness (aparigraha), renunciation of all possessions (sarvatyaga), tranquillity (śama), sense-control (dama), withdrawal of the senses from their objects (uparati), study of the scriptures (svādhyāya), austerities (tapas), cleanliness or purity of body and mind (śauca), discrimination of the self from the not-self (viveka), fixation of mind (dhāraṇā), meditation (dhyāna), concentration of mind on Brahman with devotion (samādhi), and the like are auxiliary to integral experience.[3] Truthfulness consists in eschewing falsehood, deceit, hypocrisy, pride, and boastfulness. Non-deceit and non-crookedness in speech, body, and mind constitute truthfulness. It is better than a thousand Aśvamedha sacrifices. It is the foundation of the knowledge of Brahman.[4] Celibacy destroys afflictions and purifies the mind. It aids the dawn of perfect knowledge (samyag jñāna).[5] Truthfulness and renunciation of desires lead to the attainment of the highest good.[5] When the mind is purged of attachment, aversion, delusion, and

---

[1] SV., pp. 59, 403-04; Urquhart: *Pantheism and the Value of Life*, ch. xi; *The Vedanta and Modern Thought*, p. 173.

[2] SBS., i. 1. 1; SB., Bṛ. Up., iv. 4. 23; VPB., pp. 429-30.

[3] SB., Bṛ. Up., iv. 5. 15; SB., Muṇḍ. Up., iii. 1. 2; iii. 2. 5; SB., Tait. Up., i. 11; SB., Pr. Up., v. 1.

[4] SB., Muṇḍ. Up., iii. 1. 6; SB., Kena Up., iv. 8.

[5] *Ibid*, iii. 1. 5.

other afflictions, it can have pure knowledge and intuition of Brahman.[1] The mind purified by instructions of the scriptures and preceptors, tranquillity, sense-control, and the like is the organ of the intuition of the Ātman.[2] The saving knowledge is preceded by purity of mind and purity of conduct. Morality is an indispensable precondition of higher knowledge. Therefore Saṁkara's ethics is not intellectualistic.

Hearing the scriptural texts regarding Identity (śravaṇa), reflection (manana), and meditation (nididhyāsana) on them remove hindrances to higher knowledge (vidyā) and aid its manifestation.[3] They should be repeated till the dawn of intuition. They end in mystic vision (darśana).[4] The mind is inclined towards śravaṇa, manana, and nididhyāsana, when it is purified by sacrifices, charity, and austerities. They can manifest vidyā, if there are no hindrances in the shape of fruits of other works.[5] Sacrifices, charity, and austerities done without attachment and desire for fruits purify the mind. They are obligatory duties (nitya karma). They ought to be performed by those who have not yet destroyed avidya.[6]

Courage (abhīrutā), penances (tapas), performance of sacrifices (yajña) spiritedness (tejas), fortitude (dhṛti), bodily and mental cleanliness (śauca), study of the scriptures (svādhyāya), knowledge of the Ātman obtained from the scriptures and preceptors (jñāna), inactivity of the cognitive organs in the presence of their objects (alolupatva), inactivity of the motor organs (acāpala), tranquillity of mind (śānti), purity of mind (sattvasaṁśuddhi), and concentration of mind (yoga) are the self-regarding virtues, which ought to be cultivated.[7] These include physical, intellectual, and moral virtues. They are auxiliary to knowledge.

Good-will and love for all creatures (adveṣa), friendship (maitra), compassion (karuṇā) for the distressed, forgiveness (kṣamā), selflessness or extinction of self-love or egoism, con-

---

[1] *Ibid,* iii. 1. 8.
[2] Śāstrācāryopadeśaśamadamādisaṁskṛtaṁ manaḥ ātmadarśane karaṇam. SBG., ii. 21.
[3] SBS., iii. 4. 38; SB., Bṛ. Up., ii. 4. 5.
[4] SBS., iv. 1. 1.
[5] SBS., iii. 4. 51.
[6] SBG., xviii. 5, 6, 7; SBS., iii. 4. 27; SB., Bṛ. Up., iv. 4. 22.
[7] BG., xvi, 1-3.

quest of enmity to all creatures, universal benevolence, equal treatment with all, charity, and pursuit of the welfare of humanity (lokasaṁgraha) are the social virtues, which ought to be cultivated. These include justice, benevolence, and love.[1] Love thy enemy as thyself. The Ātman exists in friend and foe alike.[2] Causing anxiety, fear, and pain to others should be eschewed.[3] Charity (dāna), self-sacrifice (tyāga), straightforwardness (ārjava), non-killing or non-injury (ahiṁsā), tenderness (mārdava), non-malevolence (adroha), non-cavilling (apaiśuna), pacification of anger (akrodha), non-self-glorification (amānitva), non-hypocrisy (adambhitva), modesty (hrī) are the other social virtues which ought to be cultivated. Social virtues spring from true knowledge (jñāna). Social vices spring from ignorance (ajñāna). The former counteract the latter.[4] Religions hypocrisy (dambha), pride (darpa) of wealth, learning, and noble birth, and harshness of words (pāruṣya) are vices.[5] Those, who perpetrate cruelty and violence, are enemies of mankind because they destroy the social order.[6] Egoism is due to ignorance (avidyā) or confusion of the Self with the mind-body-complex.[7] But the Ātman is one infinite Spirit. It exists in all creatures. When avidyā is destroyed by the knowledge of the Ātman, egoism is eradicated. Altruism is the inevitable consequence of the realization of all-selfless (sarvātmabhāva). Social virtues are not intrinsic values. They purify the mind, and aid self-realization.[8]

Mokṣa is eternal. It cannot be produced by works (karma), which spring from ignorance (avidyā). Works are antagonistic to knowledge (vidyā). Vidyā is knowledge of one undifferenced Ātman. Works are due to false knowledge of difference of actors, actions, fruits, means and ends.[9] They are due to egoism or confusion of the Self with the body.[10] Knowledge of Brahman results in realization of all-selfness.[11] Desires cannot spring from it.[12] When avidyā is destroyed by Brahmavidyā, nothing but the Ātman exists.[13] Works can never lead to knowledge of Brahman,

---

1 BG., xii. 4, 13; xi. 55; ii. 11.
2 BG., xii. 18.
3 SBG., xii. 15.
4 SBG., xiii. 7, 11; xvi. 1-4.
5 SBG., xvi. 4.
6 SBG., xvi. 9.
7 SBG., xiii. 2.
8 SBG., xiii. 11.
9 SB., Ch. Up., ii. 23. 1.
10 SB., Tait. Up., i. 11.
11 SB., Bṛ. Up., i. 4. 10; ii. 1. 20.
12 SB., Bṛ. Up., i. 5. 2.
13 SB., Bṛ. Up., ii. 4. 14.

since they are antagonistic to each other like light and darkness.[1] Works devoid of knowledge spring from desires due to avidyā, and therefore give rise to misery.[2]

Śaṁkara maintains that knowledge combined with works (jñānakarmasamuccaya) cannot lead to liberation, since they are antagonistic to each other. Knowledge is vidyā. Works are avidyā. When vidyā dawns, avidyā is dispelled. They cannot co-exist with each other.[3] Mokṣa can be attained by knowledge only. It can never be attained by knowledge combined with works.[4] Knowledge dispels avidyā, and ends in liberation (kaivalya). Mokṣa is the eternal reality. It is the essential nature of Ātman or Brahman. It cannot be produced by knowledge or works, or both together. It is only revealed by knowledge. It is not produced by voluntary actions motived by desire for an end.[5] Knowledge of identity of Ātman with Brahman cannot be combined with works even in dream.[6] Karma is the path of action (pravṛtti). Jñāna is the path of renunciation of action (nivṛtti).[7]

But empirical duties (kāmya karma) and prohibited acts (niṣiddha karma) should not be performed.[8] Empirical duties are selfish prudential acts for the fulfilment of desires due to avidyā. They are not auxiliary to knowledge.[9] Daily obligatory duties (nitya karma), *e.g.*, ablutions and prayers arrest production of sins, destroy accumulated demerits, remove hindrances, produce purity of mind (sattvaśuddhi), and aid the emergence of knowledge. They are not prompted by desires. They are acts of reason. They are auxiliary to knowledge.[10] They ought to be performed without desire for fruits by those who have not destroyed avidyā[11] Occasional duties (naimittika karma) also ought to be performed by them on particular occasions in order

---

[1] Na hi karmaṇi brahmaniṣṭhatā sambhavati, karmātmajñānayor virodhāt. SB., Maṇḍ. Up., i. 1. 12.

[2] SB., Muṇḍ. Up., i. 1. 7.

[3] Karmaṇo vidyāvirodhitvāt. SB., Īśa Up., 9. Vidyākarmaṇośca samuccayo na. *Ibid.*, 18; SB., Tait. Up. i. 11; SB., Muṇḍ., Introduction; SB., Bṛ. Up., iii. 5. 1.

[4] Kevalādeva jñānāt mokṣaḥ. SBG., iii. 1. SB., Ch. Up., ii. 23. 1. Kayapi yuktyā na samuccayo jñānakarmaṇoḥ. SBG., ii. 3.

[5] SBG., xviii. 66.

[6] SB., Muṇḍ. Up., Introduction.

[7] SB., Īśa Up., 2.

[8] SBG., xviii. 2, 7.

[9] SBG., iv. 1. 7.

[10] SBS., iv. 1. 8; SBG., xviii. 10, 16; SB., Bṛ. Up., iv. 4. 22; iii. 3. 1.

[11] SBG., xviii. 2, 7, 9.

to avoid demerits. They also are acts of reason. But they produce special karmas without the agent's knowledge, which demand retribution in a new birth.[1] Holy works indirectly lead to mokṣa. They aid the emergence of knowledge which manifests the self's intrinsic freedom.[2] Non-performance of empirical duties leads to non-production of desired bodies. Non-commission of prohibited acts leads to non-production of undesired bodies. Performance of daily obligatory duties and occasional duties leads to non-attainment of sins of omission. They ought to be performed by those who are subject to false knowledge.[3] Integral experience only can consume all merits and demerits, which have not yet begun to bear fruits.[4] Empirical duties and prohibited acts cannot be completely renounced till the dawn of integral experience, which consumes all desires. There is no other means of liberation than knowledge (jñāna) or expansion of the finite individual self into the infinite universal Self (sarvātmabhāva). When the saving knowledge dawns, the absolute good is realized.[5] Integral experience is the highest consummation of morality. We rise from prohibited acts to empirical duties prompted by desire. We rise from these acts of desire to acts of reason, and perform daily obligatory duties and occasional duties, and cultivate altruistic virtues. We rise from these acts of reason to the integral experience of the Ātman or infinite universal Spirit. Integral experience presupposes transformation of will.

The duties pertaining to castes (varṇa) and stages of life (āśrama) lead to attainment of heaven.[6] They cannot achieve liberation, since they are due to false knowledge of difference of actors, acts, and fruits.[7] Vidyā does not depend on duties of different stages of life in order to accomplish mokṣa.[8] But if they are performed with a desire to know Brahman, they are indirect means to the production of knowledge. But they do not aid knowledge to produce liberation.[9] Ritualistic acts done with a desire to know Brahman (vividiṣā) are external aids to the production of knowledge. But sense-control, control of mind,

---

[1] SBS., iv. 3. 14.
[2] SBG., xviii. 66.
[3] Puruṣārthasamāptir buddhyutpatteḥ. SBS., iv. 3. 14.
[4] SBS., iv. 1. 6.
[5] SBG., ii. 51.
[6] SBS., xviii. 44.
[7] SB., Bṛ. Up., ii. 4. 5.
[8] SBS., iii. 4. 26.
[9] SBS., iii. 4. 25, 26.

and the like are the internal means to it. Śaṁkara stresses the inner purity of mind more than external observance of customary rules of conduct. Ritualistic acts done without desire for fruits are the means of knowledge of those, who are desirous of achieving liberation.[1]

Duties of different stages of life (āśrama karma) are auxiliary to knowledge, since they purify the mind. When the mind is purified, it acquires the saving knowledge.[2] Recitation of mantras (japa), fasting, and prayer can be performed by all. Knowledge dawns upon a mind purified by duties of stages of life performed even in a previous birth.[3] The rules of stages of life are binding on all. A student's (brahmacārin) duties, a householder's (gṛhastha) duties, and a forester's (vānaprastha) duties lead to heaven. But the duties of an ascetic (sannyāsin) lead to immortality (amṛtatva). The duties of the first three stages of life cannot lead to immortality, since their non-performance generates sins of omission. But the ascetic has renounced all works, and therefore sins of omission do not accrue to him due to non-performance of duties. His moral duties of sense-restraint, tranquillity of mind, and the like are contributory to realization of Brahman (brahmasaṁsthā). They are not antagonistic to it. An individual can, therefore, attain salvation only in the stage of asceticism.[4] Extirpation of all desires, renunciation of all works, and integral experience are the means of release.[5] The wise should adopt an ascetic's life. Those, who are in quest of true knowledge, also should adopt it.[6] Devotion to knowledge culminates in release. It must be preceded by renunciation of all works. Integral experience of the Ātman or Brahman is the culmination of knowledge.[7] There can be no release without complete renunciation of all works (naiṣkarmya) coupled with intuition of the Ātman.[8] Śaṁkara over-emphasizes the importance of the last stage of sannyāsa which only directly leads to release through true insight. But in the first three stages of life duties are performed, which involve false knowledge (avidyā) of actors, actions, and objects,

[1] SBS., iii. 4. 27.
[2] SBS., iii. 4. 33.
[3] SBS., iii. 4. 38.
[4] SBS., iii. 4. 20.
[5] SB., Īśa Up., 15; SB., Bṛ. Up., iv. 4. 7.
[6] SB., Bṛ. Up., iv. 5. 15.
[7] SBG., xviii. 55, 56.
[8] SBG., xviii. 49, 66, 12; ii. 69; v. 9.

and generate re-birth as gods, men, or animals.[1] They cannot bring about release, since they cannot destroy avidyā.[2]

The rules of caste morality also are binding on all. They preserve the social order. Tranquillity, sense-restraint, purity of body and mind, forgiveness, straightness, knowledge, and faith in the scriptures are the duties of a Brāhmaṇa.[3] Heroism, spiritedness, fortitude, efficiency, bravery in fighting, charity, and supremacy are the duties of a Kṣatriya.[4] Agriculture, tending cattle, trade, and commerce are the duties of a Vaiśya. Service is the duty of a Śudra.[5] These caste duties well performed lead to attainment of heaven. They remove impurities of the body and the senses, and make the mind fit for acquiring knowledge.[6] Brāhmaṇas are specially fit for knowledge of Brahman, when they renounce all.[7] A Brāhmaṇa should renounce eruditeness (pāṇḍitya) and adopt childlike simplicity (bālya) ; he should renounce it and adopt saintliness (mauna) ; then he should renounce saintliness and have direct experience of Brahman. Then he becomes a true Brāhmaṇa.[8] Brāhmaṇas, who have destroyed false knowledge and desires for sons, wealth and enjoyment on earth and in heaven, should beg alms for bare subsistence and only cultivate knowledge of the Ātman.[9]

The liberated souls, who have acquired integral experience, renounce all actions for egoistic ends, and engage in actions only for the good of humanity (lokasaṁgraha) without attachment and desire for fruits. Their actions are, in reality, not actions because they spring from integral experience of the Ātman or Brahman.[10] Those, who perform actions for solidarity of mankind, are not bound by them, because they are selfless acts and unmotived by avidyā and egoism.[11] Those, who have acquired knowledge of the Ātman, ought to do works for the welfare of mankind. But those, who have not acquired it, ought to do works for purification of their minds.[12] If they have a strong desire for liberation, unmotived desireless works (niṣkāma karma) cause purification of mind (sattavaśuddhi).[13]

[1] SBG., xviii. 12.
[2] SB., Bṛ. Up., iii. 3. 1.
[3] SBG., xviii. 42.
[4] SBG., xviii. 43.
[5] SBG., xviii. 44.
[6] SBG., xviii. 45.
[7] SB., Muṇḍ. Up., i. 1. 12.
[8] SB., Bṛ. Up., iv. 4. 23; SBS., iii. 4. 47.
[9] SBG., iii. 17.
[10] SBG., iv. 19, 20, 24.
[11] SBG., v. 7; SBS., ii. 3. 48.
[12] SBG., iv. 15.
[13] SB., Kena Up., Introduction.

Śaṁkara prescribes niṣkāma karma for purification of mind, which is necessary for the attainment of true knowledge. But it cannot directly lead to liberation. Duties performed without attachment and aversion, and desire for fruits are niṣkāma karma. They are not actuated by egoism (ahaṁkāra). They are devoid of the sense of 'I' and 'mine'. They are dedicated to God. They are done for the good of mankind. They are service to God for the welfare of humanity.[1] They produce purification of mind (sattvaśuddhi) and aid the production of true knowledge. They are auxiliary to knowledge. They indirectly help the achievement of the highest good.[2] Śaṁkara is never tired of repeating that the highest good can be achieved by the knowledge of the Ātman only preceded by renunciation of all works.[3] He underestimates the active life of morality. He prescribes unmotived works to those only, who are devoid of integral experience, for purification of their minds. Those, who have acquired integral experience, are compelled to do works for the welfare of mankind under the influence of karmas of past births.[4]

Śaṁkara advocates ethics of asceticism. Extirpation of all primal egoistic desires (eṣaṇā) is indispensable for achievement of eternal and absolute life (amṛtatva). Desire for sons (puttraiṣaṇā), desire for wealth (vittaiṣaṇā), and desire for enjoyment here and hereafter (lokaiṣaṇā) must be extirpated.[5] Works (karma) are actuated by desires (kāma) which are due to avidyā. They generate merits and demerits. They produce happiness and misery. So destruction of all desires due to avidyā is auxiliary to realization of identity of the Ātman with Brahman.[6] The empirical world of birth and death is impure, non-eternal, full of activity involving means and ends, fraught with misery, and a sphere of avidyā. Detachment from the world is the first condition of the quest for Brahman.[7] The mind engrossed in the world does not feel the necessity for knowing the Absolute. Until natural attachment to the world is counteracted by dis-

---

[1] SBG., ii. 11, 47, 48; iii. 19, 20; iv. 14; v. 11, 12; xiii. 25; vi. 1, 2.

[2] SBG., Introduction; iii. 19, 20; ii. 11, 48.

[3] Tat sarvakarmasaṁnyāsapūrvakād ātmajñānaniṣṭhārūpād dharmād bhavati. SBG., Introduction.

[4] SBG., iii. 20.

[5] SBG., ii. 11; SB., Kena Up., 1, 2; SB., Kaṭha Up. ii. 1. 2.

[6] SB., Kaṭha Up., ii. 3. 14; SB., Bṛ. Up., i. 4. 17.

[7] SB., Bṛ. Up., i. 5. 2

passion for it, desire for knowledge of Brahman does not arise.[1] Discontent with the world, extinction of desires for happiness, and renunciation of all works prepare the mind for the knowledge of Brahman.[2] Suppression of natural impulses (svabhāvapravṛttinirodha) is absolutely necessary for it.[3] Dispassion for earthly and celestial happiness generates purity of mind, and makes it fit for the direct experience of the Ātman.[4] An ascetic, who has completely destroyed all desires for empirical pleasure, realizes eternal bliss springing from the knowledge of the Ātman.[5] Avidyā and its effects, attachment, aversion, delusion, and other emotions, obscure the bliss of the Ātman. They are destroyed by direct experience of the Ātman.[6] An ascetic should destroy these afflictions, root out desires for external objects of enjoyment, achieve erudition, childlike simplicity, and sainthood, transcend the waking condition, dream, and sleep, and attain superconscious trance, and know Brahman.[7] If he sheds all desires for external objects, and renounces duties of stages of life, he can know Brahman.[8] A wandering monk, abstaining from all works and cultivating knowledge of identity, is grounded in Brahman.[9] Asceticism is the predominant note of Śaṁkara's ethics. But altruistic emotions of universal goodwill, love, amity, forgiveness, and selfless desires and acts of universal benevolence and moralizing the social order (lokasaṁgraha),[10] and uplifting humanity (lokānugraha)[11] are inculcated. The perfect man takes upon himself the task of redeeming sinful men swerving from the path of rectitude and establishing a moral order. To bring the Kingdom of God on earth is his mission.[12] So Śaṁkara's ethics is not entirely ethics of asceticism. It permits selfless acts of universal benevolence and service of humanity enlightened by integral experience.[13]

Happiness (preyas) and self-realization (śreyas) are the two ends of human life.[14] Avidyā impels a person to seek happiness.

---

[1] SB., Kena Up., Introduction.
[2] SBG., xii. 1; SB., Kena Up., iv. 7.
[3] SB., Kaṭha Up., ii. 1. 1.
[4] *Ibid*, i. 2. 20.
[5] *Ibid*, ii. 2. 14.
[6] SBG., xii. 2, 20; SB., Kaṭha Up., ii. 2. 12.
[7] SB., Māṇḍ. K., iv. 90; SB., Bṛ. Up., iv. 4. 23.
[8] SB., Ch. Up., viii. 12. 1.
[9] *Ibid*, ii. 23. 1.
[10] SBG., ii. 11; iii. 20; iv. 24.
[11] SBG., Introduction.
[12] SBG., iv. 7, 8.
[13] Kirtikar: *Studies in Vedanta*, Ch. VII.
[14] SB., Kaṭha Up., i. 2. 1.

Vidyā impels him to seek self-realization. Duties of castes and stages of life lead to happiness on earth and heaven. They are prompted by avidyā. But quest for the Self is prompted by vidyā. It directly leads to mokṣa. A non-discriminating person runs after the phantom of happiness which is perishing. But a discriminating person strives for self-realization which is abiding.[1] Happiness is due to avidyā. Self-realization is due to vidyā. Happiness is empirical pleasure. It is derived from empirical objects. It is transient and sensuous. It ends in bondage (saṁsāra). Self-realization ends in absolute freedom (mokṣa).[2] The self is permanent and eternal. It is the end of all our striving. It is the absolute good. Ephemeral empirical objects of pleasure cannot yield the eternal and absolute good.[3] Extroverts (bahirmukha) aim at happiness and extinction of misery. They are engrossed in the empirical world. They can never attain absolute good (ātyantika puruṣārtha). Actions of the mind-body-complex on external objects of enjoyment are natural and instinctive. But until the mind is withdrawn from them, and fixed on the inner Self, self-realization is not possible.[4] Introversion must replace extroversion in the quest for the Self. Śaṁkara's ethics is anti-hedonistic.

Dharma is two-fold, positive (pravṛtti) and negative (nivṛtti). It sustains the world. Happiness (abhyudaya) and self-realization (niḥśreyasa) are the ends of human beings.[5] Dharma generates happiness. Adharma generates suffering. They sustain the round of saṁsāra.[6] Virtue and vice both lead to bondage. First virtue should replace vice. Then both should be transcended in order to realize the transcendental Ātman. Virtue and vice, happiness and misery affect the mind-body-complex only. They cannot affect the disembodied supramental Spirit. So virtue and vice, good and evil both should be transcended. The liberated person realizes transcendental perfection of the Ātman beyond good and evil.[7] Integral experience only is the means to realization of supreme perfection. It is not a condition of transformed will but willless bliss.[8] Will is empirical; it is a mode of the mind. The Ātman is beyond mind and will.

---

[1] *Ibid*, i. 2. 1.
[2] *Ibid*, i. 2. 4.
[3] *Ibid*, i. 2. 10.
[4] SBS., i. 1. 4.
[5] SBG., Introduction.
[6] SBG., ii. 11.
[7] SBG., ii. 50, 51; iv. 20.
[8] *The System of Vedantic Thought and Culture*, p. 236.

It is pure consciousness and supreme bliss. The Ātman is the dearest of all. Wife, sons, and wealth are dear to us for the sake of the Ātman, which exists in them all.[1] The infinite bliss of the Self is imperfectly reflected in transient empirical pleasures. They should be abjured. The eternal fountain of them in the inner Self should be sought. The highest state is neither a condition of unconsciousness as the Nyāya-Vaiśeṣika maintains, nor absolute knowledge only as the Sāṁkhya-Yoga maintains, but absolute knowledge and bliss. It is free from will and activity. Śaṁkara's ethics, therefore, is not pessimistic, though it is predominantly ascetic in character. It is Transcendental Eudæmonism.[2]

33. *Ethical Thought: Dharma, Adharma, Niyoga, Springs of Action, and Freedom of the Will*

Virtue (dharma) and vice (adharma) are independent of time, space, and causality. They are supersensuous. They can be known from the Vedas only.[3] They cannot be perceived by the senses. Nor can they be inferred. They cannot be known by reason.[4] The scriptures are the only source of knowing them. This is authoritarianism. But the scriptures are embodiments of intuitions. They are not irrational, but supra-rational. Dharma and adharma can be known by reason subordinate to the scriptures.[5]

What is dharma in one place and time and under certain circumstances, is adharma in another place and time and under other circumstances.[6] What is duty for one with certain innate aptitudes, is not duty for another with other native endowments.[7] Ethical good (hita) and ethical evil (ahita) are relative. They are not absolute. They are not ontological verities. They are due to avidyā or dualistic vision. They spring from non-discrimination between the Ātman and the mind-body-complex. They are valid in the empirical world of appearance. They are determined by knowledge of difference. They do not hold good

---

[1] Bṛ. Up., i. 4. 8.
[2] S. K. Maitra: *Ethics of the Hindus*, p. 315.
[3] SBS. iii. 1. 25.
[4] SBS., ii. 1. 13.
[5] SBS., ii. 1. 11.
[6] SBS., iii. 1. 25.
[7] SBG., xviii. 47. 48; iii. 35.

in the ontological reality, when knowledge of identity dawns.[1] Dharma and adharma deal with works. All works, secular and scriptural, belong to the empirical world. They are due to avidyā. They do not belong to the Ātman, which transcends them.[2] They are objects of lower knowledge, while the Ātman is grasped by higher knowledge.[3]

Actions, which are enjoined by the scriptures, are right (dharma). Those, which are forbidden by them, are wrong (adharma).[4] Dharma produces good (artha) or happiness. Adharma produces evil (anartha) or unhappiness. Happiness and unhappiness are experienced through different kinds of mind-body-complexes. Different degrees of happiness and unhappiness are experienced by different grades of creatures, animals, men, and gods. They are due to different degrees of dharma and adharma.[5]

The Vedas are revealed by Īśvara. The injunctions (vidhi) and prohibitions (niṣedha) are creations of God. The individual selves (jīva) have relative freedom to perform enjoined acts or commit prohibited acts. God awards good (artha) to those who perform right acts (dharma), and evil (anartha) to those who commit wrong acts (adharma). The jīvas have freedom of choice (puruṣakāra). If God were absolutely independent in awarding good and evil to them, their free exertions would be unavailing.[6] Śaṁkara does not deny relative empirical freedom of the will.

Dharma is a categorical imperative. It is an Ought. It ought to be done. It ought to be brought into existence by the effort and activity of a person. Secular and scriptural duties may be done, undone, or wrongly done by him. Dharma does not depend upon apprehension (anubhava). Śruti is the source of its knowledge. Anubhava is not a means of knowing it.[7] The scriptures give us categorical imperatives in the form of injunctions and prohibitions.[8] They are binding on the jīvas.

---

[1] Avidyāpratyupasthāpitanāmarūpakṛtakāryakaraṇasaṁghātopādhyavivekakṛtā hi bhrāntiḥ, hitāhitakaraṇādilakṣaṇaḥ saṁsāro na tu paramārthato'sti. SBS., ii. 1. 22.

[2] SB., Kaṭha Up., i. 2. 14. Anātmajñaviṣaya eva dharmādharmādilakṣaṇaḥ saṁsāro na brahmajñasya, dharmādharmādyanupapatteḥ. *Ibid.* i. 2. 19. SB., Muṇḍ. Up., i. 1. 2; i. 2. 12. SB., Māṇḍ. K., ii. 32.

[3] Parā ca paramātmavidyā, aparā ca dharmādharmasādhanatatphalaviṣayā. SB., Muṇḍ. Up., i. 1. 4.

[4] SBG., xviii. 15.

[5] SBS., i. 1. 2.

[6] SBS., ii. 3. 43.

[7] SBS., i. 1. 4.

[8] SBS., i. 1. 2.

They are under moral obligation to abide by them. Dharma is characterized by moral impulsion (codanā). It impels the jīvas to carry it out.[1] Dharma relates to acts. It ought to be done. Adharma ought to be avoided.[2] Dharma is an imperative (vidhi). It depends upon the activity of a person. It is an Ought. It is not an existent fact. It does not exist at the time of knowing it. It is brought into existence by a person's activity.[3] Moral Law or duty (vidhi) is different from knowledge. It depends on a person's activity. But knowledge depends on an existent fact. It represents an object as it really is. It does not depend on a person's activity. Knowledge of truth of an object does not depend upon a person's intellect. It depends upon the existent object. The object is not a creation of knowledge. Knowledge is determined by the object.[4] Śaṁkara rejects subjective idealism, and advocates empirical realism.

Brahman is absolute existence. It is an accomplished fact (pariniṣṭhita vastu).[5] It is not an Ought which can be realized by voluntary action.[6] There can be no imperative (vidhi) about it, since imperative relates to actions. Brahman is the Absolute Truth which can be known only. It is the Absolute Good. Immediate experience of Brahman is the highest good. It destroys avidyā and all afflictions, which obscure the knowledge of Brahman.[7] Direct experience of Brahman does not depend upon a command (niyoga). It depends upon instructions which annul avidyā. The jīva cannot be under moral obligation (niyoga), since it will be destroyed by the knowledge of Brahman. It appears to be different from Brahman, but really is non-different from it. The scripture dispels its avidyā, and induces knowledge of its intrinsic Brahmanhood. Brahman is indeterminate and inactive. It is the eternally realized absolute Good. It cannot be under moral obligation. So there is no niyoga because there is no agent under moral obligation. Knowledge of Brahman cannot be achieved by Moral Law (niyoga). Knowledge is determined by its object. It is not determined by activity. The scriptural texts pertaining to

---

[1] SBS., i. 1. 1.
[2] SBS., i. 3. 30.
[3] Bhavyaś ca dharmo na jñānakāle asti, puruṣavyāpāratnatratvāt. SBS., i. 1. 1.
[4] SBS., i. 1. 2.
[5] SBS., i. 1. 3.
[6] SBS., iii. 2. 20.
[7] SBS., i. 1. 2.

Brahman are not commands to be executed. They are instructions conveying the knowledge of Brahman.[1]

Vidyāraṇya also shows the ontological unreality of niyoga. It is a moral command. It is an obligation imposed by a superior person on an inferior person. The Vedas are impersonal (apauruṣeya), and cannot therefore impose moral obligation on persons. If the niyoga itself be said to reside in the object that ought to be done and oblige a person to execute it, then the object of the moral act (kārya) is either related to volition (kṛtisaṁsṛṣta), or capable of being accomplished by volition (kṛtiyogya), or extraordinary (alaukika), different from actor, act, and fruition, though capable of being accomplished by volition. The first alternative is not possible. Volition is activity of an empirical self. The object of activity (kārya) is caused by activity. Therefore, the object related to activity cannot be the cause of activity. Volition abides in the empirical self. What abides in the agent cannot impel it to act. The second alternative also is not tenable. An undesirable object also is capable of being accomplished by voluntary action. But it does not oblige a person to achieve it. The third alternative also is not possible. An extraordinary object is unknowable, indescribable, and inexplicable. It cannot be established by the scripture. A desirable object (iṣṭasādhana) capable of being aocomplished obliges a person to act. Vidyāraṇya admits that an object which is a means to the good (iṣṭasādhana) and capable of being accomplished (kṛtiyogya) is an object of moral obligation (kārya). The same object is an object of moral duty because it ought to be brought about by a voluntary action and it is a means to the good because it fulfils a rational desire. Even a future object can be known to be a means to fulfilment of a rational desire just as a past object, food or drink, is known to be a means to fulfilment of a desire. So a vidhi is not a command (niyoga). It is capable of being accomplished and a means to the good.[2] Even a vidhi, in this sense, is not possible in the Vedānta. It dispels avidyā and manifests intrinsic freedom of the individual self. Knowledge of identity of the Ātman with

[1] Avagatiniṣṭhānyeva brahmavākyāni na niyoganiṣṭhāni. SBS., iii. 2. 20.

[2] Kṛtiyogyeṣṭasādhanam eva vidhyartho na tu niyogaḥ. VPS., p. 238.

Brahman is the means of realization of freedom. The Vedānta is a means to the knowledge of Identity. The Ātman or Brahman transcends the distinction between means and ends.[1]

The Moral Laws (vidhi) are commands of Īśvara, which are communicated to men through the Vedas. But they are empirical and relative, and not true in an absolute sense. They are transcended by the realization of Identity. The moral codes are known as commands of God on the plane of empirical knowledge. But with the dawn of Identity consciousness, they are known as stepping stones to its realization. The Moral Laws are an appearance of the eternal consciousness (cidābhāsa). Morality is transcended in spiritual realization, though it is its indispensable precondition. Identity consciousness or mystic vision of Brahman is the highest consummation of morality.[2]

Śaṁkara maintains that avidyā is the root of all desires (kāma) for enjoyment. Desires are manifold. They are the springs of actions (karma). Actions produce residual impressions (saṁskāra) or subconscious predispositions (vāsanā). They are imbedded in the subtle body which clings to the empirical self (jīva). They are carried over by it to the next life. Good innate predispositions are assets. Bad innate predispositions are liabilities. Some are born with an innate predisposition for unworldliness. They have natural aversion to the world fraught with misery. Others are born with an innate predisposition for worldly enjoyments. They have insatiable thirst for empirical pleasures.[3] But all desires, conscious and subconscious, native and acquired, can be counteracted and eradicated by free volitions.

Śaṃkara mentions three primal egoistic desires. They are desire for wife and sons, desire for wealth, and desire for happiness here and hereafter. They should be supplanted by desire for the knowledge of Brahman (brahmajijñāsā). Empirical desires for happiness are natural. But non-empirical desire for the knowledge of the Self or Absolute also is hidden in human nature. The former are prompted by avidyā. The latter is prompted by implicit vidyā. The former are due to man's finitude. The latter are due to his potential infinitude. The

---

[1] VPS., pp. 237-38.
[2] S. K. Maitra: *The Ethics of the Hindus*, pp. 329-30.
[3] SBG., iii. 33; xvii. 2; xviii. 41.

realization of infinitude and absoluteness is the appointed destiny of man.[1]

Mahādevānanda Sarasvatī gives the following division of the springs of action. Vāsanās are spontaneous, instinctive, unreflective desires. They are of two kinds, impure (aśuddha) and pure (śuddha). Impure desires are the cause of bondage. They produce birth and death. Pure desires are the cause of liberation. They destroy rebirth. Impure desires are threefold: (1) desire for bodily pleasures (dehavāsanā); (2) desire for popularity or social applause (lokavāsanā); and (3) desire for piety (śāstravāsanā). Desires for wife, sons, and objects for enjoyment are impure bodily pleasures. Desire for popularity also binds the jīva to the empirical world. Desire for piety is threefold: (1) passion for study of the scriptures (pāṭhavyasana); (2) passion for good (arthavyasana); and (3) passion for holy works (anuṣṭhānavyasana). They are impure because they do not completely destroy avidyā. Boastfulness (dambha), pride (darpa), self-conceit (abhimāna), anger (krodha), harshness (pāruṣya), and ignorance (ajñāna) are impure mental desires (mānasa vāsanā). Sympathy for the happiness of others (maitrī), compassion for the misery of others (karuṇā), rejoicing at the holiness of virtuous persons (muditā), and indifference to the wickedness of vicious persons (upekṣā) are pure desires. Impure mental desires are counteracted by pure mental desires. Vices are counteracted by practice of the opposite virtues (pratipakṣabhāvanā). The Advaita Vedānta agrees with Buddhism, Jainism, and the Yoga in this respect. Impure desires are counteracted by cultivation of virtues and pure desires, discrimative knowledge of their impurity, company of the holy, and renunciation. Attachment, aversion, envy, pride, intolerance, and other vices are conquered by universal friendliness, compassion, cheerfulness, and indifference. The afflictions are attenuated by the knowledge of the unreality of the empirical objects separate from the Ātman. Impure desires are eradicated by practice of knowledge of the Ātman (bodhābhāsa). Desires relating to consciousness (cinmātravāsanā) are either desires relating to pure consciousness limited by the agent, object, and internal organs, or desires relating to pure consciousness un-

---

[1] SBS., i. 1. 1; ii. 1. 14. Sarvapravṛttīnāṁ ātmāvagatyavasānārthatvāt.

limited by the adjuncts. The former are replaced by the latter. Impure desires are destroyed by these pure desires. Eradication of impure desires is aided by conscious trance (samprajñāta samādhi) and superconscious trance (asamprajñāta samādhi). Conscious trance is aided by restraints (yama), observances (niyama), bodily postures (āsana), breath-control (prāṇāyāma), withdrawal of the senses from their objects (pratyāhāra), which are external aids, and fixation of mind (dhāraṇā), meditation (dhyāna), and trance (samādhi), which are internal aids. Non-killing or non-injury (ahiṁsā), truthfulness (satya), non-stealing (asteya), celibacy (brahmacarya), and non-covetousness or non-possession (aparigraha) are the restraints. Bodily and mental purity (śauca), contentment (santoṣa), austerities (tapas), study of the scriptures (svādhyāya), and devotion to God are the observances. Superconscious trance is aided by supreme detachment (paravairāgya) and devotion to God (īśvarapraṇidhāna) or recitation of His symbol (*Om*). Practice of the trance makes the mind extremely subtle. Immediate experience of Absoluteness (brahmatvasākṣātkāra) of the self is achieved through the subtle mind. The pure witness consciousness (sākṣin) is reflected in the subtle mind, and directly experienced. Thus the Advaita Vedānta presses the eightfold Yoga practice into its service.[1]

Śaṁkara believes in relative freedom of the will. The question of determination or freedom of the self is irrelevant. The Ātman is willless and inactive (niṣkriya) in its essential nature. It is devoid of will and activity. They belong to the empirical self (jīva). Egoism (ahaṁkāra) is an adjunct of it. Activity is a function of egoism. It is determined by the law of causation. The will of egoism is determined by natural impulses, sattva, rajas, and tamas, and passions of attachment, aversion, and delusion springing from them. Pleasure is a quality of sattva. Pain is a quality of rajas. Delusion is a quality of tamas. Man naturally seeks pleasure and shuns pain driven by natural impulses. He has natural attachment to pleasure and aversion to pain. This is psychical determination or empirical necessity. But the natural impulses and desires are counteracted by reason (buddhi) according to the moral laws or injunctions and prohibitions of the scriptures, which are commands of God. Reason

[1] *Advaitacintākaustubha* and *Tattvānusandhānavyākhyāna*, B. I., pp. 366-403.

can suppress all natural desires (svābhāvikapravṛttinirodha). It can turn the mind away from external objects of enjoyment, and concentrate it on the inner Self (pratyagātman). It can introvert the naturally extroverted mind. It can regulate natural impure desires, and supplant them by pure rational desires. This is moral freedom of the will or its rational determination. It is empirical freedom of the will. The Śāstras convey the knowledge of right and wrong. But they do not coerce a person to do what is right and refrain from doing what is wrong. "Man is not a thing to be passively moulded and shaped from outside. He may be persuaded from the inner side. Man chooses his end according to his own light. The Śāstras only present before him the lower and higher lines of conduct, but do not compel him to select a particular course of action[1]." They do not mould a person from without into accord with the Moral Law. He has freedom of choice. The scriptural injunctions and prohibitions present to him different courses of action. He is free to choose any of them according to his light. They do not determine his choice which is free.[2] When a person controls attachment and aversion by reason according to the moral codes laid down by the Śāstras, he is free from subjection to unregenerate nature.[3] Freedom of the will is rational determination of it according to the Moral Law, as distinguished from its psychical determination by natural impulses and desires. This is empirical freedom. A person should transcend it, and realize noumenal freedom of the spirit. He should rise above empirical determination by reason (buddhi), and realize the transcendental freedom of Being. The Ātman is autonomous and free. It is absolutely free from empirical determination. The empirical reality is governed by the law of causation. But the ontological reality, the Ātman, the infinite and eternal Spirit, is absolutely free. "Man's freedom is not essentially the freedom of will,

---

[1] Jñāpakaṁ hi śāstraṁ, na kārakam. Na tu śāstraṁ bhṛtyān iva balāt nivārtayati niyojayati vā. Puruṣāḥ svayam eva yathāruci sādhanaviśeṣeṣu pravartante. Yasya yathāvabhāsa sa tathārūpam puruṣarthaṁ paśyati, tadanurūpāṇi sādhanāni upāditsate. SB., Bṛ. Up., ii. 1. 20. *An Introduction to Advaita Philosophy*, p. 155. Cp. *Indian Philosophy*, Vol. II, p. 618.

[2] Puruṣasya vidhiniṣedhādhīnapravṛttinivṛttyor api svātantryam. *Bhāmatī*. SBS., i. 1. 2.

[3] Yada punā rāgadveṣau tatpratipakṣeṇa niyamayati tadā śāstradṛṣṭir eva puruṣo bhavati na prakṛtivaśaḥ. SBG., iii. 34.

far less of action, but it is the freedom of Being[1]." Real freedom is true knowledge. It is extinction of avidyā and desires. It is the mystic vision of the Ātman as absolute being, consciousness, and bliss. This is transcendental freedom (svārājya).

Man is the architect of his own destiny. His free actions in conformity with, or in violation of, the Vedic injunctions produce karmas or merits and demerits. Accumulated (sañcita) karmas of past births and those acquired by free actions in the present birth (kriyamāṇa) are consumed by freely acquired integral experience. Only karmas of past births, which have begun to bear fruits, are worn off by enjoyments and sufferings in this life. Man forges the fetters of karmas by his free actions. He breaks them also by his free actions. He can do and undo them. He freely binds himself to saṁsāra by thraldom to avidyā and natural impulses, desires, and actions (avidyā-kāma-karma). He freely achieves liberation by counteracting them by rational desires, cultivating altrustic virtues, transcending virtue (dharma) and vice (adharma), and acquiring integral experience of the Ātman. God awards fruits of actions to men in accordance with their karmas. If He did so independently of them, human free exertions (puruṣakāra) would be unavailing.[2]

34. *Religion*

Religion is a means to self-realization. It is relative and empirical. It involves false knowledge of duality of God and the worshipper. Pure, non-dual Self or the Absolute is the ontological reality. All differences of the worshipped and the worshipper are false.[3] Brahman is indeterminate and unqualified. But it appears to be personal God with attributes owing to the adjunct (upādhi) of Māyā. Identity is the ontological truth. Difference of God and the finite self is empirical.[4] Identity of Brahman (brahmaikyasvabhāvatā) underlies the

[1] *The System of Vedantic Thought and Culture*, p. 268.

[2] SBS., ii. 1. 34. Niravayavam aparatantram ātmatattvam. SBG., xviii. 17. SBG., ii. 51, 59, 64, 71, 72; iii. 34, 43; v. 7, 28; vi. 1, 5, 6. *The System of Vedantic Thought and Culture*, pp. 265-72. *Introduction to Advaita Philosophy*, pp. 131-41.

[3] Upāsyopāsanādibhedajātaṁ sarvaṁ vitathaṁ, kevalaścātmā advayaḥ paramārthaḥ. SB., Māṇḍ. K., iii. 1.

[4] Bhedasya upāsanārthatvāt abhede tātparyāt. SBS., iii. 2. 12.

empirical difference between the jīva and the Lord.[1] Brahman is formless. But it appears to have different forms due to avidyā.[2] Its forms are not real. They are empirical and intended for prayer (upāsanā) of the worshippers, who have not attained integral experience of indeterminate Brahman.[3] One unqualified Brahman is worshipped (upāsya). But different qualities are attributed to indeterminate Brahman by the worshippers. But they do not really exist in it. It is undifferenced and unqualified.[4] The Lord and the jīva ruled by Him are empirical realities. They have validity in empirical life only.[5] Brahman is an accomplished fact. It is not an object of imperative which relates to actions.[6] Worship is an activity. It involves the duality of act and object of activity. But Brahman is non-dual. So it cannot be an object of the act of worship.[7] Nirguṇa Brahman is the only reality. But it is conceived to be saguṇa for the sake of worship. It appears to be endowed with qualities through the limiting adjuncts of names and forms.[8] Brahman is devoid of difference and qualities. So it does not admit of increase or decrease of qualities. Different qualities are attributed to it by finite individuals for the sake of prayer and worship to suit their different temperaments.[9]

Different kinds of worship are mentioned in the Upaniṣads. They all are means of the intuition of Brahman.[10] Each worshipper should select one mode of worship according to his temperament, which will lead him to experience of the Deity (upāsyaviṣayasākṣātkaraṇa). No other mode of worship is necessary for him. He should not combine all the different modes of worship, which will end in confusion. The worshipper experiences his identity with the Deity. He is mentally trans-

---

[1] SBS., iii. 2. 13.

[2] Upādhikṛtatvāt ākārabhedasya. SBS., iii. 2. 12.

[3] Ākāravadbrahmaviṣayāṇi vākyāni upāsanāvidhipradhānāni. Anākāram eva brahma. SBS., iii. 2. 14.

[4] Upāsyaikatve'pi upāsanabhede dharmavyavasthā ca bhavati. SBS., iii. 3. 12.

[5] Vyavahārāvasthāyām śrutau api īśvarādivyavahāraḥ. SBS., ii. 1. 14.

[6] SBS., i. 1. 3.

[7] Na ca pariniṣṭhitavastusvarūpe vidhiḥ sambhavati kriyāviṣayatvāt vidheḥ. SBS., i. 1. 3. Na tu brahmaṇaḥ upāsanāvidhiśeṣatvam sambhavati. SBS., i. 1. 4.

[8] SBS., i. 2. 14.

[9] SBS., iii. 3. 12.

[10] SBS., iii. 3. 5.

formed into Him (tadbhāvabhāvita). He possesses Him, and is possessed by Him. Distinction between him and the Deity vanishes. Communion ends in identity. Religious identity culminates in integral experience of infinite and impersonal Brahman.[1] Worship of personal God contains the consciousness of 'I' as the agent of worship.[2] But it vanishes in integral experience of indeterminate Brahman. It can be attained by prayer (saṁrādhana), which consists in devotion, meditation, and worship.[3]

Religious consciousness of God is transcended by philosophical consciousness of the Absolute. Religion is empirical, relative and dualistic. It involves avidyā. But it leads to mystic experience of Identity, in which all distinction and relativity are extinguished. Religion is a means of spiritual realization like morality. Morality consists in the performance of duties, cultivation of virtues, and purification of the mind. But religion consists in prayer, meditation, and worship of God with devotion. Religion implies morality. But both are relative and empirical, which are transcended by integral experience or all-selfness.

Śaṁkara believes in the grace of God. Devotion to him brings his grace.[4] But it does not lead to liberation. It aids the production of higher knowledge (vidyā), which directly leads to release. Man has to work out his own salvation. Nothing but his true insight can bring about his release. Grace implies the reality of God and the jīva. Both are mere appearances. They are not metaphysically real. So prayer and grace of God have no ultimate significance. Worship of personal God leads to attainment of heaven and gradual release (kramamukti). But integral experience leads to embodied release here and now (sadyomukti).[5]

Śaṁkara believed in Vedic gods, and regarded them as personifications of natural forces. They are spiritual beings endowed with ruling power. They are presiding agents of different functions of life. Agni is the presiding deity of speech; Vāya, of breath ; Āditya, of eye. They simply aid these life functions. The supreme Lord creates gods, men, and lower

[1] SBS., iii. 3. 59.
[2] SBS., iv. 1. 16.
[3] SBS., iii. 2. 24.
[4] SBS., iii. 2. 5.
[5] SBS., i. 1. 11.

animals according to their merits and demerits. Gods enjoy relative immortality in heaven. They are born again when their merits are exhausted. They acquire the saving knowledge and achieve their liberation. Their sovereignty depends on God. They occupy certain ranks, and are species rather than individuals.[1] They are superior to men, but not equal to the Lord. Godhood (Devatva) in heaven, or even Divinity or Lordship (īśvaratva) is not the highest Good. Brahmanhood is the *summum bonum* of life.

35. *Criticism of Śaṁkara*

Śaṁkara's non-dualism (advaitavāda) or absolutism is severely criticized by Rāmānuja, Madhva, Vallabha, Nimbārka and others who are advocates of theistic Vaiṣṇava Vedānta. Śaṁkara's indeterminate and unqualified Brahman and indefinable Māyā, the individuating principle, are the targets of criticism. The relation of Brahman to Māyā is the crux of his philosophy. But Śaṁkara dismisses it lightly as an illegitimate question (atipraśna). Māyā is not real. Brahman alone is real. So the question of the relation of Brahman to Māyā does not arise. He relegates Īśvara, jīvas, and the world to the realm of appearances. Īśvara is Brahman conditioned by cosmic nescience (māyā) with pure sattva. A jīva is Brahman conditioned by the mind-body-complex generated by impure individual nescience (avidyā). The world is an appearance (prapañca), which is not illusory but empirically real. Śaṁkara refutes mentalism or subjective idealism. He recognizes degrees of empirical reality in which knowledge and bliss of Brahman are manifested in different degrees owing to different degrees of avidyā. He regards the jīvas and the world as non-different from Brahman. The world is a modification (pariṇāma) of Māyā composed of sattva, rajas and tamas. But it is an appearance (vivarta) of Brahman. Īśvara is the material cause and the efficient cause of the world. He is its Creator, Preserver, and Destroyer. He is the Moral Governor. He adapts the material world to the individual selves according to their merits and demerits. He is the promulgator of the moral codes through the Vedas. He is the object of prayer and worship. He is the source of morality

[1] SV., pp. 66-68. Cp. *Indian Philosophy,* Vol. II, p. 651.

and religion. Leaving out Brahman, we can interrelate Īśvara, jīvas, and the world to one another. But they are only appearances. They are only empirical realities. Their ontological reality is Brahman, which is undifferenced and unqualified, absolute Being, Consciousness, and Bliss. It is supreme Brahman (para Brahman). God is subordinate Brahman (apara Brahman). Indeterminate Brahman appears to be determinate, qualified, personal God to the intellect which is infected with avidyā. Brahman is Absolute. God is relative. Śaṁkara sometimes speaks of Īśvara as identical with Brahman. Sometimes he clearly distinguishes them from each other. Brahman is the ontological reality of Īśvara. He has no reality distinct from that of Brahman. He is identical with Brahman in essential reality. But still Brahman is the ontological reality while Īśvara is an empirical reality. Brahman is conceived by intellect to be personal Īśvara for the sake of religious communion. The distinction between Brahman and Īśvara, the Absolute and God, is indefensible and irrational. If they are identified with each other, Śaṁkara's absolutism becomes rational and acceptable. If Īśvara be regarded as an empirical appearance of Brahman due to its adjunct, māyā, cosmic nescience, His rôle as a Creator, Preserver, and Destroyer of the world, and Moral Governor of the jīvas and the world becomes a magic play devoid of real worth and meaning. Brahman, the unqualified and indeterminate Absolute, one without difference, is not an adequate explanation of the world of multiplicity. One and many are related to each other. But one alone is real according to Śaṁkara. Many are mere appearances, though not illusions. Many cannot be derived from One. Māyā is the individuating principle. The Absolute appears to be manifold jīvas and world-appearance through its limiting adjunct, māyā. Brahman is one, universal, eternal, undifferenced consciousness. Māyā is cosmic nescience, which hides Brahman and projects the appearance of multiplicity. Śaṁkara assumes that One cannot be many, and posits an indefinable, inexplicable, mysterious principle, māya, between One and many. Brahman is Knowledge. Māyā is ignorance. How did ignorance arise from Absolute Knowledge? Māyā is the power of Īśvara. It depends on Him. It is not independent of Him. But Īśvara is a mere appearance of Brahman. How can māyā be power of an appearance, which explains the multiplicity of the jīvas and the world-appearance? Māyā is avidyā. It is nescience. Is it subjective or objective? Does it abide in consciousness or outside consciousness? Brahman is the only ontological reality. It is Absolute Consciousness. Its Being is Consciousness. Nescience cannot exist in it. There is no reality outside Brahman. So necience cannot exist outside Absolute Consciousness. Even if it springs mysteriously, it cannot hide the nature of Brahman, which is perfect, and project the plurality of appearances. Māyā is a mysterious principle in Brahman, which explains plurality. The legitimate conclusion of Śaṁkara's philosophy is that Brahman contains within itself the principle and explanation of plurality, that it is not an undifferentiated unity. Nescience cannot subsist in Īśvara or jīvas because they are appearances due to limitation of Brahman by nescience. If nescience abides in jīvas only, Īśvara, jīvas, and the world become subjective creations of the jīvas. Śaṁkara's absolutism becomes subjectivism or mentalism, which he severely condemns. Śaṁkara's doctrine is elusive because he recognizes the empirical reality of Īśvara, jīvas, and the world for practical purposes of life, but he dismisses them as unreal appearances when philosophical wisdom (vidyā) dawns. All appearances vanish in the dazzling light of integral experience. They are real to the intellect only, infected with avidyā, which views the reality through the finite categories of time, space, and causality. Intellect gives relative knowledge. Intuition gives absolute knowledge. Intellect gives dualistic and pluralistic knowledge. Intuition gives monistic and mystic vision. Intellect is transcended by intuition. It is subordinate to intuition. Śaṁkara is wrong in holding that intellect falsifies reality, which is grasped by intuition only. Intellect gives duality, plurality, and distinctions which are unreal. Intuition gives non-dual, non-plural, distinctionless One. He opposes intuition to intellect as radically different from each other. But really vague intuition precedes and sustains intellect, and intellect finally leads to perfect intuition, which transfigures and transforms multiplicity into aspects of Unity. Intuition views the multiplicity of finite selves and finite objects as rooted in Brahman. They are real. They are not appearances. They are manifestations of Brahman. The world is an expression of Brahman. The jīvas are members of Brahman. The world and the jīvas are inseparable from each other as the known objects and the knowing subjects. They are also inseparable from Brahman from which they derive their reality. The jīvas and the world are inseparable from Brahman, which is identity-in-difference. Brahman is Īśvara. It is determinate and qualified. Īśvara is identical with Brahman. He is the ground of morality. He is morally perfect and holy. He is the Deity to be worshipped. He is the consummation of religious aspiration. Morality and religion are real and ultimate. They are not empirical. Śaṁkara does not discard morality and religion, but he degrades them to a lower plane of avidyā. But morality is real and absolute and grounded in God. Religion also is a real aspiration of the finite self to be in eternal communion with God. Integral experience does not annul the jīvas and the world, but bathes them in the flood of Divine Radiance. Śaṁkara's indeterminate Brahman is neither philosophically satisfactory nor adequate to moral needs and religious aspirations.

CHAPTER VIII

THE BACK-GROUND OF THE THEISTIC VEDĀNTA

1. *The Philosophy of the Bhagavadgītā*

The *Bhagavadgītā* is a part of the *Mahābhārata*. It is attributed to Vyāsa. It is regarded as one of the most sacred books of the Hindus. It has exerted profound influence on their minds. Śaṁkara, Ānandagiri, Madhusūdana Sarasvatī, Rāmānuja, Madhva, Śrīdhara, and others wrote commentaries on it. Bāl Gaṅgādhara Tilak's *Gītārahasya,* Mahatma Gandhi's *Anāsaktiyogo,* and Sri Aurabinda's *Essays on the Gītā* are contemporary works on the *Gītā*. Dr. S. N. Das Gupta opines that the *Bhagavadgītā* is the earliest work on the Bhāgavata school written long before the composition of the *Mahābhārata,* which was incorporated into it during one of its revisions.[1] Otto separates the original *Gītā* from the *Bhagavad Gītā*.[2] There is no doubt that it was written before the Sūtras of the different systems of philosophy were composed and after the earlier Upaniṣads were composed. It was probably written about 500 B.C. The philosophy of the *Bhagavadgītā* is a type of theism which combines the Absolutism of the Upaniṣads with the Sāṁkhya dualism of prakṛti and puruṣas, which prevailed before the *Sāṁkhyakārikā* was written by Īśvarakṛṣṇa. Its theistic idealism is similar to that of the *Śvetāśvatara Upaniṣad.* It is difficult to make out a consistent philosophical system from the texts. Some concepts have not been systemically connected with one another. They have been mentioned incidentally in giving an exposition of ethics. The *Gītā* is more a book on ethics than one on metaphysics. Even as a treatise on ethics it is not a compact philosophical work. It is an inspired poetical work with a philosophical theme. It is rightly called the *Song Divine*.

(1) *Ontology.*—The *Gītā* teaches theism, and regards Īśvara as the supreme reality. Īśvara is higher than Brahman.

---

[1] HIP., Vol. II, pp. 548, 552.

[2] *The Original Gītā,* Ch. I.

God is the foundation of the immortal, infinite Absolute. He is the ground of the eternal moral order. He is the fountain of eternal bliss.[1] He is the Supreme Reality. He is unequalled and unexcelled.[2] He is infinite, eternal, and immutable.[3] He is unborn and immortal.[4] He is omnipresent, omniscient, and omnipotent.[5] He knows the past, the present, and the future.[6] He is ancient and without beginning, middle, and end.[7] He is the First Cause. He is the ultimate ground of the universe. He is the upholder of the eternal moral order.[8] He is holy.[9] He is the creator, preserver, and destroyer of the universe.[10] He is the infinite seed of all creatures.[11] He is their Lord.[12] He is their Moral Governor.[13] He is father, mother, friend, witness, preceptor, master, and refuge of all beings.[14] He is the Supreme Being. There is no other higher Being.[15] He is one in many.[16] He is existent and non-existent. He is death and deathlessness.[17] He is transcendental existence. He is empirical existence. He is immutable Being. He is mutation and becoming.[18] He is beautiful and terrific. He is the destructive Time-Spirit.[19] Īśvara is the Supreme Person. This is theism. Vāsudeva is Īśvara.[20] His manifestations (vyūha) are not mentioned.

God is the supreme Brahman (para brahma), which is unborn and eternal, neither existent nor non-existent. It is not existent as an empirical being, nor non-existent as a transcendental reality.[21] It pervades the world, but is not exhausted in it. It is immanent in it, and transcends it.[22] It is trans-empirical and devoid of sattva, rajas, and tamas (nirguṇa). It is conscious of the empirical world composed of the guṇas (guṇabhoktṛ). It is detached (asakta) and sustains the relative world. It is devoid of all external and internal sense-organs. Still it

---

[1] Brahmaṇo hi pratiṣṭhāham amṛtasyāvyayasya ca. Śāśvatasya ca dharmasya sukhasyaikāntikasya ca. BG., xiv. 27.

[2] BG., xi. 43.

[3] BG., iv. 6; x. 12; xi. 18.

[4] BG., iv. 6; xiii. 27.

[5] BG., x. 12; vii. 6, 26; xiii. 13; xi. 40, 43.

[6] BG., vii. 26.

[7] BG., iv. 31; xi. 18, 19, 38.

[8] Śāśvatadharmagoptā. BG., xi. 18.

[9] BG., x. 12.

[10] BG., ix. 18; x. 8; xiii. 16.

[11] BG., ix. 18; x. 39.

[12] BG., iv. 6; ix. 11; x. 15.

[13] BG., ix. 17; x. 33.

[14] BG., ix. 17, 18; xi. 43, 44.

[15] BG., vii. 7.

[16] BG., ix. 15.

[17] BG., ix. 19.

[18] BG., ix. 19.

[19] BG., ix. 10, 11, 23-32.

[20] BG., vii. 19.

[21] BG., xiii. 12.

[22] BG., xiii. 13.

knows all sensible and intelligible objects.[1] Brahman is moving and unmoving, remote and near, inside and outside the creatures.[2] It is non-spatial, and yet extended in space. It is the immobile Spirit and the moving universe. It is transcendent and immanent. It is subtle and unknowable by the senses, mind, and intellect.[3] It is the supreme light of lights. It illumines all objects. It is the indwelling Spirit in the hearts of all beings.[4] Brahman is the impersonal Absolute. It is an aspect of the Supreme Person or God. It is not equal to Īśvara, the ultimate Reality.

The *Gītā* lays stress on the immanence of God in the universe in some verses. He is the indwelling Spirit in all creatures. He is their origin, middle, and end. He is the best of all things, beings, and qualities.[5] He is the source of good and evil. He is the gambling of the dice of fraudulent gamblers. He is the heroism of the heroes. He is the victory of the victorious, determination of the resolute, and moral qualities of all moral men.[6] He is the knower and the known.[7]

But the *Gītā* does not teach pantheism. It teaches panentheism. God is not the world. The world is not God. But the world exists in God. All creatures exist in Him. He pervades them all as their inner guide.[8] He is the eternal and imperishable essence abiding in perishing creatures.[9] He is the immanent essence in all finite things and spirits as a thread running through beads.[10] He is the life of all creatures. He is their seed.[11] All creatures exist in Him. But He is not identical with them. He pervades the universe by His unmanifest form (avyakta-mūrti). He is the invisible Spirit in the visible world.[12] He is not affected by empirical objects and selves. He transcends the empirical objects and finite spirits entangled in them. He is the creator, sustainer, and destroyer of all creatures. They issue from Him, are maintained by Him, and reabsorbed in Him.[13] He supports the entire universe by pervading it with His single fragment.[14] He is incorporeal, partless, undivided,

---

[1] BG., xiii. 13.
[2] BG., xiii. 15.
[3] BG., xiii. 15.
[4] BG., xiii. 17, 33; xv. 6, 12.
[5] BG., x. 20-40; xv. 13-15.
[6] BG., x. 36.
[7] BG., xi. 38.
[8] BG., vi. 31; ix. 6; viii. 22.
[9] BG., viii. 20.
[10] BG., vii. 7.
[11] BG., vii. 9-10.
[12] BG., ix. 4.
[13] BG., ix. 5-7, 18.
[14] BG., x. 42.

infinite Spirit. The entire universe is a manifestation of a single fraction of Him. He transcends it to infinite Beyond, and exists in immeasurable perfection. He is immanent in the universe. He is transcendent to it.[1] This is panentheism.

There are two puruṣas in the universe, the perishable (kṣara) Puruṣa and the imperishable (akṣara) Puruṣa. All created things and beings constitute the Kṣara Puruṣa. The immutable Puruṣa underlying them is the Akṣara Puruṣa.[2] Śaṁkara regards the Kṣara Puruṣa as the totality of the mutable universe, and the Akṣara Puruṣa as Īśvara's power of māyā.[3] It is the creative matrix of the entire world of mutable phenomena. Madhusūdana also holds the same view. Rāmānuja regards the Kṣara Puruṣa as the totality of bound finite spirits connected with unconscious matter or embodied in organisms, and the Akṣara Puruṣa as the totality of disembodied liberated puruṣas dissociated from unconscious matter.[4] Śrīdhara regards the Kṣara Puruṣa as the totality of mutable bodies of created beings, and the Akṣara Puruṣa as the conscious experiencer of the entire universe of mutable phenomena, which is an immutable and imperishable Spirit. He also suggests that the Akṣara Puruṣa is the totality of conscious finite spirits (cetanavarga), and that the Kṣara Puruṣa is the totality of unconscious material objects (jaḍavarga).[5] Sri Aurabinda regards the Kṣara Puruṣa as the universal soul immanent in the mutable cosmic phenomena, and the Akṣara Puruṣa as the immutable and transcendent Spirit.[6] The Akṣara Puruṣa is the eternal, inactive, immobile, and immutable self of all, yet unmoved and indifferent. It is timeless in time, spaceless in space, and non-causal in producing effects. The Kṣara Puruṣa is the dynamic, active, mutable, immanent, universal Soul of the world. The Akṣara Puruṣa is the transcendent, inactive, immutable Self of all, from which proceeds mutation of things. The Kṣara Puruṣa corresponds to the Kṣara Brahman, and the Akṣara Puruṣa, to the Akṣara Brahman of the Upaniṣads.[7]

---

[1] BG., x. 20; xi. 38, 41; vii. 7; xv. 1, 2, 3, 13, 15.
[2] BG., xv. 16.
[3] Bhagavato māyāśaktiḥ. SBG., xv. 6.
[4] RBG., xv. 6.
[5] Commentary on BG., xv. 16, 18.
[6] *Essays on the Gītā*, Second Series, p. 219.
[7] Kaṭha Up., i. 2. 16.

The Puruṣottama, Supreme Person, transcends the totality of mutable or empirical selves and the perishing material objects. He transcends the entire mutable universe and the immutable and imperishable Self of the world. He transcends the active, dynamic universal Soul of nature, and its eternal, immutable, static, inactive, immobile Self, and integrates them together in his supreme unity. He is immobile in his mobility, inactive and indifferent in his activity, and immutable in his mutation and becoming. He is infinite. He inspires and informs the three worlds, and sustains and maintains them. He transcends the Kṣara Puruṣa and the Akṣara Puruṣa. He is the supreme, infinite Person.[1] The Kṣara Puruṣa is the Soul immanent in the universe. The Akṣara Puruṣa is transcendent to it. It is indefinable, inconceivable, immutable, immobile, eternal, and unmanifest (avyakta). This is the transcendent Self of the universe.[2] The Puruṣottama is superior to both the immanent Soul and the transcendent Self, the mutable and the immutable. The Divine Person is higher than the Absolute. This is theism.

The *Gītā* anticipates the Sāṁkhya doctrine of Satkāryavāda. It teaches that there is neither production of the non-existent nor destruction of the existent.[3] It believes in prakṛti and puruṣas or individual souls like the Sāṁkhya. Prakṛti and puruṣas are eternal.[4] But it believes in parā prakṛti and aparā prakṛti. The former is superior. The latter is inferior. Parā prakṛti is the source of conscious spirits. Aparā prakṛti is the source of the material world, living organisms, sense-organs, manas, buddhi, and ahaṁkāra. Sattva, rajas, and tamas are products of prakṛti. They are not constituents of prakṛti as the Sāṁkhya maintains. The *Gītā* regards Prakṛti or Māyā as the power of Īśvara. But the Sāṁkhya does not believe in God. It regards prakṛti as an independent principle. It believes in the dualism of prakṛti and puruṣas. It advocates atheistic dualism. But the *Gītā* advocates theistic monism.

Prakṛti (mahad brahma) is the mother of the whole universe. Īśvara is the father, who fertilizes her, and produces the entire universe through her.[5] Prakṛti is Māyā. It is the power of

---

[1] BG., xv. 17, 18.
[2] BG., xii. 3; viii. 20, 21.
[3] BG., ii. 16.
[4] BG., xiii. 19.
[5] BG., xiv. 3, 4.

Īśvara. It is the Divine power inseparable from God.[1] Prakṛti supervised by God produces all animate and inanimate creatures.[2] They are re-absorbed in the Divine power or prakṛti in dissolution.[3] Prakṛti is unmanifest (avyakta). All manifest (vyakta) objects, inanimate and animate, spring from unmanifest prakṛti and dissolve in it.[4] Prakṛti is controlled by God, who creates all creatures through her.[5] It is the power of God. It is real. It is not indefinable (aniravacanīya) as Śaṁkara maintains. The world produced by God through his power or prakṛti is real. It is mutable and perishable. But it is not an unreal appearance. Theistic idealism of the *Gītā* recognizes the reality of the world, which is informed by the Divine Spirit.

Īśvara has parā (higher) prakṛti and aparā (lower) prakṛti. The former constitutes the universe of animate and sentient creatures (jīvabhūta). It is conscious prakṛti, which sustains the world of conscious living beings.[6] The latter is eightfold ; it is composed of the five elements of earth, water, fire, air, and ether, and the three internal organs of manas, buddhi, and ahaṁkāra.[7] The five subtle essences (tanmātra) and atoms are not mentioned. They were conceived later by the Sāṁkhya philosophy. The lower prakṛti comprises the physical and the psychical universe. It comprehends all objects of knowledge (kṣetra). The higher prakṛti comprises the knowing subjects (kṣetrajña).[8] Parā prakṛti is conscious. Aparā prakṛti is unconscious.

Sattva, rajas, and tamas are products of prakṛti. They are evidently products of aparā prakṛti. They delude the individual souls, and bind them to saṁsāra.[9] They bind the incorporeal souls to their corporeal bodies.[10] Sattva is pure, transparent, and free from trouble ; it manifests objects. It produces knowledge and pleasure in the finite souls, and binds them to the world through them.[11] Rajas is of the nature of attachment. It springs from desire and association. It produces action in the finite souls, and binds them to the world through action.[12]

---

[1] Daivī hyeṣā guṇamayī mama māyā duratyayā. BG., vii. 14.
[2] BG., ix. 10.
[3] BG., ix. 7.
[4] BG., viii. 18, 19.
[5] BG., ix. 8.
[6] BG., vii. 5.
[7] BG., vii. 4, 5.
[8] SBG., vii. 5, 6.
[9] BG., vii. 13.
[10] BG., xiv. 5.
[11] BG., xiv. 6
[12] BG., xiv. 7.

It is the cause of desire and anger.[1] Tamas springs from ignorance. It deludes all finite souls. It produces carelessness, laziness, and sleep in them, and binds them to the world.[2] Sattva attaches them to pleasure ; rajas, to action ; and tamas, to negligence.[3] The *Gītā* describes sattva, rajas, and tamas as the primordial elements in the psychical nature. It does not treat them as the primordial cosmic substances, as the Sāṁkhya does. Sometimes sattva overcomes rajas and tamas, and becomes predominant. Sometimes rajas and tamas also overcome the other two ; and become predominant.[4] Sattva is the cause of knowledge. Rajas is the cause of greed, desire for enjoyment, enterprise, action, and continuation of action.[5] An action prompted by sattva produces pure pleasure ; that prompted by rajas produces pain ; that prompted by tamas produces ignorance.[6] The guṇas constitute the internal organs, manas, buddhi, and ahaṁkāra. They move the individual selves to action. The universal self immanent in them is the indifferent spectator of these actions.[7] The prakṛti, which produces sattva, rajas, and tamas, seems to be identical with the aparā prakṛti which comprises manas, buddhi, and ahaṁkāra.

The *Gītā* divides the universe into the knowers (kṣetrajña) and the known objects (kṣetra). The kṣetra is the unconscious field of objects. It is known by the finite spirits. They are knowers of the field (kṣetrajña). They cannot be reduced to each other. Subjects and objects are irreducible elements of the reality. The *Gītā* advocates neither mentalism nor materialism. The kṣetra is the field of objects of knowledge. It comprises all mutable things, physical and psychical. It includes the unmanifest prakṛti, the five material elements, the ten sense-organs, mind (manas), intellect (buddhi), and egoism (ahaṁkara). It includes all sensible objects. It includes also desire and aversion, pleasure and pain, the organism, intelligence, and the power of endurance. All mental functions are included in the field of objects. They are unconscious objects of knowledge.[8] God is immanent in finite subjects and objects. He is the knower (vettṛ) and the known (vedya). He mani-

---

[1] BG., iii. 37.
[2] BG., xiv. 8.
[3] BG., xiv. 9.
[4] BG., xiv. 10.
[5] BG., xiv. 11-13, 17.
[6] BG., xiv. 16.
[7] BG., xiv. 19, 20, 23.
[8] BG., xiii. 1, 3, 5, 6.

fests all finite subjects and all finite objects even as the sun illumines the entire universe. Subjects and objects are not independent principles. They are real as intimately related to God.[1]

Prakṛti and puruṣa both are uncaused. Īśvara is eternal. So his twofold nature also is eternal. He is the creator, preserver, and destroyer of the universe through his twofold nature (prakṛti), subjective and objective.[2] Prakṛti is the material cause of all physical and psychical phenomena. It is the ground of all causes and effects. Puruṣa, the finite self, is the enjoyer of pleasure and pain. It is the experiencer of all physical and psychical objects.[3] It enjoys sattva, rajas, and tamas, the products of prakṛti through the psychophysical organism. Its attachment to the guṇas binds it to saṁsāra, and makes it transmigrate from one body to another.[4] This is the individual self. But there is the supreme Self (paramātman) immanent in it. It is the indifferent spectator, permitter, sustainer, and witness of all actions of the individual self.[5] The *Gītā* agrees with the Kaṭha Upaniṣad[6] that the individual self in the body is the enjoyer of fruits of actions, while the supreme Self is the witness of them. The former is the doer. The latter is the spectator. Actions are done by the individual self made of the guṇas. The pure self is not the doer.[7] It is the supreme self (paramātman). It is the eternal, infinite, trans-empirical (nirguṇa) self. It does not do any actions. It is not affected by them, because it transcends the guṇas.[8] It is not moved by them. They are the cause of actions. The guṇas constitute the empirical nature of the individual self. The universal self immanent in it transcends them.[9] It is the self of all creatures (sarvabhūtantarātmā). It is not active. It is not touched by actions of the individual self.[10] It neither acts nor apprehends objects. The sense-organs act on their proper objects.[11] Here it is suggested that the guṇas constitute the sensible objects and the sense-organs. They are not the natural psychical impulses only. Egoism (ahaṁkāra) is made of the guṇas. The self deter-

[1] BG., xi. 38; xiii. 2, 33.
[2] BG., SBG., xiii. 19.
[3] BG., xiii. 20.
[4] BG., xiii. 21.
[5] BG., xiii. 22.
[6] I. 3. 7.
[7] BG., xiii. 29.
[8] BG., xiii. 31.
[9] BG., xiv. 19, 20, 23.
[10] BG., v. 7.
[11] Guṇā guṇeṣu vartante. BG., SBG., iii. 28.

mined by egoism wrongly thinks itself to be a free doer.[1] Īśvara dwells in the hearts of all creatures. He moves them to action by his Māyā, and guides them as his instruments.[2] The individual soul (jīva) is an eternal part of God.[3] Śaṁkara explains it thus: The jīva is an apparent part of God. But it is evident from the text that it is a real eternal part of God. The *Gītā* says that prakṛti and puruṣa or the individual soul both are eternal.[4] God being eternal, his power, prakṛti, is eternal. The individual souls are eternal parts of God. They are eternal members of the Divine Spirit, the Infinite Person. The soul in the body is unborn, eternal, permanent, ancient, indestructible and immortal.[5] It is inexhaustible.[6] It is omnipresent, stable, immobile, incorporeal, unproduced, and indestructible.[7] It is incorruptible and immutable.[8] It is self-established.[9] It is unthinkable, insensible, and unmanifest.[10] The self is rational and sentient. The rational self can control, regulate, and conquer the sentient self.[11] The lower self should be delivered from saṁsāra by the higher self.[12] This implies freedom of the will. Every individual acts according to his psychical disposition (prakṛti) made of sattva, rajas, and tamas. His actions spring from his inner nature, and conform to it.[13] But he is not completely determined by his empirical nature. He has the power of counteracting his natural impulses and desires, and realizing his supra-organic, supra-mental, spiritual nature.[14] The severe ethical discipline enjoined by the *Gītā* implies human freedom. It appears to recognize empirical necessity and spiritual freedom of the human soul.

The *Gītā* lays stress on monism in some verses. God exists in all created existences undivided, but appears to be divided.[15] But pure monism is not the purport of the *Gītā*. The sāttvika knowledge is that of undivided God in divided existences.[16]

---

[1] Ahaṁkāravimūḍhātmā kartāham iti manyate. BG., iii. 27.
[2] BG., xviii. 61.
[3] Mamaivāṁśo jīvaloke jīvabhutaḥ sanātanaḥ. BG., xv. 7.
[4] BG., xiii. 19.
[5] BG., ii. 18, 20, 21.
[6] BG., ii. 21.
[7] BG., ii. 24.
[8] BG., ii. 25.
[9] SBG., ii. 18.
[10] BG., ii. 25.
[11] BG., vi. 6.
[12] BG., vi. 5.
[13] BG., iii. 33.
[14] BG., iii. 34; vi. 7.
[15] Avibhaktaṁ ca bhūteṣu vibhaktam iva ca sthitam. BG., xiii. 16.
[16] B.G., xviii. 20.

Both one and many are real. One is divided into many.[1] The finite souls are real. They are unborn and eternal. They exist in God. He exists in them. One exists in many. Many exist in one. One is not an aggregate of many. Many are not appearances of One. Both are inseparably related to each other.[2] God and the finite souls are co-eternal with each other. Affinity (sādharmya) with God is the highest consummation of man.[3] The individual soul is an eternal part of God.[4]

The *Gītā* teaches the doctrine of Divine Incarnation (avatāra). Though he is unborn, eternal, and infinite, he finitizes himself by his māyā, the principle of individuation, and assumes a human form. He creates himself a Man-God through his prakṛti.[5] Whenever there is triumph of unrighteousness and decline of righteousness, God incarnates in a human form.[6] He incarnates in different cycles for deliverance of the righteous and destruction of the unrighteous and establishment of a moral order.[7] He is perfect. He has no unfulfilled desires. He has no duties to perform. But he acts for the solidarity of mankind (lokasaṁgraha),—the moral upliftment of the unrighteous.[8] He is the Perfect Man. He is followed by all men in their conduct. He is the embodiment of moral perfection. He is their Moral Ideal completely realized.[9] He is consciously infinite in a finite form. He is the Divine in a human form. Men deluded by ignorance fail to know his divine nature (paraṁ bhāvam), and despise his human form, though he is the supreme Lord of all creatures.[10] They do not know his real nature because he is covered by his yogamāyā.[11] His divinity can be known only through his grace.[12] An Avatāra is the descent of God to man. He is not the ascent of man to God.

(2) *Ethics and Religion.*—The *Gītā* is not a book on metaphysics, but essentially one on ethics and religion. It lays down the different paths of realization of God. Its teaching is universal and intended for all persons of different temperaments. Some are predominantly men of action. They ought to follow the path of action (karmayoga). Some are predominantly

---

[1] BG., ix. 15.
[2] BG., xiv. 2.
[3] BG., vi. 29-31; ix. 4, 6, 29.
[4] BG., xv. 7.
[5] BG., iv. 6.
[6] BG., iv. 7.
[7] BG., iv. 8.
[8] BG., SBG., iii. 20-23.
[9] BG., iv. 11; iii. 2, 3.
[10] BG., ix. 11.
[11] BG., vii. 25.
[12] BG., xi. 47, 48.

emotional. They ought to follow the path of devotion (bhaktiyoga). Some are predominantly intellectual. They ought to follow the path of knowledge (jñānayoga).[1] Action, devotion, and knowledge lead to union (yoga) with God, the innermost essence of our being. God-realization or self-realization is the highest good. It is the supreme end of human life. No relative good can satisfy the aspirations of a finite soul, which is informed by the Divine Spirit. Morality is religion.

The *Gītā* uses the term *yoga* in the sense of union with God. It does not use it in the sense of complete suppression of mental functions like Patañjali.[2] It teaches the paths of union through works (karmayoga), knowledge (jñānayoga), and devotion (bhaktiyoga). Voluntary actions are due to five conditions, the active individual self or doer (kartṛ), the organism (adhiṣṭhāna), the sense-organs (karaṇa), various conscious efforts and bodily movements (ceṣṭā), and providence (daiva).[3] Śrīdhara maintains that though human effort is free, there is an unseen cosmic force or providence which guides the free human effort, moulds the action, and leads it to its fruit. The Divine Will, the inner controller, is the mover of the sense-organs.[4] Voluntary actions are either right or wrong. They are either bodily, verbal or mental. They are willed and purposive actions. They are due to the five conditions.[5] Śaṁkara maintains that non-voluntary actions are due to merits and demerits acquired in the previous births.[6] The individual self alone is not the sole cause of action. It is a knower and an active agent. God, the inner controller, guides it in its free actions. The human soul freely does right and wrong actions, for which they are responsible. If human actions were not free, rightness and wrongness would be meaningless. The activity of the free individual self depends upon the permission of God as a prior condition. This is the view of Rāmānuja.[7] Śaṁkara holds that the empirical self determined by egoism is the doer, but that the pure self is not the doer. It is incorporeal, indivisible, free (aparatantra), immutable, and inactive. It is the witness of the actions of the empirical self.[8]

---

[1] GB., iii. 3.
[2] YS., i. 1.
[3] BG., xviii. 14.
[4] Commentary on BG., xviii. 14.
[5] BG., xviii. 15.
[6] SBG., xviii. 15.
[7] RBG., xviii. 16, 17.
[8] SBG., xviii. 17.

Man cannot remain inactive for a single moment. He is compelled to do actions by sattva, rajas, and tamas, which are products of prakṛti.[1] They are primordial psychical impulses. Even the maintenance of the organism depends upon actions. So action (karma) is certainly better than inaction (akarma).[2] The *Gītā* does not teach inactivism and asceticism. It regards the performance of duties (karmayoga) as better than renunciation of actions (karmasannyāsa).[3] Renunciation of works never leads to liberation.[4] Selfless works for the welfare of mankind lead to it.[5] There is a ring of modernism in the *Gītā* ethics of action. It inculcates selfless, disinterested actions (niṣkāma karma) dedicated to God. Duties performed without attachment lead to mokṣa.[6] Works should not be actuated by attachment, aversion, and other emotions. They should not be motivated by egoistic desires.[7] They should be free from egoism. They should be devoid of the sense of 'I' (ahaṁkāra) and 'mine' (mamakāra).[8] They should be free from prudential considerations of fruits or consequences.[9] They ought to be performed without consideration of success or failure, victory or defeat, good or evil, pleasure or pain, which they will bring.[10] Their fruits should be resigned to God. "All work is worship." All works should be done as service to God. They should be dedicated to him. They should be done for the sake of God.[11] Disinterested works dedicated to him and enlightened by knowledge do not lead to bondage.[12] The karmayogin's individual will should be surrendered to the Divine Will.[13] His will is a pulsation of the Will of God. His mind is constantly fixed on him. His life is dedicated to him.[14] He is a perfect instrument of God, which consciously wills the Divine Will.[15] The karma-

---

[1] BG., iii. 5; xviii. 11, 59, 60; v. 14; xiii. 19; iii. 27, 28, 29.
[2] BG., iii. 8.
[3] BG., v. 2.
[4] BG., iii. 4.
[5] BG., iii. 20.
[6] BG., iii. 19.
[7] BG., ii. 47, 48; iii. 7, 9, 25; iv. 19, 21, 23; v. 3, 10, 11; vi. 4; xviii. 6, 9, 23, 26. Cp. Kant).
[8] BG., ii. 71; iii. 33; xii. 13; xviii. 17, 26, 53.
[9] BG., ii. 47-49, 51; iv. 20; v. 12; xvii. 15; xviii. 6, 11, 23. Cp. Kant.
[10] BG., ii. 38, 48, 57; iv. 22.
[11] BG., iii. 9, 30; iv. 41; v. 10, 13; ix. 27; xii. 10; xviii. 57. Contrast Kant.
[12] BG., ii. 51; iii. 9; iv. 41; v. 12.
[13] BG., vi. 2, 4.
[14] BG., xviii. 57.
[15] Sarvabhūtātmabhūtātmā. BG., v. 7.

yogin is a God-doer.[1] His every action is an integral action in union with God. It is service to God. It is selfless service of humanity. It is selfless work for the moral and spiritual welfare of mankind (lokasaṁgraha).[2] It aims at the good of the entire sentient creation (sarvabhūtahita).[3] The doer of good of mankind (kalyāṇakṛt) never suffers here or hereafter.[4] The path of work (karmayoga) is selfless pursuit of the moral good of mankind as service to God. Sannyāsa is said to consist in renunciation of empirical duties (kāmya karma) for the fulfilment of egoistic desires. But it really consists in renunciation of fruits of all actions.[5] We have right to works, but not to their fruits.[6] They are in the hands of God. He leads works to their fruits. We ought to do our duties *as* duties without craving for success or failure.[7] Those who crave for the attainment of fruits of actions are objects of pity.[8] Yoga is skill in actions.[9] We should do our duties efficiently. Sometimes disinterested actions for the good of mankind are regarded as the direct means of liberation.[10] Sometimes they are described as the means of self-purification (ātmaśuddhi) or purification of the mind.[11] Sometimes they are said to result in the dawn of integral knowledge.[12]

The *Gītā,* like Buddhism, does not enjoin the performance of ritualistic acts. Empirical duties (kāmya karma) are intended for the fulfilment of egoistic desires. They aim at enjoyment and sovereignty. They lead to happiness in heaven. They lead to rebirth. They are not the means of liberation. The Vedas prescribe duties relating to satta, rajas, and tamas. But mokṣa is a state of the soul, which transcends the guṇas. It cannot be attained by Vedic rituals.[13] All egoistic desires should be extirpated. Empirical transient pleasures spring from their fulfilment. But realization of the self (ātman) yields supreme bliss, which is permanent.[14] Actions motived by desires for fruits lead

---

[1] *Essays on the Gītā*, Second Series, p. 388.
[2] BG., iii. 20, 25. Lokasyonmārgapravṛttinivāraṇaṁ lokasaṁgrahaḥ SBG., iii. 20.
[3] BG., v. 25.
[4] BG., vi. 41.
[5] BG., vi. 1; xviii. 2.
[6] BG., ii. 47.
[7] BG., ii. 48; iv. 22.
[8] BG., ii. 49.
[9] Yogaḥ karmasu kauśalam. BG., ii. 50.
[10] BG., iii. 20; ii. 51.
[11] BG., v. 11.
[12] BG., iv. 33.
[13] BG., ii. 43, 44, 45.
[14] BG., ii. 55, 70, 71; iii. 13, 42; v. 21, 22, 24.

to bondage. But if they are performed without such desires, they yield permanent peace.[1] Vedic rituals are not necessary for liberation. The specific duties of an individual ought to be performed without any desire for fruits.[2] Desires ought to be surrendered to God. When all desires are resigned to him, and duties are performed in a disinterested spirit by an aspirant, he is said to be a yogin.[3] The *Gītā* agrees with Buddhism in inculcating the morality of altruism or selflessness. Egoism ought to be eradicated. Both emphasize the purity of inner life. Both condemn ritualistic morality. Buddhism stresses eradication of passions. The *Gītā* stresses the performance of duties as service to God. It condemns renunciation of works. It enjoins on us an active life dedicated to God for the moral welfare of humanity. But it is emphatic on the eradication of egoistic desires and evil passions like attachment, aversion, fear, lust, anger, greed, egoism, hypocrisy, pride, self-conceit, sorrow, melancholy, and the like.[4] It inculcates the cultivation of the virtues of fearlessness, purity of mind, concentration of the mind on knowledge of the self, charity, sense-control, sacrifice, study of the scriptures, penance, straightforwardness, non-injury, truthfulness, conquest of anger, renunciation, tranquillity, absence of fault-finding, kindness to creatures, greedlessness, softness, modesty, non-fickleness or firmness, courage, forgiveness, endurance, cleanliness, non-malevolence, non-conceit, steadfastness, and self-control.[5] Temperance in eating, walking, efforts in activities, sleep, and waking leads to happiness.[6] Equanimity (samatva) or imperturbability in joy and sorrow, gain and loss, victory and defeat, success and failure, is called yoga.[7] Love and hatred, lust and anger, fear and disgust, greed and delusion, pride and envy should be conquered.[8] Enmity should be completely discarded. Good-will and amity for all should be cultivated.[9] Reverence for gods, Brāhmaṇas, preceptors, and wise men, cleanliness, straightness, celibacy, non-injury, truthfulness, study of the scriptures, tran-

[1] BG., v. 12.
[2] BG., vi. 1.
[3] BG., vi. 2, 4, 18, 24.
[4] BG., ii. 56, 57, 62, 64, 70, 71; iii. 34, 37; iv. 19, 21; v. 23, 26; xviii. 23; xvi. 4; vi. 14; xviii. 35.
[5] BG., xiii. 7; xvi. 1-3.
[6] BG., iv. 30; vi. 17.
[7] BG., ii. 38, 48; iv. 22; v. 3; xiii. 9; vii. 13.
[8] BG., ii. 57, 62, 63; iii. 34; v. 3, 18.
[9] BG., iv. 22; xii. 13.

quillity of mind, contentment, silence, self-control, and purity of heart should be cultivated.[1]

Self-control is the foundation of moral life. It means restraint of the external cognitive and motor sense-organs and the mind. Attachment arises from meditation on objects of enjoyment. Attachment gives rise to desire. Desire gives rise to anger, when it is obstructed or baffled. Anger gives rise to delusion or non-discrimination between right and wrong. Delusion leads to lapse of memory, which destroys wisdom. Harmony of spirit (prasāda) or bliss springs from the proper enjoyment of objects by the sense-organs completely controlled by the self, supervised by the mind purged of love and hatred and other passions. Inner harmony or natural state of the soul[2] destroys all miseries, and quickly steadies the flame of knowledge.[3] Experience of proper sense-objects and performance of appointed works (niyata karma) are not forbidden. All desires should be directed to the Ātman, which is unruffled by them, and thus sublimated and purified.[4] Mere conformity to the moral law in external conduct is not morality. The mind must be purged of evil passions. If the mind meditates on improper sense-objects and enjoys them within, external conformity to the moral law is hypocrisy (mithyācāra).[5] The cognitive senses should be withdrawn from improper objects. The motor senses should not be allowed to indulge in improper activities. The external sense-organs should be controlled by the mind.[6] The mind is always restless and unsteady. It can be controlled by steadfast practice (abhyāsa) and detachment (vairāgya).[7] The mind should be fixed on the Ātman and steadied like an unflickering flame of light. Then it is cleansed of all unrighteous desires.[8] Duties should be performed with a pure mind free from immoral desires and passions.

Persons are divided into four castes (varṇa) according to their qualities (guṇa). Their vocations (karma) are appropriate to their qualities. The members of the society are divided into four castes according to their qualities and functions.[9] The

---

[1] BG., xvii. 14-16.
[2] Prasādaḥ prasannatā svāsthyam. SBG., ii. 64.
[3] BG., ii. 62-65.
[4] BG., ii. 70.
[5] BG., iii. 6, 7.
[6] BG., iv. 26, 27; vi. 24.
[7] BG., vi. 34.
[8] BG., vi. 18, 19, 24, 25, 26.
[9] BG., iv. 13.

castes may not be hereditary. The duties of the Brāhmaṇas, the Kṣatriyas, the Vaiśyas, and the Śūdras have been mentioned under the ethics of Śaṁkara's Advaita Vedānta. They ought to perform their specific duties (svadharma) in conformity with their native endowments (svabhāva). Their duties are appropriate to their station in society.[1] Their specific duties, which accord with their innate psychical dispositions (svabhāva) constitute their svadharma. They are prescribed (niyata, kārya) for them. They are their natural (sahaja) duties.[2] An individual should never give up his natural and specific duties (svadharma), and try to perform those of another person (paradharma). They do not fit in with his natural aptitudes. So they may be pernicious to him. They are not his natural duties, and therefore they will fail to fulfil his mission, and attune him with God. Svadharma ill-done is always better than paradharma well-done.[3] An individual attains fulfilment of his being (saṁsiddhi) by performing his own specific duties (svakarma).[4] Sin does not accrue to him, when he performs his own natural and specific duties.[5] Dedication of them to God leads to his liberation.[6] He should always do the duties prescribed for him.[7] If he does not perform them, he commits sin.[8] It is the duty of a Kṣatriya to fight the enemy for the preservation of society. He has no better duty than to fight a just battle (dharmya yuddha).[9]

A karmayogin should dedicate all his actions to God. Whatever he does, whatever he eats, whatever he offers in a sacrifice, whatever gifts he makes, and whatever penance he undergoes, he should dedicate to him. His acts of duty are consecrated to him. They bring him in complete union with God. Divine energy flows into him, and actuates all his actions. He becomes an instrument of divine action. He is a God-doer.

The *Gītā* teaches the path of knowledge (jñānayoga). The lowest knowledge (tāmasa jñāna) is the knowledge of one single effect, for instance, an image as God, the complete reality. The higher knowledge (rājasa jñāna) is the knowledge of different objects as separate from and unconnected with one

---

[1] BG., xviii. 41. cp. Bradley : My Station and its Duties.
[2] BG., vi. 1; xviii. 13.
[3] BG., xviii. 47; iii. 35.
[4] BG., xviii. 45.
[5] Svabhāvaniyataṁ karma. BG., xviii. 47.
[6] BG., xviii. 46.
[7] BG., iii. 8.
[8] BG., ii. 33.
[9] BG., ii. 31.

another. This is popular unscientific knowledge. The highest knowledge (sāttvika jñāna) is the knowledge of one undivided infinite spirit in the divided existences. One God is immanent in all finite existences. This is the philosophical knowledge of One in many.[1] Śaṁkara interprets the sāttvika jñāna as the integral knowledge of one Ātman or Brahman in all the multiplicity of appearances.[2] But this interpretation does not accord with the theism of the *Gītā,* which recognizes the reality of both One and many. An aspirant, whose mind is concentrated on Brahman, sees the Self (ātman) in all beings, and all beings in the Self. He sees God in all beings, and all beings in God. He who, established in oneness, worships God in all beings, abides in him, in whatever condition he lives. God is never lost to him, and he is never lost to God.[3] God and the finite soul are coeternal with each other. The individual soul with integral knowledge of God in all beings is united with him, and is not lost in him. The aspirant who sees God in all beings, sees them all as equal to himself. He sees them all alike, and treats them all alike (samadarśana). Equality (sāmya) of treatment follows from the mystic vision of God in all beings.[4] He sees a learned and modest Brāhmaṇa, a cow, an elephant, a dog, and an outcaste alike.[5] He who is contented with knowledge (jñāna) and intuition (vijñāna) of God, treats a clod, a stone, and a piece of gold alike. He knows a friend and a foe, a saint and a sinner, as equal, since God abides in them all.[6] The integral knowledge of God in all beings is expressed in universal benevolence to all without discrimination. It is expressed in love and respect for all human beings. It purifies the emotion, and moulds the will into the divine pattern. It transmutes the whole being of man into a perfect instrument of God.

Jñāna is knowledge of the Ātman derived from the scriptures. It is indirect knowledge. Vijñāna is direct and immediate knowledge, mystic vision, or intuition (anubhava) of the Ātman. The Ātman is Brahman. Jñāna is intellectual knowledge. Vijñāna is intuition. Śaṁkara interprets jñāna and vijñāna in this way.[7] Madhusūdana and Śrīdhara also give the

---

[1] BG., SBG., xviii. 22; BG., SBG., xviii. 21; BG., RBG., xviii. 20.
[2] SBG., xviii. 20.
[3] BG., vi. 29-31.
[4] BG., vi. 32.
[5] BG., v. 18.
[6] BG., vi. 8, 9.
[7] SBG., iii. 41 ; vi. 8.

same interpretation. But Rāmānuja takes jñāna in the sense of the knowledge of the essential nature of the self (ātmasvarūpa), and vijñāna in the sense of discriminative knowledge of the self (ātmaviveka), as different from prakṛti.[1] Faith (śraddhā) is a precondition of knowledge (jñāna). It can be acquired from the wise, who have a vision of Truth, through humility and reverence (praṇipāta), investigation (paripraśna), and service (sevā).[2] One devoid of faith and knowledge, and tossed in doubt perishes. He knows no happiness. Knowledge dispels doubt, and destroys ignorance and sins.[3] Intuition due to yoga dispels non-discrimination, and fixes the mind on the self.[4]

Self-control is the indispensable condition of acquisition of knowledge. Desire (kāma) and anger (krodha) are great enemies. They obscure knowledge as smoke covers fire. Knowledge is obscured by insatiable desire. Unrighteous desires, which spring from rajas, hinder knowledge. They spring from the external senses, manas, and buddhi. So they must be restrained in order to destroy unrighteous desires, which destroy knowledge and intuition (jñānavijñānanāśana). The senses should be controlled by the mind ; the mind should be controlled by the intellect ; the intellect should be controlled by the self. The lower sentient self should be controlled by the higher rational self. Unrighteous desires can be extirpated by the self by complete sense-restraint and control of mind and intellect. Without absolute self-control knowledge and intuition cannot be acquired.[5]

The wisdom (prajñā) of an aspirant becomes firm and steady, when all unrighteous desires for sensuous pleasures are extirpated, when the mind is not perturbed by love and hatred, fear and anger attachment and aversion, joy and sorrow, when the external sense-organs are withdrawn from their improper objects of enjoyment, when the senses completely controlled by the self devoid of attachment and aversion enjoy their proper objects, and the mind remains perfectly calm in adversity and prosperity, happiness and misery, and is fixed on God as the supreme goal of life. When the individual self is consecrated to God, and all its activities are dedicated to him (matpara), its wisdom becomes

---

[1] RBG., iii. 41 ; vi. 8.
[2] BG., iv. 39, 34.
[3] BG., iv. 41, 42 ; v. 16, 17.
[4] BG., ii. 52, 53.
[5] BG., iii. 37-43.

steady. When all desires are directed to the self, in which God is immanent, they are sublimated and purified. They are withdrawn from the external sense-objects and fixed on the spiritual self untouched by the natural and psychical modes of sattva, rajas, and tamas. When the mind is tranquillized by the eradication of emotions and passions, it can be fixed on the self. When it is fixed on the self, wisdom due to meditative trance becomes firm, and brings about supreme bliss in the self. The harmony of spirit (prasāda) due to equanimity of the mind, stilling of riotous emotions and desires, complete sense-control, and fixation of mind on God destroys egoism and brings eternal peace.[1] Mystic vision of God due to knowledge and intuition destroys attachment (rasa) to all sense-objects. They cease to attract the mind and the senses.[2]

Constancy in the knowledge of the self and God and insight into the goal of the knowledge of reality constitute true knowledge. The supreme Brahman is the object of true knowledge. It leads to immortality.[3] There is nothing purer than integral knowledge of God in the universe and the finite beings. It purges all works of impurities and purifies them.[4] It enlightens devotion to God, and unites the devotee with him for ever.[5] It leads to eternal peace or mokṣa. The knower of Brahman abides in Brahman. The God-knower (jñānayogin) abides in God.[6]

The *Gītā* teaches the path of devotion (bhaktiyoga). Bhakti is undivided, single-minded, unswerving, integral love of God. It completely unites the individual self with God. The bhaktiyogin is a God-lover. There are four kinds of devotees, distressed (ārta), inquisitive (jijñāsu), selfish (arthārthin), and wise (jñānin). The distressed devotee prays to God for deliverance from distress. The inquisitive devotee prays to him for knowledge of his nature. The selfish devotee prays to him for wealth and other objects of sense-gratification. The wise devotee knows the nature of God, and prays to him for his sake. He has single-minded devotion to him. He is always united with him. He is exceedingly fond of God. God also is fond of him. All kinds of devotees are pure and noble souls. They are dear to God. But the wise devotee is excessively dear to

[1] BG., ii. 55-61, 64-71.
[2] BG., ii. 59.
[3] BG., xiii. 11, 12.
[4] BG., iv. 37, 38.
[5] BG., vii. 16, 17.
[6] BG., iv. 39; v. 17, 19, 20.)

him. He is united with God, and realizes the supreme goal of life. After many births he seeks refuge in God, thinking that God is all (Vāsudevaḥ sarvam).[1] Those who throw themselves at the mercy of God, completely surrender themselves to him, and take shelter in him, cross the ocean of māyā, made of sattva, rajas, and tamas. They can transcend the guṇas, conquer the natural impulses and desires, and acquire transcendental (guṇātīta) perfection. Those who are deluded by ignorance, are puffed up by egoism, and do not take refuge in God.[2] Those who are attached to God, and take shelter in him, know him entirely. Those who take refuge in him, and make incessant efforts for release from old age and death, know the supreme Brahman. Even sinners realize the supreme goal of life by taking shelter in God, not to speak of holy persons. The devotee dedicates all his works to God, takes refuge in him, and realizes the infinite and eternal status through his grace. He fixes his mind on God, dedicates all his works to him, makes him the only end of his life, and overcomes all difficulties through his grace.[3] Complete surrender to God (prapatti) and taking refuge in him (śaraṇāgati) are essential to the cult of devotion. The grace of God is its cardinal doctrine. God can be seen through the spiritual eye by his grace. He cannot be seen in his infinite majesty through the study of the Vedas, performance of sacrifices, charity, rituals, and severe austerities. He can be known and seen in his real nature by undivided devotion. The devotee dedicates all his works to God, cleanses his mind of attachment and enmity to all creatures, makes him the only end of his life, enters into him, and attains him.[4] The path of devotion requires sense-control and purity of mind. It requires performance of works with devotion.

Those who are deluded by ignorance worship other gods with faith in accordance with their natural desires. God makes their faith firm, and fulfils their desires. But the fruit of their worship is temporary. The worshippers of gods go to them. The worshippers of the manes go to them. But those who worship God with devotion go to him.[5] The noble souls with their godlike nature (daivī prakṛti) worship him with single-

---

[1] BG., vii. 16-19. [2] BG., vii. 14, 15.
[3] BG., vii. 1, 29; ix. 32, 33; xviii. 56-58.
[4] BG., xi. 47, 48, 53-55. [5] BG., vii. 20-23; ix. 25.

minded devotion. They cultivate sense-control, tranquillity, kindness, non-injury, and other virtues, observe firm vows, chant the name of God, bow to him, and meditate on him. They are always united with him.[1] Those who fix their minds on God, and worship him with supreme faith, are always united with him. He delivers them from birth and death.[2] They know God in his real nature through devotion, and enter into him. They go to him through supreme devotion. They who fix their mind and intellect on him, make him the supreme end of their lives, bow to him, worship him, recite his name, and chant his glory, are united with him, and attain him.[3]

The devotee of God is always contented. His senses are controlled. He is of firm resolution. He sheds joy and sorrow, fear and anxiety. He does not cause pain to others. He is perfectly calm. He is not affected by praise and dispraise, pleasure and pain. He can endure heat and cold. He is devoid of attachment and aversion. He is pure in body and mind. He has no fixed abode. His mind is always fixed on God. He has undivided and unswerving devotion to him. He serves him with unflinching devotion, conquers and transcends his natural desires (guṇa), and attains affinity with God. He is impartial to friend and foe. He has compassion and good-will for all creatures. He possesses perfect tranquillity and equanimity. He is efficient in the performance of duties for the sake of God. He is detached from all egoistic works. He gives up works leading to good and evil. His life is dedicated to God. His mind and intellect are fixed on him. His heart burns with the integral love of God. His will is completely surrendered to him. He knows him in his real nature. He knows, loves, and wills God and nothing else. He is suffused with the Divine Spirit. There is complete union of the loving soul with the beloved Lord in integral love. They abide in each other. God abides in the loving soul, and it abides in him after death. The devoted soul is excessively dear to God.[4] Lord Kṛṣṇa says, "Take refuge in God alone with all thy being ; through his grace thou shalt get supreme peace and eternal status. Give up all dharmas and

---

[1] BG., SBG., ix. 13, 14.
[2] BG., xii. 2, 7.
[3] BG., xviii. 55, 65, 68; xii. 2, 7, 8; ix. 34; x. 9, 10.
[4] BG., xii. 13-20; xiv. 25, 26.

take shelter in me alone. I will deliver thee from all sins; grieve not:"[1] This message sums up the cult of devotion.

God accepts whatever the pure-hearted devotee offers him with devotion. He is impartial to all creatures. None is dear to him. None is hated by him. But those who worship him with devotion abide in him, and he abides in them. Even if a very vicious person worships him with undivided mind, he ought to be regarded as a saint. He is of holy determination. He quickly becomes a saint, and attains eternal peace. The devotee of God never perishes. The path of devotion is open to all, irrespective of caste or sex. God takes all his devotees into his bosom. His all-embracing love knows no distinction. Only he demands unconditional surrender to him and undivided and unflinching devotion and love for him. God looks after the welfare of his devotees, who worship him with single-minded devotion, and are always united with him.[2] He destroys their ignorance due to tamas, and illumines their minds with knowledge. He gives them knowledge which leads to attainment of him.[3] Integral love gives integral knowledge.

The *Gītā* sometimes prefers the path of meditation (yoga) to the path of works. Sometimes it prefers the path of works to the path of knowledge and meditation. Sometimes it prefers the path of knowledge to the path of devotion. Sometimes it prefers the path of devotion to the path of knowledge. Concentration of mind on God can be effected by constant practice. If constant practice is impracticable, all works should be done for the sake of God. If this also is impracticable, then fruits of all works should be renounced.[4] Wisdom is superior to constant practice; meditation is superior to wisdom; renunciation of fruits of works is superior to meditation; renunciation leads to peace or liberation.[5] Meditation is better than austerities, wisdom, and works. Single-minded devotion to God is superior to meditation; it unites the devoted soul with God for ever.[6] A wise devotee is always united with God through undivided devotion.[7] A wise person takes refuge in God after many births, and realizes him as the all-comprehending reality.[8] All works

[1] BG., xviii. 62, 66.
[2] BG., ix. 22, 26, 27, 29-31.
[3] BG., x. 10, 11.
[4] BG., xii. 9-11.
[5] BG., xii. 12.
[6] BG., vi. 46, 47.
[7] BG., vii. 17.
[8] BG., vii. 19.

culminate in the dawn of knowledge. The fire of knowledge consumes all works.[1] Faith (śraddhā) leads to knowledge. Knowledge with sense-control leads to peace. Devotion (bhakti) brings about knowledge of God.[2] The supreme status is attained by knowledge and renunciation as well as by dedication of works to God.[3] The *Gītā* thinks that any of the three main paths leads to mokṣa. Some know the Ātman by meditation, some by knowledge, and some by works ; others pass beyond death by worship.[4] Lord Kṛṣṇa says, "In whatever way men worship me I favour them in that way.[5]

The threefold paths of works, knowledge, and devotion imply one another. The aspirant who dedicates all his works to God without attachment and thought of consequences, free from egoism, knows him and loves him.[6] He who knows God in all beings and all beings in God, dedicates all his works to him, and is devoted to him.[7] He who loves God with single-minded devotion, performs all works for his sake, knows him in his real nature.[8] The three paths emphasize the different aspects of sādhanā in accordance with the temperaments of the aspirants. An enlightened intellect, a pure heart, and a holy will go together. A man does not live in compartments. His knowledge, emotion, and will are purified together. His whole being turns towards God, and is transmuted by his living presence in his soul. He has mystic vision and consuming love of God. His will pulsates with Divine Will, and works as a perfect instrument of God. He becomes a God-knower, God-lover, and God-doer.[9]

Mokṣa is the supreme goal (parā gati).[10] It is the supreme abode.[11] It is the highest status beyond good and evil.[12] It is the permanent status.[13] It is the eternal and indestructible status.[14] It is the seat free from all troubles.[15] It is free from

---

[1] BG., iv. 33, 37.
[2] BG., iv. 39; xviii. 55.
[3] BG., v. 5.
[4] BG., xii. 24, 25.
[5] Ye yatha māṁ prapadyante tāṁs tathaiva bhajāmy aham. BG., iv. 11.
[6] BG., iii. 19, 20, 30; iv. 19.
[7] B.G., v. 17.
[8] BG., ix. 34; x. 9, 10; xi. 54; iv. 10.
[9] *Essays on the Gītā*, Second Series, p. 388.
[10] BG., vi. 45; viii. 21; ix. 32.
[11] BG., viii. 21; xi. 38; xv. 6.
[12] BG., viii. 28; ix. 28.
[13] Śāśvataṁ sthānam. BG., xviii. 62.
[14] Śāśvataṁ padam avyayam. BG., xviii. 56.
[15] Anāmayaṁ padam. BG., SBG., ii. 51.

birth and death.[1] It is absolutely free from pain. Mokṣa is perfection (saṁsiddhi). It is supreme perfection (paramā saṁṣiddhi).[2] Mokṣa is trans-empirical state (nistraiguṇya). It is transcendental perfection of the individual self, which is not affected by the natural desires due to sattva, rajas, and tamas. First rajas and tamas are overcome by sattva which actuates the aspirant's mind. Then the sattva also is transcended by him. He becomes absolutely pure (guṇātīta). He rises above virtue and rice, good and evil.[3] Mokṣa is extinction in Brahman (brahmanirvāṇa).[4] It is abiding in Brahman (brahmī sthiti).[5] It is extinction of egoism in Brahman. It is not dissolution of integrity. The individual soul is an eternal part of God. Its integrity can never be lost. Mokṣa consists in being Brahman (brahmabhūta).[6] Being Brahman does not mean identity with Brahman. It means attainment of qualitative similarity (sādharmya) with Brahman or God.[7] Mokṣa is attainment of the nature of God (madbhāva).[8] Mokṣa is transcendental state of immortality (amṛtatva).[9] It is life eternal. It is the highest goal (anuttamā gati).[10] It is the attainment of God. It is inseparable union with him.[11] God abides in the individual souls devoted to him. They abide in him.[12] Mokṣa is not extinction of the individual soul in God. It is affinity with him in essential nature.

Mokṣa is supreme quietude (parā śānti).[13] It is supreme bliss (uttamaṁ sukham).[14] It springs from union with Brahman.[15] Mokṣa is inner delight and bliss. It is inner enlightenment. It is merging in Brahman. It is becoming Brahman.[16] It is delight in the self (atmarati) ; it is contentment with the self (ātmatṛpti). It is self-satisfaction and self-fulfilment. It is free from moral obligation. No duties are to be performed in this highest state.[17] It is a state of non-action

---

[1] BG., ii. 51.
[2] BG., viii. 15; xii. 10; xiv. 1; iii. 4, 20.
[3] BG., SBG., ii. 45, 48.
[4] BG., ii. 72; v. 24; xiii. 30.
[5] BG., ii. 72; v. 19, 20.
[6] BG., v. 24, 25, 26; vi. 27; xiv. 26; xviii. 53, 54.
[7] BG., xiv. 2.
[8] BG., iv. 10; xiv. 19.
[9] BG., xiv. 20, 21, 25.
[10] BG., vii. 18.
[11] BG., viii. 7, 8, 10, 16; ix. 28, 38; x. 10; xi. 55; xviii. 55, 65, 68.
[12] Mayi te teṣu cāpy aham. BG., ix. 29.
[13] BG., xviii. 62; v. 19.
[14] BG., vi. 27, 28.
[15] BG., vi. 20, 21.
[16] BG., v. 24.
[17] BG., iii. 17.

(naiṣkarmya).[1] The liberated person neither acts nor causes others to act.[2] He may work for the good of humanity without moral obligation.[3] But he has no duties to perform (kṛtakṛtya).[4] Mokṣa is perfect tranquillity (śānti) and desirelessness.[5] It is total destruction of egoism.[6] It is living in God.[7] It is transmutation of the individual soul by God. It is transformation of human life into divine life. It is assimilation of God into every fibre of man's being. It is divinizing human being. It is indissoluble union with God.

2. *The Philosophy of the Bhāgavata*

The *Bhāgavata* is the most popular work in the devotional literature in India. It enjoys popularity next to the *Bhāgavad Gītā*. It is attributed to Vyāsa, the legendary author of the Purāṇas. Rāmānuja (1017 A.D.—1137 A.D.) quotes from the *Mahābhārata*, the *Viṣṇupurāṇa*, and the other Purāṇas. But he does not refer to the *Bhāgavata-purāṇa*. But Madhva (1300 A.D.) wrote *Bhāgavata-tātparya* which embodies the main ideas of the *Bhāgavata*. So Dr. S. N. Das Gupta opines that it is not earlier than the age of Rāmānuja.[8] Many commentaries were written upon it. Śrīdhara's commentary enjoys the highest authority. The exposition of the philosophy of the *Bhāgāvata* given here is based on the texts as explained by Śrīdhara.

The *Bhagavad Gītā* emphasizes theism. It stresses the concept of the Supreme Person (puruṣottama) who is the foundation of Brahman. It recognizes the reality of the individual souls (jīva) and the world. It does not regard them as appearances. But the *Bhāgavata* emphasizes the monistic aspect of the reality. It regards the ultimate reality as one, non-dual pure consciousness, though it describes Brahman as the Supreme Person (puruṣottama). It regards the individual souls as Brahman deluded by ignorance (avidyā). They are not ultimately real. They are unreal appearances. They become Brahman when their avidyā is destroyed by devotion. The world of empirical objects is not real. It also is a false appearance. It is a transformation of māyā or prakṛti. Māyā is the power (śakti) of God

---

[1] BG., xviii. 49.
[2] BG., v. 13.
[3] BG., iii. 20, 25.
[4] BG., xv. 20.
[5] BG., ii. 71.
[6] BG., ii. 71.
[7] BG., v. 19; vi. 15, 31.
[8] HIP., Vol. IV, pp. 1-2.

or Brahman. God is the Lord of māyā. Prakṛti is composed of the guṇas, sattva, rajas, and tamas. They are transformed into the world under the guidance of God. He is the Lord of prakṛti and puruṣas or individual souls. He is the Lord of the guṇas. But he is devoid of them (nirguṇa). His pure consciousness is hidden by them, which constitute his māyā or inconceivable power. Avidyā or ignorance of the real nature of Brahman or Ātman, the essence of the jīva, is the cause of bondage. It is non-discrimination (aviveka) between the Ātman and its vestment or mind-body-aggregate produced by māyā. When avidyā is destroyed and intuition of the Ātman or Brahman dawns, the jīva becomes Brahman, and attains liberation. It is restored to its natural and essential state (svastha) in liberation. Right knowledge of Brahman is brought about by devotion to him. Bhakti is unconditional, uninterrupted, single-minded devotion to God. So the philosophy of the *Bhāgavata* is pure monism or absolutism like that of Śaṁkara. Only it identifies Brahman with God (Īśvara), and recognizes devotion as the only means of right knowledge. Its philosophy is a blend of absolutism and theism.

(1) *Ontology*.—Brahman is God. He is the supreme reality. He is non-dual, pure knowledge. He is pure and devoid of sattva, rajas, and tamas. He is the Supreme Person.[1] He is the extremely subtle, incomprehensible, eternal, and infinite reality. He is of the nature of pure consciousness.[2] He is one. He is non-dual. He is unconditioned (nirupādhika). There is no distinction of objects in him. He is existent (sat) and non-existent (asat). He is the duality of cause and effect. Conditions (vikalpa) and distinctions of guṇas are attributed to him owing to ignorance.[3] He is unborn and eternal. He is the Ātman. The self creates itself by itself in itself, and maintains it.[4] He exists in reality as pure formless consciousness or the inner Self. He is the beginingless, endless, eternal, non-dual reality. He is the perfect

[1] Nirañjanaṁ nirguṇam advayaṁ paraṁ tvāṁ jñaptimātraṁ puruṣaṁ brajāmy aham. *Bhāgavata,* x. 52, 58.

[2] Tad brahma paramaṁ sūkṣaṁ cinmātraṁ sad anantakam. *Ibid.,* x. 88, 10.

[3] Ekastvam eva sadasaddvayam advayaṁ ca iha na vastubhedaḥ. Ajñānatas tvayi janair vihito vikalpo yasmād guṇavyatikaro nirupādhikasya. *Ibid.,* viii. 12, 8.

[4] Ātmātmanyātmanātmānaṁ saṁyacchati pāti ca. *Ibid,* ii. 6, 38.

truth. He is the supreme reality. He is devoid of the guṇas. He is trans-empirical and non-objective.[1] He is formless consciousness. He creates visible forms in himself out of sattva, rajas, and tamas, which constitute his māyā. He is the knower (draṣṭṛ). The nature of the known (dṛśyatva) is attributed to him by the ignorant, even as clouds are attributed to the sky or dusts are attributed to the air.[2] God is pure consciousness (cinmātra). He is of the nature of eternal consciousness (aviluptabodhātmā).[3] He is the supreme Self or Ātman. He creates himself by himself through unfailing resolve.[4] He is the one Self of all selves. He is the knower of himself (svadṛk). He appears to be many through his māyā. He appears to be multiple selves and manifold objects through it.[5] He is of the essence of consciousness (cidātmaka). His consciousness never lapses (aviddhadṛk).[6] He is manifested in himself through māyā in creation. He becomes unmanifest in himself in dissolution. The world exists in him. It is created out of him. It is created by him. It is God himself.[7] He is the only reality. There is no reality higher or lower than he is. There is no reality equal to him.[8] He is independent (ātmatantra).[9] He is the sole Lord (ekarāt). He is really inactive and devoid of names, forms, and acts. But he appears to be active and create names, forms, and acts. He creates names as symbols (vācaka), and objects (vācya) denoted by them.[10]

Brahman is the highest reality. He is devoid of māyā in himself (nirastakuhaka). But he appears to be the real world composed of sattva, rajas, and tamas constituting his māyā. The world is the appearance of Brahman. Brahman is pure formless consciousness. He is eternal bliss. These are his essential characteristics (svarūpalakṣaṇa). Brahman is the creator,

---

[1] Viśuddhaṁ kevalaṁ jñānaṁ pratyak samyag avasthitam. Satyaṁ pūrṇam anādyantaṁ nirguṇaṁ nityam advayam. *Ibid*, ii. 6, 39.

[2] Etad rūpaṁ bhagavato hy arūpasya cidātmanaḥ. Māyāguṇair viracitaṁ mahadādibhir ātmani. Evaṁ draṣṭari dṛśyatvam āropitam abuddhibhiḥ. *Ibid.*, i. 3, 30, 31.

[3] *Ibid.*, iii. 7, 2-6.

[4] Sṛjaty amoghasaṅkalpa ātmaivātmānam ātmanā. *Ibid*, iii. 10, 10.

[5] *Ibid.*, i. 12, 47; Śrīdhara's commentary.

[6] *Ibid.*, viii. 2, 2, 4.

[7] Yasminnidaṁ yataś cedaṁ yenedaṁ ya idaṁm svayam. *Ibid*, viii. 2, 3.

[8] *Ibid.*, ii. 5, 6.

[9] *Ibid.*, ii. 9, 23.

[10] *Ibid.*, ii. 10, 36.

preserver, and destroyer of the world. The conscious Brahman is its material cause. He exists in all effects. Unconscious prakṛti and conscious souls, which depend upon him, are not its material cause. Independent (svarāt) Brahman is the cause of the world. This is the accidental characteristic (taṭasthalakṣaṇa) of Brahman.[1] The highest reality is non-dual knowledge. It is pure undifferenced consciousness. It is called Brahman, Paramātman, and Bhagavat.[2] The individual self (jīva) is a part of Brahman. Māyā is the power of Brahman. The world is the effect of Brahman. All these are nothing but Brahman. They are not different from him.[3]

God creates the world through his māyā. He is the Lord of māyā (māyeśa). He is not deluded by his māyā. He is devoid of it in himself. Māyā is prakṛti composed of sattva, rajas, and tamas. God is devoid of the guṇas (nirguṇa). His essence of pure consciousness is hidden by them.[4] He is the immutable Self (ātman) of the universe. He is the knower (draṣṭṛ). He is devoid of the guṇas. Yet he creates them through his māyā. They bind the individual souls to saṁsāra.[5] God exists in prakṛti. But he is not tainted by its guṇas, because he is trans-empirical (nirguṇa) immutable, and inactive.[6] God creates, preserves, and destroys the world through māyā in sport, but he is not attached to it. He enters into created objects as an independent Self, and experiences the sensible and intelligible objects without being attached to them.[7] Māyā cannot be manifested except through Brahman, and yet it is not manifested in Brahman. It cannot exist without Brahman, and yet it does not exist in Brahman.[8]

God is the ancient supreme person. He existed as undifferenced formless (aviśeṣa) consciousness before creation as the supra-cosmic Self. The world existed in the dormant powers of God, who is the Self of the world. Prakṛti is his own māyā or wonderful power. He created names and forms or empirical objects in his Self devoid of names and forms. He created the

[1] *Ibid*, i. 1, 1; Śrīdhara's commentary.

[2] *Ibid*, i. 2, 11.

[3] Vastuno'ṁśo jīvaḥ, vastunaḥ śaktir māyā, vastunaḥ kāryaṁ jagat; tat sarvaṁ vastu eva, na tataḥ pṛthag iti vedyam. Śrīdhara's commentary on *Bhāgavata*, i. 1, 2.

[4] *Bhāgavata*, ii. 9, 23; i. 7, 23; i. 1, 1; ii. 5, 21.

[5] *Ibid.*, ii. 5, 17, 18.

[6] *Ibid.*, iii. 27, 1, .2

[7] *Ibid.*, i. 3, 36; i. 11, 24.

[8] *Ibid.*, ii. 9, 33.

empirical world in his trans-empirical nature.[1] God transcends prakṛti. He exists in himself devoid of māyā in complete isolation by his power of consciousness.[2] He creates the world through his māyā (ātmamāyā) composed of sattva, rajas, and tamas in their subtle and gross forms (sadasadrūpa)[3] as the spider spins its web out of its own body.[4] He is independent (svarāt). He creates the animate and inanimate world through his māyā or power which abides in him. Māyā is incomprehensible by reason.[5] Māyā is subtle prakṛti. It is the power of God. He transcends and guides it. He is the Lord of māyā.[6] He creates the jīvas through his conscious power (cicchakti), and the world through his unconscious power (acicchakti).[7] He is eternal, unmanifest, and transcendental. But he creates the guṇas through his māyā, interpenetrates them, and becomes their ruler.[8] God, who transcends māyā, is the real cause of the universe. It exists in him. He interpenetrates the world, subtle and gross.[9] Māyā is the power of God, which is unmanifest and manifest (sadasadātmikā śakti). He impregnates it with his energy, and creates mahat and the other categories with the aid of time. He creates the world in himself and reabsorbs it in himself.[10] God is immutable and devoid of the guṇas. He creates the world out of his māyā made of the guṇas, maintains it, and dissolves it. Māyā is unborn (ajā). It is his inconceivable power (acintyaśakti). It cannot be conceived by reason.[11] Māyā is prakṛti. God is prakṛti composed of sattva, rajas, and tamas. He is the Lord and knower of its mutations which are energized by him. He cannot be known from the guṇas. His greatness is hidden by them which are his manifestations.[12] The world is sometimes described as real. It is a manifestation of God.

God is pure consciousness (vijñānamātra). He is the embodiment of supreme bliss (paramānandamūrti). He is calm (śānta), devoid of dualistic vision (nivṛttadvaitadṛṣṭi). He is delighted in himself (ātmārāma). He is devoid of names and forms (anāmarūpa). He is transcendental consciousness

[1] *Ibid.*, i. 11, 22.
[2] Māyāṁ vyudasya cicchaktyā kaivalye sthita ātmani. *Ibid.*, i. 7, 23.
[3] *Ibid.*, i. 2, 30.
[4] *Ibid.*, ii. 5, 6.
[5] *Ibid.*, iv. 19, 31.
[6] *Ibid.*, vi. 19, 11, 12.
[7] Vii. 3, 34.
[8] *Ibid.*, vii. 1, 6.
[9] Ātmani protabhuvanaṁ paraṁ sadasadātmakam. *Ibid*, iii. 15, 6.
[10] *Ibid.*, ii. 5, 23-28.
[11] *Ibid.*, iii. 7, 9.
[12] *Ibid.*, x. 11, 31-33.

(cinmātra). He is beyond cause and effect.[1] He is possessed of infinite qualities (aparimitaguṇagaṇa). Yet his greatness is unfathomable.[2] He is one, but appears to be many. He is the reality in all objects. He is the Lord of all. He is the first cause of the world. He is the inner Self of all. He is indicated by the manifestations of all guṇas. He is one only.[3] The empirical world is not real. It is a mere appearance which is experienced. Even the experience of it is false. This false experience is annulled by devotion to God.[4] Though objects do not exist in reality, empirical life does not cease, even as in dream persons come to grief owing to attachment to unreal dream-objects.[5] Objects are unreal. The sense-organs are unreal. So unreal objects should not be enjoyed through the unreal sense-organs. Illusory appearances are due to non-apprehension of the Ātman which is one.[6] One Ātman appears to be many empirical objects and empirical selves (jīva). Experiences of empirical objects are false like creations of imagination and dreams. The empirical life (saṁsāra) of the Ātman is false.[7]

There is one supreme self (Ātman) in all individual selves (jīva). It is known as many selves by the ignorant.[8] The pure Self is not apprehended owing to its limitation by the adjunct of the body.[9] The Ātman limited by egoism (ahaṁkāra) and deluded by avidyā is the jīva.[10] It undergoes birth and death. The Ātman is unchangeable and beyond birth and death. It is devoid of union and disunion with a body. Misery of the jīva is due to ignorance (ajñāna). It is destroyed by knowledge of the reality which restores the jīva to its essential divinity. Devotion to God leads to knowledge of him, which destroys ignorance. God brings about the highest good of the jīvas. He incarnates to redeem their sins.[11] God is the Lord of the individual souls

[1] *Ibid.*, v. 16, 19-21. [2] *Ibid.*, v. 9, 36.
[3] Sa eka eva paryavasitaḥ. *Ibid.*, v. 9, 38.
[4] *Ibid.*, iii. 7, 18. [5] *Ibid.*, xi. 22, 55.
[6] Ātmāgrahaṇanirbhātaṁ paśya vaikalpikaṁ brahma. *Ibid.*, xi. 22, 56.
[7] *Ibid.*, xi. 22, 54.
[8] Eka eva paro hyātmā sarveṣām api dehinām. Nāsau gṛhyate mūḍhaiḥ. *Ibid.*, x. 56, 44.
[9] Dehopādhinā śuddho na pratīyate. Śrīdhara's commentary on *Bhāgavata*, x. 56, 14.
[10] *Ibid*, i. 7. 24.
[11] *Ibid*, i. 7. 25.

limited by the adjunct of egoism (ahaṁkāra).[1] He is the Lord of prakṛti and puruṣas or individual souls (pradhānapuruṣeśvara).[2] He is the supreme Person (puruṣottama).[3]

God is one Self (ātman). He appears to be many jīvas through his māyā. His māyā deludes the jīvas who are endowed with avidyā.[4] God is free from saṁsāra. But he is bound by avidyā and suffers from misery. God is limited by avidyā, and becomes the jīva.[5] The self appears to have the quality of the not-self, though it does not exist,[6] even as trembling of the reflection of the moon in water is attributed to the moon, or as a person dreams of the cutting of his own head.[7] The mind-body-complex is the not-self which is known (dṛśya). It does not exist. It is an unreal appearance due to avidyā. It is attributed to the knowing self (draṣṭṛ). The Ātman, the knower, is the witness of the three layers of experience, waking, dream, and deep sleep.[8] It is God, the supreme Self. It is the ancient, eternal, omnipresent, perfect, self-luminous Self. It exists in the individual embodied souls (jīva) as their inner controller (antaryāmin). It controls them through māyā. It is God possessed of the six qualities of Lordship. It is neither the subject of knowledge nor the object of knowledge. It is direct eternal self-awareness (sāksāt svayaṁjyotiḥ).[9]

The jīvas are parts of God. Their experience of divinity is hidden by false identification with sattva, rajas, and tamas which constitute their psycho-physical organism. God is immanent in the body, the senses, vital forces, mind (manas), intellect (buddhi), egoism (ahaṁkāra), and citta. He is their essence, which is hidden by avidyā.[10] An individual soul is attached to the guṇas constructed by its own māyā or ignorance, and is deluded by them. The guṇas constitute its body. It assumes that kind of body which suits its manas impelled by karma (adṛṣṭa), even as light reflected in water disturbed by the wind

[1] *Ibid*, iii. 9. 42.
[2] *Ibid*, iii. 9. 44.
[3] *Ibid*, i. 17. 36.
[4] Ato bhagavato māyā māyinām api mohinī. *Ibid*, iii. 6, 39.
[5] Īśvarasya vimuktasya kārpaṇyam uta bandhanam. *Ibid*, iii. 7, 9.
[6] Dṛśyate' sannapi draṣṭur ātmano' nātmano guṇaḥ. *Ibid*, iii. 7, 11.
[7] *Ibid*, iii. 7, 10-11.
[8] Avasthātrayasākṣī kṣetrajña ātmā tattvam. Śrīdhara's commentary on *Bhāgavata*, v. 11, 12.
[9] *Ibid*, v. 11, 13.
[10] *Ibid*, x. 16, 42.

appears to tremble.[1] God is the reality in the jīvas. He assumes multiple forms for the good of creatures, animate and inanimate. Those who are deluded by the māyā of God see him as many. Those who are enlightened do not see him as many. God is the Ātman which is of the nature of pure consciousness (avabodha ātmā).[2] Thus the Ātman, Brahman, or God alone is real, and the jīvas and the world are unreal appearances. This is pure monism or absolutism.

God is the substratum of the individual souls (ātmāyatana).[3] He is the Self of the universe. He appears to be many jīvas in creatures.[4] He appears to be possessed of the guṇas when his māyā or unconscious power (acicchakti) composed of them is transformed into subtle elements, sense-organs, and bodies. He enters into them with his power of consciousness (cicchakti) and appears as jīvas and enjoys the guṇas in the physical objects.[5] The individual souls are deluded by māyā or avidyā, and forget their divine nature.[6] The Ātman is the supreme Self (puruṣaḥ paraḥ) of waking, dream, and sleep, which are modes of buddhi. It is their Lord.[7] It is eternal, inexhaustible, pure, one, immutable, omnipresent, detached, perfect, self-conscious (svadṛk) knower, and substratum of the world, and its cause. These are the twelve characteristics of the Ātman.[8] It is undecaying, trans-empirical, pure, self-luminous, and unobscured.[9] When it is deluded by avidyā, it is entangled in saṁsāra, and undergoes birth and death. It is liberated from bondage by right knowledge. The jīva is bound and liberated. The Ātman is not entangled in saṁsāra. It is ever liberated. Though it exists in the mind-body-complex made of the guṇas, which are mere māyā (māyāmātra) or empirical appearances, and which are not real (avastu), it is not attached to them.[10] Non-discrimination (aviveka) is the cause of saṁsāra. Proximity or relation of the Ātman to the body, the senses, and the life forces is its cause. Its false identification with the mind-body-complex is the cause of its empirical life.[11] The jīva is the Ātman limited

[1] *Ibid*, x. 1. 42, 43.
[2] *Ibid*, x. 2, 28, 29.
[3] *Ibid*, iv. 19, 29, 30.
[4] Nāneva bhāti viśvātmā bhūteṣu ca tathā pumān. *Ibid*, i. 2. 32.
[5] *Ibid*, i. 2. 31-33.
[6] Māyāmohitacetaso jīvalokasya. *Ibid*, i. 7. 24.
[7] *Ibid*, vii. 7. 25.
[8] *Ibid*, vii. 7. 19.
[9] *Ibid*, xi. 28, 11.
[10] *Ibid*, xi. 28, 2.
[11] *Ibid*, xi. 28, 12.

by the adjunct of egoism (ahaṁkāropādhi). Egoism undergoes birth and death. The Ātman transcends them.[1] The jīva or the inner self, which identifies itself with the mind-body-complex, assumes a body composed of the guṇas and their activities.[2] The jīva is attached to the guṇas because it thinks itself to be an active agent being deluded by egoism, and therefore it undergoes bondage. Its attachment to empirical objects is removed by devotion (bhakti).[3] The distinctions of pleasure and pain, birth and death, reward and punishment of the jīvas are due to their union with bodies through the sport of God. Distinctions of objects in the self are due to non-discrimination.[4] External objects are non-existent. Saṁsāra is due to false attachment to unreal objects, even as a person suffers from misery owing to false attachment to unreal objects of dream.[5] Egoism is the cause of activity. Subtle and gross forms due to avidyā are attributed to the self. When avidyā or māyā is destroyed by true knowledge, the self (jīva) becomes Brahman. Thus actions are attributed to the inactive Self, and birth is ascribed to unborn God.[6] The jīva can attain isolation (kaivalya) from the guṇas of prakṛti by intense devotion, knowledge and detachment.[7] When it annuls avidyā by devotion, it is dissociated from the guṇas, experiences no empirical objects, acquires detachment from them, and realizes its divinity and eternal bliss. It is divested of its modes, and transformed into Brahman.[8] This is pure monism. Yet the *Bhāgavata* teaches theism.

Vāsudeva, Saṁkarṣaṇa, Pradyumna, and Aniruddha are the four manifestations (vyūha) of God.[9] He incarnates as man (avatara) to redeem the sins of men and establish the kingdom of righteousness. His pure sattva is the inexhaustible seed of all divine incarnations. He creates gods, men, and beasts by a fraction of his pure sattva.[10] Kṛṣṇa is God himself. But the other Avatāras are his parts.[11] He incarnates as man through

---

[1] *Ibid*, xi. 28, 15.
[2] *Ibid*, xi. 28, 16.
[3] *Ibid*, iii. 27, 1-4.
[4] Avivekakṛtaḥ puṃsaḥ arthabheda iva ātmani. Guṇadoṣavikalpaśca bhideva sṛjivat kṛtaḥ. *Ibid*, vi. 18. 30.
[5] *Ibid*, xi. 28, 13.
[6] *Ibid*, i. 3, 33-35; iii. 28, 19.
[7] *Ibid*, iii. 8. 21, 22.
[8] Vṛttirūpatāṁ parityajya brahmākāreṇa pariṇamate. Śrīdhara's commentary on *Bhāgavata*, iii. 28, 35.
[9] *Ibid*, x. 49. 31.
[10] *Ibid*, i. 3. 3, 5.
[11] *Ibid*, i. 3. 28.

his māyā, and lives among men and women as an ordinary man.[1] Vāsudeva is Nārāyaṇa.

(2) *Ethics and Religion.*—God destroys all impurities.[2] The devotee who fixes his self on God with undivided devotion (ekāntabhakti) is liberated from saṁsāra.[3] Devotion to God is free from empirical qualities (nirguṇa), unmotived and unconditional (ahaitukī), and uninterrupted (avyavahita). It fills the soul with bliss. It produces detachment and knowledge.[4] It is enlightened by knowledge, and expressed in renunciation. Devotion combined with knowledge and renunciation with faith in God leads to the vision of him within the self.[5] Devotion gives rise to knowledge.[6] Real wisdom generates attachment to God.[7] Devotion and knowledge are interdependent on each other.[8] The whole being of the devotee is consecrated to God. All his desires are directed to him. All his sense-organs function for his worship. His body, mind, and spirit are entirely dedicated to him.[9] Actions done for the pleasure of God give rise to devotion. All actions should be surrendered to God without any desire for their fruits. The complete surrender of the soul to him is necessary for devotion. All actions should be done for his pleasure.[10] Devotion arises in a mind in which sattva predominates and overcomes rajas and tamas. It generates knowledge of God, which dissociates the soul from the guṇās.[11] Dharma consists in hearing of God, chanting his name and glory, recollection of him, company of saints, service, worship, bowing, self-surrender, and subordination (dāsya) to God, and friendship (sakhya) with him.[12] There are four kinds of devotion. If a person deluded by the false knowledge of difference shows devotion to God out of malevolence, arrogance, jealousy, or anger, his devotion is tāmasa since tamas predominates in it. If a person worships the images of God out of desire for fame, wealth, or any other object of enjoyment, his devotion is rājasa

---

[1] *Ibid,* i. 12, 35.
[2] *Ibid,* i. 15, 29.
[3] *Ibid,* i. 15. 32.
[4] *Ibid,* ii. 29, 12; i. 2, 7.
[5] *Ibid,* i. 2. 12.
[6] *Ibid,* iv. 29, 37.
[7] *Ibid,* iv. 29, 49.
[8] The author's article on *The Bhāgavata Religion : The Cult of Bhakti, The Cultural Heritage of India,* Vol. II, p. 55.
[9] *Bhāgavata,* x. 29. 15; x. 32, 43.
[10] *Ibid,* iv. 29, 49; i. 5, 35; xi. 2, 22; x. 10, 1; vii. 6, 34. *The Cultural Heritage of India,* Vol. II, p. 55.
[11] *Ibid,* i. 2. 20.
[12] *Ibid,* vii. 11, 9-12.

since rajas predominates in it. If a person shows devotion to God to burn up the roots of karma or latent dispositions, to do duty for the sake of duty, or to please God, his devotion is sāttvika since sattva predominates in it. These three kinds of devotion are secondary. They are motived by natural inclinations (guṇa) and affected by the false knowledge of difference. But the highest kind of devotion is absolutely unmotived and devoid of sattva, rajas, and tamas (nirguṇa), unconditional and immediate.[1] A devotee with this kind of primary devotion is delighted in the service of God only. He is established in the knowledge of unity. He does not accept even proximity to God (sāmīpya), equality with God (sārūpya), union with God (sāyujya), residence in the abode of God (sālokya), and super-natural powers of God (sārṣṭi), even if they are offered to him.[2] He does not care for absolute independence (kaivalya).[3] He lives, moves, and has his being in God. He gives his devotee, who adores him with single-minded devotion, his own divine nature of his own accord.[4]

The *Bhāgavata* mentions truthfulness (satya), kindness (dayā), austerities (tapas), cleanliness (śauca), endurance of heat and cold, and the like (titikṣā), sense-control (dama), tranquillity (śama), non-injury (ahiṁsā), sex-restraint (brahmacarya), renunciation (tyāga), recitation of God's name (svādhyāya), straightforwardness (ārjava), contentment (santoṣa), service to saints (samadṛksevā), absention from rustic activities (grāmyehoparama), silence (mauna), quest for the self (ātmavimarśana), discrimination (īkṣā), charity (annadāna), knowledge of equality in all creatures (bhūteṣu samabuddhi) as the virtues which ought to be cultivated.[5] Learning (śruta), knowledge (jñāna), recollection (smṛti), equality (sāmya), sense-restraint (uparati), detachment (virakti), independence (svātantrya), efficiency (kauśala), sovereignty (aiśyarya), heroism (vīrya), courage (tejas), strength (bala), beauty (kānti), patience (dhairya), softness (mārdava), greatness (prāgalbhya), courtesy (praśraya), good character (śila), energy (ojas), gravity (gāmbhīrya), steadiness (sthairya), belief in God (āstikya), glory (kīrti), respect (māna), conquest of egoism (anahaṁkṛti) are the other virtues

[1] *Ibid*, iii. 29. 11.
[2] *Ibid*, iii. 29, 13.
[3] *Ibid*, xi. 20, 34. *The Cultural Heritage of India*, Vol. II, pp. 57-58.
[4] *Ibid*, iii. 13. 49.
[5] *Ibid*, vii. 11, 9.

which are enjoined.[1] Learning, charity, austerities, and truthfulness are the pillars of dharma.[2] Egoistic and altruistic virtues, intellectual, moral, æsthetic, and religious virtues are included in the list of virtues. But the main stress is laid on the virtues that lead to the purification of character and liberation. Falsehood (anṛta), pride (mada), lust (kāma), injury (rajas), enmity (vaira),[3] greed (lobha), theft (caurya), fraudulence (vañcanā), quarrelsomeness (kalaha), and hypocrisy (dambha)[4] are mentioned as vices. Self-realization, realization of the essential divinity of the self, or God-realization is the highest good.

(3) *Cosmology.*—The cosmology of the *Bhāgavata* is akin to that of the Śaṁkhya except in that prakṛti is the power of God, which evolves under his guidance, and that the multiplicity of jīva are appearances of the one Self (puruṣa) of God.[5] Prakṛti is eternal, unmanifest, and mutable. It is of the nature of cause and effect. It is composed of sattva, rajas, and tamas. It is the homogeneous substratum of heterogeneous effects.[6] Twenty four categories are transformations of prakṛti. They are the five subtle essences (tanmātra), the five gross elements, the five cognitive senses, the five motor senses, manas, buddhi, ahaṁkāra, and citta. Time is the twenty fifth category.[7] God creates time (kāla), karma, and svabhāva through his māyā.[8] Prakṛti is the equilibrium of sattva, rajas, and tamas. Time disturbs their equilibrium. Nature (svabhāva) brings about their transformation. Karma supervised by God transforms them into mahat or cosmic intellect. Mahat is transformed into threefold ahaṁkāra or cosmic egoism. The vaikārika ahaṁkāra is transformed into manas. Assimilation (saṁkalpa) and discrimination (vikalpa) are its functions. The taijasa ahaṁkāra is transformed into buddhi, and the ten sense-organs. Doubt (saṁśaya), illusion (viparyāsa), determination (niścaya), recollection (smṛti), and sleep (svāpa) are the functions of buddhi. The tāmasa ahaṁkāra is transformed into the five subtle essences (tanmātra). They are transformed into the five gross elements. The Sāṁkhya order of evolution of the tanmātras and gross elements is followed. But all transformations are actuated and guided by

[1] *Ibid*, i. 17. 27-29.
[2] *Ibid*, i. 17. 40.
[3] HIP., vol. iv, p. 32.
[4] *Ibid*, i. 17. 32.
[5] *Ibid*, iii. 12. 41.
[6] *Bhāgavata*, iii. 26, 10.
[7] *Ibid*, iii. 26, 14-15.
[8] *Ibid*, ii. 5. 21.

the energy of God.[1] The *Bhāgavata* account of the evolution of prakṛti is different from that of the atheistic Sāṁkhya philosophy.

3. *The Philosophy of the Pañcarātra*

The *Sātvatasaṁhitā* describes Brahman as calm (śānta), partless, and undifferenced.[2] He is of the nature of consciousness (saṁvitsvarūpa).[3] He is self-luminous and peerless.[4] He is of the nature of bliss and vibration.[5] He is formless. But he assumes a form in a peerless body.[6] Though he is formless, he manifests himself in the form of Vyūhas without losing his essential nature.[7] Vāsudeva, Saṁkarṣaṇa, Pradyumna, and Aniruddha are the four Vyūhas.[8] They possess strength, knowledge, sovereignty, virility, splendour, and power in different degrees.[9] Vāsudeva is the supreme Lord. Brahman is the ground of all reality. He is omnipresent and omnipotent. He is devoid of all sense-organs. But he manifests all sensible qualities.[10] Brahman is the substrate of prakṛti. Prakṛti is interpenetrated with his rays. Brahman is interpenetrated with the rays of prakṛti. It is of the nature of Brahman.[11]

The *Jayākhyasaṁhitā* describes Brahman as the ultimate reality. He is the eternal, omnipresent, self-realized, pure consciousness. He is devoid of the guṇas, sattva, rajas, and tamas. But he is hidden by them. He enjoys their various modifications. He is immanent in them. He is transcendent to them. He is beginningless and infinite. He is omniscient, omnipotent, and self-existent. He is not limited by time and space. He pervades all conscious beings and unconscious objects, and transcends them. He is the Lord of all. He cannot be known by reason. He can be directly known by yogic intuition.[12]

The jīva is pure consciousness tinged with māya, avidyā, or guṇas. It is associated with root-instincts (vāsanā). The association of the self with root-instincts is beginningless. It is brought about by God. The root-instincts are due to avidyā. When the self is dissociated from the root-instincts and their cause, avidyā, it is merged in God. The liberated jīva abides

---

1 iii. 26, 23-33; ii. 5, 23-31.
2 Ch. ii. 62.
3 Ch. iii. 12-13.
4 Ch. ii. 42.
5 Ch. iii. 15.
6 Ch. ii. 70.
7 Ch. iii. 5-6.
8 Ch. vii. 25-28.
9 Ch. iii. 6-7.
10 Ch. xii. 63-64.
11 Ch. xii. 83.
12 HIP., Vol. iii. pp. 24-25, 27-28.

in God in a state of identity-in-difference. Bondage is due to disfavour of God. Liberation is due to his favour. He associates the jīva with avidyā and root-instincts. He dissociates it from them. He reduces its pristine omnipresence, omniscience, and omnipotence, and makes it atomic, ignorant, and impotent. He removes these fetters through his grace.[1] The jīva is freed from root-instincts through the destruction of karma, and becomes one with God. The released soul realizes its innate pure consciousness. Buddhi, an evolute of prakṛti, is intelligized by the self, and appears to be conscious in the state of bondage.

Prakṛti is material and unconscious. Sattva, rajas, and tamas exist in it in inseparable unity. Buddhi is evolved from prakṛti. Ahaṁkāra is evolved from buddhi. The five organs of knowledge and manas are evolved from sāttvika ahaṁkāra. The five organs of action are evolved from rājasa ahaṁkāra. The five tanmātras are evolved from tāmasa ahaṁkāra. The five gross elements are evolved from them.[2]

Lakṣmī is the great power of Viṣṇu. They are identical with each other, though they are distinct. The great power was not distinguished from the motionless ocean of the Absolute. Then it appeared as action (kriyā) and becoming (bhūti), force and matter. Even in dissolution Lakṣmī and Viṣṇu remain distinct from each other. There is an inseparable relation between them, like that of an attribute and a substance. Viṣṇu is the inactive, transcendent Absolute. Lakṣmī is the active, dynamic, immanent principle. Her action is the expression of of the Lord's desire. The power of action (kriyāśakti) of Lakṣmī is identical with Viṣṇu's will-to-be. It is the sudarśana portion of Lakṣmī. It is independent of space and time. It is undivided. It is more powerful than power of becoming (bhūtiśakti). Sudarśana is the instrument of Viṣṇu. Viṣṇu is the efficient cause, power of action the instrumental cause, and power of becoming the material cause of the world. The transcendent aspect of Viṣṇu or the supreme Absolute (paraṁ brahma) does not play any part in creation. Lakṣmī is one force. She, as Bhūti, creates the world, and as Kriyā, vitalizes and governs it.

---

[1] Schraeder: *Introduction to the Pāñcarātra*, pp. 88-89.
[2] HIP., Vol. iii, p. 25.

Pure creation (śuddhasṛṣṭi) is the first phase of the manifestation of Lakṣmī. It consists in the manifestation of the attributes of God, which are supernatural (aprākṛta). They are knowledge, strength, sovereignty, virility, power, and splendour. Knowledge (jñāna) is non-inert, self-conscious, eternal, all-comprehensive, *e.g.*, omniscience. It is the essence of Viṣṇu and Lakṣmī. Strength (bala) is absence of fatigue in creating and sustaining the world. Sovereignty (aiśvarya) is unimpeded activity. Virility (vīrya) is immutability in spite of being modified into the world. Power (śakti) is the capacity of becoming the material cause of the world. Splendour (tejas) is self-sufficiency or power of overpowering others. These attributes are the material of pure creation, in their totality, and by pairs. They constitute the supernatural body of Vāsudeva, the highest personal God, and that of his consort, Lakṣmī.

The *Pañcarātra* believes in emanation. It is a process in which the cause produces an effect without undergoing any change. Four Vyūhas emanate from Viṣṇu, Vāsudeva, Saṁkarṣaṇa, Pradyumna, and Aniruddha. Each Vyūha is possessed of the six attributes of Viṣṇu, of which, two only are manifest. Knowledge and strength are manifest in Saṁkarṣaṇa. Sovereignty and virility are manifest in Pradyumna. Power and splendour are manifest in Aniruddha. Each Vyūha has two activities, creative and moral, which are mediated by his two manifest qualities. Vāsudeva is the author of pure creation. Saṁkarṣaṇa makes non-pure creation dimly manifest. He creates a chaotic mass without internal distinctions. Pradyumna differentiates Puruṣa from Prakṛti. He creates the Group Soul, primordial matter, and subtle time. Aniruddha creates manifest matter and gross time. He is the author of mixed creation (miśra ṣṛṣṭi). He becomes the ruler of the universe. The Vyūhas create, preserve, and destroy it. They have moral activities. Saṁkarṣaṇa teaches the Śāstras or theory of monotheism (ekāntamārga). Pradyumna executes it in action (tatkriyā). Aniruddha grants liberation (tatkriyāphala)[1] God as supreme (para) is sometimes identified with, and sometimes distinguished from, the Vyūha Vāsudeva. When they are dis-

[1] *Introduction to the Pāñcarātra*, pp. 36-38.

tinguished, the Vyūha Vāsudeva is said to emanate from the Para Vāsudeva.

Pradyumna is the author of intermediate or mixed creation. He creates the Kūṭastha Puruṣa and the Māyā Śakti. The Kuṭastha Puruṣa or the Group Soul is the matrix of the souls. He is the Soul of souls. He is the source of all disembodied and non-liberated souls bound by karma prior to creation of the non-pure universe. He is pure in himself, but impure on account of his association with the root-instincts (vāsanā) of the individual souls. He is of a mixed nature. The Māyā Śakti is the matrix of the material universe. The Bhūti Śakti of Lakṣmī is manifested as the Kuṭastha Puruṣa and the Māyā Śakti. Pradyumna is the creator of moral law (niyati), time (kāla), and the guṇas. Niyati regulates positions in space, and intellectual, emotional, and practical activities of the jīvas. It is a conscious and moral principle. It is the Law of Karma. Kāla originates from Niyati. It is a mysterious power which exists in time. It is a subtle force which conditions time. It gives rise to the guṇas and urges them to action. There are three kinds of time: (1) time as effect (kārya kāla), (2) causal or subtle time, which is created, and yet relatively eternal, and (3) the highest time existing in pure creation.[1]

[1] *Ibid*, p. 66.

CHAPTER IX

THE PHILOSOPHY OF VIŚIṢṬĀDVAITA

1. *Introduction*

Rāmānuja was the chief propounder of the doctrine of qualified monism or non-dualism (viśiṣṭādvaitavāda). He criticized Śaṁkara's monism or absolutism, and established the ontological reality of God, the individual souls, and the world, and regarded the souls and the world as attributes or modes of God. The germs of theistic Vedānta are found in the theistic Upaniṣads, the Nārāyaṇīya section of the *Mahābhārata*, the *Bhagavad Gītā*, and the *Pañcarātra Āgamas*. Rāmānūja refers to Bodhāyana, Taṅka, Dramiḍa, Guhadeva, Kapardin, and Bhāruci as his predecessors who propounded qualified monism. Bodhāyana's *Vṛtti* on *Brahmasūtra* has been lost.

Nāthamuni (1000 A.D.) wrote *Nyāyatattva* and *Yogarahasya*. He was a disciple of the last of the Āḷvārs. Yāmunācārya, a teacher of Rāmānuja, wrote *Āgamaprāmāṇya Siddhitraya, Mahāpuruṣanirṇaya*, and *Gītārthasaṁgraha*. *Siddhitraya* is an important work. Rāmānuja (1017 A.D.—1137 A.D.) wrote a commentary on the *Brahmasūtra*, known as the *Śrībhāṣya*, a commentary on the *Bhagavad Gītā*, *Vedāntadīpa*, *Vedāntasāra*, *Vedārthasaṁgraha*, *Gadyatraya*, and *Bhagavadārādhanakrama*. Sudarśana wrote *Śrutaprakāśikā*, a subcommentary on *Śrībhāṣya*. Lokācārya's *Tattvatraya* is an important work on the Viśiṣṭādvaita ontology. Veṅkaṭanātha or Vedāntadeśika (1300 A.D.) wrote *Nyāyapariśuddhi*, which is an important work on Epistomology and Logic. His *Nyāyasiddhāñjana*, *Tattvamuktākalāpa*, and its commentary, *Sarvārthasiddhi* are useful works on ontology. Śrīnivāsācārya's (1700 A.D.) *Yatīndramatadīpikā* is a valuable work. *Śrībhāṣyavārtika* is a summary of *Śrībhāṣya* in verse.

2. *Bhāskara's Bhedābhedavāda*

Bhāskara (900 A.D.) wrote a commentary on the *Brahmasūtra*, and propounded the doctrine of unity and difference (bhedābhedavāda) in it. Unity and plurality both are equally real. Brahman is not pure consciousness. He is not attributeless (nirguṇa), but possessed of auspicious attributes (saguṇa). Brahman is God or divine personality. He is transformed into the world (brahmapariṇāmavāda) in his unconscious part. It is not an appearance of Brahman.[1] The doctrine of Māyā owes

[1] *Sarvārthasiddhi*, iii. 27.

its origin to Buddhism. The world is real. It is a transformation of Brahman. It is essentially spiritual. "Reality is both one and many. The one is the unconditioned Absolute, but the manifold is the Absolute conditioned by the upādhis or the delimiting adjuncts".[1] In the causal state Brahman is one; in the effected state he becomes many.[2] Both cause and effect are real. The effect is a modification of its cause. It is both identical with it and different from it.[3] It is not an unreal appearance of its cause. It is real. Though Brahman is partless, he transforms himself into the world, and remains unchanged in himself. He is immanent in the world, and transcends it. He becomes the enjoyable world (bhogya) and the enjoying souls (bhoktṛ), but he does not lose his identity in them.[4] Brahman is one and many. He is neither absolute identity nor absolute difference. Just as the sea is identical with its waves, which are its modifications, and yet different from them, so Brahman is identical with the world, which is his real modification, and yet different from it. There is difference as well as non-difference or identity between power (śakti) and the possessor of power (śaktimat). Hence the reality is characterized by unity and multiplicity, and it is definable as neither absolute identity nor absolute difference.[5] Transcendent Brahman apart from the world, his immanent forms, is a cosmic and formless (niṣprapañca). He is infinite, pure being and consciousness. He is characterized by these qualities. He does not become different by virtue of them. There is no substance without qualities. There are no qualities without substance.[6] Brahman is not attributeless (nirguṇa). He is possessed of excellent qualities (saguṇa). The relation between Brahman and the world is difference and non-difference or identity. The individual self (jīva) is Brahman limited by the adjuncts (upādhi) of ignorance (avidyā), desires (kāma), and actions (karma). The adjuncts are real. The formless Brahman is finitised by the body, the vital forces, manas, buddhi, and ahaṁkāra, and becomes the finite self. The mind-body-complex is due to avidyā-kāma-karma, which can be destroyed by the combination of true knowledge and performance of duties (jñānakarmasamuccaya). True knowledge unaided by right actions cannot lead to liberation. There is no embodied release (jīvanmukti). There is disembodied release (videhamukti) in which the finite self becomes one with the Absolute, and realizes its infinitude and absoluteness. It is identity with Brahman (ekībhāva). The relation between the jīva and Brahman is essential non-difference or identity, but non-essential difference. The identity between them is essential. Their difference is due to the limiting adjuncts.[7] The jīva is a part (aṁśa)

---

[1] P. N. Srinivasachari : *The Philosophy of Bhedābheda*, p. 8.
[2] *Bhāskarabhāṣya*, i. 1. 4.
[3] *Ibid*, ii. 1. 14.
[4] *Ibid*, ii. 1. 27.
[5] Sarvam ekānekātmakaṁ nātyatyam abhinnaṁ bhinnaṁ vā. *Ibid*, ii. 1. 18.
[6] *Ibid*, iii. 2. 23.
[7] Jīvaparayośca svābhāviko 'bhedaḥ, aupādhikas tu bhedaḥ. *Ibid*, iv. 4. 4.

of Brahman. It is a self-limitation of the Absolute. It is neither absolutely different from Brahman nor absolutely identical with him.[1] Its bondage is due to desire for enjoyment of worldly objects. Its liberation is due to its desire for Brahman. The jīva is, in its essential nature, unborn, immortal, and eternal. But it undergoes birth and death on account of its adjuncts.[2] Just as the rays come out of the sun, and return to it, so the jīvas are radiations or self-limitations of Brahman, and become one with him. Just as sparks are different and non-different from fire, so jīvas are different and non-different from Brahman. Just as space enclosed in a vessel is essentially non-different from space, so jīvas limited by the mind-body-complexes are essentially non-different from Brahman. The jīva is a knower, enjoyer, and active agent. It has freedom of the will and responsibility. Its freedom is subject to the divine freedom. The jīva is monadic or atomic, and resides in the heart. When its limiting adjuncts are destroyed it becomes infinite and absolute. Bhāskara rejects māyāvāda of Śaṁkara. The so-called avidyā, which projects the sensible world of plurality and practical life, cannot be said to be indescribable. It is self-contradictory to hold that avidyā is both existent (sat) and non-existent (asat). If it is mere negation, it cannot cause bondage. It must be a positive entity, since it causes bondage. So it must exist along with Brahman. This is dualism. If it is beginningless, it must be endless. Then there can be no liberation. If the knowledge of duality or difference is false, the knowledge of unity or identity also must be false, because it is knowledge. Knowledge of the world cannot be false, like the knowledge of dreams, since dreams also are real experiences. They are not absolutely false like hare's horns. Śaṁkara's doctrine of Māyā is an unwarranted hypothesis.[3] Rāmānuja criticized Bhāskara.

3. *Yādavaprakāśa's Bhedābhedavāda*

Yādavaprakāśa (1100 A.D.) maintains that Brahman is transformed into unconscious matter (acit), conscious souls (cit), and God (Īśvara). He is modified into enjoyed objects (bhogya), enjoying souls (bhoktṛ), and their controller (niyantṛ) or God. But he remains unchanged in his modifications. This is the doctrine of Brahmapariṇāma. Brahman is not attributeless (nirguṇa), but possessed of perfections (saguṇa). Brahman, in the causal state, is mere non-different Being (sanmātra) and universal (jāti). But, in the effected state, he is different and particular (vyakti). Brahman and the world are both non-different and different from each other, even as the sea and its waves are both non-different and different from each other.[4] Matter, souls, and God are modifications of Brahman. They are not ultimate realities. They are self-differentiations of Brahman, the supreme reality. For Bhāskara, identity is the ultimate reality and difference is adventitious, but for Yādavaprakāśa difference

[1] Sa ca bhinnābhinnasvarūpaḥ. ii. 3. 43.
[2] *Sarvārthasiddhi*, iii. 27.
[3] HIP., Vol. III, pp. 4-5. *The Philosophy of Bhedābheda*, Ch. V.
[4] *Sarvārthasiddhi*, iii. 27.

is as real as identity.[1] For Bhāskara matter and souls are parallel expressions of Brahman, but for Yādavaprakāśa matter (acit) is a phase in the manifestation of spirit (cit), and essentially spiritual. There is no qualitative distinction between them. Matter is spirit in an unmanifested state.[2] Rāmānuja criticized Yādavaprakāśa.

II. Epistemology

4. *The Sources of Knowledge*

Śrīnivāsa defines valid knowledge as the knowledge, which apprehends an object as it really exists, and which prompts fruitful activity.[3] Knowledge accords with a real object, and initiates action which leads to its practical use. Perfect knowledge is coherent. It is in harmony with the reality as an organic whole. Rāmānuja recognizes the realistic test of correspondence, the pragmatic test of workability, and the idealistic test of coherence. These are the tests of truth. Pramāṇa is the means of valid knowledge (pramā). Perception, inference, and testimony are the three sources of knowledge.

Perception is the means of immediate valid knowledge. Perceptual knowledge is immediate (sākṣātkāra). It is different from inferential knowledge which is mediate. It is different from illusion which is produced by the vitiated sense-organs. Perception is indeterminate (nirvikalpa) and determinate (savikalpa). Indeterminate perception is perception of the first individual of a class, endowed with qualities and a particular arrangement of parts. Determinate perception is the perception of the second individual and the like, qualified by attributes and a particular configuration, which involves recollection. Indeterminate perception is a presentative process. Determinate perception is a presentative-representative process. Both apprehend qualified objects (viśiṣṭaviṣaya). Knowledge of an unqualified object is impossible.[4] Perception, again, is sensuous or non-sensuous. Non-sensuous perception is yogic intuition or supra-mundane intuition due to the grace of God. Perceptions of the released souls, the eternally released souls, and God also are non-sensuous.[5] Memory depends upon previous perception.

---

[1] *The Philosophy of Bhedābheda*, p. 171.
[2] *Ibid*, pp. 4, 171.
[3] Yathāvasthitavyavahārānuguṇajñānaṁ pramā. *Yatīndramatadīpikā*, p. 2.
[4] IPP., pp. 49-52.
[5] *Yatīndramatadīpikā*, p. 3.

It is knowledge produced by the subconscious impression of previous perception only. So it is not an independent source of knowledge. It is included in perception.[1]

Inference is valid knowledge of a specific instance of the probandum on recollection of the pervasion of the probans by the probandum. A particular fire is inferred from the perception of smoke which is always pervaded by fire. The probans is the reason or the middle term. The probandum is the major term. The middle term is not of wider extent in space and time than the major term. The major term is not of narrower extent in space and time than the middle term. The middle term is invariably accompanied by the major term. The major term is the inseparable correlate of the middle term. Vyāpti is the invariable concomitance of the middle term with the major term, not vitiated by conditions (upādhi). For instance, wherever there is smoke there is fire. Vyāpti is known by observation of a large number of instances of their co-existence (bhuyodarśana). The Nyāya syllogism consists of five members, proposition (pratijñā), reason (hetu), example (udāharaṇa), application (upanaya), and conclusion (nigamana). Rāmānuja maintains that the example or universal major premise and the application or minor premise are enough for intelligent persons. The conclusion also is necessary for less intelligent persons. All the five members are necessary for dull persons. Rāmānuja recognizes the two kinds of inference, Kevalānvayi and Anvayavyatireki. He rejects Kevalavyatireki inference. He admits the five fallacies of Asiddha, Viruddha, Anaikāntika, Prakaraṇasama, and Kālātyayopadiṣṭa.[2]

Comparison (upamāna) is the knowledge of a wild cow (gavaya) as similar to a cow perceived already on the strength of a statement of a forester. It is included in inference, since it depends upon the knowledge of invariable concomitance between words and objects denoted by them. It is included in perception, since recollection of similarity of a wild cow with a cow depends upon previous perception of it. It is included in testimony, since it is produced by the statement of a reliable person. So comparison is not an independent source of knowledge. Presumption also is included in inference.[3]

---

[1] *Ibid*, p. 4.

[2] *Ibid*, pp. 7-10.

[3] *Ibid*, p. 10.

Testimony is either secular or scriptural. Secular testimony is knowledge produced by a sentence uttered by a reliable person. It is not vitiated by the defects of its cause, and not sublated by contradicting knowledge. Expectancy, mutual fitness, and proximity of the constituent words are necessary for a sentence. Scriptural testimony is knowledge of supersensible objects, produced by sentences which are not uttered by trustworthy persons. The Vedas are eternal and impersonal. They are not composed by persons. They are revealed by God at the beginning of each cycle. The entire Vedas are valid.[1] Brahman is not perceived.[2] He cannot be proved or disproved by reason.[3] He is proved by the Vedas only.[4] They are the only source of our knowledge of supersensible objects. Reason may be employed to confirm them.[5] The Smṛtis and the Purāṇas, which are in accord with the Vedas, are sources of valid knowledge. The *Pañcarātra Āgama* uttered by Vāsudeva is in complete harmony with the Vedas, and therefore authoritative.[6] Both secular testimony and Vedic testimony apprehend qualified objects possessed of distinctions.[7]

All knowledge is true, and apprehends qualified objects. Unqualified objects are never apprehended.[8] All knowledge apprehends the reality.[9] Knowledge reveals a real object.[10] It has intrinsic validity. It is valid in itself. Its validity is not due to extraneous conditions. Even illusion apprehends a real object. Rāmānuja advocates the doctrine of Satkhyāti. A shell is perceived as silver. There is the element of silver in a shell. So the perception is valid. But the element of silver is so scanty that it cannot be an object of practical use. So it is illusory. It is sublated by the knowledge of preponderance of the element of shell in it. Rāmānuja harnesses the doctrine of quintuplication to the service of his theory of error or illusion. The five elements of earth, water, fire, air, and ether are present in various proportions in all material objects. This is the

---

[1] *Ibid*, pp. 12-14.
[2] RBS., i. 1. 3.
[3] RBS., i. 2. 23.
[4] RBS., i. 2. 1.
[5] RBS., ii. 1. 12.
[6] *Yatīndramatadīpikā*, p. 13.
[7] *Ibid*, p. 14.
[8] Sarvaṁ jñānaṁ satyaṁ saviśeṣaviṣayaṁ ca. Nirviśeṣavastuno 'grahaṇāt. *Ibid*, p. 5.
[9] Sarvaṁ vijñānajātaṁ yathārtham. RBS., i. 1. 1.
[10] Arthaprakaśo buddhiḥ. *Yatīndramatadīpikā*, p. 26.

doctrine of quintuplication (pañcīkaraṇa).[1] Dreams also are true. God creates dream-objects for the enjoyment and suffering of individuals in accordance with their merits and demerits.[2] Rāmānuja explains away error.

The subject and the predicate of a judgment are distinct. But a judgment affirms the identity of them, though they are distinct. It implies identity in difference. Identity is a relation. It requires two terms to be related to each other. If the subject and the predicate are not distinct, they cannot be related to each other. If there is no difference between them, identity between them cannot be established. Identity presupposes difference. Rāmānuja maintains that every judgment implies identity in and through difference. In the judgment 'the lotus is blue' the lotus and blueness are not identical ; nor are they entirely different. The quality of blueness is attributed to the subject, lotus, which is given in sense-perception. The predicate 'blue' qualifies and amplifies the meaning of the subject 'lotus'. The substance 'lotus' and the attribute 'blue' are different from each other. Yet there is inseparable relation between them. They subsist together. Every judgment is affirmation of reality which is identity in and through difference. It is not apprehension of identity devoid of difference. Śaṁkara maintains that in the judgment 'that thou art' there is real identity between the subject and the predicate ; but that there is apparent difference between them. But Rāmānuja maintains that there is real identity as well as difference between them.

II. Ontology

35. *Brahman* : *God*

Brahman is the Supreme Person (puruṣottama) endowed with innumerable supreme and auspicious qualities and devoid of all impure qualities. He is the infinite reality by nature and qualities. There is no other supreme reality. He is possessed of truth or reality (satya), knowledge (jñāna), and bliss (ānanda). He is the eternal and changeless reality. He is self-

---

[1] *Ibid, pp.* 4-5. IPP., pp. 294-95.
[2] *Ibid,* p. 5.

luminous. He is not manifested by any other agent. He is infinite. He is not limited by time, space, and other objects. Brahman is the determinate whole (saviśeṣa). All qualities coinhere in the divine substance. Brahman is identical with God (īśvara). There is no distinction between the indeterminate Brahman (nirguṇa brahma) and the determinate Brahman (saguṇa brahma). There is no indeterminate Brahman. Brahman is said to be attributeless (nirguṇa) because he is devoid of the impure qualities derived from prakṛti. The supreme (para) Brahman is eternal, omnipresent, subtle, immanent in all, infinite, inexhaustible, omniscient, omnipotent, and endowed with many auspicious qualities. He is the creator, preserver, and destroyer of the world. He is its material cause and efficient cause. He is the ground of all.[1] He is the inner controller of all. He is the Lord. He is the goal. He is the chief. He is the giver of the supreme ends of life. He is the giver of the fruits of actions. He is the Lord of Karma. He is the refuge of his devotees. He is of the nature of infinite knowledge and bliss. His knowledge is of the nature of bliss. His auspicious qualities are eternal, unlimited, innumerable, unconditional, flawless, unequalled, and unexcelled.[2] He is the inner Self of unconscious matter and conscious souls. He is their ground, controller, and principal (śeṣin).[3] He is immanent in unconscious matter and conscious souls. He is transcendent to them. He is the inner Self of all souls.[4] He is worshipped and attained by them.[5] He is the bridge (setu) that leads them to immortality.[6] He is infinite (bhūmā). He exists in his own greatness. He is the Self of all. He is the cause of all effects. He is the First Cause.[7] He is eternal, unborn, immortal, infinite, identical in essence, and immaculate.[8] He is infinite in the sense that he is eternal and immanent in all conscious souls and unconscious matter, and their inner controller (antaryāmin). But he is not tainted with their impurities.[9] He is possessed of supreme knowledge (jñāna), power (śakti) of creating, preserv-

---

[1] RBS., i. 1, 1; *Vedāntadīpa*, i. 2, 1; i. 1, 30-31; i. 2, 4-5; *Vedārthasaṃgraha*, pp. 11, 16, 25, 32, 134, 183, 185.

[2] *Tattvatraya*, pp. 85-91.

[3] *Vedāntadīpa*, p. 1.

[4] *Ibid*, i. 2. 19, 25.

[5] *Ibid*, i. 2, 12; i. 3. 2.

[6] *Ibid*, i. 3, 1.

[7] *Ibid*, i. 3, 8.

[8] *Vedārthasaṃgraha*, p. 183.

[9] *Tattvatraya* and commentary on it, pp. 88-89.

ing, and destroying the world, strength (bala) or absence of fatigue in creating and sustaining it, lordship (aiśvarya), capacity for regulating all objects and spirits, or independence (śvātantrya), virility (vīrya) or unchangeability in the midst of changes in his body, or immutability in spite of his being the material cause of the world, and self-sufficiency (tejas) or power of acting without auxiliary conditions. He gives knowledge to the ignorant, power to the powerless, forgiveness to the guilty, mercy to the miserable, tenderness to the impure, honesty to the dishonest, straightness to the crooked, goodness to the vicious, softness to the bereaved, and fruition to the aspirant.[1] He is the Lord of all, the ground of all, the chief of all, the cause of all effects, the soul of all jīvas and unconscious objects which constitute his body, the giver of fruits of actions, the object of worship through all actions dedicated to him.[2] He controls the entire universe of conscious souls and unconscious matter which are his powers, parts, manifestations, forms, attributes (viśeṣaṇa), modes (prakāra), or body. They are his body. He is their soul. They coinhere in him. He is their ground and substance. He is different from his attributes or modes.[3] There is inseparable relation (apṛthaksiddhi) between them.[4] There is unity in plurality in him. There is plurality in unity in him.[5] The nature of Brahman is inconceivable (acintya). Though one only as the ruler, he enters into the multiplicity of jīvas and unconscious objects as their inner Self, and makes the souls do many actions freely, and makes material things assume various forms. He assumes multiform nature in spite of his unity. He does not lose his integrity in the midst of diversity of his manifestations. He abides in them as the supreme Lord.[6] Brahman is devoid of homogeneous difference (sajātīyabheda) and heterogeneous difference (vijātīyabheda). There is no other reality like him or unlike him. But there is internal difference (svagatabheda) in him. There is no contradiction between his unity and internal diversity. He is different from all. He is the ground of all. He has infinite powers. He can assume infinite forms. He can retain his unity,

---

[1] *Ibid*, pp. 95-96.
[2] *Yatīndramatadīpikāa*, p. 37.
[3] *Vedārthasaṃgraha*, pp. 11, 34.
[4] *Ibid*, p. 35.
[5] Ekatve sati nānātvaṁ nānātve sati caikatā. *Ibid*, p. 27.
[6] *Ibid*, p. 127.

identity, and integrity by his infinite wonderful power. He harmonizes all multiplicity in his all-embracing unity.[1] He is one in many. He is unity-in-difference. He is one in the sense that he is the inner Self of all which coinhere in him. He is devoid of plurality in the sense that plurality of souls and material objects are his body or modes. He is different from them.[2] They are the creations of his manifold powers. God is perfect. He creates the world in sport out of his fullness.[3] He does not realize any extraneous end in creating the world. He creates the creatures with unequal lots in accordance with their karmas. He adjusts the manifold world to the moral deserts of the jīvas.[4]

God assumes an embodiment (vigraha). It is, like his essence, eternal, identical, made of pure sattva, and endowed with a conscious body which does not veil his essence of knowledge. It manifests the essence of his divine Self. It is made of supreme effulgence. It is endowed with tenderness and other auspicious qualities. It is the object of meditation by the yogins, the enchanter of the whole world, the producer of detachment from all worldly enjoyments, the destroyer of all miseries, the root of all incarnations, the protector of all, and the refuge of all. He is beautiful and terrific. He is decorated with ornaments. He is armed with weapons. He is apprehended by the eternally released souls.[5]

God's essence is fivefold, the eternal manifestation (parā vibhūti), the fourfold manifestations (vyūha), Vāsudeva, Saṁkarṣaṇa, Pradyumna, and Aniruddha, incarnations (vibhava), the inner controller (antaryāmin), and images (arcāvatāra). The supreme manifestation is non-temporal and full of infinite bliss. It is enjoyed by the eternally released souls. God manifests himself as Vāsudeva, Saṁkarṣaṇa, Pradyumna, and Aniruddha for creation, preservation, and destruction of the world, protection of the souls in bondage, and showing favour to the devotees. Vāsudeva is possessed of the six qualities of Lordship in perfection. Saṁkarṣaṇa is possessed of knowledge and strength, and presides over the individual souls. Pradyumna is possessed of rulership and virility, and presides over the mind

[1] *Ibid*, p. 129.
[2] *Ibid*, p. 134.
[3] *Vedāntadīpa*, ii. 1, 31-33.
[4] RBS., ii. 1, 33-34.
[5] *Tattvatraya*, pp. 118-19.

(manas). Aniruddha is possessed of power and self-sufficiency, and presides over the egoism (ahaṁkāra). Saṁkarṣaṇa differentiates the souls from prakṛti, and reveals the scriptures. Pradyumna is the instructor of dharma, and the author of pure creation. Aniruddha is the giver of true knowledge, the creator of time, and the author of mixed creation. He is the preserver of the world. Pradyumna is the destroyer of it. Incarnations (vibhava) are either chief or subordinate. The chief incarnations are God's transcendental and supernatural embodiments. They are worshipped by all aspirants for liberation. The subordinate incarnations such as Vyāsa, Arjuna, and the like, should not be worshipped by aspirants for liberation, since they supervise the jīvas endowed with egoism. They are manifestations of God in men, beasts, and inanimate things. Avatāras are divine descents for protection of the virtuous, destruction of the vicious, and establishment of the moral order. God enters into conscious souls and material objects, and controls them from within. The existence of God in objects of worship such as images is called arcāvatāra. It creates attachment for God. It does good to the devotees. It is the refuge of all. It is apprehended by all. It is a concrete image through which God can be worshipped.[1]

Matter and souls are attributes (viśeṣaṇa), modes (prakāra), or parts (aṁśa) of Brahman. They are accessory (śeṣa) to him. There are changes in his parts or modes. But he remains unchanged in them. There is no change in the divine substance.[2] The conscious and unconscious modes constitute his body. He is their soul. There is an inseparable relation (apṛthaksiddhi) between them. They cannot exist apart from him. They abide in him. They are controlled by him. They are means to him.[3] He is identity-in-difference. He remains identical in the midst of diverse modes. He harmonizes the plurality of modes within his unity.[4] He is their Lord, chief, and ground. He is their Self. He is perfect and immutable. He is different from them.[5]

The text 'That art thou' (tat tvam asi) means that the individual soul is identical in essence with Brahman. The soul presiding over a body is a mode of Brahman. It is his body.

---

[1] *Tattvatraya*, pp. 121-42.
[2] *Vedārthasaṁgraha*, p. 114.
[3] *Ibid*, p. 116.
[4] *Ibid*, p. 127.
[5] *Ibid*, p. 134.

It cannot exist apart from him. It is not a mere appearance. It is real and eternal. It is an eternal part of Brahman.[1] It is finite and dependent. But Brahman is infinite and independent. He is perfect, unchangeable, and endowed with all auspicious qualities. The soul is identical in essential nature with Brahman. The souls and Brahman both are real and distinct. They have coinherence in the same ground or substance.[2] Brahman is an organic whole of different souls and material objects. He is a synthetic whole of inter-related modes or parts. He is a determinate whole. He is not an undifferenced unity. He is not indeterminate Absolute.[3] He is the Supreme Person (puruṣottama). He is not the sumtotal of finite persons. He is the perfect Person. All souls are co-eternal members with him. He is the Soul, Lord, Controller, and Chief of the community of finite souls. He is immanent in them. He is transcendent to them.[4] Though he is immanent in them, he is not affected by their joys and sorrows, since he is devoid of merits and demerits (karma). The souls experience them as fruits of their actions.[5] Brahman is unaffected by modifications of matter and imperfections of the souls. Matter and souls are dependent on him as his inseparable attributes.[6]

6. *The Jīva: Self and Consciousness*

The jīva is the individual self. It is different from the body, life, the sense-organs, manas and buddhi. It is different from the psychophysical organism. It is the knower, enjoyer, and active agent. It is not inert. It is self-luminous. It manifests itself without the aid of knowledge. It is not manifested by knowledge. It is the abode of knowledge. It has attributive consciousness. It is the subject or substrate of consciousness. It is of the nature of bliss. It is eternal. It persists in all times. It is unborn and immortal. It is not affected by birth and death. Birth is its union with body. Death is its disjunction from body. The jīva is atomic or monadic (aṇu). It resides in the heart. It pervades the world with its knowledge, even as the light of a lamp pervades a room. It is imperceptible. It cannot be perceived through the sense-organs. It is inconceivable. It can-

---

[1] *Vedāntasāra*, i. 1, 2.
[2] *Ibid*, p. 35.
[3] *Ibid*, p. 41.
[4] *Ibid*, p. 116.
[5] *Vedāntasāra*, ii. 1, 14; RBS., ii. 1. 9.
[6] P. N. Srinivasachari: *The Philosophy of Viśiṣṭādvaita*, p. 87.

not be thought as similar to matter. It is an ego. It cannot be thought as a non-ego. It is not composed of parts. It is simple. It is not an aggregate of constituents. It is a simple, immaterial spirit. It is immutable. It remains identical with itself without undergoing modifications. The body changes, but the self does not. The jīva is said to be of the nature of knowledge, since it manifests itself without knowledge. Knowledge is its essential property (nirūpakadharma). The jīva is controlled (niyāmya) by God. Its freedom is subject to the divine will. The jīva is grounded (dhārya) in God. It is sustained by him. It cannot exist apart from him. It is his attribute (viśeṣaṇa) or mode (prakāra). It is inseparably related to him. God is the ground of all jīvas. There is a relation of a master and a servant between a jīva and God. The jīva is an accessory (śeṣa) to God, who is the Lord. It is dependent on him.[1]

Self-luminosity, consciousness, self-hood, and agency are common to the jīva and God. The jīva manifests itself to itself. It is conscious. It is the substrate of knowledge. It is the self embodied in an organism. It is an active agent. It is the substrate of volition. These are the general characteristics of the self. The jīva is monadic. It is a spiritual monad. It is an accessory (śeṣa) to God. It subsists in him. It is dependent on him. These are its special characteristics. It is permanent, since it recollects its past experiences. Its essence is eternal. The jīva is a soul in relation to its body. But it is a body in relation to God. The jīva is self-luminous. It is endued with attributive knowledge. Consciousness, atomicity, purity, and the like are its essential properties.[2] The self is of the nature of knowledge, bliss, and purity. Ignorance, pain, and impurity are due to its connection with prakṛti or its product, the mind-body-complex. Its essential properties are not due to karmas due to its connection with prakṛti.[3] Brahman exists in all selves in his essence, free from all taint of imperfections due to connection with prakṛti. All souls have the essential properties of knowledge and bliss. They are homogeneous (ekarasa), accessory to God, controlled by him, subsist in him, and constitute his body. Their bondage is due to connection with prakṛti due to karmas.[4]

---

[1] *Tattvatraya*, pp. 5-15, 22-26.
[2] *Yatīndramatadīpikā*, pp. 31-32.
[3] *Vedārthasaṁgraha*, p. 124.
[4] *Ibid*, pp. 125-26.

The jīva's birth is due to avidyā. Avidyā is false identification of the self with the body. It is beginningless. It generates karmas in the shape of merits and demerits. Avidyā obscures the essential nature of the self and its affinity with God, its inner controller. When avidyā is destroyed by meditation on God, its essential nature is manifested, and it experiences the infinite bliss of Brahman.[1] Rāmānuja recognizes avidyā in the jīvas, which veils their essential nature and kinship with Brahman. But he does not admit avidyā which projects the plurality of world-appearance.

Knowledge and bliss constitute the essence of the jīvas. The differences among them are due to their bodies, which are modifications of prakṛti. They are due to karmas, which are due to avidyā. When avidyā is destroyed, the jīvas are divested of these differences due to modes of prakṛti, and experience their essential knowledge and bliss. They are common to all jīvas. They have similarity (sāmya) with God in their liberated state.[2]

The jīva acquires avidyā, actions (karma), dispositions (vāsanā), and desires (ruci) in connection with unconscious matter. When connection with it is destroyed, avidyā and its products are destroyed.[3] The jīva experiences pleasure and pain owing to its karmas. Its pleasures and pains are not due to its connection with the body. They are due to its karmas. God is devoid of them. So he does not experience pleasures and pains.[4] The self is of the nature of bliss. Knowledge, in its manifest condition, is pleasant. All objects are of the nature of Brahman. So they are essentially agreeable. Their disagreeable nature is due to accidental conditions. It is due to false identification of the self with the body.[5]

The jīvas are subordinate knowers. God is the principal knower. The knowledge of the jīvas is eternal, immaterial, and blissful. It is an attribute of the self, and yet it is a substance, since it contracts and expands. The essence of the self neither contracts nor expands. It manifests itself to itself. It is atomic. But knowledge is its attribute. It is subject to contraction and expansion. It does not manifest itself. It manifests an object.

---

[1] *Ibid*, p. 7.
[2] *Ibid*, p. 9
[3] *Tattvatraya*, p. 29.
[4] *Vedāntadīpa*, i. 2. 8; ii. 1, 14.
[5] *Tattvatraya*, pp. 38-39.

It is pervasive. Some selves always have pervasive knowledge. Others always have non-pervasive knowledge. Others sometimes have pervasive knowledge.[1] Knowledge of the self is eternal. But it appears to be produced, when it issues through the sense-organs and apprehends objects, and it appears to be destroyed, when it withdraws from objects. One eternal knowledge appears to be many cognitions because it expands to different objects.[2] Knowledge is a substance because it is the substrate of quality and activity, and because it manifests objects. It does not manifest objects in deep sleep and swoon, since it does not extend to objects at that time because it is overcome by tamas.[3] Knowledge manifests itself when the self in which it subsists apprehends objects. But it is not manifested in deep sleep because it is obscured by tamas and because the self does not apprehend objects.[4] The self experiences the whole body through its knowledge, even as a gem manifests a large area through its light.[5]

The self is the substrate of consciousness. Consciousness abides in the self, and apprehends an object. Śaṁkara recognizes subject-objectless consciousness. But Rāmānuja denies its existence. He maintains that there is no consciousness, which does not apprehend objects, since such consciousness is never perceived.[6] The self is not mere consciousness. It is conscious. It is a knower of objects. It is conscious of objects. It is self-luminous in the sense that it manifests objects. It is not mere manifestation. It is not consciousness. It is a conscious knower.[7] Consciousness is the manifestation of an object to its substrate, the self, through its own being. Self-luminousness consists in manifestation of consciousness to the self, its abode, through its own being.[8] Manifestation prompts empirical use. 'I know a jar.' Here the knowledge manifests a jar to the self through its own being. The self is the witness (sākṣin) of all objects. Knowledge is an act. The self is the agent of the cognitive

---

[1] *Ibid*, p. 35.
[2] *Ibid*, p. 36.
[3] *Ibid*, pp. 37-38.
[4] Commentary on *Ibid*, pp. 37-38.
[5] *Vedāntasāra*, ii. 3, 26.
[6] Na ca nirviṣayā kācit saṁvid asti, anupalabdheḥ. Iha tu sakalaviṣayavirahiṇī nirāśrayā ca saṁvit niṣidhyate. RB.S., i. 1, 1.
[7] Ataḥ svayaṁprakāśo'yam ātmā jñātaiva, na prakāśamātram. *Ibid*, i. 1, 1.
[8] Svasattaiva svāśrayaṁ prati kasyacid viṣayasya prakāśanaṁ hi saṁvedanaṁ. Svayaṁprakāśatā tu svasattaiva svāśrayāya prakāśamānata. *Ibid*, i. 1, 1.

act. A thing is an object of it. The cognitive act cannot be its own object. It cannot be its own subject. The self is the subject of knowledge. A thing is an object of knowledge.[1] Knowledge is a particular property of the self. Cognitions appear and disappear. They have origin, existence, and destruction. But the self, which is their witness, is permanent. It remembers and recognizes the objects of its past experience. Therefore it must exist in the past as well as the present. Memory and recognition presuppose the existence of the permanent self.[2] 'I perceived this in the past.' This recollection shows that the self is the knower. It is not mere knowledge. There is no consciousness without a self and without an object, since it is absolutely unknown.[3] The self is conscious (jña). It is not mere consciousness (jñaptimātram). It is the subject of knowledge. It is not an object of knowledge. To argue that the self, the subject of knowledge, is the object of knowledge is as absurd as to argue that one's mother is a barren woman. The self is always a subject, ego, or knower (jñātā). It is never an object of knowledge. It is self-luminous. It manifests itself to itself. It is not manifested by any other agent. Consciousness is its essence. Its essence of consciousness constitutes its self-luminous nature. What is self-luminous is not manifested by any other agent. The self manifests itself and other objects, even as a lamp manifests itself and other objects.[4] Śaṁkara maintains that subject-objectless consciousness appears to be the knower (jñātā) owing to illusion. Rāmānuja contends that this view is wrong, since there is the apprehension 'I know',[5] but never 'I am knowledge'.[6] Knowledge subsists in the knower. There is no mere knowledge. There is a knowing self that has knowledge. Knowerhood (jñātṛtva) is not a false appearance. If the knower is false, the knowledge also is false. If the knowledge is not false, the

[1] Asya sakarmakasya kartṛdharmaviśeṣasya karmatvāvat kartṛtvam api durghaṭam. *Ibid*, i. 1, 1.

[2] RBS., i. 1, 1.

[3] Saṁvit nāma kācit nirāśrayā nirviṣayā vāatyantānupalabhdher na sambhavati. *Ibid*, i. 1, 1.

[4] Na cāsau jñātāhamartho'nyādhīnaprakāśaḥ, svayaṁprakāśatvāt. Caitanyasvabhāvatā hi svayaṁprakāśata. Yaḥ prakāśasvabhāvaḥ, so'nanyādhīnaprakāśo dīpavat. *Ibid*, i. 1, 1.

[5] Anubhavāmy aham. *Ibid*, i. 1, 1.

[6] Anubhūtir aham. *Ibid*, i. 1, 1.

knower cannot be false. The knowledge is uncontradicted and valid. So the knower must exist. Śaṁkara argues that the knower is the agent of the act of knowledge, and that the self, which is unmodifiable, cannot be the agent of the cognitive act. Activity belongs to egoism (ahaṁkāra), which is an internal organ. Egoism is non-intelligent, modifiable, and active. The self is inactive and immutable. It can never be the agent of the act of knowledge. Agency (kartṛtva) is the quality of an object, like colour. If the self were the agent of the cognitive act, it would be a not-self, an object, and a non-intelligent being. But Rāmānuja urges that this argument is invalid. Inertness, being a modification of prakṛti, knownness, externality, being a means to the self's experience, and the like are the qualities common to the body and the internal organ of egoism. But knowerhood (jñātṛtva) is a unique property of an intelligent knower or self.[1] Egoism is revealed by knowledge. It is an object of knowledge. So it can never be a subject of knowledge. Egoism cannot be a knower. Further, knowerhood consists in being a substrate of the quality of knowledge. It does not consist in undergoing a change. The self is eternal. So its essential quality of knowledge also is eternal. Knowledge constitutes its essence. It naturally subsists in the self. It is of the essence of knowledge, and yet is the substrate of knowledge, even as a lamp is of the essence of light, and yet is a substrate of light.[2] Though knowledge of the self is unlimited, it undergoes contraction and expansion due to karmas during bondage. Contracted knowledge expands to objects through the sense-organs. The origin and destruction of knowledge are due to the operation or non-operation of the sense-organs. The self is the agent of the expansion of knowledge. The sense-organs are its instruments. But this agency is not esential to the self; it is due to karmas. The self is, in its essence, immutable. Such knowerhood which does not involve any modification belongs to the self, which is of the nature of knowledge. It can never belong to the non-intelligent egoism.[3] Śaṁkara maintains that non-intelligent egoism becomes a knower owing to the reflection of consciousness

[1] Cetanāsādhāraṇasvabhāvatvāc ca jñātṛtvasya. *Ibid*, i. 1, 1.

[2] Asya jñānasvarūpasyaiva jñānāśrayatvam. *Ibid*, i. 1, 1.

[3] Avikriyātmakaṁ jñātṛtvaṁ jñānasvarūpasya ātmana eveti. *Ibid*, i. 1, 1.

due to proximity. Rāmānuja asks whether egoism is reflected on consciousness or whether consciousness is reflected on egoism. Egoism cannot be reflected on consciousness, since Śaṁkara does not admit the knowerhood of consciousness. Nor can consciousness be reflected on egoism, since egoism is non-intelligent, and cannot be a knower. Both consciousness and egoism are invisible, and cannot be reflected on each other. Egoism cannot be a knower, since it is unconscious. An unconscious entity cannot be conscious owing to proximity to consciousness. Consciousness cannot be said to be manifested by egoism. The self is self-luminous ; it cannot be manifested by non-intelligent egoism. Egoism is manifested by consciousness. But consciousness is not manifested by egoism. Hence the inner self is essentially a knower. It is not mere knowledge. If it is not a knower, knowledge also cannot manifest objects.[1] Knowerhood constitutes the essence of the self. In deep sleep it is not manifested as a knower because there are no objects of knowledge at that time. It continues to be a knower in the state of liberation.

Śaṁkara maintains that consciousness is self-luminous, and that it is never an object of another consciousness. Ramānuja disputes this view. When the self manifests an object, its consciousness is said to be self-luminous. But the self can apprehend its own past consciousness as its object. It can apprehend also the consciousness of another person. We infer the consciousness of another person from his speech and behaviour. If consciousness is apprehended as an object, it does not cease to be consciousness. The essential nature of consciousness consists in its manifesting itself to its substrate at the present moment through its own being, or in its manifesting its object through its own being. Consciousness does not lose its essential nature, when it becomes an object of another consciousness. Both unconscious things and consciousness are objects of consciousness.[2] Thus Rāmānuja differs from Śaṁkara in his views of the self and consciousness.

The jīva is a knower, enjoyer, and an active agent. Agency

---

[1] Svata eva jñātṛtayā sidhyan ahamartha eva pratyagātmā, na jñaptimātram. Ahaṁbhāvavigame tu jñapter api na pratyaktvasiddhiḥ. *Ibid*, i. 1, 1.

[2] *Ibid*, i. 1, 1.

and enjoyerhood are states of knowledge. Enjoyment is the experience of pleasure and pain. It is a state of knowledge. Volition is due to desire to act. Desire is due to knowledge of end and means. So agency, which involves desire and knowledge, is a state of knowledge.[1] The Śaṁkhya maintains that the self is not active, but that buddhi composed of sattva, rajas, and tamas is active. But this view is not tenable. If the self is not free and active, it cannot acquire merits and demerits by doing right and wrong actions laid down in the Vedas, and experience pleasures and pains. But the activity of the self in the state of bondage is due to its conjunction with the guṇas. It is not due to its essential nature. Its activity is dependent on God. Human freedom is not absolute, but relative. It is subject to divine freedom.[2] God permits the jīvas to do actions freely, and enjoy their fruits. He impels them to act freely, but he does not compel them to do so. God is the permitter (prayojaka). The jīvas are permitted (prayojya).[3] They freely do right and wrong actions. Prakṛti or buddhi does not do the actions. But the free activity of the jīva is subject to the permission of God.[4] They experience the fruits of their actions. But God, who exists and shines in them, does not experience them.[5] Rāmānuja insists on human freedom subject to the will of God.[6]

The souls are bound, released, and eternally liberated. The bound souls are in bondage to empirical life. The released souls are liberated from bondage.[7] Bondage is due to avidyā, karma, vāsanā, and ruci. Avidyā is ignorance of the soul's dependence on God. Karma is action prompted by ignorance. Vāsanā is the subconscious disposition produced by actions. Ruci is attachment produced by the dispositions. Avidyā and its products connect the soul with a mind-body-complex. They can be destroyed by the intuitive knowledge of the self as disconnected with the psychophysical organism. The knowledge can be attained by devotion, complete self-surrender to God, and moral discipline.[8] Rāmānuja takes devotion (bhakti) in the

---

[1] Commentary on *Tattvatraya,* p. 18.
[2] *Tattvatraya,* pp. 19-20.
[3] *Vedāntasāra,* i. 2, 11.
[4] Ātmanaḥ kartṛtvaṁ paramapuruṣānumatisahakṛtam. *Ibid,* i. 1. 2.
[5] *Ibid,* i. 3, 6.
[6] *Ibid,* ii. 3, 40-41; RBS., ii. 3. 41.
[7] *Tattvatraya,* p. 26.
[8] RBS., iv. 4. 2-3; *Yatīndramatadīpikā,* pp. 33-34.

sense of steady recollection of God.[1] It is a particular kind of knowledge.[2] Meditation (dhyāna) also is an uninterrupted stream of recollection. It is aided by the performance of duties relating to castes and stages of life throughout life. Service (sevā) and taking refuge in God (śaraṇāgati) are essential to devotion. Daily prayers (nitya karma) and occasional duties (naimittika karma) ought to be performed. Sacrifices, charity, penances, truthfulness, cleanliness, straightforwardness, kindness, non-injury, strength, tranquillity, sense-restraint, and other virtues should be cultivated.[3] Constant prayer, recollection, obeisance, worship, effort, chanting the name of God, hearing of his qualities, uttering them, and meditation on God are necessary for liberation.[4] Bondage and liberation depend on the will of God. The essential purity of the self is concealed by a beginningless series of karmas due to avidyā at the will of God. This is bondage. The veil of karmas is removed by devotion, meditation, and knowledge at his will. This is release.[5] It is a state of similarity (sāmya) with Brahman. It is community of nature with him (brahmaprakāratā). It is not identity with him.[6] The self does not lose its identity in Brahman in the state of release. It persists as a knower.[7] Its knowledge becomes infinite. It is not contracted by karma. It gets rid of karma, and enjoys the infinite glory of God.[8] It apprehends his nature, and enjoys his infinite bliss.[9] Though it attains community of nature with God, it cannot create and govern the world.[10] The released soul becomes autonomous (svarāt). It enjoys the infinite sport of God at will.[11] God grants it release through his grace. He, pleased with his devotion and self-surrender, destroys its avidyā in the form of accumulated karmas and releases it from birth and death.[12] The manifestation of its essential purity, infinite knowledge and enjoyment, and existence in the eternal abode of God depends upon him.[13]

---

[1] Dhruvānusmṛtireva bhaktiśabdena abhidīyate. RBS., i. 1. 1.
[2] *Vedārthasaṁgraha*, p. 248.
[3] RBS., i. 1. 1; *Vedārthasaṁgraha*, pp. 142-43.
[4] *Vedārthasaṁgraha*, p. 144.
[5] RBS., iii. 2. 4; iv. 4. 3.
[6] Muktasya svarūpaṁ brahmaṇo bhāvaḥ svabhāvaḥ, na tu svarūpaikyam. RBS., i. 1, 1.
[7] RBS., i. 1. 1.
[8] RBS., iv. 4. 15, 19.
[9] RBS., iv. 4, 22.
[10] RBS., iv. 4. 17, 20.
[11] RBS., iv. 4. 19.
[12] RBS., iv. 4, 22.
[13] RBS., iv. 4, 20.

The jīva is not identical with Brahman. The identity texts indicate the essential similarity between them. They are different from each other. Brahman is the creator, controller, preserver, destroyer, moral governor, ground, goal, and Lord. He is omniscient, independent, pure, and possessed of auspicious qualities. The embodied soul (jīva) is created, controlled, preserved, destroyed, and governed by Brahman, and subsists in him. It is ignorant, dependent, impure, and possessed of inauspicious qualities. It is accessory to the Lord. He is worshipped while the soul is the worshipper. He is attained by the soul. Therefore the jīva is different from Brahman. It is a part of Brahman,[1] even as light issuing from a luminous thing is a part of it. A part constitutes one place of a thing. An attribute is a part of the thing qualified by it. A distinction between a qualified thing and a qualifying attribute is made. Though an attribute is a part of the qualified thing, there is a difference between them. The soul is an attribute (viśeṣaṇa) of Brahman. It is a part of him. There is a difference between a part and a whole. There is a difference between an attribute and a substance. So the jīva is different from Brahman.[2] There is inseparable relation (apṛthaksiddhi) between them.[3] Brahman is not composed of parts. The souls cannot be cut out from him. The text 'that thou art' (tat tvam asi) does not show the identity of the self with Brahman. It shows that Brahman is the ground of the self. The subject and the predicate are distinct. They have identity of the ground (sāmānādhikaraṇya). They coinhere in the same substance. The jīvas are the attributes or parts of Brahman.

7. *Matter*

Matter (acit) is an unconscious, mutable object of experience. It is of three kinds: pure sattva, mixed sattva, and matter devoid of sattva. Pure matter (śuddhasattva) is unmixed with rajas and tamas. It is eternal. It produces knowledge and bliss. It is of the nature of infinite effulgence. It is a very wonderful entity. Its magnitude cannot be known definitely

[1] RBS., ii. 3, 42.
[2] RBS., ii. 3, 45; *Vedāntasāra*, i. 1, 2.
[3] RBS., iii. 2, 28.

by the liberated souls and God. It is modified into celestial palaces and various other objects by the mere will of God without any action. It constitutes his transcendental abode. It constitutes his eternal manifestation (nityavibhūti). Some call it matter. Others call it non-matter. It manifests itself without the knowledge of the eternally released souls, released souls, and God. It is not manifested to the bound souls. It is different from the self (ātman) and knowledge. It is not known as 'I'. So it is not the self. It is modified into the body. It manifests itself without objects. It possesses the qualities of sound, touch, and the like. So it is not knowledge. It is pure matter different from the self and knowledge.[1] It is śuddha sattva. It is pure sattva unmixed with rajas and tamas. It constitutes the body of God in his eternal manifestation (nityavibhūti). It is self-luminous. It manifests itself to God and the liberated souls. It is transformed into instruments and objects of their enjoyment by the will of God. It is an object (parāk). But it is different from matter composed of sattva, rajas, and tamas. Therefore it may be regarded as immaterial (ajaḍa).[2]

Prakṛti, avidyā, or māyā is mixed sattva. It consists of sattva, rajas, and tamas. It is eternal. It is the means of God's sport in līlāvibhūti or empirical manifestation. It is mutable. It is transformed into homogeneous and heterogeneous modifications in different times and places. Creation is the evolution of prakṛti from the homogeneous to the heterogeneous condition. Dissolution is the devolution of prakṛti from the heterogeneous to the homogeneous condition.[3] Prakṛti obscures knowledge and bliss of the bound souls. It produces false knowledge in them. It is a kind of matter (acidviśeṣa).[4] It is called prakṛti because it produces modifications. It is called avidyā because it counteracts right knowledge. It is called māyā because it creates the manifold universe.[5] Prakṛti is the substrate of sattva, rajas, and tamas. It is the equilibrium of the three guṇas. It is thrown into disequilibrium by the will of God. It is called avyakta in a state of disequipoise ready to be transformed into effects.[6] Sattva, rajas, and tamas are the constituents of prakṛti. They are in-

[1] *Tattvatraya,* pp. 41-45.
[2] RBS., ii. 2, 2.
[3] *Ibid,* p. 48.
[4] *Yatīndramatadīpikā,* p. 24.
[5] *Tattvatraya,* pp. 45-46.
[6] *Yatīndramatadīpikā,* p. 15.

separably related to the essence of prakṛti. They are unmanifest in the state of prakṛti. They become manifest when prakṛti is modified into mahat and the other categories. Sattva produces knowledge and pleasure, and association with them. Rajas produces attachment, desire, and action. Tamas produces false knowledge, inattention, laziness, and sleep.[1] They are not substances (dravya) because they are devoid of conjunction. They are non-eternal. They pervade prakṛti. They overcome one another, and predominate over one another. They are fit matter for creation, maintenance and dissolution of the world by God.[2]

In dissolution prakṛti exists as a power of God, consisting of the subtle constituents in the causal state, abiding in him. It is uncaused (ajā) in this sense. In creation it issues forth from the body of God and assumes a gross or effected state.[3] Prakṛti is the power of God. It exists in him, and depends upon him. It is not an independent entity as the Sāṁkhya maintains. Prakṛti, independent of God, is not the material cause of the world. God, in the causal state in which names and forms are not yet differentiated, is its material cause. In this condition he is said to be non-existent (asat) or unmanifest (avyākṛta).[4] Prior to creation prakṛti exists in a subtle state devoid of names and forms as the body of God. It assumes names and forms at the time of creation at the will of God. So God is the cause of Prakṛti.[5] It is the body of God. It is a mode (prakāra) of him. It is identical with him in its essence. He is the self (ātman) of its modifications.[6] God as the substance (prakārin) of prakṛti is immutable. But as modes (prakāra) of prakṛti he is mutable. As the substance he is the inner controller (niyantṛ) of prakṛti and its mutations.[7] Prakṛti is subtle unconscious matter. God impregnates it with his conscious power.[8] Prakṛti is unconscious. So it cannot act without being supervised by conscious Īśvara.[9]

---

[1] *Tattvatraya*, pp. 51-52.
[2] *Yatīndramatadīpikā*, p. 43.
[3] *Vedāntadīpa*, B.S.S., 1904, i. 4, 10.
[4] *Ibid*, i. 4, 14; RBS., i. 4, 14.
[5] *Vedāntasāra*, 1905, i. 4, 10; RBS., i. 4, 10.
[6] *Vedārthasaṁgraha*, Benares, 1894, p. 113.
[7] *Ibid*, p. 114.
[8] Bhūtasūkṣam acid vastu. RBS., i. 1. 1; RBG., xiii. 2.
[9] RBS., ii. 1, 1.

Prakṛti is transformed into mahat or buddhi. Determination is its quality. It is threefold, sāttvika, rājasa, and tāmasa, according as sattva, rajas, or tamas predominates in it. Buddhi is transformed into ahaṁkāra. It has the quality of egoism. Ahaṁkāra also is threefold, sāttvika, rājasa, and tāmasa. Sāttvika ahaṁkāra is transformed into the five cognitive senses, the five motor senses, and manas. Tāmasa ahaṁkāra is transformed into the five subtle essences (tanmātra), which are modified into the five gross elements. Rājasa ahaṁkāra aids sāttvika ahaṁkāra and tāmasa ahaṁkāra to produce their effects. Sāttvika ahaṁkāra produces manas without any auxiliary condition. It produces the cognitive and motor organs with the aid of the subtle essences.[1] Dik is not a separate substance. Ākāśa is the cause of occupation. It has sound. Air is devoid of colour and smell. It is neither hot nor cold. Fire is bright and hot. Water has taste and cold touch. It is devoid of smell. Earth has smell, taste, and touch. The Viśiṣṭādvaita Vedānta advocates the doctrine of quintuplication (pañcīkaraṇa) of the elements.[2]

Lokācārya maintains that time (kāla) is devoid of sattva. It is the cause of transformation of prakṛti[3] and its mutations. It is eternal. It is the body of God. It aids him in his sport. It is modified into moments, days and the like, which are due to conditions (upādhi).[4] It is the cause of all effects. Śrīnivāsa maintains that time is a kind of matter (acidviśeṣa). It is matter devoid of sattva, rajas, and tamas. It is eternal and ubiquitous. It is past, present, and future. It is the cause of the use of simultaneity and succession, soon and late, and the like. It is an object of perception through the six sense-organs.[5] It is eternal in the transcendental abode of God. It is non-eternal in the world.[6]

Unconscious material objects cannot act by themselves. They act under the supervision of God. Their physical actions are subservient to the divine will.[7] They give pleasure or pain

---

[1] *Tattvatraya*, pp. 53-62; *Yatīndramatadīpikā*, pp. 15-17.
[2] *Yatīndramatadīpikā*, pp. 17-19.
[3] Cp. *Bhāgavata*.
[4] *Tattvatraya*, p. 74; *Tattvamuktākalāpa*, i. 69.
[5] *Yatīndramatadīpikā*, p. 23.
[6] *Tattvatraya*, p. 79.
[7] RBS., ii. 2, 2.

to the individual souls in accordance with their moral deserts (karma) at the will of God in different times and places. They are the matter of the sport of God who controls them in various ways. God is free from karmas. So physical objects cannot give him pleasure or pain.[1]

8. *Causality: Satkāryavāda*

Rāmānuja advocates the doctrine of Satkāryavāda. The effect pre-exists in the cause. The cause and the effect both are real. The effect is non-different from the cause. Production is modification of the cause into the effect. Destruction is re-absorption of the effect in the cause. Production and destruction are the different states of the causal substance. Production is modification (vikāra). Modification is rearrangement of the parts of the causal substance (saṁsthānaviśeṣa). A jar is a modification of earth. It is destroyed and turned into earth. A gold ornament is a modification of gold. It is destroyed and turned into gold. Production, existence, and destruction are the different states of the causal substance, even as childhood, youth and old age are the different states of a person. There is essential identity or non-difference (ananyatva) between cause and effect, both of which are real. If the cause is real (satya) and the effect is an unreal appearance (mithyā), as Śaṁkara maintains, there cannot be identity between them. There can be no identity between a reality and an appearance.[2]

9. *Creation*

Supreme Brahman is the world-soul. Unconscious matter and conscious souls in all states constitute his body.[3] Brahman is the cause. The entire unconscious world and conscious souls are the effect. The effect is non-different from the cause. Matter and souls are not separate entities from Brahman. They are inseparable and non-different from him. They are attributes (viśeṣaṇa) of Brahman, which coinhere in him. They have coinherence (sāmānādhikaraṇya) in him. Brahman invested with subtle or causal matter and souls is the cause. Brahman invested

[1] RBS., iii. 2, 12. [2] RBS., ii. 1. 15-16.
[3] Sarvāvasthasya cidacidvastunaḥ paramātmaśarīratvaṁ paramātmanaśca ātmatvam. *Vedāntadīpa*, B.S.S., 1904, p. 3.

with gross or effected matter and souls is the effect.[1] Brahman in the causal and effected condition with his body of conscious souls and unconscious matter is the whole reality. Brahman is one in the unmanifest or undifferentiated condition. He is manifold in the manifest or differentiated condition. Subtle unconscious matter unmanifested in names and forms and subtle conscious souls are the body of the causal Brahman. Gross unconscious matter manifested in names and forms or objects and individual souls with their manifest qualities are the body of the effected Brahman.[2] Matter and souls are inseparable from God. There is inseparable relation (apṛthaksiddhi) between them. They together with God immanent in them constitute the reality.

Brahman is cause as well as effect. In the causal state he is invested with the body of subtle conscious souls and unconscious matter. In the effected state he is invested with the body of gross conscious souls and unconscious matter. So the effect is non-different from the cause.[3] Though Brahman is partless, he can transform himself into the manifold world owing to his omnipotence. One indivisible Brahman can transform himself into the manifold world of souls and matter, even as one partless universal can exist in many individuals without being divided.[4]

God's creation consists in the transformation of matter into various objects and endowing souls with bodies and sense-organs and expanding their knowledge. Maintenance consists in his entering into created objects and conserving them all. Dissolution consists in his withdrawing them into himself. Brahmā endowed with rajas is the creator. Viṣṇu endowed with sattva is the preserver. Rudra endowed with tamas is the destroyer. They are different aspects of God. As the inner controller (antaryāmin) of created objects God creates, maintains, and destroys them.[5]

---

[1] Sūkṣmacidacidvastuśarīraḥ paramātmā kāraṇaṁ, sa eva paramātmā sthūlacidacidvastuśarīraḥ kāryam. *Ibid*, pp. 3-4.

[2] Nāmarūpavibhāgānarhasūkṣmacidacidvastuśarīrakatayaikadhā'vasthitasya vibhaktanāmarūpacidacidvastuśarīrakatayā bahuprakāratā viṣayaḥ. *Ibid*, p. 4.

[3] Sūkṣmacidacidvastuśarīraṁ brahma kāraṇāvasthaṁ sthūlacidacidvastuśarīraṁ brahmaiva kāryāvastham iti kāryakāraṇayorananyatvam. *Ibid*, ii. 1. 21.

[4] *Ibid*, ii. 1. 26.

[5] *Tattvatraya*, pp. 112-15.

God is the material cause, the efficient cause and the auxiliary cause of the world. He is modified into the world by his free will. Prakṛti is his power. He transforms it into the world. Independent prakṛti is not its material cause. God creates the world by his mere will without any effort. Creation, maintenance, and dissolution are his mere sport.[1] God freely transforms himself into the world. So he is its material cause. Or God as qualified by subtle conscious souls and unconscious matter, which are his attributes (viśeṣaṇa) and which are not manifested as embodied souls and gross matter, is its material cause. He is its efficient cause because by his mere will he transforms his power (prakṛti) into the world. He as qualified by knowledge, power and the like is its auxiliary cause.[2] God as substance (viśeṣya) is immutable, because his essence does not undergo modification. But he as qualified by the attributes of conscious souls and unconscious matter is modified into the world. So there is no contradiction between his immutability and modifications.[3] God as substance (prakārin) is not modified. But his attributes or modes (prakāra) of conscious souls and unconscious matter are modified. As qualified by the two attributes God, their controller, undergoes modification in the shape of being qualified by them. So Rāmānuja admits that God is subject to change.[4]

Yādavaprakāśa maintains that one Brahman that is mere Being is transformed into the enjoying souls, the enjoyed objects, and their controller. But Rāmānuja contends that in that case Īśvara and the individual souls would be produced and non-eternal. If matter, souls, and Īśvara be said to exist as causal powers (śakti) in one Brahman, then the latter has capacity for transformation into them. Therefore Brahman is the cause, and matter, souls, and God are the effects, which are non-eternal. If the existence of God and individual souls in a subtle condition be said to constitute the causal power (śakti), it should be regarded as causal Brahman. There is no proof for the existence of Brahman as mere Being (sanmātra). Its transformation into Īśvara and souls makes them non-eternal.

[1] *Ibid*, pp. 105-07. [2] *Ibid*, commentary, p. 109.
[3] Cp. Vallabha : Avikṛtapariṇāmavāda. *Ibid*, pp. 110-11.
[4] Ubhayaprakāraviśiṣṭe niyantraṁśe tadavastha-tadubhayaviśiṣṭatārūpa vikāro bhavati; kāraṇāvasthāyā avasthāntarāpattirūpo vikāraḥ prakāradvaye prakāriṇi ca samānaḥ. RBS., ii. 3. 18.

So the subtle, unmanifest and undifferentiated condition of souls and matter existing in God prior to creation is the causal Brahman. Brahman qualified by gross matter and embodied souls is the effected Brahman. Īśvara and souls are eternal. Brahman is not transformed into them. Brahman is Īśvara. Matter and souls are co-eternal with him. They are his inseparable attributes.[1] Brahman is not mere Being. He is always omniscient, omnipotent, pure, and absolute. He is endowed with infinite knowledge, bliss, and will. He is the first cause. He is determinate (saviśeṣa). His qualities of knowledge, bliss, and other auspicious qualities are essential and eternal. They are not accidental and non-eternal. Īśvara is not a part of Brahman. He *is* Brahman. If Brahman were mere Being, and as such were the whole reality, and the Self of the universe, God, its part, would not be the whole reality and the world-soul. If God, a part of Brahman, were full (purṇa), then every object would be full, being a part of Brahman. Further, mere being cannot be a cause. There are specific causes of specific effects. If Brahman were the cause of all objects, good and bad, as mere being, there would be confusion of all good and evil. Therefore Brahman as mere Being cannot be the cause of the world. So Yādavaprakāśa's view is wrong.[2]

Śaṁkara maintains that Brahman as cause is real, that the world as effect is unreal, and that the unreal effect is non-different from the cause. But Rāmānuja urges that there cannot be non-difference between a real thing and an unreal appearance. If there could be non-difference between them, Brahman also would be unreal and the world would be real. But this is absurd. So Śaṁkara's view is wrong.

Bhāskara maintains that both cause and effect are real, that the difference between the jīva and Brahman is accidental and due to limiting adjuncts (upādhi), that the non-difference between them is essential, and that both difference and non-difference between Brahman and matter are essential. But Rāmānuja urges that this doctrine contradicts the Śruti which declares that the jīva and Brahman are distinct from each other in so far as Brahman is free from all evil and not subject to the power of karma while the jīva is impure and subject to the power of

---

[1] *Vedāntadīpa*, pp. 7-8. [2] RBS., ii. 1. 15.

karma. Bhāskara's doctrine also contradicts those texts which declare that matter undergoes modifications while Brahman is immutable. There exists nothing but Brahman and the limiting adjuncts according to him. Brahman is one and indivisible. So when Brahman enters into connection with the adjuncts, his essence undergoes modifications into inferior forms. But Brahman is unmodifiable. It cannot be argued that only the power of Brahman undergoes modifications, and not Brahman himself since Brahman and his power are non-different from each other. Therefore Bhāskara's doctrine of transformation of Brahman into the world, and his difference and non-difference from it is not tenable.[1]

God creates the world out of his fullness to realize his internal end of sport. He does not create it to realize any external end. He is perfect and fulfilled. He has no unrealized end. Creation is an act of play.[2] He creates the world of various objects of enjoyment in accordance with the moral deserts (karma) of the individual souls. He adapts the created objects to the karmas of the jīvas. He makes them happy or unhappy according to their merits or demerits. Otherwise he would be partial to happy creatures and cruel to unhappy creatures.[3] So Brahman, who is omnipotent and different from matter and souls, creates the multiform world with the aid of the karmas of the jīvas in order to realize his end of playful activity.[4]

10. *Refutation of Śaṁkara's doctrine of Avidyā*

Śaṁkara maintains that one undifferenced, indeterminate, self-luminious Brahman is real, and that Iśvara, jīvas, and the material world are unreal appearances due to some defect. The defect (doṣa) is beginningless avidyā. It is neither real nor unreal but indefinable. It conceals the real nature of Brahman, and projects the appearance of the multiform world.[5] It is not being (sat), since it is illusory and contradicted by right knowledge. Nor is it non-being (asat), since it is experienced and sublated by right knowledge. So Śaṁkara maintains that avidyā or māyā is indefinable and inexplicable.

---

[1] RBS., ii. 1, 15.
[2] *Vedāntadīpa*, ii. 1, 32-33.
[3] RBS., ii. 1, 34.
[4] RBS., ii. 1, 35.
[5] Doṣaśca svarūpatirodhāna-vividhavicitravikṣepakarī sadasadanirvacanīyānādyavidyā. RBS., i. 1, 1.

First, Rāmānuja contends that avidyā must subsist in something. It cannot abide in the individual soul (jīva), since it is a product of avidyā. The jīva is not real. It is Brahman limited by avidyā or the mind-body-complex due to avidyā. Avidyā cannot abide in Brahman, since it is self-luminous and of the nature of knowledge which is contradictory to avidyā. Avidyā is sublated by knowledge. Brahman is of the nature of pure knowledge which destroys nescience (avidyā). If avidyā conceals the nature of Brahman, nothing can destroy avidyā. The knowledge of the self-luminous nature of Brahman cannot destroy avidyā, since it is of the nature of self-luminosity like Brahman. If the self-luminous Brahman cannot destroy avidyā, its appearance in the form of knowledge of self-luminosity of Brahman can far less destroy it. If the knowledge that Brahman is of the nature of pure knowledge exists, then Brahman becomes an object of knowledge (prameya). But whatever is an object of knowledge is non-intelligent according to Śaṁkara. Therefore Brahman cannot be of the nature of pure knowledge. Both Brahman, which is of the nature of pure knowledge, and the knowledge of its essential self-luminosity are contradictory to avidyā. They are alike in this respect. So it is absurd to argue that Brahman, which is of the nature of pure knowledge, cannot destroy avidyā, but that the knowledge of its self-luminous nature can destroy it. Further, Śaṁkara admits that Brahman is of the nature of intuition (anubhavasvarūpa), which is not apprehended by any other intuition. So there is no knowledge of the self-luminous nature of Brahman. Knowledge and nescience (avidyā) are contradictory to each other. So Brahman, which is of the nature of pure knowledge or intuition, destroys avidyā, which cannot abide in Brahman. The real nature of Brahman is apprehended by its own intuition, which destroys nescience (ajñāna) of its own nature. It does not require any other knowledge to destroy avidyā. It may be argued that the knowledge of the falsity of whatever is other than Brahman, is contradictory to nescience (ajñāna). Is this knowledge of the falsity of what is other than Brahman contradictory to the nescience of the real nature of Brahman, or to the nescience which consists in the view of the reality of the world-appearance (prapañca)? It cannot be contradictory to the nescience of the real nature of Brahman, since it has a different object. Knowledge and nescience can contradict each other, if they refer to one and the same object. The knowledge of the falsity of the world-appearance cannot contradict the nescience of the real nature of Brahman. It can contradict the nescience which consists in the view of the world-appearance as real. The knowledge of the reality of the world-appearance is contradicted by the knowledge of its falsity. The nescience of the real nature of Brahman is not contradicted by it. Therefore Brahman, which is of the nature of pure knowledge, cannot be the locus or substrate of nescience. Avidyā cannot abide in any locus (āśrayānupapatti).

Secondly, avidyā cannot veil the self-luminous nature of Brahman, since self-luminosity is its essence (svarūpa), which would be destroyed. Veiling the self-luminosity of Brahman consists in either obstruction of the production of manifestation of Brahman or the destruction of its existing manifestation. The manifestation of Brahman is eternal ; it is not produced. So concealment of self-luminosity of Brahman amounts to the destruction of its manifestation. Hence avidyā is incapable of concealing the nature of Brahman (tirodhānānupapatti).

Thirdly, Śaṁkara maintains that the self-luminous consciousness, which is subjectless and objectless, apprehends itself as infinite subjects and infinite objects owing to some defect it itself. Rāmānuja asks whether this defect is real or unreal. It is not real since its reality is not admitted. Its reality contradicts monism. Nor is it unreal, since in that case it is either the knowing self, the known object, or knowledge. The knowing self and the known object are imaginary and unreal. Therefore their defect must be due to some other defect, and so on to infinity. This will lead to infinite regress. The defect cannot be of the nature of knowledge, since there is no distinction within knowledge itself. If the intuition of the absolute reality or the essence of Brahman itself be regarded as the defect, then Brahman itself is the cause of the experience of the world-appearance, and it is needless to assume the existence of avidyā like the world-appearance to account for it. Further, if Brahman itself is the defect, it is eternal like Brahman, and it makes liberation of the jīva impossible, since the defect of avidyā nnot be destroyed. If the reality of avidyā different from Brahman be not admitted, the world-appearance cannot be regarded as false. So the reality of avidyā is incapable of being proved (svarūpānupapatti).

Fourthly, avidyā is indefinable (anirvacanīya). It is neither real nor unreal. It is neither existent (sat) nor non-existent (asat). Rāmānuja urges that all objects are known through experience. All experience is either of the real or the unreal. There is no experience of anything which is neither real nor unreal. If such a thing, which is neither real nor unreal, were an object of experience, then any thing would be an object of any experience. So avidyā cannot be indefinable (anirvacanīyā-nupapatti).

Fifthly, the existence of avidyā cannot be proved by perception or inference. Śaṁkara argues that ajñāna or nescience as a positive entity is known by perception, since I experience that 'I am ignorant', or that 'I do not know myself and others'. Here positive nescience is perceived ; prior non-existence of knowledge is not perceived, since non-existence is known by non-apprehension (anupalabdhi). Even if non-existence is known by perception, the perception 'I am ignorant' cannot apprehend the non-existence of knowledge in the self, since knowledge exists in it. If knowledge did not exist in it, then there could be no knowledge of the non-existence of knowledge. But Rāmānuja urges that the perception 'I am ignorant' does not apprehend the existence of positive nescience. It apprehends the prior non-existence of knowledge. If the knowledge of the prior non-existence of knowledge be said to involve contradiction, then the knowledge of positive nescience also involves contradiction. Does the knowledge of the self exist in the perception of the positive nescience (ajñana) which abides in the self? If it does, how can nescience, which is destroyed by the knowledge of the real nature of the self, exist in the same self? If it does not exist, how can nescience be perceived without the knowledge of its object and substrate? The self is the object and substrate of nescience. If nescience be said to be indistinct knowledge, then also it may be regarded as prior non-existence of distinct knowledge. Even if nescience is positive (bhāvarūpa), it is non-knowledge (a-jñāna). It presupposes knowledge (jñāna) which is negated. Prior non-existence of knowledge also presupposes knowledge which is negated.

Nescience (ajñāna) is either non-existence of knowledge, or something other than knowledge, or counter-knowledge. All these presuppose the experience of knowledge. The existence of positive nescience (ajñāna) is never proved. Its existence as non-knowledge (a-jñāna) is proved. Hence the so-called nescience is nothing but prior non-existence of knowledge (jñānaprāgabhāva). Further, Brahman is eternally free, self-luminous, and of the nature of consciousness. It apprehends its essential nature. So it cannot perceive nescience. If it be argued that Brahman perceives nescience when its essential nature is veiled, though it is of the nature of self-luminosity, then concealment of its essential nature means its non-manifestation. But the self-luminous nature of Brahman cannot be unmanifest. If the self-luminous nature of Brahman be said to be concealed by another entity, then its essential nature is destroyed. If nescience unperceived by Brahman be said to conceal its essential nature, and then become the object of its perception, then it involves mutual dependence. Nescience is perceived when it conceals the nature of Brahman. The nature of Brahman is concealed when nescience is perceived. If nescience be said to be first perceived by Brahman, and then conceal its nature, then it is needless to assume the concealment of the nature of Brahman by nescience. It is needless to assume the existence of nescience even. If Brahman can perceive nescience before its nature is concealed, it can also perceive the world-appearance as transformation of nescience. Further, if Brahman perceives nescience, its perception is either natural or adventitious. If it is natural, then it is eternal and cannot be annulled. So liberation would not be possible. If it is adventitious, it is due to some other condition. If it is due to another nescience, it leads to infinite regress. If nescience conceals the nature of Brahman, and then is perceived by it, then it veils the nature of Brahman by its very existence, and cannot be annulled by knowledge, even as cataract covers the eye-ball, and is not removed by knowledge. It may be argued that nescience is beginningless, and so it is perceived by Brahman and conceals its nature at the same time. So there is no infinite regress. This argument is wrong. Brahman is self-luminous. It apprehends itself. It cannot perceive nescience if its nature is not concealed by nescience. If its nature is concealed by some other cause, then nescience ceases to be beginningless, and it leads to infinite regress. If Brahman perceives nescience without its nature being concealed, then it cannot be self-luminous. Further, Brahman is either entirely not manifested or partially manifested, when it is concealed by avidyā. If it becomes entirely unmanifest, it ceases to be Brahman. Brahman is self-luminous. If it becomes entirely unmanifest, it becomes a non-entity. Brahman is partless and indeterminate. It is of the nature of manifestation. So it cannot be partially manifest and partially unmanifest. It cannot be argued that Brahman, which is of the nature of undifferenced being, consciousness, and bliss, is indistinct, when it is veiled by avidyā, because a determinate entity with parts can be partly manifest and partly unmanifest, and thus become indistinct. But Brahman, which is of the nature of manifestation, can be neither distinct nor indistinct. Therefore nescience as a positive entity cannot be known by percepion. Nor can it be known by inference. 'I did not know anything during deep sleep'. Nescience is said to be inferred from the knowledge during the waking state. It is not recollection but inference. But the inference is invalid. Manifestation of an unmanifested object is the reason or probans (hetu), which seeks to prove the existence of nescience, which is the probandum. It proves that there is a certain knowledge. It does not prove the existence of nescience. So the reason is contradicted (viruddha). If the reason proves the existence of nescience which veils the nature of Brahman, then it exists in nescience of the jīva and nescience of Brahman. So it is too wide (anaikāntika). Hence nescience cannot be inferred. Moreover, arguments can be advanced against the positive nature of nescience. Nescience is non-knowledge. It cannot exist in Brahman which is of the nature of pure knowledge. It can exist in the jīva subject to error. Nescience cannot veil knowledge, since it is non-knowledge. It can veil an object. So nescience is not positive in nature, and positive nescience cannot be proved (pramāṇānupapatti).

Sixthly, Śaṁkara maintains that avidyā is destroyed by the integral knowledge of the identity of Brahman and the Self (ātman). Rāmānuja urges that bondage is not apparent but real, and that it cannot be destroyed by the knowledge of one undifferenced Brahman. Bondage is due to karmas or merits and demerits of the jīvas, which lead to embodied life and enjoyments and sufferings. Cessation of bondage can be acquired by devotional meditation on God through his grace. The duality of Brahman and the jīvas and the world is real and known by valid knowledge. So the knowledge of identity contradicts the real nature of duality, and is therefore false. It leads to increase of bondage. The knowledge of God, who is different from the jīvas, and who is their inner controller, is the means of liberation. The knowledge of identity, which seeks to terminate nescience, is itself false. So it requires another knowledge to destroy it. It may be argued that the knowledge of identity destroys all knowledge of differences and then disappears. This argument is wrong. The nature, origin, and end of the bondage-terminating knowledge are imaginary and due to avidyā. So another agency is required to terminate the knowledge and its originating avidyā. The essential nature of Brahman cannot terminate the knowledge, because in that cause the bondage-terminating knowledge (nivartaka-jñāna) would not arise at all. Brahman, its destruction, is always present. Further, who is the knower of the knowledge of the falsity of every thing other than Brahman? The superimposition (adhyāsa) of Brahman in intellect (buddhi) or avidyā cannot be its knower. It is an object of negation. So it can be an object of the avidyā-terminating knowledge. It can never be its knowing subject. If the essential nature of Brahman is the knower of the avidyā-terminating knowledge, its knowerhood (jñātṛtva) is either natural or superimposed on it. If it is natural and essential, then Brahman is a knower, and not mere knowledge as Śaṁkara maintains. If it is superimposed, the superimposition and its originating avidyā persist, since they are not objects of the avidya-terminating knowledge. If they are destroyed by another avidyā-terminating knowledge, it requires another knower, and so on to infinity. Thus it leads to infinite regress. Further, the superimposed knower cannot be the agent of the avidyā-terminating knowledge, which destroys it. None aims at destroying himself. If the essential nature of Brahman be the destroyer of the superimposed knower of the falsity of plurality, it is useless to assume plurality, experience of plurality, and its origining avidyā. Thus there can be no knowledge which can terminate avidyā (nivarttakānupapatti).

Seventhly, there can be no cessation of avidyā, since there is no knowledge which can destroy it. Avidyā of the jīva is due to karma. It cannot be removed by the knowledge of the identity of the Atman and Brahman as Śaṁkara maintains. Avidyā is the knowledge of the independence of the jīva of Brahman. It can be destroyed by constant meditation on God, the true knowledge of the self, and performance of duties relating to castes and stages of life. So there can be no destruction of avidyā by the knowledge of undifferenced Brahman as Śaṁkara supposes (nivṛttyanupapatti.)[1]

11. *Reality of the World*

Before creation the world exists in Brahman in the form of prakṛti composed of sattva, rajas, and tamas in equilibrium. Prakṛti is a power of Brahman. Individual souls also exist in Brahman prior to creation, devoid of their bodies. Prakṛti and souls, in a subtle condition, constitute the body of Brahman. The manifest world and the embodied souls also constitute his body. Matter, souls, and God constitute the reality in their inseparable relation to one another. So the world is real. It is not an unreal appearance (prapañca). God is the material cause, the efficient cause, and the auxiliary cause of the world. Both cause and effect are real. The effect is not an unreal appearance (vivarta) of the cause. It is a transformation (pariṇāma) of it. The world is a transformation of prakṛti which is a power of God. Brahman is cause as well as effect. The world is the effected Brahman (kāryabrahma). It cannot be condemned as a false appearance. The manifold world is apprehended by perception and inference. Both indeterminate perception and determinate perception apprehend objects qualified by difference. All pramāṇas prove determinate objects. There are no objectless cognitions. All cognitions abide in subjects and apprehend objects.[2] That cognition is false, which prompts unsuccessful activity. But the cognitions of various objects of the world do not lead to fruitless acts. The illusion of a snake is contradicted by the perception of a rope. But the perceptions of jars, cloths, and the like are not contradicted by one another.

[1] RBS., i. 1, 1.
[2] Saṁvit nāma kācit nirāśrayā nirviṣayā vā na sambhavati. RBS., i. 1, 1.

They prompt fruitful activities. Perceptions of various objects cannot be said to be sublated by the testimony of the scripture, since their spheres are different. Perception apprehends sensible objects. The scripture bears testimony to Brahman.[1] Objects of experience are not unreal because they do not persist. They may exist here and now, but may not exist at some other place and time. There is no contradiction between their existence in this place and time and their non-existence in some other place and time. The world is real, but its gross objects are not eternal. Distinctions are real. Identity also is real. Distincts are attributes (viśeṣaṇa) or modes (prakāra) of identity. They are inseparable from each other. They are not contradictory to each other. They are not therefore unreal appearances. They are real and coinhere in Brahman. They constitute the coherent whole in their organic unity.

---

[1] *Vedārthasaṁgraha,* pp. 87-88.

CHAPTER X

THE DVAITAVĀDA OF MADHVA

1. *Introduction*

Madhva (1199-1278 A.D.) was also known as Pūrṇaprajña and Ānandatīrtha. He wrote a commentary on the *Brahmasūtra*, and commentaries on the Upaniṣads and the *Bhāgavad Gītā* on the lines of dualism. He wrote *Anuvyākhyāna* to justify his *Brahmasūtrabhāṣya*. He wrote *Bhāgavatatātparyanirṇaya*, and many other works. *Tattvapradīpikā* of Trivikrama Paṇḍitācārya, *Sattarkadīpāvalī* of Padmanābhatirtha, and *Tattvaprakāśikā* of Jayatīrtha are subcommentaries on Madhva's *Brahmasūtrabhāṣya*. *Pramāṇapaddhati* of Jayatirtha and *Pramāṇacandrikā* of Śalāriśeṣācārya are works on Mādhva Logic.

Madhva is the founder of Dvaita Vedānta. He is a staunch advocate of dualism. He recognizes the five distinctions of God and the individual soul, God and matter, the individual soul and matter, one individual soul and another, and one material thing and another to be eternal. This is the central teaching of Madhva's dualism. It is realism, and looks upon the world as real.

2. *Epistemology*

Pramāṇa is valid knowledge which is in accord with the real nature of its object. It makes an object known as it is in itself. It makes the object known either directly or indirectly through the medium of some other knowledge. The self possessing valid knowledge is the knower (pramātṛ). The object of valid knowledge is the known (prameya). Valid knowledge is pramā. There are two kinds of valid knowledge, *viz.*, kevalapramāṇa, direct and immediate intuition of objects, and anupramāṇa, the instrument or means of valid knowledge. There are four kinds of kevalapramāṇa : (1) the knowledge of the Lord ; (2) the knowledge of Lakṣmī, his consort ; (3) the knowledge of the yogin ; and (4) the knowledge of an ordinary person. There are three kinds of anupramāṇa, *viz.*, perception, inference, and Vedic testimony.

Perception is the means of the apprehension of an object present here and now, which is proximate and unobstructed. Its range is limited to present time and space. There is no indeterminate perception. All perception is determinate. Inference is the means of the knowledge of objects which are not proximate, and which are past, future, remote, and obstructed. Vedic authority is an independent source of knowledge of innumerable objects. Perceptual knowledge is direct and immediate knowledge (sākṣātkāra). Inferential knowledge is indirect and mediate knowledge. Knowledge derived from testimony is verbal (śābda). Perceptual knowledge is of seven kinds: olfactory, gustatory, visual, tactual, auditory, mental perceptions, and intuition of the self (sākṣin). The sense-organs and the objects must be flawless. Perception is due to the fourfold contact of the self with the manas, of the manas with a sense-organ, and of a sense-organ with an object. The sense-organs are the instrumental cause (karaṇa) ; the sense-object-intercourse is the function or operation (vyāpāra) ; immediate knowledge is the result (phala) of the process of perception.[1]

Inference is flawless reasoning from a mark of inference to another property marked by it. The reason or mark of inference (liṅga) is the instrumental cause (karaṇa). The knowledge of the reason pervaded by the inferable property abiding in the subject of inference (parāmarśa) is the function or operation (vyāpara). The indirect knowledge of the property marked by the reason is the result (phala) of the inferential process. Inference depends on vyāpti. Vyāpti is invariable concomitance of the *probans* (hetu) and the *probandum* (sādhya) : 'Wherever there is smoke, there is fire.' It is an unfailing relation between the *probans* and the *probandum*. Vyāpti does not mean their co-inherence in the same substrate (sāmānādhikaraṇya). There are three kinds of inference: (1) Inference from effects ; (2) inference from causes ; and (3) inference from events which are neither causes nor effects. When an effect is the reason of inference of its cause, there is an inference from an effect. We infer the existence of fire from smoke. When a cause is the reason of inference of its effect, there is an inference from a cause. We infer a rain-fall from a dense mass of clouds.

---

[1] *Pramāṇacandrikā*, C.U., Ch. 1.

When a phenomenon, which is neither a cause nor an effect, is the reason of inference of another phenomenon, there is an inference from a phenomenon which is neither a cause nor an effect. We infer the existence of colour from the presence of taste. There is uniformity of co-existence between taste and colour. There is no uniformity of causation between them. Inference is of two kinds from another point of view: (1) Dṛṣṭa, inference of a perceivable object, as fire is inferred from smoke, and (2) Sāmānyatodṛṣṭa, inference of an unperceivable object, as the visual organ is inferred from the perception of colours. The Mādhvas reject the Naiyāyika division of inference into three kinds, *viz.*, Kevalānvayi, Kevalavyatireki, and Anvayavyatireki. Invariable co-absence cannot prove the presence of the *probandum*. Inference is again of two kinds: (1) inference for oneself (svārtha) and (2) inference for others (parārtha). The former is the cause of self-conviction. The latter is intended for convincing others. It consists of five members: (1) thesis (pratijñā); (2) reason (hetu); (3) example (udāharaṇa); (4) application (upanaya); and (5) conclusion (nigamana). Vyāpti is of two kinds: (1) Anvayavyāpti, and (2) Vyatirekavyāpti. The former is the pervasion of the *probans* by the *probandum*. The latter is the pervasion of the absence of the *probandum* by the absence of the *probans*.[1]

Testimony (*āgama*) is flawless verbal knowledge. There are two kinds of testimony: (1) personal (pauruṣeya); and (2) impersonal (apauruṣeya). The former is created; the latter is eternal. The Vedas are uncreated and eternal. They are revealed by God. They are self-evident. They are valid in themselves. They have intrinsic validity.[2] Personal testimony is not reliable. Reason is subordinate to Śruti. It cannot override the authority of the Vedas. It is of some help where Vedic statements appear to be conflicting.[3] Comparison, presumption, and non-apprehension are not independent means of valid knowledge.[4]

Knowledge is intrinsically valid. Its validity is produced by the causes which produce the knowledge. Its validity is

---

[1] *Pramāṇacandrikā*, Ch. II.
[2] MBS., ii. 1. 4.
[3] MBS., ii. 1. 26, 28.
[4] *Pramāṇacandrikā*. C.U., Ch. III.

known by the knowledge itself. The sākṣin is self-luminous ; it makes itself and its validity known by itself. Invalidity of knowledge is due to adventitious conditions. The Mādhvas believe in intrinsic validity of knowledge and extrinsic invalidity of knowledge.[1]

3. *Viśeṣa*

Madhva recognizes the reality of viśeṣa. One thing is apprehenled as manifold owing to its viśeṣa or particularity. Viśeṣa is the essence of a thing (vastusvarūpa). It is self-explanatory. It defines and specifies its own nature. There are as many viśeṣas as there are qualities in a substance. They do not require other viśeṣas to connect them with the substance. So there is no infinite regress.[2] The viśeṣas bind together the different qualities of a substance into an integral unity. The Mādhvas do not recognize inherence (samavāya) as the relation between a substance and its qualities like the Nyāya-Vaiśeṣika.[3] The Mādhva conception of viśeṣa is different from the Nyāya-Vaiśeṣika conception of viśeṣa which is the distinctive feature of eternal individual substances only. The viśeṣas of the Mādhva characterize eternal as well as non-eternal substances.

We perceive whiteness of a cloth. We do not perceive difference between the cloth and whiteness. We perceive a particularity (viśeṣa) of the cloth. If there were difference between the cloth and whiteness, then there would be difference between this difference and the cloth, and difference between it and whiteness, and so on to infinity. This would involve infinite regress. Therefore the qualities are identical with the substance.[4]

4. *God*

Madhva recognizes two kinds of reality, independent (svatantra) and dependent (paratantra). God is the independent reality. Individual souls and the world are dependent realities. God is free from all imperfections. He is possessed of infinite, excellent, spiritual qualities.[5] He is not attributeless (nirguṇa). He is free from the attributes of prakṛti.

---

[1] *Pramāṇacandrikā*, C.U., pp. 165-66.
[2] *Nyāyasudhā*, p. 106.
[3] HIP., Vol. IV, pp. 126-27.
[4] *Tattvapradīpa* (edited by B. N. Krishnamurti Sharma), p. 11.
[5] SDS., v. 1.

This is the import of the texts speaking of nirguṇa Brahman. He has being (sat), consciousness (cit), and bliss (ānanda). He has six qualities of Lordship, infinite knowledge, infinite power, infinite strength, infinite rulership, infinite vigour, and infinite glory. There is no mutual difference among the qualities of God. There is non-difference among them. There is non-difference between God and his qualities which constitute his nature. Their co-inherence in him proves their identity with him. They constitute his determinate nature on account of viśeṣas.[1] He is the cause of creation, subsistence, dissolution, control, knowledge, nescience, bondage, and liberation.[2] He is the efficient cause (nimittakāraṇa) of the world. Prakṛti is the material cause (upādānakāraṇa) of the world. God is said to be indescribable because he cannot be completely comprehended. The highest and perfect Lord is Viṣṇu. He is called the Absolute (Brahman), the Supreme Self (Paramātman), and Bhagavān (Lord). He is the Inner Ruler (Antaryāmin). He is not all. But he is the ruler of all. He is the Supreme Person (Puruṣottama).[3] He is omniscient, omnipotent, perfect, eternal, extremely subtle, and immutable. He is the cause of all beings, and dwells in them. He impels men in their activities. He is the object of knowledge. He is the goal of attainment. He reveals the Vedas which embody eternal truths.[4] He has extraordinary and inconceivable powers. He can make the impossible possible. He is the controller of all. He is partless. He is devoid of body and sense-organs. He is not subject to prakṛti.[5] The Supreme Lord is Viṣṇu. He is immanent in the souls and the world. He transcends them all. He is both immanent and transcendent. He is the abode of contrary qualities.[6]

5. *Prakṛti*

Lakṣmī, the consort of Viṣṇu, is eternally blessed and absolutely accomplished. She eternally contemplates Viṣṇu. She is eternally related to the Lord. Lakṣmī and Viṣṇu rejoice

[1] *Ibid,* pp. 12-13; MBS., ii. 2. 30. 31.
[2] MBS., i. 1. 2.
[3] MBS., i. 1. 6, 7, 11, 12, 17, 29; i. 2. 1.
[4] MBS., i. 1. 1; i. 2. 1, 20; i. 2. 7.
[5] *Ibid,* ii. 1. 29-32.
[6] *Ibid,* i. 3. 12.

in each other. They are eternally united with each other. Lakṣmī is dependent on Viṣṇu. In herself she is not.[1] She is intelligent Prakṛti. She has an eternal supernatural body. She is immortal.[2] Māyā is the eternal power or will of God, which is his essence. He creates all things by the power of his will.[3] Prakṛti is the material cause of the world. The Lord moulds various forms out of Prakṛti and exhibits himself in manifold ways. He enters into Prakṛti, and makes himself many.[4] The Lord's will is Prakṛti. He is the master of the will. His will is variously called Māyā, Avidyā, and Prakṛti. He is Puruṣa. His will is Prakṛti. He is the light. He is the support.[5] Prakṛti and the Lord (paramapuruṣa) co-exist in time and space. Prakṛti is eternally liberated. She is omnipresent, immutable, and eternal. Brahman is more subtle than Prakṛti. Knowledge, bliss, power, and authority of God are infinitely greater than those of Prakṛti. They are absolutely perfect in God. Prakṛti, like God, is all-pervading in time and space. She is absolutely free from bondage like him. Her freedom is dependent on God's grace. Prakṛti is ruled by the Lord who is absolutely free.[6]

6. *The World*

The Śruti has it: "All are known when one is known." When Brahman is known, all are known. When the cause, Brahman, is known, the effect, the world, is known. The cause and the effect both are real. Brahman is real, and the world is real. Śaṁkara is wrong in holding that Brahman is real, and that the world is an unreal appearance. This is a wrong interpretation of the text. One and all both are real. The effect is a real modification (vikāra) of the cause which remains intact (avikṛta). The world is created by God out of prakṛti which is not a false appearance. Madhva asks: Is falseness of the world-appearance real or unreal? If it is real, monism is compromised. If it is unreal, then the world-appearance is real.[7] Creation is divine sport. It is the expression of God's overflowing bliss and mercy. He has no purpose in creating the world. Creative activity is his essential nature. He creates multiplicity of forms without undergoing modification.[8]

---

[1] *Ibid*, iii. 3. 40-42.
[2] *Ibid*, iii. 2. 38.
[3] SDS., v. 33.
[4] *Ibid*, i. 4. 27.
[5] *Ibid*, i. 4. 25, 26.
[6] *Ibid*, iv. 2. 7-10.
[7] SDS., v. 36.
[8] MBS., ii. 1. 34; i. 3. 13.

7. *Reality of Difference*

Śaṁkara maintains that Brahman is devoid of homogeneous difference (sajātīya bheda), heterogeneous difference (vijātīya bheda), and internal difference (svagata bheda). But Madhva recognizes difference in the Reality. Śaṁkara advocates absolute monism. But Madhva advocates pluralistic theism. He stresses the five kinds of difference which are real and beginningless. There is difference between God and the individual souls. There is difference between God and matter. There is difference between soul and matter. There is difference between one soul and another. There is difference between one material thing and another. These are the five kinds of differences.[1] Matter, soul, and God are irreducible to one another. Madhva gives a pluralistic universe with God as its Lord. The fivefold difference is not a mere appearance (māyāmātra), since Māyā is the will of God. Māyā or Prakṛti is the knowledge (prajñapti) of God which is characterized by bliss. This knowledge apprehends all, and saves all. It cannot therefore be a false appearance. Duality cannot be an imaginary appearance. God cannot have an illusory knowledge of all, since he is omniscient, and an illusion is false knowledge due to non-perception of particular qualities of an object. God is without an equal or a superior. Therefore Śruti says: "In reality, there is non-duality." It does not mean that duality or plurality is a false appearance.[2]

Difference is real. It is perceived. We perceive blue, yellow, and the like. We perceive that blue is different from yellow. Perception apprehends the difference between blue and yellow. The Advaitist contends that perception cannot apprehend difference. For it apprehends either difference only, or difference with the distinct entities. Perception cannot apprehend difference alone without apprehending the correlate (pratiyogi) of the difference. Difference is the distinction between two distinct entities. If the distincts are not perceived, the difference between them cannot be perceived. Perception cannot apprehend difference with the distincts. If it does, either it apprehends the distincts first, and then apprehends difference between them, or it apprehends both the distincts and their

---

[1] SDS., v. 22.

[2] SDS., v. 19-21.

difference simultaneously. It cannot apprehend the distincts first, and then their difference. When perception apprehends the distincts, it ceases to function, and cannot apprehend difference between them. Difference is mutual non-existence of two things in each other. So it cannot be perceived without perception of the distincts. So distincts cannot be perceived without perception of their difference. Difference cannot be perceived without perception of the distincts. This involves mutual dependence or vicious circle. Perception cannot apprehend the distincts and their difference simultaneously. Cognition of cause and cognition of effect cannot occur at the same time. Cognition of an entity (*e.g.*, a jar) and cognition of its counter-entity (*e.g.*, a cloth) are the cause of the cognition of their difference. Therefore difference cannot be perceived.[1]

But Madhva maintains that when we perceive objects, we perceive their relations, their difference, and their individualities in one and the same act of perception. Difference is the essence of the object itself. It is the essential feature of it. Essence, difference, and individuality are apprehended in the same act of perception. Perception of difference is not illusory, since even illusion is misinterpretation of sensory data. The Advaitist cannot mention any disturbing factors which are the cause of misinterpretation. Sensory data themselves are not illusory. Perception can apprehend objects and their differences. The Sākṣin or the I—awareness can apprehend the external order of material objects and individuals with their differences directly. Difference is real. It is the foundation of Madhva's pluralistic universe. It is not a subjective construction of the mind. It is constitutive of the universe. It is directly perceived by the Sākṣin.[2]

8. *Madhva and Rāmānuja*

Madhva agrees with Rāmānuja in holding that the Vedas are impersonal and eternal, that they testify to the existence and nature of Brahman, that perception, inference, and Vedic testimony are the three kinds of valid knowledge, that knowledge has intrinsic validity, that Viṣṇu himself is the reciter of

[1] SDS., v. 3.

[2] Nagaraja Sharma : *The Reign of Realism in Indian Philosophy*, pp. 51-53.

the *Pañcarātra Āgama,* which therefore has supreme authority, that the world is real, and that the jīva is atomic. But he differs from Rāmānuja in holding that God is different from the souls and the world, that God is not related to the conscious souls (cit) and the unconscious matter (acit) as the soul to its body. Two contradictory qualities of cit and acit cannot exist in God at the same time. Rāmānuja's doctrine resembles the Jaina doctrine in so far as he advocates the existence of contradictory qualities of consciousness and unconsciousness in God at the same time.[1]

9. *The Jīva*

The individual soul (jīva) is the knower, enjoyer, and doer. It is partless and eternal. It dwells in the body and the senses. It is subject to happiness and misery.[2] It is atomic in size, and yet it can experience sensations in its entire body, even as a lamp can illumine a room by its light. The soul is eternal ; its birth and death are due to its connection with and separation from its body.[3] It has by nature perfect wisdom and bliss, but they are clouded by the influence of merits and demerits (karma). When they are worn off and its embodied existence ceases, its natural wisdom and bliss are manifested by the grace of God.[4] Though the soul is dependent on God, it is an active agent, performs right and wrong actions, and acquires merits and demerits. It freely adapts means to ends, and adopts various methods to achieve liberation. But its free activity is controlled by God. It has no absolute freedom. It is not an absolute agent. It is allowed relative freedom by its divine master. God guides the free actions of the jīvas.[5]

The jīvas are different from God. There can be no absolute identity between them. God is the worshipped master. The jīvas are his worshipping servants..[6] The Deity and the devotee are different from each other. God is omniscient, omnipotent, and perfect. The jīva has finite knowledge, limited power, and is absolutely dependent on God. God dwells in the soul. But he does not experience its joys and sorrows. He enjoys bliss

---

[1] SDS., v. 1.
[2] MBS., ii. 1. 27.
[3] MBS., ii. 3. 24, 26, 19.
[4] MBS., ii. 3. 31.
[5] MBS., ii. 3. 33-42.
[6] MBS., i. 3. 5.

only arising from its good actions. God is real; the soul is real; their difference is real.[1] One individual soul is not the ruler of another, since it would involve infinite regress. Prakṛti is not the inner ruler of the souls. God is their inner ruler.[2] The text 'Tat tvam asi' does not convey identity of the soul with God. It means that the soul has similarity in essence with God. Madhva reads 'Sa ātmā tat tvam asi' as 'Sa ātmā atat tvam asi'. 'That ātman, thou art not'. The soul is not identical with God.[3] The jīva and God are always different from each other. The knowledge of difference between them liberates a person. He is the refuge of all liberated souls. They enjoy his companionship and bliss. He is their abode. He is their final goal.[4]

God is the Moral Governor. He dispenses the fruits to the souls in accordance with their good and bad actions (karma). So he cannot be charged with partiality and cruelty. There is a beginningless series of actions and their fruits. The souls freely do right and wrong actions, and reap their fruits. God, like an impartial judge, awards fruits to them in strict conformity with their merits and demerits. He is the Lord of the Law of Karma. He does not abrogate the Moral Law which follows from his nature.[5]

There are three kinds of souls: (1) eternally free (nitya) souls, like Lakṣmī; (2) liberated (mukta) souls, like gods, ṛsis, fathers, and men; (3) the bound (baddha). Among the bound souls some are eligible for liberation (muktiyogya), some are bound to saṁsāra for ever (nityasaṁsārin), and others are intended for hell (tamoyogya). Vāyu is the mediator between God and souls.

The jīva gets release through the grace of God. Release is the original state of purity. The liberated soul attains similarity with God. It never loses its identity in him. It enjoys a small measure of the infinite bliss of God through its śuddhasattva body. Its desires are not different from those of God. They are under his control. The released soul is liable to

---

[1] MBS., i. 2. 8, 11, 12.
[2] MBS., i. 2. 17, 19, 20.
[3] SDS., v. 29-30; MBS., iii. 2. 18.
[4] MBS., i. 3. 1, 2; SDS., v. 31, 32, 34.
[5] MBS., ii. 1. 35, 36; iii. 2. 42.

experience of miseries. It does not acquire power of creating, preserving, and destroying the world.[1]

Liberation is attained through knowledge of the excellence of the qualities of God. It cannot be attained through knowledge of its identity with God. It can be attained through the knowledge of its difference from and inferiority to him. It cannot be achieved without his grace. When a devotee surrenders himself to, and takes refuge in God, he grants him saving knowledge of difference, and liberates him.[2] Devotion, knowledge, performance of duties are the means to release. Truthfulness, study of the scriptures, charity, benevolence, compassion, desire for God, meditation, righteousness, faith, devotion, and worship of God should be cultivated. Yogic practices also are enjoined.[3] Bondage is due to ignorance. Release is due to knowledge. When the soul casts off its inessential forms, and is restored to its pure spiritual essence, it attains final release.[4] Until the karmas accumulated in the past births are completely worn off, the body continues. When they are exhausted, final release is attained.[5]

10. *The Categories*

Madhva recognizes ten categories: substance (dravya), quality (guṇa), action (karma), generality (sāmānya), particularity (viśeṣa), qualified (viśiṣṭa), whole (aṁśi), power (śakti), similarity (sādṛśya), and negation (abhāva). These are twenty substances: God, Lakṣmī, souls, uncreated space, prakṛti, sattva, rajas, tamas, ahaṁkāra, buddhi, manas, the sense-organs, the elements, subtle essences (tanmātra), nescience (avidyā), uttered sounds, darkness, dispositions (vāsanā), time, and reflection (pratibimba). Uncreated space (avyākṛta ākāśa) is different from the element ākāśa (bhūtākāśa). It is eternal vacuum. It is not affected by creation and destruction. Time is co-existent with it. It is a direct product of prakṛti. It is the self-subsistent abode of all other substances. It is the generic cause of production of all

[1] MBS., i. 3. 19; iv. 2. 16; iv. 4. 4, 5, 9, 15, 17; SDS., v. 17, 18.
[2] SDS., v. 27, 39; MBS., iii. 2. 42.
[3] SDS., v. 16; MBS., iii. 3. 48, 51, 53, 54; iv. 1. 4, 5, 8, 9, 10.
[4] MBS., i. 1. 17.
[5] MBS., iii. 4. 51.

things. Prakṛti is the material cause of the world. God produces sattva, rajas, and tamas out of prakṛti. Then Mahat is produced. Then Ahaṁkāra is produced. Then buddhi, manas, ten sense-organs, five tanmātras, and five elements are produced. A substance is the material cause of modifications and manifestations. Prakṛti is subject to modifications. But God and souls cannot undergo modification ; they can be manifested only. Nescience (avidyā) veils the natural knowledge and bliss of the jīvas. Each soul has a specific nescience which veils its natural qualities, and causes its bondage. There is no generic nescience which veils the knowledge of all souls. The universals or generalities, according to Madhva, are eternal in eternal substances and non-eternal in non-eternal substances and limited to the individuals so long as they last. He does not recognize the relation of inherence between a substance and its qualities and actions in order to avoid infinite regress. But he recognizes the category of the qualified (viśiṣṭa) which binds together a substance with its qualities and actions. There is no relation of inherence between the whole and its parts. The category of the whole connects its parts with one another inseparably. Power is a separate category. Inconceivable power as what abides in God, causal power, adventitious power, and power of words are the forms of power. There are four kinds of negation: prior negation, posterior negation, mutual negation, and absolute negation.[1]

Madhva's dualism is realistic. It admits the ontological reality of God, souls, and the world. It recognizes eternal distinctions between God and souls, God and matter, souls and matter, one soul and another, and one material thing and another. It is pluralistic theism. It gives a pluralistic universe with God as its creator, preserver, and destroyer. It gives three irreducible grades of reality, matter, soul, and God. It recognizes the uniqueness of God, and the individuality of each soul and material thing. This is the distinct contribution of Madhva. He does not sacrifice the many to one like Śaṁkara. He does not regard the souls and the manifold world as appearances. He treats them as ontological realities depending on God who is the supreme, absolutely independent

[1] HIP., Vol. IV, pp. 150-60.

reality. He creates the world of matter, and preserves and destroys it, and controls the souls and guides them to their destiny. God concedes relative freedom to the souls to work out their own salvation or perdition. Madhva reconciles knowledge, devotion, and action with one another as the means to release. His pluralistic theism is the antithesis of Śaṁkara's absolute monism. The Mādhvas severely criticize Śāṁkara's theory of Ajñāna and falsity of the world-appearance.[1] Madhva ascribes an inconceivable power to God by which he harmonizes the five-fold absolute differences with one another in an integral whole. He introduces the concept of viśeṣa which holds together differences within an undivided Being. Viśeṣa is self-determining and self-explanatory. It does not require the aid of any other thing. "Madhvites claim their position to be monistic. Though they accept infinite differences, still they accentuate the integrity of Being. Their doctrine of specific particulars (viśeṣa) does not make the differences absolute, it seeks to assimilate differences in integrity. They deny differences. They accept distinctions. These distinctions are specific and cannot create division in integrity. In this way Madhvites reconcile ineffaceable differences in the Absolute."[2] But dualism and pluralism cannot be reconciled with monism.

---

[1] HIP., Vol. IV, pp. 204-304.
[2] *Comparative Studies in Vendāntism,* pp. 50-51.

CHAPTER XI

DVAITĀDVAITAVĀDA OF NIMBĀRKA

1. *Introduction*

R. G. Bhandarkara thinks that Nimbārka lived shortly after Rāmānuja. Pandit Kiśoradāsa thinks that he lived in the ninth century. But Nimbārka refers to Rāmānuja's view in his commentary on the *Brahmasūtra*. Hence he must have lived after Rāmānuja. Dr. Das Gupta dates him roughly about the middle of the fourteenth century.[1] Nimbārka wrote a commentary on the *Brahmasūtra* called *Vedāntapārijātasaurabha* which is brief and clear. He wrote ten verses called *Daśaślokī* in which he elaborated his theory of dvaitādvaita. Śrīnivāsa wrote a subcommentary on *Vedāntapārijātasaurabha* called *Vedāntakaustubha*. Keśava Kāśmirī wrote a gloss on it called *Vedāntakaustubhaprabhā*. Puruṣottama Prasāda wrote a commentary on *Daśaślokī* called *Vedāntaratnamañjuṣā*.

Nimbārka advocates the doctrine of dualistic monism (dvaitādvaitavāda). He insists on difference as well as non-difference or identity (bhedābheda) between Brahman and the individual souls and the world. He advocates the relation of identity-in-difference between them. He, like Bhāskara, advocates the doctrine of transformation of Brahman into the world (brahmapariṇāmavāda). The Bhedābhedavāda of Bhāskara and Yādavaprakāśa has already been discussed.

2. *Brahman*

Brahman is the greatest, Supreme Person (puruṣottama) possessed of infinite, inconceivable, natural essences, qualities, and powers. He is omniscient, omnipotent, and omnipresent. He is possessed of infinite excellent qualities. He is free from all taint of imperfections. He is the creator, preserver, and destroyer of the world of conscious souls (cit) and unconscious matter (acit). He is absolutely free and independent controller of all finite agents, and dispenser of the fruits of their actions. He has infinite knowledge, infinite bliss, and infinite will and

---

[1] HIP., Vol. III, pp. 399-402.

power. He is Infinite (bhūmā). He is self-subsistent and absolute. He has transcendental bliss and immortality. He is imperishable (akṣara). He is the ground of all effects in the past, the present, and the future. He is the support of the world. He is the cause of its stability and harmony. He is of the nature of eternal manifestation. He is transcendent as well as immanent. He transcends the world. He is immanent in the world.[1] He is knowable through the Vedas only. He is the final goal of human attainment. He is the supreme end of the individual souls. They share in the bliss of God. He is the inner controller (antaryāmin) of the world and the souls. He is the knower and controller of all things and beings.[2]

Brahman is the material cause and the efficient cause of the world. He transforms himself into the world by his own extraordinary power without any accessory conditions, even as milk is transformed into curd without any accessory conditions. God, who is omniscient and omnipotent, transforms himself into the world by his own power and will with his essential nature (svarūpa) unmodified (avyākṛta). He is unmodified in his essential nature and modified in his inessential nature.[3] It may be urged that if God be the material cause of the world, he, being devoid of parts, becomes entirely transformed into the world, and that if he partly transforms himself into the world, he ceases to be partless. But the Śruti says: "Brahman willed to become many; he created the world (sat) out of himself and yet remained transcendent (tyat), even as a spider spins out a cobweb out of itself." The omnipotent Supreme Lord can create the world out of himself, and yet remain transcendent.[4] The inconceivable creative power in God is the cause of the world. It is real. It is the will of God. It is not indefinable Māyā of Śaṁkara, which is neither real nor unreal. The world which is the transformation of Brahman is real. It is not a false appearance as Śaṁkara holds.

Effect is non-different from cause. It is not absolutely different from cause. When cause is perceived, effect is perceived. Effect is a transformation of cause. Hence effect is

[1] VPS., i. 1. 1, 2, 3, 4, 13; i. 3. 8, 9, 10, 11, 13, 16, 22.
[2] VPS., i. 1. 4, 18; i. 2. 20; ii. 1. 21.
[3] VPS., i. 4. 26; ii. 1. 23.
[4] VPS., ii. 1. 25-29.

non-different from cause. The effect that happens subsequently, pre-exists in the cause. If the effect were non-existent in the cause, then sprouts of barley would be produced from fire. The effect is the unfoldment of the cause, even as an unrolled cloth is the unfoldment of a folded cloth. Vital airs are inhaled and exhaled. So the effect is implicit in the cause, and becomes explicit when it assumes the form of the effect. The world pre-exists in Brahman in an implicit condition, and becomes explicit after creation.[1] Cause and effect are partly different and partly non-different from the world. Brahman is transformed into the world, which is non-different from him. Brahman is the inner controller of the world. So there is no absolute identity between them.[2] Brahman is both different and non-different from the world of unconscious matter and conscious souls, even as the sea is different and non-different from its waves, and the sun is different and non-different from its rays. The world including formed and unformed existence, material things and spiritual beings, exists in its cause, Brahman, in the relation of identity-in-difference. God is related to the world as a snake is related to its coiled form.[3] God remains unmodified in his essential nature, and only undergoes modification through his conscious energy (cit-śakti) and unconscious energy (acit-śakti).[4] This doctrine resembles Vallabha's doctrine of immutable transformation (avikṛtapariṇāma). God transcends his three natures as the world, souls, and even as God. In his pure and transcendent nature he is absolutely unaffected by changes and mutations of the world of phenomena. As noumenon he is immutable ; as phenomena he undergoes mutations. In his esoteric and essential nature he is immutable ; in his exoteric and phenomenal nature he is mutable.[5]

3. *The Jīva*

The individual soul (jīva) is not born. It is eternal. Its birth and death are due to its connection with and separation

---

[1] VPS., ii. 1. 14-19.
[2] VPS., ii. 1. 14, 21.
[3] VPS., ii. 1. 16; i. 1, 4; iii. 2. 27.
[4] *Vedāntakaustubhaprabhā*, iii. 2. 29; HIP., III, p. 416.
[5] VPS., i. 1. 2; HIP., iii, p. 413.

from its body. It is the knower or ego which possesses the essential quality of knowledge. The relation of the soul to knowledge is that of the qualified (dharmin) to its quality (dharma). There is identity-in-difference between them. The soul and knowledge, though non-distinct from each other, are related to each other as substance and attribute. The soul is an enjoyer. It feels pleasure and pain, which are the fruitions of merits and demerits. It is an active agent. It has the power of doing right and wrong actions. Its activity is controlled by God. It strives to share in the infinite bliss of God. It is atomic. But it can experience pleasure and pain through its entire body. Its seat is in the heart. It has experience through its whole body, even as the light of a lamp illumines the whole room. It is a part of Brahman. It is both different and non-different from him.[1]

There is great difference between a soul and Brahman. The soul is subject to joys and sorrows (bhoktṛ). It experiences the fruits of its actions. But Brahman does not experience fruits of actions (abhoktṛ). Brahman is the worshipped while the soul is the worshipper. Brahman is known by the soul which is the knower. The soul strives to receive the infinite bliss of God who is the giver of bliss. Brahman is the inner controller of the soul which is controlled by him. So Brahman and the soul are different from each other.[2] But they are not absolutely different from each other. The soul is a part of Brahman. It is identical with him in essence. Its natural knowledge and bliss are covered by nescience (avidyā) which is removed by the grace of God. The liberated soul acquires absolute equality with God, being purged of merits and demerits and becoming immaculate. But it does not lose its integrity in him.[3]

Brahman is not defiled by the limitations and imperfections of the souls, though he regulates their different states, waking, dream, sleep, and intuitive state. Their natural will-power is eclipsed by the superior will of God who guides them in all matters according to their past deeds. Their bondage and release are due to the will of God. He is absolutely pure in spite of his connection with their impurities. He is the inner

[1] VPS., ii. 3. 16-19, 23-28, 32, 48.
[2] VPS., i. 2. 8, 11, 12; i. 3. 7.
[3] VPS., i. 3. 2.

controller of all ; yet he does not undergo any limitation. Though he is omnipresent, he does not suffer from the limitations of the souls. Even as light reveals objects covered by darkness, so God reveals every thing, but is not affected by it. He abides in the souls, but is not affected by their changes. He is not infected with their impurities.[1] Brahman is both different from and identical with souls, even as the sun is both different from and identical with its rays for the sun and its rays are both light.[2]

4. *Nimbārka and Bhāskara*

Nimbārka, like Bhāskara, believes in the transformation of Brahman into the world (brahmapariṇāma). He recognizes, like him, the relation of identity-in-difference (bhedābheda) between Brahman and the individual souls. But Bhāskara emphasizes identity between them, their difference being due to limiting conditions (upādhi). Nimbārka stresses both identity and difference between them. His doctrine is dualistic non-dualism (dvaitādvaitavāda) which stresses identity-in-difference (bhedābheda) between God and the souls and the world.[3] Nimbārka condemns both monistic absolutism and dualism, and reconciles the identity texts with the difference texts in his doctrine of dualistic monism. The world and the souls are different from Brahman because they have real and distinct existence dependent upon him. They are non-different from Brahman because they cannot exist apart from him. 'Tat tvam asi,' or 'That thout art' means that the individual soul (tvam) is both different and non-different from Brahman (tat). There is non-difference or identity between them in their essential nature. There is difference between them because they are related to each other as part and whole, the controlled and the controller, and the worshipper and the worshipped.

5. *Nimbārka and Rāmānuja*

Rāmānuja recognizes internal difference (svagatabheda) within Brahman. He regards Brahman as the qualified (viśeṣya) substance whose attributes (viśeṣaṇa) or modes (prakāra) are

[1] VPS., iii. 2. 5, 11, 12, 15, 18; iii. 2. 20, 30.
[2] VPS., iii. 2. 28.
[3] HIP., Vol. III, p. 413.

the unconscious world of matter (acit) and conscious souls (cit). Matter and souls are adjectives of the divine substance. They co-inhere in Brahman. Their co-inherence in Brahman shows their substantial identity. They constitute the body of Brahman who is the soul. They are inseparably related to each other like body and soul. There is inseparable relation (apṛthaksiddhi) between them. Rāmānuja stresses identity or unity more than difference. But Nimbārka emphasizes identity as well as difference. The world is the transformation of the conscious energies (cit-śakti) and the unconscious energies (acit-śakti) of Brahman. The individual souls are parts of Brahman. The world and souls are real and substantial ; they are not mere adjectives of Brahman. He is immanent in them as their inner controller. But he transcends them, and is not affected by their changes and mutations. He is immutable in his essential nature.

CHAPTER XII

ŚUDDHĀDVAITAVĀDA OF VALLABHA

1. *Introduction*

Vallabha (1481-1533 A.D.) was the founder of the Śuddhādvaita school of Vedānta. He wrote a commentary on the *Brahmasūtra* called *Aṇubhāṣya,* a commentary on the *Bhāgavata* called *Subodhinī,* and many other minor works. Puruṣottama wrote a subcommentary on *Aṇubhāṣya* called *Prakāśa.* Giridhara's *Śuddhādvaitamārtaṇḍa,* Bālakṛṣṇa Bhaṭṭa's *Prameyaratnārṇava,* and Puruṣottama's *Prasthānaratnākara* are important manuals on Śuddhādvaita Vedānta. Vallabha advocates pure non-dualism.

2. *Epistemology*

Valid knowledge is determinate apprehension of the real nature of an object which was not known before.[1] Perception, inference, and Vedic testimony are the three kinds of valid knowledge. The Vedas are the highest authority. Reason is subordinate to them.[2] Perception is immediate knowledge produced by the right sense-object-intercourse.[3] There is no indeterminate perception which is non-relational consciousness. The Vallabhite, like Madhva, admits only determinate perception. All perception is determinate, and involves subject-predicate relation. There are two kinds of determinate perception : (1) viśiṣṭabuddhi ; and (2) samūhāvalambana. The former is the determinate apprehension of an object (*e.g.,* a jar) qualified by some properties. It apprehends the relation between the qualified and the qualities. The latter is the determinate apprehension of a collection of objects such as a jar, a cloth, and a pillar.[4] Inference is mediate knowledge. It is derived through the medium of some other knowledge. It depends upon the knowledge of invariable concomitance (vyāpti). Vyāpti is the unconditioned and universal co-presence and co-absence of the reason (hetu) and the probandum (sādhya). Wherever the reason

---

[1] ABS., i. 1. 2, 3; PRK., p. 18.
[2] ABS., i 1. 2, 3; ii. 1. 11; PRK., p. 38.
[3] PRK., p. 20. [4] PRK., p. 13.

is present, the probandum is present. Wherever the probandum is absent, the reason is absent. There are two kinds of inference: (1) kevalavyatireki; and (2); anvayavyatireki. Puruṣottama does not admit kevalānvayi form of inference. Inference is either for oneself (svārtha) or for others (parārtha). There are five members in a demonstrative syllogism: (1) thesis (pratijñā); (2) reason (hetu); (3) example (udāharaṇa); (4) application (upanaya); and (5) conclusion (nigamana).[1] Comparison (upamāna) is not a distinct pramāṇa. It is perception of similarity between two objects, (*e.g.*, a cow and a wild cow) with the aid of recollection of the similarity indicated by authority, determined by the knowledge of the relation of the name to the thing named. It is included in perception.[2] Presumption (arthāpatti) is a kind of kevalānvayi inference.[3] Tradition (aitihya) is authority, the source of which is not known. Therefore it is not valid knowledge. When its truth is definitely ascertained, it is included in authority. Gesture (ceṣṭā) is included in inference.[4] Non-apprehension (anupalabdhi) is not necessary to apprehend non-existence (abhāva) of an object. Non-existence is not admitted. It is identical with the locus. The so-called non-apprehension is perception of the locus.[5]

3. *Brahman*

Vallabha does not admit the reality of attributeless (nirguṇa) Brahman. He is called nirguṇa in the Śruti because he is free from the qualities of prakṛti. He is qualified (saguṇa) and determinate (saviśeṣa). He is one, formed, omnipotent, omniscient, cause of all, and possessed of being, consciousness, and bliss. He is the embodiment of bliss. He has six qualities of Lordship. He has inconceivable power of producing all things and ruling over them. He is the inherent cause (samavāyikāraṇa) and the efficient cause (nimittakāraṇa) of the world. He is the world itself. He is the direct Lord of prakṛti and souls. Prakṛti, the stuff of the world, is the power of God. The souls are eternal parts of God. They are his emanations. The universe and the souls are Brahman. Brahman is God. He is not an unreal

[1] PRK., pp. 138-39; 142-44.
[2] PRK., p. 148.
[3] PRK., p. 151.
[4] PRK., p. 153.
[5] PRK., p. 121.

appearance, a product of māyā. Māyā is his power. It is his creation. He is a knower, enjoyer, and doer. He has no body, but he can assume bodies for the benefit of his devotees in sport. He is the Supreme Person (puruṣottama). Pure Brahman is the only reality.[1]

Brahman possesses being, consciousness, and bliss. He voluntarily conceals and manifests his qualities. He conceals his bliss and qualities of Lordship in the individual souls. He conceals his consciousness also in matter. Matter is Brahman with bliss and consciousness suppressed. The jīva is Brahman with bliss suppressed. Being, consciousness, and bliss are fully manifested in Brahman. The qualities of Lordship are manifest in God only.[2] Being is manifest in matter ; consciousness is manifest in the jīva ; bliss is manifest in the inner soul (antaryāmin) in the jīva ; all these qualities are manifest in Brahman.[3] There are different degrees of reality. They represent different stages of the concealment and manifestation of the divine qualities of being, consciousness, and bliss. On account of the evolution (āvirbhāva) and involution (tirobhāva) of these qualities, matter, soul, and God are different from one another. But when consciousness and bliss are manifested by Brahman, they become Brahman. Matter and soul are identical with Brahman in their essential nature. But they are different from him, when his qualities are partly concealed in them. Creation of the world and emanation of the souls are partial self-concealment (tirobhāva) of God. Self-manifestation (āvirbhāva) of him is the fulfilment of the destiny of matter and souls. Self-concealment and self-manifestation are the unique features of Śuddhādvaitavāda. Manifestation or evolution consists in perceptibility of present things. Concealment or involution consists in their imperceptibility.[4] There is greater or less manifestation of the divine qualities in different degrees of reality. Matter, souls (jīva), and inner souls (antaryāmin) are parts of being (sadaṁśa), consciousness (cidaṁśa), and bliss (ānandāṁśa) of God respectively.[5]

---

[1] ABS., i. 1. 2-4, 8, 20, 21 ; ii. 4. 23 ; iii. 3. 47 ; SAM., SAMP., 8, 18, 19.
[2] ABS., iii. 2. 5 ; ii. 3. 43.
[3] Jaḍajīvāntaryāmiṣvekaikāṁśaprākaṭyāt. ABS., i. 1. 4.
[4] SAM., SAMP., 11, 14, 16.
[5] ABS , i. 1. 4.

God is one. He wills to become many to sport with them.[1] His creative act is an act of sport undetermined by an external end. It is a voluntary play. God conceals his consciousness and bliss and becomes the world. But he does not undergo any modification in creating the world. Creation is involution (tirobhāva). Dissolution is evolution (āvirbhāva). Creation is enfoldment. Dissolution is unfoldment. God willingly becomes the world, even as a serpent folds itself into a coil.[2] God becomes the world without undergoing any modification, even as gold is modified into various ornaments without changing its nature.[3] Vallabha advocates the doctrine of immutable transformation (avikṛtapariṇāmavāda).[4] The cause remains intact and unchanged (avikṛta), though it is modified into the effect (pariṇāma).[5] Brahman remains immutable, though he is expressed in the world. How can non-eternal material things be regarded as Brahman? Vallabha answers that they are really eternal Brahman, but that they appear to be non-eternal because consciousness and bliss are suppressed in them.[6] Material things are directly produced by God. There is no physical causation. All causation is spiritual causation. What appears to be physical causation is direct divine causation. Plurality is due to the divine will. God is the abode of contrary qualities. Plurality and contrariety are reconciled in the unity of God.[7]

God has infinite supreme powers. He causes the inherent causal potencies (śakti) in the causes to manifest themselves in their effects. Production is manifestation or evolution (āvirbhāva) of the causal powers. God causes the causal potencies in the effects to conceal themselves in their causes. Destruction is concealment or involution (tirobhāva) of the causal potencies. In involution the effect exists in the cause in a causal state. In evolution the effect exists in itself in an effected state. A jar is produced out of clay. Clay exists in the form of a jar. It is destroyed into particles of earth. It exists in earth in a causal state. In production a cause is manifested as an effect.

---

1 ABS., ii. 1. 33.
2 ABS., iii. 2. 27; SAM., 12.
3 SAM., 13.
4 M. N. Sircar: *Comparative Studies in Vedāntism*, pp. 100, 102.
5 Avikṛtameva pariṇamate. ABS., ii. 4. 26.
6 SAM., 14.
7 ABS., i. 1. 4; iii. 2. 27.

In destruction an effect is absorbed in its cause. But in production and destruction the cause does not undergo modification in its essential nature.[1] There is a casual power (śakti) in the cause to produce an effect. This power is not its nature (svabhāva). It is not its essence (svarūpa). A thing can never be divested of its nature. Its essence can never be separated from it. The nature or essence of a thing is always present. So, if the causal power were the nature or essence of the cause, it would always produce the effect. Hence the causal power different from its nature or essence must be admitted. The effect is real and non-different from its cause.[2] Vallabha's Avikṛta-pariṇāmavāda is a form of Satkāryavāda. He does not believe in Asatkāryavāda.[3] He does not admit prior non-existence (prāgabhāva), posterior non-existence (pradhvaṁsābhāva), mutual non-existence (anyonyābhāva), and absolute non-existence (atyantābhāva) recognized by the Vaiśeṣika. Prior non-existence is the causal state (kāraṇāvasthā). Posterior non-existence is absorption in the cause (tirobhāvaśakti). Absolute non-existence is concealment of the divine nature. Mutual non-existence is voluntary concealment of specific natures of God. He conceals his pot-nature in a cloth, and cloth-nature in a pot. He is the cause of all things. They are not new emergences (ārambha). They pre-exist in Brahman. They are his manifestations.[4]

4. *Reality of the World*

Śaṁkara maintains that the world is a false appearance (māyika) produced by Brahman related to Māyā. Brahman unrelated to Māyā is not its cause. The world is an appearance (prapañca), a product of nescience (ajñāna). Avidyā is a form of Māyā. Pure sattva is the chief element in Māyā. Impure sattva is the chief element in Avidyā. Brahman reflected in, or limited by Māyā, is God (īsvara). Brahman reflected in, or limited by Avidyā, is the individual soul (jīva). God and jīvas are appearances. The world is a false appearance. Therefore creatorship of Brahman is apparent.[5] Nirguṇa Brahman only is real. Saguṇa Brahman or God is an appearance.

---

1 SAM., SAMP., 15.
2 ABS., ii. 1. 14.
3 ABS., ii. 3. 35.
4 SAM., SAMP., 17.
5 SAM., SAMP., 22.

The Vallabhite disputes this view. Nirguṇa Brahman is not real. Brahman is saguṇa or qualified, and possessed of being, consciousness, bliss, and the six qualities of Lordship. He is the creator, preserver, and destroyer of the world, and the Moral Governor. God is not an appearance (māyika). He is real. Therefore the world created by him is real. The cause and the effect are equally real. God cannot be the cause of an unreal world-appearance. Nescience (ajñāna) is unreal (asat), and cannot produce any effects. If ajñāna is real, it resides in Brahman. Then he becomes ignorant and qualified. Māyā is impure and unreal. Brahman is formless. So Brahman cannot be reflected in Māyā. If he is reflected in Māyā, he becomes determinate (saviśeṣa). If Brahman appears like the world, even as a rope appears as a snake, then he has a form. The world is real ; it is a manifestation of Brahman. But his nature is not fully manifested in the world. It is apprehended by waking perceptions which are dissimilar to dreams apprehending unreal forms. Real objects are apprehended by waking perceptions. The jīva is said to be an appearance. It is destroyed when identity-consciousness dawns on it. So its liberation consists in its destruction. Jīvanmukti is impossible. When avidyā is destroyed by identity-consciousness, the body is destroyed.

Is Māyā produced or not produced? If it is produced, Brahman must be its cause. Then Brahman becomes determinate and qualified. If Māyā is not produced, it is an eternal reality besides Brahman. Then non-dualism is compromised, and occasional appearance and disappearance of the world cannot be accounted for. If Māyā is not produced, it cannot be destroyed. The doctrine of Māyā is irrational and untenable.[1]

The Vallabhite maintains that Brahman is pure and free from all relation to Māyā, and that pure Brahman unassociated with Māyā is both cause and effect. Pure Brahman is the cause of the world. The world is pure Brahman in the state of an effect. Māyā is the power of God, which is non-different from him. Jīvas are not apparent (māyika). They are pure Brahman with bliss concealed. They are real parts of Brahman. There is no Avidyā in Brahman. The world is real and identical with

---

[1] SAM., SAMP., 22-24.

Brahman as being. Jīvas are real and identical with Brahman as consciousness. Their inner souls (antaryāmin) are real and identical with Brahman as bliss. Matter and souls are of the nature of Brahman.[1]

Madhva maintains that there is difference (bheda) between God and the world. Nimbārka maintains that there is real identity-in-difference (bhedābheda) between them. Bhāskara maintains that there is identity-in-difference between them due to adjuncts (upādhi). Madhva maintains that the jīvas are parts of God separate from him. There are two kinds of parts, one's own parts (svāṁśa) and separate parts (vibhinnāṁśa). The divine incarnations are God's own parts. The jīvas are his separate parts. A part is a fragment of a whole. Or it is similar to the whole, though it is separate from it. The jīvas are God's parts in the second sense. They can never have divinity in them. Nimbārka holds that there is identity between God and the jīvas owing to similarity of consciousness. The Vallabhite maintains that there is identity (abheda) between them, and that the jīvas are God's own parts (svāṁśa). There is real non-difference or identity between the whole and its parts.[2] The world is identical with God in essence. But it is different from him as an effect. When it is dissolved, it remains in him in the causal state.[3] When consciousness of God dawns, there is no consciousness of anything else. There is consciousness of God in all things.[4] This is the doctrine of pure non-dualism.

God is the inherent cause (samavāyi kāraṇa) and the efficient cause (nimitta kāraṇa)[5] of the world. He is the direct ruler of prakṛti and souls.[6] He creates the world, and emits the souls for his own sport. He creates dravya, karma, kāla, svabhāva, and jīvas. Māyā or prakṛti is the power of God. It is the stuff (upādāna) of the world.[7] It consists of sattva, rajas, and tamas. God creates prakṛti and its guṇas. Sattva is in the nature of illumination and pleasure. It is a part of the divine being (sat). Rajas is in the nature of attachment and desire for

---

[1] ABS., i. 1. 4; ii. 3, 43; SAM., SAMP., 28, 29.
[2] SAM., SAMP., 36-39.
[3] SAM., 40.
[4] SAMP., 34.
[5] ABS., i. 1. 4; ii. 4. 23; SAM., SAMP., 72.
[6] SAM., 18.
[7] PRK., p. 163.

objects. It is not in the nature of pain as the Sāṁkhya holds. It is a part of the divine consciousness. Tamas is in the nature of delusion due to the power of veiling. It is a part of the divine bliss. The guṇas are parts of God. They are created by him. In the Sāṁkhya system they are self-existent, and they overpower one another, and transform themselves into various modifications of prakṛti. They are not controlled and guided by an intelligent agent. The Sāṁkhya doctrine involves naturalism (svabhāvavāda) and atheism (anīśvaravāda). But the guṇas are created by God according to Vallabha. God, devoid of the guṇas of prakṛti, creates them out of his nature. He assumes a lower nature at his will, and produces them as parts of his being, consciousness, and bliss. They are the material cause (upādāna kāraṇa) of the world. God is its inherent cause (samavāyi kāraṇa). If he were its material cause, he would undergo modification into the world. Therefore a distinction is made between the material cause and the inherent cause of the world.[1] Prakṛti, mahat, ahaṁkāra, tanmātras, and mahābhūtas constitute the creative order. Māyā is the potency of consciousness and bliss in God. Avidyā is a part of Māyā. It is a part of divine consciousness, which deludes jīvas into the false knowledge of plurality.[2]

Karma is destiny. It is a pervasive action which can be manifested partially by right and wrong actions. It makes them produce their fruits in time. Adṛṣṭa is not a quality of the soul. It is not necessary to enable actions to bring about their fruits.[3] Karma, one general pervasive action created by God, does the functions of the specific unseen agencies (adṛṣṭa) in the jīvas.

Real time contains being, consciousness, and bliss in itself. But empirical time is a partial manifestation of sattva part to our experience. Time upsets the equilibrium of sattva, rajas, and tamas. Karma and svabhāva are parts of time.[4]

Svabhāva is the cause of transformation. Svarūpa is the will of God in a specific form. Twenty-eight categories are evolved from svabhāva or specific volitions of God. They are not evolved by the general will of God.[5]

---

[1] HIP., iv., pp. 327-30.
[2] PRK., pp. 161, 170-72, 176.
[3] PRK., pp. 168-69.
[4] PRK., pp. 165-66.
[5] PRK., p. 169.

5. *The Jīva*

Jīvas are parts of God. They are eternal and devoid of the guṇas of prakṛti. They are superior to prakṛti. They are conscious souls. They are self-luminous. They control their bodies, sense-organs, life, and internal organs. They are apprehended by self-consciousness (ahaṁvitti). They are devoid of natural qualities in their essential nature. But they assume relationships to nature, and can divest themselves of all connection with nature, and acquire fitness for liberation.[1] They are not generated by God. They spring out of him, as sparks spring out of fire. They are emanations of God.[2] They are his parts. They are spiritual atoms (aṇu) or monads. They possess the quality of consciousness which is subject to contraction and expansion.[3]

The soul is the knower, enjoyer, and doer. Its activity is dependent on God.[4] Though it is atomic, it pervades the body through its consciousness. It feels through all parts of its body, even as sandal-paste in one part of the body produces pleasure and coolness in the whole body.[5] The souls are different from one another. They are different parts of Brahman. They are different from him owing to the suppression of bliss. They are identical with him in their essential nature. They are not appearances. They are real.[6] 'That thout art.' 'Tat tvam asi.' The soul is identical with Brahman. It is Brahman's own part (svāṁśa). There is real identity between them. There is real identity (abheda) between the whole and its parts.[7]

The souls are monads (aṇu). They are eternal. Their birth and death are in relation to the bodies ensouled by them. If they were created by God, they would be liable to destruction. They are not limitations of God by limiting adjuncts (upādhi). There is no proof for the existence of the adjuncts. If they were omnipresent like Brahman, they would not be controlled by him. They are controlled by him because they are atomic. If they were omnipresent, they would share the

---

[1] PRK., p. 173.
[2] ABS., ii. 2. 17.
[3] Cp. Rāmānuja.
[4] ABS., ii. 3. 18, 25, 33-35, 39, 43, 45.
[5] ABS., ii. 3. 23.
[6] ABS., ii. 3, 50; SAM., SAMP., 10.
[7] SAM., SAMP., 39.

experiences of one another. There are different inner controllers (antaryāmin) within different souls. They are parts of the bliss of God, whereas the jīvas are parts of his consciousness, and their bodies are parts of his being.[1]

Different souls have different lots. Some are righteous, and others are unrighteous. Their different lots are not due to their merits and demerits which are the results of their past actions (karma). If they were the cause of their different lots, God would be useless and lose his sovereignty. If God awards fruits in accordance with merits and demerits of the jīvas, then he would depend upon them, and lose his independence and Lordship. God is the directive cause (kārayitṛ) of the jīvas' actions. He concedes relative freedom to them to do right or wrong actions for his own sport. The jīvas are free agents. Their free activity is dependent on God (parādhīna). They freely follow the injunctions and prohibitions of the Vedas, which are the moral laws. But God is the ultimate directive cause (kārayitṛ) of their actions. Human freedom is a part of God's freedom and sportive activity. He impels them to do right or wrong actions freely for his sport (līlā). Vallabha would not compromise the free causality and sovereignty of God for the sake of human freedom. But he concedes a part of divine freedom to jīvas to preserve morality and religion.[2]

Saṁsāra is due to the soul's ignorance (avidyā) of its non-difference from Brahman. Avidyā is due to egotism (mamakara) or a false sense of individuality. Vallabha, like Śaṁkara, posits Avidyā in the mundane soul. Liberation is due to true knowledge of the non-difference (abheda) of the world and jivas from Brahman. Vallabha agrees with Śaṁkara on this point. Avidyā is destroyed by the true knowledge of Brahman. The liberated soul is divested of its adventitious qualities of prakṛti, and it acquires its intrinsic purity. It acquires affinity with God. It does not lose its identity in Him. It does not become God. The means (sādhana) can never be the end (sādhya). God, by his infinite grace, makes his own dependent soul attain affinity with him, and liberates it. Merciful God makes his own devotee enjoy his supreme bliss.[3]

---

[1] PRK., p. 162.
[2] ABS., ii. 1. 34; iii. 3. 29; SAM., SAMP., 44.
[3] SAM., SAMP., 83, 89; ABS., i. 1. 4.

There are three kinds of souls, pure, mundane, and liberated. Bliss and six qualities of Lordship are concealed in the jīva. A pure jīva is devoid of any relation to Avidyā. Bondage is due to relation to Avidyā. It is beginningless. The bound soul acquires, through the grace of God, fivefold vidyā, dispassion, discrimination, yoga, austerities, and devotion, and attains liberation. Liberated souls acquire affinity with God. They do not acquire Lordship of God. They are either jīvanmukta or mukta. The former are liberated in embodied life. The latter enjoy disembodied liberation.

The souls are either godly (daiva) or demoniac (āsura). Godly souls are of two kinds. Some follow the path of maryādābhakti. Others follow the path of puṣṭibhakti. The former cultivate action (karma), knowledge (jñāna), and devotion (bhakti). They attain Akṣara Brahman. The latter cultivate pure love of God. They are free from desires for all things except affinity with God. They attain the Puruṣottama, Supreme Person, through his grace.[1]

Vallabha is right in stressing the reality of qualified and determinate Brahman, the reality of the world and the jīvas, and in rejecting the indefinable Māyā of Śaṁkara, but he does not adequately inter-relate Brahman, the jīvas, and the world to one another. His virtual denial of human freedom and exaggeration of divine freedom, sovereignty, and direct causation of all things tend to make his doctrine pantheistic. Evolution (āvirbhāva) and involution (tirobhāva) of the qualities of God are its unique features. Vallabha's Śuddhādvaitavāda is the anti-thesis of the doctrine of emergent evolution. According to Alexander, life emerges out of matter, mind emerges out of life, and deity will emerge out of mind. According to Vallabha, God conceals his bliss, and becomes the soul. He conceals his consciousness, and becomes matter. There is progressive involution of the divine qualities in the jīvas and matter. The lower categories of existence can be explained by the higher, but the higher categories cannot be explained by the lower.

[1] ABS., iii. 3. 29; iv. 3. 17; *Prameyaratnārṇava*, pp. 7-9, 17.

CHAPTER XIII

THE ACINTYABHEDĀBHEDAVĀDA OF CAITANYA

1. *Caitanya's Theism*

Caitanya (1485-1533 A.D.) did not write any treatise. His philosophical doctrine is known from *Caitanyacaritāmṛta* written by Kṛṣṇadāsa Kavirāja (1616 A.D.) in Bengali. It is an authoritative biography of Caitanya, which enjoys immense popularity in Bengal. It contains the philosophy of the Caitanya school. It gives an account of Caitanya's discussion with Vāsudeva Sārvabhauma, which brings out his philosophical doctrine. God is the supreme reality. He is inconceivable. His inconceivable qualities and powers subsist in him. He is not formless and indeterminate. He is devoid of the qualities of prakṛti.[1] He is determinate (saviśeṣa). Being, consciousness, and bliss constitute his essence. He is the embodiment of bliss. He is possessed of the six powers of Lordship. He is not powerless. He is the creator, preserver, and destroyer of the world. He creates prakṛti and the material world out of it. He has supernatural mind, body, and sense-organs. He has cicchakti, jīvaśakti, and māyāśakti. They are called Viṣṇuśakti, Kṣetrajñaśakti, and Avidyāśakti. The first is the internal (antaraṅga) power. The second is the inessential (taṭastha) power. The third is the external (bahiṛṅga) power. The six powers of Lordship are manifestations of his divine energy (cicchakti), which is his essential power (svarūpaśakti). It is superior to his other two powers. His divine energy consists of power of being (sandhinī), power of consciousness (samvit), and power of bliss (hlādinī).[2] God is the Lord of māyā. The jīva is subject to it. The individual soul is a power of God (jīvaśakti). The *Bhagavadgītā* admits it.[3] The jīva is different from God. They are not identical with each other. God is transformed into the world, though he does not undergo any modification by his

---

[1] Cp. Madhva.
[2] *Caitanyacaritāmṛta,* Madhyalīlā, Ch. VIII.
[3] BG., xv. 7.

inconceivable power.[1] The world is not an appearance (vivarta) of Brahman. It is real. But it is mutable and destructible. The *Brahmasūtra* teaches the doctrine of modification (pariṇāma). But Śaṁkara wrongly ascribes the doctrine of Māyā to it. It is a false doctrine taught by the Buddhists. God is determinate. The jīvas are real. The world is real. They spring from the nature of God. They are his powers. The jīvas spring from the jīvaśakti of God. The world is a modification of the māyā-śakti of God. The former is a conscious power. The latter is energy of matter. Devotion to God is the highest good.[2]

Caitanya explains the means of attaining the highest good in course of his conversation with Rāya Rāmānanda. The performance of duties relating to castes and stages of life leads to devotion to God. Complete dedication of all works to God is superior to the performance of works. Renunciation of one's specific duties and complete surrender to God are superior to it. Devotion mixed with knowledge is superior to it. Higher than this is pure devotion unmixed with knowledge. Devotion in the form of love is the best means to the Highest Good. Servitude, friendship, tender affection, and love of a wife for a husband are the best means to attainment of God. There are various means to it. There are various degrees of attainment of him. Different aspirants have different aptitudes for different kinds of sādhanā. They are the best for them. Wifely love contains the excellences of the other kinds of love for God. Complete attainment of God is possible through it.[3]

Kṛṣṇadāsa explains the philosophy of Caitanya in different parts of his biography. Kṛṣṇa is God. He is the embodiment of bliss. He is the quintessence of love. He is infinite bliss and love. All creatures become happy by partaking of his bliss. He is the cause of their happiness.[4] His being is made of pure sattva. Love is his essence. His power is identical with him. Lakṣmī is the divine power. It is expressed in the six powers of Lordship. Rādhā is the infinite power of Kṛṣṇa. He is the infinite possessor of power. There is no difference between power and the possessor of power. Kṛṣṇa is full of pure con-

---

[1] Cp. Vallabha.
[2] *Caitanyacaritāmṛta*, Madhyalīlā, Ch. VI.
[3] *Caitanyacaritāmṛta*, Madhyalīlā, Ch. VIII.
[4] *Ibid*, Ch. IV.

sciousness, infinite joy and bliss. He is the abode of contrary qualities. He is infinite, and yet he incarnates as a finite mortal. He is absolutely independent, and yet he is subject to love. Sweetness of Kṛṣṇa attracts all men and women towards him by its inherent power. He constantly endeavours to make them taste the nectar of his infinite sweetness. Pure love (prema) binds man to God. It is unconditioned. It does not seek selfish pleasure. It seeks only the pleasure of God. The devotee has instinctive love for him. His pure love transcends all moral observances and rituals.[1]

Kṛṣṇa resides in the highest heaven which is beyond prakṛti. He is infinite, ubiquitous, and possessed of divine qualities. He is unconditioned (turīya) and free from all traces of māyā. He is manifested in Vāsudeva, Saṁkarṣana, Pradyumna, and Aniruddha. He has inconceivable power (acintyaśakti). He is in the world, and yet not in it. The world is in him, and yet not in him. He is transcendent and immanent. His powers are inconceivable.[2]

God is like the blazing sun. The jīva is a spark of him. The souls issue forth from his soul-energy (jīvaśakti). He is the possessor of this power. The jīva is a power of God, and yet different from him. It is an eternal servant of him. It forgets its essential divine nature, and is entangled in bondage to māyā. Devotion (bhakti) to God only disentangles him from the bondage, and leads him to attain him. If a person surrenders himself to God completely, he breaks the fetters of māyā. The jīvas are parts of God different from him (vibhinnāṁśa). But the four Vyūhas and Avatāras are his own parts (svāṁśa) non-different from him.[3]

Virtue (dharma), wealth (artha), happiness (kāma), liberation (mokṣa), and love of God (prema) are the five ends of life. The first four are worthless in comparison with the last. Love of God is the fifth supreme end. It is the ocean of infinite bliss of God. The bliss of Brahman, the impersonal Absolute, is not even a drop of this ocean of love of God. It can be attained by reciting and chanting his name.[4] Ignorance (avidyā) of the jīva is destroyed by the grace of God, which reveals the nature of the reality. He can be known in his real nature by devotion.

---

[1] *Ibid,* Adililā, Ch. IV.
[2] *Ibid,* Adililā, Ch. V.
[3] *Ibid,* Madhyalīlā, Ch. XXII.
[4] *Ibid.* Adililā. Ch. VII.

He can be known as Brahman only through knowledge. Brahman is an imperfect manifestation of God.[1] Karma, yoga, and knowledge lead to devotion. They cannot lead to attainment of God without devotion to him. Knowledge without devotion cannot lead to liberation. But devotion without knowledge leads to liberation. Knowledge without devotion is not pure.[2] Devotion is sweet. Knowledge is bitter. Devotion or love is the best means of the attainment of God. It is the essence of the bliss of God. A devotee does not want liberation or union with God. He wants to serve and love him for ever. God is the embodiment of transcendent beauty. He is the repository of all kinds of sentiments (rasāmṛta). He is the object of devotion of the different kinds of devotees.[3]

2. *Jīva Goswāmi's Philosophy*

Jīva Goswāmī lived shortly after Caitanya. He was the nephew of Sanātana and Rūpa, followers and companions of Caitanya. Jīva Goswāmī bases his philosophy on the *Bhāgavata*. He elaborates its philosophy in the light of Caitanya's teachings. The ultimate reality is one undifferenced consciousness (advaya jñāna). It is called Brahman, Paramātman, and Bhagavat.[4] Brahman is an imperfect manifestation of God. There is no distinction of powers and the possessor of powers in it. There is no distinction of substance and attributes in it. Brahman is the indeterminate being of God.[5] It is one, eternal, pure being-consciousness-bliss. It is beyond māyā and its mutations. It is self-luminous consciousness and unconditioned bliss. It is the transcendent reality. It is apprehended by indeterminate intuition.[6] Paramātman is the inner controller of the world and individual souls.[7] He is endowed with abundance of māyāśakti and part of power of consciousness (cicchakti). Brahman is pure consciousness which transcends powers and qualities. It is known through knowledge. Paramātman is immanent. It is the indwelling Spirit in the jīvas. It

---

[1] *Ibid*, Ādilīlā, Ch. I.
[2] *Ibid*, Madhyalīlā, Ch. VIII.
[3] *Ibid*, Madhyalīlā, Ch. XXII.
[4] *Bhāgavata*, i. 2. 11.
[5] Brahmaṇaḥ bhagavata eva nirvikalpaṣattārūpatvāt. *Bhagavatsandarbha*, edited by Sanātana Goswāmī Siddhāntaratna, Calcutta, Bangabda, 1313, p. 18.
[6] *Ibid*, p. 18.
[7] *Ibid*, p. 12.

is their Inner Self. It can be known through yoga. Bhagavat, the Lord, is the perfect Being endowed with all powers.[1] He is determinate (saviśeṣa). He is possessed of infinite pure qualities and various powers. Infinite bliss constitutes his essence. The distinction between him and his powers is manifest in him. Bliss is the substance of God. All powers are its attributes. They are the manifestations of bliss.[2] God is determinate. He can be known by devotion. Brahman is an imperfect manifestation of God. He is the perfect manifestation of Brahman. God has attributes. They are not attributed to him. Divinity is real. It is not ascribed to God.[3] He exists in his essential nature in Vaikuṇṭha through his essential power (svarūpaśakti). He exists as pure jīva-consciousness through his inessential power (taṭasthaśakti). He exists as unconscious prakṛti through his external (bahiraṅga) power of māyā. Prakṛti is evolved from it. The world is a modification of prakṛti. The jīva is an inessential power of God. It partakes of his nature.[4] It is partly similar to him. Prakṛti also is partly similar to him.[5] God is possessed of conscious power (cicchakti) and unconscious power (acicchakti). The former is Vidyā. The latter is Māyā.[6] He creates the manifold world through his māyāśakti. He conceals the knowledge of the jīva through his jīvamāyā.[7] Māyā is the power of God, which is the cause of creation, maintenance, and destruction of the world. It is not mere delusion.[8] God creates the world through his guṇamāyā.[9] He has power of being (sandhinī), power of consciousness (samvit), and power of bliss (hlādinī). Consciousness is superior to being. Bliss is superior to consciousness.[10] By means of power of being God sustains all beings, and gives them power of sustenance. By means of power of consciousness he knows all, and makes all

[1] *Kramasandarbha.*
[2] Ānandamātraṁ viśeṣyaṁ, samastāḥ śaktayo viśeṣaṇāṇi, viśiṣṭo bhagavān. *Bhagavatsandarbha*, p. 2
[3] Bhagavattā nāropitā, kintu svarūpabhūtaiva. *Ibid*, p. 28.
[4] Tadātmakatvena jīvasyaiva taṭasthaśaktitvam. *Ibid*, p. 33.
[5] *Ibid*, p. 34.
[6] Cidacicchaktir bhagavān. *Ibid*, p. 38. *Bhāgavata*, vii. 3. 34; Śrīdhara's commentary.
[7] *Ibid*, p. 40.
[8] Māyā jagat-sṛṣṭyādihetur bhagavacchaktir, na tu kāpaṭyamātram. *Ibid*, p. 23.
[9] *Ibid*, p. 39.
[10] *Ibid*, p. 251.

creatures know him. By means of power of bliss he enjoys bliss, and makes the jīvas enjoy bliss.[1] God can harmonize conflicting powers into an integral unity by his supra-logical power (acintyaśakti). The jīvas are spiritual monads. They are infinite in number. They are the energy of God (taṭastha śakti). They are pure and self-luminous in their essential nature. But their essential purity is concealed by avidyā, which is dispelled by the gracious will of God.[2]

3. *Baladeva Vidyābhūṣaṇa's Philosophy*

Baladeva (1800 A.D.) wrote *Govindabhāṣya* on the *Brahmasūtra*. He wrote *Siddhāntaratna* also. S. N. Das Gupta doubts his authorship of it. Gopināth Kavirāja ascribes it to him. The account of Baladeva's philosophy given here is based on both works. Baladeva wrote a summary of Caitanya's philosophy in *Prameyaratnāvalī*.

Baladeva was influenced by Madhva. He summarized his philosophy in *Prameyaratnāvalī*. God is the highest reality. He is known from the Śruti. The souls are real. There are various grades of souls. The differences are real. Liberation is the attainment of God. Worship of God or pure devotion is the means to it.[3] Baladeva's ontology is theistic. Brahman or God is determinate. Indeterminate Brahman is false.[4] If he is indeterminate, he cannot be perceived, inferred, or known from authority.[5] He is the embodiment of being, consciousness, and bliss. He is of the nature of knowledge, sovereignty, and power.[6] His embodiment does not differ from his essence. His essence (svarūpa) is expressed in his manifestation. It does not differ from his embodiment (vigraha). He has infinite qualities, which are not separate from his essence.[7] There is no difference between Brahman and his qualities. Nor is there identity-in-difference between them. There is non-difference between a substance and its qualities.[8] They appear to be different owing

---

[1] *Ibid*, pp. 257-58.
[2] *Ṣaṭsandarbha*, p. 266. HIP., Vol. IV, Ch. XXXIII.
[3] Introduction, 8; ix. 5.
[4] Alīkaṁ nirguṇaṁ brahma. *Ibid*, iv. 10.
[5] *Ibid*, iv. 10.
[6] *Siddhāntaratna*, p. 11.
[7] *Ibid*, pp. 10, 15.
[8] Dharmiṇo dharmānatirekaḥ. *Ibid*, p. 16.

to viśeṣa.[1] Baladeva borrows the concept of viśeṣa from Madhva in order to explain the non-difference of a substance from its qualities. Viśeṣa or a specific peculiarity reconciles a substance with its qualities, non-difference with difference. The undifferenced Brahman can have different qualities owing to viśeṣa. If there were no viśeṣa, we could not speak of existence of being, difference of difference, existence of time in all times, and existence of space in all places.[2] Viśeṣa is the intrinsic nature.[3] It is non-different. It defines its own nature. It is self-determining. It is not determined by any other viśeṣa. If it were so determined, it would involve infinite regress.[4] Viśeṣa can account for difference in an undifferenced reality.[5] Brahman is devoid of internal difference. Though he appears to be a substance (guṇin) endowed with qualities (guṇa), he has no difference within him.[6] He is supra-logical (acintya) and transcendent (alaukika). He cannot be apprehended by reason.[7]

An attributeless pure consciousness is unreal. God is attributeless (nirguṇa) in the sense that he is devoid of the qualities of prakṛti. He is possessed of attributes (saguṇa) in the sense that he has transempirical (alaukika) qualities. He has infinite good qualities, and as such he is an object of love. A being devoid of attributes cannot attract our heart.[8]

God is the supreme self. He is a knower, enjoyer, and actor. He is of the nature of 'I' (aham). He is determinate (saviśeṣa). He is directly the efficient cause of the world through his agency. He is its material cause through his power of prakṛti dependent upon him. Prakṛti is his power. It is transformed into the world under his guidance. The jīvas and the world are real. They are powers of God. They are different from him.[9] God is the creator, preserver, and destroyer of the world. He is its material cause and efficient cause. These are his essential characters (svarūpalakṣaṇa). God's causality is not due to any limiting adjuncts. His being a creator, maintainer,

[1] *Prameyaratnāvalī*, i. 16.
[2] *Siddhāntaratna*, p. 19.
[3] Svabhāvastu viśeṣātmā. *Ibid*, p. 20.
[4] *Ibid*, p. 22.
[5] Nirbhede'pi tattve bhedavyavahāro viśeṣabalāt. *Ibid*, p. 23.
[6] Contrast Rāmānuja. *Ibid*, p. 17.
[7] *Ibid*, p. 17.
[8] *Ibid*, pp. 174-75, 177.
[9] *Ibid*, p. 325.

and destroyer is not his accidental characteristic (taṭastha lakṣaṇa as Śaṁkara maintains. His powers are not due to māyā. They are real. He possesses powers of consciousness and unconscious matter. His powers are not different from his essential nature.[1] He is different from jīvas and the world.[2]

The jīva is a spiritual monad (aṇu caitanya). It is a knower, enjoyer, and active agent. Its activity and enjoyment are real, though dependent upon God.[3] Knowledge is its essence. Eternal knowledge is the essence of the jīva. It is obscured by avidyā in the state of bondage. The self is of the nature of knowledge, and yet knowledge is its quality. It is not mere knowledge.[4] It is a knower. It can never be known as an object. It manifests itself when it manifests objects. When it does not manifest objects, it can be inferred from knowledge, which is its property. There is no knowledge devoid of subject and object.[5] The jīva is of the nature of 'I' (aham) or ego. It is not a bodily ego. It is a spiritual ego. It is not an empirical ego. It is a pure ego.[6] It is a knower, though its essence is knowledge.[7] Though it is atomic, it may pervade the whole body by its quality of knowledge, even as a lamp pervades a room through its light.[8] The self is an agent.[9] Activity is its essential attribute. Prakṛti is not an agent of activity. Activity of the self depends on God.[10]

The jīvas are eternal. They do not undergo any change in their essential nature. Only their knowledge contracts and expands.[11] There are many jīvas in reality. They are not appearances. They are ontological realities.[12] They spring from the jīvaśakti of God. They are different from him. They are his parts or powers. They depend on him.[13] They are similar to one another as spiritual monads endued with knowledge. But they differ from one another owing to their karmas. Their differences of enjoyment are due to their differences of devotion.[14] Their saṁsāra is due to their turning away from God. They turn away from him owing to karmas due to māyā. They are

---

[1] *Ibid*, pp. 326-27.
[2] *Ibid*, p. 199.
[3] *Ibid*, pp. 328-29.
[4] *Ibid*, pp. 329-30.
[5] *Ibid*, pp. 323-24.
[6] *Ibid*, pp. 316, 325.
[7] *Govindabhāṣya*, ii, 3. 17; ii. 3. 27.
[8] *Ibid*, ii. 3. 18, 22.
[9] *Ibid*, ii. 3. 31.
[10] *Ibid*, ii. 3. 38, 39.
[11] *Ibid*, ii. 3. 16.
[12] *Siddhāntaratna*, p. 329.
[13] *Ibid*, pp. 325, 334.
[14] *Prameyaratnāvalī*, vi. 1, 4.

released from saṁsāra when they turn towards God, and realize their essential purity. When their karmas are dissolved by the grace of God, they are released.[1]

The jīva is said to be Brahman deluded by avidyā. This view is wrong. Brahman is omniscient, and cannot be deluded by avidyā. The jīva is said to be Brahman reflected in the adjunct of the internal organ. This view is untenable. Brahman is ubiquitous and colourless. So it cannot be reflected in any adjunct, even as the ubiquitous and colourless ākāsa cannot be reflected.[2] Śaṁkara maintains that the jīva is a part of Brahman in the sense that it is limited by the adjunct of the atomic mind. This view is wrong. Brahman is partless and indivisible. It cannot be limited by the adjuncts, and broken into real parts. Further, the jīva is unborn, and it cannot arise from the division of Brahman.[3] The jīva is said to be pure Brahman conditioned by the adjunct of the internal organ. This view is wrong. Brahman does not exist as an unconditioned reality. It exists as the inner controller of the jīvas. The jīva is said to be the internal organ directed by Brahman. This view also is wrong, because it would lead to destruction of the jīva when the internal organ is destroyed in release.[4]

Baladeva maintains that the jīva is called a part of Brahman because it is a power of him, though it is different from him.[5]

The world is real because it is permeated by the powers of God who is real. Reality is common to eternal and non-eternal entities. The world is not an eternal and independent reality. It is dependent on God. But though it is non-eternal and dependent, it is real.[6] It is created by God. It is said to be unreal because it always undergoes modifications and changes its characters. It is never perceived to be immutable and homogeneous. It is mutable but real.[7] It is said to be unreal because it is transitory, and should be treated with dispassion. The Vedas testify to the reality of the world.[8]

---

[1] *Siddhāntaratna*, p. 284.
[2] *Ibid*, p. 332.
[3] *Ibid*, pp. 330-31.
[4] *Ibid*, pp. 330-31.
[5] Sa ca tadbhinnatve 'pi tacchaktirūpatvāt tadaṁśo nigadyate. *Ibid*, p. 334.
[6] *Ibid*, pp. 241-44.
[7] *Ibid*, pp. 284-85.
[8] *Prameyaratnāvalī*, iii. 1, 4.

Śaṁkara maintains that the world is imagined by avidyā and sublated by true knowledge (vidyā). This view is untenable, since there is no agent who can imagine it. Brahman cannot imagine the world, since it would then cease to be indeterminate. It is pure indeterminate consciousness. It cannot imagine the world of distinctions. The jīva also cannot imagine it, since it is non-existent prior to creation. Nor can avidyā imagine it, since it is unconscious. Avidyā is not real, since then it would not be annulled, and involve the reality of difference. Nor is it neither real nor unreal, since there is no evidence to prove its existence. Therefore the world is not imagined by avidyā.[1]

Avidyā is said to be annulled by the knowledge of identity of the Ātman with Brahman. This view is not tenable. What kind of knowledge annuls avidyā? Brahman is pure consciousness. It is eternal. So avidyā is eternally annulled. It contradicts experience, and makes perception of the world of plurality impossible. Nor can knowledge in the form of a mental mode annul avidyā, since it would involve dualism if it is real. It cannot annul avidyā, if it is unreal. The knowledge in the nature of a mental mode cannot be said to annul avidyā and then annul itself, even as fire destroys fuel and itself, since it exists for some time and contradicts monism.[2]

Śaṁkara regards the world as a false appearance because it is superimposed (adhyasta). But if it is false, then the Vedas are invalid. They declare the world to originate from, exist in, and be reabsorbed in God. Śaṁkara may argue that the world has empirical reality, and that it is not as unreal as a sky-flower. There are three degrees of reality. Brahman has ontological reality. The world has empirical reality. Illusory silver has illusory reality. The world-appearance is false, since it has no ontological reality. This argument is invalid. The Vedas declare the reality of the world-appearance which, according to Śaṁkara, is sublated. Therefore they are invalid. Further, there is no proof of the different grades of reality. If reality means apparent or empirical reality and ontological reality, then there can be no knowledge of reality common to both.[3]

---

[1] *Siddhāntaratna*, pp. 262-63.
[2] *Ibid*, pp. 265-67.
[3] *Ibid*, p. 275.

Śaṁkara may argue that the reality of the world-appearance is nothing but the reality of Brahman, and that the world-appearance is not false in the sense that it is devoid of essence. Baladeva urges that the being of Brahman (brahmasattā) means either being abiding in Brahman, or the essential nature of Brahman, or non-difference from Brahman, or non-existence in the absence of Brahman. In the first alternative, the being of Brahman is either ontological or sublated. If it is ontological, it contradicts the Vedānta doctrine that there can be no property in Brahman, which is not sublated by the knowledge of its substratum, Brahman. Further, the world-appearance endued with the ontological reality of Brahman would be as real as Brahman. If it is endued with the reality of Brahman, it is not false. If it is false, it is not endued with the reality of Brahman. A non-existent thing endued with reality is never perceived. Being cannot be common to reality and false appearance. The second alternative also is not tenable. The reality of the world-appearance is not the essential nature (svarūpa) of Brahman, since Brahman is an uncontradicted reality, and therefore the world cannot be false. The third alternative also is not tenable. The material world-appearance cannot be non-different from the spiritual reality or Brahman, since they are contradictory to each other. The fourth alternative also is not tenable. The world and Brahman co-exist. Their co-existence is indicated by the text 'all this is Brahman'. It does not mean that the world is non-existent apart from Brahman.[1] Further, the Advaitin advocates the doctrine of Dṛṣṭisṛṣṭivāda that the objects are created as soon as they are perceived. This doctrine does not differ from the Yogācāra doctrine of subjective idealism. When the objects are perceived by the mind, they are created. They are momentary cognitions of the percipient mind. The Advaitin may argue that he affirms the reality of an eternal undifferenced consciousness as distinguished from non-eternal, momentary cognitions of the Yogācāra. But Baladeva urges that the existence of an indeterminate consciousness cannot be proved by perception, inference, or authority. Further, the Advaita doctrine does not differ from Nāgārjuna's Śūnyavāda. Existence and non-existence are not real. They are Void

---

[1] *Ibid*, pp. 276-79.

(sūnya). The world is cognition veiled by avidyā. It is destroyed by excellence of meditation, and mere cognition persists, which is Void. When effects are destroyed, the cause persists. The Śūnya is the reality. The indeterminate Brahman does not differ from the essenceless Void. The Advaitin may argue that Brahman which is self-luminous and apprehended by immediate intuition, and not by any other Being, differs from the Śūnya. But Baladeva urges that Brahman is self-luminous in the sense that it apprehends itself as an object, or that it is the object of another's cognition. It cannot apprehend itself as an object. The Advaitin does not admit it. There is no duality of subject and object in Brahman. If it be infected with duality, it would become determinate. If Brahman is known as an object, it would become a false appearance like all objects of knowledge. Nor can Brahman be the object of some other agent's knowledge. In the state of release there is identity-consciousness only. The jīva realizes its identity with Brahman. It has no separate existence. So it cannot know Brahman by direct intuition. Further, the Advaita doctrine involves the Jaina doctrine. According to the Jaina doctrine of sevenfold predication every reality is somehow possessed of the contradictory characters of existence and non-existence. The Advaitin also maintains that the world is neither real nor unreal but indefinable, and that Brahman cannot be indicated by the world 'all'. So the Advaita doctrine that the world-appearance is false is invalid.[1] The world is real. It is non-eternal. It is created by God. It is a power of God. It is a modification of the unconscious power of God.

---

[1] *Ibid*, pp. 279-82.

CHAPTER XIV

ŚAIVISM AND ŚĀKTAISM

Vācaspati mentions four schools of Māheśvaras: Śaiva, Pāśupata, Kāruṇika Siddhāntin, and Kāpālika.[1] Mādhava describes three schools of Śaivism, Nakulīśa Pāśupata, Śaiva, and Pratyabhijñā system.[2]

1. *The Pāśupata Philosophy*

Appyayadīkṣita gives a gist of the five categories recognized by the Nakulīśa Pāśupatas. They are effect, cause, yoga, vidhi, and mokṣa. The effects are of ten kinds. They are the five elements of earth, water, fire, air, and ether, and the five qualities of smell, taste, colour, touch, and sound. The causes are of thirteen kinds. They are the five organs of knowledge, the five organs of action, and the three internal organs, manas, buddhi, and ahaṁkāra. Yoga is the relation of the soul to God through the mind. It is of two kinds. It consists in activity such as recitation of mantras, meditation, and the like. It consists in consciousness of God without any activity. Vidhi is the observance which achieves virtue. Austerities such as besmearing the body with ashes, lying on ashes, recitation of mantras, and the like are the observances.[3] Mokṣa is absolute extinction of pain. It is also attainment of superhuman powers of knowledge and activity. They are supernormal vision (darśana) of subtle, remote, and hidden visible and tangible objects, supernormal hearing (śravaṇa) of all audible sounds, knowledge (manana) of all intelligible objects, complete and undoubted knowledge of the scriptures (vijñāna), and omniscience (sarvajñatva) or knowledge of all principles taken individually or collectively. These are the supernormal powers of knowledge (dṛkśakti). There are three kinds of supernormal powers of activity, excessive quickness of movements (manojavatva),

---

[1] *Bhāmatī* on SBS., ii. 2. 37.
[2] SDS., ch. vi, vii, viii.
[3] SDS., vi. 11.

assumption of innumerable bodies and sense-organs and their control and guidance by sheer will without activity (kāmarūpitva), and sovereignty over objects without the aid of the sense-organs (vikaraṇadharmitva).[1]

The Pāśupatas recognize the reality of God (pati), the individual souls (paśu), and the world. God is the Lord (pati). He has supreme power of knowledge and activity. He is the independent cause of the world. He creates it by his unrestricted and arbitrary will without the aid of karmas of the souls. His sovereignty is eternal. The souls' karmas are not useless. They bear fruits, if they are aided by the will of God. They cannot bear fruits, if they are not favoured by the will of God, even as the labours of a peasant do not bear fruits without the aid of rain.[2] God is eternally fulfilled. He does not realize any end through the karmas of the souls. It is urged that if God is the independent cause of the world, all effects would be produced simultaneously. But this argument is invalid. God has inconceivable unrestricted power of creating effects by mere will. So he may create effects gradually. His will is absolute. He is the First Cause or the cause of causes.[3]

God is independent. The souls are dependent. They are produced by him. They are eternal products.[4] They are called paśu because they are fettered by bonds (pāśa). They are either tainted (sāñjana), or untainted (nirañjana). The former are embodied. The latter are disembodied.[5]

The impurity (mala) defiling the souls is fivefold: false knowledge, demerit, attachment, causality, and lapse. It is the root of sin. It binds the souls to saṁsāra. Purity is complete extinction of the fivefold impurity. There are five means of removing impurity: observance, recitation of mantras, meditation on God, constant recollection of him, and achievement of fruits. Knowledge, austerities, constancy, stability, and purity are the fivefold fruits.[6]

Mokṣa is not mere absolute negation of pain. It is also achievement of divine sovereignty. It is proximity (sāmīpya) of God, which puts an end to rebirth.[7] The souls tainted by

---

[1] SDS., vi. 7; *Kalpataruparimala*, ii. 2. 37.
[2] *Kalpataruparimala*, ii. 2. 37; SDS., vi. 15.
[3] SDS., vi. 15.
[4] SDS., vi. 5, 14.
[5] SDS., vi. 9.
[6] SDS., vi. 2-4.
[7] SDS., vi. 14.

impurities are incapable of vision of God. They can attain release by means of true knowledge of the principles derived from the Pāśupata Śāstras only.[1] The Pāśupatas are said to be the Gujerat school of Śaivism.[2]

2. *The Śaiva Siddhānta*

The South Indian school of Śaivism is called the Śaiva Siddhānta. Mādhava's account of the Śaiva Darśana is that of the South Indian school. It is based upon twenty eight Śaiva Āgamas. Mādhava quotes from the *Mṛgendra Āgama,* the jñānapāda of the *Kāmikā,* the first of the South Indian Āgamas, the *Pauṣkara, Kiraṇa, Karaṇa,* and the other Āgamas.

There are three principles of reality: God (pati), the soul (paśu), and bond (pāśa).[3] God creates the world with the aid of karmas of souls.[4] Siva is the Lord (pati). He is independent while the souls are dependent. He is conscious while bonds are unconscious. So God is different from the souls and their bonds. The souls and God are conscious. God is the supreme reality. The souls are dependent on him. Bonds abide in them.[5]

God is omniscient, omnipotent, uncaused, pure, and formless. He assumes many forms to favour his devotees. Formless God cannot be meditated on and worshipped. But forms of God can be easily worshipped.[6] His acts are fivefold: creation, maintenance, and destruction of the world, concealment or embodiment, and liberation of the individual souls. He bestows grace on his devotees in the pure path. He breaks the bonds, which fetter their souls. He is benign and endowed with auspicious qualities.[7] Śiva is the efficient cause of the world. Śakti, his conscious energy, is its instrumental cause. Māyā is its material cause. Śakti is conscious energy. It constitutes the body of God. It is not independent of him. Māyā is the unconscious primal matter. It is omnipresent, indestructible, and possessed of manifold powers. The individual souls are eternal.

[1] SDS., vi. 16.
[2] *Indian Thought,* 1912, p. 36.
[3] SDS., vii. 1, 3.
[4] Karmādisāpekṣaḥ parameśvaraḥ kāraṇam. SDS., vii. 1.
[5] SDS., vii. 2.
[6] *Pauṣkara Āgama;* SDS., vii. 9.
[7] *Karaṇa;* SDS., vii. 10.

They are tainted by impurities, and become embodied. When they are purged of impurities, they attain absoluteness (śivatā). The world and the souls are real. They are inseparably related to God. They are his body. He is their soul.[1]

The causal-teleological argument for the existence of God is given. The world is non-eternal and composed of parts with a particular arrangement. It is an effect. So it must be produced by an intelligent agent endowed with knowledge of its constituents and their arrangement. It cannot be a finite being. So it must be God.[2] It may be objected that the world may not be produced by a cause just as a body is not found to be produced by a cause. This argument is wrong. A body is composed of parts with a particular arrangement and non-eternal like a jar. So it is an effect, and must have an intelligent cause. The world has a particular arrangement of parts. It is non-eternal. So it must have an intelligent cause. It cannot be a finite being because it has no knowledge of its constituents, and cannot arrange them in this particular manner. So it must be God.[3]

God is not the independent cause of the world as the Pāśupatas maintain. He creates the world with the aid of karmas of the souls. It does not compromise his independence, since independence of an agent is not compromised by the use of instruments. If the agent is not directed by any other agent, he is independent. The use of instruments does not make him dependent. The king makes gifts through his treasurer, but it does not impair his independence. God is the supreme Lord. He does not depend upon any other Being. He is absolutely independent. His dependence upon karmas of souls does not impair his independence. He creates the world with the aid of karmas which are his instruments.[4] God is omniscient and omnipotent. He knows the constituents of the world. He knows the karmas of the souls and their fruits. He arranges the constituents of the world into objects of their experiences in conformity with their merits and demerits. A finite being is incapable of this task with his finite knowledge and power.[5]

---

[1] Cp. Rāmānuja.
[2] SDS., vii. 4.
[3] SDS., vii. 5.
[4] SDS., vii. 6.
[5] SDS., vii. 7.

It may be objected that God cannot create the world because he is disembodied. A potter with a body can produce a pot. If God creates the world with a body, he is not omniscient, omnipotent, and free from afflictions like human beings. This argument is invalid. Even a disembodied soul can produce vibration in the body ensouled by it. So even disembodied God can create the world. He is devoid of a natural body because he is free from the web of taint and karmas. But he has a spiritual body created by his will. It is made of Śakti.[1] Śakti is the conscious energy of Śiva. It is the instrumental cause of the world. Māyā is its material cause. God is its efficient cause.

The individual soul is called paśu. It is a knower, enjoyer, and active agent. It is non-atomic. It is pervasive and eternal. It is not identical with the body as the Cārvākas maintain, since it cannot account for recollection of objects perceived in the past. It is not an object of mental perception as the Naiyāyika maintains, since it would lead to infinite regress. If the soul is manifested by knowledge, that knowledge would be manifested by some other knowledge, and so on to infinity. The soul is not co-extensive with the body as the Jaina maintains, since it is not limited by space. It is not a stream of momentary cognitions as the Buddhist maintains, since it is not limited by time. It is unlimited by space and time. It is not inactive as the Sāṁkhya maintains, since it attains infinite power of activity when it is purged of all impurities. It is not one, as the Advaita Vedānta maintains, since one soul cannot account for variety of enjoyments and sufferings undergone by different souls. There is a plurality of souls.[2] They are not created by God. They are eternal.

The soul is of the nature of knowledge and activity. It attains absoluteness when its bonds (pāśa) of impurities are broken.[3] It acquires infinite knowledge and creative power, which were obscured during bondage.

Bonds (pāśa) are of four kinds: (1) Mala or impurity due to the false notion of finitude (āṇavamala); (2) karma which unites the soul with a body; (3) māyā, the cosmic power which is the material cause of the world; (4) rodhaśakti, the

---

[1] Śāktaṁ vapuḥ prabhoḥ. *Mṛgendra Āgama;* SDS., vii. 8.
[2] SDS., vii. 11, 12.
[3] Pāśānte śivatāśruteḥ. *Mṛgendra Āgama;* SDS., vii. 12.

power which conceals the real nature of the soul. Māyā unfolds the world in creation. It withdraws it in dissolution. The world is merged in māyā as a potentiality. It is manifested in creation.[1]

There are three kinds of souls: vijñānakala, pralayākala, and sakala. The first are tainted by āṇavamala only; they are free from karma, māyā, and rodhaśakti. The second are tainted by āṇavamala, and karma. The third are tainted by āṇavamala, karma, and māyā.[2]

The souls are real. The world is real. God delivers the souls from their bonds. The world has a moral purpose. It is the field of objects, which afford enjoyments and miseries to the souls. God is its First Cause. He is the Moral Governor. He gives fruits of karmas to the souls. The Śaiva Siddhānta is realistic and theistic.

The Śaiva Siddhānta recognizes thirty six principles. There are five pure principles: (1) Śiva-tattva; (2) Śakti; (3) Sadāśiva; (4) Īśvara; and (5) Śuddhavidyā. Śivatattva is an evolute of mahāmāyā or pure māyā, as distinguished from impure māyā. Māyā is not an essential power of the Lord. He assumes this power (parigrahaśakti). Śivatattva is one, omnipresent, and eternal. Knowledge and action constitute its essential nature. It is the cause of the other pure principles. Neither Śiva nor Śakti is their cause, since neither undergoes any modification. So Śivatattva is not identical with Śiva. Śakti is an evolute of Śivatattva. It is conscious energy. Sadāśiva is an evolute of Śakti; it is the principle of being (Sadākhya), in which the powers of knowledge and action are held in equipoise. Īśvaratattva is an evolute of Sadāśiva, in which the power of knowledge is subordinated to the power of action. Śuddhavidyā is an evolute of Īśvaratattva, in which the power of action is subordinated to the power of knowledge. The pure principles are timeless. Some maintain that there is pure time in the realm of the pure principles.

Impure māyā evolves into the five sheaths (pañca-kañcuka): time (kāla), destiny (niyati), limited creative power (kalā), limited knowledge (vidyā), and interest (rāga) in particular

---

[1] SDS., vii. 21, 22.
[2] *Tattvaprakāśa;* SDS., vii. 13-15.

things. Time is manifold, non-intelligent, caused, and non-eternal. Time helps production. Destiny regulates the enjoyment of appropriate fruits of actions. It is non-intelligent and guided by the conscious energy of God (Śivaśakti). Kalā partly removes the darkness that envelopes the soul. It evolves into mūla-prakṛti, on the one hand, and into vidyā and rāga, on the other. Knowledge (jñāna) is non-intelligent. It is manifested by vidyā. Attachment (avairāgya) also is non-intelligent. It is manifested by rāga. They are actuated by Śivasakti, which is conscious energy. The puruśatattva or individual soul has experience of mūla-prakṛti as enveloped in the five sheaths. Impure (aśuddha) māyā, kāla, niyati, kalā, vidyā, rāga, and puruṣa are the seven intermediate mixed principles.

Then the twenty four impure principles of the Sāṁkhya are recognized. Prakṛti is the cause of the guṇas, sattva, rajas, and tamas. It is not mere equipoise of them. It evolves into Buddhi or cosmic intellect. Ahaṁkāra, the principle of individuation, is evolved from it. The five tanmātras are evolved from tāmasa Ahaṁkāra in which tamas predominates. The five gross elements of ether, air, fire, water, and earth are evolved from the tanmātras. Manas and the five organs of knowledge are evolved from sāttvika Ahaṁkāra, in which sattva predominates. The five organs of action are evolved from rājasa Ahaṁkāra, in which rajas predominates. Manas is the sensory-motor organ. Some recognize citta also as an internal organ. Thus Śaivism recognizes thirty six principles.[1] The Southern Śaivism is realistic.

3. *The Pratyabhijñā Philosophy*

Both Nakulīśa Pāśupata school and the South Indian school are realistic and theistic. But Kāśmīr Śaivism is monistic and idealistic. It is called the Pratyabhijñā system.

Vasugupta (800 A.D.) discovered *Śivasūtra*. He wrote *Spandakārikā*. Kallaṭa (900 A.D.) wrote a commentary on it. Somānanda's (900 A.D.) *Śivadṛṣṭi*, Utpala's (1000 A.D.) *Spandapradīpikā*, a commentary on *Spandakārikā*, Abhinava Gupta's (1100 A.D.) *Īśvarapatyabhijñāsūtravṛtti*, *Tantrasāra*, and *Tantrāloka*, and Kṣemarāja's *Śivasūtravimarśinī* are important works on the Pratyabhijñā system.

[1] Article on "The Philosophy of Saivism" in *The Cultural Heritage of India*, Vol. II, pp. 36-41; SDS., vii. 16-17.

Parama Śiva is the only ontological reality. He is pure consciousness. He is the Ātman.[1] He is universal consciousness. He is objectless self-luminous consciousness. He is omnipresent, omniscient, omnipotent, independent, infinite, eternal, formless, and possessed of infinite attributes. Independence is his unique attribute. He is pure undifferenced consciousness, unlimited by space, time, and forms. He is pure consciousness unlimited by adjuncts (upādhi). He is the supreme Self (paramātman).[2] He is the Lord of the wheel of powers. He is the goal. He is the Highest Good. He is nameless and homogeneous. But he assumes various forms by volitions. He is non-different. There is no distinction of the worshipper, the worshipped, and worship in him. He is devoid of subject and object. He is self-luminous (svābhāsa). There is no distinction of pleasure and pain in him.[3]

God is the non-dual Self (advaya Ātman) possessed of consciousness, bliss, and activity. Knowledge, activity, and independence are his essence. His knowledge is not veiled by avidyā.[4] He is the self-proved Ātman. He cannot be proved by any pramāṇa, which depends upon him. He is self-luminous. He always manifests himself. He is known by one's own intuition.[5]

God is the foundational knowledge, which is the only reality. But it appears in the triple forms of the knower, the known, and knowledge.[6] The Experiencer (pramātṛ) alone is real. The experienced objects are unreal. The world divided into subjects and objects is an appearance like a reflection in a mirror. External objects are unreal. They do not exist in themselves. They exist for knowledge. But knowledge exists for itself. External objects owe their existence to the knowledge that apprehends them. They derive their being from the knowing Self, on which they depend. They have no independent existence.[7] Internal cognitions are manifested as external

---

[1] Caitanyam ātmā. *Śivasūtra*, i. 1.

[2] *Śivasūtravimarśinī*, i. 1; *Spandapradīpikā*, V.S.S., 1898, p. 3.

[3] *Spandapradīpikā*, pp. 3-5.

[4] *Śivasūtravimarśinī*, i. 1; *Vārtika*, i. 1.

[5] Eṣa eva svānubhavaikapramāṇaḥ. *Spandapradīpikā*, p. 3. *Śivasūtravimarśinī*, i. 1. Cp. *Saṁkara*.

[6] Jñātā jñeyaṁ jñānam iti jñānasyaiva tridhā sthitiḥ. *Spandapradīpikā*, p. 39.

[7] Jñānādvaitaṁ svato'sti, na jñeyasya sattā kvacit. *Ibid*, p. 39.

objects. Cognitions and their objects are of the same nature. They are known together. So they are of the nature of consciousness. The world is of the nature of knowledge.[1] All is pure consciousness, which is self-luminous and subject-objectless.[2] An object cannot exist apart from a cognition. A cognition cannot exist apart from the Ātman. So the Ātman alone, which is of the nature of pure consciousness, exists. A cognized object does not differ from cognition. Cognition does not differ from the Ātman. So the Ātman alone is real. The difference of objects from the Self that knows them is not real.[3] This is an emphatic statement of Absolutism. The Pratyabhijñā system is idealistic monism (advaitavāda).

Parama Śiva is the only reality. He is the embodiment of self-luminous consciousness and supreme bliss. He is transcendent (viśvottīrṇa). He is immanent in the world (visvātmaka). It is non-different from him. There are no subjects or objects different from him. He is undifferenced. Yet he is manifested in the infinite variety of the universe.[4] The individual souls and the world are of the nature of consciousness. They are, in reality, Parama Śiva.[5] The world is expansion of his power.[6] His power (śakti) is of the nature of consciousness. It is his conscious energy. Its expansion consists in the manifestation (ābhāsa) of his creative power in the world.[7] It endures for some time as an external manifestation, depending on his knowledge. Its dissolution consists in its resting in the Ātman of pure consciousness. Creation, maintenance, and dissolution are evolution, continuance, and involution of the creative power of the Lord.[8] Creation is its unfoldment or expansion (unmeṣa). Dissolution is its enfoldment or contraction (nimeṣa). The world is inseparable from him. It is non-different from him.[9]

---

[1] Tattadrūpatayā jñānaṁ bahirantaḥ prakāśate. Jñānād ṛte, nārthasattā jñānarūpaṁ tato jagat. *Śivasūtravimarśinī*, iii. 30.

[2] Sarvaṁ śuddhaṁ nirālambaṁ jñānaṁ svapratyayātmakam. *Ibid*, iii. 31.

[3] Jñānaṁ na bhavato bhinnaṁ jñeyaṁ jñānāt pṛthaṅ na hi. Ato na tvitarat kiñcit tasmād bhedo na vāstavaḥ. *Ibid*, iii. 2.

[4] *Pratyabhijñāhṛdaya*, p. 8.

[5] *Śivasūtravimarśinī*, i. 1.

[6] Svaśaktipracayo 'sya viśvaṁ. *Śivasūtra*, iii. 30.

[7] *Śivasūtravimarśinī*, iii. 10, 30.

[8] *Ibid*, iii. 31.

[9] *Spandakārikā*, 1; *Spandapradīpikā*, p. 9.

Umā is the will or power of Śiva. She is the supreme and independent power of God. She delights in the sport of creation and destruction of the world.[1] The supreme power (parā śakti) is subtle, pervasive, spotless, divine, and of the nature of infinite bliss. It is the fountain of all powers. It is omniscient. It is the conscious will of God. It is the seed of the universe.[2] Parama Śiva manifests the world in himself by the sport of his own vibration.[3] It is the power of God. He is endowed with the power. The power is non-different from the possessor of power.[4] Śiva is not devoid of Śakti. Śakti is not independent of Śiva. There is no difference between them. Śakti is the infinite conscious energy of Śiva, which is non-different from him.[5]

God is called *spanda*. It is vibration excited by the power of the Ātman and enlightened by its will.[6] It is the indeterminate condition of the motionless Absolute or Ātman and its readiness to function everywhere. It is the manifestation of the intuitive consciousness of the Lord, who is of the nature of infinite and eternal consciousness common to all objects.[7]

The world is the expression of the divine will or thought. Thought is always expressed in speech (vāk) before it is expressed in an external object. Speech is of the nature of thought. Logos intervenes between God and the world. Thought is expressed in Logos. Logos is expressed in the world. It is like a ray of light of the Ātman or all-manifesting pure consciousness.[8] It is pure consciousness that is expressed in speech through the principle of life. Speech is founded in consciousness. There is no consciousness without speech. All cognitions are interpenetrated with words. The world is the expression of the thought of God. It is interpenetrated by

---

[1] *Śivasūtra,* i. 13; *Śivasūtravimarśinī,* i. 13.
[2] *Ibid,* iii. 15, 27, 43, 44.
[3] *Ibid,* iii. 9.
[4] Sā ca tadabhinnaiva. *Spandapradīpikā,* p. 11.
[5] Parāśaktirūpā citireva bhagavatī śivābhinnā. *Pratyabhijñāhṛdaya,* p. 2. No śivaḥ śaktirahito na śaktir vyatirekiṇī. *Śivadṛṣṭi,* iii. 2. 3. *Kaṣhmir Shaivism,* p. 43.
[6] Cidicchāśaktisambuddhaḥ spanda ātmabaleritaḥ. *Spandapradīpikā,* p. 37.
[7] *Ibid,* p. 3.
[8] *Ibid,* pp. 9, 37, 52.

his thought and speech.[1] The Ātman manifests all objects by sheer will without any material. They are manifested by the Lord. They exist in him ; they cannot exist apart from him. They are external manifestations of his thoughts or volitions.[2] They are limited by space, time, activity, and forms. They are mere external manifestations of the infinite and eternal Ātman.[3]

The world of conscious and unconscious creatures is a manifestation (ābhāsa) of God.[4] The finite objects are not unreal appearances (vivarta). They are not absolutely non-existent. They are aspects (ābhāsa) of God.[5] The world is known by the Ātman. So it acquires the nature of consciousness. The pure consciousness is one and indivisible. There are no objects external to the knower. They acquire the nature of the Ātman, when they are known. Subjects and objects are one reality. Consciousness is the real nature of the world.[6] Consciousness is the foundation of the world. When it is known by the Experiencer, it becomes existent. An unconscious entity cannot produce the world, which contains conscious creatures.[7]

The jīva is, in reality, identical with the Ātman. It is the Self or Ātman of the universe. It is the creator of all objects. Śiva, the Experiencer, manifests himself as objects of experience. The jīva becomes Śiva, when it recognizes its identity with him. It is nothing but the Ātman, the Self of the universe. It is the universal Experiencer.[8] But it becomes an object of experience (meya) under the influence of avidyā, and does not apprehend its essential nature. Avidyā is false (anṛta). It is not real. It neither destroys a real object nor does it modify it. It cannot change the nature of the Ātman. It is bound neither by its own nature nor by any external condition. Its bodage is neither intrinsic nor extrinsic. It is bound by avidyā. It is liberated by extinction of avidyā.[9] Saṁsāra is due to ignorance

---

[1] *Ibid*, pp. 36-37.
[2] *Ibid*, p. 38.
[3] *Ibid*, p. 25.
[4] Ābhāsarūpā eva jaḍacetanapadārthāḥ. ***Pratyabhijñāvimarśinī***, iii. 1. 1.
[5] *Kashmir Shaivism*, p. 55.
[6] **Vedakaṁ vedyam ekaṁ tattvam. Caitanyaṁ viśvasya svabhāvaḥ.** ***Śivasūtravimarśinī***, **i. 1.**
[7] ***Spandapradīpikā*, p. 35.**
[8] ***Spandakārikā*, *Spandapradīpikā*, 28-29.**
[9] **Baddho 'vidyayā jīvo muktis tasya hi tatkṣaye. *Ibid*, p. 5.**

(ajñāna). There is no bondage in reality. There being no bondage, there is no liberation. Both bondage and liberation are due to imagination (vikalpa). When the jīva realizes its essential purity and identity with God, it is liberated. Until it recognizes its identity with him, it is in bondage. Its power is contracted by avidyā, which is a beginningless impurity due to non-discrimination. It produces a desire for enjoyment. When the jīva is freed from the taint of avidyā and recognizes its innate divinity, it realizes its intrinsic omniscience, omnipotence, and independence.[1]

The finite souls are not ontologically real. They are, in their essential nature, pure consciousness. They have no differences in their essential nature. The pure consciousness is devoid of difference. It is not limited by time, space, and forms. The objects, body, sense-organs, manas, buddhi, and ahaṁkāra are unreal, when they are not manifested by consciousness. When they are manifested by it, they become identical with pure consciousness. The souls are tainted by avidyā, and become finite and embodied.[2] When they are purged of all taints, they become the Self of pure consciousness.[3] There is no plurality of souls. The Pratyabhijñā system is advaitavāda. It differs from the realistic Southern Śaiva Siddhānta.

4. *Śrīkaṇṭha's Śaiva Vedānta*

Śrīkaṇṭha wrote a commentary on the *Brahmasūtra* from the Śaiva standpoint. He was probably a contemporary of Rāmānuja.[4] His philosophy partly resembles qualified monism (viśiṣṭādvaitavāda) of Rāmānuja.

Brahman is not attributeless. He is possessed of auspicious qualities. But he is devoid of inauspicious qualities.[5] He is the cause of creation, preservation, and destruction of the world, concealment or embodiment of the souls, and bestowal of grace on them.[6] He is the supreme reality. He is unexcelled and

---

[1] *Śivasūtravimarśinī*, iii. 13.
[2] *Ibid*, i. 1.
[3] *Ibid*, iii. 34.
[4] S. S. Suryanarayana Sastri : *The Śivādvaita of Śrīkaṇṭha*, p. 27.
[5] ŚBS., ii. 2. 25.
[6] ŚBS., i. 1. 2.

unequalled.[1] He is omniscient, omnipotent, independent, contented, and endowed with eternal wisdom, and infinite energy. He is the First Cause. He is uncreated.[2] He creates all names and forms.[3] He is the material cause and the efficient cause of the world.[4] He creates himself. He transforms himself.[5] He is the author of Śruti.[6] He is the Inner Ruler of the universe.[7] He is the dispenser of fruits of actions.[8] He is immanent in the world, which is transformation of his supreme energy (parā śakti). He transcends it as its Inner Ruler. He creates the world in sport without any motive. He creates it for the good of the souls.[9]

Śiva and Śakti together are Brahman. The supreme Lord is qualified by Śakti. It cannot exist apart from Brahman. As heat is inseparable from fire, so Śakti is inseparable from Brahman.[10] The Lord's Cit-Śakti is manifested in the intelligent and unintelligent world. It constitutes his body. The world is a transformation of Māyā. The Lord possesses the power of Māyā and controls it.[11] Śakti is different from and identical with Śiva, the energiser.

Causation is transformation (pariṇāma). Brahman as qualified by Māyā is transformed into the world, and is its material cause. Unqualified by Māyā he is not subject to transformation. Transformation is a change of form. It is not a change of substance. It is development from the potential to the actual state.[12] Brahman as qualified by subtle intelligent and unintelligent beings is the cause. Brahman as qualified by gross intelligent and unintelligent beings is the effect. The relation of Brahman to the world is similar to that of the soul to the body.[13] The world is non-different from Brahman, even as a pot is non-different from clay.[14] Yet it is not absolutely identical with him. It is unintelligent while Brahman is intelligent. So it is different from him. Brahman is identity-in-difference.[15] The world is not an unreal appearance (vivarta). It is a transforma-

---

[1] ŚBS., iii. 2. 30-34.
[2] ŚBS., ii. 3. 9.
[3] ŚBS., ii. 3. 17.
[4] ŚBS., iv. 2. 16.
[5] ŚBS., i. 4. 26-27.
[6] ŚBS., i. 1. 3.
[7] ŚBS., i. 1. 2.
[8] ŚBS., iii. 3. 38-40.
[9] ŚBS., ii. 1. 32-35.
[10] ŚBS., i. 1. 5.
[11] ŚBS., i. 2. 20.
[12] *Śivādvaita of Śrīkaṇṭha*, p. 179.
[13] *Ibid*, p. 49. Cp. Rāmānuja.
[14] ŚBS., ii. 1. 15-20.
[15] *Śivādvaita of Śrīkaṇṭa*, p. 180.

tion (pariṇāma) of Cit-Śakti, which is non-different from Brahman qualified by Cit-Śakti.[1]

The jīva is a knower. Knowledge is its attribute. Its knowledge is finite due to the triple impurity. It becomes infinite, when the impurity is washed away.[2] It is a free agent of actions. But its freedom is limited. It depends on the will of the Lord. He permits it to act freely.[3] The jīva is finite, dependent, and controlled by God.[4] It is essentially pure. It is not identical with Brahman. It can attain equality with him. Equality implies distinctness. It does not imply identity.[5] The jīva is distinct from Brahman. But it can attain equality with him at the final stage.[6] The jīva is eternal. It is not created by Brahman.[7] It is a part of Brahman. It is one of his forms.[8] It is neither non-different nor different from Brahman.[9] God conceals the true nature of the jīva and entangles it in bondage. He removes the veil and grants it release. Bondage and release depend upon his will. Knowledge and action lead to release. There is identity-in-difference between the soul and God.

5. *Śāktaism*

Śāktaism advocates a position intermediate between absolute monism and qualified monism. Śiva is the static Absolute. Śakti is the conscious energy of Śiva. He creates the world through Śakti. Śiva is one Ātman. He appears to be many jīvas through the bodies. They are Brahman or Ātman. The world is constructed by the Māyā of Śiva. The jīva can attain embodied release through knowledge of its identity with Brahman. Śiva and Śakti are Brahman. They are inseparable from each other. They are non-different from each other. Śiva is static. Śakti is dynamic. Śiva is the Absolute. Śakti stands for God.

Śiva is the one supreme Being. He is Being, Consciousness, and Bliss. He is indeterminate (nirvikalpa), undifferenced (nirviśeṣa), pure consciousness (cinmātra). He is perfect and self-luminous. He is non-dual truth. He is immutable, imma-

---

[1] *Ibid*, pp. 281-82.
[2] ŚBS., ii. 3. 19.
[3] ŚBS., ii. 3. 40-41.
[4] ŚBS., i. 2. 11.
[5] ŚBS., i. 3. 21.
[6] ŚBS., i. 4, 20-21.
[7] Kaṭha Up., ii. 8; v. 13.
[8] ŚBS., ii. 3. 42-44.
[9] ŚBS., ii. 3. 49-52.

culate, immobile, and inactive. He is omnipresent, omniscient, infinite, eternal, formless, and transcendent. He is supra-rational, incomprehensible, indefinable, and inexpressible. He transcends the guṇas, sattva, rajas, and tamas. He is immanent in the world. He is its ungrounded ground. He is the universal consciousness (brahma-caitanya). He is the witness of the universe. He is the Ātman of all beings. He pervades the universe. All things are inseparable from him.[1]

One pure consciousness appears to be knowledge, knower and known through māyā. They are unreal appearances. The Ātman alone is the reality. It appears to be subject and object.[2] The Ātman is Brahman. He is the ground of the false world-appearance.[3] Brahman alone is real. The world is an imaginary construction of māyā.[3]

Being, consciousness, and bliss are the essential characters (svarūpa-lakṣana) of Brahman. He is the creator, preserver, and destroyer of the world. These are his inessential characters (taṭastha-lakṣaṇa).[4] He is the cause of the world. He is manifested in it (viśvarūpa). He is the ground of the world.[5] It is constructed by his māyā. He appears to enter into it, though he does not do so. The Ātman, the witness of all, always shines by itself.[6]

Śakti is the supreme energy (parā prakṛti) of Śiva, the supreme Self. It is conscious and omniscient. It is the fountain of all powers. It is the source of all knowledge. It is subtle and gross. It is manifest and unmanifest. It is formless and multiform.[7] Śakti creates, preserves, and destroys the world at the mere will of Brahman. Śiva creates, preserves, and destroys it through his Śakti. He is the unmoved mover or energiser of Śakti. He is the First Cause.[8]

The Ātman is homogeneous, pure consciousness. It is Brahman or Śiva. It is unborn and immortal. It is one. But it appears to be many in different bodies through Māyā, even

---

[1] *Mahānirvāṇatantra,* ii. 34-40; iii. 36, 50, 59, 60, 62, 63, 74; x. 210; xiv. 115, 129.

[2] Jñānaṁ jñeyaṁ tatha jñātā tritayaṁ bhāti māyayā. Vicāryamāṇe tritaye ātmaivaiko' vaśiṣyate. *Ibid,* xiv. 137.

[3] Asat trilokīsadbhānaṁ svarūpaṁ brahmaṇaḥ smṛtam. *Ibid,* iii. 7.

[4] *Ibid,* iii. 5, 6, 8, 60.

[5] *Ibid, iii.* 60, 63.

[6] *Ibid, xiv.* 127, 128.

[7] *Ibid,* iv. 10-15.

[8] *Ibid,* iv. 25-27; v. 1, 26, 27.

as one space appears to be many spaces when it is enclosed in jars, or as the sun appears to be many, when it is reflected in water in earthen vessels. There is ultimately no plurality of souls.[1] The Ātman is calm and inactive. The buddhi infected with ignorance becomes restless and active. Its activity is attributed to the Self.[2] The jīva is the Ātman embodied in the organism. It is never free. It is directed by the Ātman dwelling in it as its inner ruler.[3] It can become Śiva through yoga.[4]

Brahman pervades the world. All things are inseparable from him. He exists in them. They exist in him.[5] The world depends upon him. It subsists in him. All things are real with the reality of Brahman. The entire universe is interpenetrated with him.[6] He assumes its form. He is subtle and gross. He is manifested in the world.[7] He creates it through his energy (māyā). Māyā is prakṛti. It is imbedded in Śakti, which is his supreme conscious energy. Though Śakti is formless, it assumes diverse forms through Māyā.[8] Mahat is evolved from prakṛti. Ahaṁkāra is evolved from mahat. Manas, the ten sense-organs, and the five elements are evolved from ahaṁkāra.[9] Śāktaism combines absolute monism with the Sāṁkhya theory of evolution.

[1] *Ibid*, xiv. 129, 131, 133.
[2] *Ibid*, xiv. 132.
[3] *Ibid*, xiv. 122.
[4] *Ibid*, ii. 43.
[5] *Ibid*, xi. 210, 212.
[6] *Ibid*, ii. 38, 39, 46.
[7] *Ibid*, v. 195.
[8] *Ibid*, xiv. 127; iv. 34; v. 19.
[9] *Ibid*, v. 95-97; xi. 5-8.

INDEX

Abhāva, 116-7
Abhidhammabhāṣya, 319n
Abhidhammapiṭaka, 280
Abhidhammāttasaṁgaha, 291n
Abhidharmakoṣa, 291, 295n, 299n, 351n, 358n
Abhidharmakoṣabhāṣya, 315n, 319n
Abhidharmakoṣavyākhyā, 302n, 309n, 351n, 352, 356n, 357n
Abhidharmasūtra, 386n
Abhimāna, 55
Abhinava Gupta, 737
Abhiniveśa, 142-43
Abhyāsa, 159
Absolutism, 454
Acittatā, 375
Actions, three kinds of, 318.
Adharma (demerit), 38, 43; (vice), 597-99; (principle of rest), 197, 231-33, 234, 276
Adhiccasamuppāda, 340
Adhipati pratyaya, 397
Adhyavasāya, 54, 60
Ādipuruṣa, 92
Adṛṣṭajanmavedanīya, 171, 172
Advaitacintākaustubha, 522n, 530n, 603n
Advaitacintāmaṇi, 521n
Affliction, 41-44; kinds of, 141-44
Āgamaprāmāṇya, 652
Ahaṁkāra, 17, 18, 20, 23, 24, 25, 37, 41, 43, 53-57, 62, 63
Ahetuvāda, 340
Ahiṁsā, 151, 252, 255-56, 325-26; 442
Ajita Keśa Kambala, 338
Ājīvaka, 339
Ajñāna, 511, 529-31, 559, 641, 742
Akalaṁkadeva, 179
Akhyāti or *Vivekākhyāti*, 72, 134; criticism of, 563-64
Akriyāvāda, 341
Akṣara, 529
Akṣara Puruṣa, 615
Alaguddūpamāsutta, 331n
Ālambana pratyaya, 397
Ālavakasutta, 327n
Ālayavijñāna, 362-66, 368-70, 385-90, 408-09, 457
Alokākāśa, 233, 234
Alokasaṁvṛti, 395
Altruism, 324-25
Āmagandhasutta, 324n
Amalānanda, 461
Amṛta Candra Sūri, 179
Ānandacoomaraswami, his *Buddha and the Gospel of Buddha*, 284n, 285n, 323n, 334n, 336n, 346n, 389n
Ānandamaya koṣa, 434
Ānandatīrtha, 689
Anantacatuṣṭaya, 246
Anantavīrya, 179
Anekabhavika, 172
Anekāntavāda, 197-99, 413; criticism of, 274
Aṅguttaranikāya, 279, 284n, 290n, 298n, 300n, 310n-313n, 321n, 329n, 331n, 343n
Aṇimā, 167
Aniruddha, 2, 40, 62, 66, 74, 90, 91
Anirvacanīyakhyāti, 72, 560-61
Anityavāda, 284-88
Aniyatavipāka, 172
Anselm, 123n
Antaryāmin, 506, 642, 659, 661, 693
Anubhāṣya, 708, 710n-712n, 714n
Anubhava, 552, 553, 555, 598, 628
Anuprekṣā, 244, 257
Anyathākhyāti, 134, 135; criticism of, 564
Anyonyābhāva, 117
Aparigraha, 252, 256
Appyayadīkṣita, 731
Apṛthaksiddhi, 707
Āptamīmāṁsā, 179, 209n, 211n, 217n
Āptamīmāṁsāvṛtti, 200n, 208n, 209n, 210n, 211n, 213n, 265n, 275n
Ārambhavāda, 3
Āryadeva, 288n, 393
Ārya satya, 281
Asaṁskṛta dharma, 287
Āsana, 155, 443
Asaṅga, 376, 383, 384, 387
Asatkāryavāda, 3, 333
Asatkhyāti, 71, 561
Āsava, 323
Aśmarathya, 522
Asmitā, 18, 19, 142, 143
Āsrava, 240-42
Aṣṭasāhasrī, 217, 264n, 266n
Aṣṭasāhasrikāprajñāpāramitā, 348
Asteya, 252, 255-56
Āsuri, 2
Aśvaghoṣa, 359-66; *Ālayavijñāna*, 362-64; *Bhūtatathatā*, 360-61; *Dharmadhātu*, 360; enlightenment, 362-64; nescience, 361-62; non-enlightenment, 362-64; phenomena, 364; *saṁsāra*, 360-61;

Aśvaghoṣa—(*Contd.*) *Śūnyatā*, 359-61; *Tathatā*, 359, 365, 366; *Tathāgatagarbha*, 362.

Atheism, 88-92, 266-73, 304-09

Aticāra, 255-56

Ātmākhyāti, 561; criticism of, 561-62

Atom, 19, 20, 21

Ātreya, B. L., his *The Philosophy of the Yogavāśiṣṭha*, 456n-460n

Attadaṇḍasutta, 282n, 283n

Attention, 317

Atthaśālinī, 280, 29n, 319n

Attribute, 104-06, 213-16, 396

Atyantābhāva, 117

Auḍulomi, 522

Aurabindo, Sri, 615; his *Essays on the Gītā*, 612, 615n

Avadānakalpalatā, 325n

Avadhi, 189, 196, 250

Avagraha, 188

Āvaraṇaśakti, 510, 511, 530

Avatāra, 621, 644

Avāya, 188

Aversion, 37, 54, 79, 97, 142

Avidyā, 77, 118, 140-42, 289-91, 295, 334, 447, 453, 462, 506, 516, 524-31, 552, 572, 573, 577, 589, 636, 642, 648, 649, 653, 665, 670, 699, 700, 705, 724, 726, 727; *mūlā*, 530; *tūlā*, 530; Aśvaghoṣa, 361-62 ;Śaṁkara 524-31; Baladeva's criticism of, 728; Rāmānuja's criticism of, 680-87; Vallabha's criticism of, 712-14

Avidyākāmakarma, 572, 594, 653

Avijjāsava, 323

Avikṛtapariṇama, 704, 711

Aviveka, 52

Avyakta, 528, 616, 617

Bajracchedikā, 348

Bandha, 242-43

Barua, B. M., his *Pre-Buddhistic Indian Philosophy*, 339n, 340n, 341n

Bergson, 286

Bhadrabāhu, 195

Bhagavadārādhanakrama, 652

Bhagavadgītā, 7n, 612-36, 614, 616, 618, 621-25, 627-28, 630, 633, 636, 613n-636n

Bhagavadgītā Philosophy, 612-36; *Akṣara Puruṣa*, 615; *Avatāra*, 621; *Brahman*, 612-13; *guṇa*, 617-18; *Īśvara*, 612-16; *jīva*, 619-20; *Kṣara Puruṣa*, 615-16; *kṣetra*, 618-19; *kṣetrajña*, 618-19; *mokṣa*, 634-36; *prakṛti*, 616-18; *aparā*, 617; *parā*, 617; *Satkāryavāda*, 616; *yoga*, 622; *bhaktiyoga*, 630-33; *jñānayoga*, 627-30; *karmayoga*, 62-27

Bhāgavata, 636-48, 637, 644, 646, 637n-648n, 722n, 723

Bhāgavata Philosophy, 636-48; *Ātman*, 641-42; *Brahman*, 637-41; cosmology, 647-48; ethics, 645-47; God, 637-45; *jīva*, 642-44; religion, 645-47; *Vyūha*, 644-45.

Bhāgavatatātparya, 636

Bhāgavatatātparyanirṇaya, 689

Bhagavatsandarbha, 722n-724n

Bhaktiyoga, 630-33, 645-46

Bhāmanī, 506.

Bhāmatī, 469n, 486n, 493n, 494n, 504n, 522n, 530n, 557n, 731n

Bhandarkar, R. G., 702

Bhāruci, 652

Bhāskara, 652-54, 655, 702

Bhaṭṭa Bālakṛṣṇa, 708

Bhattacharya, H. D., 143n

Bhattacharya, K. C., his *Studies in the Vedānta*, 524n, 559n, 564n, 565n, 567n, 569n-571n

Bhāva, 88

Bhāvabandha, 242-43

Bhāvanā, 253-54

Bhavaṅga, 292, 313

Bhavaṅgagati, 292

Bhāvāsava, 323

Bhāvāsrava, 240-42

Bhāvendriya, 187

Bheda, 498-99, reality of, 695-96

Bhojadeva, 104, 121

Bhūtādi, 17

Bhūtakoṭi, 384

Bhūtatathatā, 360, 361, 407

Bodhyāyana, 652

Bodhi, 312, 327, 330

Bodhicaryāvatāra, 325n, 395n

Bodhicaryāvatārapañjikā, 312n, 395n

Bodhisattva, 346, 347-48

Bodhisattvabhūmi, 312n

Body, 21-22; *adhiṣṭhāna*, 23; gross, 21-22; subtle, 22, 88; kinds of, 22

Bradley, 627n

Brahmā, 456

Brahman, 426-33; *apara*, 432, 503-04; *para*, 427-31; Baladeva, 724; *Bhagavadgītā*, 612-13; *Bhāgavata*, 636-39; Bhāskara, 652-54; Caitanya, 722; Gauḍapāda, 445, 447, 449-51, 544-55; Jīva Goswāmi, 722-23; Madhva, 692-93; Nimbārka, 702-03; *Pañcarātra*, 648; Rāmānuja, 658-63; Śaṁkara,

Brahman—(*Contd.*)
495-504, 507; *Upaniṣad*, 426-32; Vallabha, 709-12; Yādavaprakāśa, 654-55; *Yogavāśiṣṭha*, 456-58
Brahma, N. K., his *Philosophy of Hindu Sādhanā*, 146n
Brahmacarya, 252, 256
Brahmadeva, 179
Brahmanimantikasutta, 304n
Brahmapariṇāma, 706
Brahmavihāra, 316-17, 322
Buddha, 282, Ch. IV
Buddhacarita, 306, 307, 348
Buddhaghoṣa, 296, 340
Buddhapālita, 393
Buddhavaṁsa, 279
Buddhi, 17, 18, 20, 23-25, 37, 43, 49, 53-55, 63
Buddhism, early, Ch. IV, 279-348; anti-metaphysical attitude, 310-11; atheism, 304-09; *Bodhisattva*, 347-48; causality, 287-89; dependent origination, 287-89; *Dharma*, 302-04; ethics, 317-28; and fatalism, 339-40, 341; Hīnayāna, 343-46; impermanence, 284-86; and inactivism, 340; and Jainism, 337-38; Karma, 298-300; Mahāyāna, 343-48; and materialism, 338-39; *nirvāṇa*, 328-33; non-materialism, 309-10; no-self (anātmavāda), 292-98; *Pratītyasamutpāda*, 287-89; psychology, 313-17; rationalism, 311-13; religion, 342-48; and Sāṁkhya, 334-36; and scepticism, 341; Theravāda, 343-46; transmigration, 300-02; and *Upaniṣad*, 280-81, 333-34; wheel of existence, 289-91; and yoga, 236-37.

Caitanya, 719-22, 722-30; *Brahman*, 722; God, 719-22; highest good, 720; *Jīva*, 719, 721; Kṛṣṇa, 720-21; means to the highest good, 720, 721; Rādhā, 720; world, 719-20
Caitanyacaritāmṛta, 719n-722n
Candraprabhacaritam, 231n
Candraprabha Sūri, 201
Chandrikā on *Sāṁkhyakārikā*, 37n, 54n, 55n
Caryāpiṭaka, 279
Cārvāka, 23, 27-30, 32, 39-40, 92-93; criticism of, 39-40, 93
Categories, 238-47, 699-700
Causation, 743; *Ārambhavāda*, 3-4, 8; *Asatkāryavāda*, *Pratītyasamutpāda*, 287-89, 358-59; *Satkāryavāda*, *Gītā*, 616; Jaina, 216-17; Nimbārka, 703-04; Rāmānuja, 676; Sāṁkhya, 3-10; Vallabha, 714-15; Yoga, 113-16; *Vivartavāda*, 3, 4, 448-52, 462-63, 542-46; phenomenal, 398-99
Cetanā (will), 292, 299, 316
Cetokhilasutta, 323n
Chakravartinayanar, A., 179n; his English translation of *Pañcāstikāyasamayasāra*, 179n, 201n, 203n, 208n, 214n-216n, 218n-220n, 221n-223n, 225n-229n, 231n-236n, 239n-249n, 251n, 260n, 277n
Chatterjee, J. C., his *Kashmir Śaivism*, 740n, 741n
Chāyāvyākhyā, 104, 105n, 114n, 116n, 122n, 129n, 132n, 136n, 137n, 142n, 143n
Childer, 280n
Cinmātra, 456, 457
Citsukha, 545; criticism of Nyāya definition of cause, 545-46
Citta, 49
Cittabhūmi, 146-47
Cittamātra, 366, 368, 375, 376
Comparison, 68-69, 566-67, 656, 659, 709
Concentration, 259-60
Consciousness, 39-40; Cārvāka view of, 39; degrees of, 314; Śaṁkara's criticism of the Cārvāka view of, 575
Conservation of energy, 15
Cullavagga, 279, 328n
Cultural Heritage of India, 424n, 426n, 654n

Das, S. K., his *A Study of the Vedānta*, 242n, 521n; his *The System of the Vedānta*, 554n
Daśabhūmīśvara, 348
Das Gupta, S. N., 636, 702; his *A History of Indian Philosophy*, Vol. I, 119n, 309n, 331n, 361n, 366n, 544n, 553; Vol. II, 622n; Vol. III, 648n, 649n, 654n, 794n; Vol. IV, 636n, 647n, 700n; his *Indian Idealism*, 385n, 386n, 388n; his *Yoga as Philosophy and Religion*, 109n, 113n, 115n, 119n, 120n, 133n, 134n, 172n; his *Yoga Philosophy*, 172n
Daśaślokī, 702
Datta, D. M., his *The Six Ways of Knowing*, 570n, 571n
Davids, T. W. Rhys, his *Buddhism*, 252n, 254n, 321n, 322n, 330n,

Davids—(*Contd.*)
333n; his *Dialogues of Buddha*, II, 339n, 340n; his *Early Buddhism*, 286n, 319n, 325n; his *The Hibbert Lectures*, 302n, 319n
Davids, Mrs. Rhys, her *Buddhism*, 285n, 288n, 292n, 298n, 301n, 329n, 331n, 332n; her *Buddhist Psychology*, 313n, 314n, 315n, 317n; her English Translation of *Dhammasangaṇi*, 299n
Davids, Mrs. Rhys, and Aung, their *Compendium of Philosophy* 292n, 314n, 317n
Demerit, 38, 54, 83, 97
Descartes, 486
Desire, 37, 54, 79, 97
Detachment, 54
Determination, 54 55
Deussen, his *The Philosophy of the Upaniṣads*, 428n, 638n, 443; his *The System of the Vedānta*, 544n, 608n
Dhamma, 302-04, 342
Dhammacakkapavattanasutta, 322n, 342n
Dhammapada, 160n, 173n, 278n, 282n, 284n, 298n, 299n, 320n, 325n-327n, 331n
Dhammikasutta, 320n, 325n
Dhaniyasutta, 311n
Dhāraṇā, 156, 189, 251, 443
Dharma (merit), 38, 43; (virtue), 588-89, 597-98, 671; (moral law), 288, 327, 598-99; (observance), 257; (principle of motion), 197, 229-31, 234, 276
Dharmadhātu, 360, 361, 363, 371, 384
Dharmakīrti, 296, 376, 377, 414
Dharmapāla, 294, 384
Dharmarājādhvarīndra, 461, 494, 521, 534n, 558, 559
Dharmatā, 407
Dharmottara, 296, 414
Dhātukathā, 280
Dhvaṁsābhāva, 117
Dīghanikāya, 279, 290n, 298n, 303n, 304n, 312n, 313n, 316n, 317n, 321n, 329n, 339n, 340n, 341n
Diṅnāga, 296, 376
Discrimination, 78, 81, 84, 86
Disposition, 38, 54, 82, 83, 88, 97
Diṭṭhāsava, 323
Dramiḍa, 652
Dravyabandha, 243-45, 249
Dravyāsrava, 240-41
Dravyendriya, 187
Dṛṣṭajanmavedanīya, 171-72
Duḥkha, 72-73, 144-45; *ādhibhautika*, 73; *ādhidaivika*, 73; *ādhyātmika*, 73; *pariṇāma*, 144; *saṁskāra*, 144; *tāpa*, 144.
Duties, 624-30
Dutt, N., his *Pañcaviṁśatisāhasrikā Prajñāpāramitā*, 393n
Dveṣa, 142

Effect, 10
Egoism, 55
Ekabhavika, 172
Ekāggatā, 316
Ekāgra, 146
Ekendriyasaṁjñā, 160
Encyclopædia of Religion and Ethics, 223n, 225n, 302n, 303n, 309n, 318n, 319n, 329n, 332n, 674n
Epistemology, 58-72, 128-31, 134-35, 183-97, 205-08, 414-17, 551-71, 655-58
Eṣaṇā, 443, 582, 594
Ethics, 147-58, 252-60, 263-66, 317-28, 325-26, 441-44, 572-77, 585-605, 622-27, 645-47
Evolution, Rāmānuja, 672-76; Śaṁkara, 546-51; Sāṁkhya, 15-23; Yoga, 119-20, 417, 656

Fallacy, 417, 656
Fetters, 323
Foundation of the Kingdom of Righteousness, 282n, 283n
Four paths, 323
Freedom of the will, 603-05

Gadyatraya, 652
Gauḍapāda, 2
Gauḍapādabhāṣya on *Sāṁkhyakārikā*, 2, 9n, 13n, 14n, 25n, 27n, 32n, 34n, 37n, 66n, 82n-84n, 87n, 88n
Gauḍapāda, 544, absolute idealism, 444-55, and Asaṅga, 448, 455; *asparśayoga*, 454; *Ātman*, 444; *Brahman*, 444-46, 447-48, 455; causality, 448-52; creation, 452-53; criticism of Sāṁkhya, 451; *dharma*, 449; empirical objects, 446-47; jīva, 444, 453-54; *jīva* and *Brahman*, 453-54; and Nāgārjuna, 454-55; and Śaṁkara, 530, 535; *Prājña*, 444; subjectivism, 446-47; *Taijasa*, 444; truth, empirical, 445; ontological, 445; and Vasubandhu, 445-46; *Viśva*, 444

Gaṇḍavyūha, 348
Gandhi, Mahatma, 612; his *Anāsaktiyoga*, 612
Ghosal, S. C., 179n; his English Translation of *Dravyasaṁgraha*, 179, 179n, 218n, 231n, 233n, 235n, 236n, 238n-243n, 245n-247n, 260n-263n, 273n
Giridhara, 798
Gītārahasya, 612
Gītārthasaṁgraha, 652
God (Īśvara), Baladeva, 724-26; *Bhagavadgītā*, 612-16; *Bhāgavata*, 636-41, 642, 643-45; Bhāskara, 653-54; Caitanya, 719-20; Gauḍpāda, 452, 455; Jīva Goswāmi, 722-23; Kṛṣṇadāsa Kavirāja, 720-21; Madhva, 692-93; Nimbārka, 702-03; *Pañcarātra*, 648-50; *Ṛg Veda*, 423-24; Rāmānuja, 658-63; Śaṁkara, 503-08; Śaivism, 733-35, 742-43; Śāktaism, 745, 746; *Upaniṣad*, 432; Vallabha, 709-12; Yoga, 123-28
Goswāmi, Jīva, 722-24; *Bhagavat*, 723-24; *Brahman*, 1722-23; *Jīva*, 723, 724; *Paramātman*, 722-23; *prakṛti*, 723; world, 723
Govindabhāṣya on *Brahmasūtra*, 724, 726n
Green, 486n
Guhadeva, 652
Guṇa, 13-15
Guṇabhadra, 366
Guṇaratna, 180
Guṇasthāna, 262-63
Gupti, 244, 256-57

Haribhadra Sūri, 179
Hartmann, 95
Hemacandra Sūri, 179, 201
Hemavatasutta, 324n
Henotheism, 418
Heraclitus, 286, 292n
Hetuvāda, 340
Hetuvādin, 349
Hinayāna, 343-48, 349, 394
Holmes, Edmond, 293; his *The Creed of Buddha*, 293n, 298n
Hume, David, 296, 545n, 546n

Īhā, 188
Illusion, 71-72, 134-35, 185, 560-64, 655-56; *Akhyāti* (*Vivekākhyāti*), 72, 563-64; *Anirvacanīyakhyāti*, 72, 560-61; *Anyathākhyāti*, 72, 134-35, 564; *Asatkhyāti*, 71, 561; *Ātmakhyāti*, 561-62; *Sadasatkhyāti*, 71, 72; *Satkhyāti*, 655-56.
Inclusion, 69
Indian Thought, 733n
Inference, 63-67, 130, 191-96, 416-17, 565-66, 656, 690-91, 708-09
Instinct, 251
Intellect, 551-53, 436-39; 553-57
Interactionism, 249
Invalid knowledge, 185
Invalidity of knowledge, intrinsic (Sāṁkhya), 70-71
Īśvara, 504-22; and *Brahman*, 507-08; and *Īśvarasākṣin*, 512; and *jīva*, 508-12; and *māyā*, 524-29, 529-31; efficient and material cause of the world, 520-22; proofs of the existence of, 512-20
Īśvarakṛṣṇa, 2, 63
Īśvarapraṇidhāna, 159
Īśvarapratyabhijñāsūtravṛtti, 737
Itivuttaka, 279, 332n

Jacobi, his edition of *Vedāntasāra*, 434n
Jain, C. R., 237n; his *Key of Knowledge*, 237n
Jain, G. R., his *Cosmology Old and New*, 231n, 233n, 235n, 237n
Jaina, J. L., 179n; his English Translation of *Gommatasāra*, 223n, 225n, 262n, 263n; his English Translation of *Tattvārthādhigamasūtra*, 179n, 187n, 196n, 213n, 214n, 218n, 221n-226n, 228n, 229n, 231n, 233n, 235n, 237n, 238n, 240n, 242n, 244n, 246n, 251n, 253n-260n; his *Outlines of Jainism*, 263n
Jaina, 24, 29, 30, 32
Jaina Philosophy, 178-278; *adharma*, 231-33; and Advaita Vedānta, 181; *anekāntavāda*, 197-99, 274; *āsrava*, 240-42; atheism, 266-73; atoms, 226-29; attributes, 209, 212-16; body, 223; *bandha*, 242-43; and Buddhism, 181, 182; categories, 238-47; causation, 216-17; critical estimate, 273-78; criticism of *anekānta* positions, 208-13; *dharma*, 229-31; distinctness, 210; dualism, 180, 274-75; emotions, 251; epistemology, 183-208; error, 185; ethics, 252-60, 263-66, 277-78; existence, 208-09; feelings, 251; generality, 211; induction, 191-92; inference, 192-96; instincts, 251; *jīva*, 217-24, 275-76; *Karma*, 224-26; knowledge, valid, 183-85; kinds of, 196-97, 250-52; mediate, 190-

Jaina Philosophy—(*Contd.*) 97; *leśya*, 224; liberation, 245-57, 261-62; matter, 226-29; means to liberation, 260-62; and Mīmāṁsā, 182; modes of consciousness, 249-52; modifications, 213-16; *mokṣa*, 245-57; *naya*, 199-205, 274; *nirjarā*, 245; *niyoga*, 265-66; non-existence, 208-09; and Nyāya-Vaiśeṣika, 182-83; ontology, 208-47; panpsychism, 276; perception, 185-90, 250-51; *pramāṇa* and *naya*, 199-200; recognition, 190-91; recollection, 190; and Sāṁkhya, 181-82; *samvara*, 244-45; *saptabhaṅgīnyāya*, 205-08; soul and body, 247-49; stages in moral progress, 262-63; substance, 209, 212, 213, 214-16, 217, 237; *syādvāda*, 205-08; testimony, 196; time, 235-38; *vyāpti*, 194, 195

Jainatarkavārtika, 179, 184n, 187n, 251n

Jātākamālā, 312n, 325n

Jāti (genus), 400; (rebirth), 291

Jayākhyasaṁhitā, 648, 648n

Jayamaṅgalā on *Sāṁkhyakārikā*, 13n

Jayanta Bhaṭṭa, 296

Jayatīrtha, 689

Jīva (individual self), Baladeva, 725-27; *Bhagavadgītā*, 619-20; *Bhāgavata*, 642-44; Bhāskara, 653-54; Buddhism (*anātmavāda*), 292-98; Chaitanya, 719-20; Gauḍapāda, 444-45, 453-54; Jaina, 217-24; Jīva Goswāmī, 723-24; Madhva, 697-99; Nimbārka, 704-05; *Pañcarātra*, 648-49; Pāśupata, 732; Pratyabhijña, 741-42; Rāmānuja, 663-72; Śaṁkara, 490-93, 508-12; Sāṁkhya, 31-40, 40-44; Śaiva Siddhānta, 735-36; Śāktaism, 745; Śrīkaṇṭha, 743-44; *Upaniṣad*, 433-36; Vallabha, 716-18; Yādavaprakāśa, 654-55; *Yogavāśiṣṭha*, 459

Jīvanayoniprayatna, 22

Jīvanmukti, 508

Jīvitendriya, 326

Jñāna, *laukika*, 373, 446; *lokottara*, 373, 384, 446; *lokottaratama*, 373; *paratantra*, 371-72, 382; *parikalpita*, 371-72, 382; *pariniṣpanna*, 371-72, 382; *pratisthāpikā buddhi*, 373; *pratyātmāryajñāna*, 374; *pravicayabuddhi*, 373; *rājasa*, 627; *sāttvika*, 628; *tāmasa*, 627

Jñānakarmasamuccaya, 500, 653

Jñānayoga, 627-30

Jung, 283n

Kaivalya, 78-84

Kāla, 235-38

Kālāmasutta, 311n

Kālāṇu, 237-38

Kallaṭa, 737

Kalpataru, 461

Kalpataruparimala, 461, 732n

Kamalaśīla, 376, 378, 379

Kāmāsava, 323

Kāmikā, 733

Kant, 623n

Kapardin, 652

Kapila, 2, 60, 63, 67, 119

Kappamāṇavapucchā, 283n

Kāraṇabrahman, 508

Kāraṇḍavyūha, 348

Karma, 85, 494, 715; *akāma*, 85; *kāmya*, 85, 590; *niṣkāma*, 85, 594; Bauddha, 298-300, 302; Jaina, 224-26, 241-43, 246; *āyuṣ*, 224-25, 241, 243, 246; *aghātīya*, 224, 246; *darśanāvaraṇīya*, 224-41, 243, 246; *ghātīya*, 224; *gotra*, 224, 246; *jñānāvaraṇīya*, 224, 241, 243, 246; *mohanīyā*, 224-25, 242, 243; *nāma*, 224, 225, 241, 243, 246; *vedanīya*, 224, 225, 243, 246; Vedānta, *naimittika*, 671; *niṣiddha*, 590; *nitya*, 671; *varṇāśrama*, 591-93

Karmādhyakṣa, 506

Karmāśaya, 171-73

Karmayoga, 623-27

Karuṇā, 254, 322, 325, 3336

Kāryabrahman, 508

Kāśakṛtsna, 522, 523

Kaṣāya, 241, 243, 251

Kāśmirī Keśava, 702

Kathāvatthu, 303n, 356n

Kathāvatthupakaraṇa, 280

Kaumudī, 494

Kavirāja Kṛṣṇadāsa, 719, 720

Kāyagupti, 256-57

Keith, A. B., his *Buddhist Philosophy*, 286n, 291n, 293n, 295n, 297n, 303n, 317, 331n, 337n, 339n, 340n, 342n, 348n, 351n, 356n, 359n, 390n

Kevalajñāna, 189, 196, 246

Kevalin, 262; *ayoga*, 263; *sayoga*, 263

Kevaṭṭasutta, 304n

Khaggavisāṇasutta, 311n, 327n

Khaṇḍanakhaṇḍakhādya, 461

Khuddanikāya, 279

Kilesa, 323-24
Kirtikar, 595n; his *Studies in Vedānta*, 595n
Kiśoridāsa, 702
Koṣa, 434
Kramamukti, 508
Kramasandarbha, 723n
Kṛti, 37
Kriyāśakti, 529
Kṣapaṇasāra, 179
Kṣara Puruṣa, 615
Kṣemarāja, 737
Kṣetra, 617
Kṣetrajña, 617
Kṣipta, 146, 147
Kumārajīva, 393
Kumāralāta, 350
Kumārila, 737
Kundakundācārya, 179, 242, 246
Kūṭastha, 485, 511

Labdhisāra, 179
Lakṣmī, 649, 693-94, 94, 698
Laṅkāvatārasūtra, 366-77, 455; *Ālayavijñāna*, 368-70; knowledge, absolute, 371-72; relative, 372-73; imaginary, 371; intellectual, 373; mundane, 373; supramundane, 373; highest supramundane, 373; meditation, 373-74; mind-only, 366-67, 375; *nirvāṇa*, 374; selflessness, 370; *Śunyatā*, 370-71; *Tathatā*, 371
Leibnitz, 276
Liberation, 78-84, 173-75; 261-62, 328-33
Life, 22-23
Locke, 353
Lokācārya, 652
Lokākāśa, 233-34
Lokānugraha, 595
Lokaprakāśa, 223n
Lokasaṁgraha, 589, 593, 621, 624
Lokasaṁvṛti, 395
Lokāyata, 339

Mackenzie, J. S., his *Manual of Ethics*, 154n
Mādhavācārya, 2, 3, 118, 121, 180, 380-82
Madhva, 733; Ch. X, 724, 725; and Rāmānuja, 696-97; categories, 699-700; difference, 695-96; dualism, 700-01; epistemology, 689-92; God, 692-93; inference, 690-91; *jīva*, 697-99; liberation, 699; perception, 690; *prakṛti*, 693-94; testimony, 691; validity of
Madhva—(*Contd.*)
knowledge, intrinsic, 691-92; *viśeṣa*, 692; world, 694
Madhvabhāṣya on *Brahmasūtra*, 689, 691n, 693n, 694n, 697n-699n
Madhusūdana, 521, 628
Mādhyamika, 349, 372, 383, 393-409
Mādhyamikakārikā, 393, 394, 395n, 396n, 398n, 400n-408n
Mādhyamikakārikāvṛtti, 394, 395n, 396n, 398n-400n, 402n, 403n, 405n, 406n-408n
Madhyāntavibhāga, 383n, 384n, 386n
Mahābhārata, 612
Mahā-assapurasutta, 298n
Mahadevan, T. M. P., his *Philosophy of Advaita*, 495n, 564n, 570n, 571n
Mahādevānanda Sarasvatī, 521, 529
Mahānidānasutta, 290n
Mahānirvāṇatantra, 745n-746n
Mahāparinibbānasutta, 284n, 286n, 290n, 299n, 343n
Mahāpuruṣanirṇaya, 652
Mahāsaṅgika, 345
Mahasatipittanasutta, 322n
Mahāsudassanasutta, 322n, 325n
Mahat, 17, 19, 20, 24, 25, 53
Mahāvīra, 178
Mahāviyūhasutta, 311n
Maitra, S. K., 597n, 601n; his *Ethics of the Hindus*, 265n, 266n, 597n, 601n
Maitrī, 254, 322, 324, 325, 337
Maitreyanātha, 376, 382-83
Majjhimanikāya, 278, 283n, 284n, 287n, 289n, 290n, 293n, 297n, 300n, 304n, 311n, 313n, 314n, 316n, 329n, 339n, 341n
Makkhali Gośāla, 338, 339, 340
Mallisena, 179
Manaḥparyāyajñāna, 189, 196, 250
Manana, 551, 553, 554, 588
Manas, 251; *bhāva*, 251; *dravya*, 251
Manasikāra, 316, 317
Māṇḍukya Kārikā, 444, 444n, 445n-455n
Māṇikyanandi, 179, 183, 184
Manomaya koṣa, 434, 445
Mati, 196, 250
Matter, 226-29, 351-52, 457-59, 672-76
Māyā, 434, 437, 444, 445, 447, 448, 462, 506, 524-31, 526, 529, 605, 606, 640, 648, 721-23, 726, 735-36; Śaṁkara, 524-31; Baladeva's criticism of, 728-30; Caitanya's criticism of, 719-20; Rāmānuja's criticism of, 680-87; Vallabha's criticism of, 712-14; Śaivism,

Māyā—(*Contd.*)
733, 735-37, 743; Śāktaism, 744-46; *Yogavāśiṣṭha*, 757
Māyāśakti, 527, 651; criticism of, 531
Meditation, 277
Mental modes, 135-41; kinds of, 138
Merit, 38, 54, 83, 97
Mettasutta, 323n, 325n
Middle term, characteristics of, 65, 191, 416
Milindapañha, 280, 295, 295n, 299n, 300n, 301n, 303n, 316n, 356n, 357n
Modes, 104-06; kinds of, 109-13
Mogharājamāṇavapucchā, 292n
Mokṣa, Aśvaghoṣa, 361, 362-64, 365-66; *Bhagavadgītā*, 634-36; *Bhāgavata*, 643-44, 645-47; Buddha, 328-33; Caitanya, 720; Gauḍapāda, 453-54; Jaina, 245-47; *bhāva-*, 245-46; *dravya-*, 245-46; *Laṅkāvatārasūtra*, 374; Madhva, 699; Mādhyamika, 405-07; Nāgārjuna, 405-07; Nimbārka, 705; *Pañcarātra*, 648-49; Rāmānuja, 670-71; Sāṁkhya, 78-84; Sautrāntika, 358, 405-06; Śaṁkara, 577-85; *Upaniṣad*, 436-39; Vaibhāṣika, 357-58; Vallabha, 717; *Yogavāśiṣṭha*, 460; Yogācāra, 390; Yoga, 173-75
Motion, 400-01
Mṛgendra Āgama, 733, 735n
Mūḍha, 146
Mukherjee, A. C., his *Nature of the Self*, 486n, 557n
Mukherjee, S. K., 295; his *The Buddhist Philosophy of Universal Flux*, 295n, 357n, 358n, 417n
Mukti, *jīvan-*, 81, 90, 508, 584, 653; *krama-*, 508, 577, 584, 607; *para-*, 81; *sadyo-*, 607; *videha-*, 81, 653; *sālokya*, 584, 646; *sāmīpya*, 646; *sārūpya*, 584, 646; *sārṣṭi*, 646; *sāyujya*, 646
Müller, Max, 253, 254, 256; his *The Six Systems of Indian Philosophy*, 422n, 424n

Nāgārjuna, 294, 296, 393-409, 532n, 556n; absolutism, 408-09; causality, 397-99; *dharma*, 407; genus, 400; *karma*, 404; knowledge, 404-05; motion, 400-01; nature, 396; *nirvāṇa*, 405-07; *pratītyasamutpāda*, 398-99; relation, 399-400; rest, 401; soul, 402-04; space, 402; substance and quality, 396; *Śūnya*, 407-08; time, 401-02; truth, absolute, 395; illusory, 395; relative, 395
Nāgasena, 200, 295, 296, 355, 356
Nāgeśa, 2, 104
Na-kaṣāya, 241, 251
Nāmarūpa, 283, 289, 290, 291, 333, 440
Narasu, P. Laksmi, his *The Essence of Buddhism*, 306n, 307n, 312n, 323n, 325n, 327n, 328n, 343n
Nārāyaṇatīrtha, 2, 104
Nāthamuni, 652
Naya, 199-205; *dravya-*, 200; *evambhūta-*, 204, 205; *naigama-*, 200-01; 205; *paryāya-*, 200; *ṛjusūtra-*, 202-03; *śabda*, 203-04, 205; *saṁgraha-*, 201-02; *vyavahāra-*, 202; criticism of, 274
Negation, 70
Nemicandra, 179, 246
Nididhyāsana, 84, 553, 588
Nigaṇṭha Nātaputta, 341
Nihilism, 349
Nimbārka, Ch. XI, 702-08; and Bhāskara, 706; *Brahman*, 702-03; causality, 703-04; *jīva*, 704-05; *jīva* and *Brahman*, 705-06; and Rāmānuja, 706-07
Nirjarā, 245; *bhāva-*, 245, 258; *dravya-*, 245
Niruddha, 146, 147
Nirvāṇa, 283, 328-33; Aśvaghoṣa, 365-66; early Buddhism, 328-33; *anupādiśeṣa-*, 332; *sa-upādiśeṣa-*, 332; *pari-*, 332; *Laṅkāvatārasūtra*, 374; Mādhyamika, 406; Nāgārjuna, 406-08; Sautrāntika, 358, 405-06; Yogācāra, 390; Vaibhāṣika, 357-58, 405
Nityavibhūti, 673
Niyama (observance), 153-54, 288, 443; (Law), 288; *bīja*,- 288; *citta-*, 288; *dhamma-*, 288; *kamma-*, 288; *utu-*, 288
Niyativāda, 289
Niyoga, 265-66, 599
Non-apprehension, 70, 568-70, 709
Non-discrimination, 78, 84, 86
Non-existence, 111-17
Non-materialism, 309-10
Nyāyapariśuddhi, 652
Nyāyasiddhāñjana, 652
Nyāyasudhā, 592n
Nyāyasūtra, 567n
Nyāyatattva, 652
Nyāyāvatāra, 179
Nyāyavindu, 414n, 416n
Nyāyavinduṭīkā, 414n, 416n

Otto, 612; his *The Original Gītā*, 612n

Padārthatattvanirṇaya, 520
Padmanābhatīrtha, 689
Pain, 37, 54, 79, 97
Pali Text Society Journal, 331n
Pañcadaśī, 496n, 511, 521n, 530n
Pañcapādikā, 461
Pañcapādikāvivaraṇa, 461, 520, 530n, 531n
Pañcarātra, 648-51
Pañcaśikha, 2, 13, 18, 45
Pañcaskandha, 314
Pancīkaraṇa, 551n
Pañcīkaraṇavārtika, 548n, 550n
Pañcīkaraṇavivaraṇa, 551n
Paṇḍitācārya, Trivikrama, 589
Panpsychism, 276
Pāpa, 171, 239, 247; *bhāva-*, 239; *dravya-*, 239
Parabhāva, 396
Paradharma, 627
Parama Puruṣa, 423, 694
Paramārtha, 359
Pāramārthika pratyakṣa, 186
Parama Śiva, 738, 739
Pāramitā, 344, 347
Pārāyanasutta, 284n
Parīkṣāmukhasūtra, 179, 183n, 184n, 186n, 187n, 190n-193n, 196n
Parīkṣāmukhasūtralaghuvṛtti, 179
Pariṇāma, 608; *avasthā-*, 19; *dharma-*, 19; *lakṣaṇa-*, 19
Pariṇāmavāda, 3, 338, 440, 520, 527, 528
Parinibbānasutta, 330n
Parīṣahajaya, 244, 257-58
Parivārapāṭha, 279
Pārśvanātha, 178
Pārthasārathi Miśra, 130, 531, 540
Passion, 241, 243, 251
Pāśupata Philosophy, 731-33; categories, 731-32; God, 732; *jīva*, 732; *mokṣa*, 732-33
Patañjali, 9, 18, 44, 103, 104, 121, 123, 125, 129, 135, 141, 144, 150, 158
Pathak, P. V., his *Heyapakṣa of Yoga*, 145n
Pāthikasutta, 304n
Paṭiccasamuppāda, 340
Paṭṭhānapakaraṇa, 280
Pauṣkara Āgama, 733, 733n
Pāyāsi, 339
Perception, 60-63, 129-30, 185-90, 414-16, 559-60, 655-56, 690, 708
Persistence of force, 15
Petavatthu, 279
Phenomenalism, 454
Pleasure, 37, 54, 79, 97
Plato, 498n
Pousin, 318; his article on *Nirvāṇa*, in *Encyclopædia of Religion and Ethics*, 331n
Prabhācandra, 179
Prabhākara, 23, 72, 116, 119, 220, 229, 296
Prāgabhāva, 117
Prajñā, 284, 322, 327, 328, 336, 444, 629
Prakaraṇapañcikā, 568n, 659n
Prakāśa on *Aṇubhāṣya*, 708
Prakāśānanda Yati, 520
Prakaṭārthavivaraṇa, 510, 511
Prakṛti, 721, 723, 725; *Bhagavadgītā*, 616-17; *Bhāgavata*, 639-40; Madhva, 693-94, 699-700; Nimbārka, 703-04; *Pañcarātra*, 649, 651; Rāmānuja, 673-75; Sāṁkhya, 10-13, 15-19, 24-28; Śaṁkara, 528; Śaivism, 745-46; Vallabha, 714-15; Yoga, 115-16; *Yogavāśiṣṭha*, 457; Gauḍapāda's criticism of, 451
Prakṛtilaya, 84
Prakruddha Kātyāyana, 338, 341
Pramāṇacaitanya, 599, 560
Pramāṇacandrikā 689, 690n, 691n, 692n
Pramāṇanayatattvālokālaṅkāra, 179, 184n, 185n, 186n, 188n-190n, 192n-194n, 196n, 200n, 202n, 204n
Pramāṇapaddhati, 689
Pramāṇaparīkṣā, 189n
Pramāṇavārtika, 378n
Pramātṛcaitanya, 559, 560
Prameyakamalamārtaṇḍa, 179, 191n, 203n, 204n
Prameyaratnārṇava, 708, 718
Prameyaratnāvalī, 724, 725n-727n
Prāṇamayakoṣa, 434
Prāṇāyāma, 155, 434, 443
Prasthānaratnākara, 708, 709n, 714n-717n
Prātibhāsika, 534
Pratyabhijñā Philosophy, 737-42; *Ātman*, 738139, 741-42; *avidyā*, 741; *jīva*, 741-42; Logos, 740; *mokṣa*, 742; *Parama Śiva*, 738-40; *saṁsāra*, 741-42; *Śakti*, 740; *Umā*, 740; world, 740-41
Pratyabhijñāna, 190-91
Pratyabhijñāhṛdaya, 739n, 740n
Pratyāhāra, 155, 443
Pravṛttivijñana, 485
Presumption, 69, 567-68, 709
Psalms of the Sisters, 332n
Psychology, 135-48, 247-52, 313-17

Psycho-physical parallelism, 249
Pudgala, 226-29
Puggalapaññati (*Paññati*), 280
Pūjyapāda, 179, 200
Puṇya, 171, 239, 247; *bhāva-*, 239; *dravya-*, 239
Pūrṇa Kāśyapa, 338, 340
Pūrṇaprajña, 689
Puruṣa, and *Buddhi*, 44-50; and *Prakṛti*, 50-53; arguments for the existence of, 32-33; nature of, 34-37; plurality of, 33-34
Puruṣottama, 496, 501, 616, 636, 642, 658, 708
Puruṣottama Prasāda, 702

Quality, 104-06
Quintuplication, 440-41, 657, 658

Rāmānuja, 652-88; bondage, 670-71; *Brahman*, 658-63; causation, 676; comparison, 659; consciousness, 663-72; creation, 676-80; criticism of Bhāskara, 679-80; criticism of Śaṁkara's doctrine of *Māyā*, 680-87; criticism of Yādavaprakāśa, 678-79; God, 658-63; inference, 656; *jīva*, 663-72; judgment, 658; matter, 672-76; perception, 655-56; *prakṛti*, 673-75; release, 670-71; *Satkhyāti*, 657-58; self, 663-72; testimony, 657; time, 675; world, 687-88
Religion, 342-48, 419-21, 424-26, 605-08, 645-47
Ṛg Veda, 418-24; ethics, 425-26; henotheism, 422; monism, 424; monotheism, 422-24; polytheism, 418-22; religion, 419-21, 424-25; *ṛta*, 422-23, 425-26

Sadānanda, 530
Sadasatkhyāti, 71, 72
Ṣaḍāyatana, 289, 291
Saddharmapuṇḍarīka, 348
Ṣaḍdarśanasaṁgraha, 3, 103n, 118n, 121n, 180, 352n, 353n, 355n, 381n, 411n, 414n, 731n, 737n
Ṣaḍdarśanasamuccaya, 55n, 179, 197n, 352n, 353n, 355n, 381n, 408n, 411n, 414n
Śaiva Siddhānta, 733-37; bond, 735-36; God, 733-35; *Māyā*, 733, 735, 736-37; *prakṛti*, 737; principles, 736-37; *Śakti*, 733, 736; *Śiva*, 733-35, 736; soul, 735-36
Śaiva Vedānta, 742-44; *Brahman*, 742-43; causation, 743; *jīva*, 743, 744; *Māyā*, 743; *Śakti*, 743; *Śiva*, 743; world, 743-44
Śaivism, 731-44
Sākṣin, 493-95, 513; *Īśvara-sākṣin*, 512, 560; *jīva-sākṣin*, 494, 560
Śāktaism, 744-46; *Ātman*, 744-46; *Brahman*, 745-46; *jīva*, 745; *Māyā*, 744-46; *prakṛti*, 745-46; *Śakti*, 744-46; *Śiva*, 744-45; world, 746
Śakti, 743, 744, 745
Śalāriśeṣācārya, 689
Sallasutta, 282n
Samādhi, 156-57, 161-66, 284, 322-23, 327-28, 336; *ānandānugata*, 163; *asamprajñāta*, 161, 165, 166, 174; *asmitānugata*, 163; *grahaṇa-*, 163; *grahītṛ-*, 163; *grāhya-*, 163; *nirvicāra*, 162-63; *nirvikalpa*, 445; *nirvitarka*, 162, 164; *samprajñāta*, 161, 162-65; *savicāra*, 162, 164; *savitarka*, 162, 164
Sāṁkhya, Ch. I, *ahaṁkāra*, 55-56; atheism, 88-92; atoms, 19-21; bodies, 21-22; bondage, 145-46; *buddhi*, 17; causation (Satkāryavāda), 3-10; comparison, 68-69; critical estimate of, 92-102; criticism of the Cārvāka doctrine of consciousness, 39-40; dualism, 12-13, 50-53, 92-94; error, 71-72; evolutes of *prakṛti*, 24-28; evolution, 15-23; future life, 86-88; *guṇas*, 13-15; inclusion, 69; inference, 63-67; *jīva*, 40-44; knowledge, factors of, 58-60; intrinsic validity and invalidity of, 70-71; source of, 60-70; liberation, 78-84; life, 22-23; *mahat*, 53-55; *manas*, 56-57; means to liberation, 84-86; middle term, 65; negation, 70; pain, three kinds of, 72-77; perception, 61-63; *prakṛti*, 10-13, 24-28; presumption, 69; psychical apparatus, 53-58; *puruṣa*, 31-40; arguments for the existence of, 32-33; *prakṛti* and, 50-53; *buddhi* and, 44-50; sense-organs, 57-58; space, 28-31; time, 28-31; teleology, 23-24; testimony, 67-68; tradition, 69-70; vital forces, 23; *vyāpti*, 64-65
Samaññaphalasutta, 330n
Samādhirāja, 348
Saṁkṣepaśārīraka, 511, 520
Samantabhadra, 179

Sāmānyalakṣaṇa, 416

Samiti, 244, 252, 256

Saṁjñā, 251, 289, 292, 293

Śaṁkara, Ch. VII, 461-611, 726-29; and Gauḍapāda, 535; and Nāgārjuna, 462, 536; and *Vijñānavādin*, 462; *Ātman*, 485-90; authority, 553-57; bondage, 572-73; *Brahman*, 495-504; *apara* and *para*, 503-04; *Brahman* and *Īśvara*, 507-08; *Brahman* and *Jīva*, 508-12, 522-24; causality, 462-63; comparison, 566-67; creation, 538, 546-51; criticism of the Bhāgavata doctrine, 473-74; criticism of the Buddhist realism, 477-82; criticism of the Buddhist subjective idealism (*Vijñānavāda*), 482-85; criticism of the doctrine of God as the efficient cause of the world, 471-73; criticism of the Jaina doctrine, 475-77; criticism of the Sāṁkhya doctrine, 467-70; criticism of the Vaiśeṣika doctrine, 463-67; ethics, 572-605; future life, 575-77; illusion, 560-64; inference, 565-66; *Īśvara*, 504-07; *Īśvara* and *Jīva*, 508-12; *Īśvara* as the efficient cause and the material cause of the world, 520-22; *Jīva*, 490-93; *Karma*, 573-75; knowledge, higher and lower, 551-53; extrinsic invalidity of, 558; intrinsic validity of, 558; liberation, 577-85; *Māyā* : *Avidyā*, 524-31; non-apprehension, 568-70; perception, 559-60; *pramāṇas*, 559-71; presumption, 567-68; proofs, theistic, 512-20; religion, 605-08; *sākṣin*, 493-95; space, 541-42; testimony, 570-71; time, 541-42; truth, 557-58; *vivartavāda*, 538; world-appearance, 531-41

Saṁsāra, 448; Aśvaghoṣa, 360-61; *Bhāgavata*, 636-37; Buddha, 290-91; Gauḍapāda, 448, 453; Jaina, 242-43; *Laṅkāvatārasūtra*, 372; Madhva, 699; Mādhyamika, 406; Nimbārka, 704-05; *Pañcarātra*, 648-49; Rāmānuja, 670-71; Sāṁkhya, 145-46; Sautrāntika, 403; Śaṁkara, 572-73; *Upaniṣad*, 437-38; Vallabha, 717; Yoga, 173; Yogācāra, 387; *Yogavāśiṣṭha*, 459-60

Śaṁkarabhāṣya, 461; *Aitareya Upaniṣad*, 488n, 506n, 508n, 526n, 531n, 532n, 547n, 551n, 573n; *Bṛhadāraṇyaka Upaniṣad*, 488n, 496n, 498n, 507n, 525n, 531n, 536n, 545n, 559n, 572n, 573n, 576n, 579n, 582n-584n, 587n, 589n-595n, 597n; *Bhagavadgītā*, 572n, 578n, 581n, 583n, 585n, 586n, 588n-598n, 601n, 604n; *Brahmasūtra*, 464n, 466n-470n, 472n-474n, 476n-479n, 481n, 482n, 484n-488n, 490n, 496n, 499n-501n, 512n-520n, 522n-525n, 527n-529n, 535n, 538n-559n, 571n-581n, 584n, 585n, 587n, 588n, 591n, 592n, 597n-600n, 602n, 604n-607n; *Chāndogya Upaniṣad*, 488n, 497n, 501n, 506n, 508n, 526n, 531n, 545n, 548n, 573n, 589n, 595n; *Īśa Upaniṣad*, 492n, 493n, 528n, 551n, 552n, 573n, 581n, 582n, 589n, 590n; *Kaṭha Upaniṣad*, 487n, 488n, 497n, 501n, 505n, 523n, 527-529n, 534n, 536n, 541n, 550n, 576n, 582n-584n, 586n, 594n, 595n, 596n, 598; *Kena Upaniṣad*, 486n, 489n, 497n, 526n, 575n, 587n, 593n-595n; *Māṇḍukya Kārikā*, 462n, 486n, 487n, 489n-493n, 500n, 501n, 523n-526n, 532n, 534n, 536n, 538n, 539n, 541n, 552n, 556n, 578n, 595n, 598n, 605n; *Māṇḍukya Upaniṣad*, 462n, 491n, 493n, 498n-500n, 532n, 533n, 536n, 541n, 573n, 590n; *Muṇḍaka Upaniṣad*, 487n, 488n, 493n, 500n, 501n, 505n, 523n, 524n, 528n, 529n, 536n, 537n, 541n, 547n, 548n, 552n, 573n, 578n, 579n, 581n, 585n, 587n, 590n, 593n, 598n; *Praśna Upaniṣad*, 488n, 497n, 524n,, 533n, 547n, 548n, 551n, 587n; *Taittirīya Upaniṣad*, 488n, 495n, 496n, 499n, 501n, 525n, 534n, 537n, 538n, 544n, 545n, 551n, 573n, 579n, 587n, 589

Sāṁkhyakārikā, 2, 2n, 9n, 11n-15n, 17n, 24n, 25n, 27n, 31n-35n, 37n, 50n-52n, 54n-57n, 60n, 63n, 70n, 82n-88n

Sāṁkhyapravacanabhāṣya, 2, 12n-15n, 18n, 21n-23n, 29n, 32n-37n, 39n, 41n, 46n, 47n, 50n, 54n-62n, 64n, 67n, 71n, 73n-83n, 85n-87n, 92n

Sāṁkhyapravacanasūtra, 2, 11n-13n, 15n, 23n, 28n, 34n-40n, 43n, 44n, 51n-58n, 61n, 64n, 65n, 67n, 70n-88n, 91n

Sāṁkhyasūtravṛtti, 2, 14n-16n, 20n-24n, 28n, 36n-44n, 51n-58n, 62n, 64n, 65n, 67n, 70n-88n, 90n, 91n
Sāṁkhyasūtravṛttisāra, 22n, 28n, 40n, 56n, 64n, 71n, 79n, 82n, 83n, 85n-87n, 91n
Sāṁkhyatattvakaumudī, 2, 4n-9n, 11n, 14n, 16n, 17n, 23n, 25n-29n, 31n-35n, 37n, 46n, 54n, 55n, 59n, 60n, 63n, 66n-70n, 73n, 82n, 84n, 88n, 90n
Sāṁkṛtyāyan Rāhul, his *Darśana-digdarśana* (Hindi), 304n, 332n, 342n, 378n, 388n
Sāṁmitīya, 402
Saṁskāra, 38, 79, 99, 289, 292, 293, 573, 585
Saṁskṛta dharma, 287
Samvara, 244, 245; *bhāva-*, 244; *dravya-*, 244
Saṁvṛti, 373, 395, 445, 446
Saṁvyavahārika pratyakṣa, 186
Saṁyuktanikāya, 278, 286n, 293n, 295n, 298n, 300n, 301n, 303n, 305n, 313n-317n, 329n, 331n, 339n, 340n
Sañjaya Velaṭṭhiputta, 338-39n, 341n
Śāntācārya, 179
Śāntarakṣita, 376, 378
Sarvajñātmamuni, 520
Sarvārthasiddhi (Pūjyapāda), 188n-200n, 201n, 203n-205n, 213n, 214n, 227n, 231n, 232n, 237n, 250n, 251n, 253n, 254n-256n, 258n, 259n
Sarvārthasiddhi (Veṅkaṭanātha), 652, 652n, 654n
Sarvāstivādin, 349, 350, 351, 355
Ṣaṭsandarbha, 724n
Śāśvatavāda, 294, 322
Satkāryavāda, 544
Satkāraṇavāda, 440, 544
Sattā, *parantara*, 383; *parikalpita*, 383; *pariniṣpanna*, 383; *pāramārthika*, 534; *prātibhāsika*, 534; *vyāvahārika*, 534
Sattarkadīpāvalī, 689
Sattva, 12, 13-15, 27, 617, 618, 624, 648
Sattvaśuddhi, 594
Satya, 252, 255, 372-73, 395, 442; *paramārtha*, 373, 395; *saṁvṛti*, 373, 395; *alokasaṁvṛti*, 395; *lokasaṁvṛti*, 395
Sātvatasaṁhitā, 645, 648n
Śauca, 153
Schopenhauer, 95
Schraeder's *Introduction to the Pañcarātra*, 649, 650n, 651
Seal, B. N., 548n; his *Positive Sciences of the Ancient Hindus*, 115n, 120n, 229n, 547-n-549n, 557; his *A Syllabus of Indian Philosophy*, 424n
Selasutta, 342n, 343n
Sense-organs, 57, 58, 62-63
Service, 259
Sharma, Nagaraja, 696n; his *The Reign of Realism in Indian Philosophy*, 696n
Sautrāntika, 349-50, 350-59; 409-14; *ākāśa*, 356-57; atoms, 355; causation, 358-59; criticism of *Vijñānavāda*, 353-55; criticized by the Vaibhāṣika, 352; momentariness, 409-14; *nirvāṇa*, 358; representationism, 352-53; time, 356
Śiva, 743-45
Śāstradīpikā, 130n, 541-42, 542n, 567n-569n
Śāstrī, Kokileśwar, his *An Introduction to Advaita Philosophy*, 534n, 551n, 575n, 604n, 605n
Sāstri, S. S. Sūrynārāyaṇa, 742; his *Śivādvaita of Śrīkaṇṭha*, 742n-744n
Ṣaṣṭitantra, 3
Siddhāntaleśasaṁgraha, 494n, 495n, 511n, 512n, 520n, 521n, 527n, 530n
Siddhāntamuktāvalī, 570n
Siddhāntaratna, 724n-730n
Siddhasena Divākara, 179
Siddhitraya, 652
Sigālovāda Sutta, 321n
Śikṣānanda, 359, 366
Śīla, 284, 322, 327, 336
Singh, R. P., his *The Vedānta of Śaṅkara*, 540n
Sinha, J., his *Introduction to Indian Philosophy*, 130n, 133n, 267n, 566n, 567n, 569n; his *Indian Realism*, 128n, 354n, 378n, 380n, 485n; his *Indian Psychology: Perception*, 494n, 560n, 561n, 564n, 655n, 658n; his article on *The Cult of Bhakti*, 645n-647n
Śikṣāsamuccaya, 348
Sinha, Nanda Lal, his *The Sāṁkhya Philosophy*, 9n, 10n
Sins, 324
Sircar, M. N., 711; his *Comparative Studies in Vedāntism*, 701n, 711n; his *The System of Vedantic Thought and Culture*, 495n, 497n, 521n, 567n, 570n, 571n, 596n, 605n
Śivadṛṣṭi, 737
Śivasūtra, 737, 738n-740n

Śivasūtravimarśinī, 737, 738n-740n
Smaraṇa, 138, 140, 190
Sogen, his *Systems of Buddhist Thought*, 286n, 288n, 294n, 300n, 357n, 360n, 361n-363n, 366n, 384n, 387n
Somānanda, 737
Space, 28-31, 233-35n, 356-57, 402, 541-42.
Spanda, 546, 457, 740
Spandakārikā, 739n, 741n
Spandapradīpikā, 737, 738n-741n
Sphoṭavāda, 131-34
Springs of action, 601-03
Śrī Bhāṣya, 657n, 659n, 661n, 663n, 666n-672n
Śrībhāṣyavārtika, 652
Śrīdhara, 296, 461, 628, 636, 638; his Commentary on *Bhāgavata*, 639n, 642n, 644n
Śrīkaṇṭha, 742
Śrīkaṇṭhabhāṣya on *Brahmasūtra*, 742n-744n
Śrīnivasachari, P. N., 653n, 663n; his *The Philosophy of Bhedābheda*, 653n-655n; his *The Philosophy of Viśiṣṭādvaita*, 663n
Śruta, 196, 250
Stcherbatsky, his *The Central Conception of Buddhism*, 288n, 300n, 351n, 355n, 356n, 399n; his *Conception of the Buddhist Nirvāṇa*, 357n, 358n, 394n, 399n, 406n, 407n
Sthaviravāda, 349
Sthaviravādin, 357
Sthiramatibhāṣya, 377n
Subhāsitasutta, 320n
Subodhinī, 708
Substance, 104-06, 213-16, 396
Sudarśana, 652
Śuddhādvaitamārtaṇḍa, 708n, 710n-714n, 716n, 717n
Śuddhādvaitamārtaṇḍaprakāśa, 701n, 712n-714n, 716n, 717n
Sukha, 135, 141, 142, 158, 224-25, 246, 254, 291-93, 314, 331, 581, 583; *niratiśaya*, 582; *sātiśaya*, 582
Sukhavatīvyūha, 348
Sumaṅgalavilāsinī, 312n, 340n
Śūnya, 407, 448
Śūnyatā, 370-71, 391-93, 407-09
Śūnyavādin, 349, 391-409
Supernatural powers, 81, 167, 169
Sūtra of Forty-two Sections, 325n
Sūtrātmā, 434
Sūtrārthabodhinī, 104
Suttanipāta, 254n
Suvarṇaprabhāsa, 348
Suzuki, Mrs. B. L., her *Mahāyāna Buddhism*, 345n, 346n, 348n, 361n, 366n
Suzuki, D. T., 366; his *The Awakening of Faith*, 360n, 363n, 365n, 366n, 456; his *Outline of Mahāyāna Buddhism*, 360n-362n, 366n; his *Studies in Laṅkāvatārasūtra*, 369n, 371n-375n
Svabhāva, 396, 627, 715
Svabhāvavāda, 289, 305, 340
Svadharma, 626-27
Svakarma, 626-27
Svalakṣaṇa, 414, 416
Svasaṁvedana, 378, 380, 415
Syādvāda, 205-07; criticism of, 207-08, 273, 475
Syādvādamañjarī, 179, 182n, 201n, 202n, 204n, 206n, 211n, 213n, 268n-274n

Tajjalān, 432, 506
Tamas, 12, 13-15, 27, 617, 618, 624, 648
Taṅka, 652
Tanmātra, 17-19, 55, 60, 617, 647
Tantrāloka, 737
Tantrasāra, 737
Tarka, 191-92
Tarkarahasyadīpikā, 180, 188n, 189n, 192n, 199n, 356n
Tathāgatagarbha, 368, 407
Tathatā, 359-66, 371, 374, 384, 385, 394, 407, 445, 456
Tātparyadīpikātātparyavṛtti, 207n, 214n, 215n, 220n, 221n, 225n, 227n, 228n, 231n, 232n, 234n, 236n, 239n, 240n, 242n-244n, 246n, 249n, 251n, 260n, 277n
Tattvamuktākalāpa, 652
Tattvānusandhānavyākhyāna, 603n
Tattvapradīpikā, 495n, 547n, 689
Tattvaprakāśa, 736n
Tattvaprakāśikā, 689
Tattvarājavārtika, 201n
Tattvārthādhigamasāra, 179, 235n, 237n, 240n, 245n, 259n, 261n, 262n
Tattvasamāsa, 2
Tattvasaṁgraha, 380n
Tattvasaṁgrahapañjikā, 380n
Tattvaślokavārtika, 179, 200n, 237n, 238n
Tattvaśuddhi, 494
Tattvatraya, 652, 659n, 660n, 661n, 662n, 664n-666n, 670n
Tattvavaiśāradī, 15n, 19n-21n, 30n, 46n, 48n, 50n, 104n, 106n-108n, 110n, 111n, 113n, 116n, 121n,

Tattvavaiśāradī—(*Contd.*)
122n 124n, 126n-132n, 135n, 136n, 138n-140n, 144n, 146n, 147n, 152n, 154n, 158n, 159n, 161n-163n
Teleology, 23-24
Testimony, 67-68, 130-31, 196, 553-57, 570-71, 657, 691
Tevijjasutta, 304n, 321n, 325n, 327n
Theravāda, 349
Thibaut, 522n
Tilak, Bālgaṅgādhar, 612
Time, 28-31, 235-38, 355-56, 401-02, 541-42, 675, 715, 736-37
Tradition, 69
Triplication, 440-41
Transmigration, 86-88
Trikāya, 344, 346; *dharmakāya*, 344, 346, 407; *nirmāṇakāya*, 344, 346; *sambhogakāya*, 344, 346
Trilokasāra, 179
Triṁśikā Kārikā, 377n, 385n, 386n
Triṁśikābhāṣya, 386n
Triṁśikāvijñaptikārikā, 375
Triratna, 247
Trivṛtkaraṇa, 440-41
Tṛṣṇā, 282-83, 289, 326-27, 329, 330, 334, 336; *bhava-*, 283; *kāma-*, 283; *vibhava*, 283
Tuvaṭakasutta, 283n, 327n

Ucchedavāda, 294, 332
Udāna, 332n
Udayana, 296
Umāsvāmī, 178, 179, 196, 242, 246, 255
Upādāna, 330, 332
Upādhyāya, Baladeva, his *Bauddha Darśana* (Hindi), 342n
Upaniṣad, 426-44; *Aitareya*, 426n; *Bṛhadāraṇyaka*, 426n-433n, 436n-440n, 443n; *Chāndogya*, 181n, 426n-434n, 438n-443n; *Īśa*, 428n, 429n, 432n, 437n, 438n, 442n; *Jāvāla*, 443; *Kaiṣītakī*, 432n, 433n, 436n; *Kaṭha*, 427n-432n, 435n, 437n-439n, 441n, 442n, 444n, 615n; *Kena*, 428, 430n, 436n, 442n; *Maitrāyaṇī*, 429n, 432n, 443n; *Maitrī*, 427n-429n, 432n, 440n; *Māṇḍukya*, 427n, 429n, 431n, 432n, 437n, 444n, 445n; *Muṇḍaka*, 428n, 430n, 431n, 435n, 436n, 438n, 439n, 444n; *Nṛsiṁhatāpanī*, 426n; *Praśna*, 429n, 431n, 441n; *Śvetāśvatara*, 427n-429n, 431n, 432n, 435n, 436n, 440n; *Taittirīya*, 430n, 432n, 434n, 438n, 439n, 442n; *Tejavindu*, 432n
Upaniṣad Philosophy, 426-44; *Ātman*, 433-35; *Brahman*, *apara*, 432; *para*, 427-31; cosmology, 439-41; creation, 439-41; ethics, 441-44; *jīva*, 433-36; intellect (*avidyā*), 436-39; intuition (*vidyā*), 436-39; sheaths of the Self, 434; triplication, 440-41
Upaśivamāṇavapucchā, 283n, 329n
Upekṣā, 322, 325, 336
Uragasatta, 286n
Urquhart, 587n; his *Pantheism and the Value of Life*, 587n; his *The Vedānta and the Modern Thought*, 587n
Utpala, 737

Vācaspati Miśra, 2, 19, 23, 30, 45, 46, 48, 49, 53, 57, 59-63, 74, 89, 91, 95, 96, 104, 121, 128, 130, 135, 147, 296, 461, 493, 521, 530, 731
Vādideva Sūri, 179, 184
Vaibhāṣika, 349-52, 355-58, 408; *ākāsa*, 356-57; causes, 358; criticism of Sautrāntika realism, 352; dualism, 351-52; *nirvāṇa*, 351-58; time, 355-56
Vairāgya, 159-61
Valid knowledge, Buddhism, 414; Jaina, 183-85; Rāmānuja, 655; Sāṁkhya, 58-60; Śaṁkara, 557-58; Vallabha, 708; Yoga, 128-29
Validity of knowledge, intrinsic, Madhva, 691-92; Sāṁkhya, 70-71; Śaṁkara, 558
Vallabha, Ch. XII, 500n; and Madhva, 714; and Nimbārka, 714; *Brahman*, 709-12; criticism of, 718; God, 709-12; *jīva*, 716-18; *karma*, 715; *mokṣa*, 717; *saṁsāra*, 717; *svabhāva*, 715; time, 715; valid knowledge, kinds of, 708-09; world, reality of, 712-15
Vaiśvānara, 434
Vāmanī, 506-07
Vardhamāna, 178
Vasalasutta, 328n
Vāsanā, 79, 146, 411, 485, 511, 573, 648, 651
Vaseṭṭhasutta, 283n, 285n, 328n
Vasubandhu, 294, 296, 377, 384-86, 439
Vasugupta, 737
Vātsiputrīya, 402
Vātsyāyana, 195
Vedanā, 289-93
Vedāntadeśika, 652
Vedāntadīpa, 652, 659n, 661n, 665n

Vedāntakaustubhaprabhā, 702
Vedāntasāra (Rāmānuja), 652, 663n, 666n, 670n, 672n
Vedāntasiddhāntamuktāvalī, 520, 546n
Vedāntakaustubhaprabhā, 702
Vedāntaparibhāṣā, 558n-561n, 570n, 571n, 582n, 587n
Vedāntapārijātasaurabha, 703n-706n
Vedāntaratnamañjuṣā, 702
Vedāntasāra (Rāmānuja), 652, 663n, 666n, 670n, 672n
Vedāntasāra (Sadānanda), 512n, 548n, 550n
Vedārthasaṁgraha, 652, 659n, 660n, 662n, 664n, 670n, 671
Vedic Hymns, 424n
Veṅkaṭanātha, 652
Vibhaṅga, 279
Vice, 54, 86-88
Videhakaivalya, 78, 83
Vidyābhūṣaṇa, Baladeva, 724-30; *Brahman*, 724; criticism of Śaṁkara, 728-30; God, 724-26; *jīva*, 726-27; *prakṛti*, 725-26; *viśeṣa*, 724-25; world, reality of, 727-30
Vidyā, 552, 572, 580, 581, 589, 607, 610
Vidyabhushan, S. C., his *History of Indian Logic*, 178n, 195n, 417n; his English Translation of *Nyāyāvatāra*, 193n, 195n, 201n, 204n
Vidyānandisvāmī, 179
Vidyāraṇya, 461, 495, 521
Vijñānavāda, 349, 376-82
Vijñānabhikṣu, 2, 17, 23, 29, 30, 41, 46, 47, 49, 50, 53, 57-60, 62, 66, 74, 91, 92, 96, 104, 120, 128, 135, 141, 142, 147, 163, 296
Vijñaptimātratā, 384-86, 388, 455, 462, 485
Vijñāna, 289, 291-93
Vijñānavādin, 349, 376-90; criticism of, 353-55, 482-85
Vijñānamātraśāstra, 387n, 390n
Vijñaptimātratāsiddhi, 386n, 388n
Vijñānamayakoṣa, 434
Vikṣipta, 146, 147
Vikṣepaśakti, 510, 511, 530
Vimānavatthu, 279
Viṁśikā, 377n
Virāt, 434
Virtues, 151-54, 442-44, 625-30, 646-47
Viṣayacaitanya, 559, 560
Viṣṇu, 649, 693
Viṣṇupurāṇa, 636
Viśva, 444
Viśvakarmā, 423
Visuddhimagga, 280, 282n, 285n, 296n, 301n
Viśeṣa, 117-18, 692
Vītarāgastuti, 201n, 204n-206n, 211n, 213n
Vivaraṇaprameyasaṁgraha, 561n-564n, 601n
Vivartavāda, 333, 440, 520, 527, 528, 544, 608
Vivekajñāna, 52
Vivekākhyāti, 84
Volition, 37, 79, 97, 317-19
Vrata, 244, 252-53; *aṇu-*, 252-53; *mahā-*, т52-53; *guṇa-*, 254-55.
Vyāpti, 64-65, 130, 192, 565, 656; *antarvyāpti*, 194-95; *bahirvyāpti*, 194-95
Vyūha, 474, 613, 644-45, 648, 650, 661, 721
Vyāsa, 10, 18, 19, 29, 31, 48, 49, 59, 95, 99, 104, 105, 107, 118, 120, 121, 128-30, 141, 146, 161, 163, 296
Vyāvahārika sattā, 534

Warren, his *Buddhism in Translations*, 300n
Whole, 107-08, 400
Winternitz, his *A History of Indian Literature*, Vol. II, 366n
World, 10-31, 109-16, 226-38, 284-89, 350-59, 366-70, 375-82, 396-402, 406-09, 409-14, 439-41, 446-47, 457-59; world-appearance, 531-51, 672-80, 687-88, 694-96, 703-04, 712-15, 719-20, 728-30, 737, 743, 745-46
World-appearance, 531-40; criticism of, 540-41

Yādavaprakāśa, 654-55, 702
Yadṛcchāvāda, 289
Yama, 255, 336, 443
Yamaka, 280
Yāmunācarya, 652
Yaśomitra, 350
Yatīndramatadīpikā, 652, 655n-658n, 660n, 664n, 670n
Yoga, *abhyāsa*, 159; action, kinds of, 170-71; path of, 148-50; afflictions (*kleśa*), 141-44; atoms, 108; attachment, 142; attention, levels of, 146-47; aversion, 142; *avidyā*, 134-35, 140-41; causation, 113-16; critical estimate, 175-77; dispositions, 145-46; egoism, 143; epistemology, 128-35; error, 134-35; 138; ethics, 147-50; God,

Yoga—(*Contd.*)
121-28; nature of, 125-28; place of, in the system, 121-22; proofs for the existence of, 123-25; imagination, 138-39, 123-25; inference, 130; *karma*, 170-73; knowledge, valid, 128-29; liberation, 173-75; mental modes, 135-41; metaphysics, 104-20; mind, 135-41; mode, 104-06; modifications, kinds of, 109-13; non-existence (*abhāva*), 116-17; pain, 144-45; particularity (*viśeṣa*), 117-18; perception, 129-30; power, 114-15; *pramāṇas*, 129-31; psychology, 135-41; *samādhi*, 161-66; and Sāṁkhya, 118-20; sleep, 139-40; *sphoṭavāda*, 131-34; substance, 104-06; supernormal powers, 166-70; testimony, 130-31; theology, 121-28; transmigration, 171-73; *vairāgya*, 159-61; *Vedas*, 123; whole and part, 107-08; *Yoga*, eightfold, 150-58

Yogācāra, 349, 353-55, 375-90; *ālaya-vijñāna*, 377, 382, 385-90; *citta*, 387; knowledge, degrees of, 382-83; *nirvāṇa*, 390; reality, degrees of, 383; *Tathatā*, 383-84; *Vijñānavāda*, 378-82; *vijñptimātratā*, 384-86

Yogācāra Vijñānavāda, 378-82; *Ālayavijñāna*, 386-90; Asaṅga, 383-85; *citta*, 387; criticism of, 482; Dharmakīrti, 377-78; Kamalaśīla, 378-90; Maitreyanātha, 382-83; *nirvāṇa*, 390; Śāntarakṣita, 378-80; *Tathatā*, 384; Vasubandhu, 377, 384-85; *Vijñaptimātratā*, 385-86, 388

Yogavāśiṣṭha Philosophy, 455-60; and Gauḍapāda, 458-59; and Nāgārjuna, 458-59; and Śaivism, 457; bondage, 459-60; *Brahman, para*, 456-57; *Brahmā*, 456-57; *jīva*, 459; liberation, 460; *māyā*, 457; *prakṛti*, 457; *puruṣa*, 457; world, 457-59

Yogabhāṣya, 10n, 15n, 17n-21n, 29n-31n, 35n, 45n, 48n, 49n, 99n, 104, 104n-110n, 112n-121n, 123n-131n, 134n-159n, 161n-174n

Yogācāra, 376-90, 485; criticism of, 353-55, 482-85

Yogācārabhūmi, 388n

Yogamaṇiprabhā, 104, 155n-158n, 161n

Yogāṅga, 150-58

Yogarahasya, 652

Yogasiddhāntacandrikā, 104

Yogaśāstra, 179

Yogasūtra, 103, 104n, 117n, 118n, 121n, 123n, 125n-127n, 129n, 131n, 134n-136n, 139n-144n, 146n, 149n-159n, 161n-171n, 173n, 174n

Yogavārtika, 47n-49n, 104, 108n, 113n, 114n, 116n, 117n, 122n, 124n, 126n, 128n, 131n, 132n, 134n, 135n, 137n, 139n, 140n, 142n-145n, 147n, 152n, 153n, 158n, 159n, 161n, 163n, 164n

Yogvaśiṣṭha, 455, 456n, 457n, 458n, 460n

Zeno, 401